We are delighted you have decided to buy the **Collins Italian Travel Dictionary** and hope you will benefit from using it whether you are travelling abroad for pleasure or on business.

This dictionary provides up-to-date coverage of all the Italian you will need, in a clear and user-friendly layout. The emphasis is on contemporary language, with numerous examples of idiomatic usage which will enable you not only to understand but also to communicate with confidence.

We hope that you enjoy using the dictionary and that you find it an ideal travelling companion.

Note on trademarks

ABBREVIAZIONI

ABBREVIATIONS

aggettivo	**a**	adjective
abbreviazione	**abbr**	abbreviation
avverbio	**ad**	adverb
amministrazione	**ADMIN**	administration
aeronautica, viaggi aerei	**AER**	flying, air travel
aggettivo	**ag**	adjective
agricoltura	**AGR**	agriculture
amministrazione	**AMM**	administration
anatomia	**ANAT**	anatomy
architettura	**ARCHIT**	architecture
astronomia, astrologia	**ASTR**	astronomy, astrology
l'automobile	**AUT**	the motor car and motoring
avverbio	**av**	adverb
aeronautica, viaggi aerei	**AVIAT**	flying, air travel
biologia	**BIOL**	biology
botanica	**BOT**	botany
inglese della Gran Bretagna	**Brit**	British English
consonante	**C**	consonant
chimica	**CHIM, CHEM**	chemistry
congiunzione	**cj**	conjunction
familiare (! da evitare)	**col(!)**	colloquial usage (! particularly offensive)
commercio, finanza, banca	**COMM**	commerce, finance, banking
informatica	**COMPUT**	computers
congiunzione	**cong**	conjunction
edilizia	**CONSTR**	building
sostantivo usato come aggettivo, non può essere usato né come attributo, né dopo il sostantivo qualificato	**cpd**	compound element: noun used as adjective and which cannot follow the noun it qualifies
cucina	**CUC, CULIN**	cookery
davanti a	**dav**	before
determinativo: articolo, aggettivo dimostrativo o indefinito etc	**det**	determiner: article, demonstrative etc
diritto	**DIR**	law
economia	**ECON**	economics
edilizia	**EDIL**	building
elettricità, elettronica	**ELETTR, ELEC**	electricity, electronics
esclamazione	**escl, excl**	exclamation
femminile	**f**	feminine
familiare (! da evitare)	**fam(!)**	colloquial usage (! particularly offensive)
ferrovia	**FERR**	railways
figurato	**fig**	figurative use
fisiologia	**FISIOL**	physiology
fotografia	**FOT**	photography
(verbo inglese) la cui particella è inseparabile dal verbo	**fus**	(phrasal verb) where the particle cannot be separated from main verb

COLLINS

ITALIAN

TRAVEL DICTIONARY

HarperCollins*Publishers*

first published in this edition 1996

©HarperCollins Publishers 1996

ISBN 0 00 471022-3

A catalogue record for this book is available from the British Library

Typeset by Morton Word Processing Ltd, Scarborough
Printed and bound in Great Britain by
Caledonian International Book Manufacturing Ltd, Glasgow, G64

ABBREVIAZIONI

ABBREVIATIONS

nella maggior parte dei sensi; generalmente	**gen**	in most or all senses; generally
geografia, geologia	**GEO**	geography, geology
geometria	**GEOM**	geometry
impersonale	**impers**	impersonal
informatica	**INFORM**	computers
insegnamento, sistema scolastico e universitario	**INS**	schooling, schools and universities
invariabile	**inv**	invariable
irregolare	**irg**	irregular
grammatica, linguistica	**LING**	grammar, linguistics
maschile	**m**	masculine
matematica	**MAT(H)**	mathematics
termine medico, medicina	**MED**	medical term, medicine
il tempo, meteorologia	**METEOR**	the weather, meteorology
maschile o femminile, secondo il sesso	**m/f**	either masculine or feminine depending on sex
esercito, lingua militare	**MIL**	military matters
musica	**MUS**	music
sostantivo	**n**	noun
nautica	**NAUT**	sailing, navigation
numerale (aggettivo, sostantivo)	**num**	numeral adjective or noun
	o.s.	oneself
peggiorativo	**peg, pej**	derogatory, pejorative
fotografia	**PHOT**	photography
fisiologia	**PHYSIOL**	physiology
plurale	**pl**	plural
politica	**POL**	politics
participio passato	**pp**	past participle
preposizione	**prep**	preposition
psicologia, psichiatria	**PSIC, PSYCH**	psychology, psychiatry
tempo passato	**pt**	past tense
sostantivo che non si usa al plurale	**q**	uncountable noun: not used in the plural
qualcosa	**qc**	
qualcuno	**qn**	
religione, liturgia	**REL**	religions, church service
sostantivo	**s**	noun
	sb	somebody
insegnamento, sistema scolastico e universitario	**SCOL**	schooling, schools and universities
singolare	**sg**	singular
soggetto (grammaticale)	**sog**	(grammatical) subject
	sth	something
congiuntivo	**sub**	subjunctive
soggetto (grammaticale)	**subj**	(grammatical) subject
termine tecnico, tecnologia	**TECN, TECH**	technical term, technology
telecomunicazioni	**TEL**	telecommunications
tipografia	**TIP**	typography, printing

ABBREVIAZIONI

ABBREVIATIONS

televisione	TV	television
tipografia	TYP	typography, printing
inglese degli Stati Uniti	US	American English
vocale	V	vowel
verbo	vb	verb
verbo o gruppo verbale con funzione intransitiva	vi	verb or phrasal verb used intransitively
verbo riflessivo	vr	reflexive verb
verbo o gruppo verbale con funzione transitiva	vt	verb or phrasal verb used transitively
zoologia	ZOOL	zoology
marchio registrato	®	registered trademark
introduce un'equivalenza culturale	≈	introduces a cultural equivalent

TRASCRIZIONE FONETICA

PHONETIC TRANSCRIPTION

CONSONANTS CONSONANTI

NB The pairing of some vowel sounds only indicates approximate equivalence/La messa in equivalenza di certi suoni indica solo una rassomiglianza approssimativa.

puppy	p	padre
baby	b	bambino
tent	t	tutto
daddy	d	dado
cork kiss chord	k	cane che
gag guess	g	gola ghiro
so rice kiss	s	sano
cousin buzz	z	svago esame
sheep sugar	ʃ	scena
pleasure beige	ʒ	
church	tʃ	pece lanciare
judge general	dʒ	giro gioco
farm raffle	f	afa faro
very rev	v	vero bravo
thin maths	θ	
that other	ð	
little ball	l	letto ala
	ʎ	gli
rat brat	r	rete arco
mummy comb	m	ramo madre
no ran	n	no fumante
	ɲ	gnomo
singing bank	ŋ	
hat reheat	h	
yet	j	buio piacere
wall bewail	w	uomo guaio
loch	x	

VOWELS VOCALI

NB p, b, t, d, k, g are not aspirated in Italian/sono seguiti da un'aspirazione in inglese.

heel bead	i: i	vino idea
hit pity	ɪ	
	e	stella edera
set tent	ɛ	epoca eccetto
apple bat	æ a	mamma amore
after car calm	ɑ:	
fun cousin	ʌ	
over above	ə	
urn fern work	ə:	
wash pot	ɔ	rosa occhio
born cork	ɔ:	
	o	ponte ognuno
full soot	u	utile zucca
boon lewd	u:	

DIPHTHONGS DITTONGHI

	ɪə	beer tier
	ɛə	tear fair there
	eɪ	date plaice day
	aɪ	life buy cry
	au	owl foul now
	əu	low no
	ɔɪ	boil boy oily
	uə	poor tour

MISCELLANEOUS

VARIE

* per l'inglese: la "r" finale viene pronunciata se seguita da una vocale.

' precedes the stressed syllable/precede la sillaba accentata.

ITALIAN PRONUNCIATION

VOWELS

Where the vowel **e** or the vowel **o** appears in a stressed syllable it can be either open [ɛ], [ɔ] or closed [e], [o]. As the open or closed pronunciation of these vowels is subject to regional variation, the distinction is of little importance to the user of this dictionary. Phonetic transcription for headwords containing these vowels will therefore only appear where other pronunciation difficulties are present.

CONSONANTS

c before "e" or "i" is pronounced *tch*.

ch is pronounced like the "k" in "kit".

g before "e" or "i" is pronounced like the "j" in "jet".

gh is pronounced like the "g" in "get".

gl before "e" or "i" is normally pronounced like the "lli" in "million", and in a few cases only like the "gl" in "glove".

gn is pronounced like the "ny" in "canyon".

sc before "e" or "i" is pronounced *sh*.

z is pronounced like the "ts" in "stetson", or like the "d's" in "bird's-eye".

Headwords containing the above consonants and consonantal groups have been given full phonetic transcription in this dictionary.

NB All double written consonants in Italian are fully sounded: eg. the *tt* in "tutto" is pronounced as in "ha*t* *t*rick".

ITALIANO - INGLESE
ITALIAN - ENGLISH

A

a prep (a + il = **al**, a + lo = **allo**, a + l' = **all'**, a + la = **alla**, a + i = **ai**, a + gli = **agli**, a + le = **alle**) 1 (stato in luogo) at; (: in) in; essere ~ casa/~ scuola/~ Roma to be at home/at school/in Rome; è ~ 10 km da qui it's 10 km from here, it's 10 km away

2 (moto a luogo) to; andare ~ casa/~ scuola to go home/to school

3 (tempo) at; (epoca, stagione) in; alle cinque at five (o'clock); ~ mezzanotte/ Natale at midnight/Christmas; al mattino in the morning; ~ maggio/ primavera in May/spring; ~ cinquant'anni at fifty (years of age); ~ domani! see you tomorrow!

4 (complemento di termine) to; dare qc ~ qn to give sth to sb

5 (mezzo, modo) with, by; ~ piedi/ cavallo on foot/horseback; fatto ~ mano made by hand, handmade; una barca ~ motore a motorboat; ~ uno ~ uno one by one; all'italiana the Italian way, in the Italian fashion

6 (rapporto) a, per; (: con prezzi) at; prendo 500.000 lire al mese I get 500,000 lire a o per month; pagato ~ ore paid by the hour; vendere qc ~ 500 lire il chilo to sell sth at 500 lire a o per kilo.

a'bate sm abbot.

abbacchi'ato, a [abbak'kjato] ag downhearted, in low spirits.

abbagli'ante [abbaʎ'ʎante] ag dazzling; ~i smpl (AUT): accendere gli ~i to put one's headlights on full (Brit) o high (US) beam.

abbagli'are [abbaʎ'ʎare] vt to dazzle; (illudere) to delude; **ab'baglio** sm blunder; prendere un abbaglio to blunder, make a blunder.

abbai'are vi to bark.

abba'ino sm dormer window; (soffitta) attic room.

abbando'nare vt to leave, abandon, desert; (trascurare) to neglect; (rinunciare a) to abandon, give up; ~rsi vr to let o.s. go; ~rsi a (ricordi, vizio) to give o.s. up to; **abban'dono** sm abandoning; neglecting; (stato) abandonment; neglect; (SPORT) withdrawal; (fig) abandon; in abbandono (edificio, giardino) neglected.

abbas'sare vt to lower; (radio) to turn down; ~rsi vr (chinarsi) to stoop; (livello, sole) to go down; (fig:

umiliarsi) to demean o.s.; ~ i fari (AUT) to dip o dim (US) one's lights.

ab'basso escl: ~ il re! down with the king!

abbas'tanza [abbas'tantsa] av (a sufficienza) enough; (alquanto) quite, rather, fairly; non è ~ furbo he's not shrewd enough; un vino ~ dolce quite a sweet wine, a fairly sweet wine; averne ~ di qn/qc to have had enough of sb/sth.

ab'battere vt (muro, casa) to pull down; (ostacolo) to knock down; (albero) to fell; (: sog: vento) to bring down; (bestie da macello) to slaughter; (cane, cavallo) to destroy, put down; (selvaggina, aereo) to shoot down; (fig: sog: malattia, disgrazia) to lay low; ~rsi vr (avvilirsi) to lose heart; **abbat'tuto, a** ag (fig) despondent, depressed.

ab'bazia [abbat'tsia] sf abbey.

abbece'dario [abbetʃe'darjo] sm primer.

abbel'lire vt to make beautiful; (ornare) to embellish.

abbeve'rare vt to water; ~rsi vr to drink.

'abbi, 'abbia, abbi'amo, 'abbiano, abbi'ate forme del vb avere.

abbicci [abbit'tʃi] sm inv alphabet; (sillabario) primer; (fig) rudiments pl.

abbi'ente ag well-to-do, well-off.

abbi'etto, a ag = abietto.

abbiglia'mento [abbiʎʎa'mento] sm dress g; (indumenti) clothes pl; (industria) clothing industry.

abbigli'are [abbiʎ'ʎare] vt to dress up.

abbi'nare vt: ~ (a) to combine (with).

abbindo'lare vt (fig) to cheat, trick.

abbocca'mento sm talks pl, meeting.

abboc'care vt (tubi, canali) to connect, join up // vi (pesce) to bite; (tubi) to join; ~ (all'amo) (fig) to swallow the bait.

abboc'cato, a ag (vino) sweetish.

abbona'mento sm subscription; (alle ferrovie etc) season ticket; fare l'~ to take out a subscription (o season ticket).

abbo'narsi vr: ~ a un giornale to take out a subscription to a newspaper; ~ al teatro/alle ferrovie to take out a season ticket for the theatre/the train; **abbo'nato, a** sm/f subscriber; season-ticket holder.

abbon'dante ag abundant, plentiful; (giacca) roomy.

abbon'danza [abbon'dantsa] sf abundance; plenty.

abbon'dare *vi* to abound, be plentiful; ~ in *o* di to be full of, abound in.

abbor'dabile *ag* (*persona*) approachable; (*prezzo*) reasonable.

abbor'dare *vt* (*nave*) to board; (*persona*) to approach; (*argomento*) to tackle; ~ una curva to take a bend.

abbotto'nare *vt* to button up, do up.

abboz'zare |abbot'tsare| *vt* to sketch, outline; (*SCULTURA*) to rough-hew; ~ un sorriso to give a hint of a smile; **ab'bozzo** *sm* sketch, outline; (*DIR*) draft.

abbracci'are |abbrat'tʃare| *vt* to embrace; (*persona*) to hug, embrace; (*professione*) to take up; (*contenere*) to include; ~rsi *vr* to hug *o* embrace (one another); **ab'braccio** *sm* hug, embrace.

abbreviazi'one |abbrevjat'tsjone| *sf* abbreviation.

abbron'zante |abbron'dzante| *ag* tanning, sun *cpd*.

abbron'zare |abbron'dzare| *vt* (*pelle*) to tan; (*metalli*) to bronze; ~rsi *vr* to tan, get a tan; **abbronza'tura** *sf* tan, suntan.

abbrusto'lire *vt* (*pane*) to toast; (*caffè*) to roast.

abbru'tire *vt* to exhaust; to degrade.

abbu'ono *sm* (*COMM*) allowance, discount; (*SPORT*) handicap.

abdi'care *vi* to abdicate; ~ a to give up, renounce.

aberrazi'one |aberrat'tsjone| *sf* aberration.

a'bete *sm* fir (tree); ~ rosso spruce.

abi'etto, a *ag* despicable, abject.

'abile *ag* (*idoneo*): ~ (a qc/a fare qc) fit (for sth/to do sth); (*capace*) able; (*astuto*) clever, (*accorto*) skilful; ~ al servizio militare fit for military service; **abilità** *sf inv* ability; cleverness; skill.

abili'tato, a *ag* qualified; (*TEL*) which has an outside line; **abilitazi'one** *sf* qualification.

a'bisso *sm* abyss, gulf.

abi'tacolo *sm* (*AER*) cockpit; (*AUT*) inside; (: *di camion*) cab.

abi'tante *sm/f* inhabitant.

abi'tare *vt* to live in, dwell in // *vi*: ~ in campagna/a Roma to live in the country/in Rome; **abi'tato, a** *ag* inhabited; lived in // *sm* (*anche*: centro abitato) built-up area; **abitazi'one** *sf* residence; house.

'abito *sm* dress *q*; (*da uomo*) suit; (*da donna*) dress; (*abitudine*, *disposizione*, *REL*) habit; ~i *smpl* clothes; in ~ da sera in evening dress.

abitu'ale *ag* usual, habitual; (*cliente*) regular.

abitu'are *vt*: ~ qn a to get sb used *o* accustomed to; ~rsi a to get used to, accustom o.s. to.

abitudi'nario, a *ag* of fixed habits //

sm/f regular customer.

abi'tudine *sf* habit; aver l'~ di fare qc to be in the habit of doing sth; d'~ usually; per ~ from *o* out of habit.

abo'lire *vt* to abolish; (*DIR*) to repeal.

abomi'nevole *ag* abominable.

abo'rigeno |abo'ridʒeno| *sm* aborigine.

abor'rire *vt* to abhor, detest.

abor'tire *vi* (*MED*: *accidentalmente*) to miscarry, have a miscarriage; (: *deliberatamente*) to have an abortion; (*fig*) to miscarry, fail; **a'borto** *sm* miscarriage; abortion; (*fig*) freak.

abrasi'one *sf* abrasion; **abra'sivo, a** *ag*, *sm* abrasive.

abro'gare *vt* to repeal, abrogate.

A'bruzzo *sm*: l'~, gli ~i the Abruzzi.

'abside *sf* apse.

a'bulico, a, ci, che *ag* lacking in will power.

abu'sare *vi*: ~ di to abuse, misuse; (*alcool*) to take to excess; (*approfittare*, *violare*) to take advantage of; **a'buso** *sm* abuse, misuse; excessive use.

a.C. *ad abbr* (= *avanti Cristo*) B.C.

'acca *sf* letter H; non capire un'~ not to understand a thing.

acca'demia *sf* (*società*) learned society; (*scuola*: *d'arte*, *militare*) academy; **acca'demico, a, ci, che** *ag* academic // *sm* academician.

acca'dere *vb impers* to happen, occur; **acca'duto** *sm*: raccontare l'accaduto to describe what has happened.

accalappi'are *vt* to catch; (*fig*) to trick, dupe.

accal'care *vt* to crowd, throng.

accal'darsi *vr* to grow hot.

accalo'rarsi *vr* (*fig*) to get excited.

accampa'mento *sm* camp.

accam'pare *vt* to encamp; (*fig*) to put forward, advance; ~rsi *vr* to camp.

accani'mento *sm* fury; (*tenacia*) tenacity, perseverance.

acca'nirsi *vr* (*infierire*) to rage; (*ostinarsi*) to persist; **acca'nito, a** *ag* (*odio*, *gelosia*) fierce, bitter; (*lavoratore*) assiduous, dogged; (*fumatore*) inveterate.

ac'canto *av* near, nearby; ~ a *prep* near, beside, close to.

accanto'nare *vt* (*problema*) to shelve; (*somma*) to set aside.

accapar'rare *vt* (*COMM*) to corner, buy up; (*versare una caparra*) to pay a deposit on; ~rsi qc (*fig*: simpatia, voti) to secure sth (for o.s.).

accapigli'arsi |akkapiʎ'ʎarsi| *vr* to come to blows; (*fig*) to quarrel.

accappa'toio *sm* bathrobe.

accappo'nare *vi*: far ~ la pelle a qn (*fig*) to bring sb out in goosepimples.

accarez'zare |akkaret'tsare| *vt* to caress, stroke, fondle; (*fig*) to toy with.

acca'sarsi *vr* to set up house; to get

married.

accasci'arsi |akkaʃ'ʃarsi| *vr* to collapse; *(fig)* to lose heart.

accat'tone, a *sm/f* beggar.

accaval'lare *vt (gambe)* to cross; **~rsi** *vr (sovrapporsi)* to overlap; *(addensarsi)* to gather.

acce'care |attʃe'kare| *vt* to blind // *vi* to go blind.

ac'cedere |at'tʃedere| *vi:* ~ a to enter; *(richiesta)* to grant, accede to.

accele'rare |attʃele'rare| *vt* to speed up // *vt (AUT)* to accelerate; ~ il passo to quicken one's pace; **accele'rato** *sm (FERR)* slow train; **accelera'tore** *sm (AUT)* accelerator; **accelerazi'one** *sf* acceleration.

ac'cendere |at'tʃendere| *vt (fuoco, sigaretta)* to light; *(luce, televisione)* to put o switch o turn on; *(COMM: conto)* to open; *(fig: suscitare)* to inflame, stir up; **~rsi** *vr (luce)* to come o go on; *(legna)* to catch fire, ignite; **accen'dino** *sm,* **accendi'sigaro** *sm* (cigarette) lighter.

accen'nare |attʃen'nare| *vt* to indicate, point out; *(MUS)* to pick out the notes of; to hum // *vi:* ~ a *(fig: alludere a)* to hint at; *(: far atto di)* to make as if; ~ un saluto *(con la mano)* to make as if to wave; *(col capo)* to half nod; **accenna a piovere** it looks as if it's going to rain.

ac'cenno |at'tʃenno| *sm (cenno)* sign; nod; *(allusione)* hint.

accensi'one |attʃen'sjone| *sf (vedi accendere)* lighting; switching on; opening; *(AUT)* ignition.

accen'tare |attʃen'tare| *vt (parlando)* to stress; *(scrivendo)* to accent.

ac'cento |at'tʃento| *sm* accent; *(FONETICA, fig)* stress; *(inflessione)* tone (of voice).

accen'trare |attʃen'trare| *vt* to centralize.

accentu'are |attʃentu'are| *vt* to stress, emphasize; **~rsi** *vr* to become more noticeable.

accerchi'are |attʃer'kjare| *vt* to surround, encircle.

accerta'mento |attʃerta'mento| *sm* check; assessment.

accer'tare |attʃer'tare| *vt* to ascertain; *(verificare)* to check; *(reddito)* to assess; **~rsi** *vr:* **~rsi (di)** to make sure (of).

ac'ceso, a |at'tʃeso| *pp di* **accendere** // *ag* lit; on; open; *(colore)* bright.

acces'sibile |attʃes'sibile| *ag (luogo)* accessible; *(persona)* approachable; *(prezzo)* reasonable; *(idea):* ~ a qn within the reach of sb.

ac'cesso |at'tʃesso| *sm (anche INFORM)* access; *(MED)* attack, fit; *(impulso violento)* fit, outburst.

acces'sorio, a |attʃes'sɔrjo| *ag* secondary, of secondary importance; **~i** *smpl*

accessories.

ac'cetta |at'tʃetta| *sf* hatchet.

accet'tabile |attʃet'tabile| *ag* acceptable.

accet'tare |attʃet'tare| *vt* to accept; ~ di fare qc to agree to do sth; **accettazi'one** *sf* acceptance; *(locale di servizio pubblico)* reception; **accettazione bagagli** *(AER)* check-in (desk).

ac'cetto, a |at'tʃetto| *ag:* (ben) ~ welcome; *(persona)* well-liked.

accezi'one |attʃet'tsjone| *sf* meaning.

acchiap'pare |akkjap'pare| *vt* to catch.

acci'acco, chi |at'tʃakko| *sm* ailment.

acciaie'ria |attʃaje'ria| *sf* steelworks *sg.*

acci'aio |at'tʃajo| *sm* steel.

acciden'tale |attʃiden'tale| *ag* accidental.

acciden'tato, a |attʃiden'tato| *ag (terreno etc)* uneven.

acci'dente |attʃi'dɛnte| *sm (caso imprevisto)* accident; *(disgrazia)* mishap; non si capisce un ~ it's as clear as mud; ~i! *(fam: per rabbia)* damn (it)!; *(: per meraviglia)* good heavens!

accigli'ato, a |attʃiʎ'ʎato| *ag* frowning.

ac'cingersi |at'tʃindʒersi| *vr:* ~ a fare to be about to do.

acciuf'fare |attʃuf'fare| *vt* to seize, catch.

acci'uga, ghe |at'tʃuga| *sf* anchovy.

accla'mare *vt (applaudire)* to applaud; *(eleggere)* to acclaim; **acclamazi'one** *sf* applause; acclamation.

acclima'tare *vt* to acclimatize; **~rsi** *vr* to become acclimatized.

ac'cludere *vt* to enclose; **ac'cluso, a** *pp di* **accludere** // *ag* enclosed.

accocco'larsi *vr* to crouch.

accogli'ente |akkoʎ'ʎɛnte| *ag* welcoming, friendly; **accogli'enza** *sf* reception; welcome.

ac'cogliere |ak'koʎʎere| *vt (ricevere)* to receive; *(dare il benvenuto)* to welcome; *(approvare)* to agree to, accept; *(con tenere)* to hold, accommodate.

accol'lato, a *ag (vestito)* high-necked.

accoltel'lare *vt* to knife, stab.

ac'colto, a *pp di* **accogliere.**

accoman'dita *sf (DIR)* limited partnership.

accomia'tare *vt* to dismiss; **~rsi** *vr:* **~rsi (da)** to take one's leave (of).

accomoda'mento *sm* agreement, settlement.

accomo'dante *ag* accommodating.

accomo'dare *vt (aggiustare)* to repair, mend; *(riordinare)* to tidy; *(conciliare)* to settle; **~rsi** *vr (sedersi)* to sit down; s'accomodi! *(venga avanti)* come in!; *(si sieda)* take a seat!

accompagna'mento |akkompaɲɲa'mento| *sm (MUS)* accompaniment.

accompa'gnare |akkompaɲ'ɲare| *vt* to accompany, come o go with; *(MUS)* to accompany; *(unire)* to couple; ~ la porta to close the door gently.

accomu'nare *vt* to pool, share; (*avvicinare*) to unite.

acconcia'tura [akkontʃa'tura] *sf* hairstyle.

accondi'scendere [akkondiʃ'ʃɛndɛrɛ] *vi*: ~ a to agree o consent to; **accondi'sceso, a** *pp di* **accondiscendere**.

acconsen'tire *vi*: ~ (a) to agree o consent (to).

acconten'tare *vt* to satisfy; ~rsi di to be satisfied with, content o.s. with.

ac'conto *sm* part payment; **pagare una somma in** ~ to pay a sum of money as a deposit.

accoppia'mento *sm* coupling, pairing off; mating; (*TECN*) coupling.

accoppi'are *vt* to couple, pair off; (*BIOL*) to mate; ~rsi *vr* to pair off; to mate.

accorci'are [akkor'tʃare] *vt* to shorten; ~rsi *vr* to become shorter.

accor'dare *vt* to reconcile; (*colori*) to match; (*MUS*) to tune; (*LING*): ~ qc con qc to make sth agree with sth; (*DIR*) to grant; ~rsi *vr* to agree, come to an agreement; (*colori*) to match.

ac'cordo *sm* agreement; (*armonia*) harmony; (*MUS*) chord; **essere d'~** to agree; **andare d'~** to get on well together; **d'~!** all right!, agreed!

ac'corgersi [ak'kordʒersi] *vr*: ~ **di** to notice; (*fig*) to realize; **accorgi'mento** *sm* shrewdness *q*; (*espediente*) trick, device.

ac'correre *vi* to run up.

ac'corto, a *pp di* **accorgersi** // *ag* shrewd; **stare** ~ to be on one's guard.

accos'tare *vt* (*avvicinare*): ~ qc a to bring sth near to, put sth near to; (*avvicinarsi a*) to approach; (*socchiudere*: *imposte*) to half-close; (: *porta*) to leave ajar // *vi* (*NAUT*) to come alongside; ~rsi a to draw near, approach; (*fig*) to support.

accovacci'arsi [akkovat'tʃarsi] *vr* to crouch.

accoz'zaglia [akkot'tsaʎʎa] *sf* (*peg*: *di idee, oggetti*) jumble, hotchpotch; (: *di persone*) odd assortment.

accredi'tare *vt* (*notizia*) to confirm the truth of; (*COMM*) to credit; (*diplomatico*) to accredit; ~rsi *vr* (*fig*) to gain credit.

ac'crescere [ak'kreʃʃere] *vt* to increase; ~rsi *vr* to increase, grow; **accresci'tivo, a** *ag, sm* (*LING*) augmentative; **accresci'uto, a** *pp di* **accrescere**.

accucci'arsi [akkut'tʃarsi] *vr* (*cane*) to lie down.

accu'dire *vt* (*anche*: *vi*: ~ a) to attend to.

accumu'lare *vt* to accumulate.

accura'tezza [akkura'tettsa] *sf* care; accuracy.

accu'rato, a *ag* (*diligente*) careful; (*preciso*) accurate.

ac'cusa *sf* accusation; (*DIR*) charge; **la pubblica** ~ the prosecution.

accu'sare *vt*: ~ qn di qc to accuse sb of sth; (*DIR*) to charge sb with sth; ~ **ricevuta di** (*COMM*) to acknowledge receipt of.

accu'sato, a *sm/f* accused; defendant.

accusa'tore, 'trice *sm/f* accuser // *sm* (*DIR*) prosecutor.

a'cerbo, a [a'tʃerbo] *ag* bitter; (*frutta*) sour, unripe; (*persona*) immature.

'acero ['atʃero] *sm* maple.

a'cerrimo, a [a'tʃerrimo] *ag* very fierce.

a'ceto [a'tʃeto] *sm* vinegar.

ace'tone [atʃe'tone] *sm* nail varnish remover.

A.C.I. ['atʃi] *sigla m* (= Automobile Club d'Italia) ≈ A.A.

'acido, a ['atʃido] *ag* (*sapore*) acid, sour; (*CHIM*) acid // *sm* (*CHIM*) acid.

'acino ['atʃino] *sm* berry; ~ **d'uva** grape.

'acne *sf* acne.

'acqua *sf* water; (*pioggia*) rain; ~e *sfpl* waters; **fare** ~ (*NAUT*) to leak, take in water; ~ **in bocca!** mum's the word!; ~ **corrente** running water; ~ **dolce** fresh water; ~ **minerale** mineral water; ~ **potabile** drinking water; ~ **salata** salt water; ~ **tonica** tonic water.

acqua'forte, pl acque'forti *sf* etching.

a'cquaio *sm* sink.

acqua'ragia [akkwa'radʒa] *sf* turpentine.

a'cquario *sm* aquarium; (*dello zodiaco*): A~ Aquarius.

acqua'santa *sf* holy water.

ac'quatico, a, ci, che *ag* aquatic; (*sport, sci*) water *cpd*.

acqua'vite *sf* brandy.

acquaz'zone [akkwat'tsone] *sm* cloudburst, heavy shower.

acque'dotto *sm* aqueduct; waterworks *pl*, water system.

'acqueo, a *ag*: **vapore** ~ water vapour.

acque'rello *sm* watercolour.

acquie'tare *vt* to appease; (*dolore*) to ease; ~rsi *vr* to calm down.

acqui'rente *sm/f* purchaser, buyer.

acqui'sire *vt* to acquire.

acquis'tare *vt* to purchase, buy; (*fig*) to gain; **a'cquisto** *sm* purchase; **fare acquisti** to go shopping.

acqui'trino *sm* bog, marsh.

acquo'lina *sf*: **far venire l'~ in bocca a qn** to make sb's mouth water.

a'cquoso, a *ag* watery.

'acre *ag* acrid, pungent; (*fig*) harsh, biting.

a'crobata, i, e *sm/f* acrobat.

acu'ire *vt* to sharpen.

a'culeo *sm* (*ZOOL*) sting; (*BOT*) prickle.

a'cume *sm* acumen, perspicacity.

a'custica *sf* (*scienza*) acoustics *sg*; (*di una sala*) acoustics *pl*.

a'cuto, a *ag* (*appuntito*) sharp, pointed; (*suono, voce*) shrill, piercing; (*MAT, LING, MED*) acute; (*MUS*) high-pitched; (*fig: dolore, desiderio*) intense; (*: perspicace*) acute, keen.

ad *prep* (*dav V*) = **a**.

adagi'are |ada'dʒarɛ| *vt* to lay *o* set down carefully; **~rsi** *vr* to lie down, stretch out.

a'dagio |a'dadʒol| *av* slowly // *sm* (*MUS*) adagio; (*proverbio*) adage, saying.

adatta'mento *sm* adaptation.

adat'tare *vt* to adapt, (*sistemare*) to fit; **~rsi** (a) (*ambiente, tempi*) to adapt (to); (*essere adatto*) to be suitable (for).

a'datto, a *ag*: ~ (a) suitable (for), right (for).

addebi'tare *vt*: ~ qc a qn to debit sb with sth; (*fig: incolpare*) to blame sb for sth.

ad'debito *sm* (*COMM*) debit.

adden'sare *vt* to thicken; **~rsi** *vr* to thicken; (*nuvole*) to gather.

adden'tare *vt* to bite into.

adden'trarsi *vr*: ~ in to penetrate, go into.

ad'dentro *av* (*fig*): essere molto ~ in qc to be well-versed in sth.

addestra'mento *sm* training.

addes'trare *vt*, **~rsi** *vr* to train; **~rsi** in qc to practise (*Brit*) *o* practice (*US*) sth.

ad'detto, a *ag*: ~ a (*persona*) assigned to; (*oggetto*) intended for // *sm* employee: (*funzionario*) attaché; ~ **commerciale/stampa** commercial/press attaché; **gli ~i ai lavori** authorized personnel; (*fig*) those in the know.

addi *av* (*AMM*): ~ 3 luglio 1978 on the 3rd of July 1978 (*Brit*), on July 3rd 1978 (*US*).

addi'accio |ad'djattʃo| *sm* (*MIL*) bivouac; **dormire all'~** to sleep in the open.

addi'etro *av* (*indietro*) behind; (*nel passato, prima*) before, ago.

ad'dio *sm, escl* goodbye, farewell.

addirit'tura *av* (*veramente*) really, absolutely; (*perfino*) even; (*direttamente*) directly, right away.

ad'dirsi *vr*: ~ a to suit, be suitable for.

addi'tare *vt* to point out; (*fig*) to expose.

addi'tivo *sm* additive.

addizio'nare |addittsjo'narɛ| *vt* (*MAT*) to add (up); **addizi'one** *sf* addition.

addob'bare *vt* to decorate; **ad'dobbo** *sm* decoration.

addol'cire |addol'tʃirɛ| *vt* (*caffè etc*) to sweeten; (*acqua, fig: carattere*) to soften; **~rsi** *vr* (*fig*) to mellow, soften.

addolo'rare *vt* to pain, grieve; **~rsi** (**per**) to be distressed (by).

ad'dome *sm* abdomen.

addomesti'care *vt* to tame.

addormen'tare *vt* to put to sleep; **~rsi** *vr* to fall asleep, go to sleep.

addos'sare *vt* (*appoggiare*): ~ qc a qc to lean sth against sth; (*fig*): ~ **la colpa a qn** to lay the blame on sb; **~rsi qc** (*responsabilità etc*) to shoulder sth.

ad'dosso *av* (*sulla persona*) on; **mettersi ~ il cappotto** to put one's coat on; **non ho soldi ~** I don't have any money on me; ~ **a** *prep* (*sopra*) on; (*molto vicino*) right next to; **stare ~ a qn** (*fig*) to breathe down sb's neck; **dare ~ a qn** (*fig*) to attack sb.

ad'durre *vt* (*DIR*) to produce; (*citare*) to cite.

adegu'are *vt*: ~ qc a to adjust *o* relate sth to; **~rsi** *vr* to adapt; **adegu'ato, a** *ag* adequate; (*conveniente*) suitable; (*equo*) fair.

a'dempiere, adem'pire *vt* to fulfil, carry out.

ade'rente *ag* adhesive; (*vestito*) close-fitting // *sm/f* follower; **ade'renza** *sf* adhesion; **aderenze** *sfpl* (*fig*) connections, contacts.

ade'rire *vi* (*stare attaccato*) to adhere, stick; ~ **a** to adhere to, stick to; (*fig: società, partito*) to join; (*: opinione*) to support; (*richiesta*) to agree to.

ades'care *vt* to lure, entice.

adesi'one *sf* adhesion; (*fig*) agreement, acceptance; **ade'sivo, a** *ag, sm* adhesive.

a'desso *av* (*ora*) now; (*or ora, poco fa*) just now; (*tra poco*) any moment now.

adia'cente |adja'tʃɛntɛ| *ag* adjacent.

adi'bire *vt* (*usare*): ~ qc a to turn sth into.

adi'rarsi *vr*: ~ (**con** *o* **contro qn per qc**) to get angry (with sb over sth).

a'dire *vt* (*DIR*): ~ **le vie legali** to take legal proceedings.

'adito *sm*: **dare ~ a** to give rise to.

adocchi'are |adok'kjarɛ| *vt* (*scorgere*) to catch sight of; (*occhieggiare*) to eye.

adole'scente |adoleʃ'ʃɛntɛ| *ag, sm/f* adolescent; **adole'scenza** *sf* adolescence.

adope'rare *vt* to use; **~rsi** *vr* to strive; **~rsi per qn/qc** to do one's best for sb/sth.

ado'rare *vt* to adore; (*REL*) to adore, worship.

adot'tare *vt* to adopt; (*decisione, provvedimenti*) to pass; **adot'tivo, a** *ag* (*genitori*) adoptive; (*figlio, patria*) adopted; **adozi'one** *sf* adoption.

adri'atico, a, ci, che *ag* Adriatic // *sm*: **l'A~, il mare A~** the Adriatic, the Adriatic Sea.

adu'lare *vt* to adulate, flatter.

adulte'rare *vt* to adulterate.

adul'terio *sm* adultery.

a'dulto, a *ag* adult; (*fig*) mature // *sm* adult, grown-up.

adu'nanza |adu'nantsa| *sf* assembly, meeting.

adu'nare *vt*, **~rsi** *vr* to assemble,

gather; **adu'nata** *sf* (*MIL*) parade, muster.

a'dunco, a, chi, che *ag* hooked.

a'ereo, a *ag* air *cpd*; (*radice*) aerial // *sm* aerial; (*aeroplano*) plane; ~ **a reazione** jet (plane); **ae'robica** *sf* aerobics *sg*; **aerodi'namico, a, ci, che** *ag* aerodynamic; (*affusolato*) streamlined // *sf* aerodynamics *sg*; **aero'nautica** *sf* (*scienza*) aeronautics *sg*; aeronautica militare air force; **aero'plano** *sm* (aero)plane (*Brit*), (air)plane (*US*); **aero'porto** *sm* airport; **aero'sol** *sm inv* aerosol.

'afa *sf* sultriness.

af'fabile *ag* affable.

affaccen'darsi [affattʃen'darsi] *vr*: ~ **intorno a qc** to busy o.s. with sth.

affacci'arsi [affat'tʃarsi] *vr*: ~ **(a)** to appear (at).

affa'mato, a *ag* starving; (*fig*): ~ **(di)** eager (for).

affan'nare *vt* to leave breathless; (*fig*) to worry; ~**rsi** *vr*: ~**rsi per qn/qc** to worry about sb/sth; **af'fanno** *sm* breathlessness; (*fig*) anxiety, worry; **affan'noso, a** *ag* (*respiro*) difficult; (*fig*) troubled, anxious.

af'fare *sm* (*faccenda*) matter, affair; (*COMM*) piece of business, (business) deal; (*occasione*) bargain; (*DIR*) case; (*fam: cosa*) thing; **~i** *smpl* (*COMM*) business *sg*; **ministro degli A~i esteri** Foreign Secretary (*Brit*), Secretary of State (*US*); **affa'rista, i** *sm* profiteer, unscrupulous businessman.

affasci'nante [affaʃʃi'nante] *ag* fascinating.

affasci'nare [affaʃʃi'nare] *vt* to bewitch; (*fig*) to charm, fascinate.

affati'care *vt* to tire; ~**rsi** *vr* (*durar fatica*) to tire o.s. out.

af'fatto *av* completely; **non ... ~** not ... at all; **niente ~** not at all.

affer'mare *vt* (*dichiarare*) to maintain, affirm; ~**rsi** *vr* to assert o.s., make one's name known; **affermazi'one** *sf* affirmation, assertion; (*successo*) achievement.

affer'rare *vt* to seize, grasp; (*fig: idea*) to grasp; ~**rsi** *vr*: ~**rsi a** to cling to.

affet'tare *vt* (*tagliare a fette*) to slice; (*ostentare*) to affect; **affet'tato, a** *ag* sliced; affected // *sm* sliced cold meat.

affet'tivo, a *ag* emotional, affective.

af'fetto *sm* affection; **affettu'oso, a** *ag* affectionate.

affezio'narsi [affettsjo'narsi] *vr*: ~ **a** to grow fond of.

affezi'one [affet'tsjone] *sf* (*affetto*) affection; (*MED*) ailment, disorder.

affian'care *vt* to place side by side; (*MIL*) to flank; (*fig*) to support; ~ **qc a qc** to place sth next to *o* beside sth; ~**rsi a qn** to stand beside sb.

affia'tarsi *vr* to get on well together.

affibbi'are *vt* (*fig: dare*) to give.

affida'mento *sm* (*DIR: di bambino*) custody; (*fiducia*): **fare ~ su qn** to rely on sb; **non dà nessun ~** he's not to be trusted.

affi'dare *vt*: ~ **qc o qn a qn** to entrust sth *o* sb to sb; ~**rsi** *vr*: ~**rsi a** to place one's trust in.

affievo'lirsi *vr* to grow weak.

af'figgere [af'fidᴣere] *vt* to stick up, post up.

affi'lare *vt* to sharpen.

affili'are *vt* to affiliate; ~**rsi** *vr*: ~**rsi a** to become affiliated to.

affi'nare *vt* to sharpen.

affinché [affin'ke] *cong* in order that, so that.

af'fine *ag* similar; **affinità** *sf inv* affinity.

affio'rare *vi* to emerge.

affissi'one *sf* billposting.

af'fisso, a *pp di* **affiggere** // *sm* bill, poster; (*LING*) affix.

affit'tare *vt* (*dare in affitto*) to let, rent (out); (*prendere in affitto*) to rent; **af'fitto** *sm* rent; (*contratto*) lease.

af'fliggere [af'flidᴣere] *vt* to torment; ~**rsi** *vr* to grieve; **af'flitto, a** *pp di* **affliggere**; **afflizi'one** *sf* distress, torment.

afflosci'arsi [affloʃ'farsi] *vr* to go limp; (*frutta*) to go soft.

afflu'ente *sm* tributary; **afflu'enza** *sf* flow; (*di persone*) crowd.

afflu'ire *vi* to flow; (*fig: merci, persone*) to pour in; **af'flusso** *sm* influx.

affo'gare *vt, vi* to drown; ~**rsi** *vr* to drown; (*deliberatamente*) to drown o.s.

affol'lare *vt*, ~**rsi** *vr* to crowd; **affol'lato, a** *ag* crowded.

affon'dare *vt* to sink.

affran'care *vt* to free, liberate; (*AMM*) to redeem; (*lettera*) to stamp; (: *meccanicamente*) to frank (*Brit*), meter (*US*); ~**rsi** *vr* to free o.s.; **affranca'tura** *sf* (*di francobollo*) stamping; franking (*Brit*), metering (*US*); (*tassa di spedizione*) postage.

af'franto, a *ag* (*esausto*) worn out; (*abbattuto*) overcome.

af'fresco, schi *sm* fresco.

affret'tare *vt* to quicken, speed up; ~**rsi** *vr* to hurry; ~**rsi a fare qc** to hurry *o* hasten to do sth.

affron'tare *vt* (*pericolo etc*) to face; (*assalire: nemico*) to confront; ~**rsi** *vr* (*reciproco*) to come to blows.

af'fronto *sm* affront, insult.

affumi'care *vt* to fill with smoke; to blacken with smoke; (*alimenti*) to smoke.

affuso'lato, a *ag* tapering.

a'foso, a *ag* sultry, close.

'Africa *sf*: l'~ Africa; **afri'cano, a** *ag*, *sm/f* African.

afrodi'siaco, a, ci, che *ag*, *sm* aphrodisiac.

a'genda [a'dʒɛnda] *sf* diary.

a'gente [a'dʒɛnte] *sm* agent; ~ **di cambio** stockbroker; ~ **di polizia** police officer; **agen'zia** *sf* agency; (*succursale*) branch; **agenzia di collocamento** employment agency; **agenzia immobiliare** estate agent's (office) (*Brit*), real estate office (*US*); **agenzia pubblicitaria/viaggi** advertising/ travel agency.

agevo'lare [adʒevo'lare] *vt* to facilitate, make easy.

a'gevole [a'dʒevole] *ag* easy; (*strada*) smooth.

agganci'are [aggan'tʃare] *vt* to hook up; (*FERR*) to couple.

ag'geggio [ad'dʒeddʒo] *sm* gadget, contraption.

agget'tivo [addʒet'tivo] *sm* adjective.

agghiacci'ante [aggjat'tʃante] *ag* (*fig*) chilling.

agghin'darsi [aggin'darsi] *vr* to deck o.s. out.

aggior'nare [addʒor'nare] *vt* (*opera*, *manuale*) to bring up-to-date; (*seduta etc*) to postpone; ~**rsi** *vr* to bring (*o* keep) o.s. up-to-date; **aggior'nato, a** *ag* up-to-date.

aggi'rare [addʒi'rare] *vt* to go round; (*fig*: *ingannare*) to trick; ~**rsi** *vr* to wander about; **il prezzo s'aggira sul milione** the price is around the million mark.

aggiudi'care [addʒudi'kare] *vt* to award; (*all'asta*) to knock down; ~**rsi qc** to win sth.

aggi'ungere [ad'dʒundʒere] *vt* to add; **aggi'unto, a** *pp di* **aggiungere** // *ag* assistant *cpd* // *sm* assistant // *sf* addition; **sindaco aggiunto** deputy mayor.

aggius'tare [addʒus'tare] *vt* (*accomodare*) to mend, repair; (*riassettare*) to adjust; (*fig*: *lite*) to settle; ~**rsi** *vr* (*arrangiarsi*) to make do; (*con senso reciproco*) to come to an agreement.

agglome'rato *sm* (*di rocce*) conglomerate; (*di legno*) chipboard; ~ **urbano** built-up area.

aggrap'parsi *vr*: ~ **a** to cling to.

aggra'vare *vt* (*aumentare*) to increase; (*appesantire*: *anche fig*) to weigh down, make heavy; (*fig*: *pena*) to make worse; ~**rsi** *vr* (*fig*) to worsen, become worse.

aggrazi'ato, a [aggrat'tsjato] *ag* graceful.

aggre'dire *vt* to attack, assault.

aggre'gare *vt*: ~ **qn a qc** to admit sb to sth; ~**rsi** *vr* to join; ~**rsi a** to join, become a member of; **aggre'gato, a** *ag* associated // *sm* aggregate; **aggregato urbano** built-up area.

aggressi'one *sf* aggression; (*atto*)

attack, assault.

aggres'sivo, a *ag* aggressive.

aggrot'tare *vt*: ~ **le sopracciglia** to frown.

aggrovigli'are [aggroviʎ'ʎare] *vt* to tangle; ~**rsi** *vr* (*fig*) to become complicated.

agguan'tare *vt* to catch, seize.

aggu'ato *sm* trap; (*imboscata*) ambush; **tendere un** ~ **a qn** to set a trap for sb.

agguer'rito, a *ag* fierce.

agi'ato, a [a'dʒato] *ag* (*vita*) easy; (*persona*) well off, well-to-do.

'agile ['adʒile] *ag* agile, nimble; **agilità** *sf* agility, nimbleness.

'agio ['adʒo] *sm* ease, comfort; ~**i** *smpl* comforts; **mettersi a proprio** ~ to make o.s. at home *o* comfortable.

a'gire [a'dʒire] *vi* to act; (*esercitare un'azione*) to take effect; (*TECN*) to work, function; ~ **contro qn** (*DIR*) to take action against sb.

agi'tare [adʒi'tare] *vt* (*bottiglia*) to shake; (*mano*, *fazzoletto*) to wave; (*fig*: *turbare*) to disturb; (*: incitare*) to stir (up); (*: dibattere*) to discuss; ~**rsi** *vr* (*mare*) to be rough; (*malato*, *dormitore*) to toss and turn; (*bambino*) to fidget; (*emozionarsi*) to get upset; (*POL*) to agitate; **agi'tato, a** *ag* rough; restless; fidgety; upset, perturbed; **agitazi'one** *sf* agitation; (*POL*) unrest, agitation; **mettere in agitazione qn** to upset *o* distress sb.

'agli ['aʎʎi] *prep* + *det vedi* **a**.

'aglio ['aʎʎo] *sm* garlic.

a'gnello [aɲ'ɲɛllo] *sm* lamb.

'ago, *pl* **aghi** *sm* needle.

ago'nia *sf* agony.

ago'nistico, a, ci, che *ag* athletic; (*fig*) competitive.

agoniz'zare [agonid'dzare] *vi* to be dying.

agopun'tura *sf* acupuncture.

a'gosto *sm* August.

a'grario, a *ag* agrarian, agricultural; (*riforma*) land *cpd* // *sf* agriculture.

a'gricolo, a *ag* agricultural, farm *cpd*; **agricol'tore** *sm* farmer; **agricol'tura** *sf* agriculture, farming.

agri'foglio [agri'fɔʎʎo] *sm* holly.

agrimen'sore *sm* land surveyor.

agritu'rismo *sm* farm holidays *pl*.

'agro, a *ag* sour, sharp; ~**dolce** *ag* bittersweet; (*salsa*) sweet and sour.

a'grume *sm* (*spesso al pl*: *pianta*) citrus; (*: frutto*) citrus fruit.

aguz'zare [agut'tsare] *vt* to sharpen; ~ **gli orecchi** to prick up one's ears.

a'guzzo, a [a'guttso] *ag* sharp.

'ai *prep* + *det vedi* **a**.

'Aia *sf*: **l'**~ the Hague.

'aia *sf* threshing-floor.

ai'rone *sm* heron.

aiu'ola *sf* flower bed.

aiu'tante *sm/f* assistant // *sm* (MIL) adjutant; (NAUT) master-at-arms; ~ **di campo** aide-de-camp.

aiu'tare *vt* to help; ~ **qn (a fare)** to help sb (to do).

ai'uto *sm* help, assistance, aid; (*aiutante*) assistant; **venire in** ~ **di qn** to come to sb's aid; ~ **chirurgo** assistant surgeon.

aiz'zare [ait'tsarε] *vt* to incite; ~ **i cani contro qn** to set the dogs on sb.

al *prep* + *det vedi* **a.**

'ala, *pl* **'ali** *sf* wing; **fare** ~ to fall back, make way; ~ **destra/sinistra** (SPORT) right/left wing.

'alacre *ag* quick, brisk.

a'lano *sm* Great Dane.

a'lare *ag* wing *cpd*.

'alba *sf* dawn.

Alba'nia *sf*: **l'**~ Albania.

'albatro *sm* albatross.

albeggi'are [albεd'dʒarε] *vi*, *vb impers* to dawn.

albera'tura *sf* (NAUT) masts *pl*.

alberghi'ero, a [albεr'gjεro] *ag* hotel *cpd*.

al'bergo, ghi *sm* hotel; ~ **della gioventù** youth hostel.

'albero *sm* tree; (NAUT) mast; (TECN) shaft; ~ **genealogico** family tree; ~ **a gomiti** crankshaft; ~ **di Natale** Christmas tree; ~ **maestro** mainmast; ~ **di trasmissione** transmission shaft.

albi'cocca, che *sf* apricot; **albi'cocco, chi** *sm* apricot tree.

'albo *sm* (*registro*) register, roll; (AMM) notice board.

'album *sm* album; ~ **da disegno** sketch book.

al'bume *sm* albumen.

'alce [altʃε] *sm* elk.

al'colico, a, ci, che *ag* alcoholic // *sm* alcoholic drink.

alcoliz'zato, a [alcolid'dzato] *sm/f* alcoholic.

'alcool *sm* alcohol; **alco'olico** *etc vedi* **alcolico** *etc*.

al'cuno, a *det* (*dav sm*: **alcun** +C, V, **alcuno** + *s impura, gn, pn, ps, x, z; dav sf*: **alcuna** +C, **alcun'** +V) (*nessuno*): **non** ... ~ no, not any; ~**i(e)** *det pl*, *pronome pl* some, a few; **non c'è** ~**a fretta** there's no hurry, there isn't any hurry; **senza alcun riguardo** without any consideration.

aldilà *sm*: **l'**~ the after-life.

a'letta *sf* (TECN) fin; tab.

alfa'beto *sm* alphabet.

alfi'ere *sm* standard-bearer; (MIL) ensign; (SCACCHI) bishop.

al'fine *av* finally, in the end.

'alga, ghe *sf* seaweed *q*, alga.

'algebra ['aldʒebra] *sf* algebra.

Alge'ria [aldʒε'ria] *sf*: **l'**~ Algeria.

ali'ante *sm* (AER) glider.

'alibi *sm inv* alibi.

a'lice [a'litʃε] *sf* anchovy.

alie'nare *vt* (DIR) to alienate, transfer; (*rendere ostile*) to alienate; ~**rsi qn** to alienate sb; **alie'nato, a** *ag* alienated; transferred; (*fuor di senno*) insane // *sm* lunatic, insane person; **alienazi'one** *sf* alienation; transfer; insanity.

ali'eno, a *ag* (*avverso*): ~ **(da)** opposed (to), averse (to) // *sm/f* alien.

alimen'tare *vt* to feed; (TECN) to feed; to supply; (*fig*) to sustain // *ag* food *cpd*; ~**i** *smpl* foodstuffs; (*anche*: **negozio di** ~**i**) grocer's shop; **alimentazi'one** *sf* feeding; supplying; sustaining; (*gli alimenti*) diet.

ali'mento *sm* food; ~**i** *smpl* food *sg*; (DIR) alimony.

a'liquota *sf* share; (*d'imposta*) rate.

alis'cafo *sm* hydrofoil.

'alito *sm* breath.

all. *abbr* (= *allegato*) encl.

'alla *prep* + *det vedi* **a.**

allacci'are [allat'tʃarε] *vt* (*scarpe*) to tie, lace (up); (*cintura*) to do up, fasten; (*due località*) to link; (*luce, gas*) to connect; (*amicizia*) to form.

alla'gare *vt*, ~**rsi** *vr* to flood.

allar'gare *vt* to widen; (*vestito*) to let out; (*aprire*) to open; (*fig: dilatare*) to extend.

allar'mare *vt* to alarm.

al'larme *sm* alarm; ~ **aereo** air-raid warning.

allar'mismo *sm* scaremongering.

allat'tare *vt* to feed.

'alle *prep* + *det vedi* **a.**

alle'anza [allε'antsa] *sf* alliance.

alle'arsi *vr* to form an alliance; **alle'ato, a** *ag* allied // *sm/f* ally.

alle'gare *vt* (*accludere*) to enclose; (DIR: *citare*) to cite, adduce; (*denti*) to set on edge; **alle'gato, a** *ag* enclosed // *sm* enclosure; **in allegato** enclosed.

allegge'rire [alleddʒε'rirε] *vt* to lighten, make lighter; (*fig: sofferenza*) to alleviate, lessen; (: *lavoro, tasse*) to reduce.

alle'gria *sf* gaiety, cheerfulness.

al'legro, a *ag* cheerful, merry; (*un po' brillo*) merry, tipsy; (*vivace: colore*) bright // *sm* (MUS) allegro.

allena'mento *sm* training.

alle'nare *vt*, ~**rsi** *vr* to train; **allena'tore** *sm* (SPORT) trainer, coach.

allen'tare *vt* to slacken; (*disciplina*) to relax; ~**rsi** *vr* to become slack; (*ingranaggio*) to work loose.

aller'gia, 'gie [allεr'dʒia] *sf* allergy; **al'lergico, a, ci, che** *ag* allergic.

alles'tire *vt* (*cena*) to prepare; (*esercito, nave*) to equip, fit out; (*spettacolo*) to stage.

allet'tare *vt* to lure, entice.

alleva'mento *sm* breeding, rearing;

(*luogo*) stock farm.

alle'vare *vt* (*animale*) to breed, rear; (*bambino*) to bring up.

allevi'are *vt* to alleviate.

alli'bire *vi* to be astounded.

allibra'tore *sm* bookmaker.

allie'tare *vt* to cheer up, gladden.

alli'evo *sm* pupil; (*apprendista*) apprentice; (*MIL.*) cadet.

alliga'tore *sm* alligator.

alline'are *vt* (*persone, cose*) to line up; (*TIP*) to align; (*fig: economia, salari*) to adjust, align; ~rsi *vr* to line up; (*fig: a idee*) ~rsi a to come into line with.

'allo *prep* + *det vedi* **a**.

al'locco, a, chi, che *sm* tawny owl // *sm/f* oaf.

allocuzi'one [allokut'tsjone] *sf* address, solemn speech.

al'lodola *sf* (sky)lark.

alloggi'are [allod'dʒare] *vt* to accommodate // *vi* to live; **al'loggio** *sm* lodging, accommodation (*Brit*), accommodations (*US*); (*appartamento*) flat (*Brit*), apartment (*US*).

allontana'mento *sm* removal; dismissal.

allonta'nare *vt* to send away, send off; (*impiegato*) to dismiss; (*pericolo*) to avert, remove; (*estraniare*) to alienate; ~rsi *vr*: ~rsi (da) to go away (from); (*estraniarsi*) to become estranged (from).

al'lora *av* (*in quel momento*) then // *cong* (*in questo caso*) well then; (*dunque*) well then, so: **la gente d'~** people then *o* in those days; **da ~ in poi** from then on.

allor'ché [allor'ke] *cong* (*formale*) when, as soon as.

al'loro *sm* laurel.

'alluce ['allutʃe] *sm* big toe.

alluci'nante [allutʃi'nante] *ag* awful; (*fam*) amazing.

allucinazi'one [allutʃinat'tsjone] *sf* hallucination.

al'ludere *vi*: ~ a to allude to, hint at.

allu'minio *sm* aluminium (*Brit*), aluminum (*US*).

allun'gare *vt* to lengthen; (*distendere*) to prolong, extend; (*diluire*) to water down; ~rsi *vr* to lengthen; (*ragazzo*) to stretch, grow taller; (*sdraiarsi*) to lie down, stretch out.

allusi'one *sf* hint, allusion.

alluvi'one *sf* flood.

al'meno *av* at least // *cong*: (**se**) ~ if only; (**se**) ~ **piovesse!** if only it would rain!

a'lone *sm* halo.

'Alpi *sfpl*: **le** ~ the Alps.

alpi'nismo *sm* mountaineering, climbing; **alpi'nista, i, e** *sm/f* mountaineer, climber.

al'pino, a *ag* Alpine; mountain *cpd*.

al'quanto *av* rather, a little; ~, **a** *det* a

certain amount of, some // *pronome* a certain amount, some; ~**i(e)** *det pl*, *pronome pl* several, quite a few.

alt *escl* halt!, stop! // *sm*: **dare l'~** to call a halt.

alta'lena *sf* (*a funi*) swing; (*in bilico*, *anche fig*) seesaw.

al'tare *sm* altar.

alte'rare *vt* to alter, change; (*cibo*) to adulterate; (*registro*) to falsify; (*persona*) to irritate; ~rsi *vr* to alter; (*cibo*) to go bad; (*persona*) to lose one's temper.

al'terco, chi *sm* altercation, wrangle.

alter'nare *vt*, ~rsi *vr* to alternate; **alterna'tivo, a** *ag* alternative // *sf* alternative; **alter'nato, a** *ag* alternate; (*ELETTR*) alternating; **alterna'tore** *sm* alternator.

al'terno, a *ag* alternate; **a giorni** ~**i** on alternate days, every other day.

al'tezza [al'tettsa] *sf* height; width, breadth; depth; pitch; (*GEO*) latitude; (*titolo*) highness; (*fig: nobiltà*) greatness; **essere all'~ di** to be on a level with; (*fig*) to be up to *o* equal to; **altez'zoso, a** *ag* haughty.

al'ticcio, a, ci, ce [al'tittʃo] *ag* tipsy.

altipi'ano *sm* = **altopiano**.

alti'tudine *sf* altitude.

'alto, a *ag* high; (*persona*) tall; (*tessuto*) wide, broad; (*sonno, acque*) deep; (*suono*) high(-pitched); (*GEO*) upper; (: *settentrionale*) northern // *sm* top (part) // *av* high; (*parlare*) aloud, loudly; **il palazzo è** ~ **20 metri** the building is 20 metres high; **il tessuto è** ~ **70 cm** the material is 70 cm wide; **ad** ~**a voce** aloud; **a notte** ~**a** in the dead of night; **in** ~ up, upwards; **at the top**; **dall'~ in** *o* **al basso** up and down; **degli** ~**i e bassi** (*fig*) ups and downs; ~**a fedeltà** high fidelity, hi-fi; ~**a moda** haute couture.

alto'forno *sm* blast furnace.

altolo'cato, a *ag* of high rank, highly placed.

altopar'lante *sm* loudspeaker.

altopi'ano *sm*, *pl* **altipiani** plateau, upland plain.

altret'tanto, a *ag*, *pronome* as much; (*pl*) as many // *av* equally; **tanti auguri!** — **grazie,** ~ all the best! — thank you, the same to you.

'altri *pronome inv* (*qualcuno*) somebody; (: *in espressioni negative*) anybody; (*un'altra persona*) another (person).

altri'menti *av* otherwise.

'altro, a ◆ *det* **1** (*diverso*) other, different; **questa è un'~a cosa** that's another *o* a different thing

2 (*supplementare*) other; **prendi un** ~ **cioccolatino** have another chocolate; **hai avuto** ~**e notizie?** have you had any more *o* any other news?

3 (*nel tempo*): **l'~ giorno** the other day;

l'altr'anno last year; l'~ ieri the day before yesterday; **domani** l'~ the day after tomorrow; **quest'~ mese** next month
4: **d'~a parte** on the other hand
◆ *pronome* **1** (*persona, cosa diversa o supplementare*): **un ~, un'~a** another (one); **lo farà un ~** someone else will do it; **~l(e)** others; **gli ~i** (*la gente*) others, other people; **l'uno e l'~** both (of them); **aiutarsi l'un l'~** to help one another; **da un giorno all'~** from one day to day; (*nel giro di 24 ore*) from one day to the next; (*da un momento all'altro*) any day now **2** (*sostantivato: solo maschile*) something else; (: *in espressioni interrogative*) anything else; **non ho ~ da dire** I have nothing else o I don't have anything else to say; **più che ~** above all; **se non ~** at least; **tra l'~** among other things; **ci mancherebbe ~!** that's all we need!; **non faccio ~ che lavorare** I do nothing but work; **contento? — ~ che!** are you pleased? — and how!; *vedi* **senza, noialtri, voialtri, tutto.**
al'**tronde** *av*: **d'~** on the other hand.
al'**trove** *av* elsewhere, somewhere else.
al'**trui** *ag inv* other people's // *sm*: **l'~** other people's belongings *pl*.
altru'**ista, i, e** *ag* altruistic.
al'**tura** *sf* (*rialto*) height, high ground; (*alto mare*) open sea; **pesca d'~** deep-sea fishing.
a'**lunno, a** *sm/f* pupil.
alve'**are** *sm* hive.
'**alveo** *sm* riverbed.
al'**zare** |al'tsarc| *vt* to raise, lift; (*issare*) to hoist; (*costruire*) to build, erect; **~rsi** *vr* to rise; (*dal letto*) to get up; (*crescere*) to grow tall (*o* taller); **~ le spalle** to shrug one's shoulders; **~rsi in piedi** to stand up, get to one's feet; **al'zata** *sf* lifting, raising; **un'alzata di spalle** a shrug.
a'**mabile** *ag* lovable; (*vino*) sweet.
a'**maca, che** *sf* hammock.
amalga'**mare** *vt,* **~rsi** *vr* to amalgamate.
a'**mante** *ag*: **~ di** (*musica etc*) fond of // *sm/f* lover/mistress.
a'**mare** *vt* to love; (*amico, musica, sport*) to like.
amareggi'**ato, a** |amared'dʒato| *ag* upset, saddened.
ama'**rena** *sf* sour black cherry.
ama'**rezza** |ama'rcttsa| *sf* bitterness.
a'**maro, a** *ag* bitter // *sm* bitterness; (*liquore*) bitters *pl*.
ambasci'**ata** |ambaʃ'fata| *sf* embassy; (*messaggio*) message; **ambascia'tore, 'trice** *sm/f* ambassador/ambassadress.
ambe'due *ag inv*: **~ i ragazzi** both boys // *pronome inv* both.
ambien'**tare** *vt* to acclimatize; (*romanzo, film*) to set; **~rsi** *vr* to get

used to one's surroundings.
ambi'**ente** *sm* environment; (*fig*: *insieme di persone*) milieu; (*stanza*) room.
am'**biguo, a** *ag* ambiguous; (*persona*) shady.
am'**bire** *vt* (*anche: vi: ~ a*) to aspire to.
'**ambito** *sm* sphere, field.
ambizi'**one** |ambit'tsjone| *sf* ambition; **ambizi'oso, a** *ag* ambitious.
'**ambo** *ag inv* both.
'**ambra** *sf* amber; **~ grigia** ambergris.
ambu'**lante** *ag* travelling, itinerant.
ambu'**lanza** |ambu'lantsa| *sf* ambulance.
ambula'**torio** *sm* (*studio medico*) surgery.
amenità *sf inv* pleasantness *q*.
a'**meno, a** *ag* pleasant; (*strano*) funny, strange; (*spiritoso*) amusing.
A'**merica** *sf*: **l'~** America; **l'~ latina** Latin America; **ameri'cano, a** *ag, sm/f* American.
ami'**anto** *sm* asbestos.
a'**mica** *sf vedi* **amico**.
ami'**chevole** |ami'kevole| *ag* friendly.
ami'**cizia** |ami't∫ittsja| *sf* friendship; **~e** *sfpl* (*amici*) friends.
a'**mico, a, ci, che** *sm/f* friend; (*amante*) boyfriend/girlfriend; **~ del cuore** *o* **intimo** bosom friend.
'**amido** *sm* starch.
ammac'**care** *vt* (*pentola*) to dent; (*persona*) to bruise; **~rsi** *vr* to bruise.
ammaes'**trare** *vt* (*animale*) to train; (*persona*) to teach.
ammai'**nare** *vt* to lower, haul down.
amma'**larsi** *vr* to fall ill; **amma'lato, a** *ag* ill, sick // *sm/f* sick person; (*paziente*) patient.
ammali'**are** *vt* (*fig*) to enchant, charm.
am'**manco, chi** *sm* (*ECON*) deficit.
ammanet'**tare** *vt* to handcuff.
ammas'**sare** *vt* (*ammucchiare*) to amass; (*raccogliere*) to gather together; **~rsi** *vr* to pile up; to gather; **am'masso** *sm* mass; (*mucchio*) pile, heap; (*ECON*) stockpile.
ammat'**tire** *vi* to go mad.
ammaz'**zare** |ammat'tsare| *vt* to kill; **~rsi** *vr* (*uccidersi*) to kill o.s.; (*rimanere ucciso*) to be killed; **~rsi di lavoro** to work o.s. to death.
am'**menda** *sf* amends *pl*; (*DIR, SPORT*) fine; **fare ~ di qc** to make amends for sth.
am'**messo, a** *pp di* **ammettere** // *cong*: **~ che** supposing that.
am'**mettere** *vt* to admit; (*riconoscere: fatto*) to acknowledge, admit; (*permettere*) to allow, accept; (*supporre*) to suppose.
ammez'**zato** |ammed'dzato| *sm* (*anche: piano ~*) mezzanine, entresol.
ammic'**care** *vi*: **~ (a)** to wink (at).
amminis'**trare** *vt* to run, manage;

(REL., DIR) to administer; **ammini-stra'tivo, a** ag administrative; **amministra'tore** sm administrator; (di condominio) flats manager; **ammini-stratore delegato** managing director; **amministrazi'one** sf management; administration.

ammiragli'ato |ammiraʎ'ʎato| sm admiralty.

ammi'raglio |ammi'raʎʎo| sm admiral.

ammi'rare vt to admire; **ammira'tore, 'trice** sm/f admirer; **ammirazi'one** sf admiration.

ammis'sibile ag admissible, acceptable.

ammissi'one sf admission; (approvazione) acknowledgment.

ammobili'are vt to furnish.

am'modo, a 'modo av properly // ag inv respectable, nice.

am'mollo sm: **lasciare in ~** to leave to soak.

ammo'niaca sf ammonia.

ammoni'mento sm warning; admonishment.

ammo'nire vt (avvertire) to warn; (rimproverare) to admonish; (DIR) to caution.

ammon'tare vi: **~ a** to amount to // sm (total) amount.

ammorbi'dente sm fabric conditioner.

ammorbi'dire vt to soften.

ammortiz'zare |ammortid'dzare| vt (ECON) to pay off, amortize; (: spese d'impianto) to write off; (AUT, TECN) to absorb, deaden; **ammortizza'tore** sm (AUT, TECN) shock-absorber.

ammucchi'are |ammuk'kjare| vt, **~rsi** vr to pile up, accumulate.

ammuf'fire vi to go mouldy (Brit) o moldy (US).

ammutina'mento sm mutiny.

ammuti'narsi vr to mutiny.

ammuto'lire vi to be struck dumb.

amnis'tia sf amnesty.

'amo sm (PESCA) hook; (fig) bait.

a'more sm love; **~i** smpl love affairs; **il tuo bambino è un ~** your baby's a darling; **fare l'~** o **all'~** to make love; **per ~** o **per forza** by hook or by crook; **amor proprio** self-esteem, pride; **amo'revole** ag loving, affectionate.

a'morfo, a ag amorphous; (fig: persona) lifeless.

amo'roso, a ag (affettuoso) loving, affectionate; (d'amore: sguardo) amorous; (: poesia, relazione) love cpd.

ampi'ezza |am'pjettsa| sf width, breadth; spaciousness; (fig: importanza) scale, size.

'ampio, a ag wide, broad; (spazioso) spacious; (abbondante: vestito) loose; (: gonna) full; (: spiegazione) ample, full.

am'plesso sm (eufemismo) embrace.

ampli'are vt (ingrandire) to enlarge; (allargare) to widen.

amplifi'care vt to amplify; (magnificare) to extol; **amplifica'tore** sm (TECN, MUS) amplifier.

am'polla sf (vasetto) cruet.

ampu'tare vt (MED) to amputate.

anabbagli'ante |anabbaʎ'ʎante| ag (AUT) dipped (Brit), dimmed (US); **~i** smpl dipped (Brit) o dimmed (US) headlights.

a'nagrafe sf (registro) register of births, marriages and deaths; (ufficio) registration office.

analfa'beta, i, e ag, sm/f illiterate.

anal'gesico, a, ci, che |anal'dʒɛziko| ag, sm analgesic.

a'nalisi sf inv analysis; (MED: esame) test; **~ grammaticale** parsing; **ana'lista, i, e** sm/f analyst; (PSIC) (psycho)analyst.

analiz'zare |analid'dzare| vt to analyse; (MED) to test.

analo'gia, 'gie |analo'dʒia| sf analogy.

a'nalogo, a, ghi, ghe ag analogous.

'ananas sm inv pineapple.

anar'chia |anar'kia| sf anarchy; **a'narchico, a, ci, che** ag anarchic(al) // sm/f anarchist.

'ANAS sigla f (= Azienda Nazionale Autonoma delle Strade) national roads department.

anato'mia sf anatomy; **ana'tomico, a, ci, che** ag anatomical; (sedile) contoured.

'anatra sf duck.

'anca, che sf (ANAT) hip; (ZOOL) haunch.

'anche |'anke| cong (inoltre, pure) also, too; (persino) even; **vengo anch'io** I'm coming too; **~ se** even if.

an'cora av still; (di nuovo) again; (di più) some more; (persino): **~ più forte** even stronger; **non ~** not yet, **~ una volta** once more, once again; **~ un po'** a little more; (di tempo) a little longer.

'ancora sf anchor; **gettare/levare l'~** to cast/weigh anchor; **anco'raggio** sm anchorage; **anco'rare** vt, **ancorarsi** vr to anchor.

anda'mento sm progress, movement; course; state.

an'dante ag (corrente) current; (di poco pregio) cheap, second-rate // sm (MUS) andante.

an'dare sm: **a lungo ~** in the long run // vi to go; (essere adatto): **~ a** to suit; (piacere): **il suo comportamento non mi va** I don't like the way he behaves; **ti va di andare al cinema?** do you feel like going to the cinema?; **andarsene** to go away; **questa camicia va lavata** this shirt needs a wash o should be washed; **~ a cavallo** to ride; **~ in macchina/aereo** to go by car/plane; **~ a fare qc** to go and do sth; **~ a pescare/sciare** to go fishing/skiing; **~ a male** to go bad; **come va?**

(*lavoro, progetto*) how are things?; **come va? — bene, grazie!** how are you? — fine, thanks!; va fatto entro oggi it's got to be done today; **ne va della nostra vita** our lives are at stake; **an'data** *sf* going; (*viaggio*) outward journey; **biglietto di sola andata** single (*Brit*) *o* one-way ticket; **biglietto di andata e ritorno** return (*Brit*) *o* round-trip (*US*) ticket; **anda'tura** *sf* (*modo di andare*) walk, gait; (*SPORT*) pace; (*NAUT*) tack.

an'dazzo |an'dattso| *sm* (*peg*): **prendere un brutto ~** to take a turn for the worse.

andirivi'eni *sm inv* coming and going.

'andito *sm* corridor, passage.

an'drone *sm* entrance hall.

a'neddoto *sm* anecdote.

ane'lare *vi*: **~ a** (*fig*) to long for, yearn for.

a'nelito *sm* (*fig*): **~ di** longing *o* yearning for.

a'nello *sm* ring; (*di catena*) link.

a'nemico, a, ci, che *ag* anaemic.

a'nemone *sm* anemone.

aneste'sia *sf* anaesthesia; **anes'tetico, a, ci, che** *ag*, *sm* anaesthetic.

anfite'atro *sm* amphitheatre.

an'fratto *sm* ravine.

an'gelico, a, ci, che |an'dʒɛliko| *ag* angelic(al).

'angelo |'andʒɛlo| *sm* angel; **~ custode** guardian angel.

anghe'ria |ange'ria| *sf* vexation.

an'gina |an'dʒina| *sf* tonsillitis; **~ pectoris** angina.

angli'cano, a *ag* Anglican.

angli'cismo |angli'tʃizmo| *sm* anglicism.

anglo'sassone *ag* Anglo-Saxon.

ango'lare *ag* angular.

angolazi'one |angolat'tsjone| *sf* (*FOT etc, fig*) angle.

'angolo *sm* corner; (*MAT*) angle.

an'goscia, sce |an'gɔʃʃa| *sf* deep anxiety, anguish *q*; **angosci'oso, a** *ag* (*d'angoscia*) anguished; (*che dà angoscia*) distressing, painful.

angu'illa *sf* eel.

an'guria *sf* watermelon.

an'gustia *sf* (*ansia*) anguish, distress; (*povertà*) poverty, want.

angusti'are *vt* to distress; **~rsi** *vr*: **~rsi (per)** to worry (about).

an'gusto, a *ag* (*stretto*) narrow; (*fig*) mean, petty.

'anice |'anitʃe| *sm* (*CUC*) aniseed; (*BOT*) anise.

a'nidride *sf* (*CHIM*): **~ carbonica/solforosa** carbon/sulphur dioxide.

'anima *sf* soul; (*abitante*) inhabitant; **non c'era ~ viva** there wasn't a living soul.

ani'male *sm, ag* animal.

ani'mare *vt* to give life to, liven up; (*incoraggiare*) to encourage; **~rsi** *vr* to become animated, come to life;

ani'mato, a *ag* animate; (*vivace*) lively, animated; (*: strada*) busy; **anima'tore, 'trice** *sm/f* guiding spirit; (*CINEMA*) animator; (*di festa*) life and soul; **animazi'one** *sf* liveliness; (*di strada*) bustle; (*CINEMA*) animation; animazione teatrale amateur dramatics.

'animo *sm* (*mente*) mind; (*cuore*) heart; (*coraggio*) courage; (*disposizione*) character, disposition; **avere in ~ di fare qc** to intend *o* have a mind to do sth; **perdersi d'~** to lose heart.

'anitra *sf* = **anatra**.

anna'cquare *vt* to water down, dilute.

annaffi'are *vt* to water; **annaffia'toio** *sm* watering can.

an'nali *smpl* annals.

annas'pare *vi* to flounder.

an'nata *sf* year; (*importo annuo*) annual amount; **vino d'~** vintage wine.

annebbi'are *vt* (*fig*) to cloud; **~rsi** *vr* to become foggy; (*vista*) to become dim.

annega'mento *sm* drowning.

anne'gare *vt, vi* to drown; **~rsi** *vr* (*accidentalmente*) to drown; (*deliberatamente*) to drown o.s.

anne'rire *vt* to blacken // *vi* to become black.

an'nesso, a *pp di* **annettere** // *ag* attached; (*POL*) annexed; **... e tutti gli ~i e connessi** ... and so on and so forth.

an'nettere *vt* (*POL*) to annex; (*accludere*) to attach.

annichi'lare, annichi'lire |anniki'lare, anniki'lire| *vt* to annihilate.

anni'darsi *vr* to nest.

annienta'mento *sm* annihilation, destruction.

annien'tare *vt* to annihilate, destroy.

anniver'sario *sm* anniversary.

'anno *sm* year.

anno'dare *vt* to knot, tie; (*fig: rapporto*) to form.

annoi'are *vt* to bore; (*seccare*) to annoy; **~rsi** *vr* to be bored; to be annoyed.

anno'tare *vt* (*registrare*) to note, note down; (*commentare*) to annotate; **annotazi'one** *sf* note; annotation.

annove'rare *vt* to number.

annu'ale *ag* annual.

annu'ario *sm* yearbook.

annu'ire *vi* to nod; (*acconsentire*) to agree.

annul'lare *vt* to annihilate, destroy; (*contratto, francobollo*) to cancel; (*matrimonio*) to annul; (*sentenza*) to quash; (*risultati*) to declare void.

annunci'are |annun'tʃare| *vt* to announce; (*dar segni rivelatori*) to herald; **annuncia'tore, 'trice** *sm/f* (*RADIO, TV*) announcer; **l'Annunciazi'one** *sf* the Annunciation.

an'nuncio |an'nuntʃo| *sm* announcement; (*fig*) sign; **~ pubblicitario**

advertisement; ~i **economici** classified advertisements, small ads.

'**annuo, a** *ag* annual, yearly.

annu'sare *vt* to sniff, smell; ~ **tabacco** to take snuff.

'**ano** *sm* anus.

anoma'lla *sf* anomaly.

a'nomalo, a *ag* anomalous.

a'nonimo, a *ag* anonymous // *sm* (*autore*) anonymous writer (*o painter etc*); **società ~a** (*COMM*) joint stock company.

anor'male *ag* abnormal // *sm/f* subnormal person; (*eufemismo*) homosexual.

ANSA *sigla f* (= *Agenzia Nazionale Stampa Associata*) press agency.

'**ansa** *sf* (*manico*) handle; (*di fiume*) bend, loop.

'**ansia, ansietà** *sf* anxiety.

ansi'mare *vi* to pant.

ansi'oso, a *ag* anxious.

'**anta** *sf* (*di finestra*) shutter; (*di armadio*) door.

antago'nismo *sm* antagonism.

an'tartico, a, ci, che *ag* Antarctic // *sm*: **l'A~** the Antarctic.

antece'dente |antetʃe'dɛnte| *ag* preceding, previous.

ante'fatto *sm* previous events *pl*; previous history.

antegu'erra *sm* pre-war period.

ante'nato *sm* ancestor, forefather.

an'tenna *sf* (*RADIO, TV*) aerial; (*ZOOL*) antenna, feeler; (*NAUT*) yard.

ante'prima *sf* preview.

anteri'ore *ag* (*ruota, zampa*) front, (*fatti*) previous, preceding.

antia'ereo, a *ag* anti-aircraft.

antia'tomico, a, ci, che *ag* antinuclear; **rifugio ~** fallout shelter.

antibi'otico, a, ci, che *ag, sm* antibiotic.

anti'camera *sf* anteroom; **fare ~** to wait (for an audience).

antichità |antiki'ta| *sf inv* antiquity; (*oggetto*) antique.

antici'pare |antitʃi'pare| *vt* (*consegna, visita*) to bring forward, anticipate; (*somma di denaro*) to pay in advance; (*notizia*) to disclose // *vi* to be ahead of time; **anticipazi'one** *sf* anticipation; (*di notizia*) advance information; (*somma di denaro*) advance; **an'ticipo** *sm* anticipation; (*di denaro*) advance; **in anticipo** early, in advance.

an'tico, a, chi, che *ag* (*quadro, mobili*) antique; (*dell'antichità*) ancient; **all'~a** old-fashioned.

anticoncezio'nale |antikontʃettsjo'nale| *sm* contraceptive.

anticonfor'mista, i, e *ag, sm/f* nonconformist.

anti'corpo *sm* antibody.

anti'furto *sm* (*anche*: **sistema ~**) antitheft device.

An'tille *sfpl*: **le ~** the West Indies.

antin'cendio |antin'tʃendjo| *ag inv* fire cpd.

antio'rario |antio'rarjo| *ag*: **in senso ~** anticlockwise.

anti'pasto *sm* hors d'œuvre.

antipa'tia *sf* antipathy, dislike; **anti'patico, a, ci, che** *ag* unpleasant, disagreeable.

antiquari'ato *sm* antique trade; **un oggetto d'~** an antique.

anti'quario *sm* antique dealer.

anti'quato, a *ag* antiquated, oldfashioned.

antise'mita, i, e *ag* anti-Semitic.

anti'settico, a, ci, che *ag, sm* antiseptic.

antista'minico, a, ci, che *ag, sm* antihistamine.

antolo'gia, 'gie |antolo'dʒia| *sf* anthology.

anu'lare *ag* ring cpd // *sm* third finger.

'**anzi** |'antsi| *av* (*invece*) on the contrary; (*o meglio*) or rather, or better still.

anzianità |antsjani'ta| *sf* old age; (*AMM*) seniority.

anzi'ano, a |an'tsjano| *ag* old; (*AMM*) senior // *sm/f* old person; senior member.

anziché |antsi'ke| *cong* rather than.

anzi'tutto |antsi'tutto| *av* first of all.

apa'tia *sf* apathy, indifference.

'**ape** *sf* bee.

aperi'tivo *sm* aperitif.

a'perto, a *pp di* **aprire** // *ag* open; **all'~** in the open (air).

oper'tura *sf* opening; (*ampiezza*) width, spread; (*POL*) approach; (*FOT*) aperture; ~ **alare** wing span.

'**apice** |'apitʃe| *sm* apex; (*fig*) height.

apicol'tore *sm* beekeeper.

ap'nea *sf*: **immergersi in ~** to dive without breathing apparatus.

a'polide *ag* stateless.

apoples'sia *sf* (*MED*) apoplexy.

a'postolo *sm* apostle.

a'postrofo *sm* apostrophe.

appa'gare *vt* to satisfy; ~**rsi** *vr*: ~**rsi di** to be satisfied with.

ap'palto *sm* (*COMM*) contract; **dare/prendere in ~ un lavoro** to let out/undertake a job on contract.

appan'nare *vt* (*vetro*) to mist; (*metallo*) to tarnish; (*vista*) to dim; ~**rsi** *vr* to mist over; to tarnish; to grow dim.

appa'rato *sm* equipment, machinery; (*ANAT*) apparatus; ~ **scenico** (*TEATRO*) props *pl*.

apparecchi'are |apparek'kjare| *vt* to prepare; (*tavola*) to set // *vi* to set the table; **apparecchia'tura** *sf* equipment; (*macchina*) machine, device.

appa'recchio |appa'rekkjo| *sm* piece of apparatus, device; (*aeroplano*) aircraft *inv*; ~ **televisivo/telefonico** television set/telephone.

appa'rente *ag* apparent; **appa'renza** *sf* appearance; **in o all'apparenza** apparently, to all appearances.

appa'rire *vi* to appear; *(sembrare)* to seem, appear; **appari'scente** *ag* *(colore)* garish, gaudy; *(bellezza)* striking.

apparta'mento *sm* flat *(Brit)*, apartment *(US)*.

appar'tarsi *vr* to withdraw; **appar'tato, a** *ag* *(luogo)* secluded.

apparte'nere *vi*: ~ **a** to belong to.

appassio'nare *vt* to thrill; *(commuovere)* to move; **~rsi a qc** to take a great interest in sth; **to be deeply moved by sth**; **appassio'nato, a** *ag* passionate; *(entusiasta)*: **appassionato (di)** keen (on).

appas'sire *vi* to wither.

appel'larsi *vr* *(ricorrere)*: ~ **a** to appeal to; *(DIR)*: ~ **contro** to appeal against; **ap'pello** *sm* roll-call; *(implorazione, DIR)* appeal; **fare appello a** to appeal to.

ap'pena *av* *(a stento)* hardly, scarcely; *(solamente, da poco)* just // *cong* as soon as; **(non)** ~ **furono arrivati ... as soon as they had arrived ...;** ~ **... che** *o* **quando** no sooner ... than.

ap'pendere *vt* to hang (up).

appen'dice [appen'ditʃe] *sf* appendix; **romanzo d'~** popular serial.

appendi'cite [appendi'tʃite] *sf* appendicitis.

Appen'nini *smpl*: **gli ~** the Apennines.

appesan'tire *vt* to make heavy; **~rsi** *vr* to grow stout.

ap'peso, a *pp di* **appendere**.

appe'tito *sm* appetite; **appeti'toso, a** *ag* appetising; *(fig)* attractive, desirable.

appia'nare *vt* to level; *(fig)* to smooth away, iron out.

appiat'tire *vt* to flatten; **~rsi** *vr* to become flatter; *(farsi piatto)* to flatten o.s.; **~rsi al suolo** to lie flat on the ground.

appic'care *vt*: ~ **il fuoco a** to set fire to, set on fire.

appicci'care [appittʃi'kare] *vt* to stick; *(fig)*: ~ **qc a qn** to palm sth off on sb; **~rsi** *vr* to stick; *(fig: persona)* to cling.

appi'eno *av* fully.

appigli'arsi [appiʎ'ʎarsi] *vr*: ~ **a** *(afferrarsi)* to take hold of; *(fig)* to cling to: **ap'piglio** *sm* hold; *(fig)* pretext.

appiso'larsi *vr* to doze off.

applau'dire *vt, vi* to applaud; **ap'plauso** *sm* applause.

appli'care *vt* to apply; *(regolamento)* to enforce; **~rsi** *vr* to apply o.s.; **applicazi'one** *sf* application; enforcement.

appoggi'are [appod'dʒare] *vt* *(mettere contro)*: ~ **qc a qc** to lean o rest sth against sth; *(fig: sostenere)* to support;

~rsi *vr*: **~rsi a** to lean against; *(fig)* to rely upon; **ap'poggio** *sm* support.

appollai'arsi *vr* *(anche fig)* to perch.

ap'porre *vt* to affix.

appor'tare *vt* to bring.

apposita'mente *av* specially; *(apposta)* on purpose.

ap'posito, a *ag* appropriate.

ap'posta *av* on purpose, deliberately.

appos'tare *vt* to lie in wait for; **~rsi** *vr* to lie in wait.

ap'prendere *vt* *(imparare)* to learn; *(comprendere)* to grasp.

appren'dista, i *sm/f* apprentice.

apprensi'one *sf* apprehension; **appren'sivo, a** *ag* apprehensive.

ap'presso *av* *(accanto, vicino)* close by, near; *(dietro)* behind; *(dopo, più tardi)* after, later // *ag inv (dopo)*: **il giorno ~** the next day; ~ **a** *prep (vicino a)* near, close to.

appres'tare *vt* to prepare, get ready; **~rsi** *vr*: **~rsi a fare qc** to prepare o get ready to do sth.

ap'pretto *sm* starch.

apprez'zabile [appret'tsabile] *ag* noteworthy, significant.

apprezza'mento [apprettsa'mento] *sm* appreciation; *(giudizio)* opinion.

apprez'zare [appret'tsare] *vt* to appreciate.

ap'proccio [ap'prɔttʃo] *sm* approach.

appro'dare *vi* *(NAUT)* to land; *(fig)*: **non** ~ **a nulla** to come to nothing; **ap'prodo** *sm* landing; *(luogo)* landing-place.

approfit'tare *vi*: ~ **di** to make the most of, profit by.

approfon'dire *vt* to deepen; *(fig)* to study in depth.

appropri'ato, a *ag* appropriate.

approssi'marsi *vr*: ~ **a** to approach.

approssima'tivo, a *ag* approximate, rough; *(impreciso)* inexact, imprecise.

appro'vare *vt* *(condotta, azione)* to approve of; *(candidato)* to pass; *(progetto di legge)* to approve; **approvazi'one** *sf* approval.

approvvigio'nare [approvvidʒo'nare] *vt* to supply; **~rsi** *vr* to lay in provisions, stock up; ~ **qn di qc** to supply sb with sth.

appunta'mento *sm* appointment; *(amoroso)* date; **darsi ~** to arrange to meet (one another).

appun'tato *sm* *(CARABINIERI)* corporal.

ap'punto *sm* note; *(rimprovero)* reproach // *av (proprio)* exactly, just; **per l'~!, ~!** exactly!

appu'rare *vt* to check, verify.

apribot'tiglie [apribot'tiʎʎe] *sm inv* bottleopener.

a'prile *sm* April.

a'prire *vt* to open; *(via, cadavere)* to open up; *(gas, luce, acqua)* to turn on // *vi* to open; **~rsi** *vr* to open; **~rsi a qn** to

confide in sb, open one's heart to sb.
apris'catole *sm inv* tin (*Brit*) *o* can opener.
a'quario *sm* = **acquario**.
'aquila *sf* (*ZOOL*) eagle; (*fig*) genius.
aqui'lone *sm* (*giocattolo*) kite; (*vento*) North wind.
A'rabia 'Saudita *sf*: **l'~** Saudi Arabia.
'arabo, a *ag, sm/f* Arab // *sm* (*LING*) Arabic.
a'rachide |a'rakide| *sf* peanut.
ara'gosta *sf* crayfish; lobster.
a'raldica *sf* heraldry
a'rancia, ce |a'rantʃa| *sf* orange; **aranci'ata** *sf* orangeade; **a'rancio** *sm* (*BOT*) orange tree; (*colore*) orange // *ag inv* (*colore*) orange; **aranci'one** *ag inv*: (*color*) **arancione** bright orange.
a'rare *vt* to plough (*Brit*), plow (*US*).
a'ratro *sm* plough (*Brit*), plow (*US*).
a'razzo |a'rattso| *sm* tapestry.
arbi'trare *vt* (*SPORT*) to referee; to umpire; (*DIR*) to arbitrate.
arbi'trario, a *ag* arbitrary.
ar'bitrio *sm* will; (*abuso, sopruso*) arbitrary act.
'arbitro *sm* arbiter, judge; (*DIR*) arbitrator; (*SPORT*) referee; (: *TENNIS, CRICKET*) umpire.
ar'busto *sm* shrub.
'arca, che *sf* (*sarcofago*) sarcophagus; **l'~ di Noè** Noah's ark.
ar'cangelo |ar'kandʒelo| *sm* archangel.
ar'cano, a *ag* arcane, mysterious.
ar'cata *sf* (*ARCHIT, ANAT*) arch; (*ordine di archi*) arcade.
archeolo'gia |arkeolo'dʒia| *sf* arch(a)eology; **arche'ologo, a, gi, ghe** *sm/f* arch(a)eologist.
ar'chetto |ar'ketto| *sm* (*MUS*) bow.
archi'tetto |arki'tetto| *sm* architect; **archi'tettura** *sf* architecture.
ar'chivio |ar'kivjo| *sm* archives *pl*; (*INFORM*) file.
arci'ere |ar'tʃere| *sm* archer.
ar'cigno, a |ar'tʃiɲɲo| *ag* grim, severe.
arci'vescovo |artʃi'veskovo| *sm* archbishop.
'arco *sm* (*arma, MUS*) bow; (*ARCHIT*) arch; (*MAT*) arc.
arcoba'leno *sm* rainbow.
arcu'ato, a *ag* curved, bent; **dalle gambe ~e** bow-legged.
ar'dente *ag* burning; (*fig*) burning, ardent.
'ardere *vt, vi* to burn.
ar'desia *sf* slate.
ar'dire *vi* to dare // *sm* daring; **ar'dito, a** *ag* brave, daring, bold; (*sfacciato*) bold.
ar'dore *sm* blazing heat; (*fig*) ardour, fervour.
'arduo, a *ag* arduous, difficult.
'area *sf* area; (*EDIL*) land, ground.
a'rena *sf* arena; (*per corride*) bullring;

(*sabbia*) sand.
are'narsi *vr* to run aground.
areo'plano *sm* = **aeroplano**.
'argano *sm* winch.
argente'ria |ardʒente'ria| *sf* silverware, silver.
argenti'ere |ardʒen'tjere| *sm* silversmith.
Argen'tina |ardʒen'tina| *sf*: **l'~** Argentina; **argen'tino, a** *ag, sm/f* Argentinian.
ar'gento |ar'dʒento| *sm* silver; **~ vivo** quicksilver.
ar'gilla |ar'dʒilla| *sf* clay.
'argine |'ardʒine| *sm* embankment, bank; (*diga*) dyke, dike.
argomen'tare *vi* to argue.
argo'mento *sm* argument; (*motivo*) motive; (*materia, tema*) subject.
argu'ire *vt* to deduce.
ar'guto, a *ag* sharp, quick-witted; **ar'guzia** *sf* wit; (*battuta*) witty remark.
'aria *sf* air; (*espressione, aspetto*) air, look; (*MUS*: *melodia*) tune; (: *di opera*) aria; **mandare all'~ qc** to ruin *o* upset sth; **all'~ aperta** in the open (air).
'arido, a *ag* arid.
arieggi'are |arjed'dʒare| *vt* (*cambiare aria*) to air; (*imitare*) to imitate.
ari'ete *sm* ram; (*MIL*) battering ram; (*dello zodiaco*): **A~** Aries.
a'ringa, ghe *sf* herring *inv*.
'arista *sf* (*CUC*) chine of pork.
aristo'cratico, a, ci, che *ag* aristocratic.
arit'metica *sf* arithmetic.
arlec'chino |arlek'kino| *sm* harlequin.
'arma, i *sf* weapon, arm; (*parte dell'esercito*) arm; **chiamare alle ~i** to call up (*Brit*), draft (*US*); **sotto le ~i** in the army (*o* forces); **alle ~i!** to arms!; **~ da fuoco** firearm.
ar'madio *sm* cupboard; (*per abiti*) wardrobe.
armamen'tario *sm* equipment, instruments *pl*.
arma'mento *sm* (*MIL*) armament; (: *materiale*) arms *pl*, weapons *pl*; (*NAUT*) fitting out; manning.
ar'mare *vt* to arm; (*arma da fuoco*) to cock; (*NAUT*: *nave*) to rig, fit out; to man; (*EDIL*: *volta, galleria*) to prop up, shore up; **~rsi** *vr* to arm o.s.; (*MIL*) to take up arms; **ar'mata** *sf* (*MIL*) army; (*NAUT*) fleet; **arma'tore** *sm* shipowner; **arma'tura** *sf* (*struttura di sostegno*) framework; (*impalcatura*) scaffolding; (*STORIA*) armour *g*, suit of armour.
armeggi'are |armed'dʒare| *vi*: **~ (intorno a qc)** to mess about (with sth).
armis'tizio |armis'tittsjo| *sm* armistice.
armo'nia *sf* harmony; **ar'monico, a, ci, che** *ag* harmonic; (*fig*) harmonious // *sf* (*MUS*) harmonica; **armoni'oso, a** *ag* harmonious.
armoniz'zare |armonid'dzare| *vt* to

harmonize; (*colori, abiti*) to match // *vi* to be in harmony; to match.

ar'nese *sm* tool, implement; (*oggetto indeterminato*) thing, contraption; **male in ~** (*malvestito*) badly dressed; (*di salute malferma*) in poor health; (*di condizioni economiche*) down-at heel.

'arnia *sf* hive.

a'roma, i *sm* aroma; fragrance; **~i** *smpl* herbs and spices; **aro'matico, a, ci, che** *ag* aromatic; (*cibo*) spicy.

'arpa *sf* (*MUS*) harp.

ar'peggio |ar'peddʒo| *sm* (*MUS*) arpeggio.

ar'pia *sf* (*anche fig*) harpy.

arpi'one *sm* (*gancio*) hook; (*cardine*) hinge; (*PESCA*) harpoon.

arrabat'tarsi *vr* to do all one can, strive.

arrabbi'are *vi* (*cane*) to be affected with rabies; **~rsi** *vr* (*essere preso dall'ira*) to get angry, fly into a rage; **arrabbi'ato, a** *ag* rabid, with rabies; furious, angry.

arraf'fare *vt* to snatch, seize; (*sottrarre*) to pinch.

arrampi'carsi *vr* to climb (up).

arran'care *vi* to limp, hobble.

arran'giare |arran'dʒare| *vt* to arrange; **~rsi** *vr* to manage, do the best one can.

arre'care *vt* to bring; (*causare*) to cause.

arreda'mento *sm* (*studio*) interior design; (*mobili etc*) furnishings *pl*.

arre'dare *vt* to furnish; **arreda'tore, 'trice** *sm/f* interior designer; **ar'redo** *sm* fittings *pl*, furnishings *pl*.

ar'rendersi *vr* to surrender.

arres'tare *vt* (*fermare*) to stop, halt; (*catturare*) to arrest; **~rsi** *vr* (*fermarsi*) to stop; **ar'resto** *sm* (*cessazione*) stopping; (*fermata*) stop; (*cattura, MED*) arrest; **subire un arresto** to come to a stop *o* standstill; **mettere agli arresti** to place under arrest; **arresti domiciliari** house arrest *sg*.

arre'trare *vt, vi* to withdraw; **arre'trato, a** *ag* (*lavoro*) behind schedule; (*paese, bambino*) backward; (*numero di giornale*) back *cpd*; **arretrati** *smpl* arrears.

arric'chire |arrik'kire| *vt* to enrich; **~rsi** *vr* to become rich.

arricci'are |arrit'tʃare| *vt* to curl; **~ il naso** to turn up one's nose.

ar'ringa, ghe *sf* harangue; (*DIR*) address by counsel.

arrischi'are |arris'kjare| *vt* to risk; **~rsi** *vr* to venture, dare; **arrischi'ato, a** *ag* risky; (*temerario*) reckless, rash.

arri'vare *vi* to arrive; (*accadere*) to happen, occur; **~ a** (*livello, grado etc*) to reach; **lui arriva a Roma alle 7** he gets to *o* arrives at Rome at 7; **non ci arrivo** I can't reach it; (*fig: non capisco*) I can't understand it.

arrive'derci |arrive'dertʃi| *escl* goodbye!

arrive'derla *escl* (*forma di cortesia*) goodbye!

arri'vista, i, e *sm/f* go-getter.

ar'rivo *sm* arrival; (*SPORT*) finish, finishing line.

arro'gante *ag* arrogant.

arro'lare *vb* = **arruolare**.

arros'sire *vi* (*per vergogna, timidezza*) to blush, flush; (*per gioia, rabbia*) to flush.

arros'tire *vt* to roast; (*pane*) to toast; (*ai ferri*) to grill.

ar'rosto *sm, ag inv* roast.

arro'tare *vt* to sharpen; (*investire con un veicolo*) to run over.

arroto'lare *vt* to roll up.

arroton'dare *vt* (*forma, oggetto*) to round; (*stipendio*) to add to; (*somma*) to round off.

arrovel'larsi *vr*: **~** (**il cervello**) to rack one's brains.

arruf'fare *vt* to ruffle; (*fili*) to tangle; (*fig: questione*) to confuse.

arruggi'nire |arruddʒi'nire| *vt* to rust; **~rsi** *vr* to rust; (*fig*) to become rusty.

arruo'lare (*MIL*) *vt* to enlist; **~rsi** *vr* to enlist, join up.

arse'nale *sm* (*MIL*) arsenal; (*cantiere navale*) dockyard.

'arso, a *pp di* **ardere** // *ag* (*bruciato*) burnt; (*arido*) dry; **ar'sura** *sf* (*calore opprimente*) burning heat; (*siccità*) drought.

'arte *sf* art; (*abilità*) skill.

arte'fatto, a *ag* (*cibo*) adulterated; (*fig: modi*) artificial.

ar'tefice |ar'tefitʃe| *sm/f* craftsman/woman; (*autore*) author.

ar'teria *sf* artery.

'artico, a, ci, che *ag* Arctic.

artico'lare *ag* (*ANAT*) of the joints, articular // *vt* to articulate; (*suddividere*) to divide, split up; **articolazi'one** *sf* articulation; (*ANAT, TECN*) joint.

ar'ticolo *sm* article; **~ di fondo** (*STAMPA*) leader, leading article.

'Artide *sm*: **l'~** the Arctic.

artifici'ale |artifi'tʃale| *ag* artificial.

arti'ficio |arti'fitʃo| *sm* (*espediente*) trick, artifice; (*ricerca di effetto*) artificiality.

artigia'nato |artidʒa'nato| *sm* craftsmanship; craftsmen *pl*.

artigi'ano, a |arti'dʒano| *sm/f* craftsman/woman.

artiglie'ria |artiʎʎe'ria| *sf* artillery.

ar'tiglio |ar'tiʎʎo| *sm* claw; (*di rapaci*) talon.

ar'tista, i, e *sm/f* artist; **ar'tistico, a, ci, che** *ag* artistic.

'arto *sm* (*ANAT*) limb.

ar'trite *sf* (*MED*) arthritis.

ar'trosi *sf* osteoarthritis.

ar'zillo, a |ar'dzillo| *ag* lively, sprightly.

a'scella |aʃ'ʃella| *sf* (*ANAT*) armpit.

ascen'dente |affen'dɛnte| *sm* ancestor; *(fig)* ascendancy; *(ASTR)* ascendant.

ascensi'one |affen'sjone| *sf (ALPI-NISMO)* ascent; *(REL)*: **l'A~** the Ascension.

ascen'sore |affen'sore| *sm* lift.

a'scesa |af'fesa| *sf* ascent; *(al trono)* accession.

a'scesso |af'fɛsso| *sm (MED)* abscess.

'ascia, *pl* **'asce** |'affa| *sf* axe.

asciugaca'polli |affugaka'pɛlli| *sm* hair drier.

asciuga'mano |affuga'mano| *sm* towel.

asciu'gare |affu'gare| *vt* to dry; ~**rsi** *vr* to dry o.s.; *(diventare asciutto)* to dry.

asci'utto, a |af'futto| *ag* dry; *(fig: magro)* lean; *(: burbero)* curt; **restare a bocca** ~**a** *(fig)* to be disappointed.

ascol'tare *vt* to listen to; **ascolta'tore, 'trice** *sm/f* listener; **as'colto** *sm*: **essere** *o* **stare in ascolto** to be listening; **dare** *o* **prestare ascolto (a)** to pay attention (to).

as'falto *sm* asphalt.

asfissi'are *vt* to suffocate, asphyxiate; *(fig)* to bore to tears.

'Asia *sf*: **l'~** Asia; **asi'atico, a, ci, che** *ag, sm/f* Asiatic, Asian.

a'silo *sm* refuge, sanctuary; ~ **(d'infanzia)** nursery(-school); ~ **nido** crèche; ~ **politico** political asylum.

'asino *sm* donkey, ass.

'asma *sf* asthma.

'asola *sf* buttonhole.

as'parago, gi *sm* asparagus *q*.

aspet'tare *vt* to wait for; *(anche COMM)* to await; *(aspettarsi)* to expect // *vi* to wait; ~**rsi** *vr* to expect; ~ **un bambino** to be expecting (a baby); **questo non me l'aspettavo** I wasn't expecting this; **aspetta'tiva** *sf* wait; expectation; **inferiore all'aspettativa** worse than expected; **essere in aspettativa** *(AMM)* to be on leave of absence.

as'petto *sm (apparenza)* aspect, appearance, look; *(punto di vista)* point of view; **di bell'~** good-looking.

aspi'rante *ag (attore etc)* aspiring // *sm/f* candidate, applicant.

aspira'polvere *sm inv* vacuum cleaner.

aspi'rare *vt (respirare)* to breathe in, inhale; *(sog: apparecchi)* to suck (up) // *vi*: ~ **a** to aspire to; **aspira'tore** *sm* extractor fan.

aspi'rina *sf* aspirin.

aspor'tare *vt (anche MED)* to remove, take away.

'aspro, a *ag (sapore)* sour, tart; *(odore)* acrid, pungent; *(voce, clima, fig)* harsh; *(superficie)* rough; *(paesaggio)* rugged.

assaggi'are |assad'dʒare| *vt* to taste.

as'sai *av (molto)* a lot, much; *(: con ag)* very; *(a sufficienza)* enough // *ag inv (quantità)* a lot of, much; *(numero)* a lot of, many; ~ **contento** very pleased.

assa'lire *vt* to attack, assail.

as'salto *sm* attack, assault.

assassi'nare *vt* to murder; to assassinate; *(fig)* to ruin; **assas'sinio** *sm* murder; assassination; **assas'sino, a** *ag* murderous // *sm/f* murderer; assassin.

'asse *sm (TECN)* axle; *(MAT)* axis // *sf* board; ~ *f* **da stiro** ironing board.

assedi'are *vt* to besiege; **as'sedio** *sm* siege.

asse'gnare |asseɲ'ɲare| *vt* to assign, allot; *(premio)* to award.

as'segno |as'seɲɲo| *sm* allowance; *(anche: ~ bancario)* cheque *(Brit)*, check *(US)*; **contro** ~ cash on delivery; ~ **circolare** bank draft; ~ **sbarrato** crossed cheque; ~ **di viaggio** traveller's cheque; ~ **a vuoto** dud cheque; ~**i familiari** ≈ child benefit *q*.

assem'blea *sf* assembly.

assen'nato, a *ag* sensible.

as'senso *sm* assent, consent.

as'sente *ag* absent; *(fig)* faraway, vacant; **as'senza** *sf* absence.

asses'sore *sm (POL)* councillor.

assesta'mento *sm (sistemazione)* arrangement; *(EDIL, GEOL)* settlement.

asses'tare *vt (mettere in ordine)* to put in order, arrange; ~**rsi** *vr* to settle in; ~ **un colpo a qn** to deal sb a blow.

asse'tato, a *ag* thirsty, parched.

as'setto *sm* order, arrangement; *(NAUT, AER)* trim; **in** ~ **di guerra** on a war footing.

assicu'rare *vt (accertare)* to ensure; *(infondere certezza)* to assure; *(fermare, legare)* to make fast, secure; *(fare un contratto di assicurazione)* to insure; ~**rsi** *vr (accertarsi)*: ~**rsi (di)** to make sure (of); *(contro il furto etc)*: ~**rsi (contro)** to insure o.s. (against); **assicu'rato, a** *ag* insured // *sf (anche: lettera assicurata)* registered letter; **assicurazi'one** *sf* assurance; insurance.

assidera'mento *sm* exposure.

assi'eme *av (insieme)* together; ~ **a** *prep* (together) with.

assil'lare *vt* to pester, torment.

as'sillo *sm (fig)* worrying thought.

as'sise *sfpl (DIR)* assizes; **Corte** *f* **d'A~** Court of Assizes, ≈ Crown Court *(Brit)*.

assis'tente *sm/f* assistant; ~ **sociale** social worker; ~ **di volo** *(AER)* steward/stewardess.

assis'tenza |assis'tɛntsa| *sf* assistance; ~ **ospedaliera** free hospital treatment; ~ **sanitaria** health service; ~ **sociale** welfare services *pl*.

as'sistere *vt (aiutare)* to assist, help; *(curare)* to treat // *vi*: ~ **(a qc)** *(essere presente)* to be present (at sth), to attend (sth).

'asso *sm* ace; **piantare qn in** ~ to leave sb in the lurch.

associ'are [asso'tʃare] vt to associate; (rendere partecipe): ~ qn a (affari) to take sb into partnership in; (partito) to make sb a member of; ~rsi vr to enter into partnership; ~rsi a to become a member of, join; (dolori, gioie) to share in; ~ qn alle carceri to take sb to prison.

associazi'one [assotʃat'tsjone] sf association; (COMM) association, society; ~ a o per delinquere (DIR) criminal association.

asso'dato, a ag well-founded.

assogget'tare [assoddʒet'tare] vt to subject, subjugate.

asso'lato, a ag sunny.

assol'dare vt to recruit.

as'solto, a pp di **assolvere**.

assoluta'mente av absolutely.

asso'luto, a ag absolute.

assoluzi'one [assolut'tsjone] sf (DIR) acquittal; (REL) absolution.

as'solvere vt (DIR) to acquit; (REL) to absolve; (adempiere) to carry out, perform.

assomigli'are [assomiʎ'ʎare] vi: ~ a to resemble, look like.

asson'nato, a ag sleepy.

asso'pirsi vr to doze off.

assor'bente ag absorbent // sm: ~ igienico sanitary towel; ~ interno tampon.

assor'bire vt to absorb; (fig: far proprio) to assimilate.

assor'dare vt to deafen.

assorti'mento sm assortment.

assor'tito, a ag assorted; matched, matching.

as'sorto, a ag absorbed, engrossed.

assottigli'are [assottiʎ'ʎare] vt to make thin, to thin; (aguzzare) to sharpen; (ridurre) to reduce; ~rsi vr to grow thin; (fig: ridursi) to be reduced.

assue'fare vt to accustom; ~rsi a to get used to, accustom o.s. to.

as'sumere vt (impiegato) to take on, engage; (responsabilità) to assume, take upon o.s.; (contegno, espressione) to assume, put on; (droga) to consume; **as'sunto, a** pp di **assumere** // sm (tesi) proposition.

assurdità sf inv absurdity; dire delle ~ to talk nonsense.

as'surdo, a ag absurd.

'asta sf pole; (modo di vendita) auction.

astante'ria sf casualty department.

aste'nersi vr: ~ (da) to abstain (from), refrain (from); (POL) to abstain (from).

aste'risco, schi sm asterisk.

'astice ['astitʃe] sm lobster.

asti'nenza [asti'nɛntsa] sf abstinence; essere in crisi di ~ to suffer from withdrawal symptoms.

'astio sm rancour, resentment.

as'tratto, a ag abstract.

'astro sm star.

'astro... prefisso: **astrolo'gia** [astrolo'dʒia] sf astrology; **as'trologo, a, ghi, ghe** sm/f astrologer; **astro'nauta, e** sm/f astronaut; **astro'nave** sf space ship; **astrono'mia** sf astronomy; **astro'nomico, a, ci, che** ag astronomic(al).

as'tuccio [as'tuttʃo] sm case, box, holder.

as'tuto, a ag astute, cunning, shrewd; **as'tuzia** sf astuteness, shrewdness; (azione) trick.

A'tene sf Athens.

ate'neo sm university.

'ateo, a ag, sm/f atheist.

at'lante sm atlas.

at'lantico, a, ci, che ag Atlantic // sm: l'A~, l'Oceano A~ the Atlantic, the Atlantic Ocean.

at'leta, i, e sm/f athlete; **at'letica** sf athletics sg; **atletica leggera** track and field events pl; **atletica pesante** weightlifting and wrestling.

atmos'fera sf atmosphere.

a'tomico, a, ci, che ag atomic; (nucleare) atomic, atom cpd, nuclear.

'atomo sm atom.

'atrio sm entrance hall, lobby.

a'troce [a'trotʃe] ag (che provoca orrore) dreadful; (terribile) atrocious.

attacca'mento sm (fig) attachment, affection.

attacca'panni sm. hook, peg; (mobile) hall stand.

attac'care vt (unire) to attach; (cucendo) to sew on; (far aderire) to stick (on); (appendere) to hang (up); (assalire: anche fig) to attack; (iniziare) to begin, start; (fig: contagiare) to pass on // vi to stick, adhere; ~rsi vr to stick, adhere; (trasmettersi per contagio) to be contagious; (afferrarsi): ~rsi (a) to cling (to); (fig: affezionarsi): ~rsi (a) to become attached (to); ~ discorso to start a conversation; **at'tacco, chi** sm (azione offensiva: anche fig) attack; (MED) attack, fit; (SCI) binding; (ELETTR) socket.

atteggia'mento [atteddʒa'mento] sm attitude.

atteggi'arsi [atted'dʒarsi] vr: ~ a to pose as.

attem'pato, a ag elderly.

at'tendere vt to wait for, await // vi: ~ a to attend to.

atten'dibile ag (storia) credible; (testimone) reliable.

atte'nersi vr: ~ a to keep o stick to.

atten'tare vi: ~ a to make an attempt on; **atten'tato** sm attack; **attentato alla vita di qn** attempt on sb's life.

at'tento, a ag attentive; (accurato) careful, thorough; **stare** ~ **a qc** to pay attention to sth // escl be careful!

attenu'ante sf (DIR) extenuating

circumstance.

attenu'are *vt* to attenuate; (*dolore, rumore*) to lessen, deaden; (*pena, tasse*) to alleviate; **~rsi** *vr* to ease, abate.

attenzi'one |atten'tsjone| *sf* attention // *escl* watch out!, be careful!

atter'raggio |atter'raddʒo| *sm* landing.

atter'rare *vt* to bring down // *vi* to land.

atter'rire *vt* to terrify.

at'teso, a *pp di* **attendere** // *sf* waiting; (*tempo trascorso aspettando*) wait; essere in attesa di qc to be waiting for sth.

attes'tato *sm* certificate.

'attico, ci *sm* attic.

at'tiguo, a *ag* adjacent, adjoining.

attil'lato, a *ag* (*vestito*) close-fitting, tight; (*persona*) dressed up.

'attimo *sm* moment; in un ~ in a moment.

atti'nente *ag*: ~ a relating to, concerning.

atti'rare *vt* to attract.

atti'tudine *sf* (*disposizione*) aptitude; (*atteggiamento*) attitude.

atti'vare *vt* to activate; (*far funzionare*) to set going, start.

attività *sf inv* activity; (*COMM*) assets *pl.*

at'tivo, a *ag* active; (*COMM*) profit-making, credit *cpd* // *sm* (*COMM*) assets *pl*; in ~ in credit.

attiz'zare |attit'tsare| *vt* (*fuoco*) to poke.

'atto *sm* act; (*azione, gesto*) action, act, deed; (*DIR: documento*) deed, document; **~i** *smpl* (*di congressi etc*) proceedings; mettere in ~ to put into action; fare ~ di fare qc to make as if to do sth.

at'tonito, a *ag* dumbfounded, astonished.

attorcigli'are |attortʃiʎ'ʎare| *vt*, **~rsi** *vr* to twist.

at'tore, 'trice *sm/f* actor/actress.

at'torno *av*, ~ a *prep* round, around, about.

at'tracco, chi *sm* (*NAUT*) docking *q*; berth.

attra'ente *ag* attractive.

at'trarre *vt* to attract; **attrat'tiva** *sf* (*fig: fascino*) attraction, charm; **at'tratto, a** *pp di* **attrarre**.

attraversa'mento *sm*: ~ pedonale pedestrian crossing.

attraver'sare *vt* to cross; (*città, bosco, fig: periodo*) to go through; (*sog: fiume*) to run through.

attra'verso *prep* through; (*da una parte all'altra*) across.

attrazi'one |attrat'tsjone| *sf* attraction.

attrez'zare |attret'tsare| *vt* to equip; (*NAUT*) to rig; **attrezza'tura** *sf* equipment *q*; rigging; **at'trezzo** *sm* tool, instrument; (*SPORT*) piece of equipment.

attribu'ire *vt*: ~ qc a qn (*assegnare*) to give o award sth to sb; (*quadro etc*) to attribute sth to sb; **attri'buto** *sm* attribute.

at'trice |at'tritʃe| *sf vedi* **attore**.

at'trito *sm* (*anche fig*) friction.

attu'ale *ag* (*presente*) present; (*di attualità*) topical; (*che è in atto*) actual; **attualità** *sf inv* topicality; (*avvenimento*) current event; **attual'mente** *av* at the moment, at present.

attu'are *vt* to carry out; **~rsi** *vr* to be realized.

attu'tire *vt* to deaden, reduce.

au'dace |au'datʃe| *ag* audacious, daring, bold; (*provocante*) provocative; (*sfacciato*) impudent, bold; **au'dacia** *sf* audacity, daring; boldness; provocativeness; impudence.

audiovi'sivo, a *ag* audiovisual.

audizi'one |audit'tsjone| *sf* hearing; (*MUS*) audition.

'auge |'audʒe| *sf*: in ~ popular.

augu'rare *vt* to wish; **~rsi** qc to hope for sth.

au'gurio *sm* (*presagio*) omen; (*voto di benessere etc*) (good) wish; essere di buon/cattivo ~ to be of good omen/be ominous; fare gli **~i** a qn to give sb one's best wishes; tanti **~i**! all the best!

'aula *sf* (*scolastica*) classroom; (*universitaria*) lecture theatre; (*di edificio pubblico*) hall.

aumen'tare *vt*, *vi* to increase; **au'mento** *sm* increase.

au'reola *sf* halo.

au'rora *sf* dawn.

ausili'are *ag*, *sm*, *sm/f* auxiliary.

aus'picio |aus'pitʃo| *sm* omen; (*protezione*) patronage; sotto gli **~i** di under the auspices of.

aus'tero, a *ag* austere.

Aus'tralia *sf*: l'~ Australia; **au'strali'ano, a** *ag*, *sm/f* Australian.

'Austria *sf*: l'~ Austria; **aus'triaco, a, ci, che** *ag*, *sm/f* Austrian.

au'tentico, a, ci, che *ag* (*quadro, firma*) authentic, genuine; (*fatto*) true, genuine.

au'tista, i *sm* driver.

'auto *sf inv* car.

autoade'sivo, a *ag* self-adhesive // *sm* sticker.

autobiogra'fia *sf* autobiography.

auto'botte *sf* tanker.

'autobus *sm inv* bus.

auto'carro *sm* lorry (*Brit*), truck.

autocorri'era *sf* coach, bus.

au'tografo, a *ag*, *sm* autograph.

auto'linea *sf* bus company.

au'toma, i *sm* automaton.

auto'matico, a, ci, che *ag* automatic // *sm* (*bottone*) snap fastener; (*fucile*) automatic.

automazi'one |automat'tsjone| *sf* automation.

auto'mezzo |auto'meddzo| *sm* motor vehicle.

auto'mobile *sf* (motor) car.

autono'mia *sf* autonomy; (di volo) range.

au'tonomo, a *ag* autonomous, independent.

autop'sia *sf* post-mortem (examination), autopsy.

auto'radio *sf inv* (apparecchio) car radio; (autoveicolo) radio car.

au'tore, 'trice *sm/f* author; l'~ del furto the person who committed the robbery.

auto'revole *ag* authoritative; (persona) influential.

autori'messa *sf* garage.

autorità *sf inv* authority.

autoriz'zare |autorid'dzare| *vt* (permettere) to authorize; (giustificare) to allow, sanction; **autorizzazi'one** *sf* authorization.

autoscu'ola *sf* driving school.

autos'top *sm* hitchhiking; **autostop'pista, i, e** *sm/f* hitchhiker.

autos'trada *sf* motorway (Brit), highway (US).

auto'treno *sm* articulated lorry (Brit), semi (trailer) (US).

autove'icolo *sm* motor vehicle.

autovet'tura *sf* (motor) car.

au'tunno *sm* autumn.

avam'braccio, *pl(f)* **cia** |avam'brattʃo| *sm* forearm.

avangu'ardia *sf* vanguard.

a'vanti *av* (stato in luogo) in front; (moto: andare, venire) forward; (tempo: prima) before // prep (luogo): ~ a before, in front of; (tempo): ~ Cristo before Christ // escl (entrate) come (o go) in!; (MIL) forward!; (coraggio) come on! // sm inv (SPORT) forward; ~ e indietro backwards and forwards; andare ~ to go forward; (continuare) to go on; (precedere) to go (on) ahead; (orologio) to be fast; essere ~ negli studi to be well advanced with one's studies.

avanza'mento |avantsa'mento| *sm* progress; promotion.

avan'zare |avan'tsare| *vt* (spostare in avanti) to move forward, advance; (domanda) to put forward; (promuovere) to promote; (essere creditore): ~ qc da qn to be owed sth by sb // vi (andare avanti) to move forward, advance; (fig: progredire) to make progress; (essere d'avanzo) to be left, remain; **avan'zata** *sf* (MIL) advance; **a'vanzo** *sm* (residuo) remains pl, leftovers pl; (MAT) remainder; (COMM) surplus; **averne d'avanzo di qc** to have more than enough of sth; **avanzo di galera** (fig) jailbird.

ava'ria *sf* (guasto) damage; (: meccanico) breakdown.

a'varo, a *ag* avaricious, miserly // *sm* miser.

a'vena *sf* oats pl.

a'vere ♦ *sm* (COMM) credit; **gli ~i** (ricchezze) wealth *sg*
♦ *vt* **1** (possedere) to have; **ha due bambini/una bella casa** she has (got) two children/a lovely house; **ha i capelli lunghi** he has (got) long hair; **non ho da mangiare/bere** I've (got) nothing to eat/drink, I don't have anything to eat/drink
2 (indossare) to wear, have on; **aveva una maglietta rossa** he was wearing o he had on a red tee-shirt; **ha gli occhiali** he wears o has glasses
3 (ricevere) to get; **hai avuto l'assegno?** did you get o have you had the cheque?
4 (età, dimensione) to be; **ha 9 anni** he is 9 (years old); **la stanza ha 3 metri di lunghezza** the room is 3 metres in length; vedi **fame, paura** etc
5 (tempo): **quanti ne abbiamo oggi?** what's the date today?; **ne hai per molto?** will you be long?
6 (fraseologia): **avercela con qn** to be angry with sb; **cos'hai?** what's wrong o what's the matter (with you)?; **non ha niente a che vedere o fare con me** it's got nothing to do with me
♦ *vb ausiliare* **1** to have; **aver bevuto/mangiato** to have drunk/eaten
2 (+ da + infinito): ~ **da fare** qc to have to do sth; **non hai che da chiederlo** you only have to ask him.

'avi *smpl* ancestors, forefathers.

avia'tore, 'trice *sm/f* aviator, pilot.

aviazi'one |avjat'tsjone| *sf* aviation; (MIL) air force.

avidità *sf* eagerness; greed.

'avido, a *ag* eager; (peg) greedy.

avo'cado *sm* avocado.

a'vorio *sm* ivory.

Avv. *abbr* = avvocato.

avvalla'mento *sm* sinking q; (effetto) depression.

avvalo'rare *vt* to confirm.

avvam'pare *vi* (incendio) to flare up.

avvantaggi'are |avvantad'dʒare| *vt* to favour; ~rsi *vr*: ~rsi negli affari/sui concorrenti to get ahead in business/of one's competitors.

avvele'nare *vt* to poison.

avve'nente *ag* attractive, charming.

avveni'mento *sm* event.

avve'nire *vi, vb impers* to happen, occur // *sm* future.

avven'tarsi *vr*: ~ su o contro qn/qc to hurl o.s. o rush at sb/sth.

avven'tato, a *ag* rash, reckless.

avven'tizio, a |avven'tittsjo| *ag* (impiegato) temporary; (guadagno) casual.

av'vento *sm* advent, coming; (REL): l'A~ Advent.

avven'tore *sm* (regular) customer.

avven'tura *sf* adventure; (*amorosa*) affair.

avventu'rarsi *vr* to venture.

avventu'roso, a *ag* adventurous.

avve'rarsi *vr* to come true.

av'verbio *sm* adverb.

avver'sario, a *ag* opposing // *sm* opponent, adversary.

av'verso, a *ag* (*contrario*) contrary; (*sfavorevole*) unfavourable.

avver'tenza [avver'tentsa] *sf* (*ammonimento*) warning; (*cautela*) care; (*premessa*) foreword; ~e *sfpl* (*istruzioni per l'uso*) instructions.

avverti'mento *sm* warning.

avver'tire *vt* (*avvisare*) to warn; (*rendere consapevole*) to inform, notify; (*percepire*) to feel.

av'vezzo, a [av'vettso] *ag*: ~ a used to.

avvia'mento *sm* (*atto*) starting; (*effetto*) start; (*AUT*) starting; (*: dispositivo*) starter; (*COMM*) goodwill.

avvi'are *vt* (*mettere sul cammino*) to direct; (*impresa, trattative*) to begin, start; (*motore*) to start; ~rsi *vr* to set off, set out.

avvicen'darsi [avvitʃen'darsi] *vr* to alternate.

avvici'nare [avvitʃi'nare] *vt* to bring near; (*trattare con: persona*) to approach; ~rsi *vr*: ~rsi (a qn/qc) to approach (sb/sth), draw near (to sb/sth).

avvi'lire *vt* (*umiliare*) to humiliate; (*degradare*) to disgrace; (*scoraggiare*) to dishearten, discourage; ~rsi *vr* (*abbattersi*) to lose heart.

avvilup'pare *vt* (*avvolgere*) to wrap up; (*ingarbugliare*) to entangle.

avvinaz'zato, a [avvinat'tsato] *ag* drunk.

av'vincere [av'vintʃere] *vt* to charm, enthral.

avvinghi'are [avvin'gjare] *vt* to clasp; ~rsi *vr*: ~rsi a to cling to.

avvi'sare *vt* (*far sapere*) to inform; (*mettere in guardia*) to warn; **av'viso** *sm* warning; (*annuncio*) announcement; (*: affisso*) notice; (*inserzione pubblicitaria*) advertisement; **a mio avviso** in my opinion.

avvis'tare *vt* to sight.

avvi'tare *vt* to screw down (*o* in).

avviz'zire [avvit'tsire] *vi* to wither.

avvo'cato, 'essa *sm/f* (*DIR*) barrister (*Brit*), lawyer; (*fig*) defender, advocate.

av'volgere [av'voldʒere] *vt* to roll up; (*avviluppare*) to wrap up; ~rsi *vr* (*avvilupparsi*) to wrap o.s. up; **avvol'gibile** *sm* roller blind (*Brit*), blind.

avvol'toio *sm* vulture.

azi'enda [ad'dzjenda] *sf* business, firm, concern; ~ **agricola** farm.

azio'nare [attsjo'nare] *vt* to activate.

azi'one [at'tsjone] *sf* action; (*COMM*) share; **azio'nista, i, e** *sm/f* (*COMM*)

shareholder.

a'zoto [ad'dzɔto] *sm* nitrogen.

azzan'nare [attsan'nare] *vt* to sink one's teeth into.

azzar'darsi [addzar'darsi] *vr*: ~ **a fare** to dare (to) do; **azzar'dato, a** *ag* (*impresa*) risky; (*risposta*) rash.

az'zardo [ad'dzardo] *sm* risk.

azzec'care [attsek'kare] *vt* (*risposta etc*) to get right.

azzuf'farsi [attsuf'farsi] *vr* to come to blows.

az'zurro, a [ad'dzurro] *ag* blue // *sm* (*colore*) blue; **gli** ~**i** (*SPORT*) the Italian national team.

B

bab'beo *sm* simpleton.

'babbo *sm* (*fam*) dad, daddy; **B~ natale** Father Christmas.

bab'buccia, ce [bab'buttʃa] *sf* slipper; (*per neonati*) bootee.

ba'bordo *sm* (*NAUT*) port side.

ba'cato, a *ag* worm-eaten, rotten.

'bacca, che *sf* berry.

baccalà *sm* dried salted cod; (*fig peg*) dummy.

bac'cano *sm* din, clamour.

bac'cello [bat'tʃello] *sm* pod.

bac'chetta [bak'ketta] *sf* (*verga*) stick, rod; (*di direttore d'orchestra*) baton; (*di tamburo*) drumstick; ~ **magica** magic wand.

baci'are [ba'tʃare] *vt* to kiss; ~rsi *vr* to kiss (one another).

baci'nella [batʃi'nella] *sf* basin.

ba'cino [ba'tʃino] *sm* basin; (*MINERALOGIA*) field, bed; (*ANAT*) pelvis; (*NAUT*) dock.

'bacio [bat'tʃo] *sm* kiss.

'baco, chi *sm* worm; ~ **da seta** silkworm.

ba'dare *vi* (*fare attenzione*) to take care, be careful; (*occuparsi di*): ~ **a** to look after, take care of; (*dar ascolto*): ~ **a** to pay attention to; **bada ai fatti tuoi!** mind your own business!

ba'dia *sf* abbey.

ba'dile *sm* shovel.

'baffi *smpl* moustache *sg*; (*di animale*) whiskers; **ridere sotto i** ~ to laugh up one's sleeve; **leccarsi i** ~ to lick one's lips.

bagagli'aio [bagaʎ'ʎajo] *sm* luggage van (*Brit*) *o* car (*US*); (*AUT*) boot (*Brit*), trunk (*US*).

ba'gagli [ba'gaʎʎi] *smpl* luggage *sg*.

bagli'ore [baʎ'ʎore] *sm* flash, dazzling light; **un** ~ **di speranza** a ray of hope.

ba'gnante [baɲ'ɲante] *sm/f* bather.

ba'gnare [baɲ'ɲare] *vt* to wet; (*inzuppare*) to soak; (*innaffiare*) to water; (*sog: fiume*) to flow through; (*: mare*) to wash, bathe; **~rsi** *vr* (*al mare*) to go swimming o bathing; (*in vasca*) to have a bath.

ba'gnato, a |baɲ'ɲato| *ag* wet.

ba'gnino |baɲ'ɲino| *sm* lifeguard.

'bagno |'baɲɲo| *sm* bath; (*locale*) bathroom; (*stabilimento*) baths; **fare il ~** to have a bath; (*nel mare*) to go swimming o bathing; **fare il ~ a qn** to give sb a bath; **mettere a ~** to soak; **~ schiuma** bubble bath.

bagnoma'ria |baɲɲoma'ria| *sm*: **cuocere a ~** to cook in a double saucepan.

'baia *sf* bay.

baio'netta *sf* bayonet.

balaus'trata *sf* balustrade.

balbet'tare *vi* to stutter, stammer; (*bimbo*) to babble // *vt* to stammer out.

balbuzi'ente |balbut'tsjɛnte| *ag* stuttering, stammering.

bal'cone *sm* balcony.

baldac'chino |baldak'kino| *sm* canopy.

bal'danza |bal'dantsa| *sf* self-confidence, boldness.

'baldo, a *ag* bold, daring.

bal'doria *sf*: **fare ~** to have a riotous time.

ba'lena *sf* whale.

bale'nare *vb impers*: **balena** there's lightning // *vi* to flash; **mi balenò un'idea** an idea flashed through my mind; **ba'leno** *sm* flash of lightning; **in un baleno** in a flash.

ba'lestra *sf* crossbow.

ba'lia *sf*: **in ~ di** at the mercy of.

'balla *sf* (*di merci*) bale; (*fandonia*) (tall) story.

bal'lare *vt, vi* to dance; **bal'lata** *sf* ballad.

balle'rina *sf* dancer; ballet dancer; (*scarpa*) ballet shoe.

balle'rino *sm* dancer; ballet dancer.

bal'letto *sm* ballet.

'ballo *sm* dance; (*azione*) dancing *q*; **essere in ~** (*fig: persona*) to be involved; (*: cosa*) to be at stake.

ballot'taggio |ballot'taddʒo| *sm* (*POL*) second ballot.

balne'are *ag* seaside *cpd*; (*stagione*) bathing.

ba'locco, chi *sm* toy.

ba'lordo, a *ag* stupid, senseless.

'balsamo *sm* (*aroma*) balsam; (*lenimento, fig*) balm.

'Baltico *sm*: **il (mar) ~** the Baltic (Sea).

balu'ardo *sm* bulwark.

'balza |'baltsa| *sf* (*dirupo*) crag; (*di stoffa*) frill.

bal'zare |bal'tsare| *vi* to bounce; (*lanciarsi*) to jump, leap; **'balzo** *sm* bounce; jump, leap; (*del terreno*) crag.

bam'bagia |bam'badʒa| *sf* (*ovatta*) cotton wool (*Brit*), absorbent cotton (*US*); (*cascame*) cotton waste.

bam'bina *ag, sf* vedi **bambino.**

bambi'naia *sf* nanny, nurse(maid).

bam'bino, a *sm/f* child.

bam'boccio |bam'bɔttʃo| *sm* plump child; (*pupazzo*) rag doll.

'bambola *sf* doll.

bambù *sm* bamboo.

ba'nale *ag* banal, commonplace.

ba'nana *sf* banana; **ba'nano** *sm* banana tree.

'banca, che *sf* bank; **~ dei dati** data bank.

banca'rella *sf* stall.

ban'cario, a *ag* banking, bank *cpd* // *sm* bank clerk.

banca'rotta *sf* bankruptcy; **fare ~** to go bankrupt.

ban'chetto |ban'ketto| *sm* banquet.

banchi'ere |ban'kjɛre| *sm* banker.

ban'china |ban'kina| *sf* (*di porto*) quay; (*per pedoni, ciclisti*) path; (*di stazione*) platform; **~ cedevole** (*AUT*) soft verge (*Brit*) o shoulder (*US*).

'banco, chi *sm* bench; (*di negozio*) counter; (*di mercato*) stall; (*di officina*) (work-)bench; (*GEO, banca*) bank; **~ di corallo** coral reef; **~ degli imputati** dock; **~ di prova** (*fig*) testing ground; **~ dei testimoni** witness box.

'Bancomat *sm inv* ® automated banking; (*tessera*) cash card.

banco'nota *sf* banknote.

'banda *sf* band; (*di stoffa*) band, stripe; (*lato, parte*) side; **~ perforata** punch tape.

banderu'ola *sf* (*METEOR*) weathercock, weathervane.

bandi'era *sf* flag, banner.

ban'dire *vt* to proclaim; (*esiliare*) to exile; (*fig*) to dispense with.

ban'dito *sm* outlaw, bandit.

bandi'tore *sm* (*di aste*) auctioneer.

'bando *sm* proclamation; (*esilio*) exile, banishment; **~ alle chiacchiere!** that's enough talk!

'bandolo *sm*: **il ~ della matassa** (*fig*) the key to the problem.

bar *sm inv* bar.

'bara *sf* coffin.

ba'racca, che *sf* shed, hut; (*peg*) hovel; **mandare avanti la ~** to keep things going.

bara'onda *sf* hubbub, bustle.

ba'rare *vi* to cheat.

'baratro *sm* abyss.

barat'tare *vt*: **~ qc con** to barter sth for, swap sth for; **ba'ratto** *sm* barter.

ba'rattolo *sm* (*di latta*) tin; (*di vetro*) jar; (*di coccio*) pot.

'barba *sf* beard; **farsi la ~** to shave; **farla in ~ a qn** (*fig*) to do sth to sb's face; **che ~!** what a bore!

barbabi'etola *sf* beetroot (*Brit*), beet (*US*); **~ da zucchero** sugar beet.

bar'barico, a, ci, che *ag* barbarian; barbaric.

'barbaro, a *ag* barbarous; **~i** *smpl* barbarians.

barbi'ere *sm* barber.

bar'bone *sm* (*cane*) poodle; (*vagabondo*) tramp.

bar'buto, a *ag* bearded.

'barca, che *sf* boat; **~ a remi** rowing boat; **barcai'olo** *sm* boatman.

barcol'lare *vi* to stagger.

bar'cone *sm* (*per ponti di barche*) pontoon.

ba'rella *sf* (*lettiga*) stretcher.

ba'rile *sm* barrel, cask.

ba'rista, i, e *sm/f* barman/maid; bar owner.

ba'ritono *sm* baritone.

bar'lume *sm* glimmer, gleam.

ba'rocco, a, chi, che *ag, sm* baroque.

ba'rometro *sm* barometer.

ba'rone *sm* baron; **baro'nessa** *sf* baroness.

'barra *sf* bar; (*NAUT*) helm; (*linea grafica*) line, stroke.

barri'care *vt* to barricade; **barri'cata** *sf* barricade.

barri'era *sf* barrier; (*GEO*) reef.

ba'ruffa *sf* scuffle.

barzel'letta [bardzel'letta] *sf* joke, funny story.

ba'sare *vt* to base, found; **~rsi** *vr*: **~rsi su** (*sog: fatti, prove*) to be based o founded on; (: *persona*) to base one's arguments on.

'basco, a, schi, sche *ag* Basque // *sm* (*copricapo*) beret.

'base- *sf* base; (*fig: fondamento*) basis; (*POL*) rank and file; **di ~** basic; **in ~ a** on the basis of, according to; **a ~ di caffè** coffee-based.

ba'setta *sf* sideburn.

ba'silica, che *sf* basilica.

ba'silico *sm* basil.

bassi'fondi *smpl* (*fig*) dregs.

'basso, a *ag* low; (*di statura*) short; (*meridionale*) southern // *sm* bottom, lower part; (*MUS*) bass; **la ~a Italia** southern Italy.

bassorili'evo *sm* bas-relief.

'basta *escl* (that's) enough!, that will do!

bas'tardo, a *ag* (*animale, pianta*) hybrid, crossbreed; (*persona*) illegitimate, bastard (*peg*) // *sm/f* illegitimate child, bastard (*peg*).

bas'tare *vi, vb impers* to be enough, be sufficient; **~ a qn** to be enough for sb; **basta chiedere** o **che chieda a un vigile** you have only to o need only ask a policeman.

basti'mento *sm* ship, vessel.

basto'nare *vt* to beat, thrash.

baston'cino [baston'tʃino] *sm* (*SCI*) ski pole.

bas'tone *sm* stick; **~ da passeggio** walking stick.

bat'taglia [bat'taʎʎa] *sf* battle; fight.

bat'taglio [bat'taʎʎo] *sm* (*di campana*) clapper; (*di porta*) knocker.

battagli'one [battaʎ'ʎone] *sm* battalion.

bat'tello *sm* boat.

bat'tente *sm* (*imposta: di porta*) wing, flap; (: *di finestra*) shutter; (*batacchio: di porta*) knocker; (: *di orologio*) hammer; **chiudere i ~i** (*fig*) to shut up shop.

'battere *vt* to beat; (*grano*) to thresh; (*percorrere*) to scour // *vi* (*bussare*) to knock; (*urtare*): **~ contro** to hit o strike against; (*pioggia, sole*) to beat down; (*cuore*) to beat; (*TENNIS*) to serve; **~rsi** *vr* to fight; **~ le mani** to clap; **~ i piedi** to stamp one's feet; **~ le ore** to strike the hours; **~ su un argomento** to hammer home an argument; **~ a macchina** to type; **~ bandiera italiana** to fly the Italian flag; **~ in testa** (*AUT*) to knock; **in un batter d'occhio** in the twinkling of an eye.

bat'teri *smpl* bacteria.

batte'ria *sf* battery; (*MUS*) drums *pl*.

bat'tesimo *sm* baptism; christening.

battez'zare [batted'dzare] *vt* to baptize; to christen.

batticu'ore *sm* palpitations *pl*; **avere il ~** to be frightened to death.

batti'mano *sm* applause.

batti'panni *sm inv* carpet-beater.

battis'tero *sm* baptistry.

battis'trada *sm inv* (*di pneumatico*) tread; (*di gara*) pacemaker.

battitap'peto *sm* upright vacuum cleaner.

'battito *sm* beat, throb; **~ cardiaco** heartbeat; **~ della pioggia/dell'orologio** beating of the rain/ticking of the clock.

bat'tuta *sf* blow; (*di macchina da scrivere*) stroke; (*MUS*) bar; beat; (*TEATRO*) cue; (*frase spiritosa*) witty remark; (*di caccia*) beating; (*POLIZIA*) combing, scouring; (*TENNIS*) service.

ba'ule *sm* trunk; (*AUT*) boot (*Brit*), trunk (*US*).

'bava *sf* (*di animale*) slaver, slobber; (*di lumaca*) slime; (*di vento*) breath.

bava'glino [bavaʎ'ʎino] *sm* bib.

ba'vaglio [ba'vaʎʎo] *sm* gag.

'bavero *sm* collar.

ba'zar [bad'dzar] *sm inv* bazaar.

baz'zecola [bad'dzekola] *sf* trifle.

bazzi'care [battsi'kare] *vt* to frequent // *vi*: **~ in/con** to frequent.

be'ato, a *ag* blessed; (*fig*) happy; **~ te!** lucky you!

bec'caccia, ce [bek'kattʃa] *sf* woodcock.

bec'care *vt* to peck; (*fig: raffreddore*) to pick up, catch; **~rsi** *vr* (*fig*) to squabble.

beccheggi'are [bekked'dʒare] *vi* to pitch.

bec'chino [bek'kino] *sm* gravedigger.

'becco, chi *sm* beak, bill; (*di caffettiera etc*) spout; lip.

Be'fana *sf* old woman who, according to legend, brings children their presents at the Epiphany; (*Epifania*) Epiphany; (*donna brutta*): b~ hag, witch.

'beffa *sf* practical joke; **farsi ~e di qn** to make a fool of sb; **bef'fardo, a** *ag* scornful, mocking; **bef'fare** *vt* (*anche:* **beffarsi di**) to make a fool of, mock.

'bega, ghe *sf* quarrel.

'begli ['bɛʎʎi], **'bei, bel** *ag vedi* **bello**.

be'lare *vi* to bleat.

'belga, ghe *ag, sm/f* Belgian.

'Belgio ['bɛldʒo] *sm*: **il ~** Belgium.

bel'lezza [bel'lettsa] *sf* beauty.

'bello, a *ag* (*dav sm.* **bel** +*C*, **bell'** +*V*, **bello** + *s impura, gn, pn, ps, x, z, pl* **bei** +*C*, **begli** + *s impura etc o V*) beautiful, fine, lovely; (*uomo*) handsome // *sm* (*bellezza*) beauty; (*tempo*) fine weather // *sf* (*SPORT*) decider // *av*: **fa ~ the** weather is fine, it's fine; **una ~a cifra** a considerable sum of money; **un bel niente** absolutely nothing; **è una truffa ~a e buona!** it's a real fraud!; **è bell'e finito** it's already finished; **adesso viene il ~** now comes the best bit; **sul più ~ at** the crucial point; **cosa fai di ~?** are you doing anything interesting?; **belle arti** fine arts.

'belva *sf* wild animal.

belve'dere *sm inv* panoramic viewpoint.

benché [ben'ke] *cong* although.

'benda *sf* bandage; (*per gli occhi*) blindfold; **ben'dare** *vt* to bandage; to blindfold.

'bene *av* well; (*completamente, affatto*): **è ben difficile** it's very difficult // *ag inv*: **gente ~** well-to-do people // *sm* good; **~i** *smpl* (*averi*) property *sg*, estate *sg*; **io sto ~/poco ~** I'm well/not very well; **va ~** all right; **volere un ~ dell'anima a qn** to love sb very much; **un uomo per ~ a** respectable man; **fare ~** to do the right thing; **fare ~ a** (*salute*) to be good for; **fare del ~ a qn** to do sb a good turn; **~i di consumo** consumer goods.

bene'detto, a *pp di* **benedire** // *ag* blessed, holy.

bene'dire *vt* to bless; to consecrate; **benedizi'one** *sf* blessing.

benedu'cato, a *ag* well-mannered.

benefi'cenza [benefi'tʃɛntsa] *sf* charity.

bene'ficio [bene'fitʃo] *sm* benefit; **con ~ d'inventario** (*fig*) with reservations.

be'nefico, a, ci, che *ag* beneficial; charitable.

beneme'renza [beneme'rɛntsa] *sf* merit.

bene'merito, a *ag* meritorious.

be'nessere *sm* well-being.

benes'tante *ag* well-to-do.

benes'tare *sm* consent, approval.

be'nevolo, a *ag* benevolent.

be'nigno, a [be'niɲɲo] *ag* kind, kindly; (*critica etc*) favourable; (*MED*) benign.

benin'teso *av* of course.

bensì *cong* but (rather).

benve'nuto, a *ag, sm* welcome; **dare il ~ a qn** to welcome sb.

ben'zina [ben'dzina] *sf* petrol (*Brit*), gas (*US*); **fare ~** to get petrol (*Brit*) o gas (*US*); **benzi'naio** *sm* petrol (*Brit*) o gas (*US*) pump attendant.

'bere *vt* to drink; **darla a ~ a qn** (*fig*) to fool sb.

ber'lina *sf* (*AUT*) saloon (car) (*Brit*), sedan (*US*).

Ber'lino *sf* Berlin.

ber'noccolo *sm* bump; (*inclinazione*) flair.

ber'retto *sm* cap.

bersagli'are [bersaʎ'ʎare] *vt* to shoot at; (*colpire ripetutamente, fig*) to bombard; **bersagliato dalla sfortuna** dogged by ill fortune.

ber'saglio [ber'saʎʎo] *sm* target.

bes'temmia *sf* curse; (*REL*) blasphemy.

bestemmi'are *vi* to curse, swear; to blaspheme // *vt* to curse, swear at; to blaspheme.

'bestia *sf* animal; **andare in ~** (*fig*) to fly into a rage; **besti'ale** *ag* beastly; animal *cpd*; (*fam*): **fa un freddo bestiale** it's bitterly cold; **besti'ame** *sm* livestock; (*bovino*) cattle *pl*.

'bettola *sf* (*peg*) dive.

be'tulla *sf* birch.

be'vanda *sf* drink, beverage.

bevi'tore, 'trice *sm/f* drinker.

be'vuto, a *pp di* **bere** // *sf* drink.

bi'ada *sf* fodder.

bianche'ria [bjanke'ria] *sf* linen; **~ intima** underwear; **~ da donna** ladies' underwear, lingerie.

bi'anco, a, chi, che *ag* white; (*non scritto*) blank // *sm* white; (*intonaco*) whitewash // *sm/f* white, white man/ woman; **in ~** (*foglio, assegno*) blank; (*notte*) sleepless; **in ~ e nero** (*TV, FOT*) black and white; **mangiare in ~** to follow a bland diet; **pesce in ~** boiled fish; **andare in ~** (*non riuscire*) to fail; **~ dell'uovo** egg-white.

biasi'mare *vt* to disapprove of, censure; **bi'asimo** *sm* disapproval, censure.

'bibbia *sf* bible.

bibe'ron *sm inv* feeding bottle.

'bibita *sf* (soft) drink.

biblio'teca, che *sf* library; (*mobile*) bookcase; **bibliote'cario, a** *sm/f* librarian.

bicarbo'nato *sm*: **~ (di sodio)** bicarbonate (of soda).

bicchi'ere [bik'kjɛre] *sm* glass.

bici'cletta [bitʃi'kletta] *sf* bicycle; **andare in ~** to cycle.

bidé *sm inv* bidet.

bi'dello, a *sm/f* (*INS*) janitor.

bi'done *sm* drum, can; (*anche:* **~ dell'immondizia**) (dust)bin; (*fam: truffa*) swindle; **fare un ~ a qn** (*fam*) to

let sb down; to cheat sb.
bien'nale *ag* biennial.
bi'ennio *sm* period of two years.
bi'etola *sf* beet.
bifor'carsi *vr* to fork; **biforcazi'one** *sf* fork.
bighello'nare |bigello'nare| *vi* to loaf (about).
bigiotte'ria |bidʒotte'ria| *sf* costume jewellery; (*negozio*) jeweller's (*selling only costume jewellery*).
bigli'ardo |biʎ'ʎardo| *sm* = **billardo.**
bigliette'ria |biʎʎette'ria| *sf* (*di stazione*) ticket office; booking office; (*di teatro*) box office.
bigli'etto |biʎ'ʎetto| *sm* (*per viaggi, spettacoli etc*) ticket; (*cartoncino*) card; (*anche:* ~ **di banca**) (bank)note; ~ **d'auguri/da visita** greetings/visiting card; ~ **d'andata e ritorno** return (ticket), round-trip ticket (*US*).
bignè |biɲ'ɲe| *sm inv* cream puff.
bigo'dino *sm* roller, curler.
bi'gotto, a *ag* over-pious // *sm/f* church fiend.
bi'lancia, ce |bi'lantʃa| *sf* (*pesa*) scales *pl;* (*: di precisione*) balance; (*dello zodiaco*): **B**~ Libra; ~ **commerciale/dei pagamenti** balance of trade/payments; **bilanci'are** *vt* (*pesare*) to weigh; (*: fig*) to weigh up; (*pareggiare*) to balance.
bi'lancio |bi'lantʃo| *sm* (*COMM*) balance(-sheet); (*statale*) budget; **fare il** ~ **di** (*fig*) to assess; ~ **consuntivo** (final) balance; ~ **preventivo** budget.
'bile *sf* bile; (*fig*) rage, anger.
bili'ardo *sm* billiards *sg;* billiard table.
'bilico, ghi *sm:* **essere in** ~ to be balanced; (*fig*) to be undecided; **tenere qn in** ~ to keep sb in suspense.
bi'lingue *ag* bilingual.
bili'one *sm* (*mille milioni*) thousand million; (*milione di milioni*) billion (*Brit*), trillion (*US*).
'bimbo, a *sm/f* little boy/girl.
bimen'sile *ag* fortnightly.
bimes'trale *ag* two-monthly, bimonthly.
bi'nario, a *ag* (*sistema*) binary // *sm* (*railway*) track *o* line; (*piattaforma*) platform; ~ **morto** dead-end track.
bi'nocolo *sm* binoculars *pl.*
bio... *prefisso:* **bio'chimica** |bio'kimika| *sf* biochemistry; **biodegra'dabile** *ag* biodegradable; **biogra'fia** *sf* biography; **biolo'gia** *sf* biology; **bio'logico, a, ci, che** *ag* biological.
bi'ondo, a *ag* blond, fair.
bir'bante *sm* rogue, rascal.
biri'chino, a |biri'kino| *ag* mischievous // *sm/f* scamp, little rascal.
bi'rillo *sm* skittle (*Brit*), pin (*US*); ~**i** *smpl* (*gioco*) skittles *sg* (*Brit*), bowling (*US*).
'biro *sf inv* ® biro ®.
'birra *sf* beer; **a tutta** ~ (*fig*) at top

speed; **birre'ria** *sf* ≈ bierkeller.
bis *escl, sm inv* encore.
bis'betico, a, ci, che *ag* ill-tempered, crabby.
bisbigli'are |bisbiʎ'ʎare| *vt, vi* to whisper.
'bisca, sche *sf* gambling-house.
'biscia, sce |'biʃʃa| *sf* snake; ~ **d'acqua** grass snake.
bis'cotto *sm* biscuit.
bises'tile *ag:* **anno** ~ leap year.
bis'lungo, a, ghi, ghe *ag* oblong.
bis'nonno, a *sm/f* great grandfather/ grandmother.
biso'gnare |bizoɲ'ɲare| *vb impers:* **bisogna che tu parta/lo faccia** you'll have to go/do it; **bisogna parlargli** we'll (*o* I'll) have to talk to him.
bi'sogno |bi'zoɲɲo| *sm* need; ~**i** *smpl:* **fare i propri** ~**i** to relieve o.s.; **avere** ~ **di qc/di fare qc** to need sth/to do sth; **al** ~, **in caso di** ~ if need be; **biso'gnoso, a** *ag* needy, poor; **bisognoso di** in need of, needing.
bis'tecca, che *sf* steak, beefsteak.
bisticci'are |bistit'tʃare| *vi,* ~**rsi** *vr* to quarrel, bicker; **bis'ticcio** *sm* quarrel, squabble; (*gioco di parole*) pun.
'bisturi *sm* scalpel.
bi'sunto, a *ag* very greasy.
'bitter *sm inv* bitters *pl.*
bi'vacco, chi *sm* bivouac.
'bivio *sm* fork; (*fig*) dilemma.
'bizza |'biddza| *sf* tantrum; **fare le** ~**e** (*bambino*) to be naughty.
biz'zarro, a |bid'dzarro| *ag* bizarre, strange.
biz'zeffe |bid'dzeffe|: **a** ~ *av* in plenty, galore.
blan'dire *vt* to soothe; to flatter.
'blando, a *ag* mild, gentle.
bla'sone *sm* coat of arms.
blate'rare *vi* to chatter, blether.
blin'dato, a *ag* armoured.
bloc'care *vt* to block; (*isolare*) to isolate, cut off; (*porto*) to blockade; (*prezzi, beni*) to freeze; (*meccanismo*) to jam; ~**rsi** *vr* (*motore*) to stall; (*freni, porta*) to jam, stick; (*ascensore*) to stop, get stuck.
'blocco, chi *sm* block; (*MIL*) blockade; (*dei fitti*) restriction; (*quadernetto*) pad; (*fig: unione*) coalition; (*il bloccare*) blocking; isolating; cutting-off; blockading; freezing; jamming; **in** ~ (*nell'insieme*) as a whole; (*COMM*) in bulk; ~ **cardiaco** cardiac arrest.
blu *ag inv, sm* dark blue.
'blusa *sf* (*camiciotto*) smock; (*camicetta*) blouse.
'boa *sm inv* (*ZOOL*) boa constrictor; (*sciarpa*) feather boa // *sf* buoy.
bo'ato *sm* rumble, roar.
bo'bina *sf* reel, spool; (*di pellicola*) spool; (*di film*) reel; (*ELETTR*) coil.

'**bocca, che** sf mouth; **in ~ al lupo!** good luck!

boc'caccia, ce |bok'kattʃa| sf (malalingua) gossip; **fare le ~ce** to pull faces.

boc'cale sm jug; **~ da birra** tankard.

boc'cetta |bot'tʃetta| sf small bottle.

boccheggi'are |bokked'dʒare| vi to gasp.

boc'chino |bok'kino| sm (di sigaretta, sigaro: cannella) cigarette-holder; cigar-holder; (di pipa, strumenti musicali) mouthpiece.

'**boccia, ce** |'bottʃa| sf bottle; (di vino) decanter, carafe; (palla) bowl; **gioco delle ~ce** bowls sg.

bocci'are |bot'tʃare| vt (proposta, progetto) to reject; (INS) to fail; (BOCCE) to hit; **boccia'tura** sf failure.

bocci'olo |bot'tʃɔlo| sm bud.

boc'cone sm mouthful, morsel.

boc'coni av face downwards.

'**boia** sm inv executioner; hangman.

boi'ata sf botch.

boicot'tare vt to boycott.

'**bolide** sm meteor; **come un ~** like a flash, at top speed.

'**bolla** sf bubble; (MED) blister; **~ papale** papal bull; **~ di consegna** (COMM) delivery note.

bol'lare vt to stamp; (fig) to brand.

bol'lente ag boiling; boiling hot.

bol'letta sf bill; (ricevuta) receipt; **essere in ~** to be hard up.

bollet'tino sm bulletin; (COMM) note; **~ di spedizione** consignment note.

bol'lire vt, vi to boil; **bol'lito** sm (CUC) boiled meat.

bolli'tore sm (CUC) kettle; (per riscaldamento) boiler.

'**bollo** sm stamp.

'**bomba** sf bomb; **tornare a ~** (fig) to get back to the point; **~ atomica** atom bomb.

bombarda'mento sm bombardment; bombing.

bombar'dare vt to bombard; (da aereo) to bomb.

bombardi'ere sm bomber.

bom'betta sf bowler (hat).

'**bombola** sf cylinder.

bo'naccia, ce |bo'nattʃa| sf dead calm.

bo'nario, a ag good-natured, kind.

bo'nifica, che sf reclamation; reclaimed land.

bo'nifico, ci sm (riduzione, abbuono) discount; (versamento a terzi) credit transfer.

bontà sf goodness; (cortesia) kindness; **aver la ~ di fare qc** to be good o kind enough to do sth.

borbot'tare vi to mumble; (stomaco) to rumble.

'**borchia** |'borkja| sf stud.

borda'tura sf (SARTORIA) border, trim.

'**bordo** sm (NAUT) ship's side; (orlo) edge; (striscia di guarnizione) border, trim; **a ~ di** (nave, aereo) aboard, on board; (macchina) in.

bor'gata sf hamlet.

bor'ghese |bor'geze| ag (spesso peg) middle-class; bourgeois; **abito ~** civilian dress; **borghe'sia** sf middle classes pl; bourgeoisie.

'**borgo, ghi** sm (paesino) village; (quartiere) district; (sobborgo) suburb.

'**boria** sf self-conceit, arrogance.

boro'talco sm talcum powder.

bor'raccia, ce |bor'rattʃa| sf canteen, water-bottle.

'**borsa** sf bag; (anche: **~ da signora**) handbag; (ECON): **la B~ (valori)** the Stock Exchange; **~ nera** black market; **~ della spesa** shopping bag; **~ di studio** grant; **borsai'olo** sm pickpocket; **borsel'lino** sm purse; **bor'setta** sf handbag; **bor'sista, i, e** sm/f (ECON) speculator; (INS) grant-holder.

bos'caglia |bos'kaʎʎa| sf woodlands pl.

boscai'olo sm woodcutter; forester.

'**bosco, schi** sm wood; **bos'coso, a** ag wooded.

'**bossolo** sm cartridge-case.

bo'tanico, a, ci, che ag botanical // botanist // sf botany.

'**botola** sf trap door.

'**botta** sf blow; (rumore) bang.

'**botte** sf barrel, cask.

bot'tega, ghe sf shop; (officina) workshop; **botte'gaio, a** sm/f shopkeeper; **botte'ghino** sm ticket office; (del lotto) public lottery office.

bot'tiglia |bot'tiʎʎa| sf bottle; **bottiglie'ria** sf wine shop.

bot'tino sm (di guerra) booty; (di rapina, furto) loot.

'**botto** sm bang; crash; **di ~** suddenly.

bot'tone sm button; **attaccare ~ a qn** (fig) to buttonhole sb.

bo'vino, a ag bovine; **~i** smpl cattle.

boxe |bɔks| sf boxing.

'**bozza** |'bɔttsa| sf draft; sketch; (TIP) proof; **boz'zetto** sm sketch.

'**bozzolo** |'bɔttsolo| sm cocoon.

BR sigla fpl = Brigate Rosse.

brac'care vt to hunt.

brac'cetto |brat'tʃetto| sm: **a ~** arm in arm.

bracci'ale |brat'tʃale| sm bracelet; (distintivo) armband; **braccia'letto** sm bracelet, bangle.

bracci'ante |brat'tʃante| sm (AGR) day labourer.

bracci'ata |brat'tʃata| sf (nel nuoto) stroke.

'**braccio** |'brattʃo| sm (pl(f) **braccia**: ANAT) arm; (pl(m) **bracci**: di gru, fiume) arm; (: di edificio) wing; **~ di mare** sound; **bracci'olo** sm (appoggio) arm.

'bracco, chi sm hound.

bracconi'ere sm poacher.

'brace |'bratʃe| sf embers pl; braci'ere sm brazier.

braci'ola |bra'tʃɔla| sf (CUC) chop.

bra'mare vt: ~ qc/di fare to long for sth/to do.

'branca, che sf branch.

'branchia |'brankja| sf (ZOOL) gill.

'branco, chi sm (di cani, lupi) pack; (di uccelli, pecore) flock; (peg: di persone) gang, pack.

branco'lare vi to grope, feel one's way.

'branda sf camp bed.

bran'dello sm scrap, shred; a ~i in tatters, in rags.

bran'dire vt to brandish.

'brano sm piece; (di libro) passage.

bra'sato sm braised beef.

Bra'sile sm: il ~ Brazil; brasili'ano, a ag, sm/f Brazilian.

'bravo, a ag (abile) clever, capable, skilful; (buono) good, honest; (: bambino) good; (coraggioso) brave; ~! well done!; (al teatro) bravo!

bra'vura sf cleverness, skill.

'breccia, ce |'brettʃa| sf breach.

bre'tella sf (AUT) link; ~e sfpl braces.

'breve ag brief, short; in ~ in short.

brevet'tare vt to patent.

bre'vetto sm patent; ~ di pilotaggio pilot's licence (Brit) o license (US).

'brezza |'breddza| sf breeze.

'bricco, chi sm jug; ~ del caffè coffee-pot.

bric'cone, a sm/f rogue, rascal.

'briciola |'britʃola| sf crumb.

'briciolo |'britʃolo| sm (specie fig) bit.

'briga, ghe sf (fastidio) trouble, bother; pigliarsi la ~ di fare qc to take the trouble to do sth.

brigadi'ere sm (dei carabinieri etc) ≈ sergeant.

brl'gante sm bandit.

bri'gata sf (MIL) brigade; (gruppo) group, party.

'briglia |'briʎʎa| sf rein; a ~ sciolta at full gallop; (fig) at full speed.

bril'lante ag bright; (anche fig) brilliant; (che luccica) shining // sm diamond.

bril'lare vi to shine; (mina) to blow up // vt (mina) to set off.

'brillo, a ag merry, tipsy.

'brina sf hoarfrost.

brin'dare vi: ~ a qn/qc to drink to o toast sb/sth.

'brindisi sm inv toast.

'brio sm liveliness, go; bri'oso, a ag lively.

bri'tannico, a, ci, che ag British.

'brivido sm shiver; (di ribrezzo) shudder; (fig) thrill.

brizzo'lato, a |brittso'lato| ag (persona) going grey; (barba, capelli) greying.

'brocca, che sf jug.

broc'cato sm brocade.

'broccolo sm broccoli sg.

'brodo sm broth; (per cucinare) stock; ~ ristretto consommé.

brogli'accio |broʎ'ʎattʃo| sm scribbling pad.

'broglio |'brɔʎʎo| sm: ~ elettorale gerrymandering.

bron'chite |bron'kite| sf (MED) bronchitis.

'broncio |'brontʃo| sm sulky expression; tenere il ~ to sulk.

'bronco, chi sm bronchial tube.

bronto'lare vi to grumble; (tuono, stomaco) to rumble.

'bronzo |'brondzo| sm bronze.

bru'care vt to browse on, nibble at.

brucia'pelo |brutʃa'pelo|: a ~ av point-blank.

bruci'are |bru'tʃare| vt to burn; (scottare) to scald // vi to burn; brucia'tore sm burner; brucia'tura sf (atto) burning q; (segno) burn; (scottatura) scald; bruci'ore sm burning o smarting sensation.

'bruco, chi sm caterpillar; grub.

brughi'era |bru'gjɛra| sf heath, moor.

bruli'care vi to swarm.

'brulio, a ag bare, bleak.

'bruma sf mist.

'bruno, a ag brown, dark; (persona) dark(-haired).

'brusco, a, schi, sche ag (sapore) sharp; (modi, persona) brusque, abrupt; (movimento) abrupt, sudden.

bru'sio sm buzz, buzzing.

bru'tale ag brutal.

'bruto, a ag (forza) brute cpd // sm brute.

brut'tezza |brut'tettsa| sf ugliness.

'brutto, a ag ugly; (cattivo) bad; (malattia, strada, affare) nasty, bad; ~ tempo bad weather; brut'tura sf (cosa brutta) ugly thing; (sudiciume) filth; (azione meschina) mean action.

Bru'xelles |bry'sɛl| sf Brussels.

'buca, che sf hole; (avvallamento) hollow; ~ delle lettere letterbox.

buca'neve sm inv snowdrop.

bu'care vt (forare) to make a hole (o holes) in; (pungere) to pierce; (biglietto) to punch; ~rsi vr (con eroina) to mainline; ~ una gomma to have a puncture.

bu'cato sm (operazione) washing; (panni) wash, washing.

'buccia, ce |'buttʃa| sf skin, peel; (corteccia) bark.

bucherel'lare |bukerel'lare| vt to riddle with holes.

'buco, chi sm hole.

bu'dello sm intestine; (fig: tubo) tube; (vicolo) alley; ~a sfpl bowels, guts.

bu'dino sm pudding.

'bue *sm* ox; (*anche:* carne di ~) beef.
'bufalo *sm* buffalo.
bu'fera *sf* storm.
'buffo, a *ag* funny; (*TEATRO*) comic.
bu'gia, 'gie |bu'dʒia| *sf* lie; (*candeliere*) candleholder; **bugi'ardo, a** *ag* lying, deceitful // *sm/f* liar.
bugi'gattolo |budʒi'gattolo| *sm* poky little room.
'buio, a *ag* dark // *sm* dark, darkness; fa ~ pesto it's pitch-dark.
'bulbo *sm* (*BOT*) bulb; ~ oculare eyeball.
Bulga'ria *sf:* la ~ Bulgaria.
bul'lone *sm* bolt.
buona'notte *escl* good night! // *sf:* dare la ~ a to say good night to.
buona'sera *escl* good evening!
buon gi'orno |bwon'dʒorno| *escl* good morning (o afternoon)!
buongus'taio, a *sm/f* gourmet.
buon'gusto *sm* good taste.
bu'ono, a *ag* (*dav sm* **buon** + *C o V*, **buono** + *s impura, gn, pn, ps, x, z; dav sf* **buon'** +*V*) good; (*benevolo*): ~ (**con**) good (to), kind (to); (*adatto*): ~ a/da fit for/to // *sm.* good; (*COMM*) voucher, coupon; **alla buona** *ag* simple // *av* in a simple way, without any fuss; **buona fortuna** good luck; **buon compleanno** happy birthday; **buon divertimento** have a nice time; **a buon mercato** cheap; **di buon'ora** early; ~ **di cassa** cash voucher; ~ **di consegna** delivery note; ~ **fruttifero** bond bearing interest; ~ a **nulla** good-for-nothing; ~ **del tesoro** Treasury bill; **buon riposo** sleep well; **buon senso** common sense; **buon viaggio** bon voyage, have a good trip.
buontem'pone, a *sm/f* jovial person.
burat'tino *sm* puppet.
'burbero, a *ag* surly, gruff.
'burla *sf* prank, trick; **bur'lare** *vt:* burlare qc/qn, burlarsi di qc/qn to make fun of sth/sb.
burocra'zia |burokrat'tsia| *sf* bureaucracy.
bur'rasca, sche *sf* storm; **burras'coso, a** *ag* stormy.
'burro *sm* butter.
bur'rone *sm* ravine.
bus'care *vt* (*anche:* ~rsi: *raffreddore*) to get, catch; **buscarle** (*fam*) to get a hiding.
bus'sare *vi* to knock.
'bussola *sf* compass; perdere la ~ (*fig*) to lose one's bearings.
'busta *sf* (*da lettera*) envelope; (*astuccio*) case; **in ~ aperta/chiusa** in an unsealed/sealed envelope; ~ **paga** pay packet.
busta'rella *sf* bribe, backhander.
'busto *sm* bust; (*indumento*) corset, girdle; **a mezzo ~** (*foto*) half-length.
but'tare *vt* to throw; (*anche:* ~ **via**) to

throw away; ~ **giù** (*scritto*) to scribble down, dash off; (*cibo*) to gulp down; (*edificio*) to pull down, demolish; (*pasta, verdura*) to put into boiling water; ~rsi **dalla finestra** to jump *o* throw o.s. out of the window.

C

ca'bina *sf* (*di nave*) cabin; (*da spiaggia*) beach hut; (*di autocarro, treno*) cab; (*di aereo*) cockpit; (*di ascensore*) cage; ~ **telefonica** call *o* (tele)phone box.
ca'cao *sm* cocoa.
'caccia |'kattʃa| *sf* hunting; (*con fucile*) shooting; (*inseguimento*) chase; (*cacciagione*) game // *sm inv* (*aereo*) fighter; (*nave*) destroyer; ~ **grossa** big-game hunting; ~ **all'uomo** manhunt.
cacciabombardi'ere |kattʃabombar-'djere| *sm* fighter-bomber.
cacciagi'one |kattʃa'dʒone| *sf* game.
cacci'are |kat'tʃare| *vt* to hunt; (*mandar via*) to chase away; (*ficcare*) to shove, stick // *vi* to hunt; ~rsi *vr* (*fam:* *mettersi*): ~rsi **tra la folla** to plunge into the crowd; **dove s'è cacciata la mia borsa?** where has my bag got to?; ~rsi **nei guai** to get into trouble; ~ **fuori** qc to whip *o* pull sth out; ~ **un urlo** to let out a yell; **caccia'tore** *sm* hunter; **cacciatore di frodo** poacher.
caccia'vite |kattʃa'vite| *sm inv* screwdriver.
'cactus *sm inv* cactus.
ca'davere *sm* (dead) body, corpse.
ca'dente *ag* falling; (*casa*) tumbledown.
ca'denza |ka'dɛntsa| *sf* cadence; (*andamento ritmico*) rhythm; (*MUS*) cadenza.
ca'dere *vi* to fall; (*denti, capelli*) to fall out; (*tetto*) to fall in; **questa gonna cade bene** this skirt hangs well; **lasciar** ~ (*anche fig*) to drop; ~ **dal sonno** to be falling asleep on one's feet; ~ **dalle nuvole** (*fig*) to be taken aback.
ca'detto, a *ag* younger; (*squadra*) junior *cpd* // *sm* cadet.
ca'duta *sf* fall; **la ~ dei capelli** hair loss.
caffè *sm inv* coffee; (*locale*) café; ~ **macchiato** coffee with a dash of milk; ~ **macinato** ground coffee.
caffel'latte *sm inv* white coffee.
caffetti'era *sf* coffeepot.
cagio'nare |kadʒo'nare| *vt* to cause, be the cause of.
cagio'nevole |kadʒo'nevole| *ag* delicate, weak.
cagli'are |kaʎ'ʎare| *vi* to curdle.
'cagna |'kaɲɲa| *sf* (*ZOOL, peg*) bitch.
ca'gnesco, a, schi, sche |kaɲ'nesko| *ag* (*fig*): **guardare qn in ~** to scowl at sb.
cala'brone *sm inv* hornet.

cala'maio *sm* inkpot; inkwell.
cala'maro *sm* squid.
cala'mita *sf* magnet.
calamità *sf inv* calamity, disaster.
ca'lare *vt* (*far discendere*) to lower;
(*MAGLIA*) to decrease // *vi* (*discendere*)
to go (o come) down; (*tramontare*) to
set, go down; ~ **di peso** to lose weight.
'calca *sf* throng, press.
cal'cagno [kal'kaɲɲo] *sm* heel.
cal'care *sm* limestone // *vt* (*premere coi
piedi*) to tread, press down; (*premere
con forza*) to press down; (*mettere in
rilievo*) to stress; ~ **la mano** to overdo
it, exaggerate.
'calce ['kaltʃe] *sm*: **in** ~ at the foot of the
page // *sf* lime; ~ **viva** quicklime.
calces'truzzo [kaltʃes'truttso] *sm* concrete.
calci'are [kal'tʃare] *vt*, *vi* to kick;
calcia'tore *sm* footballer.
cal'cina [kal'tʃina] *sf* (lime) mortar.
'calcio ['kaltʃo] *sm* (*pedata*) kick;
(*sport*) football, soccer; (*di pistola,
fucile*) butt; (*CHIM*) calcium; ~ **d'angolo**
(*SPORT*) corner (kick); ~ **di punizione**
(*SPORT*) free kick.
'calco, chi *sm* (*ARTE*) casting, moulding; cast, mould.
calco'lare *vt* to calculate, work out,
reckon; (*ponderare*) to weigh (up);
calcola'tore, 'trice *ag* calculating // *sm*
calculator; (*fig*) calculating person // *sf*
(*anche*: **macchina calcolatrice**)
calculator; **calcolatore elettronico**
computer.
'calcolo *sm* (*anche MAT*) calculation;
(*infinitesimale etc*) calculus; (*MED*)
stone; **fare i propri ~i** (*fig*) to weigh the
pros and cons; **per** ~ out of self-interest.
cal'daia *sf* boiler.
caldeggi'are [kalded'dʒare] *vt* to support.
'caldo, a *ag* warm; (*molto* ~) hot; (*fig:
appassionato*) keen; hearty // *sm* heat;
ho ~ I'm warm; I'm hot; **fa** ~ it's
warm; it's hot.
calen'dario *sm* calendar.
'calibro *sm* (*di arma*) calibre, bore;
(*TECN*) callipers *pl*; (*fig*) calibre; **di
grosso** ~ (*fig*) prominent.
'calice ['kalitʃe] *sm* goblet; (*REL*)
chalice.
ca'ligine [ka'lidʒine] *sf* fog; (*mista con
fumo*) smog.
'callo *sm* callus; (*ai piedi*) corn.
'calma *sf* calm.
cal'mante *sm* sedative, tranquillizer.
cal'mare *vt* to calm; (*lenire*) to soothe;
~**rsi** *vr* to grow calm, calm down;
(*vento*) to abate; (*dolori*) to ease.
calmi'ere *sm* controlled price.
'calmo, a *ag* calm, quiet.
'calo *sm* (*COMM: di prezzi*) fall; (*: di
volume*) shrinkage; (*: di peso*) loss.

ca'lore *sm* warmth; heat; **in** ~ (*ZOOL*)
on heat.
calo'ria *sf* calorie.
calo'roso, a *ag* warm.
calpes'tare *vt* to tread on, trample on;
"**è vietato** ~ **l'erba**" "keep off the
grass".
ca'lunnia *sf* slander; (*scritta*) libel.
cal'vario *sm* (*fig*) affliction, cross.
cal'vizie [kal'vittsje] *sf* baldness.
'calvo, a *ag* bald.
'calza ['kaltsa] *sf* (*da donna*) stocking;
(*da uomo*) sock; **fare la** ~ to knit; ~**e di
nailon** nylons, (nylon) stockings.
cal'zare [kal'tsare] *vt* (*scarpe, guanti:
mettersi*) to put on; (*: portare*) to wear
// *vi* to fit; **calza'tura** *sf* footwear.
calzet'tone [kaltset'tone] *sm* heavy
knee-length sock.
cal'zino [kal'tsino] *sm* sock.
calzo'laio [kaltso'lajo] *sm* shoemaker;
(*che ripara scarpe*) cobbler; **calzole'ria**
sf (*negozio*) shoe shop.
calzon'cini [kaltson'tʃini] *smpl* shorts.
cal'zone [kal'tsone] *sm* trouser leg;
(*CUC*) savoury turnover made with pizza
dough; ~**i** *smpl* trousers (*Brit*), pants
(*US*).
cambi'ale *sf* bill (of exchange); (*pagherò cambiario*) promissory note.
cambia'mento *sm* change.
cambi'are *vt* to change; (*modificare*) to
alter, change; (*barattare*): ~ (**qc con
qn/qc**) to exchange (sth with sb/for sth)
// *vi* to change, alter; ~**rsi** *vr* (*variare
abito*) to change; ~ **casa** to move
(house); ~ **idea** to change one's mind; ~
treno to change trains.
'cambio *sm* change; (*modifica*) alteration, change; (*scambio, COMM*) exchange; (*corso dei cambi*) rate (of exchange); (*TECN, AUT*) gears *pl*; **in** ~ **di**
in exchange for; **dare il** ~ **a qn** to take
over from sb.
'camera *sf* room; (*anche*: ~ **da letto**)
bedroom; (*POL*) chamber, house; ~
ardente mortuary chapel; ~ **d'aria** inner
tube; (*di pallone*) bladder; **C**~ **di
Commercio** Chamber of Commerce; **C**~
dei Deputati Chamber of Deputies, ≈
House of Commons (*Brit*), ≈ House of
Representatives (*US*); ~ **a gas** gas
chamber; ~ **a un letto/a due letti/
matrimoniale** single/twin-bedded/double
room; ~ **oscura** (*FOT*) dark room.
came'rata, i, e *sm/f* companion, mate //
sf dormitory.
cameri'era *sf* (*domestica*) maid; (*che
serve a tavola*) waitress; (*che fa le
camere*) chambermaid.
cameri'ere *sm* (man)servant; (*di ristorante*) waiter.
came'rino *sm* (*TEATRO*) dressing room.
'camice ['kamitʃe] *sm* (*REL*) alb; (*per
medici etc*) white coat.

cami'cetta [kami'tʃɛtta] sf blouse.
ca'micia, cie [ka'mitʃa] sf (da uomo) shirt; (da donna) blouse; ~ di forza straitjacket; **camici'otto** sm casual shirt; (per operai) smock.
cami'netto sm hearth, fireplace.
ca'mino sm chimney; (focolare) fireplace, hearth.
'camion sm inv lorry (Brit), truck (US); **camion'cino** sm van.
cam'mello sm (ZOOL) camel; (tessuto) camel hair.
cammi'nare vi to walk; (funzionare) to work, go.
cam'mino sm walk; (sentiero) path; (itinerario, direzione, tragitto) way; **mettersi in** ~ to set o start off.
camo'milla sf camomile; (infuso) camomile tea.
ca'morra sf camorra; racket.
ca'moscio [ka'moʃʃo] sm chamois.
cam'pagna [kam'paɲɲa] sf country, countryside; (POL, COMM, MIL) campaign; **in** ~ in the country; (andare in ~ to go to the country); **fare una** ~ to campaign; **campa'gnolo, a** ag country cpd // sf (AUT) cross-country vehicle.
cam'pale ag field cpd; (fig): **una giornata** ~ a hard day.
cam'pana sf bell; (anche: ~ di vetro) bell jar; **campa'nella** sf small bell; (di tenda) curtain ring; **campa'nello** sm (all'uscio, da tavola) bell.
campa'nile sm bell tower, belfry; **campani'lismo** sm parochialism.
cam'pare vi to live; (tirare avanti) to get by, manage.
cam'pato, a ag: ~ **in aria** unsound, unfounded.
campeggi'are [kamped'dʒare] vi to camp; (risaltare) to stand out; **campeggia'tore, 'trice** sm/f camper; **cam'peggio** sm camping; (terreno) camp site; **fare (del) campeggio** to go camping.
cam'pestre ag country cpd, rural.
campio'nario, a ag: **fiera** ~a trade fair // sm collection of samples.
campio'nato sm championship.
campi'one, 'essa sm/f (SPORT) champion // sm (COMM) sample.
'campo sm field; (MIL) field; (: accampamento) camp; (spazio delimitato: sportivo etc) ground; field; (di quadro) background; **i** ~**i** (campagna) the countryside; ~ **da aviazione** airfield; ~ **di concentramento** concentration camp; ~ **di golf** golf course; ~ **da tennis** tennis court; ~ **visivo** field of vision.
campo'santo, pl **campisanti** sm cemetery.
camuf'fare vt to disguise.
'Canada sm: **il** ~ Canada; **cana'dese** ag, sm/f Canadian // sf (anche: **tenda**

canadese) ridge tent.
ca'naglia [ka'naʎʎa] sf rabble, mob; (persona) scoundrel, rogue.
ca'nale sm (anche fig) channel; (artificiale) canal.
'canapa sf hemp.
cana'rino sm canary.
cancel'lare [kantʃel'lare] vt (con la gomma) to rub out, erase; (con la penna) to strike out; (annullare) to annul, cancel; (disdire) to cancel.
cancelle'ria [kantʃelle'ria] sf chancery; (quanto necessario per scrivere) stationery.
cancelli'ere [kantʃel'ljere] sm chancellor; (di tribunale) clerk of the court.
can'cello [kan'tʃɛllo] sm gate.
can'crena sf gangrene.
'cancro sm (MED) cancer; (dello zodiaco): **C~** Cancer.
can'dela sf candle; ~ **(di accensione)** (AUT) spark(ing) plug.
cande'labro sm candelabra.
candeli'ere sm candlestick.
candi'dato, a sm/f candidate; (aspirante a una carica) applicant.
'candido, a ag white as snow; (puro) pure; (sincero) sincere, candid.
can'dito, a ag candied.
can'dore sm brilliant white; purity; sincerity, candour.
'cane sm dog; (di pistola, fucile) cock; **fa un freddo** ~ it's bitterly cold; **non c'era un** ~ there wasn't a soul; ~ **da caccia/guardia** hunting/guard dog; ~ **lupo** alsatian.
ca'nestro sm basket.
cangi'ante [kan'dʒante] ag iridescent.
can'guro sm kangaroo.
ca'nile sm kennel; (di allevamento) kennels pl; ~ **municipale** dog pound.
ca'nino, a ag, sm canine.
'canna sf (pianta) reed; (: indica, da zucchero) cane; (bastone) stick, cane; (di fucile) barrel; (di organo) pipe; ~ **fumaria** chimney flue; ~ **da pesca** (fishing) rod; ~ **da zucchero** sugar cane.
can'nella sf (CUC) cinnamon.
cannel'loni smpl pasta tubes stuffed with sauce and baked.
cannocchi'ale [kannok'kjale] sm telescope.
can'none sm (MIL) gun; (: STORIA) cannon; (tubo) pipe, tube; (piega) box pleat; (fig) ace.
can'nuccia, ce [kan'nuttʃa] sf (drinking) straw.
ca'noa sf canoe.
'canone sm canon, criterion; (mensile, annuo) rent; fee.
ca'nonico, ci sm (REL) canon.
ca'noro, a ag (uccello) singing, song cpd.
canot'taggio [kanot'taddʒo] sm rowing.

canotti'era *sf* vest.

ca'notto *sm* small boat, dinghy; canoe.

cano'vaccio |kano'vattʃo| *sm* (*tela*) canvas; (*strofinaccio*) duster; (*trama*) plot.

can'tante *sm/f* singer.

can'tare *vt, vi* to sing, **cantau'tore, 'trice** *sm/f* singer-composer.

canti'ere *sm* (*EDIL*) (building) site; (*anche:* ~ **navale**) shipyard.

cantl'lena *sf* (*filastrocca*) lullaby; (*fig*) sing-song voice.

can'tina *sf* (*locale*) cellar; (*bottega*) wine shop

'canto *sm* song; (*arte*) singing; (*REL*) chant; chanting; (*poesia*) poem, lyric; (*parte di una poesia*) canto; (*parte, lato*): **da un** ~ **on the one hand**; **d'altro** ~ **on the other hand**.

canto'nata *sf* corner; **prendere una** ~ (*fig*) to blunder.

can'tone *sm* (*in Svizzera*) canton.

can'tuccio |kan'tuttʃo| *sm* corner, nook.

canzo'nare |kantso'nare| *vt* to tease.

can'zone |kan'tsone| *sf* song; (*POESIA*) canzone; **canzoni'ere** *sm* (*MUS*) song-book; (*LETTERATURA*) collection of poems.

'caos *sm inv* chaos; **ca'otico, a, ci, che** *ag* chaotic.

C.A.P. *sigla m* = **codice di avviamento postale**.

ca'pace |ka'patʃe| *ag* able, capable; (*ampio, vasto*) large, capacious; **sei** ~ **di farlo?** can you o are you able to do it?; **capacità** *sf inv* ability; (*DIR, di recipiente*) capacity; **capaci'tarsi** *vr*: **capacitarsi di** to make out, understand.

ca'panna *sf* hut.

capan'none *sm* (*AGR*) barn; (*fabbricato industriale*) (factory) shed.

ca'parbio, a *ag* stubborn.

ca'parra *sf* deposit, down payment.

ca'pello *sm* hair; ~**i** *smpl* (*capigliatura*) hair *sg*.

capez'zale |kapet'tsale| *sm* bolster; (*fig*) bedside.

ca'pezzolo |ka'pettsolo| *sm* nipple.

capi'enza |ka'pjentsa| *sf* capacity.

capiglia'tura |kapiʎʎa'tura| *sf* hair.

ca'pire *vt* to understand.

capi'tale *ag* (*mortale*) capital; (*fondamentale*) main, chief // *sf* (*città*) capital // *sm* (*ECON*) capital; **capita'lismo** *sm* capitalism; **capita'lista, i, e** *ag, sm/f* capitalist.

capi'tano *sm* captain.

capi'tare *vi* (*giungere casualmente*) to happen to go, find o.s.; (*accadere*) to happen; (*presentarsi: cosa*) to turn up, present itself // *vb impers* to happen; **mi è capitato un guaio** I've had a spot of trouble.

capi'tello *sm* (*ARCHIT*) capital.

ca'pitolo *sm* chapter.

capi'tombolo *sm* headlong fall, tumble.

'capo *sm* head; (*persona*) head, leader; (*: in ufficio*) head, boss; (*: in tribù*) chief; (*di oggetti*) head; top; end; (*GEO*) cape; **andare a** ~ to start a new paragraph; **da** ~ over again; ~ **di bestiame** head *inv* of cattle, ~ **di vestiario** item of clothing.

'capo... *prefisso*: **capocu'oco, chi** *sm* head cook; **Capo'danno** *sm* New Year; **capo'fitto**: **a capofitto** *av* headfirst, headlong; **capo'giro** *sm* dizziness *q*; **capola'voro, i** *sm* masterpiece; **capo'linea, pl capi'linea** *sm* terminus; **capo'lino** *sm*: **fare capolino** to peep out (o *in etc*); **capolu'ogo, pl ghi** *o* **capilu'oghi** *sm* chief town, administrative centre.

capo'rale *sm* (*MIL*) lance corporal (*Brit*), private first class (*US*).

'capo... *prefisso*: **capostazi'one, pl capistazi'one** *sm* station master; **capo'treno, pl capi'treno** *o* **capo'treni** *sm* guard.

capo'volgere |kapo'voldʒere| *vt* to overturn; (*fig*) to reverse; ~**rsi** *vr* to overturn; (*barca*) to capsize; (*fig*) to be reversed; **capo'volto, a** *pp di* **capovolgere**.

'cappa *sf* (*mantello*) cape, cloak; (*del camino*) hood.

cap'pella *sf* (*REL*) chapel; **cappel'lano** *sm* chaplain.

cap'pello *sm* hat.

'cappero *sm* caper.

cap'pone *sm* capon.

cap'potto *sm* (over)coat.

cappuc'cino |kapput'tʃino| *sm* (*frate*) Capuchin monk; (*bevanda*) frothy white coffee.

cap'puccio |kap'puttʃo| *sm* (*copricapo*) hood; (*della biro*) cap.

'capra *sf* (she-)goat; **ca'pretto** *sm* kid.

ca'priccio |ka'prittʃo| *sm* caprice, whim; (*bizza*) tantrum; **fare i** ~**i** to be very naughty; **caprici'oso, a** *ag* capricious, whimsical; naughty.

Capri'corno *sm* Capricorn.

capri'ola *sf* somersault.

capri'olo *sm* roe deer.

'capro *sm* billy-goat; ~ **espiatorio** (*fig*) scapegoat.

'capsula *sf* capsule; (*di arma, per bottiglie*) cap.

cap'tare *vt* (*RADIO, TV*) to ·pick up; (*cattivarsi*) to gain, win.

cara'bina *sf* rifle.

carabini'ere *sm* member of Italian military police force.

ca'raffa *sf* carafe.

cara'mella *sf* sweet.

ca'rattere *sm* character; (*caratteristica*) characteristic, trait; **avere un buon** ~ to be good-natured; **caratte'ristico, a, ci, che** *ag* characteristic // *sf* characteristic, trait, peculiarity; **caratteriz'zare** vt to characterize, distinguish.

car'bone sm coal.

carbu'rante sm (motor) fuel.

carbura'tore sm carburettor.

car'cassa sf carcass; (fig: peg: macchina etc) (old) wreck.

carce'rato, a [kartʃe'rato] sm/f prisoner.

'carcere ['kartʃere] sm prison; (pena) imprisonment.

carci'ofo [kar'tʃɔfo] sm artichoke.

car'diaco, a, ci, che ag cardiac, heart cpd.

cardi'nale ag, sm cardinal.

'cardine sm hinge.

'cardo sm thistle.

ca'renza [ka'rɛntsa] sf lack, scarcity; (vitaminica) deficiency.

cares'tia sf famine; (penuria) scarcity, dearth.

ca'rezza [ka'rettsa] sf caress; **carez'zare** vt to caress, stroke, fondle.

'carica sf vedi carico.

cari'care vt to load; (aggravare: anche fig) to weigh down; (orologio) to wind up; (batteria, MIL) to charge.

'carico, a, chi, che ag (che porta un peso): ~ di loaded o laden with; (fucile) loaded; (orologio) wound up; (batteria) charged; (colore) deep; (caffè, tè) strong // sm (il caricare) loading; (ciò che si carica) load; (fig: peso) burden, weight // sf (mansione ufficiale) office, position; (MIL, TECN, ELETTR) charge; persona a ~ dependent; essere a ~ di qn (spese etc) to be charged to sb; **ha una forte ~a di simpatia** he's very likeable.

'carie sf (dentaria) decay.

ca'rino, a ag lovely, pretty, nice; (simpatico) nice.

carità sf charity; **per ~!** (escl di rifiuto) good heavens, no!

carnagi'one [karna'dʒone] sf complexion.

car'nale ag (amore) carnal; (fratello) blood cpd.

'carne sf flesh; (bovina, ovina etc) meat; ~ di manzo/maiale/pecora beef/pork/ mutton; ~ tritata mince (Brit), hamburger meat (US), minced (Brit) o ground (US) meat.

car'nefice [kar'nefitʃe] sm executioner; hangman.

carne'vale sm carnival.

car'noso, a ag fleshy.

'caro, a ag (amato) dear; (costoso) dear, expensive.

ca'rogna [ka'roɲɲa] sf carrion; (fig: fam) swine.

caro'sello sm merry-go-round.

ca'rota sf carrot.

caro'vana sf caravan.

caro'vita sm high cost of living.

carpenti'ere sm carpenter.

car'pire vt: ~ qc a qn (segreto etc) to

get sth out of sb.

car'poni av on all fours.

car'rabile ag suitable for vehicles; "passo ~" "keep clear".

car'raio, a ag: passo ~ vehicle entrance.

carreggi'ata [karred'dʒata] sf carriageway (Brit), (road)way.

car'rello sm trolley; (AER) undercarriage; (CINEMA) dolly; (di macchina da scrivere) carriage.

carri'era sf career; **fare ~** to get on; a gran ~ at full speed.

carri'ola sf wheelbarrow.

'carro sm cart, wagon; ~ armato tank.

car'rozza [kar'rɔttsa] sf carriage, coach.

carrozze'ria [karrottse'ria] sf body, coachwork (Brit); (officina) coachbuilder's workshop (Brit), body shop.

carroz'zina [karrot'tsina] sf pram (Brit), baby carriage (US).

'carta sf paper; (al ristorante) menu; (GEO) map; plan; (documento, da gioco) card; (costituzione) charter; ~e sfpl (documenti) papers, documents; alla ~ (al ristorante) à la carte; ~ assegni bank card; ~ assorbente blotting paper; ~ bollata o da bollo official stamped paper; ~ di credito credit card; ~ (geografica) map; ~ d'identità identity card; ~ igienica toilet paper; ~ d'imbarco (AER, NAUT) boarding card; ~ da lettere writing paper; ~ libera (AMM) unstamped paper; ~ da parati wallpaper; ~ verde (AUT) green card; ~ vetrata sandpaper; ~ da visita visiting card.

cartacar'bone, pl **cartecar'bone** sf carbon paper.

car'taccia, ce [kar'tattʃa] sf waste paper.

cartamo'neta sf paper money.

carta'pecora sf parchment.

carta'pesta sf papier-mâché.

car'teggio [kar'teddʒo] sm correspondence.

car'tella sf (scheda) card; (custodia: di cartone) folder; (: di uomo d'affari etc) briefcase; (: di scolaro) schoolbag, satchel; ~ clinica (MED) case sheet.

car'tello sm sign; (pubblicitario) poster; (stradale) sign, signpost; (ECON) cartel; (in dimostrazioni) placard; **cartel'lone** sm (pubblicitario) advertising poster; (della tombola) scoring frame; (TEATRO) playbill; **tenere il cartellone** (spettacolo) to have a long run.

carti'era sf paper mill.

car'tina sf (AUT, GEO) map.

car'toccio [kar'tɔttʃo] sm paper bag.

cartole'ria sf stationer's (shop).

carto'lina sf postcard.

car'tone sm cardboard; (ARTE) cartoon; ~i animati smpl (CINEMA) cartoons.

car'tuccia, ce [kar'tuttʃa] sf cartridge.

'casa sf house; (specialmente la propria casa) home; (COMM) firm, house; essere a ~ to be at home; vado a ~ mia/tua I'm going home/to your house; ~ di cura nursing home; ~ dello studente student hostel; ~e popolari ≈ council houses (*o* flats) (*Brit*), ≈ public housing units (*US*).

ca'sacca, che *sf* military coat; (*di fantino*) blouse.

casa'lingo, a, ghi, ghe *ag* household, domestic; (*fatto a casa*) home-made; (*semplice*) homely; (*amante della casa*) home-loving // *sf* housewife; ~ghi *smpl* household articles; cucina ~a plain home cooking.

cas'care *vi* to fall; **cas'cata** *sf* fall; (*d'acqua*) cascade, waterfall.

'casco, schi *sm* helmet; (*del parrucchiere*) hair-drier; (*di banane*) bunch.

casei'ficio [kazei'fitʃo] *sm* creamery.

ca'sella *sf* pigeon-hole; ~ postale (C.P.) post office box (P.O. box).

casel'lario *sm* filing cabinet; ~ giudiziale court records *pl*.

ca'sello *sm* (*di autostrada*) toll-house.

ca'serma *sf* barracks *pl*.

ca'sino *sm* (*confusione*) row, racket; (*casa di prostituzione*) brothel.

casinò *sm inv* casino.

'caso *sm* chance; (*fatto, vicenda*) event, incident; (*possibilità*) possibility; (*MED, LING*) case; a ~ at random; per ~ by chance, by accident; in ogni ~, in tutti i ~i in any case, at any rate; al ~ should the opportunity arise; nel ~ che in case; ~ mai if by chance; ~ limite borderline case.

'cassa *sf* case, crate, box; (*bara*) coffin; (*mobile*) chest; (*involucro: di orologio etc*) case; (*macchina*) cash register; (*luogo di pagamento*) checkout (counter); (*fondo*) fund; (*istituto bancario*) bank; ~ automatica prelievi automatic telling machine, cash dispenser; ~ continua night safe; ~ integrazione: mettere in ~ integrazione ≈ to lay off; ~ mutua *o* malattia health insurance scheme; ~ di risparmio savings bank; ~ toracica (*ANAT*) chest.

cassa'forte, *pl* **casseforti** *sf* safe.

cassa'panca, *pl* **cassapanche** *o* **cassepanche** *sf* settle.

casseru'ola, casse'rola *sf* saucepan.

cas'setta *sf* box; (*per registratore*) cassette; (*CINEMA, TEATRO*) box-office takings *pl*; film di ~ box-office draw; ~ di sicurezza strongbox; ~ delle lettere letterbox.

cas'setto *sm* drawer; **casset'tone** *sm* chest of drawers.

cassi'ere, a *sm/f* cashier; (*di banca*) teller.

'casta *sf* caste.

cas'tagna [kas'taɲɲa] *sf* chestnut.

cas'tagno [kas'taɲɲo] *sm* chestnut (tree).

cas'tano, a *ag* chestnut (brown).

cas'tello *sm* castle; (*TECN*) scaffolding.

casti'gare *vt* to punish; **cas'tigo, ghi** *sm* punishment.

castità *sf* chastity.

cas'toro *sm* beaver.

cas'trare *vt* to castrate; to geld; to doctor (*Brit*), fix (*US*).

casu'ale *ag* chance *cpd*.

cata'comba *sf* catacomb.

ca'talogo, ghi *sm* catalogue.

catarifran'gente [catarifran'dʒɛnte] *sm* (*AUT*) reflector.

ca'tarro *sm* catarrh.

ca'tasta *sf* stack, pile.

ca'tasto *sm* land register; land registry office.

ca'tastrofe *sf* catastrophe, disaster.

catego'ria *sf* category.

ca'tena *sf* chain; ~ di montaggio assembly line; ~e da neve (*AUT*) snow chains; **cate'naccio** *sm* bolt.

cate'ratta *sf* cataract; (*chiusa*) sluice-gate.

cati'nella *sf*: piovere a ~e to pour, rain cats and dogs.

ca'tino *sm* basin.

ca'trame *sm* tar.

'cattedra *sf* teacher's desk; (*di università*) chair.

catte'drale *sf* cathedral.

catti'veria *sf* malice, spite; naughtiness; (*atto*) spiteful act; (*parole*) malicious *o* spiteful remark.

cattività *sf* captivity.

cat'tivo, a *ag* bad; (*malvagio*) bad, wicked; (*turbolento: bambino*) bad, naughty; (*: mare*) rough; (*odore, sapore*) nasty, bad.

cat'tolico, a, ci, che *ag, sm/f* (Roman) Catholic.

cat'tura *sf* capture.

cattu'rare *vt* to capture.

cauc'ciù [kaut'tʃu] *sm* rubber.

'causa *sf* cause; (*DIR*) lawsuit, case, action; a ~ di, per ~ di because of; fare *o* muovere ~ a qn to take legal action against sb.

cau'sare *vt* to cause.

cau'tela *sf* caution, prudence.

caute'lare *vt* to protect; ~rsi *vr*: ~rsi (da) to take precautions (against).

'cauto, a *ag* cautious, prudent.

cauzi'one [kaut'tsjone] *sf* security; (*DIR*) bail.

cav. *abbr* = **cavaliere.**

'cava *sf* quarry.

caval'care *vt* (*cavallo*) to ride; (*muro*) to sit astride; (*sog: ponte*) to span; **caval'cata** *sf* ride; (*gruppo di persone*) riding party.

cavalca'via *sm inv* flyover.

cavalcioni [kaval'tʃoni]: a ~ di *prep* astride.

cavali'ere sm rider; (feudale, titolo) knight; (soldato) cavalryman; (al ballo) partner; **cavalle'resco, a, schi, sche** ag chivalrous; **cavalle'ria** sf chivalry; (milizia a cavallo) cavalry.

cavalle'rizzo, a [kavalle'rittso] sm/f riding instructor; circus rider.

caval'letta sf grasshopper.

caval'letto sm (FOT) tripod; (da pittore) easel.

ca'vallo sm horse; (SCACCHI) knight; (AUT: anche: ~ vapore) horsepower; (dei pantaloni) crotch; a ~ on horseback; a ~ di astride, straddling; ~ di battaglia (fig) hobby-horse; ~ da corsa racehorse.

ca'vare vt (togliere) to draw out, extract, take out; (: giacca, scarpe) to take off; (: fame, sete, voglia) to satisfy; cavarsela to get away with it; to manage, get on all right.

cava'tappi sm inv corkscrew.

ca'verna sf cave.

'cavia sf guinea pig.

cavi'ale sm caviar.

ca'viglia [ka'viʎʎa] sf ankle.

ca'villo sm quibble.

'cavo, a ag hollow // sm (ANAT) cavity; (grossa corda) rope, cable; (ELETTR, TEL) cable.

cavolfi'ore sm cauliflower.

'cavolo sm cabbage; (fam): non m'importa un ~ I don't give a damn; ~ di Bruxelles Brussels sprout.

cazzu'ola [kat'tswɔla] sf trowel.

c/c abbr = conto corrente.

ce [tʃe] pronome, av vedi ci.

cece [tʃetʃe] sm chickpea.

cecità [tʃetʃi'ta] sf blindness.

Cecoslo'vacchia [tʃekozlo'vakkja] sf: la ~ Czechoslovakia; **cecoslo'vacco, a, chi, che** ag, sm/f Czechoslovakian.

'cedere [tʃedere] vt (concedere: posto) to give up; (DIR) to transfer, make over // vi (cadere) to give way, subside; ~ (a) to surrender (to), yield (to), give in (to); **ce'devole** ag (terreno) soft; (fig) yielding.

'cedola [tʃedola] sf (COMM) coupon; voucher.

'cedro [tʃedro] sm cedar; (albero da frutto, frutto) citron.

C.E.E. [tʃe] sigla f = Comunità Economica Europea.

'ceffo [tʃeffo] sm (peg) ugly mug.

cef'fone [tʃef'fone] sm slap, smack.

ce'larsi [tʃe'larsi] vr to hide.

cele'brare [tʃele'brare] vt to celebrate; **celebrazi'one** sf celebration.

'celebre [tʃelebre] ag famous, celebrated; **celebrità** sf inv fame; (persona) celebrity.

'celere [tʃelere] ag fast, swift; (corso) crash cpd.

ce'leste [tʃe'leste] ag celestial; heavenly; (colore) sky-blue.

'celibe [tʃelibe] ag single, unmarried // sm bachelor.

'cella [tʃella] sf cell.

'cellula [tʃellula] sf (BIOL, ELETTR, POL) cell.

cemen'tare [tʃemen'tare] vt (anche fig) to cement.

ce'mento [tʃe'mento] sm cement; ~ armato reinforced concrete.

'cena [tʃena] sf dinner; (leggera) supper.

ce'nare [tʃe'nare] vi to dine, have dinner.

'cencio [tʃentʃo] sm piece of cloth, rag; (per spolverare) duster.

'cenere [tʃenere] sf ash.

'cenno [tʃenno] sm (segno) sign, signal; (gesto) gesture; (col capo) nod; (con la mano) wave; (allusione) hint, mention; (breve esposizione) short account; far ~ di sì/no to nod (one's head)/shake one's head.

censi'mento [tʃensi'mento] sm census.

cen'sore [tʃen'sore] sm censor.

cen'sura [tʃen'sura] sf censorship; censor's office; (fig) censure.

cente'nario, a [tʃente'narjo] ag (che ha cento anni) hundred-year-old; (che ricorre ogni cento anni) centennial, centenary cpd // sm/f centenarian // sm centenary.

cen'tesimo, a [tʃen'tezimo] ag, sm hundredth.

cen'tigrado, a [tʃen'tigrado] ag centigrade; 20 gradi ~i 20 degrees centigrade.

cen'timetro [tʃen'timetro] sm centimetre.

centi'naio, pl(f) **aia** [tʃenti'najo] sm: un ~ (di) a hundred; about a hundred.

'cento [tʃento] num a hundred, one hundred.

cen'trale [tʃen'trale] ag central // sf: ~ telefonica (telephone) exchange; ~ elettrica electric power station; **centrali'nista** sm/f operator; **centra'lino** sm (telephone) exchange; (di albergo etc) switchboard.

cen'trare [tʃen'trare] vt to hit the centre of; (TECN) to centre.

cen'trifuga [tʃen'trifuga] sf spin-drier.

'centro [tʃentro] sm centre; ~ commerciale shopping centre; (città) commercial centre.

'ceppo [tʃeppo] sm (di albero) stump; (pezzo di legno) log.

'cera [tʃera] sf wax; (aspetto) appearance, look.

ce'ramica, che [tʃe'ramika] sf ceramic; (ARTE) ceramics sg.

cerbi'atto [tʃer'bjatto] sm (ZOOL) fawn.

'cerca [tʃerka] sf: in o alla ~ di in search of.

cer'care [tʃer'kare] vt to look for, search for // vi: ~ di fare qc to try to do sth.

'cerchia |'tʃerkja| *sf* circle.

'cerchio |'tʃerkjo| *sm* circle; (*giocattolo, di botte*) hoop.

cere'ale |tʃere'ale| *sm* cereal.

ceri'monia |tʃeri'mɔnja| *sf* ceremony; **cerimoni'oso**, a *ag* formal, ceremonious.

ce'rino |tʃe'rino| *sm* wax match.

'cernia |'tʃernja| *sf* (ZOOL) stone bass.

cerni'era |tʃer'njera| *sf* hinge; ~ lampo zip (fastener) (*Brit*), zipper (*US*).

'cernita |'tʃernita| *sf* selection.

'cero |'tʃero| *sm* (church) candle.

ce'rotto |tʃe'rɔtto| *sm* sticking plaster.

certa'mente |tʃerta'mente| *av* certainly, surely.

cer'tezza |tʃer'tettsa| *sf* certainty.

certifi'cato *sm* certificate; ~ medico/di nascita medical/birth certificate.

'certo, a |'tʃerto| ◆ *ag* (*sicuro*): ~ (di/che) certain *o* sure (of/that)
◆ *det* 1 (*tale*) certain; **un ~ signor** Smith a (certain) Mr Smith
2 (*qualche; con valore intensivo*) some; dopo un ~ tempo after some time; un fatto di una ~a importanza a matter of some importance; di una ~a età past one's prime, not so young
◆ *pronome*: ~i(e) *pl* some
◆ *av* (*certamente*) certainly; (*senz'altro*) of course; di ~ certainly; no (di) ~!, ~ che no! certainly not!; sì ~ yes indeed, certainly.

cer'tuni |tʃer'tuni| *pronome pl* some (people).

cer'vello, *pl* i (*anche: pl(f)* a *o* e) |tʃer'vello| *sm* brain.

'cervo, a |'tʃervo| *sm/f* stag/doe // *sm* deer; ~ volante stag beetle.

ce'sello |tʃe'zello| *sm* chisel.

ce'soie |tʃe'zoje| *sfpl* shears.

ces'puglio |tʃes'puʎʎo| *sm* bush.

ces'sare |tʃes'sare| *vi, vt* to stop, cease; ~ di fare qc to stop doing sth; **cessate il fuoco** *sm* ceasefire.

'cesso |'tʃesso| *sm* (*fam: gabinetto*) bog.

'cesta |'tʃesta| *sf* (large) basket.

ces'tino |tʃes'tino| *sm* basket; (*per la carta straccia*) wastepaper basket; ~ da viaggio (FERR) packed lunch (*o* dinner).

'cesto |'tʃesto| *sm* basket.

'ceto |'tʃeto| *sm* (social) class.

cetrio'lino |tʃetrio'lino| *sm* gherkin.

cetri'olo |tʃetri'ɔlo| *sm* cucumber.

cfr. *abbr* (= *confronta*) cf.

CGIL *sigla f* (= *Confederazione Generale Italiana del Lavoro*) trades union organization.

che |ke| ◆ *pronome* 1 (*relativo: persona: soggetto*) who; (*: oggetto*) whom, that; (*: cosa, animale*) which, that; il ragazzo ~ è venuto the boy who came; l'uomo ~ io vedo the man (whom) I see; il libro ~ è sul tavolo the book which *o* that is on the table; il libro ~ vedi the book (which

o that) you see; la sera ~ ti ho visto the evening I saw you
2 (*interrogativo, esclamativo*) what; ~ (cosa) fai? what are you doing?; a ~ (cosa) pensi? what are you thinking about?; non sa ~ (cosa) fare he doesn't know what to do; ma ~ dici! what are you saying!
3 (*indefinito*): quell'uomo ha un ~ di losco there's something suspicious about that man; un certo non so ~ an indefinable something
◆ *det* 1 (*interrogativo: tra tanti*) what; (*: tra pochi*) which; ~ tipo di film preferisci? what sort of film do you prefer?; ~ vestito ti vuoi mettere? what (*o* which) dress do you want to put on?
2 (*esclamativo: seguito da aggettivo*) how; (*: seguito da sostantivo*) what; ~ buono! how delicious!; ~ bel vestito! what a lovely dress!
◆ *cong* 1 (*con proposizioni subordinate*) that; credo ~ verrà I think he'll come; voglio ~ tu studi I want you to study; so ~ tu c'eri I know (that) you were there; non ~: non ~ sia sbagliato, ma ... not that it's wrong, but ...
2 (*finale*) so that; vieni qua, ~ ti veda come here, so (that) I can see you
3 (*temporale*): arrivai ~ eri già partito you had already left when I arrived; sono anni ~ non lo vedo I haven't seen him for years, it's years since I saw him
4 (*in frasi imperative, concessive*): ~ venga pure! let him come by all means!; ~ tu sia benedetto! may God bless you!
5 (*comparativo: con più, meno*) than; *vedi anche* **più, meno, così** etc.

cheti'chella |keti'kella|: alla ~ *av* stealthily, unobtrusively.

'cheto, a |'keto| *ag* quiet, silent.

chi |ki| *pronome* 1 (*interrogativo: soggetto*) who; (*: oggetto*) who, whom; ~ è? who is it?; di ~ è questo libro? whose book is this?, whose is this book? con ~ parli? who are you talking to?; a ~ pensi? who are you thinking about?; a di ~ voi? which of you?; non so a ~ rivolgermi I don't know who to ask
2 (*relativo*) whoever, anyone who; dillo a ~ vuoi tell whoever you like
3 (*indefinito*): ~ ... ~ ... some ... others ...; ~ dice una cosa, ~ dice un'altra some say one thing, others say another.

chiacchie'rare |kjakkje'rare| *vi* to chat; (*discorrere futilmente*) to chatter; (*far pettegolezzi*) to gossip; **chiacchie'rata** *sf* chat; **chi'acchiere** *sfpl*: fare due *o* quattro chiacchiere to have a chat; **chiacchie'rone, a** *ag* talkative, chatty, gossipy // *sm/f* chatterbox; gossip.

chia'mare |kja'mare| *vt* to call; (*rivolgersi a qn*) to call (in), send for; ~rsi *vr* (*aver nome*) to be called; mi

chiamo Paolo my name is Paolo, I'm called Paolo; ~ **alle armi** to call up; ~ **in giudizio** to summon; **chia'mata** sf (TEL) call; (MIL) call-up.

chia'rezza [kja'rettsa] sf clearness; clarity.

chia'rire [kja'rire] vt to make clear; (fig: spiegare) to clear up, explain; ~**rsi** vr to become clear.

chi'aro, a [‘kjaro] ag clear; (luminoso) clear, bright; (colore) pale, light.

chiaroveg'gente [kjaroved'dʒɛnte] sm/f clairvoyant.

chi'asso [‘kjasso] sm uproar, row; **chias'soso, a** ag noisy, rowdy; (vistoso) showy, gaudy.

chi'ave [‘kjave] sf key // ag inv key cpd: ~ **d'accensione** (AUT) ignition key; ~ **inglese** monkey wrench; ~ **di volta** (anche fig) keystone; **chiavis'tello** sm bolt.

chi'azza [‘kjattsa] sf stain; splash.

'chicco, chi [‘kikko] sm (di cereale, riso) grain; (di caffè) bean; ~ **d'uva** grape.

chi'edere [‘kjedere] vt (per sapere) to ask; (per avere) to ask for // vi: ~ **di qn** to ask after sb; (al telefono) to ask for o want sb; ~ **qc a qn** to ask sb sth; to ask sb for sth.

chi'erico, ci [‘kjeriko] sm cleric; altar boy.

chi'esa [‘kjeza] sf church.

chi'esto, a pp di **chiedere**.

'chiglia [‘kiʎʎa] sf keel.

'chilo [‘kilo] sm kilo; **chilo'grammo** sm kilogram(me); **chi'lometro** sm kilometre.

'chimico, a, ci, che [‘kimiko] ag chemical // sm/f chemist // sf chemistry.

'china [‘kina] sf (pendio) slope, descent; (BOT) cinchona; (inchiostro di) ~ Indian ink.

chi'nare [ki'nare] vt to lower, bend; ~**rsi** vr to stoop, bend.

chi'nino [ki'nino] sm quinine.

chi'occia, ce [‘kjɔttʃa] sf brooding hen.

chi'occiola, ce [‘kjɔttʃola] sf snail; **scala a** ~ spiral staircase.

chi'odo [‘kjɔdo] sm nail; (fig) obsession.

chi'oma [‘kjɔma] sf (capelli) head of hair; (di albero) foliage.

chi'osco, schi [‘kjɔsko] sm kiosk, stall.

chi'ostro [‘kjɔstro] sm cloister.

chiro'mante [kiro'mante] sm/f palmist.

chirur'gia [kirur'dʒia] sf surgery; **chi'rurgo, ghi** o **gi** sm surgeon.

chissà [kis'sa] av who knows, I wonder.

chi'tarra [ki'tarra] sf guitar.

chi'udere [‘kjudere] vt to close, shut; (luce, acqua) to put off, turn off; (definitivamente: fabbrica) to close down, shut down; (strada) to close; (recingere) to enclose; (porre termine) to end // vi to close, shut; to close down, shut down; to end; ~**rsi** vr to shut,

close; (ritirarsi: anche fig) to shut o.s. away; (ferita) to close up.

chi'unque [ki'unkwe] pronome (relativo) whoever; (indefinito) anyone, anybody; ~ **sia** whoever it is.

chi'uso, a [‘kjuso] pp di **chiudere** // sf (di corso d'acqua) sluice, lock; (recinto) enclosure; (di discorso etc) conclusion, ending; **chiu'sura** sf closing; shutting; closing o shutting down; enclosing; putting o turning off; ending; (dispositivo) catch; fastening; fastener.

ci [tʃi] (dav lo, la, li, le, ne diventa **ce**) ◆ pronome **1** (personale: complemento oggetto) us; (: a noi: complemento di termine) (to) us; (: riflessivo) ourselves; (: reciproco) each other, one another; (impersonale): ~ **si veste** we get dressed; ~ **ha visti** he's seen us; **non** ~ **ha dato niente** he gave us nothing; ~ **vestiamo** we get dressed; ~ **amiamo** we love one another o each other

2 (dimostrativo: di ciò, su ciò, in ciò etc) about (o on o of) it; **non so cosa far\~** I don't know what to do about it; ~ **puoi contare** you can depend on it; **che c'entro io?** what have I got to do with it? ◆ av (qui) here; (lì) there; (moto attraverso luogo): ~ **passa sopra un ponte** a bridge passes over it; **non** ~ **passa più nessuno** nobody comes this way any more; **esser\~** vedi **essere**.

C.ia abbr (= compagnia) Co.

cia'batta [tʃa'batta] sf mule, slipper.

ci'alda [‘tʃalda] sf (CUC) wafer.

ciam'bella [tʃam'bella] sf (CUC) ring-shaped cake; (salvagente) rubber ring.

ci'ao [‘tʃao] escl (all'arrivo) hello!; (alla partenza) cheerio! (Brit), bye!

ciarla'tano [tʃarla'tano] sm charlatan.

cias'cuno, a [tʃas'kuno] (dav sm: **ciascun** +C, V, **ciascuno** +s impura, gn, pn, ps, x, z; dav sf: **ciascuna** +C, **ciascun'** +V) det, pronome each.

'cibo [‘tʃibo] sm food.

ci'cala [tʃi'kala] sf cicada.

cica'trice [tʃika'tritʃe] sf scar.

'cicca [‘tʃikka] sf cigarette end.

'ciccia [‘tʃittʃa] sf (fam: carne) meat; (: grasso umano) fat, flesh.

cice'rone [tʃitʃe'rone] sm guide.

ci'clismo [tʃi'klizmo] sm cycling; **ci'clista, i, e** sm/f cyclist.

'ciclo [‘tʃiklo] sm cycle; (di malattia) course.

ciclomo'tore [tʃiklomo'tore] sm moped.

ci'clone [tʃi'klone] sm cyclone.

ci'cogna [tʃi'koɲɲa] sf stork.

ci'coria [tʃi'kɔria] sf chicory.

ci'eco, a, chi, che [‘tʃɛko] ag blind // sm/f blind man/woman.

ci'elo [‘tʃɛlo] sm sky; (REL) heaven.

'cifra [‘tʃifra] sf (numero) figure; numeral; (somma di denaro) sum, figure; (monogramma) monogram, initials pl;

(*codice*) code, cipher.

'ciglio |'tʃiʎʎo| *sm* (*margine*) edge, verge; (*pl(f)* **ciglia**: *delle palpebre*) (eye)lash; (eye)lid; (*sopracciglio*) eyebrow.

'cigno |'tʃiɲɲo| *sm* swan.

cigo'lare |tʃigo'lare| *vi* to squeak, creak.

'Cile |'tʃile| *sm*: il ~ Chile.

ci'lecca |tʃi'lekka| *sf*: far ~ to fail.

cili'egia, gie *o* **ge** |tʃi'ljedʒa| *sf* cherry; **cili'egio** *sm* cherry tree.

cilin'drata |tʃilin'drata| *sf* (*AUT*) (cubic) capacity; **una macchina di grossa ~ a** big engined car.

ci'lindro |tʃi'lindro| *sm* cylinder; (*cappello*) top hat.

'cima |'tʃima| *sf* (*sommità*) top; (*di monte*) top, summit; (*estremità*) end; in ~ a at the top of; da ~ a fondo from top to bottom; (*fig*) from beginning to end.

'cimice |'tʃimitʃe| *sf* (*ZOOL*) bug; (*puntina*) drawing pin (*Brit*), thumbtack (*US*).

cimini'era |tʃimi'njera| *sf* chimney; (*di nave*) funnel.

cimi'tero |tʃimi'tɛro| *sm* cemetery.

ci'murro |tʃi'murro| *sm* (*di cani*) distemper.

'Cina |'tʃina| *sf*: la ~ China.

cin'cin, cin cin |tʃin'tʃin| *escl* cheers!

'cinema |'tʃinema| *sm inv* cinema; **cine'presa** *sf* cine-camera.

ci'nese |tʃi'nese| *ag*, *sm/f*, *sm* Chinese *inv*.

ci'netico, a, ci, che |tʃi'netiko| *ag* kinetic.

'cingere |'tʃindʒere| *vt* (*attorniare*) to surround, encircle; ~ la vita con una cintura to put a belt round one's waist.

'cinghia |'tʃingja| *sf* strap; (*cintura*, *TECN*) belt.

cinghi'ale |tʃin'gjale| *sm* wild boar.

cinguet'tare |tʃingwet'tare| *vi* to twitter.

'cinico, a, ci, che |'tʃiniko| *ag* cynical // *sm/f* cynic; **ci'nismo** *sm* cynicism.

cin'quanta |tʃin'kwanta| *num* fifty; **cinquan'tesimo, a** *num* fiftieth.

cinquan'tina |tʃinkwan'tina| *sf* (*serie*): una ~ (di) about fifty; (*età*): essere sulla ~ to be about fifty.

'cinque |'tʃinkwe| *num* five; avere ~ anni to be five (years old); il ~ dicembre 1988 the fifth of December 1988; alle ~ (*ora*) at five (o'clock).

cinque'cento |tʃinkwe'tʃento| *num* five hundred // *sm*: il C~ the sixteenth century.

'cinto, a |'tʃinto| *pp di* cingere.

cin'tura |tʃin'tura| *sf* belt; ~ di salvataggio lifebelt (*Brit*), life preserver (*US*); ~ di sicurezza (*AUT*, *AER*) safety o seat belt.

ciò |tʃɔ| *pronome* this; that; ~ che what; ~ nonostante *o* nondimeno nevertheless, in spite of that.

ci'occa, che |'tʃɔkka| *sf* (*di capelli*) lock.

ciocco'lata |tʃokko'lata| *sf* chocolate; (*bevanda*) (hot) chocolate; **cioccola'tino** *sm* chocolate; **ciocco'lato** *sm* chocolate.

cioè |tʃo'ɛ| *av* that is (to say).

ciondo'lare |tʃondo'lare| *vi* to dangle; (*fig*) to loaf (about); **ci'ondolo** *sm* pendant.

ci'otola |'tʃɔtola| *sf* bowl.

ci'ottolo |'tʃɔttolo| *sm* pebble; (*di strada*) cobble(stone).

ci'polla |tʃi'polla| *sf* onion; (*di tulipano etc*) bulb.

ci'presso |tʃi'prɛsso| *sm* cypress (tree).

'cipria |'tʃiprja| *sf* (face) powder.

'Cipro |'tʃipro| *sm* Cyprus.

'circa |'tʃirka| *av* about, roughly // *prep* about, concerning; a mezzogiorno ~ about midday.

'circo, chi |'tʃirko| *sm* circus.

circo'lare |tʃirko'lare| *vi* to circulate; (*AUT*) to drive (along), move (along) // *ag* circular // *sf* (*AMM*) circular; (*di autobus*) circle (line); **circolazi'one** *sf* circulation; (*AUT*): la circolazione (the) traffic.

'circolo |'tʃirkolo| *sm* circle.

circon'dare |tʃirkon'dare| *vt* to surround.

circonfe'renza |tʃirkonfe'rɛntsa| *sf* circumference.

circonvallazi'one |tʃirkonvallat'tsjone| *sf* ring road (*Brit*), beltway (*US*); (*per evitare una città*) by-pass.

circos'critto, a |tʃirkos'kritto| *pp di* circoscrivere.

circos'crivere |tʃirkos'krivere| *vt* to circumscribe; (*fig*) to limit, restrict; **circoscrizi'one** *sf* (*AMM*) district, area; circoscrizione elettorale constituency.

circos'petto, a |tʃirkos'petto| *ag* circumspect, cautious.

circos'tante |tʃirkos'tante| *ag* surrounding, neighbouring.

circos'tanza |tʃirkos'tantsa| *sf* circumstance; (*occasione*) occasion.

cir'cuito |tʃir'kuito| *sm* circuit.

CISL *sigla f* (= *Confederazione Italiana Sindacati Lavoratori*) trades union organization.

'ciste |'tʃiste| *sf* = **cisti**.

cis'terna |tʃis'tɛrna| *sf* tank, cistern.

'cisti |'tʃisti| *sf* cyst.

C.I.T. |tʃit| *sigla f* = *Compagnia Italiana Turismo*.

ci'tare |tʃi'tare| *vt* (*DIR*) to summon; (*autore*) to quote; (*a esempio, modello*) to cite; **citazi'one** *sf* summons *sg*; quotation; (*di persona*) mention.

ci'tofono |tʃi'tɔfono| *sm* entry phone; (*in uffici*) intercom.

città |tʃit'ta| *sf inv* town; (*importante*) city; ~ universitaria university campus.

cittadi'nanza |tʃittadi'nantsa| *sf* citizens

pl, inhabitants *pl* of a town (o city); (*DIR*) citizenship.

citta'dino, a |t∫itta'dino| *ag* town *cpd*; city *cpd* // *sm/f* (*di uno Stato*) citizen; (*abitante di città*) townsman, city dweller.

ci'uco, a, chi, che |'t∫uko| *sm/f* ass, donkey.

ci'uffo |'t∫uffo| *sm* tuft.

ci'vetta |t∫i'vetta| *sf* (*ZOOL*) owl; (*fig: donna*) coquette, flirt // *ag inv*: auto/nave ~ decoy car/ship.

'civico, a, ci, che |'t∫iviko| *ag* civic; (*museo*) municipal, town *cpd*; municipal, city *cpd*.

ci'vile |t∫i'vile| *ag* civil; (*non militare*) civilian; (*nazione*) civilized // *sm* civilian.

civilizzazi'one |t∫iviliddzat'tsjone| *sf* civilization.

civiltà |t∫ivil'ta| *sf* civilization; (*cortesia*) civility.

'clacson *sm inv* (*AUT*) horn.

cla'more *sm* (*frastuono*) din, uproar, clamour; (*fig*) outcry; **clamo'roso, a** *ag* noisy; (*fig*) sensational.

clandes'tino, a *ag* clandestine; (*POL*) underground, clandestine // *sm/f* stowaway.

clari'netto *sm* clarinet.

'classe *sf* class; di ~ (*fig*) with class; of excellent quality.

'classico, a, ci, che *ag* classical; (*tradizionale: moda*) classic(al) // *sm* classic; classical author.

clas'sifica *sf* classification; (*SPORT*) placings *pl*.

classifi'care *vt* to classify; (*candidato, compito*) to grade; ~rsi *vr* to be placed.

'clausola *sf* (*DIR*) clause.

'clava *sf* club.

clavi'cembalo |klavi't∫embalo| *sm* harpsichord.

cla'vicola *sf* (*ANAT*) collar bone.

cle'mente *ag* merciful; (*clima*) mild; **cle'menza** *sf* mercy, clemency; mildness.

'clero *sm* clergy.

cli'ente *sm/f* customer, client; **clien'tela** *sf* customers *pl*, clientèle.

'clima, i *sm* climate; **cli'matico, a, ci, che** *ag* climatic; **stazione climatica** health resort; **climatizzazi'one** *sf* (*TECN*) air conditioning.

'clinico, a, ci, che *ag* clinical // *sm* (*medico*) clinician // *sf* (*scienza*) clinical medicine; (*casa di cura*) clinic, nursing home; (*settore d'ospedale*) clinic.

clo'aca, che *sf* sewer.

'cloro *sm* chlorine.

cloro'formio *sm* chloroform.

club *sm inv* club.

c.m. *abbr* = **corrente mese.**

coabi'tare *vi* to live together, live under the same roof.

coagu'lare *vt* to coagulate // *vi*, ~rsi *vr* to coagulate; (*latte*) to curdle.

coalizi'one |koalit'tsjone| *sf* coalition.

co'atto, a *ag* (*DIR*) compulsory, forced.

'COBAS *sigla mpl* (= *Comitati di base*) independent trades unions.

coca'ina *sf* cocaine.

cocci'nella |kott∫i'nella| *sf* ladybird (*Brit*), ladybug (*US*).

'coccio |'kɔtt∫o| *sm* earthenware; (*vaso*) earthenware pot; ~i *smpl* fragments (of pottery).

cocci'uto, a |kot't∫uto| *ag* stubborn, pigheaded.

'cocco, chi *sm* (*pianta*) coconut palm; (*frutto*): noce di ~ coconut // *sm/f* (*fam*) darling.

cocco'drillo *sm* crocodile.

cocco'lare *vt* to cuddle, fondle.

co'cente |ko't∫ente| *ag* (*anche fig*) burning.

co'comero *sm* watermelon.

co'cuzzolo |ko'kuttsolo| *sm* top; (*di capo, cappello*) crown.

'coda *sf* tail; (*fila di persone, auto*) queue (*Brit*), line (*US*); (*di abiti*) train; con la ~ dell'occhio out of the corner of one's eye; mettersi in ~ to queue (up) (*Brit*), line up (*US*); to join the queue (*Brit*) o line (*US*); ~ di cavallo (*acconciatura*) ponytail.

co'dardo, a *ag* cowardly // *sm/f* coward.

'codice |'kodit∫e| *sm* code; ~ di avviamento postale (C.A.P.) postcode (*Brit*), zip code (*US*); ~ fiscale tax code; ~ della strada highway code.

coe'rente *ag* coherent; **coe'renza** *sf* coherence.

coe'taneo, a *ag, sm/f* contemporary.

'cofano *sm* (*AUT*) bonnet (*Brit*), hood (*US*); (*forziere*) chest.

'cogli |'kɔʎʎi| *prep + det vedi* **con.**

'cogliere |'kɔʎʎere| *vt* (*fiore, frutto*) to pick, gather; (*sorprendere*) to catch, surprise; (*bersaglio*) to hit; (*fig: momento opportuno etc*) to grasp, seize, take; (: *capire*) to grasp; ~ qn in flagrante o in fallo to catch sb red-handed.

co'gnato, a |koɲ'ɲato| *sm/f* brother-/sister-in-law.

cognizi'one |koɲɲit'tsjone| *sf* knowledge.

co'gnome |koɲ'ɲome| *sm* surname.

'coi *prep + det vedi* **con.**

coinci'denza |koint∫i'dentsa| *sf* coincidence; (*FERR, AER, di autobus*) connection.

coin'cidere |koin't∫idere| *vi* to coincide; **coin'ciso, a** *pp di* **coincidere.**

coin'volgere |koin'vɔldʒere| *vt*: ~ in to involve in; **coin'volto, a** *pp di* **coinvolgere.**

col *prep + det vedi* **con.**

cola'brodo *sm inv* strainer.

cola'pasta *sm inv* colander.

co'lare *vt* (*liquido*) to strain; (*pasta*) to drain; (*oro fuso*) to pour // *vi* (*sudore*) to drip; (*botte*) to leak; (*cera*) to melt; ~ a picco *vt, vi* (*nave*) to sink.

co'lata *sf* (*di lava*) flow; (*FONDERIA*) casting.

colazi'one |kolat'tsjone| *sf* (*anche:* prima ~) breakfast; (*anche:* seconda ~) lunch; **fare** ~ to have breakfast (*o* lunch).

co'lei *pronome vedi* **colui**.

co'lera *sm* (*MED*) cholera.

'colica *sf* (*MED*) colic.

'colla *prep* + *det vedi* **con** // *sf* glue; (*di farina*) paste.

collabo'rare *vi* to collaborate; ~ a to collaborate on; (*giornale*) to contribute to; **collabora'tore, 'trice** *sm/f* collaborator; contributor.

col'lana *sf* necklace; (*collezione*) collection, series.

col'lant |kɔ'lã| *sm inv* tights *pl*.

col'lare *sm* collar.

col'lasso *sm* (*MED*) collapse.

collau'dare *vt* to test, try out; **col'laudo** *sm* testing *q*; test.

'colle *sm* hill.

col'lega, ghi, ghe *sm/f* colleague.

collega'mento *sm* connection; (*MIL*) liaison.

colle'gare *vt* to connect, join, link; ~rsi *vr* (*RADIO, TV*) to link up; ~rsi con (*TEL*) to get through to.

col'legio |kol'lɛdʒo| *sm* college; (*convitto*) boarding school; ~ **elettorale** (*POL*) constituency.

'collera *sf* anger.

col'lerico, a, ci, che *ag* quicktempered, irascible.

col'letta *sf* collection.

collettività *sf* community.

collet'tivo, a *ag* collective; (*interesse*) general, everybody's; (*biglietto, visita etc*) group *cpd* // *sm* (*POL*) (political) group.

col'letto *sm* collar.

collezio'nare |kollettsjo'nare| *vt* to collect.

collezi'one |kollet'tsjone| *sf* collection.

colli'mare *vi* to correspond, coincide.

col'lina *sf* hill.

col'lirio *sm* eyewash.

collisi'one *sf* collision.

'collo *sm* neck; (*di abito*) neck, collar; (*pacco*) parcel; ~ **del piede** instep.

colloca'mento *sm* (*impiego*) employment; (*disposizione*) placing, arrangement.

collo'care *vt* (*libri, mobili*) to place; (*persona: trovare un lavoro per*) to find a job for, place; (*COMM: merce*) to find a market for.

col'loquio *sm* conversation, talk; (*ufficiale, per un lavoro*) interview; (*INS*) preliminary oral exam.

col'mare *vt*: ~ **di** (*anche fig*) to fill with; (*dare in abbondanza*) to load *o* overwhelm with; **'colmo, a** *ag*: **colmo (di)** full (of) // *sm* summit, top; (*fig*) height; **al colmo della disperazione** in the depths of despair; **è il colmo!** it's the last straw!

co'lombo, a *sm/f* dove; pigeon.

co'lonia *sf* colony; (*per bambini*) holiday camp; (**acqua di**) ~ (**eau de**) cologne; **coloni'ale** *ag* colonial // *sm/f* colonist, settler.

co'lonna *sf* column; ~ **vertebrale** spine, spinal column.

colon'nello *sm* colonel.

co'lono *sm* (*coltivatore*) tenant farmer.

colo'rante *sm* colouring.

colo'rare *vt* to colour; (*disegno*) to colour in.

co'lore *sm* colour; a ~i in colour, colour *cpd*; **farne di tutti i** ~i to get up to all sorts of mischief.

colo'rito, a *ag* coloured; (*viso*) rosy, pink; (*linguaggio*) colourful // *sm* (*tinta*) colour; (*carnagione*) complexion.

co'loro *pronome pl vedi* **colui**.

co'losso *sm* colossus.

'colpa *sf* fault; (*biasimo*) blame; (*colpevolezza*) guilt; (*azione colpevole*) offence; (*peccato*) sin; **di chi è la** ~? whose fault is it?; **è** ~ **sua** it's his fault; **per** ~ **di** through, owing to; **col'pevole** *ag* guilty.

col'pire *vt* to hit, strike; (*fig*) to strike; **rimanere colpito da qc** to be amazed *o* struck by sth.

'colpo *sm* (*urto*) knock; (*: affettivo*) blow, shock; (*: aggressivo*) blow; (*di pistola*) shot; (*MED*) stroke; (*rapina*) raid; **di** ~ suddenly; **fare** ~ to make a strong impression; ~ **di grazia** coup de grâce; ~ **di sole** sunstroke; ~ **di Stato** coup d'état; ~ **di telefono** phone call; ~ **di testa** (sudden) impulse *o* whim; ~ **di vento** gust (of wind).

coltel'lata *sf* stab.

col'tello *sm* knife; ~ **a serramanico** clasp knife.

colti'vare *vt* to cultivate; (*verdura*) to grow, cultivate; **coltiva'tore** *sm* farmer; **coltivazi'one** *sf* cultivation; growing.

'colto, a *pp di* **cogliere** // *ag* (*istruito*) cultured, educated.

'coltre *sf* blanket.

col'tura *sf* cultivation.

co'lui, co'lei, *pl* **co'loro** *pronome* the one; ~ **che parla** the one *o* the man *o* the person who is speaking; **colei che amo** the one *o* the woman *o* the person (whom) I love.

'coma *sm inv* coma.

comanda'mento *sm* (*REL*) commandment.

coman'dante *sm* (*MIL*) commander,

commandant; (di reggimento) commanding officer; (NAUT, AER) captain.

coman'dare vi to be in command // vt to command; (imporre) to order, command; ~ a qn di fare to order sb to do; **co'mando** sm (ingiunzione) order, command; (autorità) command; (TECN) control.

co'mare sf (madrina) godmother.

combaci'are |komba'tʃare| vi to meet; (fig: coincidere) to coincide, correspond.

com'battere vt to fight; (fig) to combat, fight against // vi to fight; **combatti'mento** sm fight; fighting q; (di pugilato) match.

combi'nare vt to combine; (organizzare) to arrange; (fam: fare) to make, cause; **combinazi'one** sf combination; (caso fortuito) coincidence; **per combinazione** by chance.

combus'tibile ag combustible // sm fuel.

com'butta sf (peg): in ~ in league.

'come ♦ av 1 (alla maniera di) like; ti comporti ~ lui you behave like him o like he does; bianco ~ la neve (as) white as snow; ~ se as if, as though

2 (in qualità di) as a; lavora ~ autista he works as a driver

3 (interrogativo) how; ~ ti chiami? what's your name?; ~ sta? how are you?; com'è il tuo amico? what is your friend like?; ~? (prego?) pardon?, sorry?; ~ mai? how come?; ~ mai non ci hai avvertiti? why on earth didn't you warn us?

4 (esclamativo): ~ sei bravo! how clever you are!; ~ mi dispiace! I'm terribly sorry!

♦ cong 1 (in che modo) how; mi ha spiegato ~ l'ha conosciuto he told me how he met him

2 (correlativo) as; (con comparativi di maggioranza) than; non è bravo ~ pensavo he isn't as clever as I thought; è meglio di ~ pensassi it's better than I thought

3 (appena che, quando) as soon as; ~ arrivò, iniziò a lavorare as soon as he arrived, he set to work; vedi **così**, **tanto**.

'comico, a, ci, che ag (TEATRO) comic; (buffo) comical // sm (attore) comedian, comic actor; (comicità) comic spirit, comedy.

co'mignolo |ko'miɲɲolo| sm chimney top.

cominci'are |komin'tʃare| vt, vi to begin, start; ~ a fare/col fare to begin to do/by doing.

comi'tato sm committee.

comi'tiva sf party, group.

co'mizio |ko'mittsjo| sm (POL) meeting, assembly.

com'mando sm inv commando (squad).

commandant; (di reggimento) playing officer; (NAUT, AER) captain.

com'media sf comedy; (opera teatrale) play; (: che fa ridere) comedy; (fig) playacting q; **commedi'ante** sm/f (peg) third-rate actor/actress; (: fig) sham.

commemo'rare vt to commemorate.

commenda'tore sm official title awarded for services to one's country.

commen'tare vt to comment on; (testo) to annotate; (RADIO, TV) to give a commentary on; **commenta'tore, 'trice** sm/f commentator; **com'mento** sm comment; (a un testo, RADIO, TV) commentary.

commerci'ale |kommer'tʃale| ag commercial, trading; (peg) commercial.

commerci'ante |kommer'tʃante| sm/f trader, dealer; (negoziante) shopkeeper.

commerci'are |kommer'tʃare| vt, vi: ~ in to deal o trade in.

com'mercio |kom'mertʃo| sm trade, commerce; essere in ~ (prodotto) to be on the market o on sale; essere nel ~ (persona) to be in business; ~ all'ingrosso/al minuto wholesale/retail trade.

com'messo, a pp di **commettere** // sm/f shop assistant (Brit), sales clerk (US) // sm (impiegato) clerk // sf (COMM) order; ~ **viaggiatore** commercial traveller.

commes'tibile ag edible; ~i smpl foodstuffs.

com'mettere vt to commit.

com'miato sm leave-taking.

commi'nare vt (DIR) to threaten; to inflict.

commissari'ato sm (AMM) commissionership; (: sede) commissioner's office; (: di polizia) police station.

commis'sario sm commissioner; (di pubblica sicurezza) ≈ (police) superintendent (Brit), (police) captain (US); (SPORT) steward; (membro di commissione) member of a committee o board.

commissio'nario sm (COMM) agent, broker.

commissi'one sf (incarico) errand; (comitato, percentuale) commission; (COMM: ordinazione) order; ~i sfpl (acquisti) shopping sg.

commit'tente sm/f (COMM) purchaser, customer.

com'mosso, a pp di **commuovere**.

commo'vente ag moving.

commozi'one |kommot'tsjone| sf emozione, deep feeling; ~ **cerebrale** (MED) concussion.

commu'overe vt to move, affect; ~rsi vr to be moved.

commu'tare vt (pena) to commute; (ELETTR) to change o switch over.

comò sm inv chest of drawers.

como'dino sm bedside table.

comodità sf inv comfort; convenience.

'comodo, a ag comfortable; (facile) easy; (conveniente) convenient; (utile) useful, handy // sm comfort; convenience; **con ~** at one's convenience o leisure; **fare il proprio ~** to do as one pleases; **far ~** to be useful o handy.

compae'sano, a sm/f fellow countryman; person from the same town.

com'pagine |kom'padʒine| sf (squadra) team.

compa'gnia |kompaɲ'ɲia| sf company; (gruppo) gathering.

com'pagno, a |kom'paɲɲo| sm/f (di classe, gioco) companion; (POL) comrade; **~ di lavoro** workmate.

compa'rare vt to compare.

compara'tivo, a ag, sm comparative.

compa'rire vi to appear; **com'parso, a** pp di **comparire** // sf appearance; (TEATRO) walk-on; (CINEMA) extra.

compartecipazi'one |kompartetʃipat'tsjone| sf sharing; (quota) share; **~ agli utili** profit-sharing.

comparti'mento sm compartment; (AMM) district.

compas'sato, a ag (persona) composed.

compassi'one sf compassion, pity; **avere ~ di qn** to feel sorry for sb, to pity sb.

com'passo sm (pair of) compasses pl; callipers pl.

compa'tibile ag (scusabile) excusable; (conciliabile, INFORM) compatible.

compa'tire vt (aver compassione di) to sympathize with, feel sorry for; (scusare) to make allowances for.

com'patto, a ag compact; (roccia) solid; (folla) dense; (fig: gruppo, partito) united, close-knit.

com'pendio sm summary; (libro) compendium.

compen'sare vt (equilibrare) to compensate for, make up for; **~ qn di** (rimunerare) to pay o remunerate sb for; (risarcire) to pay compensation to sb for; (fig: fatiche, dolori) to reward sb for; **com'penso** sm compensation; payment, remuneration; reward; **in compenso** (d'altra parte) on the other hand.

'compera sf (acquisto) purchase; **fare le ~e** to do the shopping.

compe'rare vt = **comprare**.

compe'tente ag competent; (mancia) apt, suitable; **compe'tenza** sf competence; **competenze** sfpl (onorari) fees.

com'petere vi to compete, vie; (DIR: spettare): **~ a** to lie within the competence of; **competizi'one** sf competition.

compia'cente |kompja'tʃɛnte| ag courteous, obliging; **compia'cenza** sf courtesy.

compia'cere |kompja'tʃere| vi: **~ a** to gratify, please // vt to please; **~rsi** vr (provare soddisfazione): **~rsi di** o **per qc** to be delighted at sth; (rallegrarsi): **~rsi con qn** to congratulate sb; (degnarsi): **~rsi di fare** to be so good as to do; **compiaci'uto, a** pp di **compiacere**.

compi'angere |kom'pjandʒere| vt to sympathize with, feel sorry for; **compi'anto, a** pp di **compiangere**.

'compiere vt (concludere) to finish, complete; (adempiere) to carry out, fulfil; **~rsi** vr (avverarsi) to be fulfilled, come true; **~ gli anni** to have one's birthday.

com'pire vt = **compiere**.

compi'tare vt to spell out.

'compito sm (incarico) task, duty; (dovere) duty; (INS) exercise; (: a casa) piece of homework; **fare i ~i** to do one's homework.

com'pito, a ag well-mannered, polite.

comple'anno sm birthday.

complemen'tare ag complementary; (INS: materia) subsidiary.

comple'mento sm complement; (MIL) reserve (troops); **~ oggetto** (LING) direct object.

complessità sf complexity.

comples'sivo, a ag (globale) comprehensive, overall; (totale: cifra) total.

com'plesso, a ag complex // sm (PSIC, EDIL) complex; (MUS: corale) ensemble; (: orchestrina) band; (: di musica pop) group; **in** o **nel ~** on the whole.

comple'tare vt to complete.

com'pleto, a ag complete; (teatro, autobus) full // sm suit; **al ~** full; (tutti presenti) all present.

compli'care vt to complicate; **~rsi** vr to become complicated; **complicazi'one** sf complication.

'complice |'komplitʃe| sm/f accomplice.

complimen'tarsi vr: **~ con** to congratulate.

compli'mento sm compliment; **~i** smpl (cortesia eccessiva) ceremony sg; (ossequi) regards, compliments; **~i!** congratulations!; **senza ~i!** don't stand on ceremony!; make yourself at home!; help yourself!

com'plotto sm plot, conspiracy.

compo'nente sm/f member // sm component.

componi'mento sm (DIR) settlement; (INS) composition; (poetico, teatrale) work.

com'porre vt (musica, testo) to compose; (mettere in ordine) to arrange; (DIR: lite) to settle; (TIP) to set; (TEL) to dial.

comporta'mento *sm* behaviour.
compor'tare *vt* (*implicare*) to involve; (*consentire*) to permit, allow (of); ~**rsi** *vr* (*condursi*) to behave.
composi'tore, 'trice *sm/f* composer; (*TIP*) compositor, typesetter.
composizi'one [kompozit'tsjone] *sf* composition; (*DIR*) settlement.
com'posta *sf vedi* **composto**.
compos'tezza [kompos'tettsa] *sf* composure; decorum.
com'posto, a *pp di* **comporre** // *ag* (*persona*) composed, self-possessed; (*: decoroso*) dignified; (*formato da più elementi*) compound *cpd* // *sm* compound // *sf* (*CUC*) stewed fruit *q*; (*AGR*) compost.
'compra *sf* = **compera**.
com'prare *vt* to buy; **compra'tore, 'trice** *sm/f* buyer, purchaser.
com'prendere *vt* (*contenere*) to comprise, consist of; (*capire*) to understand.
comprensi'one *sf* understanding.
compren'sivo, a *ag* (*prezzo*): ~ **di** inclusive of; (*indulgente*) understanding.
com'preso, a *pp di* **comprendere** // *ag* (*incluso*) included.
com'pressa *sf vedi* **compresso**.
compressi'one *sf* compression.
com'presso, a *pp di* **comprimere** // *ag* (*vedi comprimere*) pressed; compressed; repressed // *sf* (*MED*: *garza*) compress; (*: pastiglia*) tablet.
com'primere *vt* (*premere*) to press; (*FISICA*) to compress; (*fig*) to repress.
compro'messo, a *pp di* **compromettere** // *sm* compromise.
compro'mettere *vt* to compromise.
compro'vare *vt* to confirm.
com'punto, a *ag* contrite.
compu'tare *vt* to calculate; (*addebitare*): ~ **qc a qn** to debit sb with sth.
com'puter *sm inv* computer.
computiste'ria *sf* accounting, bookkeeping.
'computo *sm* calculation.
comu'nale *ag* municipal, town *cpd*, ≈ borough *cpd*.
co'mune *ag* common; (*consueto*) common, everyday; (*di livello medio*) average; (*ordinario*) ordinary // *sm* (*AMM*) town council; (*: sede*) town hall // *sf* (*di persone*) commune; **fuori del** ~ out of the ordinary; **avere in** ~ to have in common, share; **mettere in** ~ to share.
comuni'care *vt* (*notizia*) to pass on, convey; (*malattia*) to pass on; (*ansia etc*) to communicate; (*trasmettere: calore etc*) to transmit, communicate; (*REL*) to administer communion to // *vi* to communicate; ~**rsi** *vr* (*propagarsi*): ~**rsi a** to spread to; (*REL*) to receive communion.
comuni'cato *sm* communiqué; ~ **stampa** press release.
comunicazi'one [komunikat'tsjone] *sf* communication; (*annuncio*) announcement; (*TEL*): ~ (*telefonica*) (telephone) call; **dare la** ~ **a qn** to put sb through; **ottenere la** ~ to get through.
comuni'one *sf* communion; ~ **di beni** (*DIR*) joint ownership of property.
comu'nismo *sm* communism; **comu'nista, i, e** *ag*, *sm/f* communist.
comunità *sf inv* community; **C~ Economica Europea (C.E.E.)** European Economic Community (EEC).
co'munque *cong* however, no matter how // *av* (*in ogni modo*) in any case; (*tuttavia*) however, nevertheless.
con *prep* (*nei seguenti casi* **con** *può fondersi con l'articolo definito:* **con** + **il** = **col**, **con** + **gli** = **cogli**, **con** + **i** = **coi**) with; **partire col treno** to leave by train; ~ **mio grande stupore** to my great astonishment; ~ **tutto ciò** for all that.
co'nato *sm*: ~ **di vomito** retching.
'conca, che *sf* (*GEO*) valley.
con'cedere [kon'tʃedere] *vt* (*accordare*) to grant; (*ammettere*) to admit, concede; ~**rsi qc** to treat o.s. to sth, to allow o.s. sth.
concentra'mento [kontʃentra'mento] *sm* concentration.
concen'trare [kontʃen'trare] *vt*, ~**rsi** *vr* to concentrate; **concentrazi'one** *sf* concentration.
conce'pire [kontʃe'pire] *vt* (*bambino*) to conceive; (*progetto, idea*) to conceive (of); (*metodo, piano*) to devise.
con'cernere [kon'tʃɛrnere] *vt* to concern.
concer'tare [kontʃer'tare] *vt* (*MUS*) to harmonize; (*ordire*) to devise, plan; ~**rsi** *vr* to agree.
con'certo [kon'tʃɛrto] *sm* (*MUS*) concert; (*: componimento*) concerto.
concessio'nario [kontʃessjo'narjo] *sm* (*COMM*) agent, dealer.
con'cesso, a [kon'tʃɛsso] *pp di* **concedere**.
con'cetto [kon'tʃɛtto] *sm* (*pensiero, idea*) concept; (*opinione*) opinion.
concezi'one [kontʃet'tsjone] *sf* conception.
con'chiglia [kon'kiʎʎa] *sf* shell.
'concia ['kɔntʃa] *sf* (*di pelle*) tanning; (*di tabacco*) curing; (*sostanza*) tannin.
conci'are [kon'tʃare] *vt* (*pelli*) to tan; (*tabacco*) to cure; (*fig: ridurre in cattivo stato*) to beat up; ~**rsi** *vr* (*sporcarsi*) to get in a mess; (*vestirsi male*) to dress badly.
concili'are [kontʃi'ljare] *vt* to reconcile; (*contravvenzione*) to pay on the spot; (*favorire: sonno*) to be conducive to, induce; (*procurare: simpatia*) to gain; ~**rsi qc** to gain *o* win sth (for o.s.); ~**rsi**

qn to win sb over; ~**rsi con** to be reconciled with; **conciliazi'one** sf reconciliation; (DIR) settlement.

con'cilio |kon'tʃiljo| sm (REL) council.

con'cime |kon'tʃime| sm manure; (chimico) fertilizer.

con'ciso, a |kon'tʃizo| ag concise, succinct.

conci'tato, a |kontʃi'tato| ag excited, emotional.

concitta'dino, a |kontʃitta'dino| sm/f fellow citizen.

con'cludere vt to conclude; (portare a compimento) to conclude, finish, bring to an end; (operare positivamente) to achieve // vi (essere convincente) to be conclusive; ~**rsi** vr to come to an end, close; **conclusi'one** sf conclusion; (risultato) result; **conclu'sivo, a** ag conclusive; (finale) final; **con'cluso, a** pp di **concludere**.

concor'danza |konkor'dantsa| sf (anche LING) agreement.

concor'dare vt (tregua, prezzo) to agree on; (LING) to make agree // vi to agree; **concor'dato** sm agreement; (REL) concordat.

con'corde ag (d'accordo) in agreement; (simultaneo) simultaneous.

concor'rente sm/f competitor; (INS) candidate; **concor'renza** sf competition.

con'correre vi: ~ (in) (MAT) to converge o meet (in); ~ (a) (competere) to compete (for); (: INS: a una cattedra) to apply (for); (partecipare: a un'impresa) to take part (in), contribute (to); **con'corso, a** pp di **concorrere** // sm competition; (INS) competitive examination; **concorso di colpa** (DIR) contributory negligence.

con'creto, a ag concrete.

concussi'one sf (DIR) extortion.

con'danna sf sentence; conviction; condemnation.

condan'nare vt (DIR): ~ a to sentence to; ~ **per** to convict of; (disapprovare) to condemn; **condan'nato, a** sm/f convict.

conden'sare vt, ~**rsi** vr to condense; **condensazi'one** sf condensation.

condi'mento sm seasoning; dressing.

con'dire vt to season; (insalata) to dress.

condi'videre vt to share; **condi'viso, a** pp di **condividere**.

condizio'nale |kondittsjo'nale| ag conditional // sm (LING) conditional // sf (DIR) suspended sentence.

condizio'nare |kondittsjo'nare| vt to condition; **ad aria condizionata** air-conditioned.

condizi'one |kondit'tsjone| sf condition; ~**i** sfpl (di pagamento etc) terms, conditions; **a** ~ **che** on condition that, provided that.

condogli'anze |kondoʎ'ʎantse| sfpl condolences.

condo'minio sm joint ownership; (edificio) jointly-owned building.

condo'nare vt (DIR) to remit; **con'dono** sm remission; **condono fiscale** conditional amnesty for people evading tax.

con'dotta sf vedi **condotto**.

con'dotto, a pp di **condurre** // ag: **medico** ~ local authority doctor (in country district) // sm (canale, tubo) pipe, conduit; (ANAT) duct // sf (modo di comportarsi) conduct, behaviour; (di un affare etc) handling; (di acqua) piping; (incarico sanitario) country medical practice controlled by a local authority.

condu'cente |kondu'tʃente| sm driver.

con'durre vt to conduct; (azienda) to manage; (accompagnare: bambino) to take; (automobile) to drive; (trasportare: acqua, gas) to convey, conduct; (fig) to lead // vi to lead; **condursi** vr to behave, conduct o.s.

condut'tore ag: **filo** ~ (fig) thread // sm (di mezzi pubblici) driver; (FISICA) conductor.

con'farsi vr: ~ **a** to suit, agree with.

confederazi'one |konfederat'tsjone| sf confederation.

confe'renza |konfe'rentsa| sf (discorso) lecture; (riunione) conference; ~ **stampa** press conference; **confe-renzi'ere, a** sm/f lecturer.

confe'rire vt: ~ **qc a qn** to give sth to sb, bestow sth on sb // vi to confer.

con'ferma sf confirmation.

confer'mare vt to confirm.

confes'sare vt, ~**rsi** vr to confess; **andare a** ~**rsi** (REL) to go to confession; **confessio'nale** ag, sm confessional; **confessi'one** sf confession; (setta religiosa) denomination; **confes'sore** sm confessor.

con'fetto sm sugared almond; (MED) pill.

confezio'nare |konfettsjo'nare| vt (vestito) to make (up); (merci, pacchi) to package.

confezi'one |konfet'tsjone| sf (di abiti: da uomo) tailoring; (: da donna) dressmaking; (imballaggio) packaging; ~**i** sfpl garments, clothes; ~ **regalo** gift pack.

confic'care vt: ~ **qc in** to hammer o drive sth into; ~**rsi** vr to stick.

confi'dare vi: ~ **in** to confide in, rely on // vt to confide; ~**rsi con qn** to confide in sb; **confi'dente** sm/f (persona amica) confidant/confidante; (informatore) informer; **confi'denza** sf (familiarità) intimacy, familiarity; (fiducia) trust, confidence; (rivelazione) confidence; **confi-denzi'ale** ag familiar, friendly; (segreto) confidential.

configu'rarsi *vr*: ~ a to assume the shape *o* form of.

confi'nare *vi*: ~ con to border on // *vt* (*POL*) to intern; (*fig*) to confine; ~**rsi** *vr* (*isolarsi*): ~**rsi** in to shut o.s. up in.

Confin'dustria *sigla f* (= *Confederazione Generale dell'Industria Italiana*) employers' association, ≈ CBI (*Brit*).

con'fine *sm* boundary; (*di paese*) border, frontier.

con'fino *sm* internment.

confis'care *vt* to confiscate.

con'flitto *sm* conflict.

conflu'enza [konflu'entsa] *sf* (*di fiumi*) confluence; (*di strade*) junction.

conflu'ire *vi* (*fiumi*) to flow into each other, meet; (*strade*) to meet.

con'fondere *vt* to mix up, confuse; (*imbarazzare*) to embarrass; ~**rsi** *vr* (*mescolarsi*) to mingle; (*turbarsi*) to be confused; (*sbagliare*) to get mixed up; ~ **le idee a qn** to mix sb up, confuse sb.

confor'mare *vt* (*adeguare*): ~ a to adapt *o* conform to; ~**rsi** *vr*: ~**rsi** (a) to conform (to).

conforme'mente *av* accordingly; ~ a in accordance with.

confor'tare *vt* to comfort, console; **confor'tevole** *ag* (*consolante*) comforting; (*comodo*) comfortable; **con'forto** *sm* comfort, consolation; comfort.

confron'tare *vt* to compare.

con'fronto *sm* comparison; in *o* a ~ di in comparison with, compared to; nei miei (*o* tuoi *etc*) ~**i** towards me (*o* you *etc*).

confusi'one *sf* confusion; (*chiasso*) racket, noise; (*imbarazzo*) embarrassment.

con'fuso, a *pp di* **confondere** // *ag* (*vedi confondere*) confused; embarrassed.

confu'tare *vt* to refute.

conge'dare [kondʒe'dare] *vt* to dismiss; (*MIL*) to demobilize; ~**rsi** *vr* to take one's leave; **con'gedo** *sm* (*anche MIL*) leave; **prendere congedo da qn** to take one's leave of sb; **congedo assoluto** (*MIL*) discharge.

conge'gnare [kondʒeɲ'ɲare] *vt* to construct, put together; **con'gegno** *sm* device, mechanism.

conge'lare [kondʒe'lare] *vt*, ~**rsi** *vr* to freeze; **congela'tore** *sm* freezer.

congestio'nare [kondʒestjo'nare] *vt* to congest.

congesti'one [kondʒes'tjone] *sf* congestion.

conget'tura [kondʒet'tura] *sf* conjecture, supposition.

con'giungere [kon'dʒundʒere] *vt*, ~**rsi** *vr* to join (together).

congiunti'vite [kondʒunti'vite] *sf* conjunctivitis.

congiun'tivo [kondʒun'tivo] *sm* (*LING*) subjunctive.

congi'unto, a [kon'dʒunto] *pp di* **congiungere** // *ag* (*unito*) joined // *sm/f* relative.

congiun'tura [kondʒun'tura] *sf* (*giuntura*) junction, join; (*ANAT*) joint; (*circostanza*) juncture; (*ECON*) economic situation.

congiunzi'one [kondʒun'tsjone] *sf* (*LING*) conjunction.

congi'ura [kon'dʒura] *sf* conspiracy; **congiu'rare** *vi* to conspire.

conglome'rato *sm* (*GEO*) conglomerate; (*fig*) conglomeration; (*EDIL*) concrete.

congratu'larsi *vr*: ~ con qn per qc to congratulate sb on sth.

congratulazi'oni [kongratulat'tsjoni] *sfpl* congratulations.

congrega, ghe *sf* band, bunch.

con'gresso *sm* congress.

congu'aglio [kon'gwaʎʎo] *sm* balancing, adjusting; (*somma di denaro*) balance.

coni'are *vt* to mint, coin; (*fig*) to coin.

co'niglio [ko'niʎʎo] *sm* rabbit.

coniu'gare *vt* (*LING*) to conjugate; ~**rsi** *vr* to get married; **coniu'gato, a** *ag* (*sposato*) married; **coniugazi'one** *sf* (*LING*) conjugation.

'coniuge ['kɔnjudʒe] *sm/f* spouse.

connazio'nale [konnattsjo'nale] *sm/f* fellow-countryman/woman.

connessi'one *sf* connection.

con'nesso, a *pp di* **connettere**.

con'nettere *vt* to connect, join // *vi* (*fig*) to think straight.

conni'vente *ag* conniving.

conno'tati *smpl* distinguishing marks.

'cono *sm* cone; ~ **gelato** ice-cream cone.

cono'scente [konoʃ'ʃente] *sm/f* acquaintance.

cono'scenza [konoʃ'ʃentsa] *sf* (*il sapere*) knowledge *q*; (*persona*) acquaintance; (*facoltà sensoriale*) consciousness *q*; **perdere** ~ to lose consciousness.

co'noscere [ko'noʃʃere] *vt* to know; **ci siamo conosciuti a Firenze** we (first) met in Florence; **conosci'tore, 'trice** *sm/f* connoisseur; **conosci'uto, a** *pp di* **conoscere** // *ag* well-known.

con'quista *sf* conquest.

conquis'tare *vt* to conquer; (*fig*) to gain, win.

consa'crare *vt* (*REL*) to consecrate; (*: sacerdote*) to ordain; (*dedicare*) to dedicate; (*fig: uso etc*) to sanction; ~**rsi** a to dedicate o.s. to.

consangu'ineo, a *sm/f* blood relation.

consa'pevole *ag*: ~ di aware *o* conscious of; **consapevo'lezza** *sf* awareness, consciousness.

'conscio, a, sci, sce ['kɔnʃo] *ag*: ~ di aware *o* conscious of.

consecu'tivo, a *ag* consecutive;

(*successivo: giorno*) following, next.

con'segna |kon'seɲɲa| *sf* delivery; (*merce consegnata*) consignment; (*custodia*) care, custody; (*MIL: ordine*) orders *pl*; (*: punizione*) confinement to barracks; **pagamento alla ~** cash on delivery; **dare qc in ~ a qn** to entrust sth to sb.

conse'gnare |konseɲ'ɲare| *vt* to deliver; (*affidare*) to entrust, hand over; (*MIL*) to confine to barracks.

consegu'enza |konse'gwentsa| *sf* consequence, per o di ~ consequently.

consegu'ire *vt* to achieve // *vi* to follow, result.

con'senso *sm* approval, consent.

consen'tire *vi*: **~ a** to consent o agree to // *vt* to allow, permit.

con'serva *sf* (*CUC*) preserve; **~ di frutta** jam; **~ di pomodoro** tomato purée.

conser'vare *vt* (*CUC*) to preserve; (*custodire*) to keep; (*: dalla distruzione etc*) to preserve, conserve; **~rsi** *vr* to keep.

conserva'tore, 'trice *sm/f* (*POL*) conservative.

conservazi'one |konservat'tsjone| *sf* preservation; conservation.

conside'rare *vt* to consider; (*reputare*) to consider, regard; **~ molto qn** to think highly of sb; **considerazi'one** *sf* consideration; (*stima*) regard, esteem; **prendere in considerazione** to take into consideration; **conside'revole** *ag* considerable.

consigli'are |konsiʎ'ʎare| *vt* (*persona*) to advise; (*metodo, azione*) to recommend, advise, suggest; **~rsi** *vr*: **~rsi con qn** to ask sb for advice; **consigli'ere, a** *sm/f* adviser // *sm*: **consigliere d'amministrazione** board member; **consigliere comunale** town councillor; **con'siglio** *sm* (*suggerimento*) advice q, piece of advice; (*assemblea*) council; **consiglio d'amministrazione** board; **il Consiglio dei Ministri** (*POL*) ≈ the Cabinet.

consis'tente *ag* thick; solid; (*fig*) sound, valid; **consis'tenza** *sf* consistency, thickness; solidity; validity.

con'sistere *vi*: **~ in** to consist of; **consis'tito, a** *pp di* **consistere.**

conso'lare *ag* consular // *vt* (*confortare*) to console, comfort; (*rallegrare*) to cheer up; **~rsi** *vr* to be comforted; to cheer up.

conso'lato *sm* consulate.

consolazi'one |konsolat'tsjone| *sf* consolation, comfort.

'console *sm* consul // |kon'sɔl| *sf* (*quadro di comando*) console.

conso'nante *sf* consonant.

'consono, a *ag*: **~ a** consistent with, consonant with.

con'sorte *sm/f* consort.

con'sorzio |kon'sɔrtsjo| *sm* consortium.

con'stare *vi*: **~ di** to consist of // *vb impers*: **mi consta che** it has come to my knowledge that, it appears that.

consta'tare *vt* to establish, verify; **constatazi'one** *sf* observation; **constatazione amichevole** *jointly-agreed statement for insurance purposes.*

consu'eto, a *ag* habitual, usual; **consue'tudine** *sf* habit, custom; (*usanza*) custom.

consu'lente *sm/f* consultant; **consu'lenza** *sf* consultancy.

consul'tare *vt* to consult; **~rsi** *vr*: **~rsi con qn** to seek the advice of sb; **consultazi'one** *sf* consultation; **consultazioni** *sfpl* (*POL*) talks, consultations.

consu'mare *vt* (*logorare: abiti, scarpe*) to wear out; (*usare*) to consume, use up; (*mangiare, bere*) to consume; (*DIR*) to consummate; **~rsi** *vr* to wear out; to be used up; (*anche fig*) to be consumed; (*combustibile*) to burn out; **consuma'tore** *sm* consumer; **consumazi'one** *sf* (*bibita*) drink; (*spuntino*) snack; (*DIR*) consummation; **con'sumo** *sm* consumption; wear; use.

consun'tivo *sm* (*ECON*) final balance.

con'tabile *ag* accounts *cpd*, accounting // *sm/f* accountant; **contabilità** *sf* (*attività, tecnica*) accounting, accountancy; (*insieme dei libri etc*) books *pl*, accounts *pl*; (*ufficio*) accounts department.

conta'dino, a *sm/f* countryman/woman; farm worker; (*peg*) peasant.

contagi'are |konta'dʒare| *vt* to infect.

con'tagio |kon'tadʒo| *sm* infection; (*per contatto diretto*) contagion; (*epidemia*) epidemic; **contagi'oso, a** *ag* infectious; contagious.

conta'gocce |konta'gottʃe| *sm inv* (*MED*) dropper.

contami'nare *vt* to contaminate.

con'tante *sm* cash; **pagare in ~i** to pay cash.

con'tare *vt* to count; (*considerare*) to consider // *vi* to count, be of importance; **~ su qn** to count o rely on sb; **~ di fare qc** to intend to do sth; **conta'tore** *sm* meter.

contat'tare *vt* to contact.

con'tatto *sm* contact.

'conte *sm* count.

conteggi'are |konted'dʒare| *vt* to charge, put on the bill; **con'teggio** *sm* calculation.

con'tegno |kon'teɲɲo| *sm* (*comportamento*) behaviour; (*atteggiamento*) attitude; **darsi un ~** to act nonchalant; to pull o.s. together.

contem'plare *vt* to contemplate, gaze at; (*DIR*) to make provision for.

contemporanea'mente *av* simultaneously; at the same time.

contempo'raneo, a *ag, sm/f* contemporary.

conten'dente *sm/f* opponent, adversary.

con'tendere *vi* (*competere*) to compete; (*litigare*) to quarrel // *vt*: ~ qc a qn to contend with o be in competition with sb for sth.

conte'nere *vt* to contain; **conteni'tore** *sm* container.

conten'tare *vt* to please, satisfy; ~rsi di to be satisfied with, content o.s. with.

conten'tezza [konten'tettsa] *sf* contentment.

con'tento, a *ag* pleased, glad; ~ di pleased with.

conte'nuto *sm* contents *pl*; (*argomento*) content.

con'teso, a *pp di* **contendere** // *sf* dispute, argument.

con'tessa *sf* countess.

contes'tare *vt* (*DIR*) to notify; (*fig*) to dispute; **contestazi'one** *sf* (*DIR*) notification; dispute; (*protesta*) protest.

con'testo *sm* context.

con'tiguo, a *ag*: ~ (a) adjacent (to).

continen'tale *ag, sm/f* continental.

conti'nente *ag* continent // *sm* (*GEO*) continent; (*: terra ferma*) mainland; **conti'nenza** *sf* continence.

contin'gente [kontin'dʒente] *ag* contingent // *sm* (*COMM*) quota; (*MIL*) contingent; **contin'genza** *sf* circumstance; (*ECON*) (**indennità di**) **contingenza** cost-of-living allowance.

continu'are *vt* to continue (with), go on with // *vi* to continue, go on; ~ a fare qc to go on o continue doing sth; **continuazi'one** *sf* continuation.

con'tinuo, a *ag* (*numerazione*) continuous; (*pioggia*) continual, constant; (*ELETTR*): **corrente** ~**a** direct current; **di** ~ continually.

'conto *sm* (*calcolo*) calculation; (*COMM, ECON*) account; (*di ristorante, albergo*) bill; (*fig: stima*) consideration, esteem; **fare i** ~**i con qn** to settle one's account with sb; **fare** ~ **su qn/qc** to count o rely on sb; **rendere** ~ **a qn di qc** to be accountable to sb for sth; **tener** ~ **di qn/qc** to take sb/sth into account; **per** ~ **di** on behalf of; **per** ~ **mio** as far as I'm concerned; **a** ~**i fatti, in fin dei** ~**i** all things considered; ~ **corrente** current account; ~ **alla rovescia** countdown.

con'torcere [kon'tortʃere] *vt* to twist; (*panni*) to wring (out); ~**rsi** *vr* to twist, writhe.

contor'nare *vt* to surround.

con'torno *sm* (*linea*) outline, contour; (*ornamento*) border; (*CUC*) vegetables *pl*.

con'torto, a *pp di* **contorcere**.

contrabbandi'ere, a *sm/f* smuggler.

contrab'bando *sm* smuggling, contraband; **merce di** ~ contraband, smuggled goods *pl*.

contrab'basso *sm* (*MUS*) (double) bass.

contraccambi'are *vt* (*favore etc*) to return.

contraccet'tivo, a [kontrattʃet'tivo] *ag, sm* contraceptive.

contrac'colpo *sm* rebound; (*di arma da fuoco*) recoil; (*fig*) repercussion.

con'trada *sf* street; district.

contrad'detto, a *pp di* **contraddire**.

contrad'dire *vt* to contradict; **contraddit'torio, a** *ag* contradictory; (*sentimenti*) conflicting // *sm* (*DIR*) cross-examination; **contraddizi'one** *sf* contradiction.

contraf'fare *vt* (*persona*) to mimic; (*alterare: voce*) to disguise; (*firma*) to forge, counterfeit; **contraf'fatto, a** *pp di* **contraffare** // *ag* counterfeit; **contraffazi'one** *sf* mimicking q; disguising q; forging q; (*cosa contraffatta*) forgery.

contrap'peso *sm* counterbalance, counterweight.

contrap'porre *vt*: ~ qc a qc to counter sth with sth; (*paragonare*) to compare sth with sth; **contrap'posto, a** *pp di* **contrapporre**.

contraria'mente *av*: ~ a contrary to.

contrari'are *vt* (*contrastare*) to thwart, oppose; (*irritare*) to annoy, bother; ~**rsi** *vr* to get annoyed.

contrarietà *sf* adversity; (*fig*) aversion.

con'trario, a *ag* opposite; (*sfavorevole*) unfavourable // *sm* opposite; **essere** ~ **a qc** (*persona*) to be against sth; **in caso** ~ otherwise; **avere qc in** ~ to have some objection; **al** ~ on the contrary.

con'trarre *vt, contrarsi vr* to contract.

contrasse'gnare [kontrasseɲ'ɲare] *vt* to mark; **contras'segno** *sm* (*distintivo*) distinguishing mark; **spedire in contrassegno** to send C.O.D.

contras'tare *vt* (*avversare*) to oppose; (*impedire*) to bar; (*negare: diritto*) to contest, dispute // *vi*: ~ (**con**) (*essere in disaccordo*) to contrast (with); (*lottare*) to struggle (with); **con'trasto** *sm* contrast; (*conflitto*) conflict; (*litigio*) dispute.

contrat'tacco *sm* counterattack.

contrat'tare *vt, vi* to negotiate.

contrat'tempo *sm* hitch.

con'tratto, a *pp di* **contrarre** // *sm* contract; **contrattu'ale** *ag* contractual.

contravvenzi'one [kontravven'tsjone] *sf* contravention; (*ammenda*) fine.

contrazi'one [kontrat'tsjone] *sf* contraction; (*di prezzi etc*) reduction.

contribu'ente *sm/f* taxpayer; ratepayer (*Brit*), property tax payer (*US*).

contribu'ire *vi* to contribute; **contri'buto** *sm* contribution; (*tassa*) tax.

'contro *prep* against; ~ **di me/lui** against me/him; **pastiglie** ~ **la tosse** throat lozenges; ~ **pagamento** (*COMM*) on pay-

ment // *prefisso*: **contro'battere** *vt* (*fig:
a parole*) to answer back; (: *confutare*)
to refute; **controfi'gura** *sf* (*CINEMA*)
double; **controfir'mare** *vt* to counter-
sign.

control'lare *vt* (*accertare*) to check;
(*sorvegliare*) to watch, control; (*tenere
nel proprio potere, fig: dominare*) to control; **con'trollo** *sm* check; watch; control; **controllo delle nascite** birth control;
control'lore *sm* (*FERR, AUTOBUS*) (ticket) inspector.

controprodu'cente |kontroprodu'tʃɛnte]
ag counterproductive.

contro'senso *sm* (*contraddizione*) contradiction in terms; (*assurdità*) nonsense.

controspio'naggio |kontrospio'naddʒo]
sm counterespionage.

contro'versia *sf* controversy; (*DIR*) dispute.

contro'verso, a *ag* controversial.

contro'voglia |kontro'vɔʎʎa] *av* unwill-
ingly.

contu'macia |kontu'matʃa] *sf* (*DIR*)
default.

contur'bare *vt* to disturb, upset.

contusi'one *sf* (*MED*) bruise.

convale'scente |konvaleʃ'ʃɛnte] *ag, sm/f*
convalescent; **convale'scenza** *sf* con-
valescence.

convali'dare *vt* (*AMM*) to validate; (*fig:
sospetto, dubbio*) to confirm.

con'vegno |kon'veɲɲo] *sm* (*incontro*)
meeting; (*congresso*) convention, congress; (*luogo*) meeting place.

conve'nevoli *smpl* civilities.

conveni'ente *ag* suitable; (*vantaggioso*)
profitable; (: *prezzo*) cheap; **conveni'enza** *sf* suitability; advantage; cheap-
ness; **le convenienze** *sfpl* social conventions.

conve'nire *vi* (*riunirsi*) to gather,
assemble; (*concordare*) to agree;
(*tornare utile*) to be worthwhile // *vb
impers*: **conviene fare questo** it is advisable to do this; **conviene andarsene** we
should go; **ne convengo** I agree.

con'vento *sm* (*di frati*) monastery; (*di
suore*) convent.

convenzio'nale |konventsjo'nale] *ag* con-
ventional.

convenzi'one |konven'tsjone] *sf* (*DIR*)
agreement; (*nella società*) convention;
le ~i *sfpl* social conventions.

conver'sare *vi* to have a conversation,
converse.

conversazi'one |konversat'tsjone] *sf* con-
versation; **fare ~** to chat, have a chat.

conversi'one *sf* conversion; **~ ad U**
(*AUT*) U-turn.

conver'tire *vt* (*trasformare*) to change;
(*POL, REL*) to convert; **~rsi** *vr*: **~rsi (a)**
to be converted (to); **conver'tito, a**
sm/f convert.

con'vesso, a *ag* convex.

con'vincere |kon'vintʃere] *vt* to con-
vince; **~ qn di qc** to convince sb of sth;
~ qn a fare qc to persuade sb to do sth;
con'vinto, a *pp di* **convincere**;
convinzi'one *sf* conviction, firm belief.

convis'suto, a *pp di* **convivere**.

con'vitto *sm* (*INS*) boarding school.

con'vivere *vi* to live together.

convo'care *vt* to call, convene; (*DIR*) to
summon; **convocazi'one** *sf* meeting;
summons *sg*.

convogli'are |konvoʎ'ʎare] *vt* to convey;
(*dirigere*) to direct, send; **con'voglio**
sm (*di veicoli*) convoy; (*FERR*) train.

con'vulso, a *ag* (*pianto*) violent, con-
vulsive; (*attività*) feverish.

coope'rare *vi*: **~ (a)** to cooperate (in);
coopera'tiva *sf* cooperative; **coopera-
zi'one** *sf* cooperation.

coordi'nare *vt* to coordinate; **coordi'nate** *sfpl* (*MAT, GEO*) coordi-
nates; **coordi'nati** *smpl* (*MODA*) coordi-
nates.

co'perchio |ko'pɛrkjo] *sm* cover; (*di
pentola*) lid.

co'perta *sf* cover; (*di lana*) blanket; (*da
viaggio*) rug; (*NAUT*) deck.

coper'tina *sf* (*STAMPA*) cover, jacket.

co'perto, a *pp di* **coprire** // *ag* covered;
(*cielo*) overcast // *sm* place setting; (*posto a tavola*) place; (*al ristorante*) cover
charge; **~ di** covered in *o* with.

coper'tone *sm* (*telo impermeabile*)
tarpaulin; (*AUT*) rubber tyre.

coper'tura *sf* (*anche ECON, MIL*) cover;
(*di edificio*) roofing.

'copia *sf* copy; **brutta/bella ~** rough/final
copy.

copi'are *vt* to copy; **copia'trice** *sf*
copier, copying machine.

copi'one *sm* (*CINEMA, TEATRO*) script.

'coppa *sf* (*bicchiere*) goblet; (*per frutta,
gelato*) dish; (*trofeo*) cup, trophy; **~
dell'olio** oil sump (*Brit*) *o* pan (*US*).

'coppia *sf* (*di persone*) couple; (*di
animali, SPORT*) pair.

coprifu'oco, chi *sm* curfew.

copri'letto *sm* bedspread.

co'prire *vt* to cover; (*occupare: carica,
posto*) to hold; **~rsi** *vr* (*cielo*) to cloud
over; (*vestirsi*) to wrap up, cover up;
(*ECON*) to cover o.s.; **~rsi di** (*macchie,
muffa*) to become covered in.

co'raggio |ko'raddʒo] *sm* courage,
bravery; **~!** (*forza!*) come on!;
(*animo!*) cheer up!; **coraggi'oso, a** *ag*
courageous, brave.

co'rallo *sm* coral.

co'rano *sm* (*REL*) Koran.

co'razza |ko'rattsa] *sf* armour; (*di
animali*) carapace, shell; (*MIL*)
armour(-plating); **coraz'zata** *sf* battle-
ship.

corbelle'ria *sf* stupid remark; **~e** *sfpl*

nonsense *q*.

'**corda** *sf* cord; (*fune*) rope; (*spago*, *MUS*) string; **dare ~ a qn** to let sb have his (*o her*) way; **tenere sulla ~ qn** to keep sb on tenterhooks; **tagliare la ~** to slip away, sneak off; **~e vocali** vocal cords.

cordi'ale *ag* cordial, warm // *sm* (*bevanda*) cordial.

cor'doglio [kor'dɔʎʎo] *sm* grief; (*lutto*) mourning.

cor'done *sm* cord, string; (*linea: di polizia*) cordon; **~ ombelicale** umbilical cord.

Co'rea *sf*: **la ~** Korea.

coreogra'fia *sf* choreography.

cori'andolo *sm* (*BOT*) coriander; **~i** *smpl* confetti *sg*.

cori'care *vt* to put to bed; **~rsi** *vr* to go to bed.

'**corna** *sfpl vedi* **corno**.

cor'nacchia [kor'nakkja] *sf* crow.

corna'musa *sf* bagpipes *pl*.

cor'netta *sf* (*MUS*) cornet; (*TEL*) receiver.

cor'netto *sm* (*CUC*) croissant; **~ acustico** ear trumpet.

cor'nice [kor'nitʃe] *sf* frame; (*fig*) setting, background.

'**corno** *sm* (*ZOOL*: *pl(f)* **~a**, *MUS*) horn; **fare le ~a a qn** to be unfaithful to sb; **cor'nuto, a** *ag* (*con corna*) horned; (*fam!*: *marito*) cuckolded // *sm* (*fam!*) cuckold; (*: insulto*) bastard (*!*).

Corno'vaglia [korno'vaʎʎa] *sf*: **la ~** Cornwall.

'**coro** *sm* chorus; (*REL*) choir.

co'rona *sf* crown; (*di fiori*) wreath; **coro'nare** *vt* to crown.

'**corpo** *sm* body; (*cadavere*) (dead) body; (*militare, diplomatico*) corps *inv*; (*di opere*) corpus; **prendere ~** to take shape; **a ~ a ~** hand-to-hand; **~ di ballo** corps de ballet; **~ di guardia** guard-room; **~ insegnante** teaching staff.

corpo'rale *ag* bodily; (*punizione*) corporal.

corpora'tura *sf* build, physique.

corporazi'one [korporat'tsjone] *sf* corporation.

corpu'lento, a *ag* stout.

corre'dare *vt*: **~ di** to provide *o* furnish with; **cor'redo** *sm* equipment; (*di sposa*) trousseau.

cor'reggere [kor'rɛddʒere] *vt* to correct; (*compiti*) to correct, mark.

cor'rente *ag* (*fiume*) flowing; (*acqua del rubinetto*) running; (*moneta, prezzo*) current; (*comune*) everyday // *sm*: **essere al ~ (di)** to be well-informed (about); **mettere al ~ (di)** to inform (of) // *sf* (*movimento di liquido*) current, stream; (*spiffero*) draught; (*ELETTR, METEOR*) current; (*fig*) trend, tendency; **la vostra lettera del 5 ~ mese** (*COMM*)

your letter of the 5th of this month; **corrente'mente** *av* commonly; **parlare una lingua correntemente** to speak a language fluently.

cor'rere *vi* to run; (*precipitarsi*) to rush; (*partecipare a una gara*) to race, run; (*fig: diffondersi*) to go round // *vt* (*SPORT: gara*) to compete in; (*rischio*) to run; (*pericolo*) to face; **~ dietro a qn** to run after sb; **corre voce che ... it** is rumoured that ....

cor'retto, a *pp di* **correggere** // *ag* (*comportamento*) correct, proper; **caffè ~ al cognac** coffee laced with brandy.

correzi'one [korret'tsjone] *sf* correction; marking; **~ di bozze** proofreading.

corri'doio *sm* corridor.

corri'dore *sm* (*SPORT*) runner; (*: su veicolo*) racer.

corri'era *sf* coach (*Brit*), bus.

corri'ere *sm* (*diplomatico, di guerra*) courier; (*posta*) mail, post; (*COMM*) carrier.

corrispet'tivo *sm* (*somma*) amount due.

corrispon'dente *ag* corresponding // *sm/f* correspondent.

corrispon'denza [korrispon'dɛntsa] *sf* correspondence.

corris'pondere *vi* (*equivalere*): **~ (a)** to correspond (to); (*per lettera*): **~ con** to correspond with // *vt* (*stipendio*) to pay; (*fig: amore*) to return; **corris'posto, a** *pp di* **corrispondere**.

corrobo'rare *vt* to strengthen, fortify; (*fig*) to corroborate, bear out.

cor'rodere *vt*, **~rsi** *vr* to corrode.

cor'rompere *vt* to corrupt; (*comprare*) to bribe.

corrosi'one *sf* corrosion.

cor'roso, a *pp di* **corrodere**.

cor'rotto, a *pp di* **corrompere** // *ag* corrupt.

corrucci'arsi [korrut'tʃarsi] *vr* to grow angry *o* vexed.

corru'gare *vt* to wrinkle; **~ la fronte** to knit one's brows.

corruzi'one [korrut'tsjone] *sf* corruption; bribery.

'**corsa** *sf* running *q*; (*gara*) race; (*di autobus, taxi*) journey, trip; **fare una ~** to run, dash; (*SPORT*) to run a race.

cor'sia *sf* (*AUT, SPORT*) lane; (*di ospedale*) ward.

cor'sivo *sm* cursive (writing); (*TIP*) italics *pl*.

'**corso, a** *pp di* **correre** // *sm* course; (*strada cittadina*) main street; (*di unità monetaria*) circulation; (*di titoli, valori*) rate, price; **dar libero ~ a** to give free expression to; **in ~** in progress, under way; (*annata*) current; **~ d'acqua** river, stream; (*artificiale*) waterway; **~ serale** evening class.

'**corte** *sf* (court)yard; (*DIR, regale*) court; **fare la ~ a qn** to court sb; **~**

marziale court-martial.

cor'teccia, ce |kor'tettʃa| *sf* bark.

corteggi'are |korted'dʒare| *vt* to court.

cor'teo *sm* procession.

cor'tese *ag* courteous; **corte'sia** *sf* courtesy; **per cortesia** ... excuse me, please ....

cortigi'ano, a |korti'dʒano| *sm/f* courtier // *sf* courtesan.

cor'tile *sm* (court)yard.

cor'tina *sf* curtain; (*anche fig*) screen.

'corto, a *ag* short; **essere a ~ di qc** to be short of sth; **~ circuito** short-circuit.

'corvo *sm* raven.

'cosa *sf* thing; (*faccenda*) affair, matter, business *q*; (**che**) **~?** what?; (**che**) **cos'è?** what is it?; **a ~ pensi?** what are you thinking about?; **a ~e fatte** when it's all over.

'coscia, sce |'kɔʃʃa| *sf* thigh; **~ di pollo** (*CUC*) chicken leg.

cosci'ente |koʃ'ʃɛnte| *ag* conscious; **~ di** conscious *o* aware of; **cosci'enza** *sf* conscience; (*consapevolezza*) consciousness; **coscienzi'oso, a** *ag* conscientious.

cosci'otto |koʃ'ʃɔtto| *sm* (*CUC*) leg.

cos'critto *sm* (*MIL*) conscript.

così ◆ *av* **1** (*in questo modo*) like this, (in) this way; (*in tal modo*) so; **le cose stanno ~** this is the way things stand; **non ho detto ~!** I didn't say that!; **come stai? — (e) ~ e ~** how are you? — so-so; **e ~ via and so on; per ~ dire** so to speak **2** (*tanto*) so; **~ lontano** so far away; **un ragazzo ~ intelligente** such an intelligent boy ◆ *ag inv* (*tale*): **non ho mai visto un film ~** I've never seen such a film ◆ *cong* **1** (*perciò*) so, therefore **2:** **~ ... come as ... as; non è ~ bravo come te** he's not as good as you; **~ ... che** so ... that.

cosid'detto, a *ag* so-called.

cos'metico, o, ci, che *ag, sm* cosmetic.

cos'pargere |kos'pardʒere| *vt*: **~ di** to sprinkle with; **cos'parso, a** *pp di* **cospargere**.

cos'petto *sm*: **al ~ di** in front of; **in the presence of.**

cos'picuo, a *ag* considerable, large.

cospi'rare *vi* to conspire; **cospirazi'one** *sf* conspiracy.

'costa *sf* (*tra terra e mare*) coast(line); (*litorale*) shore; (*ANAT*) rib; **la C~ Azzurra** the French Riviera.

costà *av* there.

cos'tante *ag* constant; (*persona*) steadfast // *sf* constant.

cos'tare *vi, vt* to cost; **~ caro** to be expensive, cost a lot.

cos'tata *sf* (*CUC*) large chop.

cos'tato *sm* (*ANAT*) ribs *pl*.

costeggi'are |kosted'dʒare| *vt* to be close to; to run alongside.

cos'tei *pronome vedi* **costui**.

costernazi'one |kosternat'tsjone| *sf* dismay, consternation.

costi'ero, a *ag* coastal, coast *cpd* // *sf* stretch of coast.

costitu'ire *vt* (*comitato, gruppo*) to set up, form; (*collezione*) to put together, build up; (*sog: elementi, parti: comporre*) to make up, constitute; (*rappresentare*) to constitute; (*DIR*) to appoint; **~rsi alla polizia** to give o.s. up to the police.

costituzio'nale |kostituttsjo'nale| *ag* constitutional

costituzi'one |kostitut'tsjone| *sf* setting up; building up; constitution.

'costo *sm* cost; **a ogni o qualunque ~, a tutti i ~i** at all costs.

'costola *sf* (*ANAT*) rib.

costo'letta *sf* (*CUC*) cutlet.

cos'toro *pronome pl vedi* **costui**.

cos'toso, a *ag* expensive, costly.

cos'tretto, a *pp di* **costringere**.

cos'tringere |kos'trindʒere| *vt*: **~ qn a fare qc** to force sb to do sth; **cos'trizi'one** *sf* coercion.

costru'ire *vt* to construct, build; **costruzi'one** *sf* construction, building.

cos'tui, cos'tei, *pl* **cos'toro** *pronome* (*soggetto*) he/she; *pl* they; (*complemento*) him/her; *pl* them; **si può sapere chi è ~?** (*peg*) just who is that fellow?

cos'tume *sm* (*uso*) custom; (*foggia di vestire, indumento*) costume; **~i** *smpl* morals, morality *sg*; **il buon ~** public morality; **~ da bagno** bathing *o* swimming costume (*Brit*), swimsuit; (*da uomo*) bathing *o* swimming trunks *pl*.

co'tenna *sf* bacon rind.

co'togna |ko'toɲɲa| *sf* quince.

coto'letta *sf* (*di maiale, montone*) chop; (*di vitello, agnello*) cutlet.

co'tone *sm* cotton; **~ idrofilo** cotton wool (*Brit*), absorbent cotton (*US*).

'cotta *sf* (*fam: innamoramento*) crush.

'cottimo *sm*: **lavorare a ~** to do piecework.

'cotto, a *pp di* **cuocere** // *ag* cooked; (*fam: innamorato*) head-over-heels in love.

cot'tura *sf* cooking; (*in forno*) baking; (*in umido*) stewing.

co'vare *vt* to hatch; (*fig: malattia*) to be sickening for; (*: odio, rancore*) to nurse // *vi* (*fuoco, fig*) to smoulder.

'covo *sm* den.

co'vone *sm* sheaf.

'cozza |'kɔttsa| *sf* mussel.

coz'zare |kot'tsare| *vi*: **~ contro** to bang into, collide with.

C.P. *abbr* = **casella postale.**

'crampo *sm* cramp.

'cranio *sm* skull.

cra'vatta *sf* tie.

cre'anza |kre'antsa| sf manners pl.

cre'are vt to create; **cre'ato** sm creation; **crea'tore, 'trice** ag creative // sm creator; **crea'tura** sf creature; (bimbo) baby, infant; **creazi'one** sf creation; (fondazione) foundation, establishment.

cre'dente sm/f (REL) believer.

cre'denza |kre'dentsa| sf belief; (armadio) sideboard.

credenzi'ali |kreden'tsjali| sfpl credentials.

'credere vt to believe // vi: ~ **in**, ~ **a** to believe in; ~ **qn onesto** to believe sb (to be) honest; ~ **che** to believe o think that; ~**rsi furbo** to think one is clever.

'credito sm (anche COMM) credit; (reputazione) esteem, repute; **comprare a** ~ to buy on credit.

'credo sm inv creed.

'crema sf cream; (con uova, zucchero etc) custard; ~ **solare** sun cream.

cre'mare vt to cremate.

Crem'lino sm: **il** ~ the Kremlin.

'crepa sf crack.

cre'paccio |kre'pattʃo| sm large crack, fissure; (di ghiacciaio) crevasse.

crepacu'ore sm broken heart.

cre'pare vi (fam: morire) to snuff it, kick the bucket; ~ **dalle risa** to split one's sides laughing.

crepi'tare vi (fuoco) to crackle; (pioggia) to patter.

cre'puscolo sm twilight, dusk.

'crescere |'kreʃʃere| vi to grow // vt (figli) to raise; **'crescita** sf growth; **cresci'uto, a** pp di **crescere**.

'cresima sf (REL) confirmation.

'crespo, a ag (capelli) frizzy; (tessuto) puckered // sm crêpe.

'cresta sf crest; (di polli, uccelli) crest, comb.

'creta sf chalk; clay.

cre'tino, a ag stupid // sm/f idiot, fool.

cric sm inv (TECN) jack.

'cricca, che sf clique.

'cricco, chi sm = **cric.**

crimi'nale ag, sm/f criminal.

'crimine sm (DIR) crime.

'crine sm horsehair; **crini'era** sf mane.

crisan'temo sm chrysanthemum.

'crisi sf inv crisis; (MED) attack, fit; ~ **di nervi** attack o fit of nerves.

cristalliz'zare |kristalid'dzare| vi, ~**rsi** vr to crystallize; (fig) to become fossilized.

cris'tallo sm crystal.

cristia'nesimo sm Christianity.

cristi'ano, a ag, sm/f Christian.

'Cristo sm Christ.

cri'terio sm criterion; (buon senso) (common) sense.

'critica, che sf vedi **critico.**

criti'care vt to criticize.

'critico, a, ci, che ag critical // sm critic // sf criticism; **la** ~**a** (attività) criticism; (persone) the critics pl.

cri'vello sm riddle.

'croce |'krotʃe| sf cross; **in** ~ (di traverso) crosswise; (fig) on tenterhooks; **la C**~ **Rossa** the Red Cross.

croce'figgere |krotʃe'fiddʒere| etc = **crocifiggere** etc.

croce'via |krotʃe'via| sm inv crossroads sg.

croci'ata |kro'tʃata| sf crusade.

cro'cicchio |kro'tʃikkjo| sm crossroads sg.

croci'era |kro'tʃɛra| sf (viaggio) cruise; (ARCHIT) transept.

croci'figgere |krotʃi'fiddʒere| vt to crucify; **crocifissi'one** sf crucifixion; **croci'fisso, a** pp di **crocifiggere.**

crogi'olo, crogiu'olo |kro'dʒɔlo| sm (fig) melting pot.

crol'lare vi to collapse; **'crollo** sm collapse; (di prezzi) slump, sudden fall.

cro'mato, a ag chromium-plated.

'cromo sm chrome, chromium.

cromo'soma, i sm chromosome.

'cronaca, che sf chronicle; (STAMPA) news sg; (: rubrica) column; (TV, RADIO) commentary; **fatto** o **episodio di** ~ news item; ~ **nera** crime news sg; crime column.

'cronico, a, ci, che ag chronic.

cro'nista, i sm (STAMPA) reporter, columnist.

cronolo'gia |kronolo'dʒia| sf chronology.

cro'nometro sm chronometer; (a scatto) stopwatch.

'crosta sf crust.

cros'tacei |kros'tatʃei| smpl shellfish.

cros'tata sf (CUC) tart.

cros'tino sm (CUC) croûton; (: da antipasto) canapé.

'cruccio |'kruttʃo| sm worry, torment.

cruci'verba sm inv crossword (puzzle).

cru'dele ag cruel; **crudeltà** sf cruelty.

'crudo, a ag (non cotto) raw; (aspro) harsh, severe.

cru'miro sm (peg) blackleg (Brit), scab.

'crusca sf bran.

crus'cotto sm (AUT) dashboard.

'Cuba sf Cuba.

'cubico, a, ci, che ag cubic.

'cubo, a ag cubic // sm cube; **elevare al** ~ (MAT) to cube.

cuc'cagna |kuk'kaɲɲa| sf: **paese della** ~ land of plenty; **albero della** ~ greasy pole (fig).

cuc'cetta |kut'tʃetta| sf (FERR) couchette; (NAUT) berth.

cucchiai'ata |kukkja'jata| sf spoonful.

cucchia'ino |kukkja'ino| sm teaspoon; coffee spoon.

cucchi'aio |kuk'kjajo| sm spoon.

'cuccia, ce |'kuttʃa| sf dog's bed; **a** ~**!** down!

'cucciolo |'kuttʃolo| sm cub; (di cane) puppy.

cu'cina |ku'tʃina| sf (locale) kitchen;

(*arte culinaria*) cooking, cookery; (*le vivande*) food, cooking; (*apparecchio*) cooker; ~ **componibile** fitted kitchen; **cuci'nare** *vt* to cook.

cu'cire |ku'tʃire| *vt* to sew, stitch; **cuci'trice** *sf* stapler; **cuci'tura** *sf* sewing, stitching; (*costura*) seam.

cucù *sm inv*, **cu'culo** *sm* cuckoo.

'cuffia *sf* bonnet, cap; (*da infermiera*) cap; (*da bagno*) (bathing) cap; (*per ascoltare*) headphones *pl*, headset.

cu'gino, a |ku'dʒino| *sm/f* cousin.

'cui *pronome* **1** (*nei complementi indiretti: persona*) whom; (*: oggetto, animale*) which; **la persona/le persone a** ~ **accennavi** the person/people you were referring to *o* whom you were referring; **i libri di** ~ **parlavo** the books I was talking about *o* about which I was talking; **il quartiere in** ~ **abito** the district where I live; **la ragione per** ~ the reason why
2 (*inserito tra articolo e sostantivo*) whose; **la donna i** ~ **figli sono scomparsi** the woman whose children have disappeared; **il signore, dal** ~ **figlio ho avuto il libro** the man from whose son I got the book.

culi'naria *sf* cookery.

'culla *sf* cradle.

cul'lare *vt* to rock.

culmi'nare *vi*: ~ **in** *o* **con** to culminate in.

'culmine *sm* top, summit.

'culo *sm* (*fam!*) arse (*Brit!*), ass (*US!*); (*: fig: fortuna*): **aver** ~ to have the luck of the devil.

'oulto *am* (*religione*) religion; (*adorazione*) worship, adoration, (*venerazione: anche fig*) cult.

cul'tura *sf* culture; education, learning; **cultu'rale** *ag* cultural.

cumula'tivo, a *ag* cumulative; (*prezzo*) inclusive; (*biglietto*) group *cpd*.

'cumulo *sm* (*mucchio*) pile, heap; (*METEOR*) cumulus.

'cuneo *sm* wedge.

cu'oca *sf vedi* **cuoco**.

cu'ocere |'kwɔtʃere| *vt* (*alimenti*) to cook; (*mattoni etc*) to fire // *vi* to cook; ~ **al forno** (*pane*) to bake; (*arrosto*) to roast; **cu'oco, a, chi, che** *sm/f* cook; (*di ristorante*) chef.

cu'oio *sm* leather; ~ **capelluto** scalp.

cu'ore *sm* heart; ~**i** *smpl* (*CARTE*) hearts; **avere buon** ~ to be kind-hearted; **stare a** ~ **a qn** to be important to sb.

cupi'digia |kupi'didʒa| *sf* greed, covetousness.

'cupo, a *ag* dark; (*suono*) dull; (*fig*) gloomy, dismal.

'cupola *sf* dome; cupola.

'cura *sf* care; (*MED: trattamento*) (course of) treatment; **aver** ~ **di** (*occuparsi di*) to look after; **a** ~ **di** (*li-*

bro) edited by; ~ **dimagrante** diet.

cu'rare *vt* (*malato, malattia*) to treat; (*: guarire*) to cure; (*aver cura di*) to take care of; (*testo*) to edit; ~**rsi** *vr* to take care of o.s.; (*MED*) to follow a course of treatment; ~**rsi di** to pay attention to.

cu'rato *sm* parish priest; (*protestante*) vicar, minister.

cura'tore, 'trice *sm/f* (*DIR*) trustee; (*di antologia etc*) editor.

curio'sare *vi* to look round, wander round; (*tra libri*) to browse; ~ **nei negozi** to look *o* wander round the shops.

curiosità *sf inv* curiosity; (*cosa rara*) curio, curiosity.

curi'oso, a *ag* (*che vuol sapere*) curious, inquiring; (*ficcanaso*) curious, inquisitive; (*bizzarro*) strange, curious; **essere** ~ **di** to be curious about.

cur'sore *sm* (*INFORM*) cursor.

'curva *sf* curve; (*stradale*) bend, curve.

cur'vare *vt* to bend // *vi* (*veicolo*) to take a bend; (*strada*) to bend, curve; ~**rsi** *vr* to bend; (*legno*) to warp.

'curvo, a *ag* curved; (*piegato*) bent.

cusci'netto |kuʃʃi'netto| *sm* pad; (*TECN*) bearing // *ag inv*: **stato** ~ buffer state; ~ **a sfere** ball bearing.

cu'scino |kuʃ'ʃino| *sm* cushion; (*guanciale*) pillow.

'cuspide *sf* (*ARCHIT*) spire.

cus'tode *sm/f* keeper, custodian.

cus'todia *sf* care; (*DIR*) custody; (*astuccio*) case, holder.

custo'dire *vt* (*conservare*) to keep; (*assistere*) to look after, take care of; (*fare la guardia*) to guard.

'cute *sf* (*ANAT*) skin.

cu'ticola *sf* cuticle.

C.V. *abbr* (= *cavallo vapore*) h.p.

D

da *prep* (*da* + *il* = **dal**, *da* + *lo* = **dallo**, *da* + *l'* = **dall'**, *da* + *la* = **dalla**, *da* + *i* = **dai**, *da* + *gli* = **dagli**, *da* + *le* = **dalle**) **1** (*agente*) by; **dipinto** ~ **un grande artista** painted by a great artist
2 (*causa*) with; **tremare dalla paura** to tremble with fear
3 (*stato in luogo*) at; **abito** ~ **lui** I'm living at his house *o* with him; **sono dal giornalaio/**~ **Francesco** I'm at the newsagent's/Francesco's (house)
4 (*moto a luogo*) to; (*moto per luogo*) through; **vado** ~ **Pietro/dal giornalaio** I'm going to Pietro's (house)/to the newsagent's; **sono passati dalla finestra** they came in through the window
5 (*provenienza, allontanamento*) from; **arrivare/partire** ~ **Milano** to arrive/depart from Milan; **scendere dal treno/dalla macchina** to get off the train/out of the car; **si trova a 5 km** ~ **qui** it's 5 km

from here
6 (*tempo: durata*) for; (: *a partire da: nel passato*) since; (: *nel futuro*) from; vivo qui ~ un anno I've been living here for a year; è dalle 3 che ti aspetto I've been waiting for you since 3 (o'clock); ~ oggi in poi from today onwards; ~ bambino as a child, when I (o he *etc*) was a child
7 (*modo, maniera*) like; comportarsi ~ uomo to behave like a man; l'ho fatto ~ me I did it (by) myself
8 (*descrittivo*): una macchina ~ corsa a racing car; una ragazza dai capelli biondi a girl with blonde hair; un vestito ~ 100.000 lire a 100,000 lire dress; sordo ~ un orecchio deaf in one ear.
dab'bene *ag inv* honest, decent.
dac'capo, da 'capo *av* (*di nuovo*) (once) again; (*dal principio*) all over again, from the beginning.
dacché [dak'ke] *cong* since.
'dado *sm* (*da gioco*) dice *o* die (*pl* dice); (*CUC*) stock (*Brit*) *o* bouillon (*US*) cube; (*TECN*) (screw)nut; ~i *smpl* (game of) dice.
daf'fare, da 'fare *sm* work, toil.
'dagli ['daʎʎi], **'dai** *prep* + *det vedi* **da**.
'daino *sm* (fallow) deer *inv*; (*pelle*) buckskin.
dal, dall', 'dalla, 'dalle, 'dallo *prep* + *det vedi* **da**.
dal'tonico, a, ci, che *ag* colour-blind.
'dama *sf* lady; (*nei balli*) partner; (*gioco*) draughts *sg* (*Brit*), checkers *sg* (*US*).
damigi'ana [dami'dʒana] *sf* demijohn.
da'naro *sm* = **denaro**.
da'nese *ag* Danish // *sm/f* Dane // *sm* (*LING*) Danish.
Dani'marca *sf*: la ~ Denmark.
dan'nare *vt* (*REL*) to damn; ~rsi *vr* (*fig: tormentarsi*) to be worried to death; far ~ qn to drive sb mad; **dannazi'one** *sf* damnation.
danneggi'are [danned'dʒare] *vt* to damage; (*rovinare*) to spoil; (*nuocere*) to harm.
'danno *sm* damage; (*a persona*) harm, injury; ~i *smpl* (*DIR*) damages; **dan'noso, a** *ag*: dannoso (a, per) harmful (to), bad (for).
Da'nubio *sm*: il ~ the Danube.
'danza ['dantsa] *sf*: la ~ dancing; una ~ a dance.
dan'zare [dan'tsare] *vt, vi* to dance.
dapper'tutto *av* everywhere.
dap'poco *ag inv* inept, worthless.
dap'prima *av* at first.
'dardo *sm* dart.
'dare *sm* (*COMM*) debit // *vt* to give; (*produrre: frutti, suono*) to produce // *vi* (*guardare*): ~ su to look (out) onto; ~rsi *vr*: ~rsi a to dedicate o.s. to; ~rsi al commercio to go into business; ~rsi al

bere to take to drink; ~ da mangiare a qn to give sb sth to eat; ~ per certo qc to consider sth certain; ~ per morto qn to give sb up for dead; ~rsi per vinto to give in.
'darsena *sf* dock; dockyard.
'data *sf* date; ~ di nascita date of birth.
da'tare *vt* to date // *vi*: ~ da to date from.
'dato, a *ag* (*stabilito*) given // *sm* datum; ~i *smpl* data *pl*; ~ che given that; **un** ~ di fatto a fact.
'dattero *sm* date.
dattilogra'fare *vt* to type; **dattilogra'fia** *sf* typing; **datti'lografo, a** *sm/f* typist.
da'vanti *av* in front; (*dirimpetto*) opposite // *ag inv* front // *sm* front; ~ a *prep* in front of; facing, opposite; (*in presenza di*) before, in front of.
davan'zale [davan'tsale] *sm* windowsill.
da'vanzo, d'a'vanzo [da'vantso] *av* more than enough.
dav'vero *av* really, indeed.
'dazio ['dattsjo] *sm* (*somma*) duty; (*luogo*) customs *pl*.
DC *sigla f* = *Democrazia Cristiana*.
d. C. *ad abbr* (= *dopo Cristo*) A.D.
'dea *sf* goddess.
'debito, a *ag* due, proper // *sm* debt; (*COMM: dare*) debit; a tempo ~ at the right time; **debi'tore, 'trice** *sm/f* debtor.
'debole *ag* weak, feeble; (*suono*) faint; (*luce*) dim // *sm* weakness; **debo'lezza** *sf* weakness.
debut'tare *vi* to make one's début; **de'butto** *sm* début.
deca'denza [deka'dɛntsa] *sf* decline; (*DIR*) loss, forfeiture.
decaffei'nato, a *ag* decaffeinated.
decappot'tabile *ag, sf* convertible.
dece'duto, a [detʃe'duto] *ag* deceased.
de'cennio [de'tʃennjo] *sm* decade.
de'cente [de'tʃɛnte] *ag* decent, respectable, proper; (*accettabile*) satisfactory, decent.
de'cesso [de'tʃɛsso] *sm* death; atto di ~ death certificate.
de'cidere [de'tʃidere] *vt*: ~ qc to decide on sth; (*questione, lite*) to settle sth; ~ di fare/che to decide to do/that; ~ di qc (*sog: cosa*) to determine sth; ~rsi *vr* (a fare) to decide (to do), make up one's mind (to do).
deci'frare [detʃi'frare] *vt* to decode; (*fig*) to decipher, make out.
deci'male [detʃi'male] *ag* decimal.
'decimo, a ['dɛtʃimo] *num* tenth.
de'cina [de'tʃina] *sf* ten; (*circa dieci*): una ~ (di) about ten.
decisi'one [detʃi'zjone] *sf* decision; prendere una ~ to make a decision.
de'ciso, a [de'tʃizo] *pp di* **decidere**.
declas'sare *vt* to downgrade; to lower in

status.

decli'nare vi (pendio) to slope down; (fig: diminuire) to decline; (tramontare) to set, go down // vt to decline; **de-clinazi'one** sf (LING) declension; **de'clino** sm decline.

decol'lare vi (AER) to take off; **de'collo** sm take-off.

decolo'rare vt to bleach.

decom'porre vt, **decomporsi** vr to decompose; **decom'posto, a** pp di **decomporre**.

deconge'lare |dekondʒe'lare| vt to defrost.

deco'rare vt to decorate; **decora'tore, 'trice** sm/f (interior) decorator; **decorazi'one** sf decoration.

de'coro sm decorum; **deco'roso, a** ag decorous, dignified.

de'correre vi to pass, elapse; (avere effetto) to run, have effect; **de'corso, a** pp di **decorrere** // sm (evoluzione: anche MED) course.

de'crescere |de'kreʃʃere| vi (diminuire) to decrease, diminish; (acque) to subside, go down; (prezzi) to go down; **de-cresci'uto, a** pp di **decrescere**.

de'creto sm decree; ~ **legge** decree with the force of law.

'dedalo sm maze, labyrinth.

'dedica, che sf dedication.

dedi'care vt to dedicate.

'dedito, a ag: ~ **a** (studio etc) dedicated o devoted to; (vizio) addicted to.

de'dotto, a pp di **dedurre**.

de'durre vt (concludere) to deduce; (defalcare) to deduct; **deduzi'one** sf deduction.

defal'care vt to deduct.

defe'rente ag respectful, deferential.

defe'rire vt: ~ **a** (DIR) to refer to.

defezi'one |defet'tsjone| sf defection, desertion.

defici'ente |defi't ʃɛnte| ag (mancante): ~ **di** deficient in; (insufficiente) insufficient // sm/f mental defective; (peg: cretino) idiot.

'deficit |'defitʃit| sm inv (ECON) deficit.

defi'nire vt to define; (risolvere) to settle; (definitivo, a ag definitive, final; **definizi'one** sf definition; settlement.

deflet'tore sm (AUT) quarter-light.

de'flusso sm (della marea) ebb.

defor'mare vt (alterare) to put out of shape; (corpo) to deform; (pensiero, fatto) to distort; ~**rsi** vr to lose its shape.

de'forme ag deformed; disfigured; **deformità** sf inv deformity.

defrau'dare vt: ~ **qn di qc** to defraud sb of sth, cheat sb out of sth.

de'funto, a ag late cpd // sm/f deceased.

degene'rare |dedʒene'rare| vi to degenerate; **de'genere** ag degenerate.

de'gente |de'dʒɛnte| sm/f bedridden person; (ricoverato in ospedale) inpatient.

'degli |'deʎʎi| prep + det vedi **di**.

de'gnarsi |deɲ'narsi| vr: ~ **di fare** to deign o condescend to do.

'degno, a ag dignified; ~ **di** worthy of; ~ **di lode** praiseworthy.

degra'dare vt (MIL) to demote; (privare della dignità) to degrade; ~**rsi** vr to demean o.s.

degustazi'one |degustat'tsjone| sf sampling, tasting.

'dei, del prep + det vedi **di**.

dela'tore, 'trice sm/f police informer.

'delega, ghe sf (procura) proxy.

dele'gare vt to delegate; **dele'gato** sm delegate.

del'fino sm (ZOOL) dolphin; (STORIA) dauphin; (fig) probable successor.

delibe'rare vt to come to a decision on // vi (DIR): ~ **(su qc)** to rule (on sth).

delica'tezza |delika'tettsa| sf (anche CUC) delicacy; frailty; thoughtfulness; tactfulness.

deli'cato, a ag delicate; (salute) delicate, frail; (fig: gentile) thoughtful, considerate; (: che dimostra tatto) tactful.

deline'are vt to outline; ~**rsi** vr to be outlined; (fig) to emerge.

delin'quente sm/f criminal, delinquent; **delin'quenza** sf criminality, delinquency; **delinquenza minorile** juvenile delinquency.

deli'rare vi to be delirious, rave; (fig) to rave.

de'lirio sm delirium; (ragionamento insensato) raving; (fig): **andare/mandare in ~** to go/send into a frenzy.

de'litto sm crime.

de'lizia |de'littsja| sf delight; **delizi'oso, a** ag delightful; (cibi) delicious.

dell', 'della, 'delle, 'dello prep + det vedi **di**.

delta'plano sm hang-glider; **volo col** ~ hang-gliding.

de'ludere vt to disappoint; **delusi'one** sf disappointment; **de'luso, a** pp di **deludere**.

de'manio sm state property.

de'menza |de'mentsa| sf dementia; (stupidità) foolishness.

demo'cratico, a, ci, che ag democratic.

democra'zia |demokrat'tsia| sf democracy.

democristi'ano, a ag, sm/f Christian Democrat.

demo'lire vt to demolish.

'demone sm demon.

de'monio sm demon, devil; **il D~** the Devil.

de'naro sm money.

denomi'nare vt to name; ~**rsi** vr to be named o called; **denominazi'one** sf name; denomination.

densità sf inv density.

'denso, a ag thick, dense.

den'tale ag dental.

'dente sm tooth; (di forchetta) prong; (GEO: cima) jagged peak; al ~ (CUC: pasta) cooked so as to be firm when eaten; ~i del giudizio wisdom teeth; **denti'era** sf (set of) false teeth pl.

denti'fricio [denti'fritʃo] sm toothpaste.

den'tista, i, e sm/f dentist.

'dentro av inside; (in casa) indoors; (fig: nell'intimo) inwardly // prep: ~ a (a) in; piegato in ~ folded over; qui/là ~ in here/there; ~ di sé (pensare, brontolare) to oneself.

de'nuncia, ce o **cie** [de'nuntʃa], **de'-nunzia** [de'nuntsja] sf denunciation; declaration; ~ **dei redditi** (income) tax return.

denunci'are [denun'tʃare], **denunzi'are** [denun'tsjare] vt to denounce; (dichiarare) to declare.

denutrizi'one [denutrit'tsjone] sf malnutrition.

deodo'rante sm deodorant.

depe'rire vi to waste away.

depila'torio, a ag hair-removing cpd, depilatory.

dépli'ant [depli'ã] sm inv leaflet; (opuscolo) brochure.

deplo'revole ag deplorable.

de'porre vt (depositare) to put down; (rimuovere: da una carica) to remove; (: re) to depose; (DIR) to testify.

depor'tare vt to deport.

deposi'tare vt (gen, GEO, ECON) to deposit; (lasciare) to leave; (merci) to store.

de'posito sm deposit; (luogo) warehouse; depot; (: MIL) depot; ~ **bagagli** left-luggage office.

deposizi'one [depozit'tsjone] sf deposition; (da una carica) removal.

de'posto, a pp di **deporre**.

depra'vato, a ag depraved // sm/f degenerate.

depre'dare vt to rob, plunder.

depressi'one sf depression.

de'presso, a pp di **deprimere** // ag depressed.

deprez'zare [depret'tsare] vt (ECON) to depreciate.

de'primere vt to depress.

depu'rare vt to purify.

depu'tato, a o **'essa** sm/f (POL) deputy, ≈ Member of Parliament (Brit), ≈ Member of Congress (US); **deputazi'one** sf deputation; (POL) position of deputy, ≈ parliamentary seat (Brit), ≈ seat in Congress (US).

deragli'are [deraʎ'ʎare] vi to be derailed; **far** ~ to derail.

dere'litto, a ag derelict.

dere'tano sm (fam) bottom, buttocks pl.

de'ridere vt to mock, deride; **de'riso, a** pp di **deridere**.

de'riva sf (NAUT, AER) drift; **andare alla** ~ (anche fig) to drift.

deri'vare vi: ~ **da** to derive from // vt to derive; (corso d'acqua) to divert; **derivazi'one** sf derivation; diversion.

derma'tologo, a, gi, ghe sm/f dermatologist.

der'rate sfpl commodities; ~ **alimentari** foodstuffs.

deru'bare vt to rob.

des'critto, a pp di **descrivere**.

des'crivere vt to describe; **descrizi'one** sf description.

de'serto, a ag deserted // sm (GEO) desert; **isola** ~a desert island.

deside'rare vt to want, wish for; (sessualmente) to desire; ~ **fare/che qn faccia** to want o wish to do/sb to do; **desidera fare una passeggiata?** would you like to go for a walk?

desi'derio sm wish; (più intenso, carnale) desire.

deside'roso, a ag: ~ **di** longing o eager for.

desi'nenza [dezi'nentsa] sf (LING) ending, inflexion.

de'sistere vi: ~ **da** to give up, desist from; **desis'tito, a** pp di **desistere**.

deso'lato, a ag (paesaggio) desolate; (persona: spiacente) sorry.

des'tare vt to wake (up); (fig) to awaken, arouse; ~**rsi** vr to wake (up).

desti'nare vt to destine; (assegnare) to appoint, assign; (indirizzare) to address; ~ **qc a qn** to intend to give sth to sb, intend sb to have sth; **destina'tario, a** sm/f (di lettera) addressee.

destinazi'one [destinat'tsjone] sf destination; (uso) purpose.

des'tino sm destiny, fate.

destitu'ire vt to dismiss, remove.

'desto, a ag (wide) awake.

'destra sf vedi **destro**.

destreggi'arsi [destred'dʒarsi] vr to manoeuvre (Brit), maneuver (US).

des'trezza [des'trettsa] sf skill, dexterity.

'destro, a ag right, right-hand; (abile) skilful, adroit // sf (mano) right hand; (parte) right (side); (POL): **la** ~a **the** Right; **a** ~a (essere) on the right; (andare) to the right.

dete'nere vt (incarico, primato) to hold; (proprietà) to have, possess; (in prigione) to detain, hold; **dete'nuto, a** sm/f prisoner; **detenzi'one** sf holding; possession; detention.

deter'gente [deter'dʒente] ag detergent; (crema, latte) cleansing // sm detergent.

deterio'rare vt to damage; ~**rsi** vr to deteriorate.

determi'nare vt to determine; **determinazi'one** sf determination; (decisione) decision.

deter'sivo *sm* detergent.

detes'tare *vt* to detest, hate.

de'trarre *vt*: ~ (da) to deduct (from), take away (from); **de'tratto, a** *pp di* **detrarre; detrazi'one** *sf* deduction; detrazione d'imposta tax allowance.

detri'mento *sm* detriment, harm; a ~ di to the detriment of.

de'trito *sm* (*GEO*) detritus.

dettagli'are [dettaʎ'ʎare] *vt* to detail, give full details of.

det'taglio [det'taʎʎo] *sm* detail; (*COMM*): il ~ retail; al ~ (*COMM*) retail; separately.

det'tare *vt* to dictate; ~ legge (*fig*) to lay down the law; **det'tato** *sm* dictation; **detta'tura** *sf* dictation.

'detto, a *pp di* **dire** // *ag* (*soprannominato*) called, known as; (*già nominato*) above-mentioned // *sm* saying; ~ fatto no sooner said than done.

detur'pare *vt* to disfigure; (*moralmente*) to sully.

devas'tare *vt* to devastate; (*fig*) to ravage.

devi'are *vi*: ~ (da) to turn off (from) // *vt* to divert; **deviazi'one** *sf* (*anche AUT*) diversion.

devo'luto, a *pp di* **devolvere**.

devoluzi'one [devolut'tsjone] *sf* (*DIR*) devolution, transfer.

de'volvere *vt* (*DIR*) to transfer, devolve.

de'voto, a *ag* (*REL*) devout, pious; (*affezionato*) devoted.

devozi'one [devot'tsjone] *sf* devoutness; (*anche REL*) devotion.

di *prep* (*di + il* = **del,** *di + lo* = **dello,** *di + l'* = **dell',** *di + la* = **della,** *di + i* = **dei,** *di + gli* = **degli,** *di + le* = **delle)** 1 (*possesso, specificazione*) of; (*composto da, scritto da*) by; la macchina ~ Paolo/mio fratello Paolo's/my brother's car; un amico ~ mio fratello a friend of my brother's, one of my brother's friends; un quadro ~ Botticelli a painting by Botticelli 2 (*caratterizzazione, misura*) of; una casa ~ mattoni a brick house, a house made of bricks; un orologio d'oro a gold watch; un bimbo ~ 3 anni a child of 3, a 3-year-old child 3 (*causa, mezzo, modo*) with; tremare ~ paura to tremble with fear; morire ~ cancro to die of cancer; spalmare ~ burro to spread with butter 4 (*argomento*) about, of; discutere ~ sport to talk about sport 5 (*luogo: provenienza*) from; out of; essere ~ Roma to be from Rome; uscire ~ casa to come out of *o* leave the house 6 (*tempo*) in; d'estate/d'inverno in (the) summer/winter; ~ notte by night, at night; ~ mattina/sera in the morning/evening; ~ domenica on Sundays ◆ *det* (*una certa quantità di*) some; (:

negativo) any; (: *interrogativo*) any, some; del pane (some) bread; delle caramelle (some) sweets; degli amici miei some friends of mine; vuoi del vino? do you want some *o* any wine?

dia'bete *sm* diabetes *sg*.

di'acono *sm* (*REL*) deacon.

dia'dema, i *sm* diadem; (*di donna*) tiara.

dia'framma, i *sm* (*divisione*) screen; (*ANAT, FOT, contraccettivo*) diaphragm.

di'agnosi [di'aɲɲozi] *sf* diagnosis *sg*.

diago'nale *ag, sf* diagonal.

dia'gramma, i *sm* diagram.

dia'letto *sm* dialect.

di'alogo, ghi *sm* dialogue.

dia'mante *sm* diamond.

di'ametro *sm* diameter.

di'amine *escl*: che ~ ...? what on earth ...?

diaposi'tiva *sf* transparency, slide.

di'ario *sm* diary; ~ degli esami (*SCOL*) exam timetable.

diar'rea *sf* diarrhoea.

di'avolo *sm* devil.

di'battere *vt* to debate, discuss; ~rsi *vr* to struggle; **di'battito** *sm* debate, discussion.

dicas'tero *sm* ministry.

di'cembre [di'tʃembre] *sm* December.

dice'ria [ditʃe'ria] *sf* rumour, piece of gossip.

dichia'rare [dikja'rare] *vt* to declare; **dichiarazi'one** *sf* declaration.

dician'nove [ditʃan'nɔve] *num* nineteen.

dicias'sette [ditʃas'sette] *num* seventeen.

dici'otto [di'tʃɔtto] *num* eighteen.

dici'tura [ditʃi'tura] *sf* words *pl*, wording.

di'eci ['djɛtʃi] *num* ten; **die'cina** *sf* = **decina.**

'diesel ['dizəl] *sm inv* diesel engine.

di'eta *sf* diet; essere a ~ to be on a diet.

di'etro *av* behind; (*in fondo*) at the back // *prep* behind; (*tempo: dopo*) after // *sm* back, rear // *ag inv* back *cpd*; le zampe di ~ the hind legs; ~ richiesta on demand; (*scritta*) on application.

di'fatti *cong* in fact, as a matter of fact.

di'fendere *vt* to defend; **difen'sivo, a** *ag* defensive // *sf*: stare sulla difensiva (*anche fig*) to be on the defensive; **difen'sore, a** *sm/f* defender; avvocato difensore counsel for the defence; **di'feso, a** *pp di* **difendere** // *sf* defence.

difet'tare *vi* to be defective; ~ di to be lacking in, lack; **difet'tivo, a** *ag* defective.

di'fetto *sm* (*mancanza*): ~ di lack of; shortage of; (*di fabbricazione*) fault, flaw, defect; (*morale*) fault, failing; defect; (*fisico*) defect; far ~ to be lacking; in ~ at fault; in the wrong; **difet'toso, a** *ag* defective, faulty.

diffa'mare *vt* to slander; to libel.

diffe'rente *ag* different.

diffe'renza |diffe'rɛntsa| sf difference; a ~ di unlike.

differenzi'are |differen'tsjarc| vt to differentiate; ~rsi da to differentiate o.s. from; to differ from.

diffe'rire vt to postpone, defer // vi to be different.

dif'ficile |dif'fitʃile| ag difficult; (persona) hard to please, difficult (to please); (poco probabile): è ~ che sia libero it is unlikely that he'll be free // sm difficult part; difficulty; **difficoltà** sf inv difficulty.

dif'fida sf (DIR) warning, notice.

diffi'dare vi: ~ di to be suspicious o distrustful of // vt (DIR) to warn; ~ qn dal fare qc to warn sb not to do sth, caution sb against doing sth; **diffi'dente** ag suspicious, distrustful; **diffi'denza** sf suspicion, distrust.

dif'fondere vt (luce, calore) to diffuse; (notizie) to spread, circulate; ~rsi vr to spread; **diffusi'one** sf diffusion; spread; (anche di giornale) circulation; (FISICA) scattering; **dif'fuso, a** pp di **diffondere** // ag (malattia, fenomeno) widespread.

difi'lato av (direttamente) straight, directly; (subito) straight away.

difte'rite sf (MED) diphtheria.

'diga, ghe sf dam; (portuale) breakwater.

dige'rente |didʒe'rɛnte| ag (apparato) digestive.

dige'rire |didʒe'rire| vt to digest; **digesti'one** sf digestion; **diges'tivo, a** ag digestive // sm (after-dinner) liqueur.

digi'tale |didʒi'tale| ag digital; (delle dita) finger cpd, digital // sf (BOT) foxglove.

digi'tare |didʒi'tare| vt, vi (INFORM) to key (in).

digiu'nare |didʒu'nare| vi to starve o.s.; (REL) to fast; **digi'uno, a** ag: essere digiuno not to have eaten // sm fast; a digiuno on an empty stomach.

dignità |diɲɲi'ta| sf inv dignity; **di-gni'toso, a** ag dignified.

'DIGOS |'diɡɔs| sigla f (= Divisione Investigazioni Generali e Operazioni Speciali) police department dealing with political security.

digri'gnare |digriɲ'ɲare| vt: ~ i denti to grind one's teeth.

dila'gare vi to flood; (fig) to spread.

dilani'are vt (preda) to tear to pieces.

dilapi'dare vt to squander, waste.

dila'tare vt to dilate; (gas) to cause to expand; (passaggio, cavità) to open (up); ~rsi vr to dilate; (FISICA) to expand.

dilazio'nare |dilattsjo'nare| vt to delay, defer; **dilazi'one** sf delay; (COMM: di pagamento etc) extension; (rinvio) postponement.

dileggi'are |diled'dʒare| vt to mock, deride.

dilegu'are vi, ~rsi vr to vanish, disappear.

di'lemma, i sm dilemma.

dilet'tante sm/f dilettante; (anche SPORT) amateur.

dilet'tare vt to give pleasure to, delight; ~rsi vr: ~rsi di to take pleasure in, enjoy.

di'letto, a ag dear, beloved // sm pleasure, delight.

dili'gente |dili'dʒɛnte| ag (scrupoloso) diligent; (accurato) careful, accurate; **dili'genza** sf diligence; care; (carrozza) stagecoach.

dilu'ire vt to dilute.

dilun'garsi vr (fig): ~ su to talk at length on o about.

diluvi'are vb impers to pour (down).

di'luvio sm downpour; (inondazione, fig) flood.

dima'grire vi to get thinner, lose weight.

dime'nare vt to wave, shake; ~rsi vr to toss and turn; (fig) to struggle; ~ la coda (sog: cane) to wag its tail.

dimensi'one sf dimension; (grandezza) size.

dimenti'canza |dimenti'kantsa| sf forgetfulness; (errore) oversight, slip; per ~ inadvertently.

dimenti'care vt to forget; ~rsi di qc to forget sth.

di'messo, a pp di **dimettere** // ag (voce) subdued; (uomo, abito) modest, humble.

dimesti'chezza |dimesti'kettsa| sf familiarity.

di'mettere vt: ~ qn da to dismiss sb from; (dall'ospedale) to discharge sb from; ~rsi (da) to resign (from).

dimez'zare |dimed'dzare| vt to halve.

diminu'ire vt to reduce, diminish; (prezzi) to bring down, reduce // vi to decrease, diminish; (rumore) to die down, die away; (prezzi) to fall, go down; **diminuzi'one** sf decreasing, diminishing.

dimissi'oni sfpl resignation sg; dare o presentare le ~ to resign, hand in one's resignation.

di'mora sf residence.

dimo'rare vi to reside.

dimos'trare vt to demonstrate, show; (provare) to prove, demonstrate; ~rsi vr: ~rsi molto abile to show o.s. o prove to be very clever; **dimostra 30 anni** he looks about 30 (years old); **dimostrazi'one** sf demonstration; proof.

di'namico, a, ci, che ag dynamic // sf dynamics sg.

dina'mite sf dynamite.

'dinamo sf inv dynamo.

di'nanzi |di'nantsi|: ~ a prep in front of.

dini'ego, ghi sm refusal; denial.

dinocco'lato, a ag lanky; camminare ~

to walk with a slouch.

din'torno *av* round, (round) about; ~**i** *smpl* outskirts; **nei ~i di** in the vicinity *o* neighbourhood of.

'dio, *pl* **'dei** *sm* god; **D~** God; **gli dei** the gods; **D~ mio!** my goodness!, my God!

di'ocesi |di'ɔtʃezi| *sf inv* diocese.

dipa'nare *vt* (*lana*) to wind into a ball; (*fig*) to disentangle, sort out.

diparti'mento *sm* department.

dipen'dente *ag* dependent // *sm/f* employee; **dipen'denza** *sf* dependence; **essere alle dipendenze di qn** to be employed by sb *o* in sb's employ.

di'pendere *vi*: ~ **da** to depend on; (*finanziariamente*) to be dependent on; (*derivare*) to come from, be due to; **di'peso**, **a** *pp di* **dipendere.**

di'pingere |di'pindʒere| *vt* to paint; **di'pinto**, **a** *pp di* **dipingere** // *sm* painting.

di'ploma, **i** *sm* diploma.

diplo'mare *vt* to award a diploma to, graduate (US) // *vi* to obtain a diploma, graduate (US).

diplo'matico, **a**, **ci**, **che** *ag* diplomatic // *sm* diplomat.

diploma'zia |diplomat'tsia| *sf* diplomacy.

di'porto *sm*: **imbarcazione** *f* **da** ~ pleasure craft.

dira'dare *vt* to thin (out); (*visite*) to reduce, make less frequent; ~**rsi** *vr* to disperse; (*nebbia*) to clear (up).

dira'mare *vt* to issue // *vi*, ~**rsi** *vr* (*strade*) to branch.

'dire *vt* to say; (*segreto, fatto*) to tell; ~ **qc a qn** to tell sb sth; ~ **a qn di fare qc** to tell sb to do sth; ~ **di sì/no** to say yes/no; **si dice che ...** they say that ...; **si direbbe che ...** it looks (*o* sounds) as though ...; **dica, signora?** (*in un negozio*) yes, Madam, can I help you?

diret'tissimo *sm* (*FERR*) fast (through) train.

di'retto, **a** *pp di* **dirigere** // *ag* direct // *sm* (*FERR*) through train.

diret'tore, **'trice** *sm/f* (*di azienda*) director; manager/ess; (*di scuola elementare*) head (teacher) (*Brit*), principal (US); ~ **d'orchestra** conductor.

direzi'one |diret'tsjone| *sf* board of directors; management; (*senso di movimento*) direction; **in** ~ **di** in the direction of, towards.

diri'gente |diri'dʒente| *sm/f* executive; (*POL*) leader // *ag*: **classe** ~ ruling class.

di'rigere |di'ridʒere| *vt* to direct; (*impresa*) to run, manage; (*MUS*) to conduct; ~**rsi** *vr*: ~**rsi verso** *o* **a** to make *o* head for.

dirim'petto *av* opposite; ~ **a** *prep* opposite, facing.

di'ritto, **a** *ag* straight; (*onesto*) straight, upright // *av* straight, directly; **andare** ~ to go straight on // *sm* right side;

(*TENNIS*) forehand; (*MAGLIA*) plain stitch; (*prerogativa*) right; (*leggi, scienza*): **il** ~ law; ~**i** *smpl* (*tasse*) duty *sg*; **stare** ~ to stand up straight; **aver** ~ **a qc** to be entitled to sth; ~**i d'autore** royalties.

dirit'tura *sf* (*SPORT*) straight; (*fig*) rectitude.

diroc'cato, **a** *ag* tumbledown, in ruins.

dirot'tare *vt* (*nave, aereo*) to change the course of; (*aereo: sotto minaccia*) to hijack; (*traffico*) to divert // *vi* (*nave, aereo*) to change course; **dirotta'tore**, **'trice** *sm/f* hijacker.

di'rotto, **a** *ag* (*pioggia*) torrential; (*pianto*) unrestrained; **piovere a** ~ to pour, rain cats and dogs; **piangere a** ~ to cry one's heart out.

di'rupo *sm* crag, precipice.

disabi'tato, **a** *ag* uninhabited.

disabitu'arsi *vr*: ~ **a** to get out of the habit of.

disac'cordo *sm* disagreement.

disadat'tato, **a** *ag* (*PSIC*) maladjusted.

disa'dorno, **a** *ag* plain, unadorned.

disagi'ato, **a** |diza'dʒato| *ag* poor, needy; (*vita*) hard.

di'sagio |di'zadʒo| *sm* discomfort; (*disturbo*) inconvenience; (*fig*: *imbarazzo*) embarrassment; ~**i** *smpl* hardship *sg*, poverty *sg*; **essere a** ~ to be ill at ease.

disappro'vare *vt* to disapprove of; **disapprovazi'one** *sf* disapproval.

disap'punto *sm* disappointment.

disar'mare *vt*, *vi* to disarm; **di'sarmo** *sm* (*MIL*) disarmament.

di'sastro *sm* disaster.

disat'tento, **a** *ag* inattentive; **disattenzi'one** *sf* carelessness, lack of attention.

disa'vanzo |diza'vantso| *sm* (*ECON*) deficit.

disavven'tura *sf* misadventure, mishap.

dis'brigo, **ghi** *sm* (*prompt*) clearing up *o* settlement.

dis'capito *sm*: **a** ~ **di** to the detriment of.

dis'carica, **che** *sf* (*di rifiuti*) rubbish tip *o* dump.

discen'dente |diʃʃen'dɛnte| *ag* descending // *sm/f* descendant.

di'scendere |diʃ'ʃɛndere| *vt* to go (*o* come) down // *vi* to go (*o* come) down; (*strada*) to go down; (*smontare*) to get off; ~ **da** (*famiglia*) to be descended from; ~ **dalla macchina/dal treno** to get out of the car/out of *o* off the train; ~ **da cavallo** to dismount, get off one's horse.

di'scepolo, **a** |diʃ'ʃepolo| *sm/f* disciple.

di'scernere |diʃ'ʃernere| *vt* to discern.

di'sceso, **a** |diʃ'ʃeso| *pp di* **discendere** // *sf* descent; (*pendio*) slope; **in** ~**a** (*strada*) downhill *cpd*, sloping; ~**a libera** (*SCI*) downhill (race).

disci'ogliere |diʃ'ʃɔʎʎere| *vt*, ~**rsi** *vr* to

dissolve; (*fondere*) to melt; **disci'olto, a** *pp di* **disciogliere.**

disci'plina [diʃʃi'plina] *sf* discipline; **discipli'nare** *ag* disciplinary // *vt* to discipline.

'**disco, schi** *sm* disc; (*SPORT*) discus; (*fonografico*) record; (*INFORM*) disk; ~ orario (*AUT*) parking disc; ~ rigido (*INFORM*) hard disk; ~ volante flying saucer.

discol'pare *vt* to clear of blame.

disco'noscere [disko'noʃʃere] *vt* (*figlio*) to disown; (*meriti*) to ignore, disregard; **disconosci'uto, a** *pp di* **disconoscere.**

dis'corde *ag* conflicting, clashing; **dis'cordia** *sf* discord; (*dissidio*) disagreement, clash.

dis'correre *vi*: ~ (di) to talk (about).

dis'corso, a *pp di* **discorrere** // *sm* speech; (*conversazione*) conversation, talk.

dis'costo, a *ag* faraway, distant // *av* far away; ~ da *prep* far from.

disco'teca, che *sf* (*raccolta*) record library; (*luogo di ballo*) disco(theque)..

discre'panza [diskre'pantsa] *sf* disagreement.

dis'creto, a *ag* discreet; (*abbastanza buono*) reasonable, fair; **discrezi'one** *sf* discretion; (*giudizio*) judgment, discernment; **a discrezione di** at the discretion of.

discriminazi'one [diskriminat'tsjone] *sf* discrimination.

discussi'one *sf* discussion; (*litigio*) argument.

dis'cusso, a *pp di* **discutere.**

dis'cutere *vt* to discuss, debate; (*contestare*) to question // *vi* (*conversare*): ~ (di) to discuss; (*litigare*) to argue.

disde'gnare [disdeɲ'ɲare] *vt* to scorn.

dis'detto, a *pp di* **disdire** // *sf* cancellation; (*sfortuna*) bad luck.

dis'dire *vt* (*prenotazione*) to cancel; (*DIR*): ~ **un contratto d'affitto** to give notice (to quit).

dise'gnare [diseɲ'ɲare] *vt* to draw; (*progettare*) to design; (*fig*) to outline; **disegna'tore, 'trice** *sm/f* designer.

di'segno [di'seɲɲo] *sm* drawing; design; outline.

diser'bante *sm* weed-killer.

diser'tare *vt*, *vi* to desert; **diser'tore** *sm* (*MIL*) deserter.

dis'fare *vt* to undo; (*valigie*) to unpack; (*meccanismo*) to take to pieces; (*lavoro, paese*) to destroy; (*neve*) to melt; ~rsi *vr* to come undone; (*neve*) to melt; ~ **il letto** to strip the bed; ~rsi di qn (*liberarsi*) to get rid of sb; **dis'fatto, a** *pp di* **disfare** // *sf* (*sconfitta*) rout.

dis'gelo [diz'dʒɛlo] *sm* thaw.

dis'grazia [diz'grattsja] *sf* (*sventura*) misfortune; (*incidente*) accident, mishap; **disgrazi'ato, a** *ag* unfortunate // *sm/f*

wretch.

disgre'gare *vt*, ~rsi *vr* to break up.

disgu'ido *sm*: ~ **postale** error in postal delivery.

disgus'tare *vt* to disgust; ~rsi *vr*: ~rsi di to be disgusted by.

dis'gusto *sm* disgust; **disgus'toso, a** *ag* disgusting.

disidra'tare *vt* to dehydrate.

disil'ludere *vt* to disillusion, disenchant.

disimpa'rare *vt* to forget.

disimpe'gnare [dizimpeɲ'ɲare] *vt* (*persona: da obblighi*): ~ **da** to release from; (*oggetto dato in pegno*) to redeem, get out of pawn; ~rsi *vr*: ~rsi **da** (*obblighi*) to release o.s. from, free o.s. from.

disinfet'tante *ag*, *sm* disinfectant.

disinfet'tare *vt* to disinfect.

disini'bito, a *ag* uninhibited.

disinte'grare *vt*, *vi* to disintegrate.

disinteres'sarsi *vr*: ~ **di** to take no interest in.

disinte'resse *sm* indifference; (*generosità*) unselfishness.

disintossi'care *vt* (*alcolizzato, drogato*) to treat for alcoholism (o drug addiction); ~ **l'organismo** to clear out one's system.

disin'volto, a *ag* casual, free and easy; **disinvol'tura** *sf* casualness, ease.

disles'sia *sf* dyslexia.

dislo'care *vt* to station, position.

dismi'sura *sf* excess; **a** ~ to excess, excessively.

disobbe'dire *etc* = **disubbidire** *etc*.

disoccu'pato, a *ag* unemployed // *sm/f* unemployed person; **disoccupazi'one** *sf* unemployment.

diso'nesto, a *ag* dishonest.

diso'nore *sm* dishonour, disgrace.

di'sopra *av* (*con contatto*) on top; (*senza contatto*) above; (*al piano superiore*) upstairs // *ag inv* (*superiore*) upper // *sm inv* top, upper part.

disordi'nato, a *ag* untidy; (*privo di misura*) irregular, wild.

di'sordine *sm* (*confusione*) disorder, confusion; (*sregolatezza*) debauchery.

disorien'tare *vt* to disorientate; ~rsi *vr* (*fig*) to get confused, lose one's bearings.

di'sotto *av* below, underneath; (*in fondo*) at the bottom; (*al piano inferiore*) downstairs // *ag inv* (*inferiore*) lower; bottom *cpd* // *sm inv* (*parte inferiore*) lower part; bottom.

dis'paccio [dis'pattʃo] *sm* dispatch.

'**dispari** *ag inv* odd, uneven.

dis'parte: **in** ~ *av* (*da lato*) aside, apart; **tenersi** *o* **starsene in** ~ to keep to o.s., hold aloof.

dispendi'oso, a *ag* expensive.

dis'pensa *sf* pantry, larder; (*mobile*) sideboard; (*DIR*) exemption; (*REL*) dispensation; (*fascicolo*) number, issue.

dispen'sare vt (elemosine, favori) to distribute; (esonerare) to exempt.

dispe'rare vi: ~ (di) to despair (of); ~rsi vr to despair; **dispe'rato, a** ag (persona) in despair; (caso, tentativo) desperate; **disperazi'one** sf despair.

dis'perdere vt (disseminare) to disperse; (MIL.) to scatter, rout; (fig: consumare) to waste, squander; ~rsi vr to disperse; to scatter; **dis'perso, a** pp di **disperdere** // sm/f missing person.

dis'petto sm spite q, spitefulness q; fare un ~ a qn to play a (nasty) trick on sb; a ~ di in spite of; **dispet'toso, a** ag spiteful.

dispia'cere [dispja'tʃere] sm (rammarico) regret, sorrow; (dolore) grief; ~i smpl troubles, worries // vi: ~ a to displease // vb impers: mi dispiace (che) I am sorry (that); se non le dispiace, me ne vado adesso if you don't mind, I'll go now; **dispiaci'uto, a** pp di **dispiacere** // ag sorry.

dispo'nibile ag available.

dis'porre vt (sistemare) to arrange; (preparare) to prepare; (DIR) to order; (persuadere): ~ qn a to incline o dispose sb towards // vi (decidere) to decide; (usufruire): ~ di to use, have at one's disposal; (essere dotato): ~ di to have; **disporsi** vr (ordinarsi) to place o.s., arrange o.s.; **disporsi a fare** to get ready to do.

disposi'tivo sm (meccanismo) device.

disposizi'one [dispozit'tsjone] sf arrangement, layout; (stato d'animo) mood; (tendenza) bent, inclination; (comando) order; (DIR) provision, regulation; a ~ di qn at sb's disposal.

dis'posto, a pp di **disporre**.

disprez'zare [dispret'tsare] vt to despise.

dis'prezzo [dis'prettso] sm contempt.

'disputa sf dispute, quarrel.

dispu'tare vt (contendere) to dispute, contest; (gara) to take part in // vi to quarrel; ~ di to discuss; ~rsi qc to fight for sth.

dissan'guare vt (fig: persona) to bleed white; (: patrimonio) to suck dry; ~rsi vr (MED) to lose blood; (fig: rovinarsi) to ruin o.s.

dissec'care vt, ~rsi vr to dry up.

dissemi'nare vt to scatter; (fig: notizie) to spread.

dis'senso sm dissent; (disapprovazione) disapproval.

dissente'ria sf dysentery.

dissen'tire vi: ~ (da) to disagree (with).

dissertazi'one [dissertat'tsjone] sf dissertation.

disser'vizio [disser'vittsjo] sm inefficiency.

disses'tare vt (ECON) to ruin; **dis'sesto** sm (financial) ruin.

disse'tante ag refreshing.

dis'sidio sm disagreement.

dis'simile ag different, dissimilar.

dissimu'lare vt (fingere) to dissemble; (nascondere) to conceal.

dissi'pare vt to dissipate; (scialacquare) to squander, waste.

dis'solto, a pp di **dissolvere**.

disso'lubile ag soluble.

disso'luto, a pp di **dissolvere** // ag dissolute, licentious.

dis'solvere vt to dissolve; (neve) to melt; (fumo) to disperse; ~rsi vr to dissolve; to melt; to disperse.

dissu'adere vt: ~ qn da to dissuade sb from; **dissu'aso, a** pp di **dissuadere**.

distac'care vt to detach, separate; (SPORT) to leave behind; ~rsi vr to be detached; (fig) to stand out; ~rsi da (fig: allontanarsi) to grow away from.

dis'tacco, chi sm (separazione) separation; (fig: indifferenza) detachment; (SPORT): **vincere con un ~ di ...** to win by a distance of ....

dis'tante av far away // ag: ~ (da) distant (from), far away (from).

dis'tanza [dis'tantsa] sf distance.

distanzi'are [distan'tsjare] vt to space out, place at intervals; (SPORT) to outdistance; (fig: superare) to outstrip, surpass.

dis'tare vi: **distiamo pochi chilometri da Roma** we are only a few kilometres (away) from Rome.

dis'tendere vt (coperta) to spread out; (gambe) to stretch (out); (mettere a giacere) to lay; (rilassare: muscoli, nervi) to relax; ~rsi vr (rilassarsi) to relax; (sdraiarsi) to lie down; **disten'sione** sf stretching; relaxation; (POL) détente.

dis'teso, a pp di **distendere** // sf expanse, stretch.

distil'lare vt to distil.

distille'ria sf distillery.

dis'tinguere vt to distinguish.

dis'tinta sf (nota) note; (elenco) list.

distin'tivo, a ag distinctive; distinguishing // sm badge.

dis'tinto, a pp di **distinguere** // ag (dignitoso ed elegante) distinguished; ~i saluti (in lettera) yours faithfully.

distinzi'one [distin'tsjone] sf distinction.

dis'togliere [dis'tɔʎʎere] vt: ~ da to take away from; (fig) to dissuade from; **dis'tolto, a** pp di **distogliere**.

distorsi'one sf (MED) sprain; (FISICA, OTTICA) distortion.

dis'trarre vt to distract; (divertire) to entertain, amuse; **distrarsi** vr (non fare attenzione) to be distracted, let one's mind wander; (svagarsi) to amuse o enjoy o.s.; **dis'tratto, a** pp di **distrarre** // ag absent-minded; (disattento) inattentive; **distrazi'one** sf absent-mindedness;

inattention; (svago) distraction, entertainment.

dis'tretto sm district.

distribu'ire vt to distribute; (CARTE) to deal (out); (consegnare: posta) to deliver; (lavoro) to allocate, assign; (ripartire) to share out; **distribu'tore** sm (di benzina) petrol (Brit) o gas (US) pump; (AUT, ELETTR) distributor; (automatico) vending machine; **distribuzi'one** sf distribution; delivery.

distri'care vt to disentangle, unravel.

dis'truggere [dis'truddʒɛrɛ] vt to destroy; **dis'trutto, a** pp di distruggere; **distruzi'one** sf destruction.

distur'bare vt to disturb, trouble; (sonno, lezioni) to disturb, interrupt; ~rsi vr to put o.s. out.

dis'turbo sm trouble, bother, inconvenience; (indisposizione) (slight) disorder, ailment; ~i smpl (RADIO, TV) static sg.

disubbidi'ente ag disobedient; **disubbidi'enza** sf disobedience.

disubbi'dire vi: ~ (a qn) to disobey (sb).

disugu'ale ag unequal; (diverso) different; (irregolare) uneven.

disu'mano, a ag inhuman.

di'suso sm: andare o cadere in ~ to fall into disuse.

'dita fpl di dito.

di'tale sm thimble.

'dito, pl(f) **'dita** sm finger; (misura) finger, finger's breadth; ~ (del piede) toe.

'ditta sf firm, business.

ditta'tore sm dictator.

ditta'tura sf dictatorship.

dit'tongo, ghi sm diphthong.

di'urno, a ag day cpd, daytime cpd // sm (anche: albergo ~) public toilets with washing and shaving facilities etc.

'diva sf vedi divo.

diva'gare vi to digress.

divam'pare vi to flare up, blaze up.

di'vano sm sofa; divan.

divari'care vt to open wide.

di'vario sm difference.

dive'nire vi = diventare; **dive'nuto, a** pp di divenire.

diven'tare vi to become; ~ famoso/ professore to become famous/a teacher.

di'verbio sm altercation.

di'vergere [di'vɛrdʒɛrɛ] vi to diverge.

diversifi'care vt to diversify, vary; to differentiate.

diversi'one sf diversion.

diversità sf inv difference, diversity; (varietà) variety.

diver'sivo sm diversion, distraction.

di'verso, a ag (differente): ~ (da) different (from); ~i, e det pl several, various; (COMM) sundry // pronome pl several (people), many (people).

diver'tente ag amusing.

diverti'mento sm amusement, pleasure; (passatempo) pastime, recreation.

diver'tire vt to amuse, entertain; ~rsi vr to amuse o enjoy o.s.

divi'dendo sm dividend.

di'videre vt (anche MAT) to divide; (distribuire, ripartire) to divide (up), split (up); ~rsi vr (separarsi) to separate; (strade) to fork.

divi'eto sm prohibition; "~ di sosta" (AUT) "no parking".

divinco'larsi vr to wriggle, writhe.

divinità sf inv divinity.

di'vino, a ag divine.

di'visa sf (MIL etc) uniform; (COMM) foreign currency.

divisi'one sf division.

di'viso, a pp di dividere.

'divo, a sm star.

divo'rare vt to devour.

divorzi'are [divor'tsjare] vi: ~ (da qn) to divorce (sb); **divorzi'ato, a** sm/f divorcee.

di'vorzio [di'vortsjo] sm divorce.

divul'gare vt to divulge, disclose; (rendere comprensibile) to popularize; ~rsi vr to spread.

dizio'nario [ditsjo'narjo] sm dictionary.

dizi'one [dit'tsjone] sf diction; pronunciation.

do sm (MUS) C; (: solfeggiando la scala) do(h).

DOC [dɔk] abbr (= denominazione di origine controllata) label guaranteeing the quality of wine.

'doccia, ce ['dottʃa] sf (bagno) shower; (condotto) pipe; fare la ~ to have a shower.

do'cente [do'tʃɛnte] ag teaching // sm/f teacher; (di università) lecturer; **do'cenza** sf university teaching o lecturing.

'docile ['dɔtʃile] ag docile.

documen'tare vt to document; ~rsi vr: ~rsi (su) to gather information o material (about).

documen'tario sm documentary.

docu'mento sm document; ~i smpl (d'identità etc) papers.

'dodici ['dodit∫i] num twelve.

do'gana sf (ufficio) customs pl; (tassa) (customs) duty; passare la ~ to go through customs; **doga'nale** ag customs cpd; **dogani'ere** sm customs officer.

'doglie ['dɔʎʎe] sfpl (MED) labour sg, labour pains.

'dolce ['doltʃe] ag sweet; (colore) soft; (carattere, persona) gentle, mild; (fig: mite: clima) mild; (non ripido: pendio) gentle // sm (sapore dolce) sweetness, sweet taste; (CUC: portata) sweet, dessert; (: torta) cake; **dol'cezza** sf sweetness; softness; mildness; gentleness; **dolci'umi** smpl sweets.

do'lente ag sorrowful, sad.

do'lere vi to be sore, hurt, ache; **~rsi** vr to complain; (essere spiacente): **~rsi di** to be sorry for; · **mi duole la testa** my head aches, I've got a headache.

'dollaro sm dollar.

'dolo sm (DIR) malice.

Dolo'miti sfpl: **le ~** the Dolomites.

do'lore sm (fisico) pain; (morale) sorrow, grief; **dolo'roso, a** ag painful; sorrowful, sad.

do'loso, a ag (DIR) malicious.

do'manda sf (interrogazione) question; (richiesta) demand; (: cortese) request; (DIR: richiesta scritta) application; (ECON): **la ~** demand; **fare una ~ a qn** to ask sb a question; **fare ~ (per un lavoro)** to apply (for a job).

doman'dare vt (per avere) to ask for; (per sapere) to ask; (esigere) to demand; **~rsi** vr to wonder; to ask o.s.; **~ qc a qn** to ask sb for sth; to ask sb sth.

do'mani av tomorrow // sm: **il ~** (il futuro) the future; (il giorno successivo) the next day; **~ l'altro** the day after tomorrow.

do'mare vt to tame.

domat'tina av tomorrow morning.

do'menica, che sf Sunday; **di o la ~** on Sundays; **domeni'cale** ag Sunday cpd.

do'mestica, che sf vedi domestico.

do'mestico, a, ci, che ag domestic // sm/f servant, domestic.

domi'cilio [domi'tʃiljo] sm (DIR) domicile, place of residence.

domi'nare vt to dominate; (fig: sentimenti) to control, master // vi to be in the dominant position; **~rsi** vr (controllarsi) to control o.s.; **~ su** (fig) to surpass, outclass; **dominazi'one** sf domination.

do'minio sm dominion; (fig: campo) field, domain.

do'nare vt to give, present; (per beneficenza etc) to donate // vi (fig): **~ a** to suit, become; **~ sangue** to give blood; **dona'tore, 'trice** sm/f donor; **donatore di sangue/di organi** blood/organ donor.

dondo'lare vt (cullare) to rock; **~rsi** vr to swing, sway; **'dondolo** sm: **sedia/cavallo a dondolo** rocking chair/horse.

'donna sf woman; **~ di casa** housewife; home-loving woman; **~ di servizio** maid.

donnai'olo sm ladykiller.

don'nesco, a, schi, sche ag women's, woman's.

'donnola sf weasel.

'dono sm gift.

'dopo av (tempo) afterwards; (: più tardi) later; (luogo) after, next // prep after // cong (temporale): **~ aver studiato** after having studied; **~ mangiato va a dormire** after having

eaten o after a meal he goes for a sleep // ag inv: **il giorno ~** the following day; **un anno ~** a year later; **~ di me/lui** after me/him.

dopo'barba sm inv after-shave.

dopodo'mani av the day after tomorrow.

dopogu'erra sm postwar years pl.

dopo'pranzo [dopo'prandzo] av after lunch (o dinner).

doposci [dopoʃ'ʃi] sm inv après-ski outfit.

doposcu'ola sm inv school club offering extra tuition and recreational facilities.

dopo'tutto av (tutto considerato) after all.

doppi'aggio [dop'pjaddʒo] sm (CINEMA) dubbing.

doppi'are vt (NAUT) to round; (SPORT) to lap; (CINEMA) to dub.

'doppio, a ag double; (fig: falso) double-dealing, deceitful // sm (quantità): **il ~ (di)** twice as much (o many), double the amount (o number) of; (SPORT) doubles pl // av double.

doppi'one sm duplicate (copy).

doppio'petto sm double-breasted jacket.

do'rare vt to gild; (CUC) to brown; **do'rato, a** ag golden; (ricoperto d'oro) gilt, gilded; **dora'tura** sf gilding.

dormicchi'are [dormik'kjare] vi to doze.

dormigli'one, a [dormiʎ'ʎone] sm/f sleepyhead.

dor'mire vt, vi to sleep; **dor'mita** sf: **farsi una dormita** to have a good sleep.

dormi'torio sm dormitory.

dormi'veglia [dormi'veʎʎa] sm drowsiness.

'dorso sm back; (di montagna) ridge, crest; (di libro) spine; **a ~ di cavallo** on horseback.

do'sare vt to measure out; (MED) to dose.

'dose sf quantity, amount; (MED) dose.

'dosso sm (rilievo) rise; (di strada) bump; (dorso): **levarsi di ~ i vestiti** to take one's clothes off.

do'tare vt: **~ di** to provide o supply with; (fig) to endow with; **dotazi'one** sf (insieme di beni) endowment; (di macchine etc) equipment.

'dote sf (di sposa) dowry; (assegnata a un ente) endowment; (fig) gift, talent.

Dott. abbr (= dottore) Dr.

'dotto, a ag (colto) learned // sm (sapiente) scholar; (ANAT) duct.

dotto'rato sm degree; **~ di ricerca** doctorate, doctor's degree.

dot'tore, essa sm/f doctor.

dot'trina sf doctrine.

Dott.ssa abbr (= dottoressa) Dr.

'dove ◆ av (gen) where; (in cui) where, in which; (dovunque) wherever; **~ sei?/vai?** where are you?/are you going?;

dimmi dov'è tell me where it is; di ~ sei? where are you from?; per ~ si passa? which way should we go?; la città ~ abito the town where o in which I live; siediti ~ vuoi sit wherever you like ◆ cong (*mentre, laddove*) whereas.

do'vere sm (*obbligo*) duty // vt (*essere debitore*): ~ qc (a qn) to owe (sb) sth // vi (*seguito dall'infinito: obbligo*) to have to; rivolgersi a chi di ~ to apply to the appropriate authority o person; lui deve farlo he has to do it, he must do it; è dovuto partire he had to leave; ha dovuto pagare he had to pay; (: *intenzione*): devo partire domani I'm (due) to leave tomorrow; (: *probabilità*) dev'essere tardi it must be late; come si deve (*lavorare, comportarsi*) properly; una persona come si deve a respectable person.

dove'roso, a ag (right and) proper.

do'vunque av (*in qualunque luogo*) wherever; (*dappertutto*) everywhere; ~ io vada wherever I go.

do'vuto, a ag (*causato*): ~ a due to.

doz'zina [dod'dzina] sf dozen; una ~ di uova a dozen eggs.

dozzi'nale [doddzi'nale] ag cheap, second-rate.

dra'gare vt to dredge.

'drago, ghi sm dragon.

'dramma, i sm drama; dram'matico, a, ci, che ag dramatic; dram-matiz'zare vt to dramatize; dram-ma'turgo, ghi sm playwright, dramatist.

drappeggi'are [draped'dʒare] vt to drape.

drap'pello sm (*MIL*) squad; (*gruppo*) band, group.

'drastico, a, ci, che ag drastic.

dre'naggio [dre'naddʒo] sm drainage.

dre'nare vt to drain.

'dritto, a ag, av = diritto.

driz'zare [drit'tsare] vt (*far tornare diritto*) to straighten; (*volgere: sguardo, occhi*) to turn, direct; (*innalzare: antenna, muro*) to erect; ~rsi vr: ~rsi (in piedi) to stand up; ~ le orecchie to prick up one's ears.

'droga, ghe sf (*sostanza aromatica*) spice; (*stupefacente*) drug; dro'gare vt to season, spice; to drug, dope; drogarsi vr to take drugs; dro'gato, a sm/f drug addict.

droghe'ria [droge'ria] sf grocer's shop (*Brit*), grocery (store) (*US*).

'dubbio, a ag (*incerto*) doubtful, dubious; (*ambiguo*) dubious // sm (*incertezza*) doubt; avere il ~ che to be afraid that, suspect that; mettere in ~ qc to question sth; dubbi'oso, a ag doubtful, dubious.

dubi'tare vi: ~ di to doubt; (*risultato*) to be doubtful of.

Dub'lino sf Dublin.

'duca, chi sm duke.

du'chessa [du'kessa] sf duchess.

'due num two.

due'cento [due'tʃento] num two hundred // sm: il D~ the thirteenth century.

due'pezzi [due'pettsi] sm (*costume da bagno*) two-piece swimsuit; (*abito femminile*) two-piece suit.

du'etto sm duet.

'dunque cong (*perciò*) so, therefore; (*riprendendo il discorso*) well (then) // sm inv: venire al ~ to come to the point.

du'omo sm cathedral.

'duplex sm inv (*TEL*) party line.

dupli'cato sm duplicate.

'duplice ['duplitʃe] ag double, twofold; in ~ copia in duplicate.

du'rante prep during.

du'rare vi to last; ~ fatica a to have difficulty in; du'rata sf length (of time); duration; dura'turo, a ag, du'revole ag lasting.

du'rezza [du'rettsa] sf hardness; stubbornness; harshness; toughness.

'duro, a ag (*pietra, lavoro, materasso, problema*) hard; (*persona: ostinato*) stubborn, obstinate; (: *severo*) harsh, hard; (*voce*) harsh; (*carne*) tough // sm hardness; (*difficoltà*) hard part; (*persona*) tough guy; tener ~ to stand firm, hold out; ~ d'orecchi hard of hearing.

du'rone sm hard skin.

E

e, dav V spesso ed cong and; ~ lui? what about him?; ~ compralo! well buy it then!

E. abbr (= est) E.

è vb vedi essere.

'ebano sm ebony.

eb'bene cong well (then).

eb'brezza [eb'brettsa] sf intoxication.

'ebbro, a ag drunk; ~ di (*gioia etc*) beside o.s. o wild with.

'ebete ag stupid, idiotic.

ebollizi'one [ebollit'tsjone] sf boiling; punto di ~ boiling point.

e'braico, a, ci, che ag Hebrew, Hebraic // sm (*LING*) Hebrew.

e'breo, a ag Jewish // sm/f Jew/Jewess.

'Ebridi sfpl: le (isole) ~ the Hebrides.

ecc av abbr (= eccetera) etc.

ecce'denza [ettʃe'dentsa] sf excess, surplus.

ec'cedere [et'tʃedere] vt to exceed // vi to go too far; ~ nel bere/mangiare to indulge in drink/food to excess.

eccel'lente [ettʃel'lɛnte] ag excellent; eccel'lenza sf excellence; (*titolo*) Excellency.

ec'cellere [et'tʃellere] vi: ~ (in) to excel

(at); **ec'celso, a** pp di **eccellere.**

ec'centrico, a, ci, che |ct'tʃɛntriko| ag eccentric.

ecces'sivo, a |ɛttʃes'sivo| ag excessive.

ec'cesso |ɛt'tʃɛsso| sm excess; **all'~** (gentile, generoso) to excess, excessively; **~ di velocità** (AUT) speeding.

ec'cetera |ɛt'tʃɛtera| av et cetera, and so on.

ec'cetto |ɛt'tʃɛtto| prep except, with the exception of; **~ che** cong except, other than; **~ che (non)** unless.

eccettu'are |ɛttʃettu'are| vt to except.

eccezio'nale |ɛttʃetsjo'nale| ag exceptional.

eccezi'one |ɛttʃet'tsjone| sf exception; (DIR) objection; **a ~ di** with the exception of, except for; **d'~** exceptional.

ec'cidio |ɛt'tʃidio| sm massacre.

ecci'tare |ɛttʃi'tare| vt (curiosità, interesse) to excite, arouse; (folla) to incite; **~rsi** vr to get excited; (sessualmente) to become aroused; **eccitazi'one** sf excitement.

'ecco av (per dimostrare): **~ il treno!** here's o here comes the train!; (dav pronome): **~mi!** here I am!; **~ne uno!** here's one (of them)!; (dav pp): **~ fatto!** there, that's it done!

echeggi'are |ɛked'dʒare| vi to echo.

e'clissi sf eclipse.

'eco, pl(m) **'echi** sm o f echo.

ecolo'gia |ɛkolo'dʒia| sf ecology.

econo'mia sf economy; (scienza) economics sg; (risparmio: azione) saving; **fare ~** to economize, make economies; **eco'nomico, a, ci, che** ag economic; (poco costoso) economical; **econo'mista, I** sm economist; **economiz'zare** vt, vi to save; **e'conomo, a** ag thrifty // sm/f (INS) bursar.

ed cong vedi **e.**

'edera sf ivy.

e'dicola sf newspaper kiosk o stand (US).

edifi'care vt to build; (fig: teoria, azienda) to establish; (indurre al bene) to edify.

edi'ficio |edi'fitʃo| sm building; (fig) structure.

e'dile ag building cpd; **edi'lizio, a** ag building cpd // sf building, building trade.

Edim'burgo sf Edinburgh.

edi'tore, 'trice ag publishing cpd // sm/f publisher; (curatore) editor; **edito'ria** sf publishing; **editori'ale** ag publishing cpd // sm editorial, leader.

edizi'one |edit'tsjone| sf edition; (tiratura) printing; (di manifestazioni, feste etc) production.

edu'care vt to educate; (gusto, mente) to train; **~ qn a fare** to train sb to do; **edu'cato, a** ag polite, well-mannered; **educazi'one** sf education; (familiare)

upbringing; (comportamento) (good) manners pl; **educazione fisica** (INS) physical training o education.

effemi'nato, a ag effeminate.

effet'tivo, a ag (reale) real, actual; (impiegato, professore) permanent; (MIL) regular // sm (MIL) strength; (di patrimonio etc) sum total.

ef'fetto sm effect; (COMM: cambiale) bill; (fig: impressione) impression; **in ~i** in fact, actually; **effettu'are** vt to effect, carry out.

effi'cace |effi'katʃe| ag effective.

effici'ente |effi'tʃɛnte| ag efficient; **effici'enza** sf efficiency.

ef'fimero, a ag ephemeral.

E'geo |e'dʒɛo| sm: **l'~, il mare ~** the Aegean (Sea).

E'gitto |e'dʒitto| sm: **l'~** Egypt.

egizi'ano, a |edʒit'tsjano| ag, sm/f Egyptian.

'egli |'eʎʎi| pronome he; **~ stesso** he himself.

ego'ismo sm selfishness, egoism; **ego'ista, i, e** ag selfish, egoistic // sm/f egoist.

egr. abbr = **egregio.**

e'gregio, a, gi, gie |e'grɛdʒo| ag distinguished; (nelle lettere): **E~ Signore** Dear Sir.

eguagli'anza |egwaʎ'ʎantsa| etc vedi **uguaglianza** etc.

E.I. abbr = Esercito Italiano.

elabo'rare vt (progetto) to work out, elaborate; (dati) to process; (digerire) to digest; **elabora'tore** sm (INFORM): **elaboratore elettronico** computer; **elaborazi'one** sf elaboration; digestion; **elaborazione dei dati** data processing.

e'lastico, a, ci, che ag elastic; (fig: andatura) springy; (: decisione, vedute) flexible // sm (gommino) rubber band; (per il cucito) elastic q.

ole'fante sm elephant.

ele'gante ag elegant.

e'leggere |e'lɛddʒere| vt to elect.

elemen'tare ag elementary; **le (scuole) ~i** sfpl primary (Brit) o grade (US) school.

ele'mento sm element; (parte componente) element, component, part; **~i** smpl (della scienza etc) elements, rudiments.

ele'mosina sf charity, alms pl; **chiedere l'~** to beg.

elen'care vt to list.

e'lenco, chi sm list; **~ telefonico** telephone directory.

e'letto, a pp di **eleggere** // sm/f (nominato) elected member; **elet'torale** ag electoral, election cpd; **eletto'rato** sm electorate; **elet'tore, 'trice** sm/f voter, elector.

elet'trauto sm inv workshop for car electrical repairs; (tecnico) car electrician.

elettri'cista, i |elettri'tʃista| *sm* electrician.

elettricità |elettritʃi'ta| *sf* electricity.

e'lettrico, a, ci, che *ag* electric(al).

elettriz'zare |elettrid'dzare| *vt* to electrify.

e'lettro... *prefisso*: **elettrocardio'-gramma, i** *sm* electrocardiogram; **elettrodo'mestico, a, ci, che** *ag*: apparecchi elettrodomestici domestic (electrical) appliances; **elet'trone** *sm* electron; **elet'tronico, a, ci, che** *ag* electronic // *sf* electronics *sg*.

ele'vare *vt* to raise; (*edificio*) to erect; (*multa*) to impose.

elezi'one |elet'tsjone| *sf* election; ~i *sfpl* (*POL*) election(s).

'elica, che *sf* propeller.

eli'cottero *sm* helicopter.

elimi'nare *vt* to eliminate; **elimina'toria** *sf* eliminating round.

'elio *sm* helium.

'ella *pronome* she; (*forma di cortesia*) you; ~ stessa she herself; you yourself.

el'metto *sm* helmet.

e'logio |e'lɔdʒo| *sm* (*discorso, scritto*) eulogy; (*lode*) praise (*di solito q*).

elo'quente *ag* eloquent.

e'ludere *vt* to evade; **elu'sivo, a** *ag* evasive.

ema'nare *vt* to send out, give off; (*fig: leggi, decreti*) to issue // *vi*: ~ **da** to come from.

emanci'pare |emantʃi'pare| *vt* to emancipate; ~rsi *vr* (*fig*) to become liberated o emancipated.

embri'one *sm* embryo.

emenda'mento *sm* amendment.

emen'dare *vt* to amend.

emer'genza |emer'dʒɛntsa| *sf* emergency; **in caso di** ~ in an emergency.

e'mergere |e'mɛrdʒere| *vi* to emerge; (*sommergibile*) to surface; (*fig: distinguersi*) to stand out; **e'merso, a** *pp di* **emergere**.

e'messo, a *pp di* **emettere**.

e'mettere *vt* (*suono, luce*) to give out, emit; (*onde radio*) to send out; (*assegno, francobollo, ordine*) to issue; (*fig: giudizio*) to express, voice.

emi'crania *sf* migraine.

emi'grare *vi* to emigrate; **emigrazi'one** *sf* emigration.

emi'nente *ag* eminent, distinguished.

emis'fero *sm* hemisphere; ~ **boreale**/**australe** northern/southern hemisphere.

emissi'one *sf* (*vedi emettere*) emission; sending out; issue; (*RADIO*) broadcast.

emit'tente *ag* (*banca*) issuing; (*RADIO*) broadcasting, transmitting // *sf* (*RADIO*) transmitter.

emorra'gia, **'gie** |emorra'dʒia| *sf* haemorrhage.

emo'tivo, a *ag* emotional.

emozio'nante |emottsjo'nante| *ag* exciting, thrilling.

emozio'nare |emottsjo'nare| *vt* (*appassionare*) to thrill, excite; (*commuovere*) to move; (*innervosire*) to upset; ~rsi *vr* to be excited; to be moved; to be upset.

emozi'one |emot'tsjone| *sf* emotion; (*agitazione*) excitement.

'empio, a *ag* (*sacrilego*) impious; (*spietato*) cruel, pitiless; (*malvagio*) wicked, evil.

emulsi'one *sf* emulsion.

enciclope'dia |entʃiklope'dia| *sf* encyclopaedia.

endove'noso, a *ag* (*MED*) intravenous.

'ENEL |'enel| *sigla m* (= *Ente Nazionale per l'Energia Elettrica*) ≈ C.E.G.B. (= *Central Electricity Generating Board*).

ener'gia, 'gie |ener'dʒia| *sf* (*FISICA*) energy; (*fig*) energy, strength, vigour; **e'nergico, a, ci, che** *ag* energetic, vigorous.

'enfasi *sf* emphasis; (*peg*) bombast, pomposity; **en'fatico, a, ci, che** *ag* emphatic; pompous.

'ENIT |'enit| *sigla m* = *Ente Nazionale Italiano per il Turismo*.

en'nesimo, a *ag* (*MAT, fig*) nth; **per l'~a volta** for the umpteenth time.

e'norme *ag* enormous, huge; **enormità** *sf inv* enormity, huge size; (*assurdità*) absurdity; **non dire enormità!** don't talk nonsense!

'ente *sm* (*istituzione*) body, board, corporation; (*FILOSOFIA*) being.

en'trambi, e *pronome pl* both (of them) // *ag pl*: ~ **i ragazzi** both boys, both of the boys.

en'trare *vi* to enter, go (o come) in; ~ **in** (*luogo*) to enter, go (o come) into; (*trovar posto, poter stare*) to fit into; (*essere ammesso a: club etc*) to join, become a member of; ~ **in automobile** to get into the car; **far** ~ **qn** (*visitatore etc*) to show sb in; **questo non c'entra** (*fig*) that's got nothing to do with it; **en'trata** *sf* entrance, entry; **entrate** *sfpl* (*COMM*) receipts, takings; (*ECON*) income *sg*.

'entro *prep* (*temporale*) within.

entusias'mare *vt* to excite, fill with enthusiasm; ~rsi (*per qc/qn*) to become enthusiastic (about sth/sb); **entusi-si'asmo** *sm* enthusiasm; **entusi'asta, i, e** *ag* enthusiastic // *sm/f* enthusiast; **entusi'astico, a, ci, che** *ag* enthusiastic.

enunci'are |enun'tʃare| *vt* (*teoria*) to enunciate, set out.

'epico, a, ci, che *ag* epic.

epide'mia *sf* epidemic.

epi'dermide *sf* skin, epidermis.

Epifa'nia *sf* Epiphany.

epiles'sia *sf* epilepsy.

e'pilogo, ghi sm conclusion.

epi'sodio sm episode.

e'piteto sm epithet.

'epoca, che sf (periodo storico) age, era; (tempo) time; (GEO) age.

ep'pure cong and yet, nevertheless.

epu'rare vt (POL) to purge.

equa'tore sm equator.

equazi'one [ekwat'tsjone] sf (MAT) equation.

e'questre ag equestrian.

equi'latero, a ag equilateral.

equili'brare vt to balance; **equi'librio** sm balance, equilibrium; perdere l'~ to lose one's balance.

e'quino, a ag horse cpd, equine.

equipaggi'are [ekwipad'dʒare] vt (di persone) to man; (di mezzi) to equip; **equi'paggio** sm crew.

equipa'rare vt to make equal.

equità sf equity, fairness.

equitazi'one [ekwitat'tsjone] sf (horse-) riding.

equiva'lente ag, sm equivalent; **equiva'lenza** sf equivalence.

equivo'care vi to misunderstand; **e'quivoco, a, ci, che** ag equivocal, ambiguous; (sospetto) dubious // sm misunderstanding; a scanso di equivoci to avoid any misunderstanding; giocare sull'equivoco to equivocate.

'equo, a ag fair, just.

'era sf era.

'erba sf grass; (aromatica, medicinale) herb; in ~ (fig) budding; **er'baccia, ce** sf weed.

e'rede sm/f heir; **eredità** sf (DIR) inheritance; (BIOL) heredity; lasciare qc in eredità a qn to leave o bequeath sth to sb; **eredi'tare** vt to inherit; **eredi'tario, a** ag hereditary.

ere'mita, i sm hermit.

ere'sia sf heresy; **e'retico, a, ci, che** ag heretical // sm/f heretic.

e'retto, a pp di erigere // ag erect, upright; **erezi'one** sf (FISIOL) erection.

er'gastolo sm (DIR: pena) life imprisonment.

'erica sf heather.

e'rigere [e'ridʒere] vt to erect, raise; (fig: fondare) to found.

ermel'lino sm ermine.

er'metico, a, ci, che ag hermetic.

'ernia sf (MED) hernia.

e'roe sm hero.

ero'gare vt (somme) to distribute; (: per beneficenza) to donate; (gas, servizi) to supply.

e'roico, a, ci, che ag heroic.

ero'ina sf heroine; (droga) heroin.

ero'ismo sm heroism.

erosi'one sf erosion.

e'rotico, a, ci, che ag erotic.

er'rare vi (vagare) to wander, roam; (sbagliare) to be mistaken.

er'rore sm error, mistake; (morale) error; per ~ by mistake.

'erta sf steep slope; stare all'~ to be on the alert.

erut'tare vt (sog: vulcano) to throw out, belch.

eruzi'one [erut'tsjone] sf eruption.

esacer'bare [ezatʃer'bare] vt to exacerbate.

esage'rare [ezadʒe'rare] vt to exaggerate // vi to exaggerate; (eccedere) to go too far; **esagerazi'one** sf exaggeration.

e'sagono sm hexagon.

esal'tare vt to exalt; (entusiasmare) to excite, stir; **esal'tato, a** sm/f fanatic.

e'same sm examination; (INS) exam, examination; fare o dare un ~ to sit o take an exam; ~ del sangue blood test.

esami'nare vt to examine.

e'sanime ag lifeless.

esaspe'rare vt to exasperate; to exacerbate; ~rsi vr to become annoyed o exasperated; **esasperazi'one** sf exasperation.

esatta'mente av exactly; accurately, precisely.

esat'tezza [ezat'tettsa] sf exactitude, accuracy, precision.

e'satto, a pp di esigere // ag (calcolo, ora) correct, right, exact; (preciso) accurate, precise; (puntuale) punctual.

esat'tore sm (di imposte etc) collector.

esau'dire vt to grant, fulfil.

esauri'ente ag exhaustive.

esauri'mento sm exhaustion; ~ nervoso nervous breakdown.

esau'rire vt (stancare) to exhaust, wear out; (provviste, miniera) to exhaust; ~rsi vr to exhaust o.s., wear o.s. out; (provviste) to run out; **esau'rito, a** ag exhausted; (merci) sold out; (libri) out of print; registrare il tutto esaurito (TEATRO) to have a full house; **e'sausto, a** ag exhausted.

'esca, pl 'esche sf bait.

escande'scenza [eskandeʃ'ʃentsa] sf: dare in ~e to lose one's temper, fly into a rage.

'esce, 'esci ['eʃe,'eʃi] vb vedi uscire.

eschi'mese [eski'mese] ag, sm/f Eskimo.

escla'mare vi to exclaim, cry out; **esclamazi'one** sf exclamation.

es'cludere vt to exclude.

esclu'sivo, a ag exclusive // sf (DIR, COMM) exclusive o sole rights pl.

es'cluso, a pp di escludere.

'esco, 'escono vb vedi uscire.

escursi'one sf (gita) excursion, trip; (: a piedi) hike, walk; (METEOR) range.

ese'crare vt to loathe, abhor.

esecu'tivo, a ag, sm executive.

esecu'tore, 'trice sm/f (MUS) performer; (DIR) executor.

esecuzi'one [ezekut'tsjone] sf execution, carrying out; (MUS) performance; ~

capitale execution.

esegu'ire *vt* to carry out, execute; (*MUS*) to perform, execute.

e'sempio *sm* example; **per ~** for example, for instance; **fare un ~** to give an example; **esem'plare** *ag* exemplary // *sm* example; (*copia*) copy; **esemplifi'care** *vt* to exemplify.

esen'tare *vt*: **~ qn/qc da** to exempt sb/sth from.

e'sente *ag*: **~ da** (*dispensato da*) exempt from; (*privo di*) free from; **esenzi'one** *sf* exemption.

e'sequie *sfpl* funeral rites; funeral service *sg*.

eser'cente [ezer'tʃɛnte] *sm/f* trader, dealer; shopkeeper.

eserci'tare [ezertʃi'tare] *vt* (*professione*) to practise (*Brit*), practice (*US*); (*allenare: corpo, mente*) to exercise, train; (*diritto*) to exercise; (*influenza, pressione*) to exert; **~rsi** *vr* to practise; **~rsi alla lotta** to practise fighting; **esercitazi'one** *sf* (*scolastica, militare*) exercise.

e'sercito [e'zɛrtʃito] *sm* army.

eser'cizio [ezer'tʃittsjo] *sm* practice; exercising; (*fisico, di matematica*) exercise; (*ECON*) financial year; (*azienda*) business, concern; **in ~** (*medico etc*) practising.

esi'bire *vt* to exhibit, display; (*documenti*) to produce, present; **~rsi** *vr* (*attore*) to perform; (*fig*) to show off; **esibizi'one** *sf* exhibition; (*di documento*) presentation; (*spettacolo*) show, performance.

esi'gente [ezi'dʒɛnte] *ag* demanding; **esi'genza** *sf* demand, requirement.

e'sigere [c'zidʒcrc] *vt* (*pretendere*) to demand; (*richiedere*) to demand, require; (*imposte*) to collect.

e'siguo, a *ag* small, slight.

'esile *ag* (*persona*) slender, slim; (*stelo*) thin; (*voce*) faint.

esili'are *vt* to exile; **e'silio** *sm* exile.

e'simere *vt*: **~ qn/qc da** to exempt sb/sth from; **~rsi** *vr*: **~rsi da** to get out of.

esis'tenza [ezis'tɛntsa] *sf* existence.

e'sistere *vi* to exist.

esis'tito, a *pp di* **esistere**.

esi'tare *vi* to hesitate; **esitazi'one** *sf* hesitation.

'esito *sm* result, outcome.

'esodo *sm* exodus.

esone'rare *vt*: **~ qn da** to exempt sb from.

e'sordio *sm* début.

esor'tare *vt*: **~ qn a fare** to urge sb to do.

e'sotico, a, ci, che *ag* exotic.

es'pandere *vt* to expand; (*confini*) to extend; (*influenza*) to extend, spread; **~rsi** *vr* to expand; **espansi'one** *sf* expansion; **espan'sivo, a** *ag* expansive,

communicative.

espatri'are *vi* to leave one's country.

espedi'ente *sm* expedient.

es'pellere *vt* to expel.

esperi'enza [espe'rjɛntsa] *sf* experience; (*SCIENZA: prova*) experiment.

esperi'mento *sm* experiment.

es'perto, a *ag, sm* expert.

espi'are *vt* to atone for.

espi'rare *vt, vi* to breathe out.

espli'care *vt* (*attività*) to carry out, perform.

es'plicito, a [es'plitʃito] *ag* explicit.

es'plodere *vi* (*anche fig*) to explode // *vt* to fire.

esplo'rare *vt* to explore; **esplora'tore** *sm* explorer; (*anche: giovane esploratore*) (boy) scout; (*NAUT*) scout (ship).

esplosi'one *sf* explosion; **esplo'sivo, a** *ag, sm* explosive; **es'ploso, a** *pp di* **esplodere**.

espo'nente *sm/f* (*rappresentante*) representative.

es'porre *vt* (*merci*) to display; (*quadro*) to exhibit, show; (*fatti, idee*) to explain, set out; (*porre in pericolo, FOT*) to expose.

espor'tare *vt* to export; **esportazi'one** *sf* exportation; export.

esposizi'one [espozit'tsjone] *sf* displaying; exhibiting; setting out; (*anche FOT*) exposure; (*mostra*) exhibition; (*narrazione*) explanation, exposition.

es'posto, a *pp di* **esporre** // *ag*: **~ a nord** facing north // *sm* (*AMM*) statement, account; (: *petizione*) petition.

espressi'one *sf* expression.

espres'sivo, a *ag* expressive.

es'presso, a *pp di* **esprimere** // *ag* express // *sm* (*lettera*) express letter; (*anche: treno ~*) express train; (*anche: caffè ~*) espresso.

es'primere *vt* to express; **~rsi** *vr* to express o.s.

espulsi'one *sf* expulsion; **es'pulso, a** *pp di* **espellere**.

'essa *pronome f*, **'esse** *pronome fpl vedi* **esso**.

es'senza [es'sɛntsa] *sf* essence; **essenzi'ale** *ag* essential; **l'essenziale** the main o most important thing.

'essere ◆ *sm* being; **~ umano** human being

◆ *vb copulativo* **1** (*con attributo, sostantivo*) to be; **sei giovane/simpatico** you are o you're young/nice; **è medico** he is o he's a doctor

2 (+ *di: appartenere*) to be; **di chi è la penna?** whose pen is it?; **è di Carla** it is o it's Carla's, it belongs to Carla

3 (+ *di: provenire*) to be; **è di Venezia** he is o he's from Venice

4 (*data, ora*): **è il 15 agosto/lunedì** it is o it's the 15th of August/Monday; **che ora è?, che ore sono?** what time is it?; **è**

l'una it is *o* it's one o'clock; **sono le due** it is *o* it's two o'clock

5 (*costare*): **quant'è?** how much is it?; **sono 20.000 lire** it's 20,000 lire

♦ *vb ausiliare* **1** (*attivo*): **~ arrivato/venuto** to have arrived/come; **è già partita** she has already left

2 (*passivo*) to be; **~ fatto da** to be made by; **è stata uccisa** she has been killed

3 (*riflessivo*): **si sono lavati** they washed, they got washed

4 (+ *da* + *infinito*): **è da farsi subito** it must be *o* is to be done immediately

♦ *vi* **1** (*esistere, trovarsi*) to be; **sono a casa** I'm at home; **~ in piedi/seduto** to be standing/sitting

2: **esserci**: **c'è** there is; **ci sono** there are; **che c'è?** what's the matter?, what is it?; **ci sono!** (*fig: ho capito*) I get it!; *vedi anche* **ci**

♦ *vb impers*: **è tardi/Pasqua** it's late/ Easter; **è possibile che venga** he may come; **è così** that's the way it is.

'esso, a *pronome* it; (*riferito a persona: soggetto*) he/she; (: *complemento*) him/ her; **~i, e** *pronome pl* they; (*complemento*) them.

est *sm* east.

'estasi *sf* ecstasy.

es'tate *sf* summer.

es'tatico, a, ci, che *ag* ecstatic.

es'tendere *vt* to extend; **~rsi** *vr* (*diffondersi*) to spread; (*territorio, confini*) to extend; **estensi'one** *sf* extension; (*di superficie*) expanse; (*di voce*) range.

esteri'ore *ag* outward, external.

es'terno, a *ag* (*porta, muro*) outer, outside; (*scala*) outside; (*alunno, impressione*) external // *sm* outside, exterior // *sm/f* (*allievo*) day pupil; **per uso ~** for external use only.

'estero, a *ag* foreign // *sm*: **all'~** abroad.

es'teso, a *pp di* **estendere** // *ag* extensive, large; **scrivere per ~** to write in full.

es'tetico, a, ci, che *ag* aesthetic // *sf* (*disciplina*) aesthetics *sg*; (*bellezza*) attractiveness; **este'tista, i, e** *sm/f* beautician.

'estimo *sm* valuation; (*disciplina*) surveying.

es'tinguere *vt* to extinguish, put out; (*debito*) to pay off; **~rsi** *vr* to go out; (*specie*) to become extinct; **es'tinto, a** *pp di* **estinguere**; **estin'tore** *sm* (fire) extinguisher; **estinzi'one** *sf* putting out; (*di specie*) extinction.

estir'pare *vt* (*pianta*) to uproot, pull up; (*fig: vizio*) to eradicate.

es'tivo, a *ag* summer *cpd*.

es'torcere [es'tɔrtʃere] *vt*: **~ qc (a qn)** to extort sth (from sb); **es'torto, a** *pp di* **estorcere**.

estradizi'one [estradit'tsjone] *sf* extradi-

tion.

es'traneo, a *ag* foreign; (*discorso*) extraneous, unrelated // *sm/f* stranger; **rimanere ~ a qc** to take no part in sth.

es'trarre *vt* to extract; (*minerali*) to mine; (*sorteggiare*) to draw; **es'tratto, a** *pp di* **estrarre** // *sm* extract; (*di documento*) abstract; **estratto conto** statement of account; **estratto di nascita** birth certificate; **estrazi'one** *sf* extraction; mining; drawing *q*; draw.

estremità *sf inv* extremity, end // *sfpl* (ANAT) extremities.

es'tremo, a *ag* extreme; (*ultimo: ora, tentativo*) final, last // *sm* extreme; (*di pazienza, forze*) limit, end; **~i** *smpl* (AMM: *dati essenziali*) details, particulars; **l'~ Oriente** the Far East.

'estro *sm* (*capriccio*) whim, fancy; (*ispirazione creativa*) inspiration; **es'troso, a** *ag* whimsical, capricious; inspired.

estro'verso, a *ag, sm* extrovert.

'esule *sm/f* exile.

età *sf inv* age; **all'~ di 8 anni** at the age of 8, at 8 years of age; **ha la mia ~** (*he* (*o* she) is the same age as me *o* as I am; **raggiungere la maggiore ~** to come of age; **essere in ~ minore** to be under age.

'etere *sm* ether; **e'tereo, a** *ag* ethereal.

eternità *sf* eternity.

e'terno, a *ag* eternal.

etero'geneo, a [etero'dʒeneo] *ag* heterogeneous.

'etica *sf vedi* **etico**.

eti'chetta [eti'ketta] *sf* label; (*cerimoniale*): **l'~** etiquette.

'etico, a, ci, che *ag* ethical // *sf* ethics *sg*

etimolo'gia, 'gie [etimolo'dʒia] *sf* etymology.

Eti'opia *sf*: **l'~** Ethiopia.

'Etna *sm*: **l'~** Etna.

'etnico, a, ci, che *ag* ethnic.

e'trusco, a, schi, sche *ag, sm/f* Etruscan.

'ettaro *sm* hectare (= *10,000 m²*).

'etto *sm abbr di* **ettogrammo**.

etto'grammo *sm* hectogram(me) (= *100 grams*).

Eucaris'tia *sf*: **l'~** the Eucharist.

Eu'ropa *sf*: **l'~** Europe; **euro'peo, a** *ag, sm/f* European.

evacu'are *vt* to evacuate.

e'vadere *vi* (*fuggire*): **~ da** to escape from // *vt* (*sbrigare*) to deal with, dispatch; (*tasse*) to evade.

evan'gelico, a, ci, che [evan'dʒeliko] *ag* evangelical.

evapo'rare *vi* to evaporate; **evaporazi'one** *sf* evaporation.

evasi'one *sf* (*vedi* **evadere**) escape; dispatch; **~ fiscale** tax evasion.

eva'sivo, a *ag* evasive.

e'vaso, a *pp di* **evadere** // *sm* escapee.

eveni'enza [eve'njentsa] *sf*: **pronto(a) per ogni** ~ ready for any eventuality.

e'vento *sm* event.

eventu'ale *ag* possible.

evi'dente *ag* evident, obvious; **evi'denza** *sf* obviousness; **mettere in evidenza** to point out, highlight.

evi'tare *vt* to avoid; ~ **di fare** to avoid doing; ~ **qc a qn** to spare sb sth.

'evo *sm* age, epoch.

evo'care *vt* to evoke.

evo'luto, a *pp di* **evolvere** // *ag* (*civiltà*) (highly) developed, advanced; (*persona*) independent.

evoluzi'one [evolut'tsjone] *sf* evolution.

e'volversi *vr* to evolve.

ev'viva *escl* hurrah!; ~ **il re!** long live the king!, hurrah for the king!

ex *prefisso* ex, former.

'extra *ag inv* first-rate; top-quality // *sm inv* extra; **extraconiu'gale** *ag* extramarital.

F

fa *vb vedi* **fare** // *sm inv* (*MUS*) F; (: *solfeggiando la scala*) **fa** // *av*: **10 anni** ~ 10 years ago.

fabbi'sogno [fabbi'zonno] *sm* needs *pl*, requirements *pl*.

'fabbrica *sf* factory; **fabbri'cante** *sm* manufacturer, maker; **fabbri'care** *vt* to build; (*produrre*) to manufacture, make; (*fig*) to fabricate, invent.

'fabbro *sm* (black)smith.

fac'cenda [fat'tʃenda] *sf* matter, affair; (*cosa da fare*) task, chore.

fac'chino [fak'kino] *sm* porter.

'faccia, ce ['fattʃa] *sf* face; (*di moneta, medaglia*) side; ~ **a** ~ face to face.

facci'ata [fat'tʃata] *sf* façade; (*di pagina*) side.

'faccio ['fattʃo] *vb vedi* **fare**.

fa'ceto, a [fa'tʃeto] *ag* witty, humorous.

'facile ['fatʃile] *ag* easy; (*affabile*) easy-going; (*disposto*): ~ **a** inclined to, prone to; (*probabile*): **è** ~ **che piova** it's likely to rain; **facilità** *sf* easiness; (*disposizione, dono*) aptitude; **facili'tare** *vt* to make easier.

facino'roso, a [fatʃino'roso] *ag* violent.

facoltà *sf inv* faculty; (*CHIMICA*) property; (*autorità*) power.

facolta'tivo, a *ag* optional; (*fermata d'autobus*) request *cpd*.

fac'simile *sm* facsimile.

'faggio ['faddʒo] *sm* beech.

fagi'ano [fa'dʒano] *sm* pheasant.

fagio'lino [fadʒo'lino] *sm* French (*Brit*) *o* string bean.

fagi'olo [fa'dʒɔlo] *sm* bean.

fa'gotto *sm* bundle; (*MUS*) bassoon; **far** ~ (*fig*) to pack up and go.

'fai *vb vedi* **fare**.

'falce ['faltʃe] *sf* scythe; **fal'cetto** *sm* sickle; **falci'are** *vt* to cut; (*fig*) to mow down.

'falco, chi *sm* hawk.

fal'cone *sm* falcon.

'falda *sf* layer, stratum; (*di cappello*) brim; (*di cappotto*) tails *pl*; (*di monte*) lower slope; (*di tetto*) pitch; **nevica a larghe** ~**e** the snow is falling in large flakes; **abito a** ~**e** tails *pl*.

fale'gname [fale'ŋname] *sm* joiner.

fal'lace [fal'latʃe] *ag* misleading, deceptive.

falli'mento *sm* failure; bankruptcy.

fal'lire *vi* (*non riuscire*): ~ (**in**) to fail (in); (*DIR*) to go bankrupt // *vt* (*colpo, bersaglio*) to miss; **fal'lito, a** *ag* unsuccessful; bankrupt // *sm/f* bankrupt.

'fallo *sm* error, mistake; (*imperfezione*) defect, flaw; (*SPORT*) foul; fault; **senza** ~ without fail.

falò *sm inv* bonfire.

fal'sare *vt* to distort, misrepresent; **fal'sario** *sm* forger; counterfeiter; **falsifi'care** *vt* to forge; (*monete*) to forge, counterfeit.

'falso, a *ag* false; (*errato*) wrong; (*falsificato*) forged; fake; (: *oro, gioielli*) imitation *cpd* // *sm* forgery; **giurare il** ~ to commit perjury.

'fama *sf* fame; (*reputazione*) reputation, name.

'fame *sf* hunger; **aver** ~ to be hungry; **fa'melico, a, ci, che** *ag* ravenous.

fa'miglia [fa'miʎʎa] *sf* family.

famili'are *ag* (*della famiglia*) family *cpd*; (*ben noto*) familiar; (*rapporti, atmosfera*) friendly; (*LING*) informal, colloquial // *sm/f* relative, relation; **familiarità** *sf* familiarity; friendliness; informality.

fa'moso, a *ag* famous, well-known.

fa'nale *sm* (*AUT*) light, lamp (*Brit*); (*luce stradale, NAUT*) light; (*di faro*) beacon.

fa'natico, a, ci, che *ag* fanatical; (*del teatro, calcio etc*): ~ **di** *o* **per** mad *o* crazy about // *sm/f* fanatic; (*tifoso*) fan.

fanci'ullo, a [fan'tʃullo] *sm/f* child.

fan'donia *sf* tall story; ~**e** *sfpl* nonsense *sg*.

fan'fara *sf* brass band; (*musica*) fanfare.

'fango, ghi *sm* mud; **fan'goso, a** *ag* muddy.

'fanno *vb vedi* **fare**.

fannul'lone, a *sm/f* idler, loafer.

fantasci'enza [fantaʃ'ʃentsa] *sf* science fiction.

fanta'sia *sf* fantasy, imagination; (*capriccio*) whim, caprice // *ag inv*: **vestito** ~ patterned dress.

fan'tasma, i *sm* ghost, phantom.

fan'tastico, a, ci, che *ag* fantastic; (*potenza, ingegno*) imaginative.

'fante *sm* infantryman; (*CARTE*) jack,

knave (*Brit*); **fante'ria** *sf* infantry.
fan'toccio [fan'tɔttʃo] *sm* puppet.
fara'butto *sm* crook.
far'dello *sm* bundle; (*fig*) burden.
'fare ◆ *sm* 1 (*modo di fare*): con ~ distratto absent-mindedly; **ha un** ~ **simpatico** he has a pleasant manner
2: sul far del giorno/della notte at daybreak/nightfall
◆ *vt* 1 (*fabbricare, creare*) to make; (: *casa*) to build; (: *assegno*) to make out; ~ **un pasto/una promessa/un film** to make a meal/a promise/a film; ~ **rumore** to make a noise
2 (*effettuare: lavoro, attività, studi*) to do; (: *sport*) to play; **cosa fa?** (*adesso*) what are you doing?; (*di professione*) what do you do?; ~ **psicologia/italiano** (*INS*) to do psychology/Italian; ~ **un viaggio** to go on a trip *o* journey; ~ **una passeggiata** to go for a walk; ~ **la spesa** to do the shopping
3 (*funzione*) to be; (*TEATRO*) to play, be; ~ **il medico** to be a doctor; ~ **il malato** (*fingere*) to act the invalid
4 (*suscitare: sentimenti*): ~ **paura a qn** to frighten sb; **mi fa rabbia** it makes me angry; (**non**) **fa niente** (*non importa*) it doesn't matter
5 (*ammontare*): **3 più 3 fa 6** 3 and 3 are *o* make 6; **fanno 6.000 lire** that's 6,000 lire; **Roma fa 2.000.000 di abitanti** Rome has 2,000,000 inhabitants; **che ora fai?** what time do you make it?
6 (+ *infinito*): **far** ~ **qc a qn** (*obbligare*) to make sb do sth; (*permettere*) to let sb do sth; **fammi vedere** let me see; **far partire il motore** to start (up) the engine; **far riparare la macchina/costruire una casa** to get *o* have the car repaired/a house built
7: ~**rsi**: ~**rsi una gonna** to make o.s. a skirt; ~**rsi un nome** to make a name for o.s.; ~**rsi la permanente** to get a perm; ~**rsi tagliare i capelli** to get one's hair cut; ~**rsi operare** to have an operation; **si è fatto lavare la macchina** he got somebody to wash the car
8 (*fraseologia*): **farcela** to succeed, manage; **non ce la faccio più** I can't go on; **ce la faremo** we'll make it; **me l'hanno fatta!** (*imbrogliare*) I've been done!; **lo facevo più giovane** I thought he was younger; **fare sì/no con la testa** to nod/shake one's head
◆ *vi* 1 (*agire*) to act, do; **fate come volete** do as you like; ~ **presto** to be quick; ~ **da** to act as; **non c'è niente da** ~ it's no use; **saperci** ~ **con qn/qc** to know how to deal with sb/sth; **faccia pure!** go ahead!
2 (*dire*) to say; **"davvero?" fece "really?"** he said
3: ~ **per** (*essere adatto*) to be suitable for; ~ **per** ~ **qc** to be about to do sth;

fece per andarsene he made as if to leave
4: ~**rsi: si fa così** you do it like this, this is the way it's done; **non si fa così!** (*rimprovero*) that's no way to behave!; **la festa non si fa** the party is off
5: ~ **a gara con qn** to compete *o* vie with sb; ~ **a pugni** to come to blows; ~ **in tempo a** ~ to be in time to do
◆ *vb impers*: **fa bel tempo** the weather is fine; **fa caldo/freddo** it's hot/cold; **fa notte** it's getting dark
◆ *vr*: ~**rsi** 1 (*diventare*) to become; ~**rsi prete** to become a priest; ~**rsi grande/vecchio** to grow tall/old
2 (*spostarsi*): ~**rsi avanti/indietro** to move forward/back
3 (*fam: drogarsi*) to be a junkie.
far'falla *sf* butterfly.
fa'rina *sf* flour.
farma'cia, 'cie [farma'tʃia] *sf* pharmacy; (*negozio*) chemist's (shop) (*Brit*), pharmacy; **farma'cista, i, e** *sm/f* chemist (*Brit*), pharmacist.
'farmaco, ci *o* **chi** *sm* drug, medicine.
'faro *sm* (*NAUT*) lighthouse; (*AER*) beacon; (*AUT*) headlight.
'farsa *sf* farce.
'fascia, sce ['faʃʃa] *sf* band, strip; (*MED*) bandage; (*di sindaco, ufficiale*) sash; (*parte di territorio*) strip, belt; (*contribuenti etc*) group, band; **essere in** ~**sce** (*anche fig*) to be in one's infancy; ~ **oraria** time band.
fasci'are [faʃ'ʃare] *vt* to bind; (*MED*) to bandage; (*bambino*) to put a nappy (*Brit*) *o* diaper (*US*) on.
fa'scicolo [faʃ'ʃikolo] *sm* (*di documenti*) file, dossier; (*di rivista*) issue, number; (*opuscolo*) booklet, pamphlet.
'fascino ['faʃʃino] *sm* charm, fascination.
'fascio ['faʃʃo] *sm* bundle, sheaf; (*di fiori*) bunch; (*di luce*) beam; (*POL*): **il F~** the Fascist Party.
fa'scismo [faʃ'ʃizmo] *sm* fascism.
'fase *sf* phase; (*TECN*) stroke; **fuori** ~ (*motore*) rough.
fas'tidio *sm* bother, trouble; **dare** ~ **a qn** to bother *o* annoy sb; **sento** ~ **allo stomaco** my stomach's upset; **avere** ~**i con la polizia** to have trouble *o* bother with the police; **fastidi'oso, a** *ag* annoying, tiresome; (*schifiltoso*) fastidious.
'fasto *sm* pomp, splendour.
'fata *sf* fairy.
fa'tale *ag* fatal; (*inevitabile*) inevitable; (*fig*) irresistible; **fatalità** *sf inv* inevitability; (*avversità*) misfortune; (*fato*) fate, destiny.
fa'tica, che *sf* hard work, toil; (*sforzo*) effort; (*di metalli*) fatigue; **a** ~ with difficulty; **fare** ~ **a fare qc** to have a job doing sth; **fati'care** *vi* to toil; **faticare a fare qc** to have difficulty doing sth; **fati'coso, a** *ag* tiring, exhausting;

(*lavoro*) laborious.

'**fato** *sm* fate, destiny.

'**fatto, a** *pp di* **fare** // *ag*: un uomo ~ a grown man; ~ **a mano/in casa** hand-/home-made // *sm* fact; (*azione*) deed; (*avvenimento*) event, occurrence; (*di romanzo, film*) action, story; **cogliere qn sul** ~ to catch sb red-handed; **il** ~ **sta** *o* **è che** the fact remains *o* is that; **in** ~ **di** as for, as far as ... is concerned.

fat'tore *sm* (*AGR*) farm manager; (*MAT, elemento costitutivo*) factor.

fatto'ria *sf* farm; farmhouse.

fatto'rino *sm* errand-boy; (*di ufficio*) office-boy; (*d'albergo*) porter.

fat'tura *sf* (*COMM*) invoice; (*di abito*) tailoring; (*malia*) spell.

fattu'rare *vt* (*COMM*) to invoice; (*prodotto*) to produce; (*vino*) to adulterate.

'**fatuo, a** *ag* vain, fatuous.

'**fauna** *sf* fauna.

fau'tore, trice *sm/f* advocate, supporter.

fa'vella *sf* speech.

fa'villa *sf* spark.

'**favola** *sf* (*fiaba*) fairy tale; (*d'intento morale*) fable; (*fandonia*) yarn; **favo'loso, a** *ag* fabulous; (*incredibile*) incredible.

fa'vore *sm* favour; **per** ~ please; **fare un** ~ **a qn** to do sb a favour; **favo'revole** *ag* favourable.

favo'rire *vt* to favour; (*il commercio, l'industria, le arti*) to promote, encourage; **vuole** ~? won't you help yourself?; **favorisca in salotto** please come into the sitting room; **favo'rito, a** *ag, sm/f* favourite.

fazzo'letto [fattso'letto] *sm* handkerchief; (*per la testa*) (head)scarf.

feb'braio *sm* February.

'**febbre** *sf* fever; **aver la** ~ to have a high temperature; ~ **da fieno** hay fever; **feb'brile** *ag* (*anche fig*) feverish.

'**feccia, ce** ['fettʃa] *sf* dregs *pl*.

'**fecola** *sf* potato flour.

fecondazi'one [fekondat'tsjone] *sf* fertilization; ~ **artificiale** artificial insemination.

fe'condo, a *ag* fertile.

'**fede** *sf* (*credenza*) belief, faith; (*REL*) faith; (*fiducia*) faith, trust; (*fedeltà*) loyalty; (*anello*) wedding ring; (*attestato*) certificate; **aver** ~ **in qn** to have faith in sb; **in buona/cattiva** ~ **in** good/bad faith; "**in** ~" (*DIR*) "in witness whereof"; **fe'dele** *ag*: **fedele (a)** faithful (to) // *sm/f* follower; **i fedeli** (*REL*) the faithful; **fedeltà** *sf* faithfulness; (*coniugale*) fidelity; **alta fedeltà** (*RADIO*) high fidelity.

'**federa** *sf* pillowslip, pillowcase.

fede'rale *ag* federal.

'**fegato** *sm* liver; (*fig*) guts *pl*, nerve.

'**felce** ['feltʃe] *sf* fern.

fe'lice [fe'litʃe] *ag* happy; (*fortunato*) lucky; **felicità** *sf* happiness.

felici'tarsi [felitʃi'tarsi] *vr* (*congratularsi*): ~ **con qn per qc** to congratulate sb on sth.

fe'lino, a *ag, sm* feline.

'**feltro** *sm* felt.

'**femmina** *sf* (*ZOOL, TECN*) female; (*figlia*) girl, daughter; (*spesso peg*) woman; **femmi'nile** *ag* feminine; (*sesso*) female; (*lavoro, giornale, moda*) woman's // *sm* (*LING*) feminine; **femmi'nismo** *sm* feminism.

'**fendere** *vt* to cut through; **fendi'nebbia** *sm inv* (*AUT*) fog lamp.

fe'nomeno *sm* phenomenon.

'**feretro** *sm* coffin.

feri'ale *ag* working *cpd*, work *cpd*, week *cpd*; **giorno** ~ weekday.

'**ferie** *sfpl* holidays (*Brit*), vacation *sg* (*US*); **andare in** ~ to go on holiday *o* vacation.

fe'rire *vt* to injure; (*deliberatamente: MIL etc*) to wound; (*colpire*) to hurt; **fe'rito, a** *sm/f* wounded *o* injured man/woman // *sf* injury; wound.

'**ferma** *sf* (*MIL*) (period of) service; (*CACCIA*): **cane da** ~ pointer.

fer'maglio [fer'maʎʎo] *sm* clasp; (*gioiello*) brooch; (*per documenti*) clip.

fer'mare *vt* to stop, halt; (*POLIZIA*) to detain, hold; (*bottone etc*) to fasten, fix // *vi* to stop; ~**rsi** *vr* to stop, halt; ~**rsi a fare qc** to stop to do sth.

fer'mata *sf* stop; ~ **dell'autobus** bus stop.

fer'mento *sm* (*anche fig*) ferment; (*lievito*) yeast.

fer'mezza [fer'mettsa] *sf* (*fig*) firmness, steadfastness.

'**fermo, a** *ag* still, motionless; (*veicolo*) stationary; (*orologio*) not working; (*saldo: anche fig*) firm; (*voce, mano*) steady // *escl* stop!; **keep still!** // *sm* (*chiusura*) catch, lock; (*DIR*): ~ **di polizia** police detention.

'**fermo 'posta** *ag, sm inv* poste restante (*Brit*), general delivery (*US*).

fe'roce [fe'rɔtʃe] *ag* (*animale*) wild, fierce, ferocious; (*persona*) cruel, fierce; (*fame, dolore*) raging.

ferra'gosto *sm* (*festa*) feast of the Assumption; (*periodo*) August holidays *pl*.

ferra'menta *sfpl* ironmongery *sg* (*Brit*), hardware *sg*; **negozio di** ~ ironmonger's (*Brit*), hardware shop *o* store (*US*).

fer'rato, a *ag* (*FERR*): **strada** ~**a** railway (*Brit*) *o* railroad (*US*) line; (*fig*): **essere** ~ **in** to be well up in.

'**ferreo, a** *ag* iron *cpd*.

'**ferro** *sm* iron; **una bistecca ai** ~**i** a grilled steak; ~ **battuto** wrought iron; ~ **da calza** knitting needle; ~ **di cavallo** horseshoe; ~ **da stiro** iron.

ferro'via *sf* railway (*Brit*), railroad (*US*); **ferrovi'ario, a** *ag* railway *cpd* (*Brit*), railroad *cpd* (*US*); **ferrovi'ere** *sm* railwayman (*Brit*), railroad man (*US*).

'**fertile** *ag* fertile; **fertiliz'zante** *sm* fertilizer.

'**fervido, a** *ag* fervent.

fer'vore *sm* fervour, ardour; (*punto culminante*) height.

'**fesso, a** *pp di* **fendere** // *ag* (*fam*: *sciocco*) crazy, cracked.

fes'aura *sf* crack, split; (*per gettone, moneta*) slot.

'**festa** *sf* (*religiosa*) feast; (*pubblica*) holiday; (*compleanno*) birthday; (*onomastico*) name day; (*ricevimento*) celebration, party; **far ~** to have a holiday; **to live it up; far ~ a qn** to give sb a warm welcome.

festeggi'are [fested'dʒare] *vt* to celebrate; (*persona*) to have a celebration for.

fes'tino *sm* party; (*con balli*) ball.

fes'tivo, a *ag* (*atmosfera*) festive; **giorno ~** holiday.

fes'toso, a *ag* merry, joyful.

fe'ticcio [fe'tittʃo] *sm* fetish.

'**feto** *sm* foetus (*Brit*), fetus (*US*).

'**fetta** *sf* slice.

fettuc'cine [fettut'tʃine] *sfpl* (*CUC*) ribbon-shaped pasta.

FF.SS. *abbr* = Ferrovie dello Stato.

fi'aba *sf* fairy tale.

fi'acca *sf* weariness; (*svogliatezza*) listlessness.

fiac'care *vt* to weaken.

fi'acco, a, chi, che *ag* (*stanco*) tired, weary; (*svogliato*) listless; (*debole*) weak; (*mercato*) slack.

fi'accola *sf* torch.

fi'ala *sf* phial.

fi'amma *sf* flame.

fiam'mante *ag* (*colore*) flaming; **nuovo ~** brand new.

fiammeggi'are [fjammed'dʒare] *vi* to blaze.

fiam'mifero *sm* match.

fiam'mingo, a, ghi, ghe *ag* Flemish // *sm/f* Fleming // *sm* (*LING*) Flemish; (*ZOOL*) flamingo; **i F~ghi** the Flemish.

fiancheggi'are [fjanked'dʒare] *vt* to border; (*fig*) to support, back (up); (*MIL*) to flank.

fi'anco, chi *sm* side; (*MIL*) flank; **di ~** sideways, from the side; **a ~ a ~** side by side.

fi'asco, schi *sm* flask; (*fig*) fiasco; **fare ~** to be a fiasco.

fi'ato *sm* breath; (*resistenza*) stamina; **avere il ~ grosso** to be out of breath; **prendere ~** to catch one's breath; **~i** *smpl* (*MUS*) wind instruments; **strumento a ~** wind instrument.

'**fibbia** *sf* buckle.

'**fibra** *sf* fibre; (*fig*) constitution.

fic'care *vt* to push, thrust, drive; **~rsi** *vr* (*andare a finire*) to get to.

'**fico, chi** *sm* (*pianta*) fig tree; (*frutto*) fig; **~ d'India** prickly pear; **~ secco** dried fig.

fidanza'mento [fidantsa'mento] *sm* engagement.

fidan'zarsi [fidan'tsarsi] *vr* to get engaged; **fidan'zato, a** *sm/f* fiancé/fiancée.

fi'darsi *vr*: **~ di** to trust; **fi'dato, a** *ag* reliable, trustworthy.

'**fido, a** *ag* faithful, loyal // *sm* (*COMM*) credit.

fi'ducia [fi'dutʃa] *sf* confidence, trust; **incarico di ~** position of trust, responsible position; **persona di ~** reliable person.

fi'ele *sm* (*MED*) bile; (*fig*) bitterness.

fie'nile *sm* barn; hayloft.

fi'eno *sm* hay.

fi'era *sf* fair.

fie'rezza [fje'rettsa] *sf* pride.

fi'ero, a *ag* proud; (*crudele*) fierce, cruel; (*audace*) bold.

'**fifa** *sf* (*fam*): **aver ~** to have the jitters.

'**figlia** [fiʎʎa] *sf* daughter.

figli'astro, a [fiʎ'ʎastro] *sm/f* stepson/daughter.

'**figlio** [fiʎʎo] *sm* son; (*senza distinzione di sesso*) child; **~ di papà** spoilt, wealthy young man; **~ unico** only child; **figli'occio, a, ci, ce** *sm/f* godchild, godson/daughter.

fi'gura *sf* figure; (*forma, aspetto esterno*) form, shape; (*illustrazione*) picture, illustration; **far ~** to look smart; **fare una brutta ~** to make a bad impression.

figu'rare *vi* to appear // *vt*: **~rsi qc** to imagine sth; **~rsi** *vr*: **figurati!** imagine that!; **ti do noia?** — **ma figurati!** am I disturbing you? — not at all!

figura'tivo, a *ag* figurative.

figu'rina *sf* figurine; (*cartoncino*) picture card.

'**fila** *sf* row, line; (*coda*) queue; (*serie*) series, string; **di ~** in succession; **fare la ~** to queue; **in ~ indiana** in single file.

filantro'pia *sf* philanthropy.

fi'lare *vt* to spin // *vi* (*baco, ragno*) to spin; (*formaggio fuso*) to go stringy; (*discorso*) to hang together; (*fam*: *amoreggiare*) to go steady; (*muoversi a forte velocità*) to go at full speed; (: *andarsene lestamente*) to make o.s. scarce; **~ diritto** (*fig*) to toe the line.

filas'trocca, che *sf* nursery rhyme.

filate'lia *sf* philately, stamp collecting.

fi'lato, a *ag* spun // *sm* yarn; **3 giorni ~i** 3 days running *o* on end; **fila'tura** *sf* spinning; (*luogo*) spinning mill.

fi'letto *sm* (*di vite*) thread; (*di carne*) fillet.

fili'ale *ag* filial // *sf* (*di impresa*) branch.

fili'grana *sf (in oreficeria)* filigree; *(su carta)* watermark.

film *sm inv* film; **fil'mare** *vt* to film.

'filo *sm (anche fig)* thread; *(filato)* yarn; *(metallico)* wire; *(di lama, rasoio)* edge; **per ~ e per segno** in detail; **~ d'erba** blade of grass; **~ di perle** string of pearls; **~ spinato** barbed wire; **con un ~ di voce** in a whisper.

'filobus *sm inv* trolley bus.

filon'cino |filon'tʃino| *sm* ≈ French stick.

fi'lone *sm (di minerali)* seam, vein; *(pane)* ≈ Vienna loaf; *(fig)* trend.

filoso'fia *sf* philosophy; **fi'losofo, a** *sm/f* philosopher.

fil'trare *vt, vi* to filter.

'filtro *sm* filter; **~ dell'olio** *(AUT)* oil filter.

'filza |'filtsa| *sf (anche fig)* string.

fin *av*, *prep* = **fino**.

fi'nale *ag* final // *sm (di opera)* end, ending; *(: MUS)* finale // *sf (SPORT)* final; **finalità** *sf (scopo)* aim, purpose; **final'mente** *av* finally, at last.

fi'nanza |fi'nantsa| *sf* finance; **~e** *sfpl (di individuo, Stato)* finances; **finanzi'ario, a** *ag* financial; **finanzi'ere** *sm* financier; *(guardia di finanza: doganale)* customs officer; *(: tributaria)* inland revenue official.

finché |fin'ke| *cong (per tutto il tempo che)* as long as; *(fino al momento in cui)* until; **aspetta ~ io (non) sia ritornato** wait until I get back.

'fine *ag (lamina, carta)* thin; *(capelli, polvere)* fine; *(vista, udito)* keen, sharp; *(persona: raffinata)* refined, distinguished; *(osservazione)* subtle // *sf* end // *sm* aim, purpose; *(esito)* result, outcome; **secondo ~** ulterior motive; **in o alla ~** in the end, finally; **~ settimana** *sm o f inv* weekend.

fi'nestra *sf* window; **fines'trino** *sm (di treno, auto)* window.

'fingere |'findʒere| *vt* to feign; *(supporre)* to imagine, suppose; **~rsi** *vr:* **~rsi ubriaco/pazzo** to pretend to be drunk/mad; **~ di fare** to pretend to do.

fini'mondo *sm* pandemonium.

fi'nire *vt* to finish // *vi* to finish, end; **~ di fare** *(compiere)* to finish doing; *(smettere)* to stop doing; **~ in galera** to end up *o* finish up in prison; **fini'tura** *sf* finish.

finlan'dese *ag, sm (LING)* Finnish // *sm/f* Finn.

Fin'landia *sf:* **la ~** Finland.

'fino, a *ag (capelli, seta)* fine; *(oro)* pure; *(fig: acuto)* shrewd // *av (spesso troncato in fin: pure, anche)* even // *prep (spesso troncato in fin: tempo):* **fin quando?** till when?; *(: luogo):* **fin qui** as far as here; **~ a** *(tempo)* until, till; *(luogo)* as far as, (up) to; **fin da domani** from tomorrow onwards; **fin da ieri** since

yesterday; **fin dalla nascita** from *o* since birth.

fi'nocchio |fi'nɔkkjo| *sm* fennel; *(fam peg: pederasta)* queer.

fi'nora *av* up till now.

'finto, a *pp di* **fingere** // *ag* false; artificial // *sf* pretence, sham; *(SPORT)* feint; **far ~a (di fare)** to pretend (to do).

finzi'one |fin'tsjone| *sf* pretence, sham.

fi'occo, chi *sm (di nastro)* bow; *(di stoffa, lana)* flock; *(di neve)* flake; *(NAUT)* jib; **coi ~chi** *(fig)* first-rate; **~chi di granoturco** cornflakes.

fi'ocina |'fjɔtʃina| *sf* harpoon.

fi'oco, a, chi, che *ag* faint, dim.

fi'onda *sf* catapult.

fio'raio, a *sm/f* florist.

fi'ore *sm* flower; **~i** *smpl (CARTE)* clubs; **a fior d'acqua** on the surface of the water; **avere i nervi a fior di pelle** to be on edge.

fioren'tino, a *ag* Florentine.

fio'retto *sm (SCHERMA)* foil.

fio'rire *vi (rosa)* to flower; *(albero)* to blossom; *(fig)* to flourish.

Fi'renze |fi'rentse| *sf* Florence.

'firma *sf* signature; *(reputazione)* name.

fir'mare *vt* to sign.

fisar'monica, che *sf* accordion.

fis'cale *ag* fiscal, tax *cpd*; **medico ~** doctor employed by Social Security to verify cases of sick leave.

fischi'are |fis'kjare| *vi* to whistle // *vt* to whistle; *(attore)* to boo, hiss.

'fischio |'fiskjo| *sm* whistle.

'fisco *sm* tax authorities *pl*, ≈ Inland Revenue *(Brit)*, ≈ Internal Revenue Service *(US)*.

'fisico, a, ci, che *ag* physical // *sm/f* physicist // *sm* physique // *sf* physics *sg*.

fisiolo'gia |fizjolo'dʒia| *sf* physiology.

fisiono'mia *sf* face, physiognomy.

fisiotera'pia *sf* physiotherapy.

fis'sare *vt* to fix, fasten; *(guardare intensamente)* to stare at; *(data, condizioni)* to fix, establish, set; *(prenotare)* to book; **~rsi su** *(sog: sguardo, attenzione)* to focus on; *(fig: idea)* to become obsessed with; **fissazi'one** *sf (PSIC)* fixation.

'fisso, a *ag* fixed; *(stipendio, impiego)* regular // *av:* **guardare ~ qc/qn** to stare at sth/sb.

'fitta *sf vedi* **fitto.**

fit'tizio, a *ag* fictitious, imaginary.

'fitto, a *ag* thick, dense; *(pioggia)* heavy // *sm* depths *pl*, middle; *(affitto, pigione)* rent // *sf* sharp pain.

fi'ume *sm* river.

fiu'tare *vt* to smell, sniff; *(sog: animale)* to scent; *(fig: inganno)* to get wind of, smell; **~ tabacco/cocaina** to take snuff/cocaine; **fi'uto** *sm* (sense of) smell; *(fig)* nose.

fla'gello |fla'dʒello| *sm* scourge.

fla'grante *ag* flagrant; **cogliere qn in ~** to catch sb red-handed.

fla'nella *sf* flannel.

flash |flaʃ| *sm inv (FOT)* flash; *(giornalistico)* newsflash.

'flauto *sm* flute.

'flebile *ag* faint, feeble.

'flemma *sf (calma)* coolness, phlegm; *(MED)* phlegm.

fles'sibile *ag* pliable; *(fig: che si adatta)* flexible.

'flesso, a *pp di* **flettere**.

fles'so'oo, a *ag* supple, lithe; *(andatura)* flowing, graceful.

'flettere *vt* to bend.

F.lli *abbr* (= *fratelli*) Bros.

'flora *sf* flora.

'florido, a *ag* flourishing; *(fig)* glowing with health.

'floscio, a, sci, sce |'floʃʃo| *ag (cappello)* floppy, soft; *(muscoli)* flabby.

'flotta *sf* fleet.

'fluido, a *ag, sm* fluid.

flu'ire *vi* to flow.

fluo'ro *sm* fluorine.

fluo'ruro *sm* fluoride.

'flusso *sm* flow; *(FISICA, MED)* flux; **~ e riflusso** ebb and flow.

fluttu'are *vi* to rise and fall; *(ECON)* to fluctuate.

fluvi'ale *ag* river *cpd*, fluvial.

'foca, che *sf (ZOOL)* seal.

fo'caccia, ce |fo'kattʃa| *sf kind of pizza; (dolce)* bun.

'foce |'fotʃe| *sf (GEO)* mouth.

foco'laio *sm (MED)* centre of infection; *(fig)* hotbed.

foco'lare *sm* hearth, fireside; *(TECN)* furnace.

'fodera *sf (di vestito)* lining; *(di libro, poltrona)* cover; **fode'rare** *vt* to line; to cover.

'fodero *sm (di spada)* scabbard; *(di pugnale)* sheath; *(di pistola)* holster.

'foga *sf* enthusiasm, ardour.

'foggia, ge |'foddʒa| *sf (maniera)* style; *(aspetto)* form, shape; *(moda)* fashion, style.

'foglia |'foʎʎa| *sf* leaf; **~ d'argento/d'oro** silver/gold leaf; **fogli'ame** *sm* foliage, leaves *pl*.

'foglio |'foʎʎo| *sm (di carta)* sheet (of paper); *(di metallo)* sheet; *(documento)* document; *(banconota)* (bank)note; **~ rosa** *(AUT)* provisional licence; **~ di via** *(DIR)* expulsion order; **~ volante** pamphlet.

'fogna |'foɲɲa| *sf* drain, sewer; **fo-gna'tura** *sf* drainage, sewerage.

folgo'rare *vt (sog: fulmine)* to strike down; *(: alta tensione)* to electrocute.

'folla *sf* crowd, throng.

'folle *ag* mad, insane; *(TECN)* idle; **in ~** *(AUT)* in neutral.

fol'lia *sf* folly, foolishness; foolish act;

(pazzia) madness, lunacy.

'folto, a *ag* thick.

fomen'tare *vt* to stir up, foment.

fondamen'tale *ag* fundamental, basic.

fonda'mento *sm* foundation; **~a** *sfpl (EDIL)* foundations.

fon'dare *vt* to found; *(fig: dar base):* **~ qc su** to base sth on; **fondazi'one** *sf* foundation.

'fondere *vt (neve)* to melt; *(metallo)* to fuse, melt; *(fig: colori)* to merge, blend; *(: imprese, gruppi)* to merge // *vi* to melt; **~rsi** *vr* to melt; *(fig: partiti, correnti)* to unite, merge; **fonde'ria** *sf* foundry.

'fondo, a *ag* deep // *sm (di recipiente, pozzo)* bottom; *(di stanza)* back; *(quantità di liquido che resta, deposito)* dregs *pl*; *(sfondo)* background; *(unità immobiliare)* property, estate; *(somma di denaro)* fund; *(SPORT)* long-distance race; **~i** *smpl (denaro)* funds; **a notte ~a** at dead of night; **in ~ a** at the bottom of; **at the back of;** *(strada)* at the end of; **andare a ~** *(nave)* to sink; **conoscere a ~** to know inside out; **dar ~ a** *(fig: provviste, soldi)* to use up; **in ~** *(fig)* after all, all things considered; **andare fino in ~ a** *(fig)* to examine thoroughly; **a ~ perduto** *(COMM)* without security; **~i di caffè** coffee grounds; **~i di magazzino** old *o* unsold stock *sg*.

fo'netica *sf* phonetics *sg*.

fon'tana *sf* fountain.

'fonte *sf* spring, source; *(fig)* source // *sm:* **~ battesimale** *(REL)* font.

fo'raggio |fo'raddʒo| *sm* fodder, forage.

fo'rare *vt* to pierce, make a hole in; *(pallone)* to burst; *(biglietto)* to punch; **~ una gomma** to burst a tyre *(Brit) o* tire *(US)*.

'forbici |'forbitʃi| *sfpl* scissors.

'forca, che *sf (AGR)* fork, pitchfork; *(patibolo)* gallows *sg*.

for'cella |for'tʃella| *sf (TECN)* fork; *(di monte)* pass.

for'chetta |for'ketta| *sf* fork.

for'cina |for'tʃina| *sf* hairpin.

'forcipe |'fortʃipe| *sm* forceps *pl*.

fo'resta *sf* forest.

foresti'ero, a *ag* foreign // *sm/f* foreigner.

'forfora *sf* dandruff.

'forgia, ge |'fordʒa| *sf* forge; **forgi'are** *vt* to forge.

'forma *sf* form; *(aspetto esteriore)* form, shape; *(DIR: procedura)* procedure; *(per calzature)* last; *(stampo da cucina)* mould; **~e** *sfpl (del corpo)* figure, shape; **le ~e** *(convenzioni)* appearances; **essere in ~** to be in good shape.

formag'gino |formad'dʒino| *sm* processed cheese.

for'maggio |for'maddʒo| *sm* cheese.

for'male *ag* formal; **formalità** *sf inv*

formality.

for'mare *vt* to form, shape, make; (*numero di telefono*) to dial; (*fig: carattere*) to form, mould; **~rsi** *vr* to form, take shape; **for'mato** *sm* format, size; **formazi'one** *sf* formation; (*fig: educazione*) training.

for'mica, che *sf* ant; **formi'caio** *sm* anthill.

formico'lare *vi* (*gamba, braccio*) to tingle; (*brulicare: anche fig*): **~ di** to be swarming with; **mi formicola la gamba** I've got pins and needles in my leg, my leg's tingling; **formico'lio** *sm* pins and needles *pl*; swarming.

formi'dabile *ag* powerful, formidable; (*straordinario*) remarkable.

'formula *sf* formula; **~ di cortesia** courtesy form.

formu'lare *vt* to formulate; to express.

for'nace [for'natʃe] *sf* (*per laterizi etc*) kiln; (*per metalli*) furnace.

for'naio *sm* baker.

for'nello *sm* (*elettrico, a gas*) ring; (*di pipa*) bowl.

for'nire *vt*: **~ qn di qc, ~ qc a qn** to provide *o* supply sb with sth, to supply sth to sb.

'forno *sm* (*di cucina*) oven; (*panetteria*) bakery; (*TECN: per calce etc*) kiln; (*: per metalli*) furnace.

'foro *sm* (*buco*) hole; (*STORIA*) forum; (*tribunale*) (law) court.

'forse *av* perhaps, maybe; (*circa*) about; **essere in ~** to be in doubt.

forsen'nato, a *ag* mad, insane.

'forte *ag* strong; (*suono*) loud; (*spesa*) considerable, great; (*passione, dolore*) great, deep // *av* strongly; (*velocemente*) fast; (*a voce alta*) loud(ly); (*violentemente*) hard // *sm* (*edificio*) fort; (*specialità*) forte, strong point; **essere ~ in qc** to be good at sth.

for'tezza [for'tettsa] *sf* (*morale*) strength; (*luogo fortificato*) fortress.

for'tuito, a *ag* fortuitous, chance.

for'tuna *sf* (*destino*) fortune, luck; (*buona sorte*) success, fortune; (*eredità, averi*) fortune; **per ~** luckily, fortunately; **di ~** makeshift, improvised; **atterraggio di ~** emergency landing; **fortu'nato, a** *ag* lucky, fortunate; (*coronato da successo*) successful.

forvi'are *vt, vi* = **fuorviare**.

'forza [ˈfortsa] *sf* strength; (*potere*) power; (*FISICA*) force; **~e** *sfpl* (*fisiche*) strength *sg*; (*MIL*) forces // *escl* come on!; **per ~** against one's will; (*naturalmente*) of course; **a viva ~** by force; **a ~ di** by dint of; **~ maggiore** circumstances beyond one's control; **la ~ pubblica** the police *pl*; **le ~e armate** the armed forces.

for'zare [for'tsare] *vt* to force; **~ qn a fare** to force sb to do; **for'zato, a** *ag* forced // *sm* (*DIR*) prisoner sentenced to hard labour.

fos'chia [fos'kia] *sf* mist, haze.

'fosco, a, schi, sche *ag* dark, gloomy.

'fosforo *sm* phosphorous.

'fossa *sf* pit; (*di cimitero*) grave; **~ biologica** septic tank.

fos'sato *sm* ditch; (*di fortezza*) moat.

fos'setta *sf* dimple.

'fossile *ag, sm* fossil.

'fosso *sm* ditch; (*MIL*) trench.

'foto *sf* photo // *prefisso*: **foto'copia** *sf* photocopy; **fotocopi'are** *vt* to photocopy; **fotogra'fare** *vt* to photograph; **fotogra'fia** *sf* (*procedimento*) photography; (*immagine*) photograph; **fare una fotografia** to take a photograph; **una fotografia a colori/in bianco e nero** a colour/black and white photograph; **fo'tografo, a** *sm/f* photographer; **fotoro'manzo** *sm* romantic picture story.

fra *prep* = **tra**.

fracas'sare *vt* to shatter, smash; **~rsi** *vr* to shatter, smash; (*veicolo*) to crash; **fra'casso** *sm* smash; crash; (*baccano*) din, racket.

'fradicio, a, ci, ce [ˈfraditʃo] *ag* (*molto bagnato*) soaking (wet); **ubriaco ~** blind drunk.

'fragile [ˈfradʒile] *ag* fragile; (*fig: salute*) delicate.

'fragola *sf* strawberry.

fra'gore *sm* roar; (*di tuono*) rumble.

frago'roso, a *ag* deafening.

fra'grante *ag* fragrant.

frain'tendere *vt* to misunderstand; **frain'teso, a** *pp di* **fraintendere**.

fram'mento *sm* fragment.

'frana *sf* landslide; (*fig: persona*): **essere una ~** to be useless; **fra'nare** *vi* to slip, slide down.

fran'cese [fran'tʃeze] *ag* French // *sm/f* Frenchman/woman // *sm* (*LING*) French; **i F~i** the French.

fran'chezza [fran'kettsa] *sf* frankness, openness.

'Francia [ˈfrantʃa] *sf*: **la ~** France.

'franco, a, chi, che *ag* (*COMM*) free; (*sincero*) frank, open, sincere // *sm* (*moneta*) franc; **farla ~a** (*fig*) to get off scot-free; **~ di dogana** duty-free; **~ a domicilio** delivered free of charge; **prezzo ~ fabbrica** ex-works price; **~ tiratore** *sm* sniper.

franco'bollo *sm* (postage) stamp.

fran'gente [fran'dʒente] *sm* (*onda*) breaker; (*scoglio emergente*) reef; (*circostanza*) situation, circumstance.

'frangia, ge [ˈfrandʒa] *sf* fringe.

frantu'mare *vt*, **~rsi** *vr* to break into pieces, shatter.

frap'pé *sm* milk shake.

'frasca, sche *sf* (leafy) branch.

'frase *sf* (*LING*) sentence; (*locuzione*,

espressione, MUS) phrase; ~ **fatta** set phrase.

'**frassino** *sm* ash (tree).

frastagli'ato, a |frastaʎ'ʎato| *ag* (*costa*) indented, jagged.

frastor'nare *vt* to daze; to befuddle.

frastu'ono *sm* hubbub, din.

'**frate** *sm* friar, monk.

fratel'lanza |fratel'lantsa| *sf* brotherhood; (*associazione*) fraternity.

fratel'lastro *sm* stepbrother.

fra'tello *sm* brother; ~i *smpl* brothers; (*nel senso di fratelli e sorelle*) brothers and sisters.

fra'terno, a *ag* fraternal, brotherly.

frat'tanto *av* in the meantime, meanwhile.

frat'tempo *sm*: **nel ~** in the meantime, meanwhile.

frat'tura *sf* fracture; (*fig*) split, break.

frazi'one |frat'tsjone| *sf* fraction; (*borgata*): ~ **di comune** hamlet.

'**freccia, ce** |'frettʃa| *sf* arrow; ~ **di direzione** (AUT) indicator.

fred'dare *vt* to shoot dead.

fred'dezza |fred'dettsa| *sf* coldness.

'**freddo, a** *ag, sm* cold; **fa** ~ it's cold; **aver** ~ to be cold; **a** ~ (*fig*) deliberately; **freddo'loso, a** *ag* sensitive to the cold.

fred'dura *sf* pun.

fre'gare *vt* to rub; (*fam: truffare*) to take in, cheat; (: *rubare*) to swipe, pinch; **fregarsene** (*fam!*): **chi se ne frega?** who gives a damn (about it)?

fre'gata *sf* rub; (*fam*) swindle; (NAUT) frigate.

'**fregio** |'fredʒo| *sm* (ARCHIT) frieze; (*ornamento*) decoration.

'**fremere** *vi*: ~ **di** to tremble o quiver with; '**fremito** *sm* tremor, quiver.

fre'nare *vt* (*veicolo*) to slow down; (*cavallo*) to rein in; (*lacrime*) to re strain, hold back // *vi* to brake; ~**rsi** *vr* (*fig*) to restrain o.s., control o.s.; **fre'nata** *sf*: **fare una frenata** to brake.

frene'sia *sf* frenzy.

'**freno** *sm* brake; (*morso*) bit; ~ **a disco** disc brake; ~ **a mano** handbrake; **tenere a ~** to restrain.

frequen'tare *vt* (*scuola, corso*) to attend; (*locale, bar*) to go to, frequent; (*persone*) to see (often).

fre'quente *ag* frequent; **di** ~ frequently; **fre'quenza** *sf* frequency; (INS) attendance.

fres'chezza |fres'kettsa| *sf* freshness.

'**fresco, a, schi, sche** *ag* fresh; (*temperatura*) cool; (*notizia*) recent, fresh // *sm*: **godere il** ~ to enjoy the cool air; **stare** ~ (*fig*) to be in for it; **mettere al** ~ to put in a cool place.

'**fretta** *sf* hurry, haste; **in** ~ in a hurry; **in** ~ **e furia** in a mad rush; **aver** ~ to be in a hurry; **fretto'loso, a** *ag* (*persona*) in a hurry; (*lavoro etc*) hurried, rushed.

fri'abile *ag* (*terreno*) friable; (*pasta*) crumbly.

'**friggere** |'friddʒere| *vt* to fry // *vi* (*olio etc*) to sizzle.

'**frigido, a** |'fridʒido| *ag* (MED) frigid.

'**frigo** *sm* fridge.

frigo'rifero, a *ag* refrigerating // *sm* refrigerator.

fringu'ello *sm* chaffinch.

frit'tata *sf* omelette; **fare una** ~ (*fig*) to make a mess of things.

frit'tella *sf* (CUC) pancake; (: *ripiena*) fritter.

'**fritto, a** *pp di* **friggere** // *ag* fried // *sm* fried food; ~ **misto** mixed fry.

frit'tura *sf* (CUC): ~ **di pesce** mixed fried fish.

'**frivolo, a** *ag* frivolous.

frizi'one |frit'tsjone| *sf* friction; (*di pelle*) rub, rub-down; (AUT) clutch.

friz'zante |frid'dzante| *ag* (*anche fig*) sparkling.

'**frizzo** |'friddzo| *sm* witticism.

fro'dare *vt* to defraud, cheat.

'**frode** *sf* fraud; ~ **fiscale** tax evasion.

'**frollo, a** *ag* (*carne*) tender; (: *di selvaggina*) high; (*fig: persona*) soft; **pa sta** ~**a** short(crust) pastry.

'**fronda** *sf* (leafy) branch; (*di partito politico*) internal opposition; ~**e** *sfpl* foli age *sg*.

fron'tale *ag* frontal; (*scontro*) head-on.

'**fronte** *sf* (ANAT) forehead; (*di edificio*) front, façade // *sm* (MIL, POL, METEOR) front; **a** ~, **di** ~ facing, opposite; **di** ~ **a** (*posizione*) opposite, facing, in front of; (*a paragone di*) compared with.

fronteggi'are |fronted'dʒare| *vt* (*avversari, difficoltà*) to face, stand up to; (*spese*) to cope with.

fronti'era *sf* border, frontier.

'**fronzolo** |'frondzolo| *sm* frill.

'**frottola** *sf* fib; ~**e** *sfpl* nonsense *sg*.

fru'gare *vi* to rummage // *vt* to search.

frul'lare *vt* (CUC) to whisk // *vi* (*uccelli*) to flutter; **frul'lato** *sm* milk shake; fruit drink; **frulla'tore** *sm* electric mixer; **frul'lino** *sm* whisk.

fru'mento *sm* wheat.

fru'scio |fruʃ'ʃio| *sm* rustle; rustling; (*di acque*) murmur.

'**frusta** *sf* whip; (CUC) whisk.

frus'tare *vt* to whip.

frus'tino *sm* riding crop.

frus'trare *vt* to frustrate.

'**frutta** *sf* fruit; (*portata*) dessert; ~ **candita/secca** candied/dried fruit.

frut'tare *vi* to bear dividends, give a re turn.

frut'teto *sm* orchard.

frutti'vendolo, a *sm/f* greengrocer (Brit), produce dealer (US).

'**frutto** *sm* fruit; (*fig: risultato*) re sult(s); (ECON: *interesse*) interest; (: *reddito*) income; ~**i di mare** seafood *sg*.

FS *abbr* = Ferrovie dello Stato.

fu *vb vedi* **essere** // *ag inv*: **il ~ Paolo Bianchi** the late Paolo Bianchi.

fuci'lare |futʃi'lare| *vt* to shoot; **fuci'lata** *sf* rifle shot.

fu'cile |fu'tʃile| *sm* rifle, gun; *(da caccia)* shotgun, gun.

fu'cina |fu'tʃina| *sf* forge.

'fuga *sf* escape, flight; *(di gas, liquidi)* leak; *(MUS)* fugue; **~ di cervelli** brain drain.

fu'gace |fu'gatʃe| *ag* fleeting, transient.

fug'gevole |fud'dʒevole| *ag* fleeting.

fuggi'asco, a, schi, sche |fud'dʒasko| *ag, sm/f* fugitive.

fuggi'fuggi |fuddʒi'fuddʒi| *sm* scramble, stampede.

fug'gire |fud'dʒire| *vi* to flee, run away; *(fig: passar veloce)* to fly // *vt* to avoid; **fuggi'tivo, a** *sm/f* fugitive, runaway.

ful'gore *sm* brilliance, splendour.

fu'liggine |fu'liddʒine| *sf* soot.

fulmi'nare *vt* (*sog: fulmine*) to strike; (: *elettricità*) to electrocute; (*con arma da fuoco*) to shoot dead; (*fig: con lo sguardo*) to look daggers at.

'fulmine *sm* thunderbolt; lightning *q*.

fumai'olo *sm* (*di nave*) funnel; (*di fabbrica*) chimney.

fu'mare *vi* to smoke; (*emettere vapore*) to steam // *vt* to smoke; **fu'mata** *sf* (*segnale*) smoke signal; **farsi una fumata** to have a smoke; **fuma'tore, 'trice** *sm/f* smoker.

fu'metto *sm* comic strip; **~i** *smpl* comics.

'fumo *sm* smoke; (*vapore*) steam; (*il fumare tabacco*) smoking; **~i** *smpl* fumes; **i ~i dell'alcool** the after-effects of drink; **vendere ~** to deceive, cheat; **fu'moso, a** *ag* smoky; (*fig*) muddled.

fu'nambolo, a *sm/f* tightrope walker.

'fune *sf* rope, cord; (*più grossa*) cable.

'funebre *ag* (*rito*) funeral; (*aspetto*) gloomy, funereal.

fune'rale *sm* funeral.

'fungere |'fundʒere| *vi*: **~ da** to act as.

'fungo, ghi *sm* fungus; (*commestibile*) mushroom; **~ velenoso** toadstool.

funico'lare *sf* funicular railway.

funi'via *sf* cable railway.

funzio'nare |funtsjo'nare| *vi* to work, function; (*fungere*): **~ da** to act as.

funzio'nario |funtsjo'narjo| *sm* official.

funzi'one |fun'tsjone| *sf* function; (*carica*) post, position; (*REL*) service; **in ~** (*meccanismo*) in operation; **in ~ di** (*come*) as; **fare la ~ di qn** (*farne le veci*) to take sb's place.

fu'oco, chi *sm* fire; (*fornello*) ring; (*FOT, FISICA*) focus; **dare ~ a qc** to set fire to sth; **far ~** (*sparare*) to fire; **~ d'artificio** firework.

fuorché |fwor'ke| *cong, prep* except.

fu'ori *av* outside; (*all'aperto*) outdoors,

outside; (*fuori di casa, SPORT*) out; (*esclamativo*) get out! // *prep*: **~ (di)** out of, outside // *sm* outside; **lasciar ~ qc/qn** to leave sth/sb out; **far ~ qn** (*fam*) to kill sb, do sb in; **essere ~ di sé** to be beside o.s.; **~ luogo** (*inopportuno*) out of place, uncalled for; **~ mano** out of the way, remote; **~ pericolo** out of danger; **~ uso** old-fashioned; obsolete.

fu'ori... *prefisso*: **fuori'bordo** *sm inv* speedboat (with outboard motor); outboard motor; **fuori'classe** *sm/f inv* (undisputed) champion; **fuorigi'oco** *sm* offside; **fuori'legge** *sm/f inv* outlaw; **fuori'serie** *ag inv* (*auto etc*) custom-built // *sf* custom-built car; **fuori'strada** *sm* (*AUT*) cross-country vehicle; **fuoru'scito, a, fuoriu'scito, a** *sm/f* exile; **fuorvi'are** *vt* to mislead; (*fig*) to lead astray // *vi* to go astray.

'furbo, a *ag* clever, smart; (*peg*) cunning.

fu'rente *ag*: **~ (contro)** furious (with).

fur'fante *sm* rascal, scoundrel.

fur'gone *sm* van.

'furia *sf* (*ira*) fury, rage; (*fig: impeto*) fury, violence; (*fretta*) rush; **a ~ di** by dint of; **andare su tutte le ~e** to get into a towering rage; **furi'bondo, a** *ag* furious.

furi'oso, a *ag* furious; (*mare, vento*) raging.

fu'rore *sm* fury; (*esaltazione*) frenzy; **far ~** to be all the rage.

fur'tivo, a *ag* furtive.

'furto *sm* theft; **~ con scasso** burglary.

'fusa *sfpl*: **fare le ~** to purr.

fu'sibile *sm* (*ELETTR*) fuse.

fusi'one *sf* (*di metalli*) fusion, melting; (*colata*) casting; (*COMM*) merger; (*fig*) merging.

'fuso, a *pp di* **fondere** // *sm* (*FILATURA*) spindle; **~ orario** time zone.

fus'tagno |fus'taɲɲo| *sm* corduroy.

fus'tino *sm* (*di detersivo*) tub.

'fusto *sm* stem; (*ANAT, di albero*) trunk; (*recipiente*) drum, can.

fu'turo, a *ag, sm* future.

G

gab'bare *vt* to take in, dupe; **~rsi** *vr*: **~rsi di qn** to make fun of sb.

'gabbia *sf* cage; (*DIR*) dock; (*da imballaggio*) crate; **~ dell'ascensore** lift (*Brit*) *o* elevator (*US*) shaft; **~ toracica** (*ANAT*) rib cage.

gabbi'ano *sm* (sea)gull.

gabi'netto *sm* (*MED etc*) consulting room; (*POL*) ministry; (*di decenza*) toilet, lavatory; (*INS: di fisica etc*) laboratory.

'gaffe |gaf| *sf inv* blunder.

gagli'ardo, a |gaʎ'ʎardo| *ag* strong,

vigorous.

'gaio, a *ag* cheerful, gay.

'gala *sf* (*sfarzo*) pomp; (*festa*) gala.

ga'lante *ag* gallant, courteous; (*avventura*) amorous; **galante'ria** *sf* gallantry.

galantu'omo, *pl* **galantu'omini** *sm* gentleman.

ga'lassia *sf* galaxy.

gala'teo *sm* (good) manners *pl*.

gale'otto *sm* (*rematore*) galley slave; (*carcerato*) convict.

ga'lera *sf* (*NAUT*) galley; (*prigione*) prison.

'galla *sf*: a ~ afloat; venire a ~ to surface, come to the surface; (*fig*: *verità*) to come out.

galleggi'ante [galled'dʒante] *ag* floating // *sm* (*natante*) barge; (*di pescatore, lenza, TECN*) float.

galleggi'are [galled'dʒare] *vi* to float.

galle'ria *sf* (*traforo*) tunnel; (*ARCHIT, d'arte*) gallery; (*TEATRO*) circle; (*strada coperta con negozi*) arcade.

'Galles *sm*: il ~ Wales; **gal'lese** *ag, sm* (*LING*) Welsh // *sm/f* Welshman/woman.

gal'letta *sf* cracker.

gal'lina *sf* hen.

'gallo *sm* cock.

gal'lone *sm* piece of braid; (*MIL*) stripe; (*unità di misura*) gallon.

galop'pare *vi* to gallop.

ga'loppo *sm* gallop; al *o* di ~ at a gallop.

'gamba *sf* leg; (*asta*: *di lettera*) stem; in ~ (*in buona salute*) well; (*bravo, sveglio*) bright, smart; **prendere qc sotto ~** (*fig*) to treat sth too lightly.

gambe'retto *sm* shrimp.

'gambero *sm* (*di acqua dolce*) crayfish; (*di mare*) prawn.

'gambo *sm* stem; (*di frutta*) stalk.

'gamma *sf* (*MUS*) scale; (*di colori, fig*) range.

ga'nascia, sce [ga'naʃʃa] *sf* jaw; ~sce del freno (*AUT*) brake shoes.

'gancio ['gantʃo] *sm* hook.

'gangheri ['gangeri] *smpl*: uscire dai ~ (*fig*) to fly into a temper.

'gara *sf* competition; (*SPORT*) competition; contest; match; (: *corsa*) race; fare a ~ to compete, vie.

ga'rage [ga'raʒ] *sm inv* garage.

garan'tire *vt* to guarantee; (*debito*) to stand surety for; (*dare per certo*) to assure.

garan'zia [garan'tsia] *sf* guarantee; (*pegno*) security.

gar'bato, a *ag* courteous, polite.

'garbo *sm* (*buone maniere*) politeness, courtesy; (*di vestito etc*) grace, style.

gareggi'are [gared'dʒare] *vi* to compete.

garga'rismo *sm* gargle; fare i ~i to gargle.

ga'rofano *sm* carnation; **chiodo di ~** clove.

'garza ['gardza] *sf* (*per bende*) gauze.

gar'zone [gar'dzone] *sm* (*di negozio*) boy.

gas *sm inv* gas; a tutto ~ at full speed; dare ~ (*AUT*) to accelerate.

ga'solio *sm* diesel (oil).

ga's(s)ato, a *ag* (*bibita*) aerated, fizzy.

gas'soso, a *ag* gaseous; gassy // *sf* fizzy drink.

gastrono'mia *sf* gastronomy.

gat'tino *sm* kitten.

'gatto, a *sm/f* cat, tomcat/she-cat; ~ selvatico wildcat; ~ delle nevi (*AUT, SCI*) snowcat.

gatto'pardo *sm*: ~ africano serval; ~ americano ocelot.

'gaudio *sm* joy, happiness.

ga'vetta *sf* (*MIL*) mess tin; venire dalla ~ (*MIL, fig*) to rise from the ranks.

'gazza ['gaddza] *sf* magpie.

gaz'zella [gad'dzɛlla] *sf* gazelle; (*dei carabinieri*) (high-speed) police car.

gaz'zetta [gad'dzetta] *sf* news sheet; G~ Ufficiale *official publication containing details of new laws*.

gel [dʒɛl] *sm inv* gel.

ge'lare [dʒe'lare] *vt, vi, vb impers* to freeze; **ge'lata** *sf* frost.

gelate'ria [dʒelate'ria] *sf* ice-cream shop.

gela'tina [dʒela'tina] *sf* gelatine; ~ esplosiva dynamite; ~ di frutta fruit jelly.

ge'lato, a [dʒe'lato] *ag* frozen // *sm* ice cream.

'gelido, a ['dʒɛlido] *ag* icy, ice-cold.

'gelo ['dʒɛlo] *sm* (*temperatura*) intense cold; (*brina*) frost; (*fig*) chill; **ge'lone** *sm* chilblain.

gelo'sia [dʒelo'sia] *sf* jealousy.

ge'loso, a [dʒe'loso] *ag* jealous.

'gelso ['dʒɛlso] *sm* mulberry (tree).

gelso'mino [dʒelso'mino] *sm* jasmine.

ge'mello, a [dʒe'mɛllo] *ag, sm/f* twin; ~i *smpl* (*di camicia*) cufflinks; (*dello zodiaco*) G~i Gemini *sg*.

'gemere ['dʒɛmere] *vi* to moan, groan; (*cigolare*) to creak; (*gocciolare*) to drip, ooze; **'gemito** *sm* moan, groan.

'gemma ['dʒɛmma] *sf* (*BOT*) bud; (*pietra preziosa*) gem.

gene'rale [dʒene'rale] *ag, sm* general; in ~ (*per sommi capi*) in general terms; (*di solito*) usually, in general; a ~ richiesta by popular request; **generalità** *sfpl* (*dati d'identità*) particulars; **generaliz'zare** *vt, vi* to generalize; **general'mente** *av* generally.

gene'rare [dʒene'rare] *vt* (*dar vita*) to give birth to; (*produrre*) to produce; (*causare*) to arouse; (*TECN*) to produce, generate; **genera'tore** *sm* (*TECN*) generator; **generazi'one** *sf* generation.

'genere ['dʒɛnere] *sm* kind, type, sort; (*BIOL*) genus; (*merce*) article, product; (*LING*) gender; (*ARTE, LETTERATURA*) genre; **in ~** generally, as a rule; **il ~ umano** mankind; **~i alimentari** food-stuffs.

ge'nerico, a, ci, che [dʒe'nɛriko] *ag* generic; (*vago*) vague, imprecise.

'genero ['dʒɛnero] *sm* son-in-law.

generosità [dʒenerosi'ta] *sf* generosity.

gene'roso, a [dʒene'roso] *ag* generous.

ge'netico, a, ci, che [dʒe'nɛtiko] *ag* genetic // *sf* genetics *sg*.

gen'giva [dʒen'dʒiva] *sf* (ANAT) gum.

geni'ale [dʒen'jale] *ag* (*persona*) of genius; (*idea*) ingenious, brilliant.

'genio ['dʒɛnjo] *sm* genius; **andare a ~ a qn** to be to sb's liking, appeal to sb.

geni'tale [dʒeni'tale] *ag* genital; **~i** *smpl* genitals.

geni'tore [dʒeni'tore] *sm* parent, father *o* mother; **~i** *smpl* parents.

gen'naio [dʒen'najo] *sm* January.

'Genova ['dʒɛnova] *sf* Genoa.

gen'taglia [dʒen'taʎʎa] *sf* (*peg*) rabble.

'gente ['dʒɛnte] *sf* people *pl*.

gen'tile [dʒen'tile] *ag* (*persona, atto*) kind; (: *garbato*) courteous, polite; (*nelle lettere*): **G~ Signore** Dear Sir; (: *sulla busta*): **G~ Signor Fernando Villa** Mr Fernando Villa; **genti'lezza** *sf* kindness; courtesy, politeness; **per gentilezza** (*per favore*) please.

gentilu'omo, *pl* **gentilu'omini** [dʒenti'lwɔmo] *sm* gentleman.

genu'ino, a [dʒenu'ino] *ag* (*prodotto*) natural; (*persona, sentimento*) genuine, sincere.

geogra'fia [dʒeogra'fia] *sf* geography.

geolo'gia [dʒeolo'dʒia] *sf* geology.

ge'ometra, i, e [dʒe'ɔmetra] *sm/f* (*professionista*) surveyor.

geome'tria [dʒeome'tria] *sf* geometry; **geo'metrico, a, ci, che** *ag* geometric(al).

ge'ranio [dʒe'ranjo] *sm* geranium.

gerar'chia [dʒerar'kia] *sf* hierarchy.

ge'rente [dʒe'rɛnte] *sm/f* manager/manageress.

'gergo, ghi ['dʒɛrgo] *sm* jargon; slang.

geria'tria [dʒerja'tria] *sf* geriatrics *sg*.

Ger'mania [dʒer'manja] *sf*: **la ~** Germany; **la ~ occidentale/orientale** West/East Germany.

'germe ['dʒɛrme] *sm* germ; (*fig*) seed.

germogli'are [dʒermoʎ'ʎare] *vi* to sprout; to germinate; **ger'moglio** *sm* shoot; bud.

gero'glifico, ci [dʒero'glifiko] *sm* hieroglyphic.

'gesso ['dʒɛsso] *sm* chalk; (SCULTURA, MED, EDIL) plaster; (*statua*) plaster figure; (*minerale*) gypsum.

gesti'one [dʒes'tjone] *sf* management.

ges'tire [dʒes'tire] *vt* to run, manage.

'gesto ['dʒɛsto] *sm* gesture.

ges'tore [dʒes'tore] *sm* manager.

Gesù [dʒe'zu] *sm* Jesus.

gesu'ita, i [dʒezu'ita] *sm* Jesuit.

get'tare [dʒet'tare] *vt* to throw; (*anche:* **~ via**) to throw away *o* out; (SCULTURA) to cast; (EDIL) to lay; (*acqua*) to spout; (*grido*) to utter; **~rsi** *vr*: **~rsi in** (*sog: fiume*) to flow into; **~ uno sguardo su** to take a quick look at; **get'tata** *sf* (*di cemento, gesso, metalli*) cast; (*diga*) jetty.

'getto ['dʒɛtto] *sm* (*di gas, liquido, AER*) jet; **a ~ continuo** uninterruptedly; **di ~** (*fig*) straight off, in one go.

get'tone [dʒet'tone] *sm* token; (*per giochi*) counter; (: *roulette etc*) chip; **~ telefonico** telephone token.

ghiacci'aio [gjat'tʃajo] *sm* glacier.

ghiacci'are [gjat'tʃare] *vt* to freeze; (*fig*): **~ qn** to make sb's blood run cold // *vi* to freeze, ice over; **ghiacci'ato, a** *ag* frozen; (*bevanda*) ice-cold.

ghi'accio ['gjattʃo] *sm* ice.

ghiacci'olo [gjat'tʃɔlo] *sm* icicle; (*tipo di gelato*) ice lolly (*Brit*), popsicle (*US*).

ghi'aia ['gjaja] *sf* gravel.

ghi'anda ['gjanda] *sf* (BOT) acorn.

ghi'andola ['gjandola] *sf* gland.

ghigliot'tina [giʎʎot'tina] *sf* guillotine.

ghi'gnare [giɲ'ɲare] *vi* to sneer.

ghi'otto, a ['gjotto] *ag* greedy; (*cibo*) delicious, appetizing; **ghiot'tone, a** *sm/f* glutton.

ghiri'bizzo [giri'biddzo] *sm* whim.

ghiri'goro [giri'gɔro] *sm* scribble, squiggle.

ghir'landa [gir'landa] *sf* garland, wreath.

'ghiro ['giro] *sm* dormouse.

'ghisa ['giza] *sf* cast iron.

già [dʒa] *av* already; (*ex, in precedenza*) formerly // *escl* of course!, yes indeed!

gl'acca, che ['dʒakka] *sf* jacket; **~ a vento** windcheater (*Brit*), windbreaker (*US*).

giacché [dʒak'ke] *cong* since, as.

giac'chetta [dʒak'ketta] *sf* (light) jacket.

gia'cenza [dʒa'tʃentsa] *sf*: **merce in ~** goods in stock; **capitale in ~** uninvested capital; **~e di magazzino** unsold stock.

gia'cere [dʒa'tʃere] *vi* to lie; **giaci'mento** *sm* deposit.

gia'cinto [dʒa'tʃinto] *sm* hyacinth.

gi'ada ['dʒada] *sf* jade.

giaggi'olo [dʒad'dʒɔlo] *sm* iris.

giagu'aro [dʒa'gwaro] *sm* jaguar.

gi'allo ['dʒallo] *ag* yellow; (*carnagione*) sallow // *sm* yellow; (*anche:* **romanzo ~**) detective novel; (*anche:* **film ~**) detective film; **~ dell'uovo** yolk.

giam'mai [dʒam'mai] *av* never.

Giap'pone [dʒap'pone] *sm* Japan; **giappo'nese** *ag, sm/f, sm* Japanese *inv*.

gi'ara ['dʒara] *sf* jar.

giardi'naggio [dʒardi'naddʒo] *sm* gardening.

giardi'netta [dʒardi'netta] *sf* estate car (*Brit*), station wagon (*US*).

giardini'ere, a |dʒardi'njɛrɛ| *sm/f* gardener // *sf* (*misto di sottaceti*) mixed pickles *pl*; (*automobile*) = **giardinetta**.

giar'dino |dʒar'dino| *sm* garden; ~ **d'infanzia** nursery school; ~ **pubblico** public gardens *pl*, (public) park; ~ **zoologico** zoo.

giarretti'era |dʒarret'tjɛra| *sf* garter.

giavel'lotto |dʒavel'lɔtto| *sm* javelin.

gi'gante, 'essa |dʒi'gante| *sm/f* giant // *ag* giant, gigantic; (*COMM*) giant-size; **gigan'tesco, a, schi, sche** *ag* gigantic.

'giglio |'dʒiʎʎo| *sm* lily.

gilè |dʒi'lɛ| *sm inv* waistcoat.

gin |dʒin| *sm inv* gin.

gine'cologo, a, gi, ghe |dʒine'kɔlogo| *sm/f* gynaecologist.

gi'nepro |dʒi'nepro| *sm* juniper.

gi'nestra |dʒi'nɛstra| *sf* (*BOT*) broom.

Gi'nevra |dʒi'nevra| *sf* Geneva.

gingil'larsi |dʒindʒil'larsi| *vr* to fritter away one's time; (*giocare*): ~ **con** to fiddle with.

gin'gillo |dʒin'dʒillo| *sm* plaything.

gin'nasio |dʒin'nazjo| *sm the 4th and 5th year of secondary school in Italy*.

gin'nasta, i, e |dʒin'nasta| *sm/f* gymnast; **gin'nastica** *sf* gymnastics *sg*; (*esercizio fisico*) keep-fit exercises; (*INS*) physical education.

gi'nocchio |dʒi'nɔkkjo|, *pl(m)* **gi'nocchi** o *pl(f)* **gi'nocchia** *sm* knee; **stare in** ~ to kneel, be on one's knees; **mettersi in** ~ to kneel (down); **ginocchi'oni** *av* on one's knees.

gio'care |dʒo'kare| *vt* to play; (*scommettere*) to stake, wager, bet; (*ingannare*) to take in // *vi* to play; (*a roulette etc*) to gamble; (*fig*) to play a part, be important; (*TECN: meccanismo*) to be loose; ~ **a** (*gioco, sport*) to play; (*cavalli*) to bet on; **~rsi la carriera** to put one's career at risk; **gioca'tore, 'trice** *sm/f* player; gambler.

gio'cattolo |dʒo'kattolo| *sm* toy.

gio'chetto |dʒo'ketto| *sm* (*tranello*) trick; (*fig*): **è un** ~ it's child's play.

gi'oco, chi |'dʒɔko| *sm* game; (*divertimento, TECN*) play; (*al casinò*) gambling; (*CARTE*) hand; (*insieme di pezzi etc necessari per un gioco*) set; **per** ~ for fun; **fare il doppio** ~ **con qn** to double-cross sb; ~ **d'azzardo** game of chance; ~ **della palla** football; ~ **degli scacchi** chess set; **i Giochi Olimpici** the Olympic Games.

giocoli'ere |dʒoko'ljɛrɛ| *sm* juggler.

gio'coso, a |dʒo'koso| *ag* playful, jesting.

gi'ogo, ghi |'dʒɔgo| *sm* yoke.

gi'oia |'dʒɔja| *sf* joy, delight; (*pietra preziosa*) jewel, precious stone.

gioielle'ria |dʒojelle'ria| *sf* jeweller's craft; jeweller's (shop).

gioielli'ere, a |dʒojel'ljɛrɛ| *sm/f* jeweller.

gioi'ello |dʒo'jello| *sm* jewel, piece of jewellery; ~**i** *smpl* jewellery *sg*.

gioi'oso, a |dʒo'joso| *ag* joyful.

Gior'dania |dʒor'danja| *sf*: **la** ~ Jordan.

giorna'laio, a |dʒorna'lajo| *sm/f* newsagent (*Brit*), newsdealer (*US*).

gior'nale |dʒor'nale| *sm* (news)paper; (*diario*) journal, diary; (*COMM*) journal; ~ **di bordo** log; ~ **radio** radio news *sg*.

giornali'ero, a |dʒorna'ljero| *ag* daily; (*che varia: umore*) changeable // *sm* day labourer.

giorna'lismo |dʒorna'lizmo| *sm* journalism.

giorna'lista, i, e |dʒorna'lista| *sm/f* journalist.

gior'nata |dʒor'nata| *sf* day; ~ **lavorativa** working day.

gi'orno |'dʒorno| *sm* day; (*opposto alla notte*) day, daytime; (*luce del* ~) daylight; **al** ~ per day; **di** ~ by day; **al** ~ **d'oggi** nowadays.

gi'ostra |'dʒɔstra| *sf* (*per bimbi*) merry-go-round; (*torneo storico*) joust.

gio'vane |dʒo'vane| *ag* young; (*aspetto*) youthful // *sm/f* youth/girl, young man/woman; **i** ~**i** young people; **giova'nile** *ag* youthful; (*scritti*) early; (*errore*) of youth; **giova'notto** *sm* young man.

gio'vare |dʒo'vare| *vi*: ~ **a** (*essere utile*) to be useful to; (*far bene*) to be good for // *vb impers* (*essere bene, utile*) to be useful; ~**rsi di qc** to make use of sth.

giovedì |dʒove'di| *sm inv* Thursday; **di** o **il** ~ on Thursdays.

gioventù |dʒoven'tu| *sf* (*periodo*) youth; (*i giovani*) young people *pl*, youth.

giovi'ale |dʒo'vjale| *ag* jovial, jolly.

giovi'nezza |dʒovi'nettsa| *sf* youth.

gira'dischi |dʒira'diski| *sm inv* record player.

gi'raffa |dʒi'raffa| *sf* giraffe.

gi'randola |dʒi'randola| *sf* (*fuoco d'artificio*) Catherine wheel; (*giocattolo*) toy windmill; (*banderuola*) weather vane, weathercock.

gi'rare |dʒi'rare| *vt* (*far ruotare*) to turn; (*percorrere, visitare*) to go round; (*CINEMA*) to shoot; to make; (*COMM*) to endorse // *vi* to turn; (*più veloce*) to spin; (*andare in giro*) to wander, go around; ~**rsi** *vr* to turn; ~ **attorno a** to go round; to revolve round; **far** ~ **la testa a qn** to make sb dizzy; (*fig*) to turn sb's head.

girar'rosto |dʒirar'rɔsto| *sm* (*CUC*) spit.

gira'sole |dʒira'sole| *sm* sunflower.

gi'rata |dʒi'rata| *sf* (*passeggiata*) stroll; (*con veicolo*) drive; (*COMM*) endorsement.

gira'volta |dʒira'vɔlta| *sf* twirl, turn; (*curva*) sharp bend; (*fig*) about-turn.

gi'revole |dʒi'revole| *ag* revolving, turning.

gi'rino |dʒi'rino| *sm* tadpole.

'giro |'dʒiro| *sm* (*circuito, cerchio*) circle; (*di chiave, manovella*) turn; (*viaggio*) tour, excursion; (*passeggiata*) stroll, walk; (*in macchina*) drive; (*in bicicletta*) ride; (*SPORT: della pista*) lap; (*di denaro*) circulation; (*CARTE*) hand; (*TECN*) revolution; **prendere in ~ qn** (*fig*) to pull sb's leg; **fare un ~ to go for a walk** (*o a drive o a ride*); **andare in ~** to go about, walk around; **a stretto ~ di posta** by return of post; **nel ~ di un mese** in a month's time; **essere nel ~** (*fig*) to belong to a circle (of friends); **~ d'affari** (*COMM*) turnover; **~ di parole** circumlocution; **~ di prova** (*AUT*) test drive; **~ turistico** sightseeing tour; **giro-'collo** *sm*: **a girocollo** crew-neck *cpd*.

gironzo'lare |dʒirondzo'lare| *vi* to stroll about.

'gita |'dʒita| *sf* excursion, trip; **fare una ~** to go for a trip, go on an outing.

gi'tano, a |dʒi'tano| *sm/f* gipsy.

giù |dʒu| *av* down; (*dabbasso*) downstairs; **in ~** downwards, down; **~ di lì** (*pressappoco*) thereabouts; **bambini dai 6 anni in ~** children aged 6 and under; **~ per**: **cadere ~ per le scale** to fall down the stairs; **essere ~** (*fig*: *di salute*) to be run down; (*: di spirito*) to be depressed.

giub'botto |dʒub'bɔtto| *sm* jerkin; **~ antiproiettile** bulletproof vest.

gi'ubilo |'dʒubilo| *sm* rejoicing.

giudi'care |dʒudi'kare| *vt* to judge; (*accusato*) to try; (*lite*) to arbitrate in; **~ qn/qc bello** to consider sb/sth (to be) beautiful.

gi'udice |'dʒuditʃe| *sm* judge; **~ conciliatore** justice of the peace; **~ popolare** member of a jury.

giu'dizio |dʒu'dittsjo| *sm* judgment; (*opinione*) opinion; (*DIR*) judgment, sentence; (*: processo*) trial; (*: verdetto*) verdict; **aver ~** to be wise *o* prudent; **citare in ~** to summons; **giudizi'oso, a** *ag* prudent, judicious.

gi'ugno |'dʒuɲo| *sm* June.

giul'lare |dʒul'lare| *sm* jester.

giu'menta |dʒu'menta| *sf* mare.

gi'unco, chi |'dʒunko| *sm* rush.

gi'ungere |'dʒundʒere| *vi* to arrive // *vt* (*mani etc*) to join; **~ a** to arrive at, reach.

gi'ungla |'dʒungla| *sf* jungle.

gi'unto, a |'dʒunto| *pp di* **giungere** // *sm* (*TECN*) coupling, joint // *sf* addition; (*organo esecutivo, amministrativo*) council, board; **per ~a** into the bargain, in addition; **~a militare** military junta; **giun'tura** *sf* joint.

giuo'care |dʒwo'kare| *vt, vi* = **giocare**; **giu'oco** *sm* = **gioco**.

giura'mento |dʒura'mento| *sm* oath; **~ falso** perjury.

giu'rare |dʒu'rare| *vt* to swear // *vi* to swear, take an oath; **giu'rato, a** *ag*: **nemico giurato** sworn enemy // *sm/f* juror, juryman/woman.

giu'ria |dʒu'ria| *sf* jury.

giu'ridico, a, ci, che |dʒu'ridiko| *ag* legal.

giustifi'care |dʒustifi'kare| *vt* to justify; **giustificazi'one** *sf* justification; (*INS*) (note of) excuse.

gius'tizia |dʒus'tittsja| *sf* justice; **giustizi'are** *vt* to execute, put to death; **giustizi'ere** *sm* executioner.

gi'usto, a |'dʒusto| *ag* (*equo*) fair, just; (*vero*) true, correct; (*adatto*) right, suitable; (*preciso*) exact, correct // *av* (*esattamente*) exactly, precisely; (*per l'appunto, appena*) just; **arrivare ~** to arrive just in time; **ho ~ bisogno di te** you're just the person I need.

glaci'ale |gla'tʃale| *ag* glacial.

'giandola *sf* = **ghiandola**.

gli |ʎi| *det mpl* (*dav V, s impura, gn, pn, ps, x, z*) the // *pronome* (*a lui*) to him; (*a esso*) to it; (*in coppia con lo, la, li, le, ne: a lui, a lei, a loro etc*): **gliele do** I'm giving them to him (*o* her *o* them).

gli'ela |'ʎela| *etc vedi* **gli**.

glo'bale *ag* overall.

'globo *sm* globe.

'globulo *sm* (*ANAT*): **~ rosso/bianco** red/white corpuscle.

'gloria *sf* glory; **glori'oso, a** *ag* glorious.

glos'sario *sm* glossary.

'gnocchi |'ɲɔkki| *smpl* (*CUC*) small dumplings made of semolina pasta or potato.

'gobba *sf* (*ANAT*) hump; (*protuberanza*) bump.

'gobbo, a *ag* hunchbacked; (*ricurvo*) round-shouldered // *sm/f* hunchback.

'goccia, ce |'gottʃa| *sf* drop; **goccio'lare** *vi, vt* to drip.

go'dere *vi* (*compiacersi*): **~ (di)** to be delighted (at), rejoice (at); (*trarre vantaggio*): **~ di** to enjoy, benefit from // *vt* to enjoy; **~rsi la vita** to enjoy life; **~sela** to have a good time, enjoy o.s.; **godi'mento** *sm* enjoyment.

'goffo, a *ag* clumsy, awkward.

'gola *sf* (*ANAT*) throat; (*golosità*) gluttony, greed; (*di camino*) flue; (*di monte*) gorge; **fare ~** (*anche fig*) to tempt.

golf *sm inv* (*SPORT*) golf; (*maglia*) cardigan.

'golfo *sm* gulf.

go'loso, a *ag* greedy.

'gomito *sm* elbow; (*di strada etc*) sharp bend.

go'mitolo *sm* ball.

'gomma *sf* rubber; (*colla*) gum; (*per cancellare*) rubber, eraser; (*di veicolo*) tyre (*Brit*), tire (*US*); **~ a terra** flat tyre (*Brit*) *o* tire (*US*); **gommapi'uma** *sf* ®

foam rubber.

'gondola _sf_ gondola; **gondoli'ere** _sm_ gondolier.

gonfa'lone _sm_ banner.

gonfi'are _vt_ (_pallone_) to blow up, inflate; (_dilatare, ingrossare_) to swell; (_fig: notizia_) to exaggerate; ~**rsi** _vr_ to swell; (_fiume_) to rise; **'gonfio, a** _ag_ swollen; (_stomaco_) bloated; (_vela_) full; **gonfi'ore** _sm_ swelling.

gongo'lare _vi_ to look pleased with o.s.; ~ **di gioia** to be overjoyed.

'gonna _sf_ skirt; ~ **pantalone** culottes _pl_

'gonzo ['gondzo] _sm_ simpleton, fool.

gorgheggi'are [gorged'dʒare] _vi_ to warble; to trill.

'gorgo, ghi _sm_ whirlpool.

gorgogli'are [gorgoʎ'ʎare] _vi_ to gurgle.

go'rilla _sm inv_ gorilla; (_guardia del corpo_) bodyguard.

'gotta _sf_ gout.

gover'nante _sm/f_ ruler // _sf_ (_di bambini_) governess; (_donna di servizio_) housekeeper.

gover'nare _vt_ (_stato_) to govern, rule; (_pilotare, guidare_) to steer; (_bestiame_) to tend, look after; **governa'tivo, a** _ag_ government _cpd_; **governa'tore** _sm_ governor.

go'verno _sm_ government.

gozzovigli'are [gottsoviʎ'ʎare] _vi_ to make merry, carouse.

gracchi'are [grak'kjare] _vi_ to caw.

graci'dare [gratʃi'dare] _vi_ to croak.

'gracile ['gratʃile] _ag_ frail, delicate.

gra'dasso _sm_ boaster.

gradazi'one [gradat'tsjone] _sf_ (_sfumatura_) gradation; ~ **alcolica** alcoholic content, strength.

gra'devole _ag_ pleasant, agreeable.

gradi'mento _sm_ pleasure, satisfaction; è **di suo** ~? is it to your liking?

gradi'nata _sf_ flight of steps; (_in teatro, stadio_) tiers _pl_.

gra'dino _sm_ step; (_ALPINISMO_) foothold.

gra'dire _vt_ (_accettare con piacere_) to accept; (_desiderare_) to wish, like; **gradisce una tazza di tè?** would you like a cup of tea?; **gra'dito, a** _ag_ pleasing; welcome.

'grado _sm_ (_MAT, FISICA etc_) degree; (_stadio_) degree, level; (_MIL, sociale_) rank; **essere in** ~ **di fare** to be in a position to do.

gradu'ale _ag_ gradual.

gradu'are _vt_ to grade; **gradu'ato, a** _ag_ (_esercizi_) graded; (_scala, termometro_) graduated // _sm_ (_MIL_) non-commissioned officer.

'graffa _sf_ (_gancio_) clip; (_segno grafico_) brace.

graffi'are _vt_ to scratch.

'graffio _sm_ scratch.

gra'fia _sf_ spelling; (_scrittura_) handwriting.

'grafico, a, ci, che _ag_ graphic // _sm_ graph; (_persona_) graphic designer // _sf_ graphic arts _pl_.

gra'migna [gra'miɲɲa] _sf_ weed; couch grass.

gram'matica, che _sf_ grammar; **grammati'cale** _ag_ grammatical.

'grammo _sm_ gram(me).

gran _ag vedi_ **grande.**

'grana _sf_ (_granello, di minerali, corpi spezzati_) grain; (_fam: seccatura_) trouble; (: _soldi_) cash // _sm inv_ Parmesan (cheese).

gra'naio _sm_ granary, barn.

gra'nata _sf_ (_frutto_) pomegranate; (_pietra preziosa_) garnet; (_proiettile_) grenade.

Gran Bre'tagna [granbre'taɲɲa] _sf_: **la** ~ Great Britain.

'granchio ['grankjo] _sm_ crab; (_fig_) blunder; **prendere un** ~ (_fig_) to blunder.

grandango'lare _sm_ wide-angle lens _sg_.

'grande, _qualche volta_ **gran** +_C_, **grand'** +_V ag_ (_grosso, largo, vasto_) big, large; (_alto_) tall; (_lungo_) long; (_in sensi astratti_) great // _sm/f_ (_persona adulta_) adult, grown-up; (_chi ha ingegno e potenza_) great man/woman; **fare le cose in** ~ to do things in style; **una gran bella donna** a very beautiful woman; **non è una gran cosa** _o_ **un gran che** it's nothing special; **non ne so gran che** I don't know very much about it.

grandeggi'are [granded'dʒare] _vi_ (_emergere per grandezza_): ~ **su** to tower over; (_darsi arie_) to put on airs.

gran'dezza [gran'dettsa] _sf_ (_dimensione_) size; magnitude; (_fig_) greatness; **in** ~ **naturale** lifesize.

grandi'nare _vb impers_ to hail.

'grandine _sf_ hail.

gran'duca, chi _sm_ grand duke.

gra'nello _sm_ (_di cereali, uva_) seed; (_di frutta_) pip; (_di sabbia, sale etc_) grain.

gra'nita _sf_ kind of water ice.

gra'nito _sm_ granite.

'grano _sm_ (_in quasi tutti i sensi_) grain; (_frumento_) wheat; (_di rosario, collana_) bead; ~ **di pepe** peppercorn.

gran'turco _sm_ maize.

'granulo _sm_ granule; (_MED_) pellet.

'grappa _sf_ rough, strong brandy.

'grappolo _sm_ bunch, cluster.

gras'setto _sm_ (_TIP_) bold (type).

'grasso, a _ag_ fat; (_cibo_) fatty; (_pelle_) greasy; (_terreno_) rich; (_fig: guadagno, annata_) plentiful; (: _volgare_) coarse, lewd // _sm_ (_di persona, animale_) fat; (_sostanza che unge_) grease; **gras'soccio, a, ci, ce** _ag_ plump.

'grata _sf_ grating.

gra'ticola _sf_ grill.

gra'tifica, che _sf_ bonus.

'gratis _av_ free, for nothing.

grati'tudine _sf_ gratitude.

'grato, a ag grateful; (gradito) pleasant, agreeable.

gratta'capo sm worry, headache.

grattaci'elo [gratta'tʃɛlo] sm skyscraper.

grat'tare vt (pelle) to scratch; (raschiare) to scrape; (pane, formaggio, carote) to grate; (fam: rubare) to pinch // vi (stridere) to grate; (AUT) to grind; ~rsi vr to scratch o.s.

grat'tugia, gie [grat'tudʒa] sf grater; **grattugi'are** vt to grate; **pane grattugiato** breadcrumbs pl.

gra'tuito, a ag free; (fig) gratuitous.

gra'vame sm tax; (fig) burden, weight.

gra'vare vt to burden // vi: ~ su to weigh on.

'grave ag (danno, pericolo, peccato etc) grave, serious; (responsabilità) heavy, grave; (contegno) grave, solemn; (voce, suono) deep, low-pitched; (LING): **accento** ~ grave accent; **un malato** ~ a person who is seriously ill.

gravi'danza [gravi'dantsa] sf pregnancy.

'gravido, a ag pregnant.

gravità sf seriousness; (anche FISICA) gravity.

gra'voso, a ag heavy, onerous.

'grazia ['grattsja] sf grace; (favore) favour; (DIR) pardon; **grazi'are** vt (DIR) to pardon.

'grazie ['grattsje] escl thank you!; ~ **mille!** o **tante!** o **infinite!** thank you very much!; ~ a thanks to.

grazi'oso, a [grat'tsjoso] ag charming, delightful; (gentile) gracious.

'Grecia ['grɛtʃa] sf: la ~ Greece; **'greco, a, ci, che** ag, sm/f, sm Greek.

'gregge, pl(f) **i** ['greddʒe] sm flock.

'greggio, a, gi, ge ['greddʒo] ag raw, unrefined; (diamante) rough, uncut; (tessuto) unbleached // sm (anche: pe-trolio ~) crude (oil).

grembi'ule sm apron; (sopravveste) overall.

'grembo sm lap; (ventre della madre) womb.

gre'mito, a ag: ~ (di) packed o crowded (with).

'gretto, a ag mean, stingy; (fig) narrow-minded.

'greve ag heavy.

'grezzo, a ['grɛddzo] ag = **greggio.**

gri'dare vi (per chiamare) to shout, cry (out); (strillare) to scream, yell // vt to shout (out), yell (out); ~ **aiuto** to cry o shout for help.

'grido, pl(m) **i** o pl(f) **a** sm shout, cry; scream, yell; (di animale) cry; **di** ~ famous.

'grigio, a, gi, gie ['gridʒo] ag, sm grey.

'griglia ['griʎʎa] sf (per arrostire) grill; (ELETTR) grid; (inferriata) grating; **alla** ~ (CUC) grilled; **grigli'ata** sf (CUC) grill.

gril'letto sm trigger.

'grillo sm (ZOOL) cricket; (fig) whim.

grimal'dello sm picklock.

'grinta sf grim expression; (SPORT) fighting spirit.

'grinza ['grintsa] sf crease, wrinkle; (ruga) wrinkle; **non fare una** ~ (fig: ragionamento) to be faultless; **grin'zoso, a** ag creased; wrinkled.

grip'pare vi (TECN) to seize.

gris'sino sm bread-stick.

'gronda sf eaves pl.

gron'daia sf gutter.

gron'dare vi to pour; (essere bagnato): ~ **di** to be dripping with // vt to drip with.

'groppa sf (di animale) back, rump; (fam: dell'uomo) back, shoulders pl.

'groppo sm tangle; **avere un** ~ **alla gola** (fig) to have a lump in one's throat.

gros'sezza [gros'settsa] sf size; thickness.

gros'sista, i, e sm/f (COMM) wholesaler.

'grosso, a ag big, large; (di spessore) thick; (grossolano: anche fig) coarse; (grave, insopportabile) serious, great; (tempo, mare) rough // sm: **il** ~ **di** the bulk of; **un pezzo** ~ (fig) a VIP, a bigwig; **farla** ~a to do something very stupid; **dirle** ~e to tell tall stories; **sbagliarsi di** ~ to be completely wrong.

grosso'lano, a ag rough, coarse; (fig) coarse, crude; (: errore) stupid.

grosso'modo av roughly.

'grotta sf cave; grotto.

grot'tesco, a, schi, sche ag grotesque.

grovi'era sm o f gruyère (cheese).

gro'viglio [gro'viʎʎo] sm tangle; (fig) muddle.

gru sf inv crane.

'gruccia, ce ['gruttʃa] sf (per camminare) crutch; (per abiti) coat-hanger.

gru'gnire [gruɲ'ɲire] vi to grunt; **gru'gnito** sm grunt.

'grugno ['gruɲɲo] sm snout; (fam: faccia) mug.

'grullo, a ag silly, stupid.

'grumo sm (di sangue) clot; (di farina etc) lump.

'gruppo sm group; ~ **sanguigno** blood group.

gruvi'era sm o f = **groviera.**

guada'gnare [gwadaɲ'ɲare] vt (ottenere) to gain; (soldi, stipendio) to earn; (vincere) to win; (raggiungere) to reach.

gua'dagno [gwa'daɲɲo] sm earnings pl; (COMM) profit; (vantaggio, utile) advantage, gain; ~ **lordo/netto** gross/net earnings pl.

gu'ado sm ford; **passare a** ~ to ford.

gu'ai escl: ~ **a te** (o lui etc)! woe betide you (o him etc)!

gua'ina sf (fodero) sheath; (indumento per donna) girdle.

gu'aio sm trouble, mishap; (inconveniente) trouble, snag.

gua'ire vi to whine, yelp.

gu'ancia, ce ['gwantʃa] sf cheek.

guanci'ale [gwan'tʃale] sm pillow.

gu'anto sm glove.

gu'arda... prefisso: ~'**boschi** sm inv forester; ~'**caccia** sm inv gamekeeper; ~'**coste** sm inv coastguard; (nave) coastguard patrol vessel; ~'**linee** sm inv (SPORT) lineman.

guar'dare vt (con lo sguardo: osservare) to look at; (film, televisione) to watch; (custodire) to look after, take care of // vi to look; (badare): ~ a to pay attention to; (luoghi: esser orientato): ~ a to face; ~rsi vr to look at o.s.; ~rsi da (astenersi) to refrain from; (stare in guardia) to beware of; ~rsi dal fare to take care not to do; guarda di non sbagliare try not to make a mistake; ~ a vista qn to keep a close watch on sb.

guarda'roba sm inv wardrobe; (locale) cloakroom; **guardarobi'ere, a** sm/f cloakroom attendant.

gu'ardia sf (individuo, corpo) guard; (sorveglianza) watch; fare la ~ a qc/qn to guard sth/sb; stare in ~ (fig) to be on one's guard; di ~ (medico) on call; ~ carceraria (prison) warder; ~ del corpo bodyguard; ~ di finanza (corpo) customs pl; (persona) customs officer; ~ medica emergency doctor service.

guardi'ano, a sm/f (di carcere) warder; (di villa etc) caretaker; (di museo) custodian; (di zoo) keeper; ~ notturno night watchman.

guar'dingo, a, ghi, ghe ag wary, cautious.

guardi'ola sf porter's lodge; (MIL) lookout tower.

guarigi'one [gwari'dʒone] sf recovery.

gua'rire vt (persona, malattia) to cure; (ferita) to heal // vi to recover, be cured; to heal (up).

guarnigi'one [gwarni'dʒone] sf garrison.

guar'nire vt (ornare: abiti) to trim; (CUC) to garnish; **guarnizi'one** sf trimming; garnish; (TECN) gasket.

guasta'feste sm/f inv spoilsport.

guas'tare vt to spoil, ruin; (meccanismo) to break; ~rsi vr (cibo) to go bad; (meccanismo) to break down; (tempo) to change for the worse; (amici) to quarrel, fall out.

gu'asto, a ag (non funzionante) broken; (: telefono etc) out of order; (andato a male) bad, rotten; (: dente) decayed, bad; (fig: corrotto) depraved // sm breakdown; (avaria) failure; ~ al motore engine failure.

guazza'buglio [gwattsa'buʎʎo] sm muddle.

gu'ercio, a, ci, ce ['gwertʃo] ag cross-eyed.

gu'erra sf war; (tecnica: atomica, chimica etc) warfare; **fare la ~** (a) to wage war (against); ~ **mondiale** world war; **guerreggi'are** vi to wage war; **guerri'ero, a** ag warlike // sm warrior; **guer'riglia** sf guerrilla warfare; **guerri-gli'ero** sm guerrilla.

'**gufo** sm owl.

gu'ida sf guide; (comando, direzione) guidance, direction; (AUT) driving; (: sterzo) steering; (tappeto, di tenda, cassetto) runner; ~ **a destra/sinistra** (AUT) right-/left-hand drive; ~ **telefonica** telephone directory.

gui'dare vt to guide; (condurre a capo) to lead; (auto) to drive; (aereo, nave) to pilot; **sai** ~? can you drive?; **guida'tore, trice** sm/f (conducente) driver.

guin'zaglio [gwin'tsaʎʎo] sm leash, lead.

gu'isa sf: a ~ di like, in the manner of.

guiz'zare [gwit'tsare] vi to dart; to flicker; to leap; ~ **via** (fuggire) to slip away.

'**guscio** ['guʃʃo] sm shell.

gus'tare vt (cibi) to taste; (: assaporare con piacere) to enjoy, savour; (fig) to enjoy, appreciate // vi: ~ a to please; non mi gusta affatto I don't like it at all.

'**gusto** sm taste; (sapore) flavour; (godimento) enjoyment; al ~ di fragola strawberry-flavoured; mangiare di ~ to eat heartily; prenderci ~: ci ha preso ~ he's acquired a taste for it, he's got to like it; **gus'toso, a** ag tasty; (fig) agreeable.

H

h abbr = ora, altezza.

ha, 'hai [a, ai] vb vedi avere.

hall [hɔl] sf inv hall, foyer.

'**handicap** ['handikap] sm inv handicap; **handicap'pato, a** ag handicapped // sm/f handicapped person, disabled person.

'**hanno** ['anno] vb vedi avere.

'**hascisc** ['haʃiʃ] sm hashish.

'**herpes** ['ɛrpes] sm (MED) herpes sg; ~ zoster shingles sg.

ho [ɔ] vb vedi avere.

'**hobby** ['hɔbi] sm inv hobby.

'**hockey** ['hɔki] sm hockey; ~ **su ghiaccio** ice hockey.

'**hostess** ['houstis] sf inv air hostess (Brit) o stewardess.

ho'tel sm inv hotel.

I

i det mpl the.

i'ato sm hiatus.

ibernazi'one |ibɛrnat'tsjone| *sf* hibernation.

'ibrido, a *ag*, *sm* hybrid.

Id'dio *sm* God.

i'dea *sf* idea; (*opinione*) opinion, view; (*ideale*) ideal; **dare l'~ di** to seem, look like; **~ fissa** obsession; **neanche** *o* **neppure per ~!** certainly not!

ide'ale *ag*, *sm* ideal.

ide'are *vt* (*immaginare*) to think up, conceive; (*progettare*) to plan.

i'dentico, a, ci, che *ag* identical.

identifi'care *vt* to identify; **identificazi'one** *sf* identification.

identità *sf inv* identity.

idi'oma, i *sm* idiom, language; **idio'-matico, a, ci, che** *ag* idiomatic; **frase idiomatica** idiom.

idi'ota, i, e *ag* idiotic // *sm/f* idiot.

idola'trare *vt* to worship; (*fig*) to idolize.

'idolo *sm* idol.

idoneità *sf* suitability.

i'doneo, a *ag*: **~ a** suitable for, fit for; (*MIL*) fit for; (*qualificato*) qualified for.

i'drante *sm* hydrant.

i'draulico, a, ci, che *ag* hydraulic // *sm* plumber // *sf* hydraulics *sg*.

idroe'lettrico, a, ci, che *ag* hydroelectric.

i'drofilo, a *ag vedi* **cotone**.

idrofo'bia *sf* rabies *sg*.

i'drogeno |i'drɔdʒeno| *sm* hydrogen.

idros'calo *sm* seaplane base.

idrovo'lante *sm* seaplane.

i'ena *sf* hyena.

i'eri *av*, *sm* yesterday; **il giornale di ~** yesterday's paper; **~ l'altro** the day before yesterday; **~ sera** yesterday evening.

igi'ene |i'dʒɛne| *sf* hygiene; **~ pubblica** public health; **igi'enico, a, ci, che** *ag* hygienic; (*salubre*) healthy.

i'gnaro, a |iɲ'ɲaro| *ag*: **~ di** unaware of, ignorant of.

i'gnobile |iɲ'ɲɔbile| *ag* despicable, vile.

igno'rante |iɲɲo'rante| *ag* ignorant.

igno'rare |iɲɲo'rare| *vt* (*non sapere, conoscere*) to be ignorant o unaware of, not to know; (*fingere di non vedere, sentire*) to ignore.

i'gnoto, a |iɲ'ɲɔto| *ag* unknown.

il *det m* (*pl* (*m*) **i**; *diventa* **lo** (*pl* **gli**) *davanti a s impura, gn, pn, ps, x, z*; *f* **la** (*pl* **le**) **1** the; **~ libro/lo studente/l'acqua** the book/the student/the water; **gli scolari** the pupils

2 (*astrazione*): **~ coraggio/l'amore/la giovinezza** courage/love/youth

3 (*tempo*): **~ mattino/la sera** in the morning/evening; **~ venerdì** *etc* (*abitualmente*) on Fridays *etc*; (*quel giorno*) on (the) Friday *etc*; **la settimana prossima** next week

4 (*distributivo*) a, an; **2.500 lire ~ chilo/paio** 2,500 lire a *o* per kilo/pair; **110 km**

l'ora 110 km an *o* per hour

5 (*partitivo*) some, any; **hai messo lo zucchero?** have you added sugar?; **hai comprato ~ latte?** did you buy (some *o* any) milk?

6 (*possesso*): **aprire gli occhi** to open one's eyes; **rompersi la gamba** to break one's leg; **avere i capelli neri/~ naso rosso** to have dark hair/a red nose; **mettiti le scarpe** put your shoes on

7 (*con nomi propri*): **~ Petrarca** Petrarch; **~ Presidente Reagan** President Reagan; **dov'è la Francesca?** where's Francesca?

8 (*con nomi geografici*): **~ Tevere** the Tiber; **l'Italia** Italy; **~ Regno Unito** the United Kingdom; **l'Everest** Everest; **le Alpi** the Alps.

'ilare *ag* cheerful; **ilarità** *sf* hilarity, mirth.

illangui'dire *vi* to grow weak *o* feeble.

illazi'one |illat'tsjone| *sf* inference, deduction.

ille'gale *ag* illegal.

illeg'gibile |illed'dʒibile| *ag* illegible.

ille'gittimo, a |ille'dʒittimo| *ag* illegitimate.

il'leso, a *ag* unhurt, unharmed.

illette'rato, a *ag* illiterate.

illi'bato, a *ag*: **donna ~a** virgin.

illimi'tato, a *ag* boundless; unlimited.

ill.mo *abbr* = **illustrissimo**.

il'ludere *vt* to deceive, delude; **~rsi** *vr* to deceive o.s., delude o.s.

illumi'nare *vt* to light up, illuminate; (*fig*) to enlighten; **~rsi** *vr* to light up; **~ a giorno** to floodlight; **illuminazi'one** *sf* lighting; illumination; floodlighting; (*fig*) flash of inspiration.

illusi'one *sf* illusion; **farsi delle ~i** to delude o.s.

illusio'nismo *sm* conjuring.

il'luso, a *pp di* **illudere**.

illus'trare *vt* to illustrate; **illustra'tivo, a** *ag* illustrative; **illustrazi'one** *sf* illustration.

il'lustre *ag* eminent, renowned; **illus'trissimo, a** *ag* (*negli indirizzi*) very revered.

imbacuc'care *vt*, **~rsi** *vr* to wrap up.

imbal'laggio |imbal'laddʒo| *sm* packing *q*.

imbal'lare *vt* to pack; (*AUT*) to race; **~rsi** *vr* (*AUT*) to race.

imbalsa'mare *vt* to embalm.

imbambo'lato, a *ag* (*sguardo*) vacant, blank.

imban'dire *vt*: **~ un pranzo** to prepare a lavish meal.

imbaraz'zare |imbarat'tsare| *vt* (*mettere a disagio*) to embarrass; (*ostacolare: movimenti*) to hamper; (: *stomaco*) to lie heavily on.

imba'razzo |imba'rattso| *sm* (*disagio*) embarrassment; (*perplessità*) puzzlement, bewilderment; ~ **di stomaco** indigestion.

imbarca'dero *sm* landing stage.

imbar'care *vt* (*passeggeri*) to embark; (*merci*) to load; ~**rsi** *vr*: ~**rsi su** to board; ~**rsi per l'America** to sail for America; ~**rsi in** (*fig: affare etc*) to embark on.

imbarcazl'one [imbarkat'tsjone] *sf* (small) boat, (small) craft *inv*; ~ **di salvataggio** lifeboat.

im'barco, chi *sm* embarkation; loading; boarding; (*banchina*) landing stage.

imbas'tire *vt* (*cucire*) to tack; (*fig: abbozzare*) to sketch, outline.

im'battersi *vr*: ~ **in** (*incontrare*) to bump *o* run into.

imbat'tibile *ag* unbeatable, invincible.

imbavagli'are [imbavaʎ'ʎare] *vt* to gag.

imbec'cata *sf* (*TEATRO*) prompt.

imbe'cille [imbe'tʃille] *ag* idiotic // *smf* idiot; (*MED*) imbecile.

imbel'lire *vt* to adorn, embellish // *vi* to grow more beautiful.

im'berbe *ag* beardless.

im'bevere *vt* to soak; ~**rsi** *vr*: ~**rsi di** to soak up, absorb.

imbian'care *vt* to whiten; (*muro*) to whitewash // *vi* to become *o* turn white.

imbian'chino [imbjan'kino] *sm* (house) painter, painter and decorator.

imboc'care *vt* (*bambino*) to feed; (*entrare: strada*) to enter, turn into // *vi*: ~ **in** (*sog: strada*) to lead into; (: *fiume*) to flow into.

imbocca'tura *sf* mouth; (*di strada, porto*) entrance; (*MUS, del morso*) mouthpiece.

im'bocco, chi *sm* entrance.

imbos'care *vt* to hide; ~**rsi** *vr* (*MIL*) to evade military service.

imbos'cata *sf* ambush.

imbottigli'are [imbottiʎ'ʎare] *vt* to bottle; (*NAUT*) to blockade; (*MIL*) to hem in; ~**rsi** *vr* to be stuck in a traffic jam.

imbot'tire *vt* to stuff; (*giacca*) to pad; **imbot'tita** *sf* quilt; **imbotti'tura** *sf* stuffing; padding.

imbrat'tare *vt* to dirty, smear, daub.

imbrigli'are [imbriʎ'ʎare] *vt* to bridle.

imbroc'care *vt* (*fig*) to guess correctly.

imbrogli'are [imbroʎ'ʎare] *vt* to mix up; (*fig: raggirare*) to deceive, cheat; (: *confondere*) to confuse, mix up; ~**rsi** *vr* to get tangled; (*fig*) to become confused; **im'broglio** *sm* (*groviglio*) tangle; (*situazione confusa*) mess; (*truffa*) swindle, trick; **imbrogli'one, a** *smf* cheat, swindler.

imbronci'are [imbron'tʃare] *vi* (*anche*: ~**rsi**) to sulk; **imbronci'ato, a** *ag* sulky.

imbru'nire *vi, vb impers* to grow dark; **all'~** at dusk.

imbrut'tire *vt* to make ugly // *vi* to become ugly.

imbu'care *vt* to post.

imbur'rare *vt* to butter.

im'buto *sm* funnel.

imi'tare *vt* to imitate; (*riprodurre*) to copy; (*assomigliare*) to look like; **imitazi'one** *sf* imitation.

immaco'lato, a *ag* spotless; immaculate.

immagazzi'nare [immagaddzi'nare] *vt* to store.

immagi'nare [immadʒi'nare] *vt* to imagine; (*supporre*) to suppose; (*inventare*) to invent; **s'immagini!** don't mention it!, not at all!; **immagi'nario, a** *ag* imaginary; **immaginazi'one** *sf* imagination; (*cosa immaginata*) fancy.

im'magine [im'madʒine] *sf* image; (*rappresentazione grafica, mentale*) picture.

imman'cabile *ag* certain; unfailing.

immangi'abile [imman'dʒabile] *ag* inedible.

immatrico'lare *vt* to register; ~**rsi** *vr* (*INS*) to matriculate, enrol; **immatricolazi'one** *sf* registration; matriculation, enrolment.

imma'turo, a *ag* (*frutto*) unripe; (*persona*) immature; (*prematuro*) premature.

immedesi'marsi *vr*: ~ **in** to identify with.

immediata'mente *av* immediately, at once.

immedi'ato, a *ag* immediate.

im'memore *ag*: ~ **di** forgetful of.

im'menso, a *ag* immense.

im'mergere [im'mɛrdʒere] *vt* to immerse, plunge; ~**rsi** *vr* to plunge; (*sommergibile*) to dive, submerge; (*dedicarsi a*): ~**rsi in** to immerse o.s. in.

immeri'tato, a *ag* undeserved.

immeri'tevole *ag* undeserving, unworthy.

immersi'one *sf* immersion; (*di sommergibile*) submersion, dive; (*di palombaro*) dive.

im'merso, a *pp di* **immergere**.

im'mettere *vt*: ~ (**in**) to introduce (into); ~ **dati in un computer** to enter data on a computer.

immi'grato, a *smf* immigrant; **immigrazi'one** *sf* immigration.

immi'nente *ag* imminent.

immischi'are [immis'kjare] *vt*: ~ **qn in** to involve sb in; ~**rsi in** to interfere *o* meddle in.

immissi'one *sf* (*di aria, gas*) intake; ~ **di dati** (*INFORM*) data entry.

im'mobile *ag* motionless, still; (**beni**) ~**i** *smpl* real estate *sg*; **immobili'are** *ag* (*DIR*) property *cpd*; **immobilità** *sf* stillness; immobility.

immo'desto, a *ag* immodest.

immo'lare *vt* to sacrifice, immolate.

immon'dizia [immon'dittsja] *sf* dirt,

filth; (*spesso al pl: spazzatura, rifiuti*) rubbish *q*, refuse *q*.

im'mondo, a *ag* filthy, foul.

immo'rale *ag* immoral.

immor'tale *ag* immortal.

im'mune *ag* (*esente*) exempt; (*MED, DIR*) immune; **immunità** *sf* immunity; **immunità parlamentare** parliamentary privilege.

immu'tabile *ag* immutable; unchanging.

impacchet'tare [impakket'tare] *vt* to pack up.

impacci'are [impat'tʃare] *vt* to hinder, hamper; **impacci'ato, a** *ag* awkward, clumsy; (*imbarazzato*) embarrassed; **im'paccio** *sm* obstacle; (*imbarazzo*) embarrassment; (*situazione imbarazzante*) awkward situation.

im'pacco, chi *sm* (*MED*) compress.

impadro'nirsi *vr*: ~ **di** to seize, take possession of; (*fig: apprendere a fondo*) to master.

impa'gabile *ag* priceless.

impagi'nare [impadʒi'nare] *vt* (*TIP*) to paginate, page (up).

impagli'are [impaʎ'ʎare] *vt* to stuff (with straw).

impa'lato, a *ag* (*fig*) stiff as a board.

impalca'tura *sf* scaffolding.

impalli'dire *vi* to turn pale; (*fig*) to fade.

impa'nare *vt* (*CUC*) to dip in breadcrumbs.

impanta'narsi *vr* to sink (in the mud); (*fig*) to get bogged down.

impappi'narsi *vr* to stammer, falter.

impa'rare *vt* to learn.

impareggi'abile [impared'dʒabile] *ag* incomparable.

imparen'tarsi *vr*: ~ **con** to marry into.

'impari *ag inv* (*disuguale*) unequal; (*dispari*) odd.

impar'tire *vt* to bestow, give.

imparzi'ale [impar'tsjale] *ag* impartial, unbiased.

impas'sibile *ag* impassive.

impas'tare *vt* (*pasta*) to knead; (*colori*) to mix.

im'pasto *sm* (*l'impastare: di pane*) kneading; (: *di cemento*) mixing; (*pasta*) dough; (*anche fig*) mixture.

im'patto *sm* impact.

impau'rire *vt* to scare, frighten // *vi* (*anche*: ~**rsi**) to become scared *o* frightened.

impazi'ente [impat'tsjɛnte] *ag* impatient; **impazi'enza** *sf* impatience.

impaz'zata [impat'tsata] *sf*: **all'~** (*precipitosamente*) at breakneck speed.

impaz'zire [impat'tsire] *vi* to go mad; ~ **per qn/qc** to be crazy about sb/sth.

impec'cabile *ag* impeccable.

impedi'mento *sm* obstacle, hindrance.

impe'dire *vt* (*vietare*): ~ **a qn di fare** to

prevent sb from doing; (*ostruire*) to obstruct; (*impacciare*) to hamper, hinder.

impe'gnare [impeɲ'ɲare] *vt* (*dare in pegno*) to pawn; (*onore etc*) to pledge; (*prenotare*) to book, reserve; (*obbligare*) to oblige; (*occupare*) to keep busy; (*MIL: nemico*) to engage; ~**rsi** *vr* (*vincolarsi*): ~**rsi a fare** to undertake to do; (*mettersi risolutamente*): ~**rsi in qc** to devote o.s. to sth; ~**rsi con qn** (*accordarsi*) to come to an agreement with sb; **impegna'tivo, a** *ag* binding; (*lavoro*) demanding, exacting; **impe'gnato, a** *ag* (*occupato*) busy; (*fig: romanzo, autore*) committed, engagé.

im'pegno [im'peɲɲo] *sm* (*obbligo*) obligation; (*promessa*) promise, pledge; (*zelo*) diligence, zeal; (*compito, d'autore*) commitment.

impel'lente *ag* pressing, urgent.

impene'trabile *ag* impenetrable.

impen'narsi *vr* (*cavallo*) to rear up; (*AER*) to nose up; (*fig*) to bridle.

impen'sato, a *ag* unforeseen, unexpected.

impensie'rire *vt*, ~**rsi** *vr* to worry.

impe'rare *vi* (*anche fig*) to reign, rule.

impera'tivo, a *ag*, *sm* imperative.

impera'tore, 'trice *sm/f* emperor/ empress.

imperdo'nabile *ag* unforgivable, unpardonable.

imper'fetto, a *ag* imperfect // *sm* (*LING*) imperfect (tense); **imperfezi'one** *sf* imperfection.

imperi'ale *ag* imperial.

imperi'oso, a *ag* (*persona*) imperious; (*motivo, esigenza*) urgent, pressing.

impe'rizia [impe'rittsja] *sf* lack of experience.

imperma'lirsi *vr* to take offence.

imperme'abile *ag* waterproof // *sm* raincoat.

imperni'are *vt*: ~ **qc su** to hinge sth on; (*fig*) to base sth on; ~**rsi** *vr* (*fig*): ~**rsi su** to be based on.

im'pero *sm* empire; (*forza, autorità*) rule, control.

imperscru'tabile *ag* inscrutable.

imperso'nale *ag* impersonal.

imperso'nare *vt* to personify; (*TEATRO*) to play, act (the part of).

imperter'rito, a *ag* fearless, undaunted; impassive.

imperti'nente *ag* impertinent.

imperver'sare *vi* to rage.

'impeto *sm* (*moto, forza*) force, impetus; (*assalto*) onslaught; (*fig: impulso*) impulse; (: *slancio*) transport; **con** ~ energetically; vehemently.

impet'tito, a *ag* stiff, erect.

impetu'oso, a *ag* (*vento*) strong, raging; (*persona*) impetuous.

impian'tare *vt* (*motore*) to install; (*azienda, discussione*) to establish, start.

impi'anto *sm* (*installazione*) installation; (*apparecchiature*) plant; (*sistema*) system; ~ **elettrico** wiring; ~ **sportivo** sports complex; ~**i di risalita** (*SCI*) ski lifts.

impias'trare, impiastricci'are [impjastrit'tʃare] *vt* to smear, dirty.

impi'astro *sm* poultice.

impic'care *vt* to hang; ~**rsi** *vr* to hang o.s.

impicci'are [impit'tʃare] *vt* to hinder, hamper; ~**rsi** *vr* to meddle, interfere; **im'piccio** *sm* (*ostacolo*) hindrance; (*seccatura*) trouble, bother; (*affare imbrogliato*) mess; **essere d'impiccio** to be in the way.

impie'gare *vt* (*usare*) to use, employ; (*assumere*) to employ, take on; (*spendere: denaro, tempo*) to spend; (*investire*) to invest; ~**rsi** *vr* to get a job, obtain employment; **impie'gato, a** *sm/f* employee.

impi'ego, ghi *sm* (*uso*) use; (*occupazione*) employment; (*posto di lavoro*) (regular) job, post; (*ECON*) investment.

impieto'sire *vt* to move to pity; ~**rsi** *vr* to be moved to pity.

impie'trire *vt* (*fig*) to petrify.

impigli'are [impiʎ'ʎare] *vt* to catch, entangle; ~**rsi** *vr* to get caught up o entangled.

impi'grire *vt* to make lazy // *vi* (*anche*: ~**rsi**) to grow lazy.

impli'care *vt* to imply; (*coinvolgere*) to involve; ~**rsi** *vr*: ~ (**in**) to become involved (in); **implicazi'one** *sf* implication.

im'plicito, a [im'plitʃito] *ag* implicit.

impolve'rare *vt* to cover with dust; ~**rsi** *vr* to get dusty.

impo'nente *ag* imposing, impressive.

impo'nibile *ag* taxable // *sm* taxable income.

impopo'lare *ag* unpopular.

im'porre *vt* to impose; (*costringere*) to force, make; (*far valere*) to impose, enforce; **imporsi** *vr* (*persona*) to assert o.s.; (*cosa: rendersi necessario*) to become necessary; (*aver successo: moda, attore*) to become popular; ~ **a qn di fare** to force sb to do, make sb do.

impor'tante *ag* important; **impor'tanza** *sf* importance; **dare importanza a qc** to attach importance to sth; **darsi importanza** to give o.s. airs.

impor'tare *vt* (*introdurre dall'estero*) to import // *vi* to matter, be important // *vb impers* (*essere necessario*) to be necessary; (*interessare*) to matter; **non importa!** it doesn't matter!; **non me ne importa!** I don't care!; **importazi'one** *sf* importation; (*merci importate*)

imports *pl*.

im'porto *sm* (total) amount.

importu'nare *vt* to bother.

impor'tuno, a *ag* irksome, annoying.

imposizi'one [impozit'tsjone] *sf* imposition; order, command; (*onere, imposta*) tax.

imposses'sarsi *vr*: ~ **di** to seize, take possession of.

impos'sibile *ag* impossible; **fare l'~** to do one's utmost, do all one can; **impossibilità** *sf* impossibility; **essere nell'impossibilità di fare qc** to be unable to do sth.

im'posta *sf* (*di finestra*) shutter; (*tassa*) tax; ~ **sul reddito** income tax; ~ **sul valore aggiunto (I.V.A.)** value added tax (VAT) (*Brit*), sales tax (*US*).

impos'tare *vt* (*imbucare*) to post; (*preparare*) to plan, set out; (*avviare*) to begin, start off; (*voce*) to pitch.

im'posto, a *pp di* **imporre**.

impo'tente *ag* weak, powerless; (*anche MED*) impotent.

impove'rire *vt* to impoverish // *vi* (*anche*: ~**rsi**) to become poor.

imprati'cabile *ag* (*strada*) impassable; (*campo da gioco*) unplayable.

imprati'chire [imprati'kire] *vt* to train; ~**rsi in qc** to practise (*Brit*) o practice (*US*) sth.

impre'gnare [impreɲ'ɲare] *vt*: ~ (**di**) (*imbevere*) to soak o impregnate (with); (*riempire: anche fig*) to fill (with).

imprendi'tore *sm* (*industriale*) entrepreneur; (*appaltatore*) contractor; **piccolo ~** small businessman.

im'presa *sf* (*iniziativa*) enterprise; (*azione*) exploit; (*azienda*) firm, concern.

impre'sario *sm* (*TEATRO*) manager, impresario; ~ **di pompe funebri** funeral director.

imprescin'dibile [impreʃʃin'dibile] *ag* not to be ignored.

impressio'nante *ag* impressive; upsetting.

impressio'nare *vt* to impress; (*turbare*) to upset; (*FOT*) to expose; ~**rsi** *vr* to be easily upset.

impressi'one *sf* impression; (*fig: sensazione*) sensation, feeling; (*stampa*) printing; **fare** ~ (*colpire*) to impress; (*turbare*) to frighten, upset; **fare buona/cattiva** ~ **a** to make a good/bad impression on.

im'presso, a *pp di* **imprimere**.

impres'tare *vt*: ~ **qc a qn** to lend sth to sb.

impreve'dibile *ag* unforeseeable; (*persona*) unpredictable.

imprevi'dente *ag* lacking in foresight.

impre'visto, a *ag* unexpected, unforeseen // *sm* unforeseen event; **salvo** ~**i** unless anything unexpected happens.

imprigio'nare [impridʒo'nare] *vt* to imprison.

im'primere *vt* (*anche fig*) to impress, stamp; (*comunicare: movimento*) to transmit, give.

impro'babile *ag* improbable, unlikely.

im'pronta *sf* imprint, impression, sign; (*di piede, mano*) print; (*fig*) mark, stamp; ~ **digitale** fingerprint.

impro'perio *sm* insult; ~**i** *smpl* abuse *sg*.

im'proprio, a *ag* improper; **arma** ~**a** offensive weapon.

improvvisa'mente *av* suddenly; unexpectedly.

improvvi'sare *vt* to improvise; ~**rsi** *vr*: ~**rsi cuoco** to (decide to) act as cook; **improvvi'sata** *sf* (pleasant) surprise.

improv'viso, a *ag* (*imprevisto*) unexpected; (*subitaneo*) sudden; **all'**~ unexpectedly; suddenly.

impru'dente *ag* unwise, rash.

impu'dente *ag* impudent.

impu'dico, a, chi, che *ag* immodest.

impu'gnare [impuɲ'ɲare] *vt* to grasp, grip; (*DIR*) to contest; **impugna'tura** *sf* grip, grasp; (*manico*) handle; (*: di spada*) hilt.

impul'sivo, a *ag* impulsive.

im'pulso *sm* impulse.

impun'tarsi *vr* to stop dead, refuse to budge; (*fig*) to be obstinate.

impu'tare *vt* (*ascrivere*): ~ **qc a** to attribute sth to; (*DIR: accusare*): ~ **qn di** to charge sb with, accuse sb of; **impu'tato, a** *sm/f* (*DIR*) accused, defendant; **imputazi'one** *sf* (*DIR*) charge.

imputri'dire *vi* to rot.

in (*in* + *il* = **nel**, *in* + *lo* = **nello**, *in* + *l'* = **nell'**, *in* + *la* = **nella**, *in* + *i* = **nei**, *in* + *gli* = **negli**, *in* + *le* = **nelle**) *prep* **1** (*stato in luogo*) in; vivere ~ **Italia/città** to live in Italy/town; essere ~ **casa/ufficio** to be at home/the office; **se fossi** ~ **te** if I were you

2 (*moto a luogo*) to; (*: dentro*) into; **andare** ~ **Germania/città** to go to Germany/town; **andare** ~ **ufficio** to go to the office; **entrare** ~ **macchina/casa** to get into the car/go into the house

3 (*tempo*) in; **nel 1989** in 1989; ~ **giugno/estate** in June/summer

4 (*modo, maniera*) in; ~ **silenzio** in silence; ~ **abito da sera** in evening dress; ~ **guerra** at war; ~ **vacanza** on holiday; **Maria Bianchi** ~ **Rossi** Maria Rossi née Bianchi

5 (*mezzo*) by; **viaggiare** ~ **autobus/treno** to travel by bus/train

6 (*materia*) made of; ~ **marmo** made of marble, marble *cpd*; **una collana** ~ **oro** a gold necklace

7 (*misura*) in; **siamo** ~ **quattro** there are four of us; ~ **tutto** in all

8 (*fine*): **dare** ~ **dono** to give as a gift; **spende tutto** ~ **alcool** he spends all his money on drink; ~ **onore di** in honour of.

i'nabile *ag*: ~ **a** incapable of; (*fisicamente, MIL*) unfit for; **inabilità** *sf* incapacity.

inabi'tabile *ag* uninhabitable.

inacces'sibile [inattʃes'sibile] *ag* (*luogo*) inaccessible; (*persona*) unapproachable; (*mistero*) unfathomable.

inaccet'tabile [inattʃet'tabile] *ag* unacceptable.

ina'datto, a *ag*: ~ **(a)** unsuitable o unfit (for).

inadegu'ato, a *ag* inadequate.

inadempi'enza [inadem'pjentsa] *sf*: ~ **(a)** non-fulfilment (of).

inaffer'rabile *ag* elusive; (*concetto, senso*) difficult to grasp.

ina'lare *vt* to inhale.

inalbe'rare *vt* (*NAUT*) to hoist, raise; ~**rsi** *vr* (*fig*) to flare up, fly off the handle.

inalte'rabile *ag* unchangeable; (*colore*) fast, permanent; (*affetto*) constant.

inalte'rato, a *ag* unchanged.

inami'dato, a *ag* starched.

inani'mato, a *ag* inanimate; (*senza vita: corpo*) lifeless.

inappa'gabile *ag* insatiable.

inappel'labile *ag* (*decisione*) final, irrevocable; (*DIR*) final, not open to appeal.

inappe'tenza [inappe'tentsa] *sf* (*MED*) lack of appetite.

inappun'tabile *ag* irreproachable, flawless.

inar'care *vt* (*schiena*) to arch; (*sopracciglia*) to raise; ~**rsi** *vr* to arch.

inari'dire *vt* to make arid, dry up // *vi* (*anche*: ~**rsi**) to dry up, become arid.

inaspet'tato, a *ag* unexpected.

inas'prire *vt* (*disciplina*) to tighten up, make harsher; (*carattere*) to embitter; ~**rsi** *vr* to become harsher; to become bitter; to become worse.

inattac'cabile *ag* (*anche fig*) unassailable; (*alibi*) cast-iron.

inatten'dibile *ag* unreliable.

inat'teso, a *ag* unexpected.

inattu'abile *ag* impracticable.

inau'dito, a *ag* unheard of.

inaugu'rare *vt* to inaugurate, open; (*monumento*) to unveil.

inavve'duto, a *ag* careless, inadvertent.

inavver'tenza [inavver'tentsa] *sf* carelessness, inadvertence.

incagli'are [inkaʎ'ʎare] *vi* (*NAUT: anche*: ~**rsi**) to run aground.

incal'lito, a *ag* calloused; (*fig*) hardened, inveterate; (*: insensibile*) hard.

incal'zare [inkal'tsare] *vt* to follow o pursue closely; (*fig*) to press // *vi* (*urgere*) to be pressing; (*essere imminente*) to be imminent.

incame'rare vt (DIR) to expropriate.

incammi'nare vt (fig: avviare) to start up; ~**rsi** vr to set off.

incande'scente [inkande∫'∫ente] ag incandescent, white-hot.

incan'tare vt to enchant, bewitch; ~**rsi** vr (rimanere intontito) to be spellbound; to be in a daze; (meccanismo: bloccarsi) to jam; **incanta'tore, 'trice** ag enchanting, bewitching // sm/f enchanter/ enchantress; **incan'tesimo** sm spell, charm; **incan'tevole** ag charming, enchanting.

in'canto sm spell, charm, enchantment; (asta) auction; come per ~ as if by magic; **mettere all'**~ to put up for auction.

incanu'tire vi to go white.

inca'pace [inka'pat∫e] ag incapable; **incapacità** sf inability; (DIR) incapacity.

incapo'nirsi vr to be stubborn, be determined.

incap'pare vi: ~ in qc/qn (anche fig) to run into sth/sb.

incapricci'arsi [inkaprit't∫arsi] vr: ~ di to take a fancy to o for.

incapsu'lare vt (dente) to crown.

incarce'rare [inkart∫e'rare] vt to imprison.

incari'care vt: ~ qn di fare to give sb the responsibility of doing; ~**rsi di** to take care o charge of; **incari'cato, a** ag: **incaricato (di)** in charge (of), responsible (for) // sm/f delegate, representative; **professore incaricato** teacher with a temporary appointment; **incaricato d'affari** (POL) chargé d'affaires.

in'carico, chi sm task, job.

incar'nare vt to embody; ~**rsi** vr to be embodied; (REL) to become incarnate.

incarta'mento sm dossier, file.

incar'tare vt to wrap (in paper).

incas'sare vt (merce) to pack (in cases); (gemma: incastonare) to set; (ECON: riscuotere) to collect; (PUGILATO: colpi) to take, stand up to; **in'casso** sm cashing, encashment; (introito) takings pl.

incasto'nare vt to set; **incastona'tura** sf setting.

incas'trare vt to fit in, insert; (fig: intrappolare) to catch; ~**rsi** vr (combaciare) to fit together; (restare bloccato) to become stuck; **in'castro** sm slot, groove; (punto di unione) joint.

incate'nare vt to chain up.

incatra'mare vt to tar.

incatti'vire vt to make wicked; ~**rsi** vr to turn nasty.

in'cauto, a ag imprudent, rash.

inca'vare vt to hollow out; **inca'vato, a** ag hollow; (occhi) sunken; **in'cavo** sm hollow; (solco) groove.

incendi'are [int∫en'djare] vt to set fire to; ~**rsi** vr to catch fire, burst into flames.

incendi'ario, a [int∫en'djarjo] ag incendiary // sm/f arsonist.

in'cendio [in't∫endjo] sm fire.

incene'rire [int∫ene'rire] vt to burn to ashes, incinerate; (cadavere) to cremate; ~**rsi** vr to be burnt to ashes.

in'censo [in't∫enso] sm incense.

incensu'rato, a [int∫ensu'rato] ag (DIR): **essere** ~ to have a clean record.

incen'tivo [int∫en'tivo] sm incentive.

incep'pare [int∫ep'pare] vt to obstruct, hamper; ~**rsi** vr to jam.

ince'rata [int∫e'rata] sf (tela) tarpaulin; (impermeabile) oilskins pl.

incer'tezza [int∫er'tettsa] sf uncertainty.

in'certo, a [in't∫erto] ag uncertain; (irresoluto) undecided, hesitating // sm uncertainty.

in'cetta [in't∫etta] sf buying up; **fare** ~ **di** qc to buy up sth.

inchi'esta [in'kjesta] sf investigation, inquiry.

inchi'nare [inki'nare] vt to bow; ~**rsi** vr to bend down; (per riverenza) to bow; (: donna) to curtsy; **in'chino** sm bow; curtsy.

inchio'dare [inkjo'dare] vt to nail (down); ~ **la macchina** (AUT) to jam on the brakes.

inchi'ostro [in'kjɔstro] sm ink; ~ **simpatico** invisible ink.

inciam'pare [int∫am'pare] vi to trip, stumble.

inci'ampo [in't∫ampo] sm obstacle; **essere d'**~ **a qn** (fig) to be in sb's way.

inciden'tale [int∫iden'tale] ag incidental.

inci'dente [int∫i'dente] sm accident; ~ **d'auto** car accident.

inci'denza [int∫i'dentsa] sf incidence; **avere una forte** ~ **su** qc to affect sth greatly.

in'cidere [in't∫idere] vi: ~ **su** to bear upon, affect // vt (tagliare incavando) to cut into; (ARTE) to engrave; to etch; (canzone) to record.

in'cinta [in't∫inta] ag f pregnant.

incipri'are [int∫i'prjare] vt to powder.

in'circa [in't∫irka] av: **all'**~ more or less, very nearly.

incisi'one [int∫i'zjone] sf cut; (disegno) engraving; etching; (registrazione) recording; (MED) incision.

in'ciso, a [in't∫izo] pp di **incidere** // sm: **per** ~ incidentally, by the way.

inci'vile [int∫i'vile] ag uncivilized; (villano) impolite.

incivi'lire [int∫ivi'lire] vt to civilize.

incl. abbr (= incluso) encl.

incli'nare vt to tilt // vi (fig): ~ **a qc/a fare** to incline towards sth/doing; to tend towards sth/to do; ~**rsi** vr (barca) to list; (aereo) to bank; **incli'nato, a** ag sloping; **inclinazi'one** sf slope; (fig) inclination, tendency; **in'cline** ag: incline a inclined to.

in'cludere vt to include; (accludere) to enclose; **inclu'sivo, a** ag: inclusivo di inclusive of; **in'cluso, a** pp di **includere** // include; enclosed.

incoe'rente ag incoherent; (contraddittorio) inconsistent.

in'cognito, a [in'kɔɲɲito] ag unknown // sm: in ~ incognito // sf (MAT, fig) unknown quantity.

incol'lare vt to glue, gum; (unire con colla) to stick together.

incolon'nare vt to draw up in columns.

inco'lore ag colourless.

incol'pare vt: ~ qn di to charge sb with.

in'colto, a ag (terreno) uncultivated; (trascurato: capelli) neglected; (persona) uneducated.

in'colume ag safe and sound, unhurt.

in'combere vi (sovrastare minacciando): ~ su to threaten, hang over.

incominci'are [inkomin'tʃare] vi, vt to begin, start.

in'comodo, a ag uncomfortable; (inopportuno) inconvenient // sm inconvenience, bother.

incompe'tente ag incompetent.

incompi'uto, a ag unfinished, incomplete.

incom'pleto, a ag incomplete.

incompren'sibile ag incomprehensible.

incom'preso, a ag not understood; misunderstood.

inconce'pibile [inkontʃe'pibile] ag inconceivable.

inconcili'abile [inkontʃi'ljabile] ag irreconcilable.

inconclu'dente ag inconclusive; (persona) ineffectual.

incondizio'nato, a [inkondittsjo'nato] ag unconditional.

inconfu'tabile ag irrefutable.

incongru'ente ag inconsistent.

in'congruo, a ag incongruous.

inconsa'pevole ag: ~ di unaware of, ignorant of.

in'conscio, a, sci, sce [in'kɔnʃo] ag unconscious // sm (PSIC): l'~ the unconscious.

inconsis'tente ag insubstantial; unfounded.

inconsu'eto, a ag unusual.

incon'sulto, a ag rash.

incon'trare vt to meet; (difficoltà) to meet with; ~rsi vr to meet.

incontras'tabile ag incontrovertible, indisputable.

in'contro av: ~ a (verso) towards // sm meeting; (SPORT) match; meeting; ~ di calcio football match.

inconveni'ente sm drawback, snag.

incoraggia'mento [inkoraddʒa'mento]

sm encouragement.

incoraggi'are [inkorad'dʒare] vt to encourage.

incornici'are [inkorni'tʃare] vt to frame.

incoro'nare vt to crown; **incoronazi'one** sf coronation.

incorpo'rare vt to incorporate; (fig: annettere) to annex.

in'correre vi: ~ in to meet with, run into.

incosci'ente [inkoʃ'ʃɛnte] ag (inconscio) unconscious; (irresponsabile) reckless, thoughtless; **incosci'enza** sf unconsciousness; recklessness, thoughtlessness.

incre'dibile ag incredible, unbelievable.

in'credulo, a ag incredulous, disbelieving.

incremen'tare vt to increase; (dar sviluppo a) to promote.

incre'mento sm (sviluppo) development; (aumento numerico) increase, growth.

incres'parsi vr (acqua) to ripple; (capelli) to go frizzy; (pelle, tessuto) to wrinkle.

incrimi'nare vt (DIR) to charge.

incri'nare vt to crack; (fig: rapporti, amicizia) to cause to deteriorate; ~rsi vr to crack; to deteriorate; **incrina'tura** sf crack; (fig) rift.

incroci'are [inkro'tʃare] vt to cross; (incontrare) to meet // vi (NAUT, AER) to cruise; ~rsi vr (strade) to cross, intersect; (persone, veicoli) to pass each other; ~ le braccia/le gambe to fold one's arms/cross one's legs; **incrocia'tore** sm cruiser.

in'crocio [in'krotʃo] sm (anche FERR) crossing; (di strade) crossroads.

incros'tare vt to encrust.

incuba'trice [inkuba'tritʃe] sf incubator.

'incubo sm nightmare.

in'cudine sf anvil.

incu'rante ag: ~ (di) heedless (of), careless (of).

incurio'sire vt to make curious; ~rsi vr to become curious.

incursi'one sf raid.

incur'vare vt, ~rsi vr to bend, curve.

in'cusso, a pp di **incutere**.

incusto'dito, a ag unguarded, unattended.

in'cutere vt to arouse; ~ timore/rispetto a qn to strike fear into sb/command sb's respect.

'indaco sm indigo.

indaffa'rato, a ag busy.

inda'gare vt to investigate.

in'dagine [in'dadʒine] sf investigation, inquiry; (ricerca) research, study.

indebi'tarsi vr to run o get into debt.

in'debito, a ag undue; undeserved.

indebo'lire vt, vi (anche: ~rsi) to weaken.

inde'cente |inde'tʃɛnte| *ag* indecent; **inde'cenza** *sf* indecency.

inde'ciso, a |inde'tʃizo| *ag* indecisive; (*irresoluto*) undecided.

inde'fesso, a *ag* untiring, indefatigable.

indefi'nito, a *ag* (*anche* LING) indefinite; (*impreciso, non determinato*) undefined.

in'degno, a |in'deɲɲo| *ag* (*atto*) shameful; (*persona*) unworthy.

indelica'tezza |indelika'tettsa| *sf* tactlessness.

indemoni'ato, a *ag* possessed (by the devil).

in'denne *ag* unhurt, uninjured; **indennità** *sf inv* (*rimborso: di spese*) allowance; (*: di perdita*) compensation, indemnity; **indennità di contingenza** cost-of-living allowance; **indennità di trasferta** travel expenses *pl*.

indenniz'zare |indenniʣ'dzare| *vt* to compensate; **inden'nizzo** *sm* (*somma*) compensation, indemnity.

indero'gabile *ag* binding.

'India *sf*: **l'~** India; **indi'ano, a** *ag* Indian // *sm/f* (*d'India*) Indian; (*d'America*) Red Indian.

indiavo'lato, a *ag* possessed (by the devil); (*vivace, violento*) wild.

indi'care *vt* (*mostrare*) to show, indicate; (*: col dito*) to point to, point out; (*consigliare*) to suggest, recommend; **indica'tivo, a** *ag* indicative // *sm* (LING) indicative (mood); **indica'tore** *sm* (*elenco*) guide; directory; (TECN) gauge; indicator; **cartello indicatore** sign; **indicatore di velocità** (AUT) speedometer; **indicatore della benzina** fuel gauge; **indicazi'one** *sf* indication; (*informazione*) piece of information; **indicazioni per l'uso** instructions for use.

'indice |'inditʃe| *sm* (ANAT: *dito*) index finger, forefinger; (*lancetta*) needle, pointer; (*fig: indizio*) sign; (TECN, MAT, *nei libri*) index; **~ di gradimento** (RADIO, TV) popularity rating.

indi'cibile |indi'tʃibile| *ag* inexpressible.

indietreggi'are |indietred'dʒare| *vi* to draw back, retreat.

indi'etro *av* back; (*guardare*) behind, back; (*andare, cadere: anche:* **all'~**) backwards; **rimanere ~** to be left behind; **essere ~** (*col lavoro*) to be behind; (*orologio*) to be slow; **rimandare qc ~** to send sth back.

indi'feso, a *ag* (*città etc*) undefended; (*persona*) defenceless.

indiffe'rente *ag* indifferent; **indiffe'renza** *sf* indifference.

in'digeno, a |in'didʒeno| *ag* indigenous, native // *sm/f* native.

indi'gente |indi'dʒɛnte| *ag* poverty-stricken, destitute; **indi'genza** *sf* extreme poverty.

indigesti'one |indidʒes'tjone| *sf* indigestion.

indi'gesto, a |indi'dʒɛsto| *ag* indigestible.

indi'gnare |indiɲ'ɲare| *vt* to fill with indignation; **~rsi** *vr* to be (*o* get) indignant.

indimenti'cabile *ag* unforgettable.

indipen'dente *ag* independent; **indipen'denza** *sf* independence.

in'dire *vt* (*concorso*) to announce; (*elezioni*) to call.

indi'retto, a *ag* indirect.

indiriz'zare |indirit'tsare| *vt* (*dirigere*) to direct; (*mandare*) to send; (*lettera*) to address.

indi'rizzo |indi'rittso| *sm* address; (*direzione*) direction; (*avvio*) trend, course.

indis'creto, a *ag* indiscreet.

indis'cusso, a *ag* unquestioned.

indispen'sabile *ag* indispensable, essential.

indispet'tire *vt* to irritate, annoy // *vi* (*anche:* **~rsi**) to get irritated *o* annoyed.

in'divia *sf* endive.

individu'ale *ag* individual; **individualità** *sf* individuality.

individu'are *vt* (*dar forma distinta a*) to characterize; (*determinare*) to locate; (*riconoscere*) to single out.

indi'viduo *sm* individual.

indizi'are |indit'tsjare| *vt*: **~ qn di qc** to cast suspicion on sb for sth; **indizi'ato, a** *ag* suspected // *sm/f* suspect.

in'dizio |in'dittsjo| *sm* (*segno*) sign, indication; (POLIZIA) clue; (DIR) piece of evidence.

'indole *sf* nature, character.

indolen'zito, a |indolen'tsito| *ag* stiff, aching; (*intorpidito*) numb.

indo'lore *ag* painless.

indo'mani *sm*: **l'~** the next day, the following day.

Indo'nesia *sf*: **l'~** Indonesia.

indos'sare *vt* (*mettere indosso*) to put on; (*avere indosso*) to have on; **indossa'tore, 'trice** *sm/f* model.

in'dotto, a *pp di* **indurre**.

indottri'nare *vt* to indoctrinate.

indovi'nare *vt* (*scoprire*) to guess; (*immaginare*) to imagine, guess; (*il futuro*) to foretell; **indovi'nato, a** *ag* successful; (*scelta*) inspired; **indovi'nello** *sm* riddle; **indo'vino, a** *sm/f* fortuneteller.

indubbia'mente *av* undoubtedly.

in'dubbio, a *ag* certain, undoubted.

indugi'are |indu'dʒare| *vi* to take one's time, delay.

in'dugio |in'dudʒo| *sm* (*ritardo*) delay; **senza ~** without delay.

indul'gente |indul'dʒɛnte| *ag* indulgent; (*giudice*) lenient; **indul'genza** *sf* indulgence; leniency.

in'dulgere |in'duldʒere| *vi*: **~ a** (*accondiscendere*) to comply with;

(*abbandonarsi*) to indulge in; **in'dulto, a** *pp di* **indulgere** // *sm* (*DIR*) pardon.

indu'mento *sm* article of clothing, garment; ~**i** *smpl* clothes.

indu'rire *vt* to harden // *vi* (*anche:* ~**rsi**) to harden, become hard.

in'durre *vt:* ~ **qn a fare qc** to induce *o* persuade sb to do sth; ~ **qn in errore** to mislead sb.

in'dustria *sf* industry; **industri'ale** *ag* industrial // *sm* industrialist.

industri'arsi *vr* to do one's best, try hard.

industri'oso, a *ag* industrious, hardworking.

induzi'one [indut'tsjone] *sf* induction.

inebe'tito, a *ag* dazed, stunned.

inebri'are *vt* (*anche fig*) to intoxicate; ~**rsi** *vr* to become intoxicated.

inecce'pibile [inettfe'pibile] *ag* unexceptionable.

i'nedia *sf* starvation.

i'nedito, a *ag* unpublished.

ineffi'cace [ineffi'katfe] *ag* ineffective.

ineffici'ente [ineffi'tfɛnte] *ag* inefficient.

inegu'ale *ag* unequal; (*irregolare*) uneven.

ine'rente *ag:* ~ **a** concerning, regarding.

i'nerme *ag* unarmed; defenceless.

inerpi'carsi *vr:* ~ (**su**) to clamber (up).

i'nerte *ag* inert; (*inattivo*) indolent, sluggish; **i'nerzia** *sf* inertia; indolence, sluggishness.

ine'satto, a *ag* (*impreciso*) inexact; (*erroneo*) incorrect; (*AMM: non riscosso*) uncollected.

inesis'tente *ag* non-existent.

inesperi'enza [inespe'rjɛntsa] *sf* inexperience.

ines'perto, a *ag* inexperienced.

i'netto, a *ag* (*incapace*) inept; (*che non ha attitudine*): ~ (**a**) unsuited (to).

ine'vaso, a *ag* (*ordine, corrispondenza*) outstanding.

inevi'tabile *ag* inevitable.

i'nezia [i'nɛttsja] *sf* trifle, thing of no importance.

infagot'tare *vt* to bundle up, wrap up; ~**rsi** *vr* to wrap up.

infal'libile *ag* infallible.

infa'mare *vt* to defame.

in'fame *ag* infamous; (*fig: cosa, compito*) awful, dreadful.

infan'tile *ag* child *cpd*; childlike; (*adulto, azione*) childish; **letteratura** ~ children's books *pl.*

in'fanzia [in'fantsja] *sf* childhood; (*bambini*) children *pl*; **prima** ~ babyhood, infancy.

infari'nare *vt* to cover with (*o* sprinkle with *o* dip in) flour; ~ **di zucchero** to sprinkle with sugar; **infarina'tura** *sf* (*fig*) smattering.

in'farto *sm* (*MED*): ~ (**cardiaco**) coronary.

infasti'dire *vt* to annoy, irritate; ~**rsi** *vr* to get annoyed *o* irritated.

infati'cabile *ag* tireless, untiring.

in'fatti *cong* as a matter of fact, in fact, actually.

infatu'arsi *vr:* ~ **di** *o* **per** to become infatuated with, fall for; **infatuazi'one** *sf* infatuation.

in'fausto, a *ag* unpropitious, unfavourable.

infe'condo, a *ag* infertile.

infe'dele *ag* unfaithful; **infedeltà** *sf* infidelity.

infe'lice [infe'litfe] *ag* unhappy; (*sfortunato*) unlucky, unfortunate; (*inopportuno*) inopportune, ill-timed; (*mal riuscito: lavoro*) bad, poor; **infelicità** *sf* unhappiness.

inferi'ore *ag* lower; (*per intelligenza, qualità*) inferior // *smlf* inferior; ~ **a** (*numero, quantità*) less *o* smaller than; (*meno buono*) inferior to; ~ **alla media** below average; **inferiorità** *sf* inferiority.

inferme'ria *sf* infirmary; (*di scuola, nave*) sick bay.

infermi'ere, a *smlf* nurse.

infermità *sf inv* illness; infirmity.

in'fermo, a *ag* (*ammalato*) ill; (*debole*) infirm.

infer'nale *ag* infernal; (*proposito, complotto*) diabolical.

in'ferno *sm* hell.

inferri'ata *sf* grating.

infervo'rare *vt* to arouse enthusiasm in; ~**rsi** *vr* to get excited, get carried away.

infet'tare *vt* to infect; ~**rsi** *vr* to become infected; **infet'tivo, a** *ag* infectious; **in'fetto, a** *ag* infected; (*acque*) polluted, contaminated; **infezi'one** *sf* infection.

infiac'chire [infjak'kire] *vt* to weaken // *vi* (*anche:* ~**rsi**) to grow weak.

infiam'mabile *ag* inflammable.

infiam'mare *vt* to set alight; (*fig, MED*) to inflame; ~**rsi** *vr* to catch fire; (*MED*) to become inflamed; (*fig*): ~**rsi di** to be fired with; **infiammazi'one** *sf* (*MED*) inflammation.

in'fido, a *ag* unreliable, treacherous.

infie'rire *vi:* ~ **su** (*fisicamente*) to attack furiously; (*verbalmente*) to rage at; (*epidemia*) to rage over.

in'figgere [in'fiddʒere] *vt:* ~ **qc in** to thrust *o* drive sth into.

infi'lare *vt* (*ago*) to thread; (*mettere: chiave*) to insert; (*: anello, vestito*) to slip *o* put on; (*strada*) to turn into, take; ~**rsi** *vr:* ~**rsi in** to slip into; (*indossare*) to slip on; ~ **l'uscio** to slip in; to slip out.

infil'trarsi *vr* to penetrate, seep through; (*MIL*) to infiltrate; **infiltrazi'one** *sf* infiltration.

infil'zare [infil'tsare] *vt* (*infilare*) to string together; (*trafiggere*) to pierce.

'infimo, a *ag* lowest.

in'fine *av* finally; (*insomma*) in short.

infinità *sf* infinity; (*in quantità*): **un'~ di** an infinite number of.

infi'nito, a *ag* infinite; (*LING*) infinitive // *sm* infinity; (*LING*) infinitive; **all'~** (*senza fine*) endlessly.

infinocchi'are [infinok'kjare] *vt* (*fam*) to hoodwink.

infischi'arsi [infis'kjarsi] *vr*: **~ di** not to care about.

in'fisso, a *pp di* **infiggere** // *sm* fixture; (*di porta, finestra*) frame.

infit'tire *vt*, *vi* (*anche:* ~rsi) to thicken.

inflazi'one [inflat'tsjone] *sf* inflation.

in'fliggere [in'flidd3ere] *vt* to inflict; **in'flitto, a** *pp di* **infliggere**.

influ'ente *ag* influential; **influ'enza** *sf* influence; (*MED*) influenza, flu.

influ'ire *vi*: **~ su** to influence.

in'flusso *sm* influence.

infol'tire *vt*, *vi* to thicken.

infon'dato, a *ag* unfounded, groundless.

in'fondere *vt*: **~ qc in qn** to instill sth in sb.

infor'care *vt* to fork (up); (*bicicletta, cavallo*) to get on; (*occhiali*) to put on.

infor'mare *vt* to inform, tell; **~rsi** *vr*: **~rsi (di o su)** to inquire (about).

infor'matica *sf* computer science.

informa'tivo, a *ag* informative.

informa'tore *sm* informer.

informazi'one [informat'tsjone] *sf* piece of information; **~i** *sfpl* information *sg*; **chiedere un'~** to ask for (some) information.

in'forme *ag* shapeless.

informico'larsi, informico'lirsi *vr* to have pins and needles.

infor'tunio *sm* accident; **~ sul lavoro** industrial accident, accident at work.

infos'sarsi *vr* (*terreno*) to sink; (*guance*) to become hollow; **infos'sato, a** *ag* hollow; (*occhi*) deep-set; (*: per malattia*) sunken.

in'frangere [in'frand3ere] *vt* to smash; (*fig: legge, patti*) to break; **~rsi** *vr* to smash, break; **infran'gibile** *ag* unbreakable; **in'franto, a** *pp di* **infrangere** // broken.

infrazi'one [infrat'tsjone] *sf*: **~ a** breaking of, violation of.

infredda'tura *sf* slight cold.

infreddo'lito, a *ag* cold, chilled.

infruttu'oso, a *ag* fruitless.

infu'ori *av* out; **all'~** outwards; **all'~ di** (*eccetto*) except, with the exception of.

infuri'are *vi* to rage; **~rsi** *vr* to fly into a rage.

infusi'one *sf* infusion.

in'fuso, a *pp di* **infondere** // *sm* infusion; **~ di camomilla** camomile tea.

Ing. *abbr* = **ingegnere**.

ingabbi'are *vt* to cage.

ingaggi'are [ingad'd3are] *vt* (*assumere con compenso*) to take on, hire; (*SPORT*)

to sign on; (*MIL*) to engage; **in'gaggio** *sm* hiring; signing on.

ingan'nare *vt* to deceive; (*coniuge*) to be unfaithful to; (*fisco*) to cheat; (*eludere*) to dodge, elude; (*fig: tempo*) to while away // *vi* (*apparenza*) to be deceptive; **~rsi** *vr* to be mistaken, be wrong; **ingan'nevole** *ag* deceptive.

in'ganno *sm* deceit, deception; (*azione*) trick; (*menzogna, frode*) cheat, swindle; (*illusione*) illusion.

ingarbugli'are [ingarbuʎ'ʎare] *vt* to tangle; (*fig*) to confuse, muddle; **~rsi** *vr* to become confused o muddled.

inge'gnarsi [indʒeɲ'ɲarsi] *vr* to do one's best, try hard; **~ per vivere** to live by one's wits.

inge'gnere [indʒeɲ'ɲere] *sm* engineer; **~ civile/navale** civil/naval engineer; **ingegne'ria** *sf* engineering.

in'gegno [in'dʒeɲɲo] *sm* (*intelligenza*) intelligence; brains *pl*; (*capacità creativa*) ingenuity; (*disposizione*) talent; **inge'gnoso, a** *ag* ingenious, clever.

ingelo'sire [indʒelo'zire] *vt* to make jealous // *vi* (*anche:* ~rsi) to become jealous.

in'gente [in'dʒente] *ag* huge, enormous.

ingenuità [indʒenui'ta] *sf* ingenuousness.

in'genuo, a [in'dʒenuo] *ag* ingenuous, naïve.

inges'sare [indʒes'sare] *vt* (*MED*) to put in plaster; **ingessa'tura** *sf* plaster.

Inghil'terra [ingil'terra] *sf*: **l'~** England.

inghiot'tire [ingjot'tire] *vt* to swallow.

ingial'lire [indʒal'lire] *vi* to go yellow.

ingigan'tire [indʒigan'tire] *vt* to enlarge, magnify // *vi* to become gigantic o enormous.

inginocchi'arsi [indʒinok'kjarsi] *vr* to kneel (down).

ingiù [in'dʒu] *av* down, downwards.

ingi'uria [in'dʒurja] *sf* insult; (*fig: danno*) damage; **ingiuri'are** *vt* to insult, abuse; **ingiuri'oso, a** *ag* insulting, abusive.

ingius'tizia [indʒus'tittsja] *sf* injustice.

ingi'usto, a [in'dʒusto] *ag* unjust, unfair.

in'glese *ag* English // *sm/f* Englishman/ woman // *sm* (*LING*) English; **gli I~i** the English; **andarsene o filare all'~** to take French leave.

ingoi'are *vt* to gulp (down); (*fig*) to swallow (up).

ingol'fare *vt*, **~rsi** *vr* (*motore*) to flood.

ingom'brare *vt* (*strada*) to block; (*stanza*) to clutter up; **in'gombro, a** *ag* (*strada, passaggio*) blocked // *sm* obstacle; **essere d'ingombro** to be in the way.

in'gordo, a *ag*: **~ di** greedy for; (*fig*) greedy o avid for.

ingor'garsi *vr* to be blocked up, be choked up.

in'gorgo, ghi *sm* blockage, obstruction; (*anche:* ~ **stradale**) traffic jam.

ingoz'zare [ingot'tsare] *vt* (*animali*) to fatten; (*fig: persona*) to stuff; ~**rsi** *vr:* ~**rsi (di)** to stuff o.s. (with).

ingra'naggio [ingra'naddʒo] *sm* (*TECN*) gear; (*di orologio*) mechanism; **gli ~i della burocrazia** the bureaucratic machinery.

ingra'nare *vi* to mesh, engage // *vt* to engage; ~ **la marcia** to get into gear.

ingrandi'mento *sm* enlargement; extension.

ingran'dire *vt* (*anche FOT*) to enlarge; (*estendere*) to extend; (*OTTICA, fig*) to magnify // *vi* (*anche:* ~**rsi**) to become larger o bigger; (*aumentare*) to grow, increase; (*espandersi*) to expand.

ingras'sare *vt* to make fat; (*animali*) to fatten; (*AGR: terreno*) to manure; (*lubrificare*) to oil, lubricate // *vi* (*anche:* ~**rsi**) to get fat, put on weight.

in'grato, a *ag* ungrateful; (*lavoro*) thankless, unrewarding.

ingrazi'are [ingrat'tsjare] *vt:* ~**rsi qn** to ingratiate o.s. with sb.

ingredi'ente *sm* ingredient.

in'gresso *sm* (*porta*) entrance; (*atrio*) hall; (*l'entrare*) entrance, entry; (*facoltà di entrare*) admission; "~ libero" "admission free".

ingros'sare *vt* to increase; (*folla, livello*) to swell // *vi* (*anche:* ~**rsi**) to increase; to swell.

in'grosso *av:* all'~ (*COMM*) wholesale; (*all'incirca*) roughly, about.

ingual'cibile [ingwal'tʃibile] *ag* crease-resistant.

ingua'ribile *ag* incurable.

'inguine *sm* (*ANAT*) groin.

ini'bire *vt* to forbid, prohibit; (*PSIC*) to inhibit; **inibizi'one** *sf* prohibition; inhibition.

iniet'tare *vt* to inject; ~**rsi** *vr:* ~**rsi di sangue** (*occhi*) to become bloodshot; **iniezi'one** *sf* injection.

inimi'carsi *vr:* ~ **con qn** to fall out with sb.

inimi'cizia [inimi'tʃittsja] *sf* animosity.

ininter'rotto, a *ag* unbroken; uninterrupted.

iniquità *sf inv* iniquity; (*atto*) wicked action.

inizi'ale [init'tsjale] *ag, sf* initial.

inizi'are [init'tsjare] *vi, vt* to begin, start; ~ **qn a** to initiate sb into; (*pittura etc*) to introduce sb to; ~ **a fare qc** to start doing sth.

inizia'tiva [inittsja'tiva] *sf* initiative; ~ **privata** private enterprise.

i'nizio [i'nittsjo] *sm* beginning; all'~ at the beginning, at the start; **dare** ~ **a qc** to start sth, get sth going.

innaffi'are *etc* = **annaffiare** *etc*.

innal'zare [innal'tsare] *vt* (*sollevare,*

alzare) to raise; (*rizzare*) to erect; ~**rsi** *vr* to rise.

innamo'rare *vt* to enchant, charm; ~**rsi** *vr:* ~**rsi (di qn)** to fall in love (with sb); **innamo'rato, a** *ag* (*che nutre amore*): **innamorato (di)** in love (with); (*appassionato*): **innamorato di** very fond of // *sm/f* lover; sweetheart.

in'nanzi [in'nantsi] *av* (*stato in luogo*) in front, ahead; (*moto a luogo*) forward, on; (*tempo: prima*) before // *prep* (*prima*) before; ~ **a** in front of.

in'nato, a *ag* innate.

innatu'rale *ag* unnatural.

inne'gabile *ag* undeniable.

innervo'sire *vt:* ~ **qn** to get on sb's nerves; ~**rsi** *vr* to get irritated o upset.

innes'care *vt* to prime; **in'nesco, schi** *sm* primer.

innes'tare *vt* (*BOT, MED*) to graft; (*TECN*) to engage; (*inserire: presa*) to insert; **in'nesto** *sm* graft; grafting *q*; (*TECN*) clutch; (*ELETTR*) connection.

'inno *sm* hymn; ~ **nazionale** national anthem.

inno'cente [inno'tʃɛnte] *ag* innocent; **inno'cenza** *sf* innocence.

in'nocuo, a *ag* innocuous, harmless.

inno'vare *vt* to change, make innovations in.

innume'revole *ag* innumerable.

ino'doro, a *ag* odourless.

inol'trare *vt* (*AMM*) to pass on, forward; ~**rsi** *vr* (*addentrarsi*) to advance, go forward.

i'noltre *av* besides, moreover.

inon'dare *vt* to flood; **inondazi'one** *sf* flooding *q*; flood.

inope'roso, a *ag* inactive, idle.

inoppor'tuno, a *ag* untimely, ill-timed; inappropriate; (*momento*) inopportune.

inorgo'glire [inorgoʎ'ʎire] *vt* to make proud // *vi* (*anche:* ~**rsi**) to become proud; ~**rsi di qc** to pride o.s. on sth.

inorri'dire *vt* to horrify // *vi* to be horrified.

inospi'tale *ag* inhospitable.

inosser'vato, a *ag* (*non notato*) unobserved; (*non rispettato*) not observed, not kept.

inossi'dabile *ag* stainless.

inqua'drare *vt* (*foto, immagine*) to frame; (*fig*) to situate, set.

inquie'tare *vt* (*turbare*) to disturb, worry; ~**rsi** *vr* to worry, become anxious; (*impazientirsi*) to get upset.

inqui'eto, a *ag* restless; (*preoccupato*) worried, anxious; **inquie'tudine** *sf* anxiety, worry.

inqui'lino, a *sm/f* tenant.

inquina'mento *sm* pollution.

inqui'nare *vt* to pollute.

inqui'sire *vt, vi* to investigate; **inquisi'tore, 'trice** *ag* (*sguardo*) inquiring; **inquisizi'one** *sf* (*STORIA*) inquisition.

insabbi'are vt (fig: pratica) to shelve; ~rsi vr (arenarsi: barca) to run aground; (fig: pratica) to be shelved.

insac'cati smpl (CUC) sausages.

insa'lata sf salad; ~ mista mixed salad; **insalati'era** sf salad bowl.

insa'lubre ag unhealthy.

insa'nabile ag (piaga) which cannot be healed; (situazione) irremediable; (odio) implacable.

insangui'nare vt to stain with blood.

insa'puta sf: all'~ di qn without sb knowing.

insce'nare [infe'narc] vt (TEATRO) to stage, put on; (fig) to stage.

insedi'are vt to install; ~rsi vr to take up office; (popolo, colonia) to settle.

in'segna [in'senna] sf sign; (emblema) sign, emblem; (bandiera) flag, banner; ~e sfpl (decorazioni) insignia pl.

insegna'mento [insenna'mento] sm teaching.

inse'gnante [insen'nante] ag teaching // sm/f teacher.

inse'gnare [insen'nare] vt, vi to teach; ~ a qn qc to teach sb sth; ~ a qn a fare qc to teach sb (how) to do sth.

insegui'mento sm pursuit, chase.

insegu'ire vt to pursue, chase.

inselvati'chire [inselvati'kire] vi (anche: ~rsi) to grow wild.

insena'tura sf inlet, creek.

insen'sato, a ag senseless, stupid.

insen'sibile ag (nervo) insensible; (persona) indifferent.

inse'rire vt to insert; (ELETTR) to connect; (allegare) to enclose; (annuncio) to put in, place; ~rsi vr (fig): ~rsi in to become part of; **in'serto** sm (pubblicazione) insert.

inservi'ente sm/f attendant.

inserzi'one [inser'tsjone] sf insertion; (avviso) advertisement; fare un'~ sul giornale to put an advertisement in the paper.

insetti'cida, i [insetti'tʃida] sm insecticide.

in'setto sm insect.

in'sidia sf snare, trap; (pericolo) hidden danger; **insidi'are** vt: ~ la vita di qn to make an attempt on sb's life.

insi'eme av together // prep: ~ a o con together with // sm whole; (MAT, servizio, assortimento) set; (MODA) ensemble, outfit; tutti ~ all together; tutto ~ all together; (in una volta) at one go; nell'~ on the whole; d'~ (veduta etc) overall.

insignifi'cante [insinnifi'kante] ag insignificant.

insi'gnire [insin'nire] vt: ~ qn di to honour o decorate sb with.

insin'cero, a [insin'tʃero] ag insincere.

insinda'cabile ag unquestionable.

insinu'are vt (introdurre): ~ qc in to slip o slide sth into; (fig) to insinuate, imply; ~rsi vr: ~rsi in to seep into; (fig) to creep into; to worm one's way into.

insis'tente ag insistent; persistent.

in'sistere vi: ~ su qc to insist on sth; ~ in qc/a fare (perseverare) to persist in sth/in doing; **insis'tito, a** pp di **insistere**.

insoddis'fatto, a ag dissatisfied.

insoffe'rente ag intolerant.

insolazi'one [insola'tsjone] sf (MED) sunstroke.

inso'lente ag insolent; **insolen'tire** vi to grow insolent // vt to insult, be rude to.

in'solito, a ag unusual, out of the ordinary.

inso'luto, a ag (non risolto) unsolved; (non pagato) unpaid, outstanding.

insol'vibile ag insolvent.

in'somma av (in breve, in conclusione) in short; (dunque) well // escl for heaven's sake!

in'sonne ag sleepless; **in'sonnia** sf insomnia, sleeplessness.

insonno'lito, a ag sleepy, drowsy.

insoppor'tabile ag unbearable.

in'sorgere [in'sordzere] vi (ribellarsi) to rise up, rebel; (apparire) to come up, arise.

in'sorto, a pp di **insorgere** // sm/f rebel, insurgent.

insospet'tire vt to make suspicious // vi (anche: ~rsi) to become suspicious.

inspi'rare vt to breathe in, inhale.

in'stabile ag (carico, indole) unstable; (tempo) unsettled; (equilibrio) unsteady.

instal'lare vt to install; ~rsi vr (sistemarsi) ~rsi in to settle in; **installazi'one** sf installation.

instan'cabile ag untiring, indefatigable.

instau'rare vt to introduce, institute.

instra'dare vt: ~ (verso) to direct (towards).

insuc'cesso [insut'tʃesso] sm failure, flop.

insudici'are [insudi'tʃare] vt to dirty; ~rsi vr to get dirty.

insuffici'ente [insuffi'tʃente] ag insufficient; (compito, allievo) inadequate; **insuffici'enza** sf insufficiency; inadequacy; (INS) fail.

insu'lare ag insular.

insu'lina sf insulin.

in'sulso, a ag (sciocco) inane, silly; (persona) dull, insipid.

insul'tare vt to insult, affront.

in'sulto sm insult, affront.

insussis'tente ag non-existent.

intac'care vt (fare tacche) to cut into; (corrodere) to corrode; (fig: cominciare ad usare: risparmi) to break into; (: ledere) to damage.

intagli'are [inta/'/arc] *vt* to carve; **in'taglio** *sm* carving.

intan'gibile [intan'dʒibilc] *ag* untouchable; inviolable.

in'tanto *av* (*nel frattempo*) meanwhile, in the meantime; (*per cominciare*) just to begin with; ~ **che** *cong* while.

in'tarsio *sm* inlaying *q*, marquetry *q*; inlay.

inta'sare *vt* to choke (up), block (up); (*AUT*) to obstruct, block; ~**rsi** *vr* to become choked *o* blocked.

intas'care *vt* to pocket.

in'tatto, a *ag* intact; (*puro*) unsullied.

intavo'lare *vt* to start, enter into.

inte'grale *ag* complete; (*pane, farina*) wholemeal (*Brit*), whole-wheat (*US*); (*MAT*): **calcolo** ~ integral calculus.

inte'grante *ag*: **parte** ~ integral part.

inte'grare *vt* to complete; (*MAT*) to integrate; ~**rsi** *vr* (*persona*) to become integrated.

integrità *sf* integrity.

'integro, a *ag* (*intatto, intero*) complete, whole; (*retto*) upright.

intelaia'tura *sf* frame; (*fig*) structure, framework.

intel'letto *sm* intellect; **intellettu'ale** *ag, sm/f* intellectual.

intelli'gente [intelli'dʒɛnte] *ag* intelligent; **intelli'genza** *sf* intelligence.

intem'perie *sfpl* bad weather *sg*.

intempes'tivo, a *ag* untimely.

inten'dente *sm*: ~ **di Finanza** inland (*Brit*) *o* internal (*US*) revenue officer; **inten'denza** *sf*: **intendenza di Finanza** inland (*Brit*) *o* internal (*US*) revenue office.

in'tendere *vt* (*avere intenzione*): ~ **fare qc** to intend *o* mean to do sth; (*comprendere*) to understand; (*udire*) to hear; (*significare*) to mean; ~**rsi** *vr* (*conoscere*): ~**rsi di** to know a lot about, be a connoisseur of; (*accordarsi*) to get on (well); **intendersela con qn** (*avere una relazione amorosa*) to have an affair with sb; **intendi'mento** *sm* (*intelligenza*) understanding; (*proposito*) intention; **intendi'tore, 'trice** *sm/f* connoisseur, expert.

intene'rire *vt* (*fig*) to move (to pity); ~**rsi** *vr* (*fig*) to be moved.

inten'sivo, a *ag* intensive.

in'tenso, a *ag* intense.

in'tento, a *ag* (*teso, assorto*): ~ **(a)** intent (on), absorbed (in) // *sm* aim, purpose.

intenzio'nale [intentsjo'nalc] *ag* intentional.

intenzi'one [inten'tsjonc] *sf* intention; (*DIR*) intent; **avere** ~ **di fare qc** to intend to do sth, have the intention of doing sth.

interca'lare *sm* pet phrase, stock phrase // *vt* to insert.

interca'pedine *sf* gap, cavity.

intercet'tare [intertʃet'tarc] *vt* to intercept.

inter'detto, a *pp di* **interdire** // *ag* forbidden, prohibited; (*sconcertato*) dumbfounded // *sm* (*REL*) interdict.

inter'dire *vt* to forbid, prohibit, ban; (*REL*) to interdict; (*DIR*) to deprive of civil rights; **interdizi'one** *sf* prohibition, ban.

interessa'mento *sm* interest.

interes'sante *ag* interesting; **essere in stato** ~ to be expecting (a baby).

interes'sare *vt* to interest; (*concernere*) to concern, be of interest to; (*far intervenire*): ~ **qn a** to draw sb's attention to // *vi*: ~ **a** to interest, matter to; ~**rsi** *vr* (*mostrare interesse*): ~**rsi a** to take an interest in, be interested in; (*occuparsi*): ~**rsi di** to take care of.

inte'resse *sm* (*anche COMM*) interest.

inter'faccia, ce [inter'fattʃa] *sf* (*INFORM*) interface.

interfe'renza [interfe'rɛntsa] *sf* interference.

interfe'rire *vi* to interfere.

interiezi'one [interjet'tsjone] *sf* exclamation, interjection.

interi'ora *sfpl* entrails.

interi'ore *ag* interior, inner, inside, internal; (*fig*) inner.

inter'ludio *sm* (*MUS*) interlude.

inter'medio, a *ag* intermediate.

inter'mezzo [inter'mɛddzo] *sm* (*intervallo*) interval; (*breve spettacolo*) intermezzo.

inter'nare *vt* (*arrestare*) to intern; (*MED*) to commit (to a mental institution).

internazio'nale [internattsjo'nale] *ag* international.

in'terno, a *ag* (*di dentro*) internal, interior, inner; (*: mare*) inland; (*nazionale*) domestic; (*allievo*) boarding // *sm* inside, interior; (*di paese*) interior; (*fodera*) lining; (*di appartamento*) flat (number); (*TEL*) extension // *sm/f* (*INS*) boarder; ~**i** *smpl* (*CINEMA*) interior shots; **all'**~ inside; **Ministero degli I~i** Ministry of the Interior, ≈ Home Office (*Brit*), Department of the Interior (*US*).

in'tero, a *ag* (*integro, intatto*) whole, entire; (*completo, totale*) complete; (*numero*) whole; (*non ridotto: biglietto*) full.

interpel'lare *vt* to consult.

inter'porre *vt* (*ostacolo*): ~ **qc a qc** to put sth in the way of sth; (*influenza*) to use; ~ **appello** (*DIR*) to appeal; **interporsi** *vr* to intervene; **interporsi fra** (*mettersi in mezzo*) to come between; **inter'posto, a** *pp di* **interporre**.

interpre'tare *vt* to interpret; **in'terprete** *sm/f* interpreter; (*TEATRO*) actor/actress, performer; (*MUS*) performer.

interro'gare vt to question; (INS) to test; **interroga'tivo, a** ag (occhi, sguardo) questioning, inquiring; (LING) interrogative // sm question; (fig) mystery; **interroga'torio, a** ag interrogatory, questioning // sm (DIR) questioning q; **interrogazi'one** sf questioning q; (INS) oral test.

inter'rompere vt to interrupt; (studi, trattative) to break off, interrupt; ~rsi vr to break off, stop; **inter'rotto, a** pp di **interrompere**.

interrut'tore sm switch.

interruzi'one [interrut'tsjone] sf interruption; break.

interse'care vt, ~rsi vr to intersect.

inter'stizio [inter'stittsjo] sm interstice, crack.

interur'bano, a ag inter-city; (TEL: chiamata) trunk cpd, long-distance; (: telefono) long-distance // sf trunk call, long-distance call.

inter'vallo sm interval; (spazio) space, gap.

interve'nire vi (partecipare): ~ a to take part in; (intromettersi: anche POL) to intervene; (MED: operare) to operate; **inter'vento** sm participation; (intromissione) intervention; (MED) operazione; fare un intervento nel corso di (dibattito, programma) to take part in.

inter'vista sf interview; **intervis'tare** vt to interview.

in'teso, a pp di **intendere** // ag agreed // sf understanding; (accordo) agreement, understanding; non darsi per ~ di qc to take no notice of sth.

intes'tare vt (lettera) to address; (proprietà): ~ a to register in the name of; ~ un assegno a qn to make out a cheque to sb; **intestazi'one** sf heading; (su carta da lettere) letterhead; (registrazione) registration.

intes'tino, a ag (lotte) internal, civil // sm (ANAT) intestine.

inti'mare vt to order, command; **intimazi'one** sf order, command.

intimi'dire vt to intimidate // vi (anche: ~rsi) to grow shy.

intimità sf intimacy; privacy; (familiarità) familiarity.

'intimo, a ag intimate; (affetti, vita) private; (fig: profondo) inmost // sm (persona) intimate o close friend; (dell'animo) bottom, depths pl; **parti ~e** (ANAT) private parts.

intimo'rire vt to frighten; ~rsi vr to become frightened.

in'tingolo sm sauce; (pietanza) stew.

intiriz'zire [intirid'dzire] vt to numb // vi (anche: ~rsi) to go numb.

intito'lare vt to give a title to; (dedicare) to dedicate.

intolle'rabile ag intolerable.

intolle'rante ag intolerant.

in'tonaco, ci o **chi** sm plaster.

into'nare vt (canto) to start to sing; (armonizzare) to match; ~rsi vr (colori) to go together; ~rsi a (carnagione) to suit; (abito) to go with, match.

inton'tire vt to stun, daze // vi, ~rsi vr to be stunned o dazed.

in'toppo sm stumbling block, obstacle.

in'torno av around; ~ a prep (attorno a) around; (riguardo, circa) about.

intorpi'dire vt to numb; (fig) to make sluggish // vi (anche: ~rsi) to grow numb; (fig) to become sluggish.

intossi'care vt to poison; **intossicazi'one** sf poisoning.

intralci'are [intral'tʃare] vt to hamper, hold up.

in'transi'tivo, a ag, sm intransitive.

intrapren'dente ag enterprising, goahead.

intra'prendere vt to undertake.

intrat'tabile ag intractable.

intratte'nere vt to entertain; to engage in conversation; ~rsi vr to linger; ~rsi su qc to dwell on sth.

intrave'dere vt to catch a glimpse of; (fig) to foresee.

intrecci'are [intret'tʃare] vt (capelli) to plait, braid; (intessere: anche fig) to weave, interweave, intertwine; ~rsi vr to intertwine, become interwoven; ~ le mani to clasp one's hands; **in'treccio** sm (fig: trama) plot, story.

intri'gare vi to manoeuvre (Brit), maneuver (US), scheme; **in'trigo, ghi** sm plot, intrigue.

in'trinseco, a, ci, che ag intrinsic.

in'triso, a ag: ~ (di) soaked (in).

intro'durre vt to introduce; (chiave etc): ~ qc in to insert sth into; (persone: far entrare) to show in; introdursi vr (moda, tecniche) to be introduced; introdursi in (persona: penetrare) to enter; (: entrare furtivamente) to steal o slip into; **introduzi'one** sf introduction.

in'troito sm income, revenue.

intro'mettersi vr to interfere, meddle; (interporsi) to intervene.

in'truglio [in'truʎʎo] sm concoction.

intrusi'one sf intrusion; interference.

in'truso, a sm/f intruder.

intu'ire vt to perceive by intuition; (rendersi conto) to realize; **in'tuito** sm intuition; (perspicacia) perspicacity; **intuizi'one** sf intuition.

inu'mano, a ag inhuman.

inumi'dire vt to dampen, moisten; ~rsi vr to become damp o wet.

i'nutile ag useless; (superfluo) pointless, unnecessary; **inutilità** sf uselessness; pointlessness.

inva'dente ag (fig) interfering, nosey.

in'vadere vt to invade; (affollare) to

swarm into, overrun; (sog: acque) to flood; **invadi'trice** ag vedi **invasore**.

inva'ghirsi |inva'girsi| vr: ~ **di** to take a fancy to.

invalidità sf infirmity; disability; (DIR) invalidity.

in'valido, a ag (infermo) infirm, invalid; (al lavoro) disabled; (DIR: nullo) invalid // sm/f invalid; disabled person.

in'vano av in vain.

invasi'one sf invasion.

in'vaso, a pp di **invadere**.

inva'sore, invadi'trice |invadi'tritʃe| ag invading // sm invader.

invecchi'are |invek'kjare| vi (persona) to grow old; (vino, popolazione) to age; (moda) to become dated // vt to age; (far apparire più vecchio) to make look older.

in'vece |in'vetʃe| av instead; (al contrario) on the contrary; ~ **di** prep instead of.

inve'ire vi: ~ **contro** to rail against.

inven'tare vt to invent; (pericoli, pettegolezzi) to make up, invent.

inven'tario sm inventory; (COMM) stocktaking q.

inven'tivo, a ag inventive // sf inventiveness.

inven'tore sm inventor.

invenzi'one |inven'tsjone| sf invention; (bugia) lie, story.

inver'nale ag winter cpd; (simile all'inverno) wintry.

in'verno sm winter.

invero'simile ag unlikely.

inversi'one sf inversion; reversal; "divieto d'~" (AUT) "no U-turns".

in'verso, a ag opposite; (MAT) inverse // sm contrary, opposite; **in senso** ~ in the opposite direction; **in ordine** ~ in reverse order.

inver'tire vt to invert, reverse; ~ **la marcia** (AUT) to do a U-turn; **inver'tito, a** sm/f homosexual.

investi'gare vt, vi to investigate; **investiga'tore, trice** sm/f investigator, detective; **investigazi'one** sf investigation, inquiry.

investi'mento sm (ECON) investment; (scontro, urto) crash, collision; (incidente stradale) road accident.

inves'tire vt (denaro) to invest; (sog: veicolo: pedone) to knock down; (: altro veicolo) to crash into; (apostrofare) to assail; (incaricare): ~ **qn di** to invest sb with.

invi'are vt to send; **invi'ato, a** sm/f envoy; (STAMPA) correspondent.

in'vidia sf envy; **invidi'are** vt: ~ **qn (per qc)** to envy sb for sth; ~ **qc a qn** to envy sb sth; **invidi'oso, a** ag envious.

in'vio, 'vii sm sending; (insieme di merci) consignment.

invipe'rito, a ag furious.

invischi'are |invis'kjare| vt (fig): ~ **qn** in

to involve sb in; ~**rsi** vr: ~**rsi (con qn/in qc)** to get mixed up o involved (with sb/ in sth).

invi'sibile ag invisible.

invi'tare vt to invite; ~ **qn a fare** to invite sb to do; **invi'tato, a** sm/f guest; **in'vito** sm invitation.

invo'care vt (chiedere: aiuto, pace) to cry out for; (appellarsi: la legge, Dio) to appeal to, invoke.

invogli'are |invoʎ'ʎare| vt: ~ **qn a fare** to tempt sb to do, induce sb to do.

involon'tario, a ag (errore) unintentional; (gesto) involuntary.

invol'tino sm (CUC) roulade.

in'volto sm (pacco) parcel; (fagotto) bundle.

in'volucro sm cover, wrapping.

involuzi'one |involut'tsjone| sf (di stile) convolutedness; (regresso): **subire un'~** to regress.

inzacche'rare |intsakke'rare| vt to spatter with mud.

inzup'pare |intsup'pare| vt to soak; ~**rsi** vr to get soaked.

'io pronome I // sm inv: **l'~** the ego, the self; ~ **stesso(a)** I myself.

i'odio sm iodine.

i'ogurt sm inv = **yoghurt**.

I'onio sm: **lo ~, il mar ~** the Ionian (Sea).

ipermer'cato sm hypermarket.

ipertensi'one sf high blood pressure, hypertension.

ip'nosi sf hypnosis; **ipno'tismo** sm hypnotism; **ipnotiz'zare** vt to hypnotize.

ipocri'sia sf hypocrisy.

i'pocrita, i, e ag hypocritical // sm/f hypocrite.

ipo'teca, che sf mortgage; **ipote'care** vt to mortgage.

i'potesi sf inv hypothesis; **ipo'tetico, a, ci, che** ag hypothetical.

'ippico, a, ci, che ag horse cpd // sf horseracing.

ippocas'tano sm horse chestnut.

ip'podromo sm racecourse.

ippo'potamo sm hippopotamus.

'ira sf anger, wrath.

l'ran sm: **l'~** Iran.

l'raq sm: **l'~** Iraq.

'iride sf (arcobaleno) rainbow; (ANAT, BOT) iris.

Ir'landa sf: **l'~** Ireland; **l'~ del Nord** Northern Ireland, Ulster; **la Repubblica d'~** Eire, the Republic of Ireland; **irlan'dese** ag Irish // sm/f Irishman/ woman; **gli Irlandesi** the Irish.

iro'nia sf irony; **i'ronico, a, ci, che** ag ironic(al).

irradi'are vt to radiate; (sog: raggi di luce: illuminare) to shine on // vi (diffondersi: anche: ~**rsi**) to radiate; **irradiazi'one** sf radiation.

irragio'nevole |irradʒo'nevole| ag irrational; unreasonable.

irrazio'nale [irrattsjo'nale] *ag* irrational.

irre'ale *ag* unreal.

irrecupe'rabile *ag* irretrievable; *(fig: person)* irredeemable.

irrecu'sabile *ag (offerta)* not to be refused; *(prova)* irrefutable.

irrego'lare *ag* irregular; *(terreno)* uneven.

irremo'vibile *ag (fig)* unshakeable, unyielding.

irrepa'rabile *ag* irreparable; *(fig)* inevitable.

irrepe'ribile *ag* nowhere to be found.

irrequi'eto, a *ag* restless.

irresis'tibile *ag* irresistible.

irrespon'sabile *ag* irresponsible.

irridu'cibile [irridu'tʃibile] *ag* irreducible; *(fig)* indomitable.

irri'gare *vt (annaffiare)* to irrigate; *(sog: fiume etc)* to flow through; **irrigazi'one** *sf* irrigation.

irrigi'dire [irridʒi'dire] *vt*, ~**rsi** *vr* to stiffen.

irri'sorio, a *ag* derisory.

irri'tare *vt (mettere di malumore)* to irritate, annoy; *(MED)* to irritate; ~**rsi** *vr (stizzirsi)* to become irritated *o* annoyed; *(MED)* to become irritated; **irritazi'one** *sf* irritation; annoyance.

ir'rompere *vi*: ~ **in** to burst into.

irro'rare *vt* to sprinkle; *(AGR)* to spray.

irru'ente *ag (fig)* impetuous, violent.

irruzi'one [irrut'tsjone] *sf*: **fare** ~ **in** to burst into; *(sog: polizia)* to raid.

'irto, a *ag* bristly; ~ **di** bristling with.

is'critto, a *pp di* **iscrivere** // *sm/f* member; **per o in** ~ in writing.

is'crivere *vt* to register, enter; *(persona)*: ~ **(a)** to register (in), enrol (in); ~**rsi** *vr*: ~**rsi (a)** *(club, partito)* to join; *(università)* to register *o* enrol (at); *(esame, concorso)* to register *o* enter (for); **iscrizi'one** *sf (epigrafe etc)* inscription; *(a scuola, società)* enrolment, registration; *(registrazione)* registration.

Is'lam *sm*: **l'**~ Islam.

Is'landa *sf*: **l'**~ Iceland.

'isola *sf* island; ~ **pedonale** *(AUT)* pedestrian precinct.

isola'mento *sm* isolation; *(TECN)* insulation.

iso'lante *ag* insulating // *sm* insulator.

iso'lare *vt* to isolate; *(TECN)* to insulate; *(: acusticamente)* to soundproof; **iso'lato, a** *ag* isolated; insulated // *sm (edificio)* block.

ispetto'rato *sm* inspectorate.

ispet'tore *sm* inspector.

ispezio'nare [ispettsjo'nare] *vt* to inspect.

ispezi'one [ispet'tsjone] *sf* inspection.

'ispido, a *ag* bristly, shaggy.

ispi'rare *vt* to inspire; ~**rsi** *vr*: ~**rsi a** to

draw one's inspiration from.

Isra'ele *sm*: **l'**~ Israel; **israeli'ano, a** *ag, sm/f* Israeli.

is'sare *vt* to hoist.

istan'taneo, a *ag* instantaneous // *sf (FOT)* snapshot.

is'tante *sm* instant, moment; **all'**~, **sull'**~ instantly, immediately.

is'tanza [is'tantsa] *sf* petition, request.

is'terico, a, ci, che *ag* hysterical.

iste'rismo *sm* hysteria.

isti'gare *vt* to incite; **istigazi'one** *sf* incitement; **istigazione a delinquere** *(DIR)* incitement to crime.

is'tinto *sm* instinct.

istitu'ire *vt (fondare)* to institute, found; *(porre: confronto)* to establish; *(intraprendere: inchiesta)* to set up.

isti'tuto *sm* institute; *(di università)* department; *(ente, DIR)* institution; ~ **di bellezza** beauty salon.

istituzi'one [istitut'tsjone] *sf* institution.

'istmo *sm (GEO)* isthmus.

istra'dare *vt* = **instradare**.

'istrice ['istritʃe] *sm* porcupine.

istri'one *sm (peg)* ham actor.

istru'ire *vt (insegnare)* to teach; *(ammaestrare)* to train; *(informare)* to instruct, inform; *(DIR)* to prepare; **istrut'tore, 'trice** *sm/f* instructor // *ag*: **giudice istruttore** examining *(Brit) o* committing *(US)* magistrate; **istrut'toria** *sf (DIR)* (preliminary) investigation and hearing; **istruzi'one** *sf* education; training; *(direttiva)* instruction; *(DIR)* = **istruttoria**; **istruzioni per l'uso** instructions (for use).

l'talia *sf*. **l'**~ Italy.

itali'ano, a *ag* Italian // *sm/f* Italian // *sm (LING)* Italian; **gli** l~i the Italians.

itine'rario *sm* itinerary.

itte'rizia [itte'rittsja] *sf (MED)* jaundice.

'ittico, a, ci, che *ag* fish *cpd*; fishing *cpd*.

Iugos'lavia *sf* = **Jugoslavia**.

iugos'lavo, a *ag, sm/f* = **jugoslavo, a**.

i'uta *sf* jute.

I.V.A. ['iva] *sigla f* = **imposta sul valore aggiunto**.

J

jazz [dʒaz] *sm* jazz.

jeans [dʒinz] *smpl* jeans.

Jugos'lavia [jugoz'lavja] *sf*: **la** ~ Yugoslavia; **jugos'lavo, a** *ag, sm/f* Yugoslav(ian).

'juta ['juta] *sf* = **iuta**.

K

K *abbr (INFORM)* K.

k *abbr (= kilo)* k.

karatè *sm* karate.
Kg *abbr* (= *chilogrammo*) kg.
'killer *sm inv* gunman, hired gun.
km *abbr* (= *chilometro*) km.
'krapfen *sm inv* (*CUC*) doughnut.

L

l' *det vedi* **la, lo.**
la *det f* (*dav V* **l'**) the // *pronome* (*dav V* **l'**) (*oggetto: persona*) her; (: *cosa*) it; (: *forma di cortesia*) you // *sm inv* (*MUS*) A; (: *solfeggiando la scala*) la.
là *av* there; di ~ (*da quel luogo*) from there; (*in quel luogo*) in there; (*dall'altra parte*) over there; di ~ di beyond; per di ~ that way; più in ~ further on; (*tempo*) later on; fatti in ~ move up; ~ dentro/sopra/sotto in/up (*o* on)/under there; *vedi* **quello.**
'labbro *sm* (*pl(f)*: **labbra**: *solo nel senso ANAT*) lip.
labi'rinto *sm* labyrinth, maze.
labora'torio *sm* (*di ricerca*) laboratory; (*di arti, mestieri*) workshop; ~ linguistico language laboratory.
labori'oso, a *ag* (*faticoso*) laborious; (*attivo*) hard-working.
labu'rista, i, e *ag* Labour (*Brit*) *cpd* // *sm/f* Labour Party member (*Brit*).
'lacca, che *sf* lacquer.
'laccio ['lattʃo] *sm* noose; (*legaccio, tirante*) lasso; (*di scarpa*) lace; ~ emostatico tourniquet.
lace'rare [latʃe'rare] *vt* to tear to shreds, lacerate; ~rsi *vr* to tear; **'lacero, a** *ag* (*logoro*) torn, tattered; (*MED*) lacerated.
'lacrima *sf* tear; in ~e in tears; **lacri'mare** *vi* to water; **lacri'mogeno, a** *ag*: **gas lacrimogeno** tear gas.
la'cuna *sf* (*fig*) gap.
'ladro *sm* thief; **ladro'cinio** *sm* theft, larceny.
laggiù [lad'dʒu] *av* down there; (*di là*) over there.
la'gnarsi [laɲ'ɲarsi] *vr*: ~ (di) to complain (about).
'lago, ghi *sm* lake.
'lagrima *etc* = **lacrima** *etc*.
la'guna *sf* lagoon.
'laico, a, ci, che *ag* (*apostolato*) lay; (*vita*) secular; (*scuola*) nondenominational // *sm/f* layman/woman // *sm* lay brother.
'lama *sf* blade // *sm inv* (*ZOOL*) llama; (*REL*) lama.
lambic'care *vt* to distil; ~rsi **il cervello** to rack one's brains.
lam'bire *vt* to lick; to lap.
la'mella *sf* (*di metallo etc*) thin sheet, thin strip; (*di fungo*) gill.
lamen'tare *vt* to lament; ~rsi *vr* (*emettere lamenti*) to moan, groan; (*rammaricarsi*): ~rsi (di) to complain

(about); **lamen'tela** *sf* complaining *q*; **lamen'tevole** *ag* (*voce*) complaining, plaintive; (*destino*) pitiful; **la'mento** *sm* moan, groan; wail; **lamen'toso, a** *ag* plaintive.
la'metta *sf* razor blade.
lami'era *sf* sheet metal.
'lamina *sf* (*lastra sottile*) thin sheet (*o* layer *o* plate); ~ d'oro gold leaf; gold foil; **lami'nare** *vt* to laminate; **lami'nato, a** *ag* laminated; (*tessuto*) lamé // *sm* laminate.
'lampada *sf* lamp; ~ a gas gas lamp; ~ a spirito blow lamp (*Brit*), blow torch (*US*); ~ da tavolo table lamp.
lampa'dario *sm* chandelier.
lampa'dina *sf* light bulb; ~ tascabile pocket torch (*Brit*) *o* flashlight (*US*).
lam'pante *ag* (*fig: evidente*) crystal clear, evident.
lampeggi'are [lamped'dʒare] *vi* (*luce, fari*) to flash // *vb impers*: **lampeggia** there's lightning; **lampeggia'tore** *sm* (*AUT*) indicator.
lampi'one *sm* street light *o* lamp (*Brit*).
'lampo *sm* (*METEOR*) flash of lightning; (*di luce, fig*) flash; ~i *smpl* lightning *q* // *ag inv*: **cerniera** ~ zip (fastener) (*Brit*), zipper (*US*); **guerra** ~ blitzkrieg.
lam'pone *sm* raspberry.
'lana *sf* wool; ~ d'acciaio steel wool; pura ~ vergine pure new wool; ~ di vetro glass wool.
lan'cetta [lan'tʃetta] *sf* (*indice*) pointer, needle; (*di orologio*) hand.
'lancia ['lantʃa] *sf* (*arma*) lance; (: *picca*) spear; (*di pompa antincendio*) nozzle; (*imbarcazione*) launch.
lanciafi'amme [lantʃa'fjamme] *sm inv* flamethrower.
lanci'are [lan'tʃare] *vt* to throw, hurl, fling; (*SPORT*) to throw; (*far partire: automobile*) to get up to full speed; (*bombe*) to drop; (*razzo, prodotto, moda*) to launch; ~rsi *vr*: ~rsi contro/su to throw *o* hurl *o* fling o.s. against/on; ~rsi in (*fig*) to embark on.
lanci'nante [lantʃi'nante] *ag* (*dolore*) shooting, throbbing; (*grido*) piercing.
'lancio ['lantʃo] *sm* throwing *q*; throw; dropping *q*; drop; launching *q*; launch; ~ del peso putting the shot.
'landa *sf* (*GEO*) moor.
'languido, a *ag* (*fiacco*) languid, weak; (*tenero, malinconico*) languishing.
langu'ore *sm* weakness, languor.
lani'ficio [lani'fitʃo] *sm* woollen mill.
la'noso, a *ag* woolly.
lan'terna *sf* lantern; (*faro*) lighthouse.
la'nugine [la'nudʒine] *sf* down.
lapi'dare *vt* to stone.
lapi'dario, a *ag* (*fig*) terse.
'lapide *sf* (*di sepolcro*) tombstone; (*commemorativa*) plaque.
'lapis *sm inv* pencil.

Lap'ponia *sf* Lapland.

'lapsus *sm inv* slip.

'lardo *sm* bacon fat, lard.

lar'ghezza [lar'gettsa] *sf* width; breadth; looseness; generosity; ~ **di vedute** broad-mindedness.

'largo, a, ghi, ghe *ag* wide; broad; *(maniche)* wide; *(abito: troppo ampio)* loose; *(fig)* generous // *sm* width; breadth; *(mare aperto)*: **il ~** the open sea // *sf*: **stare** o **tenersi alla ~a (da** qn/ qc**)** to keep one's distance (from sb/sth), keep away (from sb/sth); ~ **due metri** two metres wide; ~ **di spalle** broad-shouldered; **di ~ghe vedute** broad-minded; **su ~a scala** on a large scale; **di manica ~a** generous, open-handed; **al ~ di Genova** off (the coast of) Genoa; **farsi ~ tra la folla** to push one's way through the crowd.

'larice ['laritʃe] *sm (BOT)* larch.

larin'gite [larin'dʒite] *sf* laryngitis.

'larva *sf* larva; *(fig)* shadow.

la'sagne [la'zanne] *sfpl* lasagna *sg*.

lasci'are [laʃ'ʃare] *vt* to leave; *(abbandonare)* to leave, abandon, give up; *(cessare di tenere)* to let go of // *vb ausiliare*: ~ **fare** qn to let sb do // *vi*: ~ **di fare** *(smettere)* to stop doing; **~rsi** andare/**truffare** to let o.s. go/be cheated; ~ **andare** o **correre** o **perdere** to let things go their own way; ~ **stare** qc/qn to leave sth/sb alone.

'lascito ['laʃʃito] *sm (DIR)* legacy.

'laser ['lazer] *ag, sm inv*: (raggio) ~ laser (beam).

lassa'tivo, a *ag, sm* laxative.

'lasso *sm*: ~ **di tempo** interval, lapse of time.

lassù *av* up there.

'lastra *sf (di pietra)* slab; *(di metallo, FOT)* plate; *(di ghiaccio, vetro)* sheet; *(radiografica)* X-ray (plate).

lastri'care *vt* to pave; **lastri'cato, 'lastrico, ci** o **chi** *sm* paving.

late'rale *ag* lateral, side *cpd*; *(uscita, ingresso etc)* side *cpd* // *sm (CALCIO)* half-back.

late'rizio [late'rittsjo] *sm* (perforated) brick.

lati'fondo *sm* large estate.

la'tino, a *ag, sm* Latin; **~-ameri'cano** *a ag* Latin-American.

lati'tante *sm/f* fugitive (from justice).

lati'tudine *sf* latitude.

'lato, a *ag (fig)* wide, broad // *sm* side; *(fig)* aspect, point of view; **in senso ~** broadly speaking.

la'trare *vi* to bark.

latro'cinio [latro'tʃinjo] *sm* = **ladrocinio**.

'latta *sf* tin (plate); *(recipiente)* tin, can.

lat'taio, a *sm/f* milkman/woman; dairyman/woman.

lat'tante *ag* unweaned.

'latte *sm* milk; ~ **detergente** cleansing milk o lotion; ~ **secco** o **in polvere** dried o powdered milk; ~ **scremato** skimmed milk; **'latteo, a** *ag* milky; *(dieta, prodotto)* milk *cpd*; **latte'ria** *sf* dairy; **latti'cini** *smpl* dairy products.

lat'tina *sf (di birra etc)* can.

lat'tuga, ghe *sf* lettuce.

'laurea *sf* degree; **laure'ando, a** *sm/f* final-year student; **laure'are** *vt* to confer a degree on; **laurearsi** *vr* to graduate; **laure'ato, a** *ag, sm/f* graduate.

'lauro *sm* laurel.

'lauto, a *ag (pranzo, mancia)* lavish.

'lava *sf* lava.

la'vabo *sm* washbasin.

la'vaggio [la'vaddʒo] *sm* washing *q*; ~ **del cervello** brainwashing *q*.

la'vagna [la'vaɲɲa] *sf (GEO)* slate; *(di scuola)* blackboard.

la'vanda *sf (anche MED)* wash; *(BOT)* lavender; **lavan'daia** *sf* washerwoman; **lavande'ria** *sf* laundry; **lavanderia automatica** launderette; **lavanderia a secco** dry-cleaner's; **lavan'dino** *sm* sink.

lavapi'atti *sm/f* dishwasher.

la'vare *vt* to wash; **~rsi** *vr* to wash, have a wash; ~ **a secco** to dry-clean; **~rsi le mani/i denti** to wash one's hands/clean one's teeth.

lava'secco *sm* o *f inv* drycleaner's.

lavasto'viglie [lavasto'viʎʎe] *sm* o *f inv (macchina)* dishwasher.

lava'toio *sm* (public) washhouse.

lava'trice [lava'tritʃe] *sf* washing machine.

lava'tura *sf* washing *q*; ~ **di piatti** dishwater.

lavo'rante *sm/f* worker.

lavo'rare *vi* to work; *(fig: bar, studio etc)* to do good business // *vt* to work; **~rsi** qn *(persuaderlo)* to work on sb; ~ **a** to work on; ~ **a maglia** to knit; **lavora'tivo, a** *ag* working; **lavora'tore, 'trice** *sm/f* worker // *ag* working; **lavorazi'one** *sf (gen)* working; *(di legno, pietra)* carving; *(di film)* making; *(di prodotto)* manufacture; *(modo di esecuzione)* workmanship; **lavo'rio** *sm* intense activity.

la'voro *sm* work; *(occupazione)* job, work *q*; *(opera)* piece of work, job; *(ECON)* labour; **~i forzati** hard labour *sg*; **~i pubblici** public works.

le *det fpl* the // *pronome (oggetto)* them; *(: a lei, a essa)* (to) her; *(: forma di cortesia)* (to) you.

le'ale *ag* loyal; *(sincero)* sincere; *(onesto)* fair; **lealtà** *sf* loyalty; sincerity; fairness.

'lebbra *sf* leprosy.

'lecca 'lecca *sm inv* lollipop.

leccapi'edi *sm/f inv (peg)* toady, bootlicker.

lec'care vt to lick; (sog: gatto: latte etc) to lick o lap up; (fig) to flatter; ~rsi i baffi to lick one's lips; **lec'cata** sf lick.

'leccio ['lɛttʃo] sm holm oak, ilex.

leccor'nia sf titbit, delicacy.

'lecito, a ['lɛtʃito] ag permitted, allowed.

'ledere vt to damage, injure.

'lega, ghe sf league; (di metalli) alloy.

le'gaccio [le'gattʃo] sm string, lace.

le'gale ag legal // sm lawyer; **legaliz'zare** vt to authenticate; (regolarizzare) to legalize.

le'game sm (corda, fig: affettivo) tie, bond; (nesso logico) link, connection.

le'gare vt (prigioniero, capelli, cane) to tie (up); (libro) to bind; (CHIM) to alloy; (fig: collegare) to bind, join // vi (far lega) to unite; (fig) to get on well.

lega'tario, a sm/f (DIR) legatee.

le'gato sm (REL) legate; (DIR) legacy, bequest.

lega'tura sf (di libro) binding; (MUS) ligature.

le'genda [le'dʒɛnda] sf (di carta geografica etc) = **leggenda**.

'legge ['lɛddʒe] sf law.

leg'genda [led'dʒɛnda] sf (narrazione) legend; (di carta geografica etc) key, legend.

'leggere ['lɛddʒere] vt, vi to read.

legge'rezza [ledʒe'rettsa] sf lightness; thoughtlessness, fickleness.

leg'gero, a [led'dʒero] ag light; (agile, snello) nimble, agile, light; (tè, caffè) weak; (fig: non grave, piccolo) slight; (: spensierato) thoughtless; (: incostante) fickle; free and easy; **alla** ~a thoughtlessly.

leggi'adro, a [led'dʒadro] ag pretty, lovely; (movimenti) graceful.

leg'gio, gii [led'dʒio] sm lectern; (MUS) music stand.

legisla'tura [ledʒizla'tura] sf legislature.

legislazi'one [ledʒizlat'tsjone] sf legislation.

le'gittimo, a [le'dʒittimo] ag legitimate; (fig: giustificato, lecito) justified, legitimate; ~a difesa (DIR) self-defence.

'legna ['leɲɲa] sf firewood; **le'gname** sm wood, timber.

'legno ['leɲɲo] sm wood; (pezzo di ~) piece of wood; **di** ~ wooden; ~ **compensato** plywood; **le'gnoso, a** ag wooden; woody; (carne) tough.

le'gumi smpl (BOT) pulses.

'lei pronome (soggetto) she; (oggetto: per dare rilievo, con preposizione) her; (forma di cortesia: anche: L~) you // sm: dare del ~ a qn to address sb as "lei"; ~ stessa she herself; you yourself.

'lembo sm (di abito, strada) edge; (striscia sottile: di terra) strip.

'lemma, i sm headword.

'lemme 'lemme av (very) very slowly.

'lena sf (fig) energy, stamina.

le'nire vt to soothe.

'lente sf (OTTICA) lens sg; ~ **d'ingrandimento** magnifying glass; ~**i a contatto** o **corneali** contact lenses.

len'tezza [len'tettsa] sf slowness.

len'ticchia [len'tikkja] sf (BOT) lentil.

len'tiggine [len'tiddʒine] sf freckle.

'lento, a ag slow; (molle: fune) slack; (non stretto: vite, abito) loose // sm (ballo) slow dance.

'lenza ['lɛntsa] sf fishing-line.

lenzu'olo [len'tswɔlo] sm sheet; ~**a** sfpl pair of sheets.

le'one sm lion; (dello zodiaco): L~ Leo.

lepo'rino, a ag: labbro ~ harelip.

'lepre sf hare.

'lercio, a, ci, cie ['lɛrtʃo] ag filthy.

'lesbica, che sf lesbian.

lesi'nare vt to be stingy with // vi: ~ (su) to skimp (on), be stingy (with).

lesi'one sf (MED) lesion; (DIR) injury, damage; (EDIL) crack.

'leso, a pp di **ledere** // ag (offeso) injured; parte ~a (DIR) injured party.

les'sare vt (CUC) to boil.

'lessico, ci sm vocabulary; lexicon.

'lesso, a ag boiled // sm boiled meat.

'lesto, a ag quick; (agile) nimble; ~ **di mano** (per rubare) light-fingered; (per picchiare) free with one's fists.

le'tale ag lethal; fatal.

leta'maio sm dunghill.

le'tame sm manure, dung.

le'targo, ghi sm lethargy; (ZOOL) hibernation.

le'tizia [le'tittsja] sf joy, happiness.

'lettera sf letter; ~**e** sfpl (letteratura) literature sg; (studi umanistici) arts (subjects); **alla** ~ literally; **in** ~**e** in words, in full; **lette'rale** ag literal.

lette'rario, a ag literary.

lette'rato, a ag well-read, scholarly.

lettera'tura sf literature.

let'tiga, ghe sf (portantina) litter; (barella) stretcher.

let'tino sm cot (Brit), crib (US).

'letto, a pp di **leggere** // sm bed; **andare a** ~ to go to bed; ~ **a castello** bunk beds pl; ~ **a una piazza/a due piazze** o **matrimoniale** single/double bed.

let'tore, 'trice sm/f reader; (INS) (foreign language) assistant (Brit); (foreign) teaching assistant (US) // sm (TECN): ~ **ottico** optical character reader.

let'tura sf reading.

leuce'mia [leutʃe'mia] sf leukaemia.

'leva sf lever; (MIL) conscription; far ~ **su qn** to work on sb; ~ **del cambio** (AUT) gear lever.

le'vante sm east; (vento) East wind; il L~ the Levant.

le'vare vt (occhi, braccio) to raise; (sollevare, togliere: tassa, divieto) to lift; (indumenti) to take off, remove;

(*rimuovere*) to take away; (: *dal di sopra*) to take off; (: *dal di dentro*) to take out; ~**rsi** *vr* to get up; (*sole*) to rise; **le'vata** *sf* (*di posta*) collection.

leva'toio, a *ag:* ~**ponte** ~ drawbridge.

leva'tura *sf* intelligence, mental capacity.

levi'gare *vt* to smooth; (*con carta vetrata*) to sand.

levri'ere *sm* greyhound.

lezi'one [let'tsjone] *sf* lesson; (*all'università, sgridata*) lecture; **fare** ~ to teach; to lecture.

lezi'oso, a [let'tsjoso] *ag* affected; simpering.

'**lezzo** ['leddzo] *sm* stench, stink.

li *pronome pl* (*oggetto*) them.

lì *av* there; **di** *o* **da** ~ from there; **per di** ~ that way; **di** ~ **a pochi giorni** a few days later; ~ **per** ~ there and then; at first; **essere** ~ (~) **per** fare to be on the point of doing, be about to do; ~ **dentro** in there; ~ **sotto** under there; ~ **sopra** on there; up there; *vedi* **quello**.

Ilba'nese *ag, sm/f* Lebanese *inv*.

Li'bano *sm*: **il** ~ **the Lebanon**.

'**libbra** *sf* (*peso*) pound.

li'beccio [li'bettʃo] *sm* south-west wind.

li'bello *sm* libel.

li'bellula *sf* dragonfly.

libe'rale *ag, sm/f* liberal.

liberaliz'zare [liberalid'dzare] *vt* to liberalize.

libe'rare *vt* (*rendere libero: prigioniero*) to release; (: *popolo*) to free, liberate; (*sgombrare: passaggio*) to clear; (: *stanza*) to vacate; (*produrre: energia*) to release; ~**rsi** *vr*: ~**rsi di qc/qn** to get rid of sth/sb; **libera'tore, 'trice** *ag* liberating // *sm/f* liberator; **liberazi'one** *sf* liberation, freeing; release; rescuing.

'**libero, a** *ag* free; (*strada*) clear; (*non occupato: posto etc*) vacant; not taken; empty; not engaged; ~ **di fare qc free to do sth**; ~ **da** free from; ~ **arbitrio** free will; ~ **professionista** self-employed professional person; ~ **scambio** free trade; **libertà** *sf inv* freedom; (*tempo disponibile*) free time // *sfpl* (*licenza*) liberties; **in libertà provvisoria/vigilata** released without bail/on probation; **libertà di riunione** right to hold meetings.

'**Libia** *sf*: **la** ~ **Libya**; '**libico, a, ci, che** *ag, sm/f* **Libyan**.

li'bidine *sf* lust.

li'braio *sm* bookseller.

li'brario, a *ag* book *cpd*.

li'brarsi *vr* to hover.

libre'ria *sf* (*bottega*) bookshop; (*stanza*) library; (*mobile*) bookcase.

li'bretto *sm* booklet; (*taccuino*) notebook; (*MUS*) libretto; ~ **degli assegni** cheque book; ~ **di circolazione** (*AUT*) logbook; ~ **di risparmio** (savings) bank-book, passbook; ~ **universitario** student's report book.

'**libro** *sm* book; ~ **bianco** (*POL*) white paper; ~ **di cassa** cash book; ~ **mastro** ledger; ~ **paga** payroll.

li'cenza [li'tʃɛntsa] *sf* (*permesso*) permission, leave; (*di pesca, caccia, circolazione*) permit, licence; (*MIL*) leave; (*INS*) school leaving certificate; (*libertà*) liberty; licence; licentiousness; **andare in** ~ (*MIL*) to go on leave.

licenzia'mento [litʃentsja'mento] *sm* dismissal.

licenzi'are [litʃen'tsjare] *vt* (*impiegato*) to dismiss; (*INS*) to award a certificate to; ~**rsi** *vr* (*impiegato*) to resign, hand in one's notice; (*INS*) to obtain one's school-leaving certificate.

li'ceo [li'tʃɛo] *sm* (*INS*) secondary (*Brit*) *o* high (*US*) school (*for 14- to 19-year-olds*).

'**lido** *sm* beach, shore.

li'eto, a *ag* happy, glad; "**molto** ~" (*nelle presentazioni*) "pleased to meet you".

li'eve *ag* light; (*di poco conto*) slight; (*sommesso: voce*) faint, soft.

lievi'tare *vi* (*anche fig*) to rise // *vt* to leaven.

li'evito *sm* yeast; ~ **di birra** brewer's yeast.

'**ligio, a, gi, gie** ['lidʒo] *ag* faithful, loyal.

'**lilla, lillà** *sm inv* lilac.

'**lima** *sf* file.

limacci'oso, a [limat'tʃoso] *ag* slimy; muddy.

li'mare *vt* to file (down); (*fig*) to polish.

'**limbo** *sm* (*REL*) limbo.

li'metta *sf* nail file.

limi'tare *vt* to limit, restrict; (*circoscrivere*) to bound, surround; **limita'tivo, a** *ag* limiting, restricting; **limi'tato, a** *ag* limited, restricted.

'**limite** *sm* limit; (*confine*) border, boundary; ~ **di velocità** speed limit.

li'mitrofo, a *ag* neighbouring.

limo'nata *sf* lemonade (*Brit*), (lemon) soda (*US*); lemon squash (*Brit*), lemonade (*US*).

li'mone *sm* (*pianta*) lemon tree; (*frutto*) lemon.

'**limpido, a** *ag* clear; (*acqua*) limpid, clear.

'**lince** ['lintʃe] *sf* lynx.

linci'are *vt* to lynch.

'**lindo, a** *ag* tidy, spick and span; (*biancheria*) clean.

'**linea** *sf* line; (*di mezzi pubblici di trasporto: itinerario*) route; (: *servizio*) service; **a grandi** ~**e** in outline; **mantenere la** ~ to look after one's figure; **di** ~: **aereo di** ~ airliner; **nave di** ~ liner; **volo di** ~ scheduled flight; ~ **aerea** airline; ~ **di partenza/d'arrivo**

(SPORT) starting/finishing line; ~ **di tiro** line of fire.

linea'menti smpl features; (fig) outlines.

line'are ag linear; (fig) coherent, logical.

line'etta sf (trattino) dash; (d'unione) hyphen.

lin'gotto sm ingot, bar.

'lingua sf (ANAT, CUC) tongue; (idioma) language; **mostrare la ~** to stick out one's tongue; **di ~ italiana** Italian-speaking; **~ madre** mother tongue; **una ~ di terra** a spit of land.

lingu'aggio [lin'gwaddʒo] sm language.

lingu'etta sf (di strumento) reed; (di scarpa, TECN) tongue; (di busta) flap.

lingu'istica sf linguistics sg.

'lino sm (pianta) flax; (tessuto) linen.

li'noleum sm inv linoleum, lino.

lique'fare vt (render liquido) to liquefy; (fondere) to melt; **~rsi** vr to liquefy; to melt.

liqui'dare vt (società, beni; persona: uccidere) to liquidate; (persona: sbarazzarsene) to get rid of; (conto, problema) to settle; (COMM: merce) to sell off, clear; **liquidazi'one** sf liquidation; settlement; clearance sale.

liquidità sf liquidity.

'liquido, a ag, sm liquid; **~ per freni** brake fluid.

liqui'rizia [likwi'rittsja] sf liquorice.

li'quore sm liqueur.

'lira sf (unità monetaria) lira; (MUS) lyre; **~ sterlina** pound sterling.

'lirico, a, ci, che ag lyric(al); (MUS) lyric // sf (poesia) lyric poetry; (componimento poetico) lyric; (MUS) opera; **cantante/teatro ~** opera singer/house.

'lisca, sche (di pesce) fishbone.

lisci'are [liʃ'ʃare] vt to smooth; (fig) to flatter.

'liscio, a, sci, sce ['liʃʃo] ag smooth; (capelli) straight; (mobile) plain; (bevanda alcolica) neat; (fig) straightforward, simple // av: **andare ~** to go smoothly; **passarla ~a** to get away with it.

'liso, a ag worn out, threadbare.

'lista sf (striscia) strip; (elenco) list; **~ elettorale** electoral roll; **~ delle vivande** menu.

lis'tino sm list; **~ dei cambi** (foreign) exchange rate; **~ dei prezzi** price list.

'lite sf quarrel, argument; (DIR) lawsuit.

liti'gare vi to quarrel; (DIR) to litigate.

li'tigio [li'tidʒo] sm quarrel; **litigi'oso, a** ag quarrelsome; (DIR) litigious.

litogra'fia sf (sistema) lithography; (stampa) lithograph.

lito'rale ag coastal, coast cpd // sm coast.

'litro sm litre.

livel'lare vt to level, make level; **~rsi** vr to become level; (fig) to level out, balance out.

li'vello sm level; (fig) level, standard; **ad alto ~** (fig) high-level; **~ del mare** sea level.

'livido, a ag livid; (per percosse) bruised, black and blue; (cielo) leaden // sm bruise.

li'vore sm malice, spite.

Li'vorno sf Livorno, Leghorn.

li'vrea sf livery.

'lizza ['littsa] sf lists pl; **scendere in ~** (anche fig) to enter the lists.

lo det m (dav s impura, gn, pn, ps, x, z; dav V l') the // pronome (dav V l') (oggetto: persona) him; (: cosa) it; **~ sapevo** I knew it; **~ so** I know; **sii buono, anche se lui non ~ è** be good, even if he isn't.

lo'cale ag local // sm room; (luogo pubblico) premises pl; **~ notturno** nightclub; **località** sf inv locality; **localiz'zare** vt (circoscrivere) to confine, localize; (accertare) to locate, place.

lo'canda sf inn; **locandi'ere, a** sm/f innkeeper.

loca'tario, a sm/f tenant.

loca'tore, 'trice sm/f landlord/lady.

locazi'one [lokat'tsjone] sf (da parte del locatario) renting q; (da parte del locatore) renting out q, letting q; (contratto di) **~ lease**; (canone di) **~ rent**; **dare in ~** to rent out, let.

locomo'tiva sf locomotive.

locomo'tore sm electric locomotive.

locomozi'one [lokomot'tsjone] sf locomotion; **mezzi di ~** vehicles, means of transport.

lo'custa sf locust.

locuzi'one [lokut'tsjone] sf phrase, expression.

lo'dare vt to praise.

'lode sf praise; (INS): **laurearsi con 110 e ~ ≈** to graduate with a first-class honours degree (Brit), graduate summa cum laude (US).

'loden sm inv (stoffa) loden; (cappotto) loden overcoat.

lo'devole ag praiseworthy.

loga'ritmo sm logarithm.

'loggia, ge ['lɔddʒa] sf (ARCHIT) loggia; (circolo massonico) lodge; **loggi'one** sm (di teatro): **il loggione** the Gods sg.

'logico, a, ci, che ['lɔdʒiko] ag logical // sf logic.

logo'rare vt to wear out; (sciupare) to waste; **~rsi** vr to wear out; (fig) to wear o.s. out.

logo'rio sm wear and tear; (fig) strain.

'logoro, a ag (stoffa) worn out, threadbare; (persona) worn out.

lom'baggine [lom'baddʒine] sf lumbago.

Lombar'dia sf: **la ~** Lombardy.

lom'bata sf (taglio di carne) loin.

'lombo sm (ANAT) loin.

lom'brico, chi *sm* earthworm.
londi'nese *ag* London *cpd* // *sm/f* Londoner.
'Londra *sf* London.
lon'gevo, a |lon'dʒevo| *ag* long-lived.
longi'tudine |londʒi'tudine| *sf* longitude.
lonta'nanza |lonta'nantsa| *sf* distance; absence.
lon'tano, a *ag* *(distante)* distant, far-away; *(assente)* absent; *(vago: sospetto)* slight, remote; *(tempo: remoto)* far-off, distant; *(parente)* distant, remote // *av* far; è ~a la casa? is it far to the house?, is the house far from here?; è ~ un chilometro it's a kilometre away *o* a kilometre from here; più ~ farther; da *o* di ~ from a distance; ~ da a long way from; alla ~a slightly, vaguely.
'lontra *sf* otter.
lo'quace |lo'kwatʃe| *ag* talkative, loquacious; *(fig: gesto etc)* eloquent.
'lordo, a *ag* dirty, filthy; *(peso, stipendio)* gross.
'loro *pronome pl* *(oggetto, con preposizione)* them; *(complemento di termine)* to them; *(soggetto)* they; *(forma di cortesia: anche:* L~) you; to you; il(la) ~, i(le) ~ *det* their; *(forma di cortesia: anche:* L~) your // *pronome* theirs; *(forma di cortesia: anche:* L~) yours; ~ stessi(e) they themselves; you yourselves.
'losco, a, schi, sche *ag* *(fig)* shady, suspicious.
'lotta *sf* struggle, fight; *(SPORT)* wrestling; ~ libera all-in wrestling; **lot'tare** *vi* to fight, struggle; to wrestle; **lotta'tore, trice** *sm/f* wrestler.
lotte'ria *sf* lottery; *(di gara ippica)* sweepstake.
'lotto *sm* *(gioco)* (state) lottery; *(parte)* lot; *(EDIL)* site.
lozi'one |lot'tsjone| *sf* lotion.
lubrifi'cante *sm* lubricant.
lubrifi'care *vt* to lubricate.
luc'chetto |luk'ketto| *sm* padlock.
lucci'care |luttʃi'kare| *vi* to sparkle, glitter, twinkle.
'luccio |'luttʃo| *sm* *(ZOOL)* pike.
'lucciola |'luttʃola| *sf* *(ZOOL)* firefly; glowworm.
'luce |'lutʃe| *sf* light; *(finestra)* window; alla ~ di by the light of; fare ~ su qc *(fig)* to shed *o* throw light on sth; ~ del sole/della luna sun/moonlight; **lu'cente** *ag* shining.
lu'cerna |lu'tʃerna| *sf* oil-lamp.
lucer'nario |lutʃer'narjo| *sm* skylight.
lu'certola |lu'tʃertola| *sf* lizard.
luci'dare |lutʃi'dare| *vt* to polish; *(ricalcare)* to trace.
lucida'trice |lutʃida'tritʃe| *sf* floor polisher.
'lucido, a |'lutʃido| *ag* shining, bright;

(lucidato) polished; *(fig)* lucid // *sm* shine, lustre; *(per scarpe etc)* polish; *(disegno)* tracing.
'lucro *sm* profit, gain; **lu'croso, a** *ag* lucrative, profitable.
lu'dibrio *sm* mockery *q*; *(oggetto di scherno)* laughing-stock.
'luglio |'luʎʎo| *sm* July.
'lugubre *ag* gloomy.
'lui *pronome* *(soggetto)* he; *(oggetto: per dare rilievo, con preposizione)* him; ~ stesso he himself.
lu'maca, che *sf* slug; *(chiocciola)* snail.
'lume *sm* light; *(lampada)* lamp; *(fig)*: chiedere ~i a qn to ask sb for advice; a ~ di naso *(fig)* by rule of thumb.
lumi'naria *sf* *(per feste)* illuminations *pl*.
lumi'noso, a *ag* *(che emette luce)* luminous; *(cielo, colore, stanza)* bright; *(sorgente)* of light, light *cpd*; *(fig: sorriso)* bright, radiant.
'luna *sf* moon; ~ nuova/piena new/full moon; ~ di miele honeymoon.
'luna park *sm inv* amusement park, funfair.
lu'nare *ag* lunar, moon *cpd*.
lu'nario *sm* almanac; sbarcare il ~ to make ends meet.
lu'natico, a, ci, che *ag* whimsical, temperamental.
lunedì *sm inv* Monday; di *o* il ~ on Mondays.
lun'gaggine |lun'gaddʒine| *sf* slowness; ~i della burocrazia red tape.
lun'ghezza |lun'gettsa| *sf* length; ~ d'onda *(FISICA)* wavelength.
'lungi |'lundʒi|: ~ da *prep* far from.
'lungo, a, ghi, ghe *ag* long; *(lento: persona)* slow; *(diluito: caffè, brodo)* weak, watery, thin // *sm* length // *prep* along; ~ 3 metri 3 metres long; a ~ for a long time; a ~ andare in the long run; di gran ~a *(molto)* by far; andare in ~ *o* per le lunghe to drag on; saperla ~a to know what's what; in ~ e in largo far and wide, all over; ~ il corso dei secoli throughout the centuries.
lungo'mare *sm* promenade.
lu'notto *sm* *(AUT)* rear *o* back window.
lu'ogo, ghi *sm* place; *(posto: di incidente etc)* scene, site; *(punto, passo di libro)* passage; in ~ di instead of; in primo ~ in the first place; aver ~ to take place; dar ~ a to give rise to; ~ comune commonplace; ~ di nascita birthplace; *(AMM)* place of birth; ~ di provenienza place of origin.
luogote'nente *sm* *(MIL)* lieutenant.
lu'para *sf* sawn-off shotgun.
'lupo, a *sm/f* wolf.
'luppolo *sm* *(BOT)* hop.
'lurido, a *ag* filthy.
lu'singa, ghe *sf* *(spesso al pl)* flattery *q*.

lusin'gare vt to flatter; **lusinghi'ero, a** ag flattering, gratifying.

lus'sare vt (MED) to dislocate.

Lussem'burgo sm (stato): il ~ Luxembourg // sf (città) Luxembourg.

'lusso sm luxury; **di** ~ luxury cpd; **lussu'oso, a** ag luxurious.

lussureggi'are [lussured'dʒare] vi to be luxuriant.

lus'suria sf lust.

lus'trare vt to polish, shine.

lustras'carpe sm/f inv shoeshine.

lus'trino sm sequin.

'lustro, a ag shiny; (pelliccia) glossy // sm shine, gloss; (fig) prestige, glory; (quinquennio) five-year period.

'lutto sm mourning; essere in/portare il ~ to be in/wear mourning; **luttu'oso, a** ag mournful, sad.

M

ma cong but; ~ **insomma!** for goodness sake!; ~ **no!** of course not!

'macabro, a ag gruesome, macabre.

macché [mak'ke] escl not at all!, certainly not!

macche'roni [makke'roni] smpl macaroni sg.

'macchia ['makkja] sf stain, spot; (chiazza di diverso colore) spot; splash, patch; (tipo di boscaglia) scrub; **alla** ~ (fig) in hiding; **macchi'are** vt (sporcare) to stain, mark; **macchiarsi** vr (persona) to get o.s. dirty; (stoffa) to stain; to get stained o marked.

'macchina ['makkina] sf machine; (motore, locomotiva) engine; (automobile) car; (fig: meccanismo) machinery; **andare in** ~ (AUT) to go by car; (STAMPA) to go to press; ~ **da cucire** sewing machine; ~ **fotografica** camera; ~ **da presa** cine o movie camera; ~ **da scrivere** typewriter; ~ **a vapore** steam engine.

macchi'nare [makki'nare] vt to plot.

macchi'nario [makki'narjo] sm machinery.

macchi'netta [makki'netta] sf (fam: caffettiera) percolator; (: accendino) lighter.

macchi'nista, i [makki'nista] sm (di treno) engine-driver; (di nave) engineer; (TEATRO, TV) stagehand.

macchi'noso, a [makki'noso] ag complex, complicated.

mace'donia [matʃe'dɔnja] sf fruit salad.

macel'laio [matʃel'lajo] sm butcher.

macel'lare [matʃel'larɛ] vt to slaughter, butcher; **macelle'ria** sf butcher's (shop); **ma'cello** sm (mattatoio) slaughterhouse, abattoir (Brit); (fig) slaughter, massacre; (: disastro) shambles sg.

mace'rare [matʃe'rarɛ] vt to macerate; (CUC) to marinate; ~**rsi** vr (fig): ~**rsi in** to be consumed with.

ma'cerie [ma'tʃerje] sfpl rubble sg, debris sg.

ma'cigno [ma'tʃiɲɲo] sm (masso) rock, boulder.

maci'lento, a [matʃi'lɛnto] ag emaciated.

'macina ['matʃina] sf (pietra) millstone; (macchina) grinder; **macinacaffè** sm inv coffee grinder; **macina'pepe** sm inv peppermill.

maci'nare [matʃi'narɛ] vt to grind; (carne) to mince (Brit), grind (US); **maci'nato** sm meal, flour; (carne) minced (Brit) o ground (US) meat.

maci'nino [matʃi'nino] sm coffee grinder; peppermill.

'madido, a ag: ~ (di) wet o moist (with).

Ma'donna sf (REL) Our Lady.

mador'nale ag enormous, huge.

'madre sf mother; (matrice di bolletta) counterfoil // ag inv mother cpd; ragazza ~ unmarried mother; scena ~ (TEATRO) principal scene; (fig) terrible scene.

madre'lingua sf mother tongue, native language.

madre'perla sf mother-of-pearl.

ma'drina sf godmother.

maestà sf inv majesty; **maes'toso, a** ag majestic.

ma'estra sf vedi maestro.

maes'trale sm north-west wind, mistral.

maes'tranze [maes'trantse] sfpl workforce sg.

maes'tria sf mastery, skill.

ma'estro, a sm/f (INS: anche: ~ di scuola o elementare) primary (Brit) o grade school (US) teacher; (esperto) expert // sm (artigiano, fig: guida) master; (MUS) maestro // ag (principale) main; (di grande abilità) masterly, skilful; ~**a d'asilo** nursery teacher; ~ **di cerimonie** master of ceremonies.

'mafia sf Mafia; **mafi'oso** sm member of the Mafia.

'maga sf sorceress.

ma'gagna [ma'gaɲɲa] sf defect, flaw, blemish; (noia, guaio) problem.

ma'gari escl (esprime desiderio): ~ **fosse vero!** if only it were true!; ti piacerebbe andare in Scozia? — ~! would you like to go to Scotland? — and how! // av (anche) even; (forse) perhaps.

magaz'zino [magad'dzino] sm warehouse; grande ~ department store.

'maggio ['maddʒo] sm May.

maggio'rana [maddʒo'rana] sf (BOT) (sweet) marjoram.

maggio'ranza [maddʒo'rantsa] sf majority.

maggio'rare [maddʒo'rare] *vt* to increase, raise.

maggior'domo [maddʒor'dɔmo] *sm* butler.

maggi'ore [mad'dʒore] *ag* (*comparativo*: *più grande*) bigger, larger; taller; greater; (: *più vecchio*: *sorella, fratello*) older, elder; (: *di grado superiore*) senior; (: *più importante, MIL, MUS*) major; (*superlativo*) biggest, largest; tallest; greatest; oldest, eldest // *sm/f* (*di grado*) superior; (*di età*) elder; (*MIL*) major; (: *AER*) squadron leader; **la maggior parte** the majority; **andare per la ~** (*cantante etc*) to be very popular; **maggio'renne** *ag* of age // *sm/f* person who has come of age; **maggior'mente** *av* much more; (*con senso superlativo*) most.

ma'gia [ma'dʒia] *sf* magic; **'magico, a, ci, che** *ag* magic; (*fig*) fascinating, charming, magical.

'magio ['madʒo] *sm* (*REL*): **i re Magi** the Magi, the Three Wise Men.

magis'tero [madʒis'tero] *sm* teaching; (*fig: maestria*) skill; (*INS*): **facoltà di M~** ≈ teachers' training college; **magis'trale** *ag* primary (*Brit*) o grade school (*US*) teachers', primary (*Brit*) o grade school (*US*) teaching *cpd*; skilful.

magis'trato [madʒis'trato] *sm* magistrate; **magistra'tura** *sf* magistrature; (*magistrati*): **la magistratura** the Bench.

'maglia ['maʎʎa] *sf* stitch; (*lavoro ai ferri*) knitting *q*; (*tessuto, SPORT*) jersey; (*maglione*) jersey, sweater; (*di catena*) link; (*di rete*) mesh; **~ diritta/rovescia** plain/purl, **maglie'ria** *sf* knit wear; (*negozio*) knitwear shop; **ma-gli'etta** *sf* (*canottiera*) vest; (*tipo camicia*) T-shirt; **magli'ficio** *sm* knitwear factory.

'maglio ['maʎʎo] *sm* mallet; (*macchina*) power hammer.

ma'gnete [maɲ'ɲete] *sm* magnet; **ma'gnetico, a, ci, che** *ag* magnetic.

magne'tofono [maɲɲe'tɔfono] *sm* tape recorder.

ma'gnifico, a, ci, che [maɲ'ɲifiko] *ag* magnificent, splendid; (*ospite*) generous.

'magno, a ['maɲɲo] *ag*: **aula ~a** main hall.

ma'gnolia [maɲ'ɲɔlja] *sf* magnolia.

'mago, ghi *sm* (*stregone*) magician, wizard; (*illusionista*) magician.

ma'grezza [ma'grettsa] *sf* thinness.

'magro, a *ag* (*very*) thin, skinny; (*carne*) lean; (*formaggio*) low-fat; (*fig: scarso, misero*) meagre, poor; (: *meschino: scusa*) poor, lame; **mangiare di ~** not to eat meat.

'mai *av* (*nessuna volta*) never; (*talvolta*) ever; **non ... ~** never; **~ più** never again; **come ~?** why (o how) on earth?; **chi/dove/quando ~?** whoever/wherever/ whenever?

mai'ale *sm* (*ZOOL*) pig; (*carne*) pork.

maio'nese *sf* mayonnaise.

'mais *sm inv* maize.

mai'uscolo, a *ag* (*lettera*) capital; (*fig*) enormous, huge // *sf* capital letter.

mal *av, sm vedi* **male**.

malac'corto, a *ag* rash, careless.

mala'fede *sf* bad faith.

mala'mente *av* badly; dangerously.

malan'dato, a *ag* (*persona: di salute*) in poor health; (: *di condizioni finanziarie*) badly off; (*trascurato*) shabby.

ma'lanno *sm* (*disgrazia*) misfortune; (*malattia*) ailment.

mala'pena *sf*: **a ~** hardly, scarcely.

ma'laria *sf* (*MED*) malaria.

mala'sorte *sf* bad luck.

mala'ticcio, a [mala'tittʃo] *ag* sickly.

ma'lato, a *ag* ill, sick; (*gamba*) bad; (*pianta*) diseased // *sm/f* sick person; (*in ospedale*) patient; **malat'tia** *sf* (*infettiva etc*) illness, disease; (*cattiva salute*) illness, sickness; (*di pianta*) disease.

malau'gurio *sm* bad o ill omen.

mala'vita *sf* underworld.

mala'voglia [mala'vɔʎʎa] *sf*: **di ~** unwillingly, reluctantly.

mal'concio, a, ci, ce [mal'kontʃo] *ag* in a sorry state.

malcon'tento *sm* discontent.

malcos'tume *sm* immorality.

mal'destro, a *ag* (*inabile*) inexpert, inexperienced; (*goffo*) awkward.

maldi'cenza [maldi'tʃentsa] *sf* malicious gossip.

maldis'posto, a *ag*: **~ (verso)** ill-disposed (towards).

'male *av* badly // *sm* (*ciò che è ingiusto, disonesto*) evil; (*danno, svantaggio*) harm; (*sventura*) misfortune; (*dolore fisico, morale*) pain, ache; **di ~ in peggio** from bad to worse; **sentirsi ~** to feel ill; **far ~** (*dolere*) to hurt; **far ~ alla salute** to be bad for one's health; **far del ~ a qn** to hurt o harm sb; **restare o rimanere ~** to be sorry; to be disappointed; to be hurt; **andare a ~** to go bad; **come va? — non c'è ~** how are you? — not bad; **mal di mare** seasickness; **avere mal di gola/testa** to have a sore throat/a headache; **aver ~ ai piedi** to have sore feet.

male'detto, a *pp di* **maledire** // *ag* cursed, damned; (*fig: fam*) damned, blasted.

male'dire *vt* to curse; **maledizi'one** *sf* curse; **maledizione!** damn it!

maledu'cato, a *ag* rude, ill-mannered.

male'fatta *sf* misdeed.

male'ficio [male'fitʃo] *sm* witchcraft.

ma'lefico, a, ci, che *ag* (*aria, cibo*) harmful, bad; (*influsso, azione*) evil.

ma'lessere *sm* indisposition, slight illness; (*fig*) uneasiness.

ma'levolo, a *ag* malevolent.

malfa'mato, a *ag* notorious.

mal'fatto, a *ag* (*persona*) deformed; (*oggetto*) badly made; (*lavoro*) badly done.

malfat'tore, 'trice *sm/f* wrongdoer.

mal'fermo, a *ag* unsteady, shaky; (*salute*) poor, delicate.

malformazi'one [malformat'tsjone] *sf* malformation.

malgo'verno *sm* maladministration.

mal'grado *prep* in spite of, despite // *cong* although; **mio (o tuo etc) ~** against my (o your *etc*) will.

ma'lia *sf* spell; (*fig: fascino*) charm.

mali'gnare [malip'pare] *vi:* **~ su** to malign, speak ill of.

ma'ligno, a [ma'lippo] *ag* (*malvagio*) malicious, malignant; (*MED*) malignant.

malinco'nia *sf* melancholy, gloom; **malin'conico, a, ci, che** *ag* melancholy.

malincu'ore: a ~ *av* reluctantly, unwillingly.

malintenzio'nato, a [malintentsjo'nato] *ag* ill-intentioned.

malin'teso, a *ag* misunderstood; (*riguardo, senso del dovere*) mistaken, wrong // *sm* misunderstanding.

ma'lizia [ma'littsja] *sf* (*malignità*) malice; (*furbizia*) cunning; (*espediente*) trick; **malizi'oso, a** *ag* malicious; cunning; (*vivace, birichino*) mischievous.

malme'nare *vt* to beat up; (*fig*) to ill-treat.

mal'messo, a *ag* shabby.

malnu'trito, a *ag* undernourished; **malnutrizi'one** *sf* malnutrition.

ma'locchio [ma'lokkjo] *sm* evil eye.

ma'lora *sf:* **andare in ~** to go to the dogs.

ma'lore *sm* (sudden) illness.

mal'sano, a *ag* unhealthy.

malsi'curo, a *ag* unsafe.

'Malta *sf:* **la ~** Malta.

'malta *sf* (*EDIL*) mortar.

mal'tempo *sm* bad weather.

'malto *sm* malt.

maltrat'tare *vt* to ill-treat.

malu'more *sm* bad mood; (*irritabilità*) bad temper; (*discordia*) ill feeling; **di ~** in a bad mood.

mal'vagio, a, gi, gie [mal'vad3o] *ag* wicked, evil.

malversazi'one [malversat'tsjone] *sf* (*DIR*) embezzlement.

mal'visto, a *ag:* **~ (da)** disliked (by), unpopular (with).

malvi'vente *sm* criminal.

malvolenti'eri *av* unwillingly, reluctantly.

'mamma *sf* mummy, mum; **~ mia!** my goodness!

mam'mella *sf* (*ANAT*) breast; (*di vacca, capra etc*) udder.

mam'mifero *sm* mammal.

'mammola *sf* (*BOT*) violet.

ma'nata *sf* (*colpo*) slap; (*quantità*) handful.

'manca *sf* left (hand); **a destra e a ~** left, right and centre, on all sides.

man'canza [man'kantsa] *sf* lack; (*carenza*) shortage, scarcity; (*fallo*) fault; (*imperfezione*) failing, shortcoming; **per ~ di tempo** through lack of time; **in ~ di meglio** for lack of anything better.

man'care *vi* (*essere insufficiente*) to be lacking; (*venir meno*) to fail; (*sbagliare*) to be wrong, make a mistake; (*non esserci*) to be missing, not to be there; (*essere lontano*): **~ (da)** to be away (from) // *vt* to miss; **~ di** to lack; **~ a** (*promessa*) to fail to keep; **tu mi manchi** I miss you; **mancò poco che morisse** he very nearly died; **mancano ancora 10 sterline** we're still £10 short; **manca un quarto alle 6** it's a quarter to 6; **man'cato, a** *ag* (*tentativo*) unsuccessful; (*artista*) failed.

'mancia, ce ['mantʃa] *sf* tip; **~ competente** reward.

manci'ata [man'tʃata] *sf* handful.

man'cino, a [man'tʃino] *ag* (*braccio*) left; (*persona*) left-handed; (*fig*) underhand.

'manco *av* (*nemmeno*): **~ per sogno** *o* **per idea!** not on your life!

man'dare *vt* to send; (*far funzionare: macchina*) to drive; (*emettere*) to send out; (*: grido*) to give, utter, let out; **~ a chiamare qn** to send for sb; **~ avanti** (*fig: famiglia*) to provide for; (*: fabbrica*) to run, look after; **~ giù** to send down; (*anche fig*) to swallow; **~ via** to send away; (*licenziare*) to fire.

manda'rino *sm* mandarin (orange); (*cinese*) mandarin.

man'data *sf* (*quantità*) lot, batch; (*di chiave*) turn; **chiudere a doppia ~** to double-lock.

manda'tario *sm* (*DIR*) representative, agent.

man'dato *sm* (*incarico*) commission; (*DIR: provvedimento*) warrant; (*di deputato etc*) mandate; (*ordine di pagamento*) postal *o* money order; **~ d'arresto** warrant for arrest.

man'dibola *sf* mandible, jaw.

'mandorla *sf* almond; **'mandorlo** *sm* almond tree.

'mandria *sf* herd.

maneggi'are [maned'd3are] *vt* (*creta, cera*) to mould, work, fashion; (*arnesi, utensili*) to handle; (*: adoperare*) to use; (*fig: persone, denaro*) to handle, deal with; **ma'neggio** *sm* moulding; handling; use; (*intrigo*) plot, scheme; (*per cavalli*) riding school.

ma'nesco, a, schi, sche *ag* free with one's fists.

ma'nette sfpl handcuffs.

manga'nello sm club.

manga'nese sm manganese.

mange'reccio, a, ci, ce [mandʒe'rettʃo] ag edible.

mangia'dischi [mandʒa'diski] sm inv record player.

mangi'are [man'dʒare] vt to eat; (intaccare) to eat into o away; (CARTE, SCACCHI etc) to take // vi to eat // sm eating; (cibo) food; (cucina) cooking; ~rsi le parole to mumble; ~rsi le unghie to bite one's nails; **mangia'toia** sf feeding-trough.

man'gime [man'dʒime] sm fodder.

'mango, ghi sm mango.

ma'nia sf (PSIC) mania; (fig) obsession, craze; **ma'niaco, a, ci, che** ag suffering from a mania; **maniaco** (di) obsessed (by), crazy (about).

'manica sf sleeve; (fig: gruppo) gang, bunch; (GEO): la M~, il Canale della M~ the (English) Channel; essere di ~ larga/stretta to be easy-going/strict; ~ a vento (AER) wind sock.

mani'chino [mani'kino] sm (di sarto, vetrina) dummy.

'manico, ci sm handle; (MUS) neck.

mani'comio sm mental hospital; (fig) madhouse.

mani'cotto sm muff; (TECN) coupling; sleeve.

mani'cure sm o f inv manicure // sf inv manicurist.

mani'era sf way, manner; (stile) style, manner; ~e sfpl manners; in ~ che so that; in ~ da so as to; in tutte le ~e at all costs.

manie'rato, a ag affected.

manifat'tura sf (lavorazione) manufacture; (stabilimento) factory.

manifes'tare vt to show, display; (esprimere) to express; (rivelare) to reveal, disclose // vi to demonstrate; ~rsi vr to show o.s.; ~rsi amico to prove o.s. (to be) a friend; **manifestazi'one** sf show, display; expression; (sintomo) sign, symptom; (dimostrazione pubblica) demonstration; (cerimonia) event.

mani'festo, a ag obvious, evident // sm poster, bill; (scritto ideologico) manifesto.

ma'niglia [ma'niʎʎa] sf handle; (sostegno: negli autobus etc) strap.

manipo'lare vt to manipulate; (alterare: vino) to adulterate; **manipolazi'one** sf manipulation; adulteration.

manis'calco, chi sm blacksmith.

'manna sf (REL) manna.

man'naia sf (del boia) (executioner's) axe; (per carni) cleaver.

man'naro: lupo ~ sm werewolf.

'mano, i sf hand; (strato: di vernice etc) coat; **di prima ~** (notizia) first-hand; **di seconda ~** second-hand; **man ~** little by little, gradually; **man ~ che** as; **darsi o stringersi la ~** to shake hands; **mettere le ~i avanti** (fig) to safeguard o.s.; **restare a ~i vuote** to be left empty-handed; **venire alle ~i** to come to blows; **a ~ by hand**; ~l in alto! hands up!

mano'dopera sf labour.

mano'messo, a pp di **manomettere**.

ma'nometro sm gauge, manometer.

mano'mettere vt (alterare) to tamper with; (aprire indebitamente) to break open illegally.

ma'nopola sf (dell'armatura) gauntlet; (guanto) mitt; (di impugnatura) hand-grip; (pomello) knob.

manos'critto, a ag handwritten // sm manuscript.

mano'vale sm labourer.

mano'vella sf handle; (TECN) crank.

ma'novra sf manoeuvre (Brit), maneuver (US); (FERR) shunting; **mano'vrare** vt (veicolo) to manoeuvre (Brit), maneuver (US); (macchina, congegno) to operate; (fig: persona) to manipulate // vi to manoeuvre.

manro'vescio [manro'veʃʃo] sm slap (with back of hand).

man'sarda sf attic.

mansi'one sf task, duty, job.

mansu'eto, a ag gentle, docile.

man'tello sm cloak; (fig: di neve etc) blanket, mantle; (TECN: involucro) casing, shell; (ZOOL) coat.

mante'nere vt to maintain; (adempiere: promesse) to keep, abide by; (provvedere a) to support, maintain; ~rsi vr: ~rsi calmo/giovane to stay calm/young; **manteni'mento** sm maintenance.

'mantice ['mantitʃe] sm bellows pl; (di carrozza, automobile) hood.

'manto sm cloak; ~ stradale road surface.

manu'ale ag manual // sm (testo) manual, handbook.

ma'nubrio sm handle; (di bicicletta etc) handlebars pl; (SPORT) dumbbell.

manu'fatto sm manufactured article.

manutenzi'one [manuten'tsjone] sf maintenance, upkeep; (d'impianti) maintenance, servicing.

'manzo ['mandzo] sm (ZOOL) steer; (carne) beef.

'mappa sf (GEO) map; **mappa'mondo** sm map of the world; (globo girevole) globe.

ma'rasma, i sm (fig) decay, decline.

mara'tona sf marathon.

'marca, che sf mark; (bollo) stamp; (COMM: di prodotti) brand; (contrassegno, scontrino) ticket, check; **prodotto di ~** (di buona qualità) high-class product; ~ **da bollo** official stamp.

mar'care vt (munire di contrassegno) to

mark; (a fuoco) to brand; (SPORT: gol) to score; (: avversario) to mark; (accentuare) to stress; ~ **visita** (MIL) to report sick.

'**Marche** ['marke] sfpl: le ~ the Marches (region of central Italy).

mar'chese, a [mar'keze] sm/f marquis o marquess/marchioness.

marchi'are [mar'kjare] vt to brand; '**marchio** sm (di bestiame, COMM, fig) brand; **marchio depositato** registered trademark; **marchio di fabbrica** trademark.

'**marcia, ce** ['martʃa] sf (anche MUS, MIL) march; (funzionamento) running; (il camminare) walking; (AUT) gear; mettere in ~ to start; mettersi in ~ to get moving; far ~ **indietro** (AUT) to reverse; (fig) to back-pedal.

marciapi'ede [martʃa'pjede] sm (di strada) pavement (Brit), sidewalk (US); (FERR) platform.

marci'are [mar'tʃare] vi to march; (andare: treno, macchina) to go; (funzionare) to run, work.

'**marcio, a, ci, ce** ['martʃo] ag (frutta, legno) rotten, bad; (MED) festering; (fig) corrupt, rotten.

mar'cire [mar'tʃire] vi (andare a male) to go bad, rot; (suppurare) to fester; (fig) to rot, waste away.

'**marco, chi** sm (unità monetaria) mark.

'**mare** sm sea; in ~ at sea; **andare al** ~ (in vacanza etc) to go to the seaside; il M~ **del Nord** the North Sea.

ma'rea sf tide; **alta/bassa** ~ high/low tide.

mareggi'ata [mared'dʒata] sf heavy sea.

ma'remma sf (GEO) maremma, swampy coastal area.

mare'moto sm seaquake.

maresci'allo [mareʃ'ʃallo] sm (MIL) marshal; (: sottufficiale) warrant officer.

marga'rina sf margarine.

marghe'rita [marge'rita] sf (ox-eye) daisy, marguerite; (di stampante) daisy wheel; **margheri'tina** sf daisy.

'**margine** ['mardʒine] sm margin; (di bosco, via) edge, border.

ma'rina sf navy; (costa) coast; (quadro) seascape; ~ **militare/mercantile** navy/ merchant navy (Brit) o marine (US).

mari'naio sm sailor.

mari'nare vt (CUC) to marinate; ~ **la scuola** to play truant; **mari'nata** sf marinade.

ma'rino, a ag sea cpd, marine.

mario'netta sf puppet.

mari'tare vt to marry; ~**rsi** vr: ~**rsi a** o **con qn** to marry sb, get married to sb.

ma'rito sm husband.

ma'rittimo, a ag maritime, sea cpd.

mar'maglia [mar'maʎʎa] sf mob, riffraff.

marmel'lata sf jam; (di agrumi) marmalade.

mar'mitta sf (recipiente) pot; (AUT) silencer.

'**marmo** sm marble.

mar'mocchio [mar'mɔkkjo] sm (fam) tot, kid.

mar'motta sf (ZOOL) marmot.

Ma'rocco sm: il ~ Morocco.

ma'roso sm breaker.

mar'rone ag inv brown // sm (BOT) chestnut.

mar'sala sm inv (vino) Marsala.

mar'sina sf tails pl, tail coat.

martedì sm inv Tuesday; di o il ~ on Tuesdays; ~ **grasso** Shrove Tuesday.

martel'lare vt to hammer // vi (pulsare) to throb; (: cuore) to thump.

mar'tello sm hammer; (di uscio) knocker.

marti'netto sm (TECN) jack.

'**martire** sm/f martyr; **mar'tirio** sm martyrdom; (fig) agony, torture.

'**martora** sf marten.

martori'are vt to torment, torture.

mar'xista, i, e ag, sm/f Marxist.

marza'pane [martsa'pane] sm marzipan.

'**marzo** ['martso] sm March.

mascal'zone [maskal'tsone] sm rascal, scoundrel.

ma'scella [maʃ'ʃella] sf (ANAT) jaw.

'**maschera** ['maskera] sf mask; (travestimento) disguise; (: per un ballo etc) fancy dress; (TEATRO, CINEMA) usher/usherette; (personaggio del teatro) stock character; **masche'rare** vt to mask; (travestire) to disguise; to dress up; (fig: celare) to hide, conceal; (MIL) to camouflage; ~**rsi da** to disguise o.s. as; to dress up as; (fig) to masquerade as.

mas'chile [mas'kile] ag masculine; (sesso, popolazione) male; (abiti) men's; (per ragazzi: scuola) boys'.

'**maschio, a** ['maskjo] ag (BIOL) male; (virile) manly // sm (anche ZOOL, TECN) male; (uomo) man; (ragazzo) boy; (figlio) son.

masco'lino, a ag masculine.

'**massa** sf mass; (di errori etc): **una** ~ **di** heaps of, masses of; (di gente) mass, multitude; (ELETTR) earth; in ~ (COMM) in bulk; (tutti insieme) en masse; **adunata in** ~ mass meeting; di ~ (cultura, manifestazione) mass cpd; **la** ~ **del popolo** the masses pl.

mas'sacro sm massacre, slaughter; (fig) mess, disaster.

mas'saggio [mas'saddʒo] sm massage.

mas'saia sf housewife.

masse'rizie [masse'rittsje] sfpl (household) furnishings.

mas'siccio, a, ci, ce [mas'sittʃo] ag (oro, legno) solid; (palazzo) massive; (corporatura) stout // sm (GEO) massif.

'massima *sf vedi* **massimo**.

massi'male *sm* maximum.

'massimo, a *ag, sm* maximum // *sf* (*sentenza, regola*) maxim; (*METEOR*) maximum temperature; **al ~ at (the)** most; **in linea di ~a** generally speaking.

'masso *sm* rock, boulder.

mas'sone *sm* freemason; **massone'ria** *sf* freemasonry.

masti'care *vt* to chew.

'mastice ['mastitʃe] *sm* mastic; (*per vetri*) putty.

mas'tino *sm* mastiff.

ma'tassa *sf* skein.

mate'matico, a, ci, che *ag* mathematical // *sm/f* mathematician // *sf* mathematics *sg*.

mate'rasso *sm* mattress; **~ a molle** spring *o* interior-sprung mattress.

ma'teria *sf* (*FISICA*) matter; (*TECN, COMM*) material, matter *q*; (*disciplina*) subject; (*argomento*) subject matter, material; **~e prime raw materials; in ~ di** (*per quanto concerne*) on the subject of; **materi'ale** *ag* material; (*fig: grossolano*) rough, rude // *sm* material; (*insieme di strumenti etc*) equipment *q*, materials *pl*.

maternità *sf* motherhood, maternity; (*clinica*) maternity hospital.

ma'terno, a *ag* (*amore, cura etc*) maternal, motherly; (*nonno*) maternal; (*lingua, terra*) mother *cpd*.

ma'tita *sf* pencil.

ma'trice [ma'tritʃe] *sf* matrix; (*COMM*) counterfoil; (*fig: origine*) background.

ma'tricola *sf* (*registro*) register; (*numero*) registration number; (*nell'università*) freshman, fresher.

ma'trigna [ma'triɲɲa] *sf* stepmother.

matrimoni'ale *ag* matrimonial, marriage *cpd*.

matri'monio *sm* marriage, matrimony; (*durata*) marriage, married life; (*cerimonia*) wedding.

ma'trona *sf* (*fig*) matronly woman.

mat'tina *sf* morning; **matti'nata** *sf* morning; (*spettacolo*) matinée, afternoon performance; **mattini'ero, a** *ag*: **essere mattiniero** to be an early riser; **mat'tino** *sm* morning.

'matto, a *ag* mad, crazy; (*fig: falso*) false, imitation; (: *opaco*) matt, dull // *sm/f* madman/woman; **avere una voglia ~a di qc** to be dying for sth.

mat'tone *sm* brick; (*fig*): **questo libro/ film è un ~** this book/film is heavy going.

matto'nella *sf* tile.

matu'rare *vi* (*anche:* **~rsi**) (*frutta, grano*) to ripen; (*ascesso*) to come to a head; (*fig: persona, idea, ECON*) to mature // *vt* to ripen; to (make) mature.

maturità *sf* maturity; (*di frutta*) ripeness, maturity; (*INS*) school-leaving examination, ≈ GCE A-levels (*Brit*).

ma'turo, a *ag* mature; (*frutto*) ripe, mature.

'mazza ['mattsa] *sf* (*bastone*) club; (*martello*) sledge-hammer; (*SPORT: da golf*) club; (: *da baseball, cricket*) bat.

maz'zata [mat'tsata] *sf* (*anche fig*) heavy blow.

'mazzo ['mattso] *sm* (*di fiori, chiavi etc*) bunch; (*di carte da gioco*) pack.

me *pronome* me; **~ stesso(a)** myself; **sei bravo quanto ~** you are as clever as I (am) *o* as me.

me'andro *sm* meander.

M.E.C. [mɛk] *sigla m* (= *Mercato Comune Europeo*) EEC.

mec'canico, a, ci, che *ag* mechanical // *sm* mechanic // *sf* mechanics *sg*; (*attività tecnologica*) mechanical engineering; (*meccanismo*) mechanism.

mecca'nismo *sm* mechanism.

me'daglia [me'daʎʎa] *sf* medal; **medagli'one** *sm* (*ARCHIT*) medallion; (*gioiello*) locket.

me'desimo, a *ag* same; (*in persona*): **io ~ I myself.**

'media *sf vedi* **medio**.

medi'ano, a *ag* median; (*valore*) mean // *sm* (*CALCIO*) half-back.

medi'ante *prep* by means of.

medi'are *vt* (*fare da mediatore*) to act as mediator in; (*MAT*) to average.

media'tore, 'trice *sm/f* mediator; (*COMM*) middle man, agent.

medica'mento *sm* medicine, drug.

medi'care *vt* to treat; (*ferita*) to dress; **medicazi'one** *sf* treatment, medication; dressing.

medi'cina [medi'tʃina] *sf* medicine; **~ legale** forensic medicine; **medici'nale** *ag* medicinal // *sm* drug, medicine.

'medico, a, ci, che *ag* medical // *sm* doctor; **~ generico** general practitioner, GP.

medie'vale *ag* medieval.

'medio, a *ag* average; (*punto, ceto*) middle; (*altezza, statura*) medium // *sm* (*dito*) middle finger // *sf* average; (*MAT*) mean; (*INS: voto*) end-of-term average; **in ~a** on average; **licenza ~a** *leaving certificate awarded at the end of 3 years of secondary education*; **scuola ~a** *first 3 years of secondary school*.

medi'ocre *ag* mediocre, poor.

medioe'vale *ag* = **medievale**.

medio'evo *sm* Middle Ages *pl*.

medi'tare *vt* to ponder over, meditate on; (*progettare*) to plan, think out // *vi* to meditate.

mediter'raneo, a *ag* Mediterranean; **il (mare) M~ the Mediterranean (Sea).**

me'dusa *sf* (*ZOOL*) jellyfish.

me'gafono *sm* megaphone.

'meglio ['mɛʎʎo] *av, ag inv* better; (*con senso superlativo*) best // *sm* (*la cosa migliore*): **il ~ the best (thing); faresti**

~ ad andartene you had better leave; alla ~ as best one can; andar di bene in ~ to get better and better; fare del proprio ~ to do one's best; per il ~ for the best; aver la ~ su qn to get the better of sb.

'mela *sf* apple; ~ cotogna quince.

mela'grana *sf* pomegranate.

melan'zana [melan'dzana] *sf* aubergine (*Brit*), eggplant (*US*).

me'lassa *sf* molasses *sg*, treacle.

me'lenso, a *ag* dull, stupid.

mel'lifluo, a *ag* (*peg*) sugary, honeyed.

'melma *sf* mud, mire.

'melo *sm* apple tree.

melo'dia *sf* melody.

me'lone *sm* (musk)melon.

'membra *sfpl vedi* **membro**.

'membro *sm* member; (*pl(f)* ~a: *arto*) limb.

memo'randum *sm inv* memorandum.

me'moria *sf* memory; ~e *sfpl* (*opera autobiografica*) memoirs; a ~ (*imparare, sapere*) by heart; a ~ d'uomo within living memory; **memori'ale** *sm* (*raccolta di memorie*) memoirs *pl*; (*DIR*) memorial.

mena'dito: a ~ *av* perfectly, thoroughly; sapere qc a ~ to have sth at one's fingertips.

me'nare *vt* to lead; (*picchiare*) to hit, beat; (*dare: colpi*) to deal; ~ la coda (*cane*) to wag its tail.

mendi'cante *sm/f* beggar.

mendi'care *vt* to beg for // *vi* to beg.

'meno ◆ *av* 1 (*in minore misura*) less; dovresti mangiare ~ you should eat less, you shouldn't eat so much
2 (*comparativo*): ~ ... di not as ... as, less ... than; sono ~ alto di te I'm not as tall as you (are), I'm less tall than you (are); ~ ... che not as ... as, less ... than; ~ che mai less than ever; è ~ intelligente che ricco he's more rich than intelligent; ~ fumo più mangio the less I smoke the more I eat
3 (*superlativo*) least; il ~ dotato degli studenti the least gifted of the students; è quello che compro ~ spesso it's the one I buy least often
4 (*MAT*) minus; 8 ~ 5 8 minus 5, 8 take away 5; sono le 8 ~ un quarto it's a quarter to 8; ~ 5 gradi 5 degrees below zero, minus 5 degrees; mille lire in ~ a thousand lire less
5 (*fraseologia*): quanto ~ poteva telefonare he could at least have phoned; non so se accettare o ~ I don't know whether to accept or not; fare a ~ di qc/ qn to do without sth/sb; non potevo fare a ~ di ridere I couldn't help laughing; ~ male! thank goodness!; ~ male che sei arrivato it's a good job that you've come ◆ *ag inv* (*tempo, denaro*) less; (*errori, persone*) fewer; ha fatto ~ errori di tutti

he made fewer mistakes than anyone, he made the fewest mistakes of all
◆ *sm inv* 1: il ~ (*il minimo*) the least; parlare del più e del ~ to talk about this and that
2 (*MAT*) minus
◆ *prep* (*eccetto*) except (for), apart from; a ~ che, a ~ di unless; a ~ che non piova unless it rains; non posso, a ~ di prendere ferie I can't, unless I take some leave.

meno'mare *vt* (*danneggiare*) to maim, disable.

meno'pausa *sf* menopause.

'mensa *sf* (*locale*) canteen; (: *MIL*) mess; (: *nelle università*) refectory.

men'sile *ag* monthly // *sm* (*periodico*) monthly (magazine); (*stipendio*) monthly salary.

'mensola *sf* bracket; (*ripiano*) shelf; (*ARCHIT*) corbel.

'menta *sf* mint; (*anche*: ~ piperita) peppermint; (*bibita*) peppermint cordial; (*caramella*) mint, peppermint.

men'tale *ag* mental; mentalità *sf inv* mentality.

'mente *sf* mind; imparare/sapere qc a ~ to learn/know sth by heart; avere in ~ qc to have sth in mind; passare di ~ a qn to slip sb's mind.

men'tire *vi* to lie.

'mento *sm* chin.

men'tolo *sm* menthol.

'mentre *cong* (*temporale*) while; (*avversativo*) whereas.

menzio'nare [mentsjo'nare] *vt* to mention.

menzi'one [men'tsjone] *sf* mention; fare ~ di to mention.

men'zogna [men'tsɔɲɲa] *sf* lie.

mera'viglia [mera'viʎʎa] *sf* amazement, wonder; (*persona, cosa*) marvel, wonder; a ~ perfectly, wonderfully; meravigli'are *vt* to amaze, astonish; meravigliarsi (di) to marvel (at); (*stupirsi*) to be amazed (at), be astonished (at); meravigli'oso, a *ag* wonderful, marvellous.

mer'cante *sm* merchant; ~ d'arte art dealer; ~ di cavalli horse dealer; mercanteggi'are *vt* (*onore, voto*) to sell // *vi* to bargain, haggle; mercan'tile *ag* commercial, mercantile; (*nave, marina*) merchant *cpd* // *sm* (*nave*) merchantman; mercan'zia *sf* merchandise, goods *pl*.

mer'cato *sm* market; ~ dei cambi exchange market; M~ Comune (Europeo) (European) Common Market; ~ nero black market.

'merce ['mertʃe] *sf* goods *pl*, merchandise; ~ deperibile perishable goods *pl*.

mercé |mer'tʃe| *sf* mercy.

merce'nario, a |mertʃe'narjo| *ag*, *sm*

mercenary.
merce'ria [mertʃe'ria] *sf* (*articoli*) haberdashery (*Brit*), notions *pl* (*US*); (*bottega*) haberdasher's shop (*Brit*), notions store (*US*).
mercoledì *sm inv* Wednesday; di *o* il ~ on Wednesdays; ~ delle Ceneri Ash Wednesday.
mer'curio *sm* mercury.
'merda *sf* (*fam!*) shit (*!*).
me'renda *sf* afternoon snack.
meridi'ano, a *ag* meridian; midday *cpd*, noonday // *sm* meridian // *sf* (*orologio*) sundial.
meridio'nale *ag* southern // *sm/f* southerner.
meridi'one *sm* south.
me'ringa, ghe *sf* (*CUC*) meringue.
meri'tare *vt* to deserve, merit // *vb impers*: merita andare it's worth going.
meri'tevole *ag* worthy.
'merito *sm* merit; (*valore*) worth; in ~ a as regards, with regard to; dare ~ a qn to give sb credit for; finire a pari ~ to finish joint first (*o* second *etc*); to tie; **meri'torio, a** *ag* praiseworthy.
mer'letto *sm* lace.
'merlo *sm* (*ZOOL*) blackbird; (*ARCHIT*) battlement.
mer'luzzo [mer'luttso] *sm* (*ZOOL*) cod.
mes'chino, a [mes'kino] *ag* wretched; (*scarso*) scanty, poor; (*persona*: *gretta*) mean; (: *limitata*) narrow-minded, petty.
mesco'lanza [mesko'lantsa] *sf* mixture.
mesco'lare *vt* to mix; (*vini, colori*) to blend; (*mettere in disordine*) to mix up, muddle up; (*carte*) to shuffle; ~rsi *vr* to mix; to blend; to get mixed up; (*fig*): ~rsi in to get mixed up in, meddle in.
'mese *sm* month.
'messa *sf* (*REL*) mass; (*il mettere*): ~ in moto starting; ~ in piega set; ~ a punto (*TECN*) adjustment; (*AUT*) tuning; (*fig*) clarification; ~ in scena = messinscena.
messag'gero [messad'dʒero] *sm* messenger.
mes'saggio [mes'saddʒo] *sm* message.
mes'sale *sm* (*REL*) missal.
'messe *sf* harvest.
Mes'sia *sm inv* (*REL*): il ~ the Messiah.
'Messico *sm*: il ~ Mexico.
messin'scena [messin'ʃena] *sf* (*TEATRO*) production.
'messo, a *pp di* **mettere** // *sm* messenger.
mesti'ere *sm* (*professione*) job; (: *manuale*) trade; (: *artigianale*) craft; (*fig*: *abilità nel lavoro*) skill, technique; essere del ~ to know the tricks of the trade.
'mesto, a *ag* sad, melancholy.
'mestola *sf* (*CUC*) ladle; (*EDIL*) trowel.
'mestolo *sm* (*CUC*) ladle.

mestruazi'one [mestruat'tsjone] *sf* menstruation.
'meta *sf* destination; (*fig*) aim, goal.
metà *sf inv* half; (*punto di mezzo*) middle; dividere qc a o per ~ to divide sth in half, halve sth; fare a ~ (di qc con qn) to go halves (with sb in sth); a ~ prezzo at half price; a ~ strada halfway.
me'tafora *sf* metaphor.
me'tallico, a, ci, che *ag* (*di metallo*) metal *cpd*; (*splendore, rumore etc*) metallic.
me'tallo *sm* metal.
metalmec'canico, a, ci, che *ag* engineering *cpd* // *sm* engineering worker.
me'tano *sm* methane.
meteorolo'gia [meteorolo'dʒia] *sf* meteorology; **meteoro'logico, a, ci, che** *ag* meteorological, weather *cpd*.
me'ticcio, a, ci, ce [me'tittʃo] *sm/f* half-caste, half-breed.
me'todico, a, ci, che *ag* methodical.
'metodo *sm* method; (*manuale*) tutor (*Brit*), manual.
'metrico, a, ci, che *ag* metric; (*POESIA*) metrical // *sf* metrics *sg*.
'metro *sm* metre; (*nastro*) tape measure; (*asta*) (metre) rule.
metropoli'tano, a *ag* metropolitan // *sf* underground, subway.
'mettere *vt* to put; (*abito*) to put on; (: *portare*) to wear; (*installare*: *telefono*) to put in; (*fig*: *provocare*): ~ fame/ allegria a qn to make sb hungry/happy; (*supporre*): mettiamo che ... let's suppose o say that ... ; ~rsi *vr* (*persona*) to put o.s.; (*oggetto*) to go; (*disporsi*: *faccenda*) to turn out; ~rsi a sedere to sit down; ~rsi a letto to get into bed; (*per malattia*) to take to one's bed; ~rsi il cappello to put on one's hat; ~rsi a (*cominciare*) to begin to, start to; ~rsi al lavoro to set to work; ~rsi con qn (*in società*) to team up with sb; (*in coppia*) to start going out with sb; ~rci: ~rci molta cura/molto tempo to take a lot of care/a lot of time; ci ho messo 3 ore per venire it's taken me 3 hours to get here; ~rcela tutta to do one's best; ~ a tacere qn/qc to keep sb/sth quiet; ~ su casa to set up house; ~ su un negozio to start a shop; ~ via to put away.
mez'zadro [med'dzadro] *sm* (*AGR*) sharecropper.
mezza'luna [meddza'luna] *sf* half-moon; (*dell'islamismo*) crescent; (*coltello*) (semicircular) chopping knife.
mezza'nino [meddza'nino] *sm* mezzanine (floor).
mez'zano, a [med'dzano] *ag* (*medio*) average, medium; (*figlio*) middle *cpd* // *sm/f* (*intermediario*) go-between; (*ruffiano*) pimp.
mezza'notte [meddza'nɔtte] *sf* midnight.

'**mezzo, a** |'mɛddzo| *ag* half; **un ~ litro/ panino** half a litre/roll // *av* half-; **~ morto** half-dead // *sm* (*metà*) half; (*parte centrale: di strada etc*) middle; (*per raggiungere un fine*) means *sg*; (*veicolo*) vehicle; (*nell'indicare l'ora*): **le nove e ~** half past nine; **mezzogiorno e ~** half past twelve // *sf*: **la ~a** half-past twelve (*in the afternoon*); **~i** *smpl* (*possibilità economiche*) means; **di ~a età** middle-aged; **un soprabito di ~a stagione** a spring (*o* autumn) coat; **di ~ middle**, in the middle; **andarci di ~** (*patir danno*) to suffer; **levarsi** *o* **togliersi di ~** to get out of the way; **in ~ a** in the middle of; **per** *o* **a ~ di** by means of; **~i di comunicazione di massa** mass media *pl*; **~i pubblici** public transport *sg*; **~i di trasporto** means of transport.

mezzogi'orno |meddzo'dʒorno| *sm* midday, noon; (GEO) south; **a ~** at 12 (o'clock) *o* midday *o* noon; **il ~ d'Italia** southern Italy.

mez'z'ora, mez'zora |med'dzora| *sf* half-hour, half an hour.

mi *pronome* (*dav lo, la, li, le, ne diventa* **me**) (*oggetto*) me; (*complemento di termine*) to me; (*riflessivo*) myself // *sm* (*MUS*) E; (: *solfeggiando la scala*) mi.

'**mia** *vedi* **mio.**

miago'lare *vi* to miaow, mew.

'**mica** *sf* (CHIM) mica // *av* (*fam*): **non ... ~** not ... at all; **non sono ~ stanco** I'm not a bit tired; **non sarà ~ partito?** he wouldn't have left, would he?; **~ male** not bad.

'**miccia, ce** |'mittʃa| *sf* fuse.

micidi'ale |mitʃi'djale| *ag* fatal; (*dannosissimo*) deadly.

mi'crofono *sm* microphone.

micros'copio *sm* microscope.

mi'dollo, *pl(f)* **~a** *sm* (ANAT) marrow.

'**mie, mi'ei** *vedi* **mio.**

mi'ele *sm* honey.

mi'etere *vt* (AGR) to reap, harvest; (*fig: vite*) to take, claim.

migli'aio |miʎ'ʎajo|, *pl(f)* **~a** *sm* thousand; **un ~ (di)** about a thousand; **a ~a** by the thousand, in thousands.

'**miglio** |'miʎʎo| *sm* (BOT) millet; (*pl(f)* **~a:** *unità di misura*) mile; **~ marino** *o* **nautico** nautical mile.

migliora'mento |miʎʎora'mento| *sm* improvement.

miglio'rare |miʎʎo'rare| *vt, vi* to improve.

migli'ore |miʎ'ʎore| *ag* (*comparativo*) better; (*superlativo*) best // *sm*: **il ~** the best (thing) // *sm/f*: **il(la) ~** the best (person); **il miglior vino di questa regione** the best wine in this area.

'**mignolo** |'miɲɲolo| *sm* (ANAT) little finger, pinkie; (: *dito del piede*) little toe.

mi'grare *vi* to migrate.

'**mila** *pl di* **mille.**

Mi'lano *sf* Milan.

miliar'dario, a *sm/f* millionaire.

mili'ardo *sm* thousand million, billion (US).

mili'are *ag*: **pietra ~** milestone.

mili'one *sm* million; **un ~ di lire** a million lire.

mili'tante *ag, sm/f* militant.

mili'tare *vi* (MIL) to be a soldier, serve; (*fig: in un partito*) to be a militant // *ag* military // *sm* serviceman; **fare il ~** to do one's military service.

'**milite** *sm* soldier.

millanta'tore, 'trice *sm/f* boaster.

'**mille** *num* (*pl* **mila**) **a** *o* **one thousand; dieci mila** ten thousand.

mille'foglie |mille'fɔʎʎe| *sm inv* (CUC) cream *o* vanilla slice.

mil'lennio *sm* millennium.

millepi'edi *sm inv* centipede.

mil'lesimo, a *ag, sm* thousandth.

milli'grammo *sm* milligram(me).

mil'limetro *sm* millimetre.

'**milza** |'miltsa| *sf* (ANAT) spleen.

mimetiz'zare |mimetid'dzare| *vt* to camouflage; **~rsi** *vr* to camouflage o.s.

'**mimica** *sf* (*arte*) mime.

'**mimo** *sm* (*attore, componimento*) mime.

mi'mosa *sf* mimosa.

'**mina** *sf* (*esplosiva*) mine; (*di matita*) lead.

mi'naccia, ce |mi'nattʃa| *sf* threat; **minacci'are** *vt* to threaten; **minacciare qn di morte** to threaten to kill sb; **minacciare di fare qc** to threaten to do sth; **minacci'oso, a** *ag* threatening.

mi'nare *vt* (MIL) to mine; (*fig*) to undermine.

mina'tore *sm* miner.

mina'torio, a *ag* threatening.

mine'rale *ag, sm* mineral.

mine'rario, a *ag* (*delle miniere*) mining; (*dei minerali*) ore *cpd*.

mi'nestra *sf* soup; **~ in brodo/di verdure** noodle/vegetable soup; **mines'trone** *sm* thick vegetable and pasta soup.

mingher'lino, a |minger'lino| *ag* thin, slender.

'**mini** *ag inv* mini // *sf inv* miniskirt.

minia'tura *sf* miniature.

mini'era *sf* mine.

mini'gonna *sf* miniskirt.

'**minimo, a** *ag* minimum, least, slightest; (*piccolissimo*) very small, slight; (*il più basso*) lowest, minimum // *sm* minimum; **al ~** at least; **girare al ~** (AUT) to idle.

minis'tero *sm* (POL, REL) ministry; (*governo*) government; **~ delle Finanze** Ministry of Finance, ≈ Treasury.

mi'nistro *sm* (POL, REL) minister; **~ delle Finanze** Minister of Finance, ≈ Chancellor of the Exchequer.

mino'ranza |mino'rantsa| *sf* minority.

mino'rato, a *ag* handicapped // *sm/f* physically (*o* mentally) handicapped person.

mi'nore *ag* (*comparativo*) less; (*più piccolo*) smaller; (*numero*) lower; (*inferiore*) lower, inferior; (*meno importante*) minor; (*più giovane*) younger; (*superlativo*) least; smallest; lowest; youngest // *sm/f* (*minorenne*) minor, person under age.

mino'renne *ag* under age // *sm/f* minor, person under age.

mi'nuscolo, a *ag* (*scrittura, carattere*) small; (*piccolissimo*) tiny // *sf* small letter.

mi'nuta *sf* rough copy, draft.

mi'nuto, a *ag* tiny, minute; (*pioggia*) fine; (*corporatura*) delicate, fine; (*lavoro*) detailed // *sm* (*unità di misura*) minute; **al ~** (*COMM*) retail.

'mio, 'mia, mi'ei, 'mie *det*: **il ~, la mia** *etc* my // *pronome*: **il ~, la mia** *etc* mine; **i miei** my family; **un ~ amico** a friend of mine.

'miope *ag* short-sighted.

'mira *sf* (*anche fig*) aim; **prendere la ~** to take aim; **prendere di ~ qn** (*fig*) to pick on sb.

mi'rabile *ag* admirable, wonderful.

mi'racolo *sm* miracle.

mi'raggio |mi'raddʒo| *sm* mirage.

mi'rare *vi*: **~ a** to aim at.

mi'rino *sm* (*TECN*) sight; (*FOT*) viewer, viewfinder.

mir'tillo *sm* bilberry (*Brit*), blueberry (*US*), whortleberry.

mi'scela |miʃ'ʃela| *sf* mixture; (*di caffè*) blend.

miscel'lanea |miʃʃel'lanea| *sf* miscellany.

'mischia |'miskja| *sf* scuffle; (*RUGBY*) scrum, scrummage.

mischi'are |mis'kjare| *vt*, **~rsi** *vr* to mix, blend.

mis'cuglio |mis'kuʎʎo| *sm* mixture, hotchpotch, jumble.

mise'rabile *ag* (*infelice*) miserable, wretched; (*povero*) poverty-stricken; (*di scarso valore*) miserable.

mi'seria *sf* extreme poverty; (*infelicità*) misery; **~e** *sfpl* (*del mondo etc*) misfortunes, troubles; **porca ~!** (*fam*) blast!, damn!

miseri'cordia *sf* mercy, pity.

'misero, a *ag* miserable, wretched; (*povero*) poverty-stricken; (*insufficiente*) miserable.

mis'fatto *sm* misdeed, crime.

mi'sogino |mi'zɔdʒino| *sm* misogynist.

'missile *sm* missile.

missio'nario, a *ag*, *sm/f* missionary.

missi'one *sf* mission.

misteri'oso, a *ag* mysterious.

mis'tero *sm* mystery.

mistifi'care *vt* to fool, bamboozle.

'misto, a *ag* mixed; (*scuola*) mixed, coeducational // *sm* mixture.

mis'tura *sf* mixture.

mi'sura *sf* measure; (*misurazione, dimensione*) measurement; (*taglia*) size; (*provvedimento*) measure, step; (*moderazione*) moderation; (*MUS*) time; (: *divisione*) bar; (*fig*: *limite*) bounds *pl*, limit; **nella ~ in cui** inasmuch as, insofar as; **su ~** made to measure.

misu'rare *vt* (*ambiente, - stoffa*) to measure; (*terreno*) to survey; (*abito*) to try on; (*pesare*) to weigh; (*fig*: *parole etc*) to weigh up; (: *spese, cibo*) to limit // *vi* to measure; **~rsi** *vr*: **~rsi con qn** to have a confrontation with sb; to compete with sb; **misu'rato, a** *ag* (*ponderato*) measured; (*prudente*) cautious; (*moderato*) moderate.

'mite *ag* mild; (*prezzo*) moderate, reasonable.

miti'gare *vt* to mitigate, lessen; (*lenire*) to soothe, relieve; **~rsi** *vr* (*odio*) to subside; (*tempo*) to become milder.

'mito *sm* myth; **mitolo'gia, 'gie** *sf* mythology.

'mitra *sf* (*REL*) mitre // *sm inv* (*arma*) sub-machine gun.

mitraglia'trice |mitraʎʎa'tritʃe| *sf* machine gun.

mit'tente *sm/f* sender.

'mobile *ag* mobile; (*parte di macchina*) moving; (*DIR: bene*) movable, personal // *sm* (*arredamento*) piece of furniture; **~i** *smpl* furniture *sg*.

mo'bilia *sf* furniture.

mobili'are *ag* (*DIR*) personal, movable.

mo'bilio *sm* = **mobilia**.

mobili'tare *vt* to mobilize.

mocas'sino *sm* moccasin.

'moccolo *sm* (*di candela*) candle-end; (*fam*: *bestemmia*) oath; (: *moccio*) snot; **reggere il ~** to play gooseberry (*Brit*), act as chaperon.

'moda *sf* fashion; **alla ~, di ~** fashionable, in fashion.

modalità *sf inv* formality.

mo'della *sf* model.

model'lare *vt* (*creta*) to model, shape; **~rsi** *vr*: **~rsi su** to model o.s. on.

mo'dello *sm* model; (*stampo*) mould // *ag inv* model *cpd*.

'modem *sm inv* modem.

mode'rare *vt* to moderate; **~rsi** *vr* to restrain o.s.; **mode'rato, a** *ag* moderate.

modera'tore, 'trice *sm/f* moderator.

mo'derno, a *ag* modern.

mo'destia *sf* modesty.

mo'desto, a *ag* modest.

'modico, a, ci, che *ag* reasonable, moderate.

mo'difica, che *sf* modification.

modifi'care *vt* to modify, alter; **~rsi** *vr*

to alter, change.

mo'dista *sf* milliner.

'**modo** *sm* way, manner; (*mezzo*) means, way; (*occasione*) opportunity; (*LING*) mood; (*MUS*) mode; ~i *smpl* manners; a suo ~, a ~ suo in his own way; ad *o* in ogni ~ anyway; di *o* in ~ che so that; in ~ da so as to; in tutti i ~i at all costs; (*comunque sia*) anyway; (*in ogni caso*) in any case; in qualche ~ somehow or other; ~ di dire turn of phrase; per ~ di dire so to speak.

modu'lare *vt* to modulate; **modulazi'one** *sf* modulation; modulazione di frequenza frequency modulation.

'**modulo** *sm* (*modello*) form; (*ARCHIT, lunare, di comando*) module.

'**mogano** *sm* mahogany.

'**mogio, a, gi, gie** ['mɔdʒo] *ag* down in the dumps, dejected.

'**moglie** ['moʎʎe] *sf* wife.

mo'ine *sfpl* cajolery *sg*; (*leziosità*) affectation *sg*.

'**mola** *sf* millstone; (*utensile abrasivo*) grindstone.

mo'lare *sm* (*dente*) molar.

'**mole** *sf* mass; (*dimensioni*) size; (*edificio grandioso*) massive structure.

moles'tare *vt* to bother, annoy; **mo'lestia** *sf* annoyance, bother; recar molestia a qn to bother sb; **mo'lesto, a** *ag* annoying.

'**molla** *sf* spring; ~e *sfpl* tongs.

mol'lare *vt* to release, let go; (*NAUT*) to ease; (*fig: ceffone*) to give // *vi* (*cedere*) to give in.

'**molle** *ag* soft; (*muscoli*) flabby; (*fig: debole*) weak, feeble.

mol'letta *sf* (*per capelli*) hairgrip; (*per panni stesi*) clothes peg; ~e *sfpl* (*per zucchero*) tongs.

'**mollica, che** *sf* crumb, soft part.

mol'lusco, schi *sm* mollusc.

'**molo** *sm* mole, breakwater; jetty.

mol'teplice [mol'teplitʃe] *ag* (*formato di più elementi*) complex; ~i *pl* (*svariati: interessi, attività*) numerous, various.

moltipli'care *vt* to multiply; ~rsi *vr* to multiply; to increase in number; **moltiplicazi'one** *sf* multiplication.

'**molto, a** ◆ *det* (*quantità*) a lot of, much; (*numero*) a lot of, many; ~ pane/carbone a lot of bread/coal; ~a gente a lot of people, many people; ~i libri a lot of books, many books; non ho ~ tempo I haven't got much time; per ~ (tempo) for a long time
◆ *av* 1 a lot, (very) much; viaggia ~ he travels a lot; non viaggia ~ he doesn't travel much *o* a lot
2 (*intensivo: con aggettivi, avverbi*) very; (: *con participio passato*) (very) much; ~ buono very good; ~ migliore, ~ meglio much *o* a lot better

◆ *pronome* much, a lot; ~i(e) *pronome pl* many, a lot; ~i pensano che ... many (people) think ....

momen'taneo, a *ag* momentary, fleeting.

mo'mento *sm* moment; da un ~ all'altro at any moment; (*all'improvviso*) suddenly; al ~ di fare just as I was (*o* you were *o* he was *etc*) doing; per il ~ for the time being; dal ~ che ever since; (*dato che*) since; a ~i (*da un ~ all'altro*) any time *o* moment now; (*quasi*) nearly.

'**monaca, che** *sf* nun.

'**Monaco** *sf* Monaco; ~ (**di Baviera**) Munich.

'**monaco, ci** *sm* monk.

mo'narca, chi *sm* monarch; **monar'chia** *sf* monarchy.

monas'tero *sm* (*di monaci*) monastery; (*di monache*) convent; **mo'nastico, a, ci, che** *ag* monastic.

'**monco, a, chi, che** *ag* maimed; (*fig*) incomplete; ~ d'un braccio one-armed.

mon'dana *sf* prostitute.

mon'dano, a *ag* (*anche fig*) worldly; (*dell'alta società*) society *cpd*; fashionable.

mon'dare *vt* (*frutta, patate*) to peel; (*piselli*) to shell; (*pulire*) to clean.

mondi'ale *ag* (*campionato, popolazione*) world *cpd*; (*influenza*) world-wide.

'**mondo** *sm* world; (*grande quantità*): un ~ di lots of, a host of; il bel ~ high society.

mo'nello, a *sm/f* street urchin; (*ragazzo vivace*) scamp, imp.

mo'neta *sf* coin; (*ECON: valuta*) currency; (*denaro spicciolo*) (small) change; ~ estera foreign currency; ~ legale legal tender; **mone'tario, a** *ag* monetary.

mongo'loide *ag*, *sm/f* (*MED*) mongol.

'**monito** *sm* warning.

'**monitor** *sm inv* (*TECN, TV*) monitor.

monoco'lore *ag* (*POL*): governo ~ one-party government.

mono'polio *sm* monopoly.

mo'notono, a *ag* monotonous.

monsi'gnore [monsiɲ'ɲore] *sm* (*REL: titolo*) Your (*o* His) Grace.

mon'sone *sm* monsoon.

monta'carichi [monta'kariki] *sm inv* hoist, goods lift.

mon'taggio [mon'taddʒo] *sm* (*TECN*) assembly; (*CINEMA*) editing.

mon'tagna [mon'taɲɲa] *sf* mountain; (*zona montuosa*): la ~ the mountains *pl*; andare in ~ to go to the mountains; ~e russe roller coaster *sg*, big dipper *sg* (*Brit*); **monta'gnoso, a** *ag* mountainous.

monta'naro, a *ag* mountain *cpd* // *sm/f* mountain dweller.

mon'tano, a *ag* mountain *cpd*; alpine.

mon'tare vt to go (o come) up; (cavallo) to ride; (apparecchiatura) to set up, assemble; (CUC) to whip; (ZOOL) to cover; (incastonare) to mount, set; (CINEMA) to edit; (FOT) to mount // vi to go (o come) up; (a cavallo): ~ bene/male to ride well/badly; (aumentare di livello, volume) to rise; ~rsi vr to become big-headed; ~ qc to exaggerate sth; ~ qn o la testa a qn to turn sb's head; ~ in bicicletta/macchina/treno to get on a bicycle/into a car/on a train; ~ a cavallo to get on o mount a horse.

monta'tura sf assembling q; (di occhiali) frames pl; (di gioiello) mounting, setting; (fig): ~ pubblicitaria publicity stunt.

'**monte** sm mountain; a ~ upstream; mandare a ~ qc to upset sth, cause sth to fail; il M~ Bianco Mont Blanc; ~ di pietà pawnshop.

mon'tone sm (ZOOL) ram; carne di ~ mutton.

montu'oso, a ag mountainous.

monu'mento sm monument.

'**mora** sf (del rovo) blackberry; (del gelso) mulberry; (DIR) delay; (: somma) arrears pl.

mo'rale ag moral // sf (scienza) ethics sg, moral philosophy; (complesso di norme) moral standards pl, morality; (condotta) morals pl; (insegnamento morale) moral // sm morale; essere giù di ~ to be feeling down; **moralità** sf morality; (condotta) morals pl.

'**morbido, a** ag soft; (pelle) soft, smooth

mor'billo sm (MED) measles sg.

'**morbo** sm disease.

mor'boso, a ag (fig) morbid.

mor'dace [mor'datʃe] ag biting, cutting.

mor'dente sm (fig: di satira, critica) bite; (: di persona) drive.

'**mordere** vt to bite; (addentare) to bite into; (corrodere) to eat into.

mori'bondo, a ag dying, moribund.

morige'rato, a [moridʒe'rato] ag of good morals.

mo'rire vi to die; (abitudine, civiltà) to die out; ~ di fame to die of hunger; (fig) to be starving; ~ di noia/paura to be bored/scared to death; fa un caldo da ~ it's terribly hot.

mormo'rare vi to murmur; (brontolare) to grumble.

'**moro, a** ag dark(-haired); dark(-complexioned); i M~i smpl (STORIA) the Moors.

mo'roso, a ag in arrears // sm/f (fam: innamorato) sweetheart.

'**morsa** sf (TECN) vice; (fig: stretta) grip.

morsi'care vt to nibble (at), gnaw (at); (sog: insetto) to bite.

'**morso, a** pp di **mordere** // sm bite; (di insetto) sting; (parte della briglia) bit; ~i della fame pangs of hunger.

mor'taio sm mortar.

mor'tale ag, sm mortal; **mortalità** sf mortality, death rate.

'**morte** sf death.

mortifi'care vt to mortify.

'**morto, a** pp di **morire** // ag dead // sm/f dead man/woman; i ~i the dead; fare il ~ (nell'acqua) to float on one's back; il Mar M~ the Dead Sea.

mor'torio sm (anche fig) funeral.

mo'saico, ci sm mosaic.

'**mosca, sche** sf fly; ~ cieca blind-man's-buff.

'**Mosca** sf Moscow.

mos'cato sm muscatel (wine).

mosce'rino [moʃʃe'rino] sm midge, gnat.

mos'chea [mos'kɛa] sf mosque.

mos'chetto [mos'ketto] sm musket.

'**moscio, a, sci, sce** ['mɔʃʃo] ag (fig) lifeless.

mos'cone sm (ZOOL) bluebottle; (barca) pedalo; (: a remi) kind of pedalo with oars.

'**mossa** sf movement; (nel gioco) move.

'**mosso, a** pp di **muovere** // ag (mare) rough; (capelli) wavy; (FOT) blurred; (ritmo, prosa) animated.

mos'tarda sf mustard.

'**mostra** sf exhibition, show; (ostentazione) show; in ~ on show; far ~ di (fingere) to pretend; far ~ di sé to show off.

mos'trare vt to show // vi: ~ di fare to pretend to do; ~rsi vr to appear.

'**mostro** sm monster; **mostru'oso, a** ag monstrous.

mo'tel sm inv motel.

moti'vare vt (causare) to cause; (giustificare) to justify, account for; **motivazi'one** sf justification; motive; (PSIC) motivation.

mo'tivo sm (causa) reason, cause; (movente) motive; (letterario) (central) theme; (disegno) motif, design, pattern; (MUS) motif; per quale ~? why?, for what reason?

'**moto** sm (anche FISICA) motion; (movimento, gesto) movement; (esercizio fisico) exercise; (sommossa) rising, revolt; (commozione) feeling, impulse // sf inv (motocicletta) motorbike; mettere in ~ to set in motion; (AUT) to start up.

motoci'cletta [mototʃi'kletta] sf motorcycle; **motoci'clismo** sm motorcycling, motorcycle racing; **motoci'clista, i, e** sm/f motorcyclist.

mo'tore, 'trice ag motor; (TECN) driving // sm engine, motor; a ~ motor cpd, power-driven; ~ a combustione interna/a reazione internal combustion/jet engine;

moto'rino sm moped; **motorino di avviamento** (AUT) starter; **motoriz'zato, a** ag (truppe) motorized; (persona) having a car o transport.

motos'cafo sm motorboat.

mot'teggio |mot'tedd3o| sm banter.

'motto sm (battuta scherzosa) witty remark; (frase emblematica) motto, maxim.

mo'vente sm motive.

movimen'tare vt to liven up.

movi'mento sm movement; (fig) activity, hustle and bustle; (MUS) tempo, movement.

mozi'one |mot'tsjone| sf (POL) motion.

moz'zare |mot'tsare| vt to cut off; (coda) to dock; ~ il fiato o il respiro a qn (fig) to take sb's breath away.

mozza'rella |mottsa'rɛlla| sf mozzarella (a moist Neapolitan curd cheese).

mozzi'cone |mottsi'kone| sm stub, butt, end; (anche: ~ di sigaretta) cigarette end.

'mozzo sm |'mɔddzo| (MECCANICA) hub; |'mottso| (NAUT) ship's boy; ~ di stalla stable boy.

'mucca, che sf cow.

'mucchio |'mukkjo| sm pile, heap; (fig): un ~ di lots of, heaps of.

'muco, chi sm mucus.

'muffa sf mould, mildew.

mug'gire |mud'd3ire| vi (vacca) to low, moo; (toro) to bellow; (fig) to roar; **mug'gito** sm low, moo; bellow; roar.

mu'ghetto |mu'getto| sm lily of the valley.

mu'gnaio, a |muɲ'ɲajo| sm/f miller.

mugo'lare vi (cane) to whimper, whine; (fig: persona) to moan.

muli'nare vi to whirl, spin (round and round).

muli'nello sm (moto vorticoso) eddy, whirl; (di canna da pesca) reel; (NAUT) windlass.

mu'lino sm mill; ~ a vento windmill.

'mulo sm mule.

'multa sf fine; **mul'tare** vt to fine.

'multiplo, a ag, sm multiple.

'mummia sf mummy.

'mungere |'mund3ere| vt (anche fig) to milk.

munici'pale |munitʃi'pale| ag municipal; town cpd.

muni'cipio |muni'tʃipjo| sm town council, corporation; (edificio) town hall.

mu'nire vt: ~ qc/qn di to equip sth/sb with.

munizi'oni |munit'tsjoni| sfpl (MIL) ammunition sg.

'munto, a pp di **mungere**.

mu'overe vt to move; (ruota, macchina) to drive; (sollevare: questione, obiezione) to raise, bring up; (: accusa) to make, bring forward; **~rsi** vr to move; **muoviti!** hurry up!, get a move on!

'mura sfpl vedi **muro**.

mu'raglia |mu'raʎʎa| sf (high) wall.

mu'rale ag wall cpd; mural.

mu'rare vt (persona, porta) to wall up.

mura'tore sm mason; bricklayer.

'muro sm wall; ~a sfpl (cinta cittadina) walls; a ~ wall cpd; (armadio etc) built-in; ~ del suono sound barrier; mettere al ~ (fucilare) to shoot o execute (by firing squad).

'muschio |'muskjo| sm (ZOOL) musk; (BOT) moss.

musco'lare ag muscular, muscle cpd.

'muscolo sm (ANAT) muscle.

mu'seo sm museum.

museru'ola sf muzzle.

'musica sf music; ~ da ballo/camera dance/chamber music; **musi'cale** ag musical; **musi'cista, i, e** sm/f musician.

'muso sm muzzle; (di auto, aereo) nose; tenere il ~ to sulk; **mu'sone, a** sm/f sulky person.

'mussola sf muslin.

'muta sf (di animali) moulting; (di serpenti) sloughing; (per immersioni subacquee) diving suit; (gruppo di cani) pack.

muta'mento sm change.

mu'tande sfpl (da uomo) (under)pants; **mutan'dine** sfpl (da donna, bambino) pants (Brit), briefs; **mutandine di plastica** plastic pants.

mu'tare vt, vi to change, alter; **mutazi'one** sf change, alteration; (BIOL) mutation; **mu'tevole** ag changeable.

muti'lare vt to mutilate, maim; (fig) to mutilate, deface; **muti'lato, a** sm/f disabled person (through loss of limbs).

mu'tismo sm (MED) mutism; (atteggiamento) (stubborn) silence.

'muto, a ag (MED) dumb; (emozione, dolore, CINEMA) silent; (LING) silent, mute; (carta geografica) blank; ~ per lo stupore etc speechless with amazement etc.

'mutua sf (anche: cassa ~) health insurance scheme.

mutu'are vt (fig) to borrow.

mutu'ato, a sm/f member of a health insurance scheme.

'mutuo, a ag (reciproco) mutual // sm (ECON) (long-term) loan.

N

N. abbr (= nord) N.

'nacchere |'nakkere| sfpl castanets.

'nafta sf naphtha; (per motori diesel) diesel oil.

nafta'lina sf (CHIM) naphthalene; (tarmicida) mothballs pl.

'naia sf (ZOOL) cobra; (MIL) slang term

for national service.

'nailon *sm* nylon.

'nanna *sf (linguaggio infantile)*: andare a ~ to go to beddy-byes.

'nano, a *ag, sm/f* dwarf.

napole'tano, a *ag, sm/f* Neapolitan.

'Napoli *sf* Naples.

'nappa *sf* tassel.

nar'ciso [nar'tʃizo] *sm* narcissus.

nar'cosi *sf* narcosis.

nar'cotico, ci *sm* narcotic.

na'rice [na'ritʃe] *sf* nostril.

nar'rare *vt* to tell the story of, recount; **narra'tivo, a** *ag* narrative // *sf (branca letteraria)* fiction; **narra'tore, 'trice** *sm/f* narrator; **narrazi'one** *sf* narration; *(racconto)* story, tale.

na'sale *ag* nasal.

'nascere ['naʃʃere] *vi (bambino)* to be born; *(pianta)* to come *o* spring up; *(fiume)* to rise, have its source; *(sole)* to rise; *(dente)* to come through; *(fig: derivare, conseguire)*: ~ **da** to arise from, be born out of; **è nata nel 1952** she was born in 1952; **'nascita** *sf* birth.

nas'condere *vt* to hide, conceal; **~rsi** *vr* to hide; **nascon'diglio** *sm* hiding place; **nascon'dino** *sm (gioco)* hide-and-seek; **nas'costo, a** *pp di* **nascondere** // *ag* hidden; **di nascosto** secretly.

na'sello *sm (ZOOL)* hake.

'naso *sm* nose.

'nastro *sm* ribbon; *(magnetico, isolante, SPORT)* tape; ~ **adesivo** adhesive tape; ~ **trasportatore** conveyor belt.

nas'turzio [nas'turtsjo] *sm* nasturtium.

na'tale *ag* of one's birth // *sm (REL)*: **N~** Christmas; *(giorno della nascita)* birthday; **natalità** *sf* birth rate; **nata'lizio, a** *ag (del Natale)* Christmas *cpd*.

na'tante *sm* craft *inv*, boat.

'natica, che *sf (ANAT)* buttock.

na'tio, a, 'tii, 'tie *ag* native.

Nativitá *sf (REL)* Nativity.

na'tivo, a *ag, sm/f* native.

'nato, a *pp di* **nascere** // *ag*: **un attore ~** a born actor; **~a Pieri** née Pieri.

na'tura *sf* nature; **pagare in ~** to pay in kind; ~ **morta** still life.

natu'rale *ag* natural; **natura'lezza** *sf* naturalness; **natura'lista, i, e** *sm/f* naturalist.

naturaliz'zare [naturalid'dzare] *vt* to naturalize.

natural'mente *av* naturally; *(certamente, sì)* of course.

naufra'gare *vi (nave)* to be wrecked; *(persona)* to be shipwrecked; *(fig)* to fall through; **nau'fragio** *sm* shipwreck; *(fig)* ruin, failure; **'naufrago, ghi** *sm* castaway, shipwreck victim.

'nausea *sf* nausea; **nausea'bondo, a** *ag* nauseating, sickening; **nause'are** *vt* to nauseate, make (feel) sick.

'nautico, a, ci, che *ag* nautical // *sf* (art of) navigation.

na'vale *ag* naval.

na'vata *sf (anche: ~ centrale)* nave; *(anche: ~ laterale)* aisle.

'nave *sf* ship, vessel; ~ **cisterna** tanker; ~ **da guerra** warship; ~ **passeggeri** passenger ship; ~ **spaziale** spaceship.

na'vetta *sf* shuttle; *(servizio di collegamento)* shuttle (service).

navi'cella [navi'tʃella] *sf (di aerostato)* gondola.

navi'gabile *ag* navigable.

navi'gare *vi* to sail; **navigazi'one** *sf* navigation.

na'viglio [na'viʎʎo] *sm* fleet, ships *pl*; *(canale artificiale)* canal; ~ **da pesca** fishing fleet.

nazio'nale [nattsjo'nale] *ag* national // *sf (SPORT)* national team; **naziona'lismo** *sm* nationalism; **nazionalità** *sf inv* nationality.

nazi'one [nat'tsjone] *sf* nation.

ne ◆ *pronome* **1** *(di lui, lei, loro)* of him/her/them; about him/her/them; ~ **riconosco la voce** I recognize his (o her) voice **2** *(di questa, quella cosa)* of it; about it; ~ **voglio ancora** I want some more (of it *o* them); **non parliamone più!** let's not talk about it any more!
3 *(con valore partitivo)*: **hai dei libri? — sì, ~ ho** have you any books? — yes, I have (some); **hai del pane? — no, non ~ ho** have you any bread? — no, I haven't any; **quanti anni hai? — ~ ho 17** how old are you? — I'm 17
◆ *av (moto da luogo: da lì)* from there; ~ **vengo ora** I've just come from there.

né *cong*: ~ ... ~ neither ... nor; ~ **l'uno ~ l'altro lo vuole** neither of them wants it; **non parla ~ l'italiano ~ il tedesco** he speaks neither Italian nor German, he doesn't speak either Italian or German; **non piove ~ nevica** it isn't raining or snowing.

ne'anche [ne'anke] *av, cong* not even; **non ... ~** not even; ~ **se volesse potrebbe venire** he couldn't come even if he wanted to; **non l'ho visto — ~ io** I didn't see him — neither did I *o* I didn't either; ~ **per idea** *o* **sogno!** not on your life!

'nebbia *sf* fog; *(foschia)* mist; **nebbi'oso, a** *ag* foggy; misty.

nebu'loso, a *ag (atmosfera)* hazy; *(fig)* hazy, vague.

necessaria'mente [netʃessarja'mente] *av* necessarily.

neces'sario, a [netʃes'sarjo] *ag* necessary.

necessità [netʃessi'ta] *sf inv* necessity; *(povertà)* need, poverty; **necessi'tare** *vt* to require // *vi (aver bisogno)*: **necessitare di** to need.

necro'logio [nekro'lɔdʒo] *sm* obituary notice; *(registro)* register of deaths.

ne'fando, a *ag* infamous, wicked.

ne'fasto, a *ag* inauspicious, ill-omened.
ne'gare *vt* to deny; (*rifiutare*) to deny, refuse; ~ **di aver fatto/che** to deny having done/that; **nega'tivo, a** *ag, sf, sm* negative; **negazi'one** *sf* negation.
ne'gletto, a [ne'gletto] *ag* (*trascurato*) neglected.
'negli ['neʎʎi] *prep + det vedi* **in**.
negli'gente [negli'dʒente] *ag* negligent, careless; **negli'genza** *sf* negligence, carelessness.
negozi'ante [negot'tsjante] *sm/f* trader, dealer; (*bottegaio*) shopkeeper (*Brit*), storekeeper (*US*).
negozi'are [negot'tsjare] *vt* to negotiate // *vi:* ~ **in** to trade *o* deal in; **negozi'ato** *sm* negotiation.
ne'gozio [ne'gɔttsjo] *sm* (*locale*) shop (*Brit*), store (*US*); (*affare*) (piece of) business *q*.
'negro, a *ag, sm/f* Negro.
'nei, nel, nell', 'nella, 'nelle, 'nello *prep + det vedi* **in**.
'nembo *sm* (*METEOR*) nimbus.
ne'mico, a, ci, che *ag* hostile; (*MIL*) enemy *cpd* // *sm/f* enemy; **essere** ~ **di** to be strongly averse *o* opposed to.
nem'meno *av, cong* = **neanche**.
'nenia *sf* dirge; (*motivo monotono*) monotonous tune.
'neo *sm* mole; (*fig*) (slight) flaw.
'neo... *prefisso* neo... .
'neon *sm* (*CHIM*) neon.
neo'nato, a *ag* newborn // *sm/f* newborn baby.
neozelan'dese [neoddzelan'dese] *ag* New Zealand *cpd* // *sm/f* New Zealander.
nep'pure *av, cong* = **neanche**.
'nerbo *sm* lash; (*fig*) strength, backbone; **nerbo'ruto, a** *ag* muscular; robust.
ne'retto *sm* (*TIP*) bold type.
'nero, a *ag* black; (*scuro*) dark // *sm* black; **il Mar N~** the Black Sea.
nerva'tura *sf* (*ANAT*) nervous system; (*BOT*) veining; (*ARCHIT, TECN*) rib.
'nervo *sm* (*ANAT*) nerve; (*BOT*) vein; **avere i** ~**i** to be on edge; **dare sui** ~**i a qn** to get on sb's nerves; **ner'voso, a** *ag* nervous; (*irritabile*) irritable // *sm* (*fam*): **far venire il nervoso a qn** to get on sb's nerves.
'nespola *sf* (*BOT*) medlar; (*fig*) blow, punch; **'nespolo** *sm* medlar tree.
'nesso *sm* connection, link.
nes'suno, a *det* (*dav sm* **nessun** + *C, V*, **nessuno** + *s impura, gn, pn, ps, x, z*; *dav sf* **nessuna** + *C*, **nessun'** + *V*) (*non uno*) no, *espressione negativa* + any; (*qualche*) any // *pronome* (*non uno*) no one, nobody, *espressione negativa* + any(one); (*: cosa*) none, *espressione negativa* + any; (*qualcuno*) anyone, anybody; (*qualcosa*) anything; **non c'è nessun libro** there isn't any book, there

is no book; **hai** ~**a obiezione?** do you have any objections?; ~ **è venuto, non è venuto** ~ nobody came; **nessun altro** no one else, nobody else; **nessun'altra cosa** nothing else; **in nessun luogo** nowhere.
net'tare *vt* to clean // *sm* ['nettare] nectar.
net'tezza [net'tettsa] *sf* cleanness, cleanliness; ~ **urbana** cleansing department.
'netto, a *ag* (*pulito*) clean; (*chiaro*) clear, clear-cut; (*deciso*) definite; (*ECON*) net.
nettur'bino *sm* dustman (*Brit*), garbage collector (*US*).
neu'rosi *sf* = **nevrosi**.
neu'trale *ag* neutral; **neutralità** *sf* neutrality; **neutraliz'zare** *vt* to neutralize.
'neutro, a *ag* neutral; (*LING*) neuter // *sm* (*LING*) neuter.
ne'vaio *sm* snowfield.
'neve *sf* snow; **nevi'care** *vb impers* to snow; **nevi'cata** *sf* snowfall.
ne'vischio [ne'viskjo] *sm* sleet.
ne'voso, a *ag* snowy; snow-covered.
nevral'gia [nevral'dʒia] *sf* neuralgia.
nevras'tenico, a, ci, che *ag* (*MED*) neurasthenic; (*fig*) hot-tempered.
ne'vrosi *sf* neurosis.
'nibbio *sm* (*ZOOL*) kite.
'nicchia ['nikkja] *sf* niche; (*naturale*) cavity, hollow.
nicchi'are [nik'kjare] *vi* to shilly-shally, hesitate.
'nichel ['nikel] *sm* nickel.
nico'tina *sf* nicotine.
'nido *sm* nest; **a** ~ **d'ape** (*tessuto etc*) honeycomb *cpd*.
ni'ente ♦ *pronome* **1** (*nessuna cosa*) nothing; ~ **può fermarlo** nothing can stop him; ~ **di** ~ absolutely nothing; **nient'altro** nothing else; **nient'altro che** nothing but, just, only; ~ **affatto** not at all, not in the least; **come se** ~ **fosse** as if nothing had happened; **cose da** ~ trivial matters; **per** ~ (*gratis, invano*) for nothing
2 (*qualcosa*): **hai bisogno di** ~? do you need anything?
3: **non ... ** ~ nothing, *espressione negativa* + anything; **non ho visto** ~ I saw nothing, I didn't see anything; **non ho** ~ **da dire** I have nothing *o* haven't anything to say
♦ *sm* nothing; **un bel** ~ absolutely nothing; **basta un** ~ **per farla piangere** the slightest thing is enough to make her cry
♦ *av* (*in nessuna misura*): **non ...** ~ not ... at all; **non è (per)** ~ **buono** it isn't good at all.
nientedi'meno, niente'meno *av* actually, even // *escl* really!, I say!
'Nilo *sm*: **il** ~ **the Nile**.
'ninfa *sf* nymph.
nin'fea *sf* water lily.

ninna-'nanna sf lullaby.

'ninnolo sm (balocco) plaything; (gingillo) knick-knack.

ni'pote smf (di zii) nephew/niece; (di nonni) grandson/daughter, grandchild.

'nitido, a ag clear; (specchio) bright.

ni'trato sm nitrate.

'nitrico, a, ci, che ag nitric.

ni'trire vi to neigh.

ni'trito sm (di cavallo) neighing q; neigh; (CHIM) nitrite.

nitroglice'rina [nitroglitʃe'rina] sf nitroglycerine.

'niveo, a ag snow-white.

no av (risposta) no; vieni o ~? are you coming or not?; perché ~? why not?; lo conosciamo? — tu ~ ma io sì do we know him? — you don't but I do; verrai, ~? you'll come, won't you?

'nobile ag noble // smf noble, nobleman/woman; **nobili'are** ag noble; **nobiltà** sf nobility; (di azione etc) nobleness.

'nocca, che sf (ANAT) knuckle.

nocci'ola [nŏt'tʃɔla] ag inv (colore) hazel, light brown // sf hazelnut.

'nocciolo ['nɔttʃolo] sm (di frutto) stone; (fig) heart, core; [nŏt'tʃɔlo] (albero) hazel.

'noce ['notʃe] sm (albero) walnut tree // sf (frutto) walnut; ~ moscata nutmeg.

no'civo, a [no'tʃivo] ag harmful, noxious.

'nodo sm (di cravatta, legname, NAUT) knot; (AUT, FERR) junction; (MED, ASTR, BOT) node; (fig: legame) bond, tie; (: punto centrale) heart, crux; avere un ~ alla gola to have a lump in one's throat; **no'doso, a** ag (tronco) gnarled.

'noi pronome (soggetto) we; (oggetto: per dare rilievo, con preposizione) us; ~ stessi(e) we ourselves; (oggetto) ourselves.

'noia sf boredom; (disturbo, impaccio) bother q, trouble q; avere qn/qc a ~ not to like sb/sth; mi è venuto a ~ I'm tired of it; dare ~ a to annoy; avere delle ~e con qn to have trouble with sb.

noi'altri pronome we.

noi'oso, a ag boring; (fastidioso) annoying, troublesome.

noleggi'are [noled'dʒare] vt (prendere a noleggio) to hire (Brit), rent; (dare a noleggio) to hire out (Brit), rent (out); (aereo, nave) to charter; **no'leggio** sm hire (Brit), rental; charter.

'nolo sm hire (Brit), rental; charter; (per trasporto merci) freight; **prendere/dare a** ~ qc to hire/hire out sth.

'nomade ag nomadic // smf nomad.

'nome sm name; (LING) noun; **in/a** ~ **di** in the name of; **di** o **per** ~ (chiamato) called, named; **conoscere qn di** ~ to know sb by name; ~ **d'arte** stage name; ~ **di battesimo** Christian name; ~ **depositato** trade name; ~ **di famiglia** surname.

no'mea sf notoriety.

no'mignolo [no'miɲɲolo] sm nickname.

'nomina sf appointment.

nomi'nale ag nominal; (LING) noun cpd.

nomi'nare vt to name; (eleggere) to appoint; (citare) to mention.

nomina'tivo, a ag (LING) nominative; (ECON) registered // sm (LING: anche: caso ~) nominative (case); (AMM) name.

non av not // prefisso non ; vedi **affatto, appena** etc

nonché [non'ke] cong (tanto più, tanto meno) let alone; (e inoltre) as well as.

noncu'rante ag: ~ (di) careless (of), indifferent (to); **noncu'ranza** sf carelessness, indifference.

nondi'meno cong (tuttavia) however; (nonostante) nevertheless.

'nonno, a smf grandfather/mother; (in senso più familiare) grandma/grandpa; ~i smpl grandparents.

non'nulla sm inv: **un** ~ nothing, a trifle.

'nono, a ag, sm ninth.

nonos'tante prep in spite of, notwithstanding // cong although, even though.

nontiscordardimé sm inv (BOT) forget-me-not.

nord sm North // ag inv north; northern; **il Mare del N**~ the North Sea; **nor'dest** sm north-east; **'nordico, a, ci, che** ag nordic, northern European; **nor'dovest** sm north-west.

'norma sf (principio) norm; (regola) regulation, rule; (consuetudine) custom, rule; **a** ~ **di legge** according to law, as laid down by law.

nor'male ag normal; standard cpd; **normalità** sf normality; **normaliz'zare** vt to normalize, bring back to normal.

normal'mente av normally.

norve'gese [norve'dʒese] ag, smf, sm Norwegian.

Nor'vegia [nor'vedʒa] sf: **la** ~ Norway.

nostal'gia [nostal'dʒia] sf (di casa, paese) homesickness; (del passato) nostalgia; **nos'talgico, a, ci, che** ag homesick; nostalgic.

nos'trano, a ag local; national; home-produced.

'nostro, a det: **il(la)** ~(a) etc our // pronome: **il(la)** ~(a) etc ours // sm: **il** ~ our money; our belongings; **i** ~i our family; our own people; **è dei** ~i he's one of us.

'nota sf (segno) mark; (comunicazione scritta, MUS) note; (fattura) bill; (elenco) list; **degno di** ~ noteworthy, worthy of note.

no'tabile ag notable; (persona) important // sm prominent citizen.

no'taio sm notary.

no'tare vt (segnare: errori) to mark;

(*registrare*) to note (down), write down; (*rilevare, osservare*) to note, notice; **farsi ~** to get o.s. noticed.

notazi'one [notat'tsjonc] *sf* (*MUS*) notation.

no'tevole *ag* (*talento*) notable, remarkable; (*peso*) considerable.

no'tifica, che *sf* notification.

notifi'care *vt* (*DIR*): **~ qc a qn** to notify sb of sth, give sb notice of sth.

no'tizia [no'tittsja] *sf* (piece of) news *sg*; (*informazione*) piece of information; **~e** *sfpl* news *sg*; information *sg*; **notizi'ario** *sm* (*RADIO, TV, STAMPA*) news *sg*.

'noto, a *ag* (well-)known.

notorietà *sf* fame; notoriety.

no'torio, a *ag* well-known; (*peg*) notorious.

not'tambulo, a *sm/f* night-bird (*fig*).

not'tata *sf* night.

'notte *sf* night; **di ~** at night; (*durante la notte*) in the night, during the night; **peggio che andar di ~** worse than ever; **~ bianca** sleepless night; **notte'tempo** *av* at night; during the night.

not'turno, a *ag* nocturnal; (*servizio, guardiano*) night *cpd*.

no'vanta *num* ninety; **novan'tesimo, a** *num* ninetieth; **novan'tina** *sf*: **una novantina (di)** about ninety.

'nove *num* nine.

nove'cento [nove'tʃɛnto] *num* nine hundred // *sm*: **il N~** the twentieth century.

no'vella *sf* (*LETTERATURA*) short story.

novel'lino, a *ag* (*pivello*) green, inexperienced.

no'vello, a *ag* (*piante, patate*) new; (*insalata, verdura*) early; (*sposo*) newly-married.

no'vembre *sm* November.

novi'lunio *sm* (*ASTR*) new moon.

novità *sf inv* novelty; (*innovazione*) innovation; (*cosa originale, insolita*) something new; (*notizia*) (piece of) news *sg*; **le ~ della moda** the latest fashions.

novizi'ato [novit'tsjato] *sm* (*REL*) novitiate; (*tirocinio*) apprenticeship.

no'vizio, a [no'vittsjo] *sm/f* (*REL*) novice; (*tirocinante*) beginner, apprentice.

nozi'one [not'tsjone] *sf* notion, idea; **~i** *sfpl* basic knowledge *sg*, rudiments.

'nozze [ˈnɔttse] *sfpl* wedding *sg*, marriage *sg*; **~ d'argento/d'oro** silver/golden wedding *sg*.

ns. *abbr* (*COMM*) = **nostro**.

'nube *sf* cloud; **nubi'fragio** *sm* cloudburst.

'nubile *ag* (*donna*) unmarried, single.

'nuca *sf* nape of the neck.

nucle'are *ag* nuclear.

'nucleo *sm* nucleus; (*gruppo*) team, unit, group; (*MIL, POLIZIA*) squad; **il ~ familiare** the family unit.

nu'dista, i, e *sm/f* nudist.

'nudo, a *ag* (*persona*) bare, naked, nude; (*membra*) bare, naked; (*montagna*) bare // *sm* (*ARTE*) nude.

'nugolo *sm*: **un ~ di** a whole host of.

'nulla *pronome, av* = **niente** // *sm*: **il ~** nothing.

nulla'osta *sm inv* authorization.

nullità *sf inv* nullity; (*persona*) nonentity.

'nullo, a *ag* useless, worthless; (*DIR*) null (and void); (*SPORT*): **incontro ~** draw.

nume'rale *ag, sm* numeral.

nume'rare *vt* to number; **numerazi'one** *sf* numbering; (*araba, decimale*) notation.

nu'merico, a, ci, che *ag* numerical.

'numero *sm* number; (*romano, arabo*) numeral; (*di spettacolo*) act, turn; **~ civico** house number; **nume'roso, a** *ag* numerous, many; (*con sostantivo sg: adunanza etc*) large.

'nunzio [ˈnuntsjo] *sm* (*REL*) nuncio.

nu'ocere [ˈnwɔtʃere] *vi*: **~ a** to harm, damage; **nuoci'uto, a** *pp di* **nuocere**.

nu'ora *sf* daughter-in-law.

nuo'tare *vi* to swim; (*galleggiare: oggetti*) to float; **nuota'tore, 'trice** *sm/f* swimmer; **'nuoto** *sm* swimming.

nu'ova *sf vedi* **nuovo**.

nuova'mente *av* again.

Nu'ova Ze'landa [-dze'landa] *sf*: **la ~** New Zealand.

nu'ovo, a *ag* new // *sf* (*notizia*) (piece of) news *sg*; **di ~** again; **~ fiammante** *o* **di zecca** brand-new.

nutri'ente *ag* nutritious, nourishing.

nutri'mento *sm* food, nourishment.

nu'trire *vt* to feed; (*fig: sentimenti*) to harbour, nurse; **nutri'tivo, a** *ag* nutritional; (*alimento*) nutritious; **nutrizi'one** *sf* nutrition.

'nuvola *sf* cloud; **'nuvolo, a** *ag*, **nuvo'loso, a** *ag* cloudy.

nuzi'ale [nut'tsjale] *ag* nuptial; wedding *cpd*.

O

o *cong* (*dav V spesso* **od**) or; **~ ... ~** either ... or; **~ l'uno ~ l'altro** either (of them).

O. *abbr* (= *ovest*) W.

'oasi *sf inv* oasis.

obbedi'ente *etc vedi* **ubbidiente** *etc*.

obbli'gare *vt* (*costringere*): **~ qn a fare** to force *o* oblige sb to do; (*DIR*) to bind; **~rsi** *vr*: **~rsi a fare** to undertake to do; **obbli'gato, a** *ag* (*costretto, grato*) obliged; (*percorso, tappa*) set, fixed; **ob-bliga'torio, a** *ag* compulsory, obligatory; **obbligazi'one** *sf* obligation; (*COMM*) bond, debenture; **'obbligo, ghi**

sm obligation; (*dovere*) duty; **avere l'obbligo di fare, essere nell'obbligo di fare** to be obliged to do; **essere d'obbligo** (*discorso, applauso*) to be called for.

ob'brobrio *sm* disgrace; (*fig*) mess, eyesore.

o'beso, a *ag* obese.

obiet'tare *vt*: ~ **che** to object that; ~ **su qc** to object to sth, raise objections concerning sth.

obiet'tivo, a *ag* objective // *sm* (*OTTICA, FOT*) lens *sg*, objective; (*MIL, fig*) objective.

obiet'tore *sm* objector; ~ **di coscienza** conscientious objector.

obiezi'one [objet'tsjone] *sf* objection.

obi'torio *sm* morgue, mortuary.

o'bliquo, a *ag* oblique; (*inclinato*) slanting; (*fig*) devious, underhand; **sguardo** ~ sidelong glance.

oblò *sm inv* porthole.

o'blungo, a, ghi, ghe *ag* oblong.

'oboe *sm* (*MUS*) oboe.

obsole'scenza [obsole∫'∫entsa] *sf* (*ECON*) obsolescence.

'oca, pl 'oche *sf* goose.

occasi'one *sf* (*caso favorevole*) opportunity; (*causa, motivo, circostanza*) occasion; (*COMM*) bargain; **d'~** (*a buon prezzo*) bargain *cpd*; (*usato*) secondhand.

occhi'aia [ok'kjaja] *sf* eye socket; ~**e** *sfpl* shadows (under the eyes).

occhi'ali [ok'kjali] *smpl* glasses, spectacles; ~ **da sole** sunglasses.

occhi'ata [ok'kjata] *sf* look, glance; **dare un'~ a** to have a look at.

occhieggi'are [okkjed'dʒare] *vi* (*apparire qua e là*) to peep (out).

occhi'ello [ok'kjello] *sm* buttonhole; (*asola*) eyelet.

'occhio ['okkjo] *sm* eye; ~**!** careful!, watch out!; **a** ~ **nudo** with the naked eye; **a quattr'~i** privately, tête-à-tête; **dare all'~ o nell'~ a qn** to catch sb's eye; **fare l'~ a qc** to get used to sth; **tenere d'~ qn** to keep an eye on sb; **vedere di buon/mal ~ qc** to look favourably/unfavourably on sth.

occhio'lino [okkjo'lino] *sm*: **fare l'~ a qn** to wink at sb.

occiden'tale [ott∫iden'tale] *ag* western // *sm/f* Westerner.

occi'dente [ott∫i'dente] *sm* west; (*POL*): **l'O~** the West; **a ~** in the west.

oc'cipite [ot't∫ipite] *sm* back of the head, occiput.

oc'cludere *vt* to block; **occlusi'one** *sf* blockage, obstruction; **oc'cluso, a** *pp di* **occludere**.

occor'rente *ag* necessary // *sm* all that is necessary.

occor'renza [okkor'rentsa] *sf* necessity, need; **all'~** in case of need.

oc'correre *vi* to be needed, be required //

vb impers: **occorre farlo** it must be done; **occorre che tu parta** you must leave, you'll have to leave; **mi occorrono i soldi** I need the money; **oc'corso, a** *pp di* **occorrere**.

occul'tare *vt* to hide, conceal.

oc'culto, a *ag* hidden, concealed; (*scienze, forze*) occult.

occu'pare *vt* to occupy; (*manodopera*) to employ; (*ingombrare*) to occupy, take up; ~**rsi** *vr* to occupy o.s., keep o.s. busy; (*impiegarsi*) to get a job; ~**rsi di** (*interessarsi*) to take an interest in; (*prendersi cura di*) to look after, take care of; **occu'pato, a** *ag* (*MIL, POL*) occupied; (*persona: affaccendato*) busy; (*posto, sedia*) taken; (*toilette, TEL*) engaged; **occupazi'one** *sf* occupation; (*impiego, lavoro*) job; (*ECON*) employment.

o'ceano [o't∫eano] *sm* ocean.

'ocra *sf* ochre.

ocu'lare *ag* ocular, eye *cpd*; **testimone ~** eye witness.

ocu'lato, a *ag* (*attento*) cautious, prudent; (*accorto*) shrewd.

ocu'lista, i, e *sm/f* eye specialist, oculist.

'ode *sf* ode.

odi'are *vt* to hate, detest.

odi'erno, a *ag* today's, of today; (*attuale*) present.

'odio *sm* hatred; **avere in ~ qc/qn** to hate o detest sth/sb; **odi'oso, a** *ag* hateful, odious.

odo'rare *vt* (*annusare*) to smell; (*profumare*) to perfume, scent // *vi*: ~ (**di**) to smell (of); **odo'rato** *sm* sense of smell.

o'dore *sm* smell; **gli ~i** *smpl* (*CUC*) (aromatic) herbs; **odo'roso, a** *ag* sweet-smelling.

of'fendere *vt* to offend; (*violare*) to break, violate; (*insultare*) to insult; (*ferire*) to hurt; ~**rsi** *vr* (*con senso reciproco*) to insult one another; (*risentirsi*): ~**rsi** (**di**) to take offence (at), be offended (by); **offen'sivo, a** *ag*, *sf* offensive.

offe'rente *sm* (*in aste*): **al maggior ~** to the highest bidder.

of'ferto, a *pp di* **offrire** // *sf* offer; (*donazione, anche REL*) offering; (*in gara d'appalto*) tender; (*in aste*) bid; (*ECON*) supply; "~**e d'impiego**" "situations vacant"; **fare un'~a** to make an offer; to tender; to bid.

of'feso, a *pp di* **offendere** // *ag* offended; (*fisicamente*) hurt, injured // *sm/f* offended party // *sf* insult, affront; (*MIL*) attack; (*DIR*) offence; **essere ~ con qn** to be annoyed with sb; **parte ~a** (*DIR*) plaintiff.

offi'cina [offi't∫ina] *sf* workshop.

of'frire *vt* to offer; ~**rsi** *vr* (*proporsi*) to

offer (o.s.), volunteer; (*occasione*) to present itself; (*esporsi*): ~**rsi a** to expose o.s. to; **ti offro da bere** I'll buy you a drink.

offus'care *vt* to obscure, darken; (*fig: intelletto*) to dim, cloud; (: *fama*) to obscure, overshadow; ~**rsi** *vr* to grow dark; to cloud, grow dim; to be obscured.

of'talmico, a, ci, che *ag* ophthalmic.

oggettività |oddʒettivi'ta| *sf* objectivity.

ogget'tivo, a |odd3et'tivo| *ag* objective.

og'getto |od'dʒetto| *sm* object; (*materia, argomento*) subject (matter); ~**i smarriti** lost property *sg*.

'oggi |'ɔddʒi| *av, sm* today; ~ **a otto** a week today; **oggigi'orno** *av* nowadays.

o'giva |o'dʒiva| *sf* ogive, pointed arch.

'ogni |'oɲɲi| *det* every, each; (*tutti*) all; (*con valore distributivo*) every; ~ **uomo è mortale** all men are mortal; **viene** ~ **due giorni** he comes every two days; ~ **cosa** everything; **ad** ~ **costo** at all costs, at any price; **in** ~ **luogo** everywhere; ~ **tanto** every so often; ~ **volta che** every time that.

Ognis'santi |oɲɲis'santi| *sm* All Saints' Day.

o'gnuno |oɲ'ɲuno| *pronome* everyone, everybody.

'ohi *escl* oh!; (*esprimente dolore*) ow!

ohimè *escl* oh dear!

O'landa *sf*: **l'**~ Holland; **olan'dese** *ag* Dutch // *sm* (*LING*) Dutch // *sm/f* Dutchman/woman; **gli Olandesi** the Dutch.

oleo'dotto *sm* oil pipeline.

ole'oso, a *ag* oily; (*che contiene olio*) oil-yielding.

ol'fatto *sm* sense of smell.

oli'are *vt* to oil.

oli'era *sf* oil cruet.

olim'piadi *sfpl* Olympic games; **o'limpico, a, ci, che** *ag* Olympic.

'olio *sm* oil; **sott'**~ (*CUC*) in oil; ~ **di fegato di merluzzo** cod liver oil; ~ **d'oliva** olive oil; ~ **di semi** vegetable oil.

o'liva *sf* olive; **oli'vastro, a** *ag* olive(-coloured); (*carnagione*) sallow; **oli'veto** *sm* olive grove; **o'livo** *sm* olive tree.

'olmo *sm* elm.

oltraggi'are |oltrad'dʒare| *vt* to outrage; to offend gravely.

ol'traggio |ol'traddʒo| *sm* outrage; offence, insult; ~ **a pubblico ufficiale** (*DIR*) insulting a public official; ~ **al pudore** (*DIR*) indecent behaviour; **oltraggi'oso, a** *ag* offensive.

ol'tralpe *av* beyond the Alps.

ol'tranza |ol'trantsa| *sf*: **a** ~ **to** the last, to the bitter end.

'oltre *av* (*più in là*) further; (*di più: aspettare*) longer, more // *prep* (*di là da*) beyond, over, on the other side of; (*più di*) more than, over; (*in aggiunta a*) besides; (*eccetto*): ~ **a** except, apart from; **oltre'mare** *av* overseas; **oltrepas'sare** *vt* to go beyond, exceed.

o'maggio |o'maddʒo| *sm* (*dono*) gift; (*segno di rispetto*) homage, tribute; ~**i** *smpl* (*complimenti*) respects; **rendere** ~ **a** to pay homage o tribute to; **in** ~ (*copia, biglietto*) complimentary.

ombeli'cale *ag* umbilical.

ombe'lico, chi *sm* navel.

'ombra *sf* (*zona non assolata, fantasma*) shade; (*sagoma scura*) shadow; **sedere all'**~ to sit in the shade; **restare nell'**~ (*fig*) to remain in obscurity.

ombreggi'are |ombred'dʒare| *vt* to shade.

om'brello *sm* umbrella; **ombrel'lone** *sm* beach umbrella.

om'bretto *sm* eyeshadow.

om'broso, a *ag* shady, shaded; (*cavallo*) nervous, skittish; (*persona*) touchy, easily offended.

ome'lia *sf* (*REL*) homily, sermon.

omeopa'tia *sf* homoeopathy.

omertà *sf* conspiracy of silence.

o'messo, a *pp di* omettere.

o'mettere *vt* to omit, leave out; ~ **di fare** to omit o fail to do.

omi'cida, i, e |omi'tʃida| *ag* homicidal, murderous // *sm/f* murderer/eress.

omi'cidio |omi'tʃidjo| *sm* murder; ~ **colposo** culpable homicide.

omissi'one *sf* omission; ~ **di soccorso** (*DIR*) failure to stop and give assistance.

omogeneiz'zato |omodʒeneid'dzato| *sm* baby food.

omo'geneo, a |omo'dʒɛneo| *ag* homogeneous.

omolo'gare *vt* to approve, recognize; to ratify.

o'monimo, a *sm/f* namesake // *sm* (*LING*) homonym.

omosessu'ale *ag, sm/f* homosexual.

'oncia, ce |'ontʃa| *sf* ounce.

'onda *sf* wave; **mettere** o **mandare in** ~ (*RADIO, TV*) to broadcast; **andare in** ~ (*RADIO, TV*) to go on the air; ~**e corte/ medie/lunghe** short/medium/long wave; **on'data** *sf* wave, billow; (*fig*) wave, surge; **a ondate** in waves; **ondata di caldo** heatwave.

'onde *cong* (*affinché: con il congiuntivo*) so that, in order that; (: *con l'infinito*) so as to, in order to.

ondeggi'are |onded'dʒare| *vi* (*acqua*) to ripple; (*muoversi sulle onde: barca*) to rock, roll; (*fig: muoversi come le onde, barcollare*) to sway; (: *essere incerto*) to waver.

ondula'torio, a *ag* undulating; (*FISICA*) undulatory, wave *cpd*.

ondulazi'one |ondulat'tsjone| *sf* undulation; (*acconciatura*) wave.

'onere *sm* burden; ~**i fiscali** taxes; **one'roso, a** *ag* (*fig*) heavy, onerous.

onestà *sf* honesty.

o'nesto, a *ag* (*probo, retto*) honest; (*giusto*) fair; (*casto*) chaste, virtuous.

'onice ['ɔnitʃe] *sf* onyx.

onnipo'tente *ag* omnipotent.

onnisci'ente [onniʃ'ʃɛnte] *ag* omniscient.

onniveg'gente [onnived'dʒɛnte] *ag* all-seeing.

ono'mastico, ci *sm* name-day.

ono'ranze [ono'rantse] *sfpl* honours.

ono'rare *vt* to honour; (*far onore a*) to do credit to; ~**rsi** *vr*: ~**rsi di** to feel honoured at, be proud of.

ono'rario, a *ag* honorary // *sm* fee.

o'nore *sm* honour; **in** ~ **di** in honour of; **fare gli** ~**i di casa** to play host (*o* hostess); **fare** ~ **a** to honour; (*pranzo*) to do justice to; (*famiglia*) to be a credit to; **farsi** ~ to distinguish o.s.; **ono'revole** *ag* honourable // *sm/f* (*POL*) ≈ Member of Parliament (*Brit*), ≈ Congressman/woman (*US*); **onorifi'cenza** *sf* honour; decoration; **ono'rifico, a, ci, che** *ag* honorary.

'onta *sf* shame, disgrace.

'O.N.U. ['ɔnu] *sigla f* (= *Organizzazione delle Nazioni Unite*) UN, UNO.

o'paco, a, chi, che *ag* (*vetro*) opaque; (*metallo*) dull, matt.

o'pale *sm o f* opal.

'opera *sf* work; (*azione rilevante*) action, deed, work; (*MUS*) work; opus; (: *melodramma*) opera; (: *teatro*) opera house; (*ente*) institution, organization; ~ **d'arte** work of art; ~ **lirica** (grand) opera; ~**e pubbliche** public works.

ope'raio, a *ag* working-class; workers' // *sm/f* worker; **classe** ~**a** working class.

ope'rare *vt* to carry out, make; (*MED*) to operate on // *vi* to operate, work; (*rimedio*) to act, work; (*MED*) to operate; ~**rsi** *vr* to occur, take place; (*MED*) to have an operation; ~**rsi d'appendicite** to have one's appendix out; **opera'tivo, a** *ag* operative, operating; **opera'tore, 'trice** *sm/f* operator; (*TV, CINEMA*) cameraman; **operatore economico** agent, broker; **operatore turistico** tour operator; **opera'torio, a** *ag* (*MED*) operating; **operazi'one** *sf* operation.

ope'retta *sf* (*MUS*) operetta, light opera.

ope'roso, a *ag* busy, active, hard-working.

opi'ficio [opi'fitʃo] *sm* factory, works *pl*.

opini'one *sf* opinion.

'oppio *sm* opium.

oppo'nente *ag* opposing // *sm/f* opponent.

op'porre *vt* to oppose; **opporsi** *vr*: **opporsi (a qc)** to oppose (sth); to object (to sth); ~ **resistenza/un rifiuto** to offer resistance/refuse.

opportu'nista, i, e *sm/f* opportunist.

opportunità *sf inv* opportunity; (*convenienza*) opportuneness, timeliness.

oppor'tuno, a *ag* timely, opportune.

opposi'tore, 'trice *sm/f* opposer, opponent.

opposizi'one [oppozit'tsjone] *sf* opposition; (*DIR*) objection.

op'posto, a *pp di* **opporre** // *ag* opposite; (*opinioni*) conflicting // *sm* opposite, contrary; **all'~** on the contrary.

oppressi'one *sf* oppression.

oppres'sivo, a *ag* oppressive.

op'presso, a *pp di* **opprimere**.

oppres'sore *sm* oppressor.

op'primere *vt* (*premere, gravare*) to weigh down; (*estenuare: sog: caldo*) to suffocate, oppress; (*tiranneggiare: popolo*) to oppress.

oppu'gnare [oppuɲ'ɲare] *vt* (*fig*) to refute.

op'pure *cong* or (else).

op'tare *vi*: ~ **per** to opt for.

o'puscolo *sm* booklet, pamphlet.

opzi'one [op'tsjone] *sf* option.

'ora *sf* (*60 minuti*) hour; (*momento*) time; **che** ~ **è?, che** ~**e sono?** what time is it?; **non veder l'**~ **di fare** to long to do, look forward to doing; **di buon'**~ early; **alla buon'**~! at last!; ~ **legale** *o* **estiva** summer time (*Brit*), daylight saving time (*US*); ~ **locale** local time; ~ **di punta** (*AUT*) rush hour // *av* (*adesso*) now; (*poco fa*): **è uscito proprio** ~ he's just gone out; (*tra poco*) presently, in a minute; (*correlativo*): ~ ... ~ now ... now; **d'**~ **in avanti** *o* **poi** from now on; **or** ~ just now, a moment ago; **5 anni or sono** 5 years ago; ~ **come** ~ right now, at present.

o'racolo *sm* oracle.

'orafo *sm* goldsmith.

o'rale *ag, sm* oral.

ora'mai *av* = **ormai**.

o'rario, a *ag* hourly; (*fuso, segnale*) time *cpd*; (*velocità*) per hour // *sm* timetable, schedule; (*di ufficio, visite etc*) hours *pl*, time(s *pl*).

ora'tore, 'trice *sm/f* speaker; orator.

ora'torio, a *ag* oratorical // *sm* (*REL*) oratory; (*MUS*) oratorio // *sf* (*arte*) oratory.

orazi'one [orat'tsjone] *sf* (*REL*) prayer; (*discorso*) speech, oration.

or'bene *cong* so, well (then).

'orbita *sf* (*ASTR, FISICA*) orbit; (*ANAT*) (eye-)socket.

or'chestra [or'kɛstra] *sf* orchestra; **or'chestrale** *ag* orchestral // *sm/f* orchestra player; **orches'trare** *vt* to orchestrate; (*fig*) to mount, stage-manage.

orchi'dea [orki'dɛa] *sf* orchid.

'orco, chi *sm* ogre.

'orda *sf* horde.

or'digno [or'diɲɲo] *sm* (*esplosivo*) explosive device.

ordi'nale *ag, sm* ordinal.

ordina'mento *sm* order, arrangement; (*regolamento*) regulations *pl*, rules *pl*; ~ scolastico/giuridico education/legal system.

ordi'nanza [ordi'nantsa] *sf* (*DIR, MIL*) order; (*persona: MIL*) orderly, batman; d'~ (*MIL*) regulation *cpd*.

ordi'nare *vt* (*mettere in ordine*) to arrange, organize; (*COMM*) to order; (*prescrivere: medicina*) to prescribe; (*comandare*): ~ a qn di fare qc to order *o* command sb to do sth; (*REL*) to ordain.

ordi'nario, a *ag* (*comune*) ordinary; everyday; standard; (*grossolano*) coarse, common // *sm* ordinary; (*INS: di università*) full professor.

ordi'nato, a *ag* tidy, orderly.

ordinazi'one [ordinat'tsjone] *sf* (*COMM*) order; (*REL*) ordination; eseguire qc su ~ to make sth to order.

'ordine *sm* order; (*carattere*): d'~ pratico of a practical nature; all'~ (*COMM: assegno*) to order; di prim'~ first-class; fino a nuovo ~ until further notice; essere in ~ (*documenti*) to be in order; (*stanza, persona*) to be tidy; mettere in ~ to put in order, tidy (up); ~ del giorno (*di seduta*) agenda; (*MIL*) order of the day; ~ di pagamento (*COMM*) order for payment; l'~ pubblico law and order; ~i (sacri) (*REL*) holy orders.

or'dire *vt* (*fig*) to plot, scheme; **or'dito** *sm* (*di tessuto*) warp.

orec'chino [orek'kino] *sm* earring.

o'recchio [o'rekkjo], *pl(f)* **o'recchie** *sm* (*ANAT*) ear.

orecchi'oni [orek'kjoni] *smpl* (*MED*) mumps *sg*.

o'refice [o'refitʃe] *sm* goldsmith; jeweller; **orefice'ria** *sf* (*arte*) goldsmith's art; (*negozio*) jeweller's (shop).

'orfano, a *ag* orphan(ed) // *sm/f* orphan; ~ di padre/madre fatherless/motherless; **orfano'trofio** *sm* orphanage.

orga'netto *sm* barrel organ; (*fam: armonica a bocca*) mouth organ; (: *fisarmonica*) accordion.

or'ganico, a, ci, che *ag* organic // *sm* personnel, staff.

organi'gramma, i *sm* organization chart.

orga'nismo *sm* (*BIOL*) organism; (*corpo umano*) body; (*AMM*) body, organism.

organiz'zare [organid'dzare] *vt* to organize; ~rsi *vr* to get organized; **organizza'tore, 'trice** *ag* organizing // *sm/f* organizer; **organizzazi'one** *sf* organization.

'organo *sm* organ; (*di congegno*) part; (*portavoce*) spokesman, mouthpiece.

or'gasmo *sm* (*FISIOL*) orgasm; (*fig*) agitation, anxiety.

'orgia, ge ['ɔrdʒa] *sf* orgy.

or'goglio [or'gɔʎʎo] *sm* pride; **orgogli'oso, a** *ag* proud.

orien'tale *ag* oriental; eastern; east.

orienta'mento *sm* positioning; orientation; direction; senso di ~ sense of direction; perdere l'~ to lose one's bearings; ~ professionale careers guidance.

orien'tare *vt* (*situare*) to position; (*fig*) to direct, orientate; ~rsi *vr* to find one's bearings; (*fig: tendere*) to tend, lean; (: *indirizzarsi*): ~rsi verso to take up, go in for.

ori'ente *sm* east; l'O~ the East, the Orient; a ~ in the east.

o'rigano *sm* oregano.

origi'nale [oridʒi'nale] *ag* original; (*bizzarro*) eccentric // *sm* original; **originalità** *sf* originality; eccentricity.

origi'nare [oridʒi'nare] *vt* to bring about, produce // *vi*: ~ da to arise *o* spring from.

origi'nario, a [oridʒi'narjo] *ag* original; essere ~ di to be a native of; (*provenire da*) to originate from; to be native to.

o'rigine [o'ridʒine] *sf* origin; all'~ originally; d'~ inglese of English origin; dare ~ a to give rise to.

origli'are [oriʎ'ʎare] *vi*: ~ (a) to eavesdrop (on).

o'rina *sf* urine; **ori'nale** *sm* chamberpot.

ori'nare *vi* to urinate // *vt* to pass; **orina'toio** *sm* (public) urinal.

ori'undo, a *ag*: essere ~ di Milano *etc* to be of Milanese *etc* extraction *o* origin // *sm/f* person of foreign extraction *o* origin.

orizzon'tale [oriddzon'tale] *ag* horizontal.

oriz'zonte [orid'dzonte] *sm* horizon.

or'lare *vt* to hem.

'orlo *sm* edge, border; (*di recipiente*) rim, brim; (*di vestito etc*) hem.

'orma *sf* (*di persona*) footprint; (*di animale*) track; (*impronta, traccia*) mark, trace.

or'mai *av* by now, by this time; (*adesso*) now; (*quasi*) almost, nearly.

ormeggi'are [ormed'dʒare] *vt* (*NAUT*) to moor; **or'meggio** *sm* (*atto*) mooring *q*; (*luogo*) moorings *pl*.

or'mone *sm* hormone.

ornamen'tale *ag* ornamental, decorative.

orna'mento *sm* ornament, decoration.

or'nare *vt* to adorn, decorate; ~rsi *vr*: ~rsi (di) to deck o.s. (out) (with); **or'nato, a** *ag* ornate.

ornitolo'gia [ornitolo'dʒia] *sf* ornithology.

'oro *sm* gold; d'~, in ~ gold *cpd*; d'~ (*colore, occasione*) golden; (*persona*) marvellous.

orologe'ria [orolodʒe'ria] *sf* watchmaking *q*; watchmaker's (shop); clockmaker's (shop); **bomba a ~** time bomb.

orologi'aio [orolo'dʒajo] *sm* watch-maker; clockmaker.

oro'logio [oro'lɔdʒo] *sm* clock; (*da tasca, da polso*) watch; **~ da polso** wrist-watch; **~ al quarzo** quartz watch; **~ a sveglia** alarm clock.

o'roscopo *sm* horoscope.

or'rendo, a *ag* (*spaventoso*) horrible, awful; (*bruttissimo*) hideous.

or'ribile *ag* horrible.

'orrido, a *ag* fearful, horrid.

orripi'lante *ag* hair-raising, horrifying.

or'rore *sm* horror; **avere in ~** qn/qc to loathe *o* detest sb/sth; **mi fanno ~** I loathe *o* detest them.

orsacchi'otto [orsak'kjɔtto] *sm* teddy bear.

'orso *sm* bear; **~ bruno/bianco** brown/polar bear.

or'taggio [or'taddʒo] *sm* vegetable.

or'tica, che *sf* (stinging) nettle.

orti'caria *sf* nettle rash.

orticol'tura *sf* horticulture.

'orto *sm* vegetable garden, kitchen garden; (*AGR*) market garden (*Brit*), truck farm (*US*).

orto'dosso, a *ag* orthodox.

ortogra'fia *sf* spelling.

orto'lano, a *smf* (*venditore*) green-grocer (*Brit*), produce dealer (*US*).

ortope'dia *sf* orthopaedics *sg*; **orto'pedico, a, ci, che** *ag* orthopaedic // *sm* orthopaedic specialist.

orzai'olo [ordza'jɔlo] *sm* (*MED*) stye.

or'zata [or'dzata] *sf* barley water.

'orzo ['ordzo] *sm* barley.

o'sare *vt, vi* to dare; **~ fare** to dare (to) do.

oscenità [oʃʃeni'ta] *sf inv* obscenity.

o'sceno, a [oʃ'ʃeno] *ag* obscene; (*ripugnante*) ghastly.

oscil'lare [oʃʃil'lare] *vi* (*pendolo*) to swing; (*dondolare: al vento etc*) to rock; (*variare*) to fluctuate; (*TECN*) to oscillate; (*fig*): **~ fra** to waver *o* hesitate between; **oscillazi'one** *sf* oscillation; (*di prezzi, temperatura*) fluctuation.

oscura'mento *sm* darkening; obscur-ing; (*in tempo di guerra*) blackout.

oscu'rare *vt* to darken, obscure; (*fig*) to obscure; **~rsi** *vr* (*cielo*) to darken, cloud over; (*persona*): **si oscurò in volto** his face clouded over.

os'curo, a *ag* dark; (*fig*) obscure; humble, lowly // *sm*: **all'~** in the dark; **tenere qn all'~ di qc** to keep sb in the dark about sth.

ospe'dale *sm* hospital; **ospedali'ero, a** *ag* hospital *cpd*.

ospi'tale *ag* hospitable; **ospitalità** *sf* hospitality.

ospi'tare *vt* to give hospitality to; (*sog: albergo*) to accommodate.

'ospite *smf* (*persona che ospita*) host/

hostess; (*persona ospitata*) guest.

os'pizio [os'pittsjo] *sm* (*per vecchi etc*) home.

'ossa *sfpl vedi* **osso**.

ossa'tura *sf* (*ANAT*) skeletal structure, frame; (*TECN, fig*) framework.

'osseo, a *ag* bony; (*tessuto etc*) bone *cpd*.

os'sequio *sm* deference, respect; **~i** *smpl* (*saluto*) respects, regards; **ossequi'oso, a** *ag* obsequious.

osser'vanza [osser'vantsa] *sf* observance.

osser'vare *vt* to observe, watch; (*esaminare*) to examine; (*notare, rilevare*) to notice, observe; (*DIR: la legge*) to observe, respect; (*mantenere: silenzio*) to keep, observe; **far ~ qc a qn** to point sth out to sb; **osserva'tore, 'trice** *ag* observant, perceptive // *smf* observer; **osserva'torio** *sm* (*ASTR*) observatory; (*MIL*) observation post; **osservazi'one** *sf* observation; (*di legge etc*) observance; (*considerazione critica*) observation, remark; (*rimprovero*) re-proof; **in osservazione** under observation.

ossessio'nare *vt* to obsess, haunt; (*tormentare*) to torment, harass.

ossessi'one *sf* obsession.

os'sesso, a *ag* (*spiritato*) possessed.

os'sia *cong* that is, to be precise.

ossi'dare *vt*, **~rsi** *vr* to oxidize.

'ossido *sm* oxide; **~ di carbonio** carbon monoxide.

ossige'nare [ossidʒe'nare] *vt* to ox-ygenate; (*decolorare*) to bleach; **acqua ossigenata** hydrogen peroxide.

os'sigeno *sm* oxygen.

'osso *sm* (*pl(f)* **ossa** *nel senso ANAT*) bone; **d'~** (*bottone etc*) of bone, bone *cpd*.

osso'buco, *pl* **ossi'buchi** *sm* (*CUC*) marrowbone; (: *piatto*) *stew made with knuckle of veal in tomato sauce*.

os'suto, a *ag* bony.

ostaco'lare *vt* to block, obstruct.

os'tacolo *sm* obstacle; (*EQUITAZIONE*) hurdle, jump.

os'taggio [os'taddʒo] *sm* hostage.

'oste, os'tessa *sm/f* innkeeper.

osteggi'are [osted'dʒare] *vt* to oppose, be opposed to.

os'tello *sm*: **~ della gioventù** youth hostel.

osten'tare *vt* to make a show of, flaunt; **ostentazi'one** *sf* ostentation, show.

oste'ria *sf* inn.

os'tessa *sf vedi* **oste**.

os'tetrico, a, ci, che *ag* obstetric // *sm* obstetrician // *sf* midwife.

'ostia *sf* (*REL*) host; (*per medicinali*) wafer.

'ostico, a, ci, che *ag* (*fig*) harsh, hard, difficult; unpleasant.

os'tile *ag* hostile; **ostilità** *sf inv* hostility // *sfpl* (*MIL*) hostilities.

osti'narsi *vr* to insist, dig one's heels in; ~ a fare to persist (obstinately) in doing; **osti'nato, a** *ag* (*caparbio*) obstinate; (*tenace*) persistent, determined; **ostinazi'one** *sf* obstinacy; persistence.

ostra'cismo [ostra'tʃizmo] *sm* ostracism.

'ostrica, che *sf* oyster.

ostru'ire *vt* to obstruct, block; **ostruzi'one** *sf* obstruction, blockage.

'otre *sm* (*recipiente*) goatskin.

ottago'nale *ag* octagonal.

ot'tagono *sm* octagon.

ot'tanta *num* eighty; **ottan'tesimo, a** *num* eightieth; **ottan'tina** *sf*: una ottantina (di) about eighty.

ot'tavo, a *num* eighth // *sf* octave.

ottempe'rare *vi*: ~ a to comply with, obey.

ottene'brare *vt* to darken; (*fig*) to cloud.

otte'nere *vt* to obtain, get; (*risultato*) to achieve, obtain.

'ottico, a, ci, che *ag* (*della vista: nervo*) optic; (*dell'ottica*) optical // *sm* optician // *sf* (*scienza*) optics *sg*; (*FOT: lenti, prismi etc*) optics *pl*.

ottima'mente *av* excellently, very well.

otti'mismo *sm* optimism; **otti'mista, i, e** *sm/f* optimist.

'ottimo, a *ag* excellent, very good.

'otto *num* eight.

ot'tobre *sm* October.

otto'cento [otto'tʃɛnto] *num* eight hundred // *sm*: l'O~ the nineteenth century.

ot'tone *sm* brass; gli ~i (*MUS*) the brass.

ot'tundere *vt* (*fig*) to dull.

ottu'rare *vt* to close (up); (*dente*) to fill; **ottura'tore** *sm* (*FOT*) shutter; (*nelle armi*) breechblock; **otturazi'one** *sf* closing (up); (*dentaria*) filling.

ot'tuso, a *pp di* **ottundere** // *ag* (*MAT, fig*) obtuse; (*suono*) dull.

o'vaia *sf*, **o'vaio** *sm* (*ANAT*) ovary.

o'vale *ag*, *sm* oval.

o'vatta *sf* cotton wool; (*per imbottire*) padding, wadding; **ovat'tare** *vt* (*fig: smorzare*) to muffle.

ovazi'one [ovat'tsjone] *sf* ovation.

'ovest *sm* west.

o'vile *sm* pen, enclosure.

o'vino, a *ag* sheep *cpd*, ovine.

ovulazi'one [ovulat'tsjone] *sf* ovulation.

'ovulo *sm* (*FISIOL*) ovum.

o'vunque *av* = **dovunque**.

ov'vero *cong* (*ossia*) that is, to be precise; (*oppure*) (or else).

ovvi'are *vi*: ~ a to obviate.

'ovvio, a *ag* obvious.

ozi'are [ot'tsjare] *vi* to laze, idle.

'ozio ['ɔttsjo] *sm* idleness; (*tempo libero*) leisure; ore d'~ leisure time; stare in ~ to be idle; **ozi'oso, a** *ag* idle.

o'zono [o'dzɔno] *sm* ozone.

P

pa'cato, a *ag* quiet, calm.

pac'chetto [pak'ketto] *sm* packet; ~ azionario (*COMM*) shareholding.

'pacco, chi *sm* parcel; (*involto*) bundle.

'pace ['patʃe] *sf* peace; darsi ~ to resign o.s.

pacifi'care [patʃifi'kare] *vt* (*riconciliare*) to reconcile, make peace between; (*mettere in pace*) to pacify.

pa'cifico, a, ci, che [pa'tʃifiko] *ag* (*persona*) peaceable; (*vita*) peaceful; (*fig: indiscusso*) indisputable; (: *ovvio*) obvious, clear // *sm*: il P~, l'Oceano P~ the Pacific (Ocean).

paci'fista, i, e [patʃi'fista] *sm/f* pacifist.

pa'della *sf* frying pan; (*per infermi*) bedpan.

padigli'one [padiʎ'ʎone] *sm* pavilion; (*AUT*) roof.

'Padova *sf* Padua.

'padre *sm* father; ~i *smpl* (*antenati*) forefathers; **pa'drino** *sm* godfather.

padro'nanza [padro'nantsa] *sf* command, mastery.

pa'drone, a *sm/f* master/mistress; (*proprietario*) owner; (*datore di lavoro*) employer; essere ~ di sé to be in control of o.s.; ~ di casa master/mistress of the house; (*per gli inquilini*) landlord/lady; **padroneggi'are** *vt* (*fig: sentimenti*) to master, control; (: *materia*) to master, know thoroughly; **padroneggiarsi** *vr* to control o.s.

pae'saggio [pae'zaddʒo] *sm* landscape.

pae'sano, a *ag* country *cpd* // *sm/f* villager; countryman/woman.

pa'ese *sm* (*nazione*) country, nation; (*terra*) country, land; (*villaggio*) village; ~ di provenienza country of origin; i P~i Bassi the Netherlands.

paf'futo, a *ag* chubby, plump.

'paga, ghe *sf* pay, wages *pl*.

paga'mento *sm* payment.

pa'gano, a *ag*, *sm/f* pagan.

pa'gare *vt* to pay; (*acquisto, fig: colpa*) to pay for; (*contraccambiare*) to repay, pay back // *vi* to pay; quanto l'hai pagato? how much did you pay for it?; ~ con carta di credito to pay by credit card; ~ in contanti to pay cash.

pa'gella [pa'dʒella] *sf* (*INS*) report card.

'paggio ['paddʒo] *sm* page(boy).

paghe'rò [page'rɔ] *sm inv* acknowledgement of a debt, IOU.

'pagina ['padʒina] *sf* page.

'paglia ['paʎʎa] *sf* straw.

pagliac'cetto [paʎʎat'tʃetto] *sm* (*per bambini*) rompers *pl*.

pagli'accio [paʎ'ʎattʃo] *sm* clown.

pagli'etta [paʎ'ʎetta] *sf* (*cappello per*

uomo) (straw) boater; (*per tegami etc*) steel wool.

pa'gnotta |paɲˈɲɔtta| *sf* round loaf.

'paio, *pl(f)* 'paia *sm* pair; un ~ di (*alcuni*) a couple of.

pai'olo, paiu'olo *sm* (copper) pot.

'pala *sf* shovel; (*di remo, ventilatore, elica*) blade; (*di ruota*) paddle.

pa'lato *sm* palate.

pa'lazzo |paˈlattso| *sm* (*reggia*) palace; (*edificio*) building; ~ di giustizia courthouse; ~ dello sport sports stadium.

pal'chetto |palˈketto| *sm* shelf.

'palco, chi *sm* (*TEATRO*) box; (*tavolato*) platform, stand; (*ripiano*) layer.

palco'scenico, ci |palkoʃˈʃɛniko| *sm* (*TEATRO*) stage.

pale'sare *vt* to reveal, disclose; ~rsi *vr* to reveal *o* show o.s.

pa'lese *ag* clear, evident.

Pales'tina *sf*: la ~ Palestine.

pa'lestra *sf* gymnasium; (*esercizio atletico*) exercise, training; (*fig*) training ground, school.

pa'letta *sf* spade; (*per il focolare*) shovel; (*del capostazione*) signalling disc.

pa'letto *sm* stake, peg; (*spranga*) bolt.

'palio *sm* (*gara*): il P~ horserace run at Siena; mettere qc in ~ to offer sth as a prize.

'palla *sf* ball; (*pallottola*) bullet; ~ canestro *sm* basketball; ~ nuoto *sm* water polo; ~ volo *sm* volleyball.

palleggi'are |palledˈdʒare| *vi* (*CALCIO*) to practise with the ball; (*TENNIS*) to knock up.

pallia'tivo *sm* palliative; (*fig*) stopgap measure.

'pallido, a *ag* pale.

pal'lina *sf* (*bilia*) marble.

pallon'cino |pallonˈtʃino| *sm* balloon; (*lampioncino*) Chinese lantern.

pal'lone *sm* (*palla*) ball; (*CALCIO*) football; (*aerostato*) balloon; gioco del ~ football.

pal'lore *sm* pallor, paleness.

pal'lottola *sf* pellet; (*proiettile*) bullet.

'palma *sf* (*ANAT*) = palmo; (*BOT, simbolo*) palm; ~ da datteri date palm.

'palmo *sm* (*ANAT*) palm; restare con un ~ di naso to be badly disappointed.

'palo *sm* (*legno appuntito*) stake; (*sostegno*) pole; fare da *o* il ~ (*fig*) to act as look-out.

palom'baro *sm* diver.

pa'lombo *sm* (*pesce*) dogfish.

pal'pare *vt* to feel, finger.

'palpebra *sf* eyelid.

palpi'tare *vi* (*cuore, polso*) to beat; (: *più forte*) to pound, throb; (*fremere*) to quiver; 'palpito *sm* (*del cuore*) beat; (*fig: d'amore etc*) throb.

pal'tò *sm inv* overcoat.

pa'lude *sf* marsh, swamp; palu'doso, a

ag marshy, swampy.

pa'lustre *ag* marsh *cpd*, swamp *cpd*.

'pampino *sm* vine leaf.

'panca, che *sf* bench.

pan'cetta |panˈtʃetta| *sf* (*CUC*) bacon.

pan'chetto |panˈketto| *sm* stool; footstool.

pan'china |panˈkina| *sf* garden seat; (*di giardino pubblico*) (park) bench.

'pancia, ce |ˈpantʃa| *sf* belly, stomach; mettere *o* fare ~ to be getting a paunch; avere mal di ~ to have stomach ache *o* a sore stomach.

panci'otto |panˈtʃɔtto| *sm* waistcoat.

'pancreas *sm inv* pancreas.

'panda *sm inv* panda.

pande'monio *sm* pandemonium.

'pane *sm* bread; (*pagnotta*) loaf (of bread); (*forma*): un ~ di burro/cera *etc* a pat of butter/bar of wax *etc*; guadagnarsi il ~ to earn one's living; ~ a cassetta sliced bread; ~ integrale wholemeal bread; ~ tostato toast.

panette'ria *sf* (*forno*) bakery; (*negozio*) baker's (shop), bakery.

panetti'ere, a *sm/f* baker.

panet'tone *sm* a kind of spiced brioche with sultanas, eaten at Christmas.

pangrat'tato *sm* breadcrumbs *pl*.

'panico, a, ci, che *ag, sm* panic.

pani'ere *sm* basket.

pani'ficio |paniˈfitʃo| *sm* (*forno*) bakery; (*negozio*) baker's (shop), bakery.

pa'nino *sm* roll; ~ imbottito filled roll; sandwich; panino'teca *sf* sandwich bar.

'panna *sf* (*CUC*) cream; (*TECN*) = panne; ~ da cucina cooking cream; ~ montata whipped cream.

'panne *sf inv*: essere in ~ (*AUT*) to have broken down.

pan'nello *sm* panel.

'panno *sm* cloth; ~i *smpl* (*abiti*) clothes; mettiti nei miei ~i (*fig*) put yourself in my shoes.

pan'nocchia |panˈnɔkkja| *sf* (*di mais etc*) ear.

panno'lino *sm* (*per bambini*) nappy (*Brit*), diaper (*US*).

pano'rama, i *sm* panorama; pano'ramico, a, ci, che *ag* panoramic; strada panoramica scenic route.

panta'loni *smpl* trousers (*Brit*), pants (*US*), pair *sg* of trousers *o* pants.

pan'tano *sm* bog.

pan'tera *sf* panther.

pan'tofola *sf* slipper.

panto'mima *sf* pantomime.

pan'zana |panˈtsana| *sf* fib, tall story.

pao'nazzo, a |paoˈnattso| *ag* purple.

'papa, i *sm* pope.

papà *sm inv* dad(dy).

pa'pale *ag* papal.

pa'pato *sm* papacy.

pa'pavero *sm* poppy.

'papero, a *sm/f* (*ZOOL*) gosling // *sf* (*fig*)

slip of the tongue, blunder.

pa'piro *sm* papyrus.

'pappa *sf* baby cereal.

pappa'gallo *sm* parrot; (*fig: uomo*) Romeo, wolf.

pappa'gorgia, ge [pappa'gɔrdʒa] *sf* double chin.

pap'pare *vt* (*fam: anche:* ~**rsi**) to gobble up.

'para *sf:* suole di ~ crepe soles.

pa'rabola *sf* (*MAT*) parabola; (*REL*) parable.

para'brezza [para'breddza] *sm inv* (*AUT*) windscreen (*Brit*), windshield (*US*).

paraca'dute *sm inv* parachute.

para'carro *sm* kerbstone (*Brit*), curb- stone (*US*).

para'diso *sm* paradise.

parados'sale *ag* paradoxical.

para'dosso *sm* paradox.

para'fango, ghi *sm* mudguard.

paraf'fina *sf* paraffin, paraffin wax.

para'fulmine *sm* lightning conductor.

pa'raggi [pa'raddʒi] *smpl:* nei ~ in the vicinity, in the neighbourhood.

parago'nare *vt:* ~ con/a to compare with/to.

para'gone *sm* comparison; (*esempio analogo*) analogy, parallel; **reggere al** ~ to stand comparison.

pa'ragrafo *sm* paragraph.

pa'ralisi *sf* paralysis; **para'litico, a, ci, che** *ag, sm/f* paralytic.

paraliz'zare [paralid'dzare] *vt* to paralyze.

paral'lelo, a *ag* parallel // *sm* (*GEO*) parallel; (*comparazione*): fare un ~ tra to draw a parallel between // *sf* parallel (line); ~**e** *sfpl* (*attrezzo ginnico*) parallel bars.

para'lume *sm* lampshade.

pa'rametro *sm* parameter.

para'noia *sf* paranoia; **para'noico, a, ci, che** *ag, sm/f* paranoid.

para'occhi [para'ɔkki] *smpl* blinkers.

para'piglia [para'piʎʎa] *sm* commotion, uproar.

pa'rare *vt* (*addobbare*) to adorn, deck; (*proteggere*) to shield, protect; (*scansare: colpo*) to parry; (*CALCIO*) to save // *vi:* dove vuole andare a ~? what are you driving at?; ~**rsi** *vr* (*pre- sentarsi*) to appear, present o.s.

para'sole *sm inv* parasol, sunshade.

paras'sita, i *sm* parasite.

pa'rata *sf* (*SPORT*) save; (*MIL*) review, parade.

para'tia *sf* (*di nave*) bulkhead.

para'urti *sm inv* (*AUT*) bumper.

para'vento *sm* folding screen; fare da ~ a qn (*fig*) to shield sb.

par'cella [par'tʃella] *sf* account, fee (*of lawyer etc*).

parcheggi'are [parked'dʒare] *vt* to park; **par'cheggio** *sm* parking *q*; (*luogo*) car

park; (*singolo posto*) parking space.

par'chimetro [par'kimetro] *sm* parking meter.

'parco, chi *sm* park; (*spazio per deposito*) depot; (*complesso di veicoli*) fleet.

'parco, a, chi, che *ag:* ~ (in) (*sobrio*) moderate (in); (*avaro*) sparing (with).

pa'recchio, a [pa'rekkjo] *det* quite a lot of; (*tempo*) quite a lot of, a long; ~**i(e)** *det pl* quite a lot of, several // *pronome* quite a lot, quite a bit; (*tempo*) quite a while, a long time; ~**i(e)** *pronome pl* quite a lot, several // *av* (*con ag*) quite, rather; (*con vb*) quite a lot, quite a bit.

pareggi'are [pared'dʒare] *vt* to make equal; (*terreno*) to level, make level; (*bilancio, conti*) to balance // *vi* (*SPORT*) to draw; **pa'reggio** *sm* (*ECON*) balance; (*SPORT*) draw.

paren'tado *sm* relatives *pl*, relations *pl*.

pa'rente *sm/f* relative, relation.

paren'tela *sf* (*vincolo di sangue, fig*) re- lationship; (*insieme dei parenti*) rela- tions *pl*, relatives *pl*.

pa'rentesi *sf* (*segno grafico*) bracket, parenthesis; (*frase incisa*) parenthesis; (*digressione*) parenthesis, digression.

pa'rere *sm* (*opinione*) opinion; (*con- siglio*) advice, opinion; a mio ~ in my opinion // *vi* to seem, appear // *vb impers:* pare che it seems o appears that, they say that; mi pare che it seems to me that; mi pare di sì I think so; fai come ti pare do as you like; che ti pare del mio libro? what do you think of my book?

pa'rete *sf* wall.

'pari *ag inv* (*uguale*) equal, same; (*in giochi*) equal; drawn, tied; (*MAT*) even // *sm inv* (*POL: di Gran Bretagna*) peer // *sm/f inv* peer, equal; **copiato** ~ ~ copied word for word; alla ~ on the same level; ragazza alla ~ au pair girl; mettersi alla ~ con to place o.s. on the same level as; mettersi in ~ con to catch up with; andare di ~ passo con qn to keep pace with sb.

Pa'rigi [pa'ridʒi] *sf* Paris.

pa'riglia [pa'riʎʎa] *sf* pair; rendere la ~ to give tit for tat.

parità *sf* parity, equality; (*SPORT*) draw, tie.

parlamen'tare *ag* parliamentary // *sm/f* ≈ Member of Parliament (*Brit*), ≈ Congressman/woman (*US*) // *vi* to negotiate, parley.

parla'mento *sm* parliament.

parlan'tina *sf* (*fam*) talkativeness; avere una buona ~ to have the gift of the gab.

par'lare *vi* to speak, talk; (*confidare cose segrete*) to talk // *vt* to speak; ~ (a qn) di to speak o talk (to sb) about; **parla'torio** *sm* (*di carcere etc*) visiting room; (*REL*) parlour.

parmigi'ano |parmi'dʒano| *sm* (*grana*) Parmesan (cheese).

paro'dia *sf* parody.

pa'rola *sf* word; (*facoltà*) speech; ~e *sfpl* (*chiacchiere*) talk *sg*; **chiedere la ~** to ask permission to speak; **prendere la ~** to take the floor; **~ d'onore** word of honour; **~ d'ordine** (*MIL*) password; **~e incrociate** crossword (puzzle) *sg*; **paro'laccia, ce** *sf* bad word, swearword.

par'rocchia |par'rɔkkja| *sf* parish; parish church.

'parroco, ci *sm* parish priest.

par'rucca, che *sf* wig.

parrucchi'ere, a |parruk'kjɛre| *sm/f* hairdresser // *sm* barber.

parsi'monia *sf* frugality, thrift.

'parso, a *pp di* **parere**.

'parte *sf* part; (*lato*) side; (*quota spettante a ciascuno*) share; (*direzione*) direction; (*POL*) party; faction; (*DIR*) party; **a ~** *ag* separate // *av* separately; **scherzi a ~** joking aside; **a ~ ciò** apart from that; **da ~** (*in disparte*) to one side, aside; **d'altra ~** on the other hand; **da ~ di** (*per conto di*) on behalf of; **da ~ mia** as far as I'm concerned, as for me; **da ~ a ~** right through; **da ogni ~** on all sides, everywhere; (*moto da luogo*) from all sides; **da nessuna ~** nowhere; **da questa ~** (*in questa direzione*) this way; **prendere ~ a qc** to take part in sth; **mettere da ~** to put aside; **mettere qn a ~ di qc** to inform sb of sth.

parteci'pare |partetʃi'pare| *vi*: **~ a** to take part in, participate in; (*utili etc*) to share in; (*spese etc*) to contribute to; (*dolore, successo di qn*) to share (in); **partecipazi'one** *sf* participation; sharing; (*ECON*) interest; **partecipazione agli utili** profit-sharing; **partecipazioni di nozze** wedding announcement card; **par'tecipe** *ag* participating; **essere partecipe di** to take part in, participate in; to share (in); (*consapevole*) to be aware of.

parteggi'are |parted'dʒare| *vi*: **~ per** to side with, be on the side of.

par'tenza |par'tɛntsa| *sf* departure; (*SPORT*) start; **essere in ~** to be about to leave, be leaving.

parti'cella |parti'tʃella| *sf* particle.

parti'cipio |parti'tʃipjo| *sm* participle.

partico'lare *ag* (*specifico*) particular; (*proprio*) personal, private; (*speciale*) special, particular; (*caratteristico*) distinctive, characteristic; (*fuori dal comune*) peculiar // *sm* detail, particular; **in ~** in particular, particularly; **particolarità** *sf inv* particularity; detail; characteristic, feature.

partigi'ano, a |parti'dʒano| *ag* partisan // *sm* (*fautore*) supporter, champion;

(*MIL*) partisan.

par'tire *vi* to go, leave; (*allontanarsi*) to go (*o drive etc*) away *o* off; (*petardo, colpo*) to go off; (*fig*: *avere inizio, SPORT*) to start; **sono partita da Roma alle 7** I left Rome at 7; **il volo parte da Ciampino** the flight leaves from Ciampino; **a ~ da** from.

par'tita *sf* (*COMM*) lot, consignment; (*ECON*: *registrazione*) entry, item; (*CARTE, SPORT*: *gioco*) game; (: *competizione*) match, game; **~ di caccia** hunting party; **~ IVA VAT** registration number.

par'tito *sm* (*POL*) party; (*decisione*) decision, resolution; (*persona da maritare*) match.

parti'tura *sf* (*MUS*) score.

'parto *sm* (*MED*) delivery, (child)birth; labour; **parto'rire** *vt* to give birth to; (*fig*) to produce.

parzi'ale |par'tsjale| *ag* (*limitato*) partial; (*non obiettivo*) biased, partial.

'pascere |'paʃʃere| *vi* to graze // *vt* (*brucare*) to graze on; (*far pascolare*) to graze, pasture; **pasci'uto, a** *pp di* **pascere**.

pasco'lare *vt, vi* to graze.

'pascolo *sm* pasture.

'Pasqua *sf* Easter; **pas'quale** *ag* Easter *cpd*.

pas'sabile *ag* fairly good, passable.

pas'saggio |pas'saddʒo| *sm* passing *q*, passage; (*traversata*) crossing *q*, passage; (*luogo, prezzo della traversata, brano di libro etc*) passage; (*su veicolo altrui*) lift (*Brit*), ride; (*SPORT*) pass; **di ~** (*persona*) passing through; **~ pedonale/a livello** pedestrian/level (*Brit*) *o* grade (*US*) crossing.

pas'sante *sm/f* passer-by // *sm* loop.

passa'porto *sm* passport.

pas'sare *vi* (*andare*) to go; (*veicolo, pedone*) to pass (by), go by; (*fare una breve sosta*: *postino etc*) to come, call; (: *amico*: *per fare una visita*) to call *o* drop in; (*sole, aria, luce*) to get through; (*trascorrere*: *giorni, tempo*) to pass, go by; (*fig*: *proposta di legge*) to be passed; (: *dolore*) to pass, go away; (*CARTE*) to pass // *vt* (*attraversare*) to cross; (*trasmettere*: *messaggio*): **~ qc a qn** to pass sth on to sb; (*dare*): **~ qc a qn** to pass sth to sb, give sb sth; (*trascorrere*: *tempo*) to spend; (*superare*: *esame*) to pass; (*triturare*: *verdura*) to strain; (*approvare*) to pass, approve; (*oltrepassare, sorpassare*: *anche fig*) to go beyond, pass; (*fig*: *subire*) to go through; **~ da ... a** to pass from ... to; **~ di padre in figlio** to be handed down *o* to pass from father to son; **~ per** (*anche fig*) to go through; **~ per stupido/un genio** to be taken for a fool/a genius; **~ sopra** (*anche fig*) to pass over; **~ at-**

traverso (*anche fig*) to go through; ~ alla storia to pass into history; ~ a un esame to go up (to the next class) after an exam; ~ inosservato to go unnoticed; ~ di moda to go out of fashion; le passo il Signor X (*al telefono*) here is Mr X; I'm putting you through to Mr X; lasciar ~ qn/qc to let sb/sth through; passarsela: come te la passi? how are you getting on o along?

pas'sata *sf*: dare una ~ di vernice a qc to give sth a coat of paint; dare una ~ al giornale to have a look at the paper, skim through the paper.

passa'tempo *sm* pastime, hobby.

pas'sato, a *ag* past; (*sfiorito*) faded // *sm* past; (*LING*) past (tense); ~ prossimo (*LING*) present perfect; ~ remoto (*LING*) past historic; ~ di verdura (*CUC*) vegetable purée.

passaver'dura *sm inv* vegetable mill.

passeg'gero, a [passed'dʒɛro] *ag* passing // *sm/f* passenger.

passeggi'are [passed'dʒare] *vi* to go for a walk; (*in veicolo*) to go for a drive; **passeggi'ata** *sf* walk; drive; (*luogo*) promenade; fare una passeggiata to go for a walk (o drive); **passeg'gino** *sm* pushchair (*Brit*), stroller (*US*); **pas'seggio** *sm* walk, stroll; (*luogo*) promenade.

passe'rella *sf* footbridge; (*di nave, aereo*) gangway; (*pedana*) catwalk.

'passero *sm* sparrow.

pas'sibile *ag*: ~ di liable to.

passi'one *sf* passion.

pas'sivo, a *ag* passive // *sm* (*LING*) passive; (*ECON*) debit; (*: complesso dei debiti*) liabilities *pl*.

'passo *sm* step; (*andatura*) pace; (*rumore*) (foot)step; (*orma*) footprint; (*passaggio, fig: brano*) passage; (*valico*) pass; a ~ d'uomo at walking pace; ~ (a) ~ step by step; fare due o quattro ~i to go for a walk o a stroll; di questo ~ at this rate; "~ carraio" "vehicle entrance — keep clear".

'pasta *sf* (*CUC*) dough; (*: impasto per dolce*) pastry; (*: anche*: ~ alimentare) pasta; (*massa molle di materia*) paste; (*fig: indole*) nature; ~e *sfpl* (*pasticcini*) pastries; ~ in brodo noodle soup.

pastasci'utta [pastaʃ'ʃutta] *sf* pasta.

pas'tella *sf* batter.

pas'tello *sm* pastel.

pas'tetta *sf* (*CUC*) = **pastella**.

pas'ticca, che *sf* = **pastiglia**.

pasticce'ria [pastittʃe'ria] *sf* (*pasticcini*) pastries *pl*, cakes *pl*; (*negozio*) cake shop; (*arte*) confectionery.

pasticci'are [pastit'tʃare] *vt* to mess up, make a mess of // *vi* to make a mess.

pasticci'ere, a [pastit'tʃɛre] *sm/f* pastrycook; confectioner.

pas'ticcio [pas'tittʃo] *sm* (*CUC*) pie;

(*lavoro disordinato, imbroglio*) mess; trovarsi nel ~1 to get into trouble.

pasti'ficio [pasti'fitʃo] *sm* pasta factory.

pas'tiglia [pas'tiʎʎa] *sf* pastille, lozenge.

pas'tina *sf* small pasta shapes used in soup.

pasti'naca, che *sf* parsnip.

'pasto *sm* meal.

pas'tore *sm* shepherd; (*REL*) pastor, minister; (*anche*: cane ~) sheepdog.

pastoriz'zare [pastorid'dzare] *vt* to pasteurize.

pas'toso, a *ag* doughy; pasty; (*fig: voce, colore*) mellow, soft.

pas'trano *sm* greatcoat.

pas'tura *sf* pasture.

pa'tata *sf* potato; ~e fritte chips (*Brit*), French fries; **pata'tine** *sfpl* (*potato*) crisps.

pata'trac *sm* (*crollo: anche fig*) crash.

pa'tella *sf* (*ZOOL*) limpet.

pa'tema, i *sm* anxiety, worry.

pa'tente *sf* licence; (*anche*: ~ di guida) driving licence (*Brit*), driver's license (*US*).

paternità *sf* paternity, fatherhood.

pa'terno, a *ag* (*affetto, consigli*) fatherly; (*casa, autorità*) paternal.

pa'tetico, a, ci, che *ag* pathetic; (*commovente*) moving, touching.

pa'tibolo *sm* gallows *sg*, scaffold.

'patina *sf* (*su rame etc*) patina; (*sulla lingua*) fur, coating.

pa'tire *vt, vi* to suffer.

pa'tito, a *sm/f* enthusiast, fan, lover.

patolo'gia [patolo'dʒia] *sf* pathology; **pato'logico, a, ci, che** *ag* pathological.

'patria *sf* homeland.

patri'arca, chi *sm* patriarch.

pa'trigno [pa'triɲɲo] *sm* stepfather.

patri'monio *sm* estate, property; (*fig*) heritage.

patri'ota, i, e *sm/f* patriot; **patri'ottico, a, ci, che** *ag* patriotic; **patriot'tismo** *sm* patriotism.

patroci'nare [patrotʃi'nare] *vt* (*DIR: difendere*) to defend; (*sostenere*) to sponsor, support; **patro'cinio** *sm* defence; support, sponsorship.

patro'nato *sm* patronage; (*istituzione benefica*) charitable institution o society.

pa'trono *sm* (*REL*) patron saint; (*socio di patronato*) patron; (*DIR*) counsel.

'patta *sf* flap; (*dei pantaloni*) fly.

patteggi'are [patted'dʒare] *vt, vi* to negotiate.

patti'naggio [patti'naddʒo] *sm* skating.

patti'nare *vi* to skate; ~ sul ghiaccio to ice-skate; **pattina'tore, 'trice** *sm/f* skater; **'pattino** *sm* skate; (*di slitta*) runner; (*AER*) skid; (*TECN*) sliding block; **pattini** (*da ghiaccio*) (ice) skates; **pattini a rotelle** roller skates; [pat'tino] (*barca*) kind of pedalo with oars.

'patto *sm* (*accordo*) pact, agreement;

(*condizione*) term, condition; **a ~ che** on condition that.

pat'tuglia |pat'tuʎʎa| *sf* (*MIL*) patrol.

pattu'ire *vt* to reach an agreement on.

pattumi'era *sf* (dust)bin (*Brit*), ashcan (*US*).

pa'ura *sf* fear; **aver ~ di/di fare/che** to be frightened *o* afraid of/of doing/that; **far ~ a** to frighten; **per ~ di/che** for fear of/that; **pau'roso, a** *ag* (*che fa paura*) frightening; (*che ha paura*) fearful, timorous.

'pausa *sf* (*sosta*) break; (*nel parlare, MUS*) pause.

pavi'mento *sm* floor.

pa'vone *sm* peacock; **pavoneggi'arsi** *vr* to strut about, show off.

pazien'tare |pattsjen'tare| *vi* to be patient.

pazi'ente |pat'tsjɛnte| *ag, sm/f* patient; **pazi'enza** *sf* patience.

paz'zesco, a, schi, sche |pat'tsesko| *ag* mad, crazy.

paz'zia |pat'tsia| *sf* (*MED*) madness, insanity; (*azione*) folly; (*di azione, decisione*) madness, folly.

'pazzo, a |'pattso| *ag* (*MED*) mad, insane; (*strano*) wild, mad // *sm/f* madman/woman; **~ di** (*gioia, amore etc*) mad *o* crazy with; **~ per qc/qn** mad *o* crazy about sth/sb.

PCI *sigla m* = *Partito Comunista Italiano.*

'pecca, che *sf* defect, flaw, fault.

peccami'noso, a *ag* sinful.

pec'care *vi* to sin; (*fig*) to err.

pec'cato *sm* sin; **è un ~ che** it's a pity that; **che ~!** what a shame *o* pity!

pecca'tore, 'trice *sm/f* sinner.

'pece |'petʃe| *sf* pitch.

Pe'chino |pe'kino| *sf* Peking.

'pecora *sf* sheep; **peco'raio** *sm* shepherd; **peco'rino** *sm* sheep's milk cheese.

peculi'are *ag*: **~ di** peculiar to.

pe'daggio |pe'daddʒo| *sm* toll.

pedago'gia |pedago'dʒia| *sf* pedagogy, educational methods *pl.*

peda'lare *vi* to pedal; (*andare in bicicletta*) to cycle.

pe'dale *sm* pedal.

pe'dana *sf* footboard; (*SPORT: nel salto*) springboard; (: *nella scherma*) piste.

pe'dante *ag* pedantic // *sm/f* pedant.

pe'data *sf* (*impronta*) footprint; (*colpo*) kick; **prendere a ~e qn/qc** to kick sb/sth.

pede'rasta, i *sm* pederast; homosexual.

pedi'atra, i, e *sm/f* paediatrician; **pedia'tria** *sf* paediatrics *sg.*

pedi'cure *sm/f inv* chiropodist.

pe'dina *sf* (*della dama*) draughtsman (*Brit*), draftsman (*US*); (*fig*) pawn.

pedi'nare *vt* to shadow, tail.

pedo'nale *ag* pedestrian.

pe'done, a *sm/f* pedestrian // *sm*

(*SCACCHI*) pawn.

'peggio |'peddʒo| *av, ag inv* worse // *sm o f*: **il o la ~** the worst; **alla ~** at worst, if the worst comes to the worst; **peggiora'mento** *sm* worsening; **peggio'rare** *vt* to make worse, worsen // *vi* to grow worse, worsen; **peggiora'tivo, a** *ag* pejorative; **peggi'ore** *ag* (*comparativo*) worse; (*superlativo*) worst // *sm/f*: **il(la) peggiore** the worst (person).

'pegno |'peɲɲo| *sm* (*DIR*) security, pledge; (*nei giochi di società*) forfeit; (*fig*) pledge, token; **dare in ~ qc** to pawn sth.

pe'lame *sm* (*di animale*) coat, fur.

pe'lare *vt* (*spennare*) to pluck; (*spellare*) to skin; (*sbucciare*) to peel; (*fig*) to make pay through the nose; **~rsi** *vr* to go bald.

pe'lame *sm* skins *pl*, hides *pl.*

'pelle *sf* skin; (*di animale*) skin, hide; (*cuoio*) leather; **avere la ~ d'oca** to have goose pimples *o* goose flesh.

pellegri'naggio |pellegri'naddʒo| *sm* pilgrimage.

pelle'grino, a *sm/f* pilgrim.

pelle'rossa, pelli'rossa, *pl* **pelli'rosse** *sm/f* Red Indian.

pellette'ria *sf* leather goods *pl*; (*negozio*) leather goods shop.

pelli'cano *sm* pelican.

pellicce'ria |pellittʃe'ria| *sf* (*negozio*) furrier's (shop); (*quantità di pellicce*) furs *pl.*

pel'liccia, ce |pel'littʃa| *sf* (*mantello di animale*) coat, fur; (*indumento*) fur coat.

pel'licola *sf* (*membrana sottile*) film, layer; (*FOT, CINEMA*) film.

'pelo *sm* hair; (*pelame*) coat, hair; (*pelliccia*) fur; (*di tappeto*) pile; (*di liquido*) surface; **per un ~**; **per un ~ non ho perduto il treno** I very nearly missed the train; **c'è mancato un ~ che** affogasse he escaped drowning by the skin of his teeth; **pe'loso, a** *ag* hairy.

'peltro *sm* pewter.

pe'luria *sf* down.

'pena *sf* (*DIR*) sentence; (*punizione*) punishment; (*sofferenza*) sadness *q*, sorrow; (*fatica*) trouble *q*, effort; (*difficoltà*) difficulty; **far ~** to be pitiful; **mi fai ~** I feel sorry for you; **prendersi o darsi la ~ di fare** to go to the trouble of doing; **~ di morte** death sentence; **~ pecuniaria** fine; **pe'nale** *ag* penal; **penalità** *sf inv* penalty; **penaliz'zare** *vt* (*SPORT*) to penalize.

pe'nare *vi* (*patire*) to suffer; (*faticare*) to struggle.

pen'dente *ag* hanging; leaning // *sm* (*ciondolo*) pendant; (*orecchino*) drop earring; **pen'denza** *sf* slope, slant; (*grado d'inclinazione*) gradient; (*ECON*) outstanding account.

'**pendere** vi (essere appeso): ~ **da** to hang from; (essere inclinato) to lean; (fig: incombere): ~ **su** to hang over.

pen'dio, 'dii sm slope, slant; (luogo in pendenza) slope.

'**pendola** sf pendulum clock.

pendo'lare smf commuter.

'**pendolo** sm (peso) pendulum; (anche: orologio a ~) pendulum clock.

'**pene** sm penis.

pene'trante ag piercing, penetrating.

pene'trare vi to come o get in // vt to penetrate); ~ **in** to enter; (sog: proiettile) to penetrate; (: acqua, aria) to go o come into.

penicil'lina [penitfil'lina] sf penicillin.

pe'nisola sf peninsula.

peni'tenza [peni'tentsa] sf penitence; (punizione) penance.

penitenzi'ario [peniten'tsjarjo] sm prison.

'**penna** sf (di uccello) feather; (per scrivere) pen; ~**e** sfpl (CUC) quills (type of pasta); ~ **a feltro/ stilografica/a sfera** felt-tip/fountain/ballpoint pen.

penna'rello sm felt-(tip) pen.

pennel'lare vi to paint.

pen'nello sm brush; (per dipingere) (paint)brush; **a** ~ (perfettamente) to perfection, perfectly; ~ **per la barba** shaving brush.

pen'nino sm nib.

pen'none sm (NAUT) yard; (stendardo) banner, standard.

pe'nombra sf half-light, dim light.

pe'noso, a ag painful, distressing; (faticoso) tiring, laborious.

pen'sare vi to think // vt to think; (inventare, escogitare) to think out; ~ **a** to think of; (amico, vacanze) to think of o about; (problema) to think about; ~ **di fare qc** to think of doing sth; **ci penso io** I'll see to o take care of it.

pensi'ero sm thought; (modo di pensare, dottrina) thinking g; (preoccupazione) worry, care, trouble; **stare in** ~ **per qn** to be worried about sb; **pensie'roso, a** ag thoughtful.

'**pensile** ag hanging.

pensio'nante smf (presso una famiglia) lodger; (di albergo) guest.

pensio'nato, a smf pensioner.

pensi'one sf (al prestatore di lavoro) pension; (vitto e alloggio) board and lodging; (albergo) boarding house; **andare in** ~ to retire; **mezza** ~ half board; ~ **completa** full board.

pen'soso, a ag thoughtful, pensive, lost in thought.

pentapar'tito sm five-party government.

Pente'coste sf Pentecost, Whit Sunday (Brit).

penti'mento sm repentance, contrition.

pen'tirsi vr: ~ **di** to repent of; (rammaricarsi) to regret, be sorry for.

'**pentola** sf pot; ~ **a pressione** pressure cooker.

pe'nultimo, a ag last but one (Brit), next to last, penultimate.

pe'nuria sf shortage.

penzo'lare [pendzo'lare] vi to dangle, hang loosely; **penzo'loni** av dangling, hanging down; **stare penzoloni** to dangle, hang down.

'**pepe** sm pepper; ~ **macinato/in grani** ground/whole pepper.

pepe'rone sm pepper, capsicum; (piccante) chili.

pe'pita sf nugget.

per prep **1** (moto attraverso luogo) through; **i ladri sono passati** ~ **la finestra** the thieves got in (o out) through the window; **l'ho cercato** ~ **tutta la casa** I've searched the whole house o all over the house for it

2 (moto a luogo) for, to; **partire** ~ **la Germania/il mare** to leave for Germany/ the sea; **il treno** ~ **Roma** the Rome train, the train for o to Rome

3 (stato in luogo): **seduto/sdraiato** ~ **terra** sitting/lying on the ground

4 (tempo) for; ~ **anni/lungo tempo** for years/a long time; ~ **tutta l'estate** throughout the summer, all summer long; **lo rividi** ~ **Natale** I saw him again at Christmas; **lo faccio** ~ **lunedì** I'll do it for Monday

5 (mezzo, maniera) by; ~ **lettera/via aerea/ferrovia** by letter/airmail/rail; **prendere qn** ~ **un braccio** to take sb by the arm

6 (causa, scopo) for; **assente** ~ **malattia** absent because of o through o owing to illness; **ottimo** ~ **il mal di gola** excellent for sore throats

7 (limitazione) for; **è troppo difficile** ~ **lui** it's too difficult for him; ~ **quel che mi riguarda** as far as I'm concerned; ~ **poco che sia** however little it may be; ~ **questa volta ti perdono** I'll forgive you this time

8 (prezzo, misura) for; (distributivo) a, per; **venduto** ~ **3 milioni** sold for 3 million; **1000 lire** ~ **persona** 1000 lire a o per person; **uno** ~ **volta** one at a time; **uno** ~ **uno** one by one; **5** ~ **cento** 5 per cent; **3** ~ **4 fa 12** 3 times 4 equals 12; **dividere/moltiplicare 12** ~ **4** to divide/ multiply 12 by 4

9 (in qualità di) as; (al posto di) for; **avere qn** ~ **professore** to have sb as a teacher; **ti ho preso** ~ **Mario** I mistook you for Mario, I though you were Mario; **dare** ~ **morto qn** to give sb up for dead

10 (seguito da vb: finale): ~ **fare qc** (so as) to do sth, in order to do sth; (: causale): ~ **aver fatto qc** for having done sth; (: consecutivo): **è abbastanza**

grande ~ andarci da solo he's big enough to go on his own.

'pera *sf* pear.

pe'raltro *av* moreover, what's more.

per'bene *ag inv* respectable, decent // *av* (*con cura*) properly, well.

percentu'ale |pertʃentu'ale| *sf* percentage.

perce'pire |pertʃe'pire| *vt* (*sentire*) to perceive; (*ricevere*) to receive; **percezi'one** *sf* perception.

perché |per'ke| ◆ *av* why; ~ no? why not?; ~ non vuoi andarci? why don't you want to go?; spiegami ~ l'hai fatto tell me why you did it ◆ *cong* 1 (*causale*) because; non posso uscire ~ ho da fare I can't go out because o as I've a lot to do 2 (*finale*) in order that, so that; te lo do ~ tu lo legga I'm giving it to you so (that) you can read it 3 (*consecutivo*): è troppo forte ~ si possa batterlo he's too strong to be beaten ◆ *sm inv* reason; il ~ di the reason for.

perciò |per'tʃɔ| *cong* so, for this (o that) reason.

per'correre *vt* (*luogo*) to go all over; (: *paese*) to travel up and down, go all over; (*distanza*) to cover.

per'corso, a *pp di* **percorrere** // *sm* (*tragitto*) journey; (*tratto*) route.

per'cosso, a *pp di* **percuotere** // *sf* blow.

percu'otere *vt* to hit, strike.

percussi'one *sf* percussion; strumenti a ~ (*MUS*) percussion instruments.

'perdere *vt* to lose; (*lasciarsi sfuggire*) to miss; (*sprecare: tempo, denaro*) to waste; (*mandare in rovina: persona*) to ruin // *vi* to lose; (*serbatoio etc*) to leak; ~rsi *vr* (*smarrirsi*) to get lost; (*svanire*) to disappear, vanish; saper ~ to be a good loser; lascia ~! forget it!, never mind!

perdigi'orno |perdi'dʒorno| *sm/f inv* idler, waster.

'perdita *sf* loss; (*spreco*) waste; (*fuoriuscita*) leak; siamo in ~ (*COMM*) we are running at a loss; a ~ d'occhio as far as the eye can see.

perdi'tempo *sm/f inv* waster, idler.

perdo'nare *vt* to pardon, forgive; (*scusare*) to excuse, pardon.

per'dono *sm* forgiveness; (*DIR*) pardon.

perdu'rare *vi* to go on, last; (*perseverare*) to persist.

perduta'mente *av* desperately, passionately.

per'duto, a *pp di* **perdere**.

peregri'nare *vi* to wander, roam.

pe'renne *ag* eternal, perpetual, perennial; (*BOT*) perennial.

peren'torio, a *ag* peremptory; (*definitivo*) final.

per'fetto, a *ag* perfect // *sm* (*LING*) perfect (tense).

perfezio'nare |perfettsjo'nare| *vt* to improve, perfect; ~rsi *vr* to improve.

perfezi'one |perfet'tsjone| *sf* perfection.

'perfido, a *ag* perfidious, treacherous.

per'fino *av* even.

perfo'rare *vt* to perforate; to punch a hole (o holes) in; (*banda, schede*) to punch; (*trivellare*) to drill; **perfora'tore, 'trice** *sm/f* punch-card operator // *sm* (*utensile*) punch; (*INFORM*): perforatore di schede card punch // *sf* (*TECN*) boring o drilling machine; (*INFORM*) card punch; **perforazi'one** *sf* perforation; punching; drilling; (*INFORM*) punch; (*MED*) perforation.

perga'mena *sf* parchment.

perico'lante *ag* precarious.

pe'ricolo *sm* danger; mettere in ~ to endanger, put in danger; **perico'loso, a** *ag* dangerous.

perife'ria *sf* periphery; (*di città*) outskirts *pl*.

pe'rifrasi *sf* circumlocution.

pe'rimetro *sm* perimeter.

peri'odico, a, ci, che *ag* periodic(al); (*MAT*) recurring // *sm* periodical.

pe'riodo *sm* period.

peripe'zie |peripet'tsie| *sfpl* ups and downs, vicissitudes.

pe'rire *vi* to perish, die.

pe'rito, a *ag* expert, skilled // *sm/f* expert; (*agronomo, navale*) surveyor; un ~ chimico a qualified chemist.

pe'rizia |pe'rittsja| *sf* (*abilità*) ability; (*giudizio tecnico*) expert opinion; expert's report.

'perla *sf* pearl; **per'lina** *sf* bead.

perlus'trare *vt* to patrol.

perma'loso, a *ag* touchy.

perma'nente *ag* permanent // *sf* permanent wave, perm; **perma'nenza** *sf* permanence; (*soggiorno*) stay.

perma'nere *vi* to remain.

perme'are *vt* to permeate.

per'messo, a *pp di* **permettere** // *sm* (*autorizzazione*) permission, leave; (*dato a militare, impiegato*) leave; (*licenza*) licence, permit; (*MIL: foglio*) pass; ~?, è ~? (*posso entrare?*) may I come in?; (*posso passare?*) excuse me; ~ di lavoro/pesca work/fishing permit.

per'mettere *vt* to allow, permit; ~ a qn qc/di fare to allow sb sth/to do; ~rsi qc/di fare to allow o.s. sth/to do; (*avere la possibilità*) to afford sth/to do.

per'nacchia |per'nakkja| *sf* (*fam*): fare una ~ to blow a raspberry.

per'nice |per'nitʃe| *sf* partridge.

'perno *sm* pivot.

pernot'tare *vi* to spend the night, stay overnight.

'pero *sm* pear tree.

però *cong* (*ma*) but; (*tuttavia*) however,

nevertheless.

pero'rare vt (DIR, fig): ~ la causa di qn to plead sb's case.

perpendico'lare ag, sf perpendicular.

perpe'trare vt to perpetrate.

perpetu'are vt to perpetuate.

per'petuo, a ag perpetual.

per'plesso, a ag perplexed; uncertain, undecided.

perqui'sire vt to search; **perquisizi'one** sf (police) search.

persecu'tore sm persecutor.

persecuzi'one [persekut'tsjone] sf persecution.

persegu'ire vt to pursue.

persegui'tare vt to persecute.

perseve'rante ag persevering.

perseve'rare vi to persevere.

'**Persia** sf: la ~ Persia.

persi'ano, a ag, sm/f Persian // sf shutter; ~a avvolgibile Venetian blind.

'**persico, a, ci, che** ag: il golfo P~ the Persian Gulf.

per'sino av = perfino.

persis'tente ag persistent.

per'sistere vi to persist; ~ a fare to persist in doing; **persis'tito, a** pp di **persistere**.

'**perso, a** pp di **perdere**.

per'sona sf person; (qualcuno): una ~ someone, somebody; (espressione interrogativa + anyone o anybody); ~e sfpl people; **non c'è ~ che ...** there's nobody who ..., there isn't anybody who ....

perso'naggio [perso'naddʒo] sm (persona ragguardevole) personality, figure; (tipo) character, individual; (LETTERATURA) character.

perso'nale ag personal // sm staff; personnel; (figura fisica) build.

personalità sf inv personality.

personifi'care vt to personify; to embody.

perspi'cace [perspi'katʃe] ag shrewd, discerning.

persu'adere vt: ~ qn (di qc/a fare) to persuade sb (of sth/to do); **persuasi'one** sf persuasion; **persua'sivo, a** ag persuasive; **persu'aso, a** pp di **persuadere**.

per'tanto cong (quindi) so, therefore.

'**pertica, che** sf pole.

perti'nente ag: ~ (a) relevant (to), pertinent (to).

per'tosse sf whooping cough.

per'tugio [per'tudʒo] sm hole, opening.

pertur'bare vt to disrupt; (persona) to disturb, perturb; **perturbazi'one** sf disruption; perturbation; **perturbazione atmosferica** atmospheric disturbance.

per'vadere vt to pervade; **per'vaso, a** pp di **pervadere**.

perve'nire vi: ~ a to reach, arrive at, come to; (venire in possesso): gli pervenne una fortuna he inherited a fortune; far ~ qc a to have sth sent to; **perve'nuto, a** pp di **pervenire**.

per'verso, a ag depraved; perverse.

perver'tire vt to pervert.

p. es. abbr (= per esempio) e.g.

'**pesa** sf weighing q; weighbridge.

pe'sante ag heavy; (fig: noioso) dull, boring.

pe'sare vt to weigh // vi (avere un peso) to weigh; (essere pesante) to be heavy; (fig) to carry weight; ~ su (fig) to lie heavy on; to influence; to hang over; **mi pesa sgridarlo** I find it hard to scold him.

'**pesca** sf (pl pesche: frutto) peach; (il pescare) fishing; **andare a** ~ to go fishing; ~ **di beneficenza** (lotteria) lucky dip; ~ **con la lenza** angling.

pes'care vt (pesce) to fish for; to catch; (qc nell'acqua) to fish out; (fig: trovare) to get hold of, find.

pesca'tore sm fisherman; angler.

'**pesce** ['peʃʃe] sm fish gen inv; **P~i** (dello zodiaco) Pisces; ~ **d'aprile!** April Fool!; ~ **spada** swordfish; **pesce'cane** sm shark.

pesche'reccio [peske'rettʃo] sm fishing boat.

pesche'ria [peske'ria] sf fishmonger's (shop) (Brit), fish store (US).

peschi'era [pes'kjera] sf fishpond.

pesci'vendolo, a [peʃʃi'vendolo] sm/f fishmonger (Brit), fish merchant (US).

'**pesco, schi** sm peach tree.

pes'coso, a ag abounding in fish.

'**peso** sm weight; (SPORT) shot; **rubare sul** ~ to give short weight; **essere di** ~ **a qn** (fig) to be a burden to sb; ~ **lordo/netto** gross/net weight; ~ **piuma/mosca/gallo/medio/massimo** (PUGILATO) feather/fly/bantam/middle/heavyweight.

pessi'mismo sm pessimism; **pessi'mista, i, e** ag pessimistic // sm/f pessimist.

'**pessimo, a** ag very bad, awful.

pes'tare vt to tread on, trample on; (sale, pepe) to grind; (uva, aglio) to crush; (fig: picchiare): ~ **qn** to beat sb up.

'**peste** sf plague; (persona) nuisance, pest.

pes'tello sm pestle.

pesti'lenza [pesti'lentsa] sf pestilence; (fetore) stench.

'**pesto, a** ag: **c'è buio** ~ it's pitch-dark; **occhio** ~ black eye // sm (CUC) sauce made with basil, garlic, cheese and oil.

'**petalo** sm (BOT) petal.

pe'tardo sm firecracker, banger (Brit).

petizi'one [petit'tsjone] sf petition.

'**peto** sm (fam!) fart (!).

petrol'chimica [petrol'kimika] sf petrochemical industry.

petroli'era sf (nave) oil tanker.

petro'lifero, a ag oil-bearing; oil cpd.

pe'trolio *sm* oil, petroleum; (*per lampada, fornello*) paraffin.

pettego'lare *vi* to gossip.

pettego'lezzo [pettego'leddzo] *sm* gossip *q*; **fare ~i** to gossip.

pet'tegolo, a *ag* gossipy // *sm/f* gossip.

petti'nare *vt* to comb (the hair of); **~rsi** *vr* to comb one's hair; **pettina'tura** *sf* (*acconciatura*) hairstyle.

'pettine *sm* comb; (*ZOOL*) scallop.

petti'rosso *sm* robin.

'petto *sm* chest; (*seno*) breast, bust; (*CUC: di carne bovina*) brisket; (: *di pollo etc*) breast; **a doppio ~** (*abito*) double-breasted; **petto'ruto, a** *ag* broad-chested; full-breasted.

petu'lante *ag* insolent.

'pezza ['pettsa] *sf* piece of cloth; (*toppa*) patch; (*cencio*) rag, cloth.

pez'zato, a [pet'tsato] *ag* piebald.

pez'zente [pet'tsɛnte] *sm/f* beggar.

'pezzo ['pettso] *sm* (*gen*) piece; (*brandello, frammento*) piece, bit; (*di macchina, arnese etc*) part; (*STAMPA*) article; (*di tempo*): **aspettare un ~** to wait quite a while *o* some time; **in *o* a ~i** in pieces; **andare in ~i** to break into pieces; **un bel ~ d'uomo** a fine figure of a man; **abito a due ~i** two-piece suit; **~ di cronaca** (*STAMPA*) report; **~ grosso** (*fig*) bigwig; **~ di ricambio** spare part.

pia'cente [pja'tʃɛnte] *ag* attractive, pleasant.

pia'cere [pja'tʃere] *vi* to please; **una ragazza che piace** a likeable girl; **an attractive girl; ~ a: mi piace** I like it; **quei ragazzi non mi piacciono** I don't like those boys; **gli piacerebbe andare al cinema** he would like to go to the cinema // *sm* pleasure; (*favore*) favour; "**~!**" (*nelle presentazioni*) "pleased to meet you!"; **con ~** certainly, with pleasure; **per ~!** please; **fare un ~ a qn** to do sb a favour; **pia'cevole** *ag* pleasant, agreeable; **piaci'uto, a** *pp di* **piacere**.

pi'aga, ghe *sf* (*lesione*) sore; (*ferita: anche fig*) wound; (*fig: flagello*) scourge, curse; (: *persona*) pest, nuisance.

piagnis'teo [pjaɲɲis'tɛo] *sm* whining, whimpering.

piagnuco'lare [pjaɲɲuko'lare] *vi* to whimper.

pi'alla *sf* (*arnese*) plane; **pial'lare** *vt* to plane.

pi'ana *sf* stretch of level ground; (*più esteso*) plain.

pianeggi'ante [pjaned'dʒante] *ag* flat, level.

piane'rottolo *sm* landing.

pia'neta *sm* (*ASTR*) planet.

pi'angere ['pjandʒere] *vi* to cry, weep; (*occhi*) to water // *vt* to cry, weep; (*lamentare*) to bewail, lament; **~ la morte di qn** to mourn sb's death.

pianifi'care *vt* to plan; **pianificazi'one** *sf* planning.

pia'nista, i, e *sm/f* pianist.

pi'ano, a *ag* (*piatto*) flat, level; (*MAT*) plane; (*facile*) straightforward, simple; (*chiaro*) clear, plain // *av* (*adagio*) slowly; (*a bassa voce*) softly; (*con cautela*) slowly, carefully // *sm* (*MAT*) plane; (*GEO*) plain; (*livello*) level, plane; (*di edificio*) floor; (*programma*) plan; (*MUS*) piano; **pian ~** very slowly; (*poco a poco*) little by little; **in primo/secondo ~** in the foreground/background; **di primo ~** (*fig*) prominent, high-ranking.

piano'forte *sm* piano, pianoforte.

pi'anta *sf* (*BOT*) plant; (*ANAT: anche: ~ del piede*) sole (of the foot); (*grafico*) plan; (*topografica*) map; **in ~ stabile** on the permanent staff; **piantagi'one** *sf* plantation; **pian'tare** *vt* to plant; (*conficcare*) to drive *o* hammer in; (*tenda*) to put up, pitch; (*fig: lasciare*) to leave, desert; **~rsi** *vr*: **~rsi davanti a qn** to plant o.s. in front of sb; **piantala!** (*fam*) cut it out!

pianter'reno *sm* ground floor.

pi'anto, a *pp di* **piangere** // *sm* tears *pl*, crying.

pian'tone *sm* (*vigilante*) sentry, guard; (*soldato*) orderly; (*AUT*) steering column.

pia'nura *sf* plain.

pi'astra *sf* plate; (*di pietra*) slab; (*di fornello*) hotplate; **~ di registrazione** tape deck; **panino alla ~** ≈ toasted sandwich.

pias'trella *sf* tile.

pias'trina *sf* (*MIL*) identity disc.

piatta'forma *sf* (*anche fig*) platform.

piat'tino *sm* saucer.

pi'atto, a *ag* flat; (*fig: scialbo*) dull // *sm* (*recipiente, vivanda*) dish; (*portata*) course; (*parte piana*) flat (part); **~i** *smpl* (*MUS*) cymbals; **~ fondo** soup dish; **~ forte** main course; **~ del giorno** dish of the day, plat du jour; **~ del giradischi** turntable; **~i già pronti** (*CULIN*) ready-cooked dishes.

pi'azza ['pjattsa] *sf* square; (*COMM*) market; **far ~ pulita** to make a clean sweep; **~ d'armi** (*MIL*) parade ground; **piaz'zale** *sm* (large) square.

piaz'zare [pjat'tsare] *vt* to place; (*COMM*) to market, sell; **~rsi** *vr* (*SPORT*) to be placed.

piaz'zista, i [pjat'tsista] *sm* (*COMM*) commercial traveller.

piaz'zola [pjat'tsɔla] *sf* (*AUT*) lay-by.

'picca, che *sf* pike; **~che** *sfpl* (*CARTE*) spades.

pic'cante *ag* hot, pungent; (*fig*) racy; biting.

pic'carsi *vr*: **~ di fare** to pride o.s. on one's ability to do; **~ per qc** to take offence at sth.

pic'chetto |pik'kɛtto| *sm* (*MIL*, *di scioperanti*) picket.

picchi'are |pik'kjare| *vt* (*persona*: *colpire*) to hit, strike; (: *prendere a botte*) to beat (up); (*battere*) to beat; (*sbattere*) to bang // *vi* (*bussare*) to knock; (: *con forza*) to bang; (*colpire*) to hit, strike; (*sole*) to beat down; **picchi'ata** *sf* (*percosse*) beating, thrashing; (*AER*) dive.

picchiet'tare |pikkjet'tare| *vt* (*punteggiare*) to spot, dot; (*colpire*) to tap.

'picchio |'pikkjo| *sm* woodpecker.

pic'cino, a |pit'tʃino| *ag* tiny, very small.

piccio'naia |pittʃo'naja| *sf* pigeon-loft; (*TEATRO*): la ~ the gods *sg*.

picci'one |pit'tʃone| *sm* pigeon.

'picco, chi *sm* peak; a ~ vertically.

'piccolo, a *ag* small; (*oggetto, mano, di età*: *bambino*) small, little (*dav sostantivo*); (*di breve durata*: *viaggio*) short; (*fig*) mean, petty // *sm/f* child, little one; ~i *smpl* (*di animale*) young *pl*; in ~ in miniature.

pic'cone *sm* pick(-axe).

pic'cozza |pik'kɔttsa| *sf* ice-axe.

pic'nic *sm inv* picnic.

pi'docchio |pi'dɔkkjo| *sm* louse.

pi'ede *sm* foot; (*di mobile*) leg; in ~i standing; a ~i on foot; a ~i nudi barefoot; su due ~i (*fig*) at once; **prendere ~** (*fig*) to gain ground, catch on; **sul ~ di guerra** (*MIL*) ready for action; ~ **di porco** crowbar.

piedis'tallo, piedes'tallo *sm* pedestal.

pi'ega, ghe *sf* (*piegatura, GEO*) fold; (*di gonna*) pleat; (*di pantaloni*) crease; (*grinza*) wrinkle, crease; **prendere una brutta ~** (*avvenimento*) to take a turn for the worse.

pie'gare *vt* to fold; (*braccia, gambe, testa*) to bend // *vi* to bend; ~**rsi** *vr* to bend; (*fig*): ~**rsi (a)** to yield (to), submit (to); **pieghet'tare** *vt* to pleat; **pie'ghevole** *ag* pliable, flexible; (*porta*) folding; (*fig*) yielding, docile.

Pie'monte *sm*: il ~ Piedmont.

pi'ena *sf vedi* pieno.

pi'eno, a *ag* full; (*muro, mattone*) solid // *sm* (*colmo*) height, peak; (*carico*) full load // *sf* (*di fiume*) flood, spate; (*gran folla*) crowd, throng; ~ **di** full of; **in ~ giorno** in broad daylight; **fare il ~** (*di benzina*) to fill up (with petrol).

pietà *sf* pity; (*REL*) piety; **senza ~** pitiless, merciless; **avere ~ di** (*compassione*) to pity, feel sorry for; (*misericordia*) to have pity o mercy on.

pie'tanza |pje'tantsa| *sf* dish; (main) course.

pie'toso, a *ag* (*compassionevole*) pitying, compassionate; (*che desta pietà*) pitiful.

pi'etra *sf* stone; ~ **preziosa** precious

stone, gem; **pie'traia** *sf* (*terreno*) stony ground; **pietrifi'care** *vt* to petrify; (*fig*) to transfix, paralyze.

'piffero *sm* (*MUS*) pipe.

pigi'ama, i |pi'dʒama| *sm* pyjamas *pl*.

'pigia 'pigia |'pidʒa'pidʒa| *sm* crowd, press.

pigi'are |pi'dʒare| *vt* to press.

pigi'one |pi'dʒone| *sf* rent.

pigli'are |piʎ'ʎare| *vt* to take, grab; (*afferrare*) to catch.

'piglio |'piʎʎo| *sm* look, expression.

pig'meo, a *sm/f* pygmy.

'pigna |'piɲɲa| *sf* pine cone.

pi'gnolo, a |piɲ'ɲɔlo| *ag* pernickety.

pigo'lare *vi* to cheep, chirp.

pi'grizia |pi'grittsja| *sf* laziness.

'pigro, a *ag* lazy.

'pila *sf* (*catasta, di ponte*) pile; (*ELETTR*) battery; (*fam*: *torcia*) torch (*Brit*), flashlight.

pi'lastro *sm* pillar.

'pillola *sf* pill; **prendere la ~** to be on the pill.

pi'lone *sm* (*di ponte*) pier; (*di linea elettrica*) pylon.

pi'lota, i, e *sm/f* pilot; (*AUT*) driver // *ag inv* pilot *cpd*; ~ **automatico** automatic pilot; **pilo'tare** *vt* to pilot; to drive.

pi'mento *sm* pimento, allspice.

pinaco'teca, che *sf* art gallery.

pi'neta *sf* pinewood.

ping-'pong |piŋ'pɔn| *sm* table tennis.

'pingue *ag* fat, corpulent.

pingu'ino *sm* (*ZOOL*) penguin.

'pinna *sf* fin; (*di pinguino, spatola di gomma*) flipper.

'pino *sm* pine (tree); **pi'nolo** *sm* pine kernel.

'pinza |'pintsa| *sf* pliers *pl*; (*MED*) forceps *pl*; (*ZOOL*) pincer.

pinzette |pin'tsette| *sfpl* tweezers.

'pio, a, 'pii, 'pie *ag* pious; (*opere, istituzione*) charitable, charity *cpd*.

pi'oggia, ge |'pjɔddʒa| *sf* rain; ~ **acida** acid rain.

pi'olo *sm* peg; (*di scala*) rung.

piom'bare *vi* to fall heavily; (*gettarsi con impeto*): ~ **su** to fall upon, assail // *vt* (*dente*) to fill; **piomba'tura** *sf* (*di dente*) filling.

piom'bino *sm* (*sigillo*) (lead) seal; (*del filo a piombo*) plummet; (*PESCA*) sinker.

pi'ombo *sm* (*CHIM*) lead; (*sigillo*) (lead) seal; (*proiettile*) (lead) shot; **a ~** (*cadere*) straight down.

pioni'ere, a *sm/f* pioneer.

pi'oppo *sm* poplar.

pi'overe *vb impers* to rain // *vi* (*fig*: *scendere dall'alto*) to rain down; (: *affluire in gran numero*): ~ **in** to pour into; **piovigginare** *vb impers* to drizzle; **pio'voso, a** *ag* rainy.

pi'ovra *sf* octopus.

'pipa *sf* pipe.

pipì *sf* (*fam*): **fare ~** to have a wee (wee).

pipis'trello *sm* (*ZOOL*) bat.

pi'ramide *sf* pyramid.

pi'rata, i *sm* pirate; **~ della strada** hit-and-run driver.

Pire'nei *smpl*: **i ~** the Pyrenees.

'pirico, a, ci, che *ag*: **polvere ~a** gunpowder.

pi'rite *sf* pyrite.

pi'rofilo, a *ag* heat-resistant.

pi'roga, ghe *sf* dug-out canoe.

pi'romane *smf* pyromaniac, arsonist.

pi'roscafo *sm* steamer, steamship.

pisci'are [pif'fare] *vi* (*fam!*) to piss (!), **pee** (!).

pi'scina [pif'fina] *sf* (swimming) pool; (*stabilimento*) (swimming) baths *pl*.

pi'sello *sm* pea.

piso'lino *sm* nap.

'pista *sf* (*traccia*) track, trail; (*di stadio*) track; (*di pattinaggio*) rink; (*da sci*) run; (*AER*) runway; (*di circo*) ring; **~ da ballo** dance floor.

pis'tacchio [pis'takkjo] *sm* pistachio (tree); pistachio (nut).

pis'tola *sf* pistol, gun.

pis'tone *sm* piston.

pi'tone *sm* python.

pit'tore, 'trice *smf* painter; **pitto'resco, a, schi, sche** *ag* picturesque.

pit'tura *sf* painting; **pittu'rare** *vt* to paint.

più ◆ *av* 1 (*in maggiore quantità*) more; **~ del solito** more than usual; **in ~, di ~** more; **ne voglio di ~** I want some more; **ci sono 3 persone in o di ~** there are 3 more o extra people; **~ o meno** more or less; **per di ~** (*inoltre*) what's more, moreover

2 (*comparativo*) more, *aggettivo corto* + ...er; **~ ... di/che** more ... than; **lavoro ~ di te/Paola** I work harder than you/Paola; **è ~ intelligente che ricco** he's more intelligent than rich

3 (*superlativo*) most, *aggettivo corto* + ...est; **il ~ grande/intelligente** the biggest/most intelligent; **è quello che compro ~ spesso** that's the one I buy most often; **al ~ presto** as soon as possible; **al ~ tardi** at the latest

4 (*negazione*): **non ... ~** no more, no longer; **non ho ~ soldi** I've got no more money, I don't have any more money; **non lavoro ~** I'm no longer working, I don't work any more; **a ~ non posso** (*gridare*) at the top of one's voice; (*correre*) as fast as one can

5 (*MAT*) plus; **4 ~ 5 fa 9** 4 plus 5 equals 9; **~ 5 gradi** 5 degrees above freezing, plus 5

◆ *prep* plus

◆ *ag inv* 1: **~ ... (di)** more ... (than); **~ denaro/tempo** more money/time; **~**

persone di quante ci aspettassimo more people than we expected

2 (*numerosi, diversi*) several; **l'aspettai per ~ giorni** I waited for it for several days

◆ *sm* 1 (*la maggior parte*): **il ~ è fatto** most of it is done

2 (*MAT*) plus (sign)

3: **i ~** the majority.

piucchepper'fetto [pjukkepper'fetto] *sm* (*LING*) pluperfect, past perfect.

pi'uma *sf* feather; **~e** *sfpl* down *sg*; (*piumaggio*) plumage *sg*, feathers; **piu'maggio** *sm* plumage, feathers *pl*; **piu'mino** *sm* (eider)down; (*per letto*) eiderdown; (: *tipo danese*) duvet, continental quilt; (*giacca*) quilted jacket (with goose-feather padding); (*per cipria*) powder puff; (*per spolverare*) feather duster.

piut'tosto *av* rather; **~ che** (*anziché*) rather than.

pi'vello, a *smf* greenhorn.

'pizza ['pittsa] *sf* pizza; **pizze'ria** *sf* place where pizzas are made, sold or eaten.

pizzi'cagnolo, a [pittsi'kaɲnolo] *smf* specialist grocer.

pizzi'care [pittsi'kare] *vt* (*stringere*) to nip, pinch; (*pungere*) to sting; to bite; (*MUS*) to pluck // *vi* (*prudere*) to itch, be itchy; (*cibo*) to be hot o spicy.

pizziche'ria [pittsike'ria] *sf* delicatessen (shop).

'pizzico, chi ['pittsiko] *sm* (*pizzicotto*) pinch, nip; (*piccola quantità*) pinch, dash; (*d'insetto*) sting; bite.

pizzi'cotto [pittsi'kɔtto] *sm* pinch, nip.

'pizzo ['pittso] *sm* (*merletto*) lace; (*barbetta*) goatee beard.

pla'care *vt* to placate, soothe; **~rsi** *vr* to calm down.

'placca, che *sf* plate; (*con iscrizione*) plaque; (*anche*: **~ dentaria**) (dental) plaque; **plac'care** *vt* to plate; **placcato in oro/argento** gold-/silver-plated.

'placido, a ['platfido] *ag* placid, calm.

plagi'are [pla'dʒare] *vt* (*copiare*) to plagiarize; **'plagio** *sm* plagiarism.

pla'nare *vi* (*AER*) to glide.

'plancia, ce ['plantʃa] *sf* (*NAUT*) bridge.

plane'tario, a *ag* planetary // *sm* (*locale*) planetarium.

'plasma *sm* plasma.

plas'mare *vt* to mould, shape.

'plastico, a, ci, che *ag* plastic // *sm* (*rappresentazione*) relief model; (*esplosivo*): **bomba al ~** plastic bomb // *sf* (*arte*) plastic arts *pl*; (*MED*) plastic surgery; (*sostanza*) plastic.

plasti'lina *sf* ® plasticine ®.

'platano *sm* plane tree.

pla'tea *sf* (*TEATRO*) stalls *pl*.

'platino *sm* platinum.

pla'tonico, a, ci, che *ag* platonic.

plau'sibile *ag* plausible.

'plauso sm (fig) approval.

ple'baglia |ple'baʎʎa| sf (peg) rabble, mob.

'plebe sf common people; **ple'beo, a** ag plebeian; (volgare) coarse, common.

ple'nario, a ag plenary.

pleni'lunio sm full moon.

'plettro sm plectrum.

pleu'rite sf pleurisy.

'plico, chi sm (pacco) parcel; **in ~ a parte** (COMM) under separate cover.

plo'tone sm (MIL) platoon; **~ d'esecuzione** firing squad.

'plumbeo, a ag leaden.

plu'rale ag, sm plural; **pluralità** sf plurality; (maggioranza) majority.

plusva'lore sm (ECON) surplus.

pneu'matico, a, ci, che ag inflatable; pneumatic // sm (AUT) tyre (Brit), tire (US).

po' av, sm vedi **poco**.

'poco, a, chi, che ♦ ag 1 (quantità) little, not much; (numero) few, not many; **~ pane/denaro/spazio** little o not much bread/money/space; **~che persone/idee** few o not many people/ ideas; **ci vediamo tra ~** (sottinteso: tempo) see you soon

♦ av 1 (in piccola quantità) little, not much; (numero limitato) few, not many; **guadagna ~** he doesn't earn much, he earns little

2 (con ag, av) (a) little, not very; **sta ~ bene** he isn't very well; **è ~ più vecchia di lui** she's a little o slightly older than him

3 (tempo): **~ dopo/prima** shortly afterwards/before; **il film dura ~** the film doesn't last very long; **ci vediamo molto ~** we don't see each other very often, we hardly ever see each other

4: **un po'** a little, a bit; **è un po' corto** it's a little o bit short; **arriverà fra un po'** he'll arrive shortly o in a little while

5: **a dir ~** to say the least; **a ~ a ~** little by little; **per ~ non cadevo** I nearly fell; **è una cosa da ~** it's nothing, it's of no importance; **una persona da ~** a worthless person

♦ pronome (a) little; **~chi(che)** pronome pl (persone) few (people); (cose) few

♦ sm 1 little; **vive del ~ che ha** he lives on the little he has

2: **un po'** a little; **un po' di zucchero** a little sugar; **un bel po' di denaro** quite a lot of money; **un po' per ciascuno** a bit each.

po'dere sm (AGR) farm.

pode'roso, a ag powerful.

podestà sm inv (nel fascismo) podesta, mayor.

'podio sm dais, platform; (MUS) podium.

po'dismo sm (SPORT) track events pl.

po'ema, i sm poem.

poe'sia sf (arte) poetry; (componimento) poem.

po'eta, 'essa sm/f poet/poetess; **po'etico, a, ci, che** ag poetic(al).

poggi'are |pod'dʒare| vt to lean, rest; (posare) to lay, place; **poggia'testa** sm inv (AUT) headrest.

'poggio |'pɔddʒo| sm hillock, knoll.

'poi av then; (alla fine) finally, at last; **e ~** (inoltre) and besides; **questa ~ (è bella)!** (ironico) that's a good one!

poiché |poi'ke| cong since, as.

'poker sm poker.

po'lacco, a, chi, che ag Polish // sm/f Pole.

po'lare ag polar.

po'lemico, a, ci, che ag polemic(al), controversial // sf controversy.

po'lenta sf (CUC) sort of thick porridge made with maize flour.

poli'clinico, ci sm general hospital, polyclinic.

poli'estere sm polyester.

'polio(mie'lite) sf polio(myelitis).

'polipo sm polyp.

polisti'rolo sm polystyrene.

poli'tecnico, ci sm postgraduate technical college.

politiciz'zare |politit∫id'dzare| vt to politicize.

po'litico, a, ci, che ag political // sm/f politician // sf politics sg; (linea di condotta) policy.

poli'zia |polit'tsia| sf police; **~ giudiziaria** ≈ Criminal Investigation Department (CID) (Brit), ≈ Federal Bureau of Investigation (FBI) (US); **~ stradale** traffic police; **polizi'esco, a, schi, sche** ag police cpd; (film, romanzo) detective cpd; **polizi'otto** sm policeman; **cane poliziotto** police dog; **donna poliziotto** policewoman.

'polizza |'polittsa| sf (COMM) bill; **~ di assicurazione** insurance policy; **~ di carico** bill of lading.

pol'laio sm henhouse.

pol'lame sm poultry.

pol'lastro sm (ZOOL) cockerel.

'pollice |'pollit∫e| sm thumb.

'polline sm pollen.

'pollo sm chicken.

pol'mone sm lung; **polmo'nite** sf pneumonia.

'polo sm (GEO, FISICA) pole; (gioco) polo; **il ~ sud/nord** the South/North Pole.

Po'lonia sf: **la ~** Poland.

'polpa sf flesh, pulp; (carne) lean meat.

pol'paccio |pol'patt∫o| sm (ANAT) calf.

pol'petta sf (CUC) meatball; **polpet'tone** sm (CUC) meatloaf.

'polpo sm octopus.

pol'poso, a ag fleshy.

pol'sino sm cuff.

'polso sm (ANAT) wrist; (pulsazione) pulse; (fig: forza) drive, vigour.

pol'tiglia |pol'tiʎʎa| sf (composto) mash, mush; (di fango e neve) slush.

pol'trire vi to laze about.

pol'trona sf armchair; (TEATRO: posto) seat in the front stalls (Brit) o orchestra (US).

pol'trone ag lazy, slothful.

'polvere sf dust; (anche: ~ da sparo) (gun)powder; (sostanza ridotta minutissima) powder, dust; **latte in ~** dried o powdered milk; **caffè in ~** instant coffee; **sapone in ~** soap powder; **polveri'era** sf powder magazine; **polveriz'zare** vt to pulverize; (nebulizzare) to atomize; (fig) to crush, pulverize; to smash; **polve'rone** sm thick cloud of dust; **polve'roso, a** ag dusty.

po'mata sf ointment, cream.

po'mello sm knob.

pomeridi'ano, a ag afternoon cpd; **nelle ore ~e** in the afternoon.

pome'riggio |pome'riddʒo| sm afternoon.

'pomice |'pɔmitʃe| sf pumice.

'pomo sm (mela) apple; (ornamentale) knob; (di sella) pommel; **~ d'Adamo** (ANAT) Adam's apple.

pomo'doro sm tomato.

'pompa sf pump; (sfarzo) pomp (and ceremony); **~e funebri** funeral parlour sg (Brit), undertaker's sg; **pom'pare** vt to pump; (trarre) to pump out; (gonfiare d'aria) to pump up.

pom'pelmo sm grapefruit.

pompi'ere sm fireman.

pom'poso, a ag pompous.

ponde'rare vt to ponder over, consider carefully.

ponde'roso, a ag (anche fig) weighty.

po'nente sm west.

'ponte sm bridge; (di nave) deck; (: an che: ~ di comando) bridge; (impalcatura) scaffold; **fare il ~** (fig) to take the extra day off (between 2 public holidays); **governo ~** interim government; **~ aereo** airlift; **~ sospeso** suspension bridge.

pon'tefice |pon'tefitʃe| sm (REL) pontiff.

pontifi'care vi (anche fig) to pontificate.

ponti'ficio, a, ci, cie |ponti'fitʃo| ag papal.

popo'lano, a ag popular, of the people.

popo'lare ag popular; (quartiere, clientela) working-class // vt (rendere abitato) to populate; **~rsi** vr to fill with people, get crowded; **popolarità** sf popularity; **popolazi'one** sf population.

'popolo sm people; **popo'loso, a** ag densely populated.

po'pone sm melon.

'poppa sf (di nave) stern; (mammella) breast.

pop'pare vt to suck.

poppa'toio sm (feeding) bottle.

porcel'lana |portʃel'lana| sf porcelain, china; piece of china.

porcel'lino, a |portʃel'lino| sm/f piglet.

porche'ria |porke'ria| sf filth, muck; (fig: oscenità) obscenity; (: azione disonesta) dirty trick; (: cosa mal fatta) rubbish.

por'cile |por'tʃile| sm pigsty.

por'cino, a |por'tʃino| ag of pigs, pork cpd // sm (fungo) type of edible mushroom.

'porco, ci sm pig; (carne) pork.

porcos'pino sm porcupine.

'porgere |'pɔrdʒere| vt to hand, give; (tendere) to hold out.

pornogra'fia sf pornography; **porno'grafico, a, ci, che** ag pornographic.

'poro sm pore; **po'roso, a** ag porous.

'porpora sf purple.

'porre vt (mettere) to put; (collocare) to place; (posare) to lay (down), put (down); (fig: supporre): **poniamo (il caso) che ...** let's suppose that ...; **porsi** vr (mettersi): **porsi a sedere/in cammino** to sit down/set off; **~ una domanda a qn** to ask sb a question, put a question to sb.

'porro sm (BOT) leek; (MED) wart.

'porta sf door; (SPORT) goal; **~e spfl** (di città) gates; **a ~e chiuse** (DIR) in camera.

'porta... prefisso: **portaba'gagli** sm inv (facchino) porter; (AUT, FERR) luggage rack; **portabandi'era** sm inv standard bearer; **porta'cenere** sm inv ashtray; **portachi'avi** sm inv keyring; **porta'cipria** sm inv powder compact; **porta'erei** sf inv (nave) aircraft carrier // sm inv (aereo) aircraft transporter; **portafi'nestra**, pl **portefi'nestre** sf French window; **porta'foglio** sm (busta) wallet; (cartella) briefcase; (POL, BORSA) portfolio; **portafor'tuna** sm inv lucky charm; mascot; **portagi'oie** sm inv, **portagioi'elli** sm inv jewellery box.

porta'lettere sm/f inv postman/woman (Brit), mailman/woman (US).

porta'mento sm carriage, bearing.

portamo'nete sm inv purse.

por'tante ag (muro etc) supporting, load-bearing.

portan'tina sf sedan chair; (per ammalati) stretcher.

por'tare vt (sostenere, sorreggere: peso, bambino, pacco) to carry; (indossare: abito, occhiali) to wear; (: capelli lunghi) to have; (avere: nome, titolo) to have, bear; (recare): **~ qc a qn** to take (o bring) sth to sb; (fig: sentimenti) to bear; **~rsi** vr (recarsi) to go; **~ avanti** (discorso, idea) to pursue; **~ via** to take away; (rubare) to take; **~ i bambini a spasso** to take the children for a walk; **~**

fortuna to bring good luck.

portasiga'rette sm inv cigarette case.

por'tata sf (vivanda) course; (AUT) carrying (o loading) capacity; (di arma) range; (volume d'acqua) (rate of) flow; (fig: limite) scope, capability; (: importanza) impact, import; **alla ~ di tutti** (conoscenza) within everybody's capabilities; (prezzo) within everybody's means; **a/fuori ~** (di) within/out of reach (of); **a ~ di mano** within (arm's) reach.

por'tatile ag portable.

por'tato, a ag (incline): ~ **a** inclined o apt to.

porta'tore, 'trice sm/f (anche COMM) bearer; (MED) carrier.

portau'ovo sm inv eggcup.

porta'voce [porta'votʃe] sm/f inv spokesman/woman.

por'tento sm wonder, marvel.

'portico, ci sm portico.

porti'era sf (AUT) door.

porti'ere sm (portinaio) concierge, caretaker; (di hotel) porter; (nel calcio) goalkeeper.

porti'naio, a sm/f concierge, caretaker.

portine'ria sf caretaker's lodge.

'porto, a pp di **porgere** // sm (NAUT) harbour, port; (spesa di trasporto) carriage // sm inv port (wine); ~ **d'armi** (documento) gun licence.

Porto'gallo sm: **il ~** Portugal; **porto'ghese** ag, sm/f, sm Portuguese inv.

por'tone sm main entrance, main door.

portu'ale ag harbour cpd, port cpd // sm dock worker.

porzi'one [por'tsjone] sf portion, share; (di cibo) portion, helping.

'posa sf (FOT) exposure; (atteggiamento, di modello) pose.

po'sare vt to put (down), lay (down) // vi (ponte, edificio, teoria): ~ **su** to rest on; (FOT, atteggiarsi) to pose; **~rsi** vr (aereo) to land; (uccello) to alight; (sguardo) to settle.

po'sata sf piece of cutlery; **~e** sfpl cutlery sg.

po'sato, a ag serious.

pos'critto sm postscript.

posi'tivo, a ag positive.

posizi'one [pozit'tsjone] sf position; **prendere ~** (fig) to take a stand; **luci di ~** (AUT) sidelights.

posolo'gia, 'gie [pozolo'dʒia] sf dosage, directions pl for use.

pos'porre vt to place after; (differire) to postpone, defer; **pos'posto, a** pp di **posporre**.

posse'dere vt to own, possess; (qualità, virtù) to have, possess; (conoscere a fondo: lingua etc) to have a thorough knowledge of; (sog: ira etc) to possess; **possedi'mento** sm possession.

posses'sivo, a ag possessive.

pos'sesso sm ownership q; possession.

posses'sore sm owner.

pos'sibile ag possible // sm: **fare tutto il ~** to do everything possible; **nei limiti del ~** as far as possible; **al più tardi ~** as late as possible; **possibilità** sf inv possibility // sfpl (mezzi) means; **aver la possibilità di fare** to be in a position to do; to have the opportunity to do.

possi'dente sm/f landowner.

'posta sf (servizio) post, postal service; (corrispondenza) post, mail; (ufficio postale) post office; (nei giochi d'azzardo) stake; **~e** sfpl (amministrazione) post office; ~ **aerea** airmail; **ministro delle P~e e Telecomunicazioni** Postmaster General; **posta'giro** sm post office cheque, postal giro (Brit); **pos'tale** ag postal, post office cpd.

post'bellico, a, ci, che ag postwar.

posteggi'are [posted'dʒare] vt, vi to park; **pos'teggio** sm car park (Brit), parking lot (US); (di taxi) rank (Brit), stand (US).

postelegra'fonico, a, ci, che ag postal and telecommunications cpd.

posteri'ore ag (dietro) back; (dopo) later // sm (fam: sedere) behind.

pos'ticcio, a, ci, ce [pos'tittʃo] ag false // sm hairpiece.

postici'pare [postitʃi'pare] vt to defer, postpone.

pos'tilla sf marginal note.

pos'tino sm postman (Brit), mailman (US).

'posto, a pp di **porre** // sm (sito, posizione) place; (impiego) job; (spazio libero) room, space; (di parcheggio) space; (sedile: al teatro, in treno etc) seat; (MIL) post; **a ~** (in ordine) in place, tidy; (fig) settled; reliable; **al ~ di** in place of; **sul ~** on the spot; **mettere a ~** to tidy (up), put in order; (faccende) to straighten out; ~ **di blocco** roadblock; ~ **di polizia** police station.

pos'tribolo sm brothel.

'postumo, a ag posthumous; (tardivo) belated; **~i** smpl (conseguenze) after-effects, consequences.

po'tabile ag drinkable; **acqua ~** drinking water.

po'tare vt to prune.

po'tassio sm potassium.

po'tente ag (nazione) strong, powerful; (veleno, farmaco) potent, strong; **po'tenza** sf power; (forza) strength.

potenzi'ale [poten'tsjale] ag, sm potential.

po'tere ◆ sm power; **al ~** (partito etc) in power; ~ **d'acquisto** purchasing power ◆ vb ausiliare **1** (essere in grado di) can, be able to; **non ha potuto ripararlo** he couldn't o he wasn't able to repair it;

non è potuto venire he couldn't o he wasn't able to come; **spiacente di non poter aiutare** sorry not to be able to help **2** (avere il permesso) can, may, be allowed to; **posso entrare?** can o may I come in?; **si può sapere dove sei stato?** where on earth have you been? **3** (eventualità) may, might, could; **potrebbe essere vero** it might o could be true; **può aver avuto un incidente** he may o might o could have had an accident; **può darsi** perhaps; **può darsi o essere che non venga** he may o might not come **4** (augurio): **potessi almeno parlargli!** if only I could speak to him! **5** (suggerimento): **potresti almeno scusarti!** you could at least apologize! ◆ vt can, be able to; **può molto per noi** he can do a lot for us; **non ne posso più** (per stanchezza) I'm exhausted; (per rabbia) I can't take any more.

potestà sf (potere) power; (DIR) authority.

'povero, a ag poor; (disadorno) plain, bare // sm/f poor man/woman; **i ~i** the poor; **~ di** lacking in, having little; **povertà** sf poverty.

'pozza ['pottsa] sf pool.

poz'zanghera [pot'tsangera] sf puddle.

'pozzo ['pottso] sm well; (cava: di carbone) pit; (di miniera) shaft; **~ petrolifero** oil well.

pran'zare [pran'dzare] vi to dine, have dinner; to lunch, have lunch.

'pranzo ['prandzo] sm dinner; (a mezzogiorno) lunch.

'prassi sf usual procedure.

'pratica, che sf practice; (esperienza) experience; (conoscenza) knowledge, familiarity; (tirocinio) training, practice; (AMM: affare) matter, case; (: incartamento) file, dossier; **in ~** (praticamente) in practice; **mettere in ~** to put into practice.

prati'cabile ag (progetto) practicable, feasible; (luogo) passable, practicable.

prati'cante sm/f apprentice, trainee; (REL) (regular) churchgoer.

prati'care vt to practise; (SPORT: tennis etc) to play; (: nuoto, scherma etc) to go in for; (eseguire: apertura, buco) to make; **~ uno sconto** to give a discount.

'pratico, a, ci, che ag practical; **~ di** (esperto) experienced o skilled in; (familiare) familiar with.

'prato sm meadow; (di giardino) lawn.

preav'viso sm notice; **telefonata con ~** personal o person to person call.

pre'cario, a ag precarious; (INS) temporary.

precauzi'one [prekaut'tsjone] sf caution, care; (misura) precaution.

prece'dente [pretʃe'dɛnte] ag previous //

sm precedent; **il discorso/film ~** the previous o preceding speech/film; **senza ~i** unprecedented; **~i penali** criminal record sg; **prece'denza** sf priority, precedence; (AUT) right of way.

pre'cedere [pre'tʃedere] vt to precede, go (o come) before.

pre'cetto [pre'tʃetto] sm precept; (MIL) call-up notice.

precet'tore [pretʃet'tore] sm (private) tutor.

precipi'tare [pretʃipi'tare] vi (cadere) to fall headlong; (fig: situazione) to get out of control // vt (gettare dall'alto in basso) to hurl, fling; (fig: affrettare) to rush; **~rsi** vr (gettarsi) to hurl o fling o.s.; (affrettarsi) to rush; **precipitazi'one** sf (METEOR) precipitation; (fig) haste; **precipi'toso, a** ag (caduta, fuga) headlong; (fig: avventato) rash, reckless; (: affrettato) hasty, rushed.

preci'pizio [pretʃi'pittsjo] sm precipice; a **~** (fig: correre) headlong.

preci'sare [pretʃi'zare] vt to state, specify; (spiegare) to explain (in detail).

precisi'one [pretʃi'zjone] sf precision; accuracy.

pre'ciso, a [pre'tʃizo] ag (esatto) precise; (accurato) accurate, precise; (deciso: idee) precise, definite; (uguale): **2 vestiti ~i** 2 dresses exactly the same; **sono le 9 ~e** it's exactly 9 o'clock.

pre'cludere vt to block, obstruct; **pre'cluso, a** pp di **precludere**.

pre'coce [pre'kɔtʃe] ag early; (bambino) precocious; (vecchiaia) premature.

precon'cetto [prekon'tʃetto] sm preconceived idea, prejudice.

precur'sore sm forerunner, precursor.

'preda sf (bottino) booty; (animale, fig) prey; **essere ~ di** to fall prey to; **essere in ~ a** to be prey to; **preda'tore** sm predator.

predeces'sore, a [predetʃes'sore] sm/f predecessor.

predesti'nare vt to predestine.

pre'detto, a pp di **predire**.

'predica, che sf sermon; (fig) lecture, talking-to.

predi'care vt, vi to preach.

predi'cato sm (LING) predicate.

predi'letto, a pp di **prediligere** // ag, sm/f favourite.

predilezi'one [predilet'tsjone] sf fondness, partiality; **avere una ~ per qc/qn** to be partial to sth/fond of sb.

predi'ligere [predi'lidʒere] vt to prefer, have a preference for.

pre'dire vt to foretell, predict.

predis'porre vt to get ready, prepare; **~ qn a qc** to predispose sb to sth; **predis'posto, a** pp di **predisporre**.

predizi'one [predit'tsjone] sf prediction.

predomi'nare *vi* to predominate; **predo'minio** *sm* predominance; supremacy.

prefabbri'cato, a *ag* (*EDIL*) prefabricated.

prefazi'one [prefat'tsjone] *sf* preface, foreword.

prefe'renza [prefe'rɛntsa] *sf* preference; **preferenzi'ale** *ag* preferential; **corsia** ~ bus and taxi lane.

prefe'rire *vt* to prefer, like better; ~ **il caffè al tè** to prefer coffee to tea, like coffee better than tea.

pre'fetto *sm* prefect; **prefet'tura** *sf* prefecture.

pre'figgersi [pre'fiddʒersi] *vr*: ~**rsi uno scopo** to set o.s. a goal.

pre'fisso, a *pp di* **prefiggere** // *sm* (*LING*) prefix; (*TEL*) dialling (*Brit*) o dial (*US*) code.

pre'gare *vi* to pray // *vt* (*REL*) to pray to; (*implorare*) to beg; (*chiedere*): ~ **qn di fare** to ask sb to do; **farsi** ~ to need coaxing o persuading.

pre'gevole [pre'dʒevole] *ag* valuable.

preghi'era [pre'gjɛra] *sf* (*REL*) prayer; (*domanda*) request.

pregi'ato, a [pre'dʒato] *ag* (*di valore*) valuable; **vino** ~ vintage wine.

'pregio ['prɛdʒo] *sm* (*stima*) esteem, regard; (*qualità*) (good) quality, merit; (*valore*) value, worth.

pregiudi'care [predʒudi'kare] *vt* to prejudice, harm, be detrimental to; **pregiudi'cato, a** *sm/f* (*DIR*) previous offender.

pregiu'dizio [predʒu'dittsjo] *sm* (*idea errata*) prejudice; (*danno*) harm q.

'pregno, a ['preɲɲo] *ag* (*gravido*) pregnant; (*saturo*): ~ **di** full of, saturated with.

'prego *escl* (*a chi ringrazia*) don't mention it!; (*invitando qn ad accomodarsi*) please sit down!; (*invitando qn ad andare prima*) after you!

pregus'tare *vt* to look forward to.

preis'torico, a, ci, che *ag* prehistoric.

pre'lato *sm* prelate.

prele'vare *vt* (*denaro*) to withdraw; (*campione*) to take; (*sog: polizia*) to take, capture.

preli'evo *sm* (*MED*): **fare un** ~ (**di**) to take a sample (of).

prelimi'nare *ag* preliminary; ~**i** *smpl* preliminary talks; preliminaries.

pre'ludio *sm* prelude.

pré-ma'man [prema'mã] *sm inv* maternity dress.

prema'turo, a *ag* premature.

premeditazi'one [premeditat'tsjone] *sf* (*DIR*) premeditation; **con** ~ *ag* premeditated // *av* with intent.

'premere *vt* to press // *vi*: ~ **su** to press down on; (*fig*) to put pressure on; ~ **a** (*fig: importare*) to matter to.

pre'messo, a *pp di* **premettere** // *sf* introductory statement, introduction.

pre'mettere *vt* to put before; (*dire prima*) to start by saying, state first.

premi'are *vt* to give a prize to; (*fig: merito, onestà*) to reward.

'premio *sm* prize; (*ricompensa*) reward; (*COMM*) premium; (*AMM*) indennità) bonus.

premu'nirsi *vr*: ~ **di** to provide o.s. with; ~ **contro** to protect o.s. from, guard o.s. against.

pre'mura *sf* (*fretta*) haste, hurry; (*riguardo*) attention, care; **premu'roso, a** *ag* thoughtful, considerate.

prena'tale *ag* antenatal.

'prendere *vt* to take; (*andare a prendere*) to get, fetch; (*ottenere*) to get; (*guadagnare*) to get, earn; (*catturare: ladro, pesce*) to catch; (*collaboratore, dipendente*) to take on; (*passeggero*) to pick up; (*chiedere: somma, prezzo*) to charge, ask; (*trattare: persona*) to handle // *vi* (*colla, cemento*) to set; (*pianta*) to take; (*fuoco: nel camino*) to catch; (*voltare*): ~ **a destra** to turn (to the) right; ~**rsi** *vr* (*azzuffarsi*): ~**rsi a pugni** to come to blows; **prendi qualcosa?** (*da bere, da mangiare*) would you like something to eat (o drink)?; **prendo un caffè** I'll have a coffee; ~ **a fare qc** to start doing sth; ~ **qn/qc per** (*scambiare*) to take sb/sth for; ~ **fuoco** to catch fire; ~ **parte a** to take part in; ~**rsi cura di qn/qc** to look after sb/sth; **prendersela** (*adirarsi*) to get annoyed; (*preoccuparsi*) to get upset, worry.

prendi'sole *sm inv* sundress.

preno'tare *vt* to book, reserve; **prenotazi'one** *sf* booking, reservation.

preoccu'pare *vt* to worry; to preoccupy; ~**rsi** *vr*: ~**rsi di qn/qc** to worry about sb/sth; ~**rsi per qn** to be anxious for sb; **preoccupazi'one** *sf* worry, anxiety.

prepa'rare *vt* to prepare; (*esame, concorso*) to prepare for; ~**rsi** *vr* (*vestirsi*) to get ready; ~**rsi a qc/a fare** to get ready o prepare (o.s.) for sth/to do; ~ **da mangiare** to prepare a meal; **prepara'tivi** *smpl* preparations; **prepa'rato** *sm* (*prodotto*) preparation; **preparazi'one** *sf* preparation.

preposizi'one [prepozit'tsjone] *sf* (*LING*) preposition.

prepo'tente *ag* (*persona*) domineering, arrogant; (*bisogno, desiderio*) overwhelming, pressing // *sm/f* bully; **prepo'tenza** *sf* arrogance; arrogant behaviour.

'presa *sf* taking q; catching q; (*di città*) capture; (*indurimento: di cemento*) setting; (*appiglio, SPORT*) hold; (*di acqua, gas*) (supply) point; (*ELETTR*): ~ (**di corrente**) socket; (: **al muro**) point;

(piccola quantità: di sale etc) pinch; *(CARTE)* trick; **far ~** *(colla)* to set; **far ~ sul pubblico** to catch the public's imagination; **~ d'aria** air inlet; **essere alle ~e con qc** *(fig)* to be struggling with sth.

pre'sagio |pre'zadʒo| *sm* omen.

presa'gire |preza'dʒire| *vt* to foresee.

'presbite *ag* long-sighted.

presbi'terio *sm* presbytery.

pre'scindere |preʃ'ʃindere| *vi*: **~ da** to leave out of consideration; **a ~ da** apart from.

pres'critto, a *pp di* **prescrivere**.

pres'crivere *vt* to prescribe; **prescrizi'one** *sf (MED, DIR)* prescription; *(norma)* rule, regulation.

presen'tare *vt* to present; *(far conoscere)*: **~ qn (a)** to introduce sb (to); *(AMM: inoltrare)* to submit; **~rsi** *vr (recarsi, farsi vedere)* to present o.s., appear; *(farsi conoscere)* to introduce o.s.; *(occasione)* to arise; **~rsi come candidato** *(POL)* to stand as a candidate; **~rsi bene/male** to have a good/poor appearance; **presentazi'one** *sf* presentation; introduction.

pre'sente *ag* present; *(questo)* this // *sm* present; **i ~i** those present; **aver ~ qc/qn** to remember sth/sb.

presenti'mento *sm* premonition.

pre'senza |pre'zentsa| *sf* presence; *(aspetto esteriore)* appearance; **~ di spirito** presence of mind.

pre'sepio, pre'sepe *sm* crib.

preser'vare *vt* to protect; to save; **preserva'tivo** *sm* sheath, condom.

'preside *sm/f (INS)* head *(teacher)* *(Brit)*, principal *(US)*; *(di facoltà universitaria)* dean.

presi'dente *sm (POL)* president; *(di assemblea, COMM)* chairman; **~ del consiglio** prime minister; **presiden'tessa** *sf* president; president's wife; chairwoman; **presi'denza** *sf* presidency; office of president; chairmanship.

presidi'are *vt* to garrison; **pre'sidio** *sm* garrison.

presi'edere *vt* to preside over // *vi*: **~ a** to direct, be in charge of.

'preso, a *pp di* **prendere**.

'pressa *sf (TECN)* press.

pressap'poco *av* about, roughly.

pres'sare *vt* to press.

pressi'one *sf* pressure; **far ~ su qn** to put pressure on sb; **~ sanguigna** blood pressure.

'presso *av (vicino)* nearby, close at hand // *prep (vicino a)* near; *(accanto a)* beside, next to; *(in casa di)*: **~ qn** at sb's home; *(nelle lettere)* care of *(abbr c/o)*; *(alle dipendenze di)*: **lavora ~ di noi** he works for o with us // *smpl*: **nei ~i di** near, in the vicinity of.

pressuriz'zare |pressurid'dzare| *vt* to pressurize.

presta'nome *sm/f inv (peg)* figurehead.

pres'tante *ag* good-looking.

pres'tare *vt*: **~ (qc a qn)** to lend (sb sth o sth to sb); **~rsi** *vr (offrirsi)*: **~rsi a fare** to offer to do; *(essere adatto)*: **~rsi a** to lend itself to, be suitable for; **~ aiuto** to lend a hand; **~ attenzione** to pay attention; **~ fede a qc/qn** to give credence to sth/sb; **~ orecchio** to listen; **prestazi'one** *sf (TECN, SPORT)* performance; **prestazioni** *sfpl (di persona: servizi)* services.

prestigia'tore, 'trice |prestidʒa'tore| *sm/f* conjurer.

pres'tigio |pres'tidʒo| *sm (potere)* prestige; *(illusione)*: **gioco di ~** conjuring trick.

'prestito *sm* lending *q*; loan; **dar in ~** to lend; **prendere in ~** to borrow.

'presto *av (tra poco)* soon; *(in fretta)* quickly; *(di buon'ora)* early; **a ~** see you soon; **fare ~ a fare qc** to hurry up and do sth; *(non costare fatica)* to have no trouble doing sth; **si fa ~ a criticare** it's easy to criticize.

pre'sumere *vt* to presume, assume; **pre'sunto, a** *pp di* **presumere**.

presuntu'oso, a *ag* presumptuous.

presunzi'one |prezun'tsjone| *sf* presumption.

presup'porre *vt* to suppose; to presuppose.

'prete *sm* priest.

preten'dente *sm/f* pretender // *sm (corteggiatore)* suitor.

pre'tendere *vt (esigere)* to demand, require; *(sostenere)*: **~ che** to claim that; **pretende di aver sempre ragione** he thinks he's always right.

pretenzi'oso, a |preten'tsjoso| *ag* pretentious.

pre'teso, a *pp di* **pretendere** // *sf (esigenza)* claim, demand; *(presunzione, sfarzo)* pretentiousness; **senza ~e** unpretentious.

pre'testo *sm* pretext, excuse.

pre'tore *sm* magistrate.

preva'lente *ag* prevailing; **preva'lenza** *sf* predominance.

preva'lere *vi* to prevail; **pre'valso, a** *pp di* **prevalere**.

preve'dere *vt (indovinare)* to foresee; *(presagire)* to foretell; *(considerare)* to make provision for.

preve'nire *vt (anticipare)* to forestall; to anticipate; *(evitare)* to avoid, prevent; *(avvertire)*: **~ qn (di)** to warn sb (of); to inform sb (of).

preven'tivo, a *ag* preventive // *sm (COMM)* estimate.

prevenzi'one |preven'tsjone| *sf* prevention; *(preconcetto)* prejudice.

previ'dente *ag* showing foresight;

prudent; **previ'denza** sf foresight; istituto di previdenza provident institution; previdenza sociale social security (Brit), welfare (US).

previsi'one sf forecast, prediction; ~i meteorologiche o del tempo weather forecast sg.

pre'visto, a pp di **prevedere** // sm: più/meno del ~ more/less than expected.

prezi'oso, a [prɛt'tsjoso] ag precious; invaluable // sm jewel; valuable.

prez'zemolo [prɛt'tsɛmolo] sm parsley.

'prezzo ['prɛttso] sm price; ~ d'acquisto/di vendita buying/selling price.

prigi'one [pri'dʒone] sf prison; **prigio'nia** sf imprisonment; **prigioni'ero, a** ag captive // sm/f prisoner.

'prima sf vedi primo // av before; (in anticipo) in advance, beforehand; (per l'addietro) at one time, formerly; (più presto) sooner, earlier; (in primo luogo) first // cong: ~ di fare/che parta before doing/he leaves; ~ di prep before; ~ o poi sooner or later.

pri'mario, a ag primary; (principale) chief, leading, primary // sm (MED) chief physician.

pri'mate sm (REL, ZOOL) primate.

pri'mato sm supremacy; (SPORT) record.

prima'vera sf spring; **primave'rile** ag spring cpd.

primeggi'are [primed'dʒare] vi to excel, be one of the best.

primi'tivo, a ag primitive; original.

pri'mizie [pri'mittsje] sfpl early produce sg.

'primo, a ag first; (fig) initial, basic; prime // sm/f first (one) // sm (CUC) first course; (in date): il ~ luglio the first of July // sf (TEATRO) first night; (CINEMA) première; (AUT) first (gear); le ~e ore del mattino the early hours of the morning; ai ~i di maggio at the beginning of May; viaggiare in ~a to travel first-class; in ~ luogo first of all, in the first place; di prim'ordine o ~a qualità first-class, first-rate; in un ~ tempo at first; ~a donna leading lady; (di opera lirica) prima donna.

primo'genito, a [primo'dʒɛnito] ag, sm/ f firstborn.

primordi'ale ag primordial.

'primula sf primrose.

princi'pale [printʃi'pale] ag main, principal // sm manager, boss.

princi'pato [printʃi'pato] sm principality.

'principe ['printʃipe] sm prince; ~ ereditario crown prince; **princi'pessa** sf princess.

principi'ante [printʃi'pjante] sm/f beginner.

prin'cipio [prin'tʃipjo] sm (inizio) begin-

ning, start; (origine) origin, cause; (concetto, norma) principle; al o in ~ at first; per ~ on principle.

pri'ore sm (REL) prior.

priorità sf priority.

'prisma, i sm prism.

pri'vare vt: ~ qn di to deprive sb of; ~rsi di to go o do without.

priva'tiva sf (ECON) monopoly.

pri'vato, a ag private // sm/f private citizen; in ~ in private.

privazi'one [privat'tsjone] sf privation, hardship.

privilegi'are [privile'dʒare] vt to grant a privilege to.

privi'legio [privi'lɛdʒo] sm privilege.

'privo, a ag: ~ di without, lacking.

pro prep for, on behalf of // sm inv (utilità) advantage, benefit; **a che ~?** what's the use?; il ~ e il contro the pros and cons.

pro'babile ag probable, likely; **probabilità** sf inv probability.

pro'blema, i sm problem.

pro'boscide [pro'bɔʃʃide] sf (di elefante) trunk.

procacci'are [prokat'tʃare] vt to get, obtain.

pro'cedere [pro'tʃɛdere] vi to proceed; (comportarsi) to behave; (iniziare): ~ a to start; ~ contro (DIR) to start legal proceedings against; **procedi'mento** sm (modo di condurre) procedure; (di avvenimenti) course; (TECN) process; procedimento penale (DIR) criminal proceedings; **proce'dura** sf (DIR) procedure.

proces'sare [protʃes'sare] vt (DIR) to try.

processi'one [protʃes'sjone] sf procession.

pro'cesso [pro'tʃesso] sm (DIR) trial; proceedings pl; (metodo) process.

pro'cinto [pro'tʃinto] sm: in ~ di fare about to do, on the point of doing.

procla'ma, i sm proclamation.

procla'mare vt to proclaim.

procre'are vt to procreate.

pro'cura sf (DIR) proxy; power of attorney; (ufficio) attorney's office.

procu'rare vt: ~ qc a qn (fornire) to get o obtain sth for sb; (causare: noie etc) to bring o give sb sth.

procura'tore, 'trice sm/f (DIR) ≈ solicitor; (: chi ha la procura) attorney; proxy; ~ generale (in corte d'appello) public prosecutor; (in corte di cassazione) Attorney General; ~ della Repubblica (in corte d'assise, tribunale) public prosecutor.

prodi'gare vt to be lavish with; ~rsi per qn to do all one can for sb.

pro'digio [pro'didʒo] sm marvel, wonder; (persona) prodigy; **prodigi'oso, a** ag prodigious; phenomenal.

'prodigo, a, ghi, ghe *ag* lavish, extravagant.
pro'dotto, a *pp di* **produrre** // *sm* product; ~i **agricoli** farm produce *sg.*
pro'durre *vt* to produce; **produttività** *sf* productivity; **produt'tivo, a** *ag* productive; **produt'tore, 'trice** *sm/f* producer; **produzi'one** *sf* production; (*rendimento*) output.
pro'emio *sm* introduction, preface.
Prof. *abbr* (= *professore*) Prof.
profa'nare *vt* to desecrate.
pro'fano, a *ag* (*mondano*) secular; profane; (*sacrilego*) profane.
profe'rire *vt* to utter.
profes'sare *vt* to profess; (*medicina etc*) to practise.
professio'nale *ag* professional.
professi'one *sf* profession; **professio'nista, i, e** *sm/f* professional.
profes'sore, 'essa *sm/f* (*INS*) teacher; (: *di università*) lecturer; (: *titolare di cattedra*) professor.
pro'feta, i *sm* prophet; **profe'zia** *sf* prophecy.
pro'ficuo, a *ag* useful, profitable.
profi'lare *vt* to outline; (*ornare: vestito*) to edge; ~**rsi** *vr* to stand out, be silhouetted; to loom up.
pro'filo *sm* profile; (*breve descrizione*) sketch, outline; **di ~** in profile.
profit'tare *vi:* ~ **di** (*trarre profitto*) to profit by; (*approfittare*) to take advantage of.
pro'fitto *sm* advantage, profit, benefit; (*fig: progresso*) progress; (*COMM*) profit.
profondità *sf inv* depth.
pro'fondo, a *ag* deep; (*rancore, meditazione*) profound // *sm* depth(s *pl*), bottom; ~ **8 metri** 8 metres deep.
'profugo, a, ghi, ghe *sm/f* refugee.
profu'mare *vt* to perfume // *vi* to be fragrant; ~**rsi** *vr* to put on perfume o scent.
profume'ria *sf* perfumery; (*negozio*) perfume shop.
pro'fumo *sm* (*prodotto*) perfume, scent; (*fragranza*) scent, fragrance.
profusi'one *sf* profusion; **a ~** in plenty.
proget'tare [prodʒet'tare] *vt* to plan; (*TECN: edificio*) to plan, design; **pro'getto** *sm* plan, (*idea*) plan, project; **progetto di legge** bill.
pro'gramma, i *sm* programme; (*TV, RADIO*) programmes *pl*; (*INS*) syllabus, curriculum; (*INFORM*) program; **program'mare** *vt* (*TV, RADIO*) to put on; (*INFORM*) to program; (*ECON*) to plan; **programma'tore, 'trice** *sm/f* (*INFORM*) computer programmer.
progre'dire *vi* to progress, make progress.
progres'sivo, a *ag* progressive.
pro'gresso *sm* progress *q*; **fare ~i** to make progress.

proi'bire *vt* to forbid, prohibit; **proibi'tivo, a** *ag* prohibitive; **proibizi'one** *sf* prohibition.
proiet'tare *vt* (*gen, GEOM, CINEMA*) to project; (: *presentare*) to show, screen; (*luce, ombra*) to throw, cast, project; **proi'ettile** *sm* projectile, bullet (*o shell etc*); **proiet'tore** *sm* (*CINEMA*) projector; (*AUT*) headlamp; (*MIL*) searchlight; **proiezi'one** *sf* (*CINEMA*) projection; showing.
'prole *sf* children *pl*, offspring.
prole'tario, a *ag, sm* proletarian.
prolife'rare *vi* (*fig*) to proliferate.
pro'lisso, a *ag* verbose.
'prologo, ghi *sm* prologue.
pro'lunga, ghe *sf* (*di cavo elettrico etc*) extension.
prolun'gare *vt* (*discorso, attesa*) to prolong; (*linea, termine*) to extend.
prome'moria *sm inv* memorandum.
pro'messa *sf* promise.
pro'messo, a *pp di* **promettere**.
pro'mettere *vt* to promise // *vi* to be o look promising; ~ **a qn di fare** to promise sb that one will do.
promi'nente *ag* prominent.
promiscuità *sf* promiscuousness.
promon'torio *sm* promontory, headland.
pro'mosso, a *pp di* **promuovere**.
promo'tore, trice *sm/f* promoter, organizer.
promozi'one [promot'tsjone] *sf* promotion.
promul'gare *vt* to promulgate.
promu'overe *vt* to promote.
proni'pote *sm/f* (*di nonni*) great-grandchild, great-grandson/grand-daughter; (*di zii*) great-nephew/niece; ~**i** *smpl* (*discendenti*) descendants.
pro'nome *sm* (*LING*) pronoun.
pron'tezza [pron'tettsa] *sf* readiness; quickness, promptness.
'pronto, a *ag* ready; (*rapido*) fast, quick, prompt; ~**!** (*TEL*) hello!; ~ **all'ira** quick-tempered; ~ **soccorso** first aid.
prontu'ario *sm* manual, handbook.
pro'nuncia [pro'nuntʃa] *etc* = **pronunzia** *etc.*
pro'nunzia [pro'nuntsja] *sf* pronunciation; **pronunzi'are** *vt* (*parola, sentenza*) to pronounce; (*dire*) to utter; (*discorso*) to deliver; **pronunziarsi** *vr* to declare one's opinion; **pronunzi'ato, a** *ag* (*spiccato*) pronounced, marked; (*sporgente*) prominent.
propa'ganda *sf* propaganda.
propa'gare *vt* (*notizia, malattia*) to spread; (*REL, BIOL*) to propagate; ~**rsi** *vr* to spread; (*BIOL*) to propagate; (*FISICA*) to be propagated.
pro'pendere *vi:* ~ **per** to favour, lean towards; **propensi'one** *sf* inclination, propensity; **pro'penso, a** *pp di*

propendere.
propi'nare vt to administer.
pro'pizio, a |pro'pittsjo| ag favourable.
pro'porre vt (suggerire): ~ qc (a qn) to suggest sth (to sb); (candidato) to put forward; (legge, brindisi) to propose; ~ di fare to suggest o propose doing; **proporsi di fare** to propose o intend to do; **proporsi una meta** to set o.s. a goal.
proporzio'nale |proportsjo'nalc| ag proportional.
proporzio'nare |proportsjo'narc| vt: ~ qc a to proportion o adjust sth to.
proporzi'one |propor'tsjone| sf proportion; in ~ a in proportion to.
pro'posito sm (intenzione) intention, aim; (argomento) subject, matter; a ~ di regarding, with regard to; di ~ (apposta) deliberately, on purpose; a ~ by the way; **capitare a ~** (cosa, persona) to turn up at the right time.
proposizi'one |propozit'tsjone| sf (LING) clause; (: periodo) sentence.
pro'posto, a pp di **proporre** // sf proposal; (suggerimento) suggestion; ~a di legge bill.
proprietà sf inv (ciò che si possiede) property gen q, estate; (caratteristica) property; (correttezza) corrèctness; **proprie'tario, a** sm/f owner; (di albergo etc) proprietor, owner; (per l'inquilino) landlord/lady.
'**proprio, a** ag (possessivo) own; (: impersonale) one's; (esatto) exact, correct, proper; (senso, significato) literal; (LING: nome) proper; (particolare): ~ di characteristic of, peculiar to // av (precisamente) just, exactly; (davvero) really; (affatto): **non ... ~** not ... at all; **l'ha visto con i** (suoi) ~i **occhi** he saw it with his own eyes.
'**prora** sf (NAUT) bow(s pl), prow.
'**proroga, ghe** sf extension; postponement; **proro'gare** vt to extend; (differire) to postpone, defer.
pro'rompere vi to burst out; **pro'rotto, a** pp di **prorompere**.
'**prosa** sf prose; **pro'saico, a, ci, che** ag (fig) prosaic, mundane.
pro'sciogliere |proʃ'ʃɔʎʎere| vt to release; (DIR) to acquit; **prosci'olto, a** pp di **prosciogliere**.
prosciu'gare |proʃʃu'garc| vt (terreni) to drain, reclaim; ~rsi vr to dry up.
prosci'utto |proʃ'ʃutto| sm ham.
prosegui'mento sm continuation; **buon** ~! all the best!; (a chi viaggia) enjoy the rest of your journey!
prosegu'ire vt to carry on with, continue // vi to carry on, go on.
prospe'rare vi to thrive; **prosperità** sf prosperity; '**prospero, a** ag (fiorente) flourishing, thriving, prosperous; **prospe'roso, a** ag (robusto) hale and hearty; (: ragazza) buxom.

prospet'tare vt (esporre) to point out, show; ~rsi vr to look, appear.
prospet'tiva sf (ARTE) perspective; (veduta) view; (fig: previsione, possibilità) prospect.
pros'petto sm (DISEGNO) elevation; (veduta) view, prospect; (facciata) façade, front; (tabella) table; (sommario) summary.
prospici'ente |prospi'tʃɛnte| ag: ~ qc facing o overlooking sth.
prossimità sf nearness, proximity; in ~ di near (to), close to.
'**prossimo, a** ag (vicino): ~ a near (to), close to; (che viene subito dopo) next; (parente) close // sm neighbour, fellow man.
prosti'tuta sf prostitute; **prostituzi'one** sf prostitution.
pros'trare vt (fig) to exhaust, wear out; ~rsi vr (fig) to humble o.s.
protago'nista, i, e sm/f protagonist.
pro'teggere |pro'tɛddʒere| vt to protect.
prote'ina sf protein.
pro'tendere vt to stretch out; **pro'teso, a** pp di **protendere**.
pro'testa sf protest.
protes'tante ag, sm/f Protestant.
protes'tare vt, vi to protest; ~rsi vr: ~rsi innocente etc to protest one's innocence o that one is innocent etc.
protet'tivo, a ag protective.
pro'tetto, a pp di **proteggere**.
protet'tore, 'trice sm/f protector; (sostenitore) patron.
protezi'one |protet'tsjone| sf protection; (patrocinio) patronage.
protocol'lare vt to register // ag formal; of protocol.
proto'collo sm protocol; (registro) register of documents.
pro'totipo sm prototype.
pro'trarre vt (prolungare) to prolong; **pro'tratto, a** pp di **protrarre**.
protube'ranza |protube'rantsa| sf protuberance, bulge.
'**prova** sf (esperimento, cimento) test, trial; (tentativo) attempt, try; (MAT, testimonianza, documento etc) proof; (DIR) evidence q, proof; (INS) exam, test; (TEATRO) rehearsal; (di abito) fitting; a ~ di (in testimonianza di) as proof of; a ~ di fuoco fireproof; fino a ~ contraria until it is proved otherwise; mettere alla ~ to put to the test; giro di ~ test o trial run; ~ generale (TEATRO) dress rehearsal.
pro'vare vt (sperimentare) to test; (tentare) to try, attempt; (assaggiare) to try, taste; (sperimentare in sé) to experience; (sentire) to feel; (cimentare) to put to the test; (dimostrare) to prove; (abito) to try on; ~rsi vr: ~rsi (a fare) to try o attempt (to do); ~ a fare to try o attempt to do.

proveni'enza |provc'njentsa| *sf* origin, source.

prove'nire *vi*: ~ **da** to come from.

pro'venti *smpl* revenue *sg*.

prove'nuto, a *pp di* **provenire**.

pro'verbio *sm* proverb.

pro'vetta *sf* test tube; **bambino in ~** test-tube baby.

pro'vetto, a *ag* skilled, experienced.

pro'vincia, ce *o* **cie** |pro'vintʃa| *sf* province; **provinci'ale** *ag* provincial; **(strada) provinciale** main road (*Brit*), highway (*US*).

pro'vino *sm* (*CINEMA*) screen test; (*campione*) specimen.

provo'cante *ag* (*attraente*) provocative.

provo'care *vt* (*causare*) to cause, bring about; (*eccitare: riso, pietà*) to arouse; (*irritare, sfidare*) to provoke; **provoca'torio, a** *ag* provocative; **provocazi'one** *sf* provocation.

provve'dere *vi* (*disporre*): ~ **(a)** to provide (for); (*prendere un provvedimento*) to take steps, act // *vt*: ~ **qc a qn** to supply sth to sb; **~rsi** *vr*: **~rsi di** to provide o.s. with; **provvedi'mento** *sm* measure; (*di previdenza*) precaution.

provvi'denza |provvi'dentsa| *sf*: **la ~** providence; **provvidenzi'ale** *ag* providential.

provvigi'one |provvi'dʒone| *sf* (*COMM*) commission.

provvi'sorio, a *ag* temporary.

prov'vista *sf* provision, supply.

'prua *sf* (*NAUT*) = **prora**.

pru'dente *ag* cautious, prudent; (*assennato*) sensible, wise; **pru'denza** *sf* prudence, caution; wisdom.

'prudere *vi* to itch, be itchy.

'prugna |'pruɲɲa| *sf* plum; ~ **secca** prune.

prurigi'noso, a |pruridʒi'noso| *ag* itchy.

pru'rito *sm* itchiness *q*; itch.

P.S. *abbr* (= *postscriptum*) P.S.; (*POLIZIA*) = **Pubblica Sicurezza**.

pseu'donimo *sm* pseudonym.

PSI *sigla m* = *Partito Socialista Italiano*.

psicana'lista, i, e *sm/f* psychoanalyst.

'psiche |'psike| *sf* (*PSIC*) psyche.

psichi'atra, i, e |psi'kjatra| *sm/f* psychiatrist; **psichi'atrico, a, ci, che** *ag* psychiatric.

'psichico, a, ci, che |'psikiko| *ag* psychological.

psicolo'gia |psikolo'dʒia| *sf* psychology; **psico'logico, a, ci, che** *ag* psychological; **psi'cologo, a, gi, ghe** *sm/f* psychologist.

psico'patico, a, ci, che *ag* psychopathic // *sm/f* psychopath.

P.T. *abbr* = *Posta e Telegrafi*.

pubbli'care *vt* to publish.

pubblicazi'one |pubblikat'tsjone| *sf* publication; **~i (matrimoniali)** *sfpl* (marriage) banns.

pubbli'cista, i, e |pubbli'tʃista| *sm/f* (*STAMPA*) occasional contributor.

pubblicità |pubblitʃi'ta| *sf* (*diffusione*) publicity; (*attività*) advertising; (*annunci nei giornali*) advertisements *pl*; **pubblici'tario, a** *ag* advertising *cpd*; (*trovata, film*) publicity *cpd*.

'pubblico, a, ci, che *ag* public; (*statale: scuola etc*) state *cpd* // *sm* public; (*spettatori*) audience; **in ~** in public; **~ funzionario** civil servant; **P~ Ministero** Public Prosecutor's Office; **la P~a Sicurezza** the police.

'pube *sm* (*ANAT*) pubis.

pubertà *sf* puberty.

'pudico, a, ci, che *ag* modest.

pu'dore *sm* modesty.

puericul'tura *sf* paediatric nursing; infant care.

pue'rile *ag* childish.

pugi'lato |pudʒi'lato| *sm* boxing.

'pugile |'pudʒile| *sm* boxer.

pugna'lare |puɲɲa'lare| *vt* to stab.

pu'gnale |puɲ'ɲale| *sm* dagger.

'pugno |'puɲɲo| *sm* fist; (*colpo*) punch; (*quantità*) fistful.

'pulce |'pultʃe| *sf* flea.

pul'cino |pul'tʃino| *sm* chick.

pu'ledro, a *sm/f* colt/filly.

pu'leggia, ge |pu'leddʒa| *sf* pulley.

pu'lire *vt* to clean; (*lucidare*) to polish; **pu'lito, a** *ag* (*anche fig*) clean; (*ordinato*) neat, tidy // *sf* quick clean; **puli'tura** *sf* cleaning; **pulitura a secco** dry cleaning; **puli'zia** *sf* cleaning; cleanness; **fare le pulizie** to do the cleaning, do the housework.

'pullman *sm inv* coach.

pul'lover *sm inv* pullover, jumper.

pullu'lare *vi* to swarm, teem.

pul'mino *sm* minibus.

'pulpito *sm* pulpit.

pul'sante *sm* (push-)button.

pul'sare *vi* to pulsate, beat; **pulsazi'one** *sf* beat.

pul'viscolo *sm* fine dust.

'puma *sm inv* puma.

pun'gente |pun'dʒente| *ag* prickly; stinging; (*anche fig*) biting.

'pungere |'pundʒere| *vt* to prick; (*sog: insetto, ortica*) to sting; (: *freddo*) to bite.

pungigli'one |pundʒiʎ'ʎone| *sm* sting.

pu'nire *vt* to punish; **punizi'one** *sf* punishment; (*SPORT*) penalty.

'punta *sf* point; (*parte terminale*) tip, end; (*di monte*) peak; (*di costa*) promontory; (*minima parte*) touch, trace; **in ~ di piedi** on tip-toe; **ore di ~** peak hours; **uomo di ~** front-rank *o* leading man.

pun'tare *vt* (*piedi a terra, gomiti sul tavolo*) to plant; (*dirigere: pistola*) to point; (*scommettere*) to bet // *vi* (*mi-*

rare): ~ a to aim at; (*avviarsi*): ~ su to head o make for; (*fig: contare*): ~ su to count o rely on.

pun'tata *sf* (*gita*) short trip; (*scommessa*) bet; (*parte di opera*) instalment; **romanzo a ~e** serial.

punteggia'tura [punteddʒa'tura] *sf* (*LING*) punctuation.

pun'teggio [pun'teddʒo] *sm* score.

puntel'lare *vt* to support.

pun'tello *sm* prop, support.

puntigli'oso, a [puntiʎ'ʎoso] *ag* punctilious.

pun'tina *sf*: ~ **da disegno** drawing pin.

pun'tino *sm* dot; **fare qc a** ~ to do sth properly.

'punto, a *pp di* **pungere** // *sm* (*segno, macchiolina*) dot; (*LING*) full stop; (*MAT, momento, di punteggio, fig: argomento*) point; (*posto*) spot; (*a scuola*) mark; (*nel cucire, nella maglia, MED*) stitch // *av*: **non ... ~** not at all; **due ~i** *sm* (*LING*) colon; **sul ~ di fare** (just) about to do; **fare il ~** (*NAUT*) to take a bearing; (*fig*): **fare il ~ della situazione** to take stock of the situation; **to sum up the situation; alle 6 in ~ at 6 o'clock sharp** o **on the dot; essere a buon ~** to have reached a satisfactory stage; **mettere a ~** to adjust; (*motore*) to tune; (*cannocchiale*) to focus; (*fig*) to settle; **di ~ in bianco** point-blank; ~ **cardinale** point of the compass, cardinal point; ~ **debole** weak point; ~ **esclamativo/interrogativo** exclamation/question mark; ~ **di riferimento** landmark; (*fig*) point of reference; ~ **di vendita** retail outlet; ~ **e virgola** semicolon; ~ **di vista** (*fig*) point of view; ~**i di sospensione** suspension points.

puntu'ale *ag* punctual; **puntualità** *sf* punctuality.

pun'tura *sf* (*di ago*) prick; (*di insetto*) sting, bite; (*MED*) puncture; (: *iniezione*) injection; (*dolore*) sharp pain.

punzecchi'are [puntsek'kjare] *vt* to prick; (*fig*) to tease.

pun'zone [pun'tsone] *sm* (*per metalli*) stamp, die.

'pupa *sf* doll.

pu'pazzo [pu'pattso] *sm* puppet.

pu'pillo, a *sm/f* (*DIR*) ward; (*prediletto*) favourite, pet // *sf* (*ANAT*) pupil.

purché [pur'ke] *cong* provided that, on condition that.

'pure *cong* (*tuttavia*) and yet, nevertheless; (*anche se*) even if // *av* (*anche*) too, also; **pur di** (*al fine di*) just to; **faccia** ~! go ahead!, please do!

purè *sm*, **pu'rea** *sf* (*CUC*) purée; (: *di patate*) mashed potatoes.

pu'rezza [pu'rettsa] *sf* purity.

'purga, ghe *sf* (*MED*) purging *q*; purge; (*POL*) purge.

pur'gante *sm* (*MED*) purgative, purge.

pur'gare *vt* (*MED, POL*) to purge; (*pulire*) to clean.

purga'torio *sm* purgatory.

purifi'care *vt* to purify; (*metallo*) to refine.

puri'tano, a *ag, sm/f* puritan.

'puro, a *ag* pure; (*acqua*) clear, limpid; (*vino*) undiluted; **puro'sangue** *sm/f inv* thoroughbred.

pur'troppo *av* unfortunately.

'pustola *sf* pimple.

puti'ferio *sm* rumpus, row.

putre'fare *vi* to putrefy, rot; **putre'fatto, a** *pp di* **putrefare**.

'putrido, a *ag* putrid, rotten.

put'tana *sf* (*fam!*) whore (*!*).

'puzza ['puttsa] *sf* = **puzzo**.

puz'zare [put'tsare] *vi* to stink.

'puzzo ['puttso] *sm* stink, foul smell.

'puzzola ['puttsola] *sf* polecat.

puzzo'lente [puttso'lɛnte] *ag* stinking.

Q

qua *av* here; **in** ~ (*verso questa parte*) this way; **da un anno in** ~ for a year now; **da quando in** ~? since when?; **per di** ~ (*passare*) this way; **al di** ~ **di** (*fiume, strada*) on this side of; ~ **dentro/fuori** *etc* in/out here *etc*; *vedi* **questo**.

qua'derno *sm* notebook; (*per scuola*) exercise book.

qua'drante *sm* quadrant; (*di orologio*) face.

qua'drare *vi* (*bilancio*) to balance, tally; (*descrizione*) to correspond; (*fig*): ~ **a** to please, be to one's liking // *vt* (*MAT*) to square; **non mi quadra** I don't like it; **qua'drato, a** *ag* square; (*fig: equilibrato*) level-headed, sensible; (: *peg*) square // *sm* (*MAT*) square; (*PUGILATO*) ring; **5 al quadrato** 5 squared.

qua'dretto *sm*: **a** ~**i** (*tessuto*) checked; (*foglio*) squared.

quadri'foglio [kwadri'fɔʎʎo] *sm* four-leaf clover.

'quadro *sm* (*pittura*) painting, picture; (*quadrato*) square; (*tabella*) table, chart; (*TECN*) board, panel; (*TEATRO*) scene; (*fig: scena, spettacolo*) sight; (: *descrizione*) outline, description; ~**i** *smpl* (*POL*) party organizers; (*MIL*) cadres; (*COMM*) managerial staff; (*CARTE*) diamonds.

'quadruplo, a *ag, sm* quadruple.

quaggiù [kwad'dʒu] *av* down here.

'quaglia ['kwaʎʎa] *sf* quail.

'qualche ['kwalke] *det* 1 some, a few; (*in interrogative*) any; **ho comprato** ~ **libro** I've bought some o a few books; ~ **volta** sometimes; **hai** ~ **sigaretta?** have you any cigarettes? 2 (*uno*): **c'è** ~ **medico?** is there a

doctor?; **in ~ modo** somehow
3 (*un certo, parecchio*) some; **un personaggio di ~ rilievo** a figure of some importance
4: ~ cosa = **qualcosa**.

qualche'duno |kwalke'duno| *pronome* = **qualcuno**.

qual'cosa *pronome* something; (*in espressioni interrogative*) anything; **qualcos'altro** something else; anything else; **~ di nuovo** something new; anything new; **~ da mangiare** something to eat; anything to eat; **c'è ~ che non va?** is there something o anything wrong?

qual'cuno *pronome* (*persona*) someone, somebody; (: *in espressioni interrogative*) anyone, anybody; (*alcuni*) some; **~ è favorevole a noi** some are on our side; **qualcun altro** someone o somebody else; anyone o anybody else.

'quale (*spesso troncato in* **qual**) ◆ *det* **1** (*interrogativo*) what; (: *scegliendo tra due o più cose o persone*) which; **~ uomo/denaro?** what man/money?; which man/money?; **~i sono i tuoi programmi?** what are your plans?; **~ stanza preferisci?** which room do you prefer?
2 (*relativo: come*): **il risultato fu ~ ci si aspettava** the result was as expected
3 (*esclamativo*) what; **~ disgrazia!** what bad luck!
◆ *pronome* **1** (*interrogativo*) which; **~ dei due scegli?** which of the two do you want?
2 (*relativo*): **il(la) ~** (*persona: soggetto*) who; (: *oggetto, con preposizione*) whom; (*cosa*) which; (*possessivo*) whose; **suo padre, il ~ è avvocato, ...** his father, who is a lawyer, ...; **il signore con il ~ parlavo** the gentleman to whom I was speaking; **l'albergo al ~ ci siamo fermati** the hotel where we stayed o which we stayed at; **la signora della ~ ammiriamo la bellezza** the lady whose beauty we admire
3 (*relativo: in elenchi*) such as, like; **piante ~i l'edera** plants like o such as ivy; **~ sindaco di questa città** as mayor of this town.

qua'lifica, che *sf* qualification; (*titolo*) title.

qualifi'care *vt* to qualify; (*definire*): **~ qn/qc come** to describe sb/sth as; **~rsi** *vr* (*anche* SPORT) to qualify; **qualifica'tivo, a** *ag* qualifying; **qualificazi'one** *sf* qualification; **gara di qualificazione** (SPORT) qualifying event.

qualità *sf inv* quality; **in ~ di** in one's capacity as.

qua'lora *cong* in case, if.

qual'siasi, qua'lunque *det inv* any; (*quale che sia*) whatever; (*discriminativo*) whichever; (*posposto: mediocre*) poor, indifferent; ordinary; **mettiti un vestito ~** put on any old

dress; **~ cosa** anything; **~ cosa accada** whatever happens; **a ~ costo** at any cost, whatever the cost; **l'uomo ~ the man in the street**; **~ persona** anyone, anybody.

'quando *cong, av* when; **~ sarò ricco** when I'm rich; **da ~** (*dacché*) since; (*interrogativo*): **da ~ sei qui?** how long have you been here?; **quand'anche** even if.

quantità *sf inv* quantity; (*gran numero*): **una ~ di** a great deal of; a lot of; **in grande ~** in large quantities; **quanta'tivo** *sm* (COMM) amount, quantity.

'quanto, a ◆ *det* **1** (*interrogativo: quantità*) how much; (: *numero*) how many; **~ pane/denaro?** how much bread/money?; **~i libri/ragazzi?** how many books/boys?; **~ tempo?** how long?; **~i anni hai?** how old are you?
2 (*esclamativo*): **~e storie!** what a lot of nonsense!; **~ tempo sprecato!** what a waste of time!
3 (*relativo: quantità*) as much ... as; (: *numero*) as many ... as; **ho ~ denaro mi occorre** I have as much money as I need; **prendi ~i libri vuoi** take as many books as you like
◆ *pronome* **1** (*interrogativo: quantità*) how much; (: *numero*) how many; (: *tempo*) how long; **~ mi dai?** how much will you give me?; **~i me ne hai portati?** how many did you bring me?; **da ~ sei qui?** how long have you been here?; **~i ne abbiamo oggi?** what's the date today?
2 (*relativo: quantità*) as much as; (: *numero*) as many as; **farò ~ posso** I'll do as much as I can; **possono venire ~i sono stati invitati** all those who have been invited can come
◆ *av* **1** (*interrogativo: con ag, av*) how; (: *con vb*) how much; **~ stanco ti sembrava?** how tired did he seem to you?; **~ corre la tua moto?** how fast can your motorbike go?; **~ costa?** how much does it cost?; **quant'è?** how much is it?
2 (*esclamativo: con ag, av*) how; (: *con vb*) how much; **~ sono felice!** how happy I am!; **sapessi ~ abbiamo camminato!** if you knew how far we've walked!; **studierò ~ posso** I'll study as much as o all I can; **~ prima** as soon as possible
3: in ~ (*in qualità di*) as; (*perché, per il fatto che*) as, since; **(in) ~ a** (*per ciò che riguarda*) as for, as regards
4: per ~ (*nonostante, anche se*) however; **per ~ si sforzi, non ce la farà** try as he may, he won't manage it; **per ~ sia brava, fa degli errori** however good she may be, she makes mistakes; **per ~ io sappia** as far as I know.

quan'tunque *cong* although, though.

qua'ranta *num* forty.

quaran'tena *sf* quarantine.

quaran'tesimo, a *num* fortieth.

quaran'tina *sf*: **una ~ (di)** about forty.

qua'resima *sf*: **la ~** Lent.

'quarta *sf vedi* **quarto.**

quar'tetto *sm* quartet(te).

quarti'ere *sm* district, area; (*MIL*) quarters *pl*; **~ generale** headquarters *pl*, HQ.

'quarto, a *ag* fourth // *sm* fourth; (*quarta parte*) quarter // *sf* (*AUT*) fourth (gear); **le 6 e un ~** a quarter past six; **~ d'ora** quarter of an hour; **~i di finale** quarter final.

'quarzo |'kwartso] *sm* quartz.

'quasi *av* almost, nearly // *cong* (*anche*: **~ che**) as if; **(non) ... ~ mai** hardly ever; **~ ~ me ne andrei** I've half a mind to leave.

quassù *av* up here.

'quatto, a *ag* crouched, squatting; (*silenzioso*) silent; **~ ~** very quietly; stealthily.

quat'tordici |kwat'torditʃi] *num* fourteen.

quat'trini *smpl* money *sg*, cash *sg*.

'quattro *num* four; **in ~ e quattr'otto** in less than no time; **quattro'cento** *num* four hundred // *sm*: **il Quattrocento** the fifteenth century; **quattro'mila** *num* four thousand.

'quello, a ◆ *det* (*dav sm* **quel** + *C*, **quell'** + *V*, **quello** + *s impura*, *gn*, *pn*, *ps*, *x*, *z*; *pl* **quei** + *C*, **quegli** + *V o s impura*, *gn*, *pn*, *ps*, *x*, *z*; *dav sf* **quella** + *C*, **quell'** + *V*; *pl* **quelle**) that; those *pl*; **~a casa** that house; **quegli uomini** those men; **voglio ~a camicia** (lì o là) I want that shirt

◆ *pronome* **1** (*dimostrativo*) that (one); those (ones) *pl*; (*ciò*) that; **conosci ~a?** do you know that woman?; **prendo ~ bianco** I'll take the white one; **chi è ~?** who's that?; **prendiamo ~** (lì o là) let's take that one (there)

2 (*relativo*): **~(a) che** (*persona*) the one (who); (*cosa*) the one (which), the one (that); **~i(e) che** (*persone*) those who; (*cose*) those which; **è lui ~ che non voleva venire** he's the one who didn't want to come; **ho fatto ~ che potevo** I did what I could.

'quercia, ce |'kwertʃa] *sf* oak (tree); (*legno*) oak.

que'rela *sf* (*DIR*) (legal) action; **quere'lare** *vt* to bring an action against.

que'sito *sm* question, query; problem.

questio'nare *vi*: **~ di/su qc** to argue about/over sth.

questio'nario *sm* questionnaire.

questi'one *sf* problem, question; (*controversia*) issue; (*litigio*) quarrel; **in ~** in question; **fuor di ~** out of the question; **è ~ di tempo** it's a matter o question of time.

'questo, a ◆ *det* **1** (*dimostrativo*) this; these *pl*; **~ libro** (qui o qua) this book;

io prendo ~ cappotto, tu quello I'll take this coat, you take that one; **quest'oggi** today; **~a sera** this evening

2 (*enfatico*): **non fatemi più prendere di ~e paure** don't frighten me like that again

◆ *pronome* (*dimostrativo*) this (one); these (ones) *pl*; (*ciò*) this; **prendo ~** (qui o qua) I'll take this one; **preferisci ~i o quelli?** do you prefer these (ones) or those (ones)?; **~ intendevo io** this is what I meant; **vengono Paolo e Luca: ~ da Roma, quello da Palermo** Paolo and Luca are coming: the former from Palermo, the latter from Rome.

ques'tore *sm* ≈ chief constable (*Brit*), ≈ police commissioner (*US*).

'questua *sf* collection (of alms).

ques'tura *sf* police headquarters *pl*.

qui *av* here; **da o di ~** from here; **di ~ in avanti** from now on; **di ~ a poco/una settimana** in a little while/a week's time; **~ dentro/sopra/vicino** in/up/near here; *vedi* **questo.**

quie'tanza |kwje'tantsa] *sf* receipt.

quie'tare *vt* to calm, soothe.

qui'ete *sf* quiet, quietness; calmness; stillness; peace.

qui'eto, a *ag* quiet; (*notte*) calm, still; (*mare*) calm.

'quindi *av* then // *cong* therefore, so.

'quindici |'kwinditʃi] *num* fifteen; **~ giorni** a fortnight (*Brit*), two weeks.

quindi'cina |kwindi'tʃina] *sf* (*serie*): **una ~** (di) about fifteen; **fra una ~ di giorni** in a fortnight.

quin'quennio *sm* period of five years.

quin'tale *sm* quintal (*100 kg*).

'quinte *sfpl* (*TEATRO*) wings.

'quinto, a *num* fifth.

'quota *sf* (*parte*) quota, share; (*AER*) height, altitude; (*IPPICA*) odds *pl*; **prendere/perdere ~** (*AER*) to gain/lose height o altitude; **~ d'iscrizione** enrolment fee; (*ad un club*) membership fee.

quo'tare *vt* (*BORSA*) to quote; **quotazi'one** *sf* quotation.

quotidi'ano, a *ag* daily; (*banale*) everyday // *sm* (*giornale*) daily (paper).

quozi'ente |kwot'tsjɛntɛ] *sm* (*MAT*) quotient; **~ d'intelligenza** intelligence quotient, IQ.

R

ra'barbaro *sm* rhubarb.

'rabbia *sf* (*ira*) anger, rage; (*accanimento*, *furia*) fury; (*MED*: *idrofobia*) rabies *sg*.

rab'bino *sm* rabbi.

rabbi'oso, a *ag* angry, furious; (*facile all'ira*) quick-tempered; (*forze*, *acqua etc*) furious, raging; (*MED*) rabid, mad.

rabbo'nire *vt*, **~rsi** *vr* to calm down.

rabbrivi'dire vi to shudder, shiver.

rabbui'arsi vr to grow dark.

raccapez'zarsi |rakkapet'tsarsi| vr: non ~ to be at a loss.

raccapricci'ante |rakkaprit'tfante| ag horrifying.

raccatta'palle sm inv (SPORT) ballboy.

raccat'tare vt to pick up.

rac'chetta |rak'ketta| sf (per tennis) racket; (per ping-pong) bat; ~ da neve snowshoe; ~ da sci ski stick.

racchi'udere |rak'kjudere| vt to contain; **racchiuso, a** pp di **racchiudere**.

rac'cogliere |rak'kɔʎʎere| vt to collect; (raccattare) to pick up; (frutti, fiori) to pick, pluck; (AGR) to harvest; (approvazione, voti) to win; (profughi) to take in; ~rsi vr to gather; (fig) to gather one's thoughts; to meditate; **raccogli'mento** sm meditation; **raccogli'tore** sm (cartella) folder, binder; **raccoglitore a fogli mobili** loose-leaf binder.

rac'colto, a pp di **raccogliere** // ag (persona: pensoso) thoughtful; (luogo: appartato) secluded, quiet // sm (AGR) crop, harvest // sf collecting q; collection; (AGR) harvesting q, gathering q; harvest, crop; (adunata) gathering.

raccoman'dare vt to recommend; (affidare) to entrust; (esortare): ~ a qn di non fare to tell o warn sb not to do; ~rsi vr: ~rsi a qn to commend o.s. to sb; mi raccomando! don't forget!; **raccoman'data** sf (anche: lettera raccomandata) recorded-delivery letter; **raccomandazi'one** sf recommendation.

raccon'tare vt: ~ (a qn) (dire) to tell (sb); (narrare) to relate (to sb), tell (sb) about; **rac'conto** sm telling q, relating q; (fatto raccontato) story, tale.

raccorci'are |rakkor'tfare| vt to shorten.

rac'cordo sm (TECN: giunzione) connection, joint; (AUT. di autostrada) slip road (Brit), entrance (o exit) ramp (US); ~ anulare (AUT) ring road (Brit), beltway (US).

ra'chitico, a, ci, che |ra'kitiko| ag suffering from rickets; (fig) scraggy, scrawny.

racimo'lare |ratfimo'lare| vt (fig) to scrape together, glean.

'rada sf (natural) harbour.

'radar sm radar.

raddol'cire |raddol'tfire| vt (persona, carattere) to soften; ~rsi vr (tempo) to grow milder; (persona) to soften, mellow.

raddoppi'are vt, vi to double.

raddriz'zare |raddrit'tsare| vt to straighten; (fig: correggere) to put straight, correct.

'radere vt (barba) to shave off; (mento) to shave; (fig: rasentare) to graze; to skim; ~rsi vr to shave (o.s.); ~ al suolo to raze to the ground.

radi'ale ag radial.

radi'are vt to strike off.

radia'tore sm radiator.

radiazi'one |radjat'tsjone| sf (FISICA) radiation; (cancellazione) striking off.

radi'cale ag radical // sm (LING) root.

ra'dicchio |ra'dikkjo| sm chicory.

ra'dice |ra'ditfe| sf root.

'radio sf inv radio // sm (CHIM) radium; **radioat'tivo, a** ag radioactive; **radiodiffusi'one** sf (radio) broadcasting; **radiogra'fare** vt to X ray; **radio gra'fia** sf radiography; (foto) X-ray photograph.

radi'oso, a ag radiant.

radiostazi'one |radjostat'tsjone| sf radio station.

radiotera'pia sf radiotherapy.

'rado, a ag (capelli) sparse, thin; (visite) infrequent; di ~ rarely.

radu'nare vt, ~rsi vr to gather, assemble.

ra'dura sf clearing.

'rafano sm horseradish.

raffazzo'nare |raffattso'nare| vt to patch up.

raf'fermo, a ag stale.

'raffica, che sf (METEOR) gust (of wind); (di colpi: scarica) burst of gunfire.

raffigu'rare vt to represent.

raffi'nare vt to refine; **raffina'tezza** sf refinement; **raffi'nato, a** ag refined; **raffine'ria** sf refinery.

raffor'zare |raffor'tsare| vt to reinforce.

raffredda'mento sm cooling.

raffred'dare vt to cool; (fig) to dampen, have a cooling effect on; ~rsi vr to grow cool o cold; (prendere un raffreddore) to catch a cold; (fig) to cool (off).

raffred'dato, a ag (MED): essere ~ to have a cold.

raffred'dore sm (MED) cold.

raf'fronto sm comparison.

'rafia sf (fibra) raffia.

ra'gazzo, a |ra'gattso| sm/f boy/girl; (fam: fidanzato) boyfriend/girlfriend.

raggi'ante |rad'dʒante| ag radiant, shining.

'raggio |'raddʒo| sm (di sole etc) ray; (MAT, distanza) radius; (di ruota etc) spoke; ~ d'azione range; ~i X X-rays.

raggi'rare |radd3i'rare| vt to take in, trick; **rag'giro** sm trick.

raggi'ungere |rad'dʒundʒere| vt to reach; (persona: riprendere) to catch up (with); (bersaglio) to hit; (fig: meta) to achieve; **raggi'unto, a** pp di **raggiungere**.

raggomito'larsi vr to curl up.

raggranel'lare vt to scrape together.

raggrin'zare |raggrin'tsare| vt, vi (anche: ~rsi) to wrinkle.

raggrup'pare vt to group (together).

raggu'aglio |rag'gwaʎʎo| sm comparison; (informazione, relazione) piece of information.

ragguar'devole ag (degno di riguardo) distinguished, notable; (notevole: somma) considerable.

ragiona'mento |radʒona'mento| sm reasoning q; arguing q; argument.

ragio'nare |radʒo'nare| vi (usare la ragione) to reason; (discorrere): ~ (di) to argue (about).

ragi'one |ra'dʒone| sf reason; (dimostrazione, prova) argument, reason; (diritto) right; aver ~ to be right; aver ~ di qn to get the better of sb; dare ~ a qn to agree with sb; to prove sb right; perdere la ~ to become insane; (fig) to take leave of one's senses; in ~ di at the rate of; to the amount of; according to; a o con ~ rightly, justly; ~ sociale (COMM) corporate name; a ragion veduta after due consideration.

ragione'ria |radʒone'ria| sf accountancy; accounts department.

ragio'nevole |radʒo'nevole| ag reasonable.

ragioni'ere, a |radʒo'njɛre| sm/f accountant.

ragli'are |raʎ'ʎare| vi to bray.

ragna'tela |raɲɲa'tela| sf cobweb, spider's web.

'ragno |'raɲɲo| sm spider.

ragù sm inv (CUC) meat sauce; stew.

RAI-TV |raiti'vu| sigla f = Radio televisiva italiana.

rallegra'menti smpl congratulations.

ralle'grare vt to cheer up; ~rsi vr to cheer up; (provare allegrezza) to rejoice; ~rsi con qn to congratulate sb.

rallen'tare vt to slow down; (fig) to lessen, slacken // vi to slow down.

raman'zina |raman'dzina| sf lecture, telling-off.

'rame sm (CHIM) copper.

rammari'carsi vr: ~ (di) (rincrescersi) to be sorry (about), regret; (lamentarsi) to complain (about); **ram'marico, chi** sm regret.

rammen'dare vt to mend; (calza) to darn; **ram'mendo** sm mending q; darning q; mend; darn.

rammen'tare vt to remember, recall; (richiamare alla memoria): ~ qc a qn to remind sb of sth; ~rsi vr: ~rsi (di qc) to remember (sth).

rammol'lire vt to soften // vi (anche: ~rsi) to go soft.

'ramo sm branch.

ramo'scello |ramoʃ'ʃello| sm twig.

'rampa sf flight (of stairs); ~ di lancio launching pad.

rampi'cante ag (BOT) climbing.

ram'pone sm harpoon; (ALPINISMO) crampon.

'rana sf frog.

'rancido, a |'rantʃido| ag rancid.

ran'core sm rancour, resentment.

ran'dagio, a, gi, gie o **ge** |ran'dadʒo| ag (gatto, cane) stray.

ran'dello sm club, cudgel.

'rango, ghi sm (condizione sociale, MIL) riga) rank.

rannicchi'arsi |rannik'kjarsi| vr to crouch, huddle.

rannuvo'larsi vr to cloud over, become overcast.

ra'nocchio |ra'nɔkkjo| sm (edible) frog.

'rantolo sm wheeze; (di agonizzanti) death rattle.

'rapa sf (BOT) turnip.

ra'pace |ra'patʃe| ag (animale) predatory; (fig) rapacious, grasping // sm bird of prey.

ra'pare vt (capelli) to crop, cut very short.

'rapida sf vedi rapido.

rapida'mente av quickly, rapidly.

rapidità sf speed.

'rapido, a ag fast; (esame, occhiata) quick, rapid // sm (FERR) express (train) // sf (di fiume) rapid.

rapi'mento sm kidnapping; (fig) rapture.

ra'pina sf robbery; ~ a mano armata armed robbery; **rapi'nare** vt to rob; **rapina'tore, 'trice** sm/f robber.

ra'pire vt (cose) to steal; (persone) to kidnap; (fig) to enrapture, delight; **rapi'tore, 'trice** sm/f kidnapper.

rappor'tare vt (confrontare) to compare; (riprodurre) to reproduce.

rap'porto sm (resoconto) report; (legame) relationship; (MAT, TECN) ratio; ~i smpl (fra persone, paesi) relations; ~i sessuali sexual intercourse sg.

rap'prendersi vr to coagulate, clot; (latte) to curdle.

rappre'saglia |rappre'saʎʎa| sf reprisal, retaliation.

rappresen'tante sm/f representative; **rappresen'tanza** sf delegation, deputation; (COMM: ufficio, sede) agency.

rappresen'tare vt to represent; (TEATRO) to perform; **rappresenta'tivo, a** ag representative; **rappresentazi'one** sf representation; performing q; (spettacolo) performance.

rap'preso, a pp di rapprendere.

rapso'dia sf rhapsody.

rara'mente av seldom, rarely.

rare'fatto, a ag rarefied.

'raro, a ag rare.

ra'sare vt (barba etc) to shave off; (siepi, erba) to trim, cut; ~rsi vr to shave (o.s.).

raschi'are |ras'kjare| vt to scrape; (macchia, fango) to scrape off // vi to clear one's throat.

rasen'tare vt (andar rasente) to keep

close to; (*sfiorare*) to skim along (*o over*); (*fig*) to border on.

ra'sente *prep*: ~ (a) close to, very near.

'raso, a *pp di* **radere** // *ag* (*barba*) shaved; (*capelli*) cropped; (*con misure di capacità*) level; (*pieno: bicchiere*) full to the brim // *sm* (*tessuto*) satin; ~ **terra** close to the ground; **un cucchiaio** ~ **a** level spoonful.

ra'soio *sm* razor; ~ **elettrico** electric shaver *o* razor.

ras'segna [ras'seɲɲa] *sf* (*MIL*) inspection, review; (*esame*) inspection; (*resoconto*) review, survey; (*pubblicazione letteraria etc*) review; (*mostra*) exhibition, show; **passare in** ~ (*MIL*, *fig*) to review.

rasse'gnare [rasseɲ'ɲare] *vt*: ~ **le dimissioni** to resign, hand in one's resignation; **~rsi** *vr* (*accettare*): **~rsi** (**a qc/a fare**) to resign o.s. (to sth/to doing); **rassegnazi'one** *sf* resignation.

rassere'narsi *vr* (*tempo*) to clear up.

rasset'tare *vt* to tidy, put in order; (*aggiustare*) to repair, mend.

rassicu'rare *vt* to reassure.

rasso'dare *vt* to harden, stiffen.

rassomigli'anza [rassomiʎ'ʎantsa] *sf* resemblance.

rassomigli'are [rassomiʎ'ʎare] *vi*: ~ **a** to resemble, look like.

rastrel'lare *vt* to rake; (*fig: perlustrare*) to comb.

rastrelli'era *sf* rack; (*per piatti*) dish rack.

ras'trello *sm* rake.

'rata *sf* (*quota*) instalment; **pagare a** ~**e** to pay by instalments *o* on hire purchase (*Brit*).

ratifi'care *vt* (*DIR*) to ratify.

'ratto *sm* (*DIR*) abduction; (*ZOOL*) rat.

rattop'pare *vt* to patch; **rat'toppo** *sm* patching *g*; patch.

rattrap'pire *vt* to make stiff; **~rsi** *vr* to be stiff.

rattris'tare *vt* to sadden; **~rsi** *vr* to become sad.

'rauco, a, chi, che *ag* hoarse.

rava'nello *sm* radish.

ravi'oli *smpl* ravioli *sg*.

ravve'dersi *vr* to mend one's ways.

ravvici'nare [ravvitʃi'nare] *vt* (*avvicinare*): ~ **qc** a to bring sth nearer to; (: *due tubi*) to bring closer together; (*riconciliare*) to reconcile, bring together.

ravvi'sare *vt* to recognize.

ravvi'vare *vt* to revive; (*fig*) to brighten up, enliven; **~rsi** *vr* to revive; to brighten up.

razio'cinio [ratsjo'tʃinjo] *sm* reasoning *g*; reason; (*buon senso*) common sense.

razio'nale [rattsjo'nale] *ag* rational.

razio'nare [rattsjo'nare] *vt* to ration.

razi'one [rat'tsjone] *sf* ration; (*porzione*) portion, share.

'razza ['rattsa] *sf* race; (*ZOOL*) breed; (*discendenza, stirpe*) stock, race; (*sorta*) sort, kind.

raz'zia [rat'tsia] *sf* raid, foray.

razzi'ale [rat'tsjale] *ag* racial.

raz'zismo [rat'tsizmo] *sm* racism, racialism.

raz'zista, i, e [rat'tsista] *ag*, *sm/f* racist, racialist.

'razzo ['raddzo] *sm* rocket.

razzo'lare [rattso'lare] *vi* (*galline*) to scratch about.

re *sm inv* king; (*MUS*) D; (: *solfeggiando la scala*) re.

rea'gire [rea'dʒire] *vi* to react.

re'ale *ag* real; (*di, da re*) royal // *sm*: **il** ~ reality; **rea'lismo** *sm* realism; **rea'lista, i, e** *sm/f* realist; (*POL*) royalist.

realiz'zare [realid'dzare] *vt* (*progetto etc*) to realize, carry out; (*sogno, desiderio*) to realize, fulfil; (*scopo*) to achieve; (*COMM: titoli etc*) to realize; (*CALCIO etc*) to score; **~rsi** *vr* to be realized; **realizzazi'one** *sf* realization; fulfilment; achievement.

real'mente *av* really, actually.

realtà *sf inv* reality.

re'ato *sm* offence.

reat'tore *sm* (*FISICA*) reactor; (*AER: aereo*) jet; (: *motore*) jet engine.

reazio'nario, a [reattsjo'narjo] *ag* (*POL*) reactionary.

reazi'one [reat'tsjone] *sf* reaction.

'rebbio *sm* prong.

recapi'tare *vt* to deliver.

re'capito *sm* (*indirizzo*) address; (*consegna*) delivery.

re'care *vt* (*portare*) to bring; (*avere su di sé*) to carry, bear; (*cagionare*) to cause, bring; **~rsi** *vr* to go.

re'cedere [re'tʃedere] *vi* to withdraw.

recensi'one [retʃen'sjone] *sf* review; **recen'sire** *vt* to review.

re'cente [re'tʃente] *ag* recent; **di** ~ recently; **recente'mente** *av* recently.

recessi'one [retʃes'sjone] *sf* (*ECON*) recession.

re'cidere [re'tʃidere] *vt* to cut off, chop off.

reci'divo, a [retʃi'divo] *sm/f* (*DIR*) second (*o* habitual) offender, recidivist.

re'cinto [re'tʃinto] *sm* enclosure; (*ciò che recinge*) fence; surrounding wall.

recipi'ente [retʃi'pjente] *sm* container.

re'ciproco, a, ci, che [re'tʃiproko] *ag* reciprocal.

re'ciso, a [re'tʃizo] *pp di* **recidere**.

'recita ['rɛtʃita] *sf* performance.

reci'tare [retʃi'tare] *vt* (*poesia, lezione*) to recite; (*dramma*) to perform; (*ruolo*) to play *o* act (the part of); **recitazi'one** *sf* recitation; (*di attore*) acting.

recla'mare *vi* to complain // *vt*

(*richiedere*) to demand.

ré'clame |rɛ'klam| *sf inv* advertising *q*; advertisement, advert (*Brit*), ad (*fam*).

re'clamo *sm* complaint.

reclusi'one *sf* (*DIR*) imprisonment.

'recluta *sf* recruit; **reclu'tare** *vt* to recruit.

re'condito, a *ag* secluded; (*fig*) secret, hidden.

recriminazi'one |rekriminat'tsjone| *sf* recrimination.

recrude'scenza |rekrudeʃ'ʃɛntsa| *sf* fresh outbreak.

recupe'rare *vt* = **ricuperare**.

redargu'ire *vt* to rebuke.

re'datto, a *pp di* **redigere**; **redat'tore, 'trice** *sm/f* (*STAMPA*) editor; (: *di articolo*) writer; (*di dizionario etc*) compiler; **redattore capo** chief editor; **redazi'one** *sf* editing; writing; (*sede*) editorial office(s); (*personale*) editorial staff; (*versione*) version.

reddi'tizio, a |reddi'tittsjo| *ag* profitable.

'reddito *sm* income; (*dello Stato*) revenue; (*di un capitale*) yield.

re'dento, a *pp di* **redimere**.

redenzi'one |reden'tsjone| *sf* redemption.

re'digere |re'didʒɛre| *vt* to write; (*contratto*) to draw up.

re'dimere *vt* to deliver; (*REL*) to redeem.

'redini *sfpl* reins.

'reduce |'redutʃe| *ag*: ~ **da** returning from, back from // *sm/f* survivor.

refe'rendum *sm inv* referendum.

refe'renza |refe'rɛntsa| *sf* reference.

re'ferto *sm* medical report.

refet'torio *sm* refectory.

refrat'tario, a *ag* refractory.

refrige'rare |refridʒe'rare| *vt* to refrigerate; (*rinfrescare*) to cool, refresh.

rega'lare *vt* to give (as a present), make a present of.

re'gale *ag* regal.

re'galo *sm* gift, present.

re'gata *sf* regatta.

reg'gente |red'dʒɛnte| *sm/f* regent.

'reggere |'reddʒɛre| *vt* (*tenere*) to hold; (*sostenere*) to support, bear, hold up; (*portare*) to carry, bear; (*resistere*) to withstand; (*dirigere: impresa*) to manage, run; (*governare*) to rule, govern; (*LING*) to take, be followed by // *vi* (*resistere*): ~ **a** to stand up to, hold out against; (*sopportare*): ~ **a** to stand; (*durare*) to last; (*fig: teoria etc*) to hold water; ~**rsi** *vr* (*stare ritto*) to stand; (*fig: dominarsi*) to control o.s.; ~**rsi sulle gambe** *o* **in piedi** to stand up.

'reggia, ge |'reddʒa| *sf* royal palace.

reggi'calze |reddʒi'kaltse| *sm inv* suspender belt.

reggi'mento |reddʒi'mento| *sm* (*MIL*) regiment.

reggi'petto |reddʒi'pɛtto| *sm*, **reggi'seno** |reddʒi'seno| *sm* bra.

re'gia, 'gie |re'dʒia| *sf* (*TV, CINEMA etc*) direction.

re'gime |re'dʒime| *sm* (*POL*) regime; (*DIR: aureo, patrimoniale etc*) system; (*MED*) diet; (*TECN*) (engine) speed.

re'gina |re'dʒina| *sf* queen.

'regio, a, gi, gie |'redʒo| *ag* royal.

regio'nale |redʒo'nale| *ag* regional.

regi'one |re'dʒone| *sf* region; (*territorio*) region, district, area.

re'gista, i, e |re'dʒista| *sm/f* (*TV, CINEMA etc*) director.

regis'trare |redʒis'trare| *vt* (*AMM*) to register; (*COMM*) to enter; (*notare*) to note, take note of; (*canzone, conversazione, sog: strumento di misura*) to record; (*mettere a punto*) to adjust, regulate; (*bagagli*) to check in; **regis'tratore** *sm* (*strumento*) recorder, register; (*magnetofono*) tape recorder; **registratore di cassa** cash register; **registrazi'one** *sf* recording; (*AMM*) registration; (*COMM*) entry; (*di bagagli*) check-in.

re'gistro |re'dʒistro| *sm* (*libro*) register; ledger; logbook; (*DIR*) registry; (*MUS, TECN*) register.

re'gnare |reɲ'ɲare| *vi* to reign, rule; (*fig*) to reign.

'regno |'reɲɲo| *sm* kingdom; (*periodo*) reign; (*fig*) realm; **il** ~ **animale/vegetale** the animal/vegetable kingdom; **il R~ Unito** the United Kingdom.

'regola *sf* rule; **a** ~ **d'arte** duly; perfectly; **in** ~ in order.

regola'mento *sm* (*complesso di norme*) regulations *pl*; (*di debito*) settlement; ~ **di conti** (*fig*) settling of scores.

rego'lare *ag* regular; (*in regola: domanda*) in order, lawful // *vt* to regulate, control; (*apparecchio*) to adjust, regulate; (*questione, conto, debito*) to settle; ~**rsi** *vr* (*moderarsi*): ~**rsi nel bere/nello spendere** to control one's drinking/spending; (*comportarsi*) to behave, act; **regolarità** *sf inv* regularity.

'regolo *sm* ruler; ~ **calcolatore** slide rule.

reinte'grare *vt* (*energie*) to recover; (*in una carica*) to reinstate.

rela'tivo, a *ag* relative.

relazi'one |relat'tsjone| *sf* (*fra cose, persone*) relation(ship); (*resoconto, sog*) report, account; ~**i** *sfpl* (*conoscenze*) connections.

rele'gare *vt* to banish; (*fig*) to relegate.

religi'one |reli'dʒone| *sf* religion; **religi'oso, a** *ag* religious // *sm/f* monk/nun.

re'liquia *sf* relic.

re'litto *sm* wreck; (*fig*) down-and-out.

re'mare *vi* to row.

remini'scenze |rɛminiʃ'ʃɛntsɛ| *sfpl* reminiscences.

remissi'one *sf* remission.

remis'sivo, a *ag* submissive, compliant.

'remo *sm* oar.

re'moto, a *ag* remote.

'rendere *vt* (*ridare*) to return, give back; (: *saluto etc*) to return; (*produrre*) to yield, bring in; (*esprimere, tradurre*) to render; (*far diventare*): ~ **qc possibile** to make sth possible; ~ **grazie a qn** to thank sb; **~rsi utile** to make o.s. useful; **~rsi conto di qc** to realize sth.

rendi'conto *sm* (*rapporto*) report, account; (*AMM, COMM*) statement of account.

rendi'mento *sm* (*reddito*) yield; (*di manodopera, TECN*) efficiency; (*capacità di produrre*) output; (*di studenti*) performance.

'rendita *sf* (*di individuo*) private *o* unearned income; (*COMM*) revenue; ~ **annua** annuity.

'rene *sm* kidney.

'reni *sfpl* back *sg*.

reni'tente *ag* reluctant, unwilling; ~ **ai consigli di qn** unwilling to follow sb's advice; **essere** ~ **alla leva** (*MIL*) to fail to report for military service.

'renna *sf* reindeer *inv*.

'Reno *sm*: **il** ~ **the** Rhine.

'reo, a *sm/f* (*DIR*) offender.

re'parto *sm* department, section; (*MIL*) detachment.

repel'lente *ag* repulsive.

repen'taglio |rɛpɛn'taʎʎo| *sm*: **mettere a** ~ to jeopardize, risk.

repen'tino, a *ag* sudden, unexpected.

repe'rire *vt* to find, trace.

re'perto *sm* (*ARCHEOLOGIA*) find; (*MED*) report; (*DIR: anche*: ~ **giudiziario**) exhibit.

reper'torio *sm* (*TEATRO*) repertory; (*elenco*) index, (alphabetical) list.

'replica, che *sf* repetition; reply, answer; (*obiezione*) objection; (*TEATRO, CINEMA*) repeat performance; (*copia*) replica.

repli'care *vt* (*ripetere*) to repeat; (*rispondere*) to answer, reply.

repressi'one *sf* repression.

re'presso, a *pp di* **reprimere**.

re'primere *vt* to suppress, repress.

re'pubblica, che *sf* republic; **repubbli'cano, a** *ag, sm/f* republican.

repu'tare *vt* to consider, judge.

reputazi'one |rɛputat'tsjonɛ| *sf* reputation.

'requie *sf*: **senza** ~ unceasingly.

requi'sire *vt* to requisition.

requi'sito *sm* requirement.

requisizi'one |rɛkwizit'tsjonɛ| *sf* requisition.

'resa *sf* (*l'arrendersi*) surrender; (*re-* stituzione, rendimento*) return; ~ **dei conti** rendering of accounts; (*fig*) day of reckoning.

resi'dente *ag* resident; **resi'denza** *sf* residence; **residenzi'ale** *ag* residential.

re'siduo, a *ag* residual, remaining // *sm* remainder; (*CHIM*) residue.

'resina *sf* resin.

resis'tente *ag* (*che resiste*): ~ **a** resistant to; (*forte*) strong; (*duraturo*) long-lasting, durable; ~ **al caldo** heat-resistant; **resis'tenza** *sf* resistance; (*di persona: fisica*) stamina, endurance; (: *mentale*) endurance, resistance.

re'sistere *vi* to resist; ~ **a** (*assalto, tentazioni*) to resist; (*dolore, sog: pianta*) to withstand; (*non patir danno*) to be resistant to; **resis'tito, a** *pp di* **resistere**.

'reso, a *pp di* **rendere**.

reso'conto *sm* report, account.

res'pingere |rɛs'pindʒɛrɛ| *vt* to drive back, repel; (*rifiutare*) to reject; (*INS: bocciare*) to fail; **res'pinto, a** *pp di* **respingere**.

respi'rare *vi* to breathe; (*fig*) to get one's breath; to breathe again // *vt* to breathe (in), inhale; **respira'tore** *sm* respirator; **respirazi'one** *sf* breathing; **respirazione artificiale** artificial respiration; **res'piro** *sm* breathing *q*; (*singolo atto*) breath; (*fig*) respite, rest; **mandare un respiro di sollievo** to give a sigh of relief.

respon'sabile *ag* responsible // *sm/f* person responsible; (*capo*) person in charge; ~ **di** responsible for; (*DIR*) liable for; **responsabilità** *sf inv* responsibility; (*legale*) liability.

res'ponso *sm* answer.

'ressa *sf* crowd, throng.

res'tare *vi* (*rimanere*) to remain, stay; (*diventare*): ~ **orfano/cieco** to become *o* be left an orphan/become blind; (*trovarsi*): ~ **sorpreso** to be surprised; (*avanzare*) to be left, remain; ~ **d'accordo** to agree; **non resta più niente** there's nothing left; **restano pochi giorni** there are only a few days left.

restau'rare *vt* to restore; **restaurazi'one** *sf* (*POL*) restoration; **res'tauro** *sm* (*di edifici etc*) restoration.

res'tio, a, 'tii, 'tie *ag* restive; (*persona*): ~ **a** a reluctant to.

restitu'ire *vt* to return, give back; (*energie, forze*) to restore.

'resto *sm* remainder, rest; (*denaro*) change; (*MAT*) remainder; **~i** *smpl* leftovers; (*di città*) remains; **del** ~ moreover, besides; **~i mortali** (mortal) remains.

res'tringere |rɛs'trindʒɛrɛ| *vt* to reduce; (*vestito*) to take in; (*stoffa*) to shrink; (*fig*) to restrict, limit; **~rsi** *vr* (*strada*) to narrow; (*stoffa*) to shrink; **re-**

strizi'one sf restriction.

'**rete** sf net; (fig) trap, snare; (di recinzione) wire netting; (AUT, FERR, di spionaggio ecc) network; **segnare una ~** (CALCIO) to score a goal; **~ del letto** (sprung) bed base.

reti'cente |reti'tʃɛnte| ag reticent.

retico'lato sm grid; (rete metallica) wire netting; (di filo spinato) barbed wire (fence).

'**retina** sf (ANAT) retina.

re'torico, a, ci, che ag rhetorical // sf rhetoric.

retribu'ire vt to pay; (premiare) to reward; **retribuzi'one** sf payment; reward.

'**retro** sm inv back // av (dietro): **vedi ~** see over(leaf).

retro'cedere |retro'tʃɛdere| vi to withdraw // vt (CALCIO) to relegate; (MIL) to degrade.

re'trogrado, a ag (fig) reactionary, backward-looking.

retro'marcia |retro'martʃa| sf (AUT) reverse; (: dispositivo) reverse gear.

retrospet'tivo, a ag retrospective.

retrovi'sore sm (AUT) (rear-view) mirror.

'**retta** sf (MAT) straight line; (di convitto) charge for bed and board; (fig: ascolto): **dar ~ a** to listen to, pay attention to.

rettango'lare ag rectangular.

ret'tangolo, a ag right-angled // sm rectangle.

ret'tifica, che sf rectification, correction.

rettifi'care vt (curva) to straighten; (fig) to rectify, correct.

'**rettile** sm reptile.

retti'lineo, a ag rectilinear.

retti'tudine sf rectitude, uprightness.

'**retto, a** pp di **reggere** // ag straight; (MAT): **angolo ~** right angle; (onesto) honest, upright; (giusto, esatto) correct, proper, right.

ret'tore sm (REL) rector; (di università) ≈ chancellor.

reuma'tismo sm rheumatism.

reve'rendo, a ag: **il ~ padre Belli** the Reverend Father Belli.

rever'sibile ag reversible.

revisio'nare vt (conti) to audit; (TECN) to overhaul, service; (DIR: processo) to review; (componimento) to revise.

revisi'one sf auditing q; audit; servicing q; overhaul; review; revision.

revi'sore sm: **~ di conti/bozze** auditor/ proofreader.

'**revoca** sf revocation.

revo'care vt to revoke.

re'volver sm inv revolver.

riabili'tare vt to rehabilitate; (fig) to restore to favour.

rial'zare |rial'tsare| vt to raise, lift;

(alzare di più) to heighten, raise; (aumentare: prezzi) to increase, raise // vi (prezzi) to rise, increase; **ri'alzo** sm (di prezzi) increase, rise; (sporgenza) rise.

rianimazi'one |rianimat'tsjone| sf (MED) resuscitation; **centro di ~** intensive care unit.

riap'pendere vt to rehang; (TEL) to hang up.

ria'prire vt, **~rsi** vr to reopen, open again.

ri'armo sm (MIL) rearmament.

rias'setto sm (di stanza ecc) rearrangement; (ordinamento) reorganization.

rias'sumere vt (riprendere) to resume; (impiegare di nuovo) to re-employ; (sintetizzare) to summarize; **rias'sunto, a** pp di **riassumere** // sm summary.

ria'vere vt to have again; (avere indietro) to get back; (riacquistare) to recover; **~rsi** vr to recover.

riba'dire vt (fig) to confirm.

ri'balta sf flap; (TEATRO: proscenio) front of the stage; (: apparecchio d'illuminazione) footlights pl; (fig) limelight.

ribal'tabile ag (sedile) tip-up.

ribal'tare vt, vi (anche: **~rsi**) to turn over, tip over.

ribas'sare vt to lower, bring down // vi to come down, fall; **ri'basso** sm reduction, fall.

ri'battere vt to return, hit back; (confutare) to refute; **~ che** to retort that.

ribel'larsi vr: **~ (a)** to rebel (against); **ri'belle** ag (soldati) rebel; (ragazzo) rebellious // sm/f rebel; **ribelli'one** sf rebellion.

'**ribes** sm inv currant; **~ nero** blackcurrant; **~ rosso** redcurrant.

ribol'lire vi (fermentare) to ferment; (fare bolle) to bubble, boil; (fig) to seethe.

ri'brezzo |ri'breddzo| sm disgust, loathing; **far ~ a** to disgust.

ribut'tante ag disgusting, revolting.

rica'dere vi to fall again; (scendere a terra, fig: nel peccato ecc) to fall back; (vestiti, capelli ecc) to hang (down); (riversarsi: fatiche, colpe): **~ su** to fall on; **rica'duta** sf (MED) relapse.

rical'care vt (disegni) to trace; (fig) to follow faithfully.

rica'mare vt to embroider.

ricambi'are vt to change again; (contraccambiare) to repay, return; **ri'cambio** sm exchange, return; (FISIOL) metabolism; **ricambi** smpl, **pezzi di ricambio** spare parts.

ri'camo sm embroidery.

ricapito'lare vt to recapitulate, sum up.

ricari'care vt (arma, macchina fotografica) to reload; (pipa) to refill; (orologio) to rewind; (batteria) to recharge.

ricat'tare vt to blackmail; **ricatta'tore, 'trice** sm/f blackmailer; **ri'catto** sm blackmail.

rica'vare vt (estrarre) to draw out, extract; (ottenere) to obtain, gain; **ri'cavo** sm proceeds pl.

ric'chezza |rik'kettsa| sf wealth; (fig) richness; ~e sfpl (beni) wealth sg, riches.

'riccio, a |'rittʃo| ag curly // sm (ZOOL) hedgehog; (: anche: ~ di mare) sea urchin; **'ricciolo** sm curl; **ricci'uto, a** ag curly.

'ricco, a, chi, che ag rich; (persona, paese) rich, wealthy // sm/f rich man/ woman; i ~chi the rich; ~ di full of; rich in.

ri'cerca, che |ri'tʃerka| sf search; (indagine) investigation, inquiry; (studio): la ~ research; una ~ piece of research.

ricer'care |ritʃer'kare| vt (motivi, cause) to look for, try to determine; (successo, piacere) to pursue; (onore, gloria) to seek; **ricer'cato, a** ag (apprezzato) much sought-after; (affettato) studied, affected // sm/f (POLIZIA) wanted man/ woman.

ri'cetta |ri'tʃetta| sf (MED) prescription; (CUC) recipe.

ricettazi'one |ritʃettat'tsjone| sf (DIR) receiving (stolen goods).

ri'cevere |ri'tʃevere| vt to receive; (stipendio, lettera) to get, receive; (accogliere: ospite) to welcome; (vedere: cliente, rappresentante etc) to see; **ricevi'mento** sm receiving q; (trattenimento) reception; **ricevi'tore** sm (TECN) receiver; ricevitore delle imposte tax collector; **rice'vuta** sf receipt; ricevuta fiscale receipt for tax purposes; **ricezi'one** sf (RADIO, TV) reception.

richia'mare |rikja'mare| vt (chiamare indietro, ritelefonare) to call back; (ambasciatore, truppe) to recall; (rimproverare) to reprimand; (attirare) to attract, draw; ~rsi a (riferirsi a) to refer to; **richi'amo** sm call; recall; reprimand; attraction.

richi'edere |ri'kjedere| vt to ask again for; (chiedere indietro): ~ qc to ask for sth back; (chiedere: per sapere) to ask; (: per avere) to ask for; (AMM: documenti) to apply for; (esigere) to need, require; **richi'esto, a** pp di **richiedere** // sf (domanda) request; (AMM) application, request; (esigenza) demand, request; a richiesta on request.

'ricino |'ritʃino| sm: olio di ~ castor oil.

ricognizi'one |rikoɲɲit'tsjone| sf (MIL) reconnaissance; (DIR) recognition, acknowledgement.

ricomincia're |rikomin'tʃare| vt, vi to start again, begin again.

ricom'pensa sf reward.

ricompen'sare vt to reward.

riconcili'are |rikontʃi'ljare| vt to reconcile; ~rsi vr to be reconciled; **riconciliazi'one** sf reconciliation.

ricono'scente |rikonoʃ'ʃente| ag grateful; **ricono'scenza** sf gratitude.

rico'noscere |riko'noʃʃere| vt to recognize; (DIR: figlio, debito) to acknowledge; (ammettere: errore) to admit, acknowledge; **riconosci'mento** sm recognition; acknowledgement; (identificazione) identification; **ricono-sci'uto, a** pp di **riconoscere**.

rico'prire vt (coprire) to cover; (occupare: carica) to hold.

ricor'dare vt to remember, recall; (richiamare alla memoria): ~ qc a qn to remind sb of sth; ~rsi vr: ~rsi (di) to remember; ~rsi di qc/di aver fatto to remember sth/having done.

ri'cordo sm memory; (regalo) keepsake, souvenir; (di viaggio) souvenir; ~i smpl (memorie) memoirs.

ricor'rente ag recurrent, recurring; **ricor'renza** sf recurrence; (festività) anniversary.

ri'correre vi (ripetersi) to recur; ~ a (rivolgersi) to turn to; (: DIR) to appeal to; (servirsi di) to have recourse to; **ri'corso, a** pp di **ricorrere** // sm recurrence; (DIR) appeal; far ricorso a = ricorrere a.

ricostru'ire vt (casa) to rebuild; (fatti) to reconstruct; **ricostruzi'one** sf rebuilding q; reconstruction.

ri'cotta sf soft white unsalted cheese made from sheep's milk.

ricove'rare vt to give shelter to; ~ qn in ospedale to admit sb to hospital.

ri'covero sm shelter, refuge; (MIL) shelter; (MED) admission (to hospital).

ricre'are vt to recreate; (rinvigorire) to restore; (fig: distrarre) to amuse.

ricreazi'one |rikreat'tsjone| sf recreation, entertainment; (INS) break.

ri'credersi vr to change one's mind.

ricupe'rare vt (rientrare in possesso di) to recover, get back; (tempo perduto) to make up for; (NAUT) to salvage; (: naufraghi) to rescue; (delinquente) to rehabilitate; ~ lo svantaggio (SPORT) to close the gap.

ridacchi'are |ridak'kjare| vi to snigger.

ri'dare vt to return, give back.

'ridere vi to laugh; (deridere, beffare): ~ di to laugh at, make fun of.

ri'detto, a pp di **ridire**.

ri'dicolo, a ag ridiculous, absurd.

ridimensio'nare vt to reorganize; (fig) to see in the right perspective.

ri'dire vt to repeat; (criticare) to find fault with; to object to; trova sempre qualcosa da ~ he always manages to find fault.

ridon'dante ag redundant.

ri'dotto, a *pp di* **ridurre**.

ri'durre *vt (anche CHIM, MAT)* to reduce; *(prezzo, spese)* to cut, reduce; *(accorciare: opera letteraria)* to abridge; *(: RADIO, TV)* to adapt; **ridursi** *vr (diminuirsi)* to be reduced, shrink; **ridursi a** to be reduced to; **ridursi pelle e ossa** to be reduced to skin and bone; **riduzi'one** *sf* reduction; abridgement; adaptation.

riem'pire *vt* to fill (up); *(modulo)* to fill in o out; **~rsi** *vr* to fill (up); *(mangiare troppo)* to stuff o.s.; **~ qc di** to fill sth (up) with.

rien'tranza |rien'trantsa| *sf* recess; indentation.

rien'trare *vi (entrare di nuovo)* to go (o come) back in; *(tornare)* to return; *(fare una rientranza)* to go in, curve inwards; to be indented; *(riguardare)*: **~ in** to be included among, form part of; **ri'entro** *sm (ritorno)* return; *(di astronave)* re-entry.

riepilo'gare *vt* to summarize // *vi* to recapitulate.

ri'fare *vt* to do again; *(ricostruire)* to make again; *(nodo)* to tie again, do up again; *(imitare)* to imitate, copy; **~rsi** *vr (risarcirsi)*: **~rsi di** to make up for; *(vendicarsi)*: **~rsi di qc su qn** to get one's own back on sb for sth; *(riferirsi)*: **~rsi a** to go back to; to follow; **~ il letto** to make the bed; **~rsi una vita** to make a new life for o.s.; **ri'fatto, a** *pp di* **rifare**.

riferi'mento *sm* reference; **in** o **con ~ a** with reference to.

rife'rire *vt (riportare)* to report; *(ascrivere)*: **~ qc a** to attribute sth to // *vi* to do a report; **~rsi** *vr*: **~rsi a** to refer to.

rifi'nire *vt* to finish off, put the finishing touches to; **rifini'tura** *sf* finishing touch; **rifiniture** *sfpl (di mobile, auto)* finish *sg*.

rifiu'tare *vt* to refuse; **~ di fare** to refuse to do; **rifi'uto** *sm* refusal; **rifiuti** *smpl (spazzatura)* rubbish *sg*, refuse *sg*.

riflessi'one *sf (FISICA, meditazione)* reflection; *(il pensare)* thought, reflection; *(osservazione)* remark.

rifles'sivo, a *ag (persona)* thoughtful, reflective; *(LING)* reflexive.

ri'flesso, a *pp di* **riflettere** // *sm (di luce, rispecchiamento)* reflection; *(FISIOL)* reflex; **di** o **per ~** indirectly.

ri'flettere *vt* to reflect // *vi* to think; **~rsi** *vr* to be reflected; **~ su** to think over.

riflet'tore *sm* reflector; *(proiettore)* floodlight; searchlight.

ri'flusso *sm* flowing back; *(della marea)* ebb; **un'epoca di ~** an era of nostalgia.

ri'fondere *vt (rimborsare)* to refund, repay.

ri'forma *sf* reform; **la R~** *(REL)* the Reformation.

rifor'mare *vt* to re-form; *(cambiare, innovare)* to reform; *(MIL: recluta)* to declare unfit for service; *(: soldato)* to invalid out, discharge; **riforma'torio** *sm (DIR)* community home *(Brit)*, reformatory *(US)*.

riforni'mento *sm* supplying, providing; restocking; **~i** *smpl* supplies, provisions.

rifor'nire *vt (provvedere)*: **~ di** to supply o provide with; *(fornire di nuovo: casa etc)* to restock.

ri'frangere |ri'frandʒere| *vt* to refract; **ri'fratto, a** *pp di* **rifrangere**; **rifrazi'one** *sf* refraction.

rifug'gire |rifud'dʒire| *vi* to escape again; *(fig)* **~ da** to shun.

rifugi'arsi |rifu'dʒarsi| *vr* to take refuge; **rifugi'ato, a** *sm/f* refugee.

ri'fugio |ri'fudʒo| *sm* refuge, shelter; *(in montagna)* shelter; **~ antiaereo** air-raid shelter.

'riga, ghe *sf* line; *(striscia)* stripe; *(di persone, cose)* line, row; *(regola)* ruler; *(scriminatura)* parting; **mettersi in ~** to line up; **a ~ghe** *(foglio)* lined; *(vestito)* striped.

ri'gagnolo |ri'gaŋɲolo| *sm* rivulet.

ri'gare *vt (foglio)* to rule // *vi*: **~ diritto** *(fig)* to toe the line.

rigatti'ere *sm* junk dealer.

riget'tare |ridʒet'tare| *vt (gettare indietro)* to throw back; *(fig: respingere)* to reject; *(vomitare)* to bring o throw up; **ri'getto** *sm (anche MED)* rejection.

rigidità |ridʒidi'ta| *sf* rigidity; stiffness; severity, rigours *pl*; strictness.

'rigido, a |'ridʒido| *ag* rigid, stiff; *(membra etc)* indurite) stiff; *(METEOR)* harsh, severe; *(fig)* strict.

rigi'rare |ridʒi'rare| *vt* to turn; **~rsi** *vr* to turn round; *(nel letto)* to turn over; **~ qc tra le mani** to turn sth over in one's hands; **~ il discorso** to change the subject.

'rigo, ghi *sm* line; *(MUS)* staff, stave.

rigogli'oso, a |rigoʎ'ʎoso| *ag (pianta)* luxuriant; *(fig: commercio, sviluppo)* thriving.

ri'gonfio, a *ag* swollen.

ri'gore *sm (METEOR)* harshness, rigours *pl*; *(fig)* severity, strictness; *(anche: calcio di ~)* penalty; **di ~** compulsory; **a rigor di termini** strictly speaking; **rigo'roso, a** *ag (severo: persona, ordine)* strict; *(preciso)* rigorous.

rigover'nare *vt* to wash (up).

riguar'dare *vt* to look at again; *(considerare)* to regard, consider; *(concernere)* to regard, concern; **~rsi** *vr (aver cura di sé)* to look after o.s.

rigu'ardo *sm (attenzione)* care; *(considerazione)* regard, respect; **~ a** concerning, with regard to; **non aver ~i nell'agire/nel parlare** to act/speak freely.

rilasci'are |rilaʃ'ʃare| *vt (rimettere in*

libertà) to release; (*AMM: documenti*) to issue; **ri'lascio** *sm* release; issue.

rilas'sare *vt* to relax; **~rsi** *vr* to relax; (*fig: disciplina*) to become slack.

rile'gare *vt* (*libro*) to bind; **rilega'tura** *sf* binding.

ri'leggere [ri'lɛddʒere] *vt* to reread, read again; (*rivedere*) to read over.

ri'lento: a ~ *av* slowly.

rileva'mento *sm* (*topografico, statistico*) survey; (*NAUT*) bearing.

rile'vante *ag* considerable; important.

rile'vare *vt* (*ricavare*) to find; (*notare*) to notice; (*mettere in evidenza*) to point out; (*venire a conoscere: notizia*) to learn; (*raccogliere: dati*) to gather, collect; (*TOPOGRAFIA*) to survey; (*MIL*) to relieve; (*COMM*) to take over.

rili'evo *sm* (*ARTE, GEO*) relief; (*fig: rilevanza*) importance; (*osservazione*) point, remark; (*TOPOGRAFIA*) survey; **dar ~ a** *o* **mettere in ~ qc** (*fig*) to bring sth out, highlight sth.

rilut'tante *ag* reluctant; **rilut'tanza** *sf* reluctance.

'rima *sf* rhyme; (*verso*) verse.

riman'dare *vt* to send again; (*restituire, rinviare*) to send back, return; (*differire*): **~ qc (a)** to postpone sth *o* put sth off (till); (*fare riferimento*): **~ qn a** to refer sb to; **essere rimandato** (*INS*) to have to repeat one's exams; **ri'mando** *sm* (*rinvio*) return; (*dilazione*) postponement; (*riferimento*) cross-reference.

rima'nente *ag* remaining // *sm* rest, remainder; **i ~i** (*persone*) the rest of them, the others; **rima'nenza** *sf* rest, remainder; **rimanenze** *sfpl* (*COMM*) unsold stock *sg.*

rima'nere *vi* (*restare*) to remain, stay; (*avanzare*) to be left, remain; (*restare stupito*) to be amazed; (*restare, mancare*): **rimangono poche settimane a Pasqua** there are only a few weeks left till Easter; **rimane da vedere se it** remains to be seen whether; (*diventare*): **~ vedovo** to be left a widower; (*trovarsi*): **~ confuso/sorpreso** to be confused/surprised.

ri'mare *vt, vi* to rhyme.

rimargi'nare [rimardʒi'nare] *vt, vi* (*anche:* **~rsi**) to heal.

ri'masto, a *pp di* **rimanere**.

rima'sugli [rima'suʎʎi] *smpl* leftovers.

rimbal'zare [rimbal'tsare] *vi* to bounce back, rebound; (*proiettile*) to ricochet; **rim'balzo** *sm* rebound; ricochet.

rimbam'bito, a *ag* senile, in one's dotage.

rimboc'care *vt* (*orlo*) to turn up; (*coperta*) to tuck in; (*maniche, pantaloni*) to turn *o* roll up.

rimbom'bare *vi* to resound.

rimbor'sare *vt* to pay back, repay; **rim'borso** *sm* repayment.

rimedi'are *vi*: **~ a** to remedy // *vt* (*fam: procurarsi*) to get *o* scrape together.

ri'medio *sm* (*medicina*) medicine; (*cura, fig*) remedy, cure.

rimesco'lare *vt* to mix well, stir well; (*carte*) to shuffle; **sentirsi ~ il sangue** (*per paura*) to feel one's blood run cold; (*per rabbia*) to feel one's blood boil.

ri'messa *sf* (*locale: per veicoli*) garage; (: *per aerei*) hangar; (*COMM: di merce*) consignment; (: *di denaro*) remittance; (*TENNIS*) return; (*CALCIO: anche:* **~ in gioco**) throw-in.

ri'messo, a *pp di* **rimettere**.

ri'mettere *vt* (*mettere di nuovo*) to put back; (*indossare di nuovo*): **~ qc** to put sth back on, put sth on again; (*restituire*) to return, give back; (*affidare*) to entrust; (: *decisione*) to refer; (*condonare*) to remit; (*COMM: merci*) to deliver; (: *denaro*) to remit; (*vomitare*) to bring up; (*perdere: anche:* **rimetterci**) to lose; **~rsi al bello** (*tempo*) to clear up; **~rsi in salute** to get better, recover one's health.

'rimmel *sm inv* ® mascara.

rimoder'nare *vt* to modernize.

rimon'tare *vt* (*meccanismo*) to reassemble; (: *tenda*) to put up again // *vi* (*salire di nuovo*): **~ in** (*macchina, treno*) to get back into; (*SPORT*) to close the gap.

rimorchi'are [rimor'kjare] *vt* to tow; (*fig: ragazza*) to pick up; **rimorchia'tore** *sm* (*NAUT*) tug(boat).

ri'morchio [ri'mɔrkjo] *sm* tow; (*veicolo*) trailer.

ri'morso *sm* remorse.

rimozi'one [rimot'tsjone] *sf* removal; (*da un impiego*) dismissal; (*PSIC*) repression.

rim'pasto *sm* (*POL*) reshuffle.

rimpatri'are *vi* to return home // *vt* to repatriate; **rim'patrio** *sm* repatriation.

rimpi'angere [rim'pjandʒere] *vt* to regret; (*persona*) to miss; **rimpi'anto, a** *pp di* **rimpiangere** // *sm* regret.

rimpiat'tino *sm* hide-and-seek.

rimpiaz'zare [rimpjat'tsare] *vt* to replace.

rimpiccio'lire [rimpittʃo'lire] *vt* to make smaller // *vi* (*anche:* **~rsi**) to become smaller.

rimpin'zare [rimpin'tsare] *vt*: **~ di** to cram *o* stuff with.

rimprove'rare *vt* to rebuke, reprimand; **rim'provero** *sm* rebuke, reprimand.

rimugi'nare [rimudʒi'nare] *vt* (*fig*) to turn over in one's mind.

rimunerazi'one [rimunerat'tsjone] *sf* remuneration; (*premio*) reward.

rimu'overe *vt* to remove; (*destituire*) to dismiss.

Rinasci'mento [rinaʃʃi'mento] *sm*: **il ~** the Renaissance.

ri'nascita |ri'naʃʃita| *sf* rebirth, revival.

rincal'zare |rinkal'tsare| *vt* (*palo, albero*) to support, prop up; (*lenzuola*) to tuck in.

rinca'rare *vt* to increase the price of // *vi* to go up, become more expensive.

rinca'sare *vi* to go home.

rinchi'udere |rin'kjudere| *vt* to shut (o lock) up; **~rsi** *vr*: **~rsi in** to shut o.s. up in; **~rsi in se stesso** to withdraw into o.s.; **rinchi'uso, a** *pp di* **rinchiudere**.

rin'correre *vt* to chase, run after; **rin'corso, a** *pp di* **rincorrere** // *sf* short run.

rin'crescere |rin'kreʃʃere| *vb impers*: mi rincresce che/di non poter fare I'm sorry that/I can't do, I regret that/being unable to do; **rincresci'mento** *sm* regret; **rincresci'uto, a** *pp di* **rincrescere**.

rincu'lare *vi* to draw back; (*arma*) to recoil.

rinfacci'are |rinfat'tʃare| *vt* (*fig*): **~ qc a qn** to throw sth in sb's face.

rinfor'zare |rinfor'tsare| *vt* to reinforce, strengthen // *vi* (*anche:* **~rsi**) to grow stronger; **rin'forzo** *sm*: **mettere un rinforzo a** to strengthen; **di rinforzo** (*asse, sbarra*) strengthening; (*esercito*) supporting; (*personale*) extra, additional; **rinforzi** *smpl* (*MIL*) reinforcements.

rinfran'care *vt* to encourage, reassure.

rinfres'care *vt* (*atmosfera, temperatura*) to cool (down); (*abito, pareti*) to freshen up // *vi* (*tempo*) to grow cooler; **~rsi** *vr* (*ristorarsi*) to refresh o.s.; (*lavarsi*) to freshen up; **rin'fresco, schi** *sm* (*festa*) party; **rinfreschi** *smpl* refreshments.

rin'fusa *sf*: **alla ~** in confusion, higgledy-piggledy.

ringhi'are |rin'gjare| *vi* to growl, snarl.

ringhi'era |rin'gjɛra| *sf* railing; (*delle scale*) banister(s *pl*).

ringiova'nire |rindʒova'nire| *vt* (*sog: vestito, acconciatura etc*): **~ qn** to make sb look younger; (*: vacanze etc*) to rejuvenate // *vi* (*anche:* **~rsi**) to become (o look) younger.

ringrazia'mento |ringrattsja'mento| *sm* thanks *pl*.

ringrazi'are |ringrat'tsjare| *vt* to thank; **~ qn di qc** to thank sb for sth.

rinne'gare *vt* (*fede*) to renounce; (*figlio*) to disown, repudiate; **rinne'gato, a** *sm/f* renegade.

rinnova'mento *sm* renewal; (*economico*) revival.

rinno'vare *vt* to renew; (*ripetere*) to repeat, renew; **~rsi** *vr* (*fenomeno*) to be repeated, recur; **rin'novo** *sm* (*di contratto*) renewal; "**chiuso per rinnovo dei locali**" "closed for alterations".

rinoce'ronte |rinotʃe'ronte| *sm* rhinoceros.

rino'mato, a *ag* renowned, celebrated.

rinsal'dare *vt* to strengthen.

rintoc'care *vi* (*campana*) to toll; (*orologio*) to strike.

rintracci'are |rintrat'tʃare| *vt* to track down.

rintro'nare *vi* to boom, roar // *vt* (*assordare*) to deafen; (*stordire*) to stun.

ri'nuncia |ri'nuntʃa| *etc* = **rinunzia** *etc*.

ri'nunzia |ri'nuntsja| *sf* renunciation.

rinunzi'are |rinun'tsjare| *vi*: **~ a** to give up, renounce.

rinve'nire *vt* to find, recover; (*scoprire*) to discover, find out // *vi* (*riprendere i sensi*) to come round; (*riprendere l'aspetto naturale*) to revive.

rinvi'are *vt* (*rimandare indietro*) to send back, return; (*differire*): **~ qc (a)** to postpone sth o put sth off (till); to adjourn sth (till); (*fare un rimando*): **~ qn a** to refer sb to.

rinvigo'rire *vt* to strengthen.

rin'vio, 'vii *sm* (*rimando*) return; (*differimento*) postponement; (: *di seduta*) adjournment; (*in un testo*) cross-reference.

ri'one *sm* district, quarter.

riordi'nare *vt* (*rimettere in ordine*) to tidy; (*riorganizzare*) to reorganize.

riorganiz'zare |riorganid'dzare| *vt* to reorganize.

ripa'gare *vt* to repay.

ripa'rare *vt* (*proteggere*) to protect, defend; (*correggere: male, torto*) to make up for; (: *errore*) to put right; (*aggiustare*) to repair // *vi* (*mettere rimedio*): **~ a** to make up for; **~rsi** *vr* (*rifugiarsi*) to take refuge o shelter; **riparazi'one** *sf* (*di un torto*) reparation, (*di guasto, scarpe*) repairing *q*; repair; (*risarcimento*) compensation.

ri'paro *sm* (*protezione*) shelter, protection; (*rimedio*) remedy.

ripar'tire *vt* (*dividere*) to divide up; (*distribuire*) to share out // *vi* to set off again; to leave again.

ripas'sare *vi* to come (o go) back // *vt* (*scritto, lezione*) to go over (again).

ripen'sare *vi* to think; (*cambiare pensiero*) to change one's mind; (*tornare col pensiero*): **~ a** to recall.

ripercu'otersi *vr*: **~ su** (*fig*) to have repercussions on.

ripercussi'one *sf* (*fig*): **avere una ~ o delle ~i su** to have repercussions on.

ripes'care *vt* (*pesce*) to catch again; (*persona, cosa*) to fish out; (*fig: ritrovare*) to dig out.

ri'petere *vt* to repeat; (*ripassare*) to go over; **ripetizi'one** *sf* repetition; (*di lezione*) revision; **ripetizioni** *sfpl* (*INS*) private tutoring o coaching *sg*.

ripi'ano *sm* (*GEO*) terrace; (*di mobile*) shelf.

ri'picca *sf*: **per ~** out of spite.

'ripido, a *ag* steep.

ripie'gare *vt* to refold; (*piegare più volte*) to fold (up) // *vi* (*MIL*) to retreat, fall back; (*fig*: *accontentarsi*): ~ su to make do with; ~rsi *vr* to bend; **ripi'ego, ghi** *sm* expedient.

ripi'eno, a *ag* full; (*CUC*) stuffed; (: *panino*) filled // *sm* (*CUC*) stuffing.

ri'porre *vt* (*porre al suo posto*) to put back, replace; (*mettere via*) to put away; (*fiducia, speranza*): ~ qc in qn to place *o* put sth in sb.

ripor'tare *vt* (*portare indietro*) to bring (*o* take) back; (*riferire*) to report; (*citare*) to quote; (*ricevere*) to receive, get; (*vittoria*) to gain; (*successo*) to have; (*MAT*) to carry; ~rsi a (*anche fig*) to go back to; (*riferirsi a*) to refer to; ~ danni to suffer damage.

ripo'sare *vt* (*bicchiere, valigia*) to put down; (*dare sollievo*) to rest // *vi* to rest; ~rsi *vr* to rest; **ri'poso** *sm* rest; (*MIL*): riposo! at ease!; a riposo (*in pensione*) retired; giorno di riposo day off.

ripos'tiglio [ripos'tiʎʎo] *sm* lumber-room.

ri'posto, a *pp di* **riporre**.

ri'prendere *vt* (*prigioniero, fortezza*) to recapture; (*prendere indietro*) to take back; (*ricominciare: lavoro*) to resume; (*andare a prendere*) to fetch, come back for; (*assumere di nuovo: impiegati*) to take on again, re-employ; (*rimprove-rare*) to tell off; (*restringere: abito*) to take in; (*CINEMA*) to shoot; ~rsi *vr* to recover; (*correggersi*) to correct o.s.; **ri'preso, a** *pp di* **riprendere** // *sf* re-capture; resumption; (*economica, da malattia, emozione*) recovery; (*AUT*) acceleration *q*; (*TEATRO, CINEMA*) re-run; (*CINEMA: presa*) shooting *q*; shot; (*SPORT*) second half; (: *PUGILATO*) round; a più riprese on several oc-casions, several times.

ripristi'nare *vt* to restore.

ripro'durre *vt* to reproduce; riprodursi *vr* (*BIOL*) to reproduce; (*riformarsi*) to form again; **riprodut'tivo, a** *ag* re-productive; **riproduzi'one** *sf* reproduc-tion; riproduzione vietata all rights re-served.

ripudi'are *vt* to repudiate, disown.

ripu'gnante [ripuɲ'ɲante] *ag* disgusting, repulsive.

ripu'gnare [ripuɲ'ɲare] *vi*: ~ a qn to re-pel *o* disgust sb.

ripu'lire *vt* to clean up; (*sog: ladri*) to clean out; (*perfezionare*) to polish, re-fine.

ri'quadro *sm* square; (*ARCHIT*) panel.

ri'saia *sf* paddy field.

risa'lire *vi* (*ritornare in su*) to go back up; ~ a (*ritornare con la mente*) to go back to; (*datare da*) to date back to, go back to.

risal'tare *vi* (*fig: distinguersi*) to stand

out; (*ARCHIT*) to project, jut out; **ri'salto** *sm* prominence; (*sporgenza*) projection; mettere *o* porre in risalto qc to make sth stand out.

risa'nare *vt* (*guarire*) to heal, cure; (*palude*) to reclaim; (*economia*) to improve; (*bilancio*) to reorganize.

risa'puto, a *ag*: è ~ che ... everyone knows that ..., it is common knowledge that ....

risarci'mento [risartʃi'mento] *sm*: ~ (di) compensation (for).

risar'cire [risar'tʃire] *vt* (*cose*) to pay compensation for; (*persona*): ~ qn di qc to compensate sb for sth.

ri'sata *sf* laugh.

riscalda'mento *sm* heating; ~ centrale central heating.

riscal'dare *vt* (*scaldare*) to heat; (: *mani, persona*) to warm; (*minestra*) to reheat; ~rsi *vr* to warm up.

riscat'tare *vt* (*prigioniero*) to ransom, pay a ransom for; (*DIR*) to redeem; ~rsi *vr* (*da disonore*) to redeem o.s.; **ris'catto** *sm* ransom; redemption.

rischia'rare [riskja'rare] *vt* (*illuminare*) to light up; (*colore*) to make lighter; ~rsi *vr* (*tempo*) to clear up; (*cielo*) to clear; (*fig: volto*) to brighten up; ~rsi la voce to clear one's throat.

rischi'are [ris'kjare] *vt* to risk // *vi*: ~ di fare qc to risk *o* run the risk of doing sth.

'rischio ['riskjo] *sm* risk; **rischi'oso, a** *ag* risky, dangerous.

riscia'cquare [riʃʃa'kware] *vt* to rinse.

riscon'trare *vt* (*confrontare: due cose*) to compare; (*esaminare*) to check, ver-ify; (*rilevare*) to find; **ris'contro** *sm* comparison; check, verification; (*AMM*: *lettera di risposta*) reply.

riscossi'one *sf* collection.

ris'cosso, a *pp di* **riscuotere** // *sf* (*riconquista*) recovery, reconquest.

ris'cuotere *vt* (*ritirare una somma dovuta*) to collect; (: *stipendio*) to draw, collect; (*assegno*) to cash; (*fig: successo etc*) to win, earn; ~rsi *vr*: ~rsi (da) to shake o.s. (out of), rouse o.s. (from).

risenti'mento *sm* resentment.

risen'tire *vt* to hear again; (*provare*) to feel // *vi*: ~ di to feel (*o* show) the effects of; ~rsi *vr*: ~rsi di *o* per to take offence at, resent; **risen'tito, a** *ag* re-sentful.

ri'serbo *sm* reserve.

ri'serva *sf* reserve; (*di caccia, pesca*) preserve; (*restrizione, di indigeni*) re-servation; di ~ (*provviste etc*) in re-serve.

riser'vare *vt* (*tenere in serbo*) to keep, put aside; (*prenotare*) to book, reserve; ~rsi *vr*: ~rsi di fare qc to intend to do sth; **riser'vato, a** *ag* (*prenotato, fig: persona*) reserved; (*confidenziale*) confidential; **riserva'tezza** sf reserve.

risi'edere vi: ~ a o in to reside in.

'risma sf (di carta) ream; (fig) kind, sort.

'riso, a pp di **ridere** // sm (pl(f) ~a: il ridere): un ~ a laugh; il ~ laughter; (pianta) rice.

riso'lino sm snigger.

ri'solto, a pp di **risolvere**.

risolu'tezza [risolu'tettsa] sf determination.

riso'luto, a ag determined, resolute.

risoluzi'one [risolut'tsjone] sf solving q; (MAT) solution; (decisione, di immagine) resolution.

ri'solvere vt (difficoltà, controversia) to resolve; (problema) to solve; (decidere): ~ di fare to resolve to do; ~rsi vr (decidersi): ~rsi a fare to make up one's mind to do; (andare a finire): ~rsi in to end up, turn out; ~rsi in nulla to come to nothing.

riso'nanza [riso'nantsa] sf resonance; aver vasta ~ (fig: fatto etc) to be known far and wide.

riso'nare vt, vi = **risuonare**.

ri'sorgere [ri'sordʒere] vi to rise again; **risorgi'mento** sm revival; il Risorgimento (STORIA) the Risorgimento.

ri'sorsa sf expedient, resort; ~e sfpl (naturali, finanziarie etc) resources; persona piena di ~e resourceful person.

ri'sorto, a pp di **risorgere**.

ri'sotto sm (CUC) risotto.

risparmi'are vt to save; (non uccidere) to spare // vi to save; ~ qc a qn to spare sb sth.

ris'parmio sm saving q; (denaro) savings pl.

rispec'chiare [rispek'kjare] vt to reflect.

rispet'tabile ag respectable.

rispet'tare vt to respect; farsi ~ to command respect.

rispet'tivo, a ag respective.

ris'petto sm respect; ~i smpl (saluti) respects, regards; ~ a (in paragone a) compared to; (in relazione a) as regards, as for; **rispet'toso, a** ag respectful.

ris'plendere vi to shine.

ris'pondere vi to answer, reply; (freni) to respond; ~ a (domanda) to answer, reply to; (persona) to answer; (invito) to reply to; (provocazione, sog: veicolo, apparecchio) to respond to; (corrispondere a) to correspond to; (: speranze, bisogno) to answer; ~ di to answer for; **ris'posto, a** pp di **rispondere** // sf answer, reply; **in risposta a** in reply to.

'rissa sf brawl.

ristabi'lire vt to re-establish, restore; (persona: sog: riposo etc) to restore to health; ~rsi vr to recover.

rista'gnare [rista'ɲɲare] vi (acqua) to become stagnant; (sangue) to cease flowing; (fig: industria) to stagnate; **ris'tagno** sm stagnation.

ris'tampa sf reprinting q; reprint.

risto'rante sm restaurant.

risto'rarsi vr to have something to eat and drink; (riposarsi) to rest, have a rest; **ris'toro** sm (bevanda, cibo) refreshment; **servizio di ristoro** (FERR) refreshments pl.

ristret'tezza [ristret'tettsa] sf (strettezza) narrowness; (fig: scarsezza) scarcity, lack; (: meschinità) meanness; ~e sfpl (povertà) financial straits.

ris'tretto, a pp di **restringere** // ag (racchiuso) enclosed, hemmed in; (angusto) narrow; (limitato): ~ (a) restricted o limited (to); (CUC: brodo) thick; (: caffè) extra strong.

risucchi'are [risuk'kjare] vt to suck in.

risul'tare vi (dimostrarsi) to prove (to be), turn out (to be); (riuscire): ~ vincitore to emerge as the winner; ~ da (provenire) to result from, be the result of; **mi risulta che** ... I understand that ...; **non mi risulta** not as far as I know; **risul'tato** sm result.

risuo'nare vi (rimbombare) to resound.

risurrezi'one [risurret'tsjone] sf (REL) resurrection.

risusci'tare [risuʃʃi'tare] vt to resuscitate, restore to life; (fig) to revive, bring back // vi to rise (from the dead).

ris'veglio [riz've ʎʎo] sm waking up; (fig) revival.

ris'volto sm (di giacca) lapel; (di pantaloni) turn-up; (di manica) cuff; (di tasca) flap; (di libro) inside flap; (fig) implication.

ritagli'are [rita ʎ'ʎare] vt (tagliar via) to cut out; **ri'taglio** sm (di giornale) cutting, clipping; (di stoffa etc) scrap; **nei ritagli di tempo** in one's spare time.

ritar'dare vi (persona, treno) to be late; (orologio) to be slow // vt (rallentare) to slow down; (impedire) to delay, hold up; (differire) to postpone, delay; **ritarda'tario, a** sm/f latecomer.

ri'tardo sm delay; (di persona aspettata) lateness q; (fig: mentale) backwardness; **in ~** late.

ri'tegno [ri'teɲɲo] sm restraint.

rite'nere vt (trattenere) to hold back; (: somma) to deduct; (giudicare) to consider, believe; **rite'nuta** sf (sul salario) deduction.

riti'rare vt to withdraw; (POL: richiamare) to recall; (andare a prendere: pacco etc) to collect, pick up; ~rsi vr to withdraw; (da un'attività) to retire; (stoffa) to shrink; (marea) to recede; **riti'rata** sf (MIL) retreat; (latrina) lavatory; **ri'tiro** sm withdrawal; recall; collection; (luogo appartato) retreat.

'ritmo sm rhythm; (fig) rate; (: della

vita) pace, tempo.

'rito *sm* rite; **di ~** usual, customary.

ritoc'care *vt (disegno, fotografia)* to touch up; *(testo)* to alter; **ri'tocco, chi** *sm* touching up *q;* alteration.

ritor'nare *vi* to return, go *(o come)* back; *(ripresentarsi)* to recur; *(ridiventare):* **~ ricco** to become rich again // *vt (restituire)* to return, give back.

ritor'nello *sm* refrain.

ri'torno *sm* return; **essere di ~** to be back; **avere un ~ di fiamma** *(AUT)* to backfire; *(fig: persona)* to be back in love again.

ri'trarre *vt (trarre indietro, via)* to withdraw; *(distogliere: sguardo)* to turn away; *(rappresentare)* to portray, depict; *(ricavare)* to get, obtain.

ritrat'tare *vt (disdire)* to retract, take back; *(trattare nuovamente)* to deal with again.

ri'tratto, a *pp di* **ritrarre** // *sm* portrait.

ri'troso, a *ag (restio):* **~ (a)** reluctant (to); *(schivo)* shy; **andare a ~** to go backwards.

ritro'vare *vt* to find; *(salute)* to regain; *(persona)* to find; to meet again; **~rsi** *vr (essere, capitare)* to find o.s.; *(raccapezzarsi)* to find one's way; *(con senso reciproco)* to meet (again); **ri'trovo** *sm* meeting place; **ritrovo notturno** night club.

'ritto, a *ag (in piedi)* standing, on one's feet; *(levato in alto)* erect, raised; (: *capelli)* standing on end; *(posto verticalmente)* upright.

ritu'ale *ag, sm* ritual.

riuni'one *sf (adunanza)* meeting, *(riconciliazione)* reunion.

riu'nire *vt (ricongiungere)* to join *(together)*; *(riconciliare)* to reunite, bring together (again); **~rsi** *vr (adunarsi)* to meet; *(tornare a stare insieme)* to be reunited.

riu'scire |riuʃ'ʃire| *vi (uscire di nuovo)* to go out again, go back out; *(aver esito: fatti, azioni)* to go, turn out; *(aver successo)* to succeed, be successful; *(essere, apparire)* to be, prove; *(raggiungere il fine)* to manage, succeed; **~ a fare qc** to manage to do *o* succeed in doing *o* be able to do sth; **questo mi riesce nuovo** this is new to me; **riu'scita** *sf (esito)* result, outcome; *(buon esito)* success.

'riva *sf (di fiume)* bank; *(di lago, mare)* shore.

ri'vale *sm/f* rival; **rivalità** *sf* rivalry.

ri'valsa *sf (rivincita)* revenge; *(risarcimento)* compensation.

rivalu'tare *vt (ECON)* to revalue.

rivan'gare *vt (ricordi etc)* to dig up (again).

rive'dere *vt* to see again; *(ripassare)* to revise; *(verificare)* to check.

rive'lare *vt* to reveal; *(divulgare)* to reveal, disclose; *(dare indizio)* to reveal, show; **~rsi** *vr (manifestarsi)* to be revealed; **~rsi onesto** *etc* to prove to be honest *etc*; **rivela'tore** *sm (TECN)* detector; *(FOT)* developer; **rivelazi'one** *sf* revelation.

rivendi'care *vt* to claim, demand.

ri'vendita *sf (bottega)* retailer's (shop).

rivendi'tore, 'trice *sm/f* retailer; **~ autorizzato** *(COMM)* authorized dealer.

ri'verbero *sm (di luce, calore)* reflection; *(di suono)* reverberation.

rive'renza |rive'rɛntsa| *sf* reverence; *(inchino)* bow; curtsey.

rive'rire *vt (rispettare)* to revere; *(salutare)* to pay one's respects to.

river'sare *vt (anche fig)* to pour; **~rsi** *vr (fig: persone)* to pour out.

rivesti'mento *sm* covering; coating.

rives'tire *vt* to dress again; *(ricoprire)* to cover; to coat; *(fig: carica)* to hold; **~rsi** *vr* to get dressed again; to change (one's clothes).

rivi'era *sf* coast; **la ~ italiana** the Italian Riviera.

ri'vincita |ri'vintʃita| *sf (SPORT)* return match; *(fig)* revenge.

rivis'suto, a *pp di* **rivivere.**

ri'vista *sf* review; *(periodico)* magazine, review; *(TEATRO)* revue; variety show.

ri'vivere *vi (riacquistare forza)* to come alive again; *(tornare in uso)* to be revived // *vt* to relive.

ri'volgere |ri'vɔldʒere| *vt (attenzione, sguardo)* to turn, direct; *(parole)* to address; **~rsi** *vr* to turn round, *(fig: dirigersi per informazioni):* **~rsi a** to go and see, go and speak to; (: *ufficio)* to enquire at.

ri'volta *sf* revolt, rebellion.

rivol'tare *vt* to turn over; *(con l'interno all'esterno)* to turn inside out; *(disgustare: stomaco)* to upset, turn; **~rsi** *vr (ribellarsi):* **~rsi (a)** to rebel (against).

rivol'tella *sf* revolver.

ri'volto, a *pp di* **rivolgere.**

rivoluzio'nare |rivoluttsjo'nare| *vt* to revolutionize.

rivoluzio'nario, a |rivoluttsjo'narjo| *ag, sm/f* revolutionary.

rivoluzi'one |rivolut'tsjone| *sf* revolution.

riz'zare |rit'tsare| *vt* to raise, erect; **~rsi** *vr* to stand up; *(capelli)* to stand on end.

'roba *sf* stuff, things *pl;* *(possessi, beni)* belongings *pl,* things *pl,* possessions *pl;* **~ da mangiare** things *pl* to eat, food; **~ da matti** sheer madness *o* lunacy.

'robot *sm inv* robot.

ro'busto, a *ag* robust, sturdy; *(solido: catena)* strong.

'rocca, che *sf* fortress.

rocca'forte *sf* stronghold.

roc'chetto |rok'ketto| *sm* reel, spool.

'roccia, ce |'rɔttʃa| sf rock; **fare ~** (SPORT) to go rock climbing; **roc'cioso, a** ag rocky.

ro'daggio |ro'daddʒo| sm running (Brit) o breaking (US) in; **in ~** running (Brit) o breaking (US) in.

'Rodano sm: **il ~** the Rhone.

'rodere vt to gnaw (at); (distruggere poco a poco) to eat into.

rodi'tore sm (ZOOL) rodent.

rodo'dendro sm rhododendron.

'rogna |'rɔɲɲa| sf (MED) scabies sg; (fig) bother, nuisance.

ro'gnone |roɲ'ɲone| sm (CUC) kidney.

'rogo, ghi sm (per cadaveri) (funeral) pyre; (supplizio): **il ~** the stake.

rol'lio sm roll(ing).

'Roma sf Rome.

Roma'nia sf: **la ~** Romania.

ro'manico, a, ci, che ag Romanesque.

ro'mano, a ag, sm/f Roman.

romanti'cismo |romanti'tʃizmo| sm romanticism.

ro'mantico, a, ci, che ag romantic.

ro'manza |ro'mandza| sf (MUS, LETTERATURA) romance.

roman'zesco, a, schi, sche |roman'dzesko| ag (stile, personaggi) fictional; (fig) storybook cpd.

romanzi'ere |roman'dzjere| sm novelist.

ro'manzo, a |ro'mandzo| ag (LING) romance cpd // sm (medievale) romance; (moderno) novel; **~ d'appendice** serial (story).

rom'bare vi to rumble, thunder, roar.

'rombo sm rumble, thunder, roar; (MAT) rhombus; (ZOOL) turbot; brill.

ro'meno, a ag, sm/f, sm = **rumeno, a.**

'rompere vt to break; (conversazione, fidanzamento) to break off // vi to break; **~rsi** vr to break; **mi rompe le scatole** (fam) he (o she) is a pain in the neck; **~rsi un braccio** to break an arm; **rompi'capo** sm worry, headache; (indovinello) puzzle; (in enigmistica) brainteaser; **rompighi'accio** sm (NAUT) icebreaker; **rompis'catole** sm/f inv (fam) pest, pain in the neck.

'ronda sf (MIL) rounds pl, patrol.

ron'della sf (TECN) washer.

'rondine sf (ZOOL) swallow.

ron'done sm (ZOOL) swift.

ron'zare |ron'dzare| vi to buzz, hum.

ron'zino |ron'dzino| sm (peg: cavallo) nag.

'rosa sf rose // ag inv, sm pink; **ro'saio** sm (pianta) rosebush, rose tree; (giardino) rose garden; **ro'sario** sm (REL) rosary; **ro'sato, a** ag pink, rosy // sm (vino) rosé (wine); **ro'seo, a** ag (anche fig) rosy.

rosicchi'are |rosik'kjare| vt to gnaw (at); (mangiucchiare) to nibble (at).

rosma'rino sm rosemary.

'roso, a pp di **rodere.**

roso'lare vt (CUC) to brown.

roso'lia sf (MED) German measles sg, rubella.

ro'sone sm rosette; (vetrata) rose window.

'rospo sm (ZOOL) toad.

ros'setto sm (per labbra) lipstick; (per guance) rouge.

'rosso, a ag, sm, sm/f red; **il mar R~** the Red Sea; **~ d'uovo** egg yolk; **ros'sore** sm flush, blush.

rosticce'ria |rostittʃe'ria| sf shop selling roast meat and other cooked food.

'rostro sm rostrum; (becco) beak.

ro'tabile ag (percorribile): **strada ~** roadway; (FERR): **materiale m ~** rolling stock.

ro'taia sf rut, track; (FERR) rail.

ro'tare vt, vi to rotate; **rotazi'one** sf rotation.

rote'are vt, vi to whirl; **~ gli occhi** to roll one's eyes.

ro'tella sf small wheel; (di mobile) castor.

roto'lare vt, vi to roll; **~rsi** vr to roll (about).

'rotolo sm roll; **andare a ~i** (fig) to go to rack and ruin.

ro'tondo, a ag round // sf rotunda.

ro'tore sm rotor.

'rotta sf (AER, NAUT) course, route; (MIL) rout; **a ~ di collo** at breakneck speed; **essere in ~ con qn** to be on bad terms with sb.

rot'tame sm fragment, scrap, broken bit; **~i** smpl (di nave, aereo etc) wreckage sg; **~i di ferro** scrap iron sg.

'rotto, a pp di **rompere** // ag broken; (calzoni) torn, split; (persona: pratico, resistente): **~ a** accustomed o inured to; **per il ~ della cuffia** by the skin of one's teeth.

rot'tura sf breaking q; break; breaking off; (MED) fracture, break.

rou'lotte |ru'lɔt| sf caravan.

ro'vente ag red-hot.

'rovere sm oak.

rovesci'are |rovef'ʃare| vt (versare in giù) to pour; (: accidentalmente) to spill; (capovolgere) to turn upside down; (gettare a terra) to knock down; (: fig: governo) to overthrow; (piegare all'indietro: testa) to throw back; **~rsi** vr (sedia, macchina) to overturn; (barca) to capsize; (liquido) to spill; (fig: situazione) to be reversed.

ro'vescio, sci |ro'veʃʃo| sm other side, wrong side; (della mano) back; (di moneta) reverse; (pioggia) sudden downpour; (fig) setback; (MAGLIA: anche: **punto ~**) purl (stitch); (TENNIS) backhand (stroke); **a ~** upside-down; inside-out; **capire qc a ~** to misunderstand sth.

ro'vina sf ruin; **~e** sfpl ruins; **andare in ~** (andare a pezzi) to collapse; (fig) to go to rack and ruin.

rovi'nare *vi* to collapse, fall down // *vt* (*far cadere giù: casa*) to demolish; (*danneggiare*, *fig*) to ruin; **rovi'noso, a** *ag* disastrous; damaging; violent.

rovis'tare *vt* (*casa*) to ransack; (*tasche*) to rummage in (*o* through).

'rovo *sm* (*BOT*) blackberry bush, bramble bush.

'rozzo, a |'roddzo| *ag* rough, coarse.

'ruba *sf*: andare a ~ to sell like hot cakes.

ru'bare *vt* to steal; ~ qc a qn to steal sth from sb.

rubi'netto *sm* tap, faucet (*US*).

ru'bino *sm* ruby.

ru'brica, che *sf* (*STAMPA*) column; (*quadernetto*) index book; address book.

'rude *ag* tough, rough.

'rudere *sm* (*rovina*) ruins *pl*.

rudimen'tale *ag* rudimentary, basic.

rudi'menti *smpl* rudiments; basic principles; basic knowledge *sg*.

ruffi'ano *sm* pimp.

'ruga, ghe *sf* wrinkle.

'ruggine |'ruddʒine| *sf* rust.

rug'gire |rud'dʒire| *vi* to roar.

rugi'ada |ru'dʒada| *sf* dew.

ru'goso, a *ag* wrinkled.

rul'lare *vi* (*tamburo, nave*) to roll; (*aereo*) to taxi.

'rullo *sm* (*di tamburi*) roll; (*arnese cilindrico, TIP*) roller; ~ compressore steam roller; ~ di pellicola roll of film.

rum *sm* rum.

ru'meno, a *ag, sm/f, sm* Romanian.

rumi'nare *vt* (*ZOOL*) to ruminate.

ru'more *sm*: un ~ a noise, a sound; (*fig*) a rumour; il ~ noise; **rumo'roso, a** *ag* noisy.

ru'olo *sm* (*TEATRO, fig*) role, part; (*elenco*) roll, register, list; di ~ permanent, on the permanent staff.

ru'ota *sf* wheel; a ~ (*forma*) circular; ~ anteriore/posteriore front/back wheel; ~ di scorta spare wheel.

ruo'tare *vt, vi* = **rotare**.

'rupe *sf* cliff.

ru'rale *ag* rural, country *cpd*.

ru'scello |ruʃ'ʃɛllo| *sm* stream.

'ruspa *sf* excavator.

rus'sare *vi* to snore.

'Russia *sf*: la ~ Russia; **'russo, a** *ag, sm/f, sm* Russian.

'rustico, a, ci, che *ag* rustic; (*fig*) rough, unrefined.

rut'tare *vi* to belch; **'rutto** *sm* belch.

'ruvido, a *ag* rough, coarse.

ruzzo'lare |ruttso'lare| *vi* to tumble down; **ruzzo'loni** *av*: cadere ruzzoloni to tumble down; fare le scale ruzzoloni to tumble down the stairs.

S

S. *abbr* (= *sud*) S.

sa *vb vedi* **sapere**.

'sabato *sm* Saturday; di *o* il ~ on Saturdays.

'sabbia *sf* sand; ~e mobili quicksand(s); **sabbi'oso, a** *ag* sandy.

sabo'taggio |sabo'taddʒo| *sm* sabotage.

sabo'tare *vt* to sabotage.

'sacca, che *sf* bag; (*bisaccia*) haversack; (*insenatura*) inlet; ~ da viaggio travelling bag.

sacca'rina *sf* saccharin(e).

sac'cente |sat'tʃente| *sm/f* know-all (*Brit*), know-it-all (*US*).

saccheggi'are |sakked'dʒare| *vt* to sack, plunder; **sac'cheggio** *sm* sack(ing).

sac'chetto |sak'ketto| *sm* (small) bag; (small) sack.

'sacco, chi *sm* bag; (*per carbone etc*) sack; (*ANAT, BIOL*) sac; (*tela*) sacking; (*saccheggio*) sack(ing); (*fig: grande quantità*): un ~ di lots of, heaps of; ~ a pelo sleeping bag; ~ per i rifiuti bin bag.

sacer'dote |satʃer'dote| *sm* priest; **sacer'dozio** *sm* priesthood.

sacra'mento *sm* sacrament.

sacrifi'care *vt* to sacrifice; ~rsi *vr* to sacrifice o.s.; (*privarsi di qc*) to make sacrifices.

sacri'ficio |sakri'fitʃo| *sm* sacrifice.

sacri'legio |sacri'lɛdʒo| *sm* sacrilege.

'sacro, a *ag* sacred.

'sadico, a, ci, che *ag* sadistic // *sm/f* sadist.

sa'etta *sf* arrow; (*fulmine: anche fig*) thunderbolt; flash of lightning.

sa'fari *sm inv* safari.

sa'gace |sa'gatʃe| *ag* shrewd, sagacious.

sag'gezza |sad'dʒettsa| *sf* wisdom.

saggi'are |sad'dʒare| *vt* (*metalli*) to assay; (*fig*) to test.

'saggio, a, gi, ge |'saddʒo| *ag* wise // *sm* (*persona*) sage; (*operazione sperimentale*) test; (: *dell'oro*) assay; (*fig: prova*) proof; (*campione indicativo*) sample; (*ricerca, esame critico*) essay.

Sagit'tario |sadʒit'tarjo| *sm* Sagittarius.

sagoma *sf* (*profilo*) outline, profile; (*forma*) form, shape; (*TECN*) template; (*bersaglio*) target; (*fig: persona*) character.

'sagra *sf* festival.

sagres'tano *sm* sacristan; sexton.

sagres'tia *sf* sacristy; (*culto protestante*) vestry.

Sa'hara |sa'ara| *sm*: il (deserto del) ~ the Sahara (Desert).

'sai *vb vedi* **sapere**.

'sala *sf* hall; (*stanza*) room; ~ d'aspetto waiting room; ~ da ballo ballroom; ~ per concerti concert hall; ~ da gioco gaming room; ~ **operatoria** operating theatre; ~ **da pranzo** dining room.

sa'lame *sm* salami *q*, salami sausage.

sala'moia *sf* (CUC) brine.

sa'lare *vt* to salt.

salari'ato, a *sm/f* wage-earner.

sa'lario *sm* pay, wages *pl*.

sa'lato, a *ag* (*sapore*) salty; (CUC) salted, salt *cpd*; (*fig: discorso etc*) biting, sharp; (: *prezzi*) steep, stiff.

sal'dare *vt* (*congiungere*) to join, bind; (*parti metalliche*) to solder; (: *con saldatura autogena*) to weld; (*conto*) to settle, pay; **salda'tura** *sf* soldering; welding; (*punto saldato*) soldered joint; weld.

sal'dezza [sal'dettsa] *sf* firmness; strength.

'saldo, a *ag* (*resistente, forte*) strong, firm; (*fermo*) firm, steady, stable; (*fig*) firm, steadfast // *sm* (*svendita*) sale; (*di conto*) settlement; (ECON) balance.

'sale *sm* salt; (*fig*): **ha poco ~ in zucca** he doesn't have much sense; ~ **fino/grosso** table/cooking salt.

'salice ['salitʃe] *sm* willow; ~ **piangente** weeping willow.

sali'ente *ag* (*fig*) salient, main.

sali'era *sf* salt cellar.

sa'lino, a *ag* saline // *sf* saltworks *sg*.

sa'lire *vi* to go (o come) up; (*aereo etc*) to climb, go up; (*passeggero*) to get on; (*sentiero, prezzi, livello*) to go up, rise // *vt* (*scale, gradini*) to go (o come) up; ~ **su** to climb (up); ~ **sul treno/sull'autobus** to board the train/the bus; ~ **in macchina** to get into the car; **sa'lita** *sf* climb, ascent; (*erta*) hill, slope; **in salita** *ag, av* uphill.

sa'liva *sf* saliva.

'salma *sf* corpse.

'salmo *sm* psalm.

sal'mone *sm* salmon.

sa'lone *sm* (*stanza*) sitting room, lounge; (*in albergo*) lounge; (*su nave*) lounge, saloon; (*mostra*) show, exhibition; ~ **di bellezza** beauty salon.

sa'lotto *sm* lounge, sitting room; (*mobilio*) lounge suite.

sal'pare *vi* (NAUT) to set sail; (*anche*: ~ **l'ancora**) to weigh anchor.

'salsa *sf* (CUC) sauce; ~ **di pomodoro** tomato sauce.

sal'siccia, ce [sal'sittʃa] *sf* pork sausage.

sal'tare *vi* to jump, leap; (*esplodere*) to blow up, explode; (: *valvola*) to blow; (*venir via*) to pop off; (*non aver luogo: corso etc*) to be cancelled // *vt* to jump (over), leap (over); (*fig: pranzo, capitolo*) to skip, miss (out); (CUC) to sauté; **far** ~ to blow up; to burst open; ~ **fuori** (*fig: apparire all'improvviso*) to turn up.

saltel'lare *vi* to skip; to hop.

saltim'banco *sm* acrobat.

'salto *sm* jump; (SPORT) jumping; **fare un** ~ to jump, leap; **fare un** ~ **da qn** to pop over to sb's (place); ~ **in alto/lungo** high/long jump; ~ **con l'asta** pole vaulting; ~ **mortale** somersault.

saltu'ario, a *ag* occasional, irregular.

sa'lubre *ag* healthy, salubrious.

salume'ria *sf* delicatessen.

sa'lumi *smpl* salted pork meats.

salu'tare *ag* healthy; (*fig*) salutary, beneficial // *vt* (*per dire buon giorno, fig*) to greet; (*per dire addio*) to say goodbye to; (MIL) to salute.

sa'lute *sf* health; ~! (*a chi starnutisce*) bless you!; (*nei brindisi*) cheers!; **bere alla** ~ **di qn** to drink (to) sb's health.

sa'luto *sm* (*gesto*) wave; (*parola*) greeting; (MIL) salute; ~**i** *smpl* greetings; **cari** ~**i** best regards; **vogliate gradire i nostri più distinti** ~**i** Yours faithfully.

salvacon'dotto *sm* (MIL) safe-conduct.

salva'gente [salva'dʒɛnte] *sm* (NAUT) lifebuoy; (*stradale*) traffic island; ~ **a ciambella** life belt; ~ **a giubbotto** life-jacket.

salvaguar'dare *vt* to safeguard.

sal'vare *vt* to save; (*trarre da un pericolo*) to rescue; (*proteggere*) to protect; ~**rsi** *vr* to save o.s.; to escape; **salva'taggio** *sm* rescue; **salva'tore, 'trice** *sm/f* saviour.

'salve *escl* (*fam*) hi!

sal'vezza [sal'vettsa] *sf* salvation; (*sicurezza*) safety.

'salvia *sf* (BOT) sage.

'salvo, a *ag* safe, unhurt, unharmed; (*fuori pericolo*) safe, out of danger // *sm*: **in** ~ safe // *prep* (*eccetto*) except; **mettere qc in** ~ to put sth in a safe place; ~ **che** *cong* (*a meno che*) unless; (*eccetto che*) except (that); ~ **imprevisti** barring accidents.

sam'buco *sm* elder (tree).

sa'nare *vt* to heal, cure; (*economia*) to put right.

san'cire [san'tʃire] *vt* to sanction.

'sandalo *sm* (BOT) sandalwood; (*calzatura*) sandal.

'sangue *sm* blood; **farsi cattivo** ~ to fret, get in a state; ~ **freddo** (*fig*) sangfroid, calm; **a** ~ **freddo** in cold blood; **sangu'igno, a** *ag* blood *cpd*; (*colore*) blood-red; **sangui'nare** *vi* to bleed; **sangui'noso, a** *ag* bloody; **sangui'suga** *sf* leech.

sanità *sf* health; (*salubrità*) healthiness; **Ministero della** S~ Department of Health; ~ **mentale** sanity.

sani'tario, a *ag* health *cpd*; (*condizioni*) sanitary // *sm* (AMM) doctor; (*impianti*) ~**i** *smpl* bathroom *o* sanitary fittings.

'sanno *vb vedi* **sapere**.

'sano, a *ag* healthy; (*denti, costituzione*) healthy, sound; (*integro*) whole, unbroken; (*fig: politica, consigli*) sound; ~

di mente sane; di ~a pianta completely, entirely; ~ e salvo safe and sound.

santifi'care *vt* to sanctify; (*feste*) to observe.

santità *sf* sanctity; holiness; Sua/Vostra ~ (*titolo di Papa*) His/Your Holiness.

'santo, a *ag* holy; (*fig*) saintly; (*seguito da nome proprio: dan sm* **san** + *C*, **sant'** + *V*, **santo** + *s impura, gn, pn, ps, x, z*; *dav sf* **santa** + *C*, **sant'** + *V*) saint // *sm/f* saint; **la S~a Sede** the Holy See.

santu'arlo *sm* sanctuary.

sanzio'nare [santsjo'nare] *vt* to sanction.

sanzi'one [san'tsjone] *sf* sanction; (*penale, civile*) sanction, penalty.

sa'pere *vt* to know; (*essere capace di*): **so nuotare** I know how to swim, I can swim // *vi*: ~ **di** (*aver sapore*) to taste of; (*aver odore*) to smell of // *sm* knowledge: **far ~ qc a qn** to inform sb about sth, let sb know sth; **mi sa che non sia vero** I don't think that's true.

sapi'enza [sa'pjentsa] *sf* wisdom.

sa'pone *sm* soap; ~ **da bucato** washing soap; **sapo'netta** *sf* cake *o* bar *o* tablet of soap.

sa'pore *sm* taste, flavour; **sapo'rito, a** *ag* tasty.

sappi'amo *vb vedi* **sapere**.

saraci'nesca [sarat͡ʃi'neska] *sf* (*serranda*) rolling shutter.

sar'casmo *sm* sarcasm *q*; sarcastic remark.

Sar'degna [sar'deɲɲa] *sf*: **la** ~ Sardinia.

sar'dina *sf* sardine.

'sardo, a *ag, sm/f* Sardinian.

'sarto, a *sm/f* tailor/dressmaker; **sarto'ria** *sf* tailor's (shop); dressmaker's (shop); (*casa di moda*) fashion house; (*arte*) couture.

'sasso *sm* stone; (*ciottolo*) pebble; (*masso*) rock.

sas'sofono *sm* saxophone.

sas'soso, a *ag* stony; pebbly.

'Satana *sm* Satan; **sa'tanico, a, ci, che** *ag* satanic, fiendish.

sa'tellite *sm, ag* satellite.

'satira *sf* satire.

'saturo, a *ag* saturated; (*fig*): ~ **di** full of.

S.A.U.B. ['saub] *sigla f* (= *Struttura Amministrativa Unificata di Base*) state welfare system.

'sauna *sf* sauna.

Sa'voia *sf*: **la** ~ Savoy.

savoi'ardo, a *ag* of Savoy, Savoyard // *sm* (*biscotto*) sponge finger.

sazi'are [sat'tsjare] *vt* to satisfy, satiate; ~**rsi** *vr* (*riempirsi di cibo*): ~**rsi (di)** to eat one's fill (of); (*fig*): ~**rsi di** to grow tired *o* weary of.

'sazio, a ['sattsjo] *ag*: ~ **(di)** sated (with), full (of); (*fig: stufo*) fed up (with), sick (of).

sba'dato, a *ag* careless, inattentive.

sbadigli'are [zbadiʎ'ʎare] *vi* to yawn; **sba'diglio** *sm* yawn.

sbagli'are [zbaʎ'ʎare] *vt* to make a mistake in, get wrong // *vi* to make a mistake, be mistaken, be wrong; (*operare in modo non giusto*) to err; ~**rsi** *vr* to make a mistake, be mistaken, be wrong; ~ **la mira/strada** to miss one's aim/take the wrong road; **'sbaglio** *sm* mistake, error; (*morale*) error; **fare uno sbaglio** to make a mistake.

sbal'lare *vt* (*merce*) to unpack // *vi* (*nel fare un conto*) to overestimate; (*fam: gergo della droga*) to get high.

sballot'tare *vt* to toss (about).

sbalor'dire *vt* to stun, amaze // *vi* to be stunned, be amazed; **sbalordi'tivo, a** *ag* amazing; (*prezzo*) incredible, absurd.

sbal'zare [zbal'tsare] *vt* to throw, hurl // *vi* (*balzare*) to bounce; (*saltare*) to leap, bound; **'sbalzo** *sm* (*spostamento improvviso*) jolt, jerk; **a sbalzi** jerkily; (*fig*) in fits and starts; **uno sbalzo di temperatura** a sudden change in temperature.

sban'dare *vi* (*NAUT*) to list; (*AER*) to bank; (*AUT*) to skid; ~**rsi** *vr* (*folla*) to disperse; (*fig: famiglia*) to break up.

sbandie'rare *vt* (*bandiera*) to wave; (*fig*) to parade, show off.

sbaragli'are [zbaraʎ'ʎare] *vt* (*MIL*) to rout; (*in gare sportive etc*) to beat, defeat.

sba'raglio [zba'raʎʎo] *sm* rout; defeat; **gettarsi allo** ~ to risk everything.

sbaraz'zarsi [zbarat'tsarsi] *vr*: ~ **di** to get rid of, rid o.s. of.

sbar'care *vt* (*passeggeri*) to disembark; (*merci*) to unload // *vi* to disembark; **'sbarco** *sm* disembarkation; unloading; (*MIL*) landing.

'sbarra *sf* bar; (*di passaggio a livello*) barrier; (*DIR*): **presentarsi alla** ~ to appear before the court.

sbarra'mento *sm* (*stradale*) barrier; (*diga*) dam, barrage; (*MIL*) barrage.

sbar'rare *vt* (*strada etc*) to block, bar; (*assegno*) to cross; ~ **il passo** to bar the way; ~ **gli occhi** to open one's eyes wide.

'sbattere *vt* (*porta*) to slam, bang; (*tappeti, ali, CUC*) to beat; (*urtare*) to knock, hit // *vi* (*porta, finestra*) to bang; (*agitarsi: ali, vele etc*) to flap; **me ne sbatto!** (*fam*) I don't give a damn!; **sbat'tuto, a** *ag* (*viso, aria*) dejected, worn out; (*uovo*) beaten.

sba'vare *vi* to dribble; (*colore*) to smear, smudge.

sbia'dire *vi* (*anche*: ~**rsi**), *vt* to fade; **sbia'dito, a** *ag* faded; (*fig*) colourless, dull.

sbian'care *vt* to whiten; (*tessuto*) to bleach // *vi* (*impallidire*) to grow pale *o* white.

sbi'eco, a, chi, che *ag (storto)* squint, askew; **di ~: guardare qn di ~** *(fig)* to look askance at sb; **tagliare una stoffa di ~** to cut a material on the bias.

sbigot'tire *vt* to dismay, stun // *vi (anche: ~rsi)* to be dismayed.

sbilanci'are |zbilan'tʃarε| *vt* to throw off balance; **~rsi** *vr (perdere l'equilibrio)* to overbalance, lose one's balance; *(fig: compromettersi)* to compromise o.s.

sbirci'are |zbir'tʃarε| *vt* to cast sidelong glances at, eye.

'sbirro *sm (peg)* cop.

sbizzar'rirsi |zbiddzar'rirsi| *vr* to indulge one's whims.

sbloc'care *vt* to unblock, free; *(freno)* to release; *(prezzi, affitti)* to decontrol.

sboc'care *vi*: **~ in** *(fiume)* to flow into; *(strada)* to lead into; *(persona)* to come (out) into; *(fig: concludersi)* to end (up) in.

sboc'cato, a *ag (persona)* foul-mouthed; *(linguaggio)* foul.

sbocci'are |zbot'tʃarε| *vi (fiore)* to bloom, open (out).

'sbocco, chi *sm (di fiume)* mouth; *(di strada)* end; *(di tubazione, COMM)* outlet; *(uscita: anche fig)* way out; **siamo in una situazione senza ~chi** there's no way out of this for us.

sbol'lire *vi (fig)* to cool down, calm down.

'sbornia *sf (fam)*: **prendersi una ~** to get plastered.

sbor'sare *vt (denaro)* to pay out.

sbot'tare *vi*: **~ in una risata/per la collera** to burst out laughing/explode with anger.

sbotto'nare *vt* to unbutton, undo.

sbracci'ato, a |zbrat'tʃato| *ag (camicia)* sleeveless; *(persona)* bare-armed.

sbrai'tare *vi* to yell, bawl.

sbra'nare *vt* to tear to pieces.

sbricio'lare |zbritʃo'larε| *vt*, **~rsi** *vr* to crumble.

sbri'gare *vt* to deal with, get through; *(cliente)* to attend to, deal with; **~rsi** *vr* to hurry (up); **sbriga'tivo, a** *ag (persona, modo)* quick, expeditious; *(giudizio)* hasty.

sbrindel'lato, a *ag* tattered, in tatters.

sbrodo'lare *vt* to stain, dirty.

'sbronzo, a |'zbrontso| *ag (fam: ubriaco)* tight // *sf*: **prendersi una ~a** to get tight o plastered.

sbu'care *vi* to come out, emerge; *(apparire improvvisamente)* to pop out (o up).

sbucci'are |zbut'tʃarε| *vt (arancia, patata)* to peel; *(piselli)* to shell; **~rsi un ginocchio** to graze one's knee.

sbudel'larsi *vr*: **~ dalle risa** to split one's sides laughing.

sbuf'fare *vi (persona, cavallo)* to snort; *(: ansimare)* to puff, pant; *(treno)* to

puff; **'sbuffo** *sm (di aria, fumo, vapore)* puff; **maniche a sbuffo** puff(ed) sleeves.

'scabbia *sf (MED)* scabies *sg*.

sca'broso, a *ag (fig: difficile)* difficult, thorny; *(: imbarazzante)* embarrassing; *(: sconcio)* indecent.

scacchi'era |skak'kjεra| *sf* chessboard.

scacci'are |skat'tʃarε| *vt* to chase away *o* out, drive away *o* out.

'scacco, chi *sm (pezzo del gioco)* chessman; *(quadretto di scacchiera)* square; *(fig)* setback, reverse; **~chi** *smpl (gioco)* chess *sg*; **a ~chi** *(tessuto)* check(ed); **scacco'matto** *sm* checkmate.

sca'dente *ag* shoddy, of poor quality.

sca'denza |ska'dεntsa| *sf (di cambiale, contratto)* maturity; *(di passaporto)* expiry date; **a breve/lunga ~** short-/long-term; **data di ~** expiry date.

sca'dere *vi (contratto etc)* to expire; *(debito)* to fall due; *(valore, forze, peso)* to decline, go down.

sca'fandro *sm (di palombaro)* diving suit; *(di astronauta)* space-suit.

scaf'fale *sm* shelf; *(mobile)* set of shelves.

'scafo *sm (NAUT, AER)* hull.

scagio'nare |skadʒo'narε| *vt* to exonerate, free from blame.

'scaglia |'skaʎʎa| *sf (ZOOL)* scale; *(scheggia)* chip, flake.

scagli'are |skaʎ'ʎarε| *vt (lanciare: anche fig)* to hurl, fling; **~rsi** *vr*: **~rsi su** *o* contro to hurl *o* fling o.s. at; *(fig)* to rail at.

scaglio'nare |skaʎʎo'narε| *vt (pagamenti)* to space out, spread out; *(MIL)* to echelon; **scagli'one** *sm* echelon; *(GEO)* terrace; **a scaglioni** in groups.

'scala *sf (a gradini etc)* staircase, stairs *pl*; *(a pioli, di corda)* ladder; *(MUS, GEO, di colori, valori, fig)* scale; **~e** *sfpl (scalinata)* stairs; **su vasta ~/~ ridotta** on a large/small scale; **~ a libretto** stepladder; **~ mobile** escalator; *(ECON)* sliding scale; **~ mobile (dei salari)** index-linked pay scale.

sca'lare *vt (ALPINISMO, muro)* to climb, scale; *(debito)* to scale down, reduce; **sca'lata** *sf* scaling *q*, climbing *q*; *(arrampicata, fig)* climb; **scala'tore, 'trice** *sm/f* climber.

scalda'bagno |skalda'baɲɲo| *sm* water-heater.

scal'dare *vt* to heat; **~rsi** *vr* to warm up, heat up; *(al fuoco, al sole)* to warm o.s.; *(fig)* to get excited.

scal'fire *vt* to scratch.

scali'nata *sf* staircase.

sca'lino *sm (anche fig)* step; *(di scala a pioli)* rung.

'scalo *sm (NAUT)* slipway; *(: porto d'approdo)* port of call; *(AER)* stopover; **fare ~ a** *(NAUT)* to call (at), put in (at); *(AER)* to land (at), make a stop (at); ~ **merci** (FERR) goods (Brit) o freight yard.

scalop'pina sf (CUC) escalope.

scal'pello sm chisel.

scal'pore sm noise, row; **far ~** (notizia) to cause a sensation o a stir.

'scaltro, a ag cunning, shrewd.

scal'zare [skal'tsare] vt (albero) to bare the roots of; (muro, fig: autorità) to undermine.

'scalzo, a ['skaltso] ag barefoot.

scambi'are vt to exchange; (confondere): ~ **qn/qc per** to take o mistake sb/sth for; **mi hanno scambiato il cappello** they've given me the wrong hat.

scambi'evole ag mutual, reciprocal.

'scambio sm exchange; (FERR) points pl; **fare (uno) ~** to make a swap.

scampa'gnata [skampaɲ'nata] sf trip to the country.

scampa'nare vi to peal.

scam'pare vt (salvare) to rescue, save; (evitare: morte, prigione) to escape // vi: ~ **(a qc)** to survive (sth), escape (sth); **scamparla bella** to have a narrow escape.

'scampo sm (salvezza) escape; (ZOOL) prawn; **cercare ~ nella fuga** to seek safety in flight.

'scampolo sm remnant.

scanala'tura sf (incavo) channel, groove.

scandagli'are [skandaʎ'ʎare] vt (NAUT) to sound; (fig) to sound out; to probe.

scandaliz'zare [skandalid'dzare] vt to shock, scandalize; **~rsi** vr to be shocked.

'scandalo sm scandal.

Scandi'navia sf: **la ~** Scandinavia; **scandi'navo, a** ag, sm/f Scandinavian.

scan'dire vt (versi) to scan; (parole) to articulate, pronounce distinctly; **~ il tempo** (MUS) to beat time.

scan'nare vt (animale) to butcher, slaughter; (persona) to cut o slit the throat of.

'scanno sm seat, bench.

scansafa'tiche [skansafa'tike] sm/f inv idler, loafer.

scan'sare vt (rimuovere) to move (aside), shift; (schivare: schiaffo) to dodge; (sfuggire) to avoid; **~rsi** vr to move aside.

scan'sia sf shelves pl; (per libri) bookcase.

'scanso sm: **a ~ di** in order to avoid, as a precaution against.

scanti'nato sm basement.

scanto'nare vi to turn the corner; (svignarsela) to sneak off.

scapes'trato, a ag dissolute.

'scapito sm (perdita) loss; (danno) damage, detriment; **a ~ di** to the detriment of.

'scapola sf shoulder blade.

'scapolo sm bachelor.

scappa'mento sm (AUT) exhaust.

scap'pare vi (fuggire) to escape; (andare via in fretta) to rush off; **lasciarsi ~ un'occasione** to let an opportunity go by; **~ di prigione** to escape from prison; **~ di mano** (oggetto) to slip out of one's hands; **~ di mente a qn** to slip sb's mind; **mi scappò detto** I let it slip; **scap'pata** sf quick visit o call; **scappa'tella** sf escapade; **scappa'toia** sf way out.

scara'beo sm beetle.

scarabocchi'are [skarabok'kjare] vt to scribble, scrawl; **scara'bocchio** sm scribble, scrawl.

scara'faggio [skara'faddʒo] sm cockroach.

scaraven'tare vt to fling, hurl.

scarce'rare [skartʃe'rare] vt to release (from prison).

'scarica, che sf (di più armi) volley of shots; (di sassi, pugni) hail, shower; (ELETTR) discharge; **~ di mitra** burst of machine-gun fire.

scari'care vt (merci, camion etc) to unload; (passeggeri) to set down, put off; (arma) to unload; (: sparare, ELETTR) to discharge; (sog: corso d'acqua) to empty, pour; (fig: liberare da un peso) to unburden, relieve; **~rsi** vr (orologio) to run o wind down; (batteria, accumulatore) to go flat o dead; (fig: rilassarsi) to unwind; (: sfogarsi) to let off steam; **il fulmine si scaricò su un albero** the lightning struck a tree; **scarica'tore** sm loader; (di porto) docker.

'scarico, a, chi, che ag unloaded; (orologio) run down; (accumulatore) dead, flat // sm (di merci, materiali) unloading; (di immondizie) dumping, tipping (Brit); (: luogo) rubbish dump; (TECN: deflusso) draining; (: dispositivo) drain; (AUT) exhaust.

scar'latto, a ag scarlet.

'scarno, a ag thin, bony.

'scarpa sf shoe; **~e da ginnastica/tennis** gym/tennis shoes.

scar'pata sf escarpment.

scarseggi'are [skarsed'dʒare] vi to be scarce; **~ di** to be short of, lack.

scar'sezza [skar'settsa] sf scarcity, lack.

'scarso, a ag (insufficiente) insufficient, meagre; (povero: annata) poor, lean; (INS: voto) poor; **~ di** lacking in; **3 chili ~i** just under 3 kilos, barely 3 kilos.

scarta'mento sm (FERR) gauge; **~ normale/ridotto** standard/narrow gauge.

scar'tare vt (pacco) to unwrap; (idea) to reject; (MIL) to declare unfit for military service; (carte da gioco) to discard; (CALCIO) to dodge (past) // vi to swerve.

'scarto sm (cosa scartata, anche COMM) reject; (di veicolo) swerve; (differenza) gap, difference.

scassi'nare *vt* to break, force.

'scasso *sm vedi* **furto**.

scate'nare *vt* (*fig*) to incite, stir up; **~rsi** *vr* (*temporale*) to break; (*rivolta*) to break out; (*persona: infuriarsi*) to rage.

'scatola *sf* box; (*di latta*) tin (*Brit*), can; **cibi in ~** tinned (*Brit*) *o* canned foods; **~ cranica** cranium.

scat'tare *vt* (*fotografia*) to take // *vi* (*congegno, molla etc*) to be released; (*balzare*) to spring up; (*SPORT*) to put on a spurt; (*fig: per l'ira*) to fly into a rage; **~ in piedi** to spring to one's feet.

'scatto *sm* (*dispositivo*) release; (*: di arma da fuoco*) trigger mechanism; (*rumore*) click; (*balzo*) jump, start; (*SPORT*) spurt; (*fig: di ira etc*) fit; (*: di stipendio*) increment; **di ~** suddenly.

scatu'rire *vi* to gush, spring.

scaval'care *vt* (*ostacolo*) to pass (*o* climb) over; (*fig*) to get ahead of, overtake.

sca'vare *vt* (*terreno*) to dig; (*legno*) to hollow out; (*pozzo, galleria*) to bore; (*città sepolta etc*) to excavate.

'scavo *sm* excavating *q*; excavation.

'scegliere ['ʃeʎʎere] *vt* to choose, select.

sce'icco, chi [ʃe'ikko] *sm* sheik.

scelle'rato, a [ʃelle'rato] *ag* wicked, evil.

scel'lino [ʃel'lino] *sm* shilling.

'scelto, a ['ʃelto] *pp di* **scegliere** // *ag* (*gruppo*) carefully selected; (*frutta, verdura*) choice, top quality; (*MIL: specializzato*) crack *cpd*, highly skilled // *sf* choice; selection; **di prima ~a** top grade *o* quality; **frutta o formaggi a ~a** choice of fruit or cheese.

sce'mare [ʃe'mare] *vt, vi* to diminish.

'scemo, a ['ʃemo] *ag* stupid, silly.

'scempio ['ʃempjo] *sm* slaughter, massacre; (*fig*) ruin; **far ~ di** (*fig*) to play havoc with, ruin.

'scena ['ʃɛna] *sf* (*gen*) scene; (*palcoscenico*) stage; **le ~e** (*fig: teatro*) the stage; **fare una ~** to make a scene; **andare in ~** to be staged *o* put on *o* performed; **mettere in ~** to stage.

sce'nario [ʃe'narjo] *sm* scenery; (*di film*) scenario.

sce'nata [ʃe'nata] *sf* row, scene.

'scendere ['ʃendere] *vi* to go (*o* come) down; (*strada, sole*) to go down; (*notte*) to fall; (*passeggero: fermarsi*) to get out, alight; (*fig: temperatura, prezzi*) to go *o* come down, fall, drop // *vt* (*scale, pendìo*) to go (*o* come) down; **~ dalle scale** to go (*o* come) down the stairs; **~ dal treno** to get off *o* out of the train; **~ dalla macchina** to get out of the car; **~ da cavallo** to dismount, get off one's horse.

'scenico, a, ci, che ['ʃɛniko] *ag* stage *cpd*, scenic.

scervel'lato, a [ʃervel'lato] *ag* featherbrained, scatterbrained.

'sceso, a ['ʃeso] *pp di* **scendere**.

'scettico, a, ci, che ['ʃɛttiko] *ag* sceptical.

'scettro ['ʃɛttro] *sm* sceptre.

'scheda ['skɛda] *sf* (*index*) card; **~ elettorale** ballot paper; **~ perforata** punch card; **sche'dare** *vt* (*dati*) to file; (*libri*) to catalogue; (*registrare: anche POLIZIA*) to put on one's files; **sche'dario** *sm* file; (*mobile*) filing cabinet.

'scheggia, ge ['skeddʒa] *sf* splinter, sliver.

'scheletro ['skɛletro] *sm* skeleton.

'schema, i ['skɛma] *sm* (*diagramma*) diagram, sketch; (*progetto, abbozzo*) outline, plan.

'scherma ['skerma] *sf* fencing.

scher'maglia [sker'maʎʎa] *sf* (*fig*) skirmish.

'schermo ['skermo] *sm* shield, screen; (*CINEMA, TV*) screen.

scher'nire [sker'nire] *vt* to mock, sneer at; **'scherno** *sm* mockery, derision.

scher'zare [sker'tsare] *vi* to joke.

'scherzo ['skertso] *sm* joke; (*tiro*) trick; (*MUS*) scherzo; **è uno ~!** (*una cosa facile*) it's child's play!, it's easy!; **per ~** in jest; **for a joke** *o* a laugh; **fare un brutto ~ a qn** to play a nasty trick on sb; **scher'zoso, a** *ag* (*tono, gesto*) playful; (*osservazione*) facetious; **è un tipo scherzoso** he likes a joke.

schiaccia'noci [skjattʃa'notʃi] *sm inv* nutcracker.

schiacci'are [skjat'tʃare] *vt* (*dito*) to crush; (*noci*) to crack; **~ un pisolino** to have a nap.

schiaffeggi'are [skjaffed'dʒare] *vt* to slap.

schi'affo ['skjaffo] *sm* slap.

schiamaz'zare [skjamat'tsare] *vi* to squawk, cackle.

schian'tare [skjan'tare] *vt* to break, tear apart; **~rsi** *vr* to break (up), shatter; **schi'anto** *sm* (*rumore*) crash; tearing sound; **è uno schianto!** (*fam*) it's (*o* he's *o* she's) terrific!; **di schianto** all of a sudden.

schia'rire [skja'rire] *vt* to lighten, make lighter // *vi* (*anche*: **~rsi**) to grow lighter; (*tornar sereno*) to clear, brighten up; **~rsi la voce** to clear one's throat.

schiavitù [skjavi'tu] *sf* slavery.

schi'avo, a ['skjavo] *sm/f* slave.

schi'ena ['skjɛna] *sf* (*ANAT*) back; **schie'nale** *sm* (*di sedia*) back.

schi'era ['skjɛra] *sf* (*MIL*) rank; (*gruppo*) group, band.

schiera'mento [skjera'mento] *sm* (*MIL, SPORT*) formation; (*fig*) alliance.

schie'rare [skje'rare] *vt* (*esercito*) to line up, draw up, marshal; **~rsi** *vr* to line up; (*fig*): **~rsi con** *o* **dalla parte di**

contro qn to side with/oppose sb.

schi'etto, a |'skjetto| *ag* (*puro*) pure; (*fig*) frank, straightforward; sincere.

'**schifo** |'skifo| *sm* disgust; fare ~ (*essere fatto male, dare pessimi risultati*) to be awful; **mi fa ~** it makes me sick, it's disgusting; **quel libro è uno ~** that book's rotten; **schi'foso, a** *ag* disgusting, revolting; (*molto scadente*) rotten, lousy.

schioc'care |skjɔk'kare| *vt* (*frusta*) to crack; (*dita*) to snap; (*lingua*) to click; **~ le labbra** to smack one's lips.

schi'udere |'skjudere| *vt*, **~rsi** *vr* to open.

schi'uma |'skjuma| *sf* foam; (*di sapone*) lather; (*di latte*) froth; (*fig: feccia*) scum; **schiu'mare** *vt* to skim // *vi* to foam.

schi'uso, a |'skjuso| *pp di* **schiudere**.

schi'vare |ski'vare| *vt* to dodge, avoid.

'**schivo, a** |'skivo| *ag* (*ritroso*) standoffish, reserved; (*timido*) shy.

schiz'zare |skit'tsare| *vt* (*spruzzare*) to spurt, squirt; (*sporcare*) to splash, spatter; (*fig: abbozzare*) to sketch // *vi* to spurt, squirt; (*saltar fuori*) to dart up (o off *etc*).

schizzi'noso, a |skittsi'noso| *ag* fussy, finicky.

'**schizzo** |'skittso| *sm* (*di liquido*) spurt; splash, spatter; (*abbozzo*) sketch.

sci |ʃi| *sm* (*attrezzo*) ski; (*attività*) skiing; **~ nautico** water-skiing.

'**scia, pl 'scie** |'ʃia| *sf* (*di imbarcazione*) wake; (*di profumo*) trail.

scià |ʃa| *sm inv* shah.

sci'abola |'ʃabola| *sf* sabre.

scia'callo |ʃa'kallo| *sm* jackal.

sciac'quare |ʃak'kware| *vt* to rinse.

scia'gura |ʃa'gura| *sf* disaster, calamity; misfortune; **sciagu'rato, a** *ag* unfortunate; (*malvagio*) wicked.

scialac'quare |ʃalak'kware| *vt* to squander.

scia'lare |ʃa'lare| *vi* to lead a life of luxury.

sci'albo, a |'ʃalbo| *ag* pale, dull; (*fig*) dull, colourless.

sci'alle |'ʃalle| *sm* shawl.

scia'luppa |ʃa'luppa| *sf* (*NAUT*) sloop; (*anche: ~ di salvataggio*) lifeboat.

sci'ame |'ʃame| *sm* swarm.

scian'cato, a |ʃan'kato| *ag* lame; (*mobile*) rickety.

sci'are |ʃi'are| *vi* to ski.

sci'arpa |'ʃarpa| *sf* scarf; (*fascia*) sash.

scia'tore, 'trice |ʃia'tore| *sm/f* skier.

sci'atto, a |'ʃatto| *ag* (*persona: nell'aspetto*) slovenly, unkempt; (*: nel lavoro*) sloppy, careless.

scien'tifico, a, ci, che |ʃen'tifiko| *ag* scientific.

sci'enza |'ʃentsa| *sf* science; (*sapere*) knowledge; **~e** *sfpl* (*INS*) science *sg*; **~e**

naturali natural sciences; **scienzi'ato, a** *sm/f* scientist.

'**scimmia** |'ʃimmja| *sf* monkey; **scimmiot'tare** *vt* to ape, mimic.

scimpanzé |ʃimpan'tse| *sm inv* chimpanzee.

scimu'nito, a |ʃimu'nito| *ag* silly, idiotic.

'**scindere** |'ʃindere| *vt*, **~rsi** *vr* to split (up).

scin'tilla |ʃin'tilla| *sf* spark; **scintil'lare** *vi* to spark; (*acqua, occhi*) to sparkle.

scioc'chezza |ʃok'kettsa| *sf* stupidity *q*, stupid o foolish thing; **dire ~e** to talk nonsense.

sci'occo, a, chi, che |'ʃokko| *ag* stupid, foolish.

sci'ogliere |'ʃɔʎʎere| *vt* (*nodo*) to untie; (*capelli*) to loosen; (*persona, animale*) to untie, release; (*fig: persona*): **~ da** to release from; (*neve*) to melt; (*nell'acqua: zucchero etc*) to dissolve; (*fig: mistero*) to solve; (*porre fine a: contratto*) to cancel; (*: società, matrimonio*) to dissolve; (*: riunione*) to bring to an end; **~rsi** *vr* to loosen, come untied; to melt; to dissolve; (*assemblea etc*) to break up; **~ i muscoli** to limber up.

sciol'tezza |ʃol'tettsa| *sf* agility; suppleness; ease.

sci'olto, a |'ʃɔlto| *pp di* **sciogliere** // *ag* loose; (*agile*) agile, nimble; supple; (*disinvolto*) free and easy; **versi ~i** (*POESIA*) blank verse.

sciope'rante |ʃope'rante| *sm/f* striker.

sciope'rare |ʃope'rare| *vi* to strike, go on strike.

sci'opero |'ʃɔpero| *sm* strike; fare **~** to strike; **~ bianco** work-to-rule (*Brit*); slowdown (*US*); **~ selvaggio** wildcat strike; **~ a singhiozzo** on-off strike.

sci'rocco |ʃi'rɔkko| *sm* sirocco.

sci'roppo |ʃi'rɔppo| *sm* syrup.

'**scisma, i** |'ʃizma| *sm* (*REL*) schism.

scissi'one |ʃis'sjone| *sf* (*anche fig*) split, division; (*FISICA*) fission.

sci'sso, a |'ʃisso| *pp di* **scindere**.

sciu'pare |ʃu'pare| *vt* (*abito, libro, appetito*) to spoil, ruin; (*tempo, denaro*) to waste; **~rsi** *vr* to get spoilt o ruined; (*rovinarsi la salute*) to ruin one's health.

scivo'lare |ʃivo'lare| *vi* to slide o glide along; (*involontariamente*) to slip, slide; '**scivolo** *sm* slide; (*TECN*) chute.

scle'rosi |skle'rosi| *sf* sclerosis.

scoc'care *vt* (*freccia*) to shoot // *vi* (*guizzare*) to shoot up; (*battere: ora*) to strike.

scocci'are |skot'tʃare| (*fam*) *vt* to bother, annoy; **~rsi** *vr* to be bothered o annoyed.

sco'della *sf* bowl.

scodinzo'lare |skodintso'lare| *vi* to wag its tail.

scogli'era |skoʎ'ʎɛra| sf reef; cliff.

'scoglio |'skɔʎʎo| sm (al mare) rock.

scoi'attolo sm squirrel.

sco'iare ag: età ~ school age // vt to drain // vi to drip.

scola'resca sf schoolchildren pl, pupils pl.

sco'laro, a sm/f pupil, schoolboy/girl.

sco'lastico, a, ci, che ag school cpd; scholastic.

scol'lare vt (staccare) to unstick; ~rsi vr to come unstuck.

scolla'tura sf neckline.

'scolo sm drainage.

scolo'rire vt to fade; to discolour // vi (anche: ~rsi) to fade; to become discoloured; (impallidire) to turn pale.

scol'pire vt to carve, sculpt.

scombi'nare vt to mess up, upset.

scombusso'lare vt to upset.

scom'messo, a pp di **scommettere** // sf bet, wager.

scom'mettere vt, vi to bet.

scomo'dare vt to trouble, bother; to disturb; ~rsi vr to put o.s. out; ~rsi a fare to go to the bother o trouble of doing.

'scomodo, a ag uncomfortable; (sistemazione, posto) awkward, inconvenient.

scompa'rire vi (sparire) to disappear, vanish; (fig) to be insignificant; **scom'parso, a** pp di **scomparire** // sf disappearance.

scomparti'mento sm (FERR) compartment.

scom'parto sm compartment, division.

scompigli'are |skompiʎ'ʎare| vt (cassetto, capelli) to mess up, disarrange; (fig: piani) to upset; **scom'piglio** sm mess, confusion.

scom'porre vt (parola, numero) to break up; (CHIM) to decompose; **scomporsi** vr (fig) to get upset, lose one's composure; **scom'posto, a** pp di **scomporre** // ag (gesto) unseemly; (capelli) ruffled, dishevelled.

sco'munica sf excommunication.

scomuni'care vt to excommunicate.

sconcer'tare |skontʃer'tare| vt to disconcert, bewilder.

'sconcio, a, ci, ce |'skontʃo| ag (osceno) indecent, obscene // sm (cosa riprovevole, mal fatta) disgrace.

sconfes'sare vt to renounce, disavow; to repudiate.

scon'figgere |skon'fiddʒere| vt to defeat, overcome.

sconfi'nare vi to cross the border; (in proprietà privata) to trespass; (fig): ~ da to stray o digress from; **sconfi'nato, a** ag boundless, unlimited.

scon'fitto, a pp di **sconfiggere** // sf defeat.

scon'forto sm despondency.

scongiu'rare |skondʒu'rare| vt (implo-

rare) to entreat, beseech, implore; (eludere: pericolo) to ward off, avert; **scongi'uro** sm entreaty; (esorcismo) exorcism; **fare gli scongiuri** to touch wood (Brit), knock on wood (US).

scon'nesso, a ag (fig: discorso) incoherent, rambling.

sconosci'uto, a |skonoʃ'futo| ag unknown; new, strange // sm/f stranger; unknown person.

sconquas'sare vt to shatter, smash.

sconside'rato, a ag thoughtless, rash.

sconsigli'are |skonsiʎ'ʎare| vt: ~ qc a qn to advise sb against sth; ~ qn dal fare qc to advise sb not to do o against doing sth.

sconso'lato, a ag inconsolable; desolate.

scon'tare vt (COMM: detrarre) to deduct; (: debito) to pay off; (: cambiale) to discount; (pena) to serve; (colpa, errori) to pay for, suffer for.

scon'tato, a ag (previsto) foreseen, taken for granted; **dare per ~ che** to take it for granted that.

scon'tento, a ag: ~ (di) discontented o dissatisfied (with) // sm discontent, dissatisfaction.

'sconto sm discount; **fare uno ~** to give a discount.

scon'trarsi vr (treni etc) to crash, collide; (venire ad uno scontro, fig) to clash; ~ **con** to crash into, collide with.

scon'trino sm ticket.

'scontro sm clash, encounter; crash, collision.

scon'troso, a ag sullen, surly; (permaloso) touchy.

sconveni'ente ag unseemly, improper.

scon'volgere |skon'vɔldʒere| vt to throw into confusion, upset; (turbare) to shake, disturb, upset; **scon'volto, a** pp di **sconvolgere.**

'scopa sf broom; (CARTE) Italian card game; **sco'pare** vt to sweep.

sco'perto, a pp di **scoprire** // ag uncovered; (capo) uncovered, bare; (macchina) open; (MIL) exposed, without cover; (conto) overdrawn // sf discovery.

'scopo sm aim, purpose; **a che ~?** what for?

scoppi'are vi (spaccarsi) to burst; (esplodere) to explode; (fig) to break out; ~ **in pianto** o **a piangere** to burst out crying; ~ **dalle risa** o **dal ridere** to split one's sides laughing.

scoppiet'tare vi to crackle.

'scoppio sm explosion; (di tuono, arma etc) crash, bang; (fig: di risa, ira) fit, outburst; (: di guerra) outbreak; **a ~ ritardato** delayed-action.

sco'prire vt to discover; (liberare da ciò che copre) to uncover; (: monumento) to unveil; ~rsi vr to put on lighter clothes; (fig) to give o.s. away.

scoraggi'are |skorad'dʒare| *vt* to discourage; ~**rsi** *vr* to become discouraged, lose heart.

scorcia'toia |skortʃa'toja| *sf* short cut.

'scorcio |'skortʃo| *sm* (ARTE) foreshortening; (*di secolo, periodo*) end, close.

scor'dare *vt* to forget; ~**rsi** *vr*: ~**rsi di qc/di** fare to forget sth/to do.

'scorgere |'skordʒere| *vt* to make out, distinguish, see.

sco'ria *sf* (*di metalli*) slag; (*vulcanica*) scoria; ~**e radioattive** (FISICA) radioactive waste *sg*.

'scorno *sm* ignominy, disgrace.

scorpacci'ata |skorpat'tʃata| *sf*: **fare una** ~ **(di)** to stuff o.s. (with), eat one's fill (of).

scorpi'one *sm* scorpion; (*dello zodiaco*): **S~** Scorpio.

scorraz'zare |skorrat'tsare| *vi* to run about.

'scorrere *vt* (*giornale, lettera*) to run o skim through // *vi* (*liquido, fiume*) to run, flow; (*fune*) to run; (*cassetto, porta*) to slide easily; (*tempo*) to pass (by).

scor'retto, a *ag* incorrect; (*sgarbato*) impolite; (*sconveniente*) improper.

scor'revole *ag* (*porta*) sliding; (*fig*: *stile*) fluent, flowing.

scorri'banda *sf* (MIL) raid; (*escursione*) trip, excursion.

'scorso, a *pp di* **scorrere** // *ag* last // *sf* quick look, glance.

scor'soio, a *ag*: **nodo** ~ noose.

'scorta *sf* (*di personalità, convoglio*) escort; (*provvista*) supply, stock; **scor'tare** *vt* to escort.

scor'tese *ag* discourteous, rude; **scorte'sia** *sf* discourtesy, rudeness; (*azione*) discourtesy.

scorti'care *vt* to skin.

'scorto, a *pp di* **scorgere**.

'scorza |'skordza| *sf* (*di albero*) bark, (*di agrumi*) peel, skin.

sco'sceso, a |skoʃ'ʃeso| *ag* steep.

'scosso, a *pp di* **scuotere** // *ag* (*turbato*) shaken, upset // *sf* jerk, jolt, shake; (ELETTR, *fig*) shock.

scos'tante *ag* (*fig*) off-putting (*Brit*), unpleasant.

scos'tare *vt* to move (away), shift; ~**rsi** *vr* to move away.

scostu'mato, a *ag* immoral, dissolute.

scot'tare *vt* (*ustionare*) to burn; (: **con liquido bollente**) to scald // *vi* to burn; (*caffè*) to be too hot; **scotta'tura** *sf* burn; scald.

'scotto, a *ag* overcooked // *sm* (*fig*): **pagare lo** ~ **(di)** to pay the penalty (for).

sco'vare *vt* to drive out, flush out; (*fig*) to discover.

'Scozia |'skottsia| *sf*: **la** ~ Scotland; **scoz'zese** *ag* Scottish // *sm/f* Scot.

scredi'tare *vt* to discredit.

screpo'lare *vt*, ~**rsi** *vr* to crack; **screpola'tura** *sf* cracking *q*; crack.

screzi'ato, a |skret'tsjato| *ag* streaked.

'screzio |'skrettsjo| *sm* disagreement.

scricchio'lare |skrikkjo'lare| *vi* to creak, squeak.

'scricciolo |'skrittʃolo| *sm* wren.

'scrigno |'skriɲɲo| *sm* casket.

scrimina'tura *sf* parting.

'scritto, a *pp di* **scrivere** // *ag* written // *sm* writing; (*lettera*) letter, note // *sf* inscription; ~**i** *smpl* (*letterari etc*) writing *sg*; **per o in** ~ in writing.

scrit'toio *sm* writing desk.

scrit'tore, 'trice *sm/f* writer.

scrit'tura *sf* writing; (COMM) entry; (*contratto*) contract; (REL): **la Sacra S~** the Scriptures *pl*; ~**e** *sfpl* (COMM) accounts, books.

scrittu'rare *vt* (TEATRO, CINEMA) to sign up, engage; (COMM) to enter.

scriva'nia *sf* desk.

scri'vente *sm/f* writer.

'scrivere *vt* to write; **come si scrive?** how is it spelt?, how do you write it?

scroc'cone, a *sm/f* scrounger.

'scrofa *sf* (ZOOL) sow.

scrol'lare *vt* to shake; ~**rsi** *vr* (*anche fig*) to give o.s. a shake; ~ **le spalle/il capo** to shrug one's shoulders/shake one's head.

scrosci'are |skroʃ'ʃare| *vi* (*pioggia*) to pour down, pelt down; (*torrente, fig*: *applausi*) to thunder, roar; **'scroscio** *sm* pelting; thunder, roar; (*di applausi*) burst.

scros'tare *vt* (*intonaco*) to scrape off, strip; ~**rsi** *vr* to peel off, flake off.

'scrupolo *sm* scruple; (*meticolosità*) care, conscientiousness.

scru'tare *vt* to scrutinize; (*intenzioni, causa*) to examine, scrutinize.

scruti'nare *vt* (*voti*) to count; **scru'tinio** *sm* (*votazione*) ballot; (*insieme delle operazioni*) poll; (INS) (*meeting for*) *assignment of marks at end of a term or year*.

scu'cire |sku'tʃire| *vt* (*orlo etc*) to unpick, undo.

scude'ria *sf* stable.

scu'detto *sm* (SPORT) (championship) shield; (*distintivo*) badge.

'scudo *sm* shield.

scul'tore, 'trice *sm/f* sculptor.

scul'tura *sf* sculpture.

scu'ola *sf* school; ~ **elementare/materna/media** primary (*Brit*) o grade (US)/nursery/secondary (*Brit*) o high (US) school; ~ **guida** driving school; ~ **dell'obbligo** compulsory education; ~**e serali** evening classes, night school *sg*; ~ **tecnica** technical college.

scu'otere *vt* to shake; ~**rsi** *vr* to jump, be startled; (*fig*: *muoversi*) to rouse o.s., stir o.s.; (: *turbarsi*) to be shaken.

'**scure** *sf* axe.

'**scuro, a** *ag* dark; (*fig: espressione*) grim // *sm* darkness; dark colour; (*imposta*) (window) shutter; verde/rosso *etc* ~ dark green/red *etc*.

scur'rile *ag* scurrilous.

'**scusa** *sf* excuse; ~e *sfpl* apology *sg*, apologies; **chiedere** ~ **a qn** (**per**) to apologize to sb (for); **chiedo** ~ I'm sorry; (*disturbando etc*) excuse me.

scu'sare *vt* to excuse; ~**rsi** *vr*: ~**rsi** (**di**) to apologize (for); (**mi**) **scusi** I'm sorry; (*per richiamare l'attenzione*) excuse me.

sde'gnato, a [zdeɲ'ɲato] *ag* indignant, angry.

'**sdegno** ['zdeɲɲo] *sm* scorn, disdain; **sde'gnoso, a** *ag* scornful, disdainful.

sdoga'nare *vt* (*merci*) to clear through customs.

sdolci'nato, a [zdoltʃi'nato] *ag* mawkish, oversentimental.

sdoppi'are *vt* (*dividere*) to divide o split in two.

sdrai'arsi *vr* to stretch out, lie down.

'**sdraio** *sm*: **sedia a** ~ deck chair.

sdruccio'levole [zdruttʃo'levole] *ag* slippery.

se ♦ *pronome vedi* **si**
♦ *cong* **1** (*condizionale, ipotetica*) if; ~ **nevica non vengo** I won't come if it snows; **sarei rimasto** ~ **me l'avessero chiesto** I would have stayed if they'd asked me; **non puoi fare altro** ~ **non telefonare** all you can do is phone; ~ **mai** if, if ever; **siamo noi** ~ **mai che le siamo grati** it is we who should be grateful to you; ~ **no** (*altrimenti*) or (else), otherwise
2 (*in frasi dubitative, interrogative indirette*) if, whether; **non so** ~ **scrivere o telefonare** I don't know whether o if I should write or phone.

sé *pronome* (*gen*) oneself; (*esso, essa, lui, lei, loro*) itself; himself; herself; themselves; ~ **stesso(a)** *pronome* oneself; itself; himself; herself; ~ **stessi(e)** *pronome pl* themselves.

seb'bene *cong* although, though.

sec. *abbr* (= *secolo*) c.

'**secca** *sf vedi* **secco**.

sec'care *vt* to dry; (*prosciugare*) to dry up; (*fig: importunare*) to annoy, bother // *vi* to dry; to dry up; ~**rsi** *vr* to dry; to dry up; (*fig*) to grow annoyed; **secca'tura** *sf* (*fig*) bother *q*, trouble *q*.

'**secchia** ['sɛkkja] *sf* bucket, pail.

'**secco, a, chi, che** *ag* dry; (*fichi, pesce*) dried; (*foglie, ramo*) withered; (*magro: persona*) thin, skinny; (*fig: risposta, modo di fare*) curt, abrupt; (: *colpo*) clean, sharp // *sm* (*siccità*) drought // *sf* (*del mare*) shallows *pl*; **restarci** ~ (*fig: morire sul colpo*) to drop dead; **mettere in** ~ (*barca*) to beach;

rimanere in *o* **a** ~ (*NAUT*) to run aground; (*fig*) to be left in the lurch.

seco'lare *ag* age-old, centuries-old; (*laico, mondano*) secular.

'**secolo** *sm* century; (*epoca*) age.

se'conda *sf vedi* **secondo**.

secon'dario, a *ag* secondary.

se'condo, a *ag* second // *sm* second; (*di pranzo*) main course // *sf* (*AUT*) second (gear) // *prep* according to; (*nel modo prescritto*) in accordance with; ~ **me** in my opinion, to my mind; **di** ~**a classe** second-class; **di** ~**a mano** second-hand; **viaggiare in** ~**a** to travel second-class; **a** ~**a di** *prep* according to; in accordance with.

'**sedano** *sm* celery.

seda'tivo, a *ag, sm* sedative.

'**sede** *sf* seat; (*di ditta*) head office; (*di organizzazione*) headquarters *pl*; **in** ~ **di** (*in occasione di*) during; ~ **sociale** registered office.

seden'tario, a *ag* sedentary.

se'dere *vi* to sit, be seated; ~**rsi** *vr* to sit down // *sm* (*deretano*) behind, bottom.

'**sedia** *sf* chair.

sedi'cente [sedi'tʃɛnte] *ag* self-styled.

'**sedici** ['seditʃi] *num* sixteen.

se'dile *sm* seat; (*panchina*) bench.

sedizi'one [sedit'tsjone] *sf* revolt, rebellion.

se'dotto, a *pp di* **sedurre**.

sedu'cente [sedu'tʃɛnte] *ag* seductive; (*proposta*) very attractive.

se'durre *vt* to seduce.

se'duta *sf* session, sitting; (*riunione*) meeting; ~ **spiritica** séance; ~ **stante** (*fig*) immediately.

seduzi'one [sedut'tsjone] *sf* seduction; (*fascino*) charm, appeal.

'**sega, ghe** *sf* saw.

'**segale** *sf* rye.

se'gare *vt* to saw; (*recidere*) to saw off; **sega'tura** *sf* (*residuo*) sawdust.

'**seggio** ['sɛddʒo] *sm* seat; ~ **elettorale** polling station.

'**seggiola** ['sɛddʒola] *sf* chair; **seggio'lino** *sm* seat; (*per bambini*) child's chair; **seggio'lone** *sm* (*per bambini*) highchair.

seggio'via [sedo'via] *sf* chairlift.

seghe'ria [sege'ria] *sf* sawmill.

segna'lare [seɲɲa'lare] *vt* (*manovra etc*) to signal; to indicate; (*annunciare*) to announce; to report; (*fig: far conoscere*) to point out; (: *persona*) to single out; ~**rsi** *vr* (*distinguersi*) to distinguish o.s.

se'gnale [seɲ'ɲale] *sm* signal; (*cartello*): ~ **stradale** road sign; ~ **d'allarme** alarm; (*FERR*) communication cord; ~ **orario** (*RADIO*) time signal; **segna'letica** *sf* signalling, signposting; **segnaletica stradale** road signs *pl*.

se'gnare [seɲ'ɲare] *vt* to mark; (*prendere nota*) to note; (*indicare*) to indicate, mark; (SPORT: goal) to score; ~rsi vr (REL) to make the sign of the cross, cross o.s.

'segno |'seɲɲo| sm sign; (impronta, contrassegno) mark; (limite) limit, bounds pl; (bersaglio) target; fare ~ di si/no to nod (one's head)/shake one's head; fare ~ a qn di fermarsi to motion (to) sb to stop; cogliere o colpire nel ~ (fig) to hit the mark.

segre'gare vt to segregate, isolate; **segregazi'one** sf segregation.

segre'tario, a sm/f secretary; ~ comunale town clerk; ~ di Stato Secretary of State.

segrete'ria sf (di ditta, scuola) (secretary's) office; (d'organizzazione internazionale) secretariat; (POL etc: carica) office of Secretary; ~ telefonica answering service.

segre'tezza |segre'tettsa| sf secrecy.

se'greto, a ag secret // sm secret; secrecy q; in ~ in secret, secretly.

segu'ace |se'gwatʃe| sm/f follower, disciple.

segu'ente ag following, next.

segu'ire vt to follow; (frequentare: corso) to attend // vi to follow; (continuare: testo) to continue.

segui'tare vt to continue, carry on with // vi to continue, carry on.

'seguito sm (scorta) suite, retinue; (discepoli) followers pl; (favore) following; (serie) sequence, series sg; (continuazione) continuation; (conseguenza) result; di ~ at a stretch, on end; in ~ later on; in ~ a, a ~ di following; (a causa di) as a result of, owing to.

'sel vb vedi **essere** // num six.

sei'cento |sei'tʃento| num six hundred // sm: il S~ the seventeenth century.

selci'ato |sel'tʃato| sm cobbled surface.

selezio'nare |seletstsjo'nare| vt to select.

selezi'one |selet'tsjone| sf selection.

'sella sf saddle; **sel'lare** vt to saddle.

selvag'gina |selvad'dʒina| sf (animali) game.

sel'vaggio, a, gi, ge |sel'vaddʒo| ag wild; (tribù) savage, uncivilized; (fig) savage, brutal // sm/f savage.

sel'vatico, a, ci, che ag wild.

se'maforo sm (AUT) traffic lights pl.

sem'brare vi to seem // vb impers: sembra che it seems that; mi sembra che it seems to me that; I think (that); ~ di essere to seem to be.

'seme sm seed; (sperma) semen; (CARTE) suit.

se'mestre sm half-year, six-month period.

'semi... prefisso semi...; **semi'cerchio** sm semicircle; **semifi'nale** sf semifinal; **semi'freddo, a** ag (CUC) chilled // sm ice-cream cake.

'semina sf (AGR) sowing.

semi'nare vt to sow.

semi'nario sm seminar; (REL) seminary.

seminter'rato sm basement; (appartamento) basement flat.

se'mitico, a, ci, che ag semitic.

sem'mai = se mai; vedi **se.**

'semola sf bran; ~ di grano duro durum wheat.

semo'lino sm semolina.

'semplice |'semplitʃe| ag simple; (di un solo elemento) single; **semplice'mente** av simply; **semplicità** sf simplicity.

'sempre av always; (ancora) still; posso ~ tentare I can always o still try; da ~ always; per ~ forever; una volta per ~ once and for all; ~ che cong provided (that); ~ più more and more; ~ meno less and less.

sempre'verde ag, sm o f (BOT) evergreen.

'senape sf (CUC) mustard.

se'nato sm senate; **sena'tore, 'trice** sm/f senator.

'senno sm judgment, (common) sense; col ~ di poi with hindsight.

sennò av = **se no;** vedi **se.**

'seno sm (ANAT: petto, mammella) breast; (: grembo, fig) womb; (: cavità) sinus; (GEO) inlet, creek; (MAT) sine.

sen'sato, a ag sensible.

sensazio'nale |sensatsjo'nale| ag sensational.

sensazi'one |sensat'tsjone| sf feeling, sensation; avere la ~ che to have a feeling that; fare ~ to cause a sensation, create a stir.

sen'sibile ag sensitive; (ai sensi) perceptible; (rilevante, notevole) appreciable, noticeable; ~ a sensitive to; **sensibilità** sf sensitivity.

'senso sm (FISIOL, istinto) sense; (impressione, sensazione) feeling, sensation; (significato) meaning, sense; (direzione) direction; ~i smpl (coscienza) consciousness sg; (sensualità) senses; ciò non ha ~ that doesn't make sense; fare ~ a (ripugnare) to disgust, repel; ~ comune common sense; in ~ orario/antiorario clockwise/anticlockwise; a ~ unico (strada) one-way; "~ vietato" (AUT) "no entry".

sensu'ale ag sensual; sensuous; **sensualità** sf sensuality; sensuousness.

sen'tenza |sen'tentsa| sf (DIR) sentence; (massima) maxim; **sentenzi'are** vi (DIR) to pass judgment.

senti'ero sm path.

sentimen'tale ag sentimental; (vita, avventura) love cpd.

senti'mento sm feeling.

senti'nella sf sentry.

sen'tire vt (percepire al tatto, fig) to feel; (udire) to hear; (ascoltare) to listen to; (odore) to smell; (avvertire *con il gusto, assaggiare)* to taste // *vi:* ~ *di (avere sapore)* to taste of; *(avere odore)* to smell of; ~**rsi** *vr (uso reciproco)* to be in touch; ~**rsi bene/male** to feel well/unwell *o* ill; ~**rsi di fare qc** *(essere disposto)* to feel like doing sth.

sen'tito, a *ag (sincero)* sincere, warm; **per ~ dire** by hearsay.

'senza |'sɛntsa| *prep, cong* without; ~ **dir nulla** without saying a word; **fare ~ qc** to do without sth; ~ **di me** without me; ~ **che io lo sapessi** without me *o* my knowing; **senz'altro** of course, certainly; ~ **dubbio** no doubt; ~ **scrupoli** unscrupulous; ~ **amici** friendless.

sepa'rare *vt* to separate; *(dividere)* to divide; *(tenere distinto)* to distinguish; ~**rsi** *vr (coniugi)* to separate, part; *(amici)* to part, leave each other; ~**rsi da** *(coniuge)* to separate *o* part from; *(amico, socio)* to part company with; *(oggetto)* to part with; **sepa'rato, a** *ag (letti, conto etc)* separate; *(coniugi)* separated; **separazi'one** *sf* separation.

se'polcro *sm* sepulchre.

se'polto, a *pp di* **seppellire**.

seppel'lire *vt* to bury.

'seppia *sf* cuttlefish // *ag inv* sepia.

se'quenza |se'kwentsa| *sf* sequence.

seques'trare *vt* *(DIR)* to impound; *(rapire)* to kidnap; *(costringere in un luogo)* to keep, confine; **se'questro** *sm* *(DIR)* impoundment; **sequestro di persona** kidnapping.

'sera *sf* evening; **di ~** in the evening; **domani ~** tomorrow evening, tomorrow night; **se'rale** *ag* evening *cpd*; **se'rata** *sf* evening; *(ricevimento)* party.

ser'bare *vt* to keep; *(mettere da parte)* to put aside; ~ **rancore/odio verso qn** to bear sb a grudge/hate sb.

serba'toio *sm* tank; *(cisterna)* cistern.

'serbo *sm:* **mettere/tenere** *o* **avere in** ~ **qc** to put/keep sth aside.

se'reno, a *ag (tempo, cielo)* clear; *(fig)* serene, calm.

ser'gente |ser'dʒɛnte| *sm* *(MIL)* sergeant.

'serie *sf inv (successione)* series *inv*; *(gruppo, collezione: di chiavi etc)* set; *(SPORT)* division; league; *(COMM):* **modello di ~/fuori ~** standard/custom-built model; **in ~** in quick succession; *(COMM)* mass *cpd*.

serietà *sf* seriousness; reliability.

'serio, a *ag* serious; *(impiegato)* responsible, reliable; *(ditta, cliente)* reliable, dependable; **sul ~** *(davvero)* really, truly; *(seriamente)* seriously, in earnest.

ser'mone *sm* sermon.

serpeggi'are |serped'dʒare| *vi* to wind; *(fig)* to spread.

ser'pente *sm* snake; ~ **a sonagli** rattlesnake.

'serra *sf* greenhouse; hothouse.

ser'randa *sf* roller shutter.

ser'rare *vt* to close, shut; *(a chiave)* to lock; *(stringere)* to tighten; *(premere: nemico)* to close in on; ~ **i pugni/i denti** to clench one's fists/teeth; ~ **le file** to close ranks.

serra'tura *sf* lock.

'serva *sf vedi* **servo**.

ser'vire *vt* to serve; *(clienti: al ristorante)* to wait on; *(: al negozio)* to serve, attend to; *(fig: giovare)* to aid, help; *(CARTE)* to deal // *vi (TENNIS)* to serve; *(essere utile):* ~ **a qn** to be of use to sb; ~ **a qc/a fare** *(utensile etc)* to be used for sth/for doing; ~ **(a qn) da** to serve as (for sb); ~**rsi** *vr (usare):* ~**rsi di** to use; *(prendere: cibo):* ~**rsi (di)** to help o.s. (to); *(essere cliente abituale):* ~**rsi da** to be a regular customer at, go to.

servitù *sf* servitude; slavery; *(personale di servizio)* servants *pl*, domestic staff.

servizi'evole |servit'tsjevole| *ag* obliging, willing to help.

ser'vizio |ser'vittsjo| *sm* service; *(al ristorante: sul conto)* service (charge); *(STAMPA, TV, RADIO)* report; *(da tè, caffè etc)* set, service; ~**i** *smpl (di casa)* kitchen and bathroom; *(ECON)* services; **essere di ~** to be on duty; **fuori ~** *(telefono etc)* out of order; ~ **compreso** service included; ~ **militare** military service; ~**i segreti** secret service *sg*.

'servo, a *sm/f* servant.

ses'santa *num* sixty; **sessan'tesimo, a** *num* sixtieth.

sessan'tina *sf:* **una ~ (di)** about sixty.

sessi'one *sf* session.

'sesso *sm* sex; **sessu'ale** *ag* sexual, sex *cpd*.

ses'tante *sm* sextant.

'sesto, a *ag, sm* sixth.

'seta *sf* silk.

'sete *sf* thirst; **avere ~** to be thirsty.

'setola *sf* bristle.

'setta *sf* sect.

set'tanta *num* seventy; **settan'tesimo, a** *num* seventieth.

settan'tina *sf:* **una ~ (di)** about seventy.

'sette *num* seven.

sette'cento |sette'tʃento| *num* seven hundred // *sm:* **il S~** the eighteenth century.

set'tembre *sm* September.

settentrio'nale *ag* northern.

settentri'one *sm* north.

'settico, a, ci, che *ag (MED)* septic.

setti'mana *sf* week; **settima'nale** *ag, sm* weekly.

'settimo, a *ag, sm* seventh.

set'tore *sm* sector.

severità *sf* severity.

se'vero, a *ag* severe.

se'vizie |se'vittsje| *sfpl* torture *sg*;

sevizi'are vt to torture.

sezio'nare |settsjo'nare| vt to divide into sections; (MED) to dissect.

sezi'one |set'tsjone| sf section; (MED) dissection.

sfaccen'dato, a |sfattʃen'dato| ag idle.

sfacci'ato, a |sfat'tʃato| ag (maleducato) cheeky, impudent; (vistoso) gaudy.

sfa'celo |sfa'tʃelo| sm (fig) ruin, collapse.

sfal'darsi vr to flake (off).

'sfarzo |'sfartso| sm pomp, splendour.

sfasci'are |sfaʃ'ʃare| vt (ferita) to unbandage, (distruggere: porta) to smash, shatter; ~rsi vr (rompersi) to smash, shatter.

sfa'tare vt (leggenda) to explode.

sfavil'lare vi to spark, send out sparks; (risplendere) to sparkle.

sfavo'revole ag unfavourable.

'sfera sf sphere; **'sferico, a, ci, che** ag spherical.

sfer'rare vt (fig: colpo) to land, deal; (: attacco) to launch.

sfer'zare |sfer'tsare| vt to whip; (fig) to lash out at.

sfi'brare vt (indebolire) to exhaust, enervate.

'sfida sf challenge; **sfi'dare** vt to challenge; (fig) to defy, brave.

sfi'ducia |sfi'dutʃa| sf distrust, mistrust.

sfigu'rare vt (persona) to disfigure; (quadro, statua) to deface // vi (far cattiva figura) to make a bad impression.

sfi'lare vt (ago) to unthread; (abito, scarpe) to slip off // vi (truppe) to march past; (atleti) to parade; ~rsi vr (perle etc) to come unstrung; (orlo, tessuto) to fray; (calza) to run, ladder; **sfi'lata** sf march past; parade; sfilata di moda fashion show.

'sfinge |'sfindʒe| sf sphinx.

sfi'nito, a ag exhausted.

sfio'rare vt to brush (against); (argomento) to touch upon.

sfio'rire vi to wither, fade.

sfo'cato, a ag (FOT) out of focus.

sfoci'are |sfo'tʃare| vi: ~ in to flow into; (fig: malcontento) to develop into.

sfo'gare vt to vent, pour out; ~rsi vr (sfogare la propria rabbia) to give vent to one's anger; (confidarsi): ~rsi (con) to pour out one's feelings (to); non sfogarti su di me! don't take your bad temper out on me!

sfoggi'are |sfod'dʒare| vt, vi to show off.

'sfoglia |'sfoʎʎa| sf sheet of pasta dough; pasta ~ (CUC) puff pastry.

sfogli'are |sfoʎ'ʎare| vt (libro) to leaf through.

'sfogo, ghi sm outlet; (eruzione cutanea) rash; (fig) outburst; **dare ~ a** (fig) to give vent to.

sfolgo'rante ag (luce) blazing; (fig: vittoria) brilliant.

sfol'lare vt to empty, clear // vi to disperse; ~ da (città) to evacuate.

sfon'dare vt (porta) to break down; (scarpe) to wear a hole in; (cesto, scatola) to burst, knock the bottom out of; (MIL) to break through // vi (riuscire) to make a name for o.s. **'sfondo** sm background.

sfor'mato sm (CUC) type of soufflé.

sfor'nito, a ag: ~ di lacking in, without; (negozio) out of.

sfor'tuna sf misfortune, ill luck q; avere ~ to be unlucky; **sfortu'nato, a** ag unlucky; (impresa, film) unsuccessful.

sfor'zare |sfor'tsare| vt to force; (voce, occhi) to strain; ~rsi vr: ~rsi di o a o per fare to try hard to do.

'sforzo |'sfortso| sm effort; (tensione eccessiva, TECN) strain; **fare uno ~** to make an effort.

sfrat'tare vt to evict; **'sfratto** sm eviction.

sfrecci'are |sfret'tʃare| vi to shoot o flash past.

sfregi'are |sfre'dʒare| vt to slash, gash; (persona) to disfigure; (quadro) to deface; **'sfregio** sm gash; scar; (fig) insult.

sfre'nato, a ag (fig) unrestrained, unbridled.

sfron'tato, a ag shameless.

sfrutta'mento sm exploitation.

sfrut'tare vt (terreno) to overwork, exhaust; (miniera) to exploit, work; (fig: operai, occasione, potere) to exploit.

sfug'gire |sfud'dʒire| vi to escape; ~ a (custode) to escape (from); (morte) to escape; ~ a qn (dettaglio, nome) to escape sb; ~ di mano a qn to slip out of sb's hand (o hands); **sfug'gita**: di sfuggita ad (rapidamente, in fretta) in passing.

sfu'mare vt (colori, contorni) to soften, shade off // vi to shade (off), fade; (fig: svanire) to vanish, disappear; (: speranze) to come to nothing; **sfuma'tura** sf shading off q; (tonalità) shade, tone; (fig) touch, hint.

sfuri'ata sf (scatto di collera) fit of anger; (rimprovero) sharp rebuke.

sga'bello sm stool.

sgabuz'zino |sgabud'dzino| sm lumber room.

sgambet'tare vi to kick one's legs about.

sgam'betto sm: far lo ~ a qn to trip sb up; (fig) to oust sb.

sganasci'arsi |zganaʃ'ʃarsi| vr: ~ dalle risa to roar with laughter.

sganci'are |zgan'tʃare| vt to unhook; (FERR) to uncouple; (bombe: da aereo) to release, drop; (fig: fam: soldi) to fork out; ~rsi vr (fig): ~rsi (da) to get away (from).

sganghe'rato, a [zgange'rato] *ag* *(porta)* off its hinges; *(auto)* ramshackle; *(risata)* wild, boisterous.

sgar'bato, a *ag* rude, impolite.

'sgarbo *sm*: **fare uno ~ a qn** to be rude to sb.

sgattaio'lare *vi* to sneak away *o* off.

sge'lare [zdʒe'lare] *vi*, *vt* to thaw.

'sghembo, a ['zgembo] *ag* *(obliquo)* slanting; *(storto)* crooked.

sghignaz'zare [zgiɲɲat'tsare] *vi* to laugh scornfully.

sgob'bare *vi* *(fam: scolaro)* to swot; *(: operaio)* to slog.

sgoccio'lare [zgottʃo'lare] *vt* *(vuotare)* to drain (to the last drop) // *vi* *(acqua)* to drip; *(recipiente)* to drain.

sgo'larsi *vr* to talk *(o* shout *o* sing) o.s. hoarse.

sgomb(e)'rare *vt* to clear; *(andarsene da: stanza)* to vacate; *(evacuare)* to evacuate.

'sgombro, a *ag*: **~ (di)** clear (of), free (from) // *sm* *(ZOOL)* mackerel; *(anche: sgombero)* clearing; vacating; evacuation; *(: trasloco)* removal.

sgomen'tare *vt* to dismay; **~rsi** *vr* to be dismayed; **sgo'mento, a** *ag* dismayed // *sm* dismay, consternation.

sgonfi'are *vt* to let down, deflate; **~rsi** *vr* to go down.

'sgorbio *sm* blot; scribble.

sgor'gare *vi* to gush (out).

sgoz'zare [zgot'tsare] *vt* to cut the throat of.

sgra'devole *ag* unpleasant, disagreeable.

sgra'dito, a *ag* unpleasant, unwelcome.

sgra'nare *vt* *(piselli)* to shell; **~ gli occhi** to open one's eyes wide.

sgran'chirsi [zgran'kirsi] *vr* to stretch; **~ le gambe** to stretch one's legs.

sgranocchi'are [zgranok'kjare] *vt* to munch.

'sgravio *sm*: **~ fiscale** tax relief.

sgrazi'ato, a [zgrat'tsjato] *ag* clumsy, ungainly.

sgreto'lare *vt* to cause to crumble; **~rsi** *vr* to crumble.

sgri'dare *vt* to scold; **sgri'data** *sf* scolding.

sguai'ato, a *ag* coarse, vulgar.

sgual'cire [zgwal'tʃire] *vt* to crumple (up), crease.

sgual'drina *sf* *(peg)* slut.

sgu'ardo *sm* *(occhiata)* look, glance; *(espressione)* look (in one's eye).

sguaz'zare [zgwat'tsare] *vi* *(nell'acqua)* to splash about; *(nella melma)* to wallow; **~ nell'oro** to be rolling in money.

sguinzagli'are [zgwintsaʎ'ʎare] *vt* to let off the leash; *(fig: persona)*: **~ qn dietro a qn** to set sb on sb.

sgusci'are [zguʃ'ʃare] *vt* to shell // *vi*

(sfuggire di mano) to slip; **~ via** to slip *o* slink away.

'shampoo ['ʃampo] *sm inv* shampoo.

shock [ʃɔk] *sm inv* shock.

si ◆ *sm* *(MUS)* B; *(solfeggiando la scala)* ti

◆ *pronome* *(dav lo, la, li, le, ne diventa* **se**) **1** *(riflessivo: maschile)* himself; *(: femminile)* herself; *(: neutro)* itself; *(: impersonale)* oneself; *(: pl)* themselves; **lavarsi** to wash (oneself); **~ è tagliato** he has cut himself; **~ credono importanti** they think a lot of themselves

2 *(riflessivo: con complemento oggetto)*: **lavarsi le mani** to wash one's hands; **~ sta lavando i capelli** he *(o* she) is washing his *(o* her) hair

3 *(reciproco)* one another, each other; **~ amano** they love one another *o* each other

4 *(passivo)*: **~ ripara facilmente** it is easily repaired

5 *(impersonale)*: **~ dice che ...** they *o* people say that ...; **~ vede che è vecchio** one *o* you can see that it's old

6 *(noi)* we; **tra poco ~ parte** we're leaving soon.

sì *av* yes; **un giorno ~ e uno no** every other day.

'sia *cong*: **~ ... ~** *(o ... o)*: **~ che lavori, ~ che non lavori** whether he works or not; *(tanto ... quanto)*: **verranno ~ Luigi ~ suo fratello** both Luigi and his brother will be coming.

si'amo *vb vedi* **essere**.

sibi'lare *vi* to hiss; *(fischiare)* to whistle; **'sibilo** *sm* hiss; whistle.

si'cario *sm* hired killer.

sicché [sik'ke] *cong* *(perciò)* so (that), therefore; *(e quindi)* (and) so.

siccità [sittʃi'ta] *sf* drought.

sic'come *cong* since, as.

Si'cilia [si'tʃilja] *sf*: **la ~** Sicily; **sicili'ano, a** *ag, sm/f* Sicilian.

sicu'rezza [siku'rettsa] *sf* safety; security; *(fiducia)* confidence; *(certezza)* certainty; **di ~** safety *cpd*; **la ~ stradale** road safety.

si'curo, a *ag* safe; *(ben difeso)* secure; *(fiducioso)* confident; *(certo)* sure, certain; *(notizia, amico)* reliable; *(esperto)* skilled // *av* *(anche: di ~)* certainly; **essere/mettere al ~** to be safe/put in a safe place; **~ di sé** self-confident, sure of o.s.; **sentirsi ~** to feel safe *o* secure.

siderur'gia [siderur'dʒia] *sf* iron and steel industry.

'sidro *sm* cider.

si'epe *sf* hedge.

si'ero *sm* *(MED)* serum.

si'esta *sf* siesta, (afternoon) nap.

si'ete *vb vedi* **essere**.

si'filide *sf* syphilis.

si'fone *sm* siphon.

Sig. *abbr* (= *signore*) Mr.

siga'retta *sf* cigarette.

'sigaro *sm* cigar.

Sigg. *abbr* (= *signori*) Messrs.

sigil'lare |sidʒil'larc| *vt* to seal.

si'gillo |si'dʒillo| *sm* seal.

'sigla *sf* initials *pl*; acronym, abbreviation; ~ **automobilistica** *abbreviation of province on vehicle number plate*; ~ **musicale** signature tune.

si'glare *vt* to initial.

Sig.na *abbr* (= *signorina*) Miss.

signifi'care |siɲɲifi'karc| *vt* to mean; **significa'tivo, a** *ag* significant; **significato** *sm* meaning.

si'gnora |siɲ'ɲora| *sf* lady; la ~ X Mrs ['mɪsɪz] X; **buon giorno S~/Signore/Signorina** good morning; (*deferente*) good morning Madam/Sir/Madam; (*quando si conosce il nome*) good morning Mrs/Mr/Miss; **Gentile S~/Signore/Signorina** (*in una lettera*) Dear Madam/Sir/Madam; **il signor Rossi e ~** Mr Rossi and his wife; **~e e signori** ladies and gentlemen.

si'gnore |siɲ'ɲorc| *sm* gentleman; (*padrone*) lord, master; (*REL*): **il S~** the Lord; **il signor X** Mr ['mɪstə*] X; **i ~i Bianchi** (*coniugi*) Mr and Mrs Bianchi; *vedi anche* **signora**.

signo'rile |siɲɲo'rilc| *ag* refined.

signo'rina |siɲɲo'rina| *sf* young lady; la ~ X Miss X; *vedi anche* **signora**.

Sig.ra *abbr* (= *signora*) Mrs.

silenzia'tore |silentsja'torc| *sm* silencer.

si'lenzio |si'lɛntsjo| *sm* silence; **fare ~** to be quiet, stop talking; **silenzi'oso, a** *ag* silent, quiet.

si'licio |si'litʃo| *sm* silicon; **piastrina di ~** silicon chip.

'sillaba *sf* syllable.

silu'rare *vt* to torpedo, (*fig. privare del comando*) to oust.

si'luro *sm* torpedo.

simboleggi'are |simboled'dʒarc| *vt* to symbolize.

'simbolo *sm* symbol.

'simile *ag* (*analogo*) similar; (*di questo tipo*): **un uomo ~** such a man, a man like this; **libri ~i** such books; **~ a** similar to; **i suoi ~i** one's fellow men; one's peers.

simme'tria *sf* symmetry.

simpa'tia *sf* (*qualità*) pleasantness; (*inclinazione*) liking; **avere ~ per qn** to like sb, have a liking for sb; **sim'patico, a, ci, che** *ag* (*persona*) nice, pleasant, likeable; (*casa, albergo etc*) nice, pleasant.

simpatiz'zare |simpatid'dzarc| *vi:* ~ **con** to take a liking to.

sim'posio *sm* symposium.

simu'lare *vt* to sham, simulate; (*TECN*) to simulate; **simulazi'one** *sf* shamming; simulation.

simul'taneo, a *ag* simultaneous.

sina'goga, ghe *sf* synagogue.

sincerità |sintʃeri'ta| *sf* sincerity.

sin'cero, a |sin'tʃcro| *ag* sincere; genuine; heartfelt.

'sincope *sf* syncopation; (*MED*) blackout.

sinda'cale *ag* (trade-)union *cpd*; **sindaca'lista, i, e** *sm/f* trade unionist.

sinda'cato *sm* (*di lavoratori*) (trade) union; (*AMM, ECON, DIR*) syndicate, trust, pool; ~ **dei datori di lavoro** employers' association, employers' federation.

'sindaco, ci *sm* mayor.

sinfo'nia *sf* (*MUS*) symphony.

singhioz'zare |singjot'tsarc| *vi* to sob; to hiccup.

singhi'ozzo |sin'gjottso| *sm* sob; (*MED*) hiccup; **avere il ~** to have the hiccups; **a ~** (*fig*) by fits and starts.

singo'lare *ag* (*insolito*) remarkable, singular; (*LING*) singular // *sm* (*LING*) singular; (*TENNIS*): ~ **maschile/femminile** men's/women's singles.

'singolo, a *ag* single, individual // *sm* (*persona*) individual; (*TENNIS*) = **singolare**.

si'nistro, a *ag* left, left-hand; (*fig*) sinister // *sm* (*incidente*) accident // *sf* (*POL*) left (wing); **a ~a** on the left; (*direzione*) to the left.

'sino *prep* = **fino**.

si'nonimo, a *ag* synonymous // *sm* synonym; ~ **di** synonymous with.

sin'tassi *sf* syntax.

'sintesi *sf* synthesis; (*riassunto*) summary, résumé.

sin'tetico, a, ci, che *ag* synthetic.

sintetiz'zare |sintetid'dzarc| *vt* to synthesize; (*riassumere*) to summarize.

sinto'matico, a, ci, che *ag* symptomatic.

'sintomo *sm* symptom.

sinu'oso, a *ag* (*strada*) winding.

S.I.P. *sigla f* (= *Società italiana per l'esercizio telefonico*) Italian telephone company.

si'pario *sm* (*TEATRO*) curtain.

si'rena *sf* (*apparecchio*) siren; (*nella mitologia, fig*) siren, mermaid.

'Siria *sf*: la ~ Syria.

si'ringa, ghe *sf* syringe.

'sismico, a, ci, che *ag* seismic.

sis'mografo *sm* seismograph.

sis'tema, i *sm* system; method, way; ~ **di vita** way of life.

siste'mare *vt* (*mettere a posto*) to tidy, put in order; (*risolvere: questione*) to sort out, settle; (*procurare un lavoro a*) to find a job for; (*dare un alloggio a*) to settle, find accommodation for; **~rsi** *vr* (*problema*) to be settled; (*persona: trovare alloggio*) to find accommodation (*Brit*) *o* accommodations (*US*); (: *trovarsi un lavoro*) to get fixed up with a job; ti sistemo io! I'll soon sort you out!

siste'matico, a, ci, che ag systematic.

sistemazi'one |sistemat'tsjone| sf arrangement, order; settlement; employment; accommodation (Brit), accommodations (US).

'sito sm (letterario) place.

situ'are vt to site, situate; **situ'ato, a** ag: situato a/su situated at/on.

situazi'one |situat'tsjone| sf situation.

slacci'are |zlat't∫are| vt to undo, unfasten.

slanci'arsi |zlan't∫arsi| vr to dash, fling o.s.; **slanci'ato, a** ag slender; **'slancio** sm dash, leap; (fig) surge; di slancio impetuously.

sla'vato, a ag faded, washed out; (fig: viso, occhi) pale, colourless.

'slavo, a ag Slav(onic), Slavic.

sle'ale ag disloyal; (concorrenza etc) unfair.

sle'gare vt to untie.

'slitta sf sledge; (trainata) sleigh.

slit'tare vi to slip, slide; (AUT) to skid.

slo'gare vt (MED) to dislocate.

sloggi'are |zlod'dʒare| vt (inquilino) to turn out; (nemico) to drive out, dislodge // vi to move out.

smacchi'are |zmak'kjare| vt to remove stains from.

'smacco, chi sm humiliating defeat.

smagli'ante |zmaʎ'ʎante| ag brilliant, dazzling.

smaglia'tura |zmaʎʎa'tura| sf (su maglia, calza) ladder; (della pelle) stretch mark.

smalizi'ato, a |smalit'tsjato| ag shrewd, cunning.

smal'tare vt to enamel; (ceramica) to glaze; (unghie) to varnish.

smal'tire vt (merce) to sell off; (rifiuti) to dispose of; (cibo) to digest; (peso) to lose; (rabbia) to get over; ~ la sbornia to sober up.

'smalto sm (anche: di denti) enamel; (per ceramica) glaze; ~ **per unghie** nail varnish.

'smania sf agitation, restlessness; (fig): ~ **di** thirst for, craving for; **avere la** ~ **addosso** to have the fidgets; **avere la** ~ **di fare** to be desperate to do.

smantel'lare vt to dismantle.

smarri'mento sm loss; (fig) bewilderment; dismay.

smar'rire vt to lose; (non riuscire a trovare) to mislay; ~**rsi** vr (perdersi) to lose one's way, get lost; (: oggetto) to go astray; **smar'rito, a** ag (sbigottito) bewildered.

smasche'rare |zmaske'rare| vt to unmask.

smemo'rato, a ag forgetful.

smen'tire vt (negare) to deny; (testimonianza) to refute; (reputazione) to give the lie to; ~**rsi** vr to be in-

consistent; **smen'tita** sf denial; retraction.

sme'raldo sm emerald.

smerci'are |zmer't∫are| vt (COMM) to sell; (: svendere) to sell off.

sme'riglio |zme'riʎʎo| sm emery.

'smesso, a pp di **smettere.**

'smettere vt to stop; (vestiti) to stop wearing // vi to stop, cease; ~ **di fare** to stop doing.

'smilzo, a |'zmiltso| ag thin, lean.

sminu'ire vt to diminish, lessen; (fig) to belittle.

sminuz'zare |zminut'tsare| vt to break into small pieces; to crumble.

smis'tare vt (pacchi etc) to sort; (FERR) to shunt.

smisu'rato, a ag boundless, immeasurable; (grandissimo) immense, enormous.

smobili'tare vt to demobilize.

smo'dato, a ag immoderate.

smoking |'sməukıŋ| sm inv dinner jacket.

smon'tare vt (mobile, macchina etc) to take to pieces, dismantle; (fig: scoraggiare) to dishearten // vi (scendere: da cavallo) to dismount; (: da treno) to get off; (terminare il lavoro) to stop (work); ~**rsi** vr to lose heart; to lose one's enthusiasm.

'smorfia sf grimace; (atteggiamento lezioso) simpering; **fare** ~**e** to make faces; to simper; **smorfi'oso, a** ag simpering.

'smorto, a ag (viso) pale, wan; (colore) dull.

smor'zare |zmor'tsare| vt (suoni) to deaden; (colori) to tone down; (luce) to dim; (sete) to quench; (entusiasmo) to dampen; ~**rsi** vr (suono, luce) to fade; (entusiasmo) to dampen.

'smosso, a pp di **smuovere.**

smotta'mento sm landslide.

'smunto, a ag haggard, pinched.

smu'overe vt to move, shift; (fig: commuovere) to move; (: dall'inerzia) to rouse, stir; ~**rsi** vr to move, shift.

smus'sare vt (angolo) to round off, smooth; (lama etc) to blunt; ~**rsi** vr to become blunt.

snatu'rato, a ag inhuman, heartless.

'snello, a ag (agile) agile; (svelto) slender, slim.

sner'vare vt to enervate, wear out; ~**rsi** vr to become enervated.

sni'dare vt to drive out, flush out.

snob'bare vt to snub.

sno'bismo sm snobbery.

snoccio'lare |znottʃo'lare| vt (frutta) to stone; (fig: orazioni) to rattle off; (: verità) to blab.

sno'dare vt (rendere agile, mobile) to loosen; ~**rsi** vr to come loose; (articolarsi) to bend; (strada, fiume) to wind.

so vb vedi **sapere**.

so'ave ag sweet, gentle, soft.

sobbal'zare |sobbal'tsarc| vi to jolt, jerk; (trasalire) to jump, start; **sob'balzo** sm jerk, jolt; jump, start.

sobbar'carsi vr: ~ a to take on, undertake.

sob'borgo, ghi sm suburb.

sobil'lare vt to stir up, incite.

'sobrio, a ag sober.

socchi'udere |sok'kjudere| vt (porta) to leave ajar; (occhi) to half-close; **socchi'uso, a** pp di **socchiudere**.

soc'correre vt to help, assist; **soc'corso, a** pp di **soccorrere** // sm help, aid, assistance; **soccorsi** smpl relief sg, aid sg; **soccorso stradale** breakdown service.

socialdemo'cratico, a, ci, che |sotʃaldemo kratiko| sm/f Social Democrat.

soci'ale |so'tʃale| ag social; (di associazione) club cpd, association cpd.

socia'lismo |sotʃa'lizmo| sm socialism; **socia'lista, i, e** ag, sm/f socialist.

società |sotʃe'ta| sf inv society; (sportiva) club; (COMM) company; ~ per azioni (S.p.A.) limited (Brit) o incorporated (US) company; ~ a responsabilità limitata (S.r.l.) type of limited liability company.

soci'evole |so'tʃevole| ag sociable.

'socio |'sɔtʃo| sm (DIR, COMM) partner; (membro di associazione) member.

'soda sf (CHIM) soda; (acqua gassata) soda (water).

soda'lizio |soda'littsjo| sm association, society.

soddisfa'cente |soddisfa'tʃente| ag satisfactory.

soddis'fare vt, vi: ~ a to satisfy; (impegno) to fulfil, (debito) to pay off, (richiesta) to meet, comply with; (offesa) to make amends for; **soddis'fatto, a** pp di **soddisfare** // ag satisfied; **soddisfatto di** happy o satisfied with; pleased with; **soddisfazi'one** sf satisfaction.

'sodo, a ag firm, hard // av (picchiare, lavorare) hard; **dormire** ~ to sleep soundly.

sofà sm inv sofa.

soffe'renza |soffe'rɛntsa| sf suffering.

sof'ferto, a pp di **soffrire**.

soffi'are vt to blow; (notizia, segreto) to whisper // vi to blow; (sbuffare) to puff (and blow); ~rsi il naso to blow one's nose; ~ qc/qn a qn (fig) to pinch o steal sth/sb from sb; ~ via qc to blow sth away.

'soffice |'sɔffitʃe| ag soft.

'soffio sm (di vento) breath; (di fumo) puff; (MED) murmur.

sof'fitta sf attic.

sof'fitto sm ceiling.

soffo'care vi (anche: ~rsi) to suffocate, choke // vt to suffocate, choke; (fig) to stifle, suppress.

sof'friggere |sof'friddʒere| vt to fry lightly.

sof'frire vt to suffer; endure; (sopportare) to bear, stand // vi to suffer; to be in pain; ~ (di) qc (MED) to suffer from sth.

sof'fritto, a pp di **soffriggere** // sm (CUC) fried mixture of herbs, bacon and onions.

sofisti'cato, a ag sophisticated; (vino) adulterated.

sogget'tivo, a |soddʒet'tivo| ag subjective.

sog'getto, a |sod'dʒɛtto| ag: ~ a (sottomesso) subject to; (esposto: a variazioni, danni etc) subject o liable to // sm subject.

soggezi'one |soddʒet'tsjone| sf subjection; (timidezza) awe; **avere** ~ **di qn** to stand in awe of sb; to be ill at ease in sb's presence.

sogghi'gnare |soggiɲ'ɲare| vi to sneer.

soggior'nare |soddʒor'nare| vi to stay; **soggi'orno** sm (invernale, marino) stay; (stanza) living room.

sog'giungere |sod'dʒundʒere| vt to add.

'soglia |'sɔʎʎa| sf doorstep; (anche fig) threshold.

'sogliola |'sɔʎʎola| sf (ZOOL) sole.

so'gnare |soɲ'ɲare| vt, vi to dream; ~ a occhi aperti to daydream; **sogna'tore, 'trice** sm/f dreamer.

'sogno |'soɲɲo| sm dream.

'soia sf (BOT) soya.

sol sm (MUS) G; (: solfeggiando la scala) so(h).

so'laio sm (soffitta) attic.

sola'mente av only, just.

so'lare ag solar, sun cpd.

'solco, chi sm (scavo, fig: ruga) furrow; (incavo) rut, track; (di disco) groove; (scia) wake.

sol'dato sm soldier; ~ **semplice** private.

'soldo sm (fig): **non avere un** ~ to be penniless; **non vale un** ~ it's not worth a penny; ~i smpl (denaro) money sg.

'sole sm sun; (luce) sun(light); (tempo assolato) sun(shine); **prendere il** ~ to sunbathe.

soleggi'ato, a |soled'dʒato| ag sunny.

so'lenne ag solemn; **solennità** sf solemnity; (festività) holiday, feast day.

sol'fato sm (CHIM) sulphate.

soli'dale ag: **essere** ~ **(con)** to be in agreement (with).

solidarietà sf solidarity.

'solido, a ag solid; (forte, robusto) sturdy, solid; (fig: ditta) sound, solid // sm (MAT) solid.

soli'loquio sm soliloquy.

so'lista, i, e ag solo // sm/f soloist.

solita'mente av usually, as a rule.

soli'tario, a *ag* (*senza compagnia*) solitary, lonely; (*solo, isolato*) solitary, lone; (*deserto*) lonely // *sm* (*gioiello, gioco*) solitaire.

'solito, a *ag* usual; **essere ~ fare** to be in the habit of doing; **di ~** usually; **più tardi del ~** later than usual; **come al ~** as usual.

soli'tudine *sf* solitude.

solleci'tare |solletʃi'tare| *vt* (*lavoro*) to speed up; (*persona*) to urge on; (*chiedere con insistenza*) to press for, request urgently; (*stimolare*): **~ qn a fare** to urge sb to do; (*TECN*) to stress; **solle-citazi'one** *sf* entreaty, request; (*fig*) incentive; (*TECN*) stress.

sol'lecito, a |sol'letʃito| *ag* prompt, quick // *sm* (*lettera*) reminder; **solleci'tudine** *sf* promptness, speed.

solleti'care *vt* to tickle.

sol'letico *sm* tickling; **soffrire il ~** to be ticklish.

solleva'mento *sm* raising; lifting; revolt; **~ pesi** (*SPORT*) weight-lifting.

solle'vare *vt* to lift, raise; (*fig: persona: alleggerire*): **~ (da)** to relieve (of); (: *dar conforto*) to comfort, relieve; (: *questione*) to raise; (: *far insorgere*) to stir (: to revolt); **~rsi** *vr* to rise; (*fig: riprendersi*) to recover; (: *ribellarsi*) to rise up.

solli'evo *sm* relief; (*conforto*) comfort.

'solo, a *ag* alone; (*in senso spirituale: isolato*) lonely; (*unico*): **un ~ libro** only one book, a single book; (*con ag numerale*): **veniamo noi tre ~i** just *o* only the three of us are coming // *av* (*soltanto*) only, just; **non ~ ... ma anche not only ... but also; **fare qc da ~** to do sth (all) by oneself; **da me ~** single-handed, on my own.

sol'tanto *av* only.

so'lubile *ag* (*sostanza*) soluble.

soluzi'one |solut'tsjone| *sf* solution.

sol'vente *ag, sm* solvent.

'soma *sf*: **bestia da ~** beast of burden.

so'maro *sm* ass, donkey.

somigli'anza |somiʎ'ʎantsa| *sf* resemblance.

somigli'are |somiʎ'ʎare| *vi*: **~ a** to be like, resemble; (*nell'aspetto fisico*) to look like; **~rsi** *vr* to be (*o* look) alike.

'somma *sf* (*MAT*) sum; (*di denaro*) sum (of money); (*complesso di varie cose*) whole amount, sum total.

som'mare *vt* to add up; (*aggiungere*) to add; **tutto sommato** all things considered.

som'mario, a *ag* (*racconto, indagine*) brief; (*giustizia*) summary // *sm* summary.

som'mergere |som'merdʒere| *vt* to submerge.

sommer'gibile |sommer'dʒibile| *sm* submarine.

som'merso, a *pp di* **sommergere**.

som'messo, a *ag* (*voce*) soft, subdued.

somminis'trare *vt* to give, administer.

sommità *sf inv* summit, top; (*fig*) height.

'sommo, a *ag* highest; (*rispetto etc*) highest, greatest; (*poeta, artista*) great, outstanding // *sm* (*fig*) height; **per ~i capi** briefly, covering the main points.

som'mossa *sf* uprising.

so'nare *etc* = **suonare** *etc.*

son'daggio |son'daddʒo| *sm* sounding; probe; boring, drilling; (*indagine*) survey; **~ d'opinioni** opinion poll.

son'dare *vt* (*NAUT*) to sound; (*atmosfera, piaga*) to probe; (*MINERALOGIA*) to bore, drill; (*fig: opinione etc*) to survey, poll.

so'netto *sm* sonnet.

son'nambulo, a *sm/f* sleepwalker.

sonnecchi'are |sonnek'kjare| *vi* to doze, nod.

son'nifero, a *sm* sleeping draug (*o* pill).

'sonno *sm* sleep; **prendere ~** to fall asleep; **aver ~** to be sleepy.

'sono *vb vedi* **essere**.

so'noro, a *ag* (*ambiente*) resonant; (*voce*) sonorous, ringing; (*onde, film*) sound *cpd*.

sontu'oso, a *ag* sumptuous; lavish.

sopo'rifero, a *ag* soporific.

soppe'sare *vt* to weigh in one's hand(s), feel the weight of; (*fig*) to weigh up.

soppi'atto: di ~ *av* secretly; furtively.

soppor'tare *vt* (*reggere*) to support; (*subire: perdita, spese*) to bear, sustain; (*soffrire: dolore*) to bear, endure; (*sog: cosa: freddo*) to withstand; (*sog: persona: freddo, vino*) to take; (*tollerare*) to put up with, tolerate.

sop'presso, a *pp di* **sopprimere**.

sop'primere *vt* (*carica, privilegi, testimone*) to do away with; (*pubblicazione*) to suppress; (*parola, frase*) to delete.

'sopra *prep* (*gen*) on; (*al di sopra di, più in alto di*) above; over; (*riguardo a*) on, about // *av* on top; (*attaccato, scritto*) on it; (*al di sopra*) above; (*al piano superiore*) upstairs; **donne ~ i 30 anni** women over 30 (years of age); **abito di ~** I live upstairs; **dormirci ~** (*fig*) to sleep on it.

se'prabito *sm* overcoat.

soprac'ciglio |soprat'tʃiʎʎo|, *pl(f)* **soprac'ciglia** *sm* eyebrow.

sopracco'perta *sf* (*di letto*) bedspread; (*di libro*) jacket.

soprad'detto, a *ag* aforesaid.

sopraf'fare *vt* to overcome, overwhelm; **sopraf'fatto, a** *pp di* **sopraffare**.

sopraf'fino, a *ag* (*pranzo, vino*) excellent.

sopraggi'ungere |soprad'dʒundʒere| *vi* (*giungere all'improvviso*) to arrive (unexpectedly); (*accadere*) to occur (unexpectedly).

sopral'luogo, ghi *sm (di esperti)* inspection; *(di polizia)* on-the-spot investigation.

sopram'mobile *sm* ornament.

soprannatu'rale *ag* supernatural.

sopran'nome *sm* nickname.

so'prano, a *sm/f (persona)* soprano // *sm (voce)* soprano.

soprappensi'ero *av* lost in thought.

sopras'salto *sm*: di ~ with a start; suddenly.

soprasse'dere *vi*: ~ a to delay, put off.

soprat'tutto *av (anzitutto)* above all; *(specialmente)* especially.

soprav'vento *sm*: avere/prendere il ~ su to have/get the upper hand over.

sopravvis'suto, a *pp di* **sopravvivere**.

soprav'vivere *vi* to survive; *(continuare a vivere)*: ~ (in) to live on (in); ~ a *(incidente etc)* to survive; *(persona)* to outlive.

soprinten'dente *sm/f* supervisor; *(statale: di belle arti etc)* keeper; **soprinten'denza** *sf* supervision; *(ente)*: **soprintendenza alle Belle Arti** *government department responsible for monuments and artistic treasures.*

so'pruso *sm* abuse of power; **subire un** ~ to be abused.

soq'quadro *sm*: mettere a ~ to turn upside-down.

sor'betto *sm* sorbet, water ice.

sor'bire *vt* to sip; *(fig)* to put up with.

'sorcio, ci |'sortʃo| *sm* mouse.

'sordido, a *ag* sordid; *(fig: gretto)* stingy.

sor'dina *sf*: in ~ softly; *(fig)* on the sly.

sordità *sf* deafness.

'sordo, a *ag* deaf; *(rumore)* muffled; *(dolore)* dull; *(odio, rancore)* veiled // *sm/f* deaf person; **sordo'muto, a** *ag* deaf-and-dumb // *sm/f* deaf-mute.

so'rella *sf* sister; **sorel'lastra** *sf* stepsister.

sor'gente |sor'dʒɛnte| *sf (acqua che sgorga)* spring; *(di fiume, FISICA, fig)* source.

'sorgere |'sordʒere| *vi* to rise; *(scaturire)* to spring, rise; *(fig: difficoltà)* to arise.

sormon'tare *vt (fig)* to overcome, surmount.

sorni'one, a *ag* sly.

sorpas'sare *vt (AUT)* to overtake; *(fig)* to surpass; *(: eccedere)* to exceed, go beyond; ~ in altezza to be higher than; *(persona)* to be taller than.

sorpren'dente *ag* surprising.

sor'prendere *vt (cogliere: in flagrante etc)* to catch; *(stupire)* to surprise; ~rsi *vr*: ~rsi (di) to be surprised (at); **sor'preso, a** *pp di* **sorprendere** // *sf* surprise; fare una sorpresa a qn to give sb a surprise.

sor'reggere |sor'reddʒere| *vt* to support, hold up; *(fig)* to sustain; **sor'retto, a** *pp di* **sorreggere**.

sor'ridere *vi* to smile; **sor'riso, a** *pp di* **sorridere** // *sm* smile.

'sorso *sm* sip.

'sorta *sf* sort, kind; di ~ whatever, of any kind, at all.

'sorte *sf (fato)* fate, destiny; *(evento fortuito)* chance; tirare a ~ to draw lots.

sor'teggio |sor'teddʒo| *sm* draw.

sorti'legio |sorti'lɛdʒo| *sm* witchcraft *q*; *(incantesimo)* spell; fare un ~ a qn to cast a spell on sb.

sor'tita *sf (MIL)* sortie.

'sorto, a *pp di* **sorgere**.

sorvegli'anza |sorveʎ'ʎantsa| *sf* watch; supervision; *(POLIZIA, MIL)* surveillance.

sorvegli'are |sorveʎ'ʎare| *vt (bambino, bagagli, prigioniero)* to watch, keep an eye on; *(malato)* to watch over; *(territorio, casa)* to watch o keep watch over; *(lavori)* to supervise.

sorvo'lare *vt (territorio)* to fly over // *vi*: ~ su *(fig)* to skim over.

'sosia *sm inv* double.

sos'pendere *vt (appendere)* to hang (up); *(interrompere, privare di una carica)* to suspend; *(rimandare)* to defer; ~ un quadro al muro/un lampadario al soffitto to hang a picture on the wall/a chandelier from the ceiling; **sospensi'one** *sf (anche CHIM, AUT)* suspension; deferment; **sos'peso, a** *pp di* **sospendere** // *ag (appeso)*: sospeso a hanging on (o from); *(treno, autobus)* cancelled; in sospeso in abeyance; *(conto)* outstanding; tenere in sospeso *(fig)* to keep in suspense.

sospet'tare *vt* to suspect // *vi*: ~ di to suspect; *(diffidare)* to be suspicious of.

sos'petto, a *ag* suspicious // *sm* suspicion; **sospet'toso, a** *ag* suspicious.

sos'pingere |sos'pindʒere| *vt* to drive, push; **sos'pinto, a** *pp di* **sospingere**.

sospi'rare *vi* to sigh // *vt* to long for, yearn for; **sos'piro** *sm* sigh.

'sosta *sf (fermata)* stop, halt; *(pausa)* pause, break; senza ~ non-stop, without a break.

sostan'tivo *sm* noun, substantive.

sos'tanza |sos'tantsa| *sf* substance; ~e *sfpl (ricchezze)* wealth *sg*, possessions; in ~ in short, to sum up; **sostanzi'oso, a** *ag (cibo)* nourishing, substantial.

sos'tare *vi (fermarsi)* to stop (for a while), stay; *(fare una pausa)* to take a break.

sos'tegno |sos'teɲɲo| *sm* support.

soste'nere *vt* to support; *(prendere su di sé)* to take on, bear; *(resistere)* to withstand, stand up to; *(affermare)*: ~ che to maintain that; ~rsi *vr* to hold o.s. up, support o.s.; *(fig)* to keep up one's strength; ~ **gli esami** to sit exams; **so-steni'tore, 'trice** *sm/f* supporter.

sostenta'mento *sm* maintenance, support.

soste'nuto, a *ag* (*stile*) elevated; (*velocità, ritmo*) sustained; (*prezzo*) high // *sm/f:* **fare il(la) ~(a)** to be standoffish, keep one's distance.

sostitu'ire *vt* (*mettere al posto di*): ~ **qn/qc a** to substitute sb/sth for; (*prendere il posto di: persona*) to substitute for; (: *cosa*) to take the place of.

sosti'tuto, a *sm/f* substitute.

sostituzi'one |sostitut'tsjone| *sf* substitution; **in ~ di** as a substitute for, in place of.

sotta'ceti |sotta'tfeti| *smpl* pickles.

sot'tana *sf* (*sottoveste*) underskirt; (*gonna*) skirt; (*REL*) soutane, cassock.

sotter'fugio |sotter'fud3o| *sm* subterfuge.

sotter'raneo, a *ag* underground // *sm* cellar.

sotter'rare *vt* to bury.

sottigli'ezza |sottiʎ'ʎettsa| *sf* thinness; slimness; (*fig: acutezza*) subtlety; shrewdness; ~**e** *sfpl* (*pedanteria*) quibbles.

sot'tile *ag* thin; (*figura, caviglia*) thin, slim, slender; (*fine: polvere, capelli*) fine; (*fig: leggero*) light; (: *vista*) sharp, keen; (: *olfatto*) fine, discriminating; (: *mente*) subtle; shrewd // *sm:* **non andare per il ~** not to mince matters.

sottin'tendere *vt* (*intendere qc non espresso*) to understand; (*implicare*) to imply; **sottin'teso, a** *pp di* **sottintendere** // *sm* allusion; **parlare senza sottintesi** to speak plainly.

'sotto *prep* (*gen*) under; (*più in basso di*) below // *av* underneath, beneath; below; (*al piano inferiore*): (**al piano) di** ~ downstairs; ~ **forma di** in the form of; ~ **il monte** at the foot of the mountain; **siamo ~ Natale** it's nearly Christmas; ~ **la pioggia/il sole** in the rain/sun(shine); ~ **terra** underground; ~ **voce** in a low voice; **chiuso ~ vuoto** vacuum-packed.

sottoline'are *vt* to underline; (*fig*) to emphasize, stress.

sottoma'rino, a *ag* (*flora*) submarine; (*cavo, navigazione*) underwater // *sm* (*NAUT*) submarine.

sotto'messo, a *pp di* **sottomettere**.

sotto'mettere *vt* to subdue, subjugate; ~**rsi** *vr* to submit.

sottopas'saggio |sottopas'sadd3o| *sm* (*AUT*) underpass; (*pedonale*) subway, underpass.

sotto'porre *vt* (*costringere*) to subject; (*fig: presentare*) to submit; **sottoporsi** *vr* to submit; **sottoporsi a** (*subire*) to undergo; **sotto'posto, a** *pp di* **sottoporre**.

sottos'critto, a *pp di* **sottoscrivere**.

sottos'crivere *vt* to sign // *vi:* ~ **a** to subscribe to; **sottoscrizi'one** *sf* signing; subscription.

sottosegre'tario *sm:* ~ **di Stato** Under-Secretary of State (*Brit*), Assistant Secretary of State (*US*).

sotto'sopra *av* upside-down.

sotto'terra *av* underground.

sotto'titolo *sm* subtitle.

sotto'veste *sf* underskirt.

sotto'voce |sotto'votfe| *av* in a low voice.

sot'trarre *vt* (*MAT*) to subtract, take away; ~ **qn/qc a** (*togliere*) to remove sb/sth from; (*salvare*) to save o rescue sb/sth from; ~ **qc a qn** (*rubare*) to steal sth from sb; **sottrarsi** *vr:* **sottrarsi a** (*sfuggire*) to escape; (*evitare*) to avoid; **sot'tratto, a** *pp di* **sottrarre**; **sot-trazi'one** *sf* subtraction; removal.

sovi'etico, a, ci, che *ag* Soviet // *sm/f* Soviet citizen.

sovraccari'care *vt* to overload.

sovrannatu'rale *ag* = **soprannaturale**.

so'vrano, a *ag* sovereign; (*fig: sommo*) supreme // *sm/f* sovereign, monarch.

sovrap'porre *vt* to place on top of, put on top of.

sovras'tare *vi:* ~ **a**, *vt* (*vallata, fiume*) to overhang; (*fig*) to hang over, threaten.

sovrinten'dente *sm/f* = **soprinten-dente; sovrinten'denza** *sf* = **soprin-tendenza**.

sovru'mano, a *ag* superhuman.

sovvenzi'one |sovven'tsjone| *sf* subsidy, grant.

sovver'sivo, a *ag* subversive.

'sozzo, a |'sottso| *ag* filthy, dirty.

S.p.A. *abbr* = **società per azioni**.

spac'care *vt* to split, break; (*legna*) to chop; ~**rsi** *vr* to split, break; **spacca'tura** *sf* split.

spacci'are |spat'tfare| *vt* (*vendere*) to sell (off); (*mettere in circolazione*) to circulate; (*droga*) to peddle, push; ~**rsi** *vr:* ~**rsi per** (*farsi credere*) to pass o.s. off as, pretend to be; **spaccia'tore, 'trice** *sm/f* (*di droga*) pusher; (*di denaro falso*) dealer; **'spaccio** *sm* (*di merce rubata, droga*): **spaccio (di)** trafficking (in); (*in denaro falso*): **spaccio (di)** passing (of); (*vendita*) sale; (*bottega*) shop.

'spacco, chi *sm* (*fenditura*) split, crack; (*strappo*) tear; (*di gonna*) slit.

spac'cone *sm/f* boaster, braggart.

'spada *sf* sword.

spae'sato, a *ag* disorientated, lost.

spa'ghetti |spa'getti| *smpl* (*CUC*) spaghetti *sg*.

'Spagna |'spaɲɲa| *sf:* **la ~** Spain; **spa'gnolo, a** *ag* Spanish // *sm/f* Spaniard // *sm* (*LING*) Spanish; **gli Spa-gnoli** the Spanish.

'spago, ghi *sm* string, twine.
spai'ato, a *ag* (*calza, guanto*) odd.
spalan'care *vt*, ~**rsi** *vr* to open wide.
spa'lare *vt* to shovel.
'spalla *sf* shoulder; (*fig*: TEATRO) stooge; ~**e** *sfpl* (*dorso*) back; **spalleggi'are** *vt* to back up, support.
spal'letta *sf* (*parapetto*) parapet.
spalli'era *sf* (*di sedia etc*) back; (*di letto*: *da capo*) head(board); (: *da piedi*) foot(board); (GINNASTICA) wall bars *pl*.
spal'mare *vt* to spread.
'spalti *smpl* (*di stadio*) terracing.
'spandere *vt* to spread; (*versare*) to pour (out); ~**rsi** *vr* to spread; **'spanto, a** *pp di* **spandere**.
spa'rare *vt* to fire // *vi* (*far fuoco*) to fire; (*tirare*) to shoot; **spara'tore** *sm* gunman; **spara'toria** *sf* exchange of shots.
sparecchi'are |sparek'kjare| *vt*: ~ (la tavola) to clear the table.
spa'reggio |spa'reddʒo| *sm* (SPORT) play-off.
'spargere |'spardʒere| *vt* (*sparpagliare*) to scatter; (*versare: vino*) to spill; (: *lacrime, sangue*) to shed; (*diffondere*) to spread; (*emanare*) to give off (o out); ~**rsi** *vr* to spread; **spargi'mento** *sm* scattering, strewing; spilling; shedding; spargimento di sangue bloodshed.
spa'rire *vi* to disappear, vanish.
spar'lare *vi*: ~ di to run down, speak ill of.
'sparo *sm* shot.
sparpagli'are |sparpaʎ'ʎare| *vt*, ~**rsi** *vr* to scatter.
'sparso, a *pp di* **spargere** // *ag* scattered; (*sciolto*) loose.
spar'tire *vt* (*eredità, bottino*) to share out; (*avversari*) to separate.
sparti'traffico *sm inv* (AUT) central reservation (*Brit*), median (strip) (*US*).
spa'ruto, a *ag* (*viso etc*) haggard.
sparvi'ero *sm* (ZOOL) sparrowhawk.
spasi'mare *vi* to be in agony; ~ di fare (*fig*) to yearn to do; ~ per qn to be madly in love with sb.
'spasimo *sm* pang; **'spasmo** *sm* (MED) spasm; **spas'modico, a, ci, che** *ag* (*angoscioso*) agonizing; (MED) spasmodic.
spassio'nato, a *ag* dispassionate, impartial.
'spasso *sm* (*divertimento*) amusement, enjoyment; andare a ~ to go out for a walk; essere a ~ (*fig*) to be out of work; mandare qn a ~ (*fig*) to give sb the sack.
spau'racchio |spau'rakkjo| *sm* scarecrow.
spau'rire *vt* to frighten, terrify.
spa'valdo, a *ag* arrogant, bold.
spaventa'passeri *sm inv* scarecrow.
spaven'tare *vt* to frighten, scare; ~**rsi**

vr to be frightened, be scared; to get a fright; **spa'vento** *sm* fear, fright; far spavento a qn to give sb a fright; **spaven'toso, a** *ag* frightening, terrible; (*fig*: *fam*) tremendous, fantastic.
spazien'tire |spattsjen'tire| *vi* (*anche*: ~**rsi**) to lose one's patience.
'spazio |'spattsjo| *sm* space; ~ aereo airspace; **spazi'oso, a** *ag* spacious.
spazzaca'mino |spattsaka'mino| *sm* chimney sweep.
spaz'zare |spat'tsare| *vt* to sweep; (*foglie etc*) to sweep up; (*cacciare*) to sweep away; **spazza'tura** *sf* sweepings *pl*; (*immondizia*) rubbish; **spaz'zino** *sm* street sweeper.
spaz'zola |'spattsola| *sf* brush; ~ per abiti clothesbrush; ~ da capelli hairbrush; **spazzo'lare** *vt* to brush; **spazzo'lino** *sm* (*small*) brush; spazzolino da denti toothbrush.
specchi'arsi |spek'kjarsi| *vr* to look at o.s. in a mirror; (*riflettersi*) to be mirrored, be reflected.
'specchio |'spekkjo| *sm* mirror.
speci'ale |spe'tʃale| *ag* special; **specia'lista, i, e** *sm/f* specialist; **specialità** *sf inv* speciality; (*branca di studio*) special field, speciality; specializ'zarsi *vr*: specializzarsi (in) to specialize (in); **special'mente** *av* especially, particularly.
'specie |'spetʃe| *sf inv* (BIOL, BOT, ZOOL) species *inv*; (*tipo*) kind, sort // *av* especially, particularly; una ~ di a kind of; fare ~ a qn to surprise sb; la ~ umana mankind.
specifi'care |spetʃifi'kare| *vt* to specify, state.
spe'cifico, a, ci, che |spe'tʃifiko| *ag* specific.
specu'lare *vi*: ~ su (COMM) to speculate in; (*sfruttare*) to exploit; (*meditare*) to speculate on; **speculazi'one** *sf* speculation.
spe'dire *vt* to send; **spedizi'one** *sf* sending; (*collo*) consignment; (*scientifica etc*) expedition.
'spegnere |'spennere| *vt* (*fuoco, sigaretta*) to put out, extinguish; (*apparecchio elettrico*) to turn o switch off; (*gas*) to turn off; (*fig*: *suoni, passioni*) to stifle; (*debito*) to extinguish; ~**rsi** *vr* to go out; to go off; (*morire*) to pass away.
spel'lare *vt* (*scuoiare*) to skin; (*scorticare*) to graze; ~**rsi** *vr* to peel.
'spendere *vt* to spend.
spen'nare *vt* to pluck.
spensie'rato, a *ag* carefree.
'spento, a *pp di* **spegnere** // *ag* (*suono*) muffled; (*colore*) dull; (*sigaretta*) out; (*civiltà, vulcano*) extinct.
spe'ranza |spe'rantsa| *sf* hope.
spe'rare *vt* to hope for // *vi*: ~ in to trust in; ~ che/di fare to hope that/to do; lo

spero, spero di sì I hope so.
sper'duto, a ag (isolato) out-of-the-way; (persona: smarrita, a disagio) lost.
spergi'uro, a |sper'dʒuro| sm/f perjurer // sm perjury.
sperimen'tale ag experimental.
sperimen'tare vt to experiment with, test; (fig) to test, put to the test.
'sperma, i sm (BIOL) sperm.
spe'rone sm spur.
sperpe'rare vt to squander.
'spesa sf (somma di denaro) expense; (costo) cost; (acquisto) purchase; (fam: acquisto del cibo quotidiano) shopping; ~e sfpl expenses; (COMM) costs; charges; fare la ~ to do the shopping; a ~e di (a carico di) at the expense of; ~e generali overheads; ~e postali postage sg; ~e di viaggio travelling expenses.
'speso, a pp di spendere.
'spesso, a ag (fitto) thick; (frequente) frequent // av often; ~e volte frequently, often.
spes'sore sm thickness.
spet'tabile ag (abbr: Spett.: in lettere): ~ ditta X Messrs X and Co.
spet'tacolo sm (rappresentazione) performance, show; (vista, scena) sight; dare ~ di sé to make an exhibition o a spectacle of o.s.; **spettaco'loso, a** ag spectacular.
spet'tare vi: ~ a (decisione) to be up to; (stipendio) to be due to; spetta a te decidere it's up to you to decide.
spetta'tore, 'trice sm/f (CINEMA, TEATRO) member of the audience; (di avvenimento) onlooker, witness.
spetti'nare vt: ~ qn to ruffle sb's hair; ~rsi vr to get one's hair in a mess.
'spettro sm (fantasma) spectre; (FISICA) spectrum.
'spezie |'spɛttsje| sfpl (CUC) spices.
spez'zare |spet'tsare| vt (rompere) to break; (fig: interrompere) to break up; ~rsi vr to break.
spezza'tino |spettsa'tino| sm (CUC) stew.
spezzet'tare |spettset'tare| vt to break up (o chop) into small pieces.
'spia sf spy; (confidente della polizia) informer; (ELETTR) indicating light; warning light; (fessura) peep-hole; (fig: sintomo) sign, indication.
spia'cente |spja'tʃɛnte| ag sorry; essere ~ di qc/di fare qc to be sorry about sth/for doing sth.
spia'cevole |spja'tʃevole| ag unpleasant, disagreeable.
spi'aggia, ge |'spjaddʒa| sf beach.
spia'nare vt (terreno) to level, make level; (edificio) to raze to the ground; (pasta) to roll out; (rendere liscio) to smooth (out).
spi'ano sm: a tutto ~ (lavorare) non-stop, without a break; (spendere) lavishly.

spian'tato, a ag penniless, ruined.
spi'are vt to spy on; (occasione etc) to watch o wait for.
spi'azzo |'spjattso| sm open space; (radura) clearing.
spic'care vt (assegno, mandato di cattura) to issue // vi (risaltare) to stand out; ~ il volo to fly off; (fig) to spread one's wings; ~ un balzo to leap; **spic'cato, a** ag (marcato) marked, strong; (notevole) remarkable.
'spicchio |'spikkjo| sm (di agrumi) segment; (di aglio) clove; (parte) piece, slice.
spicci'arsi |spit'tʃarsi| vr to hurry up.
'spicciolo, a |'spittʃolo| ag: moneta ~a, ~i smpl (small) change.
'spicco, chi sm: di ~ outstanding; (tema) main, principal; fare ~ to stand out.
spi'edo sm (CUC) spit.
spie'gare vt (far capire) to explain; (tovaglia) to unfold; (vele) to unfurl; ~rsi vr to explain o.s., make o.s. clear; ~ qc a qn to explain sth to sb; il problema si spiega one can understand the problem; **spiegazi'one** sf explanation.
spiegaz'zare |spjegat'tsare| vt to crease, crumple.
spie'tato, a ag ruthless, pitiless.
spiffe'rare vt (fam) to blurt out, blab.
'spiga, ghe sf (BOT) ear.
spigli'ato, a |spiʎ'ʎato| ag self-possessed, self-confident.
'spigolo sm corner; (MAT) edge.
'spilla sf brooch; (da cravatta, cappello) pin.
spil'lare vt (vino, fig) to tap; ~ denaro/ notizie a qn to tap sb for money/ information.
'spillo sm pin; (spilla) brooch; ~ di sicurezza o da balia safety pin; ~ di sicurezza (MIL) (safety) pin.
spi'lorcio, a, ci, ce |spi'lortʃo| ag mean, stingy.
'spina sf (BOT) thorn; (ZOOL) spine, prickle; (di pesce) bone; (ELETTR) plug; (di botte) bunghole; birra alla ~ draught beer; ~ dorsale (ANAT) backbone.
spi'nacio |spi'natʃo| sm spinach; (CUC): ~i spinach sg.
spi'nale ag (ANAT) spinal.
'spingere |'spindʒere| vt to push; (condurre: anche fig) to drive; (stimolare): ~ qn a fare to urge o press sb to do; ~rsi vr (inoltrarsi) to push on, carry on; ~rsi troppo lontano (anche fig) to go too far.
spi'noso, a ag thorny, prickly.
'spinto, a pp di spingere // sf (urto) push; (FISICA) thrust; (fig: stimolo) incentive, spur; (: appoggio) string-pulling q; dare una ~a a qn (fig) to pull strings for sb.
spio'naggio |spio'naddʒo| sm espionage,

spying.
spi'overe vi (scorrere) to flow down; (ricadere) to hang down, fall.
'spira sf coil.
spi'raglio [spi'raʎʎo] sm (fessura) chink, narrow opening; (raggio di luce, fig) glimmer, gleam.
spi'rale sf spiral; (contraccettivo) coil; a ~ spiral(-shaped).
spi'rare vi (vento) to blow; (morire) to expire, pass away.
spiri'tato, a ag possessed; (fig: persona, espressione) wild.
spiri'tismo sm spiritualism.
'spirito sm (REL, CHIM, disposizione d'animo, di legge etc, fantasma) spirit; (pensieri, intelletto) mind; (arguzia) wit; (umorismo) humour, wit; lo S~ Santo the Holy Spirit o Ghost.
spirito'saggine [spirito'saddʒine] sf witticism; (peg) wisecrack.
spiri'toso, a ag witty.
spiritu'ale ag spiritual.
'splendere vi to shine.
'splendido, a ag splendid; (splendente) shining; (sfarzoso) magnificent, splendid.
splen'dore sm splendour; (luce intensa) brilliance, brightness.
spodes'tare vt to deprive of power; (sovrano) to depose.
'spoglia ['spɔʎʎa] sf vedi spoglio.
spogli'are [spoʎ'ʎare] vt (svestire) to undress; (privare, fig: depredare): ~ qn di qc to deprive sb of sth; (togliere ornamenti: anche fig): ~ qn/qc di to strip sb/sth of; ~rsi vr to undress, strip; ~rsi di (ricchezze etc) to deprive o.s. of, give up; (pregiudizi) to rid o.s. of; **spoglia'toio** sm dressing room; (di scuola etc) cloakroom; (SPORT) changing room; **'spoglio, a** ag (pianta, terreno) bare; (privo): spoglio di stripped of; lacking in, without // sm (di voti) counting // sf (ZOOL) skin, hide; (: di rettile) slough; **'spoglie** sfpl (salma) remains; (preda) spoils, booty sg.
'spola sf shuttle; (bobina di filo) cop; fare la ~ (fra) to go to and fro o shuttle (between).
spol'pare vt to strip the flesh off.
spolve'rare vt (anche CUC) to dust; (con spazzola) to brush; (con battipanni) to beat; (fig) to polish off // vi to dust.
'sponda sf (di fiume) bank; (di mare, lago) shore; (bordo) edge.
spon'taneo, a ag spontaneous; (persona) unaffected, natural.
spopo'lare vt to depopulate // vi (attirare folla) to draw the crowds; ~rsi vr to become depopulated.
spor'care vt to dirty, make dirty; (fig) to sully, soil; ~rsi vr to get dirty.
spor'cizia [spor'tʃittsja] sf (stato) dirtiness; (sudiciume) dirt, filth; (cosa

sporca) dirt q, something dirty; (fig: cosa oscena) obscenity.
'sporco, a, chi, che ag dirty, filthy.
spor'genza [spor'dʒɛntsa] sf projection.
'sporgere ['spɔrdʒere] vt to put out, stretch out // vi (venire in fuori) to stick out; ~rsi vr to lean out; ~ querela contro qn (DIR) to take legal action against sb.
sport sm inv sport.
'sporta sf shopping bag.
spor'tello sm (di treno, auto etc) door; (di banca, ufficio) window, counter; ~ automatico (BANCA) cash dispenser, automated telling machine.
spor'tivo, a ag (gara, giornale) sports cpd; (persona) sporty; (abito) casual; (spirito, atteggiamento) sporting.
'sporto, a pp di sporgere.
'sposa sf bride; (moglie) wife.
sposa'lizio [spoza'littsjo] sm wedding.
spo'sare vt to marry; (fig: idea, fede) to espouse; ~rsi vr to get married, marry; ~rsi con qn to marry sb, get married to sb; **spo'sato, a** ag married.
'sposo sm (bride)groom; (marito) husband; gli ~i smpl the newlyweds.
spos'sato, a ag exhausted, weary.
spos'tare vt to move, shift; (cambiare: orario) to change; ~rsi vr to move.
'spranga, ghe sf (sbarra) bar.
'sprazzo ['sprattso] sm (di sole etc) flash; (fig: di gioia etc) burst.
spre'care vt to waste; ~rsi vr (persona) to waste one's energy; **'spreco** sm waste.
spre'gevole [spre'dʒevole] ag contemptible, despicable.
spregiudi'cato, a [spredʒudi'kato] ag unprejudiced, unbiased; (peg) unscrupulous.
'spremere vt to squeeze.
spre'muta sf fresh juice; ~ d'arancia fresh orange juice.
sprez'zante [spret'tsante] ag scornful, contemptuous.
sprigio'nare [spridʒo'nare] vt to give off, emit; ~rsi vr to emanate; (uscire con impeto) to burst out.
spriz'zare [sprit'tsare] vt, vi to spurt; ~ gioia/salute to be bursting with joy/health.
sprofon'dare vi to sink; (casa) to collapse; (suolo) to give way, subside; ~rsi vr: ~rsi in (poltrona) to sink into; (fig) to become immersed o absorbed in.
spro'nare vt to spur (on).
'sprone sm (sperone etc) spur.
sproporzio'nato, a [sproportsjo'nato] ag disproportionate, out of all proportion.
sproporzi'one [sropor'tsjone] sf disproportion.
sproposi'tato, a ag (lettera, discorso) full of mistakes; (fig: costo) excessive, enormous.

spro'posito *sm* blunder; **a ~ at the wrong time**; (*rispondere, parlare*) irrelevantly.

sprovve'duto, a *ag* inexperienced, naïve.

sprov'visto, a *ag* (*mancante*): **~ di** lacking in, without; **alla ~a** unawares.

spruz'zare |sprut'tsare| *vt* (*a nebulizzazione*) to spray; (*aspergere*) to sprinkle; (*inzaccherare*) to splash; **'spruzzo** *sm* spray; splash.

'spugna |'spuɲɲa| *sf* (*ZOOL*) sponge; (*tessuto*) towelling; **spu'gnoso, a** *ag* spongy.

'spuma *sf* (*schiuma*) foam; (*bibita*) mineral water.

spu'mante *sm* sparkling wine.

spumeggi'ante |spumed'dʒante| *ag* (*birra*) foaming; (*vino, fig*) sparkling.

spu'mone *sm* (*CUC*) mousse.

spun'tare *vt* (*coltello*) to break the point of; (*capelli*) to trim // *vi* (*uscire: germogli*) to sprout; (: *capelli*) to begin to grow; (: *denti*) to come through; (*apparire*) to appear (suddenly); **~rsi** *vr* to become blunt, lose its point; **spuntarla** (*fig*) to make it, win through.

spun'tino *sm* snack.

'spunto *sm* (*TEATRO, MUS*) cue; (*fig*) starting point; **dare lo ~ a** (*fig*) to give rise to.

spur'gare *vt* (*fogna*) to clean, clear; **~rsi** *vr* (*MED*) to expectorate.

spu'tare *vt* to spit out; (*fig*) to belch (out) // *vi* to spit; **'sputo** *sm* spittle *q*, spit *q*.

'squadra *sf* (*strumento*) (set) square; (*gruppo*) team, squad; (*di operai*) gang, squad; (*MIL*) squad; (: *AER, NAUT*) squadron; (*SPORT*) team; **lavoro a ~e** teamwork.

squa'drare *vt* to square, make square; (*osservare*) to look at closely.

squa'driglia |skwa'driʎʎa| *sf* (*AER*) flight; (*NAUT*) squadron.

squa'drone *sm* squadron.

squagli'arsi |skwaʎ'ʎarsi| *vr* to melt; (*fig*) to sneak off.

squa'lifica *sf* disqualification.

squalifi'care *vt* to disqualify.

'squallido, a *ag* wretched, bleak.

squal'lore *sm* wretchedness, bleakness.

'squalo *sm* shark.

'squama *sf* scale; **squa'mare** *vt* to scale; **squamarsi** *vr* to flake *o* peel (off).

squarcia'gola |skwartfa'gola|: **a ~** *av* at the top of one's voice.

squar'tare *vt* to quarter, cut up.

squattri'nato, a *ag* penniless.

squili'brare *vt* to unbalance; **squili'brato, a** *ag* (*PSIC*) unbalanced; **squi'librio** *sm* (*differenza, sbilancio*) imbalance; (*PSIC*) unbalance.

squil'lante *ag* shrill, sharp.

squil'lare *vi* (*campanello, telefono*) to

ring (out); (*tromba*) to blare; **'squillo** *sm* ring, ringing *q*; blare; **ragazza** *f* **squillo** *inv* call girl.

squi'sito, a *ag* exquisite; (*cibo*) delicious; (*persona*) delightful.

squit'tire *vi* (*uccello*) to squawk; (*topo*) to squeak.

sradi'care *vt* to uproot; (*fig*) to eradicate.

sragio'nare |zradʒo'nare| *vi* to talk nonsense, rave.

srego'lato, a *ag* (*senza ordine: vita*) disorderly; (*smodato*) immoderate; (*dissoluto*) dissolute.

S.r.l. *abbr* = **società a responsabilità limitata**.

'stabile *ag* stable, steady; (*tempo: non variabile*) settled; (*TEATRO: compagnia*) resident // *sm* (*edificio*) building.

stabili'mento *sm* (*edificio*) establishment; (*fabbrica*) plant, factory.

stabi'lire *vt* to establish; (*fissare: prezzi, data*) to fix; (*decidere*) to decide; **~rsi** *vr* (*prendere dimora*) to settle.

stac'care *vt* (*levare*) to detach, remove; (*separare: anche fig*) to separate, divide; (*strappare*) to tear off (*o* out); (*scandire: parole*) to pronounce clearly; (*SPORT*) to leave behind; **~rsi** *vr* (*bottone etc*) to come off; (*scostarsi*): **~rsi (da)** to move away (from); (*fig: separarsi*): **~rsi da** to leave; **non ~ gli occhi da qn** not to take one's eyes off sb.

'stadio *sm* (*SPORT*) stadium; (*periodo, fase*) phase, stage.

'staffa *sf* (*di sella, TECN*) stirrup; **perdere le ~e** (*fig*) to fly off the handle.

staf'fetta *sf* (*messo*) dispatch rider; (*SPORT*) relay race.

stagio'nale |stadʒo'nale| *ag* seasonal.

stagio'nare |stadʒo'nare| *vt* (*legno*) to season; (*formaggi, vino*) to mature.

stagi'one |sta'dʒone| *sf* season; **alta/bassa ~** high/low season.

stagli'arsi |staʎ'ʎarsi| *vr* to stand out, be silhouetted.

sta'gnare |staɲ'ɲare| *vt* (*vaso, tegame*) to tin-plate; (*barca, botte*) to make watertight; (*sangue*) to stop // *vi* to stagnate.

'stagno, a |'staɲɲo| *ag* watertight; (*a tenuta d'aria*) airtight // *sm* (*acquitrino*) pond; (*CHIM*) tin.

sta'gnola |staɲ'ɲɔla| *sf* tinfoil.

'stalla *sf* (*per bovini*) cowshed; (*per cavalli*) stable.

stal'lone *sm* stallion.

sta'mani, stamat'tina *av* this morning.

'stampa *sf* (*TIP, FOT*: tecnica) printing; (*impressione, copia fotografica*) print; (*insieme di quotidiani, giornalisti etc*) press; **~e** *sfpl* printed matter.

stam'pante *sf* (*INFORM*) printer.

stam'pare *vt* to print; (*pubblicare*) to

publish; (*coniare*) to strike, coin; (*imprimere*: *anche fig*) to impress.

stampa'tello *sm* block letters *pl*.

stam'pella *sf* crutch.

'stampo *sm* mould; (*fig*: *indole*) type, kind, sort.

sta'nare *vt* to drive out.

stan'care *vt* to tire, make tired; (*annoiare*) to bore; (*infastidire*) to annoy; ~**rsi** *vr* to get tired, tire o.s. out; ~**rsi** (**di**) to grow weary (of), grow tired (of).

stan'chezza |stan'kettsa| *sf* tiredness, fatigue.

'stanco, a, chi, che *ag* tired; ~ **di** tired of, fed up with.

'stanga, ghe *sm* bar; (*di carro*) shaft.

stan'gata *sf* (*colpo*: *anche fig*) blow; (*cattivo risultato*) poor result; (*CALCIO*) shot.

sta'notte *av* tonight; (*notte passata*) last night.

'stante *prep*: **a sé** ~ (*appartamento, casa*) independent, separate.

stan'tio, a, 'tii, 'tie *ag* stale; (*burro*) rancid; (*fig*) old.

stan'tuffo *sm* piston.

'stanza |'stantsa| *sf* room; (*POESIA*) stanza; ~ **da letto** bedroom.

stanzi'are |stan'tsjare| *vt* to allocate.

stap'pare *vt* to uncork; to uncap.

'stare *vi* (*restare in un luogo*) to stay, remain; (*abitare*) to stay, live; (*essere situato*) to be, be situated; (*anche*: ~ **in piedi**) to be, stand; (*essere, trovarsi*) to be; (*dipendere*): **se stesse in me** if it were up to me, if it depended on me; (*seguito da gerundio*): **sta studiando** he's studying; **starci** (*esserci spazio*): **nel baule non ci sta più niente** there's no more room in the boot; (*accettare*) to accept; **ci stai?** is that okay with you?; ~ **a** (*attenersi a*) to follow, stick to; (*seguito dall'infinito*): **stiamo a discutere** we're talking; (*toccare a*): **sta a te giocare** it's your turn to play; ~ **per fare qc** to be about to do sth; **come sta?** how are you?; **io sto bene/male** I'm very well/not very well; ~ **a qn** (*abiti etc*) to fit sb; **queste scarpe mi stanno strette** these shoes are tight for me; **il rosso ti sta bene** red suits you.

starnu'tire *vi* to sneeze; **star'nuto** *sm* sneeze.

sta'sera *av* this evening, tonight.

sta'tale *ag* state *cpd*; government *cpd* // *sm/f* state employee, local authority employee; (*nell'amministrazione*) ≈ civil servant.

sta'tista, i *sm* statesman.

sta'tistica *sf* statistics *sg*.

'stato, a *pp di* **essere, stare** // *sm* (*condizione*) state, condition; (*POL*) state; (*DIR*) status; **essere in** ~ **d'accusa** (*DIR*) to be committed for trial; ~ **d'assedio/**

d'emergenza state of siege/emergency; ~ **civile** (*AMM*) marital status; ~ **maggiore** (*MIL*) staff; **gli S**~**i Uniti (d'America)** the United States (of America).

'statua *sf* statue.

statuni'tense *ag* United States *cpd*, of the United States.

sta'tura *sf* (*ANAT*) height, stature; (*fig*) stature.

sta'tuto *sm* (*DIR*) statute; constitution.

sta'volta *av* this time.

stazio'nario, a |stattsjo'narjo| *ag* stationary; (*fig*) unchanged.

stazi'one |stat'tsjone| *sf* station; (*balneare, termale*) resort; ~ **degli autobus** bus station; ~ **balneare** seaside resort; ~ **ferroviaria** railway (*Brit*) o railroad (*US*) station; ~ **invernale** winter sports resort; ~ **di polizia** police station (*in small town*); ~ **di servizio** service o petrol (*Brit*) o filling station.

'stecca, che *sf* stick; (*di ombrello*) rib; (*di sigarette*) carton; (*MED*) splint; (*stonatura*): **fare una** ~ to sing (o play) a wrong note.

stec'cato *sm* fence.

stec'chito, a |stek'kito| *ag* dried up; (*persona*) skinny; **lasciar** ~ **qn** (*fig*) to leave sb flabbergasted; **morto** ~ stone dead.

'stella *sf* star; ~ **alpina** (*BOT*) edelweiss; ~ **di mare** (*ZOOL*) starfish.

'stelo *sm* stem; (*asta*) rod; **lampada a** ~ standard lamp.

'stemma, i *sm* coat of arms.

stempe'rare *vt* to dilute; to dissolve; (*colori*) to mix.

sten'dardo *sm* standard.

'stendere *vt* (*braccia, gambe*) to stretch (out); (*tovaglia*) to spread (out); (*bucato*) to hang out; (*mettere a giacere*) to lay (down); (*spalmare*: *colore*) to spread; (*mettere per iscritto*) to draw up; ~**rsi** *vr* (*coricarsi*) to stretch out, lie down; (*estendersi*) to extend, stretch.

stenodatti'lografo, a *sm/f* shorthand typist (*Brit*), stenographer (*US*).

stenogra'fare *vt* to take down in shorthand; **stenogra'fia** *sf* shorthand.

sten'tare *vi*: ~ **a fare** to find it hard to do, have difficulty doing.

'stento *sm* (*fatica*) difficulty; ~**i** *smpl* (*privazioni*) hardship *sg*, privation *sg*; **a** ~ *av* with difficulty, barely.

'sterco *sm* dung.

'stereo('fonico, a, ci, che) *ag* stereo(phonic).

'sterile *ag* sterile; (*terra*) barren; (*fig*) futile, fruitless; **sterilità** *sf* sterility.

steriliz'zare |sterilid'dzare| *vt* to sterilize; **sterilizzazi'one** *sf* sterilization.

ster'lina *sf* pound (sterling).

stermi'nare *vt* to exterminate, wipe out.

stermi'nato, a *ag* immense; endless.

ster'minio *sm* extermination, destruction.

'sterno *sm* (*ANAT*) breastbone.

ster'zare [ster'tsare] *vt, vi* (*AUT*) to steer; **'sterzo** *sm* steering; (*volante*) steering wheel.

'steso, a *pp di* **stendere**.

'stesso, a *ag* same; (*rafforzativo: in persona, proprio*): il re ~ the king himself *o* in person // *pronome*: lo(la) ~(a) the same (one); i suoi ~i avversari lo ammirano even his enemies admire him; fa lo ~ it doesn't matter; per me è lo ~ it's all the same to me, it doesn't matter to me; *vedi* **io, tu** *etc*.

ste'sura *sf* drafting *q*, drawing up *q*; draft.

'stigma, i *sm* stigma.

'stigmate *sfpl* (*REL*) stigmata.

sti'lare *vt* to draw up, draft.

'stile *sm* style; **sti'lista, i** *sm* designer.

stil'lare *vi* (*trasudare*) to ooze; (*gocciolare*) to drip; **stilli'cidio** *sm* (*fig*) continual pestering (*o* moaning *etc*).

stilo'grafica, che *sf* (*anche:* **penna** ~) fountain pen.

'stima *sf* esteem; valuation; assessment, estimate.

sti'mare *vt* (*persona*) to esteem, hold in high regard; (*terreno, casa etc*) to value; (*stabilire in misura approssimativa*) to estimate, assess; (*ritenere*): ~ che to consider that; ~rsi fortunato to consider o.s. (to be) lucky.

stimo'lare *vt* to stimulate; (*incitare*): ~ qn (a fare) to spur sb on (to do).

'stimolo *sm* (*anche fig*) stimulus.

'stinco, chi *sm* shin; shinbone.

'stingere ['stindʒere] *vt, vi* (*anche:* ~rsi) to fade; **'stinto, a** *pp di* **stingere**.

sti'pare *vt* to cram, pack; ~rsi *vr* (*accalcarsi*) to crowd, throng.

sti'pendio *sm* salary.

'stipite *sm* (*di porta, finestra*) jamb.

stipu'lare *vt* (*redigere*) to draw up.

sti'rare *vt* (*abito*) to iron; (*distendere*) to stretch; (*strappare: muscolo*) to strain; ~rsi *vr* to stretch (o.s.); **stira'tura** *sf* ironing.

'stirpe *sf* birth, stock; descendants *pl*.

stiti'chezza [stiti'kettsa] *sf* constipation.

'stitico, a, ci, che *ag* constipated.

'stiva *sf* (*di nave*) hold.

sti'vale *sm* boot.

'stizza ['stittsa] *sf* anger, vexation; **stiz'zirsi** *vr* to lose one's temper; **stiz'zoso, a** *ag* (*persona*) quick-tempered, irascible; (*risposta*) angry.

stocca'fisso *sm* stockfish, dried cod.

stoc'cata *sf* (*colpo*) stab, thrust; (*fig*) gibe, cutting remark.

'stoffa *sf* material, fabric; (*fig*): aver la ~ di to have the makings of.

'stola *sf* stole.

'stolto, a *ag* stupid, foolish.

'stomaco, chi *sm* stomach; dare di ~ to vomit, be sick.

sto'nare *vt* to sing (*o* play) out of tune // *vi* to be out of tune, sing (*o* play) out of tune; (*fig*) to be out of place, jar; (: *colori*) to clash; **stona'tura** *sf* (*suono*) false note.

stop *sm inv* (*TEL*) stop; (*AUT: cartello*) stop sign; (: *fanalino d'arresto*) brakelight.

'stoppa *sf* tow.

'stoppia *sf* (*AGR*) stubble.

stop'pino *sm* wick; (*miccia*) fuse.

'storcere ['stortʃere] *vt* to twist; ~rsi *vr* to writhe, twist; ~ il naso (*fig*) to turn up one's nose; ~rsi la caviglia to twist one's ankle.

stor'dire *vt* (*intontire*) to stun, daze; ~rsi *vr*: ~rsi col bere to dull one's senses with drink; **stor'dito, a** *ag* stunned; (*sventato*) scatterbrained, heedless.

'storia *sf* (*scienza, avvenimenti*) history; (*racconto, bugia*) story; (*faccenda, questione*) business *q*; (*pretesto*) excuse, pretext; ~e *sfpl* (*smancerie*) fuss *sg*; **'storico, a, ci, che** *ag* historic(al) // *sm* historian.

stori'one *sm* (*ZOOL*) sturgeon.

stor'mire *vi* to rustle.

'stormo *sm* (*di uccelli*) flock.

stor'nare *vt* (*COMM*) to transfer.

'storno *sm* starling.

storpi'are *vt* to cripple, maim; (*fig: parole*) to mangle; (: *significato*) to twist.

'storpio, a *ag* crippled, maimed.

'storto, a *pp di* **storcere** // *ag* (*chiodo*) twisted, bent; (*gamba, quadro*) crooked; (*fig: ragionamento*) false, wrong // *sf* (*distorsione*) sprain, twist; (*recipiente*) retort.

sto'viglie [sto'viʎʎe] *sfpl* dishes *pl*, crockery.

'strabico, a, ci, che *ag* squint-eyed; (*occhi*) squint.

stra'bismo *sm* squinting.

stra'carico, a, chi, che *ag* overloaded.

stracci'are [strat'tʃare] *vt* to tear.

'straccio, a, ci, ce ['strattʃo] *ag*: carta ~a waste paper // *sm* rag; (*per pulire*) cloth, duster; **stracci'vendolo** *sm* ragman.

stra'cotto, a *ag* overcooked // *sm* (*CUC*) beef stew.

'strada *sf* road; (*di città*) street; (*cammino, via, fig*) way; farsi ~ (*fig*) to do well for o.s.; essere fuori ~ (*fig*) to be on the wrong track; ~ facendo on the way; ~ senza uscita dead end; **stra'dale** *ag* road *cpd*.

strafalci'one [strafal'tʃone] *sm* blunder, howler.

stra'fare *vi* to overdo it; **stra'fatto, a** *pp di* **strafare**.

strafot'tente *ag*: è ~ he doesn't give a

damn, he couldn't care less.

'strage |'stradʒe| sf massacre, slaughter.

stralu'nato, a ag (occhi) rolling; (persona) beside o.s., very upset.

stramaz'zare |stramat'tsare| vi to fall heavily.

'strambo, a ag strange, queer.

strampa'lato, a ag odd, eccentric.

stra'nezza |stra'nettsa| sf strangeness.

strango'lare vt to strangle; ~rsi vr to choke.

strani'ero, a ag foreign // sm/f foreigner.

'strano, a ag strange, odd.

straordi'nario, a ag extraordinary; (treno etc) special // sm (lavoro) overtime.

strapaz'zare |strapat'tsare| vt to ill-treat; ~rsi vr to tire o.s. out, overdo things; **stra'pazzo** sm strain, fatigue; da strapazzo (fig) third-rate.

strapi'ombo sm overhanging rock; a ~ overhanging.

strapo'tere sm excessive power.

strap'pare vt (gen) to tear, rip; (pagina etc) to tear off, tear out; (sradicare) to pull up; (togliere): ~ qc a qn to snatch sth from sb; (fig) to wrest sth from sb; ~rsi vr (lacerarsi) to rip, tear; (rompersi) to break; ~rsi un muscolo to tear a muscle; **'strappo** sm pull, tug; tear, rip; fare uno strappo alla regola to make an exception to the rule; strappo muscolare torn muscle.

strapun'tino sm jump o foldaway seat.

strari'pare vi to overflow.

strasci'care |straʃʃi'kare| vt to trail; (piedi) to drag; ~ le parole to drawl.

'strascico |'straʃʃiko| sm (di abito) train; (conseguenza) after-effect.

strata'gemma, i |strata'dʒemma| sm stratagem.

strate'gia, 'gie |strate'dʒia| sf strategy; **stra'tegico, a, ci, che** ag strategic.

'strato sm layer; (rivestimento) coat, coating; (GEO, fig) stratum; (METEOR) stratus.

stratos'fera sf stratosphere.

strava'gante ag odd, eccentric; **strava'ganza** sf eccentricity.

stra'vecchio, a |stra'vekkjo| ag very old.

stra'vizio |stra'vittsjo| sm excess.

stra'volgere |stra'voldʒere| vt (volto) to contort; (fig: animo) to trouble deeply; (: verità) to twist, distort; **stra'volto, a** pp di stravolgere.

strazi'are |strat'tsjare| vt to torture, torment; **'strazio** sm torture; (fig: cosa fatta male): essere uno ~ to be appalling.

'strega, ghe sf witch.

stre'gare vt to bewitch.

stre'gone sm (mago) wizard; (di tribù) witch doctor.

'stregua sf: alla ~ di by the same

standard as.

stre'mare vt to exhaust.

'stremo sm very end; essere allo ~ to be at the end of one's tether.

'strenna sf Christmas present.

'strenuo, a ag brave, courageous.

strepi'toso, a ag clamorous, deafening; (fig: successo) resounding.

stres'sante ag stressful.

'stretta sf vedi stretto.

stretta'mente av tightly; (rigorosamente) strictly.

stret'tezza |stret'tettsa| sf narrowness; ~e sfpl poverty sg, straitened circumstances.

'stretto, a pp di stringere // ag (corridoio, limiti) narrow; (gonna, scarpe, nodo, curva) tight; (intimo: parente, amico) close; (rigoroso: osservanza) strict; (preciso: significato) precise, exact // sm (braccio di mare) strait // sf (di mano) grasp; (finanziaria) squeeze; (fig: dolore, turbamento) pang; a denti ~i with clenched teeth; lo ~ necessario the bare minimum; una ~a di mano a handshake; essere alle ~e to have one's back to the wall; **stret'toia** sf bottleneck; (fig) tricky situation.

stri'ato, a ag streaked.

'stridere vi (porta) to squeak; (animale) to screech, shriek; (colori) to clash; **'strido, pl(f) strida** sm screech, shriek; **stri'dore** sm screeching, shrieking; **'stridulo, a** ag shrill.

stril'lare vt, vi to scream, shriek; **'strillo** sm scream, shriek.

stril'lone sm newspaper seller.

strimin'zito, a |strimin'tsito| ag (misero) shabby; (molto magro) skinny.

strimpel'lare vt (MUS) to strum.

'stringa, ghe sf lace.

strin'gato, a ag (fig) concise.

'stringere |'strindʒere| vt (avvicinare due cose) to press (together), squeeze (together); (tenere stretto) to hold tight, clasp, clutch; (pugno, mascella, denti) to clench; (labbra) to compress; (avvitare) to tighten; (abito) to take in; (sog: scarpe) to pinch, be tight for; (fig: concludere: patto) to make; (: accelerare: passo, tempo) to quicken // vi (essere stretto) to be tight; (tempo: incalzare) to be pressing; ~rsi vr (accostarsi): ~rsi a to press o.s. up against; ~ la mano a qn to shake sb's hand; ~ gli occhi to screw up one's eyes.

'striscia, sce |'striʃʃa| sf (di carta, tessuto etc) strip; (riga) stripe; ~sce (pedonali) zebra crossing sg.

strisci'are |striʃ'ʃare| vt (piedi) to drag; (muro, macchina) to graze // vi to crawl, creep.

'striscio |'striʃʃo| sm graze; (MED) smear; colpire di ~ to graze.

strito'lare vt to grind.

striz'zare |strit'tsare| *vt* (*arancia*) to squeeze; (*panni*) to wring (out); ~ l'occhio to wink.

'strofa *sf*, **'strofe** *sf inv* strophe.

strofi'naccio |strofi'nattʃo| *sm* duster, cloth; (*per piatti*) dishcloth; (*per pavimenti*) floorcloth.

strofi'nare *vt* to rub.

stron'care *vt* to break off; (*fig*: *ribellione*) to suppress, put down; (*: film, libro*) to tear to pieces.

stropicci'are |stropit'tʃare| *vt* to rub.

stroz'zare |strot'tsare| *vt* (*soffocare*) to choke, strangle; ~rsi *vr* to choke; **strozza'tura** *sf* (*restringimento*) narrowing; (*di strada etc*) bottleneck.

'struggere |'struddʒere| *vt* (*fig*) to consume; ~rsi *vr* (*fig*): ~rsi di to be consumed with.

strumen'tale *ag* (*MUS*) instrumental.

strumentaliz'zare |strumentalid'dzare| *vt* to exploit, use to one's own ends.

stru'mento *sm* (*arnese, fig*) instrument, tool; (*MUS*) instrument; ~ a corda *o* ad arco/a fiato stringed/wind instrument.

'strutto *sm* lard.

strut'tura *sf* structure; **struttu'rare** *vt* to structure.

'struzzo |'struttso| *sm* ostrich.

stuc'care *vt* (*muro*) to plaster; (*vetro*) to putty; (*decorare con stucchi*) to stucco.

stuc'chevole |stuk'kevole| *ag* nauseating; (*fig*) tedious, boring.

'stucco, chi *sm* plaster; (*da vetri*) putty; (*ornamentale*) stucco; rimanere di ~ (*fig*) to be dumbfounded.

stu'dente, 'essa *smf* student; (*scolaro*) pupil, schoolboy/girl; **studen'tesco, a, schi, sche** *ag* student *cpd*; school *cpd*.

studi'are *vt* to study.

'studio *sm* studying; (*ricerca, saggio, stanza*) study; (*di professionista*) office; (*di artista, CINEMA, TV, RADIO*) studio; ~i *smpl* (*INS*) studies; ~ medico doctor's surgery (*Brit*) *o* office (*US*).

studi'oso, a *ag* studious, hard- working // *sm/f* scholar.

'stufa *sf* stove; ~ elettrica electric fire *o* heater.

stu'fare *vt* (*CUC*) to stew; (*fig: fam*) to bore; **stu'fato** *sm* (*CUC*) stew; **'stufo, a** *ag* (*fam*): essere stufo di to be fed up with, be sick and tired of.

stu'oia *sf* mat.

stupefa'cente |stupefa'tʃente| *ag* stunning, astounding // *sm* drug, narcotic.

stu'pendo, a *ag* marvellous, wonderful.

stupi'daggine |stupi'daddʒine| *sf* stupid thing (to do *o* say).

stupidità *sf* stupidity.

'stupido, a *ag* stupid.

stu'pire *vt* to amaze, stun // *vi* (*anche*: ~rsi): ~ (di) to be amazed (at), be stunned (by).

stu'pore *sm* amazement, astonishment.

'stupro *sm* rape.

stu'rare *vt* (*lavandino*) to clear.

stuzzica'denti |stuttsika'denti| *sm* toothpick.

stuzzi'care |stuttsi'kare| *vt* (*ferita etc*) to poke (at), prod (at); (*fig*) to tease; (*: appetito*) to whet; (*: curiosità*) to stimulate; ~ i denti to pick one's teeth.

su ◆ *prep* (*su + il* = **sul**, *su + lo* = **sullo**, *su + l'* = **sull'**, *su + la* = **sulla**, *su + i* = **sui**, *su + gli* = **sugli**, *su + le* = **sulle**) 1 (*gen*) on; (*moto*) on(to); (*in cima a*) on (top of); mettilo sul tavolo put it on the table; un paesino sul mare a village by the sea

2 (*argomento*) about, on; un libro ~ Cesare a book on *o* about Caesar

3 (*circa*) about; costerà sui 3 milioni it will cost about 3 million; una ragazza sui 17 anni a girl of about 17 (years of age)

4: ~ misura made to measure; ~ richiesta on request; 3 casi ~ dieci 3 cases out of 10

◆ *av* 1 (*in alto, verso l'alto*) up; vieni ~ come on up; guarda ~ look up; ~ le mani! hands up!; in ~ (*verso l'alto*) up(wards); (*in poi*) onwards; dai 20 anni in ~ from the age of 20 onwards

2 (*addosso*) on; cos'hai ~? what have you got on?

◆ *escl* come on!; ~ coraggio! come on, cheer up!

'sua *vedi* **suo**.

su'bacqueo, a *ag* underwater // *sm* skindiver.

sub'buglio |sub'buʎʎo| *sm* confusion, turmoil.

subcosci'ente |subkoʃ'ʃente| *ag, sm* subconscious.

'subdolo, a *ag* underhand, sneaky.

suben'trare *vi*: ~ a qn in qc to take over sth from sb.

su'bire *vt* to suffer, endure.

subis'sare *vt* (*fig*): ~ di to overwhelm with, load with.

subi'taneo, a *ag* sudden.

'subito *av* immediately, at once, straight away.

subodo'rare *vt* (*insidia etc*) to smell, suspect.

subordi'nato, a *ag* subordinate; (*dipendente*): ~ a dependent on, subject to.

subur'bano, a *ag* suburban.

succe'daneo |suttʃe'daneo| *sm* substitute.

suc'cedere |sut'tʃedere| *vi* (*prendere il posto di qn*): ~ a to succeed; (*venire dopo*): ~ a to follow; (*accadere*) to happen; ~rsi *vr* to follow each other; ~ al trono to succeed to the throne; **successi'one** *sf* succession; **succes'sivo, a** *ag* successive; **suc'cesso, a** *pp di* **succedere** // *sm* (*esito*) outcome;

(buona riuscita) success; **di successo** *(libro, personaggio)* successful.

succhi'are |suk'kjare| *vt* to suck (up).

suc'cinto, a |sut'tʃinto| *ag (discorso)* succinct; *(abito)* brief.

'succo, chi *sm* juice; *(fig)* essence, gist; ~ **di frutta** fruit juice; **suc'coso, a** *ag* juicy; *(fig)* pithy.

succur'sale *sf* branch (office).

sud *sm* south // *ag inv* south; *(lato)* south, southern.

Su'dafrica *sm*: **il ~** South Africa; **sudafri'cano, a** *ag, sm/f* South African.

Suda'merica *sm*: **il ~** South America; **sudameri'cano, a** *ag, sm/f* South American.

su'dare *vi* to perspire, sweat; ~ **freddo** to come out in a cold sweat; **su'data** *sf* sweat; **ho fatto una bella sudata per finirlo in tempo** it was a real sweat to get it finished in time.

sud'detto, a *ag* above-mentioned.

sud'dito, a *sm/f* subject.

suddi'videre *vt* to subdivide.

su'dest *sm* south-east.

'sudicio, a, ci, ce |'suditʃo| *ag* dirty, filthy; **sudici'ume** *sm* dirt, filth.

su'dore *sm* perspiration, sweat.

su'dovest *sm* south-west.

'sue *vedi* **suo.**

suffici'ente |suffi'tʃɛnte| *ag* enough, sufficient; *(borioso)* self-important; *(INS)* satisfactory; **suffici'enza** *sf* self-importance; pass mark; **a sufficienza** *av* enough; **ne ho avuto a sufficienza!** I've had enough of this!

suf'fisso *sm (LING)* suffix.

suf'fragio |suf'fradʒo| *sm (voto)* vote; ~ **universale** universal suffrage.

suggel'lare |suddʒel'lare| *vt (fig)* to seal.

suggeri'mento |suddʒeri'mento| *sm* suggestion; *(consiglio)* piece of advice, advice *q.*

sugge'rire |suddʒe'rire| *vt (risposta)* to tell; *(consigliare)* to advise; *(proporre)* to suggest; *(TEATRO)* to prompt; **suggeri'tore, 'trice** *sm/f (TEATRO)* prompter.

suggestio'nare |suddʒestjo'nare| *vt* to influence.

suggesti'one |suddʒes'tjone| *sf (PSIC)* suggestion; *(istigazione)* instigation.

sugges'tivo, a |suddʒes'tivo| *ag (paesaggio)* evocative; *(teoria)* interesting, attractive.

'sughero |'sugero| *sm* cork.

'sugli |'suʎʎi| *prep + det vedi* **su.**

'sugo, ghi *sm (succo)* juice; *(di carne)* gravy; *(condimento)* sauce; *(fig)* gist, essence.

'sui *prep + det vedi* **su.**

sui'cida, i, e |sui'tʃida| *ag* suicidal // *sm/f* suicide.

suici'darsi |suitʃi'darsi| *vr* to commit suicide.

sui'cidio |sui'tʃidjo| *sm* suicide.

su'ino, a *ag*: **carne ~a** pork // *sm* pig; **~i** *smpl* swine *pl.*

sul, sull', 'sulla, 'sulle, 'sullo *prep + det vedi* **su.**

sulta'nina *ag f*: **(uva)** ~ sultana.

sul'tano, a *sm/f* sultan/sultana.

'sunto *sm* summary.

'suo, 'sua, 'sue, su'oi *det*: **il ~, la sua** *etc (di lui)* his; *(di lei)* her; *(di esso)* its; *(con valore indefinito)* one's, his/her; *(forma di cortesia: anche:* S~) your // *pronome*: **il ~, la sua** *etc* his; hers; yours; **i suoi** *(parenti)* his *(o her o one's o* your) family.

su'ocero, a |'swɔtʃero| *sm/f* father/mother-in-law; **i ~i** *smpl* father and mother-in-law.

su'oi *vedi* **suo.**

su'ola *sf (di scarpa)* sole.

su'olo *sm (terreno)* ground; *(terra)* soil.

suo'nare *vt (MUS)* to play; *(campana)* to ring; *(ore)* to strike; *(clacson, allarme)* to sound // *vi (di ni)* to play; *(telefono, campana)* to ring; *(ore)* to strike; *(clacson, fig: parole)* to sound.

su'ono *sm* sound.

su'ora *sf (REL)* sister.

'super *sf (anche:* **benzina** ~) ≈ four-star (petrol) *(Brit)*, premium *(US)*.

supe'rare *vt (oltrepassare: limite)* to exceed, surpass; *(percorrere)* to cover; *(attraversare: fiume)* to cross; *(sorpassare: veicolo)* to overtake; *(fig: essere più bravo di)* to surpass, outdo; *(: difficoltà)* to overcome; *(: esame)* to get through; ~ **qn in altezza/peso** to be taller/heavier than sb; **ha superato la cinquantina** he's over fifty (years of age).

su'perbia *sf* pride.

su'perbo, a *ag* proud; *(fig)* magnificent, superb.

superfici'ale |superfi'tʃale| *ag* superficial.

super'ficie, ci |super'fitʃe| *sf* surface.

su'perfluo, a *ag* superfluous.

superi'ore *ag (piano, arto, classi)* upper; *(più elevato: temperatura, livello)*: ~ **(a)** higher (than); *(migliore)*: ~ **(a)** superior (to); ~, **a** *sm/f (anche REL)* superior; **superiorità** *sf* superiority.

superla'tivo, a *ag, sm* superlative.

supermer'cato *sm* supermarket.

su'perstite *ag* surviving // *sm/f* survivor.

superstizi'one |superstit'tsjone| *sf* superstition; **superstizi'oso, a** *ag* superstitious.

su'pino, a *ag* supine.

suppel'lettile *sf* furnishings *pl.*

suppergiù |supper'dʒu| *av* more or less, roughly.

supplemen'tare *ag* extra; *(treno)* relief *cpd*; *(entrate)* additional.

supple'mento *sm* supplement.

sup'plente ag temporary; (insegnante) supply cpd (Brit), substitute cpd (US) // smlf temporary member of staff; supply (o substitute) teacher.

'supplica, che sf (preghiera) plea; (domanda scritta) petition, request.

suppli'care vt to implore, beseech.

sup'plire vi: ~ a to make up for, compensate for.

sup'plizio |sup'plittsjo| sm torture.

sup'porre vt to suppose.

sup'porto sm (sostegno) support.

sup'posta sf (MED) suppository.

sup'posto, a pp di supporre.

su'premo, a ag supreme.

surge'lare |surdʒe'lare| vt to (deep-)freeze; **surge'lati** smpl frozen food sg.

sur'plus sm inv (ECON) surplus.

surriscal'dare vt to overheat.

surro'gato sm substitute.

suscet'tibile |suʃʃet'tibile| ag (sensibile) touchy, sensitive; (soggetto): ~ di miglioramento that can be improved, open to improvement.

susci'tare |suʃʃi'tare| vt to provoke, arouse.

su'sina sf plum; **su'sino** sm plum (tree).

sussegu'ire vt to follow; ~rsi vr to follow one another.

sussidi'ario, a ag subsidiary; auxiliary.

sus'sidio sm subsidy.

sussis'tenza |sussis'tɛntsa| sf subsistence.

sus'sistere vi to exist; (essere fondato) to be valid o sound.

sussul'tare vi to shudder.

sussur'rare vt, vi to whisper, murmur; **sus'surro** sm whisper, murmur.

sutu'rare vt (MED) to stitch up, suture.

sva'gare vt (distrarre) to distract; (divertire) to amuse; ~rsi vr to amuse o.s.; to enjoy o.s.

'svago, ghi sm (riposo) relaxation; (ricreazione) amusement; (passatempo) pastime.

svaligi'are |zvali'dʒare| vt to rob, burgle (Brit), burglarize (US).

svalu'tare vt (ECON) to devalue; (fig) to belittle; ~rsi vr (ECON) to be devalued; **svalutazi'one** sf devaluation.

sva'nire vi to disappear, vanish.

svan'taggio |zvan'taddʒo| sm disadvantage; (inconveniente) drawback, disadvantage.

svapo'rare vi to evaporate.

svari'ato, a ag varied; various.

'svastica sf swastika.

sve'dese ag Swedish // smlf Swede // sm (LING) Swedish.

'sveglia |'zveʎʎa| sf waking up; (orologio) alarm (clock); **suonare la ~** (MIL) to sound the reveille.

svegli'are |zveʎ'ʎare| vt to wake up; (fig) to awaken, arouse; ~rsi vr to wake

up; (fig) to be revived, reawaken.

'sveglio, a |'zveʎʎo| ag awake; (fig) quick-witted.

sve'lare vt to reveal.

'svelto, a ag (passo) quick; (mente) quick, alert; (linea) slim, slender; **alla ~a** av quickly.

'svendita sf (COMM) (clearance) sale.

sveni'mento sm fainting fit, faint.

sve'nire vi to faint.

sven'tare vt to foil, thwart.

sven'tato, a ag (distratto) scatter-brained; (imprudente) rash.

svento'lare vt, vi to wave, flutter.

sven'trare vt to disembowel.

sven'tura sf misfortune; **sventu'rato, a** ag unlucky, unfortunate.

sve'nuto, a pp di svenire.

svergo'gnato, a |zvergoɲ'ɲato| ag shameless.

sver'nare vi to spend the winter.

sves'tire vt to undress; ~rsi vr to get undressed.

'Svezia |'zvɛttsja| sf: la ~ Sweden.

svez'zare |zvet'tsare| vt to wean.

svi'are vt to divert; (fig) to lead astray; ~rsi vr to go astray.

svi'gnarsela |zviɲ'ɲarsela| vr to slip away, sneak off.

svilup'pare vt, ~rsi vr to develop.

svi'luppo sm development.

'svincolo sm (COMM) clearance; (stradale) motorway (Brit) o expressway (US) intersection.

svisce'rare |zviʃʃe'rare| vt (fig: argomento) to examine in depth; **svisce'rato, a** ag (amore) passionate; (lodi) obsequious.

'svista sf oversight.

svi'tare vt to unscrew.

'Svizzera |'zvittsera| sf: la ~ Switzerland.

'svizzero, a |'zvittsero| ag, smlf Swiss.

svogli'ato, a |zvoʎ'ʎato| ag listless; (pigro) lazy.

svolaz'zare |zvolat'tsare| vi to flutter.

'svolgere |'zvoldʒere| vt to unwind; (srotolare) to unroll; (fig: argomento) to develop; (: piano, programma) to carry out; ~rsi vr to unwind; to unroll; (fig: aver luogo) to take place; (: procedere) to go on; **svolgi'mento** sm development; carrying out; (andamento) course.

'svolta sf (atto) turning q; (curva) turn, bend; (fig) turning-point.

svol'tare vi to turn.

'svolto, a pp di svolgere.

svuo'tare vt to empty (out).

T

tabac'caio, a smlf tobacconist.

tabacche'ria |tabakke'ria| sf tobacconist's (shop).

ta'bacco, chi *sm* tobacco.

ta'bella *sf* (*tavola*) table; (*elenco*) list.

taber'nacolo *sm* tabernacle.

tabu'lato *sm* (*INFORM*) printout.

'tacca, che *sf* notch, nick; **di mezza ~** (*fig*) mediocre.

tac'cagno, a [tak'kaɲɲo] *ag* mean, stingy.

tac'cheggio [tak'keddʒo] *sm* shoplifting.

tac'chino [tak'kino] *sm* turkey.

tacci'are [tat'tʃare] *vt*: **~ qn di** to accuse sb of.

'tacco, chi *sm* heel.

taccu'ino *sm* notebook.

ta'cere [ta'tʃere] *vi* to be silent *o* quiet; (*smettere di parlare*) to fall silent // *vt* to keep to oneself, say nothing about; **far ~ qn** to make sb be quiet; (*fig*) to silence sb.

ta'chimetro [ta'kimetro] *sm* speedometer.

'tacito, a ['tatʃito] *ag* silent; (*sottinteso*) tacit, unspoken.

ta'fano *sm* horsefly.

taffe'ruglio [taffe'ruʎʎo] *sm* brawl, scuffle.

taffettà *sm* taffeta.

'taglia ['taʎʎa] *sf* (*statura*) height; (*misura*) size; (*riscatto*) ransom; (*ricompensa*) reward.

taglia'carte [taʎʎa'karte] *sm inv* paperknife.

tagli'ando [taʎ'ʎando] *sm* coupon.

tagli'are [taʎ'ʎare] *vt* to cut; (*recidere, interrompere*) to cut off; (*intersecare*) to cut across, intersect; (*carne*) to carve; (*vini*) to blend // *vi* to cut; (*prendere una scorciatoia*) to take a short-cut; **~ corto** (*fig*) to cut short.

taglia'telle [taʎʎa'telle] *sfpl* tagliatelle *pl*.

tagli'ente [taʎ'ʎɛnte] *ag* sharp.

'taglio ['taʎʎo] *sm* cutting *q*; cut; (*parte tagliente*) cutting edge; (*di abito*) cut, style; (*di stoffa: lunghezza*) length; (*di vini*) blending; **di ~** on edge, edgeways; **banconote di piccolo/grosso ~** notes of small/large denomination.

tagli'ola [taʎ'ʎola] *sf* trap, snare.

tagliuz'zare [taʎʎut'tsare] *vt* to cut into small pieces.

'talco *sm* talcum powder.

'tale ◆ *det* **1** (*simile, così grande*) such; **un(a) ~ ...** such (a) ...; **non accetto ~i discorsi** I won't allow such talk; **è di una ~ arroganza** he is so arrogant; **fa una ~ confusione!** he makes such a mess!

2 (*persona o cosa indeterminata*) such-and-such; **il giorno ~ all'ora ~** on such-and-such a day at such-and-such a time; **la tal persona** that person; **ha telefonato una ~ Giovanna** somebody called Giovanna phoned

3 (*nelle similitudini*): **~ ... ~** like ...

like; **~ padre ~ figlio** like father, like son; **hai il vestito ~ quale il mio** your dress is just *o* exactly like mine

◆ *pronome* (*indefinito: persona*): **un(a) ~** someone; **quel (o quella) ~** that person, that man (o woman); **il tal dei ~i** what's-his-name.

ta'lento *sm* talent.

talis'mano *sm* talisman.

tallon'cino [tallon'tʃino] *sm* counterfoil.

tal'lone *sm* heel.

tal'mente *av* so.

tal'ora *av* = **talvolta**.

'talpa *sf* (*ZOOL*) mole.

tal'volta *av* sometimes, at times.

tambu'rello *sm* tambourine.

tam'buro *sm* drum.

Ta'migi [ta'midʒi] *sm*: **il ~** the Thames.

tampo'nare *vt* (*otturare*) to plug; (*urtare: macchina*) to crash *o* ram into.

tam'pone *sm* (*MED*) wad, pad; (*per timbri*) ink-pad; (*respingente*) buffer; **~ assorbente** tampon.

'tana *sf* lair, den.

'tanfo *sm* stench; musty smell.

tan'gente [tan'dʒɛnte] *ag* (*MAT*): **~ a** tangential to // *sf* tangent; (*quota*) share.

tan'tino: un ~ *av* a little, a bit.

'tanto, a ◆ *det* **1** (*molto: quantità*) a lot of, much; (: *numero*) a lot of, many; (*così ~: quantità*) so much, such a lot of; (: *numero*) so many, such a lot of; **~e volte** so many times, so often; **~i auguri!** all the best!; **~e grazie** many thanks; **~ tempo** so long, such a long time; **ogni ~i chilometri** every so many kilometres

2: **~ ... quanto** (*quantità*) as much ... as; (*numero*) as many ... as; **ho ~a pazienza quanta ne hai tu** I have as much patience as you have *o* as you; **ha ~i amici quanti nemici** he has as many friends as he has enemies

3 (*rafforzativo*) such; **ho aspettato per ~ tempo** I waited so long *o* for such a long time

◆ *pronome* **1** (*molto*) much, a lot; (*così ~*) so much, such a lot; (*così ~*) **~i(e)** many, a lot; so many, such a lot; **credevo ce ne fosse ~** I thought there was (such) a lot, I thought there was plenty

2: **~ quanto** (*denaro*) as much as; (*cioccolatini*) as many as; **ne ho ~ quanto basta** I have as much as I need; **due volte ~** twice as much

3 (*indeterminato*) so much; **~ per l'affitto, ~ per il gas** so much for the rent, so much for the gas; **costa un ~ al metro** it costs so much per metre; **di ~ in ~, ogni ~** every so often; **~ vale che ...** I (*o* we *etc*) may as well ...; **~ meglio!** so much the better!; **~ peggio per lui!** so much the worse for him!

◆ *av* **1** (*molto*) very; **vengo ~ volentieri** I'd be very glad to come; **non ci vuole ~**

a capirlo it doesn't take much to understand it

2 (così ~: con ag, av) so; (: con vb) so much, such a lot; è ~ bella! she's so beautiful!; non urlare ~ don't shout so much; sto ~ meglio adesso I'm so much better now; ~ ... che so ... (that); ~ ... da so ... as

3: ~ ... quanto as ... as; conosco ~ Carlo quanto suo padre I know both Carlo and his father; non è poi ~ complicato quanto sembri it's not as difficult as it seems; ~ più insisti, ~ più non mollerà the more you insist, the more stubborn he'll be; quanto più ... ~ meno the more ... the less

4 (solamente) just; ~ per cambiare/scherzare just for a change/a joke; una volta ~ for once

5 (a lungo) (for) long
◆ cong after all.

'tappa sf (luogo di sosta, fermata) stop, halt; (parte di un percorso) stage, leg; (SPORT) lap; a ~e in stages.

tap'pare vt to plug, stop up; (bottiglia) to cork.

tap'peto sm carpet; (anche: tappetino) rug; (di tavolo) cloth; (SPORT): andare al ~ to go down for the count; mettere sul ~ (fig) to bring up for discussion.

tappez'zare [tappet'tsare] vt (con carta) to paper; (rivestire): ~ qc (di) to cover sth (with); **tappezze'ria** sf (tessuto) tapestry; (carta da parato) wallpaper; (arte) upholstery; far da tappezzeria (fig) to be a wallflower; **tappezzi'ere** sm upholsterer.

'tappo sm stopper; (in sughero) cork.

tarchi'ato, a [tar'kjato] ag stocky, thickset.

tar'dare vi to be late // vt to delay; ~ a fare to delay doing.

'tardi av late; più ~ later (on); al più ~ at the latest; sul ~ (verso sera) late in the day; far ~ to be late; (restare alzato) to stay up late.

tar'divo, a ag (primavera) late; (rimedio) belated, tardy; (fig: bambino) retarded.

'tardo, a ag (lento, fig: ottuso) slow; (tempo: avanzato) late.

'targa, ghe sf plate; (AUT) number (Brit) o license (US) plate.

ta'riffa sf (gen) rate, tariff; (di trasporti) fare; (elenco) price list; tariff.

'tarlo sm woodworm.

'tarma sf moth.

ta'rocco, chi sm tarot card; ~chi smpl (gioco) tarot sg.

tartagli'are [tartaʎ'ʎare] vi to stutter, stammer.

'tartaro, a ag, sm (in tutti i sensi) tartar.

tarta'ruga, ghe sf tortoise; (di mare) turtle; (materiale) tortoiseshell.

tar'tina sf canapé.

tar'tufo sm (BOT) truffle.

'tasca, sche sf pocket; **tas'cabile** ag (libro) pocket cpd; **tasca'pane** sm haversack; **tas'chino** sm breast pocket.

'tassa sf (imposta) tax; (doganale) duty; (per iscrizione: a scuola etc) fee; ~ di circolazione/di soggiorno road/tourist tax.

tas'sametro sm taximeter.

tas'sare vt to tax; to levy a duty on.

tassa'tivo, a ag peremptory.

tassazi'one [tassat'tsjone] sf taxation.

tas'sello sm plug; wedge.

tassì sm inv = **taxi**; **tas'sista, i, e** sm/f taxi driver.

'tasso sm (di natalità, d'interesse etc) rate; (BOT) yew; (ZOOL) badger; ~ di cambio/d'interesse rate of exchange/interest.

tas'tare vt to feel; ~ il terreno (fig) to see how the land lies.

tasti'era sf keyboard.

'tasto sm key; (tatto) touch, feel.

tas'toni av: procedere (a) ~ to grope one's way forward.

'tattico, a, ci, che ag tactical // sf tactics pl.

'tatto sm (senso) touch; (fig) tact; duro al ~ hard to the touch; aver ~ to be tactful, have tact.

tatu'aggio [tatu'addʒo] sm tattooing; (disegno) tattoo.

tatu'are vt to tattoo.

'tavola sf table; (asse) plank, board; (lastra) tablet; (quadro) panel (painting); (illustrazione) plate; ~ calda snack bar; ~ pieghevole folding table.

tavo'lato sm boarding; (pavimento) wooden floor.

tavo'letta sf tablet, bar; a ~ (AUT) flat out.

tavo'lino sm small table; (scrivania) desk.

'tavolo sm table.

tavo'lozza [tavo'lɔttsa] sf (ARTE) palette.

'taxi sm inv taxi.

'tazza ['tattsa] sf cup; ~ da caffè/tè coffee/tea cup; una ~ di caffè/tè a cup of coffee/tea.

te pronome (soggetto: in forme comparative, oggetto) you.

tè sm inv tea; (trattenimento) tea party.

tea'trale ag theatrical.

te'atro sm theatre.

'tecnico, a, ci, che ag technical // sm/f technician // sf technique; (tecnologia) technology.

tecnolo'gia [teknolo'dʒia] sf technology.

te'desco, a, schi, sche ag, sm/f, sm German.

'tedio sm tedium, boredom.

te'game sm (CUC) pan.

'tegola sf tile.

tei'era sf teapot.

'tela sf (tessuto) cloth; (per vele, quadri)

canvas; (*dipinto*) canvas, painting; **di ~** (*calzoni*) (heavy) cotton *cpd*; (*scarpe, borsa*) canvas *cpd*; **~ cerata** oilcloth; (*copertone*) tarpaulin.

te'laio *sm* (*apparecchio*) loom; (*struttura*) frame.

tele'camera *sf* television camera.

tele'cronaca *sf* television report.

tele'ferica, che *sf* cableway.

telefo'nare *vi* to telephone, ring; to make a phone call // *vt* to telephone; **~ a** to phone up, ring up, call up.

telefo'nata *sf* (telephone) call; **~ a carico del destinatario** reverse charge (*Brit*) o collect (*US*) call.

tele'fonico, a, ci, che *ag* (tele)phone *cpd*.

telefo'nista, i, e *sm/f* telephonist; (*d'impresa*) switchboard operator.

te'lefono *sm* telephone; **~ a gettoni** ≈ pay phone.

telegior'nale [teledʒor'nale] *sm* television news (programme).

te'legrafo *sm* telegraph; (*ufficio*) telegraph office.

tele'gramma, i *sm* telegram.

tele'matica *sf* data transmission; telematics *sg*.

telepa'tia *sf* telepathy.

teles'copio *sm* telescope.

teleselezi'one [teleselet'tsjone] *sf* direct dialling.

telespetta'tore, 'trice *sm/f* (television) viewer.

televisi'one *sf* television.

televi'sore *sm* television set.

'telex *sm inv* telex.

'tema, i *sm* theme; (*INS*) essay, composition.

teme'rario, a *ag* rash, reckless.

te'mere *vt* to fear, be afraid of; (*essere sensibile a: freddo, calore*) to be sensitive to // *vi* to be afraid; (*essere preoccupato*): **~ per** to worry about, fear for; **~ di/che** to be afraid of/that.

temperama'tite *sm inv* pencil sharpener.

tempera'mento *sm* temperament.

tempe'rare *vt* (*aguzzare*) to sharpen; (*fig*) to moderate, control, temper.

tempe'rato, a *ag* moderate, temperate; (*clima*) temperate.

tempera'tura *sf* temperature.

tempe'rino *sm* penknife.

tem'pesta *sf* storm; **~ di sabbia/neve** sand/snowstorm.

tempes'tare *vt*: **~ qn di domande** to bombard sb with questions; **~ qn di colpi** to rain blows on sb.

tempes'tivo, a *ag* timely.

tempes'toso, a *ag* stormy.

'tempia *sf* (*ANAT*) temple.

'tempio *sm* (*edificio*) temple.

'tempo *sm* (*METEOR*) weather; (*cronologico*) time; (*epoca*) time, times

pl; (*di film, gioco: parte*) part; (*MUS*) time; (: *battuta*) beat; (*LING*) tense; **un ~ once**; **~ fa** some time ago; **al ~ stesso** o **a un ~** at the same time; **per ~** early; **aver fatto il suo ~** to have had its (o his *etc*) day; **primo/secondo ~** (*TEATRO*) first/second part; (*SPORT*) first/second half; **in ~ utile** in due time o course.

tempo'rale *ag* temporal // *sm* (*METEOR*) (thunder)storm.

tempo'raneo, a *ag* temporary.

temporeggi'are [tempored'dʒare] *vi* to play for time, temporize.

tem'prare *vt* to temper.

te'nace [te'natʃe] *ag* strong, tough; (*fig*) tenacious; **te'nacia** *sf* tenacity.

te'naglie [te'naʎʎe] *sfpl* pincers *pl*.

'tenda *sf* (*riparo*) awning; (*di finestra*) curtain; (*per campeggio etc*) tent.

ten'denza [ten'dentsa] *sf* tendency; (*orientamento*) trend; **avere ~ a** o **per qc** to have a bent for sth.

'tendere *vt* (*allungare al massimo*) to stretch, draw tight; (*porgere: mano*) to hold out; (*fig: trappola*) to lay, set // *vi*: **~ a qc/a fare** to tend towards sth/to do; **~ l'orecchio** to prick up one's ears; **il tempo tende al caldo** the weather is getting hot; **un blu che tende al verde** a greenish blue.

ten'dina *sf* curtain.

'tendine *sm* tendon, sinew.

'ten'done *sm* (*da circo*) tent.

'tenebre *sfpl* darkness *sg*; **tene'broso, a** *ag* dark, gloomy.

te'nente *sm* lieutenant.

te'nere *vt* to hold; (*conservare, mantenere*) to keep; (*ritenere, considerare*) to consider; (*spazio: occupare*) to take up, occupy; (*seguire: strada*) to keep to // *vi* to hold; (*colori*) to be fast; (*dare importanza*): **~ a** to care about; **~ a fare** to want to do, be keen to do; **~rsi** *vr* (*stare in una determinata posizione*) to stand; (*stimarsi*) to consider o.s.; (*aggrapparsi*): **~rsi a** to hold on to; (*attenersi*): **~rsi a** to stick to; **~ una conferenza** to give a lecture; **~ conto di qc** to take sth into consideration; **~ presente qc** to bear sth in mind.

'tenero, a *ag* tender; (*pietra, cera, colore*) soft; (*fig*) tender, loving.

'tenia *sf* tapeworm.

'tennis *sm* tennis.

te'nore *sm* (*tono*) tone; (*MUS*) tenor; **~ di vita** way of life; (*livello*) standard of living.

tensi'one *sf* tension.

ten'tare *vt* (*indurre*) to tempt; (*provare*): **~ qc/di fare** to attempt o try sth/to do; **tenta'tivo** *sm* attempt; **tentazi'one** *sf* temptation.

tenten'nare *vi* to shake, be unsteady; (*fig*) to hesitate, waver // *vt*: **~ il capo** to shake one's head.

ten'toni *av:* andare a ~ (*anche fig*) to grope one's way.

'tenue *ag* (*sottile*) fine; (*colore*) soft; (*fig*) slender, slight.

te'nuta *sf* (*capacità*) capacity; (*divisa*) uniform; (*abito*) dress; (*AGR*) estate; a ~ d'aria airtight; ~ di strada roadholding power.

teolo'gia [teolo'dʒia] *sf* theology; **te'ologo, gi** *sm* theologian.

teo'rema, i *sm* theorem.

teo'ria *sf* theory; **te'orico, a, ci, che** *ag* theoretic(al).

'tepido, a *ag* = **tiepido**.

te'pore *sm* warmth.

'teppa *sf* mob, hooligans *pl*; **tep'pismo** *sm* hooliganism; **tep'pista, i** *sm* hooligan.

tera'pia *sf* therapy.

tergicris'tallo [terdʒikris'tallo] *sm* windscreen (*Brit*) *o* windshield (*US*) wiper.

tergiver'sare [terdʒiver'sare] *vi* to shilly-shally.

'tergo *sm:* a ~ behind; vedi a ~ please turn over.

ter'male *ag* thermal; stazione *f* ~ spa.

'terme *sfpl* thermal baths.

'termico, a, ci, che *ag* thermic; (*unità*) thermal.

termi'nale *ag, sm* terminal.

termi'nare *vt* to end; (*lavoro*) to finish // *vi* to end.

'termine *sm* term; (*fine, estremità*) end; (*di territorio*) boundary, limit; contratto a ~ (*COMM*) forward contract; a breve/lungo ~ short-/long-term; parlare senza mezzi ~i to talk frankly, not to mince one's words.

ter'mometro *sm* thermometer.

termonucle'are *ag* thermonuclear.

'termos *sm inv* = **thermos**.

termosi'fone *sm* radiator; (*riscaldamento a*) ~ central heating.

ter'mostato *sm* thermostat.

'terra *sf* (*gen, ELETTR*) earth; (*sostanza*) soil, earth; (*opposto al mare*) land *q*; (*regione, paese*) land; (*argilla*) clay; ~e *sfpl* (*possedimenti*) lands, land *sg*; a *o* per ~ (*stato*) on the ground (*o* floor); (*moto*) to the ground, down; mettere a ~ (*ELETTR*) to earth.

terra'cotta *sf* terracotta; vasellame *m* di ~ earthenware.

terra'ferma *sf* dry land, terra firma; (*continente*) mainland.

terrapi'eno *sm* embankment, bank.

ter'razza [ter'rattsa] *sf*, **ter'razzo** [ter'rattso] *sm* terrace.

terre'moto *sm* earthquake.

ter'reno, a *ag* (*vita, beni*) earthly // *sm* (*suolo, fig*) ground; (*COMM*) land *q*, plot (of land); site; (*SPORT, MIL*) field.

ter'restre *ag* (*superficie*) of the earth, earth's; (*di terra: battaglia, animale*) land *cpd*; (*REL*) earthly, worldly.

ter'ribile *ag* terrible, dreadful.

terrifi'cante *ag* terrifying.

territori'ale *ag* territorial.

terri'torio *sm* territory.

ter'rore *sm* terror; **terro'rismo** *sm* terrorism; **terro'rista, i, e** *sm/f* terrorist.

'terso, a *ag* clear.

'terzo, a ['tertso] *ag* third // *sm* (*frazione*) third; (*DIR*) third party; ~i *smpl* (*altri*) others, other people; la ~a pagina (*STAMPA*) the Arts page.

'tesa *sf* brim.

'teschio ['teskjo] *sm* skull.

'tesi *sf* thesis.

'teso, a *pp di* **tendere** // *ag* (*tirato*) taut, tight; (*fig*) tense.

tesore'ria *sf* treasury.

tesori'ere *sm* treasurer.

te'soro *sm* treasure; il Ministero del T~ the Treasury.

'tessera *sf* (*documento*) card.

'tessere *vt* to weave; **'tessile** *ag, sm* textile; **tessi'tore, 'trice** *sm/f* weaver; **tessi'tura** *sf* weaving.

tes'suto *sm* fabric, material; (*BIOL*) tissue; (*fig*) web.

'testa *sf* head; (*di cose: estremità, parte anteriore*) head, front; (*di vettura etc*) front; tenere ~ a qn (*nemico etc*) to stand up to sb; fare di ~ propria to go one's own way; in ~ (*SPORT*) in the lead; ~ o croce? heads or tails?; avere la ~ dura to be stubborn; ~ di serie (*TENNIS*) seed, seeded player.

testa'mento *sm* (*atto*) will; l'Antico/il Nuovo T~ (*REL*) the Old/New Testament.

tes'tardo, a *ag* stubborn, pig-headed.

tes'tata *sf* (*parte anteriore*) head; (*intestazione*) heading.

'teste *sm/f* witness.

tes'ticolo *sm* testicle.

testi'mone *sm/f* (*DIR*) witness.

testimoni'anza [testimo'njantsa] *sf* testimony.

testimoni'are *vt* to testify; (*fig*) to bear witness to, testify to // *vi* to give evidence, testify.

'testo *sm* text; fare ~ (*opera, autore*) to be authoritative; questo libro non fa ~ this book is not essential reading; **testu'ale** *ag* textual; literal, word for word.

tes'tuggine [tes'tuddʒine] *sf* tortoise; (*di mare*) turtle.

'tetano *sm* (*MED*) tetanus.

'tetro, a *ag* gloomy.

'tetto *sm* roof; **tet'toia** *sf* roofing; canopy.

'Tevere *sm:* il ~ the Tiber.

Tg. *abbr* = **telegiornale**.

'thermos ® ['termos] *sm inv* vacuum *o* Thermos ® flask.

ti *pronome* (*dav lo, la, li, le, ne diventa* **te**) (*oggetto*) you; (*complemento di*

termine) (to) you; (*riflessivo*) yourself.
ti'ara *sf* (*REL*) tiara.
'tibia *sf* tibia, shinbone.
tic *sm inv* tic, (nervous) twitch; (*fig*)
mannerism.
ticchet'tio [tikket'tio] *sm* (*di macchina
da scrivere*) clatter; (*di orologio*) tick-
ing; (*della pioggia*) patter.
'ticchio ['tikkjo] *sm* (*ghiribizzo*) whim;
(*tic*) tic, (nervous) twitch.
ti'epido, a *ag* lukewarm, tepid.
ti'fare *vi*: ~ **per** to be a fan of;
(*parteggiare*) to side with.
'tifo *sm* (*MED*) typhus; (*fig*): **fare il ~
per** to be a fan of.
tifoi'dea *sf* typhoid.
ti'fone *sm* typhoon.
ti'foso, a *sm/f* (*SPORT etc*) fan.
'tiglio ['tiʎʎo] *sm* lime (tree), linden
(tree).
'tigre *sf* tiger.
tim'ballo *sm* (*strumento*) kettledrum;
(*CUC*) timbale.
'timbro *sm* stamp; (*MUS*) timbre, tone.
'timido, a *ag* shy; timid.
'timo *sm* thyme.
ti'mone *sm* (*NAUT*) rudder; **timoni'ere**
sm helmsman.
ti'more *sm* (*paura*) fear; (*rispetto*) awe;
timo'roso, a *ag* timid, timorous.
'timpano *sm* (*ANAT*) eardrum; (*MUS*):
~**i** *smpl* kettledrums, timpani.
'tingere ['tindʒere] *vt* to dye.
'tino *sm* vat.
ti'nozza [ti'nɔttsa] *sf* tub.
'tinta *sf* (*materia colorante*) dye;
(*colore*) colour, shade; **tinta'rella** *sf*
(*fam*) (sun)tan.
tintin'nare *vi* to tinkle.
'tinto, a *pp di* **tingere**.
tinto'ria *sf* (*officina*) dyeworks *sg*;
(*lavasecco*) dry cleaner's (shop).
tin'tura *sf* (*operazione*) dyeing; (*colorante*) dye; ~ **di iodio** tincture of iodine.
'tipico, a, ci, che *ag* typical.
'tipo *sm* type; (*genere*) kind, type;
(*fam*) chap, fellow.
tipogra'fia *sf* typography; (*procedimento*) letterpress (printing); (*officina*)
printing house; **tipo'grafico, a, ci, che**
ag typographic(al); letterpress *cpd*; **ti-
'pografo** *sm* typographer.
ti'ranno, a *ag* tyrannical // *sm* tyrant.
ti'rante *sm* (*per tenda*) guy.
ti'rare *vt* (*gen*) to pull; (*estrarre*): ~ **qc
da** to take o pull sth out of; to get sth out
of; to extract sth from; (*chiudere: tenda
etc*) to draw, pull; (*tracciare, disegnare*)
to draw, trace; (*lanciare: sasso, palla*)
to throw; (*stampare*) to print; (*pistola,
freccia*) to fire // *vi* (*pipa, camino*) to
draw; (*vento*) to blow; (*abito*) to be
tight; (*fare fuoco*) to fire; (*fare del tiro,
CALCIO*) to shoot; ~ **avanti** *vi* to struggle
on // *vt* to keep going; ~ **fuori** *vt*

(*estrarre*) to take out, pull out; ~ **giù** *vt*
(*abbassare*) to bring down; ~ **su** *vt* to
pull up; (*capelli*) to put up; (*fig:
bambino*) to bring up; ~**rsi indietro** to
move back.
tira'tore *sm* gunman; **un buon** ~ a good
shot; ~ **scelto** marksman.
tira'tura *sf* (*azione*) printing; (*di libro*)
(print) run; (*di giornale*) circulation.
'tirchio, a ['tirkjo] *ag* mean, stingy.
'tiro *sm* shooting *q*, firing *q*; (*colpo,
sparo*) shot; (*di palla: lancio*) throwing
q; throw; (*fig*) trick; **cavallo da** ~
draught (*Brit*) o draft (*US*) horse; ~ **a
segno** target shooting; (*luogo*) shooting
range.
tiro'cinio [tiro'tʃinjo] *sm* apprenticeship;
(*professionale*) training.
ti'roide *sf* thyroid (gland).
Tir'reno *sm*: **il (mar)** ~ the Tyrrhenian
Sea.
ti'sana *sf* herb tea.
tito'lare *ag* appointed; (*sovrano*) titular
// *sm/f* incumbent; (*proprietario*) owner;
(*CALCIO*) regular player.
'titolo *sm* title; (*di giornale*) headline;
(*diploma*) qualification; (*COMM*)
security; (: *azione*) share; **a che** ~? for
what reason?; **a** ~ **di amicizia** out of
friendship; **a** ~ **di premio** as a prize; ~
di credito share; ~ **di proprietà** title
deed.
titu'bante *ag* hesitant, irresolute.
'tizio, a ['tittsjo] *sm/f* fellow, chap.
tiz'zone [tit'tsone] *sm* brand.
toc'cante *ag* touching.
toc'care *vt* to touch; (*tastare*) to feel;
(*fig: riguardare*) to concern; (:
commuovere) to touch, move; (:
pungere) to hurt, wound; (: *far cenno a:
argomento*) to touch on, mention // *vi*: ~
a (*accadere*) to happen to; (*spettare*) to
be up to; ~ (**il fondo**) (*in acqua*) to
touch the bottom; **tocca a te difenderci**
it's up to you to defend us; **a chi tocca?**
whose turn is it?; **mi toccò pagare** I had
to pay.
'tocco, chi *sm* touch; (*ARTE*) stroke,
touch.
'toga, ghe *sf* toga; (*di magistrato,
professore*) gown.
'togliere ['tɔʎʎere] *vt* (*rimuovere*) to
take away (o off), remove; (*riprendere,
non concedere più*) to take away, remove; (*MAT*) to take away, subtract;
(*liberare*) to free; ~ **qc a qn** to take sth
(away) from sb; **ciò non toglie che**
nevertheless, be that as it may; ~**rsi il
cappello** to take off one's hat.
toi'lette [twa'lɛt] *sf inv*, **to'letta** *sf* toilet; (*mobile*) dressing table.
tolle'ranza [tolle'rantsa] *sf* tolerance.
tolle'rare *vt* to tolerate.
'tolto, a *pp di* **togliere**.
to'maia *sf* (*di scarpa*) upper.

'tomba *sf* tomb.

tom'bino *sm* manhole cover.

'tombola *sf* (*gioco*) tombola; (*ruzzolone*) tumble.

'tomo *sm* volume.

'tonaca, che *sf* (*REL*) habit.

to'nare *vi* = **tuonare**.

'tondo, a *ag* round.

'tonfo *sm* splash; (*rumore sordo*) thud; (*caduta*): **fare un** ~ to take a tumble.

'tonico, a, ci, che *ag, sm* tonic.

tonifi'care *vt* (*muscoli, pelle*) to tone up; (*irrobustire*) to invigorate, brace.

tonnel'laggio |tonnel'laddʒo| *sm* (*NAUT*) tonnage.

tonnel'lata *sf* ton.

'tonno *sm* tuna (fish).

'tono *sm* (*gen*) tone; (*MUS: di pezzo*) key; (*di colore*) shade, tone.

ton'silla *sf* tonsil; **tonsil'lite** *sf* tonsillitis.

'tonto, a *ag* dull, stupid.

to'pazio |to'pattsjo| *sm* topaz.

'topo *sm* mouse.

topogra'fia *sf* topography.

'toppa *sf* (*serratura*) keyhole; (*pezza*) patch.

to'race |to'ratʃe| *sm* chest.

'torba *sf* peat.

'torbido, a *ag* (*liquido*) cloudy; (: *fiume*) muddy; (*fig*) dark; troubled // *sm*: **pescare nel** ~ (*fig*) to fish in troubled water.

'torcere |'tɔrtʃere| *vt* to twist; (*biancheria*) to wring (out); ~**rsi** *vr* to twist, writhe.

torchi'are |tor'kjare| *vt* to press; **'torchio** *sm* press; **torchio tipografico** printing press.

'torcia, ce |'tɔrtʃa| *sf* torch; ~ **elettrica** torch (*Brit*), flashlight (*US*).

torci'collo |tortʃi'kɔllo| *sm* stiff neck.

'tordo *sm* thrush.

To'rino *sf* Turin.

tor'menta *sf* snowstorm.

tormen'tare *vt* to torment; ~**rsi** *vr* to fret, worry o.s.; **tor'mento** *sm* torment.

torna'conto *sm* advantage, benefit.

tor'nado *sm* tornado.

tor'nante *sm* hairpin bend.

tor'nare *vi* to return, go (*o* come) back; (*ridiventare: anche fig*) to become (again); (*riuscire giusto, esatto: conto*) to work out; (*risultare*) to turn out (to be), prove (to be); ~ **utile** to prove *o* turn out (to be) useful; ~ **a casa** to go (*o* come) home.

torna'sole *sm inv* litmus.

tor'neo *sm* tournament.

'tornio *sm* lathe.

'toro *sm* bull; (*dello zodiaco*): **T~** Taurus.

tor'pedine *sf* torpedo; **torpedini'era** *sf* torpedo boat.

'torre *sf* tower; (*SCACCHI*) rook, castle;

~ **di controllo** (*AER*) control tower.

torrefazi'one |torrefat'tsjone| *sf* roasting.

tor'rente *sm* torrent.

tor'retta *sf* turret.

torri'one *sm* keep.

tor'rone *sm* nougat.

torsi'one *sf* twisting; torsion.

'torso *sm* torso, trunk; (*ARTE*) torso.

'torsolo *sm* (*di cavolo etc*) stump; (*di frutta*) core.

'torta *sf* cake.

'torto, a *pp di* **torcere** // *ag* (*ritorto*) twisted; (*storto*) twisted, crooked // *sm* (*ingiustizia*) wrong; (*colpa*) fault; **a** ~ wrongly; **aver** ~ to be wrong.

'tortora *sf* turtle dove.

tortu'oso, a *ag* (*strada*) twisting; (*fig*) tortuous.

tor'tura *sf* torture; **tortu'rare** *vt* to torture.

'torvo, a *ag* menacing, grim.

tosa'erba *sm o f inv* (lawn)mower.

to'sare *vt* (*pecora*) to shear; (*siepe*) to clip, trim.

Tos'cana *sf*: **la** ~ Tuscany; **tos'cano, a** *ag, sm/f* Tuscan // *sm* (*sigaro*) strong Italian cigar.

'tosse *sf* cough.

'tossico, a, ci, che *ag* toxic.

tossicodipen'dente, tossi'comane *sm/f* drug addict.

tos'sire *vi* to cough.

tosta'pane *sm inv* toaster.

tos'tare *vt* to toast; (*caffè*) to roast.

'tosto, a *ag*: **faccia** ~**a** cheek.

to'tale *ag, sm* total; **totalità** *sf*: **la totalità di** all of, the total amount (*o* number) of; **the whole** + *sg*; **totaliz'zare** *vt* to total; (*SPORT: punti*) to score.

toto'calcio |toto'kaltʃo| *sm* gambling pool betting on football results, ≈ (football) pools *pl* (*Brit*).

to'vaglia |to'vaʎʎa| *sf* tablecloth; **tova-gli'olo** *sm* napkin.

'tozzo, a |'tɔttso| *ag* squat // *sm*: ~ **di pane** crust of bread.

tra *prep* (*di due persone, cose*) between; (*di più persone, cose*) among(st); (*tempo: entro*) within, in; ~ **5 giorni** in 5 days' time; **sia detto** ~ **noi** ... between you and me ...; **litigano** ~ (*di*) **loro** they're fighting amongst themselves; ~ **breve** soon; ~ **sé e sé** (*parlare etc*) to oneself.

trabal'lare *vi* to stagger, totter.

traboc'care *vi* to overflow.

traboc'chetto |trabok'ketto| *sm* (*fig*) trap.

tracan'nare *vt* to gulp down.

'traccia, ce |'trattʃa| *sf* (*segno, striscia*) trail, track; (*orma*) tracks *pl*; (*residuo, testimonianza*) trace, sign; (*abbozzo*) outline.

tracci'are |trat'tʃare| *vt* to trace, mark

(out); (*disegnare*) to draw; (*fig: abbozzare*) to outline; **tracci'ato** *sm* (*grafico*) layout, plan.

tra'chea |tra'kεa| *sf* windpipe, trachea.

tra'colla *sf* shoulder strap; **borsa a ~** shoulder bag.

tra'collo *sm* (*fig*) collapse, crash.

traco'tante *ag* overbearing, arrogant.

tradi'mento *sm* betrayal; (*DIR, MIL*) treason.

tra'dire *vt* to betray; (*coniuge*) to be unfaithful to; (*doveri: mancare*) to fail in; (*rivelare*) to give away, reveal; **tradi'tore, 'trice** *sm/f* traitor.

tradizio'nale |tradittsjo'nalε| *ag* traditional.

tradizi'one |tradit'tsjone| *sf* tradition.

tra'dotto, a *pp di* **tradurre**.

tra'durre *vt* to translate; (*spiegare*) to render, convey; **tradut'tore, 'trice** *sm/f* translator; **traduzi'one** *sf* translation.

tra'ente *sm/f* (*ECON*) drawer.

trafe'lato, a *ag* out of breath.

traffi'cante *sm/f* dealer; (*peg*) trafficker.

traffi'care *vi* (*commerciare*): **~ (in)** to trade (in), deal (in); (*affaccendarsi*) to busy o.s. // *vt* (*peg*) to traffic in.

'traffico, ci *sm* traffic; (*commercio*) trade, traffic.

tra'figgere |tra'fiddʒεrε| *vt* to run through, stab; (*fig*) to pierce; **tra'fitto, a** *pp di* **trafiggere**.

trafo'rare *vt* to bore, drill; **tra'foro** *sm* (*azione*) boring, drilling; (*galleria*) tunnel.

tra'gedia |tra'dʒεdja| *sf* tragedy.

tra'ghetto |tra'gεtto| *sm* crossing; (*barca*) ferry(boat).

'tragico, a, ci, che |'tradʒiko| *ag* tragic.

tra'gitto |tra'dʒitto| *sm* (*passaggio*) crossing; (*viaggio*) journey.

tragu'ardo *sm* (*SPORT*) finishing line; (*fig*) goal, aim.

traiet'toria *sf* trajectory.

trai'nare *vt* to drag, haul; (*rimorchiare*) to tow; **'traino** *sm* (*carro*) wagon; (*slitta*) sledge; (*carico*) load.

tralasci'are |tralaʃ'ʃarε| *vt* (*studi*) to neglect; (*dettagli*) to leave out, omit.

'tralcio |'traltʃo| *sm* (*BOT*) shoot.

tra'liccio |tra'littʃo| *sm* (*tela*) ticking; (*struttura*) trellis; (*ELETTR*) pylon.

tram *sm inv* tram.

'trama *sf* (*filo*) weft, woof; (*fig: argomento, maneggio*) plot.

traman'dare *vt* to pass on, hand down.

tra'mare *vt* (*fig*) to scheme, plot.

tram'busto *sm* turmoil.

trames'tio *sm* bustle.

tramez'zino |tramed'dzino| *sm* sandwich.

tra'mezzo |tra'meddzo| *sm* (*EDIL*) partition.

'tramite *prep* through.

tramon'tare *vi* to set, go down; **tra'monto** *sm* setting; (*del sole*) sunset.

tramor'tire *vi* to faint // *vt* to stun.

trampo'lino *sm* (*per tuffi*) springboard, diving board; (*per lo sci*) ski-jump.

'trampolo *sm* stilt.

tramu'tare *vt*: **~ in** to change into, turn into.

tra'nello *sm* trap.

trangugi'are |trangu'dʒarε| *vt* to gulp down.

'tranne *prep* except (for), but (for); **~ che** *cong* unless.

tranquil'lante *sm* (*MED*) tranquillizer.

tranquillità *sf* calm, stillness; quietness; peace of mind.

tranquilliz'zare |trankwillid'dzarε| *vt* to reassure.

tran'quillo, a *ag* calm, quiet; (*bambino, scolaro*) quiet; (*sereno*) with one's mind at rest; **sta' ~** don't worry.

transat'lantico, a, ci, che *ag* transatlantic // *sm* transatlantic liner.

tran'satto, a *pp di* **transigere**.

transazi'one |transat'tsjone| *sf* compromise; (*DIR*) settlement; (*COMM*) transaction, deal.

tran'senna *sf* barrier.

tran'sigere |tran'sidʒεrε| *vi* (*DIR*) to reach a settlement; (*venire a patti*) to compromise, come to an agreement.

tran'sistor *sm*, **transis'tore** *sm* transistor.

transi'tabile *ag* passable.

transi'tare *vi* to pass.

transi'tivo, a *ag* transitive.

'transito *sm* transit; **di ~** (*merci*) in transit; (*stazione*) transit *cpd*; "**divieto di ~**" "no entry".

transi'torio, a *ag* transitory, transient; (*provvisorio*) provisional.

tran'via *sf* tramway (*Brit*), streetcar line (*US*).

'trapano *sm* (*utensile*) drill; (*: MED*) trepan.

trapas'sare *vt* to pierce.

tra'passo *sm* passage.

trape'lare *vi* to leak, drip; (*fig*) to leak out.

tra'pezio |tra'pεttsjo| *sm* (*MAT*) trapezium; (*attrezzo ginnico*) trapeze.

trapian'tare *vt* to transplant; **trapi'anto** *sm* transplanting; (*MED*) transplant.

'trappola *sf* trap.

tra'punta *sf* quilt.

'trarre *vt* to draw, pull; (*portare*) to take; (*prendere, tirare fuori*) to take (out), draw; (*derivare*) to obtain; **~ origine da qc** to have its origins *o* originate in sth.

trasa'lire *vi* to start, jump.

trasan'dato, a *ag* shabby.

trasbor'dare *vt* to transfer; (*NAUT*) to tran(s)ship // *vi* (*NAUT*) to change ship;

(AER) to change plane; (FERR) to change (trains).

trasci'nare |traʃʃi'nare| vt to drag; ~rsi vr to drag o.s. along; (fig) to drag on.

tras'correre vt (tempo) to spend, pass // vi to pass; **tras'corso, a** pp di trascorrere.

tras'critto, a pp di trascrivere.

tras'crivere vt to transcribe.

trascu'rare vt to neglect; (non considerare) to disregard; **trascura'tezza** sf carelessness, negligence; **trascu'rato, a** ag (casa) neglected; (persona) careless, negligent.

traseco'lato, a ag astounded, amazed.

trasferi'mento sm transfer; (trasloco) removal, move.

trasfe'rire vt to transfer; ~rsi vr to move; **tras'ferta** sf transfer; (indennità) travelling expenses pl; (SPORT) away game.

trasfigu'rare vt to transfigure.

trasfor'mare vt to transform, change.

trasfusi'one sf (MED) transfusion.

trasgre'dire vt to disobey, contravene.

tras'lato, a ag metaphorical, figurative.

traslo'care vt to move, transfer; ~rsi vr to move; **tras'loco, chi** sm removal.

tras'messo, a pp di trasmettere.

tras'mettere vt (passare): ~ qc a qn to pass sth on to sb; (mandare) to send; (TECN, TEL, MED) to transmit; (TV, RADIO) to broadcast; **trasmetti'tore** sm transmitter; **trasmissi'one** sf (gen, FISICA, TECN) transmission; (passaggio) transmission, passing on; (TV, RADIO) broadcast; **trasmit'tente** sf transmitting o broadcasting station.

traso'gnato, a |trasoɲ'ɲato| ag dreamy.

traspa'rente ag transparent.

traspa'rire vi to show (through).

traspi'rare vi to perspire; (fig) to come to light, leak out; **traspirazi'one** sf perspiration.

traspor'tare vt to carry, move; (merce) to transport, convey; **lasciarsi** ~ (da qc) (fig) to let o.s. be carried away (by sth); **tras'porto** sm transport.

trastul'lare vt to amuse; ~rsi vr to amuse o.s.

trasu'dare vi (filtrare) to ooze; (sudare) to sweat // vt to ooze with.

trasver'sale ag transverse, cross(-); running at right angles.

trasvo'lare vt to fly over.

'tratta sf (ECON) draft; (di persone): la ~ delle bianche the white slave trade.

tratta'mento sm treatment; (servizio) service.

trat'tare vt (gen) to treat; (commerciare) to deal in; (svolgere: argomento) to discuss, deal with; (negoziare) to negotiate // vi: ~ di to deal with; ~ con (persona) to deal with; si tratta di ... it's about ...; **tratta'tive**

sfpl negotiations; **trat'tato** sm (testo) treatise; (accordo) treaty; **trattazi'one** sf treatment.

tratteggi'are |tratted'dʒare| vt (disegnare: a tratti) to sketch, outline; (: col tratteggio) to hatch.

tratte'nere vt (far rimanere: persona) to detain; (intrattenere: ospiti) to entertain; (tenere, frenare, reprimere) to hold back, keep back; (astenersi dal consegnare) to hold, keep; (detrarre: somma) to deduct; ~rsi vr (astenersi) to restrain o.s., stop o.s.; (soffermarsi) to stay, remain.

tratteni'mento sm entertainment; (festa) party.

tratte'nuta sf deduction.

trat'tino sm dash; (in parole composte) hyphen.

'tratto, a pp di trarre // sm (di penna, matita) stroke; (parte) part, piece; (di strada) stretch; (di mare, cielo) expanse; (di tempo) period (of time); ~i smpl (caratteristiche) features; (modo di fare) ways, manners; a un ~, d'un ~ suddenly.

trat'tore sm tractor.

tratto'ria sf restaurant.

'trauma, i sm trauma; **trau'matico, a, ci, che** ag traumatic.

tra'vaglio |tra'vaʎʎo| sm (angoscia) pain, suffering; (MED) pains pl; ~ di parto labour pains.

trava'sare vt to decant.

'trave sf beam.

tra'versa sf (trave) crosspiece; (via) sidestreet; (FERR) sleeper (Brit), (railroad) tie (US); (CALCIO) crossbar.

traver'sare vt to cross; **traver'sata** sf crossing; (AER) flight, trip.

traver'sie sfpl mishaps, misfortunes.

traver'sina sf (FERR) sleeper (Brit), (railroad) tie (US).

tra'verso, a ag oblique; **di** ~ ag askew // av sideways; **andare di** ~ (cibo) to go down the wrong way; **guardare di** ~ to look askance at.

travesti'mento sm disguise.

traves'tire vt to disguise; ~rsi vr to disguise o.s.

travi'are vt (fig) to lead astray.

travi'sare vt (fig) to distort, misrepresent.

tra'volgere |tra'voldʒere| vt to sweep away, carry away; (fig) to overwhelm; **tra'volto, a** pp di travolgere.

tre num three.

trebbi'are vt to thresh.

'treccia, ce |'trettʃa| sf plait, braid.

tre'cento |tre'tʃento| num three hundred // sm: il T~ the fourteenth century.

'tredici |'treditʃi| num thirteen.

'tregua sf truce; (fig) respite.

tre'mare vi: ~ di (freddo etc) to shiver o tremble with; (paura, rabbia) to shake

o tremble with.
tre'mendo, a *ag* terrible, awful.
tre'mila *num* three thousand.
'tremito *sm* trembling *q*; shaking *q*; shivering *q*.
tremo'lare *vi* to tremble; (*luce*) to flicker; (*foglie*) to quiver.
tre'more *sm* tremor.
'treno *sm* train; ~ **di gomme** set of tyres (*Brit*) *o* tires (*US*); ~ **merci** goods (*Brit*) *o* freight train; ~ **viaggiatori** passenger train.
'trenta *num* thirty, **tren'tesimo, a** *num* thirtieth; **tren'tina** *sf*: **una trentina** (**di**) thirty or so, about thirty.
'trepido, a *ag* anxious.
treppi'ede *sm* tripod; (*CUC*) trivet.
'tresca, coho *sf* (*fig*) intrigue; (*: relazione amorosa*) affair.
'trespolo *sm* trestle.
tri'angolo *sm* triangle.
tribù *sf inv* tribe.
tri'buna *sf* (*podio*) platform; (*in aule etc*) gallery; (*di stadio*) stand.
tribu'nale *sm* court.
tribu'tare *vt* to bestow.
tri'buto *sm* tax; (*fig*) tribute.
tri'checo, chi [tri'kɛko] *sm* (*ZOOL*) walrus.
tri'ciclo [tri'tʃiklo] *sm* tricycle.
trico'lore *ag* three-coloured // *sm* tricolour; (*bandiera italiana*) Italian flag.
tri'dente *sm* trident.
tri'foglio [tri'fɔʎʎo] *sm* clover.
'triglia ['triʎʎa] *sf* red mullet.
tril'lare *vi* (*MUS*) to trill.
tri'mestre *sm* period of three months; (*INS*) term, quarter (*US*); (*COMM*) quarter.
'trina *sf* lace.
trin'cea [trin'tʃea] *sf* trench; **trince'rare** *vt* to entrench.
trinci'are [trin'tʃare] *vt* to cut up.
trion'fare *vi* to triumph, win; ~ **su** to triumph over, overcome; **tri'onfo** *sm* triumph.
tripli'care *vt* to triple.
'triplice ['triplitʃe] *ag* triple; **in** ~ **copia** in triplicate.
'triplo, a *ag* triple; treble // *sm*: **il** ~ (**di**) three times as much (as); **la spesa è** ~**a** it costs three times as much.
'tripode *sm* tripod.
'trippa *sf* (*CUC*) tripe.
'triste *ag* sad; (*luogo*) dreary, gloomy; **tris'tezza** *sf* sadness; gloominess.
trita'carne *sm inv* mincer, grinder (*US*).
tri'tare *vt* to mince, grind (*US*).
'trito, a *ag* (*tritato*) minced, ground (*US*); ~ **e ritrito** (*fig*) trite, hackneyed.
'trittico, ci *sm* (*ARTE*) triptych.
trivel'lare *vt* to drill.
trivi'ale *ag* vulgar, low.
tro'feo *sm* trophy.

'trogolo *sm* (*per maiali*) trough.
'tromba *sf* (*MUS*) trumpet; (*AUT*) horn; ~ **d'aria** whirlwind; ~ **delle scale** stairwell.
trom'bone *sm* trombone.
trom'bosi *sf* thrombosis.
tron'care *vt* to cut off; (*spezzare*) to break off.
'tronco, a, chi, che *ag* cut off; broken off; (*LING*) truncated; (*fig*) cut short // *sm* (*BOT*, *ANAT*) trunk; (*fig: tratto*) section; (*: pezzo: di lancia*) stump; **licenziare qn in** ~ to fire sb on the spot.
troneggi'are [troned'dʒare] *vi*: ~ (**su**) to tower (over).
'tronfio, a *ag* conceited.
'trono *sm* throne.
tropi'cale *ag* tropical.
'tropico, ci *sm* tropic; ~**ci** *smpl* tropics.
'troppo, a ♦ *det* (*in eccesso: quantità*) too much; (*: numero*) too many; **c'era** ~**a gente** there were too many people; **fa** ~ **caldo** it's too hot
♦ *pronome* (*in eccesso: quantità*) too much; (*: numero*) too many; **ne hai messo** ~ you've put in too much; **meglio** ~**i che pochi** better too many than too few
♦ *av* (*eccessivamente: con ag, av*) too; (*: con vb*) too much; ~ **amaro/tardi** too bitter/late; **lavora** ~ he works too much; **di** ~ too much; too many; **qualche tazza di** ~ **a few cups too many; 3000 lire di** ~ **3000 lire too much; essere di** ~ **to be in the way.**
'trota *sf* trout.
trot'tare *vi* to trot; **trotterel'lare** *vi* to trot along; (*bambino*) to toddle; **'trotto** *sm* trot.
'trottola *sf* spinning top.
tro'vare *vt* to find; (*giudicare*): **trovo che** I find *o* think that; ~**rsi** *vr* (*reciproco: incontrarsi*) to meet; (*essere, stare*) to be; (*arrivare, capitare*) to find o.s.; **andare a** ~ **qn** to go and see sb; ~ **qn colpevole** to find sb guilty; ~**rsi bene** (*in un luogo, con qn*) to get on well; **tro'vata** *sf* good idea.
truc'care *vt* (*falsare*) to fake; (*attore etc*) to make up; (*travestire*) to disguise; (*SPORT*) to fix; (*AUT*) to soup up; ~**rsi** *vr* to make up (one's face); **trucca'tore, 'trice** *sm/f* (*CINEMA, TEATRO*) make-up artist.
'trucco, chi *sm* trick; (*cosmesi*) make-up.
'truce ['trutʃe] *ag* fierce.
truci'dare [trutʃi'dare] *vt* to slaughter.
'truciolo ['trutʃolo] *sm* shaving.
'truffa *sf* fraud, swindle; **truf'fare** *vt* to swindle, cheat.
'truppa *sf* troop.
tu *pronome* you; ~ **stesso(a)** you yourself; **dare del** ~ **a qn** to address sb as "tu".

'tua vedi **tuo.**

'tuba sf (MUS) tuba; (cappello) top hat.

tu'bare vi to coo.

tuba'tura sf, **tubazi'one** |tubat'tsjone| sf piping q, pipes pl.

tu'betto sm tube.

'tubo sm tube; pipe; ~ **digerente** (ANAT) alimentary canal, digestive tract; ~ **di scappamento** (AUT) exhaust pipe.

'tue vedi **tuo.**

tuf'fare vt to plunge, dip; **~rsi** vr to plunge, dive; **'tuffo** sm dive; (breve bagno) dip.

tu'gurio sm hovel.

tuli'pano sm tulip.

tume'farsi vr (MED) to swell.

'tumido, a ag swollen.

tu'more sm (MED) tumour.

tu'multo sm uproar, commotion; (sommossa) riot; (fig) turmoil; **tumul-tu'oso, a** ag rowdy, unruly; (fig) turbulent, stormy.

'tunica, che sf tunic.

Tuni'sia sf: la ~ Tunisia.

'tuo, 'tua, tu'oi, 'tue det: il ~, la tua etc your // pronome: il ~, la tua etc yours.

tuo'nare vi to thunder; **tuona** it is thundering, there's some thunder.

tu'ono sm thunder.

tu'orlo sm yolk.

tu'racciolo |tu'rattʃolo| sm cap, top; (di sughero) cork.

tu'rare vt to stop, plug; (con sughero) to cork; **~rsi** il naso to hold one's nose.

turba'mento sm disturbance; (di animo) anxiety, agitation.

tur'bante sm turban.

tur'bare vt to disturb, trouble.

turbi'nare vi to whirl.

'turbine sm whirlwind; ~ **di neve** swirl of snow; ~ **di polvere/sabbia** dust/sandstorm.

turbo'lento, a ag turbulent; (ragazzo) boisterous, unruly.

turbo'lenza |turbo'lɛntsa| sf turbulence.

tur'chese |tur'kese| sf turquoise.

Tur'chia |tur'kia| sf: la ~ Turkey.

tur'chino, a |tur'kino| ag deep blue.

'turco, a, chi, che ag Turkish // sm/f Turk/Turkish woman // sm (LING) Turkish; **parlare** ~ (fig) to talk double-dutch.

tu'rismo sm tourism; tourist industry; **tu'rista, i, e** sm/f tourist; **tu'ristico, a, ci, che** ag tourist cpd.

'turno sm turn; (di lavoro) shift; **di** ~ (soldato, medico, custode) on duty; **a** ~ (rispondere) in turn; (lavorare) in shifts; **fare a** ~ **a fare qc** to take turns to do sth; **è il suo** ~ it's your (o his etc) turn.

'turpe ag filthy, vile; **turpi'loquio** sm obscene language.

'tuta sf overalls pl; (SPORT) tracksuit.

tu'tela sf (DIR: di minore) guardianship; (: protezione) protection; (difesa) defence; **tute'lare** vt to protect, defend.

tu'tore, 'trice sm/f (DIR) guardian.

tutta'via cong nevertheless, yet.

'tutto, a ◆ det **1** (intero) all; ~ **il latte** all the milk; **~a la notte** all night, the whole night; ~ **il libro** the whole book; **~a una bottiglia** a whole bottle

2 (pl, collettivo) all; every; **~i i libri** all the books; **~e le notti** every night; **~i i venerdì** every Friday; **~i gli uomini** all the men; (collettivo) all men; **~i e due** both o each of us (o them o you); **~i e cinque** all five of us (o them o you)

3 (completamente): **era ~a sporca** she was all dirty; **tremava** ~ he was trembling all over; **è ~a sua madre** she's just o exactly like her mother

4: **a tutt'oggi** so far, up till now; **a ~a velocità** at full o top speed

◆ pronome **1** (ogni cosa) everything, all; (qualsiasi cosa) anything; **ha mangiato** ~ he's eaten everything; ~ **considerato** all things considered; **in** ~: **10.000 lire in** ~ 10,000 lire in all; **in** ~ **eravamo 50** there were 50 of us in all

2: **~i(e)** (ognuno) all, everybody; **vengono ~i** they are all coming, everybody's coming; **~i quanti** all and sundry

◆ av (completamente) entirely, quite; **è** ~ **il contrario** it's quite o exactly the opposite; **tutt'al più**: **saranno stati tutt'al più una cinquantina** there were about fifty of them at (the very) most; **tutt'al più possiamo prendere un treno** if the worst comes to the worst we can take a train; **tutt'altro** on the contrary; **è tutt'altro che felice** he's anything but happy; **tutt'a un tratto** suddenly

◆ sm: **il** ~ the whole lot, all of it.

tutto'fare ag inv: **domestica** ~ general maid; **ragazzo** ~ office boy // sm/f inv handyman/woman.

tut'tora av still.

U

ubbidi'ente ag obedient; **ubbidi'enza** sf obedience.

ubbi'dire vi to obey; ~ **a** to obey; (sog: veicolo, macchina) to respond to.

ubiquità sf: **non ho il dono dell'**~ I can't be everywhere at once.

ubria'care vt: ~ **qn** to get sb drunk; (sog: alcool) to make sb drunk; (fig) to make sb's head spin o reel; **~rsi** vr to get drunk; **~rsi di** (fig) to become intoxicated with.

ubri'aco, a, chi, che ag, sm/f drunk.

uccelli'era |uttʃel'ljɛra| sf aviary.

uccel'lino |uttʃel'lino| sm baby bird, chick.

uc'cello |ut'tʃɛllo| sm bird.

uc'cidere |ut'tʃidere| vt to kill; **~rsi** vr

(*suicidarsi*) to kill o.s.; (*perdere la vita*) to be killed; **uccisi'one** *sf* killing; **uc'ciso, a** *pp di* **uccidere; ucci'sore, uccidi'trice** *sm/f* killer.

udi'enza |u'djentsa| *sf* audience; (*DIR*) hearing; **dare ~ (a)** to grant an audience (to).

u'dire *vt* to hear; **udi'tivo, a** *ag* auditory; **u'dito** *sm* (sense of) hearing; **udi'tore, 'trice** *sm/f* listener; (*INS*) un-registered student (*attending lectures*); **udi'torio** *sm* (*persone*) audience.

uffa *escl* tut!

uffici'ale |uffi'tʃale| *ag* official // *sm* (*AMM*) official, officer; (*MIL*) officer; **~ di stato civile** registrar.

uf'ficio |uf'fitʃo| *sm* (*gen*) office; (*dovere*) duty; (*mansione*) task, func-tion, job; (*agenzia*) agency, bureau; (*REL*) service; **d'~** *ag* office *cpd*; official // *av* officially; **~ di collocamento** employment office; **~ informazioni** in-formation bureau; **~ oggetti smarriti** lost property office (*Brit*), lost and found (*US*); **~ postale** post office.

uffici'oso, a |uffi'tʃoso| *ag* unofficial.

'ufo: a **~** *av* free, for nothing.

uggi'oso, a |ud'dʒoso| *ag* tiresome; (*tempo*) dull.

uguagli'anza |ugwaʎ'ʎantsa| *sf* equality.

uguagli'are |ugwaʎ'ʎare| *vt* to make equal; (*essere uguale*) to equal, be equal to; (*livellare*) to level; **~rsi a** *o* **con qn** (*paragonarsi*) to compare o.s. to sb.

ugu'ale *ag* equal; (*identico*) identical, the same; (*uniforme*) level, even // *av*: **costano ~** they cost the same; **sono bravi ~** they're equally good, **ugual'mente** *av* equally; (*lo stesso*) all the same.

'ulcera |'ultʃera| *sf* ulcer.

u'liva *etc* = **oliva** etc.

ulteri'ore *ag* further.

ulti'mare *vt* to finish, complete.

'ultimo, a *ag* (*finale*) last; (*estremo*) farthest, utmost; (*recente: notizia, mo-da*) latest; (*fig: sommo, fondamen-tale*) ultimate // *sm/f* last (one); **fino all'~** to the last, until the end; **da ~, in ~** in the end; **abitare all'~ piano** to live on the top floor; **per ~** (*entrare, arrivare*) last.

ulu'lare *vi* to howl; **ulu'lato** *sm* howling *q*; howl.

umanità *sf* humanity; **umani'tario, a** *ag* humanitarian.

u'mano, a *ag* human; (*comprensivo*) humane.

umbi'lico *sm* = **ombelico**.

umet'tare *vt* to dampen, moisten.

umidità *sf* dampness; humidity.

'umido, a *ag* damp; (*mano, occhi*) moist; (*clima*) humid // *sm* dampness, damp; **carne in ~** stew.

'umile *ag* humble.

umili'are *vt* to humiliate; **~rsi** *vr* to

humble o.s.; **umiliazi'one** *sf* humilia-tion.

umiltà *sf* humility, humbleness.

u'more *sm* (*disposizione d'animo*) mood; (*carattere*) temper; **di buon/cattivo ~** in a good/bad mood.

umo'rismo *sm* humour; **avere il senso dell'~** to have a sense of humour; **umo'rista, i, e** *sm/f* humorist; **umo'ristico, a, ci, che** *ag* humorous, funny.

un, un', una *vedi* **uno.**

u'nanime *ag* unanimous; **unanimità** *sf* unanimity; **all'unanimità** unanimously.

unci'netto |untʃi'netto| *sm* crochet hook.

un'cino |un'tʃino| *sm* hook.

'undici |'unditʃi| *num* eleven.

'ungere |'undʒere| *vt* to grease, oil; (*REL*) to anoint; (*fig*) to flatter, butter up; **~rsi** *vr* (*sporcarsi*) to get covered in grease; **~rsi con la crema** to put on cream.

unghe'rese |unge'rese| *ag, sm/f, sm* Hungarian.

Unghe'ria |unge'ria| *sf:* **l'~** Hungary.

'unghia |'ungja| *sf* (*ANAT*) nail; (*di animale*) claw; (*di rapace*) talon; (*di cavallo*) hoof; **unghi'ata** *sf* (*graffio*) scratch.

ungu'ento *sm* ointment.

'unico, a, ci, che *ag* (*solo*) only; (*ineguagliabile*) unique; (*singolo: bina-rio*) single; **figlio(a) ~(a)** only son/daughter, only child.

unifi'care *vt* to unite, unify; (*sistemi*) to standardize; **unificazi'one** *sf* uniting; unification; standardization.

uni'forme *ag* uniform; (*superficie*) even // *sf* (*divisa*) uniform.

unilate'rale *ag* one-sided; (*DIR*) uni-lateral.

uni'one *sf* union; (*fig: concordia*) unity, harmony; **l'U~ Sovietica** the Soviet Union.

u'nire *vt* to unite; (*congiungere*) to join, connect; (*: ingredienti, colori*) to combine; (*in matrimonio*) to unite, join together; **~rsi** *vr* to unite; (*in ma-trimonio*) to be joined together; **~ qc a** to unite sth with; **to join** *o* **connect sth with;** to combine sth with; **~rsi a** (*gruppo, società*) to join.

unità *sf inv* (*unione, concordia*) unity; (*MAT, MIL, COMM, di misura*) unit; **uni'tario, a** *ag* unitary; **prezzo unitario** price per unit.

u'nito, a *ag* (*paese*) united; (*amici, famiglia*) close; **in tinta ~a** plain, self-coloured.

univer'sale *ag* universal; general.

università *sf inv* university; **universi'tario, a** *ag* university *cpd* // *sm/f* (*studente*) university student; (*in-segnante*) academic, university lecturer.

uni'verso *sm* universe.

'uno, a (*dav sm* **un** + *C, V,* **uno** + *s impura, gn, pn, ps, x, z; dav sf* **un'** + *V,* **una** + *C*) ◆ *articolo indefinito* **1** a; (*dav vocale*) an; **un bambino** a child; **~a strada** a street; **~ zingaro** a gypsy **2** (*intensivo*): **ho avuto ~a paura!** I got such a fright!
◆ *pronome* **1** one; **prendine ~** take one (of them); **l'~ o l'altro** either (of them); **l'~ e l'altro** both (of them); **aiutarsi l'un l'altro** to help one another o each other; **sono entrati l'~ dopo l'altro** they came in one after the other
2 (*un tale*) someone, somebody
3 (*con valore impersonale*) one, you; **se ~ vuole** if one wants, if you want
◆ *num* one; **~a mela e due pere** one apple and two pears; **~ più ~ fa due** one plus one equals two, one and one are two
◆ *sf:* **è l'~a** it's one (o'clock).

'unto, a *pp di* **ungere** // *ag* greasy, oily // *sm* grease; **untu'oso, a** *ag* greasy, oily.

u'omo, *pl* **u'omini** *sm* man; **da ~** (*abito, scarpe*) men's, for men; **~ d'affari** businessman; **~ di paglia** stooge; **~ rana** frogman.

u'opo *sm:* **all'~** if necessary.

u'ovo, *pl(f)* **u'ova** *sm* egg; **~ affogato** poached egg; **~ bazzotto/sodo** soft-/hard-boiled egg; **~ alla coque** boiled egg; **~ di Pasqua** Easter egg; **uova strapazzate** scrambled eggs.

ura'gano *sm* hurricane.

urba'nistica *sf* town planning.

ur'bano, a *ag* urban, city *cpd*, town *cpd*; (*TEL:* **chiamata**) local; (*fig*) urbane.

ur'gente [ur'dʒɛnte] *ag* urgent; **ur'genza** *sf* urgency; **in caso d'urgenza** (in case of) an emergency; **d'urgenza** *ag* emergency // *av* urgently, as a matter of urgency.

'urgere ['urdʒere] *vi* to be urgent; to be needed urgently.

u'rina *sf* = **orina**.

ur'lare *vi* (*persona*) to scream, yell; (*animale, vento*) to howl // *vt* to scream, yell.

'urlo, *pl(m)* **'urli,** *pl(f)* **'urla** *sm* scream, yell; howl.

'urna *sf* urn; (*elettorale*) ballot-box; **andare alle ~e** to go to the polls.

urrà *escl* hurrah!

U.R.S.S. *abbr f:* **l'~** the USSR.

ur'tare *vt* to bump into, knock against; (*fig: irritare*) to annoy // *vi:* **~ contro** o **in** to bump into, knock against, crash into; (*fig: imbattersi*) to come up against; **~rsi** *vr* (*reciproco: scontrarsi*) to collide; (*: fig*) to clash; (*irritarsi*) to get annoyed; **'urto** *sm* (*colpo*) knock, bump; (*scontro*) crash, collision; (*fig*) clash.

U.S.A. ['uza] *smpl:* **gli ~** the USA.

u'sanza [u'zantsa] *sf* custom; (*moda*) fashion.

u'sare *vt* to use, employ // *vi* (*servirsi*): **~ di** to use; (*: diritto*) to exercise; (*essere di moda*) to be fashionable; (*essere solito*): **~ fare** to be in the habit of doing, be accustomed to doing // *vb impersonale:* **qui usa così** it's the custom round here; **u'sato, a** *ag* used; (*consumato*) worn; (*di seconda mano*) used, second-hand // *sm* second-hand goods *pl*.

usci'ere [uʃ'ʃɛre] *sm* usher.

'uscio ['uʃʃo] *sm* door.

u'scire [uʃ'ʃire] *vi* (*gen*) to come out; (*partire, andare a passeggio, a uno spettacolo etc*) to go out; (*essere sorteggiato: numero*) to come up; **~ da** (*gen*) to leave; (*posto*) to go (o come) out of, leave; (*solco, vasca etc*) to come out of; (*muro*) to stick out of; (*competenza etc*) to be outside; (*infanzia, adolescenza*) to leave behind; (*famiglia nobile etc*) to come from; **~ da** o **di casa** to go out; (*fig*) to leave home; **~ in automobile** to go out in the car, go for a drive; **~ di strada** (*AUT*) to go off o leave the road.

u'scita [uʃ'ʃita] *sf* (*passaggio, varco*) exit, way out; (*per divertimento*) outing; (*ECON: somma*) expenditure; (*TEATRO*) entrance; (*fig: battuta*) witty remark; **~ di sicurezza** emergency exit.

usi'gnolo [uzin'ɲɔlo] *sm* nightingale.

U.S.L. [uzl] *sigla f* (= *unità sanitaria locale*) local health centre.

'uso *sm* (*utilizzazione*) use; (*esercizio*) practice; (*abitudine*) custom; **a ~ di** for (the use of); **d'~** (*corrente*) in use; **fuori ~** out of use.

usti'one *sf* burn.

usu'ale *ag* common, everyday.

u'sura *sf* usury; (*logoramento*) wear (and tear).

uten'sile *sm* tool, implement; **~i da cucina** kitchen utensils.

u'tente *sm/f* user.

'utero *sm* uterus.

'utile *ag* useful // *sm* (*vantaggio*) advantage, benefit; (*ECON: profitto*) profit; **utilità** *sf* usefulness o; use; (*vantaggio*) benefit; **utili'tario, a** *ag* utilitarian // *sf* (*AUT*) economy car.

utiliz'zare [utilid'dzare] *vt* to use, make use of, utilize.

'uva *sf* grapes *pl*; **~ passa** raisins *pl*; **~ spina** gooseberry.

V

v. *abbr* (= *vedi*) v.

va *vb vedi* **andare**.

va'cante *ag* vacant.

va'canza [va'kantsa] *sf* (*l'essere vacante*) vacancy; (*riposo, ferie*) holiday(s *pl*)

(*Brit*), vacation (*US*); (*giorno di permesso*) day off, holiday; **~e** *sfpl* (*periodo di ferie*) holidays (*Brit*), vacation *sg* (*US*); **essere/andare in ~** to be/go on holiday *o* vacation; **~e estive** summer holiday(s) *o* vacation.

'vacca, che *sf* cow.

vacci'nare [vattʃi'nare] *vt* to vaccinate.

vacil'lare [vatʃil'lare] *vi* to sway, wobble; (*luce*) to flicker; (*fig: memoria, coraggio*) to be failing, falter.

'vacuo, a *ag* (*fig*) empty, vacuous // *sm* vacuum.

'vado *vb vedi* **andare.**

vaga'bondo, a *sm/f* tramp, vagrant; (*fannullone*) idler, loafer.

va'gare *vi* to wander.

vagheggi'are [vaged'dʒare] *vt* to long for, dream of.

va'gina [va'dʒina] *sf* vagina.

va'gire [va'dʒire] *vi* to whimper.

'vaglia ['vaʎʎa] *sm inv* money order; **~ postale** postal order.

vagli'are [vaʎ'ʎare] *vt* to sift; (*fig*) to weigh up; **'vaglio** *sm* sieve.

'vago, a, ghi, ghe *ag* vague.

va'gone *sm* (*FERR: per passeggeri*) coach; (: *per merci*) truck, wagon; **~ letto** sleeper, sleeping car; **~ ristorante** dining *o* restaurant car.

'vai *vb vedi* **andare.**

vai'olo *sm* smallpox.

va'langa, ghe *sf* avalanche.

va'lente *ag* able, talented.

va'lere *vi* (*avere forza, potenza*) to have influence; (*essere valido*) to be valid; (*avere vigore, autorità*) to hold, apply; (*essere capace: poeta, studente*) to be good, be able // *vt* (*prezzo, sforzo*) to be worth; (*corrispondere*) to correspond to; (*procurare*): **~ qc a qn** to earn sb sth; **~rsi di** to make use of, take advantage of; **far ~** (*autorità etc*) to assert; **vale a dire** that is to say; **~ la pena** to be worth the effort *o* worth it.

va'levole *ag* valid.

vali'care *vt* to cross.

'valico, chi *sm* (*passo*) pass.

'valido, a *ag* valid; (*rimedio*) effective; (*aiuto*) real; (*persona*) worthwhile.

valige'ria [validʒe'ria] *sf* leather goods *pl*; leather goods factory; leather goods shop.

va'ligia, gie *o* **ge** [va'lidʒa] *sf* (suit)case; **fare le ~gie** to pack (up); **~ diplomatica** diplomatic bag.

val'lata *sf* valley.

'valle *sf* valley; **a ~** (*di fiume*) downstream; **scendere a ~** to go downhill.

val'letto *sm* valet.

va'lore *sm* (*gen*) value; (*merito*) merit, worth; (*coraggio*) valour, courage; (*COMM: titolo*) security; **~i** *smpl* (*oggetti preziosi*) valuables.

valoriz'zare [valorid'dzare] *vt* (*terreno*)

to develop; (*fig*) to make the most of.

'valso, a *pp di* **valere.**

va'luta *sf* currency, money; (*BANCA*): **~ 15 gennaio** interest to run from January 15th.

valu'tare *vt* (*casa, gioiello, fig*) to value; (*stabilire: peso, entrate, fig*) to estimate; **valutazi'one** *sf* valuation; estimate.

'valvola *sf* (*TECN, ANAT*) valve; (*ELETTR*) fuse.

'valzer ['valtser] *sm inv* waltz.

vam'pata *sf* (*di fiamma*) blaze; (*di calore*) blast; (: *al viso*) flush.

vam'piro *sm* vampire.

vanda'lismo *sm* vandalism.

'vandalo *sm* vandal.

vaneggi'are [vaned'dʒare] *vi* to rave.

'vanga, ghe *sf* spade; **van'gare** *vt* to dig.

van'gelo [van'dʒelo] *sm* gospel.

va'niglia [va'niʎʎa] *sf* vanilla.

vanità *sf* vanity; (*di promessa*) emptiness; (*di sforzo*) futility; **vani'toso, a** *ag* vain, conceited.

'vanno *vb vedi* **andare.**

'vano, a *ag* vain // *sm* (*spazio*) space; (*apertura*) opening; (*stanza*) room.

van'taggio [van'taddʒo] *sm* advantage; **essere/portarsi in ~** (*SPORT*) to be in/take the lead; **vantaggi'oso, a** *ag* advantageous; favourable.

van'tare *vt* to praise, speak highly of; **~rsi** *vr*: **~rsi** (di/di aver fatto) to boast *o* brag (about/about having done); **vante'ria** *sf* boasting; **'vanto** *sm* boasting; (*merito*) virtue, merit; (*gloria*) pride.

'vanvera *sf*: **a ~** haphazardly; **parlare a ~** to talk nonsense.

va'pore *sm* vapour; (*anche:* **~ acqueo**) steam; (*nave*) steamer; **a ~** (*turbina etc*) steam *cpd*; **al ~** (*CUC*) steamed; **vapo'retto** *sm* steamer; **vapori'era** *sf* (*FERR*) steam engine; **vaporiz'zare** *vt* to vaporize; **vapo'roso, a** *ag* (*tessuto*) filmy; (*capelli*) soft and full.

va'rare *vt* (*NAUT, fig*) to launch; (*DIR*) to pass.

var'care *vt* to cross.

'varco, chi *sm* passage; **aprirsi un ~ tra la folla** to push one's way through the crowd.

vari'abile *ag* variable; (*tempo, umore*) changeable, variable // *sf* (*MAT*) variable.

vari'are *vt, vi* to vary; **~ di opinione** to change one's mind; **variazi'one** *sf* variation; change.

va'rice [va'ritʃe] *sf* varicose vein.

vari'cella [vari'tʃɛlla] *sf* chickenpox.

vari'coso, a *ag* varicose.

varie'gato, a *ag* variegated.

varietà *sf inv* variety // *sm inv* variety show.

'vario, a *ag* varied; (*parecchi: col so-*

stantivo al pl) various; *(mutevole: umore)* changeable; **vario'pinto, a** *ag* multicoloured.

'**varo** *sm* (NAUT, *fig*) launch; *(di leggi)* passing.

va'saio *sm* potter.

'**vasca, sche** *sf* basin; *(anche: ~ da bagno)* bathtub, bath.

va'scello [vaʃˈʃɛllo] *sm* (NAUT) vessel, ship.

vase'lina *sf* vaseline.

vasel'lame *sm* (*stoviglie*) crockery; (: *di porcellana)* china; **~ d'oro/d'argento** gold/silver plate.

'**vaso** *sm* (*recipiente*) pot; (: *barattolo)* jar; (: *decorativo*) vase; (ANAT) vessel; **~ da fiori** vase; (*per piante*) flowerpot.

vas'soio *sm* tray.

'**vasto, a** *ag* vast, immense.

Vati'cano *sm*: **il ~** the Vatican.

ve *pronome, av vedi* **vi**.

vecchi'aia [vekˈkjaja] *sf* old age.

'**vecchio, a** [ˈvekkjo] *ag* old // *sm/f* old man/woman; **i ~i** the old.

'**vece** [ˈvetʃe] *sf*: **in ~ di** in the place of, for; **fare le ~i di qn** to take sb's place.

ve'dere *vt, vi* to see; **~rsi** *vr* to meet, see one another; **avere a che ~ con** to have something to do with; **far ~ qc a qn** to show sb sth; **farsi ~** to show o.s.; (*farsi vivo*) to show one's face; **vedi di non farlo** make sure *o* see you don't do it; **non (ci) si vede** (*è buio etc*) you can't see a thing; **non lo posso ~** (*fig*) I can't stand him.

ve'detta *sf* (*sentinella, posto*) look-out; (NAUT) patrol boat.

'**vedovo, a** *sm/f* widower/widow.

ve'duta *sf* view.

vee'mente *ag* vehement; violent.

vege'tale [vedʒeˈtale] *ag, sm* vegetable.

vegetari'ano, a [vedʒetaˈrjano] *ag, sm/f* vegetarian.

'**vegeto, a** [ˈvedʒeto] *ag* (*pianta*) thriving; (*persona*) strong, vigorous.

'**veglia** [ˈveʎʎa] *sf* wakefulness; (*sorveglianza*) watch; (*trattenimento*) evening gathering; **fare la ~ a un malato** to watch over a sick person.

vegli'are [veʎˈʎare] *vi* to be awake; to stay *o* sit up; (*stare vigile*) to watch; to keep watch // *vt* (*malato, morto*) to watch over, sit up with.

ve'icolo *sm* vehicle; **~ spaziale** spacecraft *inv*.

'**vela** *sf* (NAUT: *tela*) sail; (*sport*) sailing.

ve'lare *vt* to veil; **~rsi** *vr* (*occhi, luna*) to mist over; (*voce*) to become husky; **~rsi il viso** to cover one's face (with a veil); **ve'lato, a** *ag* veiled.

veleggi'are [veledˈdʒare] *vi* to sail; (AER) to glide.

ve'leno *sm* poison; **vele'noso, a** *ag* poisonous.

veli'ero *sm* sailing ship.

ve'lina *sf* (*anche*: **carta ~**: *per imballare*) tissue paper; (: *per copie*) flimsy paper; (*copia*) carbon copy.

ve'livolo *sm* aircraft.

velleità *sf inv* vain ambition, vain desire.

'**vello** *sm* fleece.

vel'luto *sm* velvet; **~ a coste** cord.

'**velo** *sm* veil; (*tessuto*) voile.

ve'loce [veˈlotʃe] *ag* fast, quick // *av* fast, quickly; **velo'cista, i, e** *sm/f* (SPORT) sprinter; **velocità** *sf* speed; **a forte velocità** at high speed; **velocità di crociera** cruising speed.

ve'lodromo *sm* velodrome.

'**vena** *sf* (*gen*) vein; (*filone*) vein, seam; (*fig: ispirazione*) inspiration; (: *umore*) mood; **essere in ~ di qc** to be in the mood for sth.

ve'nale *ag* (*prezzo, valore*) market *cpd*; (*fig*) venal; mercenary.

ven'demmia *sf* (*raccolta*) grape harvest; (*quantità d'uva*) grape crop, grapes *pl*; (*vino ottenuto*) vintage; **vendemmi'are** *vt* to harvest // *vi* to harvest the grapes.

'**vendere** *vt* to sell; "**vendesi**" "for sale".

ven'detta *sf* revenge.

vendi'care *vt* to avenge; **~rsi** *vr*: **~rsi (di)** to avenge o.s. (for); (*per rancore*) to take one's revenge (for); **~rsi su qn** to revenge o.s. on sb; **vendica'tivo, a** *ag* vindictive.

'**vendita** *sf* sale; **la ~** (*attività*) selling; (*smercio*) sales *pl*; **in ~** on sale; **~ all'asta** sale by auction; **vendi'tore** *sm* seller, vendor; (*gestore di negozio*) trader, dealer.

ve'nefico, a, ci, che *ag* poisonous.

vene'rabile *ag*, **vene'rando, a** *ag* venerable.

vene'rare *vt* to venerate.

venerdì *sm inv* Friday; **di** *o* **il ~** on Fridays; **V~ Santo** Good Friday.

ve'nereo, a *ag* venereal.

'**veneto, a** *ag, sm/f* Venetian.

Ve'nezia [veˈnettsja] *sf* Venice; **venezi'ano, a** *ag, sm/f* Venetian.

veni'ale *ag* venial.

ve'nire *vi* to come; (*riuscire: dolce, fotografia*) to turn out; (*come ausiliare: essere*): **viene ammirato da tutti** he is admired by everyone; **~ da** to come from; **quanto viene?** how much does it cost?; **far ~** (*mandare a chiamare*) to send for; **~ giù** to come down; **~ meno** (*svenire*) to faint; **~ meno a qc** not to fulfil sth; **~ su** to come up; **~ a trovare qn** to come and see sb; **~ via** to come away.

ven'taglio [venˈtaʎʎo] *sm* fan.

ven'tata *sf* gust (of wind).

ven'tenne *ag*: **una ragazza ~ a** twenty-year-old girl, a girl of twenty.

ven'tesimo, a *num* twentieth.

'venti *num* twenty.

venti'lare *vt* (*stanza*) to air, ventilate; (*fig: idea, proposta*) to air; **ventila'tore** *sm* ventilator, fan.

ven'tina *sf:* una ~ (di) around twenty, twenty or so.

venti'sette *num* twenty-seven; il ~ (*giorno di paga*) (monthly) pay day.

'vento *sm* wind.

'ventola *sf* (*AUT, TECN*) fan.

ven'tosa *sf* (*ZOOL*) sucker; (*di gomma*) suction pad.

ven'toso, a *ag* windy.

'ventre *sm* stomach.

ven'tura *sf:* andare alla ~ to trust to luck; soldato di ~ mercenary.

ven'turo, a *ag* next, coming.

ve'nuto, a *pp di* venire // *sf* coming, arrival.

vera'mente *av* really.

ver'bale *ag* verbal // *sm* (*di riunione*) minutes *pl*.

'verbo *sm* (*LING*) verb; (*parola*) word; (*REL*): il V~ the Word.

'verde *ag, sm* green; essere al ~ to be broke; ~ bottiglia/oliva *ag inv* bottle/olive green.

verde'rame *sm* verdigris.

ver'detto *sm* verdict.

ver'dura *sf* vegetables *pl*.

vere'condo, a *ag* modest.

'verga, ghe *sf* rod.

ver'gato, a *ag* (*foglio*) ruled.

'vergine ['verdʒine] *sf* virgin; (*dello zodiaco*): V~ Virgo // *ag* virgin; (*ragazza*): essere ~ to be a virgin.

ver'gogna [ver'goɲɲa] *sf* shame; (*timidezza*) shyness, embarrassment; **vergo'gnarsi** *vr*: vergognarsi (di) to be o feel ashamed (of); to be shy (about), be embarrassed (about); **vergo'gnoso, a** *ag* ashamed; (*timido*) shy, embarrassed; (*causa di vergogna: azione*) shameful.

ve'rifica, che *sf* checking *q*, check.

verifi'care *vt* (*controllare*) to check; (*confermare*) to confirm, bear out.

verità *sf inv* truth.

veriti'ero, a *ag* (*che dice la verità*) truthful; (*conforme a verità*) true.

'verme *sm* worm.

vermi'celli [vermi'tʃɛlli] *smpl* vermicelli *sg*.

ver'miglio [ver'miʎʎo] *sm* vermilion, scarlet.

'vermut *sm inv* vermouth.

ver'nice [ver'nitʃe] *sf* (*coloratione*) paint; (*trasparente*) varnish; (*pelle*) patent leather; "~ fresca" "wet paint"; **vernici'are** *vt* to paint; to varnish.

'vero, a *ag* (*veridico: fatti, testimonianza*) true; (*autentico*) real // *sm* (*verità*) truth; (*realtà*) (real) life; un ~ e proprio delinquente a real criminal, an out-and-out criminal.

vero'simile *ag* likely, probable.

ver'ruca, che *sf* wart.

versa'mento *sm* (*pagamento*) payment; (*deposito di denaro*) deposit.

ver'sante *sm* slopes *pl*, side.

ver'sare *vt* (*fare uscire: vino, farina*) to pour (out); (*spargere: lacrime, sangue*) to shed; (*rovesciare*) to spill; (*ECON*) to pay; (: *depositare*) to deposit, pay in; ~rsi *vr* (*rovesciarsi*) to spill; (*fiume, folla*): ~rsi (in) to pour (into).

versa'tile *ag* versatile.

ver'setto *sm* (*REL*) verse.

versi'one *sf* version; (*traduzione*) translation.

'verso *sm* (*di poesia*) verse, line; (*di animale, uccello, venditore ambulante*) cry; (*direzione*) direction; (*modo*) way; (*di foglio di carta*) verso; (*di moneta*) reverse; ~i *smpl* (*poesia*) verse *sg*; non c'è ~ di persuaderlo there's no way of persuading him, he can't be persuaded // *prep* (*in direzione di*) toward(s); (*nei pressi di*) near, around (about); (*in senso temporale*) about, around; (*nei confronti di*) for; ~ di me towards me; ~ sera towards evening.

verti'cale *ag, sf* vertical.

'vertice ['vertitʃe] *sm* summit, top; (*MAT*) vertex; conferenza al ~ (*POL*) summit conference.

ver'tigine [ver'tidʒine] *sf* dizziness *q*; dizzy spell; (*MED*) vertigo; avere le ~i to feel dizzy; **vertigi'noso, a** *ag* (*altezza*) dizzy; (*fig*) breathtakingly high (*o deep etc*).

ve'scica, che [veʃ'ʃika] *sf* (*ANAT*) bladder; (*MED*) blister.

'vescovo *sm* bishop.

'vespa *sf* wasp.

'vespro *sm* (*REL*) vespers *pl*.

ves'sillo *sm* standard; (*bandiera*) flag.

ves'taglia [ves'taʎʎa] *sf* dressing gown.

'veste *sf* garment; (*rivestimento*) covering; (*qualità, facoltà*) capacity; ~i *sfpl* clothes, clothing *sg*; in ~ ufficiale (*fig*) in an official capacity; in ~ di in the guise of, as; **vesti'ario** *sm* wardrobe, clothes *pl*.

ves'tibolo *sm* (*entrance*) hall.

ves'tire *vt* (*bambino, malato*) to dress; (*avere indosso*) to have on, wear; ~rsi *vr* to dress, get dressed; **ves'tito, a** *ag* dressed // *sm* garment; (*da donna*) dress; (*da uomo*) suit; vestiti *smpl* clothes; vestito di bianco dressed in white.

Ve'suvio *sm*: il ~ Vesuvius.

vete'rano, a *ag, sm/f* veteran.

veteri'nario, a *ag* veterinary // *sm* veterinary surgeon (*Brit*), veterinarian (*US*), vet // *sf* veterinary medicine.

'veto *sm inv* veto.

ve'traio *sm* glassmaker; glazier.

ve'trato, a *ag* (*porta, finestra*) glazed;

(*che contiene vetro*) glass *cpd* // *sf* glass door (*o* window); (*di chiesa*) stained glass window.

vetre'ria *sf* (*stabilimento*) glassworks *sg*; (*oggetti di vetro*) glassware.

ve'trina *sf* (*di negozio*) (shop) window; (*armadio*) display cabinet; **vetri'nista, i, e** *sm/f* window dresser.

vetri'olo *sm* vitriol.

'vetro *sm* glass; (*per finestra, porta*) pane (of glass).

'vetta *sf* peak, summit, top.

vet'tore *sm* (MAT, FISICA) vector; (*chi trasporta*) carrier.

vetto'vaglie [vetto'vaʎʎe] *sfpl* supplies.

vet'tura *sf* (*carrozza*) carriage; (FERR) carriage (*Brit*), car (*US*); (*auto*) car (*Brit*), automobile (*US*).

vezzeggi'are [vettsed'dʒare] *vt* to fondle, caress; **vezzeggia'tivo** *sm* (LING) term of endearment.

'vezzo ['vettso] *sm* habit; ~**i** *smpl* (*smancerie*) affected ways; (*leggiadria*) charms; **vez'zoso, a** *ag* (*grazioso*) charming, pretty; (*lezioso*) affected.

vi, *dav* **lo, la, li, le, ne** *diventa* **ve** *pronome* (*oggetto*) you; (*complemento di termine*) (to) you; (*riflessivo*) yourselves; (*reciproco*) each other // *av* (*lì*) there; (*qui*) here; (*per questo/quel luogo*) through here/there; ~ **è/sono** there is/are.

'via *sf* (*gen*) way; (*strada*) street; (*sentiero, pista*) path, track; (AMM: *procedimento*) channels *pl* // *prep* (*passando per*) via, by way of // *av* away // *escl* go away!; (*suvvia*) come on!; (SPORT) go! // *sm* (SPORT) starting signal; **in** ~ **di guarigione** on the road to recovery; **per** ~ **di** (*a causa di*) because of, on account of; **in** *o* **per** ~ on the way; **per** ~ **aerea** by air; (*lettere*) by airmail; **andare/essere** ~ to go/be away; ~ ~ **che** (*a mano a mano*) as; **dare il** ~ (SPORT) to give the starting signal; **dare il** ~ **a** (*fig*) to start; **V~ lattea** (ASTR) Milky Way; ~ **di mezzo** middle course; **in** ~ **provvisoria** provisionally.

viabilità *sf* (*di strada*) practicability; (*rete stradale*) roads *pl*, road network.

via'dotto *sm* viaduct.

viaggi'are [viad'dʒare] *vi* to travel; **viaggia'tore, 'trice** *ag* travelling // *sm* traveller; (*passeggero*) passenger.

vi'aggio ['vjaddʒo] *sm* travel(ling); (*tragitto*) journey, trip; **buon** ~! have a good trip!; ~ **di nozze** honeymoon.

vi'ale *sm* avenue.

via'vai *sm* coming and going, bustle.

vi'brare *vi* to vibrate; (*agitarsi*): ~ (**di**) to quiver (with).

vi'cario *sm* (*apostolico etc*) vicar.

'vice ['vitʃe] *sm/f* deputy // *prefisso*: ~**'console** *sm* vice-consul; ~**diret'tore** *sm* assistant manager.

vi'cenda [vi'tʃɛnda] *sf* event; **a** ~ in turn; **vicen'devole** *ag* mutual, reciprocal.

vice'versa [vitʃe'vɛrsa] *av* vice versa; **da Roma a Pisa e** ~ from Rome to Pisa and back.

vici'nanza [vitʃi'nantsa] *sf* nearness, closeness; ~**e** *sfpl* neighbourhood, vicinity.

vici'nato [vitʃi'nato] *sm* neighbourhood; (*vicini*) neighbours *pl*.

vi'cino, a [vi'tʃino] *ag* (*gen*) near; (*nello spazio*) near, nearby; (*accanto*) next; (*nel tempo*) near, close at hand // *sm/f* neighbour // *av* near, close; **da** ~ (*guardare*) close up; (*esaminare, seguire*) closely; (*conoscere*) well, intimately; ~ **a** *prep* near (to), close to; (*accanto a*) beside; ~ **di casa** neighbour.

'vicolo *sm* alley; ~ **cieco** blind alley.

'video *sm* *inv* (TV: *schermo*) screen; ~**cas'setta** *sf* videocassette; ~**regi-stra'tore** *sm* video (recorder).

vie'tare *vt* to forbid; (AMM) to prohibit; ~ **a qn di fare** to forbid sb to do; to prohibit sb from doing; "**vietato fumare/l'ingresso**" "no smoking/admittance".

Viet'nam *sm*: **il** ~ Vietnam; **vietna'mita, i, e** *ag, sm/f, sm* Vietnamese *inv*.

vi'gente [vi'dʒɛnte] *ag* in force.

vigi'lante [vidʒi'lante] *ag* vigilant, watchful.

vigi'lare [vidʒi'lare] *vt* to watch over, keep an eye on; ~ **che** to make sure that, see to it that.

'vigile ['vidʒile] *ag* watchful // *sm* (*anche*: ~ **urbano**) policeman (*in towns*); ~ **del fuoco** fireman.

vi'gilia [vi'dʒilja] *sf* (*giorno antecedente*) eve; **la** ~ **di Natale** Christmas Eve.

vigli'acco, a, chi, che [viʎ'ʎakko] *ag* cowardly // *sm/f* coward.

'vigna ['viɲɲa] *sf*, **vi'gneto** [viɲ'ɲeto] *sm* vineyard.

vi'gnetta [viɲ'ɲetta] *sf* cartoon.

vi'gore *sm* vigour; (DIR): **essere/entrare in** ~ to be in/come into force; **vigo'roso, a** *ag* vigorous.

'vile *ag* (*spregevole*) low, mean, base; (*codardo*) cowardly.

vili'pendio *sm* contempt, scorn; public insult.

'villa *sf* villa.

vil'laggio [vil'laddʒo] *sm* village.

villa'nia *sf* rudeness, lack of manners; **fare** (*o* **dire**) **una** ~ **a qn** to be rude to sb.

vil'lano, a *ag* rude, ill-mannered // *sm* boor.

villeggia'tura [villeddʒa'tura] *sf* holiday(s *pl*) (*Brit*), vacation (*US*).

vil'lino *sm* small house (with a garden), cottage.

vil'loso, a *ag* hairy.

viltà sf cowardice q; cowardly act.

'vimine sm wicker; **mobili di ~i** wicker furniture sg.

'vincere |'vintʃere| vt (in guerra, al gioco, a una gara) to defeat, beat; (premio, guerra, partita) to win; (fig) to overcome, conquer // vi to win; **~ qn in bellezza** to be better-looking than sb; **'vincita** sf win; (denaro vinto) winnings pl; **vinci'tore** sm winner; (MIL) victor.

vinco'lare vt to bind; (COMM: denaro) to tie up; **'vincolo** sm (fig) bond, tie; (DIR: servitù) obligation.

vi'nicolo, a ag wine cpd.

'vino sm wine; **~ bianco/rosso** white/red wine.

'vinto, a pp di **vincere**.

vi'ola sf (BOT) violet; (MUS) viola // ag, sm inv (colore) purple.

vio'lare vt (chiesa) to desecrate, violate; (giuramento, legge) to violate.

violen'tare vt to use violence on; (donna) to rape.

vio'lento, a ag violent; **vio'lenza** sf violence; **violenza carnale** rape.

vio'letto, a ag, sm (colore) violet // sf (BOT) violet.

violi'nista, i, e sm/f violinist.

vio'lino sm violin.

violon'cello |violon'tʃɛllo| sm cello.

vi'ottolo sm path, track.

'vipera sf viper, adder.

vi'raggio |vi'raddʒo| sm (NAUT, AER) turn; (FOT) toning.

vi'rare vt (NAUT) to haul (in), heave (in) // vi (NAUT, AER) to turn; (FOT) to tone; **~ di bordo** (NAUT) to tack.

'virgola sf (LING) comma; (MAT) point; **virgo'lette** spl inverted commas, quotation marks.

vi'rile ag (proprio dell'uomo) masculine; (non puerile, da uomo) manly, virile.

virtù sf inv virtue; **in o per ~ di** by virtue of, by.

virtu'ale ag virtual.

virtu'oso, a ag virtuous // sm/f (MUS etc) virtuoso.

'virus sm inv virus.

'viscere |'viʃʃere| sm (ANAT) internal organ // sfpl (di animale) entrails pl; (fig) bowels pl.

'vischio |'viskjo| sm (BOT) mistletoe; (pania) birdlime; **vischi'oso, a** ag sticky.

'viscido, a |'viʃʃido| ag slimy.

vi'sibile ag visible.

visi'bilio sm: **andare in ~** to go into raptures.

visibilità sf visibility.

visi'era sf (di elmo) visor; (di berretto) peak.

visi'one sf vision; **prendere ~ di qc** to examine sth, look sth over; **prima/seconda ~** (CINEMA) first/second showing.

'visita sf visit; (MED) visit, call; (: esame) examination; **visi'tare** vt to visit; (MED) to visit, call on; (: esaminare) to examine; **visita'tore, 'trice** sm/f visitor.

vi'sivo, a ag visual.

'viso sm face.

vi'sone sm mink.

'vispo, a ag quick, lively.

vis'suto, a pp di **vivere** // ag (aria, modo di fare) experienced.

'vista sf (facoltà) (eye)sight; (fatto di vedere): **la ~ di** the sight of; (veduta) view; **sparare a ~** to shoot on sight; **in ~** in sight; **perdere qn di ~** to lose sight of sb; (fig) to lose touch with sb; **a ~ d'occhio** as far as the eye can see; (fig) before one's very eyes; **far ~ di fare** to pretend to do.

'visto, a pp di **vedere** // sm visa; **~ che** cong seeing (that).

vis'toso, a ag gaudy, garish; (ingente) considerable.

visu'ale ag visual; **visualizza'tore** sm (INFORM) visual display unit, VDU.

'vita sf life; (ANAT) waist; **a ~ for life.**

vi'tale ag vital; **vita'lizio, a** ag life cpd // sm life annuity.

vita'mina sf vitamin.

'vite sf (BOT) vine; (TECN) screw.

vi'tello sm (ZOOL) calf; (carne) veal; (pelle) calfskin.

vi'ticcio |vi'tittʃo| sm (BOT) tendril.

viticol'tore sm wine grower; **viticol'tura** sf wine growing.

'vitreo, a ag vitreous; (occhio, sguardo) glassy.

'vittima sf victim.

'vitto sm food; (in un albergo etc) board; **~ e alloggio** board and lodging.

vit'toria sf victory.

'viva escl: **~ il re!** long live the king!

vi'vace |vi'vatʃe| ag (vivo, animato) lively; (: mente) lively, sharp; (colore) bright; **vivacità** sf vivacity; liveliness; brightness.

vi'vaio sm (di pesci) hatchery; (AGR) nursery.

vi'vanda sf food; (piatto) dish.

vi'vente ag living, alive; **i ~i** the living.

'vivere vi to live // vt to live; (passare: brutto momento) to live through, go through; (sentire: gioie, pene di qn) to share // sm life; (anche: modo di ~) way of life; **~i** smpl food sg, provisions; **~ di** to live on.

'vivido, a ag (colore) vivid, bright.

'vivo, a ag (vivente) alive, living; (: animale) live; (fig) (anche: colore) bright, brilliant; **i ~i** the living; **~ e vegeto** hale and hearty; **farsi ~** to show one's face; **to be heard from; ritrarre dal ~** to paint from life; **pungere qn nel ~** (fig) to cut sb to the quick.

vizi'are |vit'tsjare| vt (bambino) to spoil;

(*corrompere moralmente*) to corrupt;
vizi'ato, a *ag* spoilt; (*aria, acqua*)
polluted.

'vizio ['vittsjo] *sm* (*morale*) vice; (*cattiva abitudine*) bad habit; (*imperfezione*) flaw, defect; (*errore*) fault, mistake; **vizi'oso, a** *ag* depraved; defective; (*inesatto*) incorrect, wrong.

vocabo'lario *sm* (*dizionario*) dictionary; (*lessico*) vocabulary.

vo'cabolo *sm* word.

vo'cale *ag* vocal // *sf* vowel.

vocazi'one [vokat'tsjone] *sf* vocation; (*fig*) natural bent.

'voce ['votʃe] *sf* voice; (*diceria*) rumour; (*di un elenco, in bilancio*) item; aver ~ in capitolo (*fig*) to have a say in the matter.

voci'are [vo'tʃare] *vi* to shout, yell.

'voga *sf* (*NAUT*) rowing; (*usanza*): essere in ~ to be in fashion *o* in vogue.

vo'gare *vi* to row.

'voglia ['vɔʎʎa] *sf* desire, wish; (*macchia*) birthmark; aver ~ di qc/di fare to feel like sth/like doing; (*più forte*) to want sth/to do.

'voi *pronome* you; **voi'altri** *pronome* you.

vo'lano *sm* (*SPORT*) shuttlecock; (*TECN*) flywheel.

vo'lante *ag* flying // *sm* (steering) wheel.

volan'tino *sm* leaflet.

vo'lare *vi* (*uccello, aereo, fig*) to fly; (*cappello*) to blow away *o* off, fly away *o* off; ~ via to fly away *o* off.

vo'latile *ag* (*CHIM*) volatile // *sm* (*ZOOL*) bird.

volente'roso, a *ag* willing.

volenti'eri *av* willingly; "~" "with pleasure", "I'd be glad to".

vo'lere ♦ *sm* will, wish(es); contro il ~ di against the wishes of; per ~ di qn in obedience to sb's will *o* wishes
♦ *vt* 1 (*esigere, desiderare*) to want; voler fare/che qn faccia to want to do/sb to do; volete del caffè? would you like *o* do you want some coffee?; vorrei questo/fare I would *o* I'd like this/to do; come vuoi as you like; senza ~ (*inavvertitamente*) without meaning to, unintentionally
2 (*consentire*): vogliate attendere, per piacere please wait; vogliamo andare? shall we go?; vuole essere così gentile da ...? would you be so kind as to ...?; non ha voluto ricevermi he wouldn't see me
3: volerci (*essere necessario: materiale, attenzione*) to need; (: *tempo*) to take; quanta farina ci vuole per questa torta? how much flour do you need for this cake?; ci vuole un'ora per arrivare a Venezia it takes an hour to get to Venice
4: voler bene a qn (*amore*) to love sb; (*affetto*) to be fond of sb, like sb very much; voler male a qn to dislike sb;

volerne a qn to bear sb a grudge; **voler dire** to mean.

vol'gare *ag* vulgar; **volgariz'zare** *vt* to popularize.

'volgere ['vɔldʒere] *vt* to turn // *vi* to turn; (*tendere*): ~ a: il tempo volge al brutto the weather is breaking; un rosso che volge al viola a red verging on purple; ~rsi *vr* to turn; ~ al peggio to take a turn for the worse; ~ al termine to draw to an end.

'volgo *sm* common people.

voli'era *sf* aviary.

voli'tivo, a *ag* strong-willed.

'volo *sm* flight; al ~: colpire qc al ~ to hit sth as it flies past; capire al ~ to understand straight away.

volontà *sf* will; a ~ (*mangiare, bere*) as much as one likes; **buona/cattiva ~** goodwill/lack of goodwill.

volon'tario, a *ag* voluntary // *sm* (*MIL*) volunteer.

'volpe *sf* fox.

'volta *sf* (*momento, circostanza*) time; (*turno, giro*) turn; (*curva*) turn, bend; (*ARCHIT*) vault; (*direzione*): partire alla ~ di to set off for; a mia (*o* tua *etc*) ~ in turn; una ~ once; una ~ sola only once; due ~e twice; una cosa per ~ one thing at a time; una ~ per tutte once and for all; a ~e at times, sometimes; una ~ che (*temporale*) once; (*causale*) since; 3 ~e 4 3 times 4.

volta'faccia [volta'fattʃa] *sm inv* (*fig*) volte-face.

vol'taggio [vol'taddʒo] *sm* (*ELETTR*) voltage.

vol'tare *vt* to turn; (*girare: moneta*) to turn over; (*rigirare*) to turn round // *vi* to turn; ~rsi *vr* to turn; to turn over; to turn round.

volteggi'are [volted'dʒare] *vi* (*volare*) to circle; (*in equitazione*) to do trick riding; (*in ginnastica*) to vault; to perform acrobatics.

'volto, a *pp di* **volgere** // *sm* face.

vo'lubile *ag* changeable, fickle.

vo'lume *sm* volume; **volumi'noso, a** *ag* voluminous, bulky.

voluttà *sf* sensual pleasure *o* delight; **voluttu'oso, a** *ag* voluptuous.

vomi'tare *vt, vi* to vomit; **'vomito** *sm* vomiting *o* vomit.

'vongola *sf* clam.

vo'race [vo'ratʃe] *ag* voracious, greedy.

vo'ragine [vo'radʒine] *sf* abyss, chasm.

'vortice ['vɔrtitʃe] *sm* whirlwind; whirlpool; (*fig*) whirl.

'vostro, a *det*: il(la) ~(a) *etc* your // *pronome*: il(la) ~(a) *etc* yours.

vo'tante *sm/f* voter.

vo'tare *vi* to vote // *vt* (*sottoporre a votazione*) to take a vote on; (*approvare*) to vote for; (*REL*): ~ qc a to dedicate sth to; **votazi'one** *sf* vote, voting; **votazioni** *sfpl* (*POL*) votes; (*INS*) marks.

'voto *sm* (*POL*) vote; (*INS*) mark; (*REL*) vow; (: *offerta*) votive offering; **aver ~i belli/brutti** (*INS*) to get good/bad marks.

vs. *abbr* (*COMM*) = **vostro.**

vul'cano *sm* volcano.

vulne'rabile *ag* vulnerable.

vuo'tare *vt*, **~rsi** *vr* to empty.

vu'oto, a *ag* empty; (*fig: privo*): **~ di** (*senso etc*) devoid of // *sm* empty space, gap; (*spazio in bianco*) blank; (*FISICA*) vacuum; (*fig: mancanza*) gap, void; **a mani ~e** empty-handed; **~ d'aria** air pocket; **~ a rendere** returnable bottle.

W X Y

watt [vat] *sm inv* watt.

'weekend ['wi:kend] *sm inv* weekend.

'whisky ['wiski] *sm inv* whisky.

'xeres ['ksɛres] *sm inv* sherry.

xero'copia [ksero'kɔpja] *sf* xerox ®, photocopy.

xi'lofono [ksi'lɔfono] *sm* xylophone.

yacht [jɔt] *sm inv* yacht.

'yoghurt ['jɔgurt] *sm inv* yoghourt.

Z

zabai'one [dzaba'jone] *sm dessert made of egg yolks, sugar and marsala.*

zaf'fata [tsaf'fata] *sf* (*tanfo*) stench.

zaffe'rano [dzaffe'rano] *sm* saffron.

zaf'firo [dzaf'firo] *sm* sapphire.

'zaino ['dzaino] *sm* rucksack.

'zampa ['tsampa] *sf* (*di animale: gamba*) leg; (: *piede*) paw; **a quattro ~e** on all fours.

zampil'lare [tsampil'lare] *vi* to gush, spurt; **zam'pillo** *sm* gush, spurt.

zam'pogna [tsam'poɲɲa] *sf instrument similar to bagpipes.*

'zanna ['tsanna] *sf* (*di elefante*) tusk; (*di carnivoro*) fang.

zan'zara [dzan'dzara] *sf* mosquito; **zanzari'era** *sf* mosquito net.

'zappa ['tsappa] *sf* hoe; **zap'pare** *vt* to hoe.

zar, za'rina [tsar, tsa'rina] *sm/f* tsar/tsarina.

'zattera ['dzattera] *sf* raft.

za'vorra [dza'vɔrra] *sf* ballast.

'zazzera ['tsattsera] *sf* shock of hair.

'zebra ['dzɛbra] *sf* zebra; **~e** *sfpl* (*AUT*) zebra crossing *sg* (*Brit*), crosswalk *sg* (*US*).

'zecca, che ['tsekka] *sf* (*ZOOL*) tick; (*officina di monete*) mint.

'zelo ['dzɛlo] *sm* zeal.

'zenit ['dzɛnit] *sm* zenith.

'zenzero ['dzendzero] *sm* ginger.

'zeppa ['tseppa] *sf* wedge.

'zeppo, a ['tseppo] *ag:* **~ di** crammed *o* packed with.

zer'bino [dzer'bino] *sm* doormat.

'zero ['dzɛro] *sm* zero, nought; **vincere per tre a ~** (*SPORT*) to win three-nil.

'zeta ['dzɛta] *sm o f* zed, (the letter) z.

'zia ['tsia] *sf* aunt.

zibel'lino [dzibel'lino] *sm* sable.

'zigomo ['dzigomo] *sm* cheekbone.

zig'zag [dzig'dzag] *sm inv* zigzag; **andare a ~** to zigzag.

zim'bello [dzim'bɛllo] *sm* (*oggetto di burle*) laughing-stock.

'zinco ['dzinko] *sm* zinc.

'zingaro, a ['dzingaro] *sm/f* gipsy.

'zio ['tsio], *pl* **'zii** *sm* uncle; **zii** *smpl* (*zio e zia*) uncle and aunt.

zi'tella [dzi'tɛlla] *sf* spinster; (*peg*) old maid.

'zitto, a ['tsitto] *ag* quiet, silent; **sta' ~!** be quiet!

ziz'zania [dzid'dzanja] *sf* (*fig*): **gettare o seminare ~** to sow discord.

'zoccolo ['tsɔkkolo] *sm* (*calzatura*) clog; (*di cavallo etc*) hoof; (*basamento*) base; plinth.

zo'diaco [dzo'diako] *sm* zodiac.

'zolfo ['tsolfo] *sm* sulphur.

'zolla ['dzɔlla] *sf* clod (of earth).

zol'letta [dzol'letta] *sf* sugar lump.

'zona ['dzɔna] *sf* zone, area; **~ di depressione** (*METEOR*) trough of low pressure; **~ pedonale** pedestrian precinct; **~ verde** (*di abitato*) green area.

'zonzo ['dzondzo]: **a ~** *av:* **andare a ~** to wander about, stroll about.

zoo ['dzɔo] *sm inv* zoo.

zoolo'gia [dzoolo'dʒia] *sf* zoology.

zoppi'care [tsoppi'kare] *vi* to limp; to be shaky, rickety.

'zoppo, a ['tsɔppo] *ag* lame; (*fig: mobile*) shaky, rickety.

zoti'cone [dzoti'kone] *sm* lout.

'zucca, che ['tsukka] *sf* (*BOT*) marrow; pumpkin.

zucche'rare [tsukke'rare] *vt* to put sugar in; **zucche'rato, a** *ag* sweet, sweetened.

zuccheri'era [tsukke'rjɛra] *sf* sugar bowl.

zuccheri'ficio [tsukkeri'fitʃo] *sm* sugar refinery.

zucche'rino, a [tsukke'rino] *ag* sugary, sweet.

'zucchero ['tsukkero] *sm* sugar.

zuc'china [tsuk'kina] *sf*, **zuc'chino** [tsuk'kino] *sm* courgette (*Brit*), zucchini (*US*).

'zuffa ['tsuffa] *sf* brawl.

'zuppa ['tsuppa] *sf* soup; (*fig*) mixture, muddle; **~ inglese** (*CUC*) dessert made with sponge cake, custard and chocolate, ≈ trifle (*Brit*); **zuppi'era** *sf* soup tureen.

'zuppo, a ['tsuppo] *ag:* **~ (di)** drenched (with), soaked (with).

ENGLISH - ITALIAN
INGLESE - ITALIANO

A

A [eɪ] n (MUS) la m; (AUT): ~ **road** ≈ strada statale.

a indefinite article (before vowel or silent h: an) [eɪ, ə, æn, ən, n] **1** un (uno + s impure, gn, pn, ps, x, z), f una (un' + vowel); ~ **book** un libro; ~ **mirror** uno specchio; **an apple** una mela; **she's** ~ **doctor** è medico
2 (instead of the number 'one') un(o), f una; ~ **year ago** un anno fa; ~ **hundred/thousand** etc **pounds** cento/mille etc sterline
3 (in expressing ratios, prices etc) a, per; **3** ~ **day/week** 3 al giorno/alla settimana; **10 km an hour** 10 km all'ora; **£5** ~ **person** 5 sterline a persona or per persona.

A.A. n abbr (= Alcoholics Anonymous) AA; (Brit: = Automobile Association) ≈ A.C.I. m.

A.A.A. n abbr (US: = American Automobile Association) ≈ A.C.I. m.

aback [ə'bæk] ad: **to be taken** ~ essere sbalordito(a).

abandon [ə'bændən] vt abbandonare // n abbandono; **with** ~ sfrenatamente, spensieratamente.

abashed [ə'bæʃt] a imbarazzato(a).

abate [ə'beɪt] vi culmarsi.

abattoir ['æbətwɑ:*] n (Brit) mattatoio.

abbey ['æbɪ] n abbazia, badia.

abbot ['æbət] n abate m.

abbreviation [əbri.vɪ'eɪʃən] n abbreviazione f.

abdicate ['æbdɪkeɪt] vt abdicare a // vi abdicare.

abdomen ['æbdəmən] n addome m.

abduct [æb'dʌkt] vt rapire.

aberration [æbə'reɪʃən] n aberrazione f.

abet [ə'bɛt] vt see **aid**.

abeyance [ə'beɪəns] n: **in** ~ (law) in disuso; (matter) in sospeso.

abide [ə'baɪd] vt: **I can't** ~ **it/him** non lo posso soffrire or sopportare; **to** ~ **by** vt fus conformarsi a.

ability [ə'bɪlɪtɪ] n abilità f inv.

abject ['æbdʒɛkt] a (poverty) abietto(a); (apology) umiliante.

ablaze [ə'bleɪz] a in fiamme.

able ['eɪbl] a capace; **to be** ~ **to do sth** essere capace di fare qc, poter fare qc; **ably** ad abilmente.

abnormal [æb'nɔ:məl] a anormale.

aboard [ə'bɔ:d] ad a bordo // prep a bordo di.

abode [ə'bəud] n: **of no fixed** ~ senza fissa dimora.

abolish [ə'bolɪʃ] vt abolire.

abominable [ə'bomɪnəbl] a abominevole.

aborigine [æbə'rɪdʒɪnɪ] n aborigeno/a.

abort [ə'bɔ:t] vt abortire; ~**ion** [ə'bɔ:ʃən] n aborto; **to have an** ~**ion** abortire; ~**ive** a abortivo(a).

abound [ə'baund] vi abbondare; **to** ~ **in** abbondare di.

about [ə'baut] ♦ ad **1** (approximately) circa, quasi; ~ **a hundred/thousand** etc un centinaio/migliaio etc, circa cento/mille etc; **it takes** ~ **10 hours** ci vogliono circa 10 ore; **at** ~ **2 o'clock** verso le 2; **I've just** ~ **finished** ho quasi finito
2 (referring to place) qua e là, in giro; **to leave things lying** ~ lasciare delle cose in giro; **to run** ~ correre qua e là; **to walk** ~ camminare
3: **to be** ~ **to do sth** stare per fare qc
♦ prep **1** (relating to) su, di; **a book** ~ **London** un libro su Londra; **what is it** ~? di che si tratta?; (book, film etc) di cosa tratta?; **we talked** ~ **it** ne abbiamo parlato; **what or how** ~ **doing this?** che ne dici di fare questo?
2 (referring to place): **to walk** ~ **the town** camminare per la città; **her clothes were scattered** ~ **the room** i suoi vestiti erano sparsi or in giro per tutta la stanza.

about-face [ə'baut'feɪs] n, **about-turn** [ə'baut'tə:n] n dietro front m inv.

above [ə'bʌv] ad, prep sopra; **mentioned** ~ suddetto; ~ **all** soprattutto; ~**board** a aperto(a); onesto(a).

abrasive [ə'breɪzɪv] a abrasivo(a); (fig) caustico(a).

abreast [ə'brɛst] ad di fianco; **to keep** ~ **of** tenersi aggiornato su.

abridge [ə'brɪdʒ] vt ridurre.

abroad [ə'brɔ:d] ad all'estero.

abrupt [ə'brʌpt] a (steep) erto(a); (sudden) improvviso(a); (gruff, blunt) brusco(a).

abscess ['æbsɪs] n ascesso.

abscond [əb'skɔnd] vi scappare.

absence ['æbsəns] n assenza.

absent ['æbsənt] a assente; ~**ee** [-'ti:] n assente m/f; ~**-minded** a distratto(a).

absolute ['æbsəlu:t] a assoluto(a); ~**ly** [-'lu:tlɪ] ad assolutamente.

absolve [əb'zɔlv] vt: **to** ~ **sb** (from) (sin) assolvere qn (da); (oath) sciogliere qn (da).

absorb [əb'zɔ:b] vt assorbire; **to be** ~**ed**

in a book essere immerso in un libro; ~ent cotton n (US) cotone m idrofilo.

absorption [əb'sɔ:pʃən] n assorbimento.

abstain [əb'steɪn] vi: to ~ (from) astenersi (da).

abstemious [əb'sti:mɪəs] a astemio(a).

abstract ['æbstrækt] a astratto(a).

absurd [əb'sɔ:d] a assurdo(a).

abuse n [ə'bju:s] abuso; (insults) ingiurie fpl // vt [ə'bju:z] abusare di; **abusive** a ingiurioso(a).

abysmal [ə'bɪzməl] a spaventoso(a).

abyss [ə'bɪs] n abisso.

AC abbr (= alternating current) c.a.

academic [ækə'dɛmɪk] a accademico(a); (pej: issue) puramente formale // n universitario/a.

academy [ə'kædəmɪ] n (learned body) accademia; (school) scuola privata; ~ of music conservatorio.

accelerate [æk'sɛləreɪt] vt, vi accelerare; **accelerator** n acceleratore m.

accent ['æksɛnt] n accento.

accept [ək'sɛpt] vt accettare; ~able a accettabile; ~ance n accettazione f.

access ['æksɛs] n accesso; ~ible [æk'sɛsəbl] a accessibile.

accessory [æk'sɛsərɪ] n accessorio; toilet accessories npl articoli mpl da toilette.

accident ['æksɪdənt] n incidente m; (chance) caso; by ~ per caso; ~al [-'dɛntl] a accidentale; ~ally [-'dɛntəlɪ] ad per caso; ~-prone a: he's very ~-prone è un vero passaguai.

acclaim [ə'kleɪm] vt acclamare // n acclamazione f.

accommodate [ə'kɔmədeɪt] vt alloggiare; (oblige, help) favorire.

accommodating [ə'kɔmədeɪtɪŋ] a compiacente.

accommodation [əkɔmə'deɪʃən] n (US: ~s) alloggio.

accompany [ə'kʌmpənɪ] vt accompagnare.

accomplice [ə'kʌmplɪs] n complice m/f.

accomplish [ə'kʌmplɪʃ] vt compiere; ~ed a (person) esperto(a); ~ment n compimento; realizzazione f; ~ments npl doti fpl.

accord [ə'kɔ:d] n accordo // vt accordare; of his own ~ di propria iniziativa; ~ance n: in ~ance with in conformità con; ~ing to prep secondo; ~ingly ad in conformità.

accordion [ə'kɔ:dɪən] n fisarmonica.

accost [ə'kɔst] vt avvicinare.

account [ə'kaunt] n (COMM) conto; (report) descrizione f; ~s npl (COMM) conti mpl; of little ~ di poca importanza; on ~ in acconto; on no ~ per nessun motivo; on ~ of a causa di; to take into ~, take ~ of tener conto di; to ~ for spiegare; giustificare; ~able a responsabile.

accountancy [ə'kauntənsɪ] n ragioneria.

accountant [ə'kauntənt] n ragioniere/a.

account number n numero di conto.

accumulate [ə'kju:mjuleɪt] vt accumulare // vi accumularsi.

accuracy ['ækjurəsɪ] n precisione f.

accurate ['ækjurɪt] a preciso(a); ~ly ad precisamente.

accusation [ækju'zeɪʃən] n accusa.

accuse [ə'kju:z] vt accusare; ~d n accusato/a.

accustom [ə'kʌstəm] vt abituare; ~ed a (usual) abituale; ~ed to abituato(a) a.

ace [eɪs] n asso.

ache [eɪk] n male m, dolore m // vi (be sore) far male, dolere; my head ~s mi fa male la testa.

achieve [ə'tʃi:v] vt (aim) raggiungere; (victory, success) ottenere; (task) compiere; ~ment n compimento; successo.

acid ['æsɪd] a acido(a) // n acido; ~ rain n pioggia acida.

acknowledge [ək'nɔlɪdʒ] vt (letter: also: ~ receipt of) confermare la ricevuta di; (fact) riconoscere; ~ment n conferma; riconoscimento.

acne ['æknɪ] n acne f.

acorn ['eɪkɔ:n] n ghianda.

acoustic [ə'ku:stɪk] a acustico(a); ~s n, npl acustica.

acquaint [ə'kweɪnt] vt: to ~ sb with sth far sapere qc a qn; to be ~ed with (person) conoscere; ~ance n conoscenza; (person) conoscente m/f.

acquiesce [ækwɪ'ɛs] vi: to ~ (in) acconsentire (a).

acquire [ə'kwaɪə*] vt acquistare.

acquisition [ækwɪ'zɪʃən] n acquisto.

acquit [ə'kwɪt] vt assolvere; to ~ o.s. well comportarsi bene; ~tal n assoluzione f.

acre ['eɪkə*] n acro (= 4047 m²).

acrid ['ækrɪd] a acre; pungente.

acrimonious [ækrɪ'məunɪəs] a astioso(a).

acrobat ['ækrəbæt] n acrobata m/f.

across [ə'krɔs] prep (on the other side) dall'altra parte di; (crosswise) attraverso // ad dall'altra parte; in larghezza; to walk ~ (the road) attraversare (la strada); ~ from di fronte a.

acrylic [ə'krɪlɪk] a acrilico(a) // n acrilico.

act [ækt] n atto; (in music-hall etc) numero; (LAW) decreto // vi agire; (THEATRE) recitare; (pretend) fingere // vt (part) recitare; to ~ as agire da; ~ing a che fa le funzioni di // n (of actor) recitazione f; (activity): to do some ~ing fare del teatro (or del cinema).

action ['ækʃən] n azione f; (MIL) combattimento; (LAW) processo; out of ~ fuori combattimento; fuori servizio; to take ~ agire; ~ replay n (TV) replay m *inv.*

activate ['æktɪveɪt] *vt* (*mechanism*) fare funzionare; (*CHEM, PHYSICS*) rendere attivo(a).

active ['æktɪv] *a* attivo(a); ~**ly** *ad* (*participate*) attivamente; (*discourage, dislike*) vivamente.

activity [æk'tɪvɪtɪ] *n* attività *f inv.*

actor ['æktə*] *n* attore *m.*

actress ['æktrɪs] *n* attrice *f.*

actual ['æktjuəl] *a* reale, vero(a); ~**ly** *ad* veramente; (*even*) addirittura.

acumen ['ækjumən] *n* acume *m.*

acute [ə'kju:t] *a* acuto(a); (*mind, person*) perspicace.

ad [æd] *n abbr* = **advertisement.**

A.D. *ad abbr* (= *Anno Domini*) d.C.

adamant ['ædəmənt] *a* irremovibile.

adapt [ə'dæpt] *vt* adattare // *vi*: to ~ (to) adattarsi (a); ~**able** *a* (*device*) adattabile; (*person*) che sa adattarsi; ~**er** *or* ~**or** *n* (*ELEC*) adattatore *m.*

add [æd] *vt* aggiungere; (*figures: also:* to ~ up) addizionare // *vi*: to ~ to (*increase*) aumentare; it doesn't ~ up (*fig*) non quadra, non ha senso.

adder ['ædə*] *n* vipera.

addict ['ædɪkt] *n* tossicomane *m/f*; (*fig*) fanatico/a; ~**ed** [ə'dɪktɪd] *a*: to be ~**ed** to (*drink etc*) essere dedito a; (*fig: football etc*) essere tifoso di; ~**ion** [ə'dɪkʃən] *n* (*MED*) tossicomania; ~**ive** [ə'dɪktɪv] *a* che dà assuefazione.

addition [ə'dɪʃən] *n* addizione *f*; in ~ inoltre; in ~ to oltre; ~**al** *a* supplementare.

additive ['ædɪtɪv] *n* additivo.

address [ə'drɛs] *n* indirizzo; (*talk*) discorso // *vt* indirizzare; (*speak to*) fare un discorso a.

adept ['ædɛpt] *a*: ~ at esperto(a) in.

adequate ['ædɪkwɪt] *a* adeguato(a); sufficiente.

adhere [əd'hɪə*] *vi*: to ~ to aderire a; (*fig: rule, decision*) seguire.

adhesion [əd'hi:ʒən] *n* adesione *f.*

adhesive [əd'hi:zɪv] *a* adesivo(a) // *n* adesivo; ~ **tape** *n* (*Brit: for parcels etc*) nastro adesivo; (*US: MED*) cerotto adesivo.

adjective ['ædʒɛktɪv] *n* aggettivo.

adjoining [ə'dʒɔɪnɪŋ] *a* accanto *inv*, adiacente.

adjourn [ə'dʒə:n] *vt* rimandare // *vi* essere aggiornato(a); (*go*) spostarsi.

adjudicate [ə'dʒu:dɪkeɪt] *vt* (*contest*) giudicare; (*claim*) decidere su.

adjust [ə'dʒʌst] *vt* aggiustare; (*COMM*) rettificare // *vi*: to ~ (to) adattarsi (a); ~**able** *a* regolabile.

ad-lib [æd'lɪb] *vt, vi* improvvisare // *ad*: ad lib a piacere, a volontà.

administer [əd'mɪnɪstə*] *vt* amministrare; (*justice*) somministrare.

administration [ədmɪnɪs'treɪʃən] *n*

amministrazione *f.*

administrative [əd'mɪnɪstrətɪv] *a* amministrativo(a).

admiral ['ædmərəl] *n* ammiraglio; **A~ty** *n* (*Brit: also:* **A~ty Board**) Ministero della Marina.

admiration [ædmə'reɪʃən] *n* ammirazione *f.*

admire [əd'maɪə*] *vt* ammirare.

admission [əd'mɪʃən] *n* ammissione *f*; (*to exhibition, night club etc*) ingresso; (*confession*) confessione *f.*

admit [əd'mɪt] *vt* ammettere; far entrare; (*agree*) riconoscere; to ~ to riconoscere; ~**tance** *n* ingresso; ~**tedly** *ad* bisogna pur riconoscere (che).

admonish [əd'mɔnɪʃ] *vt* ammonire.

ad nauseam [æd'nɔ:sɪæm] *ad* fino alla nausea, a non finire.

ado [ə'du:] *n*: without (any) more ~ senza più indugi.

adolescence [ædəu'lɛsns] *n* adolescenza.

adolescent [ædəu'lɛsnt] *a, n* adolescente (*m/f*).

adopt [ə'dɔpt] *vt* adottare; ~**ed** *a* adottivo(a); ~**ion** [ə'dɔpʃən] *n* adozione *f.*

adore [ə'dɔ:*] *vt* adorare.

Adriatic (Sea) [eɪdrɪ'ætɪk('si:)] *n* Adriatico.

adrift [ə'drɪft] *ad* alla deriva.

adroit [ə'drɔɪt] *a* abile, destro(a).

adult ['ædʌlt] *n* adulto/a.

adultery [ə'dʌltərɪ] *n* adulterio.

advance [əd'vɑ:ns] *n* avanzamento; (*money*) anticipo // *vt* avanzare; (*date, money*) anticipare // *vi* avanzare; in ~ in anticipo; ~**d** *a* avanzato(a); (*SCOL: studies*) superiore.

advantage [əd'vɑ:ntɪdʒ] *n* (*also TENNIS*) vantaggio; to take ~ of approfittarsi di.

advent ['ædvənt] *n* avvento; **A~** Avvento.

adventure [əd'vɛntʃə*] *n* avventura.

adverb ['ædvə:b] *n* avverbio.

adverse ['ædvə:s] *a* avverso(a); ~ to contrario(a) a.

advert ['ædvə:t] *n abbr* (*Brit*) = **advertisement.**

advertise ['ædvətaɪz] *vi* (*vt*) fare pubblicità *or* réclame // *vi*; fare un'inserzione (per vendere); to ~ for (*staff*) mettere un annuncio sul giornale per trovare.

advertisement [əd'və:tɪsmənt] *n* (*COMM*) réclame *f inv*, pubblicità *f inv*; (*in classified ads*) inserzione *f.*

advertiser ['ædvətaɪzə*] *n* (*in newspaper etc*) inserzionista *m/f.*

advertising ['ædvətaɪzɪŋ] *n* pubblicità.

advice [əd'vaɪs] *n* consigli *mpl*; (*notification*) avviso; piece of ~ consiglio; to take legal ~ consultare un avvocato.

advisable [əd'vaɪzəbl] *a* consigliabile.

advise [əd'vaɪz] *vt* consigliare; to ~ sb of sth informare qn di qc; to ~ sb against sth/doing sth sconsigliare qc a qn/a qn di fare qc; **~dly** [-ədlɪ] ad (*deliberately*) di proposito; **~r** n consigliere/a; **advisory** [-əɪɪ] a consultivo(a).

advocate n ['ædvəkɪt] (*upholder*) sostenitore/trice; (*LAW*) avvocato (difensore) // vt ['ædvəkeɪt] propugnare; to be an ~ of essere a favore di.

aerial ['ɛərɪəl] n antenna // a aereo(a).

aerobics [ɛə'rəʊbɪks] n aerobica.

aeroplane ['ɛərəpleɪn] n (*Brit*) aeroplano.

aerosol ['ɛərəsɒl] n (*Brit*) aerosol m inv.

aesthetic [ɪs'θɛtɪk] a estetico(a).

afar [ə'fɑː] ad: from ~ da lontano.

affair [ə'fɛə] n affare m; (*also*: love ~) relazione f amorosa.

affect [ə'fɛkt] vt toccare; (*feign*) fingere; **~ed** a affettato(a).

affection [ə'fɛkʃən] n affezione f; **~ate** a affettuoso(a).

affirmation [æfə'meɪʃən] n affermazione f.

affix [ə'fɪks] vt apporre; attaccare.

afflict [ə'flɪkt] vt affliggere.

affluence ['æfluəns] n abbondanza; opulenza.

affluent ['æfluənt] a abbondante; opulente; (*person*) ricco(a).

afford [ə'fɔːd] vt permettersi; (*provide*) fornire.

afield [ə'fiːld] ad: far ~ lontano.

afloat [ə'fləʊt] a, ad a galla.

afoot [ə'fʊt] ad: there is something ~ si sta preparando qualcosa.

afraid [ə'freɪd] a impaurito(a); to be ~ of or to aver paura di; I am ~ that I'll be late mi dispiace, ma farò tardi.

afresh [ə'frɛʃ] ad di nuovo.

Africa ['æfrɪkə] n Africa; **~n** a, n africano(a).

aft [ɑːft] ad a poppa, verso poppa.

after ['ɑːftə] prep, ad dopo // cj dopo che; **what/who are you ~?** che/chi cerca?; ~ **he left/having done** dopo che se ne fu andato/dopo aver fatto; ~ all dopo tutto; ~ you! dopo di lei!; **~- effects** npl conseguenze fpl; (*of illness*) postumi mpl; **~life** n vita dell'al di là; **~math** n conseguenze fpl; in the **~math** of nel periodo dopo; **~noon** n pomeriggio; **~s** n (*col: dessert*) dessert m inv; **~-sales service** n (*Brit*) servizio assistenza clienti; **~-shave (lotion)** n dopobarba m inv; **~thought** n: as an **~thought** come aggiunta; **~wards** ad dopo.

again [ə'gɛn] ad di nuovo; to begin/ see ~ ricominciare/rivedere; not ... ~ non ... più; ~ and ~ ripetutamente.

against [ə'gɛnst] prep contro; ~ a blue background su uno sfondo azzurro.

age [eɪdʒ] n età f inv // vt, vi invecchiare; it's been **~s** since sono secoli che; he is 20 years of ~ ha 20 anni; to

come of ~ diventare maggiorenne; **~d 10** di 10 anni; **the ~d** ['eɪdʒɪd] gli anziani; ~ **group** n generazione f; ~ **limit** n limite m d'età.

agency ['eɪdʒənsɪ] n agenzia; **through** or by the ~ of grazie a.

agenda [ə'dʒɛndə] n ordine m del giorno.

agent ['eɪdʒənt] n agente m.

aggregate ['ægrɪgeɪt] n aggregato.

aggressive [ə'grɛsɪv] a aggressivo(a).

aggrieved [ə'griːvd] a addolorato(a).

aghast [ə'gɑːst] a sbigottito(a).

agitate ['ædʒɪteɪt] vt turbare; agitare; to ~ for agitarsi per.

ago [ə'gəʊ] ad: 2 days ~ 2 giorni fa; not long ~ poco tempo fa; how long ~? quanto tempo fa?

agog [ə'gɒg] a ansioso(a), emozionato(a).

agonizing ['ægənaɪzɪŋ] a straziante.

agony ['ægənɪ] n agonia.

agree [ə'griː] vt (*price*) pattuire // vi: to ~ (with) essere d'accordo (con); (*LING*) concordare (con); to ~ to sth/to do sth accettare qc/di fare qc; to ~ that (*admit*) ammettere che; to ~ on sth accordarsi su qc; garlic doesn't ~ with me l'aglio non mi va; **~able** a gradevole; (*willing*) disposto(a); are you ~able to this? è d'accordo con questo?; **~d** a (*time, place*) stabilito(a); **~ment** n accordo; in **~ment** d'accordo.

agricultural [ægrɪ'kʌltʃərəl] a agricolo(a).

agriculture ['ægrɪkʌltʃə] n agricoltura.

aground [ə'graʊnd] ad: to run ~ arenarsi.

ahead [ə'hɛd] ad avanti; davanti; ~ of davanti a; (*fig: schedule etc*) in anticipo su; ~ of time in anticipo; go right or straight ~ tiri diritto; they were (right) ~ of us erano (proprio) davanti a noi.

aid [eɪd] n aiuto // vt aiutare; in ~ of a favore di; to ~ and abet (*LAW*) essere complice di.

aide [eɪd] n (*person*) aiutante m.

AIDS [eɪdz] n abbr (= *acquired immune deficiency syndrome*) AIDS m.

ailing ['eɪlɪŋ] a sofferente.

ailment ['eɪlmənt] n indisposizione f.

aim [eɪm] vt: to ~ sth at (*such as gun*) mirare qc a, puntare qc a; (*camera, remark*) rivolgere qc a; (*missile*) lanciare qc contro; (*blow etc*) tirare qc a // vi (*also*: to take ~) prendere la mira // n mira; to ~ at mirare; to ~ to do aver l'intenzione di fare; **~less** a senza scopo.

ain't [eɪnt] (*col*) = **am not; aren't; isn't**.

air [ɛə] n aria // vt aerare; (*grievances, ideas*) esprimere pubblicamente // cpd (*currents*) d'aria; (*attack*) aereo(a); to throw sth into the ~ lanciare qc in aria; by ~ (*travel*) in aereo; on the ~ (*RADIO, TV*) in onda; **~bed** n (*Brit*) materassino; **~borne** *a* in volo; aerotrasportato(a); **~ conditioning** *n* condizionamento d'aria; **~craft** *n* (*pl inv*) apparecchio; **~craft carrier** *n* portaerei *f inv*; **~field** *n* campo d'aviazione; **A~ Force** *n* aviazione *f* militare; **~ freshener** *n* deodorante *m* per ambienti; **~gun** *n* fucile *m* ad aria compressa; **~hostess** *n* (*Brit*) hostess *f inv*; **~ letter** *n* (*Brit*) aerogramma *m*; **~lift** *n* ponte *m* aereo; **~line** *n* linea aerea; **~liner** *n* aereo di linea; **~lock** *n* camera d'aria; **~mail** *n*: by ~mail per via aerea; **~ mattress** *n* materassino; **~plane** *n* (*US*) aeroplano; **~port** *n* aeroporto; **~ raid** *n* incursione *f* aerea; **~sick** *a* che ha il mal d'aereo; **~space** *n* spazio aereo; **~strip** *n* pista d'atterraggio; **~ terminal** *n* air-terminal *m inv*; **~tight** *a* ermetico(a); **~ traffic controller** *n* controllore *m* del traffico aereo; **~y** *a* arioso(a); (*manners*) noncurante.

aisle [aɪl] *n* (*of church*) navata laterale; navata centrale; (*of plane*) corridoio.

ajar [əˈdʒɑː*] *a* socchiuso(a).

akin [əˈkɪn] *a*: ~ to simile a.

alacrity [əˈlækrɪtɪ] *n*: with ~ con prontezza.

alarm [əˈlɑːm] *n* allarme *m* // *vt* allarmare; ~ **clock** *n* sveglia.

alas [əˈlæs] *excl* ohimè!, ahimè!

albeit [ɔːlˈbiːɪt] *cj* sebbene+ *sub*, benché + *sub*.

album [ˈælbəm] *n* album *m inv*; (*L.P.*) 33 giri *m inv*, L.P. *m inv*.

alcohol [ˈælkəhɒl] *n* alcool *m*; **~ic** [-ˈhɒlɪk] *a* alcolico(a) // *n* alcolizzato/a.

alderman [ˈɔːldəmən] *n* consigliere *m* comunale.

ale [eɪl] *n* birra.

alert [əˈlɜːt] *a* vivo(a); (*watchful*) vigile // *n* allarme *m* // *vt* avvertire; mettere in guardia; on the ~ all'erta.

algebra [ˈældʒɪbrə] *n* algebra.

alias [ˈeɪlɪəs] *ad* alias // *n* pseudonimo, falso nome *m*.

alibi [ˈælɪbaɪ] *n* alibi *m inv*.

alien [ˈeɪlɪən] *n* straniero/a // *a*: ~ (to) estraneo(a) (a); **~ate** *vt* alienare.

alight [əˈlaɪt] *a* acceso(a) // *vi* scendere; (*bird*) posarsi.

align [əˈlaɪn] *vt* allineare.

alike [əˈlaɪk] *a* simile // *ad* sia ... sia; to look ~ assomigliarsi.

alimony [ˈælɪmənɪ] *n* (*payment*) alimenti *mpl*.

alive [əˈlaɪv] *a* vivo(a); (*active*) attivo(a).

all [ɔːl] ♦ *a* tutto(a); ~ **day** tutto il giorno; ~ **night** tutta la notte; ~ **men** tutti gli uomini; ~ **five** came sono venuti tutti e cinque; ~ **the books** tutti i libri; ~ **the food** tutto il cibo; ~ **the time** sempre; tutto il tempo; ~ **his life** tutta la vita

♦ *pronoun* **1** tutto(a); I ate it ~, I ate ~ of it l'ho mangiato tutto; ~ of us went tutti noi siamo andati; ~ of the boys went tutti i ragazzi sono andati

2 (*in phrases*): above ~ soprattutto; after ~ dopotutto; at ~: not at ~ (*in answer to question*) niente affatto; (*in answer to thanks*) prego!, di niente!, s'immagini!; I'm not at ~ tired non sono affatto stanco(a); anything at ~ will do andrà bene qualsiasi cosa; ~ in ~ tutto sommato

♦ *ad*: ~ alone tutto(a) solo(a); it's not as hard as ~ that non è poi così difficile; ~ the more/the better tanto più/meglio; ~ but quasi; the score is two ~ il punteggio è di due a due.

allay [əˈleɪ] *vt* (*fears*) dissipare.

all clear *n* (*also fig*) segnale *m* di cessato allarme.

allegation [ælɪˈgeɪʃən] *n* asserzione *f*.

allege [əˈledʒ] *vt* asserire; **~dly** [əˈledʒɪdlɪ] *ad* secondo quanto si asserisce.

allegiance [əˈliːdʒəns] *n* fedeltà.

allergic [əˈlɜːdʒɪk] *a*: ~ to allergico(a) a.

allergy [ˈælədʒɪ] *n* allergia.

alleviate [əˈliːvɪeɪt] *vt* sollevare.

alley [ˈælɪ] *n* vicolo; (*in garden*) vialetto.

alliance [əˈlaɪəns] *n* alleanza.

allied [ˈælaɪd] *a* alleato(a).

all-in [ˈɔːlɪn] *a* (*Brit: also ad: charge*) tutto compreso; ~ **wrestling** *n* lotta americana.

all-night [ˈɔːlˈnaɪt] *a* aperto(a) (*or* che dura) tutta la notte.

allocate [ˈæləkeɪt] *vt* (*share out*) distribuire; (*duties, sum, time*): to ~ sth to assegnare qc a; to ~ sth for stanziare qc per.

allot [əˈlɒt] *vt* (*share out*) spartire; to ~ sth to (*time*) dare qc a; (*duties*) assegnare qc a; **~ment** *n* (*share*) spartizione *f*; (*garden*) lotto di terra.

all-out [ˈɔːlaut] *a* (*effort etc*) totale // *ad*: to go all out for mettercela tutta per.

allow [əˈlau] *vt* (*practice, behaviour*) permettere; (*sum to spend etc*) accordare; (*sum, time estimated*) dare; (*concede*): to ~ that ammettere che; to ~ sb to do permettere a qn di fare; he is ~ed to lo può fare; **to ~ for** *vt fus* tener conto di; **~ance** *n* (*money received*) assegno; indennità *f inv*; (*TAX*) detrazione *f* di imposta; **to make ~ances for** tener conto di.

alloy [ˈælɔɪ] *n* lega.

all right *ad* (*feel, work*) bene; (*as answer*) va bene.

all-round [ˈɔːlˈraund] *a* completo(a).

all-time [ˈɔːlˈtaɪm] *a* (*record*) assoluto(a).

allude [əˈluːd] *vi*: to ~ to alludere a.

alluring [əˈljuərɪŋ] *a* seducente.

ally ['ælaɪ] *n* alleato.
almighty [ɔ:l'maɪtɪ] *a* onnipotente.
almond ['ɑ:mənd] *n* mandorla.
almost ['ɔ:lməust] *ad* quasi.
alms [ɑ:mz] *npl* elemosina *sg*.
aloft [ə'lɔft] *ad* in alto; (*NAUT*) sull'alberatura.
alone [ə'ləun] *a*, *ad* solo(a); **to leave sb ~** lasciare qn in pace; **to leave sth ~** lasciare stare qc; **let ~ ...** figuriamoci poi ..., tanto meno ... .
along [ə'lɔŋ] *prep* lungo // *ad*: **is he coming ~?** viene con noi?; **he was hopping/limping ~** veniva saltellando/zoppicando; **~ with** insieme con; **all ~** (*all the time*) sempre, fin dall'inizio; **~side** *prep* accanto a; lungo // *ad* accanto.
aloof [ə'lu:f] *a* distaccato(a) // *ad*: **to stand ~** tenersi a distanza *or* in disparte.
aloud [ə'laud] *ad* ad alta voce.
alphabet ['ælfəbet] *n* alfabeto.
alpine ['ælpaɪn] *a* alpino(a).
Alps [ælps] *npl*: **the ~** le Alpi.
already [ɔ:l'rɛdɪ] *ad* già.
alright ['ɔ:l'raɪt] *ad* (*Brit*) = **all right**.
Alsatian [æl'seɪʃən] *n* (*Brit*: *dog*) pastore *m* tedesco, (cane *m*) lupo.
also ['ɔ:lsəu] *ad* anche.
altar ['ɔltə*] *n* altare *m*.
alter ['ɔltə*] *vt*, *vi* alterare.
alternate *a* [ɔl'tə:nɪt] alterno(a) // *vb* ['ɔltə:neɪt] *vi*: **to ~ (with)** alternarsi (a) // *vt* alternare; **on ~ days** ogni due giorni; **alternating** *a* (*current*) alternato(a).
alternative [ɔl'tə:nətɪv] *a* (*solutions*) alternativo(a); (*solution*) altro(a) // *n* (*choice*) alternativa; (*other possibility*) altra possibilità; **~ly** *ad* alternativamente.
alternator ['ɔltə:neɪtə*] *n* (*AUT*) alternatore *m*.
although [ɔ:l'ðəu] *cj* benché + *sub*, sebbene + *sub*.
altitude ['æltɪtju:d] *n* altitudine *f*.
alto ['æltəu] *n* contralto; (*male*) contraltino.
altogether [ɔ:ltə'gɛðə*] *ad* del tutto, completamente; (*on the whole*) tutto considerato; (*in all*) in tutto.
aluminium [æljuˈmɪnɪəm], (*US*) **aluminum** [ə'lu:mɪnəm] *n* alluminio.
always ['ɔ:lweɪz] *ad* sempre.
am [æm] *vb see* **be**.
a.m. *ad abbr* (= *ante meridiem*) della mattina.
amalgamate [ə'mælgəmeɪt] *vt* amalgamare // *vi* amalgamarsi.
amateur ['æmətə*] *n* dilettante *m/f* // *a* (*SPORT*) dilettante; **~ish** *a* (*pej*) da dilettante.
amaze [ə'meɪz] *vt* stupire; **to be ~d (at)** essere sbalordito (da); **~ment** *n* stupore *m*; **amazing** *a* sorprendente, sbalorditivo(a); (*bargain*) sensazionale.

ambassador [æm'bæsədə*] *n* ambasciatore/trice.
amber ['æmbə*] *n* ambra; **at ~** (*Brit AUT*) giallo.
ambiguous [æm'bɪgjuəs] *a* ambiguo(a).
ambition [æm'bɪʃən] *n* ambizione *f*.
ambitious [æm'bɪʃəs] *a* ambizioso(a).
amble ['æmbl] *vi* (*gen*: **to ~ along**) camminare tranquillamente.
ambulance ['æmbjuləns] *n* ambulanza.
ambush ['æmbuʃ] *n* imboscata // *vt* fare un'imboscata a.
amenable [ə'mi:nəbl] *a*: **~ to** (*advice etc*) ben disposto(a) a.
amend [ə'mɛnd] *vt* (*law*) emendare; (*text*) correggere // *vi* emendarsi; **to make ~s** fare ammenda.
amenities [ə'mi:nɪtɪz] *npl* attrezzature *fpl* ricreative e culturali.
America [ə'mɛrɪkə] *n* America; **~n** *a*, *n* americano(a).
amiable ['eɪmɪəbl] *a* amabile, gentile.
amicable ['æmɪkəbl] *a* amichevole.
amid(st) [ə'mɪd(st)] *prep* fra, tra, in mezzo a.
amiss [ə'mɪs] *a*, *ad*: **there's something ~** c'è qualcosa che non va bene; **don't take it ~** non prendertela (a male).
ammonia [ə'məunɪə] *n* ammoniaca.
ammunition [æmju'nɪʃən] *n* munizioni *fpl*.
amok [ə'mɔk] *ad*: **to run ~** diventare pazzo(a) furioso(a).
among(st) [ə'mʌŋ(st)] *prep* fra, tra, in mezzo a.
amorous ['æmərəs] *a* amoroso(a).
amount [ə'maunt] *n* somma; ammontare *m*; quantità *f inv* // *vi*: **to ~ to** (*total*) ammontare a; (*be same as*) essere come.
amp(ère) ['æmp(ɛə*)] *n* ampère *m inv*.
ample ['æmpl] *a* ampio(a); spazioso(a); (*enough*): **this is ~** questo è più che sufficiente; **to have ~ time/room** avere assai tempo/posto.
amplifier ['æmplɪfaɪə*] *n* amplificatore *m*.
amuck [ə'mʌk] *ad* = **amok**.
amuse [ə'mju:z] *vt* divertire; **~ment** *n* divertimento; **~ment arcade** *n* sala giochi.
an [æn, ən, n] *indefinite article see* **a**.
anaemic [ə'ni:mɪk] *a* anemico(a).
anaesthetic [ænɪs'θɛtɪk] *a* anestetico(a) // *n* anestetico.
analog(ue) ['ænəlɔg] *a* (*watch, computer*) analogico(a).
analyse ['ænəlaɪz] *vt* (*Brit*) analizzare.
analysis, *pl* **analyses** [ə'næləsɪs, -si:z] *n* analisi *f inv*.
analyst ['ænəlɪst] *n* (*POL etc*) analista *m/f*; (*US*) (psic)analista *m/f*.
analyze ['ænəlaɪz] *vt* (*US*) = **analyse**.
anarchist ['ænəkɪst] *a*, *n* anarchico(a).
anarchy ['ænəkɪ] *n* anarchia.

anathema [ə'næθɪmə] *n*: that is ~ to him non vuole nemmeno sentirne parlare.

anatomy [ə'nætəmɪ] *n* anatomia.

ancestor ['ænsɪstə*] *n* antenato/a.

ancestral [æn'sɛstrəl] *a* avito(a).

anchor ['æŋkə*] *n* ancora // *vi* (*also*: to drop ~) gettare l'ancora // *vt* ancorare; to weigh ~ salpare *or* levare l'ancora.

anchovy ['æntʃəvɪ] *n* acciuga.

ancient ['eɪnʃənt] *a* antico(a); (*fig*) anziano(a).

ancillary [æn'sɪlərɪ] *a* ausiliario(a).

and [ænd] *cj* e (*often* əd *before vowel*); ~ so on e così via; try ~ come cerca di venire; he talked ~ talked non la finiva di parlare; better ~ better sempre meglio.

anew [ə'njuː] *ad* di nuovo.

angel ['eɪndʒəl] *n* angelo.

anger ['æŋgə*] *n* rabbia // *vt* arrabbiare.

angina [æn'dʒaɪnə] *n* angina pectoris.

angle ['æŋgl] *n* angolo; from their ~ dal loro punto di vista; ~r *n* pescatore *m* con la lenza.

Anglican ['æŋglɪkən] *a*, *n* anglicano(a).

angling ['æŋglɪŋ] *n* pesca con la lenza.

Anglo- ['æŋgləʊ] *prefix* anglo....

angry ['æŋgrɪ] *a* arrabbiato(a), furioso(a); to be ~ with sb/at sth essere in collera con qn/per qc; to get ~ arrabbiarsi; to make sb ~ fare arrabbiare qn.

anguish ['æŋgwɪʃ] *n* angoscia.

animal ['ænɪməl] *a*, *n* animale (*m*).

animate *vt* ['ænɪmeɪt] animare // *a* ['ænɪmɪt] animato(a); ~d *a* animato(a).

aniseed ['ænɪsiːd] *n* semi *mpl* di anice.

ankle ['æŋkl] *n* caviglia; ~ sock *n* calzino.

annex *n* ['ænɛks] (*also*: *Brit*: annexe) edificio annesso // *vt* [ə'nɛks] annettere.

annihilate [ə'naɪəleɪt] *vt* annientare.

anniversary [ænɪ'vɜːsərɪ] *n* anniversario.

announce [ə'naʊns] *vt* annunciare; ~ment *n* annuncio; (*letter*, *card*) partecipazione *f*; ~r *n* (*RADIO*, *TV*: *between programmes*) annunciatore/ trice; (: *in a programme*) presentatore/ trice.

annoy [ə'nɔɪ] *vt* dare fastidio a; don't get ~ed! non irritarti!; ~ance *n* fastidio; (*cause of* ~ance) noia; ~ing *a* noioso(a).

annual ['ænjʊəl] *a* annuale // *n* (*BOT*) pianta annua; (*book*) annuario.

annul [ə'nʌl] *vt* annullare; (*law*) rescindere.

annum ['ænəm] *n see* per.

anonymous [ə'nɒnɪməs] *a* anonimo(a).

anorak ['ænəræk] *n* giacca a vento.

another [ə'nʌðə*] *a*: ~ book (*one more*) un altro libro, ancora un libro; (*a different one*) un altro libro // *pronoun* un altro(un'altra), ancora uno(a); *see also* one.

answer ['ɑːnsə*] *n* risposta; soluzione *f* // *vi* rispondere // *vt* (*reply to*) rispondere a; (*problem*) risolvere; (*prayer*) esaudire; to ~ the phone rispondere (al telefono); in ~ to your letter in risposta alla sua lettera; to ~ the bell rispondere al campanello; to ~ the door aprire la porta; to ~ back *vi* ribattere; to ~ for *vt fus* essere responsabile di; to ~ to *vt fus* (*description*) corrispondere a; ~able *a*: ~able (to sb/for sth) responsabile (verso qn/di qc); ~ing machine *n* segreteria (telefonica) automatica.

ant [ænt] *n* formica.

antagonism [æn'tægənɪzəm] *n* antagonismo.

antagonize [æn'tægənaɪz] *vt* provocare l'ostilità di.

Antarctic [ænt'ɑːktɪk] *n*: the ~ l'Antartide *f* // *a* antartico(a).

antenatal ['æntɪ'neɪtl] *a* prenatale; ~ clinic *n* assistenza medica preparto.

anthem ['ænθəm] *n* antifona; national ~ inno nazionale.

anthology [æn'θɒlədʒɪ] *n* antologia.

antibiotic ['æntɪbaɪ'ɒtɪk] *a* antibiotico(a) // *n* antibiotico.

antibody ['æntɪbɒdɪ] *n* anticorpo.

anticipate [æn'tɪsɪpeɪt] *vt* prevedere; pregustare; (*wishes*, *request*) prevenire.

anticipation [æntɪsɪ'peɪʃən] *n* anticipazione *f*; (*expectation*) aspettative *fpl*.

anticlimax ['æntɪ'klaɪmæks] *n*: it was an ~ fu una completa delusione.

anticlockwise ['æntɪ'klɒkwaɪz] *a*, *ad* in senso antiorario.

antics ['æntɪks] *npl* buffonerie *fpl*.

antifreeze ['æntɪ'friːz] *n* anticongelante *m*.

antihistamine [æntɪ'hɪstəmɪn] *n* antistaminico.

antiquated ['æntɪkweɪtɪd] *a* antiquato(a).

antique [æn'tiːk] *n* antichità *f inv* // *a* antico(a); ~ shop *n* negozio d'antichità.

antiquity [æn'tɪkwɪtɪ] *n* antichità *f inv*.

anti-Semitism ['æntɪ'sɛmɪtɪzəm] *n* antisemitismo.

antiseptic [æntɪ'sɛptɪk] *a* antisettico(a) // *n* antisettico.

antisocial ['æntɪ'səʊʃəl] *a* asociale; (*against society*) antisociale.

antlers ['æntləz] *npl* palchi *mpl*.

anvil ['ænvɪl] *n* incudine *f*.

anxiety [æŋ'zaɪətɪ] *n* ansia; (*keenness*): ~ to do smania di fare.

anxious ['æŋkʃəs] *a* ansioso(a), inquieto(a); (*keen*): ~ to do/that impaziente di fare/che + *sub*.

any ['ɛnɪ] ◆ *a* 1 (*in questions etc*): have you ~ butter? hai del burro?, hai un po' di burro?; have you ~ children? hai bambini?; if there are ~ tickets left se ci sono ancora (dei) biglietti, se c'è ancora

qualche biglietto
2 (*with negative*): I haven't ~ money/
books non ho soldi/libri
3 (*no matter which*) qualsiasi,
qualunque; choose ~ **book you like** scegli
un libro qualsiasi
4 (*in phrases*): in ~ case in ogni caso;
~ day now da un giorno all'altro; at ~
moment in qualsiasi momento, da un
momento all'altro; at ~ rate ad ogni
modo
◆ *pronoun* **1** (*in questions, with
negative*): have you got ~? ne hai?; can
~ of you sing? qualcuno di voi sa
cantare?; I haven't ~ (of them) non ne
ho
2 (*no matter which one(s)*): take ~ of
those books (you like) prendi uno
qualsiasi di quei libri
◆ *ad* **1** (*in questions etc*): do you want
~ more soup/sandwiches? vuoi ancora un
po' di minestra/degli altri panini?; are
you feeling ~ better? ti senti meglio?
2 (*with negative*): I can't hear him ~
more non lo sento più; don't wait ~ longer non aspettare più.

anybody ['ɛnɪbɔdɪ] *pronoun* (*in questions
etc*) qualcuno, nessuno; (*with negative*)
nessuno; (*no matter who*) chiunque; can
you see ~? vedi qualcuno *or* nessuno?; if
~ should phone ... se telefona qualcuno
...; I can't see ~ non vedo nessuno; ~
could do it chiunque potrebbe farlo.

anyhow ['ɛnɪhau] *ad* (*at any rate*) ad
ogni modo, comunque; (*haphazard*) do
it ~ you like fallo come ti pare; I shall
go ~ ci andrò lo stesso *or* comunque; she
leaves things just ~ lascia tutto come
capita.

anyone ['ɛnɪwʌn] *pronoun* = anybody.

anything ['ɛnɪθɪŋ] *pronoun* (*in question
etc*) qualcosa, niente; (*with negative*)
niente; (*no matter what*): you can say ~
you like puoi dire quello che ti pare; can
you see ~? vedi niente *or* qualcosa?; if
~ happens to me ... se mi dovesse
succedere qualcosa ...; I can't see ~ non
vedo niente; ~ will do va bene qualsiasi
cosa *or* tutto.

anyway ['ɛnɪweɪ] *ad* (*at any rate*) ad
ogni modo, comunque; (*besides*) ad ogni
modo.

anywhere ['ɛnɪwɛə*] *ad* (*in questions
etc*) da qualche parte; (*with negative*)
da nessuna parte; (*no matter where*) da
qualsiasi *or* qualunque parte, dovunque;
can you see him ~? lo vedi da qualche
parte?; I can't see him ~ non lo vedo da
nessuna parte; ~ in the world dovunque
nel mondo.

apart [ə'pɑːt] *ad* (*to one side*) a parte;
(*separately*) separatamente; with one's
legs ~ con le gambe divaricate; 10 miles
~ a 10 miglia di distanza (l'uno dall'altro); to take ~ smontare; ~ from *prep* a

parte, eccetto.
apartheid [ə'pɑːteɪt] *n* apartheid *f*.
apartment [ə'pɑːtmənt] *n* (*US*)
appartamento; ~ **building** *n* (*US*)
stabile *m*, caseggiato.
apathetic [æpə'θɛtɪk] *a* apatico(a).
ape [eɪp] *n* scimmia // *vt* scimmiottare.
aperture ['æpətʃjuə*] *n* apertura.
apex ['eɪpɛks] *n* apice *m*.
apiece [ə'piːs] *ad* ciascuno(a).
apologetic [əpɔlə'dʒɛtɪk] *a* (*tone, letter*)
di scusa.
apologize [ə'pɔlədʒaɪz] *vi*: to ~ (for sth
to sb) scusarsi (di qc a qn), chiedere
scusa (a qn per qc).
apology [ə'pɔlədʒɪ] *n* scuse *fpl*.
apostle [ə'pɔsl] *n* apostolo.
apostrophe [ə'pɔstrəfɪ] *n* (*sign*) apo-
strofo.
appalling [ə'pɔːlɪŋ] *a* spaventoso(a).
apparatus [æpə'reɪtəs] *n* apparato; (*in
gymnasium*) attrezzatura.
apparel [ə'pærl] *n* (*US*) abbigliamento,
confezioni *fpl*.
apparent [ə'pærənt] *a* evidente; ~ly *ad*
evidentemente.
apparition [æpə'rɪʃən] *n* apparizione *f*.
appeal [ə'piːl] *vi* (*LAW*) appellarsi alla
legge // *n* (*LAW*) appello; (*request*) richiesta; (*charm*) attrattiva; to ~ for
chiedere (con insistenza); to ~ to (*subj:
person*) appellarsi a; (*subj: thing*)
piacere a; to ~ to sb for mercy chiedere
pietà a qn; it doesn't ~ to me mi dice
poco; ~ing *a* (*nice*) attraente; (*touching*) commovente.
appear [ə'pɪə*] *vi* apparire; (*LAW*)
comparire; (*publication*) essere pub-
blicato(a); (*seem*) sembrare; it would ~
that sembra che; to ~ in Hamlet
recitare nell'Amleto; to ~ on TV
presentarsi in televisione; ~ance *n*
apparizione *f*; apparenza; (*look, aspect*)
aspetto.
appease [ə'piːz] *vt* calmare, appagare.
appendage [ə'pɛndɪdʒ] *n* aggiunta.
appendicitis [əpɛndɪ'saɪtɪs] *n* appendicite
f.
appendix, *pl* **appendices** [ə'pɛndɪks,
-siːz] *n* appendice *f*.
appetite ['æpɪtaɪt] *n* appetito.
appetizer ['æpɪtaɪzə*] *n* stuzzichino.
applaud [ə'plɔːd] *vt*, *vi* applaudire.
applause [ə'plɔːz] *n* applauso.
apple ['æpl] *n* mela; ~ **tree** *n* melo.
appliance [ə'plaɪəns] *n* apparecchio.
applicant ['æplɪkənt] *n* candidato/a.
application [æplɪ'keɪʃən] *n* applicazione
f; (*for a job, a grant etc*) domanda; ~
form *n* modulo per la domanda.
applied [ə'plaɪd] *a* applicato(a).
apply [ə'plaɪ] *vt*: to ~ (to) (*paint,
ointment*) dare (a); (*theory, technique*)
applicare (a) // *vi*: to ~ to (*ask*)
rivolgersi a; (*be suitable for, relevant*

to) riguardare, riferirsi a; **to ~ (for)** *(permit, grant, job)* fare domanda (per); **to ~ the brakes** frenare; **to ~ o.s. to** dedicarsi a.

appoint [ə'pɔɪnt] *vt* nominare; **~ment** *n* nomina; *(arrangement to meet)* appuntamento; **to make an ~ment (with)** prendere un appuntamento (con).

appraisal [ə'preɪzl] *n* valutazione *f*.

appreciate [ə'priːʃɪeɪt] *vt (like)* apprezzare; *(be grateful for)* essere riconoscente di; *(be aware of)* rendersi conto di // *vi (FINANCE)* aumentare.

appreciation [əpriːʃɪ'eɪʃən] *n* apprezzamento; *(FINANCE)* aumento del valore.

appreciative [ə'priːʃɪətɪv] *a (person)* sensibile; *(comment)* elogiativo(a).

apprehend [æprɪ'hɛnd] *vt (arrest)* arrestare.

apprehension [æprɪ'hɛnʃən] *n (fear)* inquietudine *f*.

apprehensive [æprɪ'hɛnsɪv] *a* apprensivo(a).

apprentice [ə'prɛntɪs] *n* apprendista *m/f*; **~ship** *n* apprendistato.

approach [ə'prəʊtʃ] *vi* avvicinarsi // *vt (come near)* avvicinarsi a; *(ask, apply to)* rivolgersi a; *(subject, passer-by)* avvicinare // *n* approccio; accesso; *(to problem)* modo di affrontare; **~able** *a* accessibile.

appropriate *a* [ə'prəʊprɪɪt] appropriato(a); adatto(a) // *vt* [ə'prəʊprɪeɪt] *(take)* appropriarsi.

approval [ə'pruːvəl] *n* approvazione *f*; **on ~ (COMM)** in prova, in esame.

approve [ə'pruːv] *vt, vi* approvare; **to ~ of** *vt fus* approvare; **~d school** *n (Brit)* riformatorio.

approximate *a* [ə'prɒksɪmɪt] approssimativo(a); **~ly** *ad* circa.

apricot ['eɪprɪkɒt] *n* albicocca.

April ['eɪprəl] *n* aprile *m*; **~ fool!** pesce d'aprile!

apron ['eɪprən] *n* grembiule *m*.

apt [æpt] *a (suitable)* adatto(a); *(able)* capace; *(likely)*: **to be ~ to do** avere tendenza a fare.

aptitude ['æptɪtjuːd] *n* abilità *f inv*.

aqualung ['ækwəlʌŋ] *n* autorespiratore *m*.

aquarium [ə'kwɛərɪəm] *n* acquario.

Aquarius [ə'kwɛərɪəs] *n* Acquario.

Arab ['ærəb] *n* arabo/a.

Arabian [ə'reɪbɪən] *a* arabo(a).

Arabic ['ærəbɪk] *a* arabico(a) // *n* arabo; **~ numerals** numeri *mpl* arabi, numerazione *f* araba.

arbitrary ['ɑːbɪtrərɪ] *a* arbitrario(a).

arbitration [ɑːbɪ'treɪʃən] *n (LAW)* arbitrato; *(INDUSTRY)* arbitraggio.

arcade [ɑː'keɪd] *n* portico; *(passage with shops)* galleria.

arch [ɑːtʃ] *n* arco; *(of foot)* arco plantare

// *vt* inarcare // *a* malizioso(a).

archaeologist [ɑːkɪ'ɒlədʒɪst] *n* archeologo/a.

archaeology [ɑːkɪ'ɒlədʒɪ] *n* archeologia.

archbishop [ɑːtʃ'bɪʃəp] *n* arcivescovo.

arch-enemy ['ɑːtʃ'ɛnəmɪ] *n* arcinemico/a.

archeology [ɑːkɪ'ɒlədʒɪ] *etc* = **archaeology** *etc*.

archer ['ɑːtʃə*] *n* arciere *m*; **~y** *n* tiro all'arco.

architect ['ɑːkɪtɛkt] *n* architetto; **~ure** ['ɑːkɪtɛktʃə*] *n* architettura.

archives ['ɑːkaɪvz] *npl* archivi *mpl*.

archway ['ɑːtʃweɪ] *n* arco.

Arctic ['ɑːktɪk] *a* artico(a) // *n*: **the ~** l'Artico.

ardent ['ɑːdənt] *a* ardente.

are [ɑː*] *vb see* **be**.

area ['ɛərɪə] *n (GEOM)* area; *(zone)* zona; *(: smaller)* settore *m*.

aren't [ɑːnt] = **are not**.

Argentina [ɑːdʒən'tiːnə] *n* Argentina; **Argentinian** [-'tɪnɪən] *a, n* argentino(a).

arguably ['ɑːgjuəblɪ] *ad*: **it is ~ ...** si può sostenere che sia ....

argue ['ɑːgjuː] *vi (quarrel)* litigare; *(reason)* ragionare; **to ~ that** sostenere che.

argument ['ɑːgjumənt] *n (reasons)* argomento; *(quarrel)* lite *f*; *(debate)* discussione *f*; **~ative** [ɑːgju'mɛntətɪv] *a* litigioso(a).

Aries ['ɛəriːz] *n* Ariete *m*.

arise, *pt* **arose**, *pp* **arisen** [ə'raɪz, -'rəʊz, -'rɪzn] *vi* alzarsi; *(opportunity, problem)* presentarsi; **to ~ from** risultare da.

aristocrat ['ærɪstəkræt] *n* aristocratico/a.

arithmetic [ə'rɪθmətɪk] *n* aritmetica.

ark [ɑːk] *n*: **Noah's A~** l'arca di Noè.

arm [ɑːm] *n* braccio // *vt* armare; **~s** *npl (weapons)* armi *fpl*; **~ in ~** a braccetto.

armaments ['ɑːməmənts] *npl* armamenti *mpl*.

arm: **~chair** *n* poltrona; **~ed** *a* armato(a); **~ed robbery** *n* rapina a mano armata.

armour, *(US)* **armor** ['ɑːmə*] *n* armatura; *(also:* **~-plating)** corazza, blindatura; *(MIL: tanks)* mezzi *mpl* blindati; **~ed car** *n* autoblinda *f inv*; **~y** *n* arsenale *m*.

armpit ['ɑːmpɪt] *n* ascella.

armrest ['ɑːmrɛst] *n* bracciolo.

army ['ɑːmɪ] *n* esercito.

aroma [ə'rəʊmə] *n* aroma.

arose [ə'rəʊz] *pt of* **arise**.

around [ə'raʊnd] *ad* attorno, intorno // *prep* intorno a; *(fig: about)*: **~ £5/3 o'clock** circa 5 sterline/le 3; **is he ~?** è in giro?

arouse [ə'raʊz] *vt (sleeper)* svegliare; *(curiosity, passions)* suscitare.

arrange [ə'reɪndʒ] *vt* sistemare; *(programme)* preparare; **to ~ to do sth**

mettersi d'accordo per fare qc; **~ment** n sistemazione f; (*plans etc*): **~ments** progetti mpl, piani mpl.

array [ə'reɪ] n: **~ of** fila di.

arrears [ə'rɪəz] npl arretrati mpl; **to be in ~ with one's rent** essere in arretrato con l'affitto.

arrest [ə'rɛst] vt arrestare; (*sb's attention*) attirare // n arresto; **under ~** in arresto.

arrival [ə'raɪvəl] n arrivo; (*person*) arrivato/a; **a new ~** un nuovo venuto; (*baby*) un neonato.

arrive [ə'raɪv] vi arrivare; **to ~ at** vt fus (*fig*) raggiungere.

arrogant ['ærəgənt] a arrogante.

arrow ['ærəʊ] n freccia.

arse [ɑːs] n (*col!*) culo (!).

arson ['ɑːsn] n incendio doloso.

art [ɑːt] n arte f; (*craft*) mestiere m; **A~s** npl (*SCOL*) Lettere fpl.

artefact ['ɑːtɪfækt] n manufatto.

artery ['ɑːtərɪ] n arteria.

art gallery n galleria d'arte.

arthritis [ɑː'θraɪtɪs] n artrite f.

artichoke ['ɑːtɪtʃəʊk] n carciofo; **Jerusalem ~** topinambur m inv.

article ['ɑːtɪkl] n articolo; (*Brit LAW: training*): **~s** npl contratto di tirocinio; **~ of clothing** capo di vestiario.

articulate a [ɑː'tɪkjulɪt] (*person*) che si esprime forbitamente; (*speech*) articolato(a) // vi [ɑː'tɪkjuleɪt] articolare; **~d lorry** n (*Brit*) autotreno.

artificial [ɑːtɪ'fɪʃəl] a artificiale; **~ respiration** n respirazione f artificiale.

artillery [ɑː'tɪlərɪ] n artiglieria.

artisan ['ɑːtɪzæn] n artigiano/a.

artist ['ɑːtɪst] n artista m/f; **~ic** [ɑː'tɪstɪk] a artistico(a); **~ry** n arte f.

artless ['ɑːtlɪs] a semplice, ingenuo(a).

art school n scuola d'arte.

as [æz] ♦ cj **1** (*referring to time*) mentre; **~ the years went by** col passare degli anni; **he came in ~ I was leaving** arrivò mentre stavo uscendo; **~ from tomorrow** da domani

2 (*in comparisons*): **~ big ~ grande** come; **twice ~ big ~** due volte più grande di; **~ much/many ~** tanto quanto/tanti quanti; **~ soon ~ possible** prima possibile

3 (*since, because*) dal momento che, siccome

4 (*referring to manner, way*) come; **do ~ you wish** fa' come vuoi; **~ she said** come ha detto lei

5 (*concerning*): **~ for** or **to that** per quanto riguarda or quanto a quello

6: **~ if** or **though** come se; **he looked ~ if he was ill** sembrava stare male; *see also* **long, such, well**

♦ prep: **he works ~ a driver** fa l'autista; **~ chairman of the company, he ...** come presidente della compagnia, lui ...;

he gave me it ~ a present me lo ha regalato.

a.s.a.p. abbr (= *as soon as possible*) prima possibile.

ascend [ə'sɛnd] vt salire.

ascent [ə'sɛnt] n salita.

ascertain [æsə'teɪn] vt accertare.

ash [æʃ] n (*dust*) cenere f; (*also: ~ tree*) frassino.

ashamed [ə'ʃeɪmd] a vergognoso(a); **to be ~ of** vergognarsi di.

ashen ['æʃn] a (*pale*) livido(a).

ashore [ə'ʃɔː*] ad a terra.

ashtray ['æʃtreɪ] n portacenere m.

Ash Wednesday n mercoledì m inv delle Ceneri.

Asia ['eɪʃə] n Asia; **~n a**, n asiatico(a).

aside [ə'saɪd] ad da parte // n a parte m.

ask [ɑːsk] vt (*request*) chiedere; (*question*) domandare; (*invite*) invitare; **to ~ sb sth/sb to do sth** chiedere qc a qn/a qn di fare qc; **to ~ sb about sth** chiedere a qn di qc; **to ~ (sb) a question** fare una domanda (a qn); **to ~ sb out to dinner** invitare qn a mangiare fuori; **to ~ after** vt fus chiedere di; **to ~ for** vt fus chiedere.

askance [ə'skɑːns] ad: **to look ~ at sb** guardare qn di traverso.

askew [ə'skjuː] ad di traverso, storto.

asleep [ə'sliːp] a addormentato(a); **to be ~** dormire; **to fall ~** addormentarsi.

asparagus [əs'pærəgəs] n asparagi mpl.

aspect ['æspɛkt] n aspetto.

aspersions [əs'pɜːʃənz] npl: **to cast ~ on** diffamare.

asphyxiation [æsfɪksɪ'eɪʃən] n asfissia.

aspire [əs'paɪə*] vi: **to ~ to** aspirare a.

aspirin ['æsprɪn] n aspirina.

ass [æs] n asino; (*col*) scemo/a; (*US col!*) culo (!).

assailant [ə'seɪlənt] n assalitore m.

assassinate [ə'sæsɪneɪt] vt assassinare; **assassination** [əsæsɪ'neɪʃən] n assassinio.

assault [ə'sɔːlt] n (*MIL*) assalto; (*gen: attack*) aggressione f // vt assaltare; aggredire; (*sexually*) violentare.

assemble [ə'sɛmbl] vt riunire; (*TECH*) montare // vi riunirsi.

assembly [ə'sɛmblɪ] n (*meeting*) assemblea; (*construction*) montaggio; **~ line** n catena di montaggio.

assent [ə'sɛnt] n assenso, consenso.

assert [ə'sɜːt] vt asserire; (*insist on*) far valere.

assess [ə'sɛs] vt valutare; **~ment** n valutazione f.

asset ['æsɛt] n vantaggio; **~s** npl beni mpl; disponibilità fpl; attivo.

assign [ə'saɪn] vt: **to ~ (to)** (*task*) assegnare (a); (*resources*) riservare (a); (*cause, meaning*) attribuire (a); **to ~ a date to sth** fissare la data di qc; **~ment** n compito.

assist [ə'sıst] *vt* assistere, aiutare; **~ance** *n* assistenza, aiuto; **~ant** *n* assistente *m/f*; (*Brit: also:* **shop ~ant**) commesso/a.

associate [ə'səufııt] *a* associato(a); (*member*) aggiunto(a) // *n* collega *m/f*; (*in business*) socio/a // *vb* [ə'səufıeıt] *vt* associare // *vi:* **to ~ with sb** frequentare qn.

association [əsəusı'eıfən] *n* associazione *f*.

assorted [ə'sɔːtıd] *a* assortito(a).

assortment [ə'sɔːtmənt] *n* assortimento.

assume [ə'çjuːm] *vt* supporre; (*responsibilities etc*) assumere; (*attitude, name*) prendere; **~d name** *n* nome *m* falso.

assumption [ə'sʌmpfən] *n* supposizione *f*, ipotesi *f inv*.

assurance [ə'fuərəns] *n* assicurazione *f*; (*self-confidence*) fiducia in se stesso.

assure [ə'fuə*] *vt* assicurare.

astern [ə'stəːn] *ad* a poppa.

asthma ['æsmə] *n* asma.

astonish [ə'stɔnıf] *vt* stupire; **~ment** *n* stupore *m*.

astound [ə'staund] *vt* sbalordire.

astray [ə'streı] *ad:* **to go ~** smarrirsi; (*fig*) traviarsi.

astride [ə'straıd] *prep* a cavalcioni di.

astrology [əs'trɔlədʒı] *n* astrologia.

astronaut ['æstrənɔːt] *n* astronauta *m/f*.

astronomy [əs'trɔnəmı] *n* astronomia.

astute [əs'tjuːt] *a* astuto(a).

asylum [ə'saıləm] *n* asilo; (*building*) manicomio.

at [æt] *prep* **1** (*referring to position, direction*) a; **~** the top in cima; **~** the desk al banco, alla scrivania; **~** home/school a casa/scuola; **~** the baker's dal panettiere; **to look ~** sth guardare qc; **to throw sth ~** sb lanciare qc a qn
2 (*referring to time*) a; **~** 4 o'clock alle 4; **~** night di notte; **~** Christmas a Natale; **~** times a volte
3 (*referring to rates, speed etc*) a; **~** £1 a kilo a 1 sterlina al chilo; **two ~** a time due alla volta, due per volta; **~** 50 km/h a 50 km/h
4 (*referring to manner*): **~** a stroke d'un solo colpo; **~** peace in pace
5 (*referring to activity*): **to be ~** work essere al lavoro; **to play ~** cowboys giocare ai cowboy; **to be good ~** sth/doing sth essere bravo in qc/a fare qc
6 (*referring to cause*): **shocked/surprised/annoyed ~** sth colpito da/sorpreso da/arrabbiato per qc; **I went ~** his suggestion ci sono andato dietro suo consiglio.

ate [eıt] *pt of* **eat**.

atheist ['eıθııst] *n* ateo/a.

Athens ['æθınz] *n* Atene *f*.

athlete ['æθliːt] *n* atleta *m/f*.

athletic [æθ'letık] *a* atletico(a); **~s** *n* atletica.

Atlantic [ət'læntık] *a* atlantico(a) // *n:* **the ~** (**Ocean**) l'Atlantico, l'Oceano Atlantico.

atlas ['ætləs] *n* atlante *m*.

atmosphere ['ætməsfıə*] *n* atmosfera.

atom ['ætəm] *n* atomo; **~ic** [ə'tɔmık] *a* atomico(a); **~(ic) bomb** *n* bomba atomica; **~izer** ['ætəmaızə*] *n* atomizzatore *m*.

atone [ə'təun] *vi:* **to ~ for** espiare.

atrocious [ə'trəufəs] *a* pessimo(a), atroce.

attach [ə'tætf] *vt* attaccare; (*document, letter*) allegare; (*MIL: troops*) assegnare; **to be ~ed to** sb/ sth (*to like*) essere affezionato(a) a qn/qc.

attaché case [ə'tæfeı-] *n* valigetta per documenti.

attachment [ə'tætfmənt] *n* (*tool*) accessorio; (*love*): **~ (to)** affetto (per).

attack [ə'tæk] *vt* attaccare; (*task etc*) iniziare; (*problem*) affrontare // *n* attacco; (*also:* **heart ~**) infarto.

attain [ə'teın] *vt* (*also:* **to ~ to**) arrivare a, raggiungere; **~ments** *npl* cognizioni *fpl*.

attempt [ə'tempt] *n* tentativo // *vt* tentare; **to make an ~ on** sb's life attentare alla vita di qn.

attend [ə'tend] *vt* frequentare; (*meeting, talk*) andare a; (*patient*) assistere; **to ~ to** *vt fus* (*needs, affairs etc*) prendersi cura di; (*customer*) occuparsi di; **~ance** *n* (*being present*) presenza; (*people present*) gente *f* presente; **~ant** *n* custode *m/f*; persona di servizio // *a* concomitante.

attention [ə'tenfən] *n* attenzione *f*; **~!** (*MIL*) attenti!; **for the ~ of** (*ADMIN*) per l'attenzione di.

attentive [ə'tentıv] *a* attento(a); (*kind*) premuroso(a).

attic ['ætık] *n* soffitta.

attitude ['ætıtjuːd] *n* atteggiamento; posa.

attorney [ə'təːnı] *n* (*lawyer*) avvocato; (*having proxy*) mandatario; **A~ General** *n* (*Brit*) Procuratore *m* Generale; (*US*) Ministro della Giustizia.

attract [ə'trækt] *vt* attirare; **~ion** [ə'trækfən] *n* (*gen pl: pleasant things*) attrattiva; (*PHYSICS, fig: towards sth*) attrazione *f*; **~ive** *a* attraente.

attribute *n* ['ætrıbjuːt] attributo // *vt* [ə'trıbjuːt]: **to ~ sth to** attribuire qc a.

attrition [ə'trıfən] *n:* **war of ~** guerra di logoramento.

aubergine ['əubəʒiːn] *n* melanzana.

auburn ['ɔːbən] *a* tizianesco(a).

auction ['ɔːkfən] *n* (*also:* **sale by ~**) asta // *vt* (*also:* **to sell by ~**) vendere all'asta; (*also:* **to put up for ~**) mettere all'asta; **~eer** [-'nıə*] *n* banditore *m*.

audible ['ɔːdıbl] *a* udibile.

audience ['ɔ:dɪəns] n (*people*) pubblico; spettatori mpl; ascoltatori mpl; (*interview*) udienza.

audio-typist ['ɔ:dɪəu'taɪpɪst] n dattilografo/a che trascrive da nastro.

audio-visual [ɔ:dɪəu'vɪzjuəl] a audiovisivo(a); ~ **aid** n sussidio audiovisivo.

audit ['ɔ:dɪt] vt rivedere, verificare.

audition [ɔ:'dɪʃən] n audizione f.

auditor ['ɔ:dɪtə*] n revisore m.

augment [ɔ:g'mɛnt] vt, vi aumentare.

augur ['ɔ:gə*] vi: it ~s well promette bene.

August ['ɔ:gəst] n agosto.

aunt [ɑ:nt] n zia; ~**ie**, ~**y** n zietta.

au pair ['əu'pɛə*] n (*also*: ~ **girl**) (ragazza f) alla pari inv.

aura ['ɔ:rə] n aura.

auspicious [ɔ:s'pɪʃəs] a propizio(a).

austerity [ɔs'tɛrɪtɪ] n austerità.

Australia [ɔs'treɪlɪə] n Australia; ~**n** a, n australiano(a).

Austria ['ɔstrɪə] n Austria; ~**n** a, n austriaco(a).

authentic [ɔ:'θɛntɪk] a autentico(a).

author ['ɔ:θə*] n autore/trice.

authoritarian [ɔ:θɔrɪ'tɛərɪən] a autoritario(a).

authoritative [ɔ:'θɔrɪtətɪv] a (*account etc*) autorevole; (*manner*) autoritario(a).

authority [ɔ:'θɔrɪtɪ] n autorità f inv; (*permission*) autorizzazione f; the authorities npl le autorità.

authorize ['ɔ:θəraɪz] vt autorizzare.

auto ['ɔ:təu] n (*US*) auto f inv.

autobiography [ɔ:təbaɪ'ɔgrəfɪ] n autobiografia.

autograph ['ɔ:təgrɑ:f] n autografo // vt firmare.

automatic [ɔ:tə'mætɪk] a automatico(a) // n (*gun*) arma automatica; (*Brit* AUT) automobile f con cambio automatico; ~**ally** ad automaticamente.

automation [ɔ:tə'meɪʃən] n automazione f.

automaton, pl **automata** [ɔ:'tɔmətən, -tə] n automa m.

automobile ['ɔ:təməbi:l] n (*US*) automobile f.

autonomy [ɔ:'tɔnəmɪ] n autonomia.

autumn ['ɔ:təm] n autunno.

auxiliary [ɔ:g'zɪlɪərɪ] a ausiliario(a) // n ausiliare m/f.

Av. abbr = **avenue**.

avail [ə'veɪl] vt: to ~ o.s. of servirsi di; approfittarsi di // n: to no ~ inutilmente.

available [ə'veɪləbl] a disponibile.

avalanche ['ævəlɑ:nʃ] n valanga.

avant-garde ['ævɑ̃'gɑ:d] a d'avanguardia.

Ave. abbr = **avenue**.

avenge [ə'vɛndʒ] vt vendicare.

avenue ['ævənju:] n viale m.

average ['ævərɪdʒ] n media // a medio(a) // vt (*a certain figure*) fare di or in media; on ~ in media; **to** ~ **out** vi: to ~ out at aggirarsi in media su, essere in media di.

averse [ə'və:s] a: to be ~ to sth/doing essere contrario a qc/a fare.

avert [ə'və:t] vt evitare, prevenire; (*one's eyes*) distogliere.

aviary ['eɪvɪərɪ] n voliera, uccelliera.

avocado [ævə'kɑ:dəu] n (*also*: Brit: ~ **pear**) avocado m inv.

avoid [ə'vɔɪd] vt evitare.

await [ə'weɪt] vt aspettare.

awake [ə'weɪk] a sveglio(a) // vb (*pt* **awoke**, pp **awoken**, **awaked**) vt svegliare // vi svegliarsi; ~**ing** [ə'weɪknɪŋ] n risveglio.

award [ə'wɔ:d] n premio; (*LAW*) decreto // vt assegnare; (*LAW*: *damages*) decretare.

aware [ə'wɛə*] a: ~ of (*conscious*) conscio(a) di; (*informed*) informato(a) di; to become ~ of accorgersi di; ~**ness** n consapevolezza.

awash [ə'wɔʃ] a: ~ (with) inondato(a) (da).

away [ə'weɪ] a, ad via; lontano(a); two kilometres ~ a due chilometri di distanza; two hours ~ by car a due ore di distanza in macchina; the holiday was two weeks ~ mancavano due settimane alle vacanze; ~ from lontano da; he's ~ for a week è andato via per una settimana; he was working/pedalling etc ~ la particella indica la continuità e l'energia dell'azione: lavorava/pedalava etc più che poteva; to fade/wither etc ~ la particella rinforza l'idea della diminuzione; ~ game n (*SPORT*) partita fuori casa.

awe [ɔ:] n timore m; ~-**inspiring**, ~**some** a imponente.

awful ['ɔ:fəl] a terribile; ~**ly** ad (*very*) terribilmente.

awhile [ə'waɪl] ad (per) un po'.

awkward ['ɔ:kwəd] a (*clumsy*) goffo(a); (*inconvenient*) scomodo(a); (*embarrassing*) imbarazzante.

awning ['ɔ:nɪŋ] n (*of shop, hotel etc*) tenda.

awoke, awoken [ə'wəuk, -kən] pt, pp of **awake**.

awry [ə'raɪ] ad di traverso // a storto(a); to go ~ andare a monte.

axe, (*US*) **ax** [æks] n scure f // vt (*project etc*) abolire; (*jobs*) sopprimere.

axis, pl **axes** ['æksɪs, -si:z] n asse m.

axle ['æksl] n (*also*: ~-**tree**) asse m.

ay(e) [aɪ] excl (*yes*) sì.

B

B |bi:| n (MUS) si m.

B.A. n abbr = **Bachelor of Arts.**

baby |'beɪbɪ| n bambino/a; ~ **carriage** n (US) carrozzina; **~-sit** vi fare il (or la) babysitter; **~-sitter** n baby-sitter m/f inv.

bachelor |'bætʃələ*| n scapolo; B~ of Arts/Science (B.A./B.Sc.) ≈ laureato/a in lettere/scienze.

back |bæk| n (of person, horse) dorso, schiena; (of hand) dorso; (of house, car) didietro; (of train) coda; (of chair) schienale m; (of page) rovescio; (FOOTBALL) difensore m // vt (candidate: also: ~ up) appoggiare; (horse: at races) puntare su; (car) guidare a marcia indietro // vi indietreggiare; (car etc) fare marcia indietro // a (in compounds) posteriore, di dietro; ~ **seats/wheels** (AUT) sedili mpl/ruote fpl posteriori; ~ **payments** arretrati mpl // ad (not forward) indietro; (returned): he's ~ è tornato; he ran ~ tornò indietro di corsa; (restitution): throw the ball ~ ritira la palla; can I have it ~? posso riaverlo?; (again): he called ~ ha richiamato; **to ~ down** vi fare marcia indietro; **to ~ out** vi (of promise) tirarsi indietro; **to ~ up** vt (support) appoggiare, sostenere; (COMPUT) fare una copia di riserva di; **~bencher** n (Brit) membro del Parlamento senza potere amministrativo; **~bone** n spina dorsale; **~cloth** n scena di sfondo; **~date** vt (letter) retrodatare; **~dated** pay rise aumento retroattivo; **~drop** n = **~cloth**; **~fire** vi (AUT) dar ritorni di fiamma; (plans) fallire; **~ground** n sfondo; (of events) background m inv; (basic knowledge) base f; (experience) esperienza; family **~ground** ambiente m familiare; **~hand** n (TENNIS: also: **~hand stroke**) rovescio; **~handed** a (fig) ambiguo(a); **~hander** n (Brit: bribe) bustarella; **~ing** n (fig) appoggio; **~lash** n contraccolpo, ripercussione f; **~log** n: **~log of work** lavoro arretrato; **~ number** n (of magazine etc) numero arretrato; **~pack** n zaino; ~ **pay** n arretrato di paga; **~side** n (col) sedere m; **~stage** ad nel retroscena; **~stroke** n nuoto sul dorso; **~up** a (train, plane) supplementare; (COMPUT) di riserva // n (support) appoggio, sostegno; (also: **~up file**) file m inv di riserva; **~ward** a (movement) indietro inv; (person) tardivo(a); (country) arretrato(a); **~wards** ad indietro; (fall, walk) all'indietro; **~water** n (fig) posto morto; **~yard** n cortile m dietro la casa.

bacon |'beɪkən| n pancetta.

bad |bæd| a cattivo(a); (child) cattivello(a); (meat, food) andato(a) a male; his ~ leg la sua gamba malata; to go ~ andare a male.

bade |bæd| pt of **bid.**

badge |bædʒ| n insegna; (of policeman) stemma m.

badger |'bædʒə*| n tasso.

badly |'bædlɪ| ad (work, dress etc) male; ~ **wounded** gravemente ferito; he needs it ~ ne ha gran bisogno; ~ **off** a povero(a).

badminton |'bædmɪntən| n badminton m.

bad-tempered |'bæd'tempəd| a irritabile; di malumore.

baffle |'bæfl| vt (puzzle) confondere.

bag |bæg| n sacco; (handbag etc) borsa; (of hunter) carniere m; bottino // vt (col: take) mettersi in tasca; prendersi; **~s of** (col: lots of) un sacco di; **~gage** n bagagli mpl; **~gy** a largo(a), sformato(a); **~pipes** npl cornamusa.

bail |beɪl| n cauzione f // vt (prisoner: also: **grant ~ to**) concedere la libertà provvisoria su cauzione a; (boat: also: ~ **out**) aggottare; **on ~** (accused person) in libertà provvisoria su cauzione; **to ~ out** vt (prisoner) ottenere la libertà provvisoria su cauzione di; see also **bale.**

bailiff |'beɪlɪf| n usciere m; fattore m.

bait |beɪt| n esca // vt (fig) tormentare.

bake |beɪk| vt cuocere al forno // vi cuocersi al forno; **~d beans** npl fagioli mpl all'uccelletto; **~r** n fornaio/a, panettiere/a; **~ry** n panetteria; **baking** n cottura (al forno).

balance |'bæləns| n equilibrio; (COMM: sum) bilancio; (scales) bilancia // vt tenere in equilibrio; (pros and cons) soppesare; (budget) far quadrare; (account) pareggiare; (compensate) contrappesare; ~ **of trade/payments** bilancia commerciale/dei pagamenti; **~d** a (personality, diet) equilibrato(a); ~ **sheet** n bilancio.

balcony |'bælkənɪ| n balcone m.

bald |bɔːld| a calvo(a).

bale |beɪl| n balla; **to ~ out** vi (of a plane) gettarsi col paracadute.

baleful |'beɪlful| a funesto(a).

ball |bɔːl| n palla; (football) pallone m; (for golf) pallina; (dance) ballo.

ballast |'bæləst| n zavorra.

ball bearings npl cuscinetti a sfere.

ballerina |bælə'riːnə| n ballerina.

ballet |'bæleɪ| n balletto; (art) danza classica.

balloon |bə'luːn| n pallone m; (in comic strip) fumetto.

ballot |'bælət| n scrutinio.

ball-point pen |'bɔːlpɔɪnt-| n penna a sfera.

ballroom ['bɔːlrum] *n* sala da ballo.
balm [bɑːm] *n* balsamo.
ban [bæn] *n* interdizione *f* // *vt* interdire.
banana [bə'nɑːnə] *n* banana.
band [bænd] *n* banda; (*at a dance*) orchestra; (*MIL*) fanfara; **to ~ together** *vi* collegarsi.
bandage ['bændɪdʒ] *n* benda.
bandaid ['bændeɪd] *n* (*US*) cerotto.
bandwagon ['bændwægən] *n*: **to jump on the ~** (*fig*) seguire la corrente.
bandy ['bændɪ] *vt* (*jokes, insults*) scambiare.
bandy-legged ['bændɪ'legɪd] *a* dalle gambe storte.
bang [bæŋ] *n* botta; (*of door*) lo sbattere; (*blow*) colpo // *vt* battere (violentemente); (*door*) sbattere // *vi* scoppiare; sbattere.
bangle ['bæŋgl] *n* braccialetto.
bangs [bæŋz] *npl* (*US: fringe*) frangia, frangetta.
banish ['bænɪʃ] *vt* bandire.
banister(s) ['bænɪstə(z)] *n*(*pl*) ringhiera.
bank [bæŋk] *n* banca, banco; (*of river, lake*) riva, sponda; (*of earth*) banco // *vi* (*AVIAT*) inclinarsi in virata; **to ~ on** *vt fus* contare su; **~ account** *n* conto in banca; **~ card** *n* carta *f* assegni *inv*; **~er** *n* banchiere *m*; **~er's card** *n* (*Brit*) = **~ card**; **B~ holiday** *n* (*Brit*) giorno di festa (*in cui le banche sono chiuse*); **~ing** *n* attività bancaria; professione *f* di banchiere; **~note** *n* banconota; **~ rate** *n* tasso bancario.
bankrupt ['bæŋkrʌpt] *a* fallito(a); **to go ~** fallire; **~cy** *n* fallimento.
bank statement *n* estratto conto.
banner ['bænə*] *n* bandiera.
banns [bænz] *npl* pubblicazioni *fpl* di matrimonio.
baptism ['bæptɪzəm] *n* battesimo.
bar [bɑː*] *n* barra; (*of window etc*) sbarra; (*of chocolate*) tavoletta; (*fig*) ostacolo; restrizione *f*; (*pub*) bar *m inv*; (*counter: in pub*) banco; (*MUS*) battuta // *vt* (*road, window*) sbarrare; (*person*) escludere; (*activity*) interdire; **~ of soap** saponetta; **the B~** (*LAW*) l'Ordine *m* degli avvocati; **behind ~s** (*prisoner*) dietro le sbarre; **~ none** senza eccezione.
barbaric [bɑː'bærɪk] *a* barbarico(a).
barbecue ['bɑːbɪkjuː] *n* barbecue *m inv*.
barbed wire ['bɑːbd-] *n* filo spinato.
barber ['bɑːbə*] *n* barbiere *m*.
bar code *n* (*on goods*) codice *m* a barre.
bare [bɛə*] *a* nudo(a) // *vt* scoprire, denudare; (*teeth*) mostrare; **~back** *ad* senza sella; **~faced** *a* sfacciato(a); **~foot** *a*, *ad* scalzo(a); **~ly** *ad* appena.
bargain ['bɑːgɪn] *n* (*transaction*) contratto; (*good buy*) affare *m* // *vi* trattare; **into the ~** per giunta; **to ~ for** *vt fus*: **he got more than he ~ed for** gli è andata peggio di quel che si aspettasse

or che avesse calcolato.
barge [bɑːdʒ] *n* chiatta; **to ~ in** *vi* (*walk in*) piombare dentro; (*interrupt talk*) intromettersi a sproposito; **to ~ into** *vt fus* urtare contro.
bark [bɑːk] *n* (*of tree*) corteccia; (*of dog*) abbaio // *vi* abbaiare.
barley ['bɑːlɪ] *n* orzo.
barmaid ['bɑːmeɪd] *n* cameriera al banco.
barman ['bɑːmən] *n* barista *m*.
barn [bɑːn] *n* granaio.
barometer [bə'rɔmɪtə*] *n* barometro.
baron ['bærən] *n* barone *m*; **~ess** *n* baronessa.
barracks ['bærəks] *npl* caserma.
barrage ['bærɑːʒ] · *n* (*MIL, dam*) sbarramento; (*fig*) fiume *m*.
barrel ['bærəl] *n* barile *m*; (*of gun*) canna.
barren ['bærən] *a* sterile; (*soil*) arido(a).
barricade [bærɪ'keɪd] *n* barricata.
barrier ['bærɪə*] *n* barriera.
barring ['bɑːrɪŋ] *prep* salvo.
barrister ['bærɪstə*] *n* (*Brit*) avvocato/essa (*con diritto di parlare davanti a tutte le corti*).
barrow ['bærəu] *n* (*cart*) carriola.
bartender ['bɑːtendə*] *n* (*US*) barista *m*.
barter ['bɑːtə*] *n* baratto // *vt*: **to ~ sth for** barattare qc con.
base [beɪs] *n* base *f* // *vt*: **to ~ sth on** basare qc su // *a* vile.
baseball ['beɪsbɔːl] *n* baseball *m*.
basement ['beɪsmənt] *n* seminterrato; (*of shop*) interrato.
bases [beɪsiːz] *npl of* **basis**; ['beɪsɪz] *npl of* **base**.
bash [bæʃ] *vt* (*col*) picchiare.
bashful ['bæʃful] *a* timido(a).
basic ['beɪsɪk] *a* rudimentale; essenziale; **~ally** [-lɪ] *ad* fondamentalmente; sostanzialmente.
basil ['bæzl] *n* basilico.
basin ['beɪsn] *n* (*vessel, also GEO*) bacino; (*also:* **wash~**) lavabo.
basis, *pl* **bases** ['beɪsɪs, -siːz] *n* base *f*.
bask [bɑːsk] *vi*: **to ~ in the sun** crogiolarsi al sole.
basket ['bɑːskɪt] *n* cesta; (*smaller*) cestino; (*with handle*) paniere *m*; **~ball** *n* pallacanestro *f*.
bass [beɪs] *n* (*MUS*) basso.
bassoon [bə'suːn] *n* fagotto.
bastard ['bɑːstəd] *n* bastardo/a; (*col!*) stronzo (*!*).
bat [bæt] *n* pipistrello; (*for baseball etc*) mazza; (*Brit: for table tennis*) racchetta // *vt*: **he didn't ~ an eyelid** non battè ciglio.
batch [bætʃ] *n* (*of bread*) infornata; (*of papers*) cumulo.
bated ['beɪtɪd] *a*: **with ~ breath** col fiato sospeso.
bath [bɑːθ, *pl* bɑːðz] *n* (*see also* **baths**)

bagno; (*bathtub*) vasca da bagno // *vt* far fare il bagno a; **to have a ~** fare un bagno.

bathe [beɪð] *vi* fare il bagno // *vt* bagnare.

bathing ['beɪðɪŋ] *n* bagni *mpl*; **~ cap** *n* cuffia da bagno; **~ costume**, (*US*) **~ suit** *n* costume *m* da bagno.

bath: **~robe** *n* accappatoio; **~room** *n* stanza da bagno.

baths [bɑːðz] *npl* bagni *mpl* pubblici.

bath towel *n* asciugamano da bagno.

baton ['bætən] *n* (*MUS*) bacchetta, (*club*) manganello.

batter ['bætə*] *vt* battere // *n* pastetta; **~ed** *a* (*hat*) sformato(a); (*pan*) ammaccato(a).

battery ['bætərɪ] *n* batteria; (*of torch*) pila.

battle ['bætl] *n* battaglia // *vi* battagliare, lottare; **~field** *n* campo di battaglia; **~ship** *n* nave *f* da guerra.

bawdy ['bɔːdɪ] *a* piccante.

bawl [bɔːl] *vi* urlare.

bay [beɪ] *n* (*of sea*) baia; **to hold sb at ~** tenere qn a bada.

bay window *n* bovindo.

bazaar [bə'zɑː*] *n* bazar *m inv*; vendita di beneficenza.

b. & b., B. & B. *abbr* = **bed and breakfast**.

BBC *n abbr* (= *British Broadcasting Corporation*) rete nazionale di radiotelevisione in Gran Bretagna.

B.C. *ad abbr* (= *before Christ*) a.C.

be [biː], *pt* **was**, **were**, *pp* **been** ◆ *auxiliary vb* 1 (*with present participle: forming continuous tenses*): **what are you doing?** che fa?, che sta facendo?; **they're coming tomorrow** vengono domani; **I've been waiting for her for hours** sono ore che l'aspetto

2 (*with pp: forming passives*) essere; **to ~ killed** essere *or* venire ucciso(a); **the box had been opened** la scatola era stata aperta; **the thief was nowhere to ~ seen** il ladro non si trovava da nessuna parte

3 (*in tag questions*): **it was fun, wasn't it?** è stato divertente, no?; **he's good-looking, isn't he?** è un bell'uomo, vero?; **she's back, is she?** così è tornata, eh?

4 (*+ to + infinitive*): **the house is to ~ sold** abbiamo (*or* hanno *etc*) intenzione di vendere casa; **you're to ~ congratulated for all your work** dovremo farvi i complimenti per tutto il vostro lavoro; **he's not to open it** non deve aprirlo

◆ *vb + complement* 1 (*gen*) essere; **I'm English** sono inglese; **I'm tired** sono stanco(a); **I'm hot/cold** ho caldo/freddo; **he's a doctor** è medico; **2 and 2 are 4** 2 più 2 fa 4; **~ careful!** sta attento(a)!; **~ good** sii buono(a)

2 (*of health*) stare; **how are you?** come

sta?; **he's very ill** sta molto male

3 (*of age*): **how old are you?** quanti anni hai?; **I'm sixteen (years old)** ho sedici anni

4 (*cost*) costare; **how much was the meal?** quant'era *or* quanto costava il pranzo?; **that'll ~ £5, please** (fa) 5 sterline, per favore

◆ *vi* 1 (*exist, occur etc*) essere, esistere; **the best singer that ever was** il migliore cantante mai esistito *or* di tutti tempi; **~ that as it may** comunque sia, sia come sia, so ~ it sia pure, e sia

2 (*referring to place*) essere, trovarsi; **I won't ~ here tomorrow** non ci sarò domani; **Edinburgh is in Scotland** Edimburgo si trova in Scozia

3 (*referring to movement*): **where have you been?** dov'è stato?; **I've been to China** sono stato in Cina

◆ *impersonal vb* 1 (*referring to time, distance*) essere; **it's 5 o'clock** sono le 5; **it's the 28th of April** è il 28 aprile; **it's 10 km to the village** di qui al paese sono 10 km

2 (*referring to the weather*) fare; **it's too hot/cold** fa troppo caldo/freddo; **it's windy** c'è vento

3 (*emphatic*): **it's me** sono io; **it was Maria who paid the bill** è stata Maria che ha pagato il conto.

beach [biːtʃ] *n* spiaggia // *vt* tirare in secco.

beacon ['biːkən] *n* (*lighthouse*) faro; (*marker*) segnale *m*.

bead [biːd] *n* perlina.

beak [biːk] *n* becco.

beaker ['biːkə*] *n* coppa.

beam [biːm] *n* trave *f*; (*of light*) raggio // *vi* brillare.

bean [biːn] *n* fagiolo; (*of coffee*) chicco; **runner ~** fagiolino; **broad ~** fava; **~sprouts** *npl* germogli *mpl* di soia.

bear [bɛə*] *n* orso // *vb* (*pt* **bore**, *pp* **borne**) *vt* portare; (*endure*) sopportare // *vi*: **to ~ right/left** piegare a destra/sinistra; **to ~ out** *vt* (*suspicions*) confermare, convalidare; (*person*) dare il proprio appoggio a; **to ~ up** *vi* (*person*) fare buon viso a cattiva sorte.

beard [bɪəd] *n* barba.

bearer ['bɛərə*] *n* portatore *m*.

bearing ['bɛərɪŋ] *n* portamento; (*connection*) rapporto; **~s** *npl* (*also*: **ball ~s**) cuscinetti *mpl* a sfere; **to take a ~** fare un rilevamento; **to find one's ~s** orientarsi.

beast [biːst] *n* bestia; **~ly** *a* meschino(a); (*weather*) da cani.

beat [biːt] *n* colpo; (*of heart*) battito; (*MUS*) tempo; battuta; (*of policeman*) giro // *vt* (*pt* **beat**, *pp* **beaten**) battere; **off the ~en track** fuori mano; **to ~ time** battere il tempo; **~ it!** (*col*) fila!, fuori dai piedi!; **to ~ off** *vt* respingere; **to ~**

up vt (col: person) picchiare; (eggs) sbattere; ~ing n bastonata.

beautiful ['bju:tiful] a bello(a); ~ly ad splendidamente.

beauty ['bju:tɪ] n bellezza; ~ salon n istituto di bellezza; ~ spot n neo; (Brit: TOURISM) luogo pittoresco.

beaver ['bi:və*] n castoro.

became [bɪ'keɪm] pt of become.

because [bɪ'kɔz] cj perché; ~ of prep a causa di.

beck [bɛk] n: to be at sb's ~ and call essere a completa disposizione di qn.

beckon ['bɛkən] vt (also: ~ to) chiamare con un cenno.

become [bɪ'kʌm] vt (irg: like come) diventare; to ~ fat/thin ingrassarsi/dimagrire; what has ~ of him? che gli è successo?

becoming [bɪ'kʌmɪŋ] a (behaviour) che si conviene; (clothes) grazioso(a).

bed [bɛd] n letto; (of flowers) aiuola; (of coal, clay) strato; single/double ~ letto a una piazza/a due piazze or matrimoniale; ~ and breakfast (b. & b.) n (place) ≈ pensione f familiare; (terms) camera con colazione; ~clothes npl biancheria e coperte fpl da letto; ~ding n coperte e lenzuola fpl.

bedlam ['bɛdləm] n baraonda.

bedraggled [bɪ'dræɡld] a fradicio(a).

bed: ~ridden a costretto(a) a letto; ~room n camera da letto; ~side n: at sb's ~side al capezzale di qn; ~sit(ter) n (Brit) monolocale m; ~spread n copriletto; ~time n: it's ~time è ora di andare a letto.

bee [bi:] n ape f.

beech [bi:tʃ] n faggio.

beef [bi:f] n manzo; roast ~ arrosto di manzo; ~burger n hamburger m inv; ~eater n guardia della Torre di Londra.

beehive ['bi:haɪv] n alveare m.

beeline ['bi:laɪn] n: to make a ~ for buttarsi a capo fitto verso.

been [bi:n] pp of be.

beer [bɪə*] n birra.

beetle ['bi:tl] n scarafaggio; coleottero.

beetroot ['bi:tru:t] n (Brit) barbabietola.

before [bɪ'fɔ:*] prep (in time) prima di; (in space) davanti a // cj prima che + sub; prima di // ad prima; ~ going prima di andare; ~ she goes prima che vada; the week ~ la settimana prima; I've seen it ~ l'ho già visto; I've never seen it ~ è la prima volta che lo vedo; ~hand ad in anticipo.

beg [bɛɡ] vi chiedere l'elemosina // vt chiedere in elemosina; (favour) chiedere; (entreat) pregare.

began [bɪ'ɡæn] pt of begin.

beggar ['bɛɡə*] n mendicante m/f.

begin [bɪ'ɡɪn], pt began, pp begun vt, vi cominciare; to ~ doing or to do sth incominciare a fare qc; ~ner

n principiante m/f; ~ning n inizio, principio.

begun [bɪ'ɡʌn] pp of begin.

behalf [bɪ'hɑ:f] n: on ~ of per conto di; a nome di.

behave [bɪ'heɪv] vi comportarsi; (well: also: ~ o.s.) comportarsi bene.

behaviour, (US) **behavior** [bɪ'heɪvjə*] n comportamento, condotta.

behead [bɪ'hɛd] vt decapitare.

beheld [bɪ'hɛld] pt, pp of behold.

behind [bɪ'haɪnd] prep dietro; (followed by pronoun) dietro di; (time) in ritardo con // ad dietro; in ritardo // n didietro; to be ~ (schedule) essere in ritardo rispetto al programma; ~ the scenes (fig) dietro le quinte.

behold [bɪ'həuld] vt (irg: like hold) vedere, scorgere.

beige [beɪʒ] a beige inv.

being ['bi:ɪŋ] n essere m; to come into ~ cominciare ad esistere.

belated [bɪ'leɪtɪd] a tardo(a).

belch [bɛltʃ] vi ruttare // vt (gen: ~ out: smoke etc) eruttare.

belfry ['bɛlfrɪ] n campanile m.

Belgian ['bɛldʒən] a, n belga (m/f).

Belgium ['bɛldʒəm] n Belgio.

belie [bɪ'laɪ] vt smentire.

belief [bɪ'li:f] n (opinion) opinione f, convinzione f; (trust, faith) fede f; (acceptance as true) credenza.

believe [bɪ'li:v] vt, vi credere; to ~ in (God) credere in; (ghosts) credere a; (method) avere fiducia in; ~r n (REL) credente m/f; (in idea, activity): to be a ~r in credere in.

belittle [bɪ'lɪtl] vt sminuire.

bell [bɛl] n campana; (small, on door, electric) campanello.

bellow ['bɛləu] vi muggire.

bellows ['bɛləuz] npl soffietto.

belly ['bɛlɪ] n pancia.

belong [bɪ'lɔŋ] vi: to ~ to appartenere a; (club etc) essere socio di; this book ~s here questo libro va qui; ~ings npl cose fpl, roba.

beloved [bɪ'lʌvɪd] a adorato(a).

below [bɪ'ləu] prep sotto, al di sotto di // ad sotto, di sotto; giù; see ~ vedi sotto or oltre.

belt [bɛlt] n cintura; (TECH) cinghia // vt (thrash) picchiare // vi (col) filarsela; ~way n (US AUT: ring road) circonvallazione f; (: motorway) autostrada.

bemused [bɪ'mju:zd] a perplesso(a), stupito(a).

bench [bɛntʃ] n panca; (in workshop) banco; the B~ (LAW) la Corte.

bend [bɛnd] vb (pt, pp bent) vt curvare; (leg, arm) piegare // vi curvarsi; piegarsi // n (Brit: in road) curva; (in pipe, river) gomito; to ~ down vi chinarsi; to ~ over vi piegarsi.

beneath |bɪ'niːθ| *prep* sotto, al di sotto di; (*unworthy of*) indegno(a) di // *ad* sotto, di sotto.

benefactor |'benɪfæktə*| *n* benefattore *m*.

beneficial |benɪ'fɪʃəl| *a* che fa bene; vantaggioso(a).

benefit |'benɪfɪt| *n* beneficio, vantaggio; (*allowance of money*) indennità *f inv* // *vt* far bene a // *vi*: he'll ~ from it ne trarrà beneficio *or* profitto.

benevolent |bɪ'nevələnt| *a* benevolo(a).

benign |bɪ'naɪn| *a* (*person, smile*) benevolo(a); (*MED*) benigno(a).

bent |bent| *pt, pp of* **bend** // *n* inclinazione *f* // *a* (col: *dishonest*) losco(a); to be ~ on essere deciso(a) a.

bequest |bɪ'kwest| *n* lascito.

bereaved |bɪ'riːvd| *n*: the ~ i familiari in lutto.

beret |'bereɪ| *n* berretto.

berm |bəːm| *n* (*US AUT*) corsia d'emergenza.

berry |'berɪ| *n* bacca.

berserk |bə'səːk| *a*: to go ~ montare su tutte le furie.

berth |bəːθ| *n* (*bed*) cuccetta; (*for ship*) ormeggio // *vi* (*in harbour*) entrare in porto; (*at anchor*) gettare l'ancora.

beseech |bɪ'siːtʃ|, *pt, pp* besought *vt* implorare.

beset, *pt, pp* beset |bɪ'set| *vt* assalire.

beside |bɪ'saɪd| *prep* accanto a; to be ~ o.s. (with anger) essere fuori di sé; that's ~ the point non c'entra.

besides |bɪ'saɪdz| *ad* inoltre, per di più // *prep* oltre a; a parte.

besiege |bɪ'siːdʒ| *vt* (*town*) assediare; (*fig*) tempestare.

besought |bɪ'sɔːt| *pt, pp of* **beseech**.

best |best| *a* migliore // *ad* meglio; the ~ part of (*quantity*) la maggior parte di; at ~ tutt'al più; to make the ~ of sth cavare il meglio possibile da qc; to do one's ~ fare del proprio meglio; to the ~ of my knowledge per quel che ne so; to the ~ of my ability al massimo delle mie capacità; ~ man *n* testimone *m* dello sposo.

bestow |bɪ'stəu| *vt* accordare; (*title*) conferire.

bet |bet| *n* scommessa // *vt, vi* (*pt, pp* bet *or* betted) scommettere.

betray |bɪ'treɪ| *vt* tradire; ~al *n* tradimento.

better |'betə*| *a* migliore // *ad* meglio // *vt* migliorare // *n*: to get the ~ of avere la meglio su; you had ~ do it è meglio che lo faccia; he thought ~ of it cambiò idea; to get ~ migliorare; ~ off *a* più ricco(a); (*fig*): you'd be ~ off this way starebbe meglio così.

betting |'betɪŋ| *n* scommesse *fpl*; ~ shop *n* (*Brit*) ufficio dell'allibratore.

between |bɪ'twiːn| *prep* tra // *ad* in mezzo, nel mezzo.

beverage |'bevərɪdʒ| *n* bevanda.

bevy |'bevɪ| *n* banda.

beware |bɪ'weə*| *vt, vi*: to ~ (of) stare attento(a) (a).

bewildered |bɪ'wɪldəd| *a* sconcertato(a), confuso(a).

bewitching |bɪ'wɪtʃɪŋ| *a* affascinante.

beyond |bɪ'jɔnd| *prep* (*in space*) oltre; (*exceeding*) al di sopra di // *ad* di là; ~ doubt senza dubbio.

bias |'baɪəs| *n* (*prejudice*) pregiudizio; (*preference*) preferenza; ~(s)ed *a* parziale.

bib |bɪb| *n* bavaglino.

Bible |'baɪbl| *n* Bibbia.

bicarbonate of soda |baɪ'kɑːbənɪt-| *n* bicarbonato (di sodio).

bicker |'bɪkə*| *vi* bisticciare.

bicycle |'baɪsɪkl| *n* bicicletta.

bid |bɪd| *n* offerta; (*attempt*) tentativo // *vb* (*pt* bade |bæd| *or* bid, *pp* bidden |'bɪdn| *or* bid) *vi* fare un'offerta // *vt* fare un'offerta di; to ~ sb good day dire buon giorno a qn; ~der *n*: the highest ~der il maggior offerente; ~ding *n* offerte *fpl*.

bide |baɪd| *vt*: to ~ one's time aspettare il momento giusto.

bier |bɪə*| *n* bara.

bifocals |baɪ'fəuklz| *npl* occhiali *mpl* bifocali.

big |bɪg| *a* grande; grosso(a).

big dipper |-'dɪpə*| *n* montagne *fpl* russe, otto *m inv* volante.

bigheaded |'bɪg'hedɪd| *a* presuntuoso(a).

bigot |'bɪgət| *n* persona gretta; ~ed *a* gretto(a); ~ry *n* grettezza.

big top *n* tendone *m* del circo.

bike |baɪk| *n* bici *f inv*.

bikini |bɪ'kiːnɪ| *n* bikini *m inv*.

bilingual |baɪ'lɪŋgwəl| *a* bilingue.

bill |bɪl| *n* conto; (*POL*) atto; (*US: banknote*) banconota; (*of bird*) becco; "post no ~s" "divieto di affissione"; to fit *or* fill the ~ (*fig*) fare al caso; ~board *n* tabellone *m*.

billet |'bɪlɪt| *n* alloggio.

billfold |'bɪlfəuld| *n* (*US*) portafoglio.

billiards |'bɪljədz| *n* biliardo.

billion |'bɪljən| *n* (*Brit*) bilione *m*; (*US*) miliardo.

bin |bɪn| *n* (*for coal, rubbish*) bidone *m*; (*for bread*) cassetta; (*dust*~) pattumiera; (*litter* ~) cestino.

bind |baɪnd|, *pt, pp* bound *vt* legare; (*oblige*) obbligare; ~ing *n* (*of book*) legatura // *a* (*contract*) vincolante.

binge |bɪndʒ| *n* (*col*): to go on a ~ fare baldoria.

bingo |'bɪŋgəu| *n* gioco simile alla tombola.

binoculars |bɪ'nɔkjuləz| *npl* binocolo.

bio... |baɪə'...| *prefix*: ~chemistry *n* biochimica; ~graphy |baɪ'ɔgrəfɪ| *n* bio-

grafia; **~logical** *a* biologico(a); **~logy**
[baɪˈɒlədʒɪ] *n* biologia.

birch [bəːtʃ] *n* betulla.

bird [bəːd] *n* uccello; (*Brit: col: girl*)
bambola; **~'s eye view** *n* vista
panoramica; **~ watcher** *n* ornitologo/a
dilettante.

Biro [ˈbaɪrəu] *n* ℞ biro *f inv* ℞.

birth [bəːθ] *n* nascita; **~ certificate** *n*
certificato di nascita; **~ control** *n* controllo delle nascite; contraccezione *f*;
~day *n* compleanno; **~ rate** *n* indice *m*
di natalità.

biscuit [ˈbɪskɪt] *n* (*Brit*) biscotto.

bisect [baɪˈsɛkt] *vt* tagliare in due
(parti).

bishop [ˈbɪʃəp] *n* vescovo.

bit [bɪt] *pt of* **bite** // *n* pezzo; (*of tool*)
punta; (*COMPUT*) bit *m inv*; (*of horse*)
morso; a ~ of un po' di; a ~ mad un po'
matto; ~ **by** ~ a poco a poco.

bitch [bɪtʃ] *n* (*dog*) cagna; (*col!*) vacca.

bite [baɪt] *vt*, *vi* (*pt* **bit** [bɪt], *pp* **bitten**
[ˈbɪtn]) mordere // *n* morso; (*insect* ~)
puntura; (*mouthful*) boccone *m*; let's
have a ~ (to eat) mangiamo un
boccone; **to** ~ **one's nails** mangiarsi le
unghie.

bitter [ˈbɪtə*] *a* amaro(a); (*wind,
criticism*) pungente // *n* (*Brit: beer*)
birra amara; **~ness** *n* amarezza; gusto
amaro.

blab [blæb] *vi* parlare troppo.

black [blæk] *a* nero(a) // *n* nero;
(*person*): B~ negro/a // *vt* (*Brit IN-
DUSTRY*) boicottare; **to give sb a ~ eye**
fare un occhio nero a qn; in the ~ (*bank
account*) in attivo; ~ **and blue** *a*
tutto(a) pesto(a); **~berry** *n* mora;
~bird *n* merlo; **~board** *n* lavagna;
~currant *n*· ribes *m inv*; **~en** *vt*
annerire; ~ **ice** *n* strato trasparente di
ghiaccio; **~leg** *n* (*Brit*) crumiro; **~list**
n lista nera; **~mail** *n* ricatto // *vt*
ricattare; ~ **market** *n* mercato nero;
~out *n* oscuramento; (*fainting*)
svenimento; **the B~ Sea** *n* il Mar
Nero; ~ **sheep** *n* pecora nera; **~smith**
n fabbro ferraio; ~ **spot** *n* (*AUT*) luogo
famigerato per gli incidenti; (*for unemployment etc*) zona critica.

bladder [ˈblædə*] *n* vescica.

blade [bleɪd] *n* lama; (*of oar*) pala; ~ **of**
grass filo d'erba.

blame [bleɪm] *n* colpa // *vt*: to ~ sb/sth
for sth dare la colpa di qc a qn/qc; who's
to ~? chi è colpevole?

bland [blænd] *a* mite; (*taste*) blando(a).

blank [blæŋk] *a* bianco(a); (*look*) di-
stratto(a) // *n* spazio vuoto; (*cartridge*)
cartuccia a salve; ~ **cheque** *n* assegno
in bianco.

blanket [ˈblæŋkɪt] *n* coperta.

blare [blɛə*] *vi* strombettare.

blasphemy [ˈblæsfɪmɪ] *n* bestemmia.

blast [blɑːst] *n* raffica di vento;
esplosione *f* // *vt* far saltare; **~-off** *n*
(*SPACE*) lancio.

blatant [ˈbleɪtənt] *a* flagrante.

blaze [bleɪz] *n* (*fire*)· incendio; (*fig*)
vampata // *vi* (*fire*) ardere,
fiammeggiare; (*fig*) infiammarsi // *vt*: to
~ a trail (*fig*) tracciare una via nuova.

blazer [ˈbleɪzə*] *n* blazer *m inv*.

bleach [bliːtʃ] *n* (*also*: **household ~**)
varechina // *vt* (*material*) candeggiare;
~ed *a* (*hair*) decolorato(a); **~ers** *npl*
(*US SPORT*) posti *mpl* di gradinata.

bleak [bliːk] *a* tetro(a).

bleary-eyed [ˈblɪərˈaɪd] *a* dagli occhi
offuscati.

bleat [bliːt] *vi* belare.

bleed, *pt*, *pp* **bled** [bliːd, blɛd] *vt*
dissanguare // *vi* sanguinare; **my nose is**
~ing mi viene fuori sangue dal naso.

bleeper [ˈbliːpə*] *n* (*device*) cicalino.

blemish [ˈblɛmɪʃ] *n* macchia.

blend [blɛnd] *n* miscela // *vt* mescolare //
vi (*colours etc*) armonizzare.

bless, *pt*, *pp* **blessed** *or* **blest** [blɛs,
blɛst] *vt* benedire; **~ing** *n* benedizione *f*;
fortuna.

blew [bluː] *pt of* **blow**.

blight [blaɪt] *n* (*of plants*) golpe *f* // *vt*
(*hopes etc*) deludere; (*life*) rovinare.

blimey [ˈblaɪmɪ] *excl* (*Brit col*) accidenti!

blind [blaɪnd] *a* cieco(a) // *n* (*for window*)
avvolgibile *m*; (*Venetian* ~) veneziana //
vt accecare; ~ **alley** *n* vicolo cieco; ~
corner *n* (*Brit*) svolta cieca; **~fold** *n*
benda // *a*, *ad* bendato(a) // *vt* bendare
gli occhi a; **~ly** *ad* ciecamente; **~ness**
n cecità; ~ **spot** *n* (*AUT etc*) punto
cieco; (*fig*) punto debole.

blink [blɪŋk] *vi* battere gli occhi; (*light*)
lampeggiare; **~ers** *npl* paraocchi *mpl*.

bliss [blɪs] *n* estasi *f*.

blister [ˈblɪstə*] *n* (*on skin*) vescica; (*on
paintwork*) bolla // *vi* (*paint*) coprirsi di
bolle.

blithely [ˈblaɪðlɪ] *ad* allegramente.

blizzard [ˈblɪzəd] *n* bufera di neve.

bloated [ˈbləutɪd] *a* gonfio(a).

blob [blɔb] *n* (*drop*) goccia; (*stain, spot*)
macchia.

bloc [blɔk] *n* (*POL*) blocco.

block [blɔk] *n* blocco; (*in pipes*) ingombro; (*toy*) cubo; (*of buildings*) isolato //
vt bloccare; **~ade** [-ˈkeɪd] *n* blocco // *vt*
assediare; **~age** *n* ostacolo; **~buster** *n*
(*film, book*) grande successo; ~ **of flats**
n (*Brit*) caseggiato; ~ **letters** *npl* stampatello.

bloke [bləuk] *n* (*Brit col*) tizio.

blonde [blɔnd] *a*, *n* biondo(a).

blood [blʌd] *n* sangue *m*; ~ **donor** *n*
donatore/trice di sangue; ~ **group** *n*
gruppo sanguigno; **~hound** *n* segugio;
~ **poisoning** *n* setticemia; ~ **pressure**
n pressione *f* sanguigna; **~shed** *n*

spargimento di sangue; ~**shot** a: ~**shot eyes** occhi iniettati di sangue; ~**stream** n flusso del sangue; ~ **test** n analisi f inv del sangue; ~**thirsty** a assetato(a) di sangue; ~**y** a sanguinoso(a); (Brit col!): **this** ~**y** ... questo maledetto ...; ~**y awful/good** (col!) veramente terribile/ forte; ~**y-minded** a (Brit col) indisponente.

bloom [blu:m] n fiore m // vi essere in fiore.

blossom ['blɔsəm] n fiore m; (with pl sense) fiori mpl // vi essere in fiore.

blot [blɔt] n macchia // vt macchiare; **to** ~ **out** vt (memories) cancellare; (view) nascondere; (nation, city) annientare.

blotchy ['blɔtʃɪ] a (complexion) coperto(a) di macchie.

blotting paper ['blɔtɪŋ-] n carta assorbente.

blouse [blauz] n (feminine garment) camicetta.

blow [bləu] n colpo // vb (pt **blew**, pp **blown** [blu:, bləun]) vi soffiare // vt (fuse) far saltare; **to** ~ **one's nose** soffiarsi il naso; **to** ~ **a whistle** fischiare; **to** ~ **away** vt portare via; **to** ~ **down** vt abbattere; **to** ~ **off** vt far volare via; **to** ~ **out** vi scoppiare; **to** ~ **over** vi calmarsi; **to** ~ **up** vi saltare in aria // vt far saltare in aria; (tyre) gonfiare; (PHOT) ingrandire; ~**dry** n messa in piega a föhn; ~**lamp** n (Brit) lampada a benzina per saldare; ~**out** n (of tyre) scoppio; ~**torch** n = ~**lamp**.

blue [blu:] a azzurro(a); ~ **film/joke** film/barzelletta pornografico(a); **out of the** ~ (fig) all'improvviso; **to have the** ~**s** essere depresso(a); ~**bottle** n moscone m; ~ **jeans** npl blue-jeans mpl; ~**print** n (fig): ~**print** (**for**) formula (di)

bluff [blʌf] vi bluffare // n bluff m inv // a (person) brusco(a); **to call sb's** ~ mettere alla prova il bluff di qn.

blunder ['blʌndə*] n abbaglio // vi prendere un abbaglio.

blunt [blʌnt] a smussato(a); spuntato(a); (person) brusco(a) // vt smussare; spuntare.

blur [blə:*] n cosa offuscata // vt offuscare.

blurb [blə:b] n trafiletto pubblicitario.

blurt [blə:t]: **to** ~ **out** vt lasciarsi sfuggire.

blush [blʌʃ] vi arrossire // n rossore m.

blustery ['blʌstərɪ] a (weather) burrascoso(a).

boar [bɔ:*] n cinghiale m.

board [bɔ:d] n tavola; (on wall) tabellone m; (committee) consiglio, comitato; (in firm) consiglio d'amministrazione // vt (ship) salire a bordo di; (train) salire su; (NAUT, AVIAT): **on** ~ a bordo; **full** ~ (Brit) pensione completa;

half ~ (Brit) mezza pensione; ~ **and lodging** vitto e alloggio; **which goes by the** ~ (fig) che viene abbandonato; **to** ~ **up** vt (door) chiudere con assi; ~**er** n pensionante m/f; (SCOL) convittore/trice; ~**ing card** n (AVIAT, NAUT) carta d'imbarco; ~**ing house** n pensione f; ~**ing school** n collegio; ~ **room** n sala del consiglio.

boast [bəust] vi: **to** ~ (**about** or **of**) vantarsi (di) // vt vantare // n vanteria; vanto.

boat [bəut] n nave f; (small) barca; ~**er** n (hat) paglietta; ~**swain** ['bəusn] n nostromo.

bob [bɔb] vi (boat, cork on water: also: ~ **up and down**) andare su e giù // n (Brit col) = **shilling**; **to** ~ **up** vi saltare fuori.

bobby ['bɔbɪ] n (Brit col) poliziotto.

bobsleigh ['bɔbsleɪ] n bob m inv.

bode [bəud] vi: **to** ~ **well/ill** (**for**) essere di buon/cattivo auspicio (per).

bodily ['bɔdɪlɪ] a fisico(a), corporale // ad corporalmente; interamente; in persona.

body ['bɔdɪ] n corpo; (of car) carrozzeria; (of plane) fusoliera; (fig: quantity) quantità f inv; **a wine with** ~ un vino corposo; ~**building** n culturismo; ~**guard** n guardia del corpo; ~**work** n carrozzeria.

bog [bɔg] n palude f // vt: **to get** ~**ged down** (fig) impantanarsi.

boggle ['bɔgl] vi: **the mind** ~**s** è incredibile.

bogus ['bəugəs] a falso(a); finto(a).

boil [bɔɪl] vt, vi bollire // n (MED) foruncolo; **to come to the** (Brit) or **a** (US) ~ raggiungere l'ebollizione; **to** ~ **down** vi (fig): **to** ~ **down to** ridursi a; **to** ~ **over** vi traboccare (bollendo); ~**ed egg** n uovo alla coque; ~**ed potatoes** npl patate fpl bollite or lesse; ~**er** n caldaia; ~**er suit** n (Brit) tuta; ~**ing point** n punto di ebollizione.

boisterous ['bɔɪstərəs] a chiassoso(a).

bold [bəuld] a audace; (child) impudente; (outline) chiaro(a); (colour) deciso(a).

bollard ['bɔləd] n (Brit AUT) colonnina luminosa.

bolster ['bəulstə*] n capezzale m; **to** ~ **up** vt sostenere.

bolt [bəult] n chiavistello; (with nut) bullone m // ad: ~ **upright** diritto(a) come un fuso // vt serrare; (food) mangiare in fretta // vi scappare via.

bomb [bɔm] n bomba // vt bombardare; ~ **disposal unit** n corpo degli artificieri; ~**er** n (AVIAT) bombardiere m; ~**shell** n (fig) notizia bomba.

bona fide ['bəunə'faɪdɪ] a sincero(a); (offer) onesto(a).

bond [bɔnd] n legame m; (binding

promise, FINANCE) obbligazione *f*; (COMM): **in ~** in attesa di sdoganamento.

bondage ['bɔndɪdʒ] *n* schiavitù *f*.

bone [bəun] *n* osso; *(of fish)* spina, lisca // *vt* disossare; togliere le spine a; **~ idle, ~ lazy** *a* pigrissimo(a).

bonfire ['bɔnfaɪə*] *n* falò *m inv*.

bonnet ['bɔnɪt] *n* cuffia; *(Brit: of car)* cofano.

bonus ['bəunəs] *n* premio.

bony ['bəunɪ] *a (arm, face,* MED: *tissue)* osseo(a); *(meat)* pieno(a) di ossi; *(fish)* pieno(a) di spine.

boo [bu:] *excl* ba! // *vt* fischiare // *n* fischio.

booby trap ['bu:bɪ-] *n* trappola.

book [buk] *n* libro; *(of stamps etc)* blocchetto // *vt (ticket, seat, room)* prenotare; *(driver)* multare; *(football player)* ammonire; **~s** *npl* (COMM) conti *mpl*; **~case** *n* scaffale *m*; **~ing office** *n (Brit* RAIL) biglietteria; *(:* THEATRE) botteghino; **~-keeping** *n* contabilità; **~let** *n* libricino; **~maker** *n* allibratore *m*; **~seller** *n* libraio; **~shop, ~ store** *n* libreria.

boom [bu:m] *n (noise)* rimbombo; *(busy period)* boom *m inv* // *vi* rimbombare; andare a gonfie vele.

boon [bu:n] *n* vantaggio.

boost [bu:st] *n* spinta // *vt* spingere; **~er** *n* (MED) richiamo.

boot [bu:t] *n* stivale *m*; *(for hiking)* scarpone *m* da montagna; *(for football etc)* scarpa; *(Brit: of car)* portabagagli *m inv* // *vt* (COMPUT) inizializzare; **to ~** *(in addition)* per giunta, in più.

booth [bu:ð] *n (at fair)* baraccone *m*; *(of cinema, telephone, voting* ~) cabina.

booty ['bu:tɪ] *n* bottino.

booze [bu:z] *n (col)* alcool *m*.

border ['bɔ:də*] *n* orlo; margine *m*; *(of a country)* frontiera; the **B~s** *la zona di confine tra l'Inghilterra e la Scozia;* **to ~ on** *vt fus* confinare con; **~line** *n (fig)* linea di demarcazione; **~line case** *n* caso limite.

bore [bɔ:*] *pt of* bear // *vt (hole)* perforare; *(person)* annoiare // *n (person)* seccatore/trice; *(of gun)* calibro; **to be ~d** annoiarsi; **~dom** *n* noia; **boring** *a* noioso(a).

born [bɔ:n] *a:* **to be ~** nascere; **I was ~ in 1960** sono nato nel 1960.

borne [bɔ:n] *pp of* bear.

borough ['bʌrə] *n* comune *m*.

borrow ['bɔrəu] *vt:* **to ~ sth (from sb)** prendere in prestito qc (da qn).

bosom ['buzəm] *n* petto; *(fig)* seno.

boss [bɔs] *n* capo // *vt* comandare; **~y** *a* prepotente.

bosun ['bəusn] *n* nostromo.

botany ['bɔtənɪ] *n* botanica.

botch [bɔtʃ] *vt (also:* **~ up)** fare un pa-

sticcio di.

both [bəuθ] *a* entrambi(e), tutt'e due // *pronoun:* **~ (of them)** entrambi(e); **~ of us went, we ~ went** ci siamo andati tutt'e due // *ad:* **they sell ~ meat and poultry** vendono insieme la carne ed il pollame.

bother ['bɔðə*] *vt (worry)* preoccupare; *(annoy)* infastidire // *vi (gen:* **~ o.s.)** preoccuparsi // *n:* **it is a ~ to have to do** è una seccatura dover fare; **it was no ~** non c'era problema; **to ~ doing sth** darsi la pena di fare qc.

bottle ['bɔtl] *n* bottiglia; *(baby's)* biberon *m inv* // *vt* imbottigliare; **to ~ up** *vt* contenere; **~neck** *n* ingorgo; **~-opener** *n* apribottiglie *m inv*.

bottom ['bɔtəm] *n* fondo; *(buttocks)* sedere *m* // *a* più basso(a); ultimo(a); **at the ~ of** in fondo a.

bough [bau] *n* ramo.

bought [bɔ:t] *pt, pp of* buy.

boulder ['bəuldə*] *n* masso (tondeggiante).

bounce [bauns] *vi (ball)* rimbalzare; *(cheque)* essere restituito(a) // *vt* far rimbalzare // *n (rebound)* rimbalzo; **~r** *n (col)* buttafuori *m inv*.

bound [baund] *pt, pp of* bind // *n (gen pl)* limite *m*; *(leap)* salto // *vt (leap)* saltare; *(limit)* delimitare // *a:* **to be ~ to do sth** *(obliged)* essere costretto(a) a fare qc; **he's ~ to fail** *(likely)* è certo di fallire; **~ for** diretto(a) a; **out of ~s** il cui accesso è vietato.

boundary ['baundrɪ] *n* confine *m*.

bourgeois ['buəʒwa:] *a, n* borghese *(m/f)*.

bout [baut] *n* periodo; *(of malaria etc)* attacco; *(*BOXING *etc)* incontro.

bow *n* [bəu] nodo; *(weapon)* arco; *(*MUS) archetto; [bau] *(with body)* inchino; *(*NAUT: *also:* **~s**) prua // *vi* [bau] inchinarsi; *(yield):* **to ~ to** *or* **before** sottomettersi a.

bowels ['bauəlz] *npl* intestini *mpl*; *(fig)* viscere *fpl*.

bowl [bəul] *n (for eating)* scodella; *(for washing)* bacino; *(ball)* boccia; *(of pipe)* fornello // *vi* (CRICKET) servire (la palla); **~s** *n* gioco delle bocce.

bow-legged ['bəu'lɛgɪd] *a* dalle gambe storte.

bowler ['bəulə*] *n* giocatore *m* di bocce; *(*CRICKET) giocatore che serve la palla; *(Brit: also:* **~ hat)** bombetta.

bowling ['bəulɪŋ] *n (game)* gioco delle bocce; **~ alley** *n* pista da bowling; **~ green** *n* campo di bocce.

bow tie *n* cravatta a farfalla.

box [bɔks] *n* scatola; *(also:* **cardboard ~)** cartone *m*; *(*THEATRE) palco // *vi* fare del pugilato; **~er** *n (person)* pugile *m*; **~ing** *n (*SPORT) pugilato; **B~ing Day** *n (Brit)* Santo Stefano; **~ing gloves** *npl* guantoni *mpl* da pugile; **~ing ring** *n* ring *m inv*; **~ office** *n* biglietteria; **~ room** *n* ripostiglio.

boy [bɔɪ] *n* ragazzo.

boycott ['bɔɪkɔt] *n* boicottaggio // *vt* boicottare.

boyfriend ['bɔɪfrɛnd] *n* ragazzo.

B.R. *abbr* = **British Rail.**

bra [brɑ:] *n* reggipetto, reggiseno.

brace [breɪs] *n* sostegno; (*on teeth*) apparecchio correttore; (*tool*) trapano // *vt* rinforzare, sostenere; **~s** *npl* (*Brit*) bretelle *fpl*; **to ~ o.s.** (*fig*) farsi coraggio.

bracelet ['breɪslɪt] *n* braccialetto.

bracing ['breɪsɪŋ] *a* invigorante.

bracken ['brækən] *n* felce *f*.

bracket ['brækɪt] *n* (*TECH*) mensola; (*group*) gruppo; (*TYP*) parentesi *f inv* // *vt* mettere fra parentesi.

brag [bræg] *vi* vantarsi.

braid [breɪd] *n* (*trimming*) passamano; (*of hair*) treccia.

brain [breɪn] *n* cervello; **~s** *npl* cervella *fpl*; **he's got ~s** è intelligente; **~child** *n* creatura, creazione *f*; **~wash** *vt* fare un lavaggio di cervello a; **~wave** *n* lampo di genio; **~y** *a* intelligente.

braise [breɪz] *vt* brasare.

brake [breɪk] *n* (*on vehicle*) freno // *vt*, *vi* frenare; **~ fluid** *n* liquido dei freni; **~light** *n* (fanalino dello) stop *m inv*.

bramble ['bræmbl] *n* rovo.

bran [bræn] *n* crusca.

branch [brɑ:ntʃ] *n* ramo; (*COMM*) succursale *f* // *vi* diramarsi.

brand [brænd] *n* marca // *vt* (*cattle*) marcare (a ferro rovente).

brand-new ['brænd'nju:] *a* nuovo(a) di zecca.

brandy ['brændɪ] *n* brandy *m inv*.

brash [bræʃ] *a* sfacciato(a).

brass [brɑ:s] *n* ottone *m*; **the ~** (*MUS*) gli ottoni; **~ band** *n* fanfara.

brassière ['bræsɪə*] *n* reggipetto, reggiseno.

brat [bræt] *n* (*pej*) marmocchio, monello/ a.

bravado [brə'vɑ:dəu] *n* spavalderia.

brave [breɪv] *a* coraggioso(a) // *n* guerriero *m* pelle rossa *inv* // *vt* affrontare; **~ry** *n* coraggio.

brawl [brɔːl] *n* rissa.

brawn [brɔːn] *n* muscolo; (*meat*) carne *f* di testa di maiale.

bray [breɪ] *vi* ragliare.

brazen ['breɪzn] *a* svergognato(a) // *vt*: **to ~ it out** fare lo sfacciato.

brazier ['breɪzɪə*] *n* braciere *m*.

Brazil [brə'zɪl] *n* Brasile *m*.

breach [bri:tʃ] *vt* aprire una breccia in // *n* (*gap*) breccia, varco; (*breaking*): **~ of contract** rottura di contratto; **~ of the peace** violazione *f* dell'ordine pubblico.

bread [brɛd] *n* pane *m*; **~ and butter** *n* pane e burro; (*fig*) mezzi *mpl* di sussi-

stenza; **~bin**, (*US*) **~box** *n* cassetta *f* portapane *inv*; **~crumbs** *npl* briciole *fpl*; (*CULIN*) pangrattato; **~line** *n*: **to be on the ~line** avere appena denaro per vivere.

breadth [brɛtθ] *n* larghezza.

breadwinner ['brɛdwɪnə*] *n* chi guadagna il pane per tutta la famiglia.

break [breɪk] *vb* (*pt* **broke** [brəuk], *pp* **broken** ['brəukən]) *vt* rompere; (*law*) violare // *vi* rompersi; (*weather*) cambiare // *n* (*gap*) breccia; (*fracture*) rottura; (*rest, also SCOL*) intervallo; (: *short*) pausa; (*chance*) possibilità *f inv*; **to ~ one's leg** *etc* rompersi la gamba *etc*; **to ~ a record** battere un primato; **to ~ the news to sb** comunicare per primo la notizia a qn; **to ~ down** *vt* (*figures, data*) analizzare // *vi* crollare; (*MED*) avere un esaurimento (nervoso); (*AUT*) guastarsi; **to ~ even** *vi* coprire le spese; **to ~ free** *or* **loose** *vi* spezzare i legami; **to ~ in** *vt* (*horse etc*) domare // *vi* (*burglar*) fare irruzione: **to ~ into** *vt fus* (*house*) fare irruzione in; **to ~ off** *vi* (*speaker*) interrompersi; (*branch*) troncarsi; **to ~ open** *vt* (*door etc*) sfondare; **to ~ out** *vi* evadere; **to ~ out in spots** coprirsi di macchie; **to ~ up** *vi* (*partnership*) sciogliersi; (*friends*) separarsi // *vt* fare in pezzi, spaccare; (*fight etc*) interrompere, far cessare; **~age** *n* rottura; **~down** *n* (*AUT*) guasto; (*in communications*) interruzione *f*; (*MED: also*: **nervous ~down**) esaurimento nervoso; **~down van** *n* (*Brit*) carro *m* attrezzi *inv*; **~er** *n* frangente *m*.

breakfast ['brɛkfəst] *n* colazione *f*.

break: **~-in** *n* irruzione *f*; **~ing and entering** *n* (*LAW*) violazione *f* di domicilio con scasso; **~-through** *n* (*MIL*) breccia; (*fig*) passo avanti; **~water** *n* frangiflutti *m inv*.

breast [brɛst] *n* (*of woman*) seno; (*chest*) petto; **~-feed** *vt*, *vi* (*irg*: *like* **feed**) allattare (al seno); **~-stroke** *n* nuoto a rana.

breath [brɛθ] *n* fiato; **out of ~** senza fiato.

Breathalyser ['brɛθəlaɪzə*] *n* ® (*Brit*) alcoltest *m inv*.

breathe [bri:ð] *vt*, *vi* respirare; **to ~ in** *vt* respirare // *vi* inspirare; **to ~ out** *vt*, *vi* espirare; **~r** *n* attimo di respiro; **breathing** *n* respiro, respirazione *f*.

breathless ['brɛθlɪs] *a* senza fiato.

breath-taking ['brɛθteɪkɪŋ] *a* sbalorditivo(a).

breed [bri:d] *vb* (*pt*, *pp* **bred** [brɛd]) *vt* allevare // *vi* riprodursi // *n* razza, varietà *f inv*; **~ing** *n* riproduzione *f*; allevamento; (*upbringing*) educazione *f*.

breeze [bri:z] *n* brezza.

breezy ['bri:zɪ] *a* arioso(a); allegro(a).

brew [bru:] *vt* (*tea*) fare un infuso di; (*beer*) fare; (*plot*) tramare // *vi* (*tea*) essere in infusione; (*beer*) essere in fermentazione; (*fig*) bollire in pentola; ~**er** *n* birraio; ~**ery** *n* fabbrica di birra.

bribe [braɪb] *n* bustarella // *vt* comprare; ~**ry** *n* corruzione *f*.

brick [brɪk] *n* mattone *m*; ~**layer** *n* muratore *m*.

bridal ['braɪdl] *a* nuziale.

bride [braɪd] *n* sposa; ~**groom** *n* sposo; ~**smaid** *n* damigella d'onore.

bridge [brɪdʒ] *n* ponte *m*; (NAUT) ponte di comando; (*of nose*) dorso; (CARDS, DENTISTRY) bridge *m inv* // *vt* (*river*) fare un ponte sopra; (*gap*) colmare.

bridle ['braɪdl] *n* briglia // *vt* tenere a freno; (*horse*) mettere la briglia a; ~ **path** *n* sentiero (per cavalli).

brief [bri:f] *a* breve // *n* (LAW) comparsa // *vt* dare istruzioni a; ~**s** *npl* mutande *fpl*; ~**case** *n* cartella; ~**ing** *n* istruzioni *fpl*; ~**ly** *ad* (*glance*) di sfuggita; (*explain, say*) brevemente.

bright [braɪt] *a* luminoso(a); (*person*) sveglio(a); (*colour*) vivace; ~**en** (*also*: ~**en up**) *vt* (*room*) rendere luminoso(a); ornare // *vi* schiarirsi; (*person*) rallegrarsi.

brilliance ['brɪljəns] *n* splendore *m*.

brilliant ['brɪljənt] *a* splendente.

brim [brɪm] *n* orlo.

brine [braɪn] *n* acqua salmastra; (CULIN) salamoia.

bring [brɪŋ], *pt, pp* **brought** *vt* portare; **to ~ about** *vt* causare; **to ~ back** *vt* riportare; **to ~ down** *vt* portare giù; abbattere; **to ~ forward** *vt* portare avanti; (*in time*) anticipare; **to ~ off** *vt* (*task, plan*) portare a compimento; **to ~ out** *vt* (*meaning*) mettere in evidenza; **to ~ round** *or* **to** *vt* (*unconscious person*) far rinvenire; **to ~ up** *vt* allevare; (*question*) introdurre; (*food: vomit*) rimettere, rigurgitare.

brink [brɪŋk] *n* orlo.

brisk [brɪsk] *a* vivace.

bristle ['brɪsl] *n* setola // *vi* rizzarsi; bristling with irto(a) di.

Britain ['brɪtən] *n* (*also*: Great ~) Gran Bretagna.

British ['brɪtɪʃ] *a* britannico(a); **the ~** *npl* i Britannici; **the ~ Isles** *npl* le Isole Britanniche; ~ **Rail (B.R.)** *n* compagnia ferroviaria britannica, ≈ Ferrovie *fpl* dello Stato (F.S.).

Briton ['brɪtən] *n* britannico/a.

brittle ['brɪtl] *a* fragile.

broach [brəʊtʃ] *vt* (*subject*) affrontare.

broad [brɔ:d] *a* largo(a); (*distinction*) generale; (*accent*) spiccato(a); **in ~ daylight** in pieno giorno; ~**cast** *n* trasmissione *f* // *vb* (*pt, pp* ~**cast**) *vt* trasmettere per radio (*or* per televisione) // *vi* fare una trasmissione; ~**en** *vt*

allargare // *vi* allargarsi; ~**ly** *ad* (*fig*) in generale; ~-**minded** *a* di mente aperta.

broccoli ['brɔkəlɪ] *n* broccoli *mpl*.

brochure ['brəʊʃjʊə*] *n* dépliant *m inv*.

broil [brɔɪl] *vt* cuocere a fuoco vivo.

broke [brəʊk] *pt of* **break** // *a* (*col*) squattrinato(a).

broken ['brəʊkn] *pp of* **break** // *a*: ~ **leg** *etc* gamba *etc* rotta; **in ~ English** in un inglese stentato; ~-**hearted** *a*: **to be ~-hearted** avere il cuore spezzato.

broker ['brəʊkə*] *n* agente *m*.

brolly ['brɔlɪ] *n* (*Brit col*) ombrello.

bronchitis [brɔŋ'kaɪtɪs] *n* bronchite *f*.

bronze [brɔnz] *n* bronzo.

brooch [brəʊtʃ] *n* spilla.

brood [bru:d] *n* covata // *vi* (*hen*) covare; (*person*) rimuginare.

brook [brʊk] *n* ruscello.

broom [brʊm] *n* scopa; ~**stick** *n* manico di scopa.

Bros. *abbr* (= *Brothers*) F.lli.

broth [brɔθ] *n* brodo.

brothel ['brɔθl] *n* bordello.

brother ['brʌðə*] *n* fratello; ~-**in-law** *n* cognato.

brought [brɔ:t] *pt, pp of* **bring**.

brow [braʊ] *n* fronte *f*; (*rare, gen*: eye~) sopracciglio; (*of hill*) cima.

brown [braʊn] *a* bruno(a), marrone // *n* (*colour*) color *m* bruno *or* marrone // *vt* (CULIN) rosolare; ~ **bread** *n* pane *m* integrale, pane nero.

brownie ['braʊnɪ] *n* giovane esploratrice *f*.

brown paper *n* carta da pacchi *or* da imballaggio.

brown sugar *n* zucchero greggio.

browse [braʊz] *vi* (*among books*) curiosare fra i libri.

bruise [bru:z] *n* ammaccatura // *vt* ammaccare.

brunette [bru:'net] *n* bruna.

brunt [brʌnt] *n*: **the ~ of** (*attack, criticism etc*) il peso maggiore di.

brush [brʌʃ] *n* spazzola; (*quarrel*) schermaglia // *vt* spazzolare; (*gen*: ~ **past, ~ against**) sfiorare; **to ~ aside** *vt* scostare; **to ~ up** *vt* (*knowledge*) rinfrescare; ~**wood** *n* macchia.

Brussels ['brʌslz] *n* Bruxelles *f*; ~ **sprout** *n* cavolo di Bruxelles.

brutal ['bru:tl] *a* brutale.

brute [bru:t] *n* bestia // *a*: **by ~ force** con la forza, a viva forza.

B.Sc. *n abbr* = **Bachelor of Science**.

bubble ['bʌbl] *n* bolla // *vi* ribollire; (*sparkle, fig*) essere effervescente; ~ **bath** *n* bagnoschiuma *m inv*.

buck [bʌk] *n* maschio (*di camoscio, caprone, coniglio etc*); (US col) dollaro // *vi* sgroppare; **to pass the ~** (**to sb**) scaricare (su di qn) la propria responsabilità; **to ~ up** *vi* (*cheer up*) rianimarsi.

bucket ['bʌkɪt] n secchio.
buckle ['bʌkl] n fibbia // vt affibbiare; (warp) deformare.
bud [bʌd] n gemma; (of flower) boccio // vi germogliare; (flower) sbocciare.
Buddhism ['budɪzəm] n buddismo.
budding ['bʌdɪŋ] a (poet etc) in erba.
buddy ['bʌdɪ] n (US) compagno.
budge [bʌdʒ] vt scostare // vi spostarsi.
budgerigar ['bʌdʒərɪgɑ:*] n pappagallino.
budget ['bʌdʒɪt] n bilancio preventivo // vi: to ~ for sth fare il bilancio per qc.
budgie ['bʌdʒɪ] n = **budgerigar**.
buff [bʌf] a color camoscio // n (enthusiast) appassionato/a.
buffalo, pl ~ or ~es ['bʌfələu] n bufalo; (US) bisonte m.
buffer ['bʌfə*] n respingente m; (COMPUT) memoria tampone, buffer m inv.
buffet n ['bufeɪ] (food, Brit: bar) buffet m inv // vt ['bʌfɪt] schiaffeggiare; scuotere; urtare; ~ car n (Brit RAIL) ~ servizio ristoro.
bug [bʌg] n (insect) cimice f; (: gen) insetto; (fig: germ) virus m inv; (spy device) microfono spia // vt mettere sotto controllo; ~bear n spauracchio.
bugle ['bju:gl] n tromba.
build [bɪld] n (of person) corporatura // vt (pt, pp built) costruire; to ~ up vt accumulare; aumentare; ~er n costruttore m; ~ing n costruzione f; edificio; (also: ~ing trade) edilizia; ~ing society n (Brit) società f inv immobiliare.
built [bɪlt] pt, pp of **build**; ~-in a (cupboard) a muro; (device) incorporato/a; ~-up area n abitato.
bulb [bʌlb] n (BOT) bulbo; (ELEC) lampadina.
bulge [bʌldʒ] n rigonfiamento // vi essere protuberante or rigonfio(a); to be bulging with essere pieno(a) or zeppo(a) di.
bulk [bʌlk] n massa, volume m; in ~ a pacchi (or cassette etc); (COMM) all'ingrosso; the ~ of il grosso di; ~y a grosso(a); voluminoso(a).
bull [bul] n toro; ~dog n bulldog m inv.
bulldozer ['buldəuzə*] n bulldozer m inv.
bullet ['bulɪt] n pallottola.
bulletin ['bulɪtɪn] n bollettino.
bulletproof ['bulɪtpru:f] a (car) blindato(a); (vest etc) antiproiettile inv.
bullfight ['bulfaɪt] n corrida; ~er n torero; ~ing n tauromachia.
bullion ['buljən] n oro or argento in lingotti.
bullock ['bulək] n giovenco.
bullring ['bulrɪŋ] n arena (per corride).
bull's-eye ['bulzaɪ] n centro del bersaglio.
bully ['bulɪ] n prepotente m // vt angariare; (frighten) intimidire.

bum [bʌm] n (col: backside) culo; (tramp) vagabondo/a.
bumblebee ['bʌmblbi:] n bombo.
bump [bʌmp] n (blow) colpo; (jolt) scossa; (on road etc) protuberanza; (on head) bernoccolo // vt battere; to ~ into vt fus scontrarsi con; ~er n paraurti m inv // a: ~er harvest raccolto eccezionale.
bumptious ['bʌmpʃəs] a presuntuoso(a).
bumpy ['bʌmpɪ] a (road) dissestato(a).
bun [bʌn] n focaccia; (of hair) crocchia.
bunch [bʌntʃ] n (of flowers, keys) mazzo; (of bananas) ciuffo; (of people) gruppo; ~ of grapes grappolo d'uva.
bundle ['bʌndl] n fascio // vt (also: ~ up) legare in un fascio; (put): to ~ sth/sb into spingere qc/qn in.
bungalow ['bʌŋgələu] n bungalow m inv.
bungle ['bʌŋgl] vt abborracciare.
bunion ['bʌnjən] n callo (al piede).
bunk [bʌŋk] n cuccetta; ~ beds npl letti mpl a castello.
bunker ['bʌŋkə*] n (coal store) ripostiglio per il carbone; (MIL, GOLF) bunker m inv.
bunny ['bʌnɪ] n (also: ~ rabbit) coniglietto.
bunting ['bʌntɪŋ] n pavesi mpl, bandierine fpl.
buoy [bɔɪ] n boa; to ~ up vt tenere a galla; (fig) sostenere; ~ant a galleggiante; (fig) vivace.
burden ['bə:dn] n carico, fardello // vt caricare; (oppress) opprimere.
bureau, pl ~x [bjuə'rəu, -z] n (Brit: writing desk) scrivania; (US: chest of drawers) cassettone m; (office) ufficio, agenzia.
bureaucracy [bjuə'rɔkrəsɪ] n burocrazia.
burglar ['bə:glə*] n scassinatore m; ~ alarm n campanello antifurto; ~y n furto con scasso.
burial ['berɪəl] n sepoltura.
burly ['bə:lɪ] a robusto(a).
Burma ['bə:mə] n Birmania.
burn [bə:n] vt, vi (pt, pp **burned** or **burnt**) bruciare // n bruciatura, scottatura; to ~ down vt distruggere col fuoco; ~er n (on cooker) fornello; (TECH) bruciatore m, becco (a gas).
burnt [bə:nt] pt, pp of **burn**.
burrow ['bʌrəu] n tana // vt scavare.
bursar ['bə:sə*] n economo/a; (Brit: student) borsista m/f; ~y n (Brit) borsa di studio.
burst [bə:st] vb (pt, pp **burst**) vt far scoppiare (or esplodere) // vi esplodere; (tyre) scoppiare // n scoppio; (also: ~ pipe) rottura nel tubo, perdita; to ~ into flames/tears scoppiare in fiamme/lacrime; to ~ out laughing scoppiare a ridere; to be ~ing with essere pronto a scoppiare di; to ~ into vt fus (room etc) irrompere in; to ~ open vi aprirsi

improvvisamente; (door) spalancarsi.

bury ['bɛrɪ] vt seppellire.

bus, **~es** [bʌs, 'bʌsɪz] n autobus m inv.

bush [buʃ] n cespuglio; (scrub land) macchia; **to beat about the ~** menare il cane per l'aia.

bushy ['buʃɪ] a cespuglioso(a).

busily ['bɪzɪlɪ] ad con impegno, alacremente.

business ['bɪznɪs] n (matter) affare m; (trading) affari mpl; (firm) azienda; (job, duty) lavoro; **to be away on ~** essere andato via per affari; **it's none of my ~** questo non mi riguarda; **he means ~** non scherza; **~like** a serio(a); efficiente; **~man/woman** n uomo/donna d'affari; **~ trip** n viaggio d'affari.

busker ['bʌskə*] n (Brit) suonatore/trice ambulante.

bus-stop ['bʌsstɔp] n fermata d'autobus.

bust [bʌst] n busto; (ANAT) seno // a (col: broken) rotto(a); **to go ~** fallire.

bustle ['bʌsl] n movimento, attività // vi darsi da fare; **bustling** a (person) indaffarato(a); (town) animato(a).

busy ['bɪzɪ] a occupato(a); (shop, street) molto frequentato(a) // vt: **to ~ o.s.** darsi da fare; **~body** n ficcanaso; **~ signal** n (US TEL) segnale m di occupato.

but [bʌt] ♦ cj ma; **I'd love to come, ~ I'm busy** vorrei tanto venire, ma ho da fare

♦ prep (apart from, except) eccetto, tranne, meno; **he was nothing ~ trouble** non dava altro che guai; **no-one ~ him can do it** nessuno può farlo tranne lui; **~ for you/your help** se non fosse per te/per il tuo aiuto; **anything ~ that** tutto ma non questo

♦ ad (just, only) solo, soltanto; **she's ~ a child** è solo una bambina; **had I ~ known** se solo avessi saputo; **I can ~ try** tentar non nuoce; **all ~ finished** quasi finito.

butcher ['butʃə*] n macellaio // vt macellare.

butler ['bʌtlə*] n maggiordomo.

butt [bʌt] n (cask) grossa botte f; (thick end) estremità f inv più grossa; (of gun) calcio; (of cigarette) mozzicone m; (Brit fig: target) oggetto // vt cozzare; **to ~ in** vi (interrupt) interrompere.

butter ['bʌtə*] n burro // vt imburrare; **~cup** n ranuncolo.

butterfly ['bʌtəflaɪ] n farfalla; (SWIMMING: also: ~ **stroke**) (nuoto a) farfalla.

buttocks ['bʌtəks] npl natiche fpl.

button ['bʌtn] n bottone m // vt (also: ~ up) abbottonare // vi abbottonarsi.

buttress ['bʌtrɪs] n contrafforte f.

buxom ['bʌksəm] a formoso(a).

buy [baɪ], pt, pp **bought** vt comprare; **to ~ sb sth/sth from sb** comprare qc per

qn/qc da qn; **to ~ sb a drink** offrire da bere a qn; **~er** n compratore/trice.

buzz [bʌz] n ronzio; (col: phone call) colpo di telefono // vi ronzare.

buzzer ['bʌzə*] n cicalino.

buzz word n (col) termine m di gran moda.

by [baɪ] ♦ prep 1 (referring to cause, agent) da; **killed ~ lightning** ucciso da un fulmine; **surrounded ~ a fence** circondato da uno steccato; **a painting ~ Picasso** un quadro di Picasso

2 (referring to method, manner, means): ~ **bus/car/train** in autobus/macchina/treno, con l'autobus/la macchina/il treno; **to pay ~ cheque** pagare con (un) assegno; **~ moonlight** al chiaro di luna; **~ saving hard, he ...** risparmiando molto, lui ...

3 (via, through) per; **we came ~ Dover** siamo venuti via Dover

4 (close to, past) accanto a; **the house ~ the river** la casa sul fiume; **a holiday ~ the sea** una vacanza al mare; **she sat ~ his bed** si sedette accanto al suo letto; **she rushed ~ me** mi è passata accanto correndo; **I go ~ the post office every day** passo davanti all'ufficio postale ogni giorno

5 (not later than) per, entro; ~ **4 o'clock** per or entro le 4; ~ **this time tomorrow** domani a quest'ora; ~ **the time I got here it was too late** quando sono arrivato era ormai troppo tardi

6 (during): ~ **day/night** di giorno/notte

7 (amount) a; ~ **the kilo/metre** a chili/metri; **paid ~ the hour** pagato all'ora; **one ~ one** uno per uno; **little ~ little** a poco a poco

8 (MATH, measure): **to divide/multiply ~ 3** dividere/moltiplicare per 3; **it's broader ~ a metre** è un metro più largo, è più largo di un metro

9 (according to) per; **to play ~ the rules** attenersi alle regole; **it's all right ~ me** per me va bene

10: (all) ~ **oneself** etc (tutto(a)) solo(a); **he did it (all) ~ himself** lo ha fatto (tutto) da solo

11: ~ **the way** a proposito; **this wasn't my idea ~ the way** tra l'altro l'idea non è stata mia

♦ ad 1 see **go**, **pass** etc

2: ~ **and** ~ (in past) poco dopo; (in future) fra breve; ~ **and large** nel complesso.

bye(-bye) ['baɪ('baɪ)] excl ciao!, arrivederci!

by(e)-law ['baɪlɔ:] n legge f locale.

by-election ['baɪɪlɛkʃən] n (Brit) elezione f straordinaria.

bygone ['baɪgɔn] a passato(a) // n: **let ~s be ~s** mettiamoci una pietra sopra.

bypass ['baɪpɑ:s] n circonvallazione f; (MED) by-pass m inv // vt fare una deviazione intorno a.

by-product |'baiprɔdʌkt| n sotto-prodotto; (fig) conseguenza secondaria.

bystander |'baistændə*| n spettatore/trice.

byte |bait| n (COMPUT) byte m inv, bicarattere m.

byword |'baiwəːd| n: to be a ~ for essere sinonimo di.

by-your-leave |'baijɔːˈliːv| n: without so much as a ~ senza nemmeno chiedere il permesso.

C

C |siː| n (MUS) do.

C.A. n abbr = **chartered accountant**.

cab |kæb| n taxi m inv; (of train, truck) cabina; (horse-drawn) carrozza.

cabaret |'kæbərei| n cabaret m inv.

cabbage |'kæbidʒ| n cavolo.

cabin |'kæbin| n capanna; (on ship) cabina.

cabinet |'kæbinit| n (POL) consiglio dei ministri; (furniture) armadietto; (also: **display** ~) vetrinetta; **~-maker** n stipettaio.

cable |'keibl| n cavo; fune f; (TEL) cablogramma m // vt telegrafare; **~-car** n funivia; ~ **television** n televisione f via cavo.

cache |kæʃ| n: a ~ of food etc un deposito segreto di viveri etc.

cackle |'kækl| vi schiamazzare.

cactus, pl **cacti** |'kæktəs, -tai| n cactus m inv.

cadet |kə'dɛt| n (MIL) cadetto.

cadge |kædʒ| vt (col) scroccare.

café |'kæfei| n caffè m inv.

cafeteria |kæfi'tiəriə| n self-service m inv.

cage |keidʒ| n gabbia.

cagey |'keidʒi| a (col) chiuso(a); guardingo(a).

cagoule |kə'guːl| n K-way m inv ®.

cajole |kə'dʒəul| vt allettare.

cake |keik| n torta; ~ of soap saponetta; **~d** a: **~d with** incrostato(a) di.

calculate |'kælkjuleit| vt calcolare; **calculation** |-'leiʃən| n calcolo; **calculator** n calcolatrice f.

calendar |'kæləndə*| n calendario; ~ **year** n anno civile.

calf |kɑːf|, pl **calves** n (of cow) vitello; (of other animals) piccolo; (also: **~skin**) (pelle f di) vitello; (ANAT) polpaccio.

calibre, (US) **caliber** |'kælibə*| n calibro.

call |kɔːl| vt (gen, also TEL) chiamare // vi chiamare; (visit: also: ~ **in**, ~ **round**): to ~ (**for**) passare a (prendere) // n (shout) grido, urlo; (visit) visita; (also: **telephone** ~) telefonata; **to be ~ed** (person, object) chiamarsi; **to be on** ~

essere a disposizione; **to** ~ **back** vi (return) ritornare; (TEL) ritelefonare, richiamare; **to** ~ **for** vt fus richiedere; **to** ~ **off** vt disdire; **to** ~ **on** vt fus (visit) passare da; (request): **to** ~ **on sb to do** chiedere a qn di fare; **to** ~ **out** vi (in pain) urlare; (to person) chiamare; **to** ~ **up** vt (MIL) richiamare; **~box** n (Brit) cabina telefonica; **~er** n persona che chiama; visitatore/trice; ~ **girl** n ragazza f squillo inv; **~-in** n (US: phone-in) trasmissione f a filo diretto con gli ascoltatori; **~ing** n vocazione f; **~ing card** n (US) biglietto da visita.

callous |'kæləs| a indurito(a), insensibile.

calm |kɑːm| a calmo(a) // n calma // vt calmare; **to** ~ **down** vi calmarsi // vt calmare.

Calor gas |'kælə*-| n ® butano.

calorie |'kæləri| n caloria.

calves |kɑːvz| npl of **calf**.

camber |'kæmbə*| n (of road) bombatura.

Cambodia |kæm'bəudjə| n Cambogia.

came |keim| pt of **come**.

camel |'kæməl| n cammello.

camera |'kæmərə| n macchina fotografica; (also: **cine-~**, **movie** ~) cinepresa; **in** ~ a porte chiuse; **~man** n cameraman m inv.

camouflage |'kæməflɑːʒ| n camuffamento; (MIL) mimetizzazione f // vt camuffare; mimetizzare.

camp |kæmp| n campeggio; (MIL) campo // vi campeggiare; accamparsi.

campaign |kæm'pein| n (MIL, POL etc) campagna // vi (also fig) fare una campagna.

campbed |'kæmp'bed| n (Brit) brandina.

camper |'kæmpə*| n campeggiatore/trice.

camping |'kæmpiŋ| n campeggio; **to go** ~ andare in campeggio.

campsite |'kæmpsait| n campeggio.

campus |'kæmpəs| n campus m inv.

can |kæn| auxiliary vb see next headword // n (of milk) scatola; (of oil) bidone m; (of water) tanica; (tin) scatola // vt mettere in scatola.

can |kæn| ◆ n, vt see previous headword ◆ auxiliary vb (negative **cannot**, **can't**; conditional and pt **could**) **1** (be able to) potere; I ~'t go any further non posso andare oltre; you ~ do it if you try sei in grado di farlo — basta provarci; I'll help you all I ~ ti aiuterò come potrò; I ~'t see you non ti vedo
2 (know how to) sapere, essere capace di; I ~ **swim** so nuotare; ~ **you speak French?** parla francese?
3 (may) potere; **could I have a word with you?** posso parlarle un momento?
4 (expressing disbelief, puzzlement etc): it ~'t **be true!** non può essere vero!; **what** CAN **he want?** cosa può mai volere?

5 (*expressing possibility, suggestion etc*): he could be in the library può darsi che sia in biblioteca; she could have been delayed può aver avuto un contrattempo.

Canada ['kænədə] n Canada m.

Canadian [kə'neɪdɪən] a, n canadese (m/f).

canal [kə'næl] n canale m.

canary [kə'nɛərɪ] n canarino.

cancel ['kænsəl] vt annullare; (*train*) sopprimere; (*cross out*) cancellare; **~lation** [-'leɪʃən] n annullamento; soppressione f; cancellazione f; (*TOURISM*) prenotazione f annullata.

cancer ['kænsə*] n cancro; C~ (*sign*) Cancro.

candid ['kændɪd] a onesto(a).

candidate ['kændɪdeɪt] n candidato/a.

candle ['kændl] n candela; (*in church*) cero; by **~light** a lume di candela; **~stick** n (*also:* ~ **holder**) bugia; (*bigger, ornate*) candeliere m.

candour, (*US*) **candor** ['kændə*] n sincerità.

candy ['kændɪ] n zucchero candito; (*US*) caramella; caramelle fpl; **~-floss** n (*Brit*) zucchero filato.

cane [keɪn] n canna; (*SCOL*) verga // vt (*Brit SCOL*) punire a colpi di verga.

canister ['kænɪstə*] n scatola metallica.

cannabis ['kænəbɪs] n canapa indiana.

canned ['kænd] a (*food*) in scatola.

cannon, pl ~ or **~s** ['kænən] n (*gun*) cannone m.

cannot ['kænɔt] = **can not.**

canny ['kænɪ] a furbo(a).

canoe [kə'nu:] n canoa; (*SPORT*) canotto.

canon ['kænən] n (*clergyman*) canonico; (*standard*) canone m.

can opener [-'əupnə*] n apriscatole m inv.

canopy ['kænəpɪ] n baldacchino.

can't [kænt] = **can not.**

cantankerous [kæn'tæŋkərəs] a stizzoso(a).

canteen [kæn'ti:n] n mensa; (*Brit: of cutlery*) portaposate m inv.

canter ['kæntə*] n piccolo galoppo.

canvas ['kænvəs] n tela.

canvassing ['kænvəsɪŋ] n (*POL*) sollecitazione f; (*COMM*) indagine f di mercato.

canyon ['kænjən] n canyon m inv.

cap [kæp] n (*also Brit FOOTBALL*) berretto; (*of pen*) coperchio; (*of bottle*) tappo // vt tappare; (*outdo*) superare.

capability [keɪpə'bɪlɪtɪ] n capacità f inv, abilità f inv.

capable ['keɪpəbl] a capace.

capacity [kə'pæsɪtɪ] n capacità f inv; (*of lift etc*) capienza.

cape [keɪp] n (*garment*) cappa; (*GEO*) capo.

capital ['kæpɪtl] n (*also:* ~ **city**) capitale f; (*money*) capitale m; (*also:* ~ **letter**) (lettera) maiuscola; ~ **gains tax** n imposta sulla plusvalenza; **~ism** n capitalismo; **~ist** a, n capitalista (m/f); **~ize: to ~ize on** vt fus trarre vantaggio da; ~ **punishment** n pena capitale.

Capricorn ['kæprɪkɔ:n] n Capricorno.

capsize [kæp'saɪz] vt capovolgere // vi capovolgersi.

capsule ['kæpsju:l] n capsula.

captain ['kæptɪn] n capitano.

caption ['kæpʃən] n leggenda.

captivate ['kæptɪveɪt] vt avvincere.

captive ['kæptɪv] a, n prigioniero(a).

captivity [kæp'tɪvɪtɪ] n prigionia; in ~ (*animal*) in cattività.

capture ['kæptʃə*] vt catturare, prendere; (*attention*) attirare // n cattura; (*data* ~) registrazione f or rilevazione f di dati.

car [ka:*] n macchina, automobile f.

carafe [kə'ræf] n caraffa.

caramel ['kærəməl] n caramello.

caravan ['kærəvæn] n (*Brit*) roulotte f inv; (*of camels*) carovana; ~ **site** n (*Brit*) campeggio per roulotte.

carbohydrates [ka:bəu'haɪdreɪts] npl (*foods*) carboidrati mpl.

carbon ['ka:bən] n carbonio; ~ **paper** n carta carbone.

carburettor, (*US*) **carburetor** [ka:bju'rɛtə*] n carburatore m.

card [ka:d] n carta; (*visiting* ~ etc) biglietto; (*Christmas* ~ etc) cartolina; **~board** n cartone m; ~ **game** n gioco di carte.

cardiac ['ka:dɪæk] a cardiaco(a).

cardigan ['ka:dɪgən] n cardigan m inv.

cardinal ['ka:dɪnl] a, n cardinale (m).

card index n schedario.

care [kɛə*] n cura, attenzione f; (*worry*) preoccupazione f // vi: to ~ **about** interessarsi di; ~ **of** (c/o) presso (c/o); in sb's ~ alle cure di qn; to take ~ (to do) fare attenzione (a fare); to take ~ of curarsi di; I don't ~ non me ne importa; to ~ **for** vt fus aver cura di; (*like*) volere bene a.

career [kə'rɪə*] n carriera // vi (*also:* ~ **along**) andare di (gran) carriera.

carefree ['kɛəfri:] a sgombro(a) di preoccupazioni.

careful ['kɛəful] a attento(a); (*cautious*) cauto(a); (**be**) ~! attenzione!; **~ly** ad con cura; cautamente.

careless ['kɛəlɪs] a negligente; (*heedless*) spensierato(a).

caress [kə'rɛs] n carezza // vt accarezzare.

caretaker ['kɛəteɪkə*] n custode m.

car-ferry ['ka:fɛrɪ] n traghetto.

cargo, pl **~es** ['ka:gəu] n carico.

car hire n autonoleggio.

Caribbean [kærɪ'bi:ən] a: **the** ~ (Sea) il Mar dei Caraibi.

caring ['kɛərɪŋ] *a* (*person*) premuroso(a); (*society, organization*) umanitario(a).

carnage ['ka:nɪdʒ] *n* carneficina.

carnation [ka:'neɪʃən] *n* garofano.

carnival ['ka:nɪvəl] *n* (*public celebration*) carnevale *m*; (*US: funfair*) luna park *m inv*.

carol ['kærəl] *n*: (Christmas) ~ canto di Natale.

carp [ka:p] *n* (*fish*) carpa; **to ~ at** *vt fus* trovare a ridire su.

car park *n* (*Brit*) parcheggio.

carpenter ['ka:pɪntə*] *n* carpentiere *m*.

carpentry ['ka:pɪntrɪ] *n* carpenteria.

carpet ['ka:pɪt] *n* tappeto // *vt* coprire con tappeto; ~ **slippers** *npl* pantofole *fpl*; ~ **sweeper** *n* scopatappeti *m inv*.

carriage ['kærɪdʒ] *n* vettura; (*of goods*) trasporto; (*of typewriter*) carrello; (*bearing*) portamento; ~ **return** *n* (*on typewriter etc*) leva (*or tasto*) del ritorno a capo; ~**way** *n* (*Brit: part of road*) carreggiata.

carrier ['kærɪə*] *n* (*of disease*) portatore/trice; (*COMM*) impresa di trasporti; (*NAUT*) portaerei *f inv*; (*on car, bicycle*) portabagagli *m inv*; ~ **bag** *n* (*Brit*) sacchetto.

carrot ['kærət] *n* carota.

carry ['kærɪ] *vt* (*subj: person*) portare; (: *vehicle*) trasportare; (*a motion, bill*) far passare; (*involve: responsibilities etc*) comportare // *vi* (*sound*) farsi sentire; **to be or get carried away** (*fig*) entusiasmarsi; **to ~ on** *vi*: **to ~ on with sth/doing** continuare qc/a fare // *vt* mandare avanti; **to ~ out** (*orders*) eseguire; (*investigation*) svolgere; ~**cot** *n* culla portabile; ~**on** *n* (*col: fuss*) casino, confusione *f*.

cart [ka:t] *n* carro // *vt* (*col*) trascinare.

carton ['ka:tən] *n* (*box*) scatola di cartone; (*of yogurt*) cartone *m*; (*of cigarettes*) stecca.

cartoon [ka:'tu:n] *n* (*PRESS*) disegno umoristico; (*satirical*) caricatura; (*comic strip*) fumetto; (*CINEMA*) disegno animato.

cartridge ['ka:trɪdʒ] *n* (*for gun, pen*) cartuccia; (*for camera*) caricatore *m*; (*music tape*) cassetta.

carve [ka:v] *vt* (*meat*) trinciare; (*wood, stone*) intagliare; **to ~ up** *vt* (*meat*) tagliare; (*fig: country*) suddividere; **carving** *n* (*in wood etc*) scultura; **carving knife** *n* trinciante *m*.

car wash *n* lavaggio auto.

case [keɪs] *n* caso; (*LAW*) causa, processo; (*box*) scatola; (*Brit: also: suit~*) valigia; **he hasn't put forward his ~ very well** non ha dimostrato bene il suo caso; **in ~ of** in caso di; **in ~ he** caso mai lui; **just in ~** in caso di bisogno.

cash [kæʃ] *n* denaro; (*coins, notes*) denaro liquido // *vt* incassare; **to pay (in)** ~ pagare in contanti; ~ **on delivery (C.O.D.)** (*COMM*) pagamento alla consegna; ~**book** *n* giornale *m* di cassa; ~ **card** *n* tesserino di prelievo; ~ **desk** *n* (*Brit*) cassa; ~ **dispenser** *n* sportello automatico.

cashew [kæ'ʃu:] *n* (*also:* ~ **nut**) anacardio.

cashier [kæ'ʃɪə*] *n* cassiere/a.

cashmere ['kæʃmɪə*] *n* cachemire *m*.

cash register *n* registratore *m* di cassa.

casing ['keɪsɪŋ] *n* rivestimento.

casino [kə'si:nəu] *n* casinò *m inv*.

cask [ka:sk] *n* botte *f*.

casket ['ka:skɪt] *n* cofanetto; (*US: coffin*) bara.

casserole ['kæsərəul] *n* casseruola; (*food*): **chicken** ~ pollo in casseruola.

cassette [kæ'sɛt] *n* cassetta; ~ **player** *n* riproduttore *m* a cassette; ~ **recorder** *n* registratore *m* a cassette.

cast [ka:st] *vt* (*pt, pp* **cast**) (*throw*) gettare; (*shed*) perdere; spogliarsi di; (*metal*) gettare, fondere; (*THEATRE*): **to ~ sb as Hamlet** scegliere qn per la parte di Amleto // *n* (*THEATRE*) complesso di attori; (*mould*) forma; (*also: plaster* ~) ingessatura; **to ~ one's vote** votare, dare il voto; **to ~ off** *vi* (*NAUT*) salpare.

castaway ['ka:stəwəɪ] *n* naufrago/a.

caster sugar ['ka:stə*-] *n* (*Brit*) zucchero semolato.

casting ['ka:stɪŋ] *a*: ~ **vote** (*Brit*) voto decisivo.

cast iron *n* ghisa.

castle ['ka:sl] *n* castello; (*fortified*) rocca.

castor ['ka:stə*] *n* (*wheel*) rotella; ~ **oil** *n* olio di ricino.

castrate [kæs'treɪt] *vt* castrare.

casual ['kæʒjul] *a* (*by chance*) casuale, fortuito(a); (*irregular: work etc*) avventizio(a); (*unconcerned*) noncurante, indifferente; ~ **wear** casual *m*; ~**ly** *ad* con disinvoltura; casualmente.

casualty ['kæʒjultɪ] *n* ferito/a; (*dead*) morto/a, vittima.

cat [kæt] *n* gatto.

catalogue, (*US*) **catalog** ['kætələg] *n* catalogo // *vt* catalogare.

catalyst ['kætəlɪst] *n* catalizzatore *m*.

catapult ['kætəpʌlt] *n* catapulta; fionda.

cataract ['kætərækt] *n* (*also MED*) cateratta.

catarrh [kə'ta:*] *n* catarro.

catastrophe [kə'tæstrəfɪ] *n* catastrofe *f*.

catch [kætʃ] *vb* (*pt, pp* **caught**) *vt* (*train, thief, cold*) acchiappare; (*ball*) afferrare; (*person: by surprise*) sorprendere; (*understand*) comprendere; (*get entangled*) impigliare // *vi* (*fire*) prendere // *n* (*fish etc caught*) retata, presa; (*trick*) inganno; (*TECH*) gancio; to ~ sb's attention *or* eye attirare l'attenzione di qn; to ~ fire prendere fuoco; to ~ sight of scorgere; to ~ on *vi* capire; (*become popular*) affermarsi, far presa; to ~ up *vi* mettersi in pari // *vt* (*also:* ~ up with) raggiungere.

catching ['kætʃɪŋ] *a* (*MED*) contagioso(a).

catchment area ['kætʃmənt-] *n* (*Brit SCOL*) circoscrizione *f* scolare; (*GEO*) bacino pluviale.

catch phrase *n* slogan *m inv*; frase *f* fatta.

catchy ['kætʃɪ] *a* orecchiabile.

category ['kætɪgərɪ] *n* categoria.

cater ['keɪtə*] *vi* (*gen:* ~ for) provvedere da mangiare (per); to ~ for *vt fus* (*Brit:* needs) provvedere a; (: *readers, consumers*) incontrare i gusti di; ~er *n* fornitore *m*; ~ing *n* approvvigionamento.

caterpillar ['kætəpɪlə*] *n* bruco; ~ track *n* catena a cingoli.

cathedral [kə'θi:drəl] *n* cattedrale *f*, duomo.

catholic ['kæθəlɪk] *a* universale; aperto(a); eclettico(a); C~ *a*, *n* (*REL*) cattolico(a).

cat's-eye [kæts'aɪ] *n* (*Brit AUT*) catarifrangente *m*.

cattle ['kætl] *npl* bestiame *m*, bestie *fpl*.

catty ['kætɪ] *a* maligno(a), dispettoso(a).

caucus ['kɔ:kəs] *n* (*POL: group*) comitato di dirigenti; (: *US*) (riunione *f* del) comitato elettorale.

caught [kɔ:t] *pt, pp of* **catch**.

cauliflower ['kɔlɪflauə*] *n* cavolfiore *m*.

cause [kɔ:z] *n* causa // *vt* causare.

caution ['kɔ:ʃən] *n* prudenza; (*warning*) avvertimento // *vt* avvertire; ammonire.

cautious ['kɔ:ʃəs] *a* cauto(a), prudente.

cavalry ['kævəlrɪ] *n* cavalleria.

cave [keɪv] *n* caverna, grotta; to ~ in *vi* (*roof etc*) crollare; ~man *n* uomo delle caverne.

caviar(e) ['kævɪɑ:*] *n* caviale *m*.

cavort [kə'vɔ:t] *vi* far capriole.

CB *n abbr* (= *Citizens' Band (Radio)*): ~ radio (set) baracchino.

CBI *n abbr* (= *Confederation of British Industries*) ≈ Confindustria.

cc *abbr* = *cubic centimetres; carbon copy.*

cease [si:s] *vt, vi* cessare; ~fire *n* cessate il fuoco *m inv*; ~less *a* incessante, continuo(a).

cedar ['si:də*] *n* cedro.

ceiling ['si:lɪŋ] *n* soffitto.

celebrate ['sɛlɪbreɪt] *vt, vi* celebrare; ~d *a* celebre; **celebration** [-'breɪʃən] *n* celebrazione *f*.

celery ['sɛlərɪ] *n* sedano.

cell [sɛl] *n* cella; (*BIOL*) cellula; (*ELEC*) elemento (di batteria).

cellar ['sɛlə*] *n* sottosuolo, cantina.

'cello ['tʃɛləu] *n* violoncello.

Celt [kɛlt, sɛlt] *n* celta *m/f*.

Celtic ['kɛltɪk, 'sɛltɪk] *a* celtico(a).

cement [sə'mɛnt] *n* cemento // *vt* cementare; ~ **mixer** *n* betoniera.

cemetery ['sɛmɪtrɪ] *n* cimitero.

censor ['sɛnsə*] *n* censore *m* // *vt* censurare; ~ship *n* censura.

censure ['sɛnʃə*] *vt* riprovare, censurare.

census ['sɛnsəs] *n* censimento.

cent [sɛnt] *n* (*US: coin*) centesimo (= *1:100 di un dollaro*); *see also* **per**.

centenary [sɛn'ti:nərɪ] *n* centenario.

center ['sɛntə*] *n, vt* (*US*) = **centre**.

centi... ['sɛntɪ] *prefix:* ~grade *a* centigrado(a); ~metre, (*US*) ~meter *n* centimetro.

centipede ['sɛntɪpi:d] *n* centopiedi *m inv*.

central ['sɛntrəl] *a* centrale; C~ **America** *n* America centrale; ~ **heating** *n* riscaldamento centrale; ~ize *vt* accentrare.

centre, (*US*) **center** ['sɛntə*] *n* centro // *vt* centrare; ~-forward *n* (*SPORT*) centroavanti *m inv*; ~-half *n* (*SPORT*) centromediano.

century ['sɛntjʊrɪ] *n* secolo; 20th ~ ventesimo secolo.

ceramic [sɪ'ræmɪk] *a* ceramico(a); ~s *npl* ceramica.

cereal ['si:rɪəl] *n* cereale *m*.

ceremony ['sɛrɪmənɪ] *n* cerimonia; to stand on ~ fare complimenti.

certain ['sə:tən] *a* certo(a); to make ~ of assicurarsi di; for ~ per certo, di sicuro; ~ly *ad* certamente, certo; ~ty *n* certezza.

certificate [sə'tɪfɪkɪt] *n* certificato; diploma *m*.

certified ['sə:tɪfaɪd]: ~ **mail** *n* (*US*) posta raccomandata con ricevuta di ritorno; ~ **public accountant (CPA)** *n* (*US*) ≈ commercialista *m/f*.

cervical ['sə:vɪkl] *a*: ~ **cancer** cancro della cervice; ~ **smear** Pap-test *m inv*.

cervix ['sə:vɪks] *n* cervice *f*.

cesspit ['sɛspɪt], **cesspool** ['sɛspu:l] *n* pozzo nero.

cf. *abbr* (= *compare*) cfr.

ch. *abbr* (= *chapter*) cap.

chafe [tʃeɪf] *vt* fregare, irritare.

chaffinch ['tʃæfɪntʃ] *n* fringuello.

chain [tʃeɪn] *n* catena // *vt* (*also:* ~ up) incatenare; ~ **reaction** *n* reazione *f* a catena; ~ **smoke** *vi* fumare una sigaretta dopo l'altra; ~ **store** *n* negozio a catena.

chair [tʃɛə*] *n* sedia; (*armchair*) poltrona; (*of university*) cattedra // *vt* (*meeting*) presiedere; ~lift *n* seggiovia; ~man *n* presidente *m*.

chalice ['tʃælɪs] *n* calice *m*.

chalk [tʃɔ:k] *n* gesso.

challenge ['tʃælɪndʒ] n sfida // vt sfidare; (statement, right) mettere in dubbio; to ~ sb to do sfidare qn a fare; **challenging** a sfidante; provocatorio(a).

chamber ['tʃeɪmbə*] n camera; ~ **of commerce** n camera di commercio; ~**maid** n cameriera; ~ **music** n musica da camera.

chamois ['ʃæmwɑ:] n camoscio; ~ **leather** ['ʃæmɪ-] n pelle f di camoscio.

champagne [ʃæm'peɪn] n champagne m inv.

champion ['tʃæmpɪən] n campione/essa; ~**ship** n campionato.

chance [tʃɑ:ns] n caso; (opportunity) occasione f; (likelihood) possibilità f inv // vt: to ~ it rischiare, provarci // a fortuito(a); to take a ~ rischiarlo; by ~ per caso.

chancellor ['tʃɑ:nsələ*] n cancelliere m; C~ **of the Exchequer** n (Brit) Cancelliere dello Scacchiere.

chandelier [ʃændə'lɪə*] n lampadario.

change [tʃeɪndʒ] vt cambiare; (transform): to ~ sb into trasformare qn in // vi cambiarsi; (be transformed): to ~ into trasformarsi in // n cambiamento; (money) resto; to ~ one's mind cambiare idea; a ~ of clothes un cambio (di vestiti); for a ~ tanto per cambiare; small ~ spiccioli mpl, moneta; ~**able** a (weather) variabile; ~ **machine** n distributore automatico di monete; ~**over** n cambiamento, passaggio.

changing ['tʃeɪndʒɪŋ] a che cambia; (colours) cangiante; ~ **room** n (Brit: in shop) camerino; (: SPORT) spogliatoio.

channel ['tʃænl] n canale m; (of river, sea) alveo // vt canalizzare; **through the usual** ~s per le solite vie; **the (English) C~** la Manica; **the C~ Islands** npl le Isole Normanne.

chant [tʃɑ:nt] n canto; salmodia // vt cantare; salmodiare.

chaos ['keɪɒs] n caos m.

chaotic [keɪ'ɒtɪk] a caotico(a).

chap [tʃæp] n (Brit col: man) tipo.

chapel ['tʃæpəl] n cappella.

chaperon ['ʃæpərəun] n accompagnatrice f // vt accompagnare.

chaplain ['tʃæplɪn] n cappellano.

chapped [tʃæpt] a (skin, lips) screpolato(a).

chapter ['tʃæptə*] n capitolo.

char [tʃɑ:*] vt (burn) carbonizzare // n (Brit) = **charlady**.

character ['kærɪktə*] n carattere m; (in novel, film) personaggio; (eccentric) originale m; ~**istic** [-'rɪstɪk] a caratteristico(a) // n caratteristica.

charade [ʃə'rɑ:d] n sciarada.

charcoal ['tʃɑ:kəul] n carbone m di legna.

charge [tʃɑ:dʒ] n accusa; (cost) prezzo; (of gun, battery, MIL: attack) carica // vt

(gun, battery, MIL: enemy) caricare; (customer) fare pagare a; (sum) fare pagare; (LAW): to ~ sb (with) accusare qn (di) // vi (gen with: up, along etc) lanciarsi // ~s npl: bank ~s commissioni fpl bancarie; is there a ~? c'è da pagare?; to reverse the ~s (TEL) fare una telefonata a carico del destinatario; to take ~ of incaricarsi di; to be in ~ of essere responsabile per; to ~ an expense (up) to sb addebitare una spesa a qn; ~ **card** n carta f clienti inv.

chariot ['tʃærɪət] n carro.

charitable ['tʃærɪtəbl] a caritatevole.

charity ['tʃærɪtɪ] n carità; (organization) opera pia.

charlady ['tʃɑ:leɪdɪ] n (Brit) domestica a ore.

charlatan ['ʃɑ:lətən] n ciarlatano.

charm [tʃɑ:m] n fascino; (on bracelet) ciondolo // vt affascinare, incantare; ~**ing** a affascinante.

chart [tʃɑ:t] n tabella; grafico; (map) carta nautica // vt fare una carta nautica di.

charter ['tʃɑ:tə*] vt (plane) noleggiare // n (document) carta; ~**ed accountant (C.A.)** n (Brit) ragioniere/a professionista; ~ **flight** n volo m charter inv.

chase [tʃeɪs] vt inseguire; (away) cacciare // n caccia.

chasm ['kæzəm] n abisso.

chassis ['ʃæsɪ] n telaio.

chastity ['tʃæstɪtɪ] n castità.

chat [tʃæt] vi (also: have a ~) chiacchierare // n chiacchierata; ~ **show** n (Brit) talk show m inv.

chatter ['tʃætə*] vi (person) ciarlare // n ciarle fpl; her teeth were ~ing batteva i denti; ~**box** n chiacchierone/a.

chatty ['tʃætɪ] a (style) familiare; (person) chiacchierino/a.

chauffeur ['ʃəufə*] n autista m.

chauvinist ['ʃəuvɪnɪst] n (male ~) maschilista m; (nationalist) sciovinista m/f.

cheap [tʃi:p] a a buon mercato; (joke) grossolano(a); (poor quality) di cattiva qualità // ad a buon mercato; ~**en** vt ribassare; (fig) avvilire; ~**er** a meno caro(a); ~**ly** ad a buon prezzo, a buon mercato.

cheat [tʃi:t] vi imbrogliare; (at school) copiare // vt ingannare; (rob) defraudare // n imbroglione m; copione m; (trick) inganno.

check [tʃek] vt verificare; (passport, ticket) controllare; (halt) fermare; (restrain) contenere // n verifica; controllo; (curb) freno; (bill) conto; (pattern: gen pl) quadretti mpl; (US) = **cheque** // a (also: ~ed: pattern, cloth) a quadretti; to ~ in vi (in hotel) registrare; (at airport) presentarsi all'accettazione // vt (luggage) depositare; to ~ out vi (in hotel) saldare il conto // vt (luggage) ritirare; **to ~ up** *vi*: to ~ up (on sth) investigare (qc); **to ~ up on sb** informarsi sul conto di qn; **~ered** *a* (*US*) = **chequered**; **~ers** *n* (*US*) dama; **~-in (desk)** *n* check-in *m inv*, accettazione *f* (bagagli *inv*); **~ing account** *n* (*US*) conto corrente; **~mate** *n* scaccomatto; **~out** *n* (*in supermarket*) cassa; **~point** *n* posto di blocco; **~room** *n* (*US*) deposito *m* bagagli *inv*; **~up** *n* (*MED*) controllo medico.

cheek [tʃiːk] *n* guancia; (*impudence*) faccia tosta; **~bone** *n* zigomo; **~y** *a* sfacciato(a).

cheep [tʃiːp] *vi* pigolare.

cheer [tʃiə*] *vt* applaudire; (*gladden*) rallegrare // *vi* applaudire // *n* (*gen pl*) applausi *mpl*; evviva *mpl*; **~s!** salute!; **to ~ up** *vi* rallegrarsi, farsi animo // *vt* rallegrare; **~ful** *a* allegro(a).

cheerio ['tʃɪərɪ'əu] *excl* (*Brit*) ciao!

cheese [tʃiːz] *n* formaggio; **~board** *n* piatto del (*or* per il) formaggio.

cheetah ['tʃiːtə] *n* ghepardo.

chef [ʃef] *n* capocuoco.

chemical ['kemɪkəl] *a* chimico(a) // *n* prodotto chimico.

chemist ['kemɪst] *n* (*Brit*: *pharmacist*) farmacista *m/f*; (*scientist*) chimico/a; **~ry** *n* chimica; **~'s (shop)** *n* (*Brit*) farmacia.

cheque [tʃek] *n* (*Brit*) assegno; **~book** *n* libretto degli assegni; **~ card** *n* carta *f* assegni *inv*.

chequered ['tʃekəd] *a* (*fig*) movimentato(a).

cherish ['tʃerɪʃ] *vt* aver caro; (*hope etc*) nutrire.

cherry ['tʃerɪ] *n* ciliegia.

chess [tʃes] *n* scacchi *mpl*; **~board** *n* scacchiera; **~man** *n* pezzo degli scacchi.

chest [tʃest] *n* petto; (*box*) cassa; **~ of drawers** *n* cassettone *m*.

chestnut ['tʃesnʌt] *n* castagna; (*also:* ~ **tree**) castagno.

chew [tʃuː] *vt* masticare; **~ing gum** *n* chewing gum *m*.

chic [ʃiːk] *a* elegante.

chick [tʃɪk] *n* pulcino; (*US col*) pollastrella.

chicken ['tʃɪkɪn] *n* pollo; **to ~ out** *vi* (*col*) avere fifa; **~pox** *n* varicella.

chicory ['tʃɪkərɪ] *n* cicoria.

chief [tʃiːf] *n* capo // *a* principale; **~ constable** *n* (*Brit*) ≈ questore *m*; **~ executive** *n* direttore *m* generale; **~ly** *ad* per lo più, soprattutto.

chilblain ['tʃɪlbleɪn] *n* gelone *m*.

child, *pl* **~ren** [tʃaɪld, 'tʃɪldrən] *n* bambino/a; **~birth** *n* parto; **~hood** *n* infanzia; **~ish** *a* puerile; **~like** *a* fanciullesco(a); **~ minder** *n* (*Brit*) bambinaia.

Chile ['tʃɪlɪ] *n* Cile *m*.

chill [tʃɪl] *n* freddo; (*MED*) infreddatura // *a* freddo(a), gelido(a) // *vt* raffreddare.

chill(i) ['tʃɪlɪ] *n* peperoncino.

chilly ['tʃɪlɪ] *a* freddo(a), fresco(a); **to feel ~** sentirsi infreddolito(a).

chime [tʃaɪm] *n* carillon *m inv* // *vi* suonare, scampanare.

chimney ['tʃɪmnɪ] *n* camino; **~ sweep** *n* spazzacamino.

chimpanzee [tʃɪmpæn'ziː] *n* scimpanzé *m inv*.

chin [tʃɪn] *n* mento.

China ['tʃaɪnə] *n* Cina.

china ['tʃaɪnə] *n* porcellana.

Chinese [tʃaɪ'niːz] *a* cinese // *n* (*pl inv*) cinese *m/f*; (*LING*) cinese *m*.

chink [tʃɪŋk] *n* (*opening*) fessura; (*noise*) tintinnio.

chip [tʃɪp] *n* (*gen pl*: *CULIN*) patatina fritta; (: *US: also:* **potato ~**) patatina; (*of wood, glass, stone*) scheggia; (*also:* **micro~**) chip *m inv* // *vt* (*cup, plate*) scheggiare; **to ~ in** *vi* (*col: contribute*) contribuire; (: *interrupt*) intromettersi.

chiropodist [kɪ'rɔpədɪst] *n* (*Brit*) pedicure *m/f inv*.

chirp [tʃəːp] *vi* cinguettare.

chisel ['tʃɪzl] *n* cesello.

chit [tʃɪt] *n* biglietto.

chivalry ['ʃɪvəlrɪ] *n* cavalleria; cortesia.

chives [tʃaɪvz] *npl* erba cipollina.

chock [tʃɔk] *n* zeppa; **~-a-block, ~-full** *a* pieno(a) zeppo(a).

chocolate ['tʃɔklɪt] *n* (*substance*) cioccolato, cioccolata; (*drink*) cioccolata; (*a sweet*) cioccolatino.

choice [tʃɔɪs] *n* scelta // *a* scelto(a).

choir ['kwaɪə*] *n* coro; **~boy** *n* corista *m* fanciullo.

choke [tʃəuk] *vi* soffocare // *vt* soffocare; (*block*) ingombrare // *n* (*AUT*) valvola dell'aria.

cholera ['kɔlərə] *n* colera *m*.

cholesterol [kə'lestərɔl] *n* colesterolo.

choose [tʃuːz], *pt* **chose**, *pp* **chosen** *vt* scegliere; **to ~ to do** decidere di fare; preferire fare.

choosy ['tʃuːzɪ] *a* schizzinoso(a).

chop [tʃɔp] *vt* (*wood*) spaccare; (*CULIN: also:* ~ **up**) tritare // *n* colpo netto; (*CULIN*) costoletta; **~s** *npl* (*jaws*) mascelle *fpl*.

chopper ['tʃɔpə*] *n* (*helicopter*) elicottero.

choppy ['tʃɔpɪ] *a* (*sea*) mosso(a).

chopsticks ['tʃɔpstɪks] *npl* bastoncini *mpl* cinesi.

choral ['kɔːrəl] *a* corale.

chord [kɔːd] *n* (*MUS*) accordo.

chore [tʃɔː*] *n* faccenda; **household ~s** faccende *fpl* domestiche.

choreographer [kɔrɪ'ɔgrəfə*] *n* coreografo/a.

chorister ['kɔrɪstə*] *n* corista *m/f*.

chortle ['tʃɔːtl] *vi* ridacchiare.

chorus ['kɔ:rəs] n coro; (repeated part of song, also fig) ritornello.

chose [tʃəuz] pt of **choose**.

chosen ['tʃəuzn] pp of **choose**.

Christ [kraist] n Cristo.

christen ['krisn] vt battezzare.

Christian ['kristiən] a, n cristiano(a); ~ity [-'æniti] n cristianesimo; ~ **name** n nome m (di battesimo).

Christmas ['krisməs] n Natale m; Merry ~! Buon Natale!; ~ **card** n cartolina di Natale; ~ **Day** n il giorno di Natale; ~ **Eve** n la vigilia di Natale; ~ **tree** n albero di Natale.

chrome [krəum], **chromium** ['krəumiəm] n cromo.

chronic ['krɔnik] a cronico(a).

chronicle ['krɔnikl] n cronaca.

chronological [krɔnə'lɔdʒikəl] a cronologico(a).

chrysanthemum [kri'sænθəməm] n crisantemo.

chubby ['tʃʌbi] a paffuto(a).

chuck [tʃʌk] vt buttare, gettare; **to ~ out** vt buttar fuori; **to ~ (up)** vt (Brit) piantare.

chuckle ['tʃʌkl] vi ridere sommessamente.

chug [tʃʌg] vi fare ciuf ciuf.

chum [tʃʌm] n compagno/a.

chunk [tʃʌŋk] n pezzo; (of bread) tocco.

church [tʃə:tʃ] n chiesa; ~**yard** n sagrato.

churlish ['tʃə:liʃ] a rozzo(a), sgarbato(a).

churn [tʃə:n] n (for butter) zangola; (for transport: also: milk ~) bidone m; **to ~ out** vt sfornare.

chute [ʃu:t] n cascata; (also: **rubbish** ~) canale m di scarico; (Brit: children's slide) scivolo.

chutney ['tʃʌtni] n salsa piccante (di frutta, zucchero e spezie).

CIA n abbr (US: = Central Intelligence Agency) CIA f.

CID n abbr (Brit: = Criminal Investigation Department) ≈ polizia giudiziaria.

cider ['saidə*] n sidro.

cigar [si'ga:*] n sigaro.

cigarette [sigə'ret] n sigaretta; ~ **case** n portasigarette m inv; ~ **end** n mozzicone m.

cinder ['sində*] n cenere f.

Cinderella [sində'relə] n Cenerentola.

cine ['sini]: ~**camera** n (Brit) cinepresa; ~**film** n (Brit) pellicola.

cinema ['sinəmə] n cinema m inv.

cinnamon ['sinəmən] n cannella.

cipher ['saifə*] n cifra; (fig: faceless employee etc) persona di nessun conto.

circle ['sə:kl] n cerchio; (of friends etc) circolo; (in cinema) galleria // vi girare in circolo // vt (surround) circondare; (move round) girare intorno a.

circuit ['sə:kit] n circuito; ~**ous** [sə:'kjuitəs] a indiretto(a).

circular ['sə:kjulə*] a, n circolare (f).

circulate ['sə:kjuleit] vi circolare // vt far circolare; **circulation** [-'leiʃən] n circolazione f; (of newspaper) tiratura.

circumstances ['sə:kəmstənsiz] npl circostanze fpl; (financial condition) condizioni fpl finanziarie.

circumvent [sə:kəm'vent] vt aggirare.

circus ['sə:kəs] n circo.

cistern ['sistən] n cisterna; (in toilet) serbatoio d'acqua.

citizen ['sitizn] n (POL) cittadino/a; (resident): the ~s of this town gli abitanti di questa città; ~**ship** n cittadinanza.

citrus fruit ['sitrəs-] n agrume m.

city ['siti] n città f inv; the C~ la Città di Londra (centro commerciale).

civic ['sivik] a civico(a); ~ **centre** n (Brit) centro civico.

civil ['sivil] a civile; ~ **engineer** n ingegnere m civile; ~**ian** [si'viliən] a, n borghese (m/f).

civilization [sivilai'zeiʃən] n civiltà f inv.

civilized ['sivilaizd] a civilizzato(a); (fig) cortese.

civil: ~ **law** n codice m civile; (study) diritto civile; ~ **servant** n impiegato/a statale; C~ **Service** n amministrazione f statale; ~ **war** n guerra civile.

clad [klæd] a: ~ (in) vestito(a) (di).

claim [kleim] vt rivendicare; sostenere, pretendere; (damages) richiedere // vi (for insurance) fare una domanda d'indennizzo // n rivendicazione f; pretesa; (right) diritto; (insurance) ~ domanda d'indennizzo; ~**ant** n (ADMIN, LAW) richiedente m/f.

clairvoyant [kleə'vɔiənt] n chiaroveggente m/f.

clam [klæm] n vongola.

clamber ['klæmbə*] vi arrampicarsi.

clammy ['klæmi] a (weather) caldo(a) umido(a); (hands) viscido(a).

clamour, (US) **clamor** ['klæmə*] vi: to ~ for chiedere a gran voce.

clamp [klæmp] n pinza; morsa // vt ammorsare; **to ~ down on** vt fus dare un giro di vite a.

clan [klæn] n clan m inv.

clang [klæŋ] n fragore m, suono metallico.

clap [klæp] vi applaudire; ~**ping** n applausi mpl.

claret ['klærət] n vino di Bordeaux.

clarify ['klærifai] vt chiarificare, chiarire.

clarinet [klæri'net] n clarinetto.

clarity ['klæriti] n clarità.

clash [klæʃ] n frastuono; (fig) scontro // vi scontrarsi; cozzare.

clasp [kla:sp] n fermaglio, fibbia // vt stringere.

class [kla:s] n classe f // vt classificare.

classic ['klæsɪk] a classico(a) // n classico; **~al** a classico(a).

classified ['klæsɪfaɪd] a (information) segreto(a), riservato(a); **~ advertisement, ~ ad** n annuncio economico.

classmate ['klɑ:smeɪt] n compagno/a di classe.

classroom ['klɑ:srum] n aula.

clatter ['klætə*] n acciottolio; scalpitio // vi acciottolare; scalpitare.

clause [klɔ:z] n clausola; (LING) proposizione f.

claw [klɔ:] n tenaglia; (of bird of prey) artiglio; (of lobster) pinza // vt (also: ~ at) graffiare; afferrare.

clay [kleɪ] n argilla.

clean [kli:n] a pulito(a); (clear, smooth) liscio(a) // vt pulire; **to ~ out** vt ripulire; **to ~ up** vi far pulizia // vt (also fig) ripulire; **~er** n (person) donna delle pulizie; (also: **dry ~er**) tintore/a; (product) smacchiatore m; **~ing** n pulizia; **~liness** ['klenlɪnɪs] n pulizia.

cleanse [klenz] vt pulire; purificare; **~r** n detergente m.

clean-shaven ['kli:n'ʃeɪvn] a sbarbato(a).

cleansing department ['klenzɪŋ-] n (Brit) nettezza urbana.

clear [klɪə*] a chiaro(a); (road, way) libero(a) // vt sgombrare; liberare; (table) sparecchiare; (COMM: goods) liquidare; (: debt) liquidare, saldare; (: cheque) fare la compensazione di; (LAW: suspect) discolpare; (obstacle) superare // vi (weather) rasserenarsi; (fog) andarsene // ad: **~ of** distante da; **to ~ up** vi schiarirsi // vt mettere in ordine; (mystery) risolvere; **~ance** n (removal) sgombro; (free space) spazio; (permission) autorizzazione f, permesso; **~-cut** a ben delineato(a), distinto(a); **~ing** n radura; **~ing bank** n (Brit) banca (che fa uso della camera di compensazione); **~ly** ad chiaramente; **~way** n (Brit) strada con divieto di sosta.

cleaver ['kli:və*] n mannaia.

clef [klef] n (MUS) chiave f.

cleft [kleft] n (in rock) crepa, fenditura.

clench [klentʃ] vt stringere.

clergy ['klə:dʒɪ] n clero; **~man** n ecclesiastico.

clerical ['klerɪkəl] a d'impiegato; (REL) clericale.

clerk [klɑ:k, (US) klə:rk] n impiegato/a; (US: sales person) commesso/a.

clever ['klevə*] a (mentally) intelligente; (deft, skilful) abile; (device, arrangement) ingegnoso(a).

click [klɪk] vi scattare // vt (heels etc) battere; (tongue) far schioccare.

client ['klaɪənt] n cliente m/f.

cliff [klɪf] n scogliera scoscesa, rupe f.

climate ['klaɪmɪt] n clima m.

climax ['klaɪmæks] n culmine m.

climb [klaɪm] vi salire; (clamber) arrampicarsi // vt salire; (CLIMBING) scalare // n salita; arrampicata; scalata; **~-down** n marcia indietro; **~er** n (also: **rock ~er**) rocciatore/trice; alpinista m/f; **~ing** n (also: **rock ~ing**) alpinismo.

clinch [klɪntʃ] vt (deal) concludere.

cling [klɪŋ], pt, pp **clung** vi: **to ~ (to)** tenersi stretto(a) (a); (of clothes) aderire strettamente (a).

clinic ['klɪnɪk] n clinica.

clink [klɪŋk] vi tintinnare.

clip [klɪp] n (for hair) forcina; (also: **paper ~**) graffetta; (holding hose etc) anello d'attacco // vt (also: **~ together**: papers) attaccare insieme; (hair, nails) tagliare; (hedge) tosare; **~pers** npl macchinetta per capelli; (also: **nail ~pers**) forbicine fpl per le unghie; **~ping** n (from newspaper) ritaglio.

clique [kli:k] n cricca.

cloak [kləuk] n mantello // vt avvolgere; **~room** n (for coats etc) guardaroba m inv; (Brit: W.C.) gabinetti mpl.

clock [klɔk] n orologio; **to ~ in** or **on** vi timbrare il cartellino (all'entrata); **to ~ off** or **out** vi timbrare il cartellino (all'uscita); **~wise** ad in senso orario; **~work** n movimento or meccanismo a orologeria or a molla.

clog [klɔg] n zoccolo // vt intasare // vi intasarsi, bloccarsi.

cloister ['klɔɪstə*] n chiostro.

clone [kləun] n clone m.

close a, ad and derivatives [kləus] a: **~ (to)** vicino(a) (a); (writing, texture) fitto(a); (watch) stretto(a); (examination) attento(a); (weather) afoso(a) // ad vicino, dappresso; **~** prep vicino a; **~ by, ~ at hand** a, ad a portata di mano; **a ~ friend** un amico intimo; **to have a ~ shave** (fig) scamparla bella // vb and derivatives [kləuz] vt chiudere // vi (shop etc) chiudere; (lid, door etc) chiudersi; (end) finire // n (end) fine f; **to ~ down** vt chiudere (definitivamente) // vi cessare (definitivamente); **~d** a chiuso(a); **~d shop** n azienda o fabbrica che impiega solo aderenti ai sindacati; **~-knit** a (family, community) molto unito(a); **~ly** ad (examine, watch) da vicino.

closet ['klɔzɪt] n (cupboard) armadio.

close-up ['kləusʌp] n primo piano.

closure ['kləuʒə*] n chiusura.

clot [klɔt] n (also: **blood ~**) coagulo; (col: idiot) scemo/a // vi coagularsi.

cloth [klɔθ] n (material) tessuto, stoffa; (also: **tea~**) strofinaccio.

clothe [kləuð] vt vestire; **~s** npl abiti mpl, vestiti mpl; **~s brush** n spazzola per abiti; **~s line** n corda (per stendere il bucato); **~s peg**, (US) **~s pin** n molletta.

clothing ['kləʊðɪŋ] n = **clothes**.

cloud [klaud] n nuvola; **~y** a nuvoloso(a); (liquid) torbido(a).

clout [klaut] vt dare un colpo a.

clove [kləuv] n chiodo di garofano; **~ of garlic** spicchio d'aglio.

clover ['kləuvə*] n trifoglio.

clown [klaun] n pagliaccio // vi (also: **~ about**, **~ around**) fare il pagliaccio.

cloying ['klɔɪɪŋ] a (taste, smell) nauseabondo(a).

club [klʌb] n (society) club m inv, circolo; (weapon, GOLF) mazza // vi bastonare // vi: **to ~ together** associarsi; **~s** npl (CARDS) fiori mpl; **~ car** n (US RAIL) vagone m ristorante; **~house** n sede f del circolo.

cluck [klʌk] vi chiocciare.

clue [klu:] n indizio; (in crosswords) definizione f; **I haven't a ~** non ho la minima idea.

clump [klʌmp] n: **~ of trees** folto d'alberi.

clumsy ['klʌmzɪ] a (person) goffo(a), maldestro(a); (object) malfatto(a), mal costruito(a).

clung [klʌŋ] pt, pp of **cling**.

cluster ['klʌstə*] n gruppo // vi raggrupparsi.

clutch [klʌtʃ] n (grip, grasp) presa, stretta; (AUT) frizione f // vt afferrare, stringere forte; **to ~ at** aggrapparsi a.

clutter ['klʌtə*] vt ingombrare.

CND n abbr = Campaign for Nuclear Disarmament.

Co. abbr = **county**; **company**.

c/o abbr (= care of) presso.

coach [kəutʃ] n (bus) pullman m inv; (horse-drawn, of train) carrozza; (SPORT) allenatore/trice // vt allenare; **~ trip** n viaggio in pullman.

coagulate [kəu'ægjuleɪt] vi coagularsi.

coal [kəul] n carbone m; **~ face** n fronte f; **~field** n bacino carbonifero.

coalition [kəuə'lɪʃən] n coalizione f.

coalman, coal merchant ['kəulmən, 'kəulmə:tʃənt] n negoziante m di carbone.

coalmine ['kəulmaɪn] n miniera di carbone.

coarse [kɔ:s] a (salt, sand etc) grosso(a); (cloth, person) rozzo(a).

coast [kəust] n costa // vi (with cycle etc) scendere a ruota libera; **~al** a costiero(a); **~guard** n guardia costiera; **~line** n linea costiera.

coat [kəut] n cappotto; (of animal) pelo; (of paint) mano f // vt coprire; **~ of arms** n stemma m; **~ hanger** n attaccapanni m inv; **~ing** n rivestimento.

coax [kəuks] vt indurre (con moine).

cob [kɔb] n see **corn**.

cobbler ['kɔblə*] n calzolaio.

cobbles, cobblestones ['kɔblz, 'kɔblstəunz] npl ciottoli mpl.

cobweb ['kɔbwɛb] n ragnatela.

cocaine [kə'keɪn] n cocaina.

cock [kɔk] n (rooster) gallo; (male bird) maschio // vt (gun) armare; **~erel** n galletto; **~-eyed** a (fig) storto(a); strampalato(a).

cockle ['kɔkl] n cardio.

cockney ['kɔknɪ] n cockney m/f inv (abitante dei quartieri popolari dell'East End di Londra).

cockpit ['kɔkpɪt] n (in aircraft) abitacolo.

cockroach ['kɔkrəutʃ] n blatta.

cocktail ['kɔkteɪl] n cocktail m inv; **~ cabinet** n mobile m bar inv; **~ party** n cocktail m inv.

cocoa ['kəukəu] n cacao.

coconut ['kəukənʌt] n noce f di cocco.

cocoon [kə'ku:n] n bozzolo.

cod [kɔd] n merluzzo.

C.O.D. abbr = **cash on delivery**.

code [kəud] n codice m.

cod-liver oil ['kɔdlɪvə*-] n olio di fegato di merluzzo.

coercion [kəu'ə:ʃən] n coercizione f.

coffee ['kɔfɪ] n caffè m inv; **~ bar** n (Brit) caffè m inv; **~ break** n pausa per il caffè; **~pot** n caffettiera; **~ table** n tavolino.

coffin ['kɔfɪn] n bara.

cog [kɔg] n dente m.

cogent ['kəudʒənt] a convincente.

coherent [kəu'hɪərənt] a coerente.

coil [kɔɪl] n rotolo; (one loop) anello; (contraceptive) spirale f // vt avvolgere.

coin [kɔɪn] n moneta // vt (word) coniare; **~age** n sistema m monetario; **~-box** n (Brit) telefono a gettoni.

coincide [kəuɪn'saɪd] vi coincidere; **~nce** [kəu'ɪnsɪdəns] n combinazione f.

coke [kəuk] n coke m.

colander ['kɔləndə*] n colino.

cold [kəuld] a freddo(a) // n freddo; (MED) raffreddore m; **it's ~** fa freddo; **to be ~** aver freddo; **to catch ~** prendere freddo; **to catch a ~** prendere un raffreddore; **in ~ blood** a sangue freddo; **~ sore** n erpete m.

coleslaw ['kəulslɔ:] n insalata di cavolo bianco.

colic ['kɔlɪk] n colica.

collapse [kə'læps] vi crollare // n crollo; (MED) collasso.

collapsible [kə'læpsəbl] a pieghevole.

collar ['kɔlə*] n (of coat, shirt) colletto; **~bone** n clavicola.

collateral [kə'lætərl] n garanzia.

colleague ['kɔli:g] n collega m/f.

collect [kə'lɛkt] vt (gen) raccogliere; (as a hobby) fare collezione di; (Brit: call and pick up) prendere; (money owed, pension) riscuotere; (donations, subscriptions) fare una colletta di // vi

adunarsi, riunirsi; ammucchiarsi; **to call
~** (US TEL) fare una chiamata a carico
del destinatario; **~ion** [kə'lɛkʃən] n
collezione f; raccolta; (for money)
colletta.

collector [kə'lɛktə*] n collezionista m/f;
(of taxes) esattore m.

college ['kɔlɪdʒ] n (Brit, US SCOL)
college m inv; (of technology etc)
istituto superiore; (body) collegio.

collide [kə'laɪd] vi: **to ~** (with) scontrarsi
(con).

collie ['kɔlɪ] n (dog) collie m inv.

colliery ['kɔlɪərɪ] n (Brit) miniera di
carbone.

collision [kə'lɪʒən] n collisione f, scontro.

colloquial [kə'ləukwɪəl] a familiare.

colon ['kəulən] n (sign) due punti mpl;
(MED) colon m inv.

colonel ['kə:nl] n colonnello.

colonial [kə'ləunɪəl] a coloniale.

colony ['kɔlənɪ] n colonia.

colour, (US) **color** ['kʌlə*] n colore m //
vt colorare; (tint, dye) tingere; (fig:
affect) influenzare // vi (blush: also: **~
up**) arrossire; **~s** npl (of party, club)
emblemi mpl; **~ bar** n discriminazione f
razziale (in locali etc); **~-blind** a
daltonico(a); **~ed** a colorato(a);
(photo) a colori // n: **~eds** gente f di
colore; **~ film** n (for camera) pellicola
a colori; **~ful** a di colore, a
vivaci colori; (personality) colorato(a);
~ing n colorazione f; (substance)
colorante m; (complexion) colorito; **~
scheme** n combinazione f di colori; **~
television** n televisione f a colori.

colt [kəult] n puledro.

column ['kɔləm] n colonna; **~ist**
['kɔləmnɪst] n articolista m/f.

coma ['kəumə] n coma m inv.

comb [kəum] n pettine m // vt (hair)
pettinare; (area) battere a tappeto.

combat ['kɔmbæt] n combattimento // vt
combattere, lottare contro.

combination [kɔmbɪ'neɪʃən] n
combinazione f.

combine vb [kəm'baɪn] vt: **to ~** (with)
combinare (con); (one quality with
another) unire (a) // vi unirsi; (CHEM)
combinarsi // n ['kɔmbaɪn] lega; (ECON)
associazione f; **~ (harvester)** n mieti-
trebbia.

come [kʌm], pt **came**, pp **come** vi
venire; arrivare; **to ~ to** (decision etc)
raggiungere; **to ~ undone** slacciarsi; **to
~ loose** allentarsi; **to ~ about** vi
succedere; **to ~ across** vt fus trovare
per caso; **to ~ along** vi = **to come
on**; **to ~ away** vi venire via;
staccarsi; **to ~ back** vi ritornare; **to ~
by** vt fus (acquire) ottenere; procurarsi;
to ~ down vi scendere; (prices)
calare; (buildings) essere demolito(a);
to ~ forward vi farsi avanti;

presentarsi; **to ~ from** vt fus venire
da; provenire da; **to ~ in** vi entrare;
to ~ in for vt fus (criticism etc)
ricevere; **to ~ into** vt fus (money)
ereditare; **to ~ off** vi (button)
staccarsi; (stain) andare via; (attempt)
riuscire; **to ~ on** vi (pupil, work,
project) fare progressi; (lights)
accendersi; (electricity) entrare in
funzione; **~ on!** avanti!, andiamo!,
forza!; **to ~ out** vi uscire; (strike) entrare in sciopero; **to ~ round** vi (after
faint, operation) riprendere conoscenza,
rinvenire; **to ~ to** vi rinvenire; **to ~
up** vi venire su; **to ~ up against** vt
fus (resistance, difficulties) urtare contro; **to ~ up with** vt fus: he came up
with an idea venne fuori con un'idea; **to
~ upon** vt fus trovare per caso; **~back**
n (THEATRE etc) ritorno.

comedian [kə'mi:dɪən] n comico.

comedown ['kʌmdaun] n rovescio.

comedy ['kɔmɪdɪ] n commedia.

comeuppance [kʌm'ʌpəns] n: **to get
one's ~** ricevere ciò che si merita.

comfort ['kʌmfət] n comodità f inv,
benessere m; (solace) consolazione f,
conforto // vt consolare, confortare; **~s**
npl comodità fpl; **~able** a comodo(a);
~ably ad (sit etc) comodamente; (live)
bene; **~ station** n (US) gabinetti mpl.

comic ['kɔmɪk] a (also: **~al**) comico(a) //
n comico; (magazine) giornaletto; **~
strip** n fumetto.

coming ['kʌmɪŋ] n arrivo // a (next)
prossimo(a); (future) futuro(a); **~(s)
and going(s)** n(pl) andirivieni m inv.

comma ['kɔmə] n virgola.

command [kə'ma:nd] n ordine m,
comando; (MIL: authority) comando;
(mastery) padronanza // vt comandare;
to ~ sb to do ordinare a qn di fare;
~eer [kɔmən'dɪə*] vt requisire; **~er** n
capo; (MIL) comandante m.

commando [kə'ma:ndəu] n commando
m inv; membro di un commando.

commemorate [kə'mɛməreɪt] vt
commemorare.

commence [kə'mɛns] vt, vi cominciare.

commend [kə'mɛnd] vt lodare;
raccomandare.

commensurate [kə'mɛnʃərɪt] a: **~ with**
proporzionato(a) a.

comment ['kɔmɛnt] n commento // vi: **to
~ (on)** fare commenti (su); **~ary**
['kɔməntərɪ] n commentario; (SPORT)
radiocronaca; telecronaca; **~ator**
['kɔmənteɪtə*] n commentatore/trice;
radiocronista m/f; telecronista m/f.

commerce ['kɔmə:s] n commercio.

commercial [kə'mə:ʃəl] a commerciale //
n (TV: also: **~ break**) pubblicità f inv.

commiserate [kə'mɪzəreɪt] vi: **to ~ with**
condolersi con.

commission [kə'mɪʃən] n commissione f

// vt (MIL) nominare (al comando); (work of art) commissionare; out of ~ (NAUT) in disarmo; **~aire** [kəmɪʃə'neə*] n (Brit: at shop, cinema etc) portiere m in livrea; **~er** n commissionario; (POLICE) questore m.

commit [kə'mɪt] vt (act) commettere; (to sb's care) affidare; to ~ o.s. (to do) impegnarsi (a fare); to ~ suicide suicidarsi; **~ment** n impegno; promessa.

committee [kə'mɪtɪ] n comitato.

commodity [kə'mɔdɪtɪ] n prodotto, articolo; (food) derrata.

common ['kɔmən] a comune; (pej) volgare; (usual) normale // n terreno comune; the C~s npl (Brit) la Camera dei Comuni; in ~ in comune; **~er** n cittadino/a (non nobile); ~ **ground** n (fig) terreno comune; ~ **law** n diritto consuetudinario; **~ly** ad comunemente, usualmente; **C~ Market** n Mercato Comune; **~place** a banale, ordinario(a); **~room** n sala di riunione; (SCOL) sala dei professori; ~ **sense** n buon senso; the **C~wealth** n il Commonwealth.

commotion [kə'məuʃən] n confusione f, tumulto.

communal ['kɔmjuːnl] a (life) comunale; (for common use) pubblico(a).

commune n ['kɔmjuːn] (group) comune f // vi [kə'mjuːn]: to ~ with mettersi in comunione con.

communicate [kə'mjuːnɪkeɪt] vt comunicare, trasmettere // vi: to ~ (with) comunicare (con).

communication [kəmjuːnɪ'keɪʃən] n comunicazione f; ~ **cord** n (Brit) segnale m d'allarme.

communion [kə'mjuːnɪən] n (also: Holy C~) comunione f.

communiqué [kə'mjuːnɪkeɪ] n comunicato.

communism ['kɔmjunɪzəm] n comunismo; **communist** a, n comunista (m/f).

community [kə'mjuːnɪtɪ] n comunità f inv; ~ **centre** n circolo ricreativo; ~ **chest** n (US) fondo di beneficenza.

commutation ticket [kɔmjuː'teɪʃən-] n (US) biglietto di abbonamento.

commute [kə'mjuːt] vi fare il pendolare // vt (LAW) commutare; **~r** n pendolare m/f.

compact a [kəm'pækt] compatto(a) // n ['kɔmpækt] (also: powder ~) portacipria m inv; ~ **disk** n compact disc m inv.

companion [kəm'pænɪən] n compagno/a; **~ship** n compagnia.

company ['kʌmpənɪ] n (also COMM, MIL, THEATRE) compagnia; to keep sb ~ tenere compagnia a qn; ~ **secretary** n (Brit) segretario/a generale.

comparative [kəm'pærətɪv] a

relativo(a); (adjective etc) comparativo(a); **~ly** ad relativamente.

compare [kəm'pɛə*] vt: to ~ sth/sb with/to confrontare qc/qn con/a // vi: to ~ (with) reggere il confronto (con); **comparison** [-'pærɪsn] n confronto.

compartment [kəm'pɑːtmənt] n compartimento; (RAIL) scompartimento.

compass ['kʌmpəs] n bussola; **~es** npl compasso.

compassion [kəm'pæʃən] n compassione f.

compatible [kəm'pætɪbl] a compatibile.

compel [kəm'pɛl] vt costringere, obbligare; **~ling** a (fig: argument) irresistibile.

compendium [kəm'pendɪəm] n compendio.

compensate ['kɔmpənseɪt] vt risarcire // vi: to ~ for compensare; **compensation** [-'seɪʃən] n compensazione f; (money) risarcimento.

compère ['kɔmpeə*] n presentatore/trice.

compete [kəm'piːt] vi (take part) concorrere; (vie): to ~ (with) fare concorrenza (a).

competence ['kɔmpɪtəns] n competenza.

competent ['kɔmpɪtənt] a competente.

competition [kɔmpɪ'tɪʃən] n gara; concorso; (ECON) concorrenza.

competitive [kəm'petɪtɪv] a (ECON) concorrenziale; (sport) agonistico(a); (person) che ha spirito di competizione; che ha spirito agonistico; ~ **exam** concorso.

competitor [kəm'petɪtə*] n concorrente m/f.

complacency [kəm'pleɪnsɪ] n compiacenza di sé.

complain [kəm'pleɪn] vi: to ~ (about) lagnarsi (di); (in shop etc) reclamare (per); **~t** n lamento; reclamo; (MED) malattia.

complement n ['kɔmplɪmənt] complemento; (especially of ship's crew etc) effettivo // vt ['kɔmplɪment] (enhance) accompagnarsi bene a; **~ary** [kɔmplɪ'mentərɪ] a complementare.

complete [kəm'pliːt] a completo(a) // vt completare; (a form) riempire; **~ly** ad completamente; **completion** n completamento.

complex ['kɔmpleks] a complesso(a) // n (PSYCH, buildings etc) complesso.

complexion [kəm'plekʃən] n (of face) carnagione f; (of event etc) aspetto.

compliance [kəm'plaɪəns] n acquiescenza; in ~ with (orders, wishes etc) in conformità con.

complicate ['kɔmplɪkeɪt] vt complicare; **~d** a complicato(a); **complication** [-'keɪʃən] n complicazione f.

compliment n ['kɔmplɪmənt] complimento // vt ['kɔmplɪment] fare un complimento a; **~s** npl complimenti mpl; rispetti *mpl*; **to pay sb a ~** fare un complimento a qn; **~ary** [-'mɛntərɪ] *a* complimentoso(a), elogiativo(a); *(free)* in omaggio; **~ary ticket** *n* biglietto d'omaggio.

comply [kəm'plaɪ] *vi*: **to ~ with** assentire a; conformarsi a.

component [kəm'pəʊnənt] *n* componente *m*.

compose [kəm'pəʊz] *vt* comporre; **to ~ o.s.** ricomporsi; **~d** *a* calmo(a); **~r** *n* (MUS) compositore/trice.

composition [kɒmpə'zɪʃən] *n* composizione *f*.

composure [kəm'pəʊʒə*] *n* calma.

compound ['kɒmpaʊnd] *n* (CHEM, LING) composto; *(enclosure)* recinto // *a* composto(a); **~ fracture** *n* frattura esposta.

comprehend [kɒmprɪ'hɛnd] *vt* comprendere, capire; **comprehension** [-'hɛnʃən] *n* comprensione *f*.

comprehensive [kɒmprɪ'hɛnsɪv] *a* comprensivo(a); **~ policy** *n* (INSURANCE) polizza che copre tutti i rischi; **~ (school)** *n* (Brit) scuola secondaria aperta a tutti.

compress *vt* [kəm'prɛs] comprimere // *n* ['kɒmprɛs] (MED) compressa.

comprise [kəm'praɪz] *vt* (also: **be ~d of**) comprendere.

compromise ['kɒmprəmaɪz] *n* compromesso // *vt* compromettere // *vi* venire a un compromesso.

compulsion [kəm'pʌlʃən] *n* costrizione *f*.

compulsive [kəm'pʌlsɪv] *a* (PSYCH) incontrollabile.

compulsory [kəm'pʌlsərɪ] *a* obbligatorio(a).

computer [kəm'pju:tə*] *n* computer *m inv*, elaboratore *m* elettronico; **~ize** *vt* computerizzare; **~ programmer** *n* programmatore/trice; **~ programming** *n* programmazione *f* di computer; **~ science, computing** *n* informatica.

comrade ['kɒmrɪd] *n* compagno/a.

con [kɒn] *vt* (col) truffare // *n* truffa.

conceal [kən'si:l] *vt* nascondere.

conceit [kən'si:t] *n* presunzione *f*, vanità; **~ed** *a* presuntuoso(a), vanitoso(a).

conceive [kən'si:v] *vt* concepire // *vi* concepire un bambino.

concentrate ['kɒnsəntreɪt] *vi* concentrarsi // *vt* concentrare.

concentration [kɒnsən'treɪʃən] *n* concentrazione *f*; **~ camp** *n* campo di concentramento.

concept ['kɒnsɛpt] *n* concetto.

conception [kən'sɛpʃən] *n* concezione *f*.

concern [kən'sə:n] *n* affare *m*; (COMM) azienda, ditta; *(anxiety)* preoccupazione *f* // *vt* riguardare; **to be ~ed (about)** preoccuparsi (di); **~ing** *prep* riguardo a, circa.

concert ['kɒnsət] *n* concerto; **~ed**

[kən'sə:tɪd] *a* concertato(a); **~ hall** *n* sala da concerti.

concertina [kɒnsə'ti:nə] *n* piccola fisarmonica // *vi* ridursi come una fisarmonica.

concerto [kən'tʃə:təʊ] *n* concerto.

conclude [kən'klu:d] *vt* concludere; **conclusion** [-'klu:ʒən] *n* conclusione *f*; **conclusive** [-'klu:sɪv] *a* conclusivo(a).

concoct [kən'kɒkt] *vt* inventare; **~ion** [-'kɒkʃən] *n* miscuglio.

concourse ['kɒnkɔ:s] *n* (hall) atrio.

concrete ['kɒnkri:t] *n* calcestruzzo // *a* concreto(a); di calcestruzzo.

concur [kən'kə:*] *vi* concordare.

concurrently [kən'kʌrntlɪ] *ad* simultaneamente.

concussion [kən'kʌʃən] *n* commozione *f* cerebrale.

condemn [kən'dɛm] *vt* condannare; **~ation** [kɒndɛm'neɪʃən] *n* condanna.

condensation [kɒndɛn'seɪʃən] *n* condensazione *f*.

condense [kən'dɛns] *vi* condensarsi // *vt* condensare; **~d milk** *n* latte *m* condensato.

condition [kən'dɪʃən] *n* condizione *f* // *vt* condizionare, regolare; **on ~ that** a condizione che + sub, a condizione di; **~al** *a* condizionale; **~er** *n* (for hair) balsamo.

condolences [kən'dəʊlənsɪz] *npl* condoglianze *fpl*.

condom ['kɒndəm] *n* preservativo.

condominium [kɒndə'mɪnɪəm] *n* (US) condominio.

condone [kən'dəʊn] *vt* condonare.

conducive [kən'dju:sɪv] *a*: **~ to** favorevole a.

conduct *n* ['kɒndʌkt] condotta // *vt* [kən'dʌkt] condurre; *(manage)* dirigere; amministrare; (MUS) dirigere; **to ~ o.s.** comportarsi; **~ed tour** *n* gita accompagnata; **~or** *n* (of orchestra) direttore *m* d'orchestra; (on bus) bigliettaio; (US: on train) controllore *m*; (ELEC) conduttore *m*; **~ress** *n* (on bus) bigliettaia.

conduit ['kɒndɪt] *n* condotto; tubo.

cone [kəʊn] *n* cono; (BOT) pigna.

confectioner [kən'fɛkʃənə*] *n* pasticciere *m*; **~'s (shop)** *n* ≈ pasticceria; **~y** *n* dolciumi *mpl*.

confer [kən'fə:*] *vt*: **to ~ sth on** conferire qc a // *vi* conferire.

conference ['kɒnfərns] *n* congresso.

confess [kən'fɛs] *vt* confessare, ammettere // *vi* confessarsi; **~ion** [-'fɛʃən] *n* confessione *f*.

confetti [kən'fɛtɪ] *n* coriandoli *mpl*.

confide [kən'faɪd] *vi*: **to ~ in** confidarsi con.

confidence ['kɒnfɪdns] *n* confidenza; *(trust)* fiducia; (also: self-~) sicurezza di sé; **in ~** (speak, write) in confidenza,

confidenzialmente; ~ **trick** n truffa;
confident a sicuro(a); sicuro(a) di sé;
confidential [kɔnfɪ'dɛnʃəl] a riservato(a).

confine [kən'faɪn] vt limitare; (shut up)
rinchiudere; ~**s** ['kɔnfaɪnz] npl confini
mpl; ~**d** a (space) ristretto(a); ~**ment**
n prigionia; (MIL) consegna; (MED)
parto.

confirm [kən'fə:m] vt confermare; (REL)
cresimare; ~**ation** [kɔnfə'meɪʃən] n
conferma; cresima; ~**ed** a
inveterato(a).

confiscate ['kɔnfɪskeɪt] vt confiscare.

conflict n ['kɔnflɪkt] conflitto // vi
[kən'flɪkt] essere in conflitto; ~**ing** a
contrastante.

conform [kən'fɔ:m] vi: to ~ (to)
conformarsi (a).

confound [kən'faund] vt confondere.

confront [kən'frʌnt] vt confrontare;
(enemy, danger) affrontare; ~**ation**
[kɔnfrən'teɪʃən] n confronto.

confuse [kən'fju:z] vt imbrogliare; (one
thing with another) confondere; ~**d** a
confuso(a); **confusing** a che fa
confondere; **confusion** [-'fju:ʒən] n
confusione f.

congeal [kən'dʒi:l] vi (blood) congelarsi.

congenial [kən'dʒi:nɪəl] a (person)
simpatico(a); (thing) congeniale.

congested [kən'dʒestɪd] a conge-
stionato(a).

congestion [kən'dʒestʃən] n congestione
f.

congratulate [kən'grætjuleɪt] vt: to ~ sb
(on) congratularsi con qn (per or di);
congratulations [-'leɪʃənz] npl auguri
mpl; (on success) complimenti mpl.

congregate ['kɔŋɡrɪɡeɪt] vi congregarsi,
riunirsi.

congress ['kɔŋɡrɛs] n congresso; ~**man**
n (US) membro del Congresso.

conjecture [kən'dʒɛktʃə*] n congettura.

conjunction [kən'dʒʌŋkʃən] n
congiunzione f.

conjunctivitis [kəndʒʌŋktɪ'vaɪtɪs] n
congiuntivite f.

conjure ['kʌndʒə*] vi fare giochi di prestigio; **to** ~ **up** vt (ghost, spirit)
evocare; (memories) rievocare; ~**r** n
prestidigitatore/trice, prestigiatore/trice.

conk out [kɔŋk-] vi (col) andare in
panne.

conman ['kɔnmæn] n truffatore m.

connect [kə'nɛkt] vt connettere,
collegare; (ELEC) collegare; (fig)
associare // vi (train): to ~ with essere
in coincidenza con; to be ~ed with
(associated) aver rapporti con; (by
birth, marriage) essere imparentato
con; ~**ion** [-ʃən] n relazione f, rapporto;
(ELEC) connessione f; (TEL)
collegamento; in ~ion with con
riferimento a.

connive [kə'naɪv] vi: to ~ at essere
connivente in.

connoisseur [kɔnɪ'sə*] n conoscitore/
trice.

conquer ['kɔŋkə*] vt conquistare;
(feelings) vincere.

conquest ['kɔŋkwɛst] n conquista.

cons [kɔnz] npl see **convenience, pro**.

conscience ['kɔnʃəns] n coscienza.

conscientious [kɔnʃɪ'ɛnʃəs] a co-
scienzioso(a).

conscious ['kɔnʃəs] a consapevole;
(MED) conscio(a); ~**ness** n
consapevolezza; coscienza.

conscript ['kɔnskrɪpt] n coscritto.

consent [kən'sɛnt] n consenso // vi: to ~
(to) acconsentire (a).

consequence ['kɔnsɪkwəns] n
conseguenza, risultato; importanza.

consequently ['kɔnsɪkwəntlɪ] ad di
conseguenza, dunque.

conservation [kɔnsə'veɪʃən] n
conservazione f.

conservative [kən'sə:vətɪv] a
conservatore(trice); (cautious) cauto(a);
C~ a, n (Brit POL) conservatore(trice).

conservatory [kən'sə:vətrɪ] n
(greenhouse) serra.

conserve [kən'sə:v] vt conservare // n
conserva.

consider [kən'sɪdə*] vt considerare;
(take into account) tener conto di; to ~
doing sth considerare la possibilità di
fare qc.

considerable [kən'sɪdərəbl] a
considerevole, notevole; **considerably**
ad notevolmente, decisamente.

considerate [kən'sɪdərɪt] a
premuroso(a).

consideration [kənsɪdə'reɪʃən] n
considerazione f; (reward)
rimunerazione f.

considering [kən'sɪdərɪŋ] prep in
considerazione di.

consign [kən'saɪn] vt consegnare; (send:
goods) spedire; ~**ment** n consegna;
spedizione f.

consist [kən'sɪst] vi: to ~ of constare di,
essere composto(a) di.

consistency [kən'sɪstənsɪ] n consistenza;
(fig) coerenza.

consistent [kən'sɪstənt] a coerente; (constant) costante; ~ with compatibile con.

consolation [kɔnsə'leɪʃən] n consolazione
f.

console vt [kən'səul] consolare // n
['kɔnsəul] quadro di comando.

consonant ['kɔnsənənt] n consonante f.

consortium [kən'sɔ:tɪəm] n consorzio.

conspicuous [kən'spɪkjuəs] a co-
spicuo(a).

conspiracy [kən'spɪrəsɪ] n congiura, cospirazione f.

constable ['kʌnstəbl] n (Brit) ≈
poliziotto, agente m di polizia.

constabulary [kən'stæbjulərɪ] n forze fpl dell'ordine.

constant ['kɔnstənt] a costante; continuo(a); ~ly ad costantemente; continuamente.

constipated ['kɔnstɪpeɪtɪd] a stitico(a).

constipation [kɔnstɪ'peɪʃən] n stitichezza.

constituency [kən'stɪtjuənsɪ] n collegio elettorale.

constituent [kən'stɪtjuənt] n elettore/trice; (part) elemento componente.

constitution [kɔnstɪ'tjuːʃən] n costituzione f; ~al a costituzionale.

constraint [kən'streɪnt] n costrizione f.

construct [kən'strʌkt] vt costruire; ~ion [-ʃən] n costruzione f; ~ive a costruttivo(a).

construe [kən'struː] vt interpretare.

consul ['kɔnsl] n console m; ~ate ['kɔnsjulɪt] n consolato.

consult [kən'sʌlt] vt consultare // vi consultarsi; ~ant n (MED) consulente m medico; (other specialist) consulente; ~ing room n (Brit) ambulatorio.

consume [kən'sjuːm] vt consumare; ~r n consumatore/trice; ~r goods npl beni mpl di consumo; ~r society n società dei consumi.

consummate ['kɔnsʌmeɪt] vt consumare.

consumption [kən'sʌmpʃən] n consumo; (MED) consunzione f.

cont. abbr = continued.

contact ['kɔntækt] n contatto; (person) conoscenza // vt mettersi in contatto con; ~ lenses npl lenti fpl a contatto.

contagious [kən'teɪdʒəs] a contagioso(a).

contain [kən'teɪn] vt contenere; to ~ o.s. contenersi; ~er n recipiente m; (for shipping etc) container m.

contaminate [kən'tæmɪneɪt] vt contaminare.

cont'd abbr = continued.

contemplate ['kɔntəmpleɪt] vt contemplare; (consider) pensare a (or di).

contemporary [kən'tempərərɪ] a contemporaneo(a); (design) moderno(a) // n contemporaneo/a.

contempt [kən'tempt] n disprezzo; ~ of court (LAW) oltraggio alla Corte; ~uous a sdegnoso(a).

contend [kən'tend] vt: to ~ that sostenere che // vi: to ~ with lottare contro; ~er n contendente m/f; concorrente m/f.

content [kən'tent] a contento(a), soddisfatto(a) // vt contentare, soddisfare // n ['kɔntent] contenuto; ~s npl contenuto; (of barrel etc: capacity) capacità f inv; (table of) ~s indice m; ~ed a contento(a), soddisfatto(a).

contention [kən'tenʃən] n contesa; (assertion) tesi f inv.

contentment [kən'tentmənt] n contentezza.

contest n ['kɔntest] lotta; (competition) gara, concorso // vt [kən'test] contestare; impugnare; (compete for) contendere; ~ant [kən'testənt] n concorrente m/f; (in fight) avversario/a.

context ['kɔntekst] n contesto.

continent ['kɔntɪnənt] n continente m; the C~ (Brit) l'Europa continentale; ~al [-'nentl] a continentale // n abitante m/f dell'Europa continentale; ~al quilt n (Brit) piumino.

contingency [kən'tɪndʒənsɪ] n eventualità f inv; ~ plan n misura d'emergenza.

continual [kən'tɪnjuəl] a continuo(a).

continuation [kəntɪnju'eɪʃən] n continuazione f; (after interruption) ripresa; (of story) seguito.

continue [kən'tɪnjuː] vi continuare // vt continuare; (start again) riprendere.

continuous [kən'tɪnjuəs] a continuo(a), ininterrotto(a); ~ stationery n carta a moduli continui.

contort [kən'tɔːt] vt contorcere.

contour ['kɔntuə*] n contorno, profilo; (also: ~ line) curva di livello.

contraband ['kɔntrəbænd] n contrabbando.

contraceptive [kɔntrə'septɪv] a contraccettivo(a) // n contraccettivo.

contract n ['kɔntrækt] contratto // vi [kən'trækt] (become smaller) contrarre; (COMM): to ~ to do sth fare un contratto per fare qc; ~ion [-ʃən] n contrazione f; ~or n imprenditore m.

contradict [kɔntrə'dɪkt] vt contraddire.

contraption [kən'træpʃən] n (pej) aggeggio.

contrary ['kɔntrərɪ] a contrario(a); (unfavourable) avverso(a), contrario(a); [kən'trɛərɪ] (perverse) bisbetico(a) // n contrario; on the ~ al contrario; unless you hear to the ~ a meno che non si disdica.

contrast n ['kɔntraːst] contrasto // vt [kən'traːst] mettere in contrasto.

contribute [kən'trɪbjuːt] vi contribuire // vt: to ~ £10/an article to dare 10 sterline/un articolo a; to ~ to contribuire a; (newspaper) scrivere per; **contribution** [kɔntrɪ'bjuːʃən] n contribuzione f; **contributor** n (to newspaper) collaboratore/trice.

contrivance [kən'traɪvəns] n congegno; espediente m.

contrive [kən'traɪv] vt inventare; escogitare // vi: to ~ to do fare in modo di fare.

control [kən'trəul] vt dominare; (firm, operation etc) dirigere; (check) controllare // n controllo; ~s npl comandi mpl; under ~ sotto controllo; to be in ~ of aver autorità su; essere responsabile di; controllare; **to go out of ~** (*car*) non rispondere ai comandi; (*situation*) sfuggire di mano; **~ panel** *n* quadro dei comandi; **~ room** *n* (*NAUT, MIL*) sala di comando; (*RADIO, TV*) sala di regia; **~ tower** *n* (*AVIAT*) torre *f* di controllo.

controversial [kɔntrə'və:ʃl] *a* controverso(a), polemico(a).

controversy ['kɔntrəvə:sɪ] *n* controversia, polemica.

convalesce [kɔnvə'lɛs] *vi* rimettersi in salute.

convene [kən'vi:n] *vt* convocare // *vi* convenire, adunarsi.

convenience [kən'vi:nɪəns] *n* comodità *f inv*; **at your ~** a suo comodo; **all modern ~s**, (*Brit*) all mod cons tutte le comodità moderne.

convenient [kən'vi:nɪənt] *a* conveniente, comodo(a).

convent ['kɔnvənt] *n* convento.

convention [kən'venʃən] *n* convenzione *f*; (*meeting*) convegno; **~al** *a* convenzionale.

conversant [kən'və:snt] *a*: **to be ~ with** essere al corrente di; essere pratico(a) di.

conversation [kɔnvə'seɪʃən] *n* conversazione *f*; **~al** *a* non formale.

converse *n* ['kɔnvə:s] contrario, opposto // *vi* [kən'və:s] conversare; **~ly** [-'və:slɪ] *ad* al contrario, per contro.

convert *vt* [kən'və:t] (*REL, COMM*) convertire; (*alter*) trasformare // *n* ['kɔnvə:t] convertito/a; **~ible** *a* (*currency*) convertibile // *n* macchina decappottabile.

convex ['kɔnvɛks] *a* convesso(a).

convey [kən'veɪ] *vt* trasportare; (*thanks*) comunicare; (*idea*) dare; **~or belt** *n* nastro trasportatore.

convict *vt* [kən'vɪkt] dichiarare colpevole // *n* ['kɔnvɪkt] carcerato/a; **~ion** [-ʃən] *n* condanna; (*belief*) convinzione *f*.

convince [kən'vɪns] *vt* convincere, persuadere; **convincing** *a* convincente.

convivial [kən'vɪvɪəl] *a* allegro(a).

convoluted [kɔnvə'lu:tɪd] *a* (*argument etc*) involuto(a).

convoy ['kɔnvɔɪ] *n* convoglio.

convulse [kən'vʌls] *vt* sconvolgere; **to be ~d with laughter** contorcersi dalle risa.

coo [ku:] *vi* tubare.

cook [kuk] *vt* cucinare, cuocere // *vi* cuocere; (*person*) cucinare // *n* cuoco/a; **~book** *n* libro di cucina; **~er** *n* fornello, cucina; **~ery** *n* cucina; **~ery book** *n* (*Brit*) = **~book**; **~ie** *n* (*US*) biscotto; **~ing** *n* cucina.

cool [ku:l] *a* fresco(a); (*not afraid*) calmo(a); (*unfriendly*) freddo(a); (*impertinent*) sfacciato(a) // *vt* raffreddare, rinfrescare // *vi* raffreddarsi, rinfrescarsi.

coop [ku:p] *n* stia // *vt*: **to ~ up** (*fig*) rin-

chiudere.

cooperate [kəu'ɔpəreɪt] *vi* cooperare, collaborare; **cooperation** [-'reɪʃən] *n* cooperazione *f*, collaborazione *f*.

cooperative [kəu'ɔpərətɪv] *a* cooperativo(a) // *n* cooperativa.

coordinate *vt* [kəu'ɔ:dɪneɪt] coordinare // *n* [kəu'ɔ:dɪnət] (*MATH*) coordinata; **~s** *npl* (*clothes*) coordinati *mpl*.

cop [kɔp] *n* (*col*) sbirro.

cope [kəup] *vi* farcela; **to ~ with** (*problems*) far fronte a.

copper ['kɔpə*] *n* rame *m*; (*col: policeman*) sbirro; **~s** *npl* spiccioli *mpl*.

coppice ['kɔpɪs] *n*, **copse** [kɔps] *n* bosco ceduo.

copulate ['kɔpjuleɪt] *vi* accoppiarsi.

copy ['kɔpɪ] *n* copia; (*book etc*) esemplare *m* // *vt* copiare; **~right** *n* diritto d'autore.

coral ['kɔrəl] *n* corallo.

cord [kɔ:d] *n* corda; (*fabric*) velluto a coste.

cordial ['kɔ:dɪəl] *a*, *n* cordiale (*m*).

cordon ['kɔ:dn] *n* cordone *m*; **to ~ off** *vt* fare cordone a.

corduroy ['kɔ:dərɔɪ] *n* fustagno.

core [kɔ:*] *n* (*of fruit*) torsolo; (*TECH*) centro // *vt* estrarre il torsolo da.

cork [kɔ:k] *n* sughero; (*of bottle*) tappo; **~screw** *n* cavatappi *m inv*.

corn [kɔ:n] *n* (*Brit: wheat*) grano; (*US: maize*) granturco; (*on foot*) callo; **~ on the cob** (*CULIN*) pannocchia cotta.

corned beef ['kɔ:nd-] *n* carne *f* di manzo in scatola.

corner ['kɔ:nə*] *n* angolo; (*AUT*) curva // *vt* intrappolare; mettere con le spalle al muro; (*COMM: market*) accaparrare // *vi* prendere una curva; **~stone** *n* pietra angolare.

cornet ['kɔ:nɪt] *n* (*MUS*) cornetta; (*Brit: of ice-cream*) cono.

cornflakes ['kɔ:nfleɪks] *npl* fiocchi *mpl* di granturco.

cornflour ['kɔ:nflauə*] *n* (*Brit*) farina finissima di granturco.

cornstarch ['kɔ:nstɑ:tʃ] *n* (*US*) = **cornflour**.

Cornwall ['kɔ:nwəl] *n* Cornovaglia.

corny ['kɔ:nɪ] *a* (*col*) trito(a).

coronary ['kɔrənərɪ] *n*: **~ (thrombosis)** trombosi *f* coronaria.

coronation [kɔrə'neɪʃən] *n* incoronazione *f*.

coroner ['kɔrənə*] *n* *magistrato incaricato di indagare la causa di morte in circostanze sospette*.

coronet ['kɔrənɪt] *n* diadema *m*.

corporal ['kɔ:pərl] *n* caporalmaggiore *m* // *a*: **~ punishment** pena corporale.

corporate ['kɔ:pərɪt] *a* costituito(a) (in corporazione); comune.

corporation [kɔ:pə'reɪʃən] *n* (*of town*) consiglio comunale; (*COMM*) ente *m*.

corps |kɔː*|, pl **corps** [kɔːz] n corpo.

corpse |kɔːps| n cadavere m.

corral |kəˈraːl| n recinto.

correct |kəˈrɛkt| a (accurate) corretto(a), esatto(a); (proper) corretto(a) // vt correggere; ~ion [-ʃən] n correzione f.

correspond |kɔrɪsˈpɔnd| vi corrispondere; ~ence n corrispondenza; ~ence course n corso per corrispondenza; ~ent n corrispondente m/f.

corridor |ˈkɔrɪdɔː*| n corridoio.

corrode |kəˈrəud| vt corrodere // vi corrodersi.

corrugated |ˈkɔrəgeɪtɪd| a increspato(a); ondulato(a); ~ **iron** n lamiera di ferro ondulata.

corrupt |kəˈrʌpt| a corrotto(a) // vt corrompere; ~ion [-ʃən] n corruzione f.

corset |ˈkɔːsɪt| n busto.

cortège |kɔːˈteɪʒ| n corteo.

cosh [kɔʃ] n (Brit) randello (corto).

cosmetic |kɔzˈmɛtɪk| n cosmetico.

cosset |ˈkɔsɪt| vt vezzeggiare.

cost [kɔst] n costo // vb (pt, pp **cost**) vi costare // vt stabilire il prezzo di; ~s npl (LAW) spese fpl; at all ~s a ogni costo. it **5 to much** costa 5 sterline/troppo; **at all** ~s a ogni costo.

co-star |ˈkəustaː*| n attore/trice della stessa importanza del protagonista.

cost-effective |kɔstɪˈfɛktɪv| a conveniente.

costly |ˈkɔstlɪ| a costoso(a), caro(a).

cost-of-living |kɔstəvˈlɪvɪŋ| a: ~ **allowance** indennità f inv di contingenza; ~ **index** indice m della scala mobile.

cost price n (Brit) prezzo all'ingrosso.

costume |ˈkɔstjuːm| n costume m; (lady's suit) tailleur m inv; (Brit: also: **swimming** ~) costume da bagno; ~ **jewellery** n bigiotteria.

cosy, (US) **cozy** |ˈkəuzɪ| a intimo(a).

cot [kɔt] n (Brit: child's) lettino; (US: campbed) brandina.

cottage |ˈkɔtɪdʒ| n cottage m inv; ~ **cheese** n fiocchi mpl di latte magro; ~ **industry** n industria artigianale basata sul lavoro a cottimo; ~ **pie** n piatto a base di carne macinata in sugo e purè di patate.

cotton |ˈkɔtn| n cotone m; **to** ~ **on to** vt fus (col) afferrare; ~ **candy** n (US) zucchero filato; ~ **wool** n (Brit) cotone idrofilo.

couch |kautʃ| n sofà m inv // vt esprimere.

couchette |kuːˈʃɛt| n (on train, boat) cuccetta.

cough |kɔf| vi tossire // n tosse f; ~ **drop** n pasticca per la tosse.

could |kud| pt of **can**; ~**n't** = **could not**.

council |ˈkaunsl| n consiglio; **city** or **town** ~ consiglio comunale; ~ **estate** n (Brit) quartiere m di case popolari; ~

house n (Brit) casa popolare; ~**lor** n consigliere/a.

counsel |ˈkaunsl| n avvocato; consultazione f; ~**lor** n consigliere/a.

count |kaunt| vt, vi contare // n conto; (nobleman) conte m; **to** ~ **on** vt fus contare su; ~**down** n conto alla rovescia.

countenance |ˈkauntɪnəns| n volto, aspetto // vt approvare.

counter |ˈkauntə*| n banco // vt opporsi a; (blow) parare // ad: ~ **to** contro; in opposizione a; ~**act** vt agire in opposizione a; (poison etc) annullare gli effetti di; ~**espionage** n controspionaggio.

counterfeit |ˈkauntəfɪt| n contraffazione f, falso // vt contraffare, falsificare // a falso(a).

counterfoil |ˈkauntəfɔɪl| n matrice f.

countermand |kauntəˈmaːnd| vt annullare.

counterpart |ˈkauntəpaːt| n (of document etc) copia; (of person) corrispondente m/f.

counter-productive |kauntəprəˈdʌktɪv| a controproducente.

countersign |ˈkauntəsaɪn| vt controfirmare.

countess |ˈkauntɪs| n contessa.

countless |ˈkauntlɪs| a innumerevole.

country |ˈkʌntrɪ| n paese m; (native land) patria; (as opposed to town) campagna; (region) regione f; ~ **dancing** n (Brit) danza popolare; ~ **house** n villa in campagna; ~**man** n (national) compatriota m; (rural) contadino; ~**side** n campagna.

county |ˈkauntɪ| n contea.

coup, ~**s** [kuː, -z] n colpo; (also: ~ d'état) colpo di Stato.

couple |ˈkʌpl| n coppia // vt (carriages) agganciare; (TECH) accoppiare; (ideas, names) associare; a ~ of un paio di.

coupon |ˈkuːpɔn| n buono; (COMM) coupon m inv.

courage |ˈkʌrɪdʒ| n coraggio.

courgette |kuəˈʒɛt| n (Brit) zucchina.

courier |ˈkurɪə*| n corriere m; (for tourists) guida.

course [kɔːs] n corso; (of ship) rotta; (for golf) campo; (part of meal) piatto; **first** ~ primo piatto; **of** ~ ad senz'altro, naturalmente; ~ **of lectures** corso di lezioni; a ~ **of treatment** (MED) una cura.

court |kɔːt| n corte f; (TENNIS) campo // vt (woman) fare la corte a; **to take to** ~ citare in tribunale.

courteous |ˈkɔːtɪəs| a cortese.

courtesan |kɔːtɪˈzæn| n cortigiana.

courtesy |ˈkɔːtəsɪ| n cortesia; **by** ~ **of** per gentile concessione di.

court-house |ˈkɔːthaus| n (US) palazzo di giustizia.

courtier ['kɔːtɪə*] n cortigiano/a.
court-martial, pl **courts-martial**
['kɔːt'mɑːʃəl] n corte f marziale.
courtroom ['kɔːtrum] n tribunale m.
courtyard ['kɔːtjɑːd] n cortile m.
cousin ['kʌzn] n cugino/a; **first** ~ cugino
di primo grado.
cove [kəuv] n piccola baia.
covenant ['kʌvənənt] n accordo.
cover ['kʌvə*] vt coprire // n (of pan)
coperchio; (over furniture) fodera; (of
book) copertina; (shelter) riparo;
(COMM, INSURANCE) copertura; **to take**
~ (shelter) ripararsi; **under** ~ al riparo;
under ~ **of darkness** protetto
dall'oscurità; **under separate** ~ (COMM)
a parte, in plico separato; **to** ~ **up for sb**
coprire qn; ~**age** n (PRESS, TV, RADIO):
to give full ~**age to sth** fare un ampio
servizio su qc; ~ **charge** n coperto;
~**ing** n copertura; ~**ing letter,** (US) ~
letter n lettera d'accompagnamento; ~
note n (INSURANCE) polizza (di
assicurazione) provvisoria.
covert ['kʌvət] a (hidden) nascosto(a);
(glance) furtivo(a).
cover-up ['kʌvərʌp] n occultamento (di
informazioni).
covet ['kʌvɪt] vt bramare.
cow [kau] n vacca // vt (person)
intimidire.
coward ['kauəd] n vigliacco/a; ~**ice** [-ɪs]
n vigliaccheria; ~**ly** a vigliacco(a).
cowboy ['kaubɔɪ] n cow-boy m inv.
cower ['kauə*] vi acquattarsi.
coxswain ['kɔksn] n (abbr: cox)
timoniere m.
coy [kɔɪ] a falsamente timido(a).
cozy ['kəuzɪ] a (US) = **cosy.**
CPA n abbr (US) = **certified public
accountant.**
crab [kræb] n granchio; ~ **apple** n mela
selvatica.
crack [kræk] n fessura, crepa; in-
crinatura; (noise) schiocco; (: of gun)
scoppio; (joke) battuta; (col: attempt):
to have a ~ **at sth** tentare qc // vt
spaccare; incrinare; (whip) schioccare;
(nut) schiacciare // a (troops) fuori
classe; **to** ~ **down on** vt fus porre
freno a; **to** ~ **up** vi crollare; ~**er** n
cracker m inv; petardo.
crackle ['krækl] vi crepitare.
cradle ['kreɪdl] n culla.
craft [krɑːft] n mestiere m; (cunning)
astuzia; (boat) naviglio; ~**sman** n
artigiano; ~**smanship** n abilità; ~**y** a
furbo(a), astuto(a).
crag [kræg] n roccia.
cram [kræm] vt (fill): **to** ~ **sth with**
riempire qc di; (put): **to** ~ **sth into**
stipare qc in // vi (for exams) prepararsi
(in gran fretta).
cramp [kræmp] n crampo; ~**ed** a ri-
stretto(a).

crampon ['kræmpən] n (CLIMBING)
rampone m.
cranberry ['krænbərɪ] n mirtillo.
crane [kreɪn] n gru f inv.
crank [kræŋk] n manovella; (person)
persona stramba; ~**shaft** n albero a
gomiti.
cranny ['krænɪ] n see **nook.**
crash [kræʃ] n fragore ~m; (of car)
incidente m; (of plane) caduta // vt
fracassare // vi (plane) fracassarsi;
(car) avere un incidente; (two cars)
scontrarsi; (fig) fallire, andare in
rovina; **to** ~ **into** scontrarsi con; ~
course n corso intensivo; ~ **helmet** n
casco; ~ **landing** n atterraggio di
fortuna.
crate [kreɪt] n gabbia.
cravat(e) [krə'væt] n fazzoletto da collo.
crave [kreɪv] vt, vi: **to** ~ (**for**) desiderare
ardentemente.
crawl [krɔːl] vi strisciare carponi; (vehicle) avanzare lentamente // n
(SWIMMING) crawl m.
crayfish ['kreɪfɪʃ] n (pl inv) (freshwater)
gambero (d'acqua dolce); (saltwater)
gambero.
crayon ['kreɪən] n matita colorata.
craze [kreɪz] n mania.
crazy ['kreɪzɪ] a matto(a); ~ **paving** n
lastricato a mosaico irregolare.
creak [kriːk] vi cigolare, scricchiolare.
cream [kriːm] n crema; (fresh) panna //
a (colour) color crema inv; ~ **cake** n
torta alla panna; ~ **cheese** n formaggio
fresco; ~**y** a cremoso(a).
crease [kriːs] n grinza; (deliberate) piega
// vt sgualcire.
create [kriː'eɪt] vt creare; **creation**
[-ʃən] n creazione f; **creative** a
creativo(a).
creature ['kriːtʃə*] n creatura.
crèche, creche [kreɪ] n asilo infantile.
credence ['kriːdns] n: **to lend** or **give** ~
to prestare fede a.
credentials [krɪ'dɛnʃlz] npl (papers)
credenziali fpl.
credit ['krɛdɪt] n credito; onore m // vt
(COMM) accreditare; (believe: also:
give ~ **to**) credere, prestar fede a; ~**s**
npl (CINEMA) titoli mpl; **to** ~ **sb with**
(fig) attribuire a qn; **to be in** ~ (person)
essere creditore(trice); (bank account)
essere coperto(a); ~ **card** n carta di
credito; ~**or** n creditore/trice.
creed [kriːd] n credo; dottrina.
creek [kriːk] n insenatura; (US) piccolo
fiume m.
creep [kriːp], pt, pp **crept** vi avanzare
furtivamente (or pian piano); (plant)
arrampicarsi; ~**er** n pianta rampicante;
~**y** a (frightening) che fa accapponare
la pelle.
cremate [krɪ'meɪt] vt cremare.
crematorium, pl **crematoria**

[kremə'tɔ:rɪəm, -'tɔ:rɪə] n forno crematorio.

crêpe [kreɪp] n crespo; ~ **bandage** n (Brit) fascia elastica.

crept [krɛpt] pt, pp of **creep**.

crescent ['krɛsnt] n (shape) mezzaluna; (street) strada semicircolare.

cress [krɛs] n crescione m.

crest [krɛst] n cresta; (of helmet) pennacchiera; (of coat of arms) cimiero; ~**fallen** a mortificato(a).

crevasse [krɪ'væs] n crepaccio.

crevice ['krɛvɪs] n fessura, crepa.

crew [kru:] n equipaggio; to have a ~**cut** avere i capelli a spazzola; ~**neck** n girocollo.

crib [krɪb] n culla; (REL) presepio // vt (col) copiare.

crick [krɪk] n crampo.

cricket ['krɪkɪt] n (insect) grillo; (game) cricket m.

crime [kraɪm] n crimine m; **criminal** ['krɪmɪnl] a, n criminale (m/f).

crimson ['krɪmzn] a color cremisi inv.

cringe [krɪndʒ] vi acquattarsi; (fig) essere servile.

crinkle ['krɪŋkl] vt arricciare, increspare.

cripple ['krɪpl] n zoppo/a // vt azzoppare.

crisis, pl **crises** ['kraɪsɪs, -si:z] n crisi f inv.

crisp [krɪsp] a croccante; (fig) frizzante; vivace; deciso(a); ~**s** npl (Brit) patatine fpl.

criss-cross ['krɪskrɔs] a incrociato(a).

criterion, pl **criteria** [kraɪ'tɪərɪən, -'tɪərɪə] n criterio.

critic ['krɪtɪk] n critico; ~**al** a critico(a); ~**ally** ad (speak etc) criticamente; ~**ally ill** gravemente malato; ~**ism** ['krɪtɪsɪzm] n critica; ~**ize** ['krɪtɪsaɪz] vt criticare.

croak [krəuk] vi gracchiare; (frog) gracidare.

crochet ['krəuʃeɪ] n lavoro all'uncinetto.

crockery ['krɔkərɪ] n vasellame m.

crocodile ['krɔkədaɪl] n coccodrillo.

crocus ['krəukəs] n croco.

croft [krɔft] n (Brit) piccolo podere m.

crony ['krəunɪ] n (col) amicone/a.

crook [kruk] n truffatore m; (of shepherd) bastone m; ~**ed** ['krukɪd] a curvo(a), storto(a); (action) disonesto(a).

crop [krɔp] n (produce) coltivazione f; (amount produced) raccolto; (riding ~) frustino; **to ~ up** vi presentarsi.

croquette [krə'kɛt] n crocchetta.

cross [krɔs] n croce f; (BIOL) incrocio // vt (street etc) attraversare; (arms, legs, BIOL) incrociare; (cheque) sbarrare // a di cattivo umore; to ~ o.s. fare il segno della croce, segnarsi; **to ~ out** vt cancellare; **to ~ over** vi attraversare; ~**bar** n traversa; ~**country (race)** n cross-country m inv; ~**-examine** vt

(LAW) interrogare in contraddittorio; ~**-eyed** a strabico(a); ~**fire** n fuoco incrociato; ~**ing** n incrocio; (sea passage) traversata; (also: **pedestrian ~ing**) passaggio pedonale; ~**ing guard** n (US) dipendente comunale che aiuta i bambini ad attraversare la strada; ~ **purposes** npl: to be at ~ **purposes** non parlare della stessa cosa; ~**-reference** n rinvio, rimando; ~**roads** n incrocio; ~ **section** n (BIOL) sezione f trasversale; (in population) settore m rappresentativo; ~**walk** n (US) strisce fpl pedonali, passaggio pedonale; ~**wind** n vento di traverso; ~**wise** ad di traverso; ~**word** n cruciverba m inv.

crotch [krɔtʃ] n (of garment) pattina.

crotchety ['krɔtʃɪtɪ] a (person) burbero(a).

crouch [krautʃ] vi acquattarsi; rannicchiarsi.

crouton ['kru:tɔn] n crostino.

crow [krəu] n (bird) cornacchia; (of cock) canto del gallo // vi (cock) cantare; (fig) vantarsi; cantar vittoria.

crowbar ['krəuba:*] n piede m di porco.

crowd [kraud] n folla // vt affollare, stipare // vi affollarsi; ~**ed** a affollato(a); ~**ed with** stipato(a) di.

crown [kraun] n corona; (of head) calotta cranica; (of hat) cocuzzolo; (of hill) cima // vt incoronare; ~ **jewels** npl gioielli mpl della Corona; ~ **prince** n principe m ereditario.

crow's feet npl zampe fpl di gallina.

crucial ['kru:ʃl] a cruciale, decisivo(a).

crucifix ['kru:sɪfɪks] n crocifisso; ~**ion** [-'fɪkʃən] n crocifissione f.

crude [kru:d] a (materials) greggio(a); non raffinato(a); (fig: basic) crudo(a), primitivo(a); (: vulgar) rozzo(a), grossolano(a); ~ **(oil)** n (petrolio) greggio.

cruel ['kruəl] a crudele; ~**ty** n crudeltà f inv.

cruet ['kru:ɪt] n ampolla.

cruise [kru:z] n crociera // vi andare a velocità di crociera; (taxi) circolare; ~**r** n incrociatore m.

crumb [krʌm] n briciola.

crumble ['krʌmbl] vt sbriciolare // vi sbriciolarsi; (plaster etc) sgretolarsi; (land, earth) franare; (building, fig) crollare; **crumbly** a friabile.

crumpet ['krʌmpɪt] n specie di frittella.

crumple ['krʌmpl] vt raggrinzare, spiegazzare.

crunch [krʌntʃ] vt sgranocchiare; (underfoot) scricchiolare // n (fig) punto or momento cruciale; ~**y** a croccante.

crusade [kru:'seɪd] n crociata.

crush [krʌʃ] n folla // vt schiacciare; (crumple) sgualcire.

crust [krʌst] n crosta.

crutch [krʌtʃ] n gruccia.

crux |krʌks| *n* nodo.
cry |kraɪ| *vi* piangere; (*shout: also:* ~ out) urlare // *n* urlo, grido; **to** ~ **off** *vi* ritirarsi.
cryptic |'krɪptɪk| *a* ermetico(a).
crystal |'krɪstl| *n* cristallo; ~-**clear** *a* cristallino(a).
cub |kʌb| *n* cucciolo; (*also:* ~ scout) lupetto.
Cuba |'kju:bə| *n* Cuba.
cubbyhole |'kʌbɪhəul| *n* angolino.
cube |kju:b| *n* cubo // *vt* (*MATH*) elevare al cubo; **cubic** *a* cubico(a); (*metre, foot*) cubo(a); **cubic capacity** *n* cilindrata.
cubicle |'kju:bɪkl| *n* scompartimento separato; cabina.
cuckoo |'kuku:| *n* cucù *m inv*; ~ **clock** *n* orologio a cucù.
cucumber |'kju:kʌmbə*| *n* cetriolo.
cuddle |'kʌdl| *vt* abbracciare, coccolare // *vi* abbracciarsi.
cue |kju:| *n* (*snooker* ~) stecca; (*THEATRE etc*) segnale *m*.
cuff |kʌf| *n* (*Brit: of shirt, coat etc*) polsino; (*US: of trousers*) risvolto; **off the** ~ *ad* improvvisando; ~**link** *n* gemello.
cuisine |kwɪ'zi:n| *n* cucina.
cul-de-sac |'kʌldəsæk| *n* vicolo cieco.
culminate |'kʌlmɪneɪt| *vi:* **to** ~ **in** culminare con; **culmination** |-'neɪʃən| *n* culmine *m*.
culottes |kju:'lɔts| *npl* gonna *f* pantalone *inv.*
culpable |'kʌlpəbl| *a* colpevole.
culprit |'kʌlprɪt| *n* colpevole *m/f.*
cult |kʌlt| *n* culto.
cultivate |'kʌltɪveɪt| *vt* (*also fig*) coltivare; **cultivation** |-'veɪʃən| *n* coltivazione *f.*
cultural |'kʌltʃərəl| *a* culturale.
culture |'kʌltʃə*| *n* (*also fig*) cultura; ~**d** *a* colto(a).
cumbersome |'kʌmbəsəm| *a* ingombrante.
cunning |'kʌnɪŋ| *n* astuzia, furberia // *a* astuto(a), furbo(a).
cup |kʌp| *n* tazza; (*prize*) coppa.
cupboard |'kʌbəd| *n* armadio.
cup-tie |'kʌptaɪ| *n* (*Brit*) partita di coppa.
curate |'kjuərɪt| *n* cappellano.
curator |kjuə'reɪtə*| *n* direttore *m* (*di museo etc*).
curb |kə:b| *vt* tenere a freno // *n* freno; (*US*) = **kerb.**
curdle |'kə:dl| *vi* cagliare.
cure |kjuə*| *vt* guarire; (*CULIN*) trattare; affumicare; essiccare // *n* rimedio.
curfew |'kə:fju:| *n* coprifuoco.
curio |'kjuərɪəu| *n* curiosità *f inv.*
curiosity |kjuərɪ'ɔsɪtɪ| *n* curiosità.
curious |'kjuərɪəs| *a* curioso(a).
curl |kə:l| *n* riccio // *vt* ondulare; (*tightly*)

arricciare // *vi* arricciarsi; **to** ~ **up** *vi* avvolgersi a spirale; rannicchiarsi; ~**er** *n* bigodino.
curly |'kə:lɪ| *a* ricciuto(a).
currant |'kʌrnt| *n* uva passa.
currency |'kʌrnsɪ| *n* moneta; **to gain** ~ (*fig*) acquistare larga diffusione.
current |'kʌrnt| *a*, *n* corrente (*f*); ~ **account** *n* (*Brit*) conto corrente; ~ **affairs** *npl* attualità *fpl;* ~**ly** *ad* attualmente.
curriculum, *pl* ~**s** *or* **curricula** |kə'rɪkjuləm, -lə| *n* curriculum *m inv;* ~ **vitae (CV)** *n* curriculum vitae *m inv.*
curry |'kʌrɪ| *n* curry *m inv* // *vt:* **to** ~ **favour with** cercare di attirarsi i favori di.
curse |kə:s| *vt* maledire // *vi* bestemmiare // *n* maledizione *f;* bestemmia.
cursor |'kə:sə*| *n* (*COMPUT*) cursore *m.*
cursory |'kə:sərɪ| *a* superficiale.
curt |kə:t| *a* secco(a).
curtail |kə:'teɪl| *vt* (*visit etc*) accorciare; (*expenses etc*) ridurre, decurtare.
curtain |'kə:tn| *n* tenda.
curts(e)y |'kə:tsɪ| *n* inchino, riverenza // *vi* fare un inchino *or* una riverenza.
curve |kə:v| *n* curva // *vi* curvarsi.
cushion |'kuʃən| *n* cuscino // *vt* (*shock*) fare da cuscinetto a.
custard |'kʌstəd| *n* (*for pouring*) crema.
custodian |kʌs'təudɪən| *n* custode *m/f.*
custody |'kʌstədɪ| *n* (*of child*) tutela; (*for offenders*) arresto.
custom |'kʌstəm| *n* costume *m,* usanza; (*LAW*) consuetudine *f;* (*COMM*) clientela; ~**ary** *a* consueto(a).
customer |'kʌstəmə*| *n* cliente *m/f.*
customized |'kʌstəmaɪzd| *a* (*car etc*) fuoriserie *inv.*
custom-made |'kʌstəm'meɪd| *a* (*clothes*) fatto(a) su misura; (*other goods*) fatto(a) su ordinazione.
customs |'kʌstəmz| *npl* dogana; ~ **officer** *n* doganiere *m.*
cut |kʌt| *vb* (*pt, pp* **cut**) *vt* tagliare; (*shape, make*) intagliare; (*reduce*) ridurre // *vi* tagliare; (*intersect*) tagliarsi // *n* taglio; (*in salary etc*) riduzione *f;* **to** ~ **a tooth** mettere un dente; **to** ~ **down** *vt* (*tree etc*) abbattere // *vt fus* (*also:* ~ **down on**) ridurre; **to** ~ **off** *vt* tagliare; (*fig*) isolare; **to** ~ **out** *vt* tagliare fuori; eliminare; ritagliare; **to** ~ **up** *vt* (*paper, meat*) tagliare a pezzi; ~**back** *n* riduzione *f.*
cute |kju:t| *a* grazioso(a); (*clever*) astuto(a).
cuticle |'kju:tɪkl| *n* (*on nail*) pellicina, cuticola.
cutlery |'kʌtlərɪ| *n* posate *fpl.*
cutlet |'kʌtlɪt| *n* costoletta.
cut: ~**out** *n* interruttore *m;* (*cardboard*

~) ritaglio; ~-**price**, (*US*) ~-**rate** *a* a prezzo ridotto; ~**throat** *n* assassino // *a* (*razor*) da barbiere; (*competition*) spietato(a).

cutting ['kʌtɪŋ] *a* tagliente; (*fig*) pungente // *n* (*Brit: from newspaper*) ritaglio (di giornale).

CV *n abbr* = **curriculum vitae.**

cwt *abbr* = **hundredweight(s).**

cyanide ['saɪənaɪd] *n* cianuro.

cycle ['saɪkl] *n* ciclo; (*bicycle*) bicicletta // *vi* andare in bicicletta.

cycling ['saɪklɪŋ] *n* ciclismo.

cyclist ['saɪklɪst] *n* ciclista *m/f*.

cygnet ['sɪgnɪt] *n* cigno giovane.

cylinder ['sɪlɪndə*] *n* cilindro; ~-**head gasket** *n* guarnizione *f* della testata del cilindro.

cymbals ['sɪmblz] *npl* cembali *mpl*.

cynic ['sɪnɪk] *n* cinico/a; ~**al** *a* cinico(a); ~**ism** ['sɪnɪsɪzəm] *n* cinismo.

Cypriot ['sɪprɪət] *a*, *n* cipriota (*m/f*).

Cyprus ['saɪprəs] *n* Cipro.

cyst [sɪst] *n* cisti *f inv*.

cystitis [sɪs'taɪtɪs] *n* cistite *f*.

czar [zɑ:*] *n* zar *m inv*.

Czech [tʃɛk] *a* ceco(a) // *n* ceco/a; (*LING*) ceco.

Czechoslovakia [tʃɛkəslə'vækɪə] *n* Cecoslovacchia; ~**n** *a*, *n* cecoslovacco(a).

D

D [di:] *n* (*MUS*) re *m*.

dab [dæb] *vt* (*eyes, wound*) tamponare; (*paint, cream*) applicare (con leggeri colpetti).

dabble ['dæbl] *vi*: to ~ in occuparsi (da dilettante) di.

dad, daddy [dæd, 'dædɪ] *n* babbo, papà *m inv*.

daffodil ['dæfədɪl] *n* trombone *m*, giunchiglia.

daft [dɑ:ft] *a* sciocco(a).

dagger ['dægə*] *n* pugnale *m*.

daily ['deɪlɪ] *a* quotidiano(a), giornaliero(a) // *n* quotidiano // *ad* tutti i giorni.

dainty ['deɪntɪ] *a* delicato(a), grazioso(a).

dairy ['dɛərɪ] *n* (*shop*) latteria; (*on farm*) caseificio // *a* caseario(a); ~ **produce** *n* latticini *mpl*.

dais ['deɪɪs] *n* pedana, palco.

daisy ['deɪzɪ] *n* margherita; ~ **wheel** *n* (*on printer*) margherita.

dale [deɪl] *n* valle *f*.

dam [dæm] *n* diga // *vt* sbarrare; costruire dighe su.

damage ['dæmɪdʒ] *n* danno, danni *mpl*; (*fig*) danno // *vt* danneggiare; (*fig*) recar danno a; ~**s** *npl* (*LAW*) danni.

damn [dæm] *vt* condannare; (*curse*) maledire // *n* (*col*): **I don't give a** ~ non me ne importa un fico // *a* (*col: also*: ~**ed**): **this** ~ ... questo maledetto ...; ~ (**it**)! accidenti!

damp [dæmp] *a* umido(a) // *n* umidità, umido // *vt* (*also*: ~**en**: *cloth, rag*) inumidire, bagnare; (*enthusiasm etc*) spegnere.

damson ['dæmzən] *n* susina damaschina.

dance [dɑ:ns] *n* danza, ballo; (*ball*) ballo // *vi* ballare; ~ **hall** *n* dancing *m inv*, sala da ballo; ~**r** *n* danzatore/trice; (*professional*) ballerino/a.

dancing ['dɑ:nsɪŋ] *n* danza, ballo.

dandelion ['dændɪlaɪən] *n* dente *m* di leone.

dandruff ['dændrəf] *n* forfora.

Dane [deɪn] *n* danese *m/f*.

danger ['deɪndʒə*] *n* pericolo; **there is a** ~ **of fire** c'è pericolo di incendio; **in** ~ in pericolo; **he was in** ~ **of falling** rischiava di cadere; ~**ous** *a* pericoloso(a).

dangle ['dæŋgl] *vt* dondolare; (*fig*) far balenare // *vi* pendolare.

Danish ['deɪnɪʃ] *a* danese // *n* (*LING*) danese *m*.

dapper ['dæpə*] *a* lindo(a).

dare [dɛə*] *vt*: to ~ **sb to do** sfidare qn a fare // *vi*: to ~ (**to**) **do sth** osare fare qc; **I** ~ **say** (*I suppose*) immagino (che); ~**devil** *n* scavezzacollo *m/f*; **daring** *a* audace, ardito(a) // *n* audacia.

dark [dɑ:k] *a* (*night, room*) buio(a), scuro(a); (*colour, complexion*) scuro(a); (*fig*) cupo(a), tetro(a), nero(a) // *n*: **in the** ~ al buio; **in the** ~ **about** (*fig*) all'oscuro di; **after** ~ a notte fatta; ~**en** *vt* (*room*) oscurare; (*photo, painting*) far scuro(a) // *vi* oscurarsi; imbrunirsi; ~ **glasses** *npl* occhiali *mpl* scuri; ~**ness** *n* oscurità, buio; ~ **room** *n* camera oscura.

darling ['dɑ:lɪŋ] *a* caro(a) // *n* tesoro.

darn [dɑ:n] *vt* rammendare.

dart [dɑ:t] *n* freccetta // *vi*: to ~ **towards** precipitarsi verso; to ~ **away** guizzare via; ~**s** *n* tiro al bersaglio (con freccette); ~**board** *n* bersaglio (per freccette).

dash [dæʃ] *n* (*sign*) lineetta; (*small quantity*) punta // *vt* (*missile*) gettare; (*hopes*) infrangere // *vi*: to ~ **towards** precipitarsi verso; to ~ **away** *or* **off** *vi* scappare via.

dashboard ['dæʃbɔ:d] *n* (*AUT*) cruscotto.

dashing ['dæʃɪŋ] *a* ardito(a).

data ['deɪtə] *npl* dati *mpl*; ~**base** *n* base *f* di dati, data base *m inv*; ~ **processing** *n* elaborazione *f* (elettronica) dei dati.

date [deɪt] *n* data; appuntamento; (*fruit*) dattero // *vt* datare; ~ **of birth** data di nascita; to ~ **ad** fino a oggi; **out of** ~ scaduto(a); (*old-fashioned*) passato(a) di moda; ~**d** *a* passato(a) di moda.

daub [dɔ:b] *vt* imbrattare.

daughter |'dɔ:tə*| n figlia; **~-in-law** n nuora.

daunt |dɔ:nt| vt intimidire; **~ing** a non invidiabile.

dawdle |'dɔ:dl| vi bighellonare.

dawn |dɔ:n| n alba // vi (day) spuntare; (fig) venire in mente; it **~ed** on him that ... gli è venuto in mente che ...

day |deɪ| n giorno; (as duration) giornata; (period of time, age) tempo, epoca; the **~** before il giorno avanti or prima; the **~** after, the following **~** il giorno dopo or seguente; the **~** after tomorrow dopodomani; the **~** before yesterday l'altroieri; by **~** di giorno; **~break** n spuntar m del giorno; **~dream** vi sognare a occhi aperti; **~light** n luce f del giorno; **~ return** n (Brit) biglietto giornaliero di andata e ritorno; **~time** n giorno; **~-to-~** a (life, organization) quotidiano(a).

daze |deɪz| vt (subject: drug) inebetire; (: blow) stordire // n: in a **~** inebetito(a); stordito(a).

dazzle |'dæzl| vt abbagliare.

DC abbr (= direct current) c.c.

deacon |'di:kən| n diacono.

dead |dɛd| a morto(a); (numb) intirizzito(a) // ad assolutamente, perfettamente; he was shot **~** fu colpito a morte; **~** on time in perfetto orario; **~** tired stanco(a) morto(a); to stop **~** fermarsi in tronco; the **~** 1 morti; **~en** vt (blow, sound) ammortire; (make numb) intirizzire; **~ end** n vicolo cieco; **~ heat** n (SPORT) to finish in a **~** heat finire alla pari; **~line** n scadenza; **~lock** n punto morto; **~ loss** n: to be a **~** loss (col: person, thing) non valere niente; **~ly** a mortale; (weapon, poison) micidiale; **~pan** a a faccia impassibile.

deaf |dɛf| a sordo(a); **~en** vt assordare; **~-mute** n sordomuto/a, **~ness** n sordità.

deal |di:l| n accordo; (business **~**) affare m // vt (pt, pp dealt |dɛlt|) (blow, cards) dare; a great **~** (of) molto(a); to **~** in vt fus occuparsi di; to **~** with vt fus (COMM) fare affari con, trattare con; (handle) occuparsi di; (be about: book etc) trattare di; **~er** n commerciante m/f; **~ings** npl (COMM) relazioni fpl; (relations) rapporti mpl.

dean |di:n| n (REL) decano; (SCOL) preside m di facoltà (or di collegio).

dear |dɪə*| a caro(a) // n: my **~** caro mio/cara mia; **~** me! Dio mio!; D**~** Sir/ Madam (in letter) Egregio Signore/ Egregia Signora; D**~** Mr/Mrs X Gentile Signor/Signora X; **~ly** ad (love) moltissimo; (pay) a caro prezzo.

death |dɛθ| n morte f; (ADMIN) decesso; **~ certificate** n atto di decesso; **~ duties** npl (Brit) imposta or tassa di successione; **~ly** a di morte; **~ penalty**

n pena di morte; **~ rate** n indice m di mortalità.

debacle |dɪ'bækl| n fiasco.

debar |dɪ'bɑ:*| vt: to **~** sb from doing impedire a qn di fare.

debase |dɪ'beɪs| vt (currency) adulterare; (person) degradare.

debatable |dɪ'beɪtəbl| a discutibile.

debate |dɪ'beɪt| n dibattito // vt dibattere; discutere.

debauchery |dɪ'bɔ:tʃərɪ| n dissolutezza.

debit |'dɛbɪt| n debito // vt: to **~** a sum to sb or to sb's account addebitare una somma a qn.

debris |'dɛbri:| n detriti mpl.

debt |dɛt| n debito; to be in **~** essere indebitato(a); **~or** n debitore/trice.

debunk |di:'bʌŋk| vt (theory, claim) smentire.

début |'deɪbju:| n debutto.

decade |'dɛkeɪd| n decennio.

decadence |'dɛkədəns| n decadenza.

decaffeinated |dɪ'kæfɪneɪtɪd| a decaffeinato(a).

decanter |dɪ'kæntə*| n caraffa.

decay |dɪ'keɪ| n decadimento; impu-tridimento; (fig) rovina; (also: tooth **~**) carie f // vi (rot) imputridire; (fig) andare in rovina.

deceased |dɪ'si:st| n defunto/a.

deceit |dɪ'si:t| n inganno; **~ful** a ingannevole, perfido(a).

deceive |dɪ'si:v| vt ingannare.

December |dɪ'sɛmbə*| n dicembre m.

decent |'di:sənt| a decente; they were very **~** about it si sono comportati da si-gnori riguardo a ciò.

deception |dɪ'sɛpʃən| n inganno.

deceptive |dɪ'sɛptɪv| a ingannevole.

decide |dɪ'saɪd| vt (person) far prendere una decisione a; (question, argument) risolvere, decidere // vi decidere, decidersi; to **~** to do/that decidere di fare/che; to **~** on decidere per; **~d** a (resolute) deciso(a); (clear, definite) netto(a), chiaro(a); **~dly** |-dɪdlɪ| ad indubbiamente; decisamente.

decimal |'dɛsɪməl| a, n decimale (m); **~ point** n ≈ virgola.

decipher |dɪ'saɪfə*| vt decifrare.

decision |dɪ'sɪʒən| n decisione f.

decisive |dɪ'saɪsɪv| a decisivo(a).

deck |dɛk| n (NAUT) ponte m; (of bus): top **~** imperiale m; (of cards) mazzo; **~chair** n sedia a sdraio.

declaration |dɛklə'reɪʃən| n di-chiarazione f.

declare |dɪ'klɛə*| vt dichiarare.

decline |dɪ'klaɪn| n (decay) declino; (lessening) ribasso // vt declinare; rifiutare // vi declinare; diminuire.

decode |di:'kəud| vt decifrare.

decompose |di:kəm'pəuz| vi decomporre.

décor |'deɪkɔ:*| n decorazione f.

decorate ['dɛkəreɪt] vt (adorn, give a medal to) decorare; (paint and paper) tinteggiare e tappezzare; **decoration** [-'reɪʃən] n (medal etc, adornment) decorazione f; **decorator** n decoratore m.

decorum [dɪ'kɔ:rəm] n decoro.

decoy ['di:kɔɪ] n zimbello.

decrease n ['di:kri:s] diminuzione f // vt, vi [di:'kri:s] diminuire.

decree [dɪ'kri:] n decreto; ~ **nisi** [-'naɪsaɪ] n sentenza provvisoria di divorzio.

dedicate ['dɛdɪkeɪt] vt consacrare; (book etc) dedicare.

dedication [dɛdɪ'keɪʃən] n (devotion) dedizione f.

deduce [dɪ'dju:s] vt dedurre.

deduct [dɪ'dʌkt] vt: to ~ sth (from) dedurre qc (da); (from wage etc) trattenere qc (da); **~ion** [dɪ'dʌkʃən] n (deducting) deduzione f; (from wage etc) trattenuta; (deducing) deduzione f, conclusione f.

deed [di:d] n azione f, atto; (LAW) atto.

deep [di:p] a profondo(a); 4 metres ~ profondo(a) 4 metri // ad: spectators stood 20 ~ c'erano 20 file di spettatori; **~en** vt (hole) approfondire // vi approfondirsi; (darkness) farsi più buio; **~freeze** n congelatore m // vt congelare; **~fry** vt friggere in olio abbondante; **~ly** ad profondamente; **~sea diving** n immersione f in alto mare.

deer [dɪə*] n (pl inv): the ~ i cervidi; (red) ~ cervo; (fallow) ~ daino; (roe) ~ capriolo.

deface [dɪ'feɪs] vt imbrattare.

default [dɪ'fɔ:lt] vi (LAW) essere contumace; (gen) essere inadempiente // n (COMPUT: also: ~ value) default m inv; by ~ (LAW) in contumacia; (SPORT) per abbandono.

defeat [dɪ'fi:t] n sconfitta // vt (team, opponents) sconfiggere; (fig: plans, efforts) frustrare; **~ist** a, n disfattista (m/f).

defect n ['di:fɛkt] difetto // vi [dɪ'fɛkt]: to ~ to the enemy passare al nemico; **~ive** [dɪ'fɛktɪv] a difettoso(a).

defence, (US) defense [dɪ'fɛns] n difesa; in ~ of in difesa di; **~less** a senza difesa.

defend [dɪ'fɛnd] vt difendere; **~ant** n imputato/a; **~er** n difensore/a.

defense [dɪ'fɛns] n (US) = **defence**.

defer [dɪ'fə:*] vt (postpone) differire, rinviare // vi: to ~ to rimettersi a.

defiance [dɪ'faɪəns] n sfida; in ~ of a dispetto di.

defiant [dɪ'faɪənt] a (attitude) di sfida; (person) ribelle.

deficiency [dɪ'fɪʃənsɪ] n deficienza; carenza.

deficit ['dɛfɪsɪt] n disavanzo.

defile vb [dɪ'faɪl] vt contaminare // vi sfilare // n ['di:faɪl] gola, stretta.

define [dɪ'faɪn] vt definire.

definite ['dɛfɪnɪt] a (fixed) definito(a), preciso(a); (clear, obvious) ben definito(a), esatto(a); (LING) determinativo(a); he was ~ about it ne era sicuro; **~ly** ad indubbiamente.

definition [dɛfɪ'nɪʃən] n definizione f.

deflate [di:'fleɪt] vt sgonfiare.

deflect [dɪ'flɛkt] vt deflettere, deviare.

deformed [dɪ'fɔ:md] a deforme.

defraud [dɪ'frɔ:d] vt defraudare.

defray [dɪ'freɪ] vt: to ~ sb's expenses sostenere le spese di qn.

defrost [di:'frɔst] vt (fridge) disgelare; **~er** n (US: demister) sbrinatore m.

deft [dɛft] a svelto(a), destro(a).

defunct [dɪ'fʌŋkt] a defunto(a).

defuse [di:'fju:z] vt disinnescare.

defy [dɪ'faɪ] vt sfidare; (efforts etc) resistere a.

degenerate vi [dɪ'dʒɛnəreɪt] degenerare // a [dɪ'dʒɛnərɪt] degenere.

degree [dɪ'gri:] n grado; (SCOL) laurea (universitaria); a (first) ~ in maths una laurea in matematica; by ~s (gradually) gradualmente, a poco a poco; to some ~ fino a un certo punto, in certa misura.

dehydrated [di:haɪ'dreɪtɪd] a disidratato(a); (milk, eggs) in polvere.

de-ice [di:'aɪs] vt (windscreen) disgelare.

deign [deɪn] vi: to ~ to do degnarsi di fare.

deity ['di:ɪtɪ] n divinità f inv.

dejected [dɪ'dʒɛktɪd] a abbattuto(a), avvilito(a).

delay [dɪ'leɪ] vt (journey, operation) ritardare, rinviare; (travellers, trains) ritardare // vi: to ~ (in doing sth) ritardare (a fare qc) // n ritardo.

delectable [dɪ'lɛktəbl] a (person, food) delizioso(a).

delegate n ['dɛlɪgɪt] delegato/a // vt ['dɛlɪgeɪt] delegare.

delete [dɪ'li:t] vt cancellare.

deliberate a [dɪ'lɪbərɪt] (intentional) intenzionale; (slow) misurato(a) // vi [dɪ'lɪbəreɪt] deliberare, riflettere; **~ly** ad (on purpose) deliberatamente.

delicacy ['dɛlɪkəsɪ] n delicatezza.

delicate ['dɛlɪkɪt] a delicato(a).

delicatessen [dɛlɪkə'tɛsn] n ≈ salumeria.

delicious [dɪ'lɪʃəs] a delizioso(a), squisito(a).

delight [dɪ'laɪt] n delizia, gran piacere m // vt dilettare; **~ed** a: **~ed (at or with)** contentissimo(a) (di), felice (di); **~ed to do** felice di fare; **~ful** a delizioso(a); incantevole.

delinquent [dɪ'lɪŋkwənt] a, n delinquente (m/f).

delirious [dɪ'lɪrɪəs] a: to be ~ delirare.

deliver [dɪ'lɪvə*] vt (mail) distribuire;

(*goods*) consegnare; (*speech*) pronunciare; (*free*) liberare; (*MED*) far partorire; **~y** *n* distribuzione *f*; consegna; (*of speaker*) dizione *f*; (*MED*) parto.

delude [dɪ'luːd] *vt* deludere, illudere.

deluge ['dɛljuːdʒ] *n* diluvio.

delusion [dɪ'luːʒən] *n* illusione *f*.

delve [dɛlv] *vi*: to ~ into frugare in; (*subject*) far ricerche in.

demand [dɪ'mɑːnd] *vt* richiedere // *n* domanda; (*ECON, claim*) richiesta; in ~ ricercato(a), richiesto(a); on ~ a richiesta; **~ing** *a* (*boss*) esigente; (*work*) impegnativo(a).

demean [dɪ'miːn] *vt*: to ~ o.s. umiliarsi.

demeanour, (*US*) **demeanor** [dɪ'miːnə*] *n* comportamento; contegno.

demented [dɪ'mɛntɪd] *a* demente, impazzito(a).

demise [dɪ'maɪz] *n* decesso.

demister [diː'mɪstə*] *n* (*AUT*) sbrinatore *m*.

demo ['dɛmɔu] *n abbr* (*col*: = *demonstration*) manifestazione *f*.

demobilize [diː'məubɪlaɪz] *vt* smobilitare.

democracy [dɪ'mɒkrəsɪ] *n* democrazia.

democrat ['dɛməkræt] *n* democratico/a; **~ic** [dɛmə'krætɪk] *a* democratico(a).

demolish [dɪ'mɒlɪʃ] *vt* demolire.

demonstrate ['dɛmənstreɪt] *vt* dimostrare, provare // *vi*: to ~ (*for/against*) dimostrare (*per/contro*), manifestare (*per/contro*); **demonstration** [-'streɪʃən] *n* dimostrazione *f*; (*POL*) manifestazione *f*, dimostrazione; **demonstrator** *n* (*POL*) dimostrante *m/f*.

demote [dɪ'məut] *vt* far retrocedere.

demure [dɪ'mjuə*] *a* contegnoso(a).

den [dɛn] *n* tana, covo.

denatured alcohol [diː'neɪtʃəd-] *n* (*US*) alcool *m inv* denaturato.

denial [dɪ'naɪəl] *n* diniego; rifiuto.

denim ['dɛnɪm] *n* tessuto di cotone ritorto; **~s** *npl* blue jeans *mpl*.

Denmark ['dɛnmɑːk] *n* Danimarca.

denomination [dɪnɒmɪ'neɪʃən] *n* (*money*) valore *m*; (*REL*) confessione *f*.

denounce [dɪ'nauns] *vt* denunciare.

dense [dɛns] *a* fitto(a); (*stupid*) ottuso(a), duro(a).

density ['dɛnsɪtɪ] *n* densità *f inv*.

dent [dɛnt] *n* ammaccatura // *vt* (*also*: make a ~ in) ammaccare.

dental ['dɛntl] *a* dentale; ~ **surgeon** *n* medico/a dentista.

dentist ['dɛntɪst] *n* dentista *m/f*; **~ry** *n* odontoiatria.

denture(s) ['dɛntʃə(z)] *n(pl)* dentiera.

deny [dɪ'naɪ] *vt* negare; (*refuse*) rifiutare.

deodorant [diː'əudərənt] *n* deodorante *m*.

depart [dɪ'pɑːt] *vi* partire; to ~ from

(*fig*) deviare da.

department [dɪ'pɑːtmənt] *n* (*COMM*) reparto; (*SCOL*) sezione *f*, dipartimento; (*POL*) ministero; ~ **store** *n* grande magazzino.

departure [dɪ'pɑːtʃə*] *n* partenza; (*fig*): ~ from deviazione *f* da; a new ~ una svolta (decisiva); ~ **lounge** *n* (*at airport*) sala d'attesa.

depend [dɪ'pɛnd] *vi*: to ~ on dipendere da; (*rely on*) contare su; it ~s dipende; ~ing on the result ... a seconda del risultato ...; **~able** *a* fidato(a); (*car etc*) affidabile; **~ant** *n* persona a carico; **~ent** *a*: to be ~ent on dipendere da; (*child, relative*) essere a carico di // *n* = **~ant**.

depict [dɪ'pɪkt] *vt* (*in picture*) dipingere; (*in words*) descrivere.

depleted [dɪ'pliːtɪd] *a* diminuito(a).

deploy [dɪ'plɔɪ] *vt* dispiegare.

depopulation ['diːpɒpju'leɪʃən] *n* spopolamento.

deport [dɪ'pɔːt] *vt* deportare; espellere.

deportment [dɪ'pɔːtmənt] *n* portamento.

depose [dɪ'pəuz] *vt* deporre.

deposit [dɪ'pɒzɪt] *n* (*COMM, GEO*) deposito; (*of ore, oil*) giacimento; (*CHEM*) sedimento; (*part payment*) acconto; (*for hired goods etc*) cauzione *f* // *vt* depositare; dare in acconto; mettere or lasciare in deposito; ~ **account** *n* conto vincolato.

depot ['dɛpəu] *n* deposito.

depreciate [dɪ'priːʃɪeɪt] *vt* svalutare // *vi* svalutarsi.

depress [dɪ'prɛs] *vt* deprimere; (*press down*) premere; **~ed** *a* (*person*) depresso(a), abbattuto(a); (*area*) depresso(a); **~ing** *a* deprimente; **~ion** [dɪ'prɛʃən] *n* depressione *f*.

deprivation [dɛprɪ'veɪʃən] *n* privazione *f*; (*loss*) perdita.

deprive [dɪ'praɪv] *vt*: to ~ sb of privare qn di; **~d** *a* disgraziato(a).

depth [dɛpθ] *n* profondità *f inv*; in the ~s of nel profondo di; nel cuore di; in the ~s of winter in pieno inverno.

deputize ['dɛpjutaɪz] *vi*: to ~ for svolgere le funzioni di.

deputy ['dɛpjutɪ] *a*: ~ head (*SCOL*) vice-preside *m/f* // *n* (*replacement*) supplente *m/f*; (*second in command*) vice *m/f*.

derail [dɪ'reɪl] *vt* far deragliare; to be **~ed** deragliare.

deranged [dɪ'reɪndʒd] *a*: to be (*mentally*) ~ essere pazzo(a).

derby ['dɜːbɪ] *n* (*US: bowler hat*) bombetta.

derelict ['dɛrɪlɪkt] *a* abbandonato(a).

deride [dɪ'raɪd] *vt* deridere.

derisory [dɪ'raɪsərɪ] *a* (*sum*) irrisorio(a); (*laughter, person*) beffardo(a).

derive [dɪ'raɪv] *vt*: to ~ sth from derivare qc da; trarre qc da // *vi*: to ~

from derivare da.

derogatory [dɪˈrɔgətərɪ] a denigratorio(a).

derrick [ˈderɪk] n gru f inv; (for oil) derrick m inv.

derv [dəːv] n (Brit) gasolio.

descend [dɪˈsɛnd] vt, vi discendere, scendere; to ~ from discendere da; ~ant n discendente m/f.

descent [dɪˈsɛnt] n discesa; (origin) discendenza, famiglia.

describe [dɪsˈkraɪb] vt descrivere; **description** [-ˈkrɪpʃən] n descrizione f; (sort) genere m, specie f.

desecrate [ˈdesɪkreɪt] vt profanare.

desert n [ˈdezət] deserto // vb [dɪˈzəːt] vt lasciare, abbandonare // vi (MIL) disertare; ~er n disertore m; ~ island n isola deserta; ~s [dɪˈzəːts] npl: to get one's just ~s avere ciò che si merita.

deserve [dɪˈzəːv] vt meritare; **deserving** a (person) meritevole, degno(a); (cause) meritorio(a).

design [dɪˈzaɪn] n (sketch) disegno; (layout, shape) linea; (pattern) fantasia; (COMM) disegno tecnico; (intention) intenzione f // vt disegnare; progettare; to have ~s on aver mire su.

designer [dɪˈzaɪnə*] n (ART, TECH) disegnatore/trice; (of fashion) modellista m/f.

desire [dɪˈzaɪə*] n desiderio, voglia // vt desiderare, volere.

desk [desk] n (in office) scrivania; (for pupil) banco; (Brit: in shop, restaurant) cassa; (in hotel) ricevimento; (at airport) accettazione f.

desolate [ˈdesəlɪt] a desolato(a).

despair [dɪsˈpɛə*] n disperazione f // vi: to ~ of disperare di.

despatch [dɪsˈpætʃ] n, vt = **dispatch**.

desperate [ˈdespərɪt] a disperato(a); (fugitive) capace di tutto; ~ly ad disperatamente; (very) terribilmente, estremamente.

desperation [despəˈreɪʃən] n disperazione f.

despicable [dɪsˈpɪkəbl] a disprezzabile.

despise [dɪsˈpaɪz] vt disprezzare, sdegnare.

despite [dɪsˈpaɪt] prep malgrado, a dispetto di, nonostante.

despondent [dɪsˈpɔndənt] a abbattuto(a), scoraggiato(a).

dessert [dɪˈzəːt] n dolce m; frutta; ~spoon n cucchiaio da dolci.

destination [destɪˈneɪʃən] n destinazione f.

destiny [ˈdestɪnɪ] n destino.

destitute [ˈdestɪtjuːt] a indigente, bisognoso(a).

destroy [dɪsˈtrɔɪ] vt distruggere; ~er n (NAUT) cacciatorpediniere m.

destruction [dɪsˈtrʌkʃən] n distruzione f.

detach [dɪˈtætʃ] vt staccare, distaccare;

~ed a (attitude) distante; ~ed house n villa; ~ment n (MIL) distaccamento; (fig) distacco.

detail [ˈdiːteɪl] n particolare m, dettaglio // vt dettagliare, particolareggiare; in ~ nei particolari; ~ed a particolareggiato(a).

detain [dɪˈteɪn] vt trattenere; (in captivity) detenere.

detect [dɪˈtekt] vt scoprire, scorgere; (MED, POLICE, RADAR etc) individuare; ~ion [dɪˈtekʃən] n scoperta; individuazione f; ~ive n investigatore/trice; private ~ive investigatore m privato; ~ive story n giallo.

detention [dɪˈtenʃən] n detenzione f; (SCOL) permanenza forzata per punizione.

deter [dɪˈtəː*] vt dissuadere.

detergent [dɪˈtəːdʒənt] n detersivo.

deteriorate [dɪˈtɪərɪəreɪt] vi deteriorarsi.

determine [dɪˈtəːmɪn] vt determinare; to ~ to do decidere di fare; ~d a (person) risoluto(a), deciso(a).

detour [ˈdiːtuə*] n deviazione f // vt (US: traffic) deviare.

detract [dɪˈtrækt] vt: to ~ from detrarre da.

detriment [ˈdetrɪmənt] n: to the ~ of a detrimento di; ~al [detrɪˈmentl] a: ~al to dannoso(a) a, nocivo(a) a.

devaluation [dɪvæljuˈeɪʃən] n svalutazione f.

devastating [ˈdevəsteɪtɪŋ] a devastatore(trice).

develop [dɪˈveləp] vt sviluppare; (habit) prendere (gradualmente) // vi svilupparsi; (facts, symptoms: appear) manifestarsi, rivelarsi; ~ing country paese m in via di sviluppo; ~ment n sviluppo.

device [dɪˈvaɪs] n (apparatus) congegno.

devil [ˈdevl] n diavolo; demonio.

devious [ˈdiːvɪəs] a (means) indiretto(a), tortuoso(a); (person) subdolo(a).

devise [dɪˈvaɪz] vt escogitare, concepire.

devoid [dɪˈvɔɪd] a: ~ of privo(a) di.

devolution [diːvəˈluːʃən] n (POL) decentramento.

devote [dɪˈvəut] vt: to ~ sth to dedicare qc a; ~d a devoto(a); to be ~d to essere molto affezionato(a) a; ~e [devəuˈtiː] n (MUS, SPORT) appassionato/a.

devotion [dɪˈvəuʃən] n devozione f, attaccamento; (REL) atto di devozione, preghiera.

devour [dɪˈvauə*] vt divorare.

devout [dɪˈvaut] a pio(a), devoto(a).

dew [djuː] n rugiada.

dexterity [deksˈterɪtɪ] n destrezza.

DHSS n abbr (= Department of Health and Social Security) ≈ ministero della Sanità e della Previdenza sociale.

diabetes [daɪəˈbiːtiːz] n diabete m; **dia-**

betic [-'bɛtɪk] *a*, *n* diabetico(a).

diabolical [daɪə'bɒlɪkl] *a* (*col: weather, behaviour*) orribile.

diagnosis, pl diagnoses [daɪəg'nəʊsɪs, -siːz] *n* diagnosi *f inv*.

diagonal [daɪ'ægənl] *a*, *n* diagonale (*f*).

diagram ['daɪəgræm] *n* diagramma *m*.

dial ['daɪəl] *n* quadrante *m*; (*on telephone*) disco combinatore // *vt* (*number*) fare.

dialect ['daɪəlɛkt] *n* dialetto.

dialling ['daɪəlɪŋ]: ~ **code**, (*US*) **dial code** *n* prefisso; ~ **tone**, (*US*) **dial tone** *n* segnale *m* di linea libera.

dialogue ['daɪəlɒg] *n* dialogo.

diameter [daɪ'æmɪtə*] *n* diametro.

diamond ['daɪəmənd] *n* diamante *m*; (*shape*) rombo; ~s *npl* (*CARDS*) quadri *mpl*.

diaper ['daɪəpə*] *n* (*US*) pannolino.

diaphragm ['daɪəfræm] *n* diaframma *m*.

diarrhoea, (*US*) **diarrhea** [daɪə'riːə] *n* diarrea.

diary ['daɪərɪ] *n* (*daily account*) diario; (*book*) agenda.

dice [daɪs] *n* (*pl inv*) dado // *vt* (*CULIN*) tagliare a dadini.

Dictaphone ['dɪktəfəʊn] *n* ® dittafono ®.

dictate *vt* [dɪk'teɪt] dettare // *n* ['dɪkteɪt] dettame *m*.

dictation [dɪk'teɪʃən] *n* dettato.

dictator [dɪk'teɪtə*] *n* dittatore *m*; ~ship *n* dittatura.

dictionary ['dɪkʃənrɪ] *n* dizionario.

did [dɪd] *pt of* do.

didn't = did not.

die [daɪ] *n* (*pl dies*) conio, matrice *f*, stampo // *vi* morire; to be dying for sth/ to do sth morire dalla voglia di qc/di fare qc; to ~ **away** *vi* spegnersi a poco a poco; to ~ **down** *vi* abbassarsi; to ~ **out** *vi* estinguersi.

diehard ['daɪhɑːd] *n* reazionario/a.

Diesel ['diːzəl]: ~ **engine** *n* motore *m* diesel *inv*; ~ **(oil)** *n* gasolio (per motori diesel).

diet ['daɪət] *n* alimentazione *f*; (*restricted food*) dieta // *vi* (*also:* be on a ~) stare a dieta.

differ ['dɪfə*] *vi*: to ~ from sth differire da qc; essere diverso(a) da qc; to ~ from sb over sth essere in disaccordo con qn su qc; ~**ence** *n* differenza; (*quarrel*) screzio; ~**ent** *a* diverso(a); ~**entiate** [-'rɛnʃɪeɪt] *vi* differenziarsi; to ~entiate between discriminare *or* fare differenza fra.

difficult ['dɪfɪkəlt] *a* difficile; ~**y** *n* difficoltà *f inv*.

diffident ['dɪfɪdənt] *a* sfiduciato(a).

dig [dɪg] *vt* (*pt, pp dug*) (*hole*) scavare; (*garden*) vangare // *n* (*prod*) gomitata; (*fig*) frecciata; to ~ **in** *vi* (*MIL: also:* ~ o.s. in) trincerarsi; (*col: eat*) attaccare

a mangiare; to ~ **into** *vt fus* (*snow, soil*) scavare; to ~ **one's nails into** conficcare le unghie in; to ~ **up** *vt* scavare; (*tree etc*) sradicare.

digest [daɪ'dʒɛst] *vt* digerire; ~**ion** [dɪ'dʒɛstʃən] *n* digestione *f*; ~**ive** *a* (*juices, system*) digerente.

digit ['dɪdʒɪt] *n* cifra; (*finger*) dito; ~**al** *a* digitale.

dignified ['dɪgnɪfaɪd] *a* dignitoso(a).

dignity ['dɪgnɪtɪ] *n* dignità.

digress [daɪ'grɛs] *vi*: to ~ from divagare da.

digs [dɪgz] *npl* (*Brit col*) camera ammobiliata.

dilapidated [dɪ'læpɪdeɪtɪd] *a* cadente.

dilemma [daɪ'lɛmə] *n* dilemma *m*.

diligent ['dɪlɪdʒənt] *a* diligente.

dilute [daɪ'luːt] *vt* diluire; (*with water*) annacquare.

dim [dɪm] *a* (*light, eyesight*) debole; (*memory, outline*) vago(a); (*stupid*) lento(a) d'ingegno // *vt* (*light*) abbassare.

dime [daɪm] *n* (*US*) = 10 cents.

dimension [daɪ'mɛnʃən] *n* dimensione *f*.

diminish [dɪ'mɪnɪʃ] *vt, vi* diminuire.

diminutive [dɪ'mɪnjutɪv] *a* minuscolo(a) // *n* (*LING*) diminutivo.

dimmers ['dɪməz] *npl* (*US AUT*) anabbaglianti *mpl*; luci *fpl* di posizione.

dimple ['dɪmpl] *n* fossetta.

din [dɪn] *n* chiasso, fracasso.

dine [daɪn] *vi* pranzare.

dinghy ['dɪŋgɪ] *n* battello pneumatico; (*also:* rubber ~) gommone *m*; (*also:* sailing ~) dinghy *m inv*.

dingy ['dɪndʒɪ] *a* grigio(a).

dining ['daɪnɪŋ] *cpd*: ~ **car** *n* (*Brit*) vagone *m* ristorante; ~ **room** *n* sala da pranzo.

dinner ['dɪnə*] *n* (*lunch*) pranzo; (*evening meal*) cena; (*public*) banchetto; ~'s ready! a tavola!; ~ **jacket** *n* smoking *m inv*; ~ **party** *n* cena; ~ **time** *n* ora di pranzo (*or* cena).

dint [dɪnt] *n*: by ~ of a forza di.

dip [dɪp] *n* discesa; (*in sea*) bagno // *vt* immergere; bagnare; (*Brit AUT: lights*) abbassare // *vi* abbassarsi.

diphthong ['dɪfθɒŋ] *n* dittongo.

diploma [dɪ'pləumə] *n* diploma *m*.

diplomacy [dɪ'pləuməsɪ] *n* diplomazia.

diplomat ['dɪpləmæt] *n* diplomatico; ~**ic** [dɪplə'mætɪk] *a* diplomatico(a).

dipstick ['dɪpstɪk] *n* (*AUT*) indicatore *m* di livello dell'olio.

dire [daɪə*] *a* terribile; estremo(a).

direct [daɪ'rɛkt] *a* diretto(a) // *vt* dirigere; can you ~ me to ...? mi può indicare la strada per ...?

direction [dɪ'rɛkʃən] *n* direzione *f*; sense of ~ senso dell'orientamento; ~s *npl* (*advice*) chiarimenti *mpl*; ~s for use istruzioni *fpl*.

directly [dɪ'rektlɪ] *ad* (*in straight line*) direttamente; (*at once*) subito.

director [dɪ'rektə*] *n* direttore/trice; amministratore/trice; (*THEATRE, CINEMA*) regista *m/f*.

directory [dɪ'rektərɪ] *n* elenco.

dirt [dɜ:t] *n* sporcizia; immondizia; ~ **cheap** *a* da due soldi; ~**y** *a* sporco(a) // *vt* sporcare; ~**y trick** *n* brutto scherzo.

disability [dɪsə'bɪlɪtɪ] *n* invalidità *f inv*; (*LAW*) incapacità *f inv*.

disabled [dɪs'eɪbld] *a* invalido(a); (*maimed*) mutilato(a); (*through illness, old age*) inabile.

disadvantage [dɪsəd'vɑ:ntɪdʒ] *n* svantaggio.

disagree [dɪsə'gri:] *vi* (*differ*) discordare; (*be against, think otherwise*): to ~ (**with**) essere in disaccordo (con), dissentire (da); ~**able** *a* sgradevole; (*person*) antipatico(a); ~**ment** *n* disaccordo.

disappear [dɪsə'pɪə*] *vi* scomparire; ~**ance** *n* scomparsa.

disappoint [dɪsə'pɔɪnt] *vt* deludere; ~**ed** *a* deluso(a); ~**ing** *a* deludente; ~**ment** *n* delusione *f*.

disapproval [dɪsə'pru:vəl] *n* disapprovazione *f*.

disapprove [dɪsə'pru:v] *vi*: to ~ of disapprovare.

disarm [dɪs'ɑ:m] *vt* disarmare; ~**ament** *n* disarmo.

disarray [dɪsə'reɪ] *n*: in ~ (*army*) in rotta; (*organization*) in uno stato di confusione; (*clothes, hair*) in disordine.

disaster [dɪ'zɑ:stə*] *n* disastro.

disband [dɪs'bænd] *vt* sbandare; (*MIL*) congedare // *vi* sciogliersi.

disbelief [dɪsbə'li:f] *n* incredulità.

disc [dɪsk] *n* disco; (*COMPUT*) = **disk**.

discard [dɪs'kɑ:d] *vt* (*old things*) scartare; (*fig*) abbandonare.

discern [dɪ'sɜ:n] *vt* discernere, distinguere; ~**ing** *a* perspicace.

discharge *vt* [dɪs'tʃɑ:dʒ] (*duties*) compiere; (*ELEC, waste etc*) scaricare; (*MED*) emettere; (*patient*) dimettere; (*employee*) licenziare; (*soldier*) congedare; (*defendant*) liberare // *n* ['dɪstʃɑ:dʒ] (*ELEC*) scarica; (*MED*) emissione *f*; (*dismissal*) licenziamento; congedo; liberazione *f*.

disciple [dɪ'saɪpl] *n* discepolo.

discipline ['dɪsɪplɪn] *n* disciplina // *vt* disciplinare; (*punish*) punire.

disc jockey *n* disc jockey *m inv*.

disclaim [dɪs'kleɪm] *vt* negare, smentire.

disclose [dɪs'kləʊz] *vt* rivelare, svelare; **disclosure** [-'kləʊʒə*] *n* rivelazione *f*.

disco ['dɪskəʊ] *n abbr* = **discothèque**.

discoloured, (*US*) **discolored** [dɪs'kʌləd] *a* scolorito(a); ingiallito(a).

discomfort [dɪs'kʌmfət] *n* disagio; (*lack of comfort*) scomodità *f inv*.

disconcert [dɪskən'sɜ:t] *vt* sconcertare.

disconnect [dɪskə'nekt] *vt* sconnettere, staccare; (*ELEC, RADIO*) staccare; (*gas, water*) chiudere.

disconsolate [dɪs'kɒnsəlɪt] *a* sconsolato(a).

discontent [dɪskən'tent] *n* scontentezza; ~**ed** *a* scontento(a).

discontinue [dɪskən'tɪnju:] *vt* smettere, cessare.

discord ['dɪskɔ:d] *n* disaccordo; (*MUS*) dissonanza.

discotheque ['dɪskəʊtek] *n* discoteca.

discount *n* ['dɪskaʊnt] sconto // *vt* [dɪs'kaʊnt] scontare.

discourage [dɪs'kʌrɪdʒ] *vt* scoraggiare.

discourteous [dɪs'kɜ:tɪəs] *a* scortese.

discover [dɪs'kʌvə*] *vt* scoprire; ~**y** *n* scoperta.

discredit [dɪs'kredɪt] *vt* screditare; mettere in dubbio.

discreet [dɪ'skri:t] *a* discreto(a).

discrepancy [dɪ'skrepənsɪ] *n* discrepanza.

discriminate [dɪ'skrɪmɪneɪt] *vi*: to ~ between distinguere tra; to ~ against discriminare contro; **discriminating** *a* fine, giudizioso(a); **discrimination** [-'neɪʃən] *n* discriminazione *f*; (*judgment*) discernimento.

discuss [dɪs'kʌs] *vt* discutere; (*debate*) dibattere; ~**ion** [dɪs'kʌʃən] *n* discussione *f*.

disdain [dɪs'deɪn] *n* disdegno.

disease [dɪ'zi:z] *n* malattia.

disembark [dɪsɪm'bɑ:k] *vt*, *vi* sbarcare.

disengage [dɪsɪn'geɪdʒ] *vt* disimpegnare; (*TECH*) distaccare; (*AUT*) clutch) disinnestare.

disfigure [dɪs'fɪgə*] *vt* sfigurare.

disgrace [dɪs'greɪs] *n* vergogna; (*disfavour*) disgrazia // *vt* disonorare, far cadere in disgrazia; ~**ful** *a* scandaloso(a), vergognoso(a).

disgruntled [dɪs'grʌntld] *a* scontento(a), di cattivo umore.

disguise [dɪs'gaɪz] *n* travestimento // *vt* travestire; in ~ travestito(a).

disgust [dɪs'gʌst] *n* disgusto, nausea // *vt* disgustare, far schifo a; ~**ing** *a* disgustoso(a); ripugnante.

dish [dɪʃ] *n* piatto; to do *or* wash the ~**es** fare i piatti; **to** ~ **up** *vt* servire; (*facts, statistics*) presentare; ~**cloth** *n* strofinaccio.

dishearten [dɪs'hɑ:tn] *vt* scoraggiare.

dishevelled [dɪ'ʃevəld] *a* arruffato(a); scapigliato(a).

dishonest [dɪs'ɒnɪst] *a* disonesto(a).

dishonour, (*US*) **dishonor** [dɪs'ɒnə*] *n* disonore *m*; ~**able** *a* disonorevole.

dish towel *n* (*US*) strofinaccio dei piatti.

dishwasher ['dɪʃwɒʃə*] *n* lavastoviglie *f inv*; (*person*) sguattero/a.

disillusion |dısı'luːʒən| vt disilludere, disingannare // n disillusione f.

disincentive |dısın'sentıv| n: to be a ~ essere demotivante; to be a ~ to sb demotivare qn.

disinfect |dısın'fekt| vt disinfettare; ~ant n disinfettante m.

disintegrate |dıs'ıntıgreıt| vi disintegrarsi.

disinterested |dıs'ıntrəstıd| a disinteressato(a).

disjointed |dıs'dʒɔıntıd| a sconnesso(a).

disk |dısk| n (COMPUT) disco; single-/ double-sided ~ disco a facciata singola/ doppia; ~ **drive** n lettore m; ~**ette** n (US) = **disk**.

dislike |dıs'laık| n antipatia, avversione f // vt: he ~s it non gli piace.

dislocate |'dısləkeıt| vt slogare; disorganizzare.

dislodge |dıs'lɔdʒ| vt rimuovere, staccare; (enemy) sloggiare.

disloyal |dıs'lɔıəl| a sleale.

dismal |'dızml| a triste, cupo(a).

dismantle |dıs'mæntl| vt smantellare, smontare; (fort, warship) disarmare.

dismay |dıs'meı| n costernazione f // vt sgomentare.

dismiss |dıs'mıs| vt congedare; (employee) licenziare; (idea) scacciare; (LAW) respingere; ~**al** n congedo; licenziamento.

dismount |dıs'maunt| vi scendere.

disobedience |dısə'biːdıəns| n disubbidienza.

disobedient |dısə'biːdıənt| a disubbidiente.

disobey |dısə'beı| vt disubbidire.

disorder |dıs'ɔːdə*| n disordine m; (rioting) tumulto; (MED) disturbo; ~**ly** a disordinato(a); tumultuoso(a).

disorientated |dıs'ɔːrıenteıtıd| a disorientato(a).

disown |dıs'əun| vt ripudiare.

disparaging |dıs'pærıdʒıŋ| a spregiativo(a), sprezzante.

dispassionate |dıs'pæʃənət| a calmo(a), freddo(a); imparziale.

dispatch |dıs'pætʃ| vt spedire, inviare // n spedizione f, invio; (MIL, PRESS) dispaccio.

dispel |dıs'pel| vt dissipare, scacciare.

dispensary |dıs'pensərı| n farmacia; (in chemist's) dispensario.

dispense |dıs'pens| vt distribuire, amministrare; **to ~ with** vt fus fare a meno di; ~**r** n (container) distributore m; **dispensing chemist** n (Brit) farmacista m/f.

disperse |dıs'pɔːs| vt disperdere; (knowledge) disseminare // vi disperdersi.

dispirited |dıs'pırıtıd| a scoraggiato(a), abbattuto(a).

displace |dıs'pleıs| vt spostare; ~**d**

person n (POL) profugo/a.

display |dıs'pleı| n mostra; esposizione f; (of feeling etc) manifestazione f; (screen) schermo; (pej) ostentazione f // vt mostrare; (goods) esporre; (results) affiggere; (departure times) indicare.

displease |dıs'pliːz| vt dispiacere a, scontentare; ~**d with** scontento di; **displeasure** |-'pleʒə*| n dispiacere m.

disposable |dıs'pəuzəbl| a (pack etc) a perdere; (income) disponibile; ~ **nappy** n pannolino di carta.

disposal |dıs'pəuzl| n (of rubbish) evacuazione f; distruzione f; at one's ~ alla sua disposizione.

dispose |dıs'pəuz| vt disporre; **to ~ of** vt (time, money) disporre di; (unwanted goods) sbarazzarsi di; (problem) eliminare; ~**d** a: ~**d to do** disposto(a) a fare; **disposition** |-'zıʃən| n disposizione f; (temperament) carattere m.

disproportionate |dısprə'pɔːʃənət| a sproporzionato(a).

disprove |dıs'pruːv| vt confutare.

dispute |dıs'pjuːt| n disputa; (also: industrial ~) controversia (sindacale) // vt contestare; (matter) discutere; (victory) disputare.

disqualify |dıs'kwɔlıfaı| vt (SPORT) squalificare; **to ~ sb from sth/from doing** rendere qn incapace a qc/a fare; squalificare qn da qc/da fare; **to ~ sb from driving** ritirare la patente a qn.

disquiet |dıs'kwaıət| n inquietudine f.

disregard |dısrı'gaːd| vt non far caso a, non badare a.

disrepair |dısrı'peə*| n cattivo stato; to fall into ~ (building) andare in rovina; (street) deteriorarsi.

disreputable |dıs'repjutəbl| a (person) di cattiva fama.

disrupt |dıs'rʌpt| vt mettere in disordine.

dissatisfaction |dıssætıs'fækʃən| n scontentezza, insoddisfazione f.

dissect |dı'sekt| vt sezionare.

dissent |dı'sent| n dissenso.

dissertation |dısə'teıʃən| n tesi f inv, dissertazione f.

disservice |dıs'sɔːvıs| n: to do sb a ~ fare un cattivo servizio a qn.

dissimilar |dı'sımılə*| a: ~ (to) dissimile or diverso(a) (da).

dissipate |'dısıpeıt| vt dissipare; ~**d** a dissipato(a).

dissolute |'dısəluːt| a dissoluto(a), licenzioso(a).

dissolution |dısə'luːʃən| n (of organization, marriage, POL) scioglimento.

dissolve |dı'zɔlv| vt dissolvere, sciogliere; (POL, marriage etc) sciogliere // vi dissolversi, sciogliersi; (fig) svanire.

distance |'dıstns| n distanza; in the ~ in lontananza.

distant |'dıstnt| a lontano(a), distante;

(manner) riservato(a), freddo(a).

distaste [dɪs'teɪst] *n* ripugnanza; **~ful** *a* ripugnante, sgradevole.

distended [dɪs'tɛndɪd] *a (stomach)* dilatato(a).

distil [dɪs'tɪl] *vt* distillare; **~lery** *n* distilleria.

distinct [dɪs'tɪŋkt] *a* distinto(a); *(preference, progress)* definito(a); **as ~ from** a differenza di; **~ion** [dɪs'tɪŋkʃən] *n* distinzione *f; (in exam)* lode *f;* **~ive** *a* distintivo(a).

distinguish [dɪs'tɪŋgwɪʃ] *vt* distinguere; discernere; **~ed** *a (eminent)* eminente; **~ing** *a (feature)* distinto(a), caratteristico(a).

distort [dɪs'tɔ:t] *vt* distorcere; *(TECH)* deformare.

distract [dɪs'trækt] *vt* distrarre; **~ed** *a* distratto(a); **~ion** [dɪs'trækʃən] *n* . strazione *f.*

distraught [dɪs'trɔ:t] *a* stravolto(a).

distress [dɪs'trɛs] *n* angoscia; *(pain)* dolore *m // vt* affliggere; **~ing** *a* doloroso(a).

distribute [dɪs'trɪbju:t] *vt* distribuire; **distribution** [-'bju:ʃən] *n* distribuzione *f;* **distributor** *n* distributore *m.*

district ['dɪstrɪkt] *n (of country)* regione *f; (of town)* quartiere *m; (ADMIN)* distretto; **~ attorney** *n (US)* ≈ sostituto procuratore *m* della Repubblica; **~ nurse** *n (Brit)* infermiera di quartiere.

distrust [dɪs'trʌst] *n* diffidenza, sfiducia *// vt* non aver fiducia in.

disturb [dɪs'tə:b] *vt* disturbare; *(inconvenience)* scomodare; **~ance** *n* disturbo; *(political etc)* tumulto; *(by drunks etc)* disordini *mpl;* **~ed** *a (worried, upset)* turbato(a); **emotionally ~ed** con turbe emotive; **~ing** *a* sconvolgente.

disuse [dɪs'ju:s] *n:* **to fall into ~** cadere in disuso.

disused [dɪs'ju:zd] *a* abbandonato(a).

ditch [dɪtʃ] *n* fossa *// vt (col)* piantare in asso.

dither ['dɪðə*] *vi* vacillare.

ditto ['dɪtəu] *ad* idem.

dive [daɪv] *n* tuffo; *(of submarine)* immersione *f; (AVIAT)* picchiata; *(pej)* buco *// vi* tuffarsi; **~r** *n* tuffatore/trice; palombaro.

diverse [daɪ'və:s] *a* vario(a).

diversion [daɪ'və:ʃən] *n (Brit AUT)* deviazione *f; (distraction)* divertimento.

divert [daɪ'və:t] *vt* deviare; *(amuse)* divertire.

divide [dɪ'vaɪd] *vt* dividere; *(separate)* separare *// vi* dividersi; **~d highway** *n (US)* strada a doppia carreggiata.

dividend ['dɪvɪdɛnd] *n* dividendo.

divine [dɪ'vaɪn] *a* divino(a).

diving ['daɪvɪŋ] *n* tuffo; **~ board** *n* trampolino.

divinity [dɪ'vɪnɪtɪ] *n* divinità *f inv;* teologia.

division [dɪ'vɪʒən] *n* divisione *f;* separazione *f.*

divorce [dɪ'vɔ:s] *n* divorzio *// vt* divorziare da; **~d** *a* divorziato(a); **~e** [-'si:] *n* divorziato/a.

D.I.Y. *n abbr (Brit)* = **do-it-yourself.**

dizzy ['dɪzɪ] *a (height)* vertiginoso(a); **to feel ~** avere il capogiro; **to make sb ~** far venire il capogiro a qn.

DJ *n abbr* = **disc jockey.**

do [du:] ♦ *n (col: party etc)* festa; **it was rather a grand ~** è stato un ricevimento piuttosto importante

♦ *vb (pt did, pp done)* **1** *(in negative constructions) non tradotto;* **I don't understand** non capisco

2 *(to form questions) non tradotto;* **didn't you know?** non lo sapevi?; **why didn't you come?** perché non sei venuto?

3 *(for emphasis, in polite expressions):* **she does seem rather late** sembra essere piuttosto in ritardo; **~ sit down** si accomodi la prego, prego si sieda; **~ take care!** mi raccomando, sta attento!

4 *(used to avoid repeating vb):* **she swims better than I ~** lei nuota meglio di me; **~ you agree? — yes, I ~/no, I don't** sei d'accordo? — sì/no; **she lives in Glasgow — so ~ I** lei vive a Glasgow — anch'io; **he asked me to help him and I did** mi ha chiesto di aiutarlo ed io l'ho fatto

5 *(in question tags):* **you like him, don't you?** ti piace, vero?; **I don't know him, ~ I?** non lo conosco, vero?

♦ *vt (gen, carry out, perform etc)* fare; **what are you ~ing tonight?** che fa stasera?; **to ~ the cooking** cucinare; **to ~ the washing-up** fare i piatti; **to ~ one's teeth** lavarsi i denti; **to ~ one's hair/nails** farsi i capelli/le unghie; **the car was ~ing 100** la macchina faceva i 100 all'ora

♦ *vi* **1** *(act, behave)* fare; **~ as I ~** faccia come me, faccia come faccio io

2 *(get on, fare)* andare; **he's ~ing well/badly at school** va bene/male a scuola; **how ~ you ~?** piacere!

3 *(suit)* andare bene; **this room will ~** questa stanza va bene

4 *(be sufficient)* bastare; **will £10 ~?** basteranno 10 sterline?; **that'll ~** basta così; **that'll ~!** *(in annoyance)* ora basta!; **to make ~ (with)** arrangiarsi (con)

to do away with *vt fus (kill)* far fuori; *(abolish)* abolire

to do up *vt (laces)* allacciare; *(dress, buttons)* abbottonare; *(renovate: room, house)* rimettere a nuovo, rifare

to do with *vt fus (need)* aver bisogno di; *(be connected):* **what has it got to ~ with you?** e tu che c'entri?; **I won't have anything to ~ with it** non voglio avere niente a che farci; **it has to ~ with money** si tratta di soldi

to do without vi fare senza ◆ vt fus fare a meno di.

dock |dɔk| n bacino; (LAW) banco degli imputati // vi entrare in bacino; **~er** n scaricatore m; **~yard** n cantiere m (navale).

doctor ['dɔktə*] n medico/a; (Ph.D. etc) dottore/essa // vt (fig) alterare, manipolare, (drink etc) adulterare; **D~ of Philosophy (Ph.D.)** n dottorato di ricerca; (person) titolare m/f di un dottorato di ricerca.

doctrine ['dɔktrɪn] n dottrina.

document ['dɔkjumənt] n documento; **~ary** [-'mɛntərɪ] a documentario(a); (evidence) documentato(a) // n documentario.

dodge |dɔdʒ| n trucco; schivata // vt schivare, eludere.

doe |dəu| n (deer) femmina di daino; (rabbit) coniglia.

does [dʌz] vb see **do**; **doesn't** = **does not**.

dog |dɔg| n cane m // vt (follow closely) pedinare; (fig: memory etc) perseguitare; **~ collar** n collare m di cane; (fig) collarino; **~-eared** a (book) con orecchie.

dogged ['dɔgɪd] a ostinato(a), tenace.

dogsbody ['dɔgzbɔdɪ] n factotum m inv.

doings ['duɪŋz] npl attività fpl.

do-it-yourself [du:ɪtjɔ:'sɛlf] n il far da sé.

doldrums ['dɔldrəmz] npl (fig): **to be in the ~** essere giù.

dole |dəul| n (Brit) sussidio di disoccupazione; **to be on the ~** vivere del sussidio; **to ~ out** vt distribuire.

doleful ['dəulful] a triste, doloroso(a).

doll |dɔl| n bambola; **to ~ o.s. up** farsi bello(a).

dollar ['dɔlə*] n dollaro.

dolphin ['dɔlfɪn] n delfino.

domain |də'meɪn| n dominio.

dome |dəum| n cupola.

domestic |də'mɛstɪk| a (duty, happiness, animal) domestico(a); (policy, affairs, flights) nazionale; **~ated** a addomesticato(a).

dominate ['dɔmɪneɪt] vt dominare.

domineering [dɔmɪ'nɪərɪŋ] a dispotico(a), autoritario(a).

dominion [də'mɪnɪən] n dominio; sovranità; dominion m inv.

domino, ~es ['dɔmɪnəu] n domino; **~es** n (game) gioco del domino.

don |dɔn| n (Brit) docente m/f universitario(a).

donate [də'neɪt] vt donare.

done [dʌn] pp of **do**.

donkey ['dɔŋkɪ] n asino.

donor ['dəunə*] n donatore/trice.

don't [dəunt] vb = **do not**.

doodle ['du:dl] vi scarabocchiare.

doom |du:m| n destino; rovina // vt: **to be ~ed (to failure)** essere predestinato(a) (a fallire); **~sday** n il giorno del Giudizio.

door [dɔ:*] n porta; **~bell** n campanello; **~man** n (in hotel) portiere m in livrea; (in block of flats) portinaio; **~mat** n stuoia della porta; **~step** n gradino della porta; **~way** n porta.

dope |dəup| n (col: drugs) roba // vt (horse etc) drogare.

dopey ['dəupɪ] a (col) inebetito(a).

dormant ['dɔ:mənt] a inattivo(a); (fig) latente.

dormitory ['dɔ:mɪtrɪ] n dormitorio.

dose [dəus] n dose f; (bout) attacco.

doss house ['dɔs-] n (Brit) asilo notturno.

dot [dɔt] n punto; macchiolina; **~ted with** punteggiato(a) di; **on the ~** in punto.

dote [dəut]: **to ~ on** vt fus essere infatuato(a) di.

dot-matrix printer [dɔt'meɪtrɪks-] n stampante f a matrice a punti.

dotted line ['dɔtɪd-] n linea punteggiata.

double ['dʌbl] a doppio(a) // ad (fold) in due, doppio; (twice): **to cost ~ (sth)** costare il doppio (di qc) // n sosia m inv; (CINEMA) controfigura // vt raddoppiare; (fold) piegare doppio or in due // vi raddoppiarsi; **on the ~**, (Brit) **at the ~** a passo di corsa; **~s** n (TENNIS) doppio; **~ bass** n contrabbasso; **~ bed** n letto matrimoniale; **~-breasted** a a doppio petto; **~cross** vt fare il doppio gioco con; **~decker** n autobus m inv a due piani; **~ glazing** n (Brit) doppi vetri mpl; **~ room** n camera per due; **doubly** ad doppiamente.

doubt [daut] n dubbio // vt dubitare di; **to ~ that** dubitare che + sub; **~ful** a dubbioso(a), incerto(a); (person) equivoco(a); **~less** ad indubbiamente.

dough [dəu] n pasta, impasto; **~nut** n bombolone m.

douse [dauz] vt (drench) inzuppare; (extinguish) spegnere.

dove [dʌv] n colombo/a.

dovetail ['dʌvteɪl] vi (fig) combaciare.

dowdy ['daudɪ] a trasandato(a); malvestito(a).

down [daun] n (fluff) piumino // ad giù, di sotto // prep giù per // vt (col: drink) scolarsi; **~ with X!** abbasso X!; **~-and-out** n barbone m; **~-at-heel** a scalcagnato(a); (fig) trasandato(a); **~cast** a abbattuto(a); **~fall** n caduta; rovina; **~hearted** a scoraggiato(a); **~hill** ad: **to go ~hill** andare in discesa // n (SKI: also: **~hill race**) discesa libera; **~ payment** n acconto; **~pour** n scroscio di pioggia; **~right** a franco(a); (refusal) assoluto(a); **~stairs** ad di sotto; al piano inferiore; **~stream** ad a valle; **~-to-earth** a pratico(a); **~town** ad in città; **~ under** ad (Australia etc) agli antipodi; **~ward** ['daunwəd] a, ad, **~wards** ['daunwədz] ad in giù, in discesa.

dowry ['dauri] n dote f.

doz. abbr = **dozen.**

doze [dəuz] vi sonnecchiare; **to ~ off** vi appisolarsi.

dozen ['dʌzn] n dozzina; **a ~ books** una dozzina di libri; **~s of** decine fpl di.

Dr. abbr = **doctor; drive** (n).

drab [dræb] a tetro(a), grigio(a).

draft [drɑ:ft] n abbozzo; (COMM) tratta; (US MIL) contingente m; (: call-up) leva // vt abbozzare; see also **draught.**

draftsman ['drɑ:ftsmən] n (US) = **draughtsman.**

drag [dræg] vt trascinare; (river) dragare // vi trascinarsi // n (col) noioso/a; noia, fatica; (women's clothing): in ~ travestito (da donna); **to ~ on** vi tirar avanti lentamente.

dragon ['drægən] n drago.

dragonfly ['drægənflai] n libellula.

drain [drein] n canale m di scolo; (for sewage) fogna; (on resources) salasso // vt (land, marshes) prosciugare; (vegetables) scolare; (reservoir etc) vuotare // vi (water) defluire (via); **~age** n prosciugamento; fognatura; **~ing board,** (US) **~board** n piano del lavello; **~pipe** n tubo di scarico.

dram [dræm] n bicchierino.

drama ['drɑ:mə] n (art) dramma m, teatro; (play) commedia; (event) dramma; **~tic** [drə'mætik] a drammatico(a); **~tist** ['dræmətist] n drammaturgo/a; **~tize** vt (events) drammatizzare; (adapt: for TV/cinema) ridurre or adattare per la televisione/lo schermo.

drank [dræŋk] pt of **drink.**

drape [dreip] vt drappeggiare; **~s** npl (US) tende fpl; **~r** n (Brit) negoziante m/f di stoffe.

drastic ['dræstik] a drastico(a).

draught, (US) **draft** [drɑ:ft] n corrente f d'aria; (NAUT) pescaggio; **~s** n (Brit) (gioco della) dama; **on ~** (beer) alla spina; **~board** n (Brit) scacchiera.

draughtsman, (US) **draftsman** ['drɑ:ftsmən] n disegnatore m.

draw [drɔ:] vb (pt **drew,** pp **drawn**) vt tirare; (attract) attirare; (picture) disegnare; (line, circle) tracciare; (money) ritirare // vi (SPORT) pareggiare // n pareggio; (in lottery) estrazione f; (attraction) attrazione f; **to ~ near** vi avvicinarsi; **to ~ out** vi (lengthen) allungarsi // vt (money) ritirare; **to ~ up** vi (stop) arrestarsi, fermarsi // vt (document) compilare; **~back** n svantaggio, inconveniente m; **~bridge** n ponte m levatoio.

drawer [drɔ:*] n cassetto; ['drɔ:ə*] (of

cheque) traente m/f.

drawing ['drɔ:iŋ] n disegno; **~ board** n tavola da disegno; **~ pin** n (Brit) puntina da disegno; **~ room** n salotto.

drawl [drɔ:l] n pronuncia strascicata.

drawn [drɔ:n] pp of **draw.**

dread [drɛd] n terrore m // vt tremare all'idea di; **~ful** a terribile.

dream [dri:m] n sogno // vt, vi (pt, pp **dreamed** or **dreamt** [drɛmt]) sognare; **~y** a sognante.

dreary ['driəri] a tetro(a); monotono(a).

dredge [drɛdʒ] vt dragare.

dregs [drɛgz] npl feccia.

drench [drɛntʃ] vt inzuppare.

dress [drɛs] n vestito; (clothing) abbigliamento // vt vestire; (wound) fasciare; (food) condire; preparare // vi vestirsi; **to get ~ed** vestirsi; **to ~ up** vi vestirsi a festa; (in fancy dress) vestirsi in costume; **~ circle** n (Brit) prima galleria; **~er** n (THEATRE) assistente m/f del camerino; (furniture) credenza; **~ing** n (MED) benda; (CULIN) condimento; **~ing gown** n (Brit) vestaglia; **~ing room** n (THEATRE) camerino; (SPORT) spogliatoio; **~ing table** n toilette f inv; **~maker** n sarta; **~ rehearsal** n prova generale; **~y** a (col) elegante.

drew [dru:] pt of **draw.**

dribble ['dribl] vi gocciolare; (baby) sbavare; (FOOTBALL) dribblare.

dried [draid] a (fruit, beans) secco(a); (eggs, milk) in polvere.

drier ['draiə*] n = **dryer.**

drift [drift] n (of current etc) direzione f; forza; (of sand etc) turbine m; (of snow) cumulo; turbine; (general meaning) senso // vi (boat) essere trasportato(a) dalla corrente; (sand, snow) ammucchiarsi; **~wood** n resti mpl della mareggiata.

drill [dril] n trapano; (MIL) esercitazione f // vt trapanare // vi (for oil) fare trivellazioni.

drink [driŋk] n bevanda, bibita // vt, vi (pt **drank,** pp **drunk**) bere; **to have a ~** bere qualcosa; **a ~ of water** un po' d'acqua; **~er** n bevitore/trice; **~ing water** n acqua potabile.

drip [drip] n goccia; gocciolamento; (MED) fleboclisi f inv // vi gocciolare; (washing) sgocciolare; (wall) trasudare; **~-dry** a (shirt) che non si stira; **~ping** n grasso d'arrosto.

drive [draiv] n passeggiata or giro in macchina; (also: **~way**) viale m d'accesso; (energy) energia; (PSYCH) impulso; bisogno; (push) sforzo eccezionale; campagna; (SPORT) drive m inv; (TECH) trasmissione f; propulsione f; presa; (also: disk ~) lettore m // vb (pt **drove,** pp **driven**) vt guidare; (nail) piantare; (push) cacciare, spingere; (TECH: motor) azionare; far funzionare // vi (AUT: at controls) guidare; (: travel) andare in macchina; **left-/right-hand** ~ guida a sinistra/destra; **to** ~ **sb mad** far impazzire qn.

drivel ['drivl] n idiozie fpl.

driven ['drivn] pp of **drive**.

driver ['draivə*] n conducente m/f; (of taxi) tassista m; (of bus) autista m; ~'s **license** n (US) patente f di guida.

driveway ['draivwei] n viale m d'accesso.

driving ['draiviŋ] a: ~ **rain** pioggia sferzante // n guida; ~ **instructor** n istruttore/trice di scuola guida; ~ **lesson** n lezione f di guida; ~ **licence** n (Brit) patente f di guida; ~ **mirror** n specchietto retrovisore; ~ **school** n scuola f guida inv; ~ **test** n esame m di guida.

drizzle ['drizl] n pioggerella.

droll [drəul] a buffo(a).

drone [drəun] n ronzio; (male bee) fuco.

drool [dru:l] vi sbavare.

droop [dru:p] vi abbassarsi; languire.

drop [drɔp] n goccia; (fall) caduta; (also: **parachute** ~) lancio; (steep incline) salto // vt lasciare cadere; (voice, eyes, price) abbassare; (set down from car) far scendere // vi cascare; ~s npl (MED) gocce fpl; **to** ~ **off** vi (sleep) addormentarsi; **to** ~ **out** vi (withdraw) ritirarsi; (student etc) smettere di studiare; ~**-out** n (from society/from university) chi ha abbandonato (la società/gli studi); ~**pings** npl sterco.

drought [draut] n siccità f inv.

drove [drəuv] pt of **drive**.

drown [draun] vt affogare // vi affogarsi.

drowsy ['drauzi] a sonnolento(a), assonnato(a).

drudgery ['drʌdʒəri] n lavoro faticoso.

drug [drʌg] n farmaco; (narcotic) droga // vt drogare; ~ **addict** n tossicomane m/f; ~**gist** n (US) persona che gestisce un drugstore; ~**store** n (US) drugstore m inv.

drum [drʌm] n tamburo; (for oil, petrol) fusto // vi tamburellare; ~s npl batteria; ~**mer** n batterista m/f.

drunk [drʌŋk] pp of **drink** // a ubriaco(a); ebbro(a) // n (also: ~ard) ubriacone/a; ~**en** a ubriaco(a); da ubriaco.

dry [drai] a secco(a); (day, clothes) asciutto(a) // vt seccare; (clothes, hair, hands) asciugare // vi asciugarsi; **to** ~ **up** vi seccarsi; ~**-cleaner's** n lavasecco m inv; ~**er** n (for hair) föhn m inv, asciugacapelli m inv; (for clothes) asciugabiancheria; (US: spin-dryer) centrifuga; ~ **goods store** n (US) negozio di stoffe; ~ **rot** n fungo del legno.

dual ['djuəl] a doppio(a); ~ **carriage-**way n (Brit) strada a doppia carreggiata.

dubbed [dʌbd] a (CINEMA) doppiato(a); (nicknamed) soprannominato(a).

dubious ['dju:biəs] a dubbio(a).

Dublin ['dʌblin] n Dublino f.

duchess ['dʌtʃis] n duchessa.

duck [dʌk] n anatra // vi abbassare la testa; ~**ling** n anatroccolo.

duct [dʌkt] n condotto; (ANAT) canale m.

dud [dʌd] n (shell) proiettile m che fa cilecca; (object, tool): **it's a** ~ è inutile, non funziona // a (Brit: cheque) a vuoto; (: note, coin) falso(a).

due [dju:] a dovuto(a); (expected) atteso(a); (fitting) giusto(a) // n dovuto // ad: ~ **north** diritto verso nord; ~s npl (for club, union) quota; (in harbour) diritti mpl di porto; **in** ~ **course** a tempo debito; finalmente; ~ **to** dovuto a; a causa di; **to be** ~ **to do** dover fare.

duet [dju:'et] n duetto.

duffel [dʌfl] a: ~ **bag** sacca da viaggio di tela; ~ **coat** montgomery m inv.

dug [dʌg] pt, pp of **dig**.

duke [dju:k] n duca m.

dull [dʌl] a (boring) noioso(a); (slow-witted) ottuso(a); (sound, pain) sordo(a); (weather, day) fosco(a), scuro(a); (blade) smussato(a) // vt (pain, grief) attutire; (mind, senses) intorpidire.

duly ['dju:li] ad (on time) a tempo debito; (as expected) debitamente.

dumb [dʌm] a muto(a); (stupid) stupido(a); ~**founded** [dʌm-'faundid] a stupito(a), stordito(a).

dummy ['dʌmi] n (tailor's model) manichino; (SPORT) finto; (Brit: for baby) tettarella // a falso(a), finto(a).

dump [dʌmp] n mucchio di rifiuti; (place) luogo di scarico; (MIL) deposito // vt (put down) scaricare; mettere giù; (get rid of) buttar via; ~**ing** n (ECON) dumping m; (of rubbish): "no ~ing" "vietato lo scarico".

dumpling ['dʌmpliŋ] n specie di gnocco.

dumpy ['dʌmpi] a tracagnotto(a).

dung [dʌŋ] n concime m.

dungarees [dʌŋgə'ri:z] npl tuta.

dungeon ['dʌndʒən] n prigione f sotterranea.

dupe [dju:p] vt gabbare, ingannare.

duplex ['dju:pleks] n (US: house) casa con muro divisorio in comune con un'altra; (: apartment) appartamento su due piani.

duplicate n ['dju:plikət] doppio // vt ['dju:plikeit] raddoppiare; (on machine) ciclostilare.

durable ['djuərəbl] a durevole; (clothes, metal) resistente.

duration [djuə'reiʃən] n durata.

duress [djuə'res] n: **under** ~ sotto costrizione.

during [ˈdjuəriŋ] *prep* durante, nel corso di.

dusk [dʌsk] *n* crepuscolo.

dust [dʌst] *n* polvere *f* // *vt* (*furniture*) spolverare; (*cake etc*): to ~ with co-spargere con; ~**bin** *n* (*Brit*) pattumiera; ~**er** *n* straccio per la polvere; ~ **jacket** *n* sopraccoperta; ~**man** *n* (*Brit*) netturbino; ~**y** *a* polveroso(a).

Dutch [dʌtʃ] *a* olandese // *n* (*LING*) olandese *m*; the ~ *npl* gli Olandesi; to go ~ fare alla romana; ~**man/woman** *n* olandese *m/f*.

dutiful [ˈdjuːtiful] *a* (*child*) rispettoso(a).

duty [ˈdjuːtɪ] *n* dovere *m*; (*tax*) dazio, tassa; **duties** *npl* mansioni *fpl*; on ~ di servizio; off ~ libero(a), fuori servizio; ~-**free** *a* esente da dazio.

duvet [ˈduːveɪ] *n* (*Brit*) piumino, piumone *m*.

dwarf [dwɔːf] *n* nano/a // *vt* far apparire piccolo.

dwell, *pt*, *pp* **dwelt** [dwel, dwelt] *vi* dimorare; **to ~ on** *vt fus* indugiare su; ~**ing** *n* dimora.

dwindle [ˈdwɪndl] *vi* diminuire, decrescere.

dye [daɪ] *n* tinta // *vt* tingere.

dying [ˈdaɪɪŋ] *a* morente, moribondo(a).

dyke [daɪk] *n* (*Brit*) diga.

dynamic [daɪˈnæmɪk] *a* dinamico(a).

dynamite [ˈdaɪnəmaɪt] *n* dinamite *f*.

dynamo [ˈdaɪnəməu] *n* dinamo *f inv*.

dysentery [ˈdɪsntrɪ] *n* dissenteria.

dyslexia [dɪsˈleksɪə] *n* dislessia.

E

E [iː] *n* (*MUS*) mi *m*.

each [iːtʃ] *a* ogni, ciascuno(a) // *pronoun* ciascuno(a), ognuno(a); ~ **one** ognuno(a); ~ **other** si (*or* ci *etc*); they hate ~ other si odiano (l'un l'altro); you are jealous of ~ other siete gelosi l'uno dell'altro; they have 2 books ~ hanno 2 libri ciascuno.

eager [ˈiːgə*] *a* impaziente; desideroso(a); ardente; **to be ~ for** essere desideroso di, aver gran voglia di.

eagle [ˈiːgl] *n* aquila.

ear [ɪə*] *n* orecchio; (*of corn*) pannocchia; ~**ache** *n* mal *m* d'orecchi; ~**drum** *n* timpano.

earl [əːl] *n* conte *m*.

earlier [ˈəːlɪə*] *a* precedente // *ad* prima.

early [ˈəːlɪ] *ad* presto, di buon'ora; (*ahead of time*) in anticipo // *a* precoce; anticipato(a); che si fa vedere di buon'ora; **to have an** ~ **night** andare a letto presto; **in the** ~ *or* ~ **in the spring/ 19th century** all'inizio della primavera/ dell'Ottocento; ~ **retirement** *n* ritiro anticipato.

earmark [ˈɪəmɑːk] *vt*: **to** ~ **sth for** destinare qc a.

earn [əːn] *vt* guadagnare; (*rest, reward*) meritare.

earnest [ˈəːnɪst] *a* serio(a); **in** ~ *ad* sul serio.

earnings [ˈəːnɪŋz] *npl* guadagni *mpl*; (*salary*) stipendio.

earphones [ˈɪəfəunz] *npl* cuffia.

earring [ˈɪərɪŋ] *n* orecchino.

earshot [ˈɪəʃɔt] *n*: **out of/within** ~ fuori portata/a portata d'orecchio.

earth [əːθ] *n* (*gen, also Brit ELEC*) terra; (*of fox etc*) tana // *vt* (*Brit ELEC*) mettere a terra; ~**enware** *n* terracotta; stoviglie *fpl* di terracotta // *a* di terracotta; ~**quake** *n* terremoto; ~**y** *a* (*fig*) grossolano(a).

ease [iːz] *n* agio, comodo // *vt* (*soothe*) calmare; (*loosen*) allentare; **to** ~ **sth out/in** tirare fuori/infilare qc con delicatezza; facilitare l'uscita/l'entrata di qc; **at** ~ a proprio agio; (*MIL*) a riposo; **to** ~ **off** *or* **up** *vi* diminuire; (*slow down*) rallentarsi; (*fig*) rilassarsi.

easel [ˈiːzl] *n* cavalletto.

east [iːst] *n* est *m* // *a* dell'est // *ad* a oriente; **the E**~ l'Oriente *m*.

Easter [ˈiːstə*] *n* Pasqua; ~ **egg** *n* uovo di Pasqua.

easterly [ˈiːstəlɪ] *a* dall'est, d'oriente.

eastern [ˈiːstən] *a* orientale, d'oriente.

East Germany *n* Germania dell'Est.

eastward(s) [ˈiːstwəd(z)] *ad* verso est, verso levante.

easy [ˈiːzɪ] *a* facile; (*manner*) disinvolto(a) // *ad*: **to take it** *or* **things** ~ prendersela con calma; ~ **chair** *n* poltrona; ~-**going** *a* accomodante.

eat, *pt* **ate**, *pp* **eaten** [iːt, eit, ˈiːtn] *vt*, *vi* mangiare; **to** ~ **into**, **to** ~ **away at** *vt fus* rodere.

eaves [iːvz] *npl* gronda.

eavesdrop [ˈiːvzdrɔp] *vi*: **to** ~ **(on a conversation)** origliare (una conversazione).

ebb [eb] *n* riflusso // *vi* rifluire; (*fig*: *also*: ~ **away**) declinare.

ebony [ˈebənɪ] *n* ebano.

eccentric [ɪkˈsentrɪk] *a*, *n* eccentrico(a).

echo, ~**es** [ˈekəu] *n* eco *m or f* // *vt* ripetere; fare eco a // *vi* echeggiare; dare un eco.

eclipse [ɪˈklɪps] *n* eclissi *f inv* // *vt* eclissare.

ecology [ɪˈkɔlədʒɪ] *n* ecologia.

economic [iːkəˈnɔmɪk] *a* economico(a); ~**al** *a* economico(a); (*person*) economo(a); ~**s** *n* economia.

economize [ɪˈkɔnəmaɪz] *vi* risparmiare, fare economia.

economy [ɪˈkɔnəmɪ] *n* economia.

ecstasy [ˈekstəsɪ] *n* estasi *f inv*.

eczema [ˈeksɪmə] *n* eczema *m*.

edge [edʒ] *n* margine *m*; (*of table, plate*,

cup) orlo; (*of knife etc*) taglio // *vt* bordare; on ~ (*fig*) = edgy; to ~ away from sgattaiolare da; ~**ways** *ad* di fianco; he couldn't get a word in ~ways non riuscì a dire una parola.

edgy ['ɛdʒɪ] *a* nervoso(a).

edible ['ɛdɪbl] *a* commestibile; (*meal*) mangiabile.

edict ['i:dɪkt] *n* editto.

Edinburgh ['ɛdɪnbərə] *n* Edimburgo *f*.

edit ['ɛdɪt] *vt* curare; ~**ion** [ɪ'dɪʃən] *n* edizione *f*; ~**or** *n* (*in newspaper*) redattore/trice; redattore/trice capo; (*of sb's work*) curatore/trice; ~**orial** [-'tɔ:rɪəl] *a* redazionale, editoriale // *n* editoriale *m*.

educate ['ɛdjukeɪt] *vt* istruire; educare.

education [ɛdju'keɪʃən] *n* educazione *f*; (*schooling*) istruzione *f*; ~**al** *a* pedagogico(a); scolastico(a); istruttivo(a).

EEC *n abbr* (= *European Economic Community*) C.E.E. *f* (= *Comunità Economica Europea*).

eel [i:l] *n* anguilla.

eerie ['ɪərɪ] *a* che fa accapponare la pelle.

effect [ɪ'fɛkt] *n* effetto // *vt* effettuare; ~**s** *npl* (*THEATRE*) effetti *mpl* scenici; to take ~ (*law*) entrare in vigore; (*drug*) fare effetto; in ~ effettivamente; ~**ive** *a* efficace; ~**ively** *ad* efficacemente; (*in reality*) effettivamente; ~**iveness** *n* efficacia.

effeminate [ɪ'fɛmɪnɪt] *a* effeminato(a).

efficiency [ɪ'fɪʃənsɪ] *n* efficienza; rendimento effettivo.

efficient [ɪ'fɪʃənt] *a* efficiente.

effort ['ɛfət] *n* sforzo.

effrontery [ɪ'frʌntərɪ] *n* sfrontatezza.

effusive [ɪ'fju:sɪv] *a* (*person*) espansivo(a); (*welcome, letter*) caloroso(a); (*thanks, apologies*) interminabile.

e.g. *ad abbr* (= *exempli gratia*) per esempio, p.es.

egg [ɛg] *n* uovo; to ~ on *vt* incitare; ~**cup** *n* portauovo *m inv*; ~**plant** *n* (*especially US*) melanzana; ~**shell** *n* guscio d'uovo.

ego ['i:gəu] *n* ego *m inv*.

egotism ['ɛgəutɪzəm] *n* egotismo.

egotist ['ɛgəutɪst] *n* egotista *m/f*.

Egypt ['i:dʒɪpt] *n* Egitto; ~**ian** [ɪ'dʒɪpʃən] *a*, *n* egiziano(a).

eiderdown ['aɪdədaun] *n* piumino.

eight [eɪt] *num* otto; ~**een** *num* diciotto; ~**h** [eɪtθ] *num* ottavo(a); ~**y** *num* ottanta.

Eire ['ɛərə] *n* Repubblica d'Irlanda.

either ['aɪðə*] *a* l'uno(a) o l'altro(a); (*both, each*) ciascuno(a); on ~ side su ciascun lato // *pronoun*: ~ (of them) (o) l'uno(a) o l'altro(a); I don't like ~ non mi piace né l'uno né l'altro // *ad* nean-

che; no, I don't ~ no, neanch'io // *cj*: ~ good or bad o buono o cattivo.

eject [ɪ'dʒɛkt] *vt* espellere; lanciare.

eke [i:k]: to ~ out *vt* far durare; aumentare.

elaborate *a* [ɪ'læbərɪt] elaborato(a), minuzioso(a) // *vb* [ɪ'læbəreɪt] *vt* elaborare // *vi* fornire i particolari.

elapse [ɪ'læps] *vi* trascorrere, passare.

elastic [ɪ'læstɪk] *a* elastico(a) // *n* elastico; ~ **band** *n* (*Brit*) elastico.

elated [ɪ'leɪtɪd] *a* pieno(a) di gioia.

elbow ['ɛlbəu] *n* gomito.

elder ['ɛldə*] *a* maggiore, più vecchio(a) // *n* (*tree*) sambuco; one's ~s i più anziani; ~**ly** *a* anziano(a) // *npl*: the ~**ly** gli anziani.

eldest ['ɛldɪst] *a*, *n*: the ~ (**child**) il(la) maggiore (dei bambini).

elect [ɪ'lɛkt] *vt* eleggere; to ~ to do decidere di fare // *a*: the president ~ il presidente designato; ~**ion** [ɪ'lɛkʃən] *n* elezione *f*; ~**ioneering** [ɪlɛkʃə'nɪərɪŋ] *n* propaganda elettorale; ~**or** *n* elettore/ trice; ~**orate** *n* elettorato.

electric [ɪ'lɛktrɪk] *a* elettrico(a); ~**al** *a* elettrico(a); ~ **blanket** *n* coperta elettrica; ~ **fire** *n* stufa elettrica.

electrician [ɪlɛk'trɪʃən] *n* elettricista *m*.

electricity [ɪlɛk'trɪsɪtɪ] *n* elettricità.

electrify [ɪ'lɛktrɪfaɪ] *vt* (*RAIL*) elettrificare; (*audience*) elettrizzare.

electrocute [ɪ'lɛktrəukju:t] *vt* fulminare.

electronic [ɪlɛk'trɒnɪk] *a* elettronico(a); ~ **mail** *n* posta elettronica; ~**s** *n* elettronica.

elegant ['ɛlɪgənt] *a* elegante.

element ['ɛlɪmənt] *n* elemento; (*of heater, kettle etc*) resistenza; ~**ary** [-'mɛntərɪ] *a* elementare.

elephant ['ɛlɪfənt] *n* elefante/essa.

elevate ['ɛlɪveɪt] *vt* elevare.

elevator ['ɛlɪveɪtə*] *n* elevatore *m*; (*US: lift*) ascensore *m*.

eleven [ɪ'lɛvn] *num* undici; ~**ses** *npl* (*Brit*) caffè *m* a metà mattina; ~**th** *a* undicesimo(a).

elicit [ɪ'lɪsɪt] *vt*: to ~ (from) trarre (da), cavare fuori (da).

eligible ['ɛlɪdʒəbl] *a* eleggibile; (*for membership*) che ha i requisiti.

ellipse [ɪ'lɪps] *n* ellisse *f*.

elm [ɛlm] *n* olmo.

elongated ['i:lɒŋgeɪtɪd] *a* allungato(a).

elope [ɪ'ləup] *vi* (*lovers*) scappare.

eloquent ['ɛləkwənt] *a* eloquente.

else [ɛls] *ad* altro; something ~ qualcos'altro; somewhere ~ altrove; everywhere ~ in qualsiasi altro luogo; nobody ~ nessun altro; where ~? in quale altro luogo?; little ~ poco altro; ~**where** *ad* altrove.

elucidate [ɪ'lu:sɪdeɪt] *vt* delucidare.

elude [ɪ'lu:d] *vt* eludere.

elusive [ɪ'lu:sɪv] *a* elusivo(a).

emaciated [ɪ'meɪsɪeɪtd] *a* emaciato(a).

emancipate [ɪ'mænsɪpeɪt] *vt* emancipare.

embankment [ɪm'bæŋkmənt] *n* (*of road*, *railway*) terrapieno; (*riverside*) argine *m*; (*dyke*) diga.

embark [ɪm'bɑːk] *vi*: to ~ (on) imbarcarsi (su) // *vt* imbarcare; to ~ on (*fig*) imbarcarsi in; ~**ation** [ɛmbɑː'keɪʃən] *n* imbarco.

embarrass [ɪm'bærəs] *vt* imbarazzare; ~**ed** *a* imbarazzato(a); ~**ing** *a* imbarazzante; ~**ment** *n* imbarazzo.

embassy ['ɛmbəsɪ] *n* ambasciata.

embed [ɪm'bɛd] *vt* conficcare, incastrare.

embellish [ɪm'bɛlɪʃ] *vt* abbellire.

embers ['ɛmbəz] *npl* braci *fpl*.

embezzle [ɪm'bɛzl] *vt* appropriarsi indebitamente di.

embitter [ɪm'bɪtə*] *vt* amareggiare; inasprire.

embody [ɪm'bɔdɪ] *vt* (*features*) racchiudere, comprendere; (*ideas*) dar forma concreta a, esprimere.

embossed [ɪm'bɔst] *a* in rilievo; goffrato(a).

embrace [ɪm'breɪs] *vt* abbracciare // *vi* abbracciarsi // *n* abbraccio.

embroider [ɪm'brɔɪdə*] *vt* ricamare; (*fig*: *story*) abbellire; ~**y** *n* ricamo.

embryo ['ɛmbrɪəʊ] *n* (*also fig*) embrione *m*.

emerald ['ɛmərəld] *n* smeraldo.

emerge [ɪ'mɜːdʒ] *vi* apparire, sorgere.

emergence [ɪ'mɜːdʒəns] *n* apparizione *f*.

emergency [ɪ'mɜːdʒənsɪ] *n* emergenza; in an ~ in caso di emergenza; ~ **cord** *n* (*US*) segnale *m* d'allarme; ~ **exit** *n* uscita di sicurezza; ~ **landing** *n* atterraggio forzato; **the** ~ **services** *npl* (*fire, police, ambulance*) servizi *mpl* di pronto intervento.

emery board ['ɛmərɪ-] *n* limetta di carta smerigliata.

emigrate ['ɛmɪgreɪt] *vi* emigrare.

eminent ['ɛmɪnənt] *a* eminente.

emit [ɪ'mɪt] *vt* emettere.

emotion [ɪ'məʊʃən] *n* emozione *f*; ~**al** *a* (*person*) emotivo(a); (*scene*) commovente; (*tone, speech*) carico(a) d'emozione.

emperor ['ɛmpərə*] *n* imperatore *m*.

emphasis, *pl* -**ases** ['ɛmfəsɪs, -siːz] *n* enfasi *f inv*; importanza.

emphasize ['ɛmfəsaɪz] *vt* (*word, point*) sottolineare; (*feature*) mettere in evidenza.

emphatic [ɛm'fætɪk] *a* (*strong*) vigoroso(a); (*unambiguous, clear*) netto(a); ~**ally** *ad* vigorosamente; nettamente.

empire ['ɛmpaɪə*] *n* impero.

employ [ɪm'plɔɪ] *vt* impiegare; ~**ee** [-'iː] *n* impiegato/a; ~**er** *n* principale *m/f*, datore *m* di lavoro; ~**ment** *n* impiego;

~**ment agency** *n* agenzia di collocamento.

empower [ɪm'paʊə*] *vt*: to ~ sb to do concedere autorità a qn di fare.

empress ['ɛmprɪs] *n* imperatrice *f*.

emptiness ['ɛmptɪnɪs] *n* vuoto.

empty ['ɛmptɪ] *a* vuoto(a); (*threat, promise*) vano(a) // *vt* vuotare // *vi* vuotarsi; (*liquid*) scaricarsi // *n* (*bottle*) vuoto; ~**-handed** *a* a mani vuote.

emulate ['ɛmjʊleɪt] *vt* emulare.

emulsion [ɪ'mʌlʃən] *n* emulsione *f*; ~ (**paint**) *n* colore *m* a tempera.

enable [ɪ'neɪbl] *vt*: to ~ sb to do permettere a qn di fare.

enact [ɪn'ækt] *vt* (*law*) emanare; (*play, scene*) rappresentare.

enamel [ɪ'næməl] *n* smalto.

encased [ɪn'keɪst] *a*: ~ in racchiuso(a) in; rivestito(a) di.

enchant [ɪn'tʃɑːnt] *vt* incantare; (*subj*: *magic spell*) catturare; ~**ing** *a* incantevole, affascinante.

encircle [ɪn'sɜːkl] *vt* accerchiare.

encl. *abbr* (= *enclosed*) all.

enclave ['ɛnkleɪv] *n* enclave *f*.

enclose [ɪn'kləʊz] *vt* (*land*) circondare, recingere; (*letter etc*): to ~ (**with**) allegare (con); **please find** ~**d** trovi qui accluso.

enclosure [ɪn'kləʊʒə*] *n* recinto; (*COMM*) allegato.

encompass [ɪn'kʌmpəs] *vt* comprendere.

encore [ɔŋ'kɔː*] *excl, n* bis (*m inv*).

encounter [ɪn'kaʊntə*] *n* incontro // *vt* incontrare.

encourage [ɪn'kʌrɪdʒ] *vt* incoraggiare; ~**ment** *n* incoraggiamento.

encroach [ɪn'krəʊtʃ] *vi*: to ~ (up)on (*rights*) usurpare; (*time*) abusare di; (*land*) oltrepassare i limiti di.

encyclop(a)edia [ɛnsaɪkləʊ'piːdɪə] *n* enciclopedia.

end [ɛnd] *n* fine *f*; (*aim*) fine *m*; (*of table*) bordo estremo // *vt* finire; (*also*: bring to an ~, put an ~ to) mettere fine a // *vi* finire; **in the** ~ alla fine; on ~ (*object*) ritto(a); to stand on ~ (*hair*) rizzarsi; for 5 hours on ~ per 5 ore di fila; to ~ up *vi*: to ~ up in finire in.

endanger [ɪn'deɪndʒə*] *vt* mettere in pericolo.

endearing [ɪn'dɪərɪŋ] *a* accattivante.

endeavour, (*US*) endeavor [ɪn'dɛvə*] *n* sforzo, tentativo // *vi*: to ~ to do cercare *or* sforzarsi di fare.

ending ['ɛndɪŋ] *n* fine *f*, conclusione *f*; (*LING*) desinenza.

endive ['ɛndaɪv] *n* (*curly*) indivia (riccia); (*smooth, flat*) indivia belga.

endless ['ɛndlɪs] *a* senza fine; (*patience, resources*) infinito(a).

endorse [ɪn'dɔːs] *vt* (*cheque*) girare; (*approve*) approvare, appoggiare; ~**ment** *n* (*on driving licence*) con-

travvenzione registrata sulla patente.

endow [ɪn'dau] *vt (provide with money)* devolvere denaro a; *(equip)*: **to ~ with** fornire di, dotare di.

endurance [ɪn'djuərəns] *n* resistenza; pazienza.

endure [ɪn'djuə*] *vt* sopportare, resistere a // *vi* durare.

enemy ['enəmɪ] *a*, *n* nemico(a).

energetic [enə'dʒetɪk] *a* energico(a); attivo(a).

energy ['enədʒɪ] *n* energia.

enforce [ɪn'fɔːs] *vt (LAW)* applicare, far osservare; **~d** a forzato(a).

engage [ɪn'geɪdʒ] *vt (hire)* assumere; *(lawyer)* incaricare; *(attention, interest)* assorbire; *(MIL)* attaccare; *(TECH)*: **to ~ gear/the clutch** innestare la marcia/la frizione // *vi (TECH)* ingranare; **to ~ in** impegnarsi in; **~d** a *(Brit: busy, in use)* occupato(a); *(betrothed)* fidanzato(a); **to get ~d** fidanzarsi; **~d tone** *n (Brit TEL)* segnale *m* di occupato; **~ment** *n* impegno, obbligo; appuntamento; *(to marry)* fidanzamento; *(MIL)* combattimento; **~ment ring** *n* anello di fidanzamento.

engaging [ɪn'geɪdʒɪŋ] *a* attraente.

engender [ɪn'dʒendə*] *vt* produrre, causare.

engine ['endʒɪn] *n (AUT)* motore *m*; *(RAIL)* locomotiva; **~ driver** *n (of train)* macchinista *m*.

engineer [endʒɪ'nɪə*] *n* ingegnere *m*; *(US RAIL)* macchinista *m*; **~ing** *n* ingegneria.

England ['ɪŋglənd] *n* Inghilterra.

English ['ɪŋglɪʃ] *a* inglese // *n (LING)* inglese *m*; **the ~** *npl* gli Inglesi; **the ~ Channel** *n* la Manica; **~man/woman** *n* inglese *m/f*.

engraving [ɪn'greɪvɪŋ] *n* incisione *f*.

engrossed [ɪn'grəust] *a*: **~ in** assorbito(a) da, preso(a) da.

engulf [ɪn'gʌlf] *vt* inghiottire.

enhance [ɪn'hɑːns] *vt* accrescere.

enjoy [ɪn'dʒɔɪ] *vt* godere; *(have: success, fortune)* avere; **to ~ o.s.** godersela, divertirsi; **~able** a piacevole; **~ment** *n* piacere *m*, godimento.

enlarge [ɪn'lɑːdʒ] *vt* ingrandire // *vi*: **to ~ on** *(subject)* dilungarsi su.

enlighten [ɪn'laɪtn] *vt* illuminare; dare schiarimenti a; **~ed** a illuminato(a); **~ment** *n*: **the E~ment** *(HISTORY)* l'Illuminismo.

enlist [ɪn'lɪst] *vt* arruolare; *(support)* procurare // *vi* arruolarsi.

enmity ['enmɪtɪ] *n* inimicizia.

enormous [ɪ'nɔːməs] *a* enorme.

enough [ɪ'nʌf] *a*, *n*: **~ time/books** assai tempo/libri; **have you got ~?** ne ha abbastanza *or* a sufficienza? // *ad*: **big ~** abbastanza grande; **he has not worked ~** non ha lavorato abbastanza; **~!** basta!; **that's ~, thanks** basta così, grazie; **I've**

had ~ of him ne ho abbastanza di lui; ... **which, funnily ~** ... che, strano a dirsi.

enquire [ɪn'kwaɪə*] *vt, vi* = **inquire.**

enrage [ɪn'reɪdʒ] *vt* fare arrabbiare.

enrich [ɪn'rɪtʃ] *vt* arricchire.

enrol [ɪn'rəul] *vt* iscrivere // *vi* iscriversi; **~ment** *n* iscrizione *f*.

ensign *n (NAUT)* ['ensən] bandiera; *(MIL)* ['ensaɪn] portabandiera *m inv*.

ensue [ɪn'sjuː] *vi* seguire, risultare.

ensure [ɪn'ʃuə*] *vt* assicurare; garantire; **to ~ that** assicurarsi che.

entail [ɪn'teɪl] *vt* comportare.

entangle [ɪn'tæŋgl] *vt* impigliare.

enter ['entə*] *vt (room)* entrare in; *(club)* associarsi a; *(army)* arruolarsi in; *(competition)* partecipare a; *(sb for a competition)* iscrivere; *(write down)* registrare; *(COMPUT)* inserire // *vi* entrare; **to ~ for** *vt fus* iscriversi a; **to ~ into** *vt fus (explanation)* cominciare a dare; *(debate)* partecipare a; *(agreement)* concludere; **to ~ (up)on** *vt fus* cominciare.

enterprise ['entəpraɪz] *n (undertaking, company)* impresa; *(spirit)* iniziativa; **free ~** liberalismo economico; **private ~** iniziativa privata.

enterprising ['entəpraɪzɪŋ] *a* intraprendente.

entertain [entə'teɪn] *vt* divertire; *(invite)* ricevere; *(idea, plan)* nutrire; **~er** *n* comico/a; **~ing** a divertente; **~ment** *n (amusement)* divertimento; *(show)* spettacolo.

enthralled [ɪn'θrɔːld] *a* affascinato(a).

enthusiasm [ɪn'θuːzɪæzəm] *n* entusiasmo.

enthusiast [ɪn'θuːzɪæst] *n* entusiasta *m/f*; **~ic** [-'æstɪk] a entusiasta, entusiastico(a); **to be ~ic about sth/sb** essere appassionato di qc/entusiasta di qn.

entice [ɪn'taɪs] *vt* allettare, sedurre.

entire [ɪn'taɪə*] *a* intero(a); **~ly** *ad* completamente, interamente; **~ty** [ɪn'taɪərətɪ] *n*: **in its ~ty** nel suo complesso.

entitle [ɪn'taɪtl] *vt (give right)*: **to ~ sb to sth/to do** dare diritto a qn a qc/a fare; **~d** a *(book)* che si intitola; **to be ~d to do** avere il diritto di fare.

entrails ['entreɪlz] *npl* interiora *fpl*.

entrance *n* ['entrns] entrata, ingresso; *(of person)* entrata // *vt* [ɪn'trɑːns] incantare, rapire; **to gain ~ to** *(university etc)* essere ammesso a; **~ examination** *n* esame *m* di ammissione; **~ fee** *n* tassa d'iscrizione; *(to museum etc)* prezzo d'ingresso; **~ ramp** *n (US AUT)* rampa di accesso.

entrant ['entrnt] *n* partecipante *m/f*; concorrente *m/f*.

entreat [en'triːt] *vt* supplicare.

entrenched [en'trentʃt] *a* radicato(a).

entrepreneur [ɔntrəprə'nəː*] *n* imprenditore *m*.

entrust [ɪn'trʌst] *vt*: to ~ sth to affidare qc a.

entry ['entrɪ] *n* entrata; (*way in*) entrata, ingresso; (*item: on list*) iscrizione *f*; (*in dictionary*) voce *f*; no ~ vietato l'ingresso; (*AUT*) divieto di accesso; ~ **form** *n* modulo d'iscrizione; ~ **phone** *n* citofono.

envelop [ɪn'vɛləp] *vt* avvolgere, avviluppare.

envelope ['ɛnvələup] *n* busta.

envious ['ɛnvɪəs] *a* invidioso(a).

environment [ɪn'vaɪərnmənt] *n* ambiente *m*; ~**al** [-'mɛntl] *a* ecologico(a); ambientale.

envisage [ɪn'vɪzɪdʒ] *vt* immaginare; prevedere.

envoy ['ɛnvɔɪ] *n* inviato/a.

envy ['ɛnvɪ] *n* invidia // *vt* invidiare; to ~ sb sth invidiare qn per qc.

epic ['ɛpɪk] *n* poema *m* epico // *a* epico(a).

epidemic [ɛpɪ'dɛmɪk] *n* epidemia.

epilepsy ['ɛpɪlɛpsɪ] *n* epilessia.

episode ['ɛpɪsəud] *n* episodio.

epistle [ɪ'pɪsl] *n* epistola.

epitome [ɪ'pɪtəmɪ] *n* epitome *f*; quintessenza; **epitomize** *vt* (*fig*) incarnare.

equable ['ɛkwəbl] *a* uniforme; equilibrato(a).

equal ['iːkwl] *a, n* uguale (*m/f*) // *vt* uguagliare; ~ to (*task*) all'altezza di; ~**ity** [iː'kwɔlɪtɪ] *n* uguaglianza; ~**ize** *vt, vi* pareggiare; ~**izer** *n* pareggio; ~**ly** *ad* ugualmente.

equanimity [ɛkwə'nɪmɪtɪ] *n* serenità.

equate [ɪ'kweɪt] *vt*: to ~ sth with considerare qc uguale a; (*compare*) paragonare qc con; **equation** [ɪ'kweɪʃən] *n* (*MATH*) equazione *f*.

equator [ɪ'kweɪtə*] *n* equatore *m*.

equilibrium [iːkwɪ'lɪbrɪəm] *n* equilibrio.

equip [ɪ'kwɪp] *vt* equipaggiare, attrezzare; to ~ sb/sth with fornire qn/qc di; to be well ~ped (*office etc*) essere ben attrezzato(a); he is well ~ped for the job ha i requisiti necessari per quel lavoro; ~**ment** *n* attrezzatura; (*electrical etc*) apparecchiatura.

equitable ['ɛkwɪtəbl] *a* equo(a), giusto(a).

equities ['ɛkwɪtɪz] *npl* (*Brit COMM*) azioni *fpl* ordinarie.

equivalent [ɪ'kwɪvələnt] *a, n* equivalente (*m*); to be ~ to equivalere a.

equivocal [ɪ'kwɪvəkl] *a* equivoco(a); (*open to suspicion*) dubbio(a).

era ['ɪərə] *n* era, età *f inv*.

eradicate [ɪ'rædɪkeɪt] *vt* sradicare.

erase [ɪ'reɪz] *vt* cancellare; ~**r** *n* gomma.

erect [ɪ'rɛkt] *a* eretto(a) // *vt* costruire; (*monument, tent*) alzare; ~**ion**

[ɪ'rɛkʃən] *n* erezione *f*.

ermine ['ɔːmɪn] *n* ermellino.

erode [ɪ'rəud] *vt* erodere; (*metal*) corrodere.

erotic [ɪ'rɔtɪk] *a* erotico(a).

err [əː*] *vi* errare; (*REL*) peccare.

errand ['ɛrnd] *n* commissione *f*.

erratic [ɪ'rætɪk] *a* imprevedibile; (*person, mood*) incostante.

error ['ɛrə*] *n* errore *m*.

erupt [ɪ'rʌpt] *vi* erompere; (*volcano*) mettersi (*or* essere) in eruzione; ~**ion** [ɪ'rʌpʃən] *n* eruzione *f*.

escalate ['ɛskəleɪt] *vi* intensificarsi.

escalator ['ɛskəleɪtə*] *n* scala mobile.

escapade [ɛskə'peɪd] *n* scappatella; avventura.

escape [ɪ'skeɪp] *n* evasione *f*; fuga; (*of gas etc*) fuga, fuoriuscita // *vi* fuggire; (*from jail*) evadere, scappare; (*fig*) sfuggire; (*leak*) uscire // *vt* sfuggire a; to ~ from sb sfuggire a qn; **escapism** *n* evasione *f* (dalla realtà).

escort *n* ['ɛskɔːt] scorta; (*male companion*) cavaliere *m* // *vt* [ɪ'skɔːt] scortare; accompagnare.

Eskimo ['ɛskɪməu] *n* eschimese *m/f*.

especially [ɪ'spɛʃlɪ] *ad* specialmente; soprattutto; espressamente.

espionage ['ɛspɪənɑːʒ] *n* spionaggio.

Esquire [ɪ'skwaɪə*] *n* (*abbr* Esq.): J. Brown, ~ Signor J. Brown.

essay ['ɛseɪ] *n* (*SCOL*) composizione *f*; (*LITERATURE*) saggio.

essence ['ɛsns] *n* essenza.

essential [ɪ'sɛnʃl] *a* essenziale; (*basic*) fondamentale // *n* elemento essenziale; ~**ly** *ad* essenzialmente.

establish [ɪ'stæblɪʃ] *vt* stabilire; (*business*) mettere su; (*one's power etc*) confermare; ~**ment** *n* stabilimento; the E~ment la classe dirigente, l'establishment *m*.

estate [ɪ'steɪt] *n* proprietà *f inv*; beni *mpl*, patrimonio; ~ **agent** *n* (*Brit*) agente *m* immobiliare; ~ **car** *n* (*Brit*) giardiniera.

esteem [ɪ'stiːm] *n* stima // *vt* (*think highly of*) stimare; (*consider*) considerare.

esthetic [ɪs'θɛtɪk] *a* (*US*) = **aesthetic**.

estimate *n* ['ɛstɪmət] stima; (*COMM*) preventivo // *vt* ['ɛstɪmeɪt] stimare, valutare; **estimation** [-'meɪʃən] *n* stima; opinione *f*.

estranged [ɪ'streɪndʒd] *a* separato(a).

etc *abbr* (= *et cetera*) etc, ecc.

etching ['ɛtʃɪŋ] *n* acquaforte *f*.

eternal [ɪ'təːnl] *a* eterno(a).

eternity [ɪ'təːnɪtɪ] *n* eternità.

ether ['iːθə*] *n* etere *m*.

ethical ['ɛθɪkl] *a* etico(a), morale.

ethics ['ɛθɪks] *n* etica // *npl* morale *f*.

Ethiopia [iːθɪ'əupɪə] *n* Etiopia.

ethnic ['ɛθnɪk] *a* etnico(a).

ethos ['iːθɔs] *n* norma di vita.

etiquette ['ɛtɪkɛt] n etichetta.
Eurocheque ['juərəutʃɛk] n eurochèque m inv.
Europe ['juərəp] n Europa; ~**an** [-'pi:ən] a, n europeo(a).
evacuate [ɪ'vækjueɪt] vt evacuare.
evade [ɪ'veɪd] vt eludere; (duties etc) sottrarsi a.
evaluate [ɪ'væljueɪt] vt valutare.
evaporate [ɪ'væpəreɪt] vi evaporare // vt far evaporare; ~**d milk** n latte m concentrato.
evasion [ɪ'veɪʒən] n evasione f.
evasive [ɪ'veɪsɪv] a evasivo(a)
eve [i:v] n: on the ~ of alla vigilia di.
even ['i:vn] a regolare; (number) pari inv // ad anche, perfino; ~ if, ~ though anche se; ~ more ancora di più; ~ so ciò nonostante; **not** ~ nemmeno; to get ~ with sb dare la pari a qn; **to** ~ **out** vi pareggiare.
evening ['i:vnɪŋ] n sera; (as duration, event) serata; in the ~ la sera; ~ **class** n corso serale; ~ **dress** n (woman's) abito da sera; **in** ~ **dress** (man) in abito scuro; (woman) in abito lungo.
event [ɪ'vɛnt] n avvenimento; (SPORT) gara; in the ~ of in caso di; ~**ful** a denso(a) di eventi.
eventual [ɪ'vɛntʃuəl] a finale; ~**ity** [-'ælɪtɪ] n possibilità f inv, eventualità f inv; ~**ly** ad finalmente.
ever ['ɛvrɪ] ad mai; (at all times) sempre; the best ~ il migliore che ci sia mai stato; have you ~ seen it? l'ha mai visto?; ~ **since** ad da allora // cj sin da quando; ~ **so** pretty così bello(a); ~**green** n sempreverde m; ~**lasting** a eterno(a).
every ['ɛvrɪ] a ogni; ~ **day** tutti i giorni, ogni giorno; ~ **other/third** day ogni due/tre giorni; ~ **other** car una macchina su due; ~ **now and then** ogni tanto, di quando in quando; ~**body** pronoun ognuno, tutti pl; ~**day** a quotidiano(a); di ogni giorno; ~**one** = ~**body**; ~**thing** pronoun tutto, ogni cosa; ~**where** ad (gen) dappertutto; (wherever) ovunque.
evict [ɪ'vɪkt] vt sfrattare.
evidence ['ɛvɪdns] n (proof) prova; (of witness) testimonianza; (sign): to show ~ of dare segni di; to give ~ deporre.
evident ['ɛvɪdnt] a evidente; ~**ly** ad evidentemente.
evil ['i:vl] a cattivo(a), maligno(a) // n male m.
evoke [ɪ'vəuk] vt evocare.
evolution [i:və'lu:ʃən] n evoluzione f.
evolve [ɪ'vɔlv] vt elaborare // vi svilupparsi, evolversi.
ewe [ju:] n pecora.
ex- [ɛks] prefix ex.
exacerbate [ɛks'æsəbeɪt] vt aggravare.
exact [ɪg'zækt] a esatto(a) // vt: to ~ sth

(from) estorcere qc (da); esigere qc (da); ~**ing** a esigente; (work) faticoso(a); ~**itude** n esattezza, precisione f; ~**ly** ad esattamente.
exaggerate [ɪg'zædʒəreɪt] vt, vi esagerare; **exaggeration** [-'reɪʃən] n esagerazione f.
exalted [ɪg'zɔ:ltɪd] a esaltato(a); elevato(a).
exam [ɪg'zæm] n abbr (SCOL) = **examination**.
examination [ɪgzæmɪ'neɪʃən] n (SCOL) esame m; (MED) controllo.
examine [ɪg'zæmɪn] vt esaminare; (LAW: person) interrogare; ~**r** n esaminatore/trice.
example [ɪg'zɑ:mpl] n esempio; **for** ~ ad or per esempio.
exasperate [ɪg'zɑ:spəreɪt] vt esasperare; **exasperating** a esasperante; **exasperation** [-'reɪʃən] n esasperazione f.
excavate ['ɛkskəveɪt] vt scavare.
exceed [ɪk'si:d] vt superare; (one's powers, time limit) oltrepassare; ~**ingly** ad eccessivamente.
excellent ['ɛksələnt] a eccellente.
except [ɪk'sɛpt] prep (also: ~ **for**, ~**ing**) salvo, all'infuori di, eccetto // vt escludere; ~ **if/when** salvo se/quando; ~ **that** salvo che; ~**ion** [ɪk'sɛpʃən] n eccezione f; to take ~**ion** to trovare a ridire su; ~**ional** [ɪk'sɛpʃənl] a eccezionale.
excerpt ['ɛksə:pt] n estratto.
excess [ɪk'sɛs] n eccesso; ~ **baggage** n bagaglio in eccedenza; ~ **fare** n supplemento; ~**ive** a eccessivo(a).
exchange [ɪks'tʃeɪndʒ] n scambio; (also: **telephone** ~) centralino // vt: to ~ (for) scambiare (con); ~ **rate** n tasso di cambio.
Exchequer [ɪks'tʃɛkə*] n: the ~ (Brit) lo Scacchiere, ≈ il ministero delle Finanze.
excise ['ɛksaɪz] n imposta, dazio.
excite [ɪk'saɪt] vt eccitare; to get ~**d** eccitarsi; ~**ment** n eccitazione f; agitazione f; **exciting** a avventuroso(a); (film, book) appassionante.
exclaim [ɪk'skleɪm] vi esclamare; **exclamation** [ɛksklə'meɪʃən] n esclamazione f; **exclamation mark** n punto esclamativo.
exclude [ɪk'sklu:d] vt escludere.
exclusive [ɪk'sklu:sɪv] a esclusivo(a); (club) selettivo(a); (district) snob inv; ~ **of VAT** I.V.A. esclusa.
excommunicate [ɛkskə'mju:nɪkeɪt] vt scomunicare.
excruciating [ɪk'skru:ʃɪeɪtɪŋ] a straziante, atroce.
excursion [ɪk'skə:ʃən] n escursione f, gita.
excuse n [ɪk'skju:s] scusa // vt [ɪk'skju:z] scusare; to ~ sb from (activity) dispensare qn da; ~ **me**! mi scusi!; **now**,

if you will ~ me ... ora, mi scusi ma ...
ex-directory ['eksdɪ'rektərɪ] a (Brit TEL): to be ~ non essere sull'elenco.
execute ['eksɪkjuːt] vt (prisoner) giustiziare; (plan etc) eseguire.
execution [eksɪ'kjuːʃən] n esecuzione f; ~**er** n boia m inv.
executive [ɪg'zekjutɪv] n (COMM) dirigente m; (POL) esecutivo // a esecutivo(a).
exemplify [ɪg'zemplɪfaɪ] vt esemplificare.
exempt [ɪg'zempt] a esentato(a) // vt: to ~ sb from esentare qn da; ~**ion** [ɪg'zempʃən] n esenzione f.
exercise ['eksəsaɪz] n esercizio // vt esercitare; (dog) portar fuori // vi fare del movimento or moto; ~ **book** n quaderno.
exert [ɪg'zɜːt] vt esercitare; to ~ o.s. sforzarsi; ~**ion** [-ʃən] n sforzo.
exhaust [ɪg'zɔːst] n (also: ~ fumes) scappamento; (also: ~ pipe) tubo di scappamento // vt esaurire; ~**ed** a esaurito(a); ~**ion** [ɪg'zɔːstʃən] n esaurimento; **nervous** ~**ion** sovraffaticamento mentale; ~**ive** a esauriente.
exhibit [ɪg'zɪbɪt] n (ART) oggetto esposto; (LAW) documento or oggetto esibito // vt esporre; (courage, skill) dimostrare; ~**ion** [eksɪ'bɪʃən] n mostra, esposizione f.
exhilarating [ɪg'zɪləreɪtɪŋ] a esilarante; stimolante.
exhort [ɪg'zɔːt] vt esortare.
exile ['eksaɪl] n esilio; (person) esiliato/a // vt esiliare.
exist [ɪg'zɪst] vi esistere; ~**ence** n esistenza; to be in ~**ence** esistere; ~**ing** a esistente.
exit ['eksɪt] n uscita // vi (THEATRE, COMPUT) uscire; ~ **ramp** n (US AUT) rampa di uscita.
exodus ['eksədəs] n esodo.
exonerate [ɪg'zɔnəreɪt] vt: to ~ from discolpare da.
exotic [ɪg'zɔtɪk] a esotico(a).
expand [ɪk'spænd] vt espandere; estendere; allargare // vi (trade etc) svilupparsi, ampliarsi; espandersi; (gas) espandersi; (metal) dilatarsi.
expanse [ɪk'spæns] n distesa, estensione f.
expansion [ɪk'spænʃən] n (gen) espansione f; (of town, economy) sviluppo; (of metal) dilatazione f.
expect [ɪk'spekt] vt (anticipate) prevedere, aspettarsi, prevedere or aspettarsi che + sub; (count on) contare su; (hope for) sperare; (require) richiedere, esigere; (suppose) supporre; (await, also baby) aspettare // vi: to be ~**ing** essere in stato interessante; to ~ sb to do aspettarsi che qn faccia; ~**ancy** n (anticipation) attesa; life ~**ancy**

probabilità fpl di vita; ~**ant mother** n gestante f; ~**ation** [ekspek'teɪʃən] n aspettativa; speranza.
expedience, expediency [ɪk'spiːdɪəns, ɪk'spiːdɪənsɪ] n convenienza.
expedient [ɪk'spiːdɪənt] a conveniente; vantaggioso(a) // n espediente m.
expedite ['ekspədaɪt] vt sbrigare; facilitare.
expedition [ekspə'dɪʃən] n spedizione f.
expel [ɪk'spel] vt espellere.
expend [ɪk'spend] vt spendere; (use up) consumare; ~**able** a sacrificabile; ~**iture** [ɪk'spendɪtʃə*] n spesa.
expense [ɪk'spens] n spesa; (high cost) costo; ~**s** npl (COMM) spese fpl, indennità fpl; at the ~ of a spese di; ~ **account** n conto m spese inv.
expensive [ɪk'spensɪv] a caro(a), costoso(a).
experience [ɪk'spɪərɪəns] n esperienza // vt (pleasure) provare; (hardship) soffrire; ~**d** a esperto(a).
experiment n [ɪk'sperɪmənt] esperimento, esperienza // vi [ɪk'sperɪment] fare esperimenti; to ~ with sperimentare.
expert ['ekspəːt] a, n esperto(a); ~**ise** [-'tiːz] n competenza.
expire [ɪk'spaɪə*] vi (period of time, licence) scadere; **expiry** n scadenza.
explain [ɪk'spleɪn] vt spiegare; **explanation** [eksplə'neɪʃən] n spiegazione f; **explanatory** [ɪk'splænətrɪ] a esplicativo(a).
explicit [ɪk'splɪsɪt] a esplicito(a); (definite) netto(a).
explode [ɪk'spləud] vi esplodere.
exploit n ['eksplɔɪt] impresa // vt [ɪk'splɔɪt] sfruttare; ~**ation** [-'teɪʃən] n sfruttamento.
exploratory [ɪk'splɔrətrɪ] a (fig: talks) esplorativo(a).
explore [ɪk'splɔː*] vt esplorare; (possibilities) esaminare; ~**r** n esploratore/trice.
explosion [ɪk'spləuʒən] n esplosione f.
explosive [ɪk'spləusɪv] a esplosivo(a) // n esplosivo.
exponent [ɪk'spəunənt] n esponente m/f.
export vt [ek'spɔːt] esportare // n ['ekspɔːt] esportazione f; articolo di esportazione // cpd d'esportazione; ~**er** n esportatore m.
expose [ɪk'spəuz] vt esporre; (unmask) smascherare; ~**d** a (position) esposto(a).
exposure [ɪk'spəuʒə*] n esposizione f; (PHOT) posa; (MED) assideramento; ~ **meter** n esposimetro.
expound [ɪk'spaund] vt esporre.
express [ɪk'spres] a (definite) chiaro(a), espresso(a); (Brit: letter etc) espresso inv // n (train) espresso // ad (send) espresso // vt esprimere; ~**ion**

|ɪk'spreʃən| n espressione f; ~**ive** a espressivo(a); ~**ly** ad espressamente; ~**way** n (US: *urban motorway*) autostrada che attraversa la città.

exquisite |ɛk'skwɪzɪt| a squisito(a).

extend |ɪk'stɛnd| vt (*visit*) protrarre; (*road, deadline*) prolungare; (*building*) ampliare; (*offer*) offrire, porgere // vi (*land*) estendersi.

extension |ɪk'stɛnʃən| n (*of road, term*) prolungamento; (*of contract, deadline*) proroga; (*building*) annesso; (*to wire, table*) prolunga; (*telephone*) interno; (: *in private house*) apparecchio supplementare.

extensive |ɪk'stɛnsɪv| a esteso(a), ampio(a); (*damage*) su larga scala; (*alterations*) notevole; (*inquiries*) esauriente; (*use*) grande; ~**ly** ad: he's travelled ~**ly** ha viaggiato molto.

extent |ɪk'stɛnt| n estensione f; to some ~ fino a un certo punto; to what ~? fino a che punto?; to the ~ of ... fino al punto di ...

extenuating |ɪks'tɛnjueɪtɪŋ| a: ~ circumstances attenuanti fpl.

exterior |ɛk'stɪərɪə*| a esteriore, esterno(a) // n esteriore m, esterno; aspetto (esteriore).

exterminate |ɪk'stə:mɪneɪt| vt sterminare.

external |ɛk'stə:nl| a esterno(a), esteriore.

extinct |ɪk'stɪŋkt| a estinto(a).

extinguish |ɪk'stɪŋgwɪʃ| vt estinguere; ~**er** n estintore m.

extort |ɪk'stɔ:t| vt: to ~ sth (from) estorcere qc (da); ~**ionate** |ɪk'stɔ:ʃnət| a esorbitante.

extra |'ɛkstrə| a extra inv, supplementare // ad (*in addition*) di più // n supplemento; (*THEATRE*) comparsa.

extra... |'ɛkstrə| prefix extra... .

extract vt |ɪk'strækt| estrarre; (*money, promise*) strappare // n |'ɛkstrækt| estratto; (*passage*) brano.

extracurricular |'ɛkstrəkə'rɪkjulə*| a parascolastico(a).

extradite |'ɛkstrədaɪt| vt estradare.

extramarital |ɛkstrə'mærɪtl| a extraconiugale.

extramural |ɛkstrə'mjuərl| a fuori dell'università.

extraordinary |ɪk'strɔ:dnrɪ| a straordinario(a).

extravagance |ɪk'strævəgəns| n sperpero; stravaganza.

extravagant |ɪk'strævəgənt| a stravagante; (*in spending*) dispendioso(a).

extreme |ɪk'stri:m| a estremo(a) // n estremo; ~**ly** ad estremamente.

extricate |'ɛkstrɪkeɪt| vt: to ~ sth (from) districare qc (da).

extrovert |'ɛkstrəvə:t| n estroverso/a.

exude |ɪg'zju:d| vt trasudare; (*fig*) emanare.

eye |aɪ| n occhio; (*of needle*) cruna // vt osservare; to keep an ~ on tenere d'occhio; ~**ball** n globo dell'occhio; ~**bath** n occhino; ~**brow** n sopracciglio; ~**brow pencil** n matita per le sopracciglia; ~**drops** npl gocce fpl oculari, collirio; ~**lash** n ciglio; ~**lid** n palpebra; ~ **liner** n eye-liner m inv; ~**opener** n rivelazione f; ~**shadow** n ombretto; ~**sight** n vista; ~**sore** n pugno nell'occhio; ~ **witness** n testimone m/f oculare.

F

F |ɛf| n (*MUS*) fa m.

fable |'feɪbl| n favola.

fabric |'fæbrɪk| n stoffa, tessuto.

fabrication |fæbrɪ'keɪʃən| n fabbricazione f; falsificazione f.

fabulous |'fæbjuləs| a favoloso(a); (*col: super*) favoloso(a), fantastico(a).

façade |fə'sɑ:d| n facciata.

face |feɪs| n faccia, viso, volto; (*expression*) faccia; (*grimace*) smorfia; (*of clock*) quadrante m; (*of building*) facciata; (*side, surface*) faccia // vt essere di fronte a; (*fig*) affrontare; ~ down a faccia in giù; to make or pull a ~ fare una smorfia; in the ~ of (*difficulties etc*) di fronte a; on the ~ of it a prima vista; to ~ ~ faccia a faccia; to ~ up to vt fus affrontare, far fronte a; ~ **cloth** n (*Brit*) guanto di spugna; ~ **cream** n crema per il viso; ~ **lift** n lifting m inv; (*of façade etc*) ripulita.

facet |'fæsɪt| n faccetta, sfaccettatura; (*fig*) sfaccettatura.

facetious |fə'si:ʃəs| a faceto(a).

face value n (*of coin*) valore m facciale or nominale; to take sth at ~ (*fig*) giudicare qc dalle apparenze.

facilities |fə'sɪlɪtɪz| npl attrezzature fpl; credit ~ facilitazioni fpl di credito.

facing |'feɪsɪŋ| prep di fronte a // n (*of wall etc*) rivestimento; (*SEWING*) paramontura.

facsimile |fæk'sɪmɪlɪ| n facsimile m inv; ~ **machine** n telecopiatrice f.

fact |fækt| n fatto; in ~ infatti.

factor |'fæktə*| n fattore m.

factory |'fæktərɪ| n fabbrica, stabilimento.

factual |'fæktjuəl| a che si attiene ai fatti.

faculty |'fækəltɪ| n facoltà f inv.

fad |fæd| n mania; capriccio.

fade |feɪd| vi sbiadire, sbiadirsi; (*light, sound, hope*) attenuarsi, affievolirsi; (*flower*) appassire.

fag |fæg| n (*col: cigarette*) cicca.

fail |feɪl| vt (*exam*) non superare; (*candidate*) bocciare; (*subj: courage,* *memory*) mancare a // *vi* fallire; (*student*) essere respinto(a); (*supplies*) mancare; (*eyesight, health, light*) venire a mancare; **to ~ to do sth** (*neglect*) mancare di fare qc; (*be unable*) non riuscire a fare qc; **without ~** senza fallo; certamente; **~ing** *n* difetto // *prep* in mancanza di; **~ure** ['feɪljə*] *n* fallimento; (*person*) fallito/a; (*mechanical etc*) guasto.

faint [feɪnt] *a* debole; (*recollection*) vago(a); (*mark*) indistinto(a) // *vi* svenire; **to feel ~** sentirsi svenire.

fair [fɛə*] *a* (*person, decision*) giusto(a), equo(a); (*hair etc*) biondo(a); (*skin, complexion*) bianco(a); (*weather*) bello(a), clemente; (*good enough*) assai buono(a); (*sizeable*) bello(a) // *ad* (*play*) lealmente // *n* fiera; (*Brit: funfair*) luna park *m inv*; **~ly** *ad* equamente; (*quite*) abbastanza; **~ness** *n* equità, giustizia; **~ play** *n* correttezza.

fairy ['fɛərɪ] *n* fata; **~ tale** *n* fiaba.

faith [feɪθ] *n* fede *f*; (*trust*) fiducia; (*sect*) religione *f*, fede *f*; **~ful** *a* fedele; **~fully** *ad* fedelmente; **yours ~fully** (*Brit: in letters*) distinti saluti.

fake [feɪk] *n* imitazione *f*; (*picture*) falso; (*person*) impostore/a // *a* falso(a) // *vt* (*accounts*) falsificare; (*illness*) fingere; (*painting*) contraffare.

falcon ['fɔːlkən] *n* falco, falcone *m*.

fall [fɔːl] *n* caduta; (*in temperature*) abbassamento; (*in price*) ribasso; (*US: autumn*) autunno // *vi* (*pt fell, pp fallen*) cadere; (*temperature, price*) abbassare; **~s** *npl* (*waterfall*) cascate *fpl*; **to ~ flat** *vi* (*on one's face*) cadere bocconi; (*joke*) fare cilecca; (*plan*) fallire; **to ~ back** *vi* (*retreat*) indietreggiare; (*MIL*) ritirarsi; **to ~ back on** *vt fus* (*remedy etc*) ripiegare su; **to ~ behind** *vi* rimanere indietro; **to ~ down** *vi* (*person*) cadere; (*building*) crollare; **to ~ for** *vt fus* (*person*) prendere una cotta per; **to ~ for a trick** (*or a story etc*) cascarci; **to ~ in** *vi* crollare; (*MIL*) mettersi in riga; **to ~ off** *vi* cadere; (*diminish*) diminuire, abbassarsi; **to ~ out** *vi* (*friends etc*) litigare; **to ~ through** *vi* (*plan, project*) fallire.

fallacy ['fæləsɪ] *n* errore *m*.

fallen ['fɔːlən] *pp* of **fall**.

fallout ['fɔːlaʊt] *n* fall-out *m*; **~ shelter** *n* rifugio antiatomico.

fallow ['fæləʊ] *a* incolto(a), a maggese.

false [fɔːls] *a* falso(a); **under ~ pretences** con l'inganno; **~ teeth** *npl* (*Brit*) denti *mpl* finti.

falter ['fɔːltə*] *vi* esitare, vacillare.

fame [feɪm] *n* fama, celebrità.

familiar [fə'mɪlɪə*] *a* familiare; (*common*) comune; (*close*) intimo(a); **to be ~ with** (*subject*) conoscere; **~ity** [fəmɪlɪ'ærɪtɪ] *n* familiarità; intimità;

~ize [fə'mɪlɪəraɪz] *vt*: **to ~ize sb with sth** far conoscere qc a qn.

family ['fæmɪlɪ] *n* famiglia.

famine ['fæmɪn] *n* carestia.

famished ['fæmɪʃt] *a* affamato(a).

famous ['feɪməs] *a* famoso(a); **~ly** *ad* (*get on*) a meraviglia.

fan [fæn] *n* (*folding*) ventaglio; (*ELEC*) ventilatore *m*; (*person*) ammiratore/trice; tifoso/a // *vt* far vento a; (*fire, quarrel*) alimentare; **to ~ out** *vi* spargersi (a ventaglio).

fanatic [fə'nætɪk] *n* fanatico/a.

fan belt *n* cinghia del ventilatore.

fanciful ['fænsɪful] *a* fantasioso(a); (*object*) di fantasia.

fancy ['fænsɪ] *n* immaginazione *f*, fantasia; (*whim*) capriccio // *a* (di) fantasia *inv* // *vt* (*feel like, want*) aver voglia di; **to take a ~ to** incapricciarsi di; **~ dress** *n* costume *m* (per maschera); **~-dress ball** *n* ballo in maschera.

fang [fæŋ] *n* zanna; (*of snake*) dente *m*.

fantastic [fæn'tæstɪk] *a* fantastico(a).

fantasy ['fæntəsɪ] *n* fantasia, immaginazione *f*; fantasticheria; chimera.

far [fɑː*] *a*: **the ~ side/end** l'altra parte/ l'altro capo // *ad* lontano; **~ away, ~ off** lontano, distante; **~ better** assai migliore; **~ from** lontano da; **by ~** di gran lunga; **go as ~ as the farm** vada fino alla fattoria; **as ~ as I know** per quel che so; **~away** *a* lontano(a).

farce [fɑːs] *n* farsa.

farcical ['fɑːsɪkəl] *a* farsesco(a).

fare [fɛə*] *n* (*on trains, buses*) tariffa; (*in taxi*) prezzo della corsa; (*food*) vitto, cibo // *vi* passarsela; **half ~** metà tariffa; **full ~** tariffa intera.

Far East *n*: **the ~** l'Estremo Oriente *m*.

farewell [fɛə'wɛl] *excl*, *n* addio.

farm [fɑːm] *n* fattoria, podere *m* // *vt* coltivare; **~er** *n* coltivatore/trice; agricoltore/trice; **~hand** *n* bracciante *m* agricolo; **~house** *n* fattoria; **~ing** *n* agricoltura; **~ worker** *n* = **~hand**; **~yard** *n* aia.

far-reaching ['fɑː'riːtʃɪŋ] *a* di vasta portata.

fart [fɑːt] (*col!*) *n* scoreggia(!) // *vi* scoreggiare (!).

farther ['fɑːðə*] *ad* più lontano // *a* più lontano(a).

farthest ['fɑːðɪst] *superlative of* **far**.

fascinate ['fæsɪneɪt] *vt* affascinare; **fascinating** *a* affascinante; **fascination** [-'neɪʃən] *n* fascino.

fascism ['fæʃɪzəm] *n* fascismo.

fascist ['fæʃɪst] *a*, *n* fascista (*m/f*).

fashion ['fæʃən] *n* moda; (*manner*) maniera, modo // *vt* foggiare, formare; **in ~** alla moda; **out of ~** passato(a) di moda; **~able** *a* alla moda, di moda; **~**

show n sfilata di moda.

fast |fɑːst| a rapido(a), svelto(a), veloce; (clock): to be ~ andare avanti; (dye, colour) solido(a) // ad rapidamente; (stuck, held) saldamente // n digiuno // vi digiunare; ~ asleep profondamente addormentato.

fasten ['fɑːsn] vt chiudere, fissare; (coat) abbottonare, allacciare // vi chiudersi, fissarsi; ~er, ~ing n fermaglio, chiusura.

fast food n fast food m.

fastidious |fæs'tɪdɪəs| a esigente, difficile.

fat |fæt| a grasso(a) // n grasso.

fatal ['feɪtl] a fatale; mortale; disastroso(a); ~ity |fə'tælɪtɪ| n (road death etc) morto/a, vittima; ~ly ad a morte.

fate |feɪt| n destino; (of person) sorte f; ~ful a fatidico(a).

father ['fɑːðə*] n padre m; ~-in-law n suocero; ~ly a paterno(a).

fathom ['fæðəm] n braccio (= 1828 mm) // vt (mystery) penetrare, sondare.

fatigue |fə'tiːg| n stanchezza; (MIL) corvé f.

fatten ['fætn] vt, vi ingrassare.

fatty ['fætɪ] a (food) grasso(a) // n (col) ciccione/a.

fatuous ['fætjʊəs] a fatuo(a).

faucet ['fɔːsɪt] n (US) rubinetto.

fault |fɔːlt| n colpa; (TENNIS) fallo; (defect) difetto; (GEO) faglia // vt criticare; it's my ~ è colpa mia; to find ~ with trovare da ridire su; at ~ in fallo; to a ~ eccessivamente; ~less a perfetto(a); senza difetto; impeccabile; ~y a difettoso(a).

fauna ['fɔːnə] n fauna.

faux pas ['fəʊ'pɑː] n gaffe f inv.

favour, (US) **favor** ['feɪvə*] n favore m, cortesia, piacere m // vt (proposition) favorire, essere favorevole a; (pupil etc) favorire; (team, horse) dare per vincente; to do sb a ~ fare un favore or una cortesia a qn; to find ~ with (subj: person) entrare nelle buone grazie di; (: suggestion) avere l'approvazione di; in ~ of in favore di; ~able a favorevole; ~ite [-rɪt] a, n favorito(a).

fawn |fɔːn| n daino // a (also: ~-coloured) marrone chiaro inv // vi: to ~ (up)on adulare servilmente.

fax |fæks| n (document) facsimile m inv, telecopia; (machine) telecopiatrice f.

FBI n abbr (US: = Federal Bureau of Investigation) F.B.I. f.

fear |fɪə*| n paura, timore m // vt aver paura di, temere; for ~ of per paura di; ~ful a pauroso(a); (sight, noise) terribile, spaventoso(a).

feasibility |fiːzə'bɪlɪtɪ| n praticabilità.

feasible ['fiːzəbl] a possibile, realizzabile.

feast |fiːst| n festa, banchetto; (REL: also: ~ day) festa // vi banchettare.

feat |fiːt| n impresa, fatto insigne.

feather ['feðə*] n penna.

feature ['fiːtʃə*] n caratteristica; (article) articolo // vt (subj: film) avere come protagonista // vi figurare; ~s npl (of face) fisionomia; ~ film n film m inv principale.

February ['februərɪ] n febbraio.

fed |fed| pt, pp of **feed**.

federal ['fedərəl] a federale.

fed-up |fed'ʌp| a: to be ~ essere stufo(a).

fee |fiː| n pagamento; (of doctor, lawyer) onorario; (for examination) tassa d'esame; **school** ~s tasse fpl scolastiche.

feeble ['fiːbl] a debole.

feed |fiːd| n (of baby) pappa; (of animal) mangime m; (on printer) meccanismo di alimentazione // vt (pt, pp **fed**) nutrire; (Brit: baby) allattare; (horse etc) dare da mangiare a; (fire, machine) alimentare; to ~ material into introdurre materiale in; to ~ data/information into inserire dati/informazioni in; to ~ on vt fus nutrirsi di; ~back n feed-back m; ~ing bottle n (Brit) biberon m inv.

feel |fiːl| n (sense of touch) tatto; (of substance) consistenza // vt (pt, pp **felt**) toccare; palpare; tastare; (cold, pain, anger) sentire; (grief) provare; (think, believe): to ~ (that) pensare che; to ~ hungry/cold aver fame/freddo; to ~ lonely/better sentirsi solo/meglio; I don't ~ well non mi sento bene; to ~ like (want) aver voglia di; to ~ about or around for cercare a tastoni; ~er n (of insect) antenna; to put out ~ers (fig) fare un sondaggio; ~ing n sensazione f; sentimento.

feet |fiːt| npl of **foot**.

feign |feɪn| vt fingere, simulare.

fell |fel| pt of **fall** // vt (tree) abbattere.

fellow ['feləʊ] n individuo, tipo; compagno; (of learned society) membro // cpd: ~ **countryman** n compatriota m; ~ **men** npl simili mpl; ~**ship** n associazione f; compagnia; specie di borsa di studio universitaria.

felony ['felənɪ] n reato, crimine m.

felt |felt| pt, pp of **feel** // n feltro; ~**-tip pen** n pennarello.

female ['fiːmeɪl] n (ZOOL) femmina; (pej: woman) donna, femmina // a femminile; (BIOL, ELEC) femmina inv; (sex, character) femminile; (vote etc) di donne.

feminine ['femɪnɪn] a, n femminile (m).

feminist ['femɪnɪst] n femminista m/f.

fence |fens| n recinto; (col: person) ricettatore/trice // vt (also: ~ in) recingere // vi schermire; **fencing** n (SPORT) scherma.

fend |fend| vi: to ~ for o.s. arrangiarsi; to ~ off vt (attack, attacker) respingere, difendersi da; (questions) eludere.

fender ['fɛndə*] n parafuoco; (US) parafango; paraurti m inv.

ferment vi [fə'mɛnt] fermentare // n ['fɜ:mɛnt] agitazione f, eccitazione f.

fern [fə:n] n felce f.

ferocious [fə'rəuʃəs] a feroce.

ferret ['fɛrɪt] n furetto.

ferry ['fɛrɪ] n (small) traghetto; (large: also: ~**boat**) nave f traghetto inv // vt traghettare.

fertile ['fə:taɪl] a fertile; (BIOL) fecondo(a); **fertilizer** ['fə:tɪlaɪzə*] n fertilizzante m.

fester ['fɛstə*] vi suppurare.

festival ['fɛstɪvəl] n (REL) festa; (ART. MUS) festival m inv.

festive ['fɛstɪv] a di festa; the ~ season (Brit: Christmas) il periodo delle feste.

festivities [fɛs'tɪvɪtɪz] npl festeggiamenti mpl.

festoon [fɛs'tu:n] vt: to ~ with ornare di.

fetch [fɛtʃ] vt andare a prendere; (sell for) essere venduto(a) per.

fetching ['fɛtʃɪŋ] a attraente.

fête [feɪt] n festa.

fetish ['fɛtɪʃ] n feticcio.

fetus ['fi:təs] n (US) = **foetus**.

feud [fju:d] n contesa, lotta // vi essere in lotta.

feudal ['fju:dl] a feudale.

fever ['fi:və*] n febbre f; ~**ish** a febbrile.

few [fju:] a pochi(e); they were ~ erano pochi; a ~ a qualche inv // pronoun alcuni(e); ~**er** a meno inv; meno numerosi(e); ~**est** a il minor numero di.

fiancé [fɪ'ã:ŋseɪ] n fidanzato; ~**e** n fidanzata.

fib [fɪb] n piccola bugia.

fibre, (US) **fiber** ['faɪbə*] n fibra; ~**glass** n fibra di vetro.

fickle ['fɪkl] a incostante, capriccioso(a).

fiction ['fɪkʃən] n narrativa, romanzi mpl; (sth made up) finzione f; ~**al** a immaginario(a).

fictitious [fɪk'tɪʃəs] a fittizio(a).

fiddle ['fɪdl] n (MUS) violino; (cheating) imbroglio; truffa // vt (Brit: accounts) falsificare, falsare; to ~ with vt fus gingillarsi con.

fidelity [fɪ'dɛlɪtɪ] n fedeltà; (accuracy) esattezza.

fidget ['fɪdʒɪt] vi agitarsi.

field [fi:ld] n campo; ~ **marshal** n feldmaresciallo; ~**work** n ricerche fpl esterne.

fiend [fi:nd] n demonio.

fierce [fɪəs] a (look, fighting) fiero(a); (wind) furioso(a); (attack) feroce; (enemy) acerrimo(a).

fiery ['faɪərɪ] a ardente; infocato(a).

fifteen [fɪf'ti:n] num quindici.

fifth [fɪfθ] num quinto(a).

fifty ['fɪftɪ] num cinquanta; ~-~ a: a ~ ~ **chance** una possibilità su due // ad fifty-fifty, metà per ciascuno.

fig [fɪg] n fico.

fight [faɪt] n zuffa, rissa; (MIL) battaglia, combattimento; (against cancer etc) lotta // vb (pt, pp **fought**) vt picchiare; combattere; (cancer, alcoholism) lottare contro, combattere // vi battersi, combattere; ~**er** n combattente m; (plane) aeroplano da caccia; ~**ing** n combattimento.

figment ['fɪgmənt] n: a ~ **of the imagination** un parto della fantasia.

figurative ['fɪgjurətɪv] a figurato(a).

figure ['fɪgə*] n (DRAWING, GEOM) figura; (number, cipher) cifra; (body, outline) forma // vi (appear) figurare; (US: make sense) spiegarsi; to ~ **out** vt riuscire a capire; calcolare; ~**head** n (NAUT) polena; (pej) prestanome m/f inv; ~ **of speech** n figura retorica.

file [faɪl] n (tool) lima; (dossier) incartamento; (folder) cartellina; (for loose leaf) raccoglitore m; (COMPUT) archivio; (row) fila // vt (nails, wood) limare; (papers) archiviare; (LAW: claim) presentare; passare agli atti; to ~ **in/out** vi entrare/uscire in fila; to ~ **past** vt fus marciare in fila davanti a.

filing ['faɪlɪŋ] n archiviare m; ~ **cabinet** n casellario.

fill [fɪl] vt riempire; (tooth) otturare; (job) coprire // n: to eat one's ~ mangiare a sazietà; to ~ **in** vt (hole) riempire; (form) compilare; to ~ **up** vt riempire // vi (AUT) fare il pieno; ~ **it up, please** (AUT) mi faccia il pieno, per piacere.

fillet ['fɪlɪt] n filetto; ~ **steak** n bistecca di filetto.

filling ['fɪlɪŋ] n (CULIN) impasto, ripieno; (for tooth) otturazione f; ~ **station** n stazione f di rifornimento.

film [fɪlm] n (CINEMA) film m inv; (PHOT) pellicola; (thin layer) velo // vt (scene) filmare; ~ **star** n divo/a dello schermo; ~ **strip** n filmina.

filter ['fɪltə*] n filtro // vt filtrare; ~ **lane** n (Brit AUT) corsia di svincolo; ~-**tipped** a con filtro.

filth [fɪlθ] n sporcizia; (fig) oscenità; ~**y** a lordo(a), sozzo(a); (language) osceno(a).

fin [fɪn] n (of fish) pinna.

final ['faɪnl] a finale, ultimo(a); definitivo(a) // n (SPORT) finale f; ~**s** npl (SCOL) esami mpl finali; ~**e** [fɪ'nɑ:lɪ] n finale m; ~**ize** vt mettere a punto; ~**ly** ad (lastly) alla fine; (eventually) finalmente.

finance [faɪ'næns] n finanza // vt finanziare; ~**s** npl finanze fpl.

financial [faɪ'nænʃəl] a finanziario(a).

financier [faɪ'nænsɪə*] n finanziatore m.

find [faɪnd] vt (pt, pp **found**) trovare;

(*lost object*) ritrovare // *n* trovata, scoperta; to ~ sb guilty (*LAW*) giudicare qn colpevole; to ~ out *vt* informarsi di; (*truth, secret*) scoprire; (*person*) cogliere in fallo; to ~ out about informarsi di; (*by chance*) scoprire; ~ings *npl* (*LAW*) sentenza, conclusioni *fpl*; (*of report*) conclusioni.

fine [faɪn] *a* bello(a); ottimo(a); (*thin, subtle*) fine // *ad* (*well*) molto bene; (*small*) finemente // *n* (*LAW*) multa // *vt* (*LAW*) multare; to be ~ (*weather*) far bello; ~ arts *npl* belle arti *fpl*.

finery ['faɪnərɪ] *n* abiti *mpl* eleganti.

finger ['fɪŋgə*] *n* dito // *vt* toccare, tastare; little/index ~ mignolo/(dito) indice *m*; ~nail *n* unghia; ~print *n* impronta digitale; ~tip *n* punta del dito.

finicky ['fɪnɪkɪ] *a* esigente, pignolo(a); minuzioso(a).

finish ['fɪnɪʃ] *n* fine *f*; (*polish etc*) finitura // *vt* finire; (*use up*) esaurire // *vi* finire; (*session*) terminare; to ~ doing sth finire di fare qc; to ~ third arrivare terzo(a); to ~ off *vt* compiere; (*kill*) uccidere; to ~ up *vi, vt* finire; ~ing line *n* linea d'arrivo; ~ing school *n* scuola privata di perfezionamento (*per signorine*).

finite ['faɪnaɪt] *a* limitato(a); (*verb*) finito(a).

Finland ['fɪnlənd] *n* Finlandia.

Finn [fɪn] *n* finlandese *m/f*; ~ish *a* finlandese // *n* (*LING*) finlandese *m*.

fir [fəː*] *n* abete *m*.

fire [taɪə*] *n* fuoco; incendio // *vt* (*discharge*); to ~ a gun scaricare un fucile; (*fig*) infiammare; (*dismiss*) licenziare // *vi* sparare, far fuoco; on ~ in fiamme; ~ alarm *n* allarme *m* d'incendio; ~arm *n* arma da fuoco; ~ brigade, (*US*) ~ department *n* (corpo dei) pompieri *mpl*; ~ engine *n* autopompa; ~ escape *n* scala di sicurezza; ~ extinguisher *n* estintore *m*; ~-man *n* pompiere *m*; ~place *n* focolare *m*; ~side *n* angolo del focolare; ~ station *n* caserma dei pompieri; ~wood *n* legna; ~work *n* fuoco d'artificio; ~works display *n* spettacolo pirotecnico.

firing ['faɪərɪŋ] *n* (*MIL*) spari *mpl*, tiro; ~ squad *n* plotone *m* d'esecuzione.

firm [fəːm] *a* fermo(a) // *n* ditta, azienda; ~ly *ad* fermamente.

first [fəːst] *a* primo(a) // *ad* (*before others*) il primo, la prima; (*before other things*) per primo; (*when listing reasons etc*) per prima cosa // *n* (*person: in race*) primo/a; (*SCOL*) laurea con lode; (*AUT*) prima; at ~ dapprima, all'inizio; ~ of all prima di tutto; ~ aid *n* pronto soccorso; ~-aid kit *n* cassetta pronto soccorso; ~-class *a* di prima classe; ~-hand *a* di prima mano; ~ lady *n* (*US*) moglie *f* del presidente; ~ly *ad* in

primo luogo; ~ name *n* prenome *m*; ~-rate *a* di prima qualità, ottimo(a).

fish [fɪʃ] *n* (*pl inv*) pesce *m* // *vi* pescare; to go ~ing andare a pesca; ~erman *n* pescatore *m*; ~ farm *n* vivaio; ~ fingers *npl* (*Brit*) bastoncini *mpl* di pesce (surgelati); ~ing boat *n* barca da pesca; ~ing line *n* lenza; ~ing rod *n* canna da pesca; ~monger *n* pescivendolo; ~monger's (shop) *n* pescheria; ~ sticks *npl* (*US*) = ~ fingers; ~y *a* (*fig*) sospetto(a).

fist [fɪst] *n* pugno.

fit [fɪt] *a* (*MED, SPORT*) in forma; (*proper*) adatto(a), appropriato(a); conveniente // *vt* (*subj: clothes*) stare bene a; (*adjust*) aggiustare; (*put in, attach*) mettere, installare; (*equip*) fornire, equipaggiare // *vi* (*clothes*) stare bene; (*parts*) andare bene, adattarsi; (*in space, gap*) entrare // *n* (*MED*) accesso, attacco; ~ to in grado di; ~ for adatto(a) a; degno(a) di; a ~ of anger un accesso d'ira; this dress is a tight/good ~ questo vestito è stretto/sta bene; by ~s and starts a sbalzi; to ~ in *vi* accordarsi; adattarsi; to ~ out *vt* (*Brit: also:* ~ up) equipaggiare; ~ful *a* saltuario(a); ~ment *n* componibile *m*; ~ness *n* (*MED*) forma fisica; (*of remark*) appropriatezza; ~ted carpet *n* moquette *f*; ~ted kitchen *n* cucina componibile; ~ter *n* aggiustatore *m or* montatore *m* meccanico; (*DRESSMAKING*) sarto/a; ~ting *a* appropriato(a) // *n* (*of dress*) prova; (*of piece of equipment*) montaggio, aggiustaggio; ~ting room *n* camerino; ~tings *npl* impianti *mpl*.

five [faɪv] *num* cinque; ~r *n* (*col: Brit*) biglietto da cinque sterline; (*: US*) biglietto da cinque dollari.

fix [fɪks] *vt* fissare; mettere in ordine; (*mend*) riparare // *n*: to be in a ~ essere nei guai; to ~ up *vt* (*meeting*) fissare; to ~ sb up with sth procurare qc a qn; ~ation *n* fissazione *f*; ~ed [fɪkst] *a* (*prices etc*) fisso(a); ~ture ['fɪkstʃə*] *n* impianto (fisso); (*SPORT*) incontro (del calendario sportivo).

fizz [fɪz] *vi* frizzare.

fizzle ['fɪzl] *vi* frizzare; to ~ out *vi* finire in nulla.

fizzy ['fɪzɪ] *a* frizzante; gassato(a).

flabbergasted ['flæbəgɑːstɪd] *a* sbalordito(a).

flabby ['flæbɪ] *a* flaccido(a).

flag [flæg] *n* bandiera; (*also:* ~stone) pietra da lastricare // *vi* stancarsi; affievolirsi; to ~ down *vt* fare segno (di fermarsi) a.

flagpole ['flægpəul] *n* albero.

flair [fleə*] *n* (*for business etc*) fiuto; (*for languages etc*) facilità.

flak [flæk] *n* (*MIL*) fuoco d'artiglieria;

(col: criticism) critiche fpl.

flake [fleɪk] n (of rust, paint) scaglia; (of snow, soap powder) fiocco // vi (also: ~ off) sfaldarsi.

flamboyant [flæm'bɔɪənt] a sgargiante.

flame [fleɪm] n fiamma.

flamingo [flə'mɪŋgəu] n fenicottero, fiammingo.

flammable ['flæməbl] a infiammabile.

flan [flæn] n (Brit) flan m inv.

flank [flæŋk] n fianco.

flannel ['flænl] n (Brit: also: face ~) guanto di spugna; (fabric) flanella; ~s npl pantaloni mpl di flanella.

flap [flæp] n (of pocket) patta; (of envelope) lembo // vt (wings) battere // vi (sail, flag) sbattere; (col: also: be in a ~) essere in agitazione.

flare [flɛə•] n razzo; (in skirt etc) svasatura; **to ~ up** vi andare in fiamme; (fig: person) infiammarsi di rabbia; (: revolt) scoppiare.

flash [flæʃ] n vampata; (also: news ~) notizia f lampo inv; (PHOT) flash m inv // vt accendere e spegnere; (send: message) trasmettere // vi brillare; (light on ambulance, eyes etc) lampeggiare; in a ~ in un lampo; to ~ one's headlights lampeggiare; he ~ed by or past ci passò davanti come un lampo; ~bulb n cubo m flash inv; ~cube n flash m inv; ~light n lampadina tascabile.

flashy ['flæʃɪ] a (pej) vistoso(a).

flask [flɑːsk] n fiasco; (CHEM) beuta; (also: vacuum ~) thermos m inv ®.

flat [flæt] a piatto(a); (tyre) sgonfio(a), a terra; (denial) netto(a); (MUS) bemolle inv; (: voice) stonato(a) // n (Brit: rooms) appartamento; (AUT) pneumatico sgonfio; (MUS) bemolle m; to work ~ out lavorare a più non posso; ~ly ad categoricamente; ~ten vt (also: ~ten out) appiattire.

flatter ['flætə•] vt lusingare; ~ing a lusinghiero(a); ~y n adulazione f.

flaunt [flɔːnt] vt fare mostra di.

flavour, (US) **flavor** ['fleɪvə•] n gusto, sapore m // vt insaporire, aggiungere sapore a; **vanilla-~ed** al gusto di vaniglia; ~ing n essenza (artificiale).

flaw [flɔː] n difetto.

flax [flæks] n lino; ~en a biondo(a).

flea [fliː] n pulce f.

fleck [flɛk] n (mark) macchiolina; (pattern) screziatura.

flee, pt, pp **fled** [fliː, flɛd] vt fuggire da // vi fuggire, scappare.

fleece [fliːs] n vello // vt (col) pelare.

fleet [fliːt] n flotta; (of lorries etc) convoglio; parco.

fleeting ['fliːtɪŋ] a fugace, fuggitivo(a); (visit) volante.

Flemish ['flɛmɪʃ] a fiammingo(a) // n (LING) fiammingo.

flesh [flɛʃ] n carne f; (of fruit) polpa; ~ **wound** n ferita superficiale.

flew [fluː] pt of **fly.**

flex [flɛks] n filo (flessibile) // vt flettere; (muscles) contrarre; ~ible a flessibile.

flick [flɪk] n colpetto; scarto; **to ~ through** vt fus sfogliare.

flicker ['flɪkə•] vi tremolare // n tremolio.

flier ['flaɪə•] n aviatore m.

flight [flaɪt] n volo; (escape) fuga; (also: ~ of steps) scalinata; ~ **attendant** n (US) steward m inv, hostess f inv; ~ **deck** n (AVIAT) cabina di controllo; (NAUT) ponte m di comando.

flimsy ['flɪmzɪ] a (fabric) inconsistente; (excuse) meschino(a).

flinch [flɪntʃ] vi ritirarsi; **to ~ from** tirarsi indietro di fronte a.

fling [flɪŋ], pt, pp **flung** vt lanciare, gettare.

flint [flɪnt] n selce f; (in lighter) pietrina.

flip [flɪp] n colpetto.

flippant ['flɪpənt] a senza rispetto, irriverente.

flipper ['flɪpə•] n pinna.

flirt [fləːt] vi flirtare // n civetta.

flit [flɪt] vi svolazzare.

float [fləut] n galleggiante m; (in procession) carro; (money) somma // vi galleggiare // vt far galleggiare; (loan, business) lanciare.

flock [flɔk] n gregge m; (of people) folla.

flog [flɔg] vt flagellare.

flood [flʌd] n alluvione m; (of words, tears etc) diluvio // vt allagare; ~ing n inondazione f; ~light n riflettore m // vt illuminare a giorno.

floor [flɔː•] n pavimento; (storey) piano; (fig: at meeting): **the ~** il pubblico // vt pavimentare; (knock down) atterrare; **on the ~** per terra; **ground ~**, (US) **first ~** pianterreno; **first ~**, (US) **second ~** primo piano; ~**board** n tavellone m di legno; ~ **show** n spettacolo di varietà.

flop [flɔp] n fiasco.

floppy ['flɔpɪ] a floscio(a), molle; ~ **(disk)** n (COMPUT) floppy disk m inv.

flora ['flɔːrə] n flora.

Florence ['flɔrəns] n Firenze f; **Florentine** ['flɔrəntaɪn] a fiorentino(a).

florid ['flɔrɪd] a (complexion) florido(a); (style) fiorito(a).

florist ['flɔrɪst] n fioraio/a.

flounce [flauns] n balzo.

flounder ['flaundə•] vi annaspare // n (ZOOL) passera di mare.

flour ['flauə•] n farina.

flourish ['flʌrɪʃ] vi fiorire // vt brandire // n abbellimento; svolazzo; (of trumpets) fanfara.

flout [flaut] vt (order) contravvenire a; (convention) sfidare.

flow [fləu] n flusso; circolazione f // vi fluire; (traffic, blood in veins) circolare; (hair) scendere; ~ **chart** n schema m di flusso.

flower ['flauə*] n fiore m // vi fiorire; ~ **bed** n aiuola; ~**pot** n vaso da fiori; ~**y** a fiorito(a).

flown [fləun] pp of **fly**.

flu [flu:] n influenza.

fluctuate ['flʌktjueɪt] vi fluttuare, oscillare.

fluency ['flu:ənsɪ] n facilità, scioltezza; his ~ in English la sua scioltezza nel parlare l'inglese.

fluent ['flu:ənt] a (speech) facile, sciolto(a); corrente; he speaks ~ Italian parla l'italiano correntemente.

fluff [flʌf] n lanugine f; ~**y** a lanuginoso(a); (toy) di peluche.

fluid ['flu:ɪd] a fluido(a) // n fluido.

fluke [flu:k] n (col) colpo di fortuna.

flung [flʌŋ] pt, pp of **fling**.

fluoride ['fluəraɪd] n fluoruro.

flurry ['flʌrɪ] n (of snow) tempesta; a ~ of activity/excitement una febbre di attività/improvvisa agitazione.

flush [flʌʃ] n rossore m; (fig) ebbrezza; (: of youth, beauty etc) rigoglio, pieno vigore // vt ripulire con un getto d'acqua // vi arrossire // a: ~ with a livello di, pari a; to ~ the toilet tirare l'acqua; to ~ out (of birds) far alzare in volo; (animals, fig) stanare; ~**ed** a tutto(a) rosso(a).

flustered ['flʌstəd] a sconvolto(a).

flute [flu:t] n flauto.

flutter ['flʌtə*] n agitazione f; (of wings) frullio // vi (bird) battere le ali.

flux [flʌks] n: in a state of ~ in continuo mutamento.

fly [flaɪ] n (insect) mosca; (on trousers: also: **flies**) bracchetta // vb (pt **flew**, pp **flown**) vt pilotare; (passengers, cargo) trasportare (in aereo); (distances) percorrere // vi volare; (passengers) andare in aereo; (escape) fuggire; (flag) sventolare; to ~ **away** or **off** vt volare via; ~**ing** n (activity) aviazione f; (action) volo // a: ~**ing visit** visita volante; **with** ~**ing colours** con risultati brillanti; ~**ing saucer** n disco volante; ~**ing start** n: to get off to a ~**ing start** partire come un razzo; ~**over** n (Brit: bridge) cavalcavia m inv; ~**sheet** n (for tent) sopratetto.

foal [fəul] n puledro.

foam [fəum] n schiuma // vi schiumare; ~ **rubber** n gommapiuma ®.

fob [fɔb] vt: to ~ **sb off with** appioppare qn con; sbarazzarsi di qn con.

focus ['fəukəs] n (pl ~**es**) fuoco; (of interest) centro // vt (field glasses etc) mettere a fuoco // vi: to ~ **on** (with camera) mettere a fuoco; (person) fissare lo sguardo su; **in** ~ a fuoco; **out of** ~ sfocato(a).

fodder ['fɔdə*] n foraggio.

foe [fəu] n nemico.

foetus, (US) **fetus** ['fi:təs] n feto.

fog [fɔg] n nebbia; ~**gy** a nebbioso(a); **it's** ~**gy** c'è nebbia; ~ **lamp** n (AUT) faro m antinebbia inv.

foil [fɔɪl] vt confondere, frustrare // n lamina di metallo; (kitchen ~) foglio di alluminio; (FENCING) fioretto.

fold [fəuld] n (bend, crease) piega; (AGR) ovile m; (fig) gregge m // vt piegare; to ~ **up** vi (business) crollare // vt (map etc) piegare, ripiegare; ~**er** n (for papers) cartella; cartellina; (brochure) dépliant m inv; ~**ing** a (chair, bed) pieghevole.

foliage ['fəulɪɪdʒ] n fogliame m.

folk [fəuk] npl gente f // a popolare; ~**s** npl famiglia; ~**lore** ['fəuklɔ:*] n folclore m; ~ **song** n canto popolare.

follow ['fɔləu] vt seguire // vi seguire; (result) conseguire, risultare; **he** ~**ed suit** lui ha fatto lo stesso; to ~ **up** vt (victory) sfruttare; (letter, offer) fare seguito a; (case) seguire; ~**er** n seguace m/f, discepolo/a; ~**ing** a seguente, successivo(a) // n seguito, discepoli mpl.

folly ['fɔlɪ] n pazzia, follia.

fond [fɔnd] a (memory, look) tenero(a), affettuoso(a); to **be** ~ **of** volere bene a.

fondle ['fɔndl] vt accarezzare.

food [fu:d] n cibo; ~ **mixer** n frullatore m; ~ **poisoning** n intossicazione f; ~ **processor** n tritatutto m inv elettrico; ~**stuffs** npl generi fpl alimentari.

fool [fu:l] n sciocco/a; (HISTORY: of king) buffone m; (CULIN) frullato // vt ingannare // vi (gen: ~ **around**) fare lo sciocco; ~**hardy** a avventato(a); ~**ish** a scemo(a), stupido(a); imprudente; ~**proof** a (plan etc) sicurissimo(a).

foot [fut] n (pl **feet**) piede m; (measure) piede (= 304 mm; 12 inches); (of animal) zampa // vt (bill) pagare; **on** ~ a piedi; ~**age** n (CINEMA: length) ≈ metraggio; (: material) sequenza; ~**ball** n pallone m; (sport: Brit) calcio; (: US) football m americano; ~**baller** n (Brit) = ~**ball player**; ~**ball ground** n campo di calcio; ~**ball player** n (Brit) calciatore m; (US) giocatore m di football americano; ~**brake** n freno a pedale; ~**bridge** n passerella; ~**hills** npl contrafforti fpl; ~**hold** n punto d'appoggio; ~**ing** n (fig) posizione f; to lose one's ~**ing** mettere un piede in fallo; ~**lights** npl luci fpl della ribalta; ~**man** n lacchè m inv; ~**note** n nota (a piè di pagina); ~**path** n sentiero; (in street) marciapiede m; ~**print** n orma, impronta; ~**step** n passo; ~**wear** n calzatura.

for [fɔ:*] ♦ prep 1 (indicating destination, intention, purpose) per; **the train** ~ **London** il treno per Londra; **he went** ~ **the paper** è andato a prendere il

giornale; it's time ~ lunch è ora di pranzo; what's it ~? a che serve?; what ~? (why) perché?
2 (on behalf of, representing) per; to work ~ sb/sth lavorare per qn/qc; I'll ask him ~ you glielo chiederò a nome tuo; G ~ George G come George
3 (because of) per, a causa di; ~ this reason per questo motivo
4 (with regard to) per; it's cold ~ July è freddo per luglio; ~ everyone who voted yes, 50 voted no per ogni voto a favore ce n'erano 50 contro
5 (in exchange for) per; I sold it ~ £5 l'ho venduto per 5 sterline
6 (in favour of) per, a favore di; are you ~ or against us? è con noi o contro di noi?; I'm all ~ it sono completamente a favore
7 (referring to distance, time) per; there are roadworks ~ 5 km ci sono lavori in corso per 5 km; he was away ~ 2 years è stato via per 2 anni; she will be away ~ a month starà via un mese; it hasn't rained ~ 3 weeks non piove da 3 settimane; can you do it ~ tomorrow? può farlo per domani?
8 (with infinitive clauses): it is not ~ me to decide non sta a me decidere; it would be best ~ you to leave sarebbe meglio che te ne andasse; there is still time ~ you to do it ha ancora tempo per farlo; ~ this to be possible ... perché ciò sia possibile ...
9 (in spite of) nonostante; ~ all his complaints, he's very fond of her nonostante tutte le sue lamentele, le vuole molto bene
◆ cj (since, as: rather formal) dal momento che, poiché.
forage ['fɔrɪdʒ] vi foraggiare.
foray ['fɔreɪ] n incursione f.
forbid, pt **forbad(e)**, pp **forbidden** [fə'bɪd, -'bæd, -'bɪdn] vt vietare, interdire; to ~ sb to do sth proibire a qn di fare qc; ~**den** a vietato(a); ~**ding** a arcigno(a), d'aspetto minaccioso.
force [fɔːs] n forza // vt forzare; the F~s npl (Brit) le forze armate; to ~ o.s. to do costringersi a fare; in ~ (in large numbers) in gran numero; (law) in vigore; to come into ~ entrare in vigore; ~**-feed** vt (animal, prisoner) sottoporre ad alimentazione forzata; ~**ful** a forte, vigoroso(a).
forceps ['fɔːsɛps] npl forcipe m.
forcibly ['fɔːsəblɪ] ad con la forza; (vigorously) vigorosamente.
ford [fɔːd] n guado // vt guadare.
fore [fɔː*] n: to the ~ in prima linea; to come to the ~ mettersi in evidenza.
forearm ['fɔːrɑːm] n avambraccio.
foreboding [fɔː'bəudɪŋ] n presagio di male.
forecast ['fɔːkɑːst] n previsione f // vt

(irg: like cast) prevedere.
forecourt ['fɔːkɔːt] n (of garage) corte f esterna.
forefathers ['fɔːfɑːðəz] npl antenati mpl, avi mpl.
forefinger ['fɔːfɪŋgə*] n (dito) indice m.
forefront ['fɔːfrʌnt] n: in the ~ of all'avanguardia in.
forego [fɔː'gəu] vt = **forgo**.
foregone ['fɔːgɔn] a: it's a ~ conclusion è una conclusione scontata.
foreground ['fɔːgraund] n primo piano.
forehead ['fɔrɪd] n fronte f.
foreign ['fɔrɪn] a straniero(a); (trade) estero(a); ~ **body** n corpo estraneo; ~**er** n straniero/a; F~ **Office** n (Brit) Ministero degli Esteri; ~ **secretary** n (Brit) ministro degli Affari esteri.
foreleg ['fɔːlɛg] n zampa anteriore.
foreman ['fɔːmən] n caposquadra m.
foremost ['fɔːməust] a principale; più in vista // ad: first and ~ innanzitutto.
forensic [fə'rɛnsɪk] a: ~ **medicine** medicina legale.
forerunner ['fɔːrʌnə*] n precursore m.
foresee, pt **foresaw**, pp **foreseen** [fɔː'siː, -'sɔː, -'siːn] vt prevedere; ~**able** a prevedibile.
foreshadow [fɔː'fædəu] vt presagire, far prevedere.
foresight ['fɔːsaɪt] n previdenza.
forest ['fɔrɪst] n foresta.
forestall [fɔː'stɔːl] vt prevenire.
forestry ['fɔrɪstrɪ] n silvicoltura.
foretaste ['fɔːteɪst] n pregustazione f.
foretell, pt, pp **foretold** [fɔː'tɛl, -'təuld] vt predire.
forever [fə'rɛvə*] ad per sempre; (fig) sempre, di continuo.
foreword ['fɔːwəːd] n prefazione f.
forfeit ['fɔːfɪt] n ammenda, pena // vt perdere; (one's happiness, health) giocarsi.
forgave [fə'geɪv] pt of **forgive**.
forge [fɔːdʒ] n fucina // vt (signature, Brit: money) contraffare, falsificare; (wrought iron) fucinare, foggiare; to ~ ahead vi tirare avanti; ~**r** n contraffattore m; ~**ry** n falso; (activity) contraffazione f.
forget [fə'gɛt], pt **forgot**, pp **forgotten** vt, vi dimenticare; ~**ful** a di corta memoria; ~**ful** of dimentico(a) di; ~**me-not** n nontiscordardimé m inv.
forgive [fə'gɪv], pt **forgave**, pp **forgiven** vt perdonare; to ~ sb for sth perdonare qc a qn; ~**ness** n perdono.
forgo [fɔː'gəu], pt **forwent**, pp **forgone** vt rinunciare a.
forgot [fə'gɔt] pt of **forget**.
forgotten [fə'gɔtn] pp of **forget**.
fork [fɔːk] n (for eating) forchetta; (for gardening) forca; (of roads) bivio; (of railways) inforcazione f // vi (road) biforcarsi; to ~ out (col: pay) vt

sborsare // vi pagare; ~-**lift truck** n carrello elevatore.

forlorn [fə'lɔ:n] a (person) sconsolato(a); (place) abbandonato(a); (attempt) disperato(a); (hope) vano(a).

form [fɔ:m] n forma; (SCOL) classe f; (questionnaire) scheda // vt formare; **in top ~** in gran forma.

formal ['fɔ:məl] a (offer, receipt) vero(a) e proprio(a); (person) cerimonioso(a); (occasion, dinner) formale, ufficiale; (ART, PHILOSOPHY) formale; ~**ly** ad ufficialmente; formalmente; cerimoniosamente.

format ['fɔ:mæt] n formato // vt (COMPUT) formattare.

formation [fɔ:'meɪʃən] n formazione f.

formative ['fɔ:mətɪv] a: ~ **years** anni mpl formativi.

former ['fɔ:mə*] a vecchio(a) (before n), ex inv (before n); the ~ ... the latter quello ... questo; ~**ly** ad in passato.

formula ['fɔ:mjulə] n formula.

forsake, pt **forsook**, pp **forsaken** [fə'seɪk, -'suk, -'seɪkən] vt abbandonare.

fort [fɔ:t] n forte m.

forth [fɔ:θ] ad in avanti; **to go back and ~** andare avanti e indietro; **and so ~** e così via; ~**coming** a prossimo(a); (character) aperto(a), comunicativo(a); ~**right** a franco(a), schietto(a); ~**with** ad immediatamente, subito.

fortify ['fɔ:tɪfaɪ] vt fortificare; **fortified wine** n vino ad alta gradazione alcolica.

fortnight ['fɔ:tnaɪt] n quindici giorni mpl, due settimane fpl; ~**ly** a bimensile // ad ogni quindici giorni.

fortress ['fɔ:trɪs] n fortezza, rocca.

fortunate ['fɔ:tʃənɪt] a fortunato(a); **it is ~ that** è una fortuna che; ~**ly** ad fortunatamente.

fortune ['fɔ:tʃən] n fortuna; ~**teller** n indovino/a.

forty ['fɔ:tɪ] num quaranta.

forum ['fɔ:rəm] n foro.

forward ['fɔ:wəd] a (ahead of schedule) in anticipo; (movement, position) in avanti; (not shy) aperto(a); diretto(a); sfacciato(a) // n (SPORT) avanti m inv // vt (letter) inoltrare; (parcel, goods) spedire; (fig) promuovere, appoggiare; **to move ~** avanzare; ~**(s)** ad avanti.

forwent [fɔ:'wɛnt] pt of **forgo**.

fossil ['fɔsl] a, n fossile (m).

foster ['fɔstə*] vt incoraggiare, nutrire; (child) avere in affidamento; ~ **child** n bambino(a) preso(a) in affidamento; ~ **mother** n madre f affidataria.

fought [fɔ:t] pt, pp of **fight**.

foul [faul] a (smell, food) cattivo(a); (weather) brutto(a); (language) osceno(a); (deed) infame // n (FOOTBALL) fallo // vt sporcare; (football player) commettere un fallo su.

found [faund] pt, pp of **find** // vt (es-

tablish) fondare; ~**ation** [-'deɪʃən] n (act) fondazione f; (base) base f; (also: ~**ation cream**) fondo tinta; ~**ations** npl (of building) fondamenta fpl.

founder ['faundə*] n fondatore/trice // vi affondare.

foundry ['faundrɪ] n fonderia.

fount [faunt] n fonte f.

fountain ['fauntɪn] n fontana; ~ **pen** n penna stilografica.

four [fɔ:*] num quattro; **on all ~s** a carponi; ~-**poster** n (also: ~-**poster bed**) letto a quattro colonne; ~**some** ['fɔ:səm] n partita a quattro; uscita in quattro; ~**teen** num quattordici; ~**th** num quarto(a).

fowl [faul] n pollame m; volatile m.

fox [fɔks] n volpe f // vt confondere.

foyer ['fɔɪeɪ] n atrio; (THEATRE) ridotto.

fraction ['frækʃən] n frazione f.

fracture ['fræktʃə*] n frattura.

fragile ['frædʒaɪl] a fragile.

fragment ['frægmənt] n frammento.

fragrant ['freɪgrənt] a fragrante, profumato(a).

frail [freɪl] a debole, delicato(a).

frame [freɪm] n (of building) armatura; (of human, animal) ossatura, corpo; (of picture) cornice f; (of door, window) telaio; (of spectacles: also: ~s) montatura; ~ **of mind** n stato d'animo; ~**work** n struttura.

France [frɑ:ns] n Francia.

franchise ['fræntʃaɪz] n (POL) diritto di voto; (COMM) concessione f.

frank [fræŋk] a franco(a), aperto(a) // vt (letter) affrancare; ~**ly** ad francamente, sinceramente.

frantic ['fræntɪk] a frenetico(a).

fraternity [frə'tə:nɪtɪ] n (club) associazione f; (spirit) fratellanza.

fraud [frɔ:d] n truffa; (LAW) frode f; (person) impostore/a.

fraught [frɔ:t] a: ~ **with** pieno(a) di, intriso(a) da.

fray [freɪ] n baruffa // vt logorare // vi logorarsi; **her nerves were ~ed** aveva i nervi a pezzi.

freak [fri:k] n fenomeno, mostro // cpd fenomenale.

freckle ['frɛkl] n lentiggine f.

free [fri:] a libero(a); (gratis) gratuito(a); (liberal) generoso(a) // vt (prisoner, jammed person) liberare; (jammed object) districare; ~ (of charge), **for ~** ad gratuitamente; ~**dom** ['fri:dəm] n libertà; ~-**for-all** n parapiglia m generale; ~ **gift** n regalo, omaggio; ~**hold** n proprietà assoluta; ~ **kick** n calcio libero; ~**lance** a indipendente; ~**ly** ad liberamente; (liberally) liberalmente; ~**mason** n massone m; ~**post** n affrancatura a carico del destinatario; ~-**range** a (hen) ruspante; (eggs) di gallina ruspante; ~ **trade** n libero scambio; ~**way** n (US) superstrada; ~**wheel** vi andare a ruota libera; ~ **will** n libero arbitrio; **of** one's own ~ **will** di spontanea volontà.

freeze [fri:z] vb (pt **froze**, pp **frozen**) vi gelare // vt gelare; (food) congelare; (prices, salaries) bloccare // n gelo; blocco; ~**-dried** a liofilizzato(a); ~**r** n congelatore m.

freezing ['fri:zɪŋ] a: I'm ~ mi sto congelando // n (also: ~ **point**) punto di congelamento; **3 degrees below** ~ 3 gradi sotto zero.

freight [freɪt] n (goods) merce f, merci fpl; (money charged) spese fpl di trasporto; ~ **train** n (US) treno m merci inv.

French [frentʃ] a francese // n (LING) francese m; **the** ~ npl i Francesi; ~ **bean** n fagiolino; ~ **fried potatoes**, (US) ~ **fries** npl patate fpl fritte; ~**man** n francese m; ~ **window** n portafinestra; ~**woman** n francese f.

frenzy ['frenzɪ] n frenesia.

frequent a ['fri:kwənt] frequente // vt [frɪ'kwent] frequentare; ~**ly** ad frequentemente, spesso.

fresco ['freskəu] n affresco.

fresh [freʃ] a fresco(a); (new) nuovo(a); (cheeky) sfacciato(a); **to** ~**en up** vi rinfrescarsi; ~**er** n (Brit SCOL: col) matricola; ~**ly** ad di recente, di fresco; ~**man** n (US) = ~**er**; ~**ness** n freschezza; ~**water** a (fish) d'acqua dolce.

fret [fret] vi agitarsi, affliggersi.

friar ['fraɪə*] n frate m.

friction ['frɪkʃən] n frizione f, attrito.

Friday ['fraɪdɪ] n venerdì m inv.

fridge [frɪdʒ] n (Brit) frigo, frigorifero.

fried [fraɪd] pt, pp of **fry** // a fritto(a).

friend [frend] n amico/a; ~**ly** a amichevole; ~**ship** n amicizia.

frieze [fri:z] n fregio.

fright [fraɪt] n paura, spavento; **to take** ~ spaventarsi; ~**en** vt spaventare, far paura a; ~**ened** a spaventato(a); ~**ening** a spaventoso(a), pauroso(a); ~**ful** a orribile.

frigid ['frɪdʒɪd] a (woman) frigido(a).

frill [frɪl] n balza.

fringe [frɪndʒ] n (Brit: of hair) frangia; (edge: of forest etc) margine m; (fig): **on the** ~ al margine; ~ **benefits** npl vantaggi mpl.

frisk [frɪsk] vt perquisire.

frisky ['frɪskɪ] a vivace, vispo(a).

fritter ['frɪtə*] n frittella; **to** ~ **away** vt sprecare.

frivolity [frɪ'vɔlɪtɪ] n frivolezza.

frivolous ['frɪvələs] a frivolo(a).

frizzy ['frɪzɪ] a crespo(a).

fro [frəu] ad: **to and** ~ avanti e indietro.

frock [frɔk] n vestito.

frog [frɔg] n rana; ~**man** n uomo m rana inv.

frolic ['frɔlɪk] vi sgambettare.

from [frɔm] prep **1** (indicating starting place, origin etc) da; **where do you come** ~?, **where are you** ~? da dove viene?, di dov'è?; ~ **London to Glasgow** da Londra a Glasgow; **a letter** ~ **my sister** una lettera da mia sorella; **tell him** ~ **me that ...** gli dica da parte mia che ...
2 (indicating time) da; ~ **one o'clock to** or **until** or **till two** dall'una alle due; ~ **January (on)** da gennaio, a partire da gennaio
3 (indicating distance) da; **the hotel is 1 km** ~ **the beach** l'albergo è a 1 km dalla spiaggia
4 (indicating price, number etc) da; **prices range** ~ **£10 to £50** i prezzi vanno dalle 10 alle 50 sterline
5 (indicating difference) da; **he can't tell red** ~ **green** non sa distinguere il rosso dal verde
6 (because of, on the basis of): ~ **what he says** da quanto dice lui; **weak** ~ **hunger** debole per la fame.

front [frʌnt] n (of house, dress) davanti m inv; (of train) testa; (of book) copertina; (promenade: also: **sea** ~) lungomare m; (MIL, POL, METEOR) fronte m; (fig: appearances) fronte f // a primo(a); anteriore, davanti inv; **in** ~ **of davanti a**; ~ **door** n porta d'entrata; (of car) sportello anteriore; ~**ier** ['frʌntɪə*] n frontiera; ~ **page** n prima pagina; ~ **room** n (Brit) salotto; ~**wheel drive** n trasmissione f anteriore.

frost [frɔst] n gelo; (also: **hoar**~) brina; ~**bite** n congelamento; ~**ed** a (glass) smerigliato(a); ~**y** a (window) coperto(a) di ghiaccio; (welcome) gelido(a).

froth ['frɔθ] n spuma; schiuma.

frown [fraun] n cipiglio // vi accigliarsi.

froze [frəuz] pt of **freeze**; ~**n** pp of **freeze** // a (food) congelato(a).

fruit [fru:t] n (pl inv) frutto; (collectively) frutta; ~**erer** n fruttivendolo; ~**erer's (shop)** n: **at the** ~**erer's (shop)** dal fruttivendolo; ~**ful** a fruttuoso(a); (plant) fruttifero(a); (soil) fertile; ~**ion** [fru:'ɪʃən] n: **to come to** ~**ion** realizzarsi; ~ **juice** n succo di frutta; ~ **machine** n (Brit) macchina f mangiasoldi inv; ~ **salad** n macedonia.

frustrate [frʌs'treɪt] vt frustrare; ~**d** a frustrato(a).

fry [fraɪ], pt, pp **fried** vt friggere; **the small** ~ i pesci piccoli; ~**ing pan** n padella.

ft. abbr = **foot, feet.**

fuddy-duddy ['fʌdɪdʌdɪ] n matusa.

fudge [fʌdʒ] n (CULIN) specie di caramella a base di latte, burro e zucchero.

fuel [fjuəl] n (for heating) combustibile

m; (*for propelling*) carburante *m*; ~ **tank** *n* deposito *m* nafta *inv*; (*on vehicle*) serbatoio (della benzina).

fugitive ['fju:dʒɪtɪv] *n* fuggitivo/a, profugo/a.

fulfil [ful'fɪl] *vt* (*function*) compiere; (*order*) eseguire; (*wish, desire*) soddisfare, appagare; **~ment** *n* (*of wishes*) soddisfazione *f*, appagamento.

full [ful] *a* pieno(a); (*details, skirt*) ampio(a) // *ad*: to know ~ well that sapere benissimo che; I'm ~ (up) sono pieno, ~ employment piena occupazione; a ~ two hours due ore intere; at ~ speed a tutta velocità; in ~ per intero; to pay in ~ pagare tutto; ~ **moon** *n* luna piena; **~-scale** *a* (*attack, war*) su larga scala; (*model*) in grandezza naturale; ~ **stop** *n* punto; **~-time** *a, ad* (*work*) a tempo pieno // *n* (*SPORT*) fine *f* partita; **~y** *ad* interamente, pienamente, completamente; **~y-fledged** *a* (*teacher, member etc*) a tutti gli effetti.

fulsome ['fulsəm] *a* (*pej: praise, gratitude*) esagerato(a).

fumble ['fʌmbl] *vi* brancolare, andare a tentoni; to ~ **with** *vt fus* trafficare.

fume [fju:m] *vi* essere furioso(a); **~s** *npl* esalazioni *fpl*, vapori *mpl*.

fumigate ['fju:mɪgeɪt] *vt* suffumicare.

fun [fʌn] *n* divertimento, spasso; to have ~ divertirsi; for ~ per scherzo; to make ~ of *vt fus* prendersi gioco di.

function ['fʌŋkʃən] *n* funzione *f*; cerimonia, ricevimento // *vi* funzionare; **~al** *a* funzionale.

fund [fʌnd] *n* fondo, cassa; (*source*) fondo; (*store*) riserva; **~s** *npl* (*money*) fondi *mpl*.

fundamental [fʌndə'mentl] *a* fondamentale.

funeral ['fju:nərəl] *n* funerale *m*; ~ **parlour** *n* impresa di pompe funebri; ~ **service** *n* ufficio funebre.

fun fair *n* (*Brit*) luna park *m inv*.

fungus, *pl* **fungi** ['fʌŋgəs, -gaɪ] *n* fungo; (*mould*) muffa.

funnel ['fʌnl] *n* imbuto; (*of ship*) ciminiera.

funny ['fʌnɪ] *a* divertente, buffo(a); (*strange*) strano(a), bizzarro(a).

fur [fə:*] *n* pelo; pelliccia; (*Brit: in kettle etc*) deposito calcare; ~ **coat** *n* pelliccia.

furious ['fjuərɪəs] *a* furioso(a); (*effort*) accanito(a).

furlong ['fə:lɔŋ] *n* = 201.17 m (*termine ippico*).

furlough ['fə:ləu] *n* congedo, permesso.

furnace ['fə:nɪs] *n* fornace *f*.

furnish ['fə:nɪʃ] *vt* ammobiliare; (*supply*) fornire; **~ings** *npl* mobili *mpl*, mobilia.

furniture ['fə:nɪtʃə*] *n* mobili *mpl*; piece of ~ mobile *m*.

furrow ['fʌrəu] *n* solco.

furry ['fə:rɪ] *a* (*animal*) peloso(a).

further ['fə:ðə*] *a* supplementare, altro(a); nuovo(a); più lontano(a) // *ad* più lontano; (*more*) di più; (*moreover*) inoltre // *vt* favorire, promuovere; **college of** ~ **education** *n* istituto statale con corsi specializzati (*di formazione professionale, aggiornamento professionale etc*); **~more** [fə:ðə'mɔ:*] *ad* inoltre, per di più.

furthest ['fə:ðɪst] *superlative of* **far**.

fury ['fjuərɪ] *n* furore *m*.

fuse [fju:z] *n* fusibile *m*; (*for bomb etc*) miccia, spoletta // *vt* fondere; (*Brit ELEC*): to ~ **the lights** far saltare i fusibili // *vi* fondersi; ~ **box** *n* cassetta dei fusibili.

fuselage ['fju:zəlɑ:ʒ] *n* fusoliera.

fuss [fʌs] *n* chiasso, trambusto, confusione *f*; (*complaining*) storie *fpl*; to make a ~ fare delle storie; **~y** *a* (*person*) puntiglioso(a), esigente; che fa le storie; (*dress*) carico(a) di fronzoli; (*style*) elaborato(a).

future ['fju:tʃə*] *a* futuro(a) // *n* futuro, avvenire *m*; (*LING*) futuro; in ~ in futuro.

fuze [fju:z] (*US*) = **fuse**.

fuzzy ['fʌzɪ] *a* (*PHOT*) indistinto(a), sfocato(a); (*hair*) crespo(a).

G

G [dʒi:] *n* (*MUS*) sol *m*.

gabble ['gæbl] *vi* borbottare; farfugliare.

gable ['geɪbl] *n* trontone *m*.

gadget ['gædʒɪt] *n* aggeggio.

Gaelic ['geɪlɪk] *a* gaelico(a) // *n* (*LING*) gaelico.

gag [gæg] *n* bavaglio; (*joke*) facezia, scherzo // *vt* imbavagliare.

gaiety ['geɪɪtɪ] *n* gaiezza.

gaily ['geɪlɪ] *ad* allegramente.

gain [geɪn] *n* guadagno, profitto // *vt* guadagnare // *vi* (*watch*) andare avanti; to ~ **in/by** aumentare di/con; to ~ **3lbs** (**in weight**) aumentare di 3 libbre.

gait [geɪt] *n* andatura.

gal. *abbr* = **gallon**.

galaxy ['gæləksɪ] *n* galassia.

gale [geɪl] *n* vento forte; burrasca.

gallant ['gælənt] *a* valoroso(a); (*towards ladies*) galante, cortese.

gall bladder ['gɔ:l-] *n* cistifellea.

gallery ['gælərɪ] *n* galleria.

galley ['gælɪ] *n* (*ship's kitchen*) cambusa; (*ship*) galea.

gallon ['gælən] *n* gallone *m* (= 8 pints; Brit = 4.543l; US = 3.785l).

gallop ['gæləp] *n* galoppo // *vi* galoppare.

gallows ['gæləuz] *n* forca.

gallstone ['gɔ:lstəun] *n* calcolo biliare.

galore [gə'lɔ:*] *ad* a iosa, a profusione.

galvanize ['gælvənaɪz] vt galvanizzare.

gambit ['gæmbɪt] n (fig): (opening) ~ prima mossa.

gamble ['gæmbl] n azzardo, rischio calcolato // vt, vi giocare; to ~ on (fig) giocare su; ~r n giocatore/trice d'azzardo; **gambling** n gioco d'azzardo.

game [geɪm] n gioco; (event) partita; (HUNTING) selvaggina // a coraggioso(a); (ready): to be ~ (for sth/to do) essere pronto(a) (a qc/a fare); **big** ~ n selvaggina grossa; ~**keeper** n guardacaccia m inv.

gammon ['gæmən] n (bacon) quarto di maiale; (ham) prosciutto affumicato.

gamut ['gæmət] n gamma.

gang [gæŋ] n banda, squadra // vi: to ~ up on sb far combutta contro qn.

gangrene ['gæŋgri:n] n cancrena.

gangster ['gæŋstə*] n gangster m inv.

gangway ['gæŋweɪ] n passerella; (Brit: of bus) corridoio.

gaol [dʒeɪl] n, vt (Brit) = **jail**.

gap [gæp] n buco; (in time) intervallo; (fig) lacuna; vuoto.

gape [geɪp] vi restare a bocca aperta; **gaping** (a hole) squarciato(a).

garage ['gæra:ʒ] n garage m inv.

garbage ['ga:bɪdʒ] n immondizie fpl, rifiuti mpl; ~ **can** n (US) bidone m della spazzatura.

garbled ['ga:bld] a deformato(a); ingarbugliato(a).

garden ['ga:dn] n giardino // vi lavorare nel giardino; ~**er** n giardiniere/a; ~**ing** n giardinaggio.

gargle ['ga:gl] vi fare gargarismi // n gargarismo.

gargoyle ['ga:gɔɪl] n gargouille f inv.

garish ['gɛərɪʃ] a vistoso(a).

garland ['ga:lənd] n ghirlanda; corona.

garlic ['ga:lɪk] n aglio.

garment ['ga:mənt] n indumento.

garrison ['gærɪsn] n guarnigione f.

garrulous ['gærjuləs] a ciarliero(a), loquace.

garter ['ga:tə*] n giarrettiera.

gas [gæs] n gas m inv; (US: gasoline) benzina // vt asfissiare con il gas; (MIL) gasare; ~ **cooker** n (Brit) cucina a gas; ~ **cylinder** n bombola del gas; ~ **fire** n radiatore m a gas.

gash [gæʃ] n sfregio // vt sfregiare.

gasket ['gæskɪt] n (AUT) guarnizione f.

gas mask n maschera f antigas inv.

gas meter n contatore m del gas.

gasoline ['gæsəli:n] n (US) benzina.

gasp [ga:sp] vi ansare, boccheggiare; (in surprise) restare senza fiato; **to ~ out** vt dire affannosamente.

gas ring n fornello a gas.

gassy ['gæsɪ] a gassoso(a).

gas tap n rubinetto del gas.

gate [geɪt] n cancello; ~**crash** vt (Brit) partecipare senza invito a; ~**way** n porta.

gather ['gæðə*] vt (flowers, fruit) cogliere; (pick up) raccogliere; (assemble) radunare; raccogliere; (understand) capire // vi (assemble) radunarsi; to ~ speed acquistare velocità; ~**ing** n adunanza.

gauche [gəuʃ] a goffo(a), maldestro(a).

gaudy ['gɔ:dɪ] a vistoso(a).

gauge [geɪdʒ] n (standard measure) calibro; (RAIL) scartamento; (instrument) indicatore m // vt misurare.

gaunt [gɔ:nt] a scarno(a); (grim, desolate) desolato(a).

gauntlet ['gɔ:ntlɪt] n (fig): to run the ~ through an angry crowd passare sotto il fuoco di una folla ostile; to throw down the ~ gettare il guanto.

gauze [gɔ:z] n garza.

gave [geɪv] pt of **give**.

gay [geɪ] a (person) gaio(a), allegro(a); (colour) vivace, vivo(a); (col) omosessuale.

gaze [geɪz] n sguardo fisso // vi: to ~ at guardare fisso.

GB abbr = **Great Britain**.

GCE n abbr (Brit: = General Certificate of Education) ≈ maturità.

GCSE n abbr (Brit) = General Certificate of Secondary Education.

gear [gɪə*] n attrezzi mpl, equipaggiamento; (belongings) roba; (TECH) ingranaggio; (AUT) marcia // vt (fig: adapt): to ~ sth to adattare qc a; in top or (US) high/low/bottom ~ in quarta (or quinta)/seconda/prima; in ~ in marcia; ~ **box** n scatola del cambio; ~ **lever**, (US) ~ **shift** n leva del cambio.

geese [gi:s] npl of **goose**.

gel [dʒɛl] n gel m inv.

gelignite ['dʒɛlɪgnaɪt] n nitroglicerina.

gem [dʒɛm] n gemma.

Gemini ['dʒɛmɪnaɪ] n Gemelli mpl.

gender ['dʒɛndə*] n genere m.

general ['dʒɛnərl] n generale m // a generale; **in** ~ in genere; ~ **delivery** n (US) fermo posta m; ~ **election** n elezioni fpl generali; ~**ize** vi generalizzare; ~**ly** ad generalmente; ~ **practitioner (G.P.)** n medico generico.

generate ['dʒɛnəreɪt] vt generare.

generation [dʒɛnə'reɪʃən] n generazione f.

generator ['dʒɛnəreɪtə*] n generatore m.

generosity [dʒɛnə'rɔsɪtɪ] n generosità.

generous ['dʒɛnərəs] a generoso(a); (copious) abbondante.

genetic [dʒɪ'nɛtɪk] a genetico(a).

Geneva [dʒɪ'ni:və] n Ginevra.

genial ['dʒi:nɪəl] a geniale, cordiale.

genitals ['dʒɛnɪtlz] npl genitali mpl.

genius ['dʒi:nɪəs] n genio.

Genoa ['dʒɛnəuə] n Genova.

gent [dʒɛnt] n abbr = **gentleman**.

genteel [dʒɛn'tiːl] *a* raffinato(a), distinto(a).

gentle ['dʒɛntl] *a* delicato(a); (*persona*) dolce.

gentleman ['dʒɛntlmən] *n* signore *m*; (*well-bred man*) gentiluomo.

gently ['dʒɛntlɪ] *ad* delicatamente.

gentry ['dʒɛntrɪ] *n* nobiltà minore.

gents [dʒɛnts] *n* W.C. *m* (per signori).

genuine ['dʒɛnjuɪn] *a* autentico(a); sincero(a).

geography [dʒɪ'ɔgrəfɪ] *n* geografia.

geology [dʒɪ'ɔlədʒɪ] *n* geologia.

geometric(al) [dʒɪə'mɛtrɪk(l)] *a* geometrico(a).

geometry [dʒɪ'ɔmətrɪ] *n* geometria.

geranium [dʒɪ'reɪnjəm] *n* geranio.

geriatric [dʒɛrɪ'ætrɪk] *a* geriatrico(a).

germ [dʒəːm] *n* (*MED*) microbo; (*BIOL*, *fig*) germe *m*.

German ['dʒəːmən] *a* tedesco(a) // *n* tedesco/a; (*LING*) tedesco; **~ measles** *n* rosolia.

Germany ['dʒəːmənɪ] *n* Germania.

gesture ['dʒɛstjə*] *n* gesto.

get [gɛt], *pt, pp* **got**, *pp* **gotten** (*US*) ◆ *vi* 1 (*become, be*) diventare, farsi; **to ~ old** invecchiare; **to ~ tired** stancarsi; **to ~ drunk** ubriacarsi; **to ~ killed** venire *or* rimanere ucciso(a); **when do I ~ paid?** quando mi pagate?; **it's ~ting late** si sta facendo tardi

2 (*go*): **to ~ to/from** andare a/da; **to ~ home** arrivare *or* tornare a casa; **how did you ~ here?** come sei venuto?

3 (*begin*) mettersi a, cominciare a; **to ~ to know sb** incominciare a conoscere qn; **let's ~ going** *or* **started** muoviamoci

4 (*modal auxiliary vb*): **you've got to do it** devi farlo

◆ *vt* 1: **to ~ sth done** (*do*) fare qc; (*have done*) far fare qc; **to ~ one's hair cut** farsi tagliare i capelli; **to ~ sb to do sth** far fare qc a qn

2 (*obtain: money, permission, results*) ottenere; (*find: job, flat*) trovare; (*fetch: person, doctor*) chiamare; (: *object*) prendere; **to ~ sth for sb** prendere *or* procurare qc a qn; **~ me Mr Jones, please** (*TEL*) mi passi il signor Jones, per favore; **can I ~ you a drink?** le posso offrire da bere?

3 (*receive: present, letter, prize*) ricevere; (*acquire: reputation*) farsi; **how much did you ~ for the painting?** quanto le hanno dato per il quadro?

4 (*catch*) prendere; (*hit: target etc*) colpire; **to ~ sb by the arm/throat** afferrare qn per un braccio/alla gola; **~ him!** prendetelo!

5 (*take, move*) portare; **to ~ sth to sb** far avere qc a qn; **do you think we'll ~ it through the door?** pensi che riusciremo a farlo passare per la porta?

6 (*catch, take: plane, bus etc*) prendere

7 (*understand*) afferrare; (*hear*) sentire; **I've got it!** ci sono arrivato!, ci sono!; **I'm sorry, I didn't ~ your name** scusi, non ho capito (*or* sentito) il suo nome

8 (*have, possess*): **to have got** avere; **how many have you got?** quanti ne ha?

to get about *vi* muoversi; (*news*) diffondersi

to get along *vi* (*agree*) andare d'accordo; (*depart*) andarsene; (*manage*) = **to get by**

to get at *vt fus* (*attack*) prendersela con; (*reach*) raggiungere, arrivare a

to get away *vi* partire, andarsene; (*escape*) scappare

to get away with *vt fus* cavarsela, farla franca

to get back *vi* (*return*) ritornare, tornare ◆ *vt* riottenere, riavere

to get by *vi* (*pass*) passare; (*manage*) farcela

to get down *vi, vt fus* scendere ◆ *vt* far scendere; (*depress*) buttare giù

to get down to *vt fus* (*work*) mettersi a (fare)

to get in *vi* entrare; (*train*) arrivare; (*arrive home*) ritornare, tornare

to get into *vt fus* entrare in; **to ~ into a rage** incavolarsi

to get off *vi* (*from train etc*) scendere; (*depart: person, car*) andare via; (*escape*) cavarsela ◆ *vt* (*remove: clothes, stain*) levare ◆ *vt fus* (*train, bus*) scendere da

to get on *vi* (*at exam etc*) andare; (*agree*): **to ~ on (with)** andare d'accordo (con) ◆ *vt fus* montare in; (*horse*) montare su

to get out *vi* uscire; (*of vehicle*) scendere ◆ *vt* tirar fuori, far uscire

to get out of *vt fus* uscire da; (*duty etc*) evitare

to get over *vt fus* (*illness*) riaversi da

to get round *vt fus* aggirare; (*fig: person*) rigirare

to get through *vi* (*TEL*) avere la linea

to get through to *vt fus* (*TEL*) parlare a

to get together *vi* riunirsi ◆ *vt* raccogliere; (*people*) adunare

to get up *vi* (*rise*) alzarsi ◆ *vt fus* salire su per

to get up to *vt fus* (*reach*) raggiungere; (*prank etc*) fare.

getaway ['gɛtəweɪ] *n* fuga.

geyser ['giːzə*] *n* scaldabagno; (*GEO*) geyser *m inv*.

Ghana ['gɑːnə] *n* Ghana *m*.

ghastly ['gɑːstlɪ] *a* orribile, orrendo(a).

gherkin ['gəːkɪn] *n* cetriolino.

ghost [gəust] *n* fantasma *m*, spettro.

giant ['dʒaɪənt] *n* gigante/essa // *a* gigante, enorme.

gibberish ['dʒɪbərɪʃ] *n* parole *fpl* senza

senso.
gibe |dʒaɪb| n frecciata.
giblets |'dʒɪblɪts| npl frattaglie fpl.
Gibraltar |dʒɪ'brɔːltə*| n Gibilterra.
giddy |'gɪdɪ| a (dizzy): to be ~ aver le vertigini; (height) vertiginoso(a).
gift |gɪft| n regalo; (donation, ability) dono; ~**ed** a dotato(a); ~ **token** or **voucher** n buono m omaggio inv.
gigantic |dʒaɪ'gæntɪk| a gigantesco(a).
giggle |'gɪgl| vi ridere scioccamente.
gill |dʒɪl| n (measure) = 0.25 pints (Brit = 0.148l, US = 0.118l).
gills |gɪlz| npl (of fish) branchie fpl.
gilt |gɪlt| n doratura // a dorato(a); ~**edged** a (COMM) della massima sicurezza.
gimmick |'gɪmɪk| n trucco.
gin |dʒɪn| n (liquor) gin m inv.
ginger |'dʒɪndʒə*| n zenzero; ~ **ale**, ~ **beer** n bibita gassosa allo zenzero; ~**bread** n pan m di zenzero.
gingerly |'dʒɪndʒəlɪ| ad cautamente.
gipsy |'dʒɪpsɪ| n zingaro/a.
giraffe |dʒɪ'rɑːf| n giraffa.
girder |'gəːdə*| n trave f.
girdle |'gəːdl| n (corset) guaina.
girl |gəːl| n ragazza; (young unmarried woman) signorina; (daughter) figlia, figliola; ~**friend** n (of girl) amica; (of boy) ragazza; ~**ish** a da ragazza.
giro |'dʒaɪrəu| n (bank ~) versamento bancario; (post office ~) postagiro.
girth |gəːθ| n circonferenza; (of horse) cinghia.
gist |dʒɪst| n succo.
give |gɪv| vb (pt **gave**, pp **given**) vt dare // vi cedere; to ~ sb sth, ~ sth to sb dare qc a qn; to ~ a cry/sigh emettere un grido/sospiro; **to ~ away** vt dare via; (give free) fare dono di; (betray) tradire; (disclose) rivelare; (bride) condurre all'altare; **to ~ back** vt rendere; **to ~ in** vi cedere // vt consegnare; **to ~ off** vt emettere; **to ~ out** vt distribuire; annunciare; **to ~ up** vi rinunciare // vt rinunciare a; to ~ up smoking smettere di fumare; to ~ o.s. up arrendersi; **to ~ way** vi cedere; (Brit AUT) dare la precedenza.
glacier |'glæsɪə*| n ghiacciaio.
glad |glæd| a lieto(a), contento(a).
gladly |'glædlɪ| ad volentieri.
glamorous |'glæmərəs| a affascinante, seducente.
glamour |'glæmə*| n fascino.
glance |glɑːns| n occhiata, sguardo // vi: to ~ at dare un'occhiata a; to ~ off (bullet) rimbalzare su; **glancing** a (blow) che colpisce di striscio.
gland |glænd| n ghiandola.
glare |glɛə*| n riverbero, luce f abbagliante; (look) sguardo furioso // vi abbagliare; to ~ at guardare male; **glaring** a (mistake) madornale.

glass |glɑːs| n (substance) vetro; (tumbler) bicchiere m; (also: **looking** ~) specchio; ~**es** npl (spectacles) occhiali mpl; ~**ware** n vetrame m; ~**y** a (eyes) vitreo(a).
glaze |gleɪz| vt (door) fornire di vetri; (pottery) smaltare // n smalto.
glazier |'gleɪzɪə*| n vetraio.
gleam |gliːm| n barlume m; raggio // vi luccicare; ~**ing** a lucente.
glean |gliːn| vt (information) racimolare.
glee |gliː| n allegrezza, gioia.
glen |glɛn| n valletta.
glib |glɪb| a dalla parola facile; facile.
glide |glaɪd| vi scivolare; (AVIAT, birds) planare; ~**r** n (AVIAT) aliante m; **gliding** n (AVIAT) volo a vela.
glimmer |'glɪmə*| vi luccicare // n barlume m.
glimpse |glɪmps| n impressione f fugace // vt vedere al volo.
glint |glɪnt| n luccichio // vi luccicare.
glisten |'glɪsn| vi luccicare.
glitter |'glɪtə*| vi scintillare // n scintillio.
gloat |gləut| vi: to ~ (over) gongolare di piacere (per).
global |'gləubl| a globale.
globe |gləub| n globo, sfera.
gloom |gluːm| n oscurità, buio; (sadness) tristezza, malinconia; ~**y** a fosco(a), triste.
glorious |'glɔːrɪəs| a glorioso(a); magnifico(a).
glory |'glɔːrɪ| n gloria; splendore m // vi: to ~ in gloriarsi di or in.
gloss |glɔs| n (shine) lucentezza; **to ~ over** vt fus scivolare su.
glossary |'glɔsərɪ| n glossario.
glossy |'glɔsɪ| a lucente.
glove |glʌv| n guanto; ~ **compartment** n (AUT) vano portaoggetti.
glow |gləu| vi ardere; (face) essere luminoso(a) // n bagliore m; (of face) colorito acceso.
glower |'glauə*| vi: to ~ (at sb) guardare (qn) in cagnesco.
glue |gluː| n colla // vt incollare.
glum |glʌm| a abbattuto(a).
glut |glʌt| n eccesso // vt saziare; (market) saturare.
glutton |'glʌtn| n ghiottone/a; a ~ for work un(a) patito(a) del lavoro.
gnarled |nɑːld| a nodoso(a).
gnat |næt| n moscerino.
gnaw |nɔː| vt rodere.
go |gəu| vb (pt **went**, pp **gone**) vi andare; (depart) partire, andarsene; (work) funzionare; (break etc) cedere; (be sold): to ~ for £10 essere venduto per 10 sterline; (fit, suit): to ~ with andare bene con; (become): to ~ pale diventare pallido(a); to ~ mouldy ammuffire // n (pl ~**es**): to have a ~ (at) provare; to be on the ~ essere in moto; whose ~ is it? a chi tocca?; he's

going to do sta per fare; **to ~ for a walk** andare a fare una passeggiata; **to ~ dancing/shopping** andare a ballare/fare la spesa; **how did it ~?** com'è andato?; **to ~ round the back/by the shop** passare da dietro/davanti al negozio; **to ~ about** vi (rumour) correre, circolare // vt fus: **how do I ~ about this?** qual'è la prassi per questo?; **to ~ ahead** vi andare avanti; **~ ahead!** faccia pure!; **to ~ along** vi andare, avanzare // vt fus percorrere; **to ~ away** vi partire, andarsene; **to ~ back** vi tornare, ritornare; (go again) andare di nuovo; **to ~ back on** vt fus (promise) non mantenere; **to ~ by** vi (years, time) scorrere // vt fus attenersi a, seguire (alla lettera); prestar fede a; **to ~ down** vi scendere; (ship) affondare; (sun) tramontare // vt fus scendere; **to ~ for** vt fus (fetch) andare a prendere; (col: like) andar matto(a) per; (attack) attaccare; saltare addosso a; **to ~ in** vi entrare; **to ~ in for** vt fus (competition) iscriversi a; (be interested in) interessarsi di; **to ~ into** vt fus entrare in; (investigate) indagare, esaminare; (embark on) lanciarsi in; **to ~ off** vi partire, andar via; (food) guastarsi; (explode) esplodere, scoppiare; (event) passare // vt fus: **I've gone off chocolate** la cioccolata non mi piace più; **the gun went off** il fucile si scaricò; **to ~ on** vi continuare; (happen) succedere; **to ~ on doing** continuare a fare; **to ~ out** vi uscire; (fire, light) spegnersi; **to ~ over** vi (ship) ribaltarsi // vt fus (check) esaminare; **to ~ through** vt fus (town etc) attraversare; **to ~ up** vi salire // vt fus salire su per; **to ~ without** vt fus fare a meno di.

goad [gəud] vt spronare.

go-ahead ['gəuəhɛd] a intraprendente // n via m.

goal [gəul] n (SPORT) gol m, rete f; (: place) porta; (fig: aim) fine m, scopo; **~keeper** n portiere m; **~-post** n palo (della porta).

goat [gəut] n capra.

gobble ['gɔbl] vt (also: ~ **down**, ~ **up**) ingoiare.

goblet ['gɔblɪt] n calice m, coppa.

god [gɔd] n dio; **G~** n Dio; **~child** n figlioccio/a; **~daughter** n figlioccia; **~dess** n dea; **~father** n padrino; **~-forsaken** a desolato(a), sperduto(a); **~mother** n madrina; **~send** n dono del cielo; **~son** n figlioccio.

goggles ['gɔglz] npl occhiali mpl (di protezione).

going ['gəuɪŋ] n (conditions) andare m, stato del terreno // a: **the ~ rate** la tariffa in vigore.

gold [gəuld] n oro // a d'oro; **~en** a

(made of gold) d'oro; (gold in colour) dorato(a); **~fish** n pesce m dorato or rosso; **~-plated** a placcato(a) oro inv; **~smith** n orefice m, orafo.

golf [gɔlf] n golf m; ~ **ball** n (for game) pallina da golf; (on typewriter) pallina; ~ **club** n circolo di golf; (stick) bastone m or mazza da golf; ~ **course** n campo di golf; **~er** n giocatore/trice di golf.

gondola ['gɔndələ] n gondola.

gone [gɔn] pp of **go** // a partito(a).

gong [gɔŋ] n gong m inv.

good [gud] a buono(a); (kind) buono(a), gentile; (child) bravo(a) // n bene m; **~s** npl (COMM etc) beni mpl; merci fpl; **~!** bene!, ottimo!; **to be ~ at** essere bravo(a) in; **to be ~ for** andare bene per; **it's ~ for you** fa bene; **would you be ~ enough to ...?** avrebbe la gentilezza di ...?; **a ~ deal (of)** molto(a), una buona quantità (di); **a ~ many** molti(e); **to make ~** vi (succeed) aver successo // vt (deficit) colmare; (losses) compensare; **it's no ~ complaining** brontolare non serve a niente; **for ~** per sempre, definitivamente; ~ **morning!** buon giorno!; ~ **afternoon/evening!** buona sera!; ~ **night!** buona notte!; **~bye** excl arrivederci!; **G~ Friday** n Venerdì Santo; **~-looking** a bello(a); **~-natured** a affabile; (discussion) amichevole, cordiale; **~ness** n (of person) bontà; **for ~ness sake!** per amor di Dio!; **~ness gracious!** santo cielo!, mamma mia!; **~s train** n (Brit) treno m merci inv; **~will** n amicizia, benevolenza; (COMM) avviamento.

goose [gu:s], pl **geese** n oca.

gooseberry ['guzbəri] n uva spina; **to play ~** tenere la candela.

gooseflesh ['gu:sflɛʃ] n, **goose pimples** npl pelle f d'oca.

gore [gɔ:*] vt incornare // n sangue m (coagulato).

gorge [gɔ:dʒ] n gola // vt: **to ~ o.s. (on)** ingozzarsi (di).

gorgeous ['gɔ:dʒəs] a magnifico(a).

gorilla [gə'rɪlə] n gorilla m inv.

gorse [gɔ:s] n ginestrone m.

gory ['gɔ:rɪ] a sanguinoso(a).

go-slow ['gəu'sləu] n (Brit) rallentamento dei lavori (per agitazione sindacale).

gospel ['gɔspl] n vangelo.

gossip ['gɔsɪp] n chiacchiere fpl; pettegolezzi mpl; (person) pettegolo/a // vi chiacchierare; (maliciously) pettegolare.

got [gɔt] pt, pp of **get**; **~ten** (US) pp of **get**.

gout [gaut] n gotta.

govern ['gʌvən] vt governare; (LING) reggere.

governess ['gʌvənɪs] n governante f.

government ['gʌvnmənt] n governo.

governor ['gʌvənə*] n (of state, bank) governatore m; (of school, hospital) amministratore m.

gown [gaun] n vestito lungo; (of teacher, Brit: of judge) toga.

G.P. n abbr = general practitioner.

grab [græb] vt afferrare, arraffare; (property, power) impadronirsi di.

grace [greɪs] n grazia // vt onorare; 5 'days' ~ dilazione f di 5 giorni; to say ~ dire il benedicite; ~ful a elegante, aggraziato(a); **gracious** ['greɪʃəs] a grazioso(a); misericordioso(a).

grade [greɪd] n (COMM) qualità f inv; classe f; categoria; (in hierarchy) grado; (US: SCOL) voto; classe // vt classificare; ordinare; graduare; ~ **crossing** n (US) passaggio a livello; ~ **school** n (US) scuola elementare.

gradient ['greɪdɪənt] n pendenza, inclinazione f.

gradual ['grædjuəl] a graduale; ~ly ad man mano, a poco a poco.

graduate n ['grædjuɪt] laureato/a // vi ['grædjueɪt] laurearsi; **graduation** [-'eɪʃən] n cerimonia del conferimento della laurea.

graffiti [grə'fi:tɪ] npl graffiti mpl.

graft [grɑːft] n (AGR, MED) innesto // vt innestare; **hard ~** n (col): by sheer hard ~ lavorando da matti.

grain [greɪn] n grano; (of sand) granello; (of wood) venatura.

gram [græm] n grammo.

grammar ['græmə*] n grammatica; ~ **school** n (Brit) ≈ liceo.

grammatical [grə'mætɪkl] a grammaticale.

gramme [græm] n = gram.

grand [grænd] a grande, magnifico(a); grandioso(a); ~**children** npl nipoti mpl; ~**dad** n (col) nonno; ~**daughter** n nipote f; ~**father** n nonno; ~**ma** n (col) nonna; ~**mother** n nonna; ~**pa** n (col) = ~dad; ~**parents** npl nonni mpl; ~ **piano** n pianoforte m a coda; ~**son** n nipote m; ~**stand** n (SPORT) tribuna.

granite ['grænɪt] n granito.

granny ['grænɪ] n (col) nonna.

grant [grɑːnt] vt accordare; (a request) accogliere; (admit) ammettere, concedere // n (SCOL) borsa; (ADMIN) sussidio, sovvenzione f; to take sth for ~ed dare qc per scontato.

granulated ['grænjuleɪtɪd] a: ~ sugar zucchero cristallizzato.

grape [greɪp] n chicco d'uva, acino.

grapefruit ['greɪpfruːt] n pompelmo.

graph [grɑːf] n grafico; ~**ic** a grafico(a); (vivid) vivido(a); ~**ics** n grafica // npl illustrazioni fpl.

grapple ['græpl] vi: to ~ with essere alle prese con.

grasp [grɑːsp] vt afferrare // n (grip) presa; (fig) potere m; comprensione f;

~**ing** a avido(a).

grass [grɑːs] n erba; ~**hopper** n cavalletta; ~**-roots** a di base; ~ **snake** n natrice f.

grate [greɪt] n graticola (del focolare) // vi cigolare, stridere // vt (CULIN) grattugiare.

grateful ['greɪtful] a grato(a), riconoscente; ~**ly** ad con gratitudine.

grater ['greɪtə*] n grattugia.

gratify ['grætɪfaɪ] vt appagare; (whim) soddisfare.

grating ['greɪtɪŋ] n (iron bars) grata // a (noise) stridente, stridulo(a).

gratitude ['grætɪtjuːd] n gratitudine f.

gratuity [grə'tjuːɪtɪ] n mancia.

grave [greɪv] n tomba // a grave, serio(a).

gravel ['grævl] n ghiaia.

gravestone ['greɪvstəun] n pietra tombale.

graveyard ['greɪvjɑːd] n cimitero.

gravity ['grævɪtɪ] n (PHYSICS) gravità; pesantezza; (seriousness) gravità, serietà.

gravy ['greɪvɪ] n intingolo della carne; salsa.

gray [greɪ] a = grey.

graze [greɪz] vi pascolare, pascere // vt (touch lightly) sfiorare; (scrape) escoriare // n (MED) escoriazione f.

grease [griːs] n (fat) grasso; (lubricant) lubrificante m // vt ingrassare; lubrificare; ~**proof paper** n (Brit) carta oleata; **greasy** a grasso(a), untuoso(a).

great [greɪt] a grande; (col) magnifico(a), meraviglioso(a); **G~ Britain** n Gran Bretagna; ~**-grandfather** n bisnonno; ~**-grandmother** n bisnonna; ~**ly** ad molto; ~**ness** n grandezza.

Greece [griːs] n Grecia.

greed [griːd] n (also: ~iness) avarizia; (for food) golosità, ghiottoneria; ~**y** a avido(a); goloso(a), ghiotto(a).

Greek [griːk] a greco(a) // n greco/a; (LING) greco.

green [griːn] a verde; (inexperienced) inesperto(a), ingenuo(a) // n verde m; (stretch of grass) prato; (also: village ~) ≈ piazza del paese; ~s npl (vegetables) verdura; ~ **belt** n (round town) cintura di verde; ~ **card** n (AUT) carta verde; ~**ery** n verde m; ~**gage** n susina Regina Claudia; ~**grocer** n (Brit) fruttivendolo/a, erbivendolo/a; ~**house** n serra.

Greenland ['griːnlənd] n Groenlandia.

greet [griːt] vt salutare; ~**ing** n saluto; ~**ing(s) card** n cartolina d'auguri.

grenade [grə'neɪd] n granata.

grew [gruː] pt of grow.

grey [greɪ] a grigio(a); ~**hound** n levriere m.

grid [grɪd] n grata; (ELEC) rete f.

grief [griːf] n dolore m.

grievance ['gri:vəns] n doglianza, lagnanza.

grieve [gri:v] vi addolorarsi; rattristarsi // vt addolorare; **to ~ for sb** (dead person) piangere qn.

grievous ['gri:vəs] a: **~ bodily harm** (LAW) aggressione f.

grill [grɪl] n (on cooker) griglia // vt (Brit) cuocere ai ferri; (question) interrogare senza sosta.

grille [grɪl] n grata; (AUT) griglia.

grim [grɪm] a sinistro(a), brutto(a).

grimace [grɪ'meɪs] n smorfia // vi fare smorfie; fare boccacce.

grime [graɪm] n sudiciume m.

grimy ['graɪmɪ] a sudicio(a).

grin [grɪn] n sorriso smagliante // vi fare un gran sorriso.

grind [graɪnd] vt (pt, pp **ground**) macinare; (make sharp) arrotare // n (work) sgobbata; **to ~ one's teeth** digrignare i denti.

grip [grɪp] n impugnatura; presa; (holdall) borsa da viaggio // vt impugnare; afferrare; **to come to ~s with** affrontare; cercare di risolvere.

gripping ['grɪpɪŋ] a avvincente.

grisly ['grɪzlɪ] a macabro(a), orrido(a).

gristle ['grɪsl] n cartilagine f.

grit [grɪt] n ghiaia; (courage) fegato // vt (road) coprire di sabbia; **to ~ one's teeth** stringere i denti.

groan [grəun] n gemito // vi gemere.

grocer ['grəusə°] n negoziante m di generi alimentari; **~ies** npl provviste fpl.

groggy ['grɔgɪ] a barcollante.

groin [grɔɪn] n inguine m.

groom [gru:m] n palafreniere m; (also: **bride~**) sposo // vt (horse) strigliare; (fig): **to ~ sb for** avviare qn a.

groove [gru:v] n scanalatura, solco.

grope [grəup] vi andare a tentoni; **to ~ for** vt fus cercare a tastoni.

gross [grəus] a grossolano(a); (COMM) lordo(a) // n (pl inv) (twelve dozen) grossa; **~ly** ad (greatly) molto.

grotesque [grəu'tɛsk] a grottesco(a).

grotto ['grɔtəu] n grotta.

ground [graund] pt, pp of **grind** // n suolo, terra; (land) terreno; (SPORT) campo; (reason: gen pl) ragione f; (US: also: ~ **wire**) terra // vt (plane) tenere a terra // vi (ship) arenarsi; **~s** npl (of coffee etc) fondi mpl; (gardens etc) terreno, giardini mpl; **on/to the ~** per/a terra; **to gain/lose ~** guadagnare/perdere terreno; **~ cloth** n (US) = **~sheet**; **~ing** n (in education) basi fpl; **~less** a infondato(a); **~sheet** n (Brit) telone m impermeabile; **~ staff** n personale m di terra; **~ swell** n maremoto; (fig) movimento d'opinione; **~work** n preparazione f.

group [gru:p] n gruppo // vt (also: **~**

together) raggruppare // vi (also: **~ together**) raggrupparsi.

grouse [graus] n (pl inv) (bird) tetraone m // vi (complain) brontolare.

grove [grəuv] n boschetto.

grovel ['grɔvl] vi (fig): **to ~ (before)** strisciare (di fronte a).

grow [grəu], pt **grew**, pp **grown** vi crescere; (increase) aumentare; (become): **to ~ rich/weak** arricchirsi/indebolirsi // vt coltivare, far crescere; **to ~ up** vi farsi grande, crescere; **~er** n coltivatore/trice, **~ing** a (fear, amount) crescente.

growl [graul] vi ringhiare.

grown [grəun] pp of **grow** // a adulto(a), maturo(a); **~-up** n adulto/a, grande m/f.

growth [grəuθ] n crescita, sviluppo; (what has grown) crescita; (MED) escrescenza, tumore m.

grub [grʌb] n larva; (col: food) roba (da mangiare).

grubby ['grʌbɪ] a sporco(a).

grudge [grʌdʒ] n rancore m // vt: **to ~ sb sth** dare qc a qn di malavoglia; invidiare qc a qn; **to bear sb a ~ (for)** serbar rancore a qn (per).

gruelling ['gruəlɪŋ] a estenuante.

gruesome ['gru:səm] a orribile.

gruff [grʌf] a rozzo(a).

grumble ['grʌmbl] vi brontolare, lagnarsi.

grumpy ['grʌmpɪ] a stizzito(a).

grunt [grʌnt] vi grugnire // n grugnito.

G-string ['dʒi:strɪŋ] n tanga m inv.

guarantee [gærən'ti:] n garanzia // vt garantire.

guard [gu:d] n guardia; (BOXING) difesa; (one man) guardia, sentinella; (Brit RAIL) capotreno // vt fare la guardia a; **~ed** a (fig) cauto(a), guardingo(a); **~ian** n custode m; (of minor) tutore/trice; **~'s van** n (Brit RAIL) vagone m di servizio.

guerrilla [gə'rɪlə] n guerrigliero; **~ warfare** n guerriglia.

guess [gɛs] vi indovinare // vt indovinare; (US) credere, pensare // n congettura; **~work** n: **I got the answer by ~work** ho azzeccato la risposta.

guest [gɛst] n ospite m/f; (in hotel) cliente m/f; **~-house** n pensione f; **~ room** n camera degli ospiti.

guffaw [gʌ'fɔ:] vi scoppiare in una risata sonora.

guidance ['gaɪdəns] n guida, direzione f.

guide [gaɪd] n (person, book etc) guida; (also: **girl ~**) giovane esploratrice f // vt guidare; **~book** n guida; **~ dog** n cane m guida inv; **~lines** npl (fig) indicazioni fpl, linee fpl direttive.

guild [gɪld] n arte f, corporazione f; associazione f.

guile [gaɪl] n astuzia.

guillotine ['gɪləti:n] n ghigliottina.

guilt [gɪlt] n colpevolezza; **~y** a

colpevole.
guinea pig ['gɪnɪ-] *n* cavia.
guise [gaɪz] *n* maschera.
guitar [gɪ'tɑ:*] *n* chitarra.
gulf [gʌlf] *n* golfo; (*abyss*) abisso.
gull [gʌl] *n* gabbiano.
gullet ['gʌlɪt] *n* gola.
gullible ['gʌlɪbl] *a* credulo(a).
gully ['gʌlɪ] *n* burrone *m*; gola; canale *m*.
gulp [gʌlp] *vi* deglutire; (*from emotion*) avere il nodo in gola // *vt* (*also*: ~ **down**) tracannare, inghiottire.
gum [gʌm] *n* (*ANAT*) gengiva; (*glue*) colla; (*sweet*) gelatina di frutta; (*also*: chewing-~) chewing-gum *m* // *vt* incollare; ~**boots** *npl* (*Brit*) stivali *mpl* di gomma.
gun [gʌn] *n* fucile *m*; (*small*) pistola, rivoltella; (*rifle*) carabina; (*shotgun*) fucile da caccia; (*cannon*) cannone *m*; ~**boat** *n* cannoniera; ~**fire** *n* spari *mpl*; ~**man** *n* bandito armato; ~**ner** *n* artigliere *m*; ~**point** *n*: at ~**point** sotto minaccia di fucile; ~**powder** *n* polvere *f* da sparo; ~**shot** *n* sparo; ~**smith** *n* armaiolo.
gurgle ['gɜ:gl] *vi* gorgogliare.
guru ['guru:] *n* guru *m inv*.
gush [gʌʃ] *vi* sgorgare; (*fig*) abbandonarsi ad effusioni.
gusset ['gʌsɪt] *n* gherone *m*.
gust [gʌst] *n* (*of wind*) raffica; (*of smoke*) buffata.
gusto ['gʌstəu] *n* entusiasmo.
gut [gʌt] *n* intestino, budello; (*MUS etc*) minugia; ~**s** *npl* (*courage*) fegato.
gutter ['gʌtə*] *n* (*of roof*) grondaia; (*in street*) cunetta.
guy [gaɪ] *n* (*also*: ~**rope**) cavo *or* corda di fissaggio; (*col: man*) tipo, elemento; (*figure*) effigie di Guy Fawkes.
guzzle ['gʌzl] *vi* gozzovigliare // *vt* tranguiare.
gym [dʒɪm] *n* (*also*: **gymnasium**) palestra; (*also*: **gymnastics**) ginnastica.
gymnast ['dʒɪmnæst] *n* ginnasta *m/f*; ~**ics** [-'næstɪks] *n*, *npl* ginnastica.
gym shoes *npl* scarpe *fpl* da ginnastica.
gym slip *n* (*Brit*) grembiule *m* da scuola (*per ragazze*).
gynaecologist, (*US*) **gynecologist** [gaɪnɪ'kɔlədʒɪst] *n* ginecologo/a.
gypsy ['dʒɪpsɪ] *n* = **gipsy.**
gyrate [dʒaɪ'reɪt] *vi* girare.

H

haberdashery ['hæbə'dæʃərɪ] *n* (*Brit*) merceria.
habit ['hæbɪt] *n* abitudine *f*; (*costume*) abito; (*REL*) tonaca.
habitation [hæbɪ'teɪʃən] *n* abitazione *f*.
habitual [hə'bɪtjuəl] *a* abituale; (*drinker,*

liar) inveterato(a); ~**ly** *ad* abitualmente, di solito.
hack [hæk] *vt* tagliare, fare a pezzi // *n* (*cut*) taglio; (*blow*) colpo; (*pej: writer*) negro.
hackneyed ['hæknɪd] *a* comune, trito(a).
had [hæd] *pt, pp of* **have.**
haddock, *pl* ~ *or* ~**s** ['hædək] *n* eglefino.
hadn't ['hædnt] = **had not.**
haemorrhage, (*US*) **hemorrhage** ['hemərɪdʒ] *n* emorragia.
haemorrhoids, (*US*) **hemorrhoids** ['hemərɔɪdz] *npl* emorroidi *fpl*.
haggard ['hægəd] *a* smunto(a).
haggle ['hægl] *vi* mercanteggiare.
Hague [heɪg] *n*: **The** ~ L'Aia.
hail [heɪl] *n* grandine *f* // *vt* (*call*) chiamare; (*greet*) salutare // *vi* grandinare; ~**stone** *n* chicco di grandine.
hair [heə*] *n* capelli *mpl*; (*single hair: on head*) capello; (: *on body*) pelo; to do one's ~ pettinarsi; ~**brush** *n* spazzola per capelli; ~**cut** *n* taglio di capelli; ~**do** ['heədu:] *n* acconciatura, pettinatura; ~**dresser** *n* parrucchiere/a; ~**-dryer** *n* asciugacapelli *m inv*; ~ **grip** *n* forcina; ~**pin** *n* forcina; ~**pin bend**, (*US*) ~**pin curve** *n* tornante *m*; ~**raising** *a* orripilante; ~ **remover** *n* crema depilatoria; ~ **spray** *n* lacca per capelli; ~**style** *n* pettinatura, acconciatura; ~**y** *a* irsuto(a); peloso(a); (*col: frightening*) spaventoso(a).
hake, *pl* ~ *or* ~**s** [heɪk] *n* nasello.
half [hɑ:f] *n* (*pl* **halves**) mezzo, metà *f inv* // *a* mezzo(a) // *ad* a mezzo, a metà; ~ **an hour** mezz'ora; ~ **a dozen** mezza dozzina; ~ **a pound** mezza libbra; **two and a** ~ due e mezzo; **a week and a** ~ una settimana e mezza; ~ (**of it**) la metà; ~ (**of**) la metà di; **to cut sth in** ~ tagliare qc in due; ~ **asleep** mezzo(a) addormentato(a); ~**-back** *n* (*SPORT*) mediano; ~**-breed**, ~**-caste** *n* meticcio/a; ~**-hearted** *a* tiepido(a); ~ **hour** *n* mezz'ora; ~**-mast** *n*: at ~**-mast** (*flag*) a mezz'asta; ~**penny** ['heɪpnɪ] *n* (*Brit*) mezzo penny *m inv*; ~**-price** *a*, *ad* a metà prezzo; ~ **term** *n* (*Brit SCOL*) vacanza *a or* di metà trimestre; ~**-time** *n* (*SPORT*) intervallo; ~**way** *ad* a metà strada.
halibut ['hælɪbət] *n* (*pl inv*) ippoglosso.
hall [hɔ:l] *n* sala, salone *m*; (*entrance way*) entrata; (*corridor*) corridoio; (*mansion*) grande villa, maniero; ~ **of residence** *n* (*Brit*) casa dello studente.
hallmark ['hɔ:lmɑ:k] *n* marchio di garanzia; (*fig*) caratteristica.
hallo [hə'ləu] *excl* = **hello.**
Hallowe'en [hæləu'i:n] *n* vigilia d'Ognissanti.
hallucination [həlu:sɪ'neɪʃən] *n*

allucinazione *f*.

hallway ['hɔ:lweɪ] *n* corridoio; *(entrance)* ingresso.

halo ['heɪləʊ] *n (of saint etc)* aureola; *(of sun)* alone *m*.

halt [hɔ:lt] *n* fermata // *vt* fermare // *vi* fermarsi.

halve [ha:v] *vt (apple etc)* dividere a metà; *(expense)* ridurre di metà.

halves [ha:vz] *npl of* **half**.

ham [hæm] *n* prosciutto.

hamburger ['hæmbə:gə*] *n* hamburger *m inv*.

hamlet ['hæmlɪt] *n* paesetto.

hammer ['hæmə*] *n* martello // *vt* martellare; *(fig)* sconfiggere duramente // *vi*: to ~ **on** *or* **at the door** picchiare alla porta.

hammock ['hæmək] *n* amaca.

hamper ['hæmpə*] *vt* impedire // *n* cesta.

hamster ['hæmstə*] *n* criceto.

hand [hænd] *n* mano *f*; *(of clock)* lancetta; *(handwriting)* scrittura; *(at cards)* mano; (: *game*) partita; *(worker)* operaio/a // *vt* dare, passare; **to give sb a ~** dare una mano a qn; **at ~** a portata di mano; **in ~** a disposizione; *(work)* in corso; **on ~** *(person)* disponibile; *(services)* pronto(a) a intervenire; **to ~** *(information etc)* a portata di mano; **on the one ~ ..., on the other ~** da un lato ..., dall'altro; **to ~ in** *vt* consegnare; **to ~ out** *vt* distribuire; **to ~ over** *vt* passare; cedere; **~bag** *n* borsetta; **~book** *n* manuale *m*; **~brake** *n* freno a mano; **~cuffs** *npl* manette *fpl*; **~ful** *n* manciata, pugno.

handicap ['hændɪkæp] *n* handicap *m inv* // *vt* handicappare; **to be physically ~ped** essere handicappato(a); **to be mentally ~ped** essere un(a) handicappato(a) mentale.

handicraft ['hændɪkrɑ:ft] *n* lavoro d'artigiano.

handiwork ['hændɪwɜ:k] *n* opera.

handkerchief ['hæŋkətʃɪf] *n* fazzoletto.

handle ['hændl] *n (of door etc)* maniglia; *(of cup etc)* ansa; *(of knife etc)* impugnatura; *(of saucepan)* manico; *(for winding)* manovella // *vt* toccare, maneggiare; *(deal with)* occuparsi di; *(treat: people)* trattare; **"~ with care"** "fragile"; **to fly off the ~** *(fig)* perdere le staffe, uscire dai gangheri; **~bar(s)** *n(pl)* manubrio.

hand: ~ **luggage** *n* bagagli *mpl* a mano; **~made** *a* fatto(a) a mano; **~out** *n (leaflet)* volantino; *(at lecture)* prospetto; **~rail** *n* corrimano; **~shake** *n* stretta di mano.

handsome ['hænsəm] *a* bello(a); *(reward)* generoso(a); *(profit, fortune)* considerevole.

handwriting ['hændraɪtɪŋ] *n* scrittura.

handy ['hændɪ] *a (person)* bravo(a);

(close at hand) a portata di mano; *(convenient)* comodo(a); **~man** *n* tuttofare *m inv*.

hang [hæŋ], *pt, pp* **hung** *vt* appendere; *(criminal: pt, pp* **hanged**) impiccare // *vi* pendere; *(hair)* scendere; *(drapery)* cadere; **to get the ~ of sth** *(col)* capire come qc funziona; **to ~ about** *vi* bighellonare, ciondolare; **to ~ on** *vi (wait)* aspettare; **to ~ up** *vi (TEL)* riattaccare // *vt* appendere.

hangar ['hæŋə*] *n* hangar *m inv*.

hanger ['hæŋə*] *n* gruccia.

hanger-on [hæŋər'ɔn] *n* parassita *m*.

hang-gliding ['hæŋglaɪdɪŋ] *n* volo col deltaplano.

hangover ['hæŋəʊvə*] *n (after drinking)* postumi *mpl* di sbornia.

hang-up ['hæŋʌp] *n* complesso.

hanker ['hæŋkə*] *vi*: **to ~ after** bramare.

hankie, hanky ['hæŋkɪ] *n abbr* = **handkerchief**.

haphazard [hæp'hæzəd] *a* a casaccio, alla carlona.

happen ['hæpən] *vi* accadere, succedere; **as it ~s** guarda caso; **~ing** *n* avvenimento.

happily ['hæpɪlɪ] *ad* felicemente; fortunatamente.

happiness ['hæpɪnɪs] *n* felicità, contentezza.

happy ['hæpɪ] *a* felice, contento(a); ~ **with** *(arrangements etc)* soddisfatto(a) di; ~ **birthday!** buon compleanno!; **~-go-lucky** *a* spensierato(a).

harangue [hə'ræŋ] *vt* arringare.

harass ['hærəs] *vt* molestare; **~ment** *n* molestia.

harbour, *(US)* **harbor** ['hɑ:bə*] *n* porto // *vt* dare rifugio a.

hard [hɑ:d] *a* duro(a) // *ad (work)* sodo; *(think, try)* bene; **to look ~ at** guardare fissamente; **to examine ~** esaminare attentamente; **no ~ feelings!** senza rancore!; **to be ~ of hearing** essere duro(a) d'orecchio; **to be ~ done by** essere trattato(a) ingiustamente; **~back** *n* libro rilegato; ~ **cash** *n* denaro in contanti; ~ **disk** *n (COMPUT)* disco rigido; **~en** *vt, vi* indurire; **~-headed** *a* pratico(a); ~ **labour** *n* lavori forzati *mpl*.

hardly ['hɑ:dlɪ] *ad (scarcely)* appena; **it's ~ the case** non è proprio il caso; **that can ~ be true** non può essere vero; ~ **anyone/anywhere** nessuno/da nessuna parte; ~ **ever** quasi mai.

hardship ['hɑ:dʃɪp] *n* avversità *f inv*; privazioni *fpl*.

hard-up [hɑ:d'ʌp] *a (col)* al verde.

hardware ['hɑ:dweə*] *n* ferramenta *fpl*; *(COMPUT)* hardware *m*; ~ **shop** *n* (negozio di) ferramenta *fpl*.

hard-wearing [hɑ:d'weərɪŋ] *a* resistente; *(shoes)* robusto(a).

hard-working [hɑ:d'wɜ:kɪŋ] *a*

lavoratore(trice).

hardy [ˈhɑːdɪ] a robusto(a); (plant) resistente al gelo.

hare [hɛəʳ] n lepre f; **~-brained** a folle; scervellato(a).

harm [hɑːm] n male m; (wrong) danno // vt (person) fare male a; (thing) danneggiare; **out of ~'s way** al sicuro; **~ful** a dannoso(a); **~less** a innocuo(a); inoffensivo(a).

harmonica [hɑːˈmɔnɪkə] n armonica.

harmonious [hɑːˈməʊnɪəs] a armonioso(a).

harmony [ˈhɑːmənɪ] n armonia.

harness [ˈhɑːnɪs] n bardatura, finimenti mpl // vt (horse) bardare; (resources) sfruttare.

harp [hɑːp] n arpa // vi: **to ~ on about** insistere tediosamente su.

harpoon [hɑːˈpuːn] n arpione m.

harrowing [ˈhærəʊɪŋ] a straziante.

harsh [hɑːʃ] a (hard) duro(a); (severe) severo(a); (unpleasant: sound) rauco(a); (: colour) chiassoso(a); violento(a); **~ly** ad duramente; severamente.

harvest [ˈhɑːvɪst] n raccolto; (of grapes) vendemmia // vt fare il raccolto di, raccogliere; vendemmiare.

has [hæz] vb see **have**.

hash [hæʃ] n (CULIN) specie di spezzatino fatto con carne già cotta; (fig: mess) pasticcio.

hashish [ˈhæʃɪʃ] n hascisc m.

hasn't [ˈhæznt] = **has not**.

hassle [ˈhæsl] n (col) sacco di problemi.

haste [heɪst] n fretta; precipitazione f; **~n** [ˈheɪsn] vt affrettare // vi affrettarsi; **hastily** ad in fretta; precipitosamente; **hasty** a affrettato(a); precipitoso(a).

hat [hæt] n cappello.

hatch [hætʃ] n (NAUT: also: ~way) boccaporto; (also: service ~) portello di servizio // vi schiudersi // vt covare.

hatchback [ˈhætʃbæk] n (AUT) tre (or cinque) porte f inv.

hatchet [ˈhætʃɪt] n accetta.

hate [heɪt] vt odiare, detestare // n odio; **~ful** a odioso(a), detestabile.

hatred [ˈheɪtrɪd] n odio.

hat trick n: **to get a ~** segnare tre punti consecutivi (or vincere per tre volte consecutive).

haughty [ˈhɔːtɪ] a altero(a), arrogante.

haul [hɔːl] vt trascinare, tirare // n (of fish) pescata; (of stolen goods etc) bottino; **~age** n trasporto; autotrasporto; **~ier**, (US) **~er** n trasportatore m.

haunch [hɔːntʃ] n anca.

haunt [hɔːnt] vt (subj: fear) pervadere; (: person) frequentare // n rifugio; a ghost ~s this house questa casa è abitata da un fantasma.

have [hæv], pt, pp **had** ♦ auxiliary vb **1** (gen) avere; essere; **to ~ arrived/gone** essere arrivato(a)/andato(a); **to ~ eaten/slept** avere mangiato/dormito; he has been kind/promoted è stato gentile/promosso; having finished or when he had finished, he left dopo aver finito, se n'è andato

2 (in tag questions): you've done it, ~n't you? l'ha fatto, (non è) vero?; he hasn't done it, has he? non l'ha fatto, vero?

3 (in short answers and questions): you've made a mistake — no I ~n't/so I ~ ha fatto un errore — ma no, niente affatto/sì, è vero; we ~n't paid — yes we ~! non abbiamo pagato — ma sì che abbiamo pagato!; I've been there before, ~ you? ci sono già stato, e lei?

♦ modal auxiliary vb (be obliged): **to ~ (got) to do sth** dover fare qc; I ~n't got or I don't ~ to wear glasses non ho bisogno di portare gli occhiali

♦ vt **1** (possess, obtain) avere; he has (got) blue eyes/dark hair ha gli occhi azzurri/i capelli scuri; do you ~ or ~ you got a car/phone? ha la macchina/il telefono?; may I ~ your address? potrebbe darmi il suo indirizzo?; you can ~ it for £5 te lo lascio per 5 sterline

2 (+ noun: take, hold etc): **to ~ breakfast/a swim/a bath** fare colazione/una nuotata/un bagno; **to ~ lunch** pranzare; **to ~ dinner** cenare; **to ~ a drink** bere qualcosa; **to ~ a cigarette** fumare una sigaretta

3: **to ~ sth done** far fare qc; **to ~ one's hair cut** farsi tagliare i capelli; **to ~ sb do sth** far fare qc a qn

4 (experience, suffer) avere; **to ~ a cold/flu** avere il raffreddore/l'influenza; she had her bag stolen le hanno rubato la borsa

5 (col: dupe): you've been had! ci sei cascato!

to have out vt: **to ~ it out with sb** (settle a problem etc) mettere le cose in chiaro con qn.

haven [ˈheɪvn] n porto; (fig) rifugio.

haven't [ˈhævnt] = **have not**.

haversack [ˈhævəsæk] n zaino.

havoc [ˈhævək] n caos m.

hawk [hɔːk] n falco.

hay [heɪ] n fieno; **~ fever** n febbre f da fieno; **~stack** n pagliaio.

haywire [ˈheɪwaɪəʳ] a (col): **to go ~** perdere la testa; impazzire.

hazard [ˈhæzəd] n azzardo, ventura; pericolo, rischio; **~ (warning) lights** npl (AUT) luci fpl di emergenza.

haze [heɪz] n foschia.

hazelnut [ˈheɪzlnʌt] n nocciola.

hazy [ˈheɪzɪ] a fosco(a); (idea) vago(a); (photograph) indistinto(a).

he [hiː] pronoun lui, egli; it is ~ who ... è lui che ....

head [hɛd] n testa, capo; (leader) capo //

vt (*list*) essere in testa a; (*group*) essere a capo di; ~s (or **tails**) testa (o croce), pari (o dispari); ~ **first** a capofitto, di testa; ~ **over heels in love** pazzamente innamorato(a); **to ~ the ball** dare di testa alla palla; **to ~ for** *vt fus* dirigersi verso; ~**ache** *n* mal *m* di testa; ~**dress** *n* (*of Indian etc*) copricapo; (*of bride*) acconciatura; ~**ing** *n* titolo; intestazione *f*; ~**lamp** *n* (*Brit*) = ~**light**; ~**land** *n* promontorio; ~**light** *n* fanale *m*; ~**line** *n* titolo; ~**long** *ad* (*fall*) a capofitto; (*rush*) precipitosamente, ~**master** *n* preside *m*; ~**mistress** *n* preside *f*; ~ **office** *n* sede *f* (centrale); ~**on** *a* (*collision*) frontale; ~**phones** *npl* cuffia; ~**quarters (HQ)** *npl* ufficio centrale; (*MIL*) quartiere *m* generale; ~**rest** *n* poggiacapo; ~**room** *n* (*in car*) altezza dell'abitacolo; (*under bridge*) altezza limite; ~**scarf** *n* foulard *m inv*; ~**strong** *a* testardo(a); ~ **waiter** *n* capocameriere *m*; ~**way** *n*: to make ~**way** fare progressi; ~**wind** *n* controvento; ~**y** *a* (*experience, period*) inebriante.

heal [hi:l] *vt, vi* guarire.

health [hɛlθ] *n* salute *f*; ~ **food(s)** *n(pl)* alimenti *mpl* integrali; **the H~ Service** *n* (*Brit*) = il Servizio Sanitario Statale; ~**y** *a* (*person*) in buona salute; (*climate*) salubre; (*food*) salutare; (*attitude etc*) sano(a).

heap [hi:p] *n* mucchio // *vt* ammucchiare.

hear, *pt*, *pp* **heard** [hɪə*, hə:d] *vt* sentire; (*news*) ascoltare; (*lecture*) assistere a // *vi* sentire; **to ~ about** avere notizie di; sentire parlare di; **to ~ from sb** ricevere notizie da qn; ~**ing** *n* (*sense*) udito; (*of witnesses*) audizione *f*; (*of a case*) udienza; ~**ing aid** *n* apparecchio acustico; ~**say** *n* dicerie *fpl*, chiacchiere *fpl*.

hearse [hə:s] *n* carro funebre.

heart [hɑ:t] *n* cuore *m*; ~**s** *npl* (*CARDS*) cuori *mpl*; at ~ in fondo; by ~ (*learn, know*) a memoria; ~ **attack** *n* attacco di cuore; ~**beat** *n* battito del cuore; ~**broken** *a*: to be ~**broken** avere il cuore spezzato; ~**burn** *n* bruciore *m* di stomaco; ~ **failure** *n* arresto cardiaco; ~**felt** *a* sincero(a).

hearth [hɑ:θ] *n* focolare *m*.

heartily [hɑ:tɪlɪ] *ad* (*laugh*) di cuore; (*eat*) di buon appetito; (*agree*) in pieno, completamente.

hearty [hɑ:tɪ] *a* caloroso(a); robusto(a), sano(a); vigoroso(a).

heat [hi:t] *n* calore *m*; (*fig*) ardore *m*; fuoco; (*SPORT: also*: **qualifying ~**) prova eliminatoria // *vt* scaldare; **to ~ up** *vi* (*liquids*) scaldarsi; (*room*) riscaldarsi // *vt* riscaldare; ~**ed** *a* riscaldato(a); (*fig*) appassionato(a); acceso(a), eccitato(a); ~**er** *n* stufa; radiatore *m*.

heath [hi:θ] *n* (*Brit*) landa.

heathen [hi:ðn] *a, n* pagano(a).

heather [hɛðə*] *n* erica.

heating [hi:tɪŋ] *n* riscaldamento.

heatstroke [hi:tstrəuk] *n* colpo di sole.

heatwave [hi:tweɪv] *n* ondata di caldo.

heave [hi:v] *vt* sollevare (con forza) // *vi* sollevarsi; (*retch*) aver conati di vomito // *n* (*push*) grande spinta.

heaven [hɛvn] *n* paradiso, cielo; ~**ly** *a* divino(a), celeste.

heavily [hɛvɪlɪ] *ad* pesantemente; (*drink, smoke*) molto.

heavy [hɛvɪ] *a* pesante; (*sea*) grosso(a); (*rain*) forte; (*drinker, smoker*) gran (*before noun*); ~ **goods vehicle (HGV)** *n* veicolo per trasporti pesanti; ~**weight** *n* (*SPORT*) peso massimo.

Hebrew [hi:bru:] *a* ebreo(a) // *n* (*LING*) ebraico.

Hebrides [hɛbrɪdi:z] *npl*: **the ~** le Ebridi.

heckle [hɛkl] *vt* interpellare e dare noia a (*un oratore*).

hectic [hɛktɪk] *a* movimentato(a).

he'd [hi:d] = **he would, he had**.

hedge [hɛdʒ] *n* siepe *f* // *vi* essere elusivo(a); **to ~ one's bets** (*fig*) coprirsi dai rischi.

hedgehog [hɛdʒhɔg] *n* riccio.

heed [hi:d] *vt* (*also*: **take ~ of**) badare a, far conto di; ~**less** *a* sbadato(a).

heel [hi:l] *n* (*ANAT*) calcagno; (*of shoe*) tacco // *vt* (*shoe*) rifare i tacchi a.

hefty [hɛftɪ] *a* (*person*) solido(a); (*parcel*) pesante; (*piece, price*) grosso(a).

heifer [hɛfə*] *n* giovenca.

height [haɪt] *n* altezza; (*high ground*) altura; (*fig: of glory*) apice *m*; (: *of stupidity*) colmo; ~**en** *vt* innalzare; (*fig*) accrescere.

heir [ɛə*] *n* erede *m*; ~**ess** *n* erede *f*; ~**loom** *n* mobile *m* (or gioiello or quadro) di famiglia.

held [hɛld] *pt, pp* of **hold**.

helicopter [hɛlɪkɔptə*] *n* elicottero.

heliport [hɛlɪpɔ:t] *n* eliporto.

helium [hi:lɪəm] *n* elio.

hell [hɛl] *n* inferno; ~! (*col*) porca miseria!, accidenti!

he'll [hi:l] = **he will, he shall**.

hellish [hɛlɪʃ] *a* infernale.

hello [hə'ləu] *excl* buon giorno!; ciao! (*to sb one addresses as "tu"*); (*surprise*) ma guarda!

helm [hɛlm] *n* (*NAUT*) timone *m*.

helmet [hɛlmɪt] *n* casco.

help [hɛlp] *n* aiuto; (*charwoman*) donna di servizio; (*assistant etc*) impiegato/a // *vt* aiutare; ~! aiuto!; ~ **yourself** (*to bread*) si serva (del pane); **he can't ~ it** non ci può far niente; ~**er** *n* aiutante *m/f*, assistente *m/f*; ~**ful** *a* di grande aiuto; (*useful*) utile; ~**ing** *n* porzione *f*;

~less a impotente; debole.
hem |hɛm| n orlo // vt fare l'orlo a; **to ~ in** vt cingere.
he-man |'hi:mæn| n fusto.
hemisphere |'hɛmɪsfɪə*| n emisfero.
hemorrhage |'hɛmərɪdʒ| n (US) = **haemorrhage**.
hemorrhoids |'hɛmərɔɪdz| npl (US) = **haemorrhoids**.
hen |hɛn| n gallina.
hence |hɛns| ad (therefore) dunque; **2 years ~** di qui a 2 anni; **~forth** ad d'ora in poi.
henchman |'hɛntʃmən| n (pej) caudatario.
henpecked |'hɛnpɛkt| a dominato dalla moglie.
hepatitis |hɛpə'taɪtɪs| n epatite f.
her |hə:*| pronoun (direct) la, l' + vowel; (indirect) le; (stressed, after prep) lei; see note at **she** // a il(la) suo(a), i(le) suoi(sue); see also **me, my**.
herald |'hɛrəld| n araldo // vt annunciare.
heraldry |'hɛrəldrɪ| n araldica.
herb |hə:b| n erba.
herd |hə:d| n mandria.
here |hɪə*| ad qui, qua // excl ehi!; **~!** (at roll call) presente!; **~ is/are** ecco; **~'s** my sister ecco mia sorella; **~ he/she is** eccolo/eccola; **~ she comes** eccola che viene; **~after** ad in futuro; dopo questo // n: the **~after** l'al di là m; **~by** ad (in letter) con la presente.
hereditary |hɪ'rɛdɪtrɪ| a ereditario(a).
heresy |'hɛrəsɪ| n eresia.
heretic |'hɛrətɪk| n eretico/a.
heritage |'hɛrɪtɪdʒ| n eredità; (fig) retaggio.
hermetically |hə:'mɛtɪklɪ| ad: **~ sealed** ermeticamente chiuso(a).
hermit |'hə:mɪt| n eremita m.
hernia |'hə:nɪə| n ernia.
hero, ~es |'hɪərəu| n eroe m.
heroin |'hɛrəuɪn| n eroina.
heroine |'hɛrəuɪn| n eroina.
heron |'hɛrən| n airone m.
herring |'hɛrɪŋ| n aringa.
hers |hə:z| pronoun il(la) suo(a), i(le) suoi(sue); see also **mine**.
herself |hə:'sɛlf| pronoun (reflexive) si; (emphatic) lei stessa; (after prep) se stessa, sé; see also **oneself**.
he's |hi:z| = **he is, he has**.
hesitant |'hɛzɪtənt| a esitante, indeciso(a).
hesitate |'hɛzɪteɪt| vi: **to ~ (about/to do)** esitare (su/a fare); **hesitation** |-'teɪʃən| n esitazione f.
heterosexual |'hɛtərəu'sɛksjuəl| a, n eterosessuale (m/f).
hexagon |'hɛksəgən| n esagono.
heyday |'heɪdeɪ| n: the **~ of** i bei giorni di, l'età d'oro di.
HGV n abbr = **heavy goods vehicle**.
hi |haɪ| excl ciao!

hiatus |haɪ'eɪtəs| n vuoto; (LING) iato.
hibernate |'haɪbəneɪt| vi ibernare.
hiccough, hiccup |'hɪkʌp| vi singhiozzare // n singhiozzo.
hide |haɪd| n (skin) pelle f // vb (pt **hid**, pp **hidden** |hɪd, 'hɪdn|) vt: **to ~ sth (from sb)** nascondere qc (a qn) // vi: **to ~ (from sb)** nascondersi (da qn); **~-and-seek** n rimpiattino; **~away** n nascondiglio.
hideous |'hɪdɪəs| a laido(a); orribile.
hiding |'haɪdɪŋ| n (beating) bastonata; **to be in ~** (concealed) tenersi nascosto(a).
hierarchy |'haɪərɑːkɪ| n gerarchia.
hi-fi |'haɪfaɪ| n stereo // a ad alta fedeltà, hi-fi inv.
high |haɪ| a alto(a); (speed, respect, number) grande; (wind) forte // ad alto, in alto; **20m ~** alto(a) 20m; **~boy** n (US: tallboy) cassettone m; **~brow** a, n intellettuale (m/f); **~chair** n seggiolone m; **~er education** n studi mpl superiori; **~-handed** a prepotente; **~jack** vt = **hijack**; **~ jump** n (SPORT) salto in alto; **the H~lands** npl le Highlands scozzesi; **~light** n (fig: of event) momento culminante // vt mettere in evidenza; **~ly** ad molto; **~ly strung** a teso(a) di nervi, eccitabile; **~ness** n altezza; **Her H~ness** Sua Altezza; **~pitched** a acuto(a); **~-rise block** n palazzone m; **~ school** n scuola secondaria; (US) istituto superiore d'istruzione; **~ season** n (Brit) alta stagione; **~ street** n (Brit) strada principale.
highway |'haɪweɪ| n strada maestra; **H~ Code** n (Brit) codice m della strada.
hijack |'haɪdʒæk| vt dirottare; **~er** n dirottatore/trice.
hike |haɪk| vi fare un'escursione a piedi // n escursione f a piedi; (in prices) aumento; **~r** n escursionista m/f.
hilarious |hɪ'lɛərɪəs| a (behaviour, event) che fa schiantare dal ridere.
hilarity |hɪ'lærɪtɪ| n ilarità.
hill |hɪl| n collina, colle m; (fairly high) montagna; (on road) salita; **~side** n fianco della collina; **~y** a collinoso(a); montagnoso(a).
hilt |hɪlt| n (of sword) elsa; **to the ~** (fig: support) fino in fondo.
him |hɪm| pronoun (direct) lo, l' + vowel; (indirect) gli; (stressed, after prep) lui; see also **me**; **~self** pronoun (reflexive) si; (emphatic) lui stesso; (after prep) se stesso, sé; see also **oneself**.
hind |haɪnd| a posteriore // n cerva.
hinder |'hɪndə*| vt ostacolare; (delay) tardare; (prevent): **to ~ sb from doing** impedire a qn di fare; **hindrance** |'hɪndrəns| n ostacolo, impedimento.
hindsight |'haɪndsaɪt| n: **with ~** con il

senno di poi.

Hindu ['hɪndu:] n indù m/f inv.

hinge [hɪndʒ] n cardine m // vi (fig): to ~ on dipendere da.

hint [hɪnt] n accenno, allusione f; (advice) consiglio // vt: to ~ that lasciar capire che // vi: to ~ at accennare a.

hip [hɪp] n anca, fianco.

hippopotamus, pl ~es or **hippopotami** [hɪpə'pɒtəməs, -'pɒtəmaɪ] n ippopotamo.

hire ['haɪə*] vt (Brit: car, equipment) noleggiare; (worker) assumere, dare lavoro a // n nolo, noleggio; for ~ da nolo; (taxi) libero(a); ~ **purchase (H.P.)** n (Brit) acquisto (or vendita) rateale.

his [hɪz] a, pronoun il(la) suo(sua), i(le) suoi(sue); see also my, mine.

hiss [hɪs] vi fischiare; (cat, snake) sibilare // n fischio; sibilo.

historic(al) [hɪ'stɔrɪk(l)] a storico(a).

history ['hɪstərɪ] n storia.

hit [hɪt] vt (pt, pp hit) colpire, picchiare; (knock against) battere; (reach: target) raggiungere; (collide with: car) urtare contro; (fig: affect) colpire; (find: problem etc) incontrare // n colpo; (success, song) successo; to ~ it off with sb andare molto d'accordo con qn; ~-**and-run driver** n pirata m della strada.

hitch [hɪtʃ] vt (fasten) attaccare; (also: ~ up) tirare su // n (difficulty) intoppo, difficoltà f inv; to ~ a lift fare l'autostop.

hitch-hike ['hɪtʃhaɪk] vi fare l'autostop; ~r n autostoppista m/f.

hi-tech ['haɪ'tɛk] a di alta tecnologia // n alta tecnologia.

hitherto [hɪðə'tu:] ad in precedenza.

hive [haɪv] n alveare m; to ~ **off** vt separare.

H.M.S. abbr = His (Her) Majesty's Ship.

hoard [hɔ:d] n (of food) provviste fpl; (of money) gruzzolo // vt ammassare.

hoarding ['hɔ:dɪŋ] n (Brit: for posters) tabellone m per affissioni.

hoarfrost ['hɔ:frɔst] n brina.

hoarse [hɔ:s] a rauco(a).

hoax [həʊks] n scherzo; falso allarme.

hob [hɒb] n piastra (con fornelli).

hobble ['hɒbl] vi zoppicare.

hobby ['hɒbɪ] n hobby m inv, passatempo; ~-**horse** n (fig) chiodo fisso.

hobo ['həʊbəʊ] n (US) vagabondo.

hockey ['hɒkɪ] n hockey m.

hoe [həʊ] n zappa.

hog [hɒg] n maiale m // vt (fig) arraffare; to go the whole ~ farlo fino in fondo.

hoist [hɔɪst] n paranco // vt issare.

hold [həʊld] vb (pt, pp held) vt tenere; (contain) contenere; (keep back) trattenere; (believe) mantenere; considerare; (possess) avere, possedere; detenere // vi (withstand pressure) tenere; (be valid) essere valido(a) // n presa; (fig) potere m; (NAUT) stiva; to ~ the line! (TEL) resti in linea!; to ~ one's own (fig) difendersi bene; to catch or get (a) ~ of afferrare; to get ~ of (fig) trovare; to ~ **back** vt trattenere; (secret) tenere celato(a); to ~ **down** vt (person) tenere a terra; (job) tenere; to ~ **off** vt tener lontano; to ~ **on** vi tener fermo; (wait) aspettare; ~ on! (TEL) resti in linea!; to ~ **on to** vt fus tenersi stretto(a) a; (keep) conservare; to ~ **out** vi offrire // vi (resist) resistere; to ~ **up** vt (raise) alzare; (support) sostenere; (delay) ritardare; ~**all** n (Brit) borsone m; ~**er** n (of ticket, title) possessore/posseditrice; (of office etc) incaricato/a; (of record) detentore/trice; ~**ing** n (share) azioni fpl, titoli mpl; (farm) podere m, tenuta; ~**up** n (robbery) rapina a mano armata; (delay) ritardo; (Brit: in traffic) blocco.

hole [həʊl] n buco, buca // vt bucare.

holiday ['hɒlədɪ] n vacanza; (day off) giorno di vacanza; (public) giorno festivo; on ~ in vacanza; ~ **camp** n (for children) colonia (di villeggiatura); (also: ~ centre) = villaggio (di vacanze); ~-**maker** n (Brit) villeggiante m/f; ~ **resort** n luogo di villeggiatura.

holiness ['həʊlɪnɪs] n santità.

Holland ['hɒlənd] n Olanda.

hollow ['hɒləʊ] a cavo(a), vuoto(a); (fig) falso(a); vano(a) // n cavità f inv; (in land) valletta, depressione f // vt: to ~ out scavare.

holly ['hɒlɪ] n agrifoglio.

holocaust ['hɒləkɔ:st] n olocausto.

holster ['həʊlstə*] n fondina (di pistola).

holy ['həʊlɪ] a santo(a); (bread) benedetto(a), consacrato(a); (ground) consacrato(a); H~ **Ghost** or **Spirit** n Spirito Santo; ~ **orders** npl ordini mpl (sacri).

homage ['hɒmɪdʒ] n omaggio; to pay ~ to rendere omaggio a.

home [həʊm] n casa; (country) patria; (institution) casa, ricovero // a familiare; (cooking etc) casalingo(a); (ECON, POL) nazionale, interno(a) // ad a casa; in patria; (right in: nail etc) fino in fondo; at ~ a casa; to go (or come) ~ tornare a casa (or in patria); make yourself at ~ si metta a suo agio; ~ **address** n indirizzo di casa; ~ **computer** n home computer m inv; ~**land** n patria; ~**less** a senza tetto; spatriato(a); ~**ly** a semplice, alla buona; accogliente; ~-**made** a casalingo(a); H~ **Office** n (Brit) ministero degli Interni; ~ **rule** n autogoverno; **H~ Secretary** n (Brit) ministro degli Interni; **~sick** a: to be **~sick** avere la nostalgia; **~ town** n città f inv natale; **~ward** ['həumwəd] a (journey) di ritorno; **~work** n compiti mpl (per casa).

homicide ['hɒmɪsaɪd] n (US) omicidio.

homoeopathy [həumɪ'ɒpəθɪ] n omeopatia.

homogeneous [hɒməu'dʒi:nɪəs] a omogeneo(a).

homosexual [hɒməu'sɛksjuəl] a, n omosessuale (m/f).

honest ['ɒnɪst] a onesto(a); sincero(a); **~ly** ad onestamente; sinceramente; **~y** n onestà.

honey ['hʌnɪ] n miele m; **~comb** n favo; **~moon** n luna di miele, viaggio di nozze; **~suckle** n (BOT) caprifoglio.

honk [hɒŋk] vi suonare il clacson.

honorary ['ɒnərərɪ] a onorario(a); (duty, title) onorifico(a).

honour, (US **honor** ['ɒnə*] vt onorare // n onore m; **~able** a onorevole; **~s degree** n (SCOL) laurea specializzata.

hood [hud] n cappuccio; (Brit AUT) capote f; (US AUT) cofano.

hoodlum ['hu:dləm] n teppista m/f.

hoodwink ['hudwɪŋk] vt infinocchiare.

hoof [hu:f], pl **~s** or **hooves** n zoccolo.

hook [huk] n gancio; (for fishing) amo // vt uncinare; (dress) agganciare.

hooligan ['hu:lɪgən] n giovinastro, teppista m.

hoop [hu:p] n cerchio.

hoot [hu:t] vi (AUT) suonare il clacson; **~er** n (Brit AUT) clacson m inv; (NAUT) sirena.

hoover ['hu:və*] ® (Brit) n aspirapolvere m inv // vt pulire con l'aspirapolvere.

hooves [hu:vz] npl of **hoof**.

hop [hɒp] vi saltellare, saltare; (on one foot) saltare su una gamba // n salto.

hope [həup] vt, vi sperare // n speranza; I **~** so/not spero di sì/no; **~ful** a (person) pieno(a) di speranza; (situation) promettente; **~fully** ad con speranza; **~fully** he will recover speriamo che si riprenda; **~less** a senza speranza, disperato(a); (useless) inutile.

hops [hɒps] npl luppoli mpl.

horde [hɔːd] n orda.

horizon [hə'raɪzn] n orizzonte m; **~tal** [hɒrɪ'zɒntl] a orizzontale.

hormone ['hɔːməun] n ormone m.

horn [hɔːn] n (ZOOL, MUS) corno; (AUT) clacson m inv.

hornet ['hɔːnɪt] n calabrone m.

horny ['hɔːnɪ] a corneo(a); (hands) calloso(a); (col) arrapato(a).

horoscope ['hɒrəskəup] n oroscopo.

horrendous [hə'rɛndəs] a orrendo(a).

horrible ['hɒrɪbl] a orribile, tremendo(a).

horrid ['hɒrɪd] a orrido(a); (person)

antipatico(a).

horrify ['hɒrɪfaɪ] vt scandalizzare.

horror ['hɒrə*] n orrore m; **~ film** n film m inv dell'orrore.

hors d'œuvre [ɔː'dəːvrə] n antipasto.

horse [hɔːs] n cavallo; **~ back**: on **~back** a cavallo; **~ chestnut** n ippocastano; **~man** n cavaliere m; **~power (h.p.)** n cavallo (vapore); **~-racing** n ippica; **~radish** n rafano; **~shoe** n ferro di cavallo; **~woman** n amazzone f.

horticulture ['hɔːtɪkʌltʃə*] n orticoltura.

hose [həuz] n (also: **~pipe**) tubo; (also: garden~) tubo per annaffiare.

hospice ['hɒspɪs] n ricovero, ospizio.

hospitable [hɒs'pɪtəbl] a ospitale.

hospital ['hɒspɪtl] n ospedale m.

hospitality [hɒspɪ'tælɪt] n ospitalità.

host [həust] n ospite m; (REL) ostia; (large number): **a ~** of una schiera di.

hostage ['hɒstɪdʒ] n ostaggio/a.

hostel ['hɒstl] n ostello; (also: **youth ~**) ostello della gioventù.

hostess ['həustɪs] n ospite f; (Brit: air **~**) hostess f inv; (in nightclub) entraîneuse f inv.

hostile ['hɒstaɪl] a ostile.

hostility [hɒ'stɪlɪtɪ] n ostilità f inv.

hot [hɒt] a caldo(a); (as opposed to only warm) molto caldo(a); (spicy) piccante; (fig) accanito(a); ardente; violento(a), focoso(a); to be **~** (person) aver caldo; (object) essere caldo(a); (weather) far caldo; **~bed** n (fig) focolaio; **~ dog** n hot dog m inv.

hotel [həu'tɛl] n albergo; **~ier** n albergatore/trice.

hot: ~headed a focoso(a), eccitabile; **~house** n serra; **~ line** n (POL) telefono rosso; **~ly** ad violentemente; **~plate** n (on cooker) piastra riscaldante; **~-water bottle** n borsa dell'acqua calda.

hound [haund] vt perseguitare // n segugio.

hour ['auə*] n ora; **~ly** a all'ora // ad ogni ora; **~ly paid** a pagato(a) a ore.

house n [haus] (pl **~s** ['hauzɪz]) (also: firm) casa; (POL) camera; (THEATRE) sala; pubblico; spettacolo // vt [hauz] (person) ospitare, alloggiare; **on the ~** (fig) offerto(a) dalla casa; **~boat** n house boat f inv; **~breaking** n furto con scasso; **~coat** n vestaglia; **~hold** n famiglia; casa; **~keeper** n governante f; **~keeping** n (work) governo della casa; **~keeping** (money) soldi mpl per le spese di casa; **~-warming party** n festa per inaugurare la casa nuova; **~wife** n massaia, casalinga; **~work** n faccende fpl domestiche.

housing ['hauzɪŋ] n alloggio; **~ development,** (Brit) **~ estate** n zona residenziale con case popolari e/o *private*.

hovel ['hɒvl] *n* casupola.

hover ['hɒvə*] *vi* (*bird*) librarsi; (*helicopter*) volare a punto fisso; **~craft** *n* hovercraft *m inv*.

how [hau] *ad* come; ~ are you? come sta?; ~ do you do? piacere!; ~ far is it to the river? quanto è lontano il fiume?; ~ long have you been here? da quando è qui?; ~ lovely!/awful! che bello!/orrore!; ~ many? quanti(e)?; ~ much? quanto(a)?; ~ much milk? quanto latte?; ~ many people? quante persone?; ~ old are you? quanti anni ha?; **~ever** *ad* in qualsiasi modo *or* maniera che; (+ *adjective*) per quanto + *sub*; (*in questions*) come // *cj* comunque, però.

howl [haul] *n* ululato // *vi* ululare.

h.p., H.P. *abbr* = **hire purchase, horsepower**.

HQ *n abbr* = **headquarters**.

hub [hʌb] *n* (*of wheel*) mozzo; (*fig*) fulcro.

hubbub ['hʌbʌb] *n* baccano.

hub cap *n* coprimozzo.

huddle ['hʌdl] *vi*: to ~ together rannicchiarsi l'uno contro l'altro.

hue [hju:] *n* tinta; ~ and cry *n* clamore *m*.

huff [hʌf] *n*: in a ~ stizzito(a).

hug [hʌg] *vt* abbracciare; (*shore, kerb*) stringere // *n* abbraccio, stretta.

huge [hju:dʒ] *a* enorme, immenso(a).

hulk [hʌlk] *n* (*ship*) nave *f* in disarmo; (*building, car*) carcassa; (*person*) mastodonte *m*.

hull [hʌl] *n* (*of ship*) scafo.

hullo [hə'ləu] *excl* = **hello**.

hum [hʌm] *vt* (*tune*) canticchiare // *vi* canticchiare; (*insect, plane, tool*) ronzare.

human ['hju:mən] *a* umano(a) // *n* essere *m* umano.

humane [hju:'meɪn] *a* umanitario(a).

humanitarian [hju:mænɪ'tɛərɪən] *a* umanitario(a).

humanity [hju:'mænɪtɪ] *n* umanità.

humble ['hʌmbl] *a* umile, modesto(a) // *vt* umiliare.

humbug ['hʌmbʌg] *n* inganno; sciocchezze *fpl*.

humdrum ['hʌmdrʌm] *a* monotono(a), tedioso(a).

humid ['hju:mɪd] *a* umido(a).

humiliate [hju:'mɪlɪeɪt] *vt* umiliare; **humiliation** [-'eɪʃən] *n* umiliazione *f*.

humility [hju:'mɪlɪtɪ] *n* umiltà.

humorous ['hju:mərəs] *a* umoristico(a); (*person*) buffo(a).

humour, (*US*) **humor** ['hju:mə*] *n* umore *m* // *vt* (*person*) compiacere; (*sb's whims*) assecondare.

hump [hʌmp] *n* gobba.

hunch [hʌntʃ] *n* gobba; (*premonition*)

intuizione *f*; **~back** *n* gobbo/a; **~ed** *a* incurvato(a).

hundred ['hʌndrəd] *num* cento; **~s of** centinaia *fpl* di; **~weight** *n* (*Brit*) = *50.8 kg; 112 lb;* (*US*) = *45.3 kg; 100 lb.*

hung [hʌŋ] *pt, pp of* **hang**.

Hungary ['hʌŋgərɪ] *n* Ungheria.

hunger ['hʌŋgə*] *n* fame *f* // *vi*: to ~ for desiderare ardentemente.

hungry ['hʌŋgrɪ] *a* affamato(a); to be ~ aver fame.

hunk [hʌŋk] *n* (*of bread etc*) bel pezzo.

hunt [hʌnt] *vt* (*seek*) cercare, (*SPORT*) cacciare // *vi* andare a caccia // *n* caccia; **~er** *n* cacciatore *m*; **~ing** *n* caccia.

hurdle ['hə:dl] *n* (*SPORT, fig*) ostacolo.

hurl [hə:l] *vt* lanciare con violenza.

hurrah, hurray [hu'rɑ:, hu'reɪ] *excl* urra!, evviva!

hurricane ['hʌrɪkən] *n* uragano.

hurried ['hʌrɪd] *a* affrettato(a); (*work*) fatto(a) in fretta; **~ly** *ad* in fretta.

hurry ['hʌrɪ] *n* fretta // *vb* (*also:* ~ up) *vi* affrettarsi // *vt* (*person*) affrettare; (*work*) far in fretta; to be in a ~ aver fretta; to do sth in a ~ fare qc in fretta; to ~ in/out entrare/uscire in fretta.

hurt [hə:t] *vb* (*pt, pp* **hurt**) *vt* (*cause pain to*) far male a; (*injure, fig*) ferire // *vi* far male // *a* ferito(a); **~ful** *a* (*remark*) che ferisce.

hurtle ['hə:tl] *vt* scagliare // *vi*: to ~ past/down passare/scendere a razzo.

husband ['hʌzbənd] *n* marito.

hush [hʌʃ] *n* silenzio, calma // *vt* zittire; ~! zitto(a)!

husk [hʌsk] *n* (*of wheat*) cartoccio; (*of rice, maize*) buccia.

husky ['hʌskɪ] *a* roco(a) // *n* cane *m* eschimese.

hustle ['hʌsl] *vt* spingere, incalzare // *n* pigia pigia *m inv*; ~ and bustle *n* trambusto.

hut [hʌt] *n* rifugio; (*shed*) ripostiglio.

hutch [hʌtʃ] *n* gabbia.

hyacinth ['haɪəsɪnθ] *n* giacinto.

hybrid ['haɪbrɪd] *a* ibrido(a) // *n* ibrido.

hydrant ['haɪdrənt] *n* (*also:* fire ~) idrante *m*.

hydraulic [haɪ'drɔ:lɪk] *a* idraulico(a).

hydroelectric [haɪdrəu'lɛktrɪk] *a* idroelettrico(a).

hydrofoil ['haɪdrəufɔɪl] *n* aliscafo.

hydrogen ['haɪdrədʒən] *n* idrogeno.

hyena [haɪ'i:nə] *n* iena.

hygiene ['haɪdʒi:n] *n* igiene *f*.

hymn [hɪm] *n* inno; cantica.

hype [haɪp] *n* (*col*) campagna pubblicitaria.

hypermarket ['haɪpəmɑ:kɪt] *n* ipermercato.

hyphen ['haɪfn] *n* trattino.

hypnotism ['hɪpnətɪzm] *n* ipnotismo.

hypnotize ['hɪpnətaɪz] *vt* ipnotizzare.

hypocrisy [hɪ'pɔkrɪsɪ] n ipocrisia.
hypocrite ['hɪpəkrɪt] n ipocrita m/f;
  hypocritical [-'krɪtɪkl] a ipocrita.
hypothermia [haɪpəu'θəːmɪə] n
  ipotermia.
hypothesis, pl **hypotheses** [haɪ'pɔθɪsɪs,
  -siːz] n ipotesi f inv.
hypothetical [haɪpəu'θetɪkl] a
  ipotetico(a).
hysterical [hɪ'sterɪkl] a isterico(a).
hysterics [hɪ'sterɪks] npl accesso di
  isteria; (laughter) attacco di riso.

I

I [aɪ] pronoun io.
ice [aɪs] n ghiaccio; (on road) gelo // vt
  (cake) glassare; (drink) mettere in fresco // vi (also: ~ over) ghiacciare;
  (also: ~ up) gelare; ~ **axe** n piccozza
  da ghiaccio; ~**berg** n iceberg m inv;
  ~**box** n (US) frigorifero; (Brit) reparto
  ghiaccio; (insulated box) frigo portatile;
  ~ **cream** n gelato; ~ **hockey** n hockey
  m su ghiaccio.
Iceland ['aɪslənd] n Islanda.
ice: ~ **lolly** n (Brit) ghiacciolo; ~ **rink**
  n pista di pattinaggio; ~ **skating** n
  pattinaggio sul ghiaccio.
icicle ['aɪsɪkl] n ghiacciolo.
icing ['aɪsɪŋ] n (AVIAT etc) patina di
  ghiaccio; (CULIN) glassa; ~ **sugar** n
  (Brit) zucchero a velo.
icy ['aɪsɪ] a ghiacciato(a); (weather,
  temperature) gelido(a).
I'd [aɪd] = **I would, I had.**
idea [aɪ'dɪə] n idea.
ideal [aɪ'dɪəl] a, n ideale (m).
identical [aɪ'dentɪkl] a identico(a).
identification [aɪdentɪfɪ'keɪʃən] n
  identificazione f; **means of** ~ carta
  d'identità.
identify [aɪ'dentɪfaɪ] vt identificare.
identikit picture [aɪ'dentɪkɪt-] n
  identikit m inv.
identity [aɪ'dentɪtɪ] n identità f inv; ~
  card n carta d'identità.
idiom ['ɪdɪəm] n idioma m; (phrase)
  espressione f idiomatica.
idiot ['ɪdɪət] n idiota m/f; ~**ic** [-'ɔtɪk] a
  idiota.
idle ['aɪdl] a inattivo(a); (lazy) pigro(a),
  ozioso(a); (unemployed) disoccupato(a);
  (question, pleasures) ozioso(a); **to lie** ~
  stare fermo, non funzionare; **to** ~
  away vt (time) sprecare, buttar via.
idol ['aɪdl] n idolo; ~**ize** vt idoleggiare.
i.e. ad abbr (= that is) cioè.
if [ɪf] cj se; ~ **I were you** ... se fossi in te
  ..., io al tuo posto ...; ~ **so** se è così; ~
  not se no; ~ **only** se solo or soltanto.
ignite [ɪg'naɪt] vt accendere // vi
  accendersi.
ignition [ɪg'nɪʃən] n (AUT) accensione f;

to switch on/off the ~ accendere/
  spegnere il motore; ~ **key** n (AUT)
  chiave f dell'accensione.
ignorant ['ɪgnərənt] a ignorante; **to be** ~
  of (subject) essere ignorante in; (events)
  essere ignaro(a) di.
ignore [ɪg'nɔː*] vt non tener conto di;
  (person, fact) ignorare.
I'll [aɪl] = **I will, I shall.**
ill [ɪl] a (sick) malato(a); (bad)
  cattivo(a) // n male m // ad: **to speak** etc
  ~ **of sb** parlare etc male di qn; **to take**
  or **be taken** ~ ammalarsi; ~-**advised** a
  (decision) poco giudizioso(a); (person)
  mal consigliato(a); ~-**at-ease** a a
  disagio.
illegal [ɪ'liːgl] a illegale.
illegible [ɪ'ledʒɪbl] a illeggibile.
illegitimate [ɪlɪ'dʒɪtɪmət] a
  illegittimo(a).
ill-fated [ɪl'feɪtɪd] a nefasto(a).
ill feeling n rancore m.
illiterate [ɪ'lɪtərət] a analfabeta,
  illetterato(a); (letter) scorretto(a).
illness ['ɪlnɪs] n malattia.
ill-treat [ɪl'triːt] vt maltrattare.
illuminate [ɪ'luːmɪneɪt] vt illuminare;
  illumination [-'neɪʃən] n illuminazione f.
illusion [ɪ'luːʒən] n illusione f; **to be**
  under the ~ **that** avere l'impressione
  che.
illustrate ['ɪləstreɪt] vt illustrare;
  illustration [-'streɪʃən] n illustrazione f.
ill will n cattiva volontà.
I'm [aɪm] = **I am.**
image ['ɪmɪdʒ] n immagine f; (public
  face) immagine (pubblica); ~**ry** n
  immagini fpl.
imaginary [ɪ'mædʒɪnərɪ] a immagina-
  rio(a).
imagination [ɪmædʒɪ'neɪʃən] n immaginazione f, fantasia.
imaginative [ɪ'mædʒɪnətɪv] a immagino-
  so(a).
imagine [ɪ'mædʒɪn] vt immaginare.
imbalance [ɪm'bæləns] n squilibrio.
imitate ['ɪmɪteɪt] vt imitare; **imitation**
  [-'teɪʃən] n imitazione f.
immaculate [ɪ'mækjulət] a
  immacolato(a); (dress, appearance)
  impeccabile.
immaterial [ɪmə'tɪərɪəl] a immateriale,
  indifferente.
immature [ɪmə'tjuə*] a immaturo(a).
immediate [ɪ'miːdɪət] a immediato(a);
  ~**ly** ad (at once) subito,
  immediatamente; ~**ly next to** proprio
  accanto a.
immense [ɪ'mens] a immenso(a);
  enorme.
immerse [ɪ'məːs] vt immergere.
immersion heater [ɪ'məːʃən-] n (Brit)
  scaldaacqua m inv a immersione.
immigrant ['ɪmɪgrənt] n immigrante m/
  f; immigrato/a.

immigration [ɪmɪˈgreɪʃən] *n* immi-
grazione *f*.
imminent [ˈɪmɪnənt] *a* imminente.
immoral [ɪˈmɔrl] *a* immorale.
immortal [ɪˈmɔːtl] *a, n* immortale *(m/f)*.
immune [ɪˈmjuːn] *a*: ~ (to) immune
(da).
immunity [ɪˈmjuːnɪtɪ] *n* immunità.
imp [ɪmp] *n* folletto, diavoletto; *(child)*
diavoletto.
impact [ˈɪmpækt] *n* impatto.
impair [ɪmˈpeə*] *vt* danneggiare.
impart [ɪmˈpɑːt] *vt (make known)*
comunicare; *(bestow)* impartire.
impartial [ɪmˈpɑːʃl] *a* imparziale.
impassable [ɪmˈpɑːsəbl] *a* insuperabile;
(road) impraticabile.
impassive [ɪmˈpæsɪv] *a* impassibile.
impatience [ɪmˈpeɪʃəns] *n* impazienza.
impatient [ɪmˈpeɪʃənt] *a* impaziente; to
get *or* grow ~ perdere la pazienza.
impeccable [ɪmˈpekəbl] *a* impeccabile.
impede [ɪmˈpiːd] *vt* impedire.
impediment [ɪmˈpedɪmənt] *n*
impedimento; *(also:* speech ~) difetto di
pronuncia.
impending [ɪmˈpendɪŋ] *a* imminente.
imperative [ɪmˈperətɪv] *a* imperativo(a);
necessario(a), urgente; *(voice)*
imperioso(a) // *n (LING)* imperativo.
imperfect [ɪmˈpəːfɪkt] *a* imperfetto(a);
(goods etc) difettoso(a).
imperial [ɪmˈpɪərɪəl] *a* imperiale;
(measure) legale.
impersonal [ɪmˈpəːsənl] *a* impersonale.
impersonate [ɪmˈpəːsəneɪt] *vt*
impersonare; *(THEATRE)* fare la mimica
di.
impertinent [ɪmˈpəːtɪnənt] *a* insolente,
impertinente.
impervious [ɪmˈpəːvɪəs] *a* impermeabile; *(fig):* ~ to insensibile a; impassibile di fronte a.
impetuous [ɪmˈpetjuəs] *a* impetuoso(a),
precipitoso(a).
impetus [ˈɪmpətəs] *n* impeto.
impinge [ɪmˈpɪndʒ]: to ~ on *vt fus*
(person) colpire; *(rights)* ledere.
implement *n* [ˈɪmplɪmənt] attrezzo; *(for
cooking)* utensile *m* // *vt* [ˈɪmplɪment]
effettuare.
implicit [ɪmˈplɪsɪt] *a* implicito(a); *(complete)* completo(a).
imply [ɪmˈplaɪ] *vt* insinuare; suggerire.
impolite [ɪmpəˈlaɪt] *a* scortese.
import *vt* [ɪmˈpɔːt] importare // *n*
[ˈɪmpɔːt] *(COMM)* importazione *f*;
(meaning) significato, senso.
importance [ɪmˈpɔːtns] *n* importanza.
important [ɪmˈpɔːtnt] *a* importante; it's
not ~ non ha importanza.
importer [ɪmˈpɔːtə*] *n* importatore/trice.
impose [ɪmˈpəuz] *vt* imporre // *vi*: to ~
on sb sfruttare la bontà di qn.
imposing [ɪmˈpəuzɪŋ] *a* imponente.

imposition [ɪmpəˈzɪʃən] *n (of tax etc)*
imposizione *f*; to be an ~ on *(person)*
abusare della gentilezza di.
impossibility [ɪmpɔsəˈbɪlɪtɪ] *n*
impossibilità.
impossible [ɪmˈpɔsɪbl] *a* impossibile.
impotent [ˈɪmpətnt] *a* impotente.
impound [ɪmˈpaund] *vt* confiscare.
impoverished [ɪmˈpɔvərɪʃt] *a*
impoverito(a).
impractical [ɪmˈpræktɪkl] *a* non
pratico(a).
impregnable [ɪmˈpregnəbl] *a (fortress)*
inespugnabile; *(fig)* inoppugnabile;
irrefutabile.
impress [ɪmˈpres] *vt* impressionare;
(mark) imprimere, stampare; to ~ sth
on sb far capire qc a qn.
impression [ɪmˈpreʃən] *n* impressione *f*;
to be under the ~ that avere l'impressione che.
impressive [ɪmˈpresɪv] *a* impressionante.
imprint [ˈɪmprɪnt] *n (PUBLISHING)* sigla
editoriale.
imprison [ɪmˈprɪzn] *vt* imprigionare;
~ment *n* imprigionamento.
improbable [ɪmˈprɔbəbl] *a* improbabile;
(excuse) inverosimile.
impromptu [ɪmˈprɔmptjuː] *a* im-
provvisato(a).
improper [ɪmˈprɔpə*] *a* scorretto(a);
(unsuitable) inadatto(a), improprio(a);
sconveniente, indecente.
improve [ɪmˈpruːv] *vt* migliorare // *vi* migliorare; *(pupil etc)* fare progressi;
~ment *n* miglioramento; progresso.
improvise [ˈɪmprəvaɪz] *vt, vi* improvvisare.
impudent [ˈɪmpjudnt] *a* impudente,
sfacciato(a).
impulse [ˈɪmpʌls] *n* impulso; on ~
d'impulso, impulsivamente.
impulsive [ɪmˈpʌlsɪv] *a* impulsivo(a).
in [ɪn] ♦ *prep* 1 *(indicating place,
position)* in; ~ the house/garden in casa/
giardino; ~ the box nella scatola; ~ the
fridge nel frigorifero; I have it ~ my
hand ce l'ho in mano; ~ town/the country in città/campagna; ~ school a
scuola; ~ here/there qui/lì dentro
2 *(with place names: of town, region,
country):* ~ London a Londra; ~
England in Inghilterra; ~ the United
States negli Stati Uniti; ~ Yorkshire
nello Yorkshire
3 *(indicating time: during, in the space
of)* in; ~ spring/summer in primavera/
estate; ~ 1988 nel 1988; ~ May in *or* a
maggio; I'll see you ~ July ci vediamo a
luglio; ~ the afternoon nel pomeriggio;
at 4 o'clock ~ the afternoon alle 4 del
pomeriggio; I did it ~ 3 hours/days l'ho
fatto in 3 ore/giorni; I'll see you ~ 2
weeks *or* ~ 2 weeks' time ci vediamo tra
2 settimane

4 (*indicating manner etc*) a; ~ a loud/ soft **voice** a voce alta/bassa; ~ **pencil** a matita; ~ **English/French** in inglese/ francese; **the boy** ~ **the blue shirt** il ragazzo con la camicia blu

5 (*indicating circumstances*): ~ **the sun** al sole; ~ **the shade** all'ombra; ~ **the rain** sotto la pioggia; **a rise** ~ **prices** un aumento dei prezzi

6 (*indicating mood, state*): ~ **tears** in lacrime; ~ **anger** per la rabbia; ~ **despair** disperato(a); ~ **good condition** in buono stato, in buone condizioni; **to live** ~ **luxury** vivere nel lusso

7 (*with ratios, numbers*): 1 ~ 10 1 su 10; **20 pence** ~ **the pound** 20 pence per sterlina; **they lined up** ~ **twos** si misero in fila a due a due

8 (*referring to people, works*) in; **the disease is common** ~ **children** la malattia è comune nei bambini; ~ (**the works of**) **Dickens** in Dickens

9 (*indicating profession etc*) in; **to be** ~ **teaching** fare l'insegnante, insegnare; **to be** ~ **publishing** essere nell'editoria

10 (*after superlative*) di; **the best** ~ **the class** il migliore della classe

11 (*with present participle*): ~ **saying** this dicendo questo, nel dire questo

◆ *ad*: **to be** ~ (*person: at home, work*) esserci; (*train, ship, plane*) essere arrivato(a); (*in fashion*) essere di moda; **to ask sb** ~ invitare qn ad entrare; **to run/limp** *etc* ~ entrare di corsa/zoppicando *etc*

◆ *n*: **the** ~**s and outs of the problem** tutti i particolari del problema.

in., ins *abbr* = **inch(es).**

inability [ɪnə'bɪlɪtɪ] *n* inabilità, incapacità.

inaccurate [ɪn'ækjurət] *a* inesatto(a), impreciso(a).

inadequate [ɪn'ædɪkwət] *a* insufficiente.

inadvertently [ɪnəd'vɜːtntlɪ] *ad* senza volerlo.

inane [ɪ'neɪn] *a* vacuo(a), stupido(a).

inanimate [ɪn'ænɪmət] *a* inanimato(a).

inappropriate [ɪnə'prəuprɪət] *a* disadatto(a); (*word, expression*) improprio(a).

inarticulate [ɪnɑː'tɪkjulət] *a* (*person*) che si esprime male; (*speech*) inarticolato(a).

inasmuch as [ɪnəz'mʌtʃæz] *ad* in quanto che; (*seeing that*) poiché.

inaudible [ɪn'ɔːdɪbl] *a* che non si riesce a sentire.

inauguration [ɪnɔːgju'reɪʃən] *n* inaugurazione *f*; insediamento in carica.

in-between [ɪnbɪ'twiːn] *a* fra i (*or* le) due.

inborn [ɪn'bɔːn] *a* (*feeling*) innato(a); (*defect*) congenito(a).

inbred [ɪn'brɛd] *a* innato(a); (*family*) connaturato(a).

Inc. *abbr* = **incorporated.**

incapable [ɪn'keɪpəbl] *a* incapace.

incapacitate [ɪnkə'pæsɪteɪt] *vt*: **to** ~ **sb from doing** rendere qn incapace di fare.

incense *n* ['ɪnsɛns] incenso // *vt* [ɪn'sɛns] (*anger*) infuriare.

incentive [ɪn'sɛntɪv] *n* incentivo.

incessant [ɪn'sɛsnt] *a* incessante; ~**ly** *ad* di continuo, senza sosta.

inch [ɪntʃ] *n* pollice *m* (= 25 mm; 12 in a foot); **within an** ~ **of** a un pelo da; **he didn't give an** ~ non ha ceduto di un millimetro; **to** ~ **forward** *vi* avanzare pian piano.

incidence ['ɪnsɪdns] *n* (*of crime, disease*) incidenza.

incident ['ɪnsɪdnt] *n* incidente *m*; (*in book*) episodio.

incidental [ɪnsɪ'dɛntl] *a* accessorio(a), d'accompagnamento; (*unplanned*) incidentale; ~ **to** marginale a; ~**ly** [-'dɛntəlɪ] *ad* (*by the way*) a proposito.

inclination [ɪnklɪ'neɪʃən] *n* inclinazione *f*.

incline *n* ['ɪnklaɪn] pendenza, pendio // *vb* [ɪn'klaɪn] *vt* inclinare // *vi*: **to** ~ **to** tendere a; **to be** ~**d to do** tendere a fare; essere propenso(a) a fare.

include [ɪn'kluːd] *vt* includere, comprendere; **including** *prep* compreso(a), incluso(a).

inclusive [ɪn'kluːsɪv] *a* incluso(a), compreso(a) // *ad*: ~ **of tax** *etc* tasse *etc* comprese.

incoherent [ɪnkəu'hɪərənt] *a* incoerente.

income ['ɪnkʌm] *n* reddito; ~ **tax** *n* imposta sul reddito.

incompetent [ɪn'kɔmpɪtnt] *a* incompetente, incapace.

incomplete [ɪnkəm'pliːt] *a* incompleto(a).

incongruous [ɪn'kɔŋgruəs] *a* poco appropriato(a); (*remark, act*) incongruo(a).

inconsiderate [ɪnkən'sɪdərət] *a* sconsiderato(a).

inconsistency [ɪnkən'sɪstənsɪ] *n* (*of actions, statement*) incoerenza; (*of work*) irregolarità.

inconspicuous [ɪnkən'spɪkjuəs] *a* incospicuo(a); (*colour*) poco appariscente; (*dress*) dimesso(a).

inconvenience [ɪnkən'viːnjəns] *n* inconveniente *m*; (*trouble*) disturbo // *vt* disturbare.

inconvenient [ɪnkən'viːnjənt] *a* scomodo(a).

incorporate [ɪn'kɔːpəreɪt] *vt* incorporare; (*contain*) contenere; ~**d** *a*: ~**d company** (*US: abbr* **Inc.**) società *f inv* anonima (S.A.).

incorrect [ɪnkə'rɛkt] *a* scorretto(a); (*statement*) impreciso(a).

increase *n* ['ɪnkriːs] aumento // *vi, vt* [ɪn'kriːs] aumentare.

increasing [ɪn'kriːsɪŋ] *a* (*number*) crescente; ~**ly** *ad* sempre più.

incredible [ɪn'krɛdɪbl] *a* incredibile.
incredulous [ɪn'krɛdjuləs] *a* incredulo(a).
increment ['ɪnkrɪmənt] *n* aumento, incremento.
incriminate [ɪn'krɪmɪneɪt] *vt* compromettere.
incubator ['ɪnkjubeɪtə*] *n* incubatrice *f*.
incumbent [ɪn'kʌmbənt] *a* titolare *m/f* // *a*: to be ~ on sb spettare a qn.
incur [ɪn'kə:*] *vt* (*expenses*) incorrere; (*anger*, *risk*) esporsi a; (*debt*) contrarre; (*loss*) subire.
indebted [ɪn'dɛtɪd] *a*: to be ~ to sb (for) essere obbligato(a) verso qn (per).
indecent [ɪn'di:snt] *a* indecente; ~ **assault** *n* (*Brit*) aggressione *f* a scopo di violenza sessuale; ~ **exposure** *n* atti *mpl* osceni in luogo pubblico.
indecisive [ɪndɪ'saɪsɪv] *a* indeciso(a); (*discussion*) non decisivo(a).
indeed [ɪn'di:d] *ad* infatti; veramente; yes ~! certamente!
indefinite [ɪn'dɛfɪnɪt] *a* indefinito(a); (*answer*) vago(a); (*period*, *number*) indeterminato(a); ~**ly** *ad* (*wait*) indefinitamente.
indemnity [ɪn'dɛmnɪtɪ] *n* (*insurance*) assicurazione *f*; (*compensation*) indennità, indennizzo.
independence [ɪndɪ'pɛndns] *n* indipendenza.
independent [ɪndɪ'pɛndnt] *a* indipendente.
index ['ɪndɛks] *n* (*pl* ~es: *in book*) indice *m*; (: *in library etc*) catalogo; (*pl* indices: *ratio*, *sign*) indice *m*; ~ **card** *n* scheda; ~ **finger** *n* (dito) indice *m*; ~**linked**, (*US*) ~ed *a* legato(a) al costo della vita.
India ['ɪndɪə] *n* India; ~n *a*, *n* indiano(a); Red ~n pellerossa *m/f*.
indicate ['ɪndɪkeɪt] *vt* indicare, **indication** [-'keɪʃən] *n* indicazione *f*, segno.
indicative [ɪn'dɪkətɪv] *a*: ~ of indicativo(a) di // *n* (*LING*) indicativo.
indicator ['ɪndɪkeɪtə*] *n* indicatore *m*.
indices ['ɪndɪsi:z] *npl of* **index**.
indictment [ɪn'daɪtmənt] *n* accusa.
indifference [ɪn'dɪfrəns] *n* indifferenza.
indifferent [ɪn'dɪfrənt] *a* indifferente; (*poor*) mediocre.
indigenous [ɪn'dɪdʒɪnəs] *a* indigeno(a).
indigestible [ɪndɪ'dʒɛstɪbl] *a* indigeribile.
indigestion [ɪndɪ'dʒɛstʃən] *n* indigestione *f*.
indignant [ɪn'dɪgnənt] *a*: ~ (at sth/with sb) indignato(a) (per qc/contro qn).
indignity [ɪn'dɪgnɪtɪ] *n* umiliazione *f*.
indirect [ɪndɪ'rɛkt] *a* indiretto(a).
indiscreet [ɪndɪ'skri:t] *a* indiscreto(a); (*rash*) imprudente.
indiscriminate [ɪndɪ'skrɪmɪnət] *a* (*person*) che non sa discernere; (*admiration*) cieco(a); (*killings*) indiscriminato(a).

indisputable [ɪndɪ'spju:təbl] *a* incontestabile, indiscutibile.
individual [ɪndɪ'vɪdjuəl] *n* individuo // *a* individuale; (*characteristic*) particolare, originale; ~**ist** *n* individualista *m/f*; ~**ity** [-'ælɪtɪ] *n* individualità.
indoctrination [ɪndɔktrɪ'neɪʃən] *n* indottrinamento.
Indonesia [ɪndə'ni:zɪə] *n* Indonesia.
indoor ['ɪndɔ:*] *a* da interno; (*plant*) d'appartamento; (*swimming pool*) coperto(a); (*sport*, *games*) fatto(a) al coperto; ~**s** [ɪn'dɔ:z] *ad* all'interno; (*at home*) in casa.
induce [ɪn'dju:s] *vt* persuadere; (*bring about*) provocare; ~**ment** *n* incitamento; (*incentive*) stimolo, incentivo.
induction [ɪn'dʌkʃən] *n* (*MED: of birth*) parto indotto; ~ **course** *n* (*Brit*) corso di avviamento.
indulge [ɪn'dʌldʒ] *vt* (*whim*) compiacere, soddisfare; (*child*) viziare // *vi*: to ~ in sth concedersi qc; abbandonarsi a qc; ~**nce** *n* lusso (che uno si permette); (*leniency*) indulgenza; ~**nt** *a* indulgente.
industrial [ɪn'dʌstrɪəl] *a* industriale; (*injury*) sul lavoro; (*dispute*) di lavoro; ~ **action** *n* azione *f* rivendicativa; ~ **estate** *n* (*Brit*) zona industriale; ~**ist** *n* industriale *m*; ~ **park** *n* (*US*) = ~ **estate**.
industrious [ɪn'dʌstrɪəs] *a* industrioso(a), assiduo(a).
industry ['ɪndʌstrɪ] *n* industria; (*diligence*) operosità.
inebriated [ɪ'ni:brɪeɪtɪd] *a* ubriaco(a).
inedible [ɪn'ɛdɪbl] *a* immangiabile.
ineffective [ɪnɪ'fɛktɪv], **ineffectual** [ɪnɪ'fɛktʃuəl] *a* inefficace; incompetente.
inefficiency [ɪnɪ'fɪʃənsɪ] *n* inefficienza.
inefficient [ɪnɪ'fɪʃənt] *a* inefficiente.
inept [ɪ'nɛpt] *a* inetto(a).
inequality [ɪnɪ'kwɔlɪtɪ] *n* ineguaglianza.
inescapable [ɪnɪ'skeɪpəbl] *a* inevitabile.
inevitable [ɪn'ɛvɪtəbl] *a* inevitabile; **inevitably** *ad* inevitabilmente.
inexact [ɪnɪg'zækt] *a* inesatto(a).
inexpensive [ɪnɪk'spɛnsɪv] *a* poco costoso(a).
inexperienced [ɪnɪks'pɪərɪənst] *a* inesperto(a), senza esperienza.
infallible [ɪn'fælɪbl] *a* infallibile.
infamous ['ɪnfəməs] *a* infame.
infancy ['ɪnfənsɪ] *n* infanzia.
infant ['ɪnfənt] *n* bambino/a; ~ **school** *n* (*Brit*) scuola elementare (*per bambini dall'età di 5 a 7 anni*).
infantry ['ɪnfəntrɪ] *n* fanteria.
infatuated [ɪn'fætjueɪtɪd] *a*: ~ with infatuato(a) di.
infatuation [ɪnfætju'eɪʃən] *n* infatuazione *f*.
infect [ɪn'fɛkt] *vt* infettare; ~**ion**

|in'fekʃən| *n* infezione *f*; ~ious |in'fekʃəs| *a* (*disease*) infettivo(a), contagioso(a); (*person*, *laughter*) contagioso(a).

infer |in'fə:*| *vt* inferire, dedurre.

inferior |in'fiəriə*| *a* inferiore; (*goods*) di qualità scadente // *n* inferiore *m/f*; (*in rank*) subalterno/a; ~ity |infiəri'ɔrəti| *n* inferiorità; ~ity **complex** *n* complesso di inferiorità.

infertile |in'fə:tail| *a* sterile.

in-fighting |'infaitiŋ| *n* lotte *fpl* intestine.

infinite |'infinit| *a* infinito(a).

infinitive |in'finitiv| *n* infinito.

infinity |in'finiti| *n* infinità; (*also MATH*) infinito.

infirmary |in'fə:məri| *n* ospedale *m*; (*in school, factory*) infermeria.

infirmity |in'fə:miti| *n* infermità *f inv*.

inflamed |in'fleimd| *a* infiammato(a).

inflammable |in'flæməbl| *a* (*Brit*) infiammabile.

inflammation |inflə'meiʃən| *n* infiammazione *f*.

inflatable |in'fleitəbl| *a* gonfiabile.

inflate |in'fleit| *vt* (*tyre, balloon*) gonfiare; (*fig*) esagerare; gonfiare; **inflation** |in'fleiʃən| *n* (*ECON*) inflazione *f*; **inflationary** |in'fleiʃnəri| *a* inflazionistico(a).

inflict |in'flikt| *vt*: **to ~ on** infliggere a.

influence |'influəns| *n* influenza // *vt* influenzare; **under the ~ of** sotto l'influenza di.

influential |influ'ɛnʃl| *a* influente.

influenza |influ'ɛnzə| *n* (*MED*) influenza.

influx |'inflʌks| *n* afflusso.

inform |in'fɔ:m| *vt*: **to ~ sb** (**of**) informare qn (di) // *vi*: **to ~ on sb** denunciare qn; **to ~ sb about** mettere qn al corrente di.

informal |in'fɔ:ml| *a* (*person, manner*) alla buona, semplice; (*visit, discussion*) informale; (*announcement, invitation*) non ufficiale; ~ity |-'mæliti| *n* semplicità, informalità; carattere *m* non ufficiale.

informant |in'fɔ:mənt| *n* informatore/trice.

information |infə'meiʃən| *n* informazioni *fpl*; particolari *mpl*; **a piece of ~** un'informazione; ~ **office** *n* ufficio *m* informazioni *inv*.

informative |in'fɔ:mətiv| *a* istruttivo(a).

informer |in'fɔ:mə*| *n* informatore/trice; **to turn ~** (*POLICE*) denunciare i complici.

infringe |in'frindʒ| *vt* infrangere // *vi*: **to ~ on** calpestare; ~**ment** *n*: ~**ment** (**of**) infrazione *f* (di).

infuriating |in'fjuərieitiŋ| *a* molto irritante.

ingenious |in'dʒi:njəs| *a* ingegnoso(a).

ingenuity |indʒi'nju:iti| *n* ingegnosità.

ingenuous |in'dʒɛnjuəs| *a* ingenuo(a).

ingot |'iŋgət| *n* lingotto.

ingrained |in'greind| *a* radicato(a).

ingratiate |in'greiʃieit| *vt*: **to ~ o.s. with sb** ingraziarsi qn.

ingredient |in'gri:diənt| *n* ingrediente *m*; elemento.

inhabit |in'hæbit| *vt* abitare.

inhabitant |in'hæbitnt| *n* abitante *m/f*.

inhale |in'heil| *vt* inalare // *vi* (*in smoking*) aspirare.

inherent |in'hiərənt| *a*: **~** (**in** *or* **to**) inerente (a).

inherit |in'herit| *vt* ereditare; ~**ance** *n* eredità.

inhibit |in'hibit| *vt* (*PSYCH*) inibire; **to ~ sb from doing** impedire a qn di fare; ~**ion** |-'biʃən| *n* inibizione *f*.

inhospitable |inhɔs'pitəbl| *a* inospitale.

inhuman |in'hju:mən| *a* inumano(a).

initial |i'niʃl| *a* iniziale // *n* iniziale *f* // *vt* siglare; ~**s** *npl* iniziali *fpl*; (*as signature*) sigla; ~**ly** *ad* inizialmente, all'inizio.

initiate |i'niʃieit| *vt* (*start*) avviare; intraprendere; iniziare; (*person*) iniziare.

initiative |i'niʃətiv| *n* iniziativa.

inject |in'dʒɛkt| *vt* (*liquid*) iniettare; (*person*) fare una puntura a; ~**ion** |in'dʒɛkʃən| *n* iniezione *f*, puntura.

injure |'indʒə*| *vt* ferire; (*wrong*) fare male *or* torto a; (*damage: reputation etc*) nuocere a; ~**d** *a* (*person, arm*) ferito(a).

injury |'indʒəri| *n* ferita; (*wrong*) torto; **~ time** *n* (*SPORT*) tempo di recupero.

injustice |in'dʒʌstis| *n* ingiustizia.

ink |iŋk| *n* inchiostro.

inkling |'iŋkliŋ| *n* sentóre *m*, vaga idea.

inlaid |'inleid| *a* incrostato(a); (*table etc*) intarsiato(a).

inland *a* |'inlənd| interno(a) // *ad* |in'lænd| all'interno; **I~ Revenue** *n* (*Brit*) Fisco.

in-laws |'inlɔ:z| *npl* suoceri *mpl*; famiglia del marito (*or* della moglie).

inlet |'inlɛt| *n* (*GEO*) insenatura, baia.

inmate |'inmeit| *n* (*in prison*) carcerato/a; (*in asylum*) ricoverato/a.

inn |in| *n* locanda.

innate |i'neit| *a* innato(a).

inner |'inə*| *a* interno(a), interiore; **~ city** *n* centro di una zona urbana; **~ tube** *n* camera d'aria.

innings |'iniŋz| *n* (*CRICKET*) turno di battuta.

innocence |'inəsns| *n* innocenza.

innocent |'inəsnt| *a* innocente.

innocuous |i'nɔkjuəs| *a* innocuo(a).

innuendo, ~**es** |inju'ɛndəu| *n* insinuazione *f*.

innumerable |i'nju:mrəbl| *a* innumerevole.

inordinately |i'nɔ:dinətli| *ad* smoderatamente.

in-patient |'inpeiʃənt| *n* ricoverato/a.

input ['input] n (ELEC) energia, potenza; (of machine) alimentazione f; (of computer) input m.

inquest ['inkwɛst] n inchiesta.

inquire [in'kwaiə*] vi informarsi // vt domandare, informarsi su; **to ~ about** vt fus informarsi di or su; **to ~ into** vt fus fare indagini su; **inquiry** n domanda; (LAW) indagine f, investigazione f; **inquiry office** n (Brit) ufficio m informazioni inv.

inquisitive [in'kwizitiv] a curioso(a).

inroad ['inrəud] n incursione f.

insane [in'sein] a matto(a), pazzo(a); (MED) alienato(a).

insanity [in'sæniti] n follia; (MED) alienazione f mentale.

inscription [in'skripʃən] n iscrizione f; dedica.

inscrutable [in'skru:təbl] a imperscrutabile.

insect ['insɛkt] n insetto; **~icide** [in'sɛktisaid] n insetticida m.

insecure [insi'kjuə*] a malsicuro(a); (person) insicuro(a)

insemination [insɛmi'neiʃən] n: **artificial ~** fecondazione f artificiale.

insensible [in'sɛnsibl] a insensibile; (unconscious) privo(a) di sensi.

insensitive [in'sɛnsitiv] a insensibile.

insert vt [in'sə:t] inserire, introdurre // n ['insə:t] inserto; **~ion** [in'sə:ʃən] n inserzione f.

in-service [in'sə:vis] a (training, course) durante l'orario di lavoro.

inshore [in'ʃɔ:*] a costiero(a) // ad presso la riva; verso la riva.

inside ['in'said] n interno, parte f interiore // a interno(a), interiore // ad dentro, all'interno // prep dentro, all'interno di; (of time): **~ 10 minutes** entro 10 minuti; **~s** npl (col) ventre m; **~ forward** n (SPORT) mezzala, interno; **~ lane** n (AUT) corsia di marcia; **~ out** ad (turn) a rovescio; (know) in fondo; to turn sth **~ out** rivoltare qc.

insight ['insait] n acume m, perspicacia; (glimpse, idea) percezione f.

insignia [in'signiə] npl insegne fpl.

insignificant [insig'nifikənt] a insignificante.

insincere [insin'siə*] a insincero(a).

insinuate [in'sinjueit] vt insinuare.

insist [in'sist] vi insistere; **to ~ on doing** insistere per fare; **to ~ that** insistere perché + sub; (claim) sostenere che; **~ent** a insistente.

insole ['insəul] n soletta.

insolent ['insələnt] a insolente.

insomnia [in'sɔmniə] n insonnia.

inspect [in'spɛkt] vt ispezionare; (ticket) controllare; **~ion** [in'spɛkʃən] n ispezione f; controllo; **~or** n ispettore/trice; (Brit: on buses, trains) controllore m.

inspire [in'spaiə*] vt ispirare.

install [in'stɔ:l] vt installare; **~ation** [instə'leiʃən] n installazione f.

instalment, (US) **installment** [in'stɔ:lmənt] n rata; (of TV serial etc) puntata; **in ~s** (pay) a rate; (receive) una parte per volta; (: publication) a fascicoli.

instance ['instəns] n esempio, caso; **for ~** per or ad esempio; **in many ~s** in molti casi; **in the first ~** in primo luogo.

instant ['instənt] n istante m, attimo // a immediato(a); urgente; (coffee, food) in polvere; **~ly** ad immediatamente, subito.

instead [in'stɛd] ad invece; **~ of** invece di; **~ of sb** al posto di qn.

instep ['instɛp] n collo del piede; (of shoe) collo della scarpa.

instil [in'stil] vt: to **~ (into)** inculcare (in).

instinct ['instiŋkt] n istinto.

institute ['institju:t] n istituto // vt istituire, stabilire; (inquiry) avviare; (proceedings) iniziare.

institution [insti'tju:ʃən] n istituzione f; istituto (d'istruzione); istituto (psichiatrico).

instruct [in'strʌkt] vt istruire; to **~ sb in sth** insegnare qc a qn; to **~ sb to do** dare ordini a qn di fare; **~ion** [in'strʌkʃən] n istruzione f; **~ions** (for use) istruzioni per l'uso; **~or** n istruttore/trice; (for skiing) maestro/a.

instrument ['instrəmənt] n strumento; **~al** [-'mɛntl] a (MUS) strumentale; **to be ~al in** essere d'aiuto in; **~ panel** n quadro m portastrumenti inv.

insufficient [insə'fiʃənt] a insufficiente.

insular ['insjulə*] a insulare; (person) di mente ristretta.

insulate ['insjuleit] vt isolare; **insulating tape** n nastro isolante; **insulation** [-'leiʃən] n isolamento.

insulin ['insjulin] n insulina.

insult n ['insʌlt] insulto, affronto // vt [in'sʌlt] insultare; **~ing** a offensivo(a), ingiurioso(a).

insuperable [in'sju:prəbl] a insormontabile, insuperabile.

insurance [in'ʃuərəns] n assicurazione f; **fire/life ~** assicurazione contro gli incendi/sulla vita; **~ policy** n polizza d'assicurazione.

insure [in'ʃuə*] vt assicurare.

intact [in'tækt] a intatto(a).

intake ['inteik] n (TECH) immissione f; (of food) consumo; (Brit: of pupils etc) afflusso.

integral ['intigrəl] a integrale; (part) integrante.

integrate ['intigreit] vt integrare.

integrity [in'tegriti] n integrità.

intellect ['intəlɛkt] n intelletto; **~ual** [-'lɛktjuəl] a, n intellettuale (m/f).

intelligence [ɪn'tɛlɪdʒəns] n intelligenza; (*MIL etc*) informazioni *fpl*.
intelligent [ɪn'tɛlɪdʒənt] a intelligente.
intend [ɪn'tɛnd] vt (*gift etc*): to ~ sth for destinare qc a; to ~ to do aver l'intenzione di fare; **~ed** a (*effect*) voluto(a).
intense [ɪn'tɛns] a intenso(a); (*person*) di forti sentimenti; **~ly** ad intensamente; profondamente.
intensive [ɪn'tɛnsɪv] a intensivo(a); ~ **care unit** n reparto terapia intensiva.
intent [ɪn'tɛnt] n intenzione f // a: ~ (on) intento(a) a, immerso(a) in; to all ~s and purposes a tutti gli effetti; to be ~ on doing sth essere deciso a fare qc.
intention [ɪn'tɛnʃən] n intenzione f; **~al** a intenzionale, deliberato(a); **~ally** ad apposta.
intently [ɪn'tɛntlɪ] ad attentamente.
inter [ɪn'tə:*] vt sotterrare.
interact [ɪntər'ækt] vi agire reciprocamente, interagire.
interchange n ['ɪntətʃeɪndʒ] (*exchange*) scambio; (*on motorway*) incrocio pluridirezionale // vt [ɪntə'tʃeɪndʒ] scambiare; sostituire l'uno(a) per l'altro(a); **~able** a intercambiabile.
intercom ['ɪntəkɔm] n interfono.
intercourse ['ɪntəkɔ:s] n rapporti mpl.
interest ['ɪntrɪst] n interesse m; (*COMM: stake, share*) interessi mpl // vt interessare; **~ed** a interessato(a); to be ~ed in interessarsi di; **~ing** a interessante; ~ **rate** n tasso di interesse.
interface ['ɪntəfeɪs] n (*COMPUT*) interfaccia.
interfere [ɪntə'fɪə*] vi: to ~ in (*quarrel, other people's business*) immischiarsi in; to ~ with (*object*) toccare; (*plans*) ostacolare; (*duty*) interferire con.
interference [ɪntə'fɪərəns] n interferenza.
interim ['ɪntərɪm] a provvisorio(a) // n: in the ~ nel frattempo.
interior [ɪn'tɪərɪə*] n interno; (*of country*) entroterra // a interiore, interno(a); ~ **designer** n arredatore/trice.
interlock [ɪntə'lɔk] vi ingranarsi // vt ingranare.
interloper ['ɪntələupə*] n intruso/a.
interlude ['ɪntəlu:d] n intervallo; (*THEATRE*) intermezzo.
intermediate [ɪntə'mi:dɪət] a intermedio(a); (*SCOL: course, level*) medio(a).
intermission [ɪntə'mɪʃən] n pausa; (*THEATRE, CINEMA*) intermissione f, intervallo.
intern vt [ɪn'tə:n] internare // n ['ɪntə:n] (*US*) medico interno.
internal [ɪn'tə:nl] a interno(a); **~ly** ad all'interno; "not to be taken ~ly" "per uso esterno"; **I~ Revenue Service (IRS)** n (*US*) Fisco.

international [ɪntə'næʃənl] a internazionale.
interplay ['ɪntəpleɪ] n azione e reazione f.
interpret [ɪn'tə:prɪt] vt interpretare // vi fare da interprete; **~er** n interprete m/f.
interrelated [ɪntərɪ'leɪtɪd] a correlato(a).
interrogate [ɪn'tɛrəugeɪt] vt interrogare; **interrogation** [-'geɪʃən] n interrogazione f; (*of suspect etc*) interrogatorio; **interrogative** [ɪntə'rɔgətɪv] a interrogativo(a).
interrupt [ɪntə'rʌpt] vt interrompere; **~ion** [-'rʌpʃən] n interruzione f.
intersect [ɪntə'sɛkt] vt intersecare // vi (*roads*) intersecarsi; **~ion** [-'sɛkʃən] n intersezione f; (*of roads*) incrocio.
intersperse [ɪntə'spə:s] vt: to ~ with costellare di.
intertwine [ɪntə'twaɪn] vt intrecciare // vi intrecciarsi.
interval ['ɪntəvl] n intervallo; at **~s** a intervalli.
intervene [ɪntə'vi:n] vi (*time*) intercorrere; (*event, person*) intervenire; **intervention** [-'vɛnʃən] n intervento.
interview ['ɪntəvju:] n (*RADIO, TV etc*) intervista; (*for job*) colloquio // vt intervistare; avere un colloquio con; **~er** n intervistatore/trice.
intestine [ɪn'tɛstɪn] n intestino.
intimacy ['ɪntɪməsɪ] n intimità.
intimate a ['ɪntɪmət] intimo(a); (*knowledge*) profondo(a) // vt ['ɪntɪmeɪt] lasciar capire.
into ['ɪntu:] prep dentro, in; come ~ the house vieni dentro la casa; ~ Italian in italiano.
intolerable [ɪn'tɔlərəbl] a intollerabile.
intolerance [ɪn'tɔlərns] n intolleranza.
intolerant [ɪn'tɔlərnt] a: ~ of intollerante di.
intoxicate [ɪn'tɔksɪkeɪt] vt inebriare; **~d** a inebriato(a); **intoxication** [-'keɪʃən] n ebbrezza.
intractable [ɪn'træktəbl] a intrattabile.
intransitive [ɪn'trænsɪtɪv] a intransitivo(a).
intravenous [ɪntrə'vi:nəs] a endovenoso(a).
in-tray ['ɪntreɪ] n contenitore m per la corrispondenza in arrivo.
intricate ['ɪntrɪkət] a intricato(a), complicato(a).
intrigue [ɪn'tri:g] n intrigo // vt affascinare // vi complottare, tramare; **intriguing** a affascinante.
intrinsic [ɪn'trɪnsɪk] a intrinseco(a).
introduce [ɪntrə'dju:s] vt introdurre; to ~ sb (to sb) presentare qn (a qn); to ~ sb to (*pastime, technique*) iniziare qn a; **introduction** [-'dʌkʃən] n introduzione f; (*of person*) presentazione f; **introductory** a introduttivo(a).
intrude [ɪn'tru:d] vi (*person*): to ~ (on)

intromettersi (in); **am I intruding?** disturbo?; **~r** n intruso/a.

intuition |ɪntju:'ɪʃən| n intuizione f.

inundate |'ɪnʌndeɪt| vt: **to ~ with** inondare di.

invade |ɪn'veɪd| vt invadere.

invalid n |'ɪnvəlɪd| malato/a; (with disability) invalido/a // a |ɪn'vælɪd| (not valid) invalido(a), non valido(a).

invaluable |ɪn'væljuəbl| a prezioso(a); inestimabile.

invariably |ɪn'vɛərɪəblɪ| ad invariabilmente; sempre.

invasion |ɪn'veɪʒən| n invasione f.

invent |ɪn'vent| vt inventare; **~ion** |ɪn'venʃən| n invenzione f; **~ive** a inventivo(a); **~or** n inventore m.

inventory |'ɪnvəntrɪ| n inventario.

invert |ɪn'vɜ:t| vt invertire; (cup, object) rovesciare; **~ed commas** npl (Brit) virgolette fpl.

invest |ɪn'vest| vt investire // vi fare investimenti.

investigate |ɪn'vestɪgeɪt| vt investigare, indagare; (crime) fare indagini su; **investigation** |-'geɪʃən| n investigazione f; (of crime) indagine f.

investment |ɪn'vestmənt| n investimento.

investor |ɪn'vestə*| n investitore/trice; azionista m/f.

invidious |ɪn'vɪdɪəs| a odioso(a); (task) spiacevole.

invigilate |ɪn'vɪdʒɪleɪt| vt, vi (in exam) sorvegliare.

invigorating |ɪn'vɪgəreɪtɪŋ| a stimolante; vivificante.

invisible |ɪn'vɪzɪbl| a invisibile; **~ ink** n inchiostro simpatico.

invitation |ɪnvɪ'teɪʃən| n invito.

invite |ɪn'vaɪt| vt invitare; (opinions etc) sollecitare; (trouble) provocare; **inviting** a invitante, attraente.

invoice |'ɪnvɔɪs| n fattura.

involuntary |ɪn'vɔləntrɪ| a involontario(a).

involve |ɪn'vɔlv| vt (entail) richiedere, comportare; (associate): **to ~ sb (in)** implicare qn (in); coinvolgere qn (in); **~d a** involuto(a), complesso(a); **to feel ~d** sentirsi coinvolto(a); **~ment (in)** implicazione f; coinvolgimento; **~ment (in)** impegno (in); partecipazione f (in).

inward |'ɪnwəd| a (movement) verso l'interno; (thought, feeling) interiore, intimo(a); **~(s)** ad verso l'interno.

I/O abbr (COMPUT: = input/output) I/O.

iodine |'aɪəʊdi:n| n iodio.

iota |aɪ'əʊtə| n (fig) briciolo.

IOU n abbr (= I owe you) pagherò m inv.

IQ n abbr (= intelligence quotient) quoziente m d'intelligenza.

IRA n abbr (= Irish Republican Army) IRA f.

Iran |ɪ'rɑ:n| n Iran m.

Iraq |ɪ'rɑ:k| n Iraq m.

Ireland |'aɪələnd| n Irlanda.

iris, ~es |'aɪrɪs, -ɪz| n iride f; (BOT) giaggiolo, iride.

Irish |'aɪrɪʃ| a irlandese // npl: **the ~** gli Irlandesi; **~man** n irlandese m; **~ Sea** n Mar m d'Irlanda; **~woman** n irlandese f.

irksome |'ɜ:ksəm| a seccante.

iron |'aɪən| n ferro; (for clothes) ferro da stiro // a di or in ferro // vt (clothes) stirare; **to ~ out** vt (crease) appianare; (fig) spianare; far sparire; **the I~ Curtain** n la cortina di ferro.

ironic(al) |aɪ'rɒnɪk(l)| a ironico(a).

ironing |'aɪənɪŋ| n (act) stirare m; (clothes) roba da stirare; **~ board** n asse f da stiro.

ironmonger |'aɪənmʌŋgə*| n (Brit) negoziante m in ferramenta; **~'s (shop)** n negozio di ferramenta.

ironworks |'aɪənwɜ:ks| n ferriera.

irony |'aɪrənɪ| n ironia.

irrational |ɪ'ræʃənl| a irrazionale; irragionevole; illogico(a).

irregular |ɪ'regjulə*| a irregolare.

irrelevant |ɪ'reləvənt| a non pertinente.

irreplaceable |ɪrɪ'pleɪsəbl| a insostituibile.

irrepressible |ɪrɪ'presbl| a irrefrenabile.

irresistible |ɪrɪ'zɪstɪbl| a irresistibile.

irrespective |ɪrɪ'spektɪv|: **~ of** prep senza riguardo a.

irresponsible |ɪrɪ'spɒnsɪbl| a irresponsabile.

irrigate |'ɪrɪgeɪt| vt irrigare; **irrigation** |-'geɪʃən| n irrigazione f.

irritable |'ɪrɪtəbl| a irritabile.

irritate |'ɪrɪteɪt| vt irritare; **irritating** a (person, sound etc) irritante; **irritation** |-'teɪʃən| n irritazione f.

IRS n abbr = **Internal Revenue Service**.

is |ɪz| vb see **be**.

Islam |'ɪzlɑ:m| n Islam m.

island |'aɪlənd| n isola; (also: traffic ~) salvagente m; **~er** n isolano/a.

isle |aɪl| n isola.

isn't |'ɪznt| = **is not**.

isolate |'aɪsəleɪt| vt isolare; **~d** a isolato(a); **isolation** |-'leɪʃən| n isolamento.

Israel |'ɪzreɪl| n Israele m; **~i** |ɪz'reɪlɪ| a, n israeliano(a).

issue |'ɪʃju:| n questione f, problema m; (outcome) esito, risultato; (of banknotes etc) emissione f; (of newspaper etc) numero; (offspring) discendenza // vt (rations, equipment) distribuire; (orders) dare; (book) pubblicare; (banknotes, cheques, stamps) emettere; **at ~** in gioco, in discussione; **to take ~ with sb (over sth)** prendere posizione contro qn (riguardo a qc).

isthmus |'ɪsməs| n istmo.

it [ɪt] *pronoun* **1** (*specific: subject*) esso(a); (: *direct object*) lo(la), l'; (: *indirect object*) gli(le); **where's my book?** — **~'s on the table** dov'è il mio libro? — è sulla tavola; **I can't find ~** non lo (*or* la) trovo; **give ~ to me** dammelo (*or* dammela); **about/from/of ~** ne; **I spoke to him about ~** gliene ho parlato; **what did you learn from ~?** quale insegnamento ne hai tratto?; **I'm proud of ~** ne sono fiero; **did you go to ~?** ci sei andato?; **put the book in ~** mettici il libro
2 (*impersonal*): **~'s raining** piove; **~'s Friday tomorrow** domani è venerdì; **~'s 6 o'clock** sono le 6; **who is ~?** — **~'s me** chi è? — sono io.

Italian [ɪ'tæljən] *a* italiano(a) // *n* italiano/a; (*LING*) italiano; **the ~s** gli Italiani.

italic [ɪ'tælɪk] *a* corsivo(a); **~s** *npl* corsivo.

Italy [ˈɪtəlɪ] *n* Italia.

itch [ɪtʃ] *n* prurito // *vi* (*person*) avere il prurito; (*part of body*) prudere; **to be ~ing to do sth** aver una gran voglia di fare qc; **~y** *a* che prude; **to be ~y** = **to ~**.

it'd [ˈɪtd] = **it would**; **it had**.

item [ˈaɪtəm] *n* articolo; (*on agenda*) punto; (*in programme*) numero; (*also: news ~*) notizia; **~ize** *vt* specificare, dettagliare.

itinerant [ɪ'tɪnərənt] *a* ambulante.

itinerary [aɪ'tɪnərərɪ] *n* itinerario.

it'll [ˈɪtl] = **it will**, **it shall**.

its [ɪts] *a* il(la) suo(a), i(le) suoi(sue).

it's [ɪts] = **it is**; **it has**.

itself [ɪt'sɛlf] *pronoun* (*emphatic*) esso(a) stesso(a); (*reflexive*) si.

ITV *n abbr* (*Brit*: = *Independent Television*) rete televisiva in concorrenza con la BBC.

I.U.D. *n abbr* (= *intra-uterine device*) spirale *f*.

I've [aɪv] = **I have**.

ivory [ˈaɪvərɪ] *n* avorio.

ivy [ˈaɪvɪ] *n* edera.

J

jab [dʒæb] *vt*: **to ~ sth into** affondare *or* piantare qc dentro // *n* colpo; (*MED*: *col*) puntura.

jack [dʒæk] *n* (*AUT*) cricco; (*CARDS*) fante *m*; **to ~ up** *vt* sollevare sul cricco.

jackal [ˈdʒækl] *n* sciacallo.

jackdaw [ˈdʒækdɔː] *n* taccola.

jacket [ˈdʒækɪt] *n* giacca; (*of book*) copertura.

jack-knife [ˈdʒæknaɪf] *vi*: **the lorry ~d** l'autotreno si è piegato su se stesso.

jack plug *n* (*ELEC*) jack *m inv*.

jackpot [ˈdʒækpɔt] *n* primo premio (in denaro).

jade [dʒeɪd] *n* (*stone*) giada.

jaded [ˈdʒeɪdɪd] *a* sfinito(a), spossato(a).

jagged [ˈdʒægɪd] *a* sbocconcellato(a); (*cliffs etc*) frastagliato(a).

jail [dʒeɪl] *n* prigione *f* // *vt* mandare in prigione; **~er** *n* custode *m* del carcere.

jam [dʒæm] *n* marmellata; (*of shoppers etc*) ressa; (*also:* **traffic ~**) ingorgo // *vt* (*passage etc*) ingombrare, ostacolare; (*mechanism, drawer etc*) bloccare; (*RADIO*) disturbare con interferenze // *vi* (*mechanism, sliding part*) incepparsi, bloccarsi; (*gun*) incepparsi; **to ~ sth into** forzare qc dentro; infilare qc a forza dentro.

Jamaica [dʒə'meɪkə] *n* Giamaica.

jangle [ˈdʒæŋgl] *vi* risuonare; (*bracelet*) tintinnare.

janitor [ˈdʒænɪtə*] *n* (*caretaker*) portiere *m*; (: *SCOL*) bidello.

January [ˈdʒænjuərɪ] *n* gennaio.

Japan [dʒə'pæn] *n* Giappone *m*; **~ese** [dʒæpə'niːz] *a* giapponese // *n* (*pl inv*) giapponese *m/f*; (*LING*) giapponese *m*.

jar [dʒɑː*] *n* (*glass*) barattolo, vasetto // *vi* (*sound*) stridere; (*colours etc*) stonare.

jargon [ˈdʒɑːgən] *n* gergo.

jasmin(e) [ˈdʒæzmɪn] *n* gelsomino.

jaundice [ˈdʒɔːndɪs] *n* itterizia; **~d** *a* (*fig*) invidioso(a) e critico(a).

jaunt [dʒɔːnt] *n* gita; **~y** *a* vivace; disinvolto(a).

javelin [ˈdʒævlɪn] *n* giavellotto.

jaw [dʒɔː] *n* mascella.

jay [dʒeɪ] *n* ghiandaia.

jaywalker [ˈdʒeɪwɔːkə*] *n* pedone(a) indisciplinato(a).

jazz [dʒæz] *n* jazz *m*; **to ~ up** *vt* rendere vivace.

jealous [ˈdʒɛləs] *a* geloso(a); **~y** *n* gelosia.

jeans [dʒiːnz] *npl* (blue-)jeans *mpl*.

jeer [dʒɪə*] *vi*: **to ~ (at)** fischiare; beffeggiare.

jelly [ˈdʒɛlɪ] *n* gelatina; **~fish** *n* medusa.

jeopardy [ˈdʒɛpədɪ] *n*: **in ~** in pericolo.

jerk [dʒɜːk] *n* sobbalzo, scossa; sussulto // *vt* dare una scossa a // *vi* (*vehicles*) sobbalzare.

jerkin [ˈdʒɜːkɪn] *n* giubbotto.

jersey [ˈdʒɜːzɪ] *n* maglia.

jest [dʒɛst] *n* scherzo.

Jesus [ˈdʒiːzəs] *n* Gesù *m*.

jet [dʒɛt] *n* (*of gas, liquid*) getto; (*AVIAT*) aviogetto; **~-black** *a* nero(a) come l'ebano, corvino(a); **~ engine** *n* motore *m* a reazione; **~ lag** *n* (problemi *mpl* dovuti allo) sbalzo dei fusi orari.

jettison [ˈdʒɛtɪsn] *vt* gettare in mare.

jetty [ˈdʒɛtɪ] *n* molo.

Jew [dʒuː] *n* ebreo.

jewel [ˈdʒuːəl] *n* gioiello; **~ler** *n* orefice

m, gioielliere/a; **~ler's (shop)** *n* oreficeria, gioielleria; **~lery** *n* gioielli *mpl*.

Jewess ['dʒu:ɪs] *n* ebrea.

Jewish ['dʒu:ɪʃ] *a* ebreo(a), ebraico(a).

jib [dʒɪb] *n* (*NAUT*) fiocco; (*of crane*) braccio.

jibe [dʒaɪb] *n* beffa.

jiffy ['dʒɪfɪ] *n* (*col*): **in a ~** in un batter d'occhio.

jig [dʒɪg] *n* giga.

jigsaw ['dʒɪgsɔ:] *n* (*also*: **~ puzzle**) puzzle *m inv*.

jilt [dʒɪlt] *vt* piantare in asso.

jingle ['dʒɪŋgl] *n* (*advert*) sigla pubblicitaria // *vi* tintinnare, scampanellare.

jinx [dʒɪŋks] *n* (*col*) iettatura; (*person*) iettatore/trice.

jitters ['dʒɪtəz] *npl* (*col*): **to get the ~** aver fifa.

job [dʒɔb] *n* lavoro; (*employment*) impiego, posto; **it's a good ~ that ...** meno male che ...; **just the ~!** proprio quello che ci vuole; **~ centre** *n* (*Brit*) ufficio di collocamento; **~less** *a* senza lavoro, disoccupato(a).

jockey ['dʒɔkɪ] *n* fantino, jockey *m inv* // *vi*: **to ~ for position** manovrare per una posizione di vantaggio.

jocular ['dʒɔkjulə*] *a* gioviale; scherzoso(a).

jog [dʒɔg] *vt* urtare // *vi* (*SPORT*) fare footing, fare jogging; **to ~ along** trottare; (*fig*) andare avanti piano piano; **~ging** *n* footing *m*, jogging *m*.

join [dʒɔɪn] *vt* unire, congiungere; (*become member of*) iscriversi a; (*meet*) raggiungere; riunirsi a // *vi* (*roads, rivers*) confluire // *n* giuntura; **to ~ in** *vi* partecipare // *vt fus* unirsi a; **to ~ up** *vi* arruolarsi.

joiner ['dʒɔɪnə*] *n* falegname *m*; **~y** *n* falegnameria.

joint [dʒɔɪnt] *n* (*TECH*) giuntura; giunto; (*ANAT*) articolazione *f*, giuntura; (*Brit CULIN*) arrosto; (*col: place*) locale *m* // *a* comune; **~ account** *n* (*at bank etc*) conto in partecipazione, conto comune; **~ly** *ad* in comune, insieme.

joist [dʒɔɪst] *n* trave *f*.

joke [dʒəuk] *n* scherzo; (*funny story*) barzelletta; (*also*: **practical ~**) beffa // *vi* scherzare; **to play a ~ on sb** fare uno scherzo a qn; **~r** *n* buffone/a, burlone/a; (*CARDS*) matta, jolly *m inv*.

jolly ['dʒɔlɪ] *a* allegro(a), gioioso(a) // *ad* (*col*) veramente, proprio.

jolt [dʒəult] *n* scossa, sobbalzo // *vt* urtare.

Jordan ['dʒɔ:dən] *n* (*country*) Giordania; (*river*) Giordano.

jostle ['dʒɔsl] *vt* spingere coi gomiti // *vi* farsi spazio coi gomiti.

jot [dʒɔt] *n*: **not one ~** nemmeno un po'; **to ~ down** *vt* annotare in fretta,

buttare giù; **~ter** *n* (*Brit*) blocco.

journal ['dʒə:nl] *n* giornale *m*; rivista; diario; **~ism** *n* giornalismo; **~ist** *n* giornalista *m/f*.

journey ['dʒə:nɪ] *n* viaggio; (*distance covered*) tragitto // *vi* viaggiare.

joy [dʒɔɪ] *n* gioia; **~ful, ~ous** *a* gioioso(a), allegro(a); **~ ride** *n* gita in automobile (*specialmente rubata*); **~stick** *n* (*AVIAT*) barra di comando; (*COMPUT*) joystick *m inv*.

J.P. *n abbr* = **Justice of the Peace**.

Jr, Jun., Junr *abbr* = **junior**.

jubilant ['dʒu:bɪlnt] *a* giubilante; trionfante.

jubilee ['dʒu:bɪli:] *n* giubileo; **silver ~** venticinquesimo anniversario.

judge [dʒʌdʒ] *n* giudice *m/f* // *vt* giudicare; **judg(e)ment** *n* giudizio; (*punishment*) punizione *f*.

judicial [dʒu:'dɪʃl] *a* giudiziale, giudiziario(a).

judiciary [dʒu:'dɪʃɪərɪ] *n* magistratura.

judo ['dʒu:dəu] *n* judo.

jug [dʒʌg] *n* brocca, bricco.

juggernaut ['dʒʌgənɔ:t] *n* (*Brit: huge truck*) bestione *m*.

juggle ['dʒʌgl] *vi* fare giochi di destrezza; **~r** *n* giocoliere/a.

Jugoslav ['ju:gəuslɑ:v] *etc* = **Yugoslav** *etc*.

juice [dʒu:s] *n* succo.

juicy ['dʒu:sɪ] *a* succoso(a).

jukebox ['dʒu:kbɔks] *n* juke-box *m inv*.

July [dʒu:'laɪ] *n* luglio.

jumble ['dʒʌmbl] *n* miscuglio // *vt* (*also*: **~ up**) mischiare; **~ sale** *n* (*Brit*) vendita di oggetti per beneficenza.

jumbo (jet) ['dʒʌmbəu-] *n* jumbo-jet *m inv*.

jump [dʒʌmp] *vi* saltare, balzare; (*start*) sobbalzare; (*increase*) rincarare // *vt* saltare // *n* salto, balzo; sobbalzo.

jumper ['dʒʌmpə*] *n* (*Brit: pullover*) maglione *m*, pullover *m inv*; (*US: dress*) scamiciato; **~ cables** *npl* (*US*) = **jump leads**.

jump leads *npl* (*Brit*) cavi *mpl* per batteria.

jumpy ['dʒʌmpɪ] *a* nervoso(a), agitato(a).

junction ['dʒʌŋkʃən] *n* (*Brit: of roads*) incrocio; (*of rails*) nodo ferroviario.

juncture ['dʒʌŋktʃə*] *n*: **at this ~** in questa congiuntura.

June [dʒu:n] *n* giugno.

jungle ['dʒʌŋgl] *n* giungla.

junior ['dʒu:nɪə*] *a, n*: **he's ~ to me (by 2 years), he's my ~ (by 2 years)** è più giovane di me (di 2 anni); **he's ~ to me** (*seniority*) è al di sotto di me, ho più anzianità di lui; **~ school** *n* (*Brit*) scuola elementare (*da 8 a 11 anni*).

junk [dʒʌŋk] *n* (*rubbish*) chincaglia; (*ship*) giunca; **~ food** *n* porcherie *fpl*;

~ **shop** n chincaglieria.
juror ['dʒuərə*] n giurato/a.
jury ['dʒuəri] n giuria.
just [dʒʌst] a giusto(a) // ad: he's ~ done
it/left lo ha appena fatto/è appena
partito; ~ as I expected proprio come
me lo aspettavo; ~ **right** proprio giusto;
~ 2 o'clock le 2 precise; she's ~ as
clever as you è in gamba proprio quanto
te; it's ~ as well that ... meno male
che ...; ~ as I arrived proprio mentre
arrivavo; it was ~ before/enough/here
era poco prima/appena assai/proprio qui;
it's ~ me sono solo io; it's ~ a mistake
non è che uno sbaglio; ~ missed/caught
appena perso/preso; ~ **listen to this**!
senta un po' questo!
justice ['dʒʌstɪs] n giustizia; **J~ of the
Peace (J.P.)** n giudice m conciliatore.
justify ['dʒʌstɪfaɪ] vt giustificare.
jut [dʒʌt] vi (also: ~ out) sporgersi.
juvenile ['dʒuːvənaɪl] a giovane,
giovanile; (court) dei minorenni;
(books) per ragazzi // n giovane m/f,
minorenne m/f.
juxtapose ['dʒʌkstəpəuz] vt giu-
stapporre.

K

K abbr (= one thousand) mille; (=
kilobyte) K.
kangaroo [kæŋgə'ruː] n canguro.
karate [kə'rɑːtɪ] n karatè m.
kebab [kə'bæb] n spiedino.
keel [kiːl] n chiglia; **on an even** ~ (fig) in
uno stato normale.
keen [kiːn] a (interest, desire) vivo(a);
(eye, intelligence) acuto(a);
(competition) serrato(a); (edge) af-
filato(a); (eager) entusiasta; **to be** ~ **to
do or on doing sth** avere una gran voglia
di fare qc; **to be** ~ **on sth** essere
appassionato(a) di qc; **to be** ~ **on sb**
avere un debole per qn.
keep [kiːp] vb (pt, pp **kept**) vt tenere;
(hold back) trattenere; (feed: one's
family etc) mantenere, sostentare; (a
promise) mantenere; (chickens, bees,
pigs etc) allevare // vi (food)
mantenersi; (remain: in a certain state
or place) restare // n (of castle) maschio; (food etc): **enough for his** ~ abbastanza per vitto e alloggio; (col): **for** ~s
per sempre; **to** ~ **doing sth** continuare a
fare qc; fare qc di continuo; **to** ~ **sb
from doing/sth from happening** impedire
a qn di fare/che qc succeda; **to** ~ **sb
busy/a place tidy** tenere qn occupato(a)/
un luogo in ordine; **to** ~ **sth to o.s.** tenere
qc per sé; **to** ~ **sth (back) from sb**
celare qc a qn; **to** ~ **time** (clock) andar
bene; **to** ~ **on** vi continuare; **to** ~ **on
doing** continuare a fare; **to** ~ **out** vt

tener fuori; "**~ out**" "vietato l'accesso";
to ~ **up** vi mantenersi // vt continuare,
mantenere; **to** ~ **up with** tener dietro a,
andare di pari passo con; (work etc)
farcela a seguire; **~er** n custode m/f,
guardiano/a; **~-fit** n ginnastica; **~ing** n
(care) custodia; **in ~ing with** in armonia
con; in accordo con; **~sake** n ricordo.
keg [kɛg] n barilotto.
kennel ['kɛnl] n canile m.
kept [kɛpt] pt, pp of **keep**.
kerb [kəːb] n (Brit) orlo del marciapiede.
kernel ['kəːnl] n nocciolo.
kettle ['kɛtl] n bollitore m.
kettle drums npl timpano.
key [kiː] n (gen, MUS) chiave f; (of piano,
typewriter) tasto // vt (also: ~ **in**)
digitare; **~board** n tastiera; **~ed up** a
(person) agitato(a); **~hole** n buco della
serratura; **~note** n (MUS) tonica; (fig)
nota dominante; **~ring** n portachiavi m
inv.
khaki ['kɑːkɪ] a, n cachi (m).
kick [kɪk] vt calciare, dare calci a // vi
(horse) tirar calci // n calcio; (of rifle)
contraccolpo; (thrill): **he does it for** ~s
lo fa giusto per il piacere di farlo; **to** ~
off vi (SPORT) dare il primo calcio.
kid [kɪd] n (col: child) ragazzino/a;
(animal, leather) capretto // vi (col)
scherzare // vt (col) prendere in giro.
kidnap ['kɪdnæp] vt rapire, sequestrare;
~per n rapitore/trice; **~ping** n sequestro (di persona).
kidney ['kɪdnɪ] n (ANAT) rene m;
(CULIN) rognone m.
kill [kɪl] vt uccidere, ammazzare; (fig)
sopprimere; sopraffare; ammazzare // n
uccisione f; **~er** n uccisore m, killer m
inv; assassino/a; **~ing** n assassinio;
(massacre) strage f; **~joy** n guastafeste
m/f inv.
kiln [kɪln] n forno.
kilo ['kiːləu] n chilo; **~byte** n (COMPUT)
kilobyte m inv; **~gram(me)**
['kɪləugræm] n chilogrammo; **~metre**,
(US) **~meter** ['kɪləmiːtə*] n chilometro;
~watt ['kɪləuwɔt] n chilowatt m inv.
kilt [kɪlt] n gonnellino scozzese.
kin [kɪn] n see **next**, **kith**.
kind [kaɪnd] a gentile, buono(a) // n sorta,
specie f; (species) genere m; **to be two
of a** ~ essere molto simili; **in** ~ (COMM)
in natura.
kindergarten ['kɪndəgɑːtn] n giardino
d'infanzia.
kind-hearted [kaɪnd'hɑːtɪd] a di buon
cuore.
kindle ['kɪndl] vt accendere, infiammare.
kindly ['kaɪndlɪ] a buono(a) di bontà,
benevolo(a) // ad con bontà, gentilmente;
will you ~... vuole ... per favore.
kindness ['kaɪndnɪs] n bontà, gentilezza.
kindred ['kɪndrɪd] a imparentato(a); ~
spirit n spirito affine.

king |kɪŋ| n re m inv; ~**dom** n regno, reame m; ~**fisher** n martin m inv pescatore; ~-**size** a super inv; gigante.

kinky |'kɪŋkɪ| a (fig) eccentrico(a); dai gusti particolari.

kiosk |'kiːɔsk| n edicola, chiosco; (Brit TEL) cabina (telefonica).

kipper |'kɪpə*| n aringa affumicata.

kiss |kɪs| n bacio // vt baciare; to ~ (each other) baciarsi.

kit |kɪt| n equipaggiamento, corredo; (set of tools etc) attrezzi mpl; (for assembly) scatola di montaggio.

kitchen |'kɪtʃɪn| n cucina; ~ **sink** n acquaio.

kite |kaɪt| n (toy) aquilone m; (ZOOL) nibbio.

kith |kɪθ| n: ~ **and kin** amici e parenti mpl.

kitten |'kɪtn| n gattino/a, micino/a.

kitty |'kɪtɪ| n (money) fondo comune.

knack |næk| n: to have the ~ of avere l'abilità di; there's a ~ to doing this c'è un trucco per fare questo.

knapsack |'næpsæk| n zaino, sacco da montagna.

knead |niːd| vt impastare.

knee |niː| n ginocchio; ~**cap** n rotula.

kneel, pt, pp **knelt** |niːl, nelt| vi (also: ~ down) inginocchiarsi.

knell |nɛl| n rintocco.

knew |njuː| pt of **know**.

knickers |'nɪkəz| npl (Brit) mutandine fpl.

knife |naɪf| n (pl **knives**) coltello // vt accoltellare, dare una coltellata a.

knight |naɪt| n cavaliere m; (CHESS) cavallo; ~**hood** n (title): to get a ~hood essere fatto cavaliere.

knit |nɪt| vt fare a maglia; (fig): to ~ together unire // vi lavorare a maglia; (broken bones) saldarsi; ~**ting** n lavoro a maglia; ~**ting needle** n ferro (da calza); ~**wear** n maglieria.

knives |naɪvz| npl of **knife**.

knob |nɔb| n bottone m; manopola.

knock |nɔk| vt colpire; urtare; (fig: col) criticare // vi (engine) battere; (at door etc): to ~ at/on bussare a // n bussata; colpo, botta; to ~ **down** vt abbattere; to ~ **off** vi (col: finish) smettere (di lavorare); to ~ **out** vt stendere; (BOXING) mettere K.O.; to ~ **over** vt (person) investire; (object) far cadere; ~**er** n (on door) battente m; ~-**kneed** a che ha le gambe ad x; ~**out** n (BOXING) knock out m inv.

knot |nɔt| n nodo // vt annodare; ~**ty** a (fig) spinoso(a).

know |nəu| vt (pt **knew**, pp **known**) sapere; (person, author, place) conoscere; to ~ how to do sapere fare; to ~ about or of sth/sb conoscere qc/qn; ~-**all** n sapientone/a; ~-**how** n tecnica; pratica; ~**ing** a (look etc) d'in-

tesa; ~**ingly** ad (purposely) consapevolmente; (smile, look) con aria d'intesa.

knowledge |'nɔlɪdʒ| n consapevolezza; (learning) conoscenza, sapere m; ~**able** a ben informato(a).

known |nəun| pp of **know**.

knuckle |'nʌkl| n nocca.

Koran |kɔ'rɑːn| n Corano.

Korea |kə'rɪə| n Corea.

kosher |'kəuʃə*| a kasher inv.

L

lab |læb| n abbr (= laboratory) laboratorio.

label |'leɪbl| n etichetta, cartellino; (brand: of record) casa // vt etichettare.

laboratory |lə'bɔrətərɪ| n laboratorio.

labour, (US) **labor** |'leɪbə*| n (task) lavoro; (workmen) manodopera; (MED) travaglio del parto, doglie fpl // vi: to ~ (at) lavorare duro (a); in ~ (MED) in travaglio; L~, the L~ party (Brit) il partito laburista, i laburisti; ~**ed** a (breathing) affannoso(a); (style) pesante; ~**er** n manovale m; (on farm) lavoratore m agricolo.

lace |leɪs| n merletto, pizzo; (of shoe etc) laccio // vt (shoe) allacciare.

lack |læk| n mancanza // vt mancare di; through or for ~ of per mancanza di; to be ~ing mancare; to be ~ing in mancare di.

lackadaisical |lækə'deɪzɪkl| a disinteressato(a), noncurante.

lacquer |'lækə*| n lacca.

lad |læd| n ragazzo, giovanotto.

ladder |'lædə*| n scala; (Brit: in tights) smagliatura // vt smagliare // vi smagliarsi.

laden |'leɪdn| a: ~ (with) carico(a) or caricato(a) (di).

ladle |'leɪdl| n mestolo.

lady |'leɪdɪ| n signora; dama; L~ Smith lady Smith; the ladies' (room) i gabinetti per signore; ~**bird**, (US) ~**bug** n coccinella; ~-**in-waiting** n dama di compagnia; ~**like** a da signora, distinto(a); ~**ship** n: your ~ship signora contessa (or baronessa etc).

lag |læg| vi (also: ~ behind) trascinarsi // vt (pipes) rivestire di materiale isolante.

lager |'lɑːgə*| n lager m inv.

lagoon |lə'guːn| n laguna.

laid |leɪd| pt, pp of **lay**; ~ **back** a (col) rilassato(a), tranquillo(a).

lain |leɪn| pp of **lie**.

lair |lɛə*| n covo, tana.

laity |'leɪətɪ| n laici mpl.

lake |leɪk| n lago.

lamb |læm| n agnello.

lame |leɪm| a zoppo(a).

lament |lə'mɛnt| n lamento // vt

lamentare, piangere.

laminated ['læmɪncɪtɪd] *a* laminato(a).

lamp [læmp] *n* lampada.

lampoon [læm'pu:n] *n* satira.

lamp: ~**post** *n* (*Brit*) lampione *m*; ~**shade** *n* paralume *m*.

lance [lɑ:ns] *n* lancia // *vt* (*MED*) incidere; ~ **corporal** *n* (*Brit*) caporale *m*.

land [lænd] *n* (*as opposed to sea*) terra (ferma); (*country*) paese *m*; (*soil*) terreno; suolo; (*estate*) terreni *mpl*, terre *fpl* // *vi* (*from ship*) sbarcare; (*AVIAT*) atterrare; (*fig: fall*) cadere // *vt* (*obtain*) acchiappare; (*passengers*) sbarcare; (*goods*) scaricare; **to ~ up** *vi* andare a finire; ~**ing** *n* sbarco; atterraggio; (*of staircase*) pianerottolo; ~**ing stage** *n* (*Brit*) pontile *m* da sbarco; ~**lady** *n* padrona *or* proprietaria di casa; ~**lord** *n* padrone *m or* proprietario di casa; (*of pub etc*) oste *m*; ~**mark** *n* punto di riferimento; (*fig*) pietra miliare; ~**owner** *n* proprietario(a) terriero(a).

landscape ['lænskeɪp] *n* paesaggio.

landslide ['lændslaɪd] *n* (*GEO*) frana; (*fig: POL*) valanga.

lane [leɪn] *n* (*in country*) viottolo; (*in town*) stradetta; (*AUT, in race*) corsia.

language ['læŋgwɪdʒ] *n* lingua; (*way one speaks*) linguaggio; **bad ~** linguaggio volgare; ~ **laboratory** *n* laboratorio linguistico.

languid ['læŋgwɪd] *a* languente; languido(a).

lank [læŋk] *a* (*hair*) liscio(a) e opaco(a).

lanky ['læŋkɪ] *a* allampanato(a).

lantern ['læntn] *n* lanterna.

lap [læp] *n* (*of track*) giro; (*of body*): **in** *or* **on one's ~** in grembo // *vt* (*also:* ~ **up**) papparsi, leccare // *vi* (*waves*) sciabordare.

lapel [lə'pɛl] *n* risvolto.

Lapland ['læplænd] *n* Lapponia.

lapse [læps] *n* lapsus *m inv*; (*longer*) caduta // *vi* (*law, act*) cadere; (*ticket, passport*) scadere; **to ~ into bad habits** pigliare cattive abitudini; ~ **of time** spazio di tempo.

larceny ['lɑ:sənɪ] *n* furto.

lard [lɑ:d] *n* lardo.

larder ['lɑ:də*] *n* dispensa.

large [lɑ:dʒ] *a* grande; (*person, animal*) grosso(a); **at ~** (*free*) in libertà; (*generally*) in generale; nell'insieme; ~**ly** *ad* in gran parte.

largesse [lɑ:'ʒɛs] *n* generosità.

lark [lɑ:k] *n* (*bird*) allodola; (*joke*) scherzo, gioco; **to ~ about** *vi* fare lo stupido.

laryngitis [lærɪn'dʒaɪtɪs] *n* laringite *f*.

laser ['leɪzə*] *n* laser *m*; ~ **printer** *n* stampante *f* laser *inv*.

lash [læʃ] *n* frustata; (*also:* eye~) ciglio // *vt* frustare; (*tie*) assicurare con una corda; **to ~ out** *vi*: **to ~ out** (at *or* against sb/sth) attaccare violentemente (qn/qc); **to ~ out** (on sth) (*col: spend*) spendere un sacco di soldi (per qc).

lass [læs] *n* ragazza.

lasso [læ'su:] *n* laccio.

last [lɑ:st] *a* ultimo(a); (*week, month, year*) scorso(a), passato(a) // *ad* per ultimo // *vi* durare; ~ **week** la settimana scorsa; ~ **night** ieri sera, la notte scorsa; **at ~** finalmente, alla fine; ~ **but one** penultimo(a); ~**-ditch** *a* (*attempt*) estremo(a); ~**ing** *a* durevole; ~**ly** *ad* infine, per finire; ~**-minute** *a* fatto(a) (*or* preso(a) *etc*) all'ultimo momento.

latch [lætʃ] *n* serratura a scatto.

late [leɪt] *a* (*not on time*) in ritardo; (*far on in day etc*) tardi *inv*; tardo(a); (*recent*) recente, ultimo(a); (*former*) ex; (*dead*) defunto(a) // *ad* tardi; (*behind time, schedule*) in ritardo; **of ~** di recente; **in the ~ afternoon** nel tardo pomeriggio; **in ~ May** verso la fine di maggio; ~**comer** *n* ritardatario/a; ~**ly** *ad* recentemente.

later ['leɪtə*] *a* (*date etc*) posteriore; (*version etc*) successivo(a) // *ad* più tardi; ~ **on** più avanti.

lateral ['lætərl] *a* laterale.

latest ['leɪtɪst] *a* ultimo(a), più recente; **at the ~** al più tardi.

lathe [leɪð] *n* tornio.

lather ['lɑ:ðə*] *n* schiuma di sapone // *vt* insaponare.

Latin ['lætɪn] *n* latino // *a* latino(a); ~ **America** *n* America Latina; ~ **American** *a* sudamericano(a).

latitude ['lætɪtju:d] *n* latitudine *f*.

latter ['lætə*] *a* secondo(a); più recente // *n*: **the ~** quest'ultimo, il secondo; ~**ly** *ad* recentemente, negli ultimi tempi.

lattice ['lætɪs] *n* traliccio; graticolato.

laudable ['lɔ:dəbl] *a* lodevole.

laugh [lɑ:f] *n* risata // *vi* ridere; **to ~ at** *vt fus* (*misfortune etc*) ridere di; **to ~ off** *vt* prendere alla leggera; ~**able** *a* ridicolo(a); ~**ing stock** *n*: **the** ~**ing stock of** lo zimbello di; ~**ter** *n* riso; risate *fpl*.

launch [lɔ:ntʃ] *n* (*of rocket etc*) lancio; (*of new ship*) varo; (*boat*) scialuppa; (*also:* **motor ~**) lancia // *vt* (*rocket*) lanciare; (*ship, plan*) varare; ~**(ing) pad** *n* rampa di lancio.

launder ['lɔ:ndə*] *vt* lavare e stirare.

launderette [lɔ:n'drɛt], (*US*) **laundromat** ['lɔ:ndrəmæt] *n* lavanderia (automatica).

laundry ['lɔ:ndrɪ] *n* lavanderia; (*clothes*) biancheria.

laureate ['lɔ:rɪət] *a see* **poet**.

laurel ['lɔrl] *n* lauro.

lava ['lɑ:və] *n* lava.

lavatory ['lævətərɪ] *n* gabinetto.

lavender ['lævəndə*] n lavanda.
lavish ['lævɪʃ] a copioso(a); abbondante; (giving freely): ~ with prodigo(a) di, largo(a) in // vt: to ~ on sb/sth (care) profondere a qn/qc.
law [lɔː] n legge f; civil/criminal ~ diritto civile/penale; ~-abiding a ubbidiente alla legge; ~ and order n l'ordine m pubblico; ~ court n tribunale m, corte f di giustizia; ~ful a legale; lecito(a).
lawn [lɔːn] n tappeto erboso; ~mower n tosaerba m or f inv; ~ tennis n tennis m su prato.
law school n facoltà f inv di legge.
lawsuit ['lɔːsuːt] n processo, causa.
lawyer ['lɔːjə*] n (consultant, with company) giurista m/f; (for sales, wills etc) ≈ notaio; (partner, in court) ≈ avvocato/essa.
lax [læks] a rilassato(a); negligente.
laxative ['læksətɪv] n lassativo.
laxity ['læksɪtɪ] n rilassatezza; negligenza.
lay [leɪ] pt of **lie** // a laico(a); secolare // vt (pt, pp **laid**) posare, mettere; (eggs) fare; (trap) tendere; (plans) fare, elaborare; to ~ the table apparecchiare la tavola; to ~ aside or by vt mettere da parte; to ~ down vt mettere giù; to ~ down the law dettar legge; to ~ off vt (workers) licenziare; to ~ on vt (water, gas) installare, mettere; (provide) fornire; (paint) applicare; to ~ out vt (design) progettare; (display) presentare; (spend) sborsare; to ~ up vt (to store) accumulare; (ship) mettere in disarmo; (subj: illness) costringere a letto; ~about n sfaccendato/a, fannullone/a; ~-by n (Brit) piazzola (di sosta).
layer ['leɪə*] n strato.
layman ['leɪmən] n laico; profano.
layout ['leɪaut] n lay-out m inv, disposizione f; (PRESS) impaginazione f.
laze [leɪz] vi oziare.
lazy ['leɪzɪ] a pigro(a).
lb. abbr = **pound** (weight).
lead [liːd] n (front position) posizione f di testa; (distance, time ahead) vantaggio; (clue) indizio; (ELEC) filo (elettrico); (for dog) guinzaglio; (THEATRE) parte f principale; [lɛd] (metal) piombo; (in pencil) mina // vb (pt, pp **led**) vt menare, guidare, condurre; (induce) indurre; (be leader of) essere a capo di; (SPORT) essere in testa a // vi condurre, essere in testa; to ~ astray vt sviare; to ~ away vt condurre via; to ~ back vt: to ~ back to ricondurre a; to ~ on vt (tease) tenere sulla corda; to ~ on to (induce) portare a; to ~ to vt fus condurre a; portare a; to ~ up to vt fus portare a.
leaden ['lɛdn] a (sky, sea) plumbeo(a); (heavy: footsteps) pesante.

leader ['liːdə*] n capo; leader m inv; (in newspaper) articolo di fondo; ~ship n direzione f; capacità di comando.
leading ['liːdɪŋ] a primo(a); principale; ~ man/lady n (THEATRE) primo attore/prima attrice; ~ light n (person) personaggio di primo piano.
leaf [liːf] n (pl **leaves**) foglia; (of table) ribalta // vi: to ~ through sfogliare qc; to turn over a new ~ cambiar vita.
leaflet ['liːflɪt] n dépliant m inv; (POL, REL) volantino.
league [liːg] n lega; (FOOTBALL) campionato; to be in ~ with essere in lega con.
leak [liːk] n (out, also fig) fuga; (in) infiltrazione f // vi (roof, bucket) perdere; (liquid) uscire; (shoes) lasciar passare l'acqua // vt (liquid) spandere; (information) divulgare; to ~ out vi uscire; (information) trapelare.
lean [liːn] a magro(a) // vb (pt, pp **leaned** or **leant** [lɛnt]) vt: to ~ sth on sth appoggiare qc su qc // vi (slope) pendere; (rest): to ~ against appoggiarsi contro; essere appoggiato(a) a; to ~ on appoggiarsi a; to ~ back/forward vi sporgersi indietro/in avanti; to ~ out vi sporgersi; to ~ over vi inclinarsi; ~ing n: ~ing (towards) propensione f (per); ~-to n (roof) tettoia; (shed) capanno con tetto a una falda.
leap [liːp] n salto, balzo // vi (pt, pp **leaped** or **leapt** [lɛpt]) saltare, balzare; ~frog n gioco della cavallina; ~ year n anno bisestile.
learn [lɜːn], pt, pp **learned** or **learnt** [lɜːn, -t] vt, vi imparare; to ~ how to do sth imparare a fare qc; ~ed ['lɜːnɪd] a erudito(a), dotto(a); ~er n principiante m/f; apprendista m/f; (Brit: also: ~er driver) guidatore/trice principiante; ~ing n erudizione f, sapienza.
lease [liːs] n contratto d'affitto // vt affittare.
leash [liːʃ] n guinzaglio.
least [liːst] a: the ~ + noun il(la) più piccolo(a), il(la) minimo(a); (smallest amount of) il(la) meno; the ~ + adjective: the ~ beautiful girl la ragazza meno bella; the ~ expensive il(la) meno caro(a); I have the ~ money ho meno denaro di tutti; at ~ almeno; not in the ~ affatto, per nulla.
leather ['lɛðə*] n cuoio // cpd di cuoio.
leave [liːv] vb (pt, pp **left**) vt lasciare; (go away from) partire da // vi partire, andarsene // n (time off) congedo; (MIL, also: consent) licenza; to be left rimanere; there's some milk left over c'è rimasto del latte; on ~ in congedo; to ~ behind vt (person, object) lasciare indietro; (: forget) dimenticare; to ~ out vt omettere, tralasciare; ~ of absence n congedo.

leaves [li:vz] *npl of* **leaf**.

Lebanon ['lebənən] *n* Libano.

lecherous ['letʃərəs] *a* lascivo(a), lubrico(a).

lecture ['lektʃə*] *n* conferenza; (SCOL) lezione *f* // *vi* fare conferenze; fare lezioni // *vt* (scold) rimproverare, fare una ramanzina a; **to ~ on** fare una conferenza su; **to give a ~ on** tenere una conferenza su.

lecturer ['lektʃərə*] *n* (speaker) conferenziere/a; (Brit: at university) professore/essa, docente *m/f*.

led [led] *pt, pp of* **lead**.

ledge [ledʒ] *n* (of window) davanzale *m*; (on wall etc) sporgenza; (of mountain) cornice *f*, cengia.

ledger ['ledʒə*] *n* libro maestro, registro.

lee [li:] *n* lato sottovento.

leech [li:tʃ] *n* sanguisuga.

leek [li:k] *n* porro.

leer [liə*] *vi:* **to ~ at sb** gettare uno sguardo voglioso (or maligno) su qn.

leeway ['li:wei] *n* (fig): **to have some ~** avere una certa libertà di agire.

left [left] *pt, pp of* **leave** // *a* sinistra(o) // *ad* a sinistra // *n* sinistra; **on the ~, to the ~** a sinistra; **the L~** (POL) la sinistra; **~-handed** a mancino(a); **~-hand side** *n* lato *or* fianco sinistro; **~ luggage (office)** *n* (Brit) deposito *m* bagagli *inv*; **~-overs** *npl* avanzi *mpl*, resti *mpl*; **~-wing** a (POL) di sinistra.

leg [leg] *n* gamba; (of animal) zampa; (of furniture) piede *m*; (CULIN: of chicken) coscia; (of journey) tappa; **1st/2nd ~** (SPORT) partita di andata/ritorno.

legacy ['legəsi] *n* eredità *f inv*.

legal ['li:gl] *a* legale; **~ holiday** *n* (US) giorno festivo, festa nazionale; **~ tender** *n* moneta legale.

legend ['ledʒənd] *n* leggenda.

legible ['ledʒəbl] *a* leggibile.

legislation [ledʒis'leiʃən] *n* legislazione *f*; **legislature** ['ledʒislətʃə*] *n* corpo legislativo.

legitimate [li'dʒitimət] *a* legittimo(a).

leg-room ['legru:m] *n* spazio per le gambe.

leisure ['leʒə*] *n* agio, tempo libero; ricreazioni *fpl*; **at ~** all'agio; a proprio comodo; **~ centre** *n* centro di ricreazione; **~ly** a tranquillo(a); fatto(a) con comodo *or* senza fretta.

lemon ['lemən] *n* limone *m*; **~ade** [-'neid] *n* limonata; **~ tea** *n* tè *m inv* al limone.

lend [lend], *pt, pp* **lent** *vt:* **to ~ sth (to sb)** prestare qc (a qn).

length [leŋθ] *n* lunghezza; (section: of road, pipe etc) pezzo, tratto; **at ~** (at last) finalmente, alla fine; (lengthily) a lungo; **~en** *vt* allungare, prolungare // *vi* allungarsi; **~ways** *ad* per il lungo; **~y** a molto lungo(a).

lenient ['li:niənt] *a* indulgente, clemente.

lens [lenz] *n* lente *f*; (of camera) obiettivo.

Lent [lent] *n* Quaresima.

lent [lent] *pt, pp of* **lend**.

lentil ['lentl] *n* lenticchia.

Leo ['li:əu] *n* Leone *m*.

leotard ['li:əta:d] *n* calzamaglia.

leper ['lepə*] *n* lebbroso/a.

leprosy ['leprəsi] *n* lebbra.

lesbian ['lezbiən] *n* lesbica.

less [les] a, pronoun, ad meno; **~ than you/ever** meno di lei/che mai; **~ than half** meno della metà; **~ and ~** sempre meno; **the ~ he works ...** meno lavora ... .

lessen ['lesn] *vi* diminuire, attenuarsi // *vt* diminuire, ridurre.

lesser ['lesə*] *a* minore, più piccolo(a); **to a ~ extent** in grado *or* misura minore.

lesson ['lesn] *n* lezione *f*.

lest [lest] *cj* per paura di + infinitive, per paura che + sub.

let, *pt, pp* **let** [let] *vt* lasciare; (Brit: lease) dare in affitto; **to ~ sb do sth** lasciar fare qc a qn, lasciare che qn faccia qc; **to ~ sb know sth** far sapere qc a qn; **he ~ me go** mi ha lasciato andare; **~'s go** andiamo; **~ him come** lo lasci venire; **"to ~"** "affittasi"; **to ~ down** *vt* (lower) abbassare; (dress) allungare; (hair) sciogliere; (disappoint) deludere; **to ~ go** *vt*, *vi* mollare; **to ~ in** *vt* lasciare entrare; (visitor etc) far entrare; **to ~ off** *vt* (allow to go) lasciare andare; (firework etc) far partire; (smell etc) emettere; **to ~ on** *vi* (col) dire; **to ~ out** *vt* lasciare uscire; (dress) allargare; (scream) emettere; **to ~ up** *vi* diminuire.

lethal ['li:θl] *a* letale, mortale.

lethargy ['leθədʒi] *n* letargia.

letter ['letə*] *n* lettera; **~ bomb** *n* lettera esplosiva; **~box** *n* (Brit) buca delle lettere; **~ing** *n* iscrizione *f*; caratteri *mpl*.

lettuce ['letis] *n* lattuga, insalata.

leukaemia, (US) **leukemia** [lu:'ki:miə] *n* leucemia.

level ['levl] *a* piatto(a), piano(a); orizzontale // *n* livello; (also: **spirit ~**) livella (a bolla d'aria) // *vt* livellare, spianare; **to be ~ with** essere alla pari di; **A ~s** *npl* (Brit) ≈ esami *mpl* di maturità; **O ~s** *npl* (Brit) esami fatti in Inghilterra all'età di 16 anni; **on the ~** piatto(a); (fig) onesto(a); **to ~ off** *or* **out** *vi* (prices etc) stabilizzarsi; **~ crossing** *n* (Brit) passaggio a livello; **~-headed** a equilibrato(a).

lever ['li:və*] *n* leva // *vt:* **to ~ up/out** sollevare/estrarre con una leva; **~age** *n:* **~age (on or with)** ascendente *m* (su).

levy ['levi] *n* tassa, imposta // *vt* imporre.

lewd [lu:d] *a* osceno(a), lascivo(a).

liability [laɪə'bɪlətɪ] *n* responsabilità *f inv*; (*handicap*) peso; **liabilities** *npl* debiti *mpl*; (*on balance sheet*) passivo.

liable ['laɪəbl] *a* (*subject*): ~ **to** soggetto(a) a; passibile di; (*responsible*): ~ **(for)** responsabile (di); (*likely*): ~ **to do** propenso(a) a fare.

liaison [liː'eɪzɒn] *n* relazione *f*; (*MIL*) collegamento.

liar ['laɪə*] *n* bugiardo/a.

libel ['laɪbl] *n* libello, diffamazione *f* // *vt* diffamare.

liberal ['lɪbərl] *a* liberale; (*generous*): **to be ~ with** distribuire liberalmente.

liberty ['lɪbətɪ] *n* libertà *f inv*; **at ~ to do** libero(a) di fare.

Libra ['liːbrə] *n* Bilancia.

librarian [laɪ'brɛərɪən] *n* bibliotecario/a.

library ['laɪbrərɪ] *n* biblioteca.

Libya ['lɪbɪə] *n* Libia.

lice [laɪs] *npl of* **louse**.

licence, (*US*) **license** ['laɪsns] *n* autorizzazione *f*, permesso; (*COMM*) licenza; (*RADIO, TV*) canone *m*, abbonamento; (*also*: **driving ~**, (*US*) **driver's ~**) patente *f* di guida; (*excessive freedom*) licenza; ~ **number** *n* numero di targa; ~ **plate** *n* targa.

license ['laɪsns] *n* (*US*) = **licence** // *vt* dare una licenza a; ~**d** *a* (*for alcohol*) che ha la licenza di vendere bibite alcoliche.

liok [lɪk] *vt* leccare.

licorice ['lɪkərɪs] *n* = **liquorice**.

lid [lɪd] *n* coperchio.

lie [laɪ] *n* bugia, menzogna // *vi* mentire, dire bugie; (*pt* **lay**, *pp* **lain**) (*rest*) giacere, star disteso(a); (*in grave*) giacere, riposare; (*of object*: *be situated*) trovarsi, essere; **to ~ low** (*fig*) latitare; **to ~ about** *vi* (*things*) essere in giro; (*person*) bighellonare; ~**-down** *n* (*Brit*): **to have a ~-down** sdraiarsi, riposarsi; ~**-in** *n* (*Brit*): **to have a ~-in** rimanere a letto.

lieutenant [lɛf'tɛnənt, (*US*) luː'tɛnənt] *n* tenente *m*.

life [laɪf] *n* (*pl* **lives**) vita // *cpd* di vita; della vita; **a vita**; ~ **assurance** *n* (*Brit*) assicurazione *f* sulla vita; ~**belt** *n* (*Brit*) salvagente *m*; ~**boat** *n* scialuppa di salvataggio; ~**guard** *n* bagnino; ~ **insurance** *n* = ~ **assurance**; ~ **jacket** *n* giubbotto di salvataggio; ~**less** *a* senza vita; ~**like** *a* verosimile; rassomigliante; ~**long** *a* per tutta la vita; ~ **preserver** *n* (*US*) salvagente *m*; giubbotto di salvataggio; ~**saver** *n* bagnino; ~ **sentence** *n* ergastolo; ~**sized** *a* a grandezza naturale; ~ **span** *n* (durata della) vita; ~**style** *n* stile *m* di vita; ~ **support system** *n* respiratore *m* automatico; ~**time** *n*: **in his ~time** durante la sua vita; **once in a ~time** una volta nella vita.

lift [lɪft] *vt* sollevare, levare; (*steal*) prendere, rubare // *vi* (*fog*) alzarsi // *n* (*Brit*: *elevator*) ascensore *m*; **to give sb a ~** (*Brit*) dare un passaggio a qn; ~**off** *n* decollo.

light [laɪt] *n* luce *f*, lume *m*; (*daylight*) luce *f*, giorno; (*lamp*) lampada; (*AUT*: *rear* ~) luce *f* di posizione; (: *headlamp*) fanale *m*; (*for cigarette etc*): **have you got a ~?** ha da accendere? // *vt* (*pt, pp* **lighted** *or* **lit**) (*candle, cigarette, fire*) accendere; (*room*) illuminare // *a* (*room, colour*) chiaro(a); (*not heavy, also fig*) leggero(a); ~**s** *npl* (*AUT*: *traffic* ~**s**) semaforo; **to come to ~** venire alla luce, emergere; **to ~ up** *vi* illuminarsi // *vt* illuminare; ~ **bulb** *n* lampadina; ~**en** *vi* schiarirsi // *vt* (*give light to*) illuminare; (*make lighter*) schiarire; (*make less heavy*) alleggerire; ~**er** *n* (*also*: **cigarette ~er**) accendino; (*boat*) chiatta; ~**-headed** *a* stordito(a); ~**-hearted** *a* gioioso(a), gaio(a); ~**house** *n* faro; ~**ing** *n* illuminazione *f*; ~**ly** *ad* leggermente; **to get off ~ly** cavarsela a buon mercato; ~**ness** *n* chiarezza; (*in weight*) leggerezza.

lightning ['laɪtnɪŋ] *n* lampo, fulmine *m*; ~ **conductor**, (*US*) ~ **rod** *n* parafulmine *m*.

light pen *n* penna ottica.

lightweight ['laɪtweɪt] *a* (*suit*) leggero(a); (*boxer*) peso leggero *inv* // *n* (*BOXING*) peso leggero.

like [laɪk] *vt* (*person*) volere bene a; (*activity, object, food*): **I ~ swimming/ that book/chocolate** mi piace nuotare/ quel libro/il cioccolato // *prep* come // *a* simile, uguale // *n*: **the ~** uno(a) uguale; **his ~s and dislikes** i suoi gusti; **I would ~, I'd ~** mi piacerebbe, vorrei; **would you ~ a coffee?** gradirebbe un caffè?; **to be/look ~ sb/sth** somigliare a qn/qc; **that's just ~ him** è proprio da lui; **do it ~ this** fallo così; **it is nothing ~ ...** non è affatto come ...; ~**able** *a* simpatico(a).

likelihood ['laɪklɪhʊd] *n* probabilità.

likely ['laɪklɪ] *a* probabile; plausibile; **he's ~ to leave** probabilmente partirà, è probabile che parta; **not ~!** neanche per sogno!

likeness ['laɪknɪs] *n* somiglianza.

likewise ['laɪkwaɪz] *ad* similmente, nello stesso modo.

liking ['laɪkɪŋ] *n*: ~ **(for)** debole *m* (per).

lilac ['laɪlək] *n* lilla *m inv* // *a* lilla *inv*.

lily ['lɪlɪ] *n* giglio; ~ **of the valley** *n* mughetto.

limb [lɪm] *n* membro.

limber ['lɪmbə*]: **to ~ up** *vi* riscaldarsi i muscoli.

limbo ['lɪmbəʊ] *n*: **to be in ~** (*fig*) essere lasciato(a) nel dimenticatoio.

lime [laɪm] *n* (*tree*) tiglio; (*fruit*) limetta; (*GEO*) calce *f*.

limelight ['laɪmlaɪt] n: in the ~ (fig) alla ribalta, in vista.

limerick ['lɪmərɪk] n poesiola umoristica di 5 versi.

limestone ['laɪmstəun] n pietra calcarea; (GEO) calcare m.

limit ['lɪmɪt] n limite m // vt limitare; **~ed** a limitato(a), ristretto(a); **to be ~ed** to limitarsi a; **~ed (liability) company (Ltd)** n (Brit) ≈ società f inv a responsabilità limitata (S.r.l.).

limp [lɪmp] n: to have a ~ zoppicare // vi zoppicare // a floscio(a), flaccido(a).

limpet ['lɪmpɪt] n patella.

line [laɪn] n linea; (rope) corda; (wire) filo; (of poem) verso; (row, series) fila, riga; coda // vt (clothes): to ~ (with) foderare (di); (box): to ~ (with) rivestire or foderare (di); (subj: trees, crowd) fiancheggiare; ~ of business settore m or ramo d'attività; in ~ with in linea con; **to ~ up** vi allinearsi, mettersi in fila // vt mettere in fila.

lined [laɪnd] a (face) rugoso(a); (paper) a righe, rigato(a).

linen ['lɪnɪn] n biancheria, panni mpl; (cloth) tela di lino.

liner ['laɪnə*] n nave f di linea.

linesman ['laɪnzmən] n guardalinee m inv.

line-up ['laɪnʌp] n allineamento, fila; (SPORT) formazione f di gioco.

linger ['lɪŋgə*] vi attardarsi; indugiare; (smell, tradition) persistere.

lingo, ~es ['lɪŋgəu] n (pej) gergo.

linguistics [lɪŋ'gwɪstɪks] n linguistica.

lining ['laɪnɪŋ] n fodera.

link [lɪŋk] n (of a chain) anello; (connection) legame m, collegamento // vt collegare, unire, congiungere; **~s** npl (GOLF) pista or terreno da golf; **to ~ up** vt collegare, unire // vi riunirsi; associarsi.

lino ['laɪnəu], **linoleum** [lɪ'nəuliəm] n linoleum m inv.

lion ['laɪən] n leone m; **~ess** n leonessa.

lip [lɪp] n labbro; (of cup etc) orlo; (insolence) sfacciataggine f; **~read** vi leggere sulle labbra; ~ **salve** n burro di cacao; ~ **service** n: to pay ~ service to sth essere favorevole a qc solo a parole; **~stick** n rossetto.

liqueur [lɪ'kjuə*] n liquore m.

liquid ['lɪkwɪd] n liquido // a liquido(a).

liquidize ['lɪkwɪdaɪz] vt (CULIN) passare al frullatore; **~r** n frullatore m (a brocca).

liquor ['lɪkə*] n alcool m.

liquorice ['lɪkərɪs] n liquirizia.

liquor store n (US) negozio di liquori.

lisp [lɪsp] n difetto nel pronunciare le sibilanti.

list [lɪst] n lista, elenco; (of ship) sbandamento // vt (write down) mettere in lista; fare una lista di; (enumerate) elencare // vi (ship) sbandare.

listen ['lɪsn] vi ascoltare; **to ~ to** ascoltare; **~er** n ascoltatore/trice.

listless ['lɪstlɪs] a apatico(a).

lit [lɪt] pt, pp of **light**.

liter ['liːtə*] n (US) = **litre**.

literacy ['lɪtərəsɪ] n il sapere leggere e scrivere.

literal ['lɪtərl] a letterale.

literary ['lɪtərərɪ] a letterario(a).

literate ['lɪtərət] a che sa leggere e scrivere.

literature ['lɪtərɪtʃə*] n letteratura; (brochures etc) materiale m.

lithe [laɪð] a agile, snello(a).

litigation [lɪtɪ'geɪʃən] n causa.

litre, (US) liter ['liːtə*] n litro.

litter ['lɪtə*] n (rubbish) rifiuti mpl; (young animals) figliata // vt sparpagliare; lasciare rifiuti in; ~ **bin** n (Brit) cestino per rifiuti; **~ed** a: **~ed with** coperto(a) di.

little ['lɪtl] a (small) piccolo(a); (not much) poco(a) // ad poco; a ~ un po' (di); a ~ **milk** un po' di latte; ~ **by** ~ a poco a poco.

live vi [lɪv] vivere; (reside) vivere, abitare // a [laɪv] (animal) vivo(a); (wire) sotto tensione; (broadcast) diretto(a); **to ~ down** vt far dimenticare (alla gente); **to ~ on** vt fus (food) vivere di // vi sopravvivere, continuare a vivere; **to ~ together** vi vivere insieme, convivere; **to ~ up to** vt fus tener fede a, non venir meno a.

livelihood ['laɪvlɪhud] n mezzi mpl di sostentamento.

lively ['laɪvlɪ] a vivace, vivo(a).

liven up ['laɪvn'ʌp] vt (discussion, evening) animare.

liver ['lɪvə*] n fegato.

livery ['lɪvərɪ] n livrea.

lives [laɪvz] npl of **life**.

livestock ['laɪvstɔk] n bestiame m.

livid ['lɪvɪd] a livido(a); (furious) livido(a) di rabbia, furibondo(a).

living ['lɪvɪŋ] a vivo(a), vivente // n: to earn or make a ~ guadagnarsi la vita; ~ **conditions** npl condizioni fpl di vita; ~ **room** n soggiorno; ~ **wage** n salario sufficiente per vivere.

lizard ['lɪzəd] n lucertola.

load [ləud] n (weight) peso; (ELEC, TECH, thing carried) carico // vt (also: ~ up): to ~ (with) (lorry, ship) caricare (di); (gun, camera, COMPUT) caricare (con); a ~ of, **~s of** (fig) un sacco di; **~ed** a (dice) falsato(a); (question) capzioso(a); (col: rich) carico(a); di soldi; (: drunk) ubriaco(a); **~ing bay** n piazzola di carico.

loaf [ləuf] n (pl **loaves**) n pane m, pagnotta // vi (also: ~ **about**, ~ **around**) bighellonare.

loan [ləun] n prestito // vt dare in prestito; on ~ in prestito.

loath [ləuθ] *a*: to be ~ to do essere restio(a) a fare.

loathe [ləuð] *vt* detestare, aborrire.

loaves [ləuvz] *npl of* **loaf**.

lobby ['lɔbɪ] *n* atrio, vestibolo; (*POL*: *pressure group*) gruppo di pressione // *vt* fare pressione su.

lobster ['lɔbstə*] *n* aragosta.

local ['ləukl] *a* locale // *n* (*Brit*: *pub*) ≈ bar *m inv* all'angolo; the ~s *npl* la gente della zona; ~ **call** *n* (*TEL*) telefonata urbana; ~ **government** *n* amministrazione *f* locale.

locality [ləu'kælɪtɪ] *n* località *f inv*; (*position*) posto, luogo.

locally ['ləukəlɪ] *ad* da queste parti; nel vicinato.

locate [ləu'keɪt] *vt* (*find*) trovare; (*situate*) collocare.

location [ləu'keɪʃən] *n* posizione *f*; on ~ (*CINEMA*) all'esterno.

loch [lɔx] *n* lago.

lock [lɔk] *n* (*of door, box*) serratura; (*of canal*) chiusa; (*of hair*) ciocca, riccio // *vt* (*with key*) chiudere a chiave; (*immobilize*) bloccare // *vi* (*door etc*) chiudersi; (*wheels*) bloccarsi, incepparsi.

locker ['lɔkə*] *n* armadietto.

locket ['lɔkɪt] *n* medaglione *m*.

locksmith ['lɔksmɪθ] *n* magnano.

lock-up ['lɔkʌp] *n* (*garage*) box *m inv*.

locomotive [ləukə'məutɪv] *n* locomotiva.

locum ['ləukəm] *n* (*MED*) medico sostituto.

locust ['ləukəst] *n* locusta.

lodge [lɔdʒ] *n* casetta, portineria // *vi* (*person*): to ~ (*with*) essere a pensione (presso *or* da) // *vt* (*appeal etc*) presentare, fare; to ~ a complaint presentare un reclamo; ~r *n* affittuario/a; (*with room and meals*) pensionante *m/f*.

lodgings ['lɔdʒɪŋz] *npl* camera d'affitto; camera ammobiliata.

loft [lɔft] *n* solaio, soffitta; (*AGR*) granaio.

lofty ['lɔftɪ] *a* alto(a); (*haughty*) altezzoso(a).

log [lɔg] *n* (*of wood*) ceppo; (*book*) = **logbook**.

logbook ['lɔgbuk] *n* (*NAUT, AVIAT*) diario di bordo; (*AUT*) libretto di circolazione; (*of lorry driver*) registro di viaggio; (*of events, movement of goods etc*) registro.

loggerheads ['lɔgəhedz] *npl*: at ~ (with) ai ferri corti (con).

logic ['lɔdʒɪk] *n* logica; ~al *a* logico(a).

loin [lɔɪn] *n* (*CULIN*) lombata.

loiter ['lɔɪtə*] *vi* attardarsi; to ~ (about) indugiare, bighellonare.

loll [lɔl] *vi* (*also*: ~ about) essere stravaccato(a).

lollipop ['lɔlɪpɔp] *n* lecca lecca *m inv*; ~ **man/lady** *n* (*Brit*) impiegato/a che aiuta i bambini ad attraversare la strada in vicinanza di scuole.

London ['lʌndən] *n* Londra; ~er *n* londinese *m/f*.

lone [ləun] *a* solitario(a).

loneliness ['ləunlɪnɪs] *n* solitudine *f*, isolamento.

lonely ['ləunlɪ] *a* solo(a); solitario(a), isolato(a).

long [lɔŋ] *a* lungo(a) // *ad* a lungo, per molto tempo // *vi*: to ~ for sth/to do desiderare qc/di fare; non veder l'ora di aver qc/di fare; so *or* as ~ as (*while*) finché; (*provided that*) sempre che + *sub*; don't be ~! fai presto!; how ~ is this river/course? quanto è lungo questo fiume/corso?; 6 metres ~ lungo 6 metri; 6 months ~ che dura 6 mesi, di 6 mesi; all night ~ tutta la notte; he no ~er comes non viene più; ~ before molto tempo prima; before ~ (+ *future*) presto, fra poco; (+ *past*) poco tempo dopo; at ~ last finalmente; ~-distance *a* (*race*) di fondo; (*call*) interurbano(a); ~-hand *n* scrittura normale; ~ing *n* desiderio, voglia, brama // *a* di desiderio; pieno(a) di nostalgia.

longitude ['lɔŋgɪtjuːd] *n* longitudine *f*.

long: ~ **jump** *n* salto in lungo; ~-**playing record (L.P.)** *n* (*disco*) 33 giri *m inv*; ~-**range** *a* a lunga portata; ~-**sighted** *a* presbite; (*fig*) lungimirante; ~-**standing** *a* di vecchia data; ~-**suffering** *a* estremamente paziente; infinitamente tollerante; ~-**term** *a* a lungo termine; ~ **wave** *n* onde *fpl* lunghe; ~-**winded** *a* prolisso(a), interminabile.

loo [luː] *n* (*Brit col*) W.C. *m inv*, cesso.

look [luk] *vi* guardare; (*seem*) sembrare, parere; (*building etc*): to ~ south/on to the sea dare a sud/sul mare // *n* sguardo; (*appearance*) aspetto, aria; ~s *npl* aspetto; bellezza; to ~ after *vt fus* occuparsi di, prendere cura di; (*keep an eye on*) guardare, badare a; to ~ at *vt fus* guardare; to ~ back *vi*: to ~ back at voltarsi a guardare; to ~ back on (*event etc*) ripensare a; to ~ down on *vt fus* (*fig*) guardare dall'alto, disprezzare; to ~ for *vt fus* cercare; to ~ forward to *vt fus* non veder l'ora di; (*in letters*): we ~ forward to hearing from you in attesa di una vostra gentile risposta; to ~ into *vt fus* esaminare; to ~ on *vi* fare da spettatore; to ~ out *vi* (*beware*): to ~ out (for) stare in guardia (per); to ~ out for *vt fus* cercare; (*watch for*): to ~ out for sb/sth guardare se arriva qn/qc; to ~ round *vi* (*turn*) girarsi, voltarsi; (*in shop*) dare un'occhiata; to ~ to *vt fus* stare attento(a) a; (*rely on*) contare su; to ~

up *vi* alzare gli occhi; (*improve*) migliorare // *vt* (*word*) cercare; (*friend*) andare a trovare; **to ~ up to** *vt fus* avere rispetto per; **~-out** *n* posto d'osservazione; guardia; **to be on the ~ out (for)** stare in guardia (per).

loom |luːm| *n* telaio // *vi* sorgere; (*fig*) minacciare.

loony |'luːnɪ| *n* (*col*) pazzo/a.

loop |luːp| *n* cappio; **~hole** *n* via d'uscita; scappatoia.

loose |luːs| *a* (*knot*) sciolto(a); (*screw*) allentato(a); (*stone*) cadente; (*clothes*) ampio(a), largo(a); (*animal*) in libertà, scappato(a); (*life, morals*) dissoluto(a); (*discipline*) allentato(a); (*thinking*) poco rigoroso(a), vago(a); **~ change** *n* spiccioli *mpl*, moneta; **~ chippings** *npl* (*on road*) ghiaino; **~ end** *n*: **to be at a ~ end** *or* (*US*) **at ~ ends** non saper che fare; **~ly** *ad* lentamente; approssimativamente; **~n** *vt* sciogliere.

loot |luːt| *n* bottino // *vt* saccheggiare.

lop |lɔp| *vt* (*also*: **~ off**) tagliare via, recidere.

lop-sided |'lɔp'saɪdɪd| *a* non equilibrato(a), asimmetrico(a).

lord |lɔːd| *n* signore *m*; **L~ Smith** lord Smith; **the L~** il Signore; **the** (**House of**) **L~s** (*Brit*) la Camera dei Lord; **~ship** *n*: **your L~ship** Sua Eccellenza.

lore |lɔː*| *n* tradizioni *fpl*.

lorry |'lɔrɪ| *n* (*Brit*) camion *m inv*; **~ driver** *n* (*Brit*) camionista *m*.

lose |luːz|, *pt*, *pp* **lost** *vt* perdere; (*pursuers*) distanziare // *vi* perdere; **to ~** (*time*) (*clock*) ritardare; **to get lost** *vi* perdersi, smarrirsi; **~r** *n* perdente *m/f*.

loss |lɔs| *n* perdita; **to be at a ~** essere perplesso(a).

lost |lɔst| *pt*, *pp* of **lose** // *a* perduto(a); **~ property**, (*US*) **~ and found** *n* oggetti *mpl* smarriti.

lot |lɔt| *n* (*at auctions*) lotto; (*destiny*) destino, sorte *f*; **the ~** tutto(a) quanto(a); tutti(e) quanti(e); **a ~** molto; **a ~ of** una gran quantità di, un sacco di; **~s of** molto(a); **to draw ~s** (**for sth**) tirare a sorte (per qc).

lotion |'ləʊʃən| *n* lozione *f*.

lottery |'lɔtərɪ| *n* lotteria.

loud |laʊd| *a* forte, alto(a); (*gaudy*) vistoso(a), sgargiante // *ad* (*speak etc*) forte; **~hailer** *n* (*Brit*) portavoce *m inv*; **~ly** *ad* fortemente, ad alta voce; **~speaker** *n* altoparlante *m*.

lounge |laʊndʒ| *n* salotto, soggiorno // *vi* oziare; starsene colle mani in mano; **~ suit** *n* (*Brit*) completo da uomo.

louse |laʊs|, *pl* **lice** *n* pidocchio.

lousy |'laʊzɪ| *a* (*fig*) orrendo(a), schifoso(a).

lout |laʊt| *n* zoticone *m*.

louvre, (*US*) **louver** |'luːvə*| *a* (*door, window*) con apertura a gelosia.

lovable |'lʌvəbl| *a* simpatico(a), carino(a); amabile.

love |lʌv| *n* amore *m* // *vt* amare; voler bene a; **to ~ to do:** **I ~ to do** mi piace fare; **to be in ~ with** essere innamorato(a) di; **to make ~** fare l'amore; "**15 ~**" (*TENNIS*) "15 a zero"; **~ affair** *n* relazione *f*; **~ life** *n* vita sentimentale.

lovely |'lʌvlɪ| *a* bello(a); (*delicious: smell, meal*) buono(a).

lover |'lʌvə*| *n* amante *m/f*; (*amateur*): **a ~ of** un(un')amante di; un(un')appassionato(a) di.

loving |'lʌvɪŋ| *a* affettuoso(a), amoroso(a), tenero(a).

low |ləʊ| *a* basso(a) // *ad* in basso // *n* (*METEOR*) depressione *f* // *vi* (*cow*) muggire; **to feel ~** sentirsi giù; **to turn** (**down**) **~** *vt* abbassare; **~-cut** *a* (*dress*) scollato(a); **~er** *vt* calare; (*reduce*) abbassare; **~-fat** *a* magro(a); **~lands** *npl* (*GEO*) pianura; **~ly** *a* umile, modesto(a); **~-lying** *a* a basso livello.

loyal |'lɔɪəl| *a* fedele, leale; **~ty** *n* fedeltà, lealtà.

lozenge |'lɔzɪndʒ| *n* (*MED*) pastiglia; (*GEOM*) losanga.

L.P. *n abbr* = **long-playing record**.

L-plates |'ɛlpleɪts| *npl* (*Brit*) cartelli sui veicoli dei guidatori principianti.

Ltd *abbr* = **limited**.

lubricant |'luːbrɪkənt| *n* lubrificante *m*.

lubricate |'luːbrɪkeɪt| *vt* lubrificare.

luck |lʌk| *n* fortuna, sorte *f*; **bad ~** sfortuna, mala sorte; **good ~!** buona fortuna!; **~ily** *ad* fortunatamente, per fortuna; **~y** *a* fortunato(a); (*number etc*) che porta fortuna.

ludicrous |'luːdɪkrəs| *a* ridicolo(a), assurdo(a).

lug |lʌg| *vt* trascinare.

luggage |'lʌgɪdʒ| *n* bagagli *mpl*; **~ rack** *n* portabagagli *m inv*.

lukewarm |'luːkwɔːm| *a* tiepido(a).

lull |lʌl| *n* intervallo di calma // *vt* (*child*) cullare; (*person, fear*) acquietare, calmare.

lullaby |'lʌləbaɪ| *n* ninnananna.

lumbago |lʌm'beɪgəʊ| *n* lombaggine *f*.

lumber |'lʌmbə*| *n* roba vecchia; **~jack** *n* boscaiolo.

luminous |'luːmɪnəs| *a* luminoso(a).

lump |lʌmp| *n* pezzo; (*in sauce*) grumo; (*swelling*) gonfiore *m* // *vt* (*also*: **~ together**) riunire, mettere insieme; **a ~ sum** una somma globale.

lunacy |'luːnəsɪ| *n* demenza, follia, pazzia.

lunar |'luːnə*| *a* lunare.

lunatic |'luːnətɪk| *a*, *n* pazzo(a), matto(a).

lunch |lʌntʃ| *n* pranzo, colazione *f*.

luncheon |'lʌntʃən| *n* pranzo; **~ meat** *n*

≈ mortadella; ~ **voucher** n buono m pasto inv.

lung [lʌŋ] n polmone m.

lunge [lʌndʒ] vi (also: ~ **forward**) fare un balzo in avanti; **to ~ at** balzare su.

lurch [lɜːtʃ] vi vacillare, barcollare // n scatto improvviso; **to leave sb in the ~** piantare in asso qn.

lure [luə*] n richiamo; lusinga // vt attirare (con l'inganno).

lurid ['luərɪd] a sgargiante; (details etc) impressionante.

lurk [lɜːk] vi stare in agguato.

luscious ['lʌʃəs] a succulento(a); delizioso(a).

lush [lʌʃ] a lussureggiante.

lust [lʌst] n lussuria; cupidigia; desiderio; (fig): ~ **for** sete f di; **to ~ after** vt fus bramare, desiderare.

lusty ['lʌstɪ] a vigoroso(a), robusto(a).

Luxembourg ['lʌksəmbɜːg] n (state) Lussemburgo m; (city) Lussemburgo f.

luxuriant [lʌg'zjuərɪənt] a lussureggiante.

luxurious [lʌg'zjuərɪəs] a sontuoso(a), di lusso.

luxury ['lʌkʃərɪ] n lusso // cpd di lusso.

lying ['laɪɪŋ] n bugie fpl, menzogne fpl.

lynch [lɪntʃ] vt linciare.

lynx [lɪŋks] n lince f.

lyric ['lɪrɪk] a lirico(a); ~**s** npl (of song) parole fpl; ~**al** a lirico(a).

M

m. abbr = **metre, mile, million.**

M.A. abbr = **Master of Arts.**

mac [mæk] n (Brit) impermeabile m.

macaroni [mækə'rəunɪ] n maccheroni mpl.

mace [meɪs] n mazza; (spice) macis m or f.

machine [mə'ʃiːn] n macchina // vt (dress etc) cucire a macchina; ~ **gun** n mitragliatrice f; ~**ry** n macchinario, macchine fpl; (fig) macchina.

mackerel ['mækrl] n (pl inv) sgombro.

mackintosh ['mækɪntɔʃ] n (Brit) impermeabile m.

mad [mæd] a matto(a), pazzo(a); (foolish) sciocco(a); (angry) furioso(a).

madam ['mædəm] n signora.

madden ['mædn] vt fare infuriare.

made [meɪd] pt, pp of **make**.

Madeira [mə'dɪərə] n (GEO) Madera; (wine) madera.

made-to-measure ['meɪdtə'mɛʒə*] a (Brit) fatto(a) su misura.

madly ['mædlɪ] ad follemente; (love) alla follia.

madman ['mædmən] n pazzo, alienato.

madness ['mædnɪs] n pazzia.

magazine [mægə'ziːn] n (PRESS) rivista; (MIL: store) magazzino, deposito; (of firearm) caricatore m.

maggot ['mægət] n baco, verme m.

magic ['mædʒɪk] n magia // a magico(a); ~**al** a magico(a); ~**ian** [mə'dʒɪʃən] n mago/a.

magistrate ['mædʒɪstreɪt] n magistrato; giudice m/f.

magnet ['mægnɪt] n magnete m, calamita; ~**ic** [-'nɛtɪk] a magnetico(a).

magnificent [mæg'nɪfɪsnt] a magnifico(a).

magnify ['mægnɪfaɪ] vt ingrandire; ~**ing glass** n lente f d'ingrandimento.

magnitude ['mægnɪtjuːd] n grandezza; importanza.

magpie ['mægpaɪ] n gazza.

mahogany [mə'hɔgənɪ] n mogano // cpd di or in mogano.

maid [meɪd] n domestica; (in hotel) cameriera; old ~ (pej) vecchia zitella.

maiden ['meɪdn] n fanciulla // a (aunt etc) nubile; (speech, voyage) inaugurale; ~ **name** n nome m nubile or da ragazza.

mail [meɪl] n posta // vt spedire (per posta); ~**box** n (US) cassetta delle lettere; ~**ing list** n elenco d'indirizzi; ~-**order** n vendita (or acquisto) per corrispondenza.

maim [meɪm] vt mutilare.

main [meɪn] a principale // n (pipe) conduttura principale; the ~s (ELEC) la linea principale; **in the ~** nel complesso, nell'insieme; ~**frame** n (COMPUT) mainframe m inv; ~**land** n continente m; ~**ly** ad principalmente, soprattutto; ~ **road** n strada principale; ~**stay** n (fig) sostegno principale; ~**stream** n (fig) corrente f principale.

maintain [meɪn'teɪn] vt mantenere; (affirm) sostenere; **maintenance** ['meɪntənəns] n manutenzione f; (alimony) alimenti mpl.

maize [meɪz] n granturco, mais m.

majestic [mə'dʒɛstɪk] a maestoso(a).

majesty ['mædʒɪstɪ] n maestà f inv.

major ['meɪdʒə*] n (MIL) maggiore m // a (greater, MUS) maggiore; (in importance) principale, importante.

Majorca [mə'jɔːkə] n Maiorca.

majority [mə'dʒɔrɪtɪ] n maggioranza.

make [meɪk] vt (pt, pp **made**) fare; (manufacture) fare, fabbricare; (cause to be): **to ~ sb sad** etc rendere qn triste etc; (force): **to ~ sb do sth** costringere qn a fare qc, far fare qc a qn; (equal): 2 **and** 2 ~ 4 2 più 2 fa 4 // n fabbricazione f; (brand) marca; **to ~ a fool of sb** far fare a qn la figura dello scemo; **to ~ a profit** realizzare un profitto; **to ~ a loss** subire una perdita; **to ~ it** (arrive) arrivare; (achieve sth) farcela; **what time do you ~ it?** che ora fai?; **to ~ do with arrangiarsi con; to ~ for** vt fus (place) avviarsi verso; **to ~ out** vt (write out) scrivere; (: cheque) emettere; (*understand*) capire; (*see*) distinguere; (: *numbers*) decifrare; **to ~ up** *vt* (*invent*) inventare; (*parcel*) fare // *vi* conciliarsi; (*with cosmetics*) truccarsi; **to ~ up for** *vt fus* compensare; ricuperare; **~-believe** *n*: a world of **~-believe** un mondo di favole; it's just **~-believe** è tutta un'invenzione; **~r** *n* fabbricante *m*; creatore/trice, autore/trice; **~shift** *a* improvvisato(a); **~-up** *n* trucco; **~-up remover** *n* struccatore *m*.

making ['meıkıŋ] *n* (*fig*): **in the ~ in** formazione; **to have the ~s of** (*actor*, *athlete etc*) avere la stoffa di.

maladjusted [mælə'dʒʌstıd] *a* disadattato(a).

malaria [mə'lɛərıə] *n* malaria.

Malaya [mə'leıə] *n* Malesia.

male [meıl] *n* (*BIOL*, *ELEC*) maschio // *a* maschile; maschio(a).

malevolent [mə'levələnt] *a* malevolo(a).

malfunction [mæl'fʌŋkʃən] *n* funzione *f* difettosa.

malice ['mælıs] *n* malevolenza; **malicious** [mə'lıʃəs] *a* malevolo(a); (*LAW*) doloso(a).

malign [mə'laın] *vt* malignare su; calunniare.

malignant [mə'lıgnənt] *a* (*MED*) maligno(a).

mall [mɔːl] *n* (*also*: **shopping ~**) centro commerciale.

mallet ['mælıt] *n* maglio.

malnutrition [mælnjuː'trıʃən] *n* denutrizione *f*.

malpractice [mæl'præktıs] *n* prevaricazione *f*; negligenza.

malt [mɔːlt] *n* malto.

Malta ['mɔːltə] *n* Malta.

mammal ['mæml] *n* mammifero.

mammoth ['mæməθ] *n* mammut *m inv* // *a* enorme, gigantesco(a).

man [mæn] *n* (*pl* **men**) uomo; (*CHESS*) pezzo; (*DRAUGHTS*) pedina // *vt* fornire d'uomini; stare a; essere di servizio a; **an old ~** un vecchio; **~ and wife** marito e moglie.

manage ['mænıdʒ] *vi* farcela // *vt* (*be in charge of*) occuparsi di; gestire; **to ~ to do sth** riuscire a far qc; **~able** *a* maneggevole; fattibile; **~ment** *n* amministrazione *f*, direzione *f*; **~r** *n* direttore *m*; (*of shop*, *restaurant*) gerente *m*; (*of artist*) manager *m inv*; **~ress** [-ə'rɛs] *n* direttrice *f*; gerente *f*; **~rial** [-ə'dʒıərıəl] *a* dirigenziale; **managing** *a*: **managing director** amministratore *m* delegato.

mandarin ['mændərın] *n* (*person*, *fruit*) mandarino.

mandatory ['mændətərı] *a* obbligatorio(a); ingiuntivo(a).

mane [meın] *n* criniera.

maneuver [mə'nuːvə*] *etc* (*US*) =

manoeuvre *etc*.

manfully ['mænfəlı] *ad* valorosamente.

mangle ['mæŋgl] *vt* straziare; mutilare // *n* strizzatoio.

mango, ~es ['mæŋgəu] *n* mango.

mangy ['meındʒı] *a* rognoso(a).

manhandle ['mænhændl] *vt* malmenare.

manhole ['mænhəul] *n* botola stradale.

manhood ['mænhud] *n* età virile; virilità.

man-hour ['mæn'auə*] *n* ora di lavoro.

manhunt ['mænhʌnt] *n* caccia all'uomo.

mania ['meınıə] *n* mania; **~c** ['meınıæk] *n* maniaco/a.

manic ['mænık] *a* (*behaviour*, *activity*) maniacale.

manicure ['mænıkjuə*] *n* manicure *f inv*; **~ set** *n* trousse *f inv* della manicure.

manifest ['mænıfest] *vt* manifestare // *a* manifesto(a), palese.

manifesto [mænı'fɛstəu] *n* manifesto.

manipulate [mə'nıpjuleıt] *vt* manipolare.

mankind [mæn'kaınd] *n* umanità, genere *m* umano.

manly ['mænlı] *a* virile; coraggioso(a).

man-made ['mæn'meıd] *a* sintetico(a); artificiale.

manner ['mænə*] *n* maniera, modo; **~s** *npl* maniere *fpl*; **~ism** *n* vezzo, tic *m inv*.

manoeuvre, (*US*) **maneuver** [mə'nuːvə*] *vt* manovrare // *vi* far manovre // *n* manovra.

manor ['mænə*] *n* (*also*: **~ house**) maniero.

manpower ['mænpauə*] *n* manodopera.

mansion ['mænʃən] *n* casa signorile.

manslaughter ['mænslɔːtə*] *n* omicidio preterintenzionale.

mantelpiece ['mæntlpiːs] *n* mensola del caminetto.

Mantua ['mæntjuə] *n* Mantova.

manual ['mænjuəl] *a* manuale // *n* manuale *m*.

manufacture [mænju'fæktʃə*] *vt* fabbricare // *n* fabbricazione *f*, manifattura; **~r** *n* fabbricante *m*.

manure [mə'njuə*] *n* concime *m*.

manuscript ['mænjuskrıpt] *n* manoscritto.

many ['menı] *a* molti(e) // *pronoun* molti(e), un gran numero; **a great ~** moltissimi(e), un gran numero (di); **~ a** ... molti(e) ..., più di un(a) ... .

map [mæp] *n* carta (geografica) // *vt* fare una carta di; **to ~ out** *vt* tracciare un piano di.

maple ['meıpl] *n* acero.

mar [mɑː*] *vt* sciupare.

marathon ['mærəθən] *n* maratona.

marauder [mə'rɔːdə*] *n* saccheggiatore *m*; predatore *m*.

marble ['mɑːbl] *n* marmo; (*toy*) pallina, bilia; **~s** *n* (*game*) palline, bilie.

March [mɑːtʃ] *n* marzo.

march [mɑ:tʃ] vi marciare; sfilare // n marcia; (*demonstration*) dimostrazione f.

mare [mɛə*] n giumenta.

margarine [mɑ:dʒə'ri:n] n margarina.

margin [mɑ:dʒɪn] n margine m; **~al** (**seat**) n (POL) seggio elettorale ottenuto con una stretta maggioranza.

marigold [ˈmærɪgəuld] n calendola.

marijuana [mærɪˈwɑ:nə] n marijuana.

marine [məˈri:n] a (*animal, plant*) marino(a); (*forces, engineering*) marittimo(a) // n fante m di marina; (*US*) marine m inv.

marital [ˈmærɪtl] a maritale, coniugale; ~ **status** stato coniugale.

mark [mɑ:k] n segno; (*stain*) macchia; (*of skid etc*) traccia; (*Brit SCOL*) voto; (*SPORT*) bersaglio; (*currency*) marco // vt segnare; (*stain*) macchiare; (*Brit SCOL*) dare un voto a; correggere; to ~ time segnare il passo; **to ~ out** vt delimitare; **~ed** a spiccato(a), chiaro(a); **~er** n (*sign*) segno; (*bookmark*) segnalibro.

market [ˈmɑ:kɪt] n mercato // vt (COMM) mettere in vendita; ~ **garden** n (*Brit*) orto industriale; ~**ing** n marketing m; ~ **place** n piazza del mercato; (COMM) piazza, mercato; ~ **research** n indagine f or ricerca di mercato; ~ **value** n valore m di mercato.

marksman [ˈmɑ:ksmən] n tiratore m scelto.

marmalade [ˈmɑ:məleɪd] n marmellata d'arance.

maroon [məˈru:n] vt (*fig*): to be ~ed (in or at) essere abbandonato(a) (in) // a bordeaux inv.

marquee [mɑ:ˈki:] n padiglione m.

marquess, marquis [ˈmɑ:kwɪs] n marchese m.

marriage [ˈmærɪdʒ] n matrimonio; ~ **bureau** n agenzia matrimoniale; ~ **certificate** n certificato di matrimonio.

married [ˈmærɪd] a sposato(a); (*life, love*) coniugale, matrimoniale.

marrow [ˈmærəu] n midollo; (*vegetable*) zucca.

marry [ˈmærɪ] vt sposare, sposarsi con; (*subj: father, priest etc*) dare in matrimonio // vi (*also*: get married) sposarsi.

Mars [mɑ:z] n (*planet*) Marte m.

marsh [mɑ:ʃ] n palude f.

marshal [ˈmɑ:ʃl] n maresciallo; (*US: fire*) capo; (*: police*) capitano // vt adunare.

martyr [ˈmɑ:tə*] n martire m/f // vt martirizzare; ~**dom** n martirio.

marvel [ˈmɑ:vl] n meraviglia // vi: to ~ (at) meravigliarsi (di); ~**lous**, (*US*) ~**ous** a meraviglioso(a).

Marxist [ˈmɑ:ksɪst] a, n marxista (m/f).

marzipan [ˈmɑ:zɪpæn] n marzapane m.

mascara [mæsˈkɑ:rə] n mascara m.

masculine [ˈmæskjulɪn] a maschile // n genere m maschile.

mashed [mæʃt] a: ~ **potatoes** purè m di patate.

mask [mɑ:sk] n maschera // vt mascherare.

mason [ˈmeɪsn] n (*also*: stone~) scalpellino; (*also*: free~) massone m; ~**ry** n muratura.

masquerade [mæskəˈreɪd] n ballo in maschera; (*fig*) mascherata // vi: to ~ as farsi passare per.

mass [mæs] n moltitudine f, massa; (PHYSICS) massa; (REL) messa // vi ammassarsi; **the ~es** le masse.

massacre [ˈmæsəkə*] n massacro.

massage [ˈmæsɑ:ʒ] n massaggio.

masseur [mæˈsə:*] n massaggiatore m; **masseuse** [-ˈsə:z] n massaggiatrice f.

massive [ˈmæsɪv] a enorme, massiccio(a).

mass media npl mass media mpl.

mass-produce [ˈmæsprəˈdju:s] vt produrre in serie.

mast [mɑ:st] n albero.

master [ˈmɑ:stə*] n padrone m; (ART etc, *teacher: in primary school*) maestro; (*: in secondary school*) professore m; (*title for boys*): M~ X Signorino X // vt domare; (*learn*) imparare a fondo; (*understand*) conoscere a fondo; ~ **key** n chiave f maestra; ~**ly** a magistrale; ~**mind** n mente f superiore // vt essere il cervello di; M~ **of Arts/Science (M.A./M.Sc.)** n Master m inv in lettere/scienze; ~**piece** n capolavoro; ~**y** n dominio; padronanza.

mat [mæt] n stuoia; (*also*: door~) stoino, zerbino // a = **matt**.

match [mætʃ] n fiammifero; (*game*) partita, incontro; (*fig*) uguale m/f; matrimonio; partito // vt intonare; (*go well with*) andare benissimo con; (*equal*) uguagliare // vi combaciare; **to be a good** ~ andare bene; ~**box** n scatola per fiammiferi; ~**ing** a ben assortito(a).

mate [meɪt] n compagno/a di lavoro; (*col: friend*) amico/a; (*animal*) compagno/a; (*in merchant navy*) secondo // vi accoppiarsi // vt accoppiare.

material [məˈtɪərɪəl] n (*substance*) materiale m, materia; (*cloth*) stoffa // a materiale; (*important*) essenziale; ~**s** npl materiali mpl.

maternal [məˈtə:nl] a materno(a).

maternity [məˈtə:nɪtɪ] n maternità; ~ **dress** n vestito m pre-maman inv; ~ **hospital** n ≈ clinica ostetrica.

math [mæθ] n (*US*) = **maths**.

mathematical [mæθəˈmætɪkl] a matematico(a).

mathematics [mæθəˈmætɪks] n matematica.

maths |mæθs|, (US) **math** |mæθ| n matematica.

matinée |'mætɪnɪi| n matinée f inv.

mating |'meɪtɪŋ| n accoppiamento.

matriculation |mətrɪkju'leɪʃən| n immatricolazione f.

matrimonial |mætrɪ'məunɪəl| a matrimoniale, coniugale.

matrimony |'mætrɪmənɪ| n matrimonio.

matron |'meɪtrən| n (in hospital) capoinfermiera; (in school) infermiera; ~ly a da matrona.

mat(t) |mæt| a opaco(a).

matted |'mætɪd| a ingarbugliato(a).

matter |'mætə*| n questione f; (PHYSICS) materia, sostanza; (content) contenuto; (MED: pus) pus m // vi importare; it doesn't ~ non importa; (I don't mind) non fa niente; what's the ~? che cosa c'è?; no ~ what qualsiasi cosa accada; as a ~ of course come cosa naturale; as a ~ of fact in verità; ~-of-fact a prosaico(a).

mattress |'mætrɪs| n materasso.

mature |mə'tjuə*| a maturo(a); (cheese) stagionato(a) // vi maturare; stagionare; (COMM) scadere.

maul |mɔ:l| vt lacerare.

mauve |məuv| a malva inv.

maxim |'mæksɪm| n massima.

maximum |'mæksɪməm| a massimo(a) // n (pl **maxima** |'mæksɪmə|) massimo.

May |meɪ| n maggio.

may |meɪ| vi (conditional: **might**) (indicating possibility): he ~ come può darsi che venga; (be allowed to): ~ I smoke? posso fumare?; (wishes): ~ God bless you! Dio la benedica!

maybe |'meɪbiː| ad forse, può darsi; ~ he'll ... può darsi che lui ... +sub, forse lui ....

May Day n il primo maggio.

mayhem |'meɪhem| n cagnara.

mayonnaise |meɪə'neɪz| n maionese f.

mayor |meə*| n sindaco; ~ess n sindaco (donna); moglie f del sindaco.

maze |meɪz| n labirinto, dedalo.

M.D. abbr = Doctor of Medicine.

me |miː| pronoun mi, m' + vowel or silent 'h'; (stressed, after prep) me; he heard ~ mi ha or m'ha sentito; give ~ a book dammi (or mi dia) un libro; it's ~ sono io; with ~ con me; without ~ senza di me.

meadow |'medəu| n prato.

meagre, (US) **meager** |'miːgə*| a magro(a).

meal |miːl| n pasto; (flour) farina; ~time n l'ora di mangiare.

mean |miːn| a (with money) avaro(a), gretto(a); (unkind) meschino(a), maligno(a); (average) medio(a) // vt (pt, pp **meant**) (signify) significare, voler dire; (intend): to ~ to do aver l'intenzione di fare // n mezzo; (MATH) media; ~s npl

mezzi mpl; by ~s of per mezzo di; (person) a mezzo di; by all ~s ma certo, prego; to be **meant** for essere destinato(a) a; do you ~ it? dice sul serio?; what do you ~? che cosa vuol dire?

meander |mɪ'ændə*| vi far meandri; (fig) divagare.

meaning |'miːnɪŋ| n significato, senso; ~ful a significativo(a); ~less a senza senso.

meant |ment| pt, pp of **mean**.

meantime |'miːntaɪm| ad, **meanwhile** |'miːnwaɪl| ad (also: in the ~) nel frattempo.

measles |'miːzlz| n morbillo.

measly |'miːzlɪ| a (col) miserabile.

measure |'meʒə*| vt, vi misurare // n misura; (ruler) metro; ~ments npl misure fpl; chest/hip ~ment giro petto/fianchi.

meat |miːt| n carne f; ~ball n polpetta di carne; ~y a che sa di carne; (fig) sostanzioso(a).

Mecca |'mekə| n Mecca.

mechanic |mɪ'kænɪk| n meccanico; ~al a meccanico(a); ~s n meccanica // npl meccanismo.

mechanism |'mekənɪzəm| n meccanismo.

medal |'medl| n medaglia; ~lion |mɪ'dælɪən| n medaglione m.

meddle |'medl| vi: to ~ in immischiarsi in, mettere le mani in; to ~ with toccare.

media |'miːdɪə| npl media mpl.

mediaeval |medɪ'iːvl| a = **medieval**.

median |'miːdɪən| n mediana; (US: also: ~ strip) banchina f spartitraffico.

mediate |'miːdɪeɪt| vi interporsi; fare da mediatore/trice.

Medicaid |'medɪkeɪd| n (US) assistenza medica ai poveri.

medical |'medɪkl| a medico(a).

Medicare |'medɪkeə*| n (US) assistenza medica agli anziani.

medication |medɪ'keɪʃən| n medicinali mpl, farmaci mpl.

medicine |'medsɪn| n medicina.

medieval |medɪ'iːvl| a medievale.

mediocre |miːdɪ'əukə*| a mediocre.

meditate |'medɪteɪt| vi: to ~ (on) meditare (su).

Mediterranean |medɪtə'reɪnɪən| a mediterraneo(a); the ~ (Sea) il (mare) Mediterraneo.

medium |'miːdɪəm| a medio(a) // n (pl media: means) mezzo; (pl **mediums**: person) medium m inv; the happy ~ una giusta via di mezzo; ~ wave n onde fpl medie.

medley |'medlɪ| n selezione f.

meek |miːk| a dolce, umile.

meet |miːt|, pt, pp **met** vt incontrare; (for the first time) fare la conoscenza di;

(fig) affrontare; soddisfare; raggiungere // *vi* incontrarsi; *(in session)* riunirsi; *(join: objects)* unirsi; I'll ~ you at the station verrò a prenderla alla stazione; **to ~ with** *vt fus* incontrare; **~ing** *n* incontro; *(session: of club etc)* riunione *f*; *(interview)* intervista; **she's at a ~ing** *(COMM)* è in riunione.

megabyte ['mɛgəbaɪt] *n (COMPUT)* megabyte *m inv.*

megaphone ['mɛgəfəun] *n* megafono.

melancholy ['mɛlənkəlɪ] *n* malinconia // *a* malinconico(a).

mellow ['mɛləu] *a (wine, sound)* ricco(a); *(person, light)* dolce; *(colour)* caldo(a); *(fruit)* maturo(a) // *vi (person)* addolcirsi.

melody ['mɛlədɪ] *n* melodia.

melon ['mɛlən] *n* melone *m.*

melt [mɛlt] *vi (gen)* sciogliersi, struggersi; *(metals)* fondersi; *(fig)* intenerirsi // *vt* sciogliere, struggere; fondere; *(person)* commuovere; **to ~ away** *vi* sciogliersi completamente; **to ~ down** *vt* fondere; **~down** *n (in nuclear reactor)* fusione *f* (dovuta a surriscaldamento); **~ing pot** *n (fig)* crogiolo.

member ['mɛmbə*] *n* membro; **M~ of the European Parliament (MEP)** *n (Brit)* eurodeputato; **M~ of Parliament (MP)** *n (Brit)* deputato; **~ship** *n* iscrizione *f*; *(number of)* iscritti *mpl*, membri *mpl*; **~ship card** *n* tessera (di iscrizione).

memento [mə'mɛntəu] *n* ricordo, souvenir *m inv.*

memo ['mɛməu] *n* appunto; *(COMM etc)* comunicazione *f* di servizio.

memoirs ['mɛmwɑ:z] *npl* memorie *fpl*, ricordi *mpl.*

memorandum, *pl* **memoranda** [mɛmə'rændəm, -də] *n* appunto; *(COMM etc)* comunicazione *f* di servizio; *(DIPLOMACY)* memorandum *m inv.*

memorial [mɪ'mɔ:rɪəl] *n* monumento commemorativo // *a* commemorativo(a).

memorize ['mɛməraɪz] *vt* imparare a memoria.

memory ['mɛmərɪ] *n (also COMPUT)* memoria; *(recollection)* ricordo.

men [mɛn] *npl of* **man.**

menace ['mɛnəs] *n* minaccia // *vt* minacciare.

menagerie [mɪ'nædʒərɪ] *n* serraglio.

mend [mɛnd] *vt* aggiustare, riparare; *(darn)* rammendare // *n* rammendo; **on the ~** in via di guarigione.

menial ['mi:nɪəl] *a* da servo, domestico(a); umile.

meningitis [mɛnɪn'dʒaɪtɪs] *n* meningite *f.*

menopause ['mɛnəupɔ:z] *n* menopausa.

menstruation [mɛnstru'eɪʃən] *n* mestruazione *f.*

mental ['mɛntl] *a* mentale.

mentality [mɛn'tælɪtɪ] *n* mentalità *f inv.*

menthol ['mɛnθɒl] *n* mentolo.

mention ['mɛnʃən] *n* menzione *f* // *vt* menzionare, far menzione di; **don't ~ it!** non c'è di che!, prego!

menu ['mɛnju:] *n (set ~, COMPUT)* menù *m inv*; *(printed)* carta.

MEP *n abbr* = **Member of the European Parliament.**

mercenary ['mə:sɪnərɪ] *a* venale // *n* mercenario.

merchandise ['mə:tʃəndaɪz] *n* merci *fpl.*

merchant ['mə:tʃənt] *n* mercante *m*, commerciante *m*; **~ bank** *n (Brit)* banca d'affari; **~ navy**, *(US)* **~ marine** *n* marina mercantile.

merciful ['mə:sɪful] *a* pietoso(a), clemente.

merciless ['mə:sɪlɪs] *a* spietato(a).

mercury ['mə:kjurɪ] *n* mercurio.

mercy ['mə:sɪ] *n* pietà; *(REL)* misericordia; **at the ~ of** alla mercé di.

mere [mɪə*] *a* semplice; **by a ~ chance** per mero caso; **~ly** *ad* semplicemente, non ... che.

merge [mə:dʒ] *vt* unire // *vi* fondersi, unirsi; *(COMM)* fondersi; **~r** *n (COMM)* fusione *f.*

meringue [mə'ræŋ] *n* meringa.

merit ['mɛrɪt] *n* merito, valore *m* // *vt* meritare.

mermaid ['mə:meɪd] *n* sirena.

merry ['mɛrɪ] *a* gaio(a), allegro(a); **M~ Christmas!** Buon Natale!; **~-go-round** *n* carosello.

mesh [mɛʃ] *n* maglia; rete *f.*

mesmerize ['mɛzməraɪz] *vt* ipnotizzare; affascinare.

mess [mɛs] *n* confusione *f*, disordine *m*; *(fig)* pasticcio; *(MIL)* mensa; **to ~ about** *or* **around** *vi (col)* trastullarsi; **to ~ about** *or* **around with** *vt fus (col)* gingillarsi con; *(: plans)* fare un pasticcio di; **to ~ up** *vt* sporcare; fare un pasticcio di; rovinare.

message ['mɛsɪdʒ] *n* messaggio.

messenger ['mɛsɪndʒə*] *n* messaggero/a.

Messrs ['mɛsəz] *abbr (on letters)* Spett.

messy ['mɛsɪ] *a* sporco(a); disordinato(a).

met [mɛt] *pt, pp of* **meet.**

metal ['mɛtl] *n* metallo; **~lic** [-'tælɪk] *a* metallico(a).

metaphor ['mɛtəfə*] *n* metafora.

mete [mi:t]: **to ~ out** *vt fus* infliggere.

meteorology [mi:tɪə'rɔlədʒɪ] *n* meteorologia.

meter ['mi:tə*] *n (instrument)* contatore *m*; *(US: unit)* = **metre.**

method ['mɛθəd] *n* metodo; **~ical** [mɪ'θɔdɪkl] *a* metodico(a).

Methodist ['mɛθədɪst] *a, n* metodista *(m/f).*

methylated spirit ['mɛθɪleɪtɪd-] *n (Brit:*

also: meths) alcool *m* denaturato.

metre, (*US*) **meter** ['mi:tə*] *n* metro.

metric ['mɛtrɪk] *a* metrico(a).

metropolitan [mɛtrə'pɔlɪtən] *a* metropolitano(a); **the M~ Police** *n* (*Brit*) la polizia di Londra.

mettle ['mɛtl] *n* coraggio.

mew [mju:] *vi* (*cat*) miagolare.

mews [mju:z] *n*: ~ **cottage** (*Brit*) *villetta ricavata da un'antica scuderia.*

Mexico ['mɛksɪkəu] *n* Messico.

miaow [mi:'au] *vi* miagolare.

mice [maɪs] *npl of* **mouse.**

micro ['maɪkrəu] *n* (*also:* ~-**computer**) microcomputer *m inv.*

microchip ['maɪkrəutʃɪp] *n* microcircuito integrato.

microfilm ['maɪkrəufɪlm] *n* microfilm *m inv* // *vt* microfilmare.

microphone ['maɪkrəfəun] *n* microfono.

microscope ['maɪkrəskəup] *n* microscopio.

microwave ['maɪkrəuweɪv] *n* (*also:* ~ oven) forno a microonde.

mid [mɪd] *a*: ~ **May** metà maggio; ~ **afternoon** metà pomeriggio; **in** ~ **air** a mezz'aria; ~**day** *n* mezzogiorno.

middle ['mɪdl] *n* mezzo; centro; (*waist*) vita // *a* di mezzo; **in the** ~ **of the night** nel bel mezzo della notte; ~-**aged** *a* di mezza età; **the M~ Ages** *npl* il Medioevo; ~-**class** *a* ≈ borghese; **the** ~ **class(es)** *n(pl)* ≈ la borghesia; **M~ East** *n* Medio Oriente *m*; ~**man** *n* intermediario; agente *m* rivenditore; ~**name** *n* secondo nome *m*; ~**weight** *n* (*BOXING*) peso medio.

middling ['mɪdlɪŋ] *a* medio(a).

midge [mɪdʒ] *n* moscerino.

midget ['mɪdʒɪt] *n* nano/a.

Midlands ['mɪdləndz] *npl* contee del centro dell'Inghilterra.

midnight ['mɪdnaɪt] *n* mezzanotte *f.*

midriff ['mɪdrɪf] *n* diaframma *m.*

midst [mɪdst] *n*: **in the** ~ **of** in mezzo a.

midsummer [mɪd'sʌmə*] *n* mezza *or* piena estate *f.*

midway [mɪd'weɪ] *a, ad*: ~ (**between**) a mezza strada (fra) .

midweek [mɪd'wi:k] *a, ad* a metà settimana.

midwife, *pl* **midwives** ['mɪdwaɪf, -vz] *n* levatrice *f*; ~**ry** [-wɪfərɪ] *n* ostetrica.

might [maɪt] *vb see* **may** // *n* potere *m*, forza; ~**y** *a* forte, potente.

migraine ['mi:greɪn] *n* emicrania.

migrant ['maɪgrənt] *a* (*bird*) migratore(trice); (*person*) nomade; (*worker*) emigrato(a).

migrate [maɪ'greɪt] *vi* migrare.

mike [maɪk] *n abbr* (= *microphone*) microfono.

Milan [mɪ'læn] *n* Milano *f.*

mild [maɪld] *a* mite; (*person, voice*) dolce; (*flavour*) delicato(a); (*illness*) leggero(a) // *n* birra leggera.

mildew ['mɪldju:] *n* muffa.

mildly ['maɪldlɪ] *ad* mitemente; dolcemente; delicatamente; leggermente; **to put it** ~ a dire poco.

mile [maɪl] *n* miglio; ~**age** *n* distanza in miglia, ≈ chilometraggio; ~**stone** *n* pietra miliare.

milieu ['mi:ljə:] *n* ambiente *m.*

militant ['mɪlɪtnt] *a, n* militante (*m/f*).

military ['mɪlɪtərɪ] *a* militare.

militate ['mɪlɪteɪt] *vi*: **to** ~ **against** essere d'ostacolo a.

milk [mɪlk] *n* latte *m* // *vt* (*cow*) mungere; (*fig*) sfruttare; ~ **chocolate** *n* cioccolato al latte; ~**man** *n* lattaio; ~ **shake** *n* frappé *m inv*; ~**y** *a* lattiginoso(a); (*colour*) latteo(a); **M~y Way** *n* Via Lattea.

mill [mɪl] *n* mulino; (*small: for coffee, pepper etc*) macinino; (*factory*) fabbrica; (*spinning* ~) filatura // *vt* macinare // *vi* (*also:* ~ **about**) formicolare.

millennium, *pl* ~**s** *or* **millennia** [mɪ'lɛnɪəm, -'lɛnɪə] *n* millennio.

miller ['mɪlə*] *n* mugnaio.

millet ['mɪlɪt] *n* miglio.

milli... ['mɪlɪ] *prefix*: ~**gram(me)** *n* milligrammo; ~**metre**, (*US*) ~**meter** *n* millimetro.

millinery ['mɪlɪnərɪ] *n* modisteria.

million ['mɪljən] *n* milione *m*; ~**aire** *n* milionario, ≈ miliardario.

millstone ['mɪlstəun] *n* macina.

milometer [maɪ'lɔmɪtə*] *n* ≈ contachilometri *m inv.*

mime [maɪm] *n* mimo // *vt, vi* mimare.

mimic ['mɪmɪk] *n* imitatore/trice // *vt* fare la mimica di; ~**ry** *n* mimica; (*ZOOL*) mimetismo.

min. *abbr* = **minute(s), minimum.**

mince [mɪns] *vt* tritare, macinare // *vi* (*in walking*) camminare a passettini // *n* (*Brit CULIN*) carne *f* tritata *or* macinata; ~**meat** *n* frutta secca tritata per uso in pasticceria; ~ **pie** *n* specie di torta con frutta secca; ~**r** *n* tritacarne *m inv.*

mind [maɪnd] *n* mente *f* // *vt* (*attend to, look after*) badare a, occuparsi di; (*be careful*) fare attenzione a, stare attento(a) a; (*object to*): **I don't** ~ **the noise** il rumore non mi dà alcun fastidio; **I don't** ~ **non m'importa; it is on my** ~ **mi preoccupa; to my** ~ **secondo me, a mio parere; to be out of one's** ~ **essere uscito(a) di mente; to keep *or* bear sth in** ~ **non dimenticare qc; to make up one's** ~ **decidersi;** ~ **you, ... sì, però va detto che ...; never** ~ **non importa, non fa niente;** "~ **the step"** "attenzione allo scalino"; ~**er** *n* (*child* ~**er**) bambinaia; (*bodyguard*) guardia del corpo; ~**ful** *a*: ~**ful of** attento(a) a; memore di; ~**less**

a idiota.

mine [maɪn] *pronoun* il(la) mio(a), *pl* i(le) miei(mie); **that book is ~** quel libro è mio; **yours is red, ~ is green** il tuo è rosso, il mio è verde; **a friend of ~** un mio amico // *n* miniera; (*explosive*) mina // *vt* (*coal*) estrarre; (*ship, beach*) minare.

miner ['maɪnə*] *n* minatore *m*.

mineral ['mɪnərəl] *a* minerale // *n* minerale *m*; **~s** *npl* (*Brit: soft drinks*) bevande *fpl* gasate; **~ water** *n* acqua minerale.

minesweeper ['maɪnswiːpə*] *n* dragamine *m inv*.

mingle ['mɪŋgl] *vi*: **to ~ with** mescolarsi a, mischiarsi con.

miniature ['mɪnətʃə*] *a* in miniatura // *n* miniatura.

minibus ['mɪnɪbʌs] *n* minibus *m inv*.

minim ['mɪnɪm] *n* (*MUS*) minima.

minimum ['mɪnɪməm] *n* (*pl* **minima** ['mɪnɪmə]) minimo // *a* minimo(a).

mining ['maɪnɪŋ] *n* industria mineraria // *a* minerario(a); di minatori.

miniskirt ['mɪnɪskɜːt] *n* minigonna.

minister ['mɪnɪstə*] *n* (*Brit POL*) ministro; (*REL*) pastore *m* // *vi*: **to ~ to sb** assistere qn; **to ~ to sb's needs** provvedere ai bisogni di qn; **~ial** [-'tɪərɪəl] *a* (*Brit POL*) ministeriale.

ministry ['mɪnɪstrɪ] *n* (*Brit POL*) ministero; (*REL*): **to go into the ~** diventare pastore.

mink [mɪŋk] *n* visone *m*.

minnow ['mɪnəʊ] *n* pesciolino d'acqua dolce.

minor ['maɪnə*] *a* minore, di poca importanza; (*MUS*) minore // *n* (*LAW*) minorenne *m/f*.

minority [maɪ'nɒrɪtɪ] *n* minoranza.

mint [mɪnt] *n* (*plant*) menta; (*sweet*) pasticca di menta // *vt* (*coins*) battere; **the (Royal) M~**, (*US*) **the (US) M~** la Zecca; **in ~ condition** come nuovo(a) di zecca.

minus ['maɪnəs] *n* (*also*: **~ sign**) segno meno // *prep* meno.

minute *a* [maɪ'njuːt] minuscolo(a); (*detail*) minuzioso(a) // *n* ['mɪnɪt] minuto; (*official record*) processo verbale, resoconto sommario; **~s** *npl* verbale *m*, verbali *mpl*.

miracle ['mɪrəkl] *n* miracolo.

mirage ['mɪrɑːʒ] *n* miraggio.

mire ['maɪə*] *n* pantano, melma.

mirror ['mɪrə*] *n* specchio // *vt* rispecchiare, riflettere.

mirth [mɜːθ] *n* gaiezza.

misadventure ['mɪsəd'ventʃə*] *n* disavventura; **death by ~** morte *f* accidentale.

misapprehension ['mɪsæprɪ'henʃən] *n* malinteso.

misbehave [mɪsbɪ'heɪv] *vi* comportarsi male.

miscarriage ['mɪskærɪdʒ] *n* (*MED*) aborto spontaneo; **~ of justice** errore *m* giudiziario.

miscellaneous [mɪsɪ'leɪnɪəs] *a* (*items*) vario(a); (*selection*) misto(a).

mischief ['mɪstʃɪf] *n* (*naughtiness*) birichineria; (*harm*) male *m*, danno; (*maliciousness*) malizia; **mischievous** *a* (*naughty*) birichino(a); (*harmful*) dannoso(a).

misconception ['mɪskən'sɛpʃən] *n* idea sbagliata.

misconduct [mɪs'kɒndʌkt] *n* cattiva condotta; **professional ~** reato professionale.

misconstrue [mɪskən'struː] *vt* interpretare male.

misdeed [mɪs'diːd] *n* misfatto.

misdemeanour, (*US*) **misdemeanor** [mɪsdɪ'miːnə*] *n* misfatto; infrazione *f*.

miser ['maɪzə*] *n* avaro.

miserable ['mɪzərəbl] *a* infelice; (*wretched*) miserabile.

miserly ['maɪzəlɪ] *a* avaro(a).

misery ['mɪzərɪ] *n* (*unhappiness*) tristezza; (*pain*) sofferenza; (*wretchedness*) miseria.

misfire [mɪs'faɪə*] *vi* far cilecca; (*car engine*) perdere colpi.

misfit ['mɪsfɪt] *n* (*person*) spostato/a.

misfortune [mɪs'fɔːtʃən] *n* sfortuna.

misgiving(s) [mɪs'gɪvɪŋ(z)] *n(pl)* dubbi *mpl*, sospetti *mpl*.

misguided [mɪs'gaɪdɪd] *a* sbagliato(a); poco giudizioso(a).

mishandle [mɪs'hændl] *vt* (*treat roughly*) maltrattare; (*mismanage*) trattare male.

mishap ['mɪshæp] *n* disgrazia.

misinterpret [mɪsɪn'tɜːprɪt] *vt* interpretare male.

misjudge [mɪs'dʒʌdʒ] *vt* giudicare male.

mislay [mɪs'leɪ] *vt irg* smarrire.

mislead [mɪs'liːd] *vt irg* sviare; **~ing** *a* ingannevole.

misnomer [mɪs'nəʊmə*] *n* termine *m* sbagliato *or* improprio.

misplace [mɪs'pleɪs] *vt* smarrire; collocare fuori posto.

misprint ['mɪsprɪnt] *n* errore *m* di stampa.

Miss [mɪs] *n* Signorina.

miss [mɪs] *vt* (*fail to get*) perdere; (*regret the absence of*): **I ~ him/it** sento la sua mancanza, lui/esso mi manca // *vi* mancare // *n* (*shot*) colpo mancato; **to ~ out** *vt* (*Brit*) omettere.

misshapen [mɪs'ʃeɪpən] *a* deforme.

missile ['mɪsaɪl] *n* (*AVIAT*) missile *m*; (*object thrown*) proiettile *m*.

missing ['mɪsɪŋ] *a* perso(a), smarrito(a); (*person*) scomparso(a); (: *after disaster, MIL*) disperso(a); **to be ~** mancare.

mission ['mɪʃən] n missione f; ~ary n missionario/a.

misspent ['mɪs'spɛnt] a: his ~ youth la sua gioventù sciupata.

mist |mɪst| n nebbia, foschia // vi (also: ~ over, ~ up) annebbiarsi; (: Brit: windows) appannarsi.

mistake |mɪs'teɪk| n sbaglio, errore m // vt (irg: like take) sbagliarsi di; fraintendere; **to make a** ~ fare uno sbaglio, sbagliare; **by** ~ per sbaglio; **to** ~ **for** prendere per; ~**n** a (idea etc) sbagliato(a); **to be** ~**n** sbagliarsi.

mister ['mɪstə*] n (col) signore m; see **Mr.**

mistletoe ['mɪsltəu] n vischio.

mistook |mɪs'tuk| pt of **mistake**.

mistress ['mɪstrɪs] n padrona; (lover) amante f; (Brit SCOL) insegnante f; see **Mrs.**

mistrust |mɪs'trʌst| vt diffidare di.

misty ['mɪstɪ] a nebbioso(a), brumoso(a).

misunderstand |mɪsʌndə'stænd| vt, vi irg capire male, fraintendere; ~**ing** n malinteso, equivoco.

misuse n |mɪs'juːs| cattivo uso; (of power) abuso // vt |mɪs'juːz| far cattivo uso di; abusare di.

mitigate ['mɪtɪgeɪt] vt mitigare.

mitt(en) ['mɪt(n)] n mezzo guanto; manopola.

mix |mɪks| vt mescolare // vi mescolarsi // n mescolanza; preparato; **to** ~ **up** vt mescolare; (confuse) confondere; ~**ed** a misto(a); ~**ed grill** n misto alla griglia; ~**ed-up** a (confused) confuso(a); ~**er** n (for food: electric) frullatore m; (: hand) frullino; (person): **he is a good** ~**er** è molto socievole; ~**ture** n mescolanza; (blend: of tobacco etc) miscela; (MED) sciroppo; ~**-up** n confusione f.

moan |məun| n gemito // vi gemere; (col: complain): **to** ~ **(about)** lamentarsi (di); ~**ing** n gemiti mpl.

moat |məut| n fossato.

mob |mɔb| n folla; (disorderly) calca; (pej): **the** ~ la plebaglia // vt accalcarsi intorno a.

mobile ['məubaɪl] a mobile; ~ **home** n grande roulotte f inv (utilizzata come domicilio).

mock |mɔk| vt deridere, burlarsi di // a falso(a); ~**ery** n derisione f.

mod |mɔd| a see **convenience**.

mode |məud| n modo.

model ['mɔdl] n modello; (person: for fashion) indossatore/trice; (: for artist) modello/a // vt modellare // vi fare l'indossatore (or l'indossatrice) // a (small-scale: railway etc) in miniatura; (child, factory) modello inv; **to** ~ **clothes** presentare degli abiti.

modem ['məudɛm] n modem m inv.

moderate a, n ['mɔdərət] moderato(a) //

vb ['mɔdəreɪt] vi moderarsi, placarsi // vt moderare.

modern ['mɔdən] a moderno(a); ~**ize** vt modernizzare.

modest ['mɔdɪst] a modesto(a); ~**y** n modestia.

modicum ['mɔdɪkəm] n: **a** ~ **of** un minimo di.

modify ['mɔdɪfaɪ] vt modificare.

mogul ['məugl] n (fig) magnate m, pezzo grosso.

mohair ['məuhɛə*] n mohair m.

moist |mɔɪst| a umido(a); ~**en** ['mɔɪsn] vt inumidire; ~**ure** ['mɔɪstʃə*] n umidità; (on glass) goccioline fpl di vapore; ~**urizer** ['mɔɪstʃəraɪzə*] n idratante f.

molar ['məulə*] n molare m.

molasses [məu'læsɪz] n molassa.

mold [məuld] n, vt (US) = **mould**.

mole |məul| n (animal) talpa; (spot) neo.

molest |məu'lɛst| vt molestare.

mollycoddle ['mɔlɪkɔdl] vt coccolare, vezzeggiare.

molt |məult| vi (US) = **moult**.

molten ['məultən] a fuso(a).

mom |mɔm| n (US) = **mum**.

moment ['məumənt] n momento, istante m; importanza; **at the** ~ al momento, in questo momento; ~**ary** a momentaneo(a), passeggero(a); ~**ous** [-'mɛntəs] a di grande importanza.

momentum [məu'mɛntəm] n velocità acquisita, slancio; (PHYSICS) momento; **to gather** ~ aumentare di velocità.

mommy ['mɔmɪ] n (US) = **mummy**.

Monaco ['mɔnəkəu] n Principato di Monaco.

monarch ['mɔnək] n monarca m; ~**y** n monarchia.

monastery ['mɔnəstərɪ] n monastero.

monastic [mə'næstɪk] a monastico(a).

Monday ['mʌndɪ] n lunedì m inv.

monetary ['mʌnɪtərɪ] a monetario(a).

money ['mʌnɪ] n denaro, soldi mpl; ~**lender** n prestatore m di denaro; ~ **order** n vaglia m inv; ~**-spinner** n (col) miniera d'oro (fig).

mongol ['mɔŋgəl] a, n (MED) mongoloide (m/f).

mongrel ['mʌŋgrəl] n (dog) cane m bastardo.

monitor ['mɔnɪtə*] n (SCOL) capoclasse m/f; (TV, COMPUT) monitor m inv // vt controllare.

monk |mʌŋk| n monaco.

monkey ['mʌŋkɪ] n scimmia; ~ **nut** n (Brit) nocciolina americana; ~ **wrench** n chiave f a rullino.

mono... ['mɔnəu] prefix: ~**chrome** a monocromo(a).

monopoly [mə'nɔpəlɪ] n monopolio.

monotone ['mɔnətəun] n pronunzia (or voce f) monotona.

monotonous [mə'nɔtənəs] *a* monotono(a).

monsoon [mɔn'su:n] *n* monsone *m*.

monster ['mɔnstə*] *n* mostro.

monstrous ['mɔnstrəs] *a* mostruoso(a).

montage [mɔn'tɑ:ʒ] *n* montaggio.

month [mʌnθ] *n* mese *m*; ~**ly** *a* mensile // *ad* al mese; ogni mese // *n* (*magazine*) rivista mensile.

monument ['mɔnjumənt] *n* monumento.

moo [mu:] *vi* muggire, mugghiare.

mood [mu:d] *n* umore *m*; to be in a good/bad ~ essere di buon/cattivo umore; ~**y** *a* (*variable*) capriccioso(a), lunatico(a); (*sullen*) imbronciato(a).

moon [mu:n] *n* luna; ~**light** *n* chiaro di luna; ~**lighting** *n* lavoro nero; ~**lit** *a*: a ~**lit night** una notte rischiarata dalla luna.

moor [muə*] *n* brughiera // *vt* (*ship*) ormeggiare // *vi* ormeggiarsi.

moorland ['muələnd] *n* brughiera.

moose [mu:s] *n* (*pl inv*) alce *m*.

mop [mɔp] *n* lavapavimenti *m* *inv*; (*also*: ~ **of hair**) zazzera // *vt* lavare con lo straccio; **to** ~ **up** *vt* asciugare con uno straccio.

mope [məup] *vi* fare il broncio.

moped ['məuped] *n* ciclomotore *m*.

moral ['mɔrl] *a* morale // *n* morale *f*; ~**s** *npl* moralità.

morale [mɔ'rɑ:l] *n* morale *m*.

morality [mə'rælɪtɪ] *n* moralità.

morass [mə'ræs] *n* palude *f*, pantano.

morbid ['mɔ:bɪd] *a* morboso(a).

more [mɔ:*] ♦ *a* 1 (*greater in number etc*) più; ~ **people/letters than we expected** più persone/lettere di quante ne aspettavamo; **I have** ~ **wine/money than you** ho più vino/soldi di te; **I have** ~ **wine than beer** ho più vino che birra
2 (*additional*) altro(a), ancora; **do you want** (*some*) ~ **tea?** vuole dell'altro tè?, vuole ancora del tè?; **I have no** *or* **I don't have any** ~ **money** non ho più soldi
♦ *pronoun* 1 (*greater amount*) più; ~ **than 10** più di 10; **it cost** ~ **than we expected** ha costato più di quanto ci aspettavamo
2 (*further or additional amount*) ancora; **is there any** ~? ce n'è ancora?; **there's no** ~ non ce n'è più; **a little** ~ ancora un po'; **many/much** ~ molti(e)/molto(a) di più
♦ *ad*: ~ **dangerous/easily** (**than**) più pericoloso/facilmente (di); ~ **and** ~ sempre di più; ~ **and** ~ **difficult** sempre più difficile; ~ **or less** più o meno; ~ **than ever** più che mai.

moreover [mɔ:'rəuvə*] *ad* inoltre, di più.

morgue [mɔ:g] *n* obitorio.

morning ['mɔ:nɪŋ] *n* mattina, mattino; (*duration*) mattinata; **in the** ~ la mattina; **7 o'clock in the** ~ le 7 di *or* della mattina.

Morocco [mə'rɔkəu] *n* Marocco.

moron ['mɔ:rɔn] *n* deficiente *m/f*.

morose [mə'rəus] *a* cupo(a), tetro(a).

Morse [mɔ:s] *n* (*also*: ~ **code**) alfabeto Morse.

morsel ['mɔ:sl] *n* boccone *m*.

mortal ['mɔ:tl] *a*, *n* mortale (*m*); ~**ity** [-'tælɪtɪ] *n* mortalità.

mortar ['mɔ:tə*] *n* (*CONSTR*) malta; (*dish*) mortaio.

mortgage ['mɔ:gɪdʒ] *n* ipoteca; (*loan*) prestito ipotecario // *vt* ipotecare; ~ **company** *n* (*US*) società *f inv* di credito immobiliare.

mortified ['mɔ:tɪfaɪd] *a* umiliato(a).

mortuary ['mɔ:tjuərɪ] *n* camera mortuaria; obitorio.

mosaic [məu'zeɪɪk] *n* mosaico.

Moscow ['mɔskəu] *n* Mosca.

Moslem ['mɔzləm] *a*, *n* = **Muslim**.

mosque [mɔsk] *n* moschea.

mosquito, ~**es** [mɔs'ki:təu] *n* zanzara.

moss [mɔs] *n* muschio.

most [məust] *a* la maggior parte di; il più di // *pronoun* la maggior parte // *ad* più; (*work*, *sleep etc*) di più; (*very*) molto, estremamente; **the** ~ (*also*: + *adjective*) il(la) più; ~ **of** la maggior parte di; ~ **of them** quasi tutti; **I saw** (**the**) ~ ho visto più io; **at the** (**very**) ~ al massimo; **to make the** ~ **of** trarre il massimo vantaggio da; **a** ~ **interesting book** un libro estremamente interessante; ~**ly** *ad* per lo più.

MOT *n abbr* (*Brit*: = *Ministry of Transport*): **the** ~ (**test**) *revisione annuale obbligatoria degli autoveicoli*.

motel [məu'tel] *n* motel *m inv*.

moth [mɔθ] *n* farfalla notturna; tarma; ~**ball** *n* pallina di naftalina.

mother ['mʌðə*] *n* madre *f* // *vt* (*care for*) fare da madre a; ~**hood** *n* maternità; ~**in-law** *n* suocera; ~**ly** *a* materno(a); ~**-of-pearl** *n* madreperla; ~**-to-be** *n* futura mamma; ~ **tongue** *n* madrelingua.

motion ['məuʃən] *n* movimento, moto; (*gesture*) gesto; (*at meeting*) mozione *f* // *vt*, *vi*: **to** ~ (**to**) **sb to do** fare cenno a qn di fare; ~**less** *a* immobile; ~ **picture** *n* film *m inv*.

motivated ['məutɪveɪtɪd] *a* motivato(a).

motive ['məutɪv] *n* motivo.

motley ['mɔtlɪ] *a* eterogeneo(a), molto vario(a).

motor ['məutə*] *n* motore *m*; (*Brit col*: *vehicle*) macchina // *a* motore(trice); ~**bike** *n* moto *f inv*; ~**boat** *n* motoscafo; ~**car** *n* (*Brit*) automobile *f*; ~**cycle** *n* motocicletta; ~**cyclist** *n* motociclista *m/f*; ~**ing** *n* (*Brit*) turismo automobilistico; ~**ist** *n* automobilista *m/f*; ~ **racing** *n* (*Brit*) corse *fpl* automobilistiche; ~**way** *n* (*Brit*) autostrada.

mottled ['mɔtld] a chiazzato(a), marezzato(a).

motto, **~es** ['mɔtəu] n motto.

mould, (US) **mold** [məuld] n forma, stampo; (mildew) muffa // vt formare; (fig) foggiare; **~er** vi (decay) ammuffire; **~y** a ammuffito(a).

moult, (US) **molt** [məult] vi far la muta.

mound [maund] n rialzo, collinetta.

mount [maunt] n monte m, montagna; (horse) cavalcatura; (for jewel etc) montatura // vt montare; (horse) montare a // vi salire, montare; (also: ~ up) aumentare.

mountain ['mauntin] n montagna // cpd di montagna; **~eer** [-'niə*] n alpinista m/f; **~eering** [-'niəriŋ] n alpinismo; **~ous** a montagnoso(a); **~side** n fianco della montagna.

mourn [mɔ:n] vt piangere, lamentare // vi: **to ~** (for sb) piangere (la morte di qn); **~er** n parente m/f or amico/a del defunto; persona venuta a rendere omaggio al defunto; **~ful** a triste, lugubre; **~ing** n lutto // cpd (dress) da lutto; **in ~ing** in lutto.

mouse [maus], pl **mice** n topo; (COMPUT) mouse m inv; **~trap** n trappola per i topi.

mousse [mu:s] n mousse f inv.

moustache [məs'ta:ʃ] n baffi mpl.

mousy ['mausi] a (person) timido(a); (hair) né chiaro(a) né scuro(a).

mouth, **~s** [mauθ, -ðz] n bocca; (of river) bocca, foce f; (opening) orifizio; **~ful** n boccata; **~ organ** n armonica; **~piece** n (of musical instrument) imboccatura, bocchino; (spokesman) portavoce m/f inv; **~wash** n collutorio; **~watering** a che fa venire l'acquolina in bocca.

movable ['mu:vəbl] a mobile.

move [mu:v] n (movement) movimento; (in game) mossa; (: turn to play) turno; (change of house) trasloco // vt muovere, spostare; (emotionally) commuovere; (POL: resolution etc) proporre // vi (gen) muoversi, spostarsi; (traffic) circolare; (also: ~ house) cambiar casa, traslocare; **to ~ towards** andare verso; **to ~ sb to do sth** indurre or spingere qn a fare qc; **to get a ~ on** affrettarsi, sbrigarsi; **to ~ about or around** vi (fidget) agitarsi; (travel) viaggiare; **to ~ along** vi muoversi avanti; **to ~ away** vi allontanarsi, andarsene; **to ~ back** vi indietreggiare; (return) ritornare; **to ~ forward** vi avanzare // vt avanzare, spostare in avanti; (people) far avanzare; **to ~ in** vi (to a house) entrare (in una nuova casa); **to ~ on** vi riprendere la strada // vt (onlookers) far circolare; **to ~ out** vi (of house) sgombrare; **to ~ over** vi spostarsi; **to ~ up** vi avanzare.

movement ['mu:vmənt] n (gen) movimento; (gesture) gesto; (of stars, water, physical) moto.

movie ['mu:vi] n film m inv; **the ~s** il cinema; **~ camera** n cinepresa.

moving ['mu:viŋ] a mobile; (causing emotion) commovente.

mow, pt **mowed**, pp **mowed** or **mown** [məu, -n] vt falciare; (lawn) mietere; **to ~ down** vt falciare; **~er** n (also: lawnmower) tagliaerba m inv.

MP n abbr = **Member of Parliament**.

m.p.h. abbr = miles per hour (60 m.p.h. = 96 km/h).

Mr, Mr. ['mistə*] n: ~ X Signor X, Sig. X.

Mrs, Mrs. ['misiz] n: ~ X Signora X, Sig.ra X.

Ms, Ms. [miz] n (= Miss or Mrs): ~ X ≈ Signora X, Sig.ra X.

M.Sc. abbr = **Master of Science**.

much [mʌtʃ] a molto(a) // ad, n or pronoun molto; **how ~ is it?** quanto costa?; **too ~** troppo.

muck [mʌk] n (mud) fango; (dirt) sporcizia; **to ~ about or around** vi (col) fare lo stupido; (: waste time) gingillarsi; **to ~ up** vt (col: ruin) rovinare.

mud [mʌd] n fango.

muddle ['mʌdl] n confusione f, disordine m; pasticcio // vt (also: ~ up) impasticciare; **to be in a ~** (person) non riuscire a raccapezzarsi; **to ~ through** vi cavarsela alla meno peggio.

muddy ['mʌdi] a fangoso(a).

mudguard ['mʌdgɑ:d] n parafango.

mudslinging ['mʌdsliŋiŋ] n (fig) denigrazione f.

muff [mʌf] n manicotto // vt (shot, catch etc) mancare, sbagliare.

muffin ['mʌfin] n specie di pasticcino soffice da tè.

muffle ['mʌfl] vt (sound) smorzare, attutire; (against cold) imbaccuccare.

muffler ['mʌflə*] n (US AUT) marmitta; (: on motorbike) silenziatore m.

mug [mʌg] n (cup) tazzone m; (for beer) boccale m; (col: face) muso; (: fool) scemo/a // vt (assault) assalire; **~ging** n assalto.

muggy ['mʌgi] a afoso(a).

mule [mju:l] n mulo.

mull [mʌl]: **to ~ over** vt rimuginare.

mulled [mʌld] a: ~ **wine** vino caldo.

multi-level ['mʌltilevl] a (US) = **multistorey**.

multiple ['mʌltipl] a multiplo(a); molteplice // n multiplo; ~ **sclerosis** n sclerosi f a placche.

multiplication [mʌltiplɪ'keiʃən] n moltiplicazione f.

multiply ['mʌltiplai] vt moltiplicare // vi moltiplicarsi.

multistorey ['mʌlti'stɔ:ri] a (Brit:

building, car park) a più piani.
mum [mʌm] *n* (*Brit*) mamma // *a*: **to keep ~** non aprire bocca.
mumble ['mʌmbl] *vt, vi* borbottare.
mummy ['mʌmɪ] *n* (*Brit: mother*) mamma; (*embalmed*) mummia.
mumps [mʌmps] *n* orecchioni *mpl*.
munch [mʌntʃ] *vt, vi* sgranocchiare.
mundane [mʌn'deɪn] *a* terra a terra *inv*.
municipal [mju:'nɪsɪpl] *a* municipale; **~ity** [-'pælɪtɪ] *n* municipio.
mural ['mjuərl] *n* dipinto murale.
murder ['mɜːdə*] *n* assassinio, omicidio // *vt* assassinare; **~er** *n* omicida *m*, assassino; **~ous** *a* micidiale.
murky ['mɜːkɪ] *a* tenebroso(a), buio(a).
murmur ['mɜːmə*] *n* mormorio // *vt, vi* mormorare.
muscle ['mʌsl] *n* muscolo; **to ~ in** *vi* immischiarsi.
muscular ['mʌskjulə*] *a* muscolare; (*person, arm*) muscoloso(a).
muse [mju:z] *vi* meditare, sognare // *n* musa.
museum [mju:'zɪəm] *n* museo.
mushroom ['mʌʃrum] *n* fungo.
music ['mju:zɪk] *n* musica; **~al** *a* musicale // *n* (*show*) commedia musicale; **~al box** *n* carillon *m inv*; **~al instrument** *n* strumento musicale; **~ hall** *n* teatro di varietà; **~ian** [-'zɪʃən] *n* musicista *m/f*.
musk [mʌsk] *n* muschio.
Muslim ['mʌzlɪm] *a, n* musulmano(a).
muslin ['mʌzlɪn] *n* mussola.
mussel ['mʌsl] *n* cozza.
must [mʌst] *auxiliary vb* (*obligation*): I **~ do** it devo farlo; (*probability*): he **~ be there by now** dovrebbe essere arrivato ormai; I **~ have made a mistake** devo essermi sbagliato // *n* cosa da non mancare; cosa d'obbligo.
mustard ['mʌstəd] *n* senape *f*, mostarda.
muster ['mʌstə*] *vt* radunare.
mustn't ['mʌsnt] = **must not**.
musty ['mʌstɪ] *a* che sa di muffa *or* di rinchiuso.
mutation [mju:'teɪʃən] *n* mutazione *f*.
mute [mju:t] *a, n* muto(a).
muted ['mju:tɪd] *a* (*noise*) attutito(a), smorzato(a); (*criticism*) attenuato(a).
mutiny ['mju:tɪnɪ] *n* ammutinamento.
mutter ['mʌtə*] *vt, vi* borbottare, brontolare.
mutton ['mʌtn] *n* carne *f* di montone.
mutual ['mju:tʃuəl] *a* mutuo(a), reciproco(a).
muzzle ['mʌzl] *n* muso; (*protective device*) museruola; (*of gun*) bocca // *vt* mettere la museruola a.
my [maɪ] *a* il(la) mio(a), *pl* i(le) miei(mie); **~ house** la mia casa; **~ books** i miei libri; **~ brother** mio fratello; I've washed **~** hair/cut **~** finger mi sono lavato i capelli/tagliato il dito.

myself [maɪ'sɛlf] *pronoun* (*reflexive*) mi; (*emphatic*) io stesso(a); (*after prep*) me; *see also* **oneself**.
mysterious [mɪs'tɪərɪəs] *a* misterioso(a).
mystery ['mɪstərɪ] *n* mistero.
mystify ['mɪstɪfaɪ] *vt* mistificare; (*puzzle*) confondere.
mystique [mɪs'ti:k] *n* fascino.
myth [mɪθ] *n* mito; **~ology** [mɪ'θɔlədʒɪ] *n* mitologia.

N

n/a *abbr* = **not applicable**.
nab [næb] *vt* (*col*) beccare, acchiappare.
nag [næg] *n* (*pej: horse*) ronzino; (: *person*) brontolone/a // *vt* tormentare // *vi* brontolare in continuazione; **~ging** *a* (*doubt, pain*) persistente.
nail [neɪl] *n* (*human*) unghia; (*metal*) chiodo // *vt* inchiodare; **to ~ sb down to a date/price** costringere qn a un appuntamento/ad accettare un prezzo; **~brush** *n* spazzolino da *or* per unghie; **~file** *n* lima da *or* per unghie; **~ polish** *n* smalto da *or* per unghie; **~ polish remover** *n* acetone *m*, solvente *m*; **~ scissors** *npl* forbici *fpl* da *or* per unghie; **~ varnish** *n* (*Brit*) = **~ polish**.
naïve [naɪ'i:v] *a* ingenuo(a).
naked ['neɪkɪd] *a* nudo(a).
name [neɪm] *n* nome *m*; (*reputation*) nome, reputazione *f* // *vt* (*baby etc*) chiamare; (*plant, illness*) nominare; (*person, object*) identificare; (*price, date*) fissare; **by ~** di nome; **she knows them all by ~** li conosce tutti per nome; **~less** *a* senza nome; **~ly** *ad* cioè; **~sake** *n* omonimo.
nanny ['nænɪ] *n* bambinaia.
nap [næp] *n* (*sleep*) pisolino; (*of cloth*) peluria; **to be caught ~ping** essere preso alla sprovvista.
nape [neɪp] *n*: **~ of the neck** nuca.
napkin ['næpkɪn] *n* (*also*: **table ~**) tovagliolo.
nappy ['næpɪ] *n* (*Brit*) pannolino; **~ rash** *n* arrossamento (causato dal pannolino).
narcissus, *pl* **narcissi** [nɑ:'sɪsəs, -saɪ] *n* narciso.
narcotic [nɑ:'kɔtɪk] *n* narcotico // *a* narcotico(a).
narrative ['nærətɪv] *n* narrativa // *a* narrativo(a).
narrow ['nærəu] *a* stretto(a); (*fig*) limitato(a), ristretto(a) // *vi* restringersi; **to have a ~ escape** farcela per un pelo; **to ~ sth down to** ridurre qc a; **~ly** *ad* per un pelo; (*time*) per poco; **~-minded** *a* meschino(a).
nasty ['nɑ:stɪ] *a* (*person, remark*) cattivo(a); (*smell, wound, situation*) brutto(a).

nation ['neɪʃən] n nazione f.

national ['næʃənl] a nazionale // n cittadino/a; ~ **dress** n costume m nazionale; **N~ Health Service (NHS)** n (Brit) servizio nazionale di assistenza sanitaria; ≈ S.A.U.B. f; **N~ Insurance** n (Brit) ≈ Previdenza Sociale; ~**ism** n nazionalismo; ~**ity** [-'nælɪtɪ] n nazionalità f inv; ~**ize** vt nazionalizzare; ~**ly** ad a livello nazionale.

nation-wide ['neɪʃənwaɪd] a diffuso(a) in tutto il paese // ad in tutto il paese.

native ['neɪtɪv] n abitante m/f del paese; (in colonies) indigeno/a // a indigeno(a); (country) natio(a); (ability) innato(a); a ~ of Russia un nativo della Russia; a ~ speaker of French una persona di madrelingua francese; ~ **language** n madrelingua.

NATO ['neɪtəu] n abbr (= North Atlantic Treaty Organization) N.A.T.O. f.

natural ['nætʃrəl] a naturale; (ability) innato(a); (manner) semplice; ~ **gas** n gas m metano; ~**ize** vt naturalizzare; to become ~**ized** (person) naturalizzarsi; ~**ly** ad naturalmente; (by nature: gifted) di natura.

nature ['neɪtʃə*] n natura; (character) natura, indole f; by ~ di natura.

naught [nɔ:t] n = nought.

naughty ['nɔ:tɪ] a (child) birichino(a), cattivello(a); (story, film) spinto(a).

nausea ['nɔ:sɪə] n (MED) nausea; (fig: disgust) schifo; ~**te** ['nɔ:sɪeɪt] vt nauseare; far schifo a.

nautical ['nɔ:tɪkl] a nautico(a).

naval ['neɪvl] a navale; ~ **officer** n ufficiale m di marina.

nave [neɪv] n navata centrale.

navel ['neɪvl] n ombelico.

navigate ['nævɪgeɪt] vt percorrere navigando // vi navigare; (AUT) fare da navigatore; **navigation** [-'geɪʃən] n navigazione f; **navigator** n (NAUT, AVIAT) ufficiale m di rotta; (explorer) navigatore m; (AUT) copilota m/f.

navvy ['nævɪ] n (Brit) manovale m.

navy ['neɪvɪ] n marina; ~**(-blue)** a blu scuro inv.

Nazi ['nɑ:tsɪ] n nazista m/f.

NB abbr (= nota bene) N.B.

near [nɪə*] a vicino(a); (relation) prossimo(a) // ad vicino // prep (also: ~ to) vicino a, presso; (: time) verso // vt avvicinarsi a; ~**by** [nɪə'baɪ] a vicino(a) // ad vicino; ~**ly** ad quasi; I ~**ly** fell per poco non sono caduto; ~ **miss** n: that was a ~ miss c'è mancato poco; ~**side** n (AUT: in Britain) lato sinistro; (: in Italy etc) lato destro; ~-**sighted** a miope.

neat [ni:t] a (person, room) ordinato(a); (work) pulito(a); (solution, plan) ben indovinato(a), azzeccato(a); (spirits) li-

scio(a); ~**ly** ad con ordine; (skilfully) abilmente.

necessarily ['nesɪsrɪlɪ] ad necessariamente.

necessary ['nesɪsrɪ] a necessario(a).

necessity [nɪ'sesɪtɪ] n necessità f inv.

neck [nek] n collo; (of garment) colletto // vi (col) pomiciare, sbaciucchiarsi; ~ **and** ~ testa a testa.

necklace ['neklɪs] n collana.

neckline ['neklaɪn] n scollatura.

necktie ['nektaɪ] n cravatta.

née [neɪ] a: ~ Scott nata Scott.

need [ni:d] n bisogno // vt aver bisogno di; to ~ to do dover fare; aver bisogno di fare; you don't ~ to go non devi andare, non c'è bisogno che tu vada.

needle ['ni:dl] n ago // vt punzecchiare.

needless ['ni:dlɪs] a inutile.

needlework ['ni:dlwɔ:k] n cucito.

needn't ['ni:dnt] = need not.

needy ['ni:dɪ] a bisognoso(a).

negative ['negətɪv] n (answer) risposta negativa; (LING) negazione f; (PHOT) negativo // a negativo(a).

neglect [nɪ'glekt] vt trascurare // n (of person, duty) negligenza; **state of** ~ stato di abbandono.

negligee ['neglɪʒeɪ] n négligé m inv.

negligence ['neglɪdʒəns] n negligenza.

negligible ['neglɪdʒɪbl] a insignificante, trascurabile.

negotiate [nɪ'gəuʃɪeɪt] vi: to ~ (with) negoziare (con) // vt (COMM) negoziare; (obstacle) superare; **negotiation** [-'eɪʃən] n negoziato, trattativa.

Negro ['ni:grəu] a, n (pl ~es) negro(a).

neigh [neɪ] vi nitrire.

neighbour, (US) **neighbor** ['neɪbə*] n vicino/a; ~**hood** n vicinato; ~**ing** a vicino(a); ~**ly** a: he is a ~**ly** person è un buon vicino.

neither ['naɪðə*] a, pronoun né l'uno(a) né l'altro(a), nessuno(a) dei(delle) due // cj neanche, nemmeno, neppure // ad: ~ good nor bad né buono né cattivo; I didn't move and ~ did Claude io non mi mossi e nemmeno Claude; ..., ~ did I refuse ..., ma non ho nemmeno rifiutato.

neon ['ni:ɔn] n neon m; ~ **light** n luce f al neon.

nephew ['nevju:] n nipote m.

nerve [nɔ:v] n nervo; (fig) coraggio; (impudence) faccia tosta; a **fit of** ~s una crisi di nervi; ~-**racking** a che spezza i nervi.

nervous ['nɔ:vəs] a nervoso(a); (anxious) agitato(a), in apprensione; ~ **breakdown** n esaurimento nervoso.

nest [nest] n nido // vi fare il nido, nidificare; ~ **egg** n (fig) gruzzolo.

nestle ['nesl] vi accoccolarsi.

net [net] n rete f // a netto(a) // vt (fish etc) prendere con la rete; (profit) ricavare un utile netto di; ~**ball** n

specie di pallacanestro; ~ **curtains** *npl* tende *fpl* di tulle.
Netherlands ['nɛðələndz] *npl*: the ~ i Paesi Bassi.
nett [nɛt] *a* = **net**.
netting ['nɛtɪŋ] *n* (*for fence etc*) reticolato.
nettle ['nɛtl] *n* ortica.
network ['nɛtwə:k] *n* rete *f*.
neurotic [njuə'rɔtɪk] *a, n* nevrotico(a).
neuter ['nju:tə*] *a* neutro(a) // *n* neutro // *vt* (*cat etc*) castrare.
neutral ['nju:trəl] *a* neutro(a); (*person, nation*) neutrale // *n* (*AUT*): **in** ~ in folle; ~**ize** *vt* neutralizzare.
never ['nɛvə*] *ad* (non...) mai; ~ **again** mai più; **I'll** ~ **go there again** non ci vado più; ~ **in my life** mai in vita mia; *see also* **mind**; ~-**ending** *a* interminabile; ~**theless** [nɛvəðə'lɛs] *ad* tuttavia, ciò nonostante, ciò nondimeno.
new [nju:] *a* nuovo(a); (*brand new*) nuovo(a) di zecca; ~**born** *a* neonato(a); ~**comer** ['nju:kʌmə*] *n* nuovo(a) venuto(a); ~**fangled** ['nju:fæŋgld] *a* (*pej*) stramoderno(a); ~-**found** *a* nuovo(a); ~**ly** *ad* di recente; ~**ly-weds** *npl* sposini *mpl*, sposi *mpl* novelli.
news [nju:z] *n* notizie *fpl*; (*RADIO*) giornale *m* radio; (*TV*) telegiornale *m*; **a piece of** ~ una notizia; ~ **agency** *n* agenzia di stampa; ~**agent** *n* (*Brit*) giornalaio; ~**caster** *n* (*RADIO, TV*) annunciatore/trice; ~**dealer** *n* (*US*) = ~**agent**; ~ **flash** *n* notizia *f* lampo *inv*; ~**letter** *n* bollettino; ~**paper** *n* giornale *m*; ~**print** *n* carta da giornale; ~**reader** *n* = ~**caster**; ~**reel** *n* cinegiornale *m*; ~ **stand** *n* edicola
newt [nju:t] *n* tritone *m*.
New Year *n* Anno Nuovo; ~**'s Day** *n* il Capodanno; ~**'s Eve** *n* la vigilia di Capodanno.
New Zealand [-'zi:lənd] *n* Nuova Zelanda; ~**er** *n* neozelandese *m/f*.
next [nɛkst] *a* prossimo(a) // *ad* accanto; (*in time*) dopo; **the** ~ **day** il giorno dopo, l'indomani; ~ **year** l'anno prossimo; **when do we meet** ~? quando ci rincontriamo?; ~ **door** *ad* accanto; ~-**of-kin** *n* parente *m/f* prossimo(a); ~ **to** *prep* accanto a; ~ **to nothing** quasi niente.
NHS *n abbr* = **National Health Service**.
nib [nɪb] *n* (*of pen*) pennino.
nibble ['nɪbl] *vt* mordicchiare.
Nicaragua [nɪkə'ræɡjuə] *n* Nicaragua *m*.
nice [naɪs] *a* (*holiday, trip*) piacevole; (*flat, picture*) bello(a); (*person*) simpatico(a), gentile; (*distinction, point*) sottile; ~-**looking** *a* bello(a); ~**ly** *ad* bene.
niceties ['naɪsɪtɪz] *npl* finezze *fpl*.
niche [ni:ʃ] *n* nicchia; (*fig*): **to find a** ~ **for o.s.** trovare la propria strada.

nick [nɪk] *n* tacca // *vt* (*col*) rubare; **in the** ~ **of time** appena in tempo.
nickel ['nɪkl] *n* nichel *m*; (*US*) *moneta da cinque centesimi di dollaro*.
nickname ['nɪkneɪm] *n* soprannome *m* // *vt* soprannominare.
niece [ni:s] *n* nipote *f*.
Nigeria [naɪ'dʒɪərɪə] *n* Nigeria.
nigger ['nɪɡə*] *n* (*col!: highly offensive*) negro/a.
niggling ['nɪɡlɪŋ] *a* pignolo(a).
night [naɪt] *n* notte *f*; (*evening*) sera; **at** ~ la sera; **by** ~ di notte; **the** ~ **before last** l'altro ieri notte (*or* sera); ~**cap** *n* bicchierino prima di andare a letto; ~ **club** *n* locale *m* notturno; ~**dress** *n* camicia da notte; ~**fall** *n* crepuscolo; ~**gown** *n*, ~**ie** ['naɪtɪ] *n* camicia da notte.
nightingale ['naɪtɪŋɡeɪl] *n* usignolo.
night life *n* vita notturna.
nightly ['naɪtlɪ] *a* di ogni notte *or* sera; (*by night*) notturno(a) // *ad* ogni notte *or* sera.
nightmare ['naɪtmɛə*] *n* incubo.
night: ~ **porter** *n* portiere *m* di notte; ~ **school** *n* scuola serale; ~ **shift** *n* turno di notte; ~-**time** *n* notte *f*.
nil [nɪl] *n* nulla *m*; (*Brit SPORT*) zero.
Nile [naɪl] *n*: **the** ~ il Nilo.
nimble ['nɪmbl] *a* agile.
nine [naɪn] *num* nove; ~**teen** *num* diciannove; ~**ty** *num* novanta.
ninth [naɪnθ] *a* nono(a).
nip [nɪp] *vt* pizzicare.
nipple ['nɪpl] *n* (*ANAT*) capezzolo.
nitrogen ['naɪtrədʒən] *n* azoto.
no [nəu] ♦ *ad* (*opposite of "yes"*) no; **are you coming?** — ~ (**I'm not**) **viene?** — no (non vengo); **would you like some more?** — ~ **thank you** ne vuole ancora un po'? — no, grazie
♦ *a* (*not any*) nessuno(a); **I have** ~ **money/time/books** non ho soldi/tempo/ libri; ~ **student would have done it** nessuno studente lo avrebbe fatto; "~ **parking**" "divieto di sosta"; "~ **smoking**" "vietato fumare"
♦ *n* (*pl* ~**es**) no *m inv*.
nobility [nəu'bɪlɪtɪ] *n* nobiltà.
noble ['nəubl] *a, n* nobile (*m*).
nobody ['nəubədɪ] *pronoun* nessuno.
nod [nɔd] *vi* accennare col capo, fare un cenno; (*sleep*) sonnecchiare // *vt*: **to** ~ **one's head** fare di sì col capo // *n* cenno; **to** ~ **off** *vi* assopirsi.
noise [nɔɪz] *n* rumore *m*; (*din, racket*) chiasso; **noisy** *a* (*street, car*) rumoroso(a); (*person*) chiassoso(a).
no man's land ['nəumænzlænd] *n* terra di nessuno.
nominal ['nɔmɪnl] *a* nominale.
nominate ['nɔmɪneɪt] *vt* (*propose*) proporre come candidato; (*elect*) nominare.

nominee [nɔmɪ'niː|] *n* persona nominata; candidato/a.

non... [nɔn] *prefix* non...; **~-alcoholic** *a* analcolico(a); **~-committal** ['nɔnkə-'mɪtl] *a* evasivo(a).

nondescript ['nɔndɪskrɪpt] *a* qualunque *inv*.

none [nʌn] *pronoun* (*not one thing*) niente; (*not one person*) nessuno(a); **~ of you** nessuno (a) di voi; **I've ~ left** non ne ho più; **he's ~ the worse for it** non ne ha risentito.

nonentity [nɔ'nɛntɪtɪ] *n* persona insignificante.

nonetheless [nʌnðə'lɛs] *ad* nondimeno.

non: ~-existent *a* inesistente; **~-fiction** *n* saggistica.

nonplussed [nɔn'plʌst] *a* sconcertato(a).

nonsense ['nɔnsəns] *n* sciocchezze *fpl*.

non: ~-smoker *n* non fumatore/trice; **~-stick** *a* antiaderente, antiadesivo(a); **~-stop** *a* continuo(a); (*train, bus*) direttissimo(a) // *ad* senza sosta.

noodles ['nuːdlz] *npl* taglierini *mpl*.

nook [nuk] *n*: **~s and crannies** angoli *mpl*.

noon [nuːn] *n* mezzogiorno.

no one ['nəuwʌn] *pronoun* = **nobody**.

noose [nuːs] *n* nodo scorsoio; (*hangman's*) cappio.

nor [nɔː*] *cj* = **neither** // *ad see* **neither**.

norm [nɔːm] *n* norma.

normal ['nɔːml] *a* normale; **~ly** *ad* normalmente.

north [nɔːθ] *n* nord *m*, settentrione *m* // *a* nord *inv*, del nord, settentrionale // *ad* verso nord; **N~ America** *n* America del Nord; **~-east** *n* nord-est *m*; **~erly** ['nɔːðəlɪ] *a* (*point, direction*) verso nord; **~ern** ['nɔːðən] *a* del nord, settentrionale; **N~ern Ireland** *n* Irlanda del Nord; **N~ Pole** *n* Polo Nord; **N~ Sea** *n* Mare *m* del Nord; **~ward(s)** ['nɔːθwəd(z)] *ad* verso nord; **~-west** *n* nord-ovest *m*.

Norway ['nɔːweɪ] *n* Norvegia.

Norwegian [nɔː'wiːdʒən] *a* norvegese // *n* norvegese *m/f*; (*LING*) norvegese *m*.

nose [nəuz] *n* naso; (*of animal*) muso *vi*: **to ~ about** aggirarsi; **~bleed** *n* emorragia nasale; **~-dive** *n* picchiata; **~y** *a* = **nosy**.

nostalgia [nɔs'tældʒɪə] *n* nostalgia.

nostril ['nɔstrɪl] *n* narice *f*; (*of horse*) frogia.

nosy ['nəuzɪ] *a* curioso(a).

not [nɔt] *ad* non; **he is ~ or isn't here** non è qui, non c'è; **you must ~ or you mustn't do that** non devi fare quello; **it's too late, isn't it or is it ~?** è troppo tardi, vero?; **~ that I don't like him** non che (lui) non mi piaccia; **~ yet/now** non ancora/ora; *see also* **all, only**.

notably ['nəutəblɪ] *ad* (*markedly*) notevolmente; (*particularly*) in particolare.

notary ['nəutərɪ] *n* (*also*: **~ public**) notaio.

notch [nɔtʃ] *n* tacca.

note [nəut] *n* nota; (*letter, banknote*) biglietto // *vt* (*also*: **~ down**) prendere nota di; **to take ~s** prendere appunti; **~book** *n* taccuino; **~d** ['nəutɪd] *a* celebre; **~pad** *n* bloc-notes *m inv*; **~paper** *n* carta da lettere.

nothing ['nʌθɪŋ] *n* nulla *m*, niente *m*; (*zero*) zero; **he does ~** non fa niente; **~ new** niente di nuovo; **for ~** per niente.

notice ['nəutɪs] *n* avviso; (*of leaving*) preavviso // *vt* notare, accorgersi di; **to take ~ of** fare attenzione a; **to bring sth to sb's ~** far notare qc a qn; **at short ~** con un breve preavviso; **until further ~** fino a nuovo avviso; **to hand in one's ~** licenziarsi; **~able** *a* evidente; **~ board** *n* (*Brit*) tabellone *m* per affissi.

notify ['nəutɪfaɪ] *vt*: **to ~ sth to sb** far sapere qc a qn; **to ~ sb of sth** avvisare qn di qc.

notion ['nəuʃən] *n* idea; (*concept*) nozione *f*.

notorious [nəu'tɔːrɪəs] *a* famigerato(a).

notwithstanding [nɔtwɪθ'stændɪŋ] *ad* nondimeno // *prep* nonostante, malgrado.

nougat ['nuːgɑː] *n* torrone *m*.

nought [nɔːt] *n* zero.

noun [naun] *n* nome *m*, sostantivo.

nourish ['nʌrɪʃ] *vt* nutrire; **~ing** *a* nutriente; **~ment** *n* nutrimento.

novel ['nɔvl] *n* romanzo // *a* nuovo(a); **~ist** *n* romanziere/a; **~ty** *n* novità *f inv*.

November [nəu'vɛmbə*] *n* novembre *m*.

novice ['nɔvɪs] *n* principiante *m/f*; (*REL*) novizio/a.

now [nau] *ad* ora, adesso // *cj*: **~ (that)** adesso che, ora che; **by ~** ormai; **just ~** proprio ora; **right ~** subito, immediatamente; **~ and then, ~ and again** ogni tanto; **from ~ on** da ora in poi; **~adays** ['nauədeɪz] *ad* oggidì.

nowhere ['nəuwɛə*] *ad* in nessun luogo, da nessuna parte.

nozzle ['nɔzl] *n* (*of hose etc*) boccaglio; (*of fire extinguisher*) lancia.

nuance ['njuːɑːns] *n* sfumatura.

nuclear ['njuːklɪə*] *a* nucleare.

nucleus, *pl* **nuclei** ['njuːklɪəs, 'njuːklɪaɪ] *n* nucleo.

nude [njuːd] *a* nudo(a) // *n* (*ART*) nudo; **in the ~** tutto(a) nudo(a).

nudge [nʌdʒ] *vt* dare una gomitata a.

nudist ['njuːdɪst] *n* nudista *m/f*.

nuisance ['njuːsns] *n*: **it's a ~** è una seccatura; **he's a ~** è uno scocciatore; **what a ~!** che seccatura!

null [nʌl] *a*: **~ and void** nullo(a).

numb [nʌm] *a* intorpidito(a); **~ with cold** intirizzito(a) (dal freddo).

number ['nʌmbə*] *n* numero // *vt*

numerare; (*include*) contare; a ~ of un certo numero di; **to be ~ed among** venire annoverato(a) tra; **they were 10 in ~** erano in tutto 10; **~ plate** *n* (*Brit* AUT) targa.

numeral ['nju:mərəl] *n* numero, cifra.

numerate ['nju:mərɪt] *a*: **to be ~** avere nozioni di aritmetica.

numerical [nju:'merɪkl] *a* numerico(a).

numerous ['nju:mərəs] *a* numeroso(a).

nun [nʌn] *n* suora, monaca.

nurse [nɜ:s] *n* infermiere/a // *vt* (*patient*, *cold*) curare; (*baby*; *Brit*) cullare; (: *US*) allattare, dare il latte a; (*hope*) nutrire.

nursery ['nɜ:sərɪ] *n* (*room*) camera dei bambini; (*institution*) asilo; (*for plants*) vivaio; **~ rhyme** *n* filastrocca; **~ school** *n* scuola materna; **~ slope** *n* (*Brit* SKI) pista per principianti.

nursing ['nɜ:sɪŋ] *n* (*profession*) professione *f* di infermiere (or di infermiera); **~ home** *n* casa di cura.

nurture ['nɜ:tʃə*] *vt* allevare; nutrire.

nut [nʌt] *n* (*of metal*) dado; (*fruit*) noce *f*; **he's ~s** (*col*) è matto; **~crackers** *npl* schiaccianoci *m inv*.

nutmeg ['nʌtmeg] *n* noce *f* moscata.

nutritious [nju:'trɪʃəs] *a* nutriente.

nutshell ['nʌtʃel] *n* guscio di noce; **in a ~** in poche parole.

nylon ['naɪlɔn] *n* nailon *m* // *a* di nailon.

nymph [nɪmf] *n* ninfa.

O

oak [əuk] *n* quercia // *a* di quercia.

O.A.P. *abbr* = **old age pensioner**.

oar [ɔ:*] *n* remo.

oasis, *pl* **oases** [əu'eɪsɪs] *n* oasi *f inv*.

oath [əuθ] *n* giuramento; (*swear word*) bestemmia.

oatmeal ['əutmi:l] *n* farina d'avena.

oats [əuts] *npl* avena.

obedience [ə'bi:dɪəns] *n* ubbidienza.

obedient [ə'bi:dɪənt] *a* ubbidiente.

obey [ə'beɪ] *vt* ubbidire a; (*instructions*, *regulations*) osservare // *vi* ubbidire.

obituary [ə'bɪtjuərɪ] *n* necrologia.

object *n* ['ɔbdʒɪkt] oggetto; (*purpose*) scopo, intento; (*LING*) complemento oggetto // *vi* [əb'dʒekt]: **to ~ to** (*attitude*) disapprovare; (*proposal*) protestare contro, sollevare delle obiezioni contro; **expense is no ~** non si bada a spese; **I ~!** mi oppongo!; **he ~ed that ...** obiettò che ...; **~ion** [əb'dʒekʃən] *n* obiezione *f*; (*drawback*) inconveniente *m*; **~ionable** [əb'dʒekʃənəbl] *a* antipatico(a); (*smell*) sgradevole; (*language*) scostumato(a); **~ive** *n* obiettivo // *a* obiettivo(a).

obligation [ɔblɪ'geɪʃən] *n* obbligo, dovere *m*; (*debt*) obbligo (di riconoscenza); **without ~** senza impegno.

oblige [ə'blaɪdʒ] *vt* (*force*): **to ~ sb to do** costringere qn a fare; (*do a favour*) fare una cortesia a; **to be ~d to sb for sth** essere grato a qn per qc; **obliging** *a* servizievole, compiacente.

oblique [ə'bli:k] *a* obliquo(a); (*allusion*) indiretto(a).

obliterate [ə'blɪtəreɪt] *vt* cancellare.

oblivion [ə'blɪvɪən] *n* oblio.

oblivious [ə'blɪvɪəs] *a*: **~ of** incurante di; inconscio(a) di.

oblong ['ɔblɔŋ] *a* oblungo(a) // *n* rettangolo.

obnoxious [əb'nɔkʃəs] *a* odioso(a), (*smell*) disgustoso(a), ripugnante.

oboe ['əubəu] *n* oboe *m*.

obscene [əb'si:n] *a* osceno(a).

obscure [əb'skjuə*] *a* oscuro(a) // *vt* oscurare; (*hide*: *sun*) nascondere.

observant [əb'zə:vnt] *a* attento(a).

observation [ɔbzə'veɪʃən] *n* osservazione *f*; (*by police etc*) sorveglianza.

observatory [əb'zə:vətrɪ] *n* osservatorio.

observe [əb'zə:v] *vt* osservare; (*remark*) fare osservare; **~r** *n* osservatore/trice.

obsess [əb'ses] *vt* ossessionare; **~ive** *a* ossessivo(a).

obsolescence [ɔbsə'lesns] *n* obsolescenza.

obsolete ['ɔbsəli:t] *a* obsoleto(a); (*word*) desueto(a).

obstacle ['ɔbstəkl] *n* ostacolo.

obstinate ['ɔbstɪnɪt] *a* ostinato(a).

obstruct [əb'strʌkt] *vt* (*block*) ostruire, ostacolare; (*halt*) fermare; (*hinder*) impedire.

obtain [əb'teɪn] *vt* ottenere // *vi* essere in uso; **~able** *a* ottenibile.

obtrusive [əb'tru:sɪv] *a* (*person*) importuno(a); (*smell*) invadente; (*building etc*) imponente e invadente.

obtuse [əb'tju:s] *a* ottuso(a).

obvious ['ɔbvɪəs] *a* ovvio(a), evidente; **~ly** *ad* ovviamente; certo.

occasion [ə'keɪʒən] *n* occasione *f*; (*event*) avvenimento // *vt* cagionare; **~al** *a* occasionale; **~ally** *ad* ogni tanto.

occupation [ɔkju'peɪʃən] *n* occupazione *f*; (*job*) mestiere *m*, professione *f*; **~al hazard** *n* rischio del mestiere.

occupier ['ɔkjupaɪə*] *n* occupante *m/f*.

occupy ['ɔkjupaɪ] *vt* occupare; **to ~ o.s. with** *or* **by doing** occuparsi a fare.

occur [ə'kə:*] *vi* accadere; (*difficulty*, *opportunity*) capitare; (*phenomenon*, *error*) trovarsi; **to ~ to sb** venire in mente a qn; **~rence** *n* caso, fatto; presenza.

ocean ['əuʃən] *n* oceano; **~-going** *a* d'alto mare.

o'clock [ə'klɔk] *ad*: **it is 5 ~** sono le 5.

OCR *n abbr* = **optical character recognition/reader**.

octave ['ɔktɪv] *n* ottavo.

October [ɔk'təubə*] *n* ottobre *m*.

octopus ['ɔktəpəs] n polpo, piovra.

odd [ɔd] a (strange) strano(a), bizzarro(a); (number) dispari inv; (left over) in più; (not of a set) spaiato(a); **60~** 60 e oltre; **at ~ times** di tanto in tanto; **the ~ one out** l'eccezione f; **~s and ends** npl avanzi mpl; **~ity** n bizzarria; (person) originale m; **~ jobs** npl lavori mpl occasionali; **~ly** ad stranamente; **~ments** npl (COMM) rimanenze fpl; **~s** npl (in betting) quota; **it makes no ~s** non importa; **at ~s in contesa**.

odometer [ɔ'dɔmɪtə*] n odometro.

odour, (US) **odor** ['əudə*] n odore m.

of [ɔv, əv] prep 1 (gen) di; **a boy ~ 10** un ragazzo di 10 anni; **a friend ~ ours** un nostro amico; **that was kind ~ you** è stato molto gentile da parte sua

2 (expressing quantity, amount, dates etc) di; **a kilo ~ flour** un chilo di farina; **how much ~ this do you need?** quanto gliene serve?; **there were 3 ~ them** (people) erano in 3; (objects) ce n'erano 3; **3 ~ us went** 3 di noi sono andati; **the 5th ~ July** il 5 luglio

3 (from, out of) di, in; **made ~ wood** (fatto) di or in legno.

off [ɔf] a, ad (engine) spento(a); (tap) chiuso(a); (Brit: food: bad) andato(a) a male; (absent) assente; (cancelled) sospeso(a) // prep da; **a poca distanza di**; **to be ~** (to leave) partire, andarsene; **to be ~ sick** essere assente per malattia; **a day ~** un giorno di vacanza; **to have an ~ day** non essere in forma; **he had his coat ~** si era tolto il cappotto; **10% ~** (COMM) con uno sconto di 10%; **~ the coast** al largo della costa; **I'm ~ meat** la carne non mi va più; (no longer eat it) non mangio più la carne; **on the ~ chance** a caso.

offal ['ɔfl] n (CULIN) frattaglie fpl.

offbeat ['ɔfbi:t] a eccentrico(a).

off-colour ['ɔf'kʌlə*] a (Brit: ill) malato(a), indisposto(a).

offence, (US) **offense** [ə'fɛns] n (LAW) contravvenzione f; (: more serious) reato; **to take ~ at** offendersi per.

offend [ə'fɛnd] vt (person) offendere; **~er** n delinquente m/f; (against regulations) contravventore/trice.

offensive [ə'fɛnsɪv] a offensivo(a); (smell etc) sgradevole, ripugnante // n (MIL) offensiva.

offer ['ɔfə*] n offerta, proposta // vt offrire; **"on ~"** (COMM) "in offerta speciale"; **~ing** n offerta.

offhand [ɔf'hænd] a disinvolto(a), noncurante // ad all'improvviso.

office ['ɔfɪs] n (place) ufficio; (position) carica; **doctor's ~** (US) studio; **to take ~** entrare in carica; **~ automation** n automazione f d'ufficio; burotica; **~ block**, (US) **~ building** n complesso di

uffici; **~ hours** npl orario d'ufficio; (US MED) orario di visite.

officer ['ɔfɪsə*] n (MIL etc) ufficiale m; (of organization) funzionario; (also: **police ~**) agente m di polizia.

office worker n impiegato/a d'ufficio.

official [ə'fɪʃl] a (authorized) ufficiale // n ufficiale m; (civil servant) impiegato/a statale; funzionario; **~dom** n burocrazia.

officiate [ə'fɪʃɪeɪt] vi presenziare; **to ~ at a marriage** celebrare un matrimonio.

officious [ə'fɪʃəs] a invadente.

offing ['ɔfɪŋ] n: **in the ~** (fig) in vista.

off: ~-licence n (Brit: shop) spaccio di bevande alcoliche; **~-line** a, ad (COMPUT) off-line inv, fuori linea; (: switched off) spento(a); **~-peak** a (ticket etc) a tariffa ridotta; (time) non di punta; **~-putting** a (Brit) sgradevole, antipatico(a); **~-season** a, ad fuori stagione.

offset ['ɔfsɛt] vt irg (counteract) controbilanciare, compensare.

offshoot ['ɔfʃu:t] n (fig) diramazione f.

offshore [ɔf'ʃɔ:*] a (breeze) di terra; (island) vicino alla costa; (fishing) costiero(a).

offside ['ɔf'saɪd] a (SPORT) fuori gioco; (AUT: in Britain) destro(a); (: in Italy etc) sinistro(a) // n (AUT) lato destro; lato sinistro.

offspring ['ɔfsprɪŋ] n prole f, discendenza.

off: ~-stage ad dietro le quinte; **~-the-peg**, (US) **~-the-rack** ad prêt-à-porter; **~-white** a bianco sporco inv.

often ['ɔfn] ad spesso; **how ~ do you go?** quanto spesso ci vai?

ogle ['əugl] vt occhieggiare.

oh [əu] excl oh!

oil [ɔɪl] n olio; (petroleum) petrolio; (for central heating) nafta // vt (machine) lubrificare; **~can** n oliatore m a mano; (for storing) latta da olio; **~field** n giacimento petrolifero; **~ filter** n (AUT) filtro dell'olio; **~ fired** a a nafta; **~ level** n livello dell'olio; **~ painting** n quadro a olio; **~ refinery** n raffineria di petrolio; **~ rig** n derrick m inv; (at sea) piattaforma per trivellazioni subacquee; **~skins** npl indumenti mpl di tela cerata; **~ tanker** n petroliera; **~ well** n pozzo petrolifero; **~y** a unto(a), oleoso(a); (food) untuoso(a).

ointment ['ɔɪntmənt] n unguento.

O.K., **okay** ['əu'keɪ] excl d'accordo! // vt approvare; **is it ~?**, **are you ~?** tutto bene?

old [əuld] a vecchio(a); (ancient) antico(a), vecchio(a); (person) vecchio(a), anziano(a); **how ~ are you?** quanti anni ha?; **he's 10 years ~** ha 10 anni; **~er brother/sister** fratello/sorella maggiore; **~ age** n vecchiaia; **~ age**

pensioner (O.A.P.) *n* (*Brit*) pensionato/a; **~-fashioned** *a* antiquato(a), fuori moda; (*person*) all'antica.

olive [ˈɔlɪv] *n* (*fruit*) oliva; (*tree*) olivo // *a* (*also*: **~-green**) verde oliva *inv*; ~ **oil** *n* olio d'oliva.

Olympic [əʊˈlɪmpɪk] *a* olimpico(a); **the ~ Games, the ~s** i giochi olimpici, le Olimpiadi.

omelet(te) [ˈɔmlɪt] *n* omelette *f inv*.

omen [ˈəʊmən] *n* presagio, augurio.

ominous [ˈɔmɪnəs] *a* minaccioso(a); (*event*) di malauguro.

omit [əʊˈmɪt] *vt* omettere.

on [ɔn] ♦ *prep* 1 (*indicating position*) su; ~ **the wall** sulla parete; ~ **the left** *a or* sulla sinistra
2 (*indicating means, method, condition etc*): ~ **foot** a piedi; ~ **the train/plane** in treno/aereo; ~ **the telephone** al telefono; ~ **the radio/television** alla radio/televisione; **to be ~ drugs** drogarsi; ~ **holiday** in vacanza
3 (*referring to time*): ~ **Friday** venerdì; ~ **Fridays** il *or* di venerdì; ~ **June 20th** il 20 giugno; ~ **Friday, June 20th** venerdì, 20 giugno; **a week ~ Friday** venerdì a otto; ~ **his arrival** al suo arrivo; ~ **seeing this** vedendo ciò
4 (*about, concerning*) su, di; **information ~ train services** informazioni sui collegamenti ferroviari; **a book ~ Goldoni/physics** un libro su Goldoni/di *or* sulla fisica
♦ *ad* 1 (*referring to dress, covering*): **to have one's coat ~** avere indosso il cappotto; **to put one's coat ~** mettersi il cappotto; **what's she got ~?** cosa indossa?; **she put her boots/gloves/hat ~** si mise gli stivali/i guanti/il cappello; **screw the lid ~ tightly** avvita bene il coperchio
2 (*further, continuously*): **to walk ~, go ~ etc** continuare, proseguire *etc*; **to read ~** continuare a leggere; **~ and off** ogni tanto
♦ *a* 1 (*in operation: machine, TV, light*) acceso(a); (: *tap*) aperto(a); (: *brake*) inserito(a); **is the meeting still ~?** (*in progress*) la riunione è ancora in corso?; (*not cancelled*) è confermato l'incontro?; **there's a good film ~ at the cinema** danno un buon film al cinema
2 (*col*): **that's not ~!** (*not acceptable*) non si fa così!; (*not possible*) non se ne parla neanche!

once [wʌns] *ad* una volta // *cj* non appena, quando; ~ **he had left/it was done** dopo che se n'era andato/fu fatto; **at ~** subito; (*simultaneously*) a un tempo; ~ **more** ancora una volta; ~ **and for all** una volta per sempre; ~ **upon a time** c'era una volta.

oncoming [ˈɔnkʌmɪŋ] *a* (*traffic*) che viene in senso opposto.

one [wʌn] ♦ *num* uno(a); ~ **hundred and fifty** centocinquanta; ~ **day** un giorno
♦ *a* 1 (*sole*) unico(a); **the ~ book which** l'unico libro che; **the ~ man who** l'unico che
2 (*same*) stesso(a); **they came in the ~ car** sono venuti nella stessa macchina
♦ *pronoun* 1: **this ~** questo/a; **that ~** quello/a; **I've already got ~/a red ~** ne ho già uno/uno rosso; ~ **by ~** uno per uno
2: ~ **another** l'un l'altro; **to look at ~ another** guardarsi
3 (*impersonal*) si: ~ **never knows** non si sa mai; **to cut ~'s finger** tagliarsi un dito; ~ **needs to eat** bisogna mangiare.

one-: **~-armed bandit** *n* slot-machine *f inv*; **~-day excursion** *n* (*US*) biglietto giornaliero di andata e ritorno; **~-man** *a* (*business*) diretto(a) *etc* da un solo uomo; **~-man band** *n* suonatore ambulante con vari strumenti; **~-off** *n* (*Brit col*) fatto eccezionale.

oneself [wʌnˈsɛlf] *pronoun* (*reflexive*) si; (*after prep*) se stesso(a), sé; **to do sth (by) ~** fare qc da sé; **to hurt ~** farsi male; **to keep sth for ~** tenere qc per sé; **to talk to ~** parlare da solo.

one-: **~-sided** *a* (*argument*) unilaterale; **~-to-~** *a* (*relationship*) univoco(a); **~-upmanship** [-ˈʌpmənʃɪp] *n* l'arte di fare sempre meglio degli altri; **~-way** *a* (*street, traffic*) a senso unico.

ongoing [ˈɔngəʊɪŋ] *a* in corso; in attuazione.

onion [ˈʌnjən] *n* cipolla.

on-line [ˈɔnlaɪn] *a*, *ad* (*COMPUT*) on-line *inv*.

onlooker [ˈɔnlʊkə*] *n* spettatore/trice.

only [ˈəʊnlɪ] *ad* solo, soltanto // *a* solo(a), unico(a) // *cj* solo che, ma; **an ~ child** un figlio unico; **not ~ ... but also** non solo ... ma anche; **I ~ took one** ne ho preso soltanto uno, non ne ho preso che uno.

onset [ˈɔnsɛt] *n* inizio; (*of winter, old age*) approssimarsi *m*.

onshore [ˈɔnʃɔ:*] *a* (*wind*) di mare.

onslaught [ˈɔnslɔ:t] *n* attacco, assalto.

onto [ˈɔntu] *prep* su, sopra.

onus [ˈəʊnəs] *n* onere *m*, peso.

onward(s) [ˈɔnwəd(z)] *ad* (*move*) in avanti.

onyx [ˈɔnɪks] *n* onice *f*.

ooze [u:z] *vi* stillare.

opaque [əʊˈpeɪk] *a* opaco(a).

OPEC [ˈəʊpɛk] *n abbr* (= *Organization of Petroleum-Exporting Countries*) O.P.E.C. *f*.

open [ˈəʊpn] *a* aperto(a); (*road*) libero(a); (*meeting*) pubblico(a); (*admiration*) evidente, franco(a); (*question*) insoluto(a); (*enemy*) dichiarato(a) // *vt* aprire // *vi* (*eyes, door, debate*) aprirsi; (*flower*) sbocciare; (*shop, bank, museum*) aprire; (*book etc*:

commence) cominciare; **in the ~ (air)** all'aperto; **to ~ on to** *vt fus* (*subj: room, door*) dare su; **to ~ up** *vt* aprire; (*blocked road*) sgombrare // *vi* aprirsi; **~ing** *n* apertura; (*opportunity*) occasione *f*, opportunità *f inv*; sbocco; (*job*) posto vacante; **~ly** *ad* apertamente; **~-minded** *a* che ha la mente aperta; **~-plan** *a* senza pareti divisorie.

opera ['ɔpərə] *n* opera; **~ house** *n* opera.

operate ['ɔpəreɪt] *vt* (*machine*) azionare, far funzionare; (*system*) usare // *vi* funzionare; (*drug*) essere efficace; **to ~ on sb (for)** (*MED*) operare qn (di).

operatic [ɔpə'rætɪk] *a* dell'opera, lirico(a).

operating ['ɔpəreɪtɪŋ] *a*: **~ table** tavolo operatorio; **~ theatre** sala operatoria.

operation [ɔpə'reɪʃən] *n* operazione *f*; **to be in ~** (*machine*) essere in azione *or* funzionamento; (*system*) essere in vigore; **to have an ~** (*MED*) subire un'operazione; **~al** *a* in funzione; d'esercizio.

operative ['ɔpərətɪv] *a* (*measure*) operativo(a).

operator ['ɔpəreɪtə*] *n* (*of machine*) operatore/trice; (*TEL*) centralinista *m/f*.

opinion [ə'pɪnɪən] *n* opinione *f*, parere *m*; **in my ~** secondo me, a mio avviso; **~ated** *a* dogmatico(a); **~ poll** *n* sondaggio di opinioni.

opium ['əupɪəm] *n* oppio.

opponent [ə'pəunənt] *n* avversario/a.

opportunist [ɔpə'tju:nɪst] *n* opportunista *m/f*.

opportunity [ɔpə'tju:nɪtɪ] *n* opportunità *f inv*, occasione *f*; **to take the ~ of doing** cogliere l'occasione per fare.

oppose [ə'pəuz] *vt* opporsi a; **~d to** *a* contrario a; **as ~d to** to in contrasto con; **opposing** *a* opposto(a); (*team*) avversario(a).

opposite ['ɔpəzɪt] *a* opposto(a); (*house etc*) di fronte // *ad* di fronte, dirimpetto // *prep* di fronte a // *n* opposto, contrario; (*of word*) contrario.

opposition [ɔpə'zɪʃən] *n* opposizione *f*.

oppress [ə'prɛs] *vt* opprimere.

opt [ɔpt] *vi*: **to ~ for** optare per; **to ~ to do** scegliere di fare; **to ~ out of** ritirarsi da.

optical ['ɔptɪkl] *a* ottico(a); **~ character recognition (OCR)** *n* lettura ottica; **~ character reader (OCR)** *n* lettore ottico.

optician [ɔp'tɪʃən] *n* ottico.

optimist ['ɔptɪmɪst] *n* ottimista *m/f*; **~ic** [-'mɪstɪk] *a* ottimistico(a).

optimum ['ɔptɪməm] *a* ottimale.

option ['ɔpʃən] *n* scelta; (*SCOL*) materia facoltativa; (*COMM*) opzione *f*; **~al** *a* facoltativo(a); (*COMM*) a scelta.

or [ɔː*] *cj* o, oppure; (*with negative*): **he hasn't seen ~ heard anything** non ha visto né sentito niente; **~ else** se no, altrimenti; oppure.

oral ['ɔːrəl] *a* orale // *n* esame *m* orale.

orange ['ɔrɪndʒ] *n* (*fruit*) arancia // *a* arancione.

orator ['ɔrətə*] *n* oratore/trice.

orbit ['ɔːbɪt] *n* orbita.

orchard ['ɔːtʃəd] *n* frutteto.

orchestra ['ɔːkɪstrə] *n* orchestra; (*US: seating*) platea; **~l** [-'kɛstrəl] *a* orchestrale; (*concert*) sinfonico(a).

orchid ['ɔːkɪd] *n* orchidea.

ordain [ɔː'deɪn] *vt* (*REL*) ordinare; (*decide*) decretare.

ordeal [ɔː'diːl] *n* prova, travaglio.

order ['ɔːdə*] *n* ordine *m*; (*COMM*) ordinazione *f* // *vt* ordinare; **in ~** in ordine; (*of document*) in regola; **in (working) ~** funzionante; **in ~ of size** in ordine di grandezza; **in ~ to do** per fare; **in ~ that** affinché +*sub*; **on ~** (*COMM*) in ordinazione; **to ~ sb to do** ordinare a qn di fare; **the lower ~s** (*pej*) i ceti inferiori; **~ form** *n* modulo d'ordinazione; **~ly** *n* (*MIL*) attendente *m* // *a* (*room*) in ordine; (*mind*) metodico(a); (*person*) ordinato(a), metodico(a).

ordinary ['ɔːdnrɪ] *a* normale, comune; (*pej*) mediocre; **out of the ~** diverso dal solito, fuori dell'ordinario.

ore [ɔː*] *n* minerale *m* grezzo.

organ ['ɔːgən] *n* organo; **~ic** [ɔː'gænɪk] *a* organico(a).

organization [ɔːgənaɪ'zeɪʃən] *n* organizzazione *f*.

organize ['ɔːgənaɪz] *vt* organizzare; **~r** *n* organizzatore/trice.

orgasm ['ɔːgæzəm] *n* orgasmo.

orgy ['ɔːdʒɪ] *n* orgia.

Orient ['ɔːrɪənt] *n*: **the ~** l'Oriente *m*; **oriental** [-'ɛntl] *a*, *n* orientale (*m/f*).

origin ['ɔrɪdʒɪn] *n* origine *f*.

original [ə'rɪdʒɪnl] *a* originale; (*earliest*) originario(a) // *n* originale *m*; **~ly** *ad* (*at first*) all'inizio.

originate [ə'rɪdʒɪneɪt] *vi*: **to ~ from** essere originario(a) di; (*suggestion*) provenire da; **to ~ in** avere origine in.

Orkneys ['ɔːknɪz] *npl*: **the ~** (*also*: **the Orkney Islands**) le Orcadi.

ornament ['ɔːnəmənt] *n* ornamento; (*trinket*) ninnolo; **~al** [-'mɛntl] *a* ornamentale.

ornate [ɔː'neɪt] *a* molto ornato(a).

orphan ['ɔːfn] *n* orfano/a // *vt*: **to be ~ed** diventare orfano; **~age** *n* orfanotrofio.

orthodox ['ɔːθədɔks] *a* ortodosso(a).

orthopaedic, (*US*) **orthopedic** [ɔːθə'piːdɪk] *a* ortopedico(a).

ostensibly [ɔs'tɛnsɪblɪ] *ad* all'apparenza.

ostentatious [ɔstɛn'teɪʃəs] *a* pretenzioso(a); ostentato(a).

ostrich |'ɔstrɪtʃ| n struzzo.

other |'ʌðə*| a altro(a) // pronoun: the ~ (one) l'altro(a); ~s (~ people) altri mpl; ~ than altro che; a parte; ~wise ad, cj altrimenti.

otter |'ɔtə*| n lontra.

ouch |autʃ| excl ohi!, ahi!

ought, pt **ought** |ɔːt| auxiliary vb: I ~ to do it dovrei farlo; this ~ to have been corrected questo avrebbe dovuto essere corretto; he ~ to win dovrebbe vincere.

ounce |auns| n oncia (= 28.35 g; 16 in a pound).

our |'auə*| a il(la) nostro(a), pl i(le) nostri(e); see also **my**; ~s pronoun il(la) nostro(a), pl i(le) nostri(e); see also **mine**; ~selves pronoun pl (reflexive) ci; (after preposition) noi; (emphatic) noi stessi(e); see also **oneself**.

oust |aust| vt cacciare, espellere.

out |aut| ad fuori; (published, not at home etc) uscito(a); (light, fire) spento(a); ~ here qui fuori; ~ there la fuori; he's ~ è uscito; (unconscious) ha perso conoscenza; to be ~ in one's calculations essersi sbagliato nei calcoli; to **run/back** etc ~ uscire di corsa/a marcia indietro etc; ~ loud ad ad alta voce; ~ of (outside) fuori di; (because of: anger etc) per; (from among): ~ of 10 su 10; (without): ~ of petrol senza benzina, a corto di benzina; ~ of order (machine etc) guasto(a); ~-and-~ a (liar, thief etc) vero(a) e proprio(a).

outback |'autbæk| n (in Australia) interno, entroterra.

outboard |'autbɔːd| n: ~ (motor) (motore m) fuoribordo.

outbreak |'autbreɪk| n scoppio; epidemia.

outburst |'autbəːst| n scoppio.

outcast |'autkɑːst| n esule m/f; (socially) paria m inv.

outcome |'autkʌm| n esito, risultato.

outcrop |'autkrɔp| n (of rock) affioramento.

outcry |'autkraɪ| n protesta, clamore m.

outdated |aut'deɪtɪd| a (custom, clothes) fuori moda; (idea) sorpassato(a).

outdo |aut'duː| vt irg sorpassare.

outdoor |aut'dɔː*| a all'aperto; ~s ad fuori; all'aria aperta.

outer |'autə*| a esteriore; ~ space n spazio cosmico.

outfit |'autfɪt| n equipaggiamento; (clothes) abito; "~ter's" (Brit) "confezioni da uomo".

outgoing |'autgəuɪŋ| a (character) socievole; ~s npl (Brit: expenses) spese fpl, uscite fpl.

outgrow |aut'grəu| vt irg (clothes) diventare troppo grande per.

outhouse |'authaus| n costruzione f annessa.

outing |'autɪŋ| n gita; escursione f.

outlandish |aut'lændɪʃ| a strano(a).

outlaw |'autlɔː| n fuorilegge m/f.

outlay |'autleɪ| n spese fpl; (investment) sborsa, spesa.

outlet |'autlet| n (for liquid etc) sbocco, scarico; (US ELEC) presa di corrente; (for emotion) sfogo; (for goods) sbocco; (also: retail ~) punto di vendita.

outline |'autlaɪn| n contorno, profilo; (summary) abbozzo, grandi linee fpl.

outlive |aut'lɪv| vt sopravvivere a.

outlook |'autluk| n prospettiva, vista.

outlying |'autlaɪɪŋ| a periferico(a).

outmoded |aut'məudɪd| a passato(a) di moda; antiquato(a).

outnumber |aut'nʌmbə*| vt superare in numero.

out-of-date |autəv'deɪt| a (passport) scaduto(a); (clothes) fuori moda inv.

out-of-the-way |'autəvðə'weɪ| a (place) fuori mano inv.

outpatient |'autpeɪʃənt| n paziente m/f esterno(a).

outpost |'autpəust| n avamposto.

output |'autput| n produzione f; (COMPUT) output m inv.

outrage |'autreɪdʒ| n oltraggio; scandalo // vt oltraggiare; ~ous |-'reɪdʒəs| a oltraggioso(a); scandaloso(a).

outright ad |aut'raɪt| completamente; schiettamente; apertamente; sul colpo // a |'autraɪt| completo(a); schietto(a) e netto(a).

outset |'autset| n inizio.

outside |aut'saɪd| n esterno, esteriore m // a esterno(a), esteriore // ad fuori, all'esterno // prep fuori di, all'esterno di; at the ~ (fig) al massimo; ~ lane n (AUT) corsia di sorpasso; ~-left/-right n (FOOTBALL) ala sinistra/destra; ~ line n (TEL) linea esterna; ~r n (in race etc) outsider m inv; (stranger) straniero/a.

outsize |'autsaɪz| a enorme; (clothes) per taglie forti.

outskirts |'autskəːts| npl sobborghi mpl.

outspoken |aut'spəukən| a molto franco(a).

outstanding |aut'stændɪŋ| a eccezionale, di rilievo; (unfinished) non completo(a); non evaso(a); non regolato(a).

outstay |aut'steɪ| vt: to ~ one's welcome diventare un ospite sgradito.

outstretched |aut'stretʃt| a (hand) teso(a); (body) disteso(a).

outstrip |aut'strɪp| vt (competitors, demand) superare.

out-tray |'auttreɪ| n contenitore m per la corrispondenza in partenza.

outward |'autwəd| a (sign, appearances) esteriore; (journey) d'andata; ~ly ad esteriormente; in apparenza.

outweigh |aut'weɪ| vt avere maggior peso di.

outwit |aut'wɪt| vt superare in astuzia.

oval ['əuvl] *a, n* ovale (*m*).

ovary ['əuvəri] *n* ovaia.

oven ['ʌvn] *n* forno; **~proof** *a* da forno.

over ['əuvə*] *ad* al di sopra // *a* (*or ad*) (*finished*) finito(a), terminato(a); (*too*) troppo; (*remaining*) che avanza // *prep* su; sopra; (*above*) al di sopra di; (*on the other side of*) di là di; (*more than*) più di; (*during*) durante; **~ here** qui; **~ there** là; **all ~** (*everywhere*) dappertutto; (*finished*) tutto(a) finito(a); **~ and ~** (**again**) più e più volte; **~ and above** oltre (a); **to ask sb ~** invitare qn (a passare).

overall *a, n* ['əuvərɔ:l] *a* totale // *n* (*Brit*) grembiule *m* // *ad* [əuvər'ɔ:l] nell'insieme, complessivamente; **~s** *npl* tuta (da lavoro).

overawe [əuvər'ɔ:] *vt* intimidire.

overbalance [əuvə'bæləns] *vi* perdere l'equilibrio.

overbearing [əuvə'bɛəriŋ] *a* imperioso(a), prepotente.

overboard ['əuvəbɔ:d] *ad* (*NAUT*) fuori bordo, in mare.

overbook [əuvə'buk] *vt*: **the hotel was ~ed** le prenotazioni all'albergo superavano i posti disponibili.

overcast ['əuvəka:st] *a* coperto(a).

overcharge [əuvə'tʃɑ:dʒ] *vt*: **to ~ sb for sth** far pagare troppo caro a qn per qc.

overcoat ['əuvəkəut] *n* soprabito, cappotto.

overcome [əuvə'kʌm] *vt irg* superare; sopraffare.

overcrowded [əuvə'kraudid] *a* sovraffollato(a).

overdo [əuvə'du:] *vt irg* esagerare; (*overcook*) cuocere troppo.

overdose ['əuvədəus] *n* dose *f* eccessiva.

overdraft ['əuvədra:ft] *n* scoperto (di conto).

overdrawn [əuvə'drɔ:n] *a* (*account*) scoperto(a).

overdue [əuvə'dju:] *a* in ritardo; (*recognition*) tardivo(a).

overestimate [əuvər'ɛstimeit] *vt* sopravvalutare.

overflow *vi* [əuvə'fləu] traboccare // *n* ['əuvəfləu] troppopieno.

overgrown [əuvə'grəun] *a* (*garden*) ricoperto(a) di vegetazione.

overhaul *vt* [əuvə'hɔ:l] revisionare // *n* ['əuvəhɔ:l] revisione *f*.

overhead *ad* [əuvə'hed] di sopra // *a* ['əuvəhed] aereo(a); (*lighting*) verticale; **~s** *npl*, (*US*) **~** *n* spese *fpl* generali.

overhear [əuvə'hiə*] *vt irg* sentire (per caso).

overheat [əuvə'hi:t] *vi* (*engine*) surriscaldare.

overjoyed [əuvə'dʒɔid] *a* pazzo(a) di gioia.

overkill ['əuvəkil] *n* (*fig*) eccessi *mpl*.

overlap [əuvə'læp] *vi* sovrapporsi.

overleaf [əuvə'li:f] *ad* a tergo.

overload [əuvə'ləud] *vt* sovraccaricare.

overlook [əuvə'luk] *vt* (*have view of*) dare su; (*miss*) trascurare; (*forgive*) passare sopra a.

overnight [əuvə'nait] *ad* (*happen*) durante la notte; (*fig*) tutto ad un tratto // *a* di notte; fulmineo(a); **he stayed there ~** ci ha passato la notte.

overpower [əuvə'pauə*] *vt* sopraffare; **~ing** *a* irresistibile; (*heat, stench*) soffocante.

overrate [əuvə'reit] *vt* sopravvalutare.

override [əuvə'raid] *vt* (*irg: like* **ride**) (*order, objection*) passar sopra a; (*decision*) annullare; **overriding** *a* preponderante.

overrule [əuvə'ru:l] *vt* (*decision*) annullare; (*claim*) respingere.

overrun [əuvə'rʌn] *vt* (*irg: like* **run**) (*country*) invadere; (*time limit*) superare.

overseas [əuvə'si:z] *ad* oltremare; (*abroad*) all'estero // *a* (*trade*) estero(a); (*visitor*) straniero(a).

overseer ['əuvəsiə*] *n* (*in factory*) caposquadra *m*.

overshadow [əuvə'ʃædəu] *vt* (*fig*) eclissare.

overshoot [əuvə'ʃu:t] *vt irg* superare.

oversight ['əuvəsait] *n* omissione *f*, svista.

oversleep [əuvə'sli:p] *vi irg* dormire troppo a lungo.

overstep [əuvə'stɛp] *vt*: **to ~ the mark** superare ogni limite.

overt [əu'və:t] *a* palese.

overtake [əuvə'teik] *vt irg* sorpassare.

overthrow [əuvə'θrəu] *vt irg* (*government*) rovesciare.

overtime ['əuvətaim] *n* (lavoro) straordinario.

overtone ['əuvətəun] *n* (*also:* **~s**) sfumatura.

overture ['əuvətʃuə*] *n* (*MUS*) ouverture *f inv*; (*fig*) approccio.

overturn [əuvə'tə:n] *vt* rovesciare // *vi* rovesciarsi.

overweight [əuvə'weit] *a* (*person*) troppo grasso(a); (*luggage*) troppo pesante.

overwhelm [əuvə'wɛlm] *vt* sopraffare; sommergere; schiacciare; **~ing** *a* (*victory, defeat*) schiacciante; (*desire*) irresistibile.

overwork [əuvə'wə:k] *vt* far lavorare troppo // *vi* lavorare troppo, strapazzarsi.

overwrought [əuvə'rɔ:t] *a* molto agitato(a).

owe [əu] *vt* dovere; **to ~ sb sth, to ~ sth to sb** dovere qc a qn.

owing to ['əuiŋtu:] *prep* a causa di.

owl [aul] *n* gufo.

own [əun] *vt* possedere // *a* proprio(a); **a room of my ~** la mia propria camera; **to**

get one's ~ back vendicarsi; on one's ~ tutto(a) solo(a); to ~ up vi confessare; ~er n proprietario/a; ~ership n possesso.

ox, pl oxen [ɔks, 'ɔksn] n bue m.

oxtail ['ɔksteɪl] n: ~ soup minestra di coda di bue.

oxygen ['ɔksɪdʒən] n ossigeno; ~ mask n maschera ad ossigeno.

oyster ['ɔɪstə*] n ostrica.

oz. abbr = ounce(s).

ozone ['əuzəun] n ozono.

P

p [pi:] abbr = penny, pence.

pa [pɑ:] n (col) papà m inv, babbo.

P.A. n abbr = personal assistant, public address system.

p.a. abbr = per annum.

pace [peɪs] n passo; (speed) passo; velocità // vi: to ~ up and down camminare su e giù; to keep ~ with camminare di pari passo a; (events) tenersi al corrente di; ~maker n (MED) segnapasso.

pacific [pə'sɪfɪk] n: the P~ (Ocean) il Pacifico, l'Oceano Pacifico.

pack [pæk] n pacco; balla; (of hounds) muta; (of thieves etc) banda; (of cards) mazzo // vt (goods) impaccare, imballare; (in suitcase etc) mettere; (box) riempire; (cram) stipare, pigiare; (press down) tamponare; turare; to ~ (one's bags) fare la valigia; to ~ off vt (person) spedire.

package ['pækɪdʒ] n pacco; balla; (also: ~ deal) pacchetto; forfait m inv; ~ tour n viaggio organizzato.

packed lunch n pranzo al sacco.

packet ['pækɪt] n pacchetto.

packing ['pækɪŋ] n imballaggio; ~ case n cassa da imballaggio.

pact [pækt] n patto, accordo; trattato.

pad [pæd] n blocco; (for inking) tampone m; (col: flat) appartamentino // vt imbottire; ~ding n imbottitura; (fig) riempitivo.

paddle ['pædl] n (oar) pagaia; (US: for table tennis) racchetta da ping-pong // vi sguazzare // vt: to ~ a canoe etc vogare con la pagaia; ~ steamer n battello a ruote; paddling pool n (Brit) piscina per bambini.

paddy field ['pædɪ-] n risaia.

padlock ['pædlɔk] n lucchetto.

paediatrics, (US) pediatrics [pi:dɪ'ætrɪks] n pediatria.

pagan ['peɪgən] a, n pagano(a).

page [peɪdʒ] n pagina; (also: ~ boy) fattorino; (at wedding) paggio // vt (in hotel etc) (far) chiamare.

pageant ['pædʒənt] n spettacolo storico; grande cerimonia; ~ry n pompa.

paid [peɪd] pt, pp of pay // a (work, official) rimunerato(a); to put ~ to (Brit) mettere fine a.

pail [peɪl] n secchio.

pain [peɪn] n dolore m; to be in ~ soffrire, aver male; to take ~s to do mettercela tutta per fare; ~ed a addolorato(a), afflitto(a); ~ful a doloroso(a), che fa male; difficile, penoso(a); ~fully ad (fig: very) fin troppo; ~killer n antalgico, antidolorifico; ~less a indolore.

painstaking ['peɪnzteɪkɪŋ] a (person) sollecito(a); (work) accurato(a).

paint [peɪnt] n vernice f, colore m // vt dipingere; (walls, door etc) verniciare; to ~ the door blue verniciare la porta di azzurro; ~brush n pennello; ~er n (artist) pittore m; (decorator) imbianchino; ~ing n pittura; verniciatura; (picture) dipinto, quadro; ~work n tinta; (of car) vernice f.

pair [pɛə*] n (of shoes, gloves etc) paio; (of people) coppia; duo m inv; a ~ of scissors/trousers un paio di forbici/ pantaloni.

pajamas [pɪ'dʒɑːməz] npl (US) pigiama m.

Pakistan [pɑːkɪ'stɑːn] n Pakistan m; ~i a, n pakistano(a).

pal [pæl] n (col) amico/a, compagno/a.

palace ['pæləs] n palazzo.

palatable ['pælɪtəbl] a gustoso(a).

palate ['pælɪt] n palato.

palatial [pə'leɪʃəl] a sontuoso(a), sfarzoso(a).

palaver [pə'lɑːvə*] n chiacchiere fpl; storie fpl.

pale [peɪl] a pallido(a) // n: to be beyond the ~ aver oltrepassato ogni limite; to grow ~ diventare pallido, impallidire.

Palestine ['pælɪstaɪn] n Palestina; Palestinian [-'tɪnɪən] a, n palestinese (m/f).

palette ['pælɪt] n tavolozza.

paling ['peɪlɪŋ] n (stake) palo; (fence) palizzata.

pall [pɔːl] n (of smoke) cappa // vi: to ~ (on) diventare noioso(a) (a).

pallet ['pælɪt] n (for goods) paletta.

pallid ['pælɪd] a pallido(a), smorto(a).

pallor ['pælə*] n pallore m.

palm [pɑːm] n (ANAT) palma, palmo; (also: ~ tree) palma // vt: to ~ sth off on sb (col) rifilare qc a qn; P~ Sunday n Domenica delle Palme.

palpable ['pælpəbl] a palpabile.

paltry ['pɔːltrɪ] a derisorio(a); insignificante.

pamper ['pæmpə*] vt viziare, accarezzare.

pamphlet ['pæmflət] n dépliant m inv.

pan [pæn] n (also: sauce~) casseruola; (also: frying ~) padella // vi (CINEMA) fare una panoramica.

panache [pə'næʃ] *n* stile *m*.

pancake ['pænkeɪk] *n* frittella.

pancreas ['pæŋkrɪəs] *n* pancreas *m inv*.

panda ['pændə] *n* panda *m inv*; ~ **car** *n* (*Brit*) auto *f* della polizia.

pandemonium [pændɪ'məʊnɪəm] *n* pandemonio.

pander ['pændə*] *vi*: to ~ to lusingare; concedere tutto a.

pane [peɪn] *n* vetro.

panel ['pænl] *n* (*of wood, cloth etc*) pannello; (*RADIO, TV*) giuria; ~**ling**, (*US*) ~**ing** *n* rivestimento a pannelli.

pang [pæŋ] *n*: ~s of hunger spasimi *mpl* della fame; ~s of conscience morsi *mpl* di coscienza.

panic ['pænɪk] *n* panico // *vi* perdere il sangue freddo; ~**ky** *a* (*person*) pauroso(a); ~**stricken** *a* (*person*) preso(a) dal panico, in preda al panico; (*look*) terrorizzato(a).

pansy ['pænzɪ] *n* (*BOT*) viola del pensiero, pensée *f inv*; (*col*) femminuccia.

pant [pænt] *vi* ansare.

panther ['pænθə*] *n* pantera.

panties ['pæntɪz] *npl* slip *m*, mutandine *fpl*.

pantihose ['pæntɪhəʊz] *n* (*US*) collant *m inv*.

pantomime ['pæntəmaɪm] *n* (*Brit*) pantomima.

pantry ['pæntrɪ] *n* dispensa.

pants [pænts] *npl* mutande *fpl*, slip *m*; (*US: trousers*) pantaloni *mpl*.

papal ['peɪpəl] *a* papale, pontificio(a).

paper ['peɪpə*] *n* carta; (*also: wall*~) carta da parati, tappezzeria; (*also: news*~) giornale *m*; (*study, article*) saggio; (*exam*) prova scritta // *a* di carta // *vt* tappezzare; ~**s** *npl* (*also: identity* ~s) carte *fpl*, documenti *mpl*; ~**back** *n* tascabile *m*; edizione *f* economica; ~ **clip** *n* graffetta, clip *f inv*; ~ **hankie** *n* fazzolettino di carta; ~ **mill** *n* cartiera; ~**weight** *n* fermacarte *m inv*; ~**work** *n* lavoro amministrativo.

papier-mâché ['pæpɪeɪ'mæʃeɪ] *n* cartapesta.

par [pɑ:*] *n* parità, pari *f*; (*GOLF*) norma; on a ~ with alla pari con.

parable ['pærəbl] *n* parabola.

parachute ['pærəʃuːt] *n* paracadute *m inv*.

parade [pə'reɪd] *n* parata; (*inspection*) rivista, rassegna // *vt* (*fig*) fare sfoggio di // *vi* sfilare in parata.

paradise ['pærədaɪs] *n* paradiso.

paradox ['pærədɔks] *n* paradosso; ~**ically** [-'dɔksɪklɪ] *ad* paradossalmente.

paraffin ['pærəfɪn] *n* (*Brit*): ~ (**oil**) paraffina.

paragon ['pærəgən] *n* modello di perfezione *or* di virtù.

paragraph ['pærəgrɑːf] *n* paragrafo.

parallel ['pærəlɛl] *a* parallelo(a); (*fig*) analogo(a) // *n* (*line*) parallela; (*fig, GEO*) parallelo.

paralysis [pə'rælɪsɪs] *n* paralisi *f inv*.

paralyze ['pærəlaɪz] *vt* paralizzare.

paramount ['pærəmaʊnt] *a*: of ~ importance di capitale importanza.

paranoid ['pærənɔɪd] *a* paranoico(a).

paraphernalia [pærəfə'neɪlɪə] *n* attrezzi *mpl*, roba.

parasol ['pærəsɔl] *n* parasole *m*.

paratrooper ['pærətruːpə*] *n* paracadutista *m* (*soldato*).

parcel ['pɑːsl] *n* pacco, pacchetto // *vt* (*also*: ~ **up**) impaccare.

parch [pɑːtʃ] *vt* riardere; ~**ed** *a* (*person*) assetato(a).

parchment ['pɑːtʃmənt] *n* pergamena.

pardon ['pɑːdn] *n* perdono; grazia // *vt* perdonare; (*LAW*) graziare; ~ me! mi scusi!; I beg your ~! scusi!; I beg your ~?, (*US*) ~ me? prego?

parent ['pɛərənt] *n* genitore *m*; ~**s** *npl* genitori *mpl*; ~**al** [pə'rɛntl] *a* dei genitori.

parentheses *pl* **parenthesis** [pə'rɛnθɪsɪs, -siːz] *n* parentesi *f inv*.

Paris ['pærɪs] *n* Parigi *f*.

parish ['pærɪʃ] *n* parrocchia; (*civil*) ≈ municipio // *a* parrocchiale.

park [pɑːk] *n* parco // *vt, vi* parcheggiare.

parka ['pɑːkə] *n* eskimo.

parking ['pɑːkɪŋ] *n* parcheggio; "no ~" "sosta vietata"; ~ **lot** *n* (*US*) posteggio, parcheggio; ~ **meter** *n* parchimetro; ~ **ticket** *n* multa per sosta vietata.

parlance ['pɑːləns] *n* gergo.

parliament ['pɑːləmənt] *n* parlamento; ~**ary** [-'mɛntərɪ] *a* parlamentare.

parlour, (*US*) **parlor** ['pɑːlə*] *n* salotto.

parochial [pə'rəʊkɪəl] *a* parrocchiale; (*pej*) provinciale.

parody ['pærədɪ] *n* parodia.

parole [pə'rəʊl] *n*: on ~ in libertà per buona condotta.

parrot ['pærət] *n* pappagallo.

parry ['pærɪ] *vt* parare.

parsley ['pɑːslɪ] *n* prezzemolo.

parsnip ['pɑːsnɪp] *n* pastinaca.

parson ['pɑːsn] *n* prete *m*; (*Church of England*) parroco.

part [pɑːt] *n* parte *f*; (*of machine*) pezzo; (*MUS*) voce *f*; parte; (*US: in hair*) scriminatura // *a* in parte // *ad* = **partly** // *vt* separare // *vi* (*people*) separarsi; (*roads*) dividersi; to take ~ in prendere parte a; for my ~ per parte mia; to take sth in good ~ prendere bene qc; to take sb's ~ parteggiare per *or* prendere le parti di qn; for the most ~ in generale; nella maggior parte dei casi; to ~ with *vt fus* separarsi da; rinunciare a; ~ **exchange** *n* (*Brit*): in ~ exchange in pagamento parziale.

partial ['pɑːʃl] *a* parziale; to be ~ to

avere un debole per.

participate [pɑːˈtɪsɪpeɪt] vi: to ~ (in) prendere parte (a), partecipare (a); **participation** [-ˈpeɪʃən] n partecipazione f.

participle [ˈpɑːtɪsɪpl] n participio.

particle [ˈpɑːtɪkl] n particella.

particular [pəˈtɪkjuləˠ] a particolare; speciale; (fussy) difficile; meticoloso(a); ~s npl particolari mpl, dettagli mpl; (information) informazioni fpl; in ~ in particolare, particolarmente; ~ly ad particolarmente; in particolare.

parting [ˈpɑːtɪŋ] n separazione f; (Brit: in hair) scriminatura // a d'addio.

partisan [pɑːtɪˈzæn] n partigiano/a // a partigiano(a); di parte.

partition [pɑːˈtɪʃən] n (POL) partizione f; (wall) tramezzo.

partly [ˈpɑːtlɪ] ad parzialmente; in parte.

partner [ˈpɑːtnəˠ] n (COMM) socio/a; (SPORT) compagno/a; (at dance) cavaliere/dama; ~ship n associazione f; (COMM) società f inv.

partridge [ˈpɑːtrɪdʒ] n pernice f.

part-time [ˈpɑːtˈtaɪm] a, ad a orario ridotto.

party [ˈpɑːtɪ] n (POL) partito; (team) squadra; gruppo; (LAW) parte f; (celebration) ricevimento; serata; festa // cpd (POL) del partito, di partito; (dress, finery) della festa; ~ line n (TEL) duplex m inv.

pass [pɑːs] vt (gen) passare; (place) passare davanti a; (exam) passare; superare; (candidate) promuovere; (overtake, surpass) sorpassare, superare; (approve) approvare // vi passare // n (permit) lasciapassare m inv; permesso; (in mountains) passo, gola; (SPORT) passaggio; (SCOL: also: ~ mark): to get a ~ prendere la sufficienza; to ~ sth through a hole etc far passare qc attraverso un buco etc; to make a ~ at sb (col) fare delle proposte or delle avances a qn; to ~ away vi morire; to ~ by vi passare // vt trascurare; to ~ on vt passare; to ~ out vi svenire; to ~ up vt (opportunity) lasciarsi sfuggire, perdere; ~able a (road) praticabile; (work) accettabile.

passage [ˈpæsɪdʒ] n (gen) passaggio; (also: ~way) corridoio; (in book) brano, passo; (by boat) traversata.

passbook [ˈpɑːsbuk] n libretto di risparmio.

passenger [ˈpæsɪndʒəˠ] n passeggero/a.

passer-by [ˈpɑːsəˈbaɪ] n passante m/f.

passing [ˈpɑːsɪŋ] a (fig) fuggevole; to mention sth in ~ accennare a qc di sfuggita; ~ place n (AUT) piazzola di sosta.

passion [ˈpæʃən] n passione f; amore m; ~ate a appassionato(a).

passive [ˈpæsɪv] a (also LING) passivo(a).

Passover [ˈpɑːsəuvəˠ] n Pasqua ebraica.

passport [ˈpɑːspɔːt] n passaporto; ~ control n controllo m passaporti inv.

password [ˈpɑːswɜːd] n parola d'ordine.

past [pɑːst] prep (further than) oltre, di là di; dopo; (later than) dopo // a passato(a); (president etc) ex inv // n passato; he's ~ forty ha più di quarant'anni; for the ~ few days da qualche giorno; in questi ultimi giorni; to run ~ passare di corsa.

pasta [ˈpæstə] n pasta.

paste [peɪst] n (glue) colla; (CULIN) pâté m inv; pasta // vt collare.

pastel [ˈpæstl] a pastello inv.

pasteurized [ˈpæstəraɪzd] a pastorizzato(a).

pastille [ˈpæstl] n pastiglia.

pastime [ˈpɑːstaɪm] n passatempo.

pastor [ˈpɑːstəˠ] n pastore m.

pastry [ˈpeɪstrɪ] n pasta.

pasture [ˈpɑːstʃəˠ] n pascolo.

pasty n [ˈpæstɪ] pasticcio di carne // a [ˈpeɪstɪ] pastoso(a); (complexion) pallido(a).

pat [pæt] vt accarezzare, dare un colpetto (affettuoso) a.

patch [pætʃ] n (of material) toppa; (spot) macchia; (of land) pezzo // vt (clothes) rattoppare; (to go through) a bad ~ (attraversare) un brutto periodo; to ~ up vt rappezzare; ~y a irregolare.

pâté [ˈpæteɪ] n pâté m inv.

patent [ˈpeɪtnt] n brevetto // vt brevettare // a patente, manifesto(a); ~ leather n cuoio verniciato.

paternal [pəˈtɜːnl] a paterno(a).

path [pɑːθ] n sentiero, viottolo; viale m; (fig) via, strada; (of planet, missile) traiettoria.

pathetic [pəˈθetɪk] a (pitiful) patetico(a); (very bad) penoso(a).

pathological [pæθəˈlɒdʒɪkl] a patologico(a).

patience [ˈpeɪʃns] n pazienza; (Brit CARDS) solitario.

patient [ˈpeɪʃnt] n paziente m/f; malato/a // a paziente.

patio [ˈpætɪəu] n terrazza.

patriot [ˈpeɪtrɪət] n patriota m/f; ~ic [pætrɪˈɒtɪk] a patriottico(a); ~ism n patriottismo.

patrol [pəˈtrəul] n pattuglia // vt pattugliare; ~ car n autoradio f inv (della polizia); ~man n (US) poliziotto.

patron [ˈpeɪtrən] n (in shop) cliente m/f; (of charity) benefattore/trice; ~ of the arts mecenate m/f; ~ize [ˈpætrənaɪz] vt essere cliente abituale di; (fig) trattare con condiscendenza.

patter [ˈpætəˠ] n picchiettio; (sales talk) propaganda di vendita.

pattern [ˈpætən] n modello; (design)

disegno, motivo; (sample) campione m.

paunch |pɔːntʃ| n pancione m.

pauper |'pɔːpə*| n indigente m/f.

pause |pɔːz| n pausa // vi fare una pausa, arrestarsi.

pave |peɪv| vt pavimentare; **to ~ the way for** aprire la via a.

pavement |'peɪvmənt| n (Brit) marciapiede m.

pavilion |pə'vɪlɪən| n padiglione m; tendone m.

paving |'peɪvɪŋ| n pavimentazione f; **~ stone** n lastra di pietra.

paw |pɔː| n zampa // vt dare una zampata a; (subj: person: pej) palpare.

pawn |pɔːn| n pegno; (CHESS) pedone m; (fig) pedina // vt dare in pegno; **~broker** n prestatore m su pegno; **~shop** n monte m di pietà.

pay |peɪ| n stipendio; paga // vb (pt, pp **paid**) vt pagare // vi pagare; (be profitable) rendere; **to ~ attention (to)** fare attenzione (a); **to ~ back** vt rimborsare; **to ~ for** vt fus pagare; **to ~ in** vt versare; **to ~ off** vt (debt) saldare; (person) pagare; (employee) pagare e licenziare // vi (scheme, decision) dare dei frutti; **to ~ up** vt saldare; **~able** a pagabile; **~ee** n beneficiario/a; **~ envelope** n (US) = **~ packet**; **~ment** n pagamento; versamento; saldamento; **advance ~ment** (part sum) anticipo, acconto; (total sum) pagamento anticipato; **~ packet** n (Brit) busta f paga inv; **~ phone** n cabina telefonica; **~roll** n ruolo (organico); **~ slip** n foglio m paga inv.

PC n abbr = **personal computer**.

p.c. abbr = **per cent**.

pea |piː| n pisello m.

peace |piːs| n pace f; (calm) calma, tranquillità; **~able** a pacifico(a); **~ful** a pacifico(a), calmo(a).

peach |piːtʃ| n pesca.

peacock |'piːkɔk| n pavone m.

peak |piːk| n (of mountain) cima, vetta; (mountain itself) picco; (fig) massimo; (: of career) acme f; **~ hours** npl ore fpl di punta.

peal |piːl| n (of bells) scampanio, carillon m inv; **~s of laughter** scoppi mpl di risa.

peanut |'piːnʌt| n arachide f, nocciolina americana.

pear |peə*| n pera.

pearl |pɜːl| n perla.

peasant |'pɛznt| n contadino/a.

peat |piːt| n torba.

pebble |'pɛbl| n ciottolo.

peck |pɛk| vt (also: **~ at**) beccare; (food) mangiucchiare // n colpo di becco; (kiss) bacetto; **~ing order** n ordine m gerarchico; **~ish** a (Brit col): **I feel ~ish** ho un languorino.

peculiar |pɪ'kjuːlɪə*| a strano(a),

bizzarro(a); peculiare; **~ to** peculiare di.

pedal |'pɛdl| n pedale m // vi pedalare.

pedantic |pɪ'dæntɪk| a pedantesco(a).

peddler |'pɛdlə*| n (US) = **pedlar**.

pedestal |'pɛdəstl| n piedestallo.

pedestrian |pɪ'dɛstrɪən| n pedone m // a pedonale; (fig) prosaico(a), pedestre; **~ crossing** n (Brit) passaggio pedonale.

pediatrics |piːdɪ'ætrɪks| n (US) = **paediatrics**.

pedigree |'pɛdɪgriː| n stirpe f; (of animal) pedigree m inv // cpd (animal) di razza.

pedlar |'pɛdlə*| n venditore m ambulante.

pee |piː| vi (col) pisciare.

peek |piːk| vi guardare furtivamente.

peel |piːl| n buccia; (of orange, lemon) scorza // vt sbucciare // vi (paint etc) staccarsi.

peep |piːp| n (Brit: look) sguardo furtivo, sbirciata; (sound) pigolio // vi (Brit) guardare furtivamente; **to ~ out** vi mostrarsi furtivamente; **~hole** n spioncino.

peer |pɪə*| vi: **to ~ at** scrutare // n (noble) pari m inv; (equal) pari m/f inv, uguale m/f; **~age** n dignità di pari; pari mpl.

peeved |piːvd| a stizzito(a).

peevish |'piːvɪʃ| a stizzoso(a).

peg |pɛg| n caviglia; (for coat etc) attaccapanni m inv; (Brit: also: **clothes ~**) molletta // vt (prices) fissare, stabilizzare.

Peking |piː'kɪŋ| n Pechino f.

pelican |'pɛlɪkən| n pellicano; **~ crossing** n (Brit AUT) attraversamento pedonale con semaforo a controllo manuale.

pellet |'pɛlɪt| n pallottola, pallina.

pelmet |'pɛlmɪt| n mantovana; cassonetto.

pelt |pɛlt| vt: **to ~ sb (with)** bombardare qn (con) // vi (rain) piovere a dirotto // n pelle f.

pelvis |'pɛlvɪs| n pelvi f inv, bacino.

pen |pɛn| n penna; (for sheep) recinto.

penal |'piːnl| a penale; **~ize** vt punire; (SPORT) penalizzare; (fig) svantaggiare.

penalty |'pɛnltɪ| n penalità f inv; sanzione f penale; (fine) ammenda; (SPORT) penalizzazione f; **~ (kick)** n (FOOTBALL) calcio di rigore.

penance |'pɛnəns| n penitenza.

pence |pɛns| npl of **penny**.

pencil |'pɛnsl| n matita; **~ case** n astuccio per matite; **~ sharpener** n temperamatite m inv.

pendant |'pɛndnt| n pendaglio.

pending |'pɛndɪŋ| prep in attesa di // a in sospeso.

pendulum |'pɛndjʊləm| n pendolo.

penetrate |'pɛnɪtreɪt| vt penetrare.

penfriend |'pɛnfrɛnd| n (Brit) corrispondente *m/f*.

penguin ['pɛŋgwɪn] *n* pinguino.

penicillin [pɛnɪ'sɪlɪn] *n* penicillina.

peninsula [pə'nɪnsjulə] *n* penisola.

penis ['pi:nɪs] *n* pene *m*.

penitent ['pɛnɪtnt] *a* penitente.

penitentiary [pɛnɪ'tɛnʃərɪ] *n* (US) carcere *m*.

penknife ['pɛnnaɪf] *n* temperino.

pen name *n* pseudonimo.

penniless ['pɛnɪlɪs] *a* senza un soldo.

penny, *pl* **pennies** *or* (Brit) **pence** ['pɛnɪ, 'pɛnɪz, pɛns] *n* penny *m* (*pl* pence); (US) centesimo.

penpal ['pɛnpæl] *n* corrispondente *m/f*.

pension ['pɛnʃən] *n* pensione *f*; ~**er** *n* (Brit) pensionato/a.

pensive ['pɛnsɪv] *a* pensoso(a).

penthouse ['pɛnthaus] *n* appartamento (di lusso) nell'attico.

pent-up ['pɛntʌp] *a* (feelings) represso(a).

people ['pi:pl] *npl* gente *f*; persone *fpl*; (citizens) popolo *m* // *n* (nation, race) popolo // *vt* popolare; **4/several** ~ came 4/parecchie persone sono venute; **the room was full of** ~ la stanza era piena di gente.

pep [pɛp] *n* (col) dinamismo; **to** ~ **up** *vt* vivacizzare; (food) rendere più gustoso(a).

pepper ['pɛpə*] *n* pepe *m*; (vegetable) peperone *m* // *vt* pepare; ~**mint** *n* (plant) menta peperita; (sweet) pasticca di menta.

peptalk ['pɛptɔ:k] *n* (col) discorso di incoraggiamento.

per [pə:*] prep per; a: ~ **hour** all'ora; ~ **kilo** etc il chilo etc; ~ **day** al giorno; ~ **annum** ad all'anno; ~ **capita** a pro capite inv.

perceive [pə'si:v] *vt* percepire; (notice) accorgersi di.

per cent [pə:'sɛnt] ad per cento.

percentage [pə'sɛntɪdʒ] *n* percentuale *f*.

perception [pə'sɛpʃən] *n* percezione *f*; sensibilità; perspicacia.

perceptive [pə'sɛptɪv] *a* percettivo(a); perspicace.

perch [pə:tʃ] *n* (fish) pesce *m* persico; (for bird) sostegno, ramo // *vi* appollaiarsi.

percolator ['pə:kəlɛɪtə*] *n* caffettiera a pressione; caffettiera elettrica.

percussion [pə'kʌʃən] *n* percussione *f*; (MUS) strumenti *mpl* a percussione.

peremptory [pə'rɛmptərɪ] *a* perentorio(a).

perennial [pə'rɛnɪəl] *a* perenne // *n* pianta perenne.

perfect *a*, *n* ['pə:fɪkt] *a* perfetto(a) // *n* (also: ~ **tense**) perfetto, passato prossimo // *vt* [pə'fɛkt] perfezionare; mettere a punto; ~**ly** ad perfettamente, alla perfezione.

perforate ['pə:fəreɪt] *vt* perforare; **perforation** [-'reɪʃən] *n* perforazione *f*; (line of holes) dentellatura.

perform [pə'fɔ:m] *vt* (carry out) eseguire, fare; (symphony etc) suonare; (play, ballet) dare; (opera) fare // *vi* suonare; recitare; ~**ance** *n* esecuzione *f*; (at theatre etc) rappresentazione *f*, spettacolo; (of an artist) interpretazione *f*; (of player etc) performance *f*; (of car, engine) prestazione *f*; ~**er** *n* artista *m/f*; ~**ing** *a* (animal) ammaestrato(a).

perfume ['pə:fju:m] *n* profumo.

perfunctory [pə'fʌŋktərɪ] *a* superficiale, per la forma.

perhaps [pə'hæps] ad forse.

peril ['pɛrɪl] *n* pericolo.

perimeter [pə'rɪmɪtə*] *n* perimetro; ~ **wall** *n* muro di cinta.

period ['pɪərɪəd] *n* periodo; (HISTORY) epoca; (SCOL) lezione *f*; (full stop) punto; (MED) mestruazioni *fpl* // *a* (costume, furniture) d'epoca; ~**ic** [-'ɔdɪk] *a* periodico(a); ~**ical** [-'ɔdɪkl] *a* periodico(a) // *n* periodico.

peripheral [pə'rɪfərəl] *a* periferico(a) // *n* (COMPUT) unità *f* inv periferica.

perish ['pɛrɪʃ] *vi* perire, morire; (decay) deteriorarsi; ~**able** *a* deperibile.

perjury ['pə:dʒərɪ] *n* spergiuro.

perk [pə:k] *n* vantaggio; **to** ~ **up** *vi* (cheer up) rianimarsi; ~**y** *a* (cheerful) vivace, allegro(a).

perm [pə:m] *n* (for hair) permanente *f*.

permanent ['pə:mənənt] *a* permanente.

permeate ['pə:mɪeɪt] *vi* penetrare // *vt* permeare.

permissible [pə'mɪsɪbl] *a* permissibile, ammissibile.

permission [pə'mɪʃən] *n* permesso.

permissive [pə'mɪsɪv] *a* tollerante; **the** ~ **society** la società permissiva.

permit *n* ['pə:mɪt] permesso // *vt* [pə'mɪt] permettere; **to** ~ **sb to do** permettere a qn di fare, dare il permesso a qn di fare.

perpendicular [pə:pən'dɪkjulə*] *a*, *n* perpendicolare (*f*).

perplex [pə'plɛks] *vt* lasciare perplesso(a).

persecute ['pə:sɪkju:t] *vt* perseguitare.

persevere [pə:sɪ'vɪə*] *vi* perseverare.

Persian ['pə:ʃən] *a* persiano(a) // *n* (LING) persiano; **the** (~) **Gulf** *n* il Golfo Persico.

persist [pə'sɪst] *vi*: **to** ~ (**in doing**) persistere (nel fare); ostinarsi (a fare); ~**ent** *a* persistente; ostinato(a).

person ['pə:sn] *n* persona; **in** ~ di *or* in persona, personalmente; ~**able** *a* di bell'aspetto; ~**al** *a* personale; individuale; ~**al assistant (P.A.)** *n* segretaria personale; ~ **computer (PC)** *n* personal computer *m* inv; ~**ality** [-'nælɪtɪ] *n* personalità *f* inv; ~**ally** ad personalmente.

personnel |pɔːsəˈnɛl| n personale m.

perspective |pəˈspɛktɪv| n prospettiva.

perspiration |pɜːspɪˈreɪʃən| n traspirazione f, sudore m.

persuade |pəˈsweɪd| vt: to ~ sb to do sth persuadere qn a fare qc.

pert |pɜːt| a (bold) sfacciato(a), impertinente.

pertaining |pəˈteɪnɪŋ|: ~ to prep che riguarda.

perturb |pəˈtɜːb| vt turbare.

peruse |pəˈruːz| vt leggere.

pervade |pəˈveɪd| vt pervadere.

perverse |pəˈvɜːs| a perverso(a).

pervert n |ˈpɜːvɜːt| pervertito/a // vt |pəˈvɜːt| pervertire.

pessimism |ˈpɛsɪmɪzəm| n pessimismo.

pessimist |ˈpɛsɪmɪst| n pessimista m/f; ~ic |-ˈmɪstɪk| a pessimistico(a).

pest |pɛst| n animale m (or insetto) pestifero; (fig) peste f.

pester |ˈpɛstə*| vt tormentare, molestare.

pet |pɛt| n animale m domestico; (favourite) favorito/a // vt accarezzare // vi (col) fare il petting.

petal |ˈpɛtl| n petalo.

peter |ˈpiːtə*|: to ~ out vi esaurirsi; estinguersi.

petite |pəˈtiːt| a piccolo(a) e aggraziato(a).

petition |pəˈtɪʃən| n petizione f.

petrified |ˈpɛtrɪfaɪd| a (fig) morto(a) di paura.

petrol |ˈpɛtrəl| n (Brit) benzina; two/four-star ~ ≈ benzina normale/super; ~ can n tanica per benzina.

petroleum |pəˈtrəʊlɪəm| n petrolio.

petrol: ~ pump n (Brit: in car, at garage) pompa di benzina; ~ station n (Brit) stazione f di rifornimento; ~ tank n (Brit) serbatoio della benzina.

petticoat |ˈpɛtɪkəʊt| n sottana.

petty |ˈpɛtɪ| a (mean) meschino(a); (unimportant) insignificante; ~ cash n piccola cassa; ~ officer n sottufficiale m di marina.

petulant |ˈpɛtjʊlənt| a irritabile.

pew |pjuː| n panca (di chiesa).

pewter |ˈpjuːtə*| n peltro.

phallic |ˈfælɪk| a fallico(a).

phantom |ˈfæntəm| n fantasma m.

pharmaceutical |fɑːməˈsjuːtɪkl| a farmaceutico(a).

pharmacy |ˈfɑːməsɪ| n farmacia.

phase |feɪz| n fase f, periodo // vt: to ~ sth in/out introdurre/eliminare qc progressivamente.

Ph.D. n abbr = **Doctor of Philosophy**.

pheasant |ˈfɛznt| n fagiano.

phenomenon, pl **phenomena** |fəˈnɒmɪnən, -nə| n fenomeno.

philanthropist |fɪˈlænθrəpɪst| n filantropo.

philately |fɪˈlætəlɪ| n filatelia.

philosophical |fɪləˈsɒfɪkl| a filosofico(a).

philosophy |fɪˈlɒsəfɪ| n filosofia.

phlegmatic |flɛgˈmætɪk| a flemmatico(a).

phobia |ˈfəʊbjə| n fobia.

phone |fəʊn| n telefono // vt telefonare; to be on the ~ avere il telefono; (be calling) essere al telefono; to ~ back vt, vi richiamare; to ~ up vt telefonare a // vi telefonare; ~ book n guida del telefono, elenco telefonico; ~ box or booth n cabina telefonica; ~ call n telefonata; ~-in n (Brit RADIO, TV) trasmissione f a filo diretto con gli ascoltatori.

phonetics |fəˈnɛtɪks| n fonetica.

phoney |ˈfəʊnɪ| a falso(a), fasullo(a) // n (person) ciarlatano.

phonograph |ˈfəʊnəgrɑːf| n (US) giradischi m inv.

phony |ˈfəʊnɪ| a = **phoney**.

phosphate |ˈfɒsfeɪt| n fosfato.

phosphorus |ˈfɒsfərəs| n fosforo.

photo |ˈfəʊtəʊ| n foto f inv.

photo... |ˈfəʊtəʊ| prefix: ~copier n fotocopiatrice f; ~copy n fotocopia // vt fotocopiare; ~graph n fotografia // vt fotografare; ~grapher |fəˈtɒgrəfə*| n fotografo; ~graphy |fəˈtɒgrəfɪ| n fotografia.

phrase |freɪz| n espressione f; (LING) locuzione f; (MUS) frase f // vt esprimere; ~ book n vocabolarietto.

physical |ˈfɪzɪkl| a fisico(a); ~ education n educazione f fisica; ~ly ad fisicamente.

physician |fɪˈzɪʃən| n medico.

physicist |ˈfɪzɪsɪst| n fisico.

physics |ˈfɪzɪks| n fisica.

physiology |fɪzɪˈɒlədʒɪ| n fisiologia.

physique |fɪˈziːk| n fisico; costituzione f.

pianist |ˈpiːənɪst| n pianista m/f.

piano |pɪˈænəʊ| n pianoforte m.

piccolo |ˈpɪkələʊ| n ottavino.

pick |pɪk| n (tool: also: ~-axe) piccone m // vt scegliere; (gather) cogliere; take your ~ scelga; the ~ of il fior fiore di; to ~ off vt (kill) abbattere (uno dopo l'altro); to ~ on vt fus (person) avercela con; to ~ out vt scegliere; (distinguish) distinguere; to ~ up vi (improve) migliorarsi // vt raccogliere; (collect) passare a prendere; (AUT: give lift to) far salire; (learn) imparare; to ~ up speed acquistare velocità; to ~ o.s. up rialzarsi.

picket |ˈpɪkɪt| n (in strike) scioperante m/f che fa parte di un picchetto; picchetto // vt picchettare.

pickle |ˈpɪkl| n (also: ~s: as condiment) sottaceti mpl // vt mettere sottaceto; mettere in salamoia.

pickpocket |ˈpɪkpɒkɪt| n borsaiolo.

pickup |ˈpɪkʌp| n (Brit: on record player) pick-up m inv; (small truck) camioncino.

picnic ['pɪknɪk] *n* picnic *m inv*.

pictorial [pɪk'tɔ:rɪəl] *a* illustrato(a).

picture ['pɪktʃə°] *n* quadro; (*painting*) pittura; (*photograph*) foto(grafia); (*drawing*) disegno; (*film*) film *m inv* // *vt* raffigurarsi; the ~s (*Brit*) il cinema; ~ **book** *n* libro illustrato.

picturesque [pɪktʃə'rɛsk] *a* pittoresco(a).

pidgin English ['pɪdʒɪn-] *n* inglese semplificato misto ad elementi indigeni.

pie [paɪ] *n* torta; (*of meat*) pasticcio.

piece [pi:s] *n* pezzo; (*of land*) appezzamento; (*item*): a ~ **of furniture/ advice** un mobile/consiglio // *vt*: to ~ **together** mettere insieme; to take to ~s smontare; ~**meal** *ad* pezzo a pezzo, a spizzicol; ~ **work** *n* (lavoro a) cottimo.

pie chart *n* grafico a torta.

pier [pɪə°] *n* molo; (*of bridge etc*) pila.

pierce [pɪəs] *vt* forare; (*with arrow etc*) trafiggere.

piercing ['pɪəsɪŋ] *a* (*cry*) acuto(a).

pig [pɪg] *n* maiale *m*, porco.

pigeon ['pɪdʒən] *n* piccione *m*; ~**hole** *n* casella.

piggy bank ['pɪgɪ-] *n* salvadanaro.

pigheaded ['pɪg'hɛdɪd] *a* caparbio(a), cocciuto(a).

piglet ['pɪglɪt] *n* porcellino.

pigskin ['pɪgskɪn] *n* cinghiale *m*.

pigsty ['pɪgstaɪ] *n* porcile *m*.

pigtail ['pɪgteɪl] *n* treccina.

pike [paɪk] *n* (*spear*) picca; (*fish*) luccio.

pilchard ['pɪltʃəd] *n* specie di sardina.

pile [paɪl] *n* (*pillar, of books*) pila; (*heap*) mucchio; (*of carpet*) pelo // *vb* (*also*: ~ **up**) *vt* ammucchiare // *vi* ammucchiarsi; to ~ **into** (*car*) stiparsi or ammucchiarsi in.

piles [paɪlz] *npl* emorroidi *fpl*.

pileup ['paɪlʌp] *n* (*AUT*) tamponamento a catena.

pilfering ['pɪlfərɪŋ] *n* rubacchiare *m*.

pilgrim ['pɪlgrɪm] *n* pellegrino/a; ~**age** *n* pellegrinaggio.

pill [pɪl] *n* pillola; the ~ la pillola.

pillage ['pɪlɪdʒ] *vt* saccheggiare.

pillar ['pɪlə°] *n* colonna; ~ **box** *n* (*Brit*) cassetta postale.

pillion ['pɪljən] *n* (*of motor cycle*) sellino posteriore.

pillory ['pɪlərɪ] *vt* mettere alla berlina.

pillow ['pɪləu] *n* guanciale *m*; ~**case** *n* federa.

pilot ['paɪlət] *n* pilota *m/f* // *cpd* (*scheme etc*) pilota *inv* // *vt* pilotare; ~ **light** *n* fiamma pilota.

pimp [pɪmp] *n* mezzano.

pimple ['pɪmpl] *n* foruncolo.

pin [pɪn] *n* spillo; (*TECH*) perno // *vt* attaccare con uno spillo; ~s and needles formicolio; to ~ **sb down** (*fig*) obbligare qn a pronunziarsi; to ~ **sth on sb** (*fig*)

addossare la colpa di qc a qn.

pinafore ['pɪnəfɔ:°] *n* grembiule *m* (senza maniche).

pinball ['pɪnbɔ:l] *n* (*also*: ~ **machine**) flipper *m inv*.

pincers ['pɪnsəz] *npl* pinzette *fpl*.

pinch [pɪntʃ] *n* pizzicotto, pizzico // *vt* pizzicare; (*col: steal*) grattare // *vi* (*shoe*) stringere; at a ~ in caso di bisogno.

pincushion ['pɪnkuʃən] *n* puntaspilli *m inv*.

pine [paɪn] *n* (*also*: ~ **tree**) pino // *vi*: to ~ **for** struggersi dal desiderio di; to ~ **away** *vi* languire.

pineapple ['paɪnæpl] *n* ananas *m inv*.

ping [pɪŋ] *n* (*noise*) tintinnio; ~-**pong** ® ping-pong *m* ®.

pink [pɪŋk] *a* rosa *inv* // *n* (*colour*) rosa *m inv*; (*BOT*) garofano.

pinpoint ['pɪnpɔɪnt] *vt* indicare con precisione.

pint [paɪnt] *n* pinta (*Brit* = 0.57*l*; *US* = 0.47*l*); (*Brit col*) ≈ birra da mezzo.

pioneer [paɪə'nɪə°] *n* pioniere/a.

pious ['paɪəs] *a* pio(a).

pip [pɪp] *n* (*seed*) seme *m*; (*Brit: time signal on radio*) segnale *m* orario.

pipe [paɪp] *n* tubo; (*for smoking*) pipa; (*MUS*) piffero // *vt* portare per mezzo di tubazione; ~s *npl* (*also*: **bag**~**s**) cornamusa (scozzese); to ~ **down** *vi* (*col*) calmarsi; ~ **cleaner** *n* scovolino; ~ **dream** *n* vana speranza; ~**line** *n* conduttura; (*for oil*) oleodotto; ~**r** *n* piffero; suonatore/trice di cornamusa.

piping ['paɪpɪŋ] *ad*: ~ **hot** caldo bollente.

pique [pi:k] *n* picca.

pirate ['paɪərət] *n* pirata *m*.

Pisces ['paɪsɪːz] *n* Pesci *mpl*.

piss [pɪs] *vi* (*col*) pisciare; ~**ed** *a* (*col: drunk*) ubriaco(a) fradicio(a).

pistol ['pɪstl] *n* pistola.

piston ['pɪstən] *n* pistone *m*.

pit [pɪt] *n* buca, fossa; (*also*: **coal** ~) miniera; (*also*: **orchestra** ~) orchestra // *vt*: to ~ **sb against sb** opporre qn a qn; ~s *npl* (*AUT*) box *im*.

pitch [pɪtʃ] *n* (*throw*) lancia; (*MUS*) tono; (*of voice*) altezza; (*Brit SPORT*) campo; (*NAUT*) beccheggio; (*tar*) pece *f* // *vt* (*throw*) lanciare // *vi* (*fall*) cascare; (*NAUT*) beccheggiare; to ~ **a tent** piantare una tenda; ~**ed battle** *n* battaglia campale.

pitcher ['pɪtʃə°] *n* brocca.

pitchfork ['pɪtʃfɔ:k] *n* forcone *m*.

piteous ['pɪtɪəs] *a* pietoso(a).

pitfall ['pɪtfɔ:l] *n* trappola.

pith [pɪθ] *n* (*of plant*) midollo; (*of orange*) parte *f* interna della scorza; (*fig*) essenza, succo; vigore *m*.

pithy ['pɪθɪ] *a* conciso(a); vigoroso(a).

pitiful ['pɪtɪful] *a* (*touching*) pietoso(a); (*contemptible*) miserabile.

pitiless |'pɪtɪlɪs| *a* spietato(a).

pittance |'pɪtns| *n* miseria, magro salario.

pity |'pɪtɪ| *n* pietà // *vt* aver pietà di; what a ~! che peccato!

pivot |'pɪvət| *n* perno.

pizza |'pi:tsə| *n* pizza.

placard |'plækɑ:d| *n* affisso.

placate |plə'keɪt| *vt* placare, calmare.

place |pleɪs| *n* posto, luogo; (*proper position, rank, seat*) posto; (*house*) casa, alloggio; (*home*): at/to his ~ a casa sua // *vt* (*object*) posare, mettere; (*identify*) riconoscere; individuare; to take ~ aver luogo; succedere; to change ~s with sb scambiare il posto con qn; out of ~ (*not suitable*) inopportuno(a); in the first ~ in primo luogo; to ~ an order dare un'ordinazione.

placid |'plæsɪd| *a* placido(a), calmo(a).

plagiarism |'pleɪdʒjərɪzm| *n* plagio.

plague |pleɪg| *n* peste *f* // *vt* tormentare.

plaice |pleɪs| *n* (*pl inv*) pianuzza.

plaid |plæd| *n* plaid *m inv.*

plain |pleɪn| *a* (*clear*) chiaro(a), palese; (*simple*) semplice; (*frank*) franco(a), aperto(a); (*not handsome*) bruttino(a); (*without seasoning etc*) scondito(a); naturale; (*in one colour*) tinta unita *inv* // *ad* francamente, chiaramente // *n* pianura; ~ **chocolate** *n* cioccolato fondente; ~ **clothes** *npl*: in ~ clothes (*police*) in borghese; ~**ly** *ad* chiaramente; (*frankly*) francamente.

plaintiff |'pleɪntɪf| *n* attore/trice.

plaintive |'pleɪntɪv| *a* (*cry, voice*) dolente, lamentoso(a).

plait |plæt| *n* treccia.

plan |plæn| *n* pianta; (*scheme*) progetto, piano // *vt* (*think in advance*) progettare; (*prepare*) organizzare // *vi* far piani *or* progetti.

plane |pleɪn| *n* (*AVIAT*) aereo; (*tree*) platano; (*tool*) pialla; (*ART, MATH etc*) piano // *a* piano(a), piatto(a) // *vt* (*with tool*) piallare.

planet |'plænɪt| *n* pianeta *m.*

plank |plæŋk| *n* tavola, asse *f.*

planner |'plænə*| *n* pianificatore/trice.

planning |'plænɪŋ| *n* progettazione *f*; family ~ pianificazione *f* delle nascite; ~ permission *n* permesso di costruzione.

plant |plɑ:nt| *n* pianta; (*machinery*) impianto; (*factory*) fabbrica // *vt* piantare; (*bomb*) mettere.

plantation |plæn'teɪʃən| *n* piantagione *f.*

plaque |plæk| *n* placca.

plaster |'plɑ:stə*| *n* intonaco; (*also:* ~ of Paris) gesso; (*Brit: also:* sticking ~) cerotto // *vt* intonacare; ingessare; (*cover*): to ~ with coprire di; in ~ (*leg etc*) ingessato(a); ~**ed** *a* (*col*) ubriaco(a) fradicio(a).

plastic |'plæstɪk| *n* plastica // *a* (*made of plastic*) di *or* in plastica; (*flexible*) pla-

stico(a), malleabile; (*art*) plastico(a); ~ **bag** *n* sacchetto di plastica.

plasticine |'plæstɪsi:n| *n* ® plastilina ®.

plastic surgery *n* chirurgia plastica.

plate |pleɪt| *n* (*dish*) piatto; (*sheet of metal*) lamiera; (*PHOT*) lastra; (*in book*) tavola.

plateau, ~**s** *or* ~**x** |'plætəu, -z| *n* altipiano.

plate glass *n* vetro piano.

platform |'plætfɔ:m| *n* (*stage, at meeting*) palco; (*RAIL*) marciapiede *m*; (*Brit: of bus*) piattaforma; ~ **ticket** *n* (*Brit*) biglietto d'ingresso ai binari.

platinum |'plætɪnəm| *n* platino.

platitude |'plætɪtju:d| *n* luogo comune.

platoon |plə'tu:n| *n* plotone *m.*

platter |'plætə*| *n* piatto.

plausible |'plɔ:zɪbl| *a* plausibile, credibile; (*person*) convincente.

play |pleɪ| *n* gioco; (*THEATRE*) commedia // *vt* (*game*) giocare a; (*team, opponent*) giocare contro; (*instrument, piece of music*) suonare; (*play, part*) interpretare // *vi* giocare; suonare; recitare; to ~ safe giocare sul sicuro; to ~ **down** *vt* minimizzare; to ~ **up** *vi* (*cause trouble*) fare i capricci; ~**boy** *n* playboy *m inv*; ~**er** *n* giocatore/trice; (*THEATRE*) attore/trice; (*MUS*) musicista *m/f*; ~**ful** *a* giocoso(a); ~**ground** *n* (*in school*) cortile *m* per la ricreazione; (*in park*) parco *m* giochi *inv*; ~**group** *n* giardino d'infanzia; ~**ing card** *n* carta da gioco; ~**ing field** *n* campo sportivo; ~**mate** *n* compagno/a di gioco; ~**-off** *n* (*SPORT*) bella; ~**pen** *n* box *m inv*; ~**school** *n* = ~**group**; ~**thing** *n* giocattolo; ~**wright** *n* drammaturgo/a.

plc *abbr* (= *public limited company*) società *per azioni a responsabilità limitata quotata in borsa.*

plea |pli:| *n* (*request*) preghiera, domanda; (*excuse*) scusa; (*LAW*) (argomento di) difesa.

plead |pli:d| *vt* patrocinare; (*give as excuse*) addurre a pretesto // *vi* (*LAW*) perorare la causa; (*beg*): to ~ with sb implorare qn.

pleasant |'plɛznt| *a* piacevole, gradevole; ~**ries** *npl* (*polite remarks*): to exchange ~ries scambiarsi i convenevoli.

please |pli:z| *vt* piacere a // *vi* (*think fit*): do as you ~ faccia come le pare; ~! per piacere!; ~ yourself! come ti (*or* le) pare!; ~**d** *a*: ~**d** (with) contento(a) (di); ~**d** to meet you! piacere!; **pleasing** *a* piacevole, che fa piacere.

pleasure |'plɛʒə*| *n* piacere *m*; "it's a ~" "prego".

pleat |pli:t| *n* piega.

plectrum |'plɛktrəm| *n* plettro.

pledge |plɛdʒ| *n* pegno; (*promise*) promessa // *vt* impegnare; promettere.

plentiful [ˈplɛntɪful] a abbondante, copioso(a).

plenty [ˈplɛntɪ] n abbondanza; ~ of tanto(a), molto(a); un'abbondanza di.

pleurisy [ˈpluərɪsɪ] n pleurite f.

pliable [ˈplaɪəbl] a flessibile; (person) malleabile.

pliers [ˈplaɪəz] npl pinza.

plight [plaɪt] n situazione f critica.

plimsolls [ˈplɪmsəlz] npl (Brit) scarpe fpl da tennis.

plinth [plɪnθ] n plinto; piedistallo.

plod [plɔd] vi camminare a stento; (fig) sgobbare; ~der n sgobbone m.

plonk [plɔŋk] (col) n (Brit: wine) vino da poco // vt: to ~ sth down buttare giù qc bruscamente.

plot [plɔt] n congiura, cospirazione f; (of story, play) trama; (of land) lotto // vt (mark out) fare la pianta di; rilevare; (: diagram etc) tracciare; (conspire) congiurare, cospirare // vi congiurare; ~ter n (instrument) plotter m inv.

plough, (US) **plow** [plau] n aratro // vt (earth) arare; **to ~ back** vt (COMM) reinvestire; **to ~ through** vt fus (snow etc) procedere a fatica in.

ploy [plɔɪ] n stratagemma m.

pluck [plʌk] vt (fruit) cogliere; (musical instrument) pizzicare; (bird) spennare // n coraggio, fegato; **to ~ up courage** farsi coraggio; ~y a coraggioso(a).

plug [plʌg] n tappo; (ELEC) spina; (AUT: also: **spark(ing) ~**) candela // vt (hole) tappare; (col: advertise) spingere; **to ~ in** vt (ELEC) attaccare a una presa.

plum [plʌm] n (fruit) susina // cpd: ~ job (col) impiego ottimo or favoloso.

plumb [plʌm] a verticale // n piombo // ad (exactly) esattamente // vt sondare.

plumber [ˈplʌmə*] n idraulico.

plumbing [ˈplʌmɪŋ] n (trade) lavoro di idraulico; (piping) tubature fpl.

plume [pluːm] n piuma, penna; (decorative) pennacchio.

plummet [ˈplʌmɪt] vi cadere a piombo.

plump [plʌmp] a grassoccio(a) // vt: to ~ sth (down) on lasciar cadere qc di peso su; **to ~ for** vt fus (col: choose) decidersi per.

plunder [ˈplʌndə*] n saccheggio // vt saccheggiare.

plunge [plʌndʒ] n tuffo // vt immergere // vi (fall) cadere, precipitare; **to take the ~** saltare il fosso; ~r n sturalavandini m inv; **plunging** a (neckline) profondo(a).

pluperfect [pluːˈpəːfɪkt] n piuc-chepperfetto.

plural [ˈpluərl] a, n plurale (m).

plus [plʌs] n (also: ~ **sign**) segno più // prep più; ten/twenty ~ più di dieci/venti.

plush [plʌʃ] a lussuoso(a).

ply [plaɪ] n (of wool) capo; (of wood) strato // vt (tool) maneggiare; (a trade)

esercitare // vi (ship) fare il servizio; **to ~ sb with drink** dare di bere continuamente a qn; ~**wood** n legno compensato.

P.M. n abbr = **prime minister**.

p.m. ad abbr (= post meridiem) del pomeriggio.

pneumatic drill [njuːˈmætɪk-] n martello pneumatico.

pneumonia [njuːˈməunɪə] n polmonite f.

poach [pəutʃ] vt (cook) affogare; (steal) cacciare (or pescare) di frodo // vi fare il bracconiere; ~**er** n bracconiere m.

P.O. Box n abbr = **Post Office Box**.

pocket [ˈpɔkɪt] n tasca // vt intascare; **to be out of ~** (Brit) rimetterci; ~**book** n (wallet) portafoglio; (notebook), taccuino; ~ **knife** n temperino; ~ **money** n paghetta, settimana.

pod [pɔd] n guscio // vt sgusciare.

podgy [ˈpɔdʒɪ] a grassoccio(a).

podiatrist [pɔˈdiːətrɪst] n (US) callista m/f, pedicure m/f.

poem [ˈpəuɪm] n poesia.

poet [ˈpəuɪt] n poeta/essa; ~**ic** [-ˈɛtɪk] a poetico(a); ~ **laureate** n poeta m laureato (nominato dalla Corte Reale); ~**ry** n poesia.

poignant [ˈpɔɪnjənt] a struggente.

point [pɔɪnt] n (gen) punto; (tip: of needle etc) punta; (in time) punto, momento; (SCOL) voto; (main idea, important part) nocciolo; (also: decimal ~): 2 ~ 3 (2.3) 2 virgola 3 (2,3) // vt (show) indicare; (gun etc): to ~ sth at puntare qc contro // vi mostrare a dito: ~s npl (AUT) puntine fpl; (RAIL) scambio; to be on the ~ of doing sth essere sul punto di or stare per fare qc; to make a ~ fare un'osservazione; to get the ~ capire; to come to the ~ venire al fatto; there's no ~ (in doing) è inutile (fare); **to ~ out** vt far notare; **to ~ to** vt fus indicare; (fig) dimostrare; ~-**blank** ad (also: at ~-blank range) a bruciapelo; (fig) categoricamente; ~**ed** a (shape) aguzzo(a), appuntito(a); (remark) specifico(a); ~**edly** ad in maniera inequivocabile; ~**er** n (stick) bacchetta; (needle) lancetta; (dog) pointer m, cane m da punta; ~**less** a inutile, vano(a); ~ **of view** n punto di vista.

poise [pɔɪz] n (balance) equilibrio; (of head, body) portamento; (calmness) calma // vt tenere in equilibrio.

poison [ˈpɔɪzn] n veleno // vt avvelenare; ~**ing** n avvelenamento; ~**ous** a velenoso(a).

poke [pəuk] vt (fire) attizzare; (jab with finger, stick etc) punzecchiare; (put): to ~ sth in(to) spingere qc dentro; **to ~ about** vi frugare.

poker [ˈpəukə*] n attizzatoio; (CARDS) poker m; ~-**faced** a dal viso impassibile.

poky ['pəʊkı] *a* piccolo(a) e stretto(a).

Poland ['pəʊlənd] *n* Polonia.

polar ['pəʊlə*] *a* polare; **~ bear** *n* orso bianco.

Pole [pəʊl] *n* polacco/a.

pole [pəʊl] *n* (*of wood*) palo; (*ELEC, GEO*) polo; **~ bean** *n* (*US: runner bean*) fagiolino; **~ vault** *n* salto con l'asta.

police [pə'li:s] *n* polizia // *vt* mantenere l'ordine in; **~ car** *n* macchina della polizia; **~man** *n* poliziotto, agente *m* di polizia; **~ station** *n* posto di polizia; **~woman** *n* donna *f* poliziotto *inv*.

policy ['pɒlısı] *n* politica; (*also: insurance* ~) polizza (d'assicurazione).

polio ['pəʊlıəʊ] *n* polio *f*.

Polish ['pəʊlıʃ] *a* polacco(a) // *n* (*LING*) polacco.

polish ['pɒlıʃ] *n* (*for shoes*) lucido; (*for floor*) cera; (*for nails*) smalto; (*shine*) lucentezza, lustro; (*fig: refinement*) raffinatezza // *vt* lucidare; (*fig: improve*) raffinare; **to ~ off** *vt* (*work*) sbrigare; (*food*) mangiarsi; **~ed** *a* (*fig*) raffinato(a).

polite [pə'laıt] *a* cortese; **~ness** *n* cortesia.

politic ['pɒlıtık] *a* diplomatico(a); **~al** [pə'lıtıkl] *a* politico(a); **~ally** *ad* politicamente; **~ian** [-'tıʃən] *n* politico; **~s** *npl* politica.

polka ['pɒlkə] *n* polca; **~ dot** *n* pois *m inv*.

poll [pəʊl] *n* scrutinio; (*votes cast*) voti *mpl*; (*also*: **opinion** ~) sondaggio (d'opinioni) // *vt* ottenere.

pollen ['pɒlən] *n* polline *m*.

pollination [pɒlı'neıʃən] *n* impollinazione *f*.

polling ['pəʊlıŋ] (*Brit*): **~ booth** *n* cabina elettorale; **~ day** *n* giorno delle elezioni; **~ station** *n* sezione *f* elettorale.

pollute [pə'lu:t] *vt* inquinare.

pollution [pə'lu:ʃən] *n* inquinamento.

polo ['pəʊləʊ] *n* polo; **~-neck** *a* a collo alto risvoltato.

polyester [pɒlı'ɛstə*] *n* poliestere *m*.

polystyrene [pɒlı'staırı:n] *n* polistirolo.

polytechnic [pɒlı'teknık] *n* (*college*) *istituto superiore ad indirizzo tecnologico*.

polythene ['pɒlıθı:n] *n* politene *m*; **~ bag** *n* sacco di plastica.

pomegranate ['pɒmıgrænıt] *n* melagrana.

pomp [pɒmp] *n* pompa, fasto.

pompom ['pɒmpɒm], **pompon** ['pɒmpɒn] *n* pompon *m inv*.

pompous ['pɒmpəs] *a* pomposo(a).

pond [pɒnd] *n* pozza; stagno.

ponder ['pɒndə*] *vt* ponderare, riflettere su; **~ous** *a* ponderoso(a), pesante.

pong [pɒŋ] *n* (*Brit col*) puzzo.

pontiff ['pɒntıf] *n* pontefice *m*.

pony ['pəʊnı] *n* pony *m inv*; **~tail** *n* coda di cavallo; **~ trekking** *n* (*Brit*) escursione *f* a cavallo.

poodle ['pu:dl] *n* barboncino, barbone *m*.

pool [pu:l] *n* (*of rain*) pozza; (*pond*) stagno; (*artificial*) vasca; (*also*: **swimming** ~) piscina; (*sth shared*) fondo comune; (*billiards*) specie di biliardo a buca // *vt* mettere in comune; **typing ~** servizio comune di dattilografia; (*football*) **~s** ≈ totocalcio.

poor [puə*] *a* povero(a); (*mediocre*) mediocre, cattivo(a) // *npl*: **the ~** i poveri; **~ly** *ad* poveramente; male // *a* indisposto(a), malato(a).

pop [pɒp] *n* (*noise*) schiocco; (*MUS*) musica pop; (*US col: father*) babbo // *vt* (*put*) mettere (in fretta) // *vi* scoppiare; (*cork*) schioccare; **to ~ in** *vi* passare; **to ~ out** *vi* fare un salto fuori; **to ~ up** *vi* apparire, sorgere; **~ concert** *n* concerto *m* pop *inv*; **~corn** *n* pop-corn *m*.

pope [pəʊp] *n* papa *m*.

poplar ['pɒplə*] *n* pioppo.

poppy ['pɒpı] *n* papavero.

popsicle ['pɒpsıkl] *n* (*US: ice lolly*) ghiacciolo.

popular ['pɒpjʊlə*] *a* popolare; (*fashionable*) in voga; **~ity** [-'lærıtı] *n* popolarità; **~ize** *vt* divulgare; (*science*) volgarizzare.

population [pɒpjʊ'leıʃən] *n* popolazione *f*.

porcelain ['pɔ:slın] *n* porcellana.

porch [pɔ:tʃ] *n* veranda.

porcupine ['pɔ:kjʊpaın] *n* porcospino.

pore [pɔ:*] *n* poro // *vi*: **to ~ over** essere immerso(a) in.

pork [pɔ:k] *n* carne *f* di maiale.

pornographic [pɔ:nə'græfık] *a* pornografico(a).

pornography [pɔ:'nɒgrəfı] *n* pornografia.

porpoise ['pɔ:pəs] *n* focena.

porridge ['pɒrıdʒ] *n* porridge *m*.

port [pɔ:t] *n* porto; (*opening in ship*) portello; (*NAUT: left side*) babordo; (*wine*) porto; **~ of call** (porto di) scalo.

portable ['pɔ:təbl] *a* portatile.

portent ['pɔ:tent] *n* presagio.

porter ['pɔ:tə*] *n* (*for luggage*) facchino, portabagagli *m inv*; (*doorkeeper*) portiere *m*, portinaio.

portfolio [pɔ:t'fəʊlıəʊ] *n* (*case*) cartella; (*POL, FINANCE*) portafoglio; (*of artist*) raccolta dei propri lavori.

porthole ['pɔ:θəʊl] *n* oblò *m inv*.

portion ['pɔ:ʃən] *n* porzione *f*.

portly ['pɔ:tlı] *a* corpulento(a).

portrait ['pɔ:treıt] *n* ritratto.

portray [pɔ:'treı] *vt* fare il ritratto di; (*character on stage*) rappresentare; (*in writing*) ritrarre.

Portugal [ˈpɔːtjugl] n Portogallo.

Portuguese [pɔːtjuˈgiːz] a portoghese // n (pl inv) portoghese m/f; (LING) portoghese m.

pose [pəuz] n posa // vi posare; (pretend): to ~ as atteggiarsi a, posare a // vt porre.

posh [pɔʃ] a (col) elegante; (family) per bene.

position [pəˈzɪʃən] n posizione f; (job) posto.

positive [ˈpɔzɪtɪv] a positivo(a); (certain) sicuro(a), certo(a); (definite) preciso(a); definitivo(a).

posse [ˈpɔsɪ] n (US) drappello.

possess [pəˈzɛs] vt possedere; ~ion [pəˈzɛʃən] n possesso; (object) bene m; ~ive a possessivo(a).

possibility [pɔsɪˈbɪlɪt] n possibilità f inv.

possible [ˈpɔsɪbl] a possibile; as big as ~ il più grande possibile.

possibly [ˈpɔsɪblɪ] ad (perhaps) forse; if you ~ can se le è possibile; I cannot ~ come proprio non posso venire.

post [pəust] n (Brit) posta; (: collection) levata; (job, situation) posto; (pole) palo // vt (Brit: send by post) impostare; (MIL) appostare; (notice) affiggere; (Brit: appoint): to ~ to assegnare a; ~age n affrancatura; ~al order n vaglia m inv postale; ~box n (Brit) cassetta postale; ~card n cartolina; ~ code n (Brit) codice m (di avviamento) postale.

poster [ˈpəustə*] n manifesto, affisso.

poste restante [pəustˈrɛstɑːnt] n (Brit) fermo posta m.

postgraduate [ˈpəustˈgrædjuət] n laureato/a che continua gli studi.

posthumous [ˈpɔstjuməs] a postumo(a).

postman [ˈpəustmən] n postino.

postmark [ˈpəustmɑːk] n bollo or timbro postale.

postmaster [ˈpəustmɑːstə*] n direttore m d'un ufficio postale.

post-mortem [pəustˈmɔːtəm] n autopsia.

post office n (building) ufficio postale; (organization): the Post Office ≈ le Poste e Telecomunicazioni; Post Office Box (P.O. Box) n casella postale (C.P.).

postpone [pəsˈpəun] vt rinviare.

postscript [ˈpəustskrɪpt] n poscritto.

posture [ˈpɔstʃə*] n portamento; (pose) posa, atteggiamento // vi posare.

postwar [ˈpəustˈwɔː*] a del dopoguerra.

posy [ˈpəuzɪ] n mazzetto di fiori.

pot [pɔt] n (for cooking) pentola; casseruola; (for plants, jam) vaso; (col: marijuana) erba // vt (plant) piantare in vaso; to go to ~ (col: work, performance) andare in malora.

potato, ~es [pəˈteɪtəu] n patata; ~ peeler n sbucciapatate m inv.

potent [ˈpəutnt] a potente, forte.

potential [pəˈtɛnʃl] a potenziale // n possibilità fpl; ~ly ad potenzialmente.

pothole [ˈpɔthəul] n (in road) buca; (Brit: underground) caverna; **potholing** n (Brit): to go potholing fare la speleologia. ·

potluck [pɔtˈlʌk] n: to take ~ tentare la sorte.

potshot [ˈpɔtʃɔt] n: to take ~s or a ~ at tirare a vanvera contro.

potted [ˈpɔtɪd] a (food) in conserva; (plant) in vaso.

potter [ˈpɔtə*] n vasaio // vi: to ~ around, ~ about lavoracchiare; ~y n ceramiche fpl.

potty [ˈpɔtɪ] a (col: mad) tocco(a) // n (child's) vasino.

pouch [pautʃ] n borsa; (ZOOL) marsupio.

poultry [ˈpəultrɪ] n pollame m.

pounce [pauns] vi: to ~ (on) balzare addosso a, piombare su // n balzo.

pound [paund] n (weight) libbra; (money) (lira) sterlina; (for dogs) canile m municipale // vt (beat) battere; (crush) pestare, polverizzare // vi (beat) battere, martellare.

pour [pɔː*] vt versare // vi riversarsi; (rain) piovere a dirotto; to ~ away or off vt vuotare; to ~ in vi (people) entrare a flotti; to ~ out vt vuotare; versare; (serve: a drink) mescere; ~ing a: ~ing rain pioggia torrenziale.

pout [paut] vi sporgere le labbra; fare il broncio.

poverty [ˈpɔvətɪ] n povertà, miseria; ~-stricken a molto povero(a), misero(a).

powder [ˈpaudə*] n polvere f // vt spolverizzare; (face) incipriare; to ~ one's nose incipriarsi il naso; ~ compact n portacipria m inv; ~ed milk n latte m in polvere; ~ puff n piumino della cipria; ~ room n toilette f inv (per signore).

power [ˈpauə*] n (strength) potenza, forza; (ability, POL: of party, leader) potere m; (MATH) potenza; (ELEC) corrente f // vt fornire di energia; to be in ~ (POL etc) essere al potere; ~ cut n (Brit) interruzione f or mancanza di corrente; ~ failure n interruzione f della corrente elettrica; ~ful a potente, forte; ~less a impotente, senza potere; ~ point n (Brit) presa di corrente; ~ station n centrale f elettrica.

p.p. abbr (= per procurationem): ~ J. Smith per J. Smith.

PR abbr = public relations.

practicable [ˈpræktɪkəbl] a (scheme) praticabile.

practical [ˈpræktɪkl] a pratico(a); ~ity [-ˈkælɪtɪ] n (no pl) (of situation etc) lato pratico; ~ joke n beffa; ~ly ad (almost) quasi.

practice [ˈpræktɪs] n pratica; (of

profession) esercizio; (*at football etc*) allenamento; (*business*) gabinetto; clientela // *vt, vi* (*US*) = **practise**; in ~ (*in reality*) in pratica; out of ~ fuori esercizio.

practise, (*US*) **practice** ['præktɪs] *vt* (*work at*: piano, one's backhand etc) esercitarsi a; (*train for*: skiing, running etc) allenarsi a; (*a sport, religion*) praticare; (*method*) usare; (*profession*) esercitare // *vi* esercitarsi; (*train*) allenarsi; **practising** *a* (*Christian etc*) praticante; (*lawyer*) che esercita la professione.

practitioner [præk'tɪʃənə*] *n* professionista *m/f.*

pragmatic [præg'mætɪk] *a* prammatico(a).

prairie ['prɛərɪ] *n* prateria.

praise [preɪz] *n* elogio, lode *f* // *vt* elogiare, lodare; ~**worthy** *a* lodevole.

pram [præm] *n* (*Brit*) carrozzina.

prance [prɑːns] *vi* (*horse*) impennarsi.

prank [præŋk] *n* burla.

prawn [prɔːn] *n* gamberetto.

pray [preɪ] *vi* pregare.

prayer [prɛə*] *n* preghiera.

preach [priːtʃ] *vt, vi* predicare.

precarious [prɪ'kɛərɪəs] *a* precario(a).

precaution [prɪ'kɔːʃən] *n* precauzione *f.*

precede [prɪ'siːd] *vt, vi* precedere.

precedence ['presɪdəns] *n* precedenza.

precedent ['presɪdənt] *n* precedente *m.*

precept ['priːsept] *n* precetto.

precinct ['priːsɪŋkt] *n* (*round cathedral*) recinto; ~**s** *npl* (*neighbourhood*) dintorni *mpl*, vicinanze *fpl*; **pedestrian** ~ (*Brit*) zona pedonale.

precious ['prɛʃəs] *a* prezioso(a).

precipitate [prɪ'sɪpɪtɪt] *a* (*hasty*) precipitoso(a).

précis, *pl* **précis** ['preɪsɪ:, -z] *n* riassunto.

precise [prɪ'saɪs] *a* preciso(a); ~**ly** *ad* precisamente.

preclude [prɪ'kluːd] *vt* precludere, impedire.

precocious [prɪ'kəʊʃəs] *a* precoce.

precondition [priːkən'dɪʃən] *n* condizione *f* necessaria.

predecessor ['priːdɪsesə*] *n* predecessore/a.

predicament [prɪ'dɪkəmənt] *n* situazione *f* difficile.

predict [prɪ'dɪkt] *vt* predire; ~**able** *a* prevedibile.

predominantly [prɪ'dɒmɪnəntlɪ] *ad* in maggior parte; soprattutto.

predominate [prɪ'dɒmɪneɪt] *vi* predominare.

preen [priːn] *vt*: to ~ itself (*bird*) lisciarsi le penne; to ~ o.s. agghindarsi.

prefab ['priːfæb] *n* casa prefabbricata.

preface ['prefəs] *n* prefazione *f.*

prefect ['priːfekt] *n* (*Brit*: *in school*) studente/essa con funzioni disciplinari;

(*in Italy*) prefetto.

prefer [prɪ'fəː*] *vt* preferire; ~**ably** ['prefrəblɪ] *ad* preferibilmente; ~**ence** ['prefrəns] *n* preferenza; ~**ential** [prefə'renʃəl] *a* preferenziale.

prefix ['priːfɪks] *n* prefisso.

pregnancy ['pregnənsɪ] *n* gravidanza.

pregnant ['pregnənt] *a* incinta *af.*

prehistoric ['priːhɪs'tɔrɪk] *a* preistorico(a).

prejudice ['predʒudɪs] *n* pregiudizio; (*harm*) torto, danno // *vt* pregiudicare, ledere; ~**d** *a* (*person*) pieno(a) di pregiudizi; (*view*) prevenuto(a).

preliminary [prɪ'lɪmɪnərɪ] *a* preliminare; **preliminaries** *npl* preliminari *mpl.*

premarital ['priː'mærɪtl] *a* prematrimoniale.

premature ['prɛmətʃuə*] *a* prematuro(a).

premier ['prɛmɪə*] *a* primo(a) // *n* (*POL*) primo ministro.

première ['prɛmɪɛə*] *n* prima.

premise ['prɛmɪs] *n* premessa; ~**s** *npl* locale *m*; on the ~**s** sul posto.

premium ['priːmɪəm] *n* premio; to be at a ~ essere ricercatissimo; ~ **bond** *n* (*Brit*) obbligazione *f* a premio.

premonition [prɛmə'nɪʃən] *n* premonizione *f.*

preoccupied [priː'ɔkjupaɪd] *a* preoccupato(a).

prep [prep] *n* (*SCOL*: *study*) studio; ~ **school** *n* = **preparatory school.**

prepaid [priː'peɪd] *a* pagato(a) in anticipo.

preparation [prepə'reɪʃən] *n* preparazione *f*; ~**s** *npl* (*for trip, war*) preparativi *mpl.*

preparatory [prɪ'pærətərɪ] *a* preparatorio(a); ~ **school** *n* scuola elementare privata.

prepare [prɪ'pɛə*] *vt* preparare // *vi*: to ~ for prepararsi a; ~**d** to pronto(a) a.

preposition [prepə'zɪʃən] *n* preposizione *f.*

preposterous [prɪ'pɔstərəs] *a* assurdo(a).

prerequisite [priː'rɛkwɪzɪt] *n* requisito indispensabile.

prescribe [prɪ'skraɪb] *vt* prescrivere; (*MED*) ordinare.

prescription [prɪ'skrɪpʃən] *n* prescrizione *f*; (*MED*) ricetta.

presence ['prezns] *n* presenza; ~ of mind presenza di spirito.

present ['preznt] *a* presente; (*wife, residence, job*) attuale // *n* regalo; (*also*: ~ tense) tempo presente // *vt* [prɪ'zent] presentare; (*give*) to ~ sb with sth offrire qc a qn; to give sb a ~ fare un regalo a qn; at ~ al momento; ~**ation** [-'teɪʃən] *n* presentazione *f*; (*gift*) regalo, dono; (*ceremony*) consegna ufficiale; ~**day** *a* attuale, d'oggigiorno; ~**er** *n*

(*RADIO*, *TV*) presentatore/trice; ~**ly** *ad*
(*soon*) fra poco, presto; (*at present*) al
momento.

preservative [prɪ'zə:vətɪv] *n* conservante
m.

preserve [prɪ'zə:v] *vt* (*keep safe*)
preservare, proteggere; (*maintain*)
conservare; (*food*) mettere in conserva //
n (*for game, fish*) riserva; (*often pl:
jam*) marmellata; (: *fruit*) frutta
sciroppata.

preside [prɪ'zaɪd] *vi* presiedere.

president ['prezɪdənt] *n* presidente *m*;
~**ial** [-'denʃl] *a* presidenziale.

press [pres] *n* (*tool, machine*) pressa;
(*for wine*) torchio; (*newspapers*)
stampa; (*crowd*) folla // *vt* (*push*)
premere, pigiare; (*squeeze*) spremere;
(: *hand*) stringere; (*clothes*: *iron*)
stirare; (*pursue*) incalzare; (*insist*): **to**
~ **sth on sb** far accettare qc da qn // *vi*
premere; accalcare; **we are** ~**ed for**
time ci manca il tempo; **to** ~ **for sth**
insistere per avere qc; **to** ~ **on** *vi*
continuare; ~ **conference** *n* conferenza
stampa; ~**ing** *a* urgente // *n* stiratura;
~ **stud** *n* (*Brit*) bottone *m* a pressione;
~-**up** *n* (*Brit*) flessione *f* sulle braccia.

pressure ['preʃə*] *n* pressione *f*; ~
cooker *n* pentola a pressione; ~ **gauge**
n manometro; ~ **group** *n* gruppo di
pressione.

prestige [pres'ti:ʒ] *n* prestigio.

presumably [prɪ'zju:məblɪ] *ad*
presumibilmente.

presume [prɪ'zju:m] *vt* supporre; **to** ~ **to**
do (*dare*) permettersi di fare.

presumption [prɪ'zʌmpʃən] *n*
presunzione *f*; (*boldness*) audacia.

presumptuous [prɪ'zʌmpʃəs] *a*
presuntuoso(a).

pretence, (US) pretense [prɪ'tens] *n*
(*claim*) pretesa; **to make a** ~ **of doing**
far finta di fare.

pretend [prɪ'tend] *vt* (*feign*) fingere // *vi*
(*feign*) far finta; (*claim*): **to** ~ **to sth**
pretendere a qc; **to** ~ **to do** far finta di
fare.

pretense [prɪ'tens] *n* (*US*) = **pretence**.

pretension [prɪ'tenʃən] *n* (*claim*)
pretesa.

pretentious [prɪ'tenʃəs] *a*
pretenzioso(a).

pretext ['pri:tekst] *n* pretesto.

pretty ['prɪtɪ] *a* grazioso(a), carino(a) //
ad abbastanza, assai.

prevail [prɪ'veɪl] *vi* (*win, be usual*)
prevalere; (*persuade*): **to** ~ (**up**)**on sb to**
do persuadere qn a fare; ~**ing** *a*
dominante.

prevalent ['prevələnt] *a* (*belief*)
predominante; (*customs*) diffuso(a);
(*fashion*) corrente; (*disease*) comune.

prevent [prɪ'vent] *vt* prevenire; **to** ~ **sb**
from doing impedire a qn di fare; ~**ion**

[-'venʃən] *n* prevenzione *f*; ~**ive** *a*
preventivo(a).

preview ['pri:vju:] *n* (*of film*) anteprima.

previous ['pri:vɪəs] *a* precedente;
anteriore; ~**ly** *ad* prima.

prewar ['pri:'wɔ:*] *a* anteguerra *inv*.

prey [preɪ] *n* preda // *vi*: **to** ~ **on** far
preda di.

price [praɪs] *n* prezzo // *vt* (*goods*) fissare
il prezzo di; valutare; ~**less** *a* inap-
prezzabile; ~ **list** *n* listino (dei) prezzi.

prick [prɪk] *n* puntura // *vt* pungere; **to** ~
up one's ears drizzare gli orecchi.

prickle ['prɪkl] *n* (*of plant*) spina;
(*sensation*) pizzicore *m*.

prickly ['prɪklɪ] *a* spinoso(a); (*fig:
person*) permaloso(a); ~ **heat** *n*
sudamina.

pride [praɪd] *n* orgoglio; superbia // *vt*: **to**
~ **o.s. on** essere orgoglioso(a) di;
vantarsi di.

priest [pri:st] *n* prete *m*, sacerdote *m*;
~**hood** *n* sacerdozio.

prig [prɪg] *n*: **he's a** ~ è compiaciuto di
se stesso.

prim [prɪm] *a* pudico(a); contegnoso(a).

primarily ['praɪmərɪlɪ] *ad* principalmente,
essenzialmente.

primary ['praɪmərɪ] *a* primario(a); (*first
in importance*) primo(a); ~ **school** *n*
(*Brit*) scuola elementare.

prime [praɪm] *a* primario(a),
fondamentale; (*excellent*) di prima
qualità // *vt* (*gun*) innescare; (*pump*)
adescare; (*fig*) mettere al corrente; **in**
the ~ **of life** nel fiore della vita; **P**~
Minister (P.M.) *n* primo ministro.

primer ['praɪmə*] *n* (*book*) testo
elementare.

primeval [praɪ'mi:vl] *a* primitivo(a).

primitive ['prɪmɪtɪv] *a* primitivo(a).

primrose ['prɪmrəuz] *n* primavera.

primus (stove) ['praɪməs(stəuv)] *n* ®
(*Brit*) fornello a petrolio.

prince [prɪns] *n* principe *m*.

princess [prɪn'ses] *n* principessa.

principal ['prɪnsɪpl] *a* principale // *n*
(*headmaster*) preside *m*.

principle ['prɪnsɪpl] *n* principio; **in** ~ **in**
linea di principio; **on** ~ per principio.

print [prɪnt] *n* (*mark*) impronta; (*letters*)
caratteri *mpl*; (*fabric*) tessuto stampato;
(*ART, PHOT*) stampa // *vt* imprimere;
(*publish*) stampare, pubblicare; (*write
in capitals*) scrivere in stampatello; **out**
of ~ esaurito(a); ~**ed matter** *n* stampe
fpl; ~**er** *n* tipografo; (*machine*)
stampante *f*; ~**ing** *n* stampa; ~-**out** *n*
(*COMPUT*) tabulato.

prior ['praɪə*] *a* precedente // *n* priore *m*;
~ **to doing** prima di fare.

priority [praɪ'ɔrɪtɪ] *n* priorità *f inv*;
precedenza.

priory ['praɪərɪ] *n* monastero.

prise [praɪz] *vt*: **to** ~ **open** forzare.

prison |'prizn| *n* prigione *f* // *cpd* (*system*) carcerario(a); (*conditions, food*) nelle *or* delle prigioni; **~er** *n* prigioniero/a.

pristine ['pristi:n] *a* immacolato(a).

privacy ['privəsi] *n* solitudine *f*, intimità.

private ['praivit] *a* privato(a); personale // *n* soldato semplice; "**~**" (*on envelope*) "riservata"; **in ~** in privato; **~ enterprise** *n* iniziativa privata; **~ eye** *n* investigatore *m* privato; **~ly** *ad* in privato; (*within oneself*) dentro di sé; **~ property** *n* proprietà privata; **privatize** *vt* privatizzare.

privet ['privit] *n* ligustro.

privilege ['privilidʒ] *n* privilegio.

privy ['privi] *a*: **to be ~ to** essere al corrente di; **~ council** *n* Consiglio della Corona.

prize [praiz] *n* premio // *a* (*example, idiot*) perfetto(a); (*bull, novel*) premiato(a) // *vt* apprezzare, pregiare; **~ giving** *n* premiazione *f*; **~winner** *n* premiato/a.

pro [prəu] *n* (*SPORT*) professionista *m/f*; **the ~s and cons** il pro e il contro.

probability [prɔbə'biliti] *n* probabilità *f inv.*

probable ['prɔbəbl] *a* probabile; **probably** *ad* probabilmente.

probation [prə'beiʃən] *n* (*in employment*) periodo di prova; (*LAW*) libertà vigilata; **on ~** (*employee*) in prova; (*LAW*) in libertà vigilata.

probe [prəub] *n* (*MED. SPACE*) sonda; (*enquiry*) indagine *f*, investigazione *f* // *vt* sondare, esplorare; indagare.

problem ['prɔbləm] *n* problema *m*.

procedure [prə'si:dʒə*] *n* (*ADMIN, LAW*) procedura; (*method*) metodo, procedimento.

proceed [prə'si:d] *vi* (*go forward*) avanzare, andare avanti; (*go about it*) procedere; (*continue*): **to ~** (*with*) continuare; **to ~ to** andare a; passare a; **to ~ to do** mettersi a fare; **~ings** *npl* misure *fpl*; (*LAW*) procedimento; (*meeting*) riunione *f*; (*records*) rendiconti *mpl*; atti *mpl*; **~s** ['prəusi:dz] *npl* profitto, incasso.

process ['prəusɛs] *n* processo; (*method*) metodo, sistema *m* // *vt* trattare; (*information*) elaborare; **~ing** *n* trattamento; elaborazione *f*.

procession [prə'sɛʃən] *n* processione *f*, corteo; **funeral ~** corteo funebre.

proclaim [prə'kleim] *vt* proclamare, dichiarare.

procrastinate [prəu'kræstineit] *vi* procrastinare.

prod [prɔd] *vt* dare un colpetto a; pungolare.

prodigal ['prɔdigl] *a* prodigo(a).

prodigy ['prɔdidʒi] *n* prodigio.

produce *n* ['prɔdju:s] (*AGR*) prodotto,

prodotti *mpl* // *vt* [prə'dju:s] produrre; (*to show*) esibire, mostrare; (*cause*) cagionare, causare; (*THEATRE*) mettere in scena; **~r** *n* (*THEATRE*) direttore/trice; (*AGR. CINEMA*) produttore *m*.

product ['prɔdʌkt] *n* prodotto.

production [prə'dʌkʃən] *n* produzione *f*; (*THEATRE*) messa in scena; **~ line** *n* catena di lavorazione.

productivity [prɔdʌk'tiviti] *n* produttività.

profane [prə'fein] *a* profano(a); (*language*) empio(a).

profession [prə'fɛʃən] *n* professione *f*; **~al** *n* (*SPORT*) professionista *m/f* // *a* professionale; (*work*) da professionista; **~alism** *n* professionismo.

professor [prə'fɛsə*] *n* professore *m* (*titolare di una cattedra*).

proficiency [prə'fiʃənsi] *n* competenza, abilità.

profile ['prəufail] *n* profilo.

profit ['prɔfit] *n* profitto; beneficio // *vi*: **to ~** (**by** *or* **from**) approfittare (di); **~ability** [-'biliti] *n* redditività; **~able** *a* redditizio(a).

profiteering [prɔfi'tiəriŋ] *n* (*pej*) affarismo.

profound [prə'faund] *a* profondo(a).

profusely [prə'fju:sli] *ad* con grande effusione.

progeny ['prɔdʒini] *n* progenie *f*; discendenti *mpl*.

programme, program (*US*) ['prəugræm] *n* programma *m* // *vt* programmare; **~r, programer** (*US*) *n* programmatore/trice.

progress *n* ['prəugrɛs] progresso // *vi* [prə'grɛs] avanzare, procedere; **in ~** in corso; **to make ~** far progressi; **~ive** [-'grɛsiv] *a* progressivo(a); (*person*) progressista *m/f*.

prohibit [prə'hibit] *vt* proibire, vietare; **~ion** [prəui'biʃən] *n* (*US*) proibizionismo, **~ive** *a* (*price etc*) proibitivo(a).

project *n* ['prɔdʒɛkt] (*plan*) piano; (*venture*) progetto; (*SCOL*) studio // *vb* [prə'dʒɛkt] *vt* proiettare // *vi* (*stick out*) sporgere.

projectile [prə'dʒɛktail] *n* proiettile *m*.

projector [prə'dʒɛktə*] *n* proiettore *m*.

prolong [prə'lɔŋ] *vt* prolungare.

prom [prɔm] *n* *abbr* = **promenade**; (*US: ball*) ballo studentesco.

promenade [prɔmə'nɑ:d] *n* (*by sea*) lungomare *m*; **~ concert** *n* concerto di musica classica.

prominent ['prɔminənt] *a* (*standing out*) prominente; (*important*) importante.

promiscuous [prə'miskjuəs] *a* (*sexually*) di facili costumi.

promise ['prɔmis] *n* promessa // *vt, vi* promettere; **promising** *a* promettente.

promote [prə'məut] *vt* promuovere; (*venture, event*) organizzare; **~r** *n* (*of* *sporting event*) organizzatore/trice; **promotion** |-'məuʃən| *n* promozione *f*.

prompt |prɔmpt| *a* rapido(a), svelto(a); puntuale; (*reply*) sollecito(a) // *ad* (*punctually*) in punto // *n* (*COMPUT*) prompt *m* // *vt* incitare; provocare; (*THEATRE*) suggerire a; **~ly** *ad* prontamente; puntualmente; **~ness** *n* prontezza; puntualità.

prone |prəun| *a* (*lying*) prono(a); **~ to** propenso(a) a, incline a.

prong |prɔŋ| *n* rebbio, punta.

pronoun |'prəunaun| *n* pronome *m*.

pronounce |prə'nauns| *vt* pronunziare // *vi*: **to ~ (up)on** pronunziare su.

pronunciation |prənʌnsɪ'eɪʃən| *n* pronunzia.

proof |pru:f| *n* prova; (*of book*) bozza; (*PHOT*) provino; (*of alcohol*) grado // *a*: **~ against** a prova di.

prop |prɔp| *n* sostegno, appoggio // *vt* (*also*: **~ up**) sostenere, appoggiare; (*lean*): **to ~ sth against** appoggiare qc contro or a.

propaganda |prɔpə'gændə| *n* propaganda.

propel |prə'pɛl| *vt* spingere (in avanti), muovere; **~ler** *n* elica; **~ling pencil** *n* (*Brit*) matita a mina.

propensity |prə'pɛnsɪtɪ| *n* tendenza.

proper |'prɔpə*| *a* (*suited, right*) adatto(a), appropriato(a); (*seemly*) decente; (*authentic*) vero(a); (*col: real*) *noun* + vero(a) e proprio(a); **~ly** *ad* (*eat, study*) bene; (*behave*) come si deve; **~ noun** *n* nome *m* proprio.

property |'prɔpətɪ| *n* (*things owned*) beni *mpl*; (*land, building*) proprietà *f inv*; (*CHEM etc: quality*) proprietà; **~ owner** *n* proprietario/a.

prophecy |'prɔfɪsɪ| *n* profezia.

prophesy |'prɔfɪsaɪ| *vt* predire.

prophet |'prɔfɪt| *n* profeta *m*.

proportion |prə'pɔ:ʃən| *n* proporzione *f*; (*share*) parte *f* // *vt* proporzionare, commisurare; **~al** *a* proporzionale; **~ate** *a* proporzionato(a).

proposal |prə'pəuzl| *n* proposta; (*plan*) progetto; (*of marriage*) proposta di matrimonio.

propose |prə'pəuz| *vt* proporre, suggerire // *vi* fare una proposta di matrimonio; **to ~ to do** proporsi di fare, aver l'intenzione di fare.

proposition |prɔpə'zɪʃən| *n* proposizione *f*.

proprietor |prə'praɪətə*| *n* proprietario/a.

propriety |prə'praɪətɪ| *n* (*seemliness*) decoro, rispetto delle convenienze sociali.

prose |prəuz| *n* prosa; (*SCOL: translation*) traduzione *f* dalla madrelingua.

prosecute |'prɔsɪkju:t| *vt* processare; **prosecution** |-'kju:ʃən| *n* processo; (*accusing side*) accusa; **prosecutor** *n*

(*also*: **public prosecutor**) ≈ procuratore *m* della Repubblica.

prospect *n* |'prɔspɛkt| prospettiva; (*hope*) speranza // *vb* |prə'spɛkt| *vt* fare assaggi in // *vi* fare assaggi; **~s** *npl* (*for work etc*) prospettive *fpl*; **prospective** |-'spɛktɪv| *a* possibile; futuro(a).

prospectus |prə'spɛktəs| *n* prospetto, programma *m*.

prosperity |prɔ'spɛrɪtɪ| *n* prosperità.

prostitute |'prɔstɪtju:t| *n* prostituta.

protect |prə'tɛkt| *vt* proteggere, salvaguardare; **~ion** *n* protezione *f*; **~ive** *a* protettivo(a).

protégé |'prəutəʒeɪ| *n* protetto; **~e** *n* protetta.

protein |'prəuti:n| *n* proteina.

protest *n* |'prəutɛst| protesta // *vt, vi* |prə'tɛst| protestare.

Protestant |'prɔtɪstənt| *a, n* protestante (*m/f*).

protester |prə'tɛstə*| *n* dimostrante *m/f*.

prototype |'prəutətaɪp| *n* prototipo.

protracted |prə'træktɪd| *a* tirato(a) per le lunghe.

protrude |prə'tru:d| *vi* sporgere.

protuberance |prə'tju:bərəns| *n* sporgenza.

proud |praud| *a* fiero(a), orgoglioso(a); (*pej*) superbo(a).

prove |pru:v| *vt* provare, dimostrare // *vi*: **to ~ correct** *etc* risultare vero(a) *etc*; **to ~ o.s.** mostrare le proprie capacità.

proverb |'prɔvə:b| *n* proverbio.

provide |prə'vaɪd| *vt* fornire, provvedere; **to ~ sb with sth** fornire or provvedere qn di qc; **to ~ for** *vt fus* provvedere a; **~d (that)** *cj* purché + *sub*, a condizione che + *sub*.

providing |prə'vaɪdɪŋ| *cj* purché + *sub*, a condizione che + *sub*.

province |'prɔvɪns| *n* provincia; **provincial** |prə'vɪnʃəl| *a* provinciale.

provision |prə'vɪʒən| *n* (*supply*) riserva; (*supplying*) provvista; rifornimento; (*stipulation*) condizione *f*; **~s** *npl* (*food*) provviste *fpl*; **~al** *a* provvisorio(a).

proviso |prə'vaɪzəu| *n* condizione *f*.

provocative |prə'vɔkətɪv| *a* (*aggressive*) provocatorio(a); (*thought-provoking*) stimolante; (*seductive*) provocante.

provoke |prə'vəuk| *vt* provocare; incitare.

prow |prau| *n* prua.

prowess |'prauɪs| *n* prodezza.

prowl |praul| *vi* (*also*: **~ about, ~ around**) aggirarsi; **~er** *n* tipo sospetto (*che s'aggira con l'intenzione di rubare, aggredire etc*).

proximity |prɔk'sɪmɪtɪ| *n* prossimità.

proxy |'prɔksɪ| *n* procura.

prudent |'pru:dnt| *a* prudente.

prudish |'pru:dɪʃ| *a* puritano(a).

prune |pru:n| *n* prugna secca // *vt* potare.

pry |praɪ| *vi*: to ~ **into** ficcare il naso in.
PS *abbr* (= *postscript*) P.S.
psalm |sɑːm| *n* salmo.
pseudo- |'sjuː:dəu| *prefix* pseudo...
pseudonym ['sjuː:dənɪm] *n* pseudonimo.
psyche ['saɪkɪ] *n* psiche *f*.
psychiatric |saɪkɪ'ætrɪk| *a* psichiatrico(a).
psychiatrist |saɪ'kaɪətrɪst| *n* psichiatra *m/f*.
psychic ['saɪkɪk] *a* (*also*: ~al) psichico(a); (*person*) dotato(a) di qualità telepatiche.
psychoanalyst |saɪkəu'ænəlɪst| *n* psicanalista *m/f*.
psychological |saɪkə'lɔdʒɪkl| *a* psicologico(a).
psychologist |saɪ'kɔlədʒɪst| *n* psicologo/a.
psychology |saɪ'kɔlədʒɪ| *n* psicologia.
psychopath ['saɪkəupæθ] *n* psicopatico/a.
P.T.O. *abbr* (= *please turn over*) v.r.
pub |pʌb| *n abbr* (= *public house*) pub *m inv*.
pubic ['pjuː:bɪk] *a* pubico(a), del pube.
public ['pʌblɪk] *a* pubblico(a) // *n* pubblico; **in** ~ in pubblico; ~ **address system (P.A.)** *n* impianto di amplificazione.
publican ['pʌblɪkən] *n* proprietario di un pub.
publication |pʌblɪ'keɪʃən| *n* pubblicazione *f*.
public: ~ **company** *n* società *f inv* per azioni (*costituita tramite pubblica sottoscrizione*); ~ **convenience** *n* (*Brit*) gabinetti *mpl*; ~ **holiday** *n* giorno festivo, festa nazionale; ~ **house** *n* (*Brit*) pub *m inv*.
publicity |pʌb'lɪsɪtɪ| *n* pubblicità.
publicize ['pʌblɪsaɪz] *vt* rendere pubblico(a).
publicly ['pʌblɪklɪ] *ad* pubblicamente.
public: ~ **opinion** *n* opinione *f* pubblica; ~ **relations (PR)** *n* pubbliche relazioni *fpl*; ~ **school** *n* (*Brit*) scuola privata; (*US*) scuola statale; ~**-spirited** *a* che ha senso civico; ~ **transport** *n* mezzi *mpl* pubblici.
publish ['pʌblɪʃ] *vt* pubblicare; ~**er** *n* editore *m*; ~**ing** *n* (*industry*) editoria; (*of a book*) pubblicazione *f*.
puck |pʌk| *n* (*ICE HOCKEY*) disco.
pucker ['pʌkə*] *vt* corrugare.
pudding ['pudɪŋ] *n* budino; (*Brit*: *dessert*) dolce *m*; **black** ~ sanguinaccio.
puddle ['pʌdl] *n* pozza, pozzanghera.
puff |pʌf| *n* sbuffo // *vt*: to ~ one's pipe tirare sboccate di fumo // *vi* uscire a sbuffi; (*pant*) ansare; to ~ **out smoke** mandar fuori sbuffi di fumo; ~**ed** *a* (*col*: *out of breath*) senza fiato; ~ **pastry** *n* pasta sfoglia; ~**y** *a* gonfio(a).
pull |pul| *n* (*tug*) to give sth a ~ tirare su qc; (*fig*) influenza // *vt* tirare; (*mus-*

cle) strappare // *vi* tirare; to ~ **to pieces** fare a pezzi; to ~ **one's punches** (*BOXING*) risparmiare l'avversario; to ~ **one's weight** dare il proprio contributo; to ~ **o.s. together** ricomporsi, riprendersi; to ~ **sb's leg** prendere in giro qn; to ~ **apart** *vt* (*break*) fare a pezzi; to ~ **down** *vt* (*house*) demolire; (*tree*) abbattere; to ~ **in** *vi* (*AUT*: *at the kerb*) accostarsi; (*RAIL*) entrare in stazione; to ~ **off** *vt* (*deal etc*) portare a compimento; to ~ **out** *vi* partire; (*AUT*: *come out of line*) spostarsi sulla mezzeria // *vt* staccare; far uscire; (*withdraw*) ritirare; to ~ **over** *vi* (*AUT*) accostare; to ~ **through** *vi* farcela; to ~ **up** *vi* (*stop*) fermarsi // *vt* (*uproot*) sradicare; (*stop*) fermare.
pulley ['pulɪ] *n* puleggia, carrucola.
pullover ['puləuvə*] *n* pullover *m inv*.
pulp |pʌlp| *n* (*of fruit*) polpa; (*for paper*) pasta per carta.
pulpit ['pulpɪt] *n* pulpito.
pulsate |pʌl'seɪt| *vi* battere, palpitare.
pulse |pʌls| *n* polso.
pummel ['pʌml] *vt* dare pugni a.
pump |pʌmp| *n* pompa; (*shoe*) scarpetta // *vt* pompare; (*fig*: *col*) far parlare; to ~ **up** *vt* gonfiare.
pumpkin ['pʌmpkɪn] *n* zucca.
pun |pʌn| *n* gioco di parole.
punch |pʌntʃ| *n* (*blow*) pugno; (*fig*: *force*) forza; (*tool*) punzone *m*; (*drink*) ponce *m* // *vt* (*hit*): to ~ **sb/sth** dare un pugno a qn/qc; to ~ **a hole** (**in**) fare un buco (in); ~ **line** *n* (*of joke*) battuta finale; ~**-up** *n* (*Brit col*) rissa.
punctual ['pʌŋktjuəl] *a* puntuale; ~**ity** [-'ælɪtɪ] *n* puntualità.
punctuation |pʌŋktju'eɪʃən| *n* interpunzione *f*, punteggiatura.
puncture ['pʌŋktʃə*] *n* foratura // *vt* forare.
pundit ['pʌndɪt] *n* sapientone/a.
pungent ['pʌndʒənt] *a* piccante; (*fig*) mordace, caustico(a).
punish ['pʌnɪʃ] *vt* punire; ~**ment** *n* punizione *f*.
punk |pʌŋk| *n* (*also*: ~ **rocker**) punk *m/f inv*; (*also*: ~ **rock**) musica punk, punk rock *m*; (*US col*: *hoodlum*) teppista *m*.
punt |pʌnt| *n* (*boat*) barchino; (*FOOTBALL*) colpo a volo.
punter ['pʌntə*] *n* (*Brit*: *gambler*) scommettitore/trice.
puny ['pjuː:nɪ] *a* gracile.
pup |pʌp| *n* cucciolo/a.
pupil ['pjuː:pl] *n* allievo/a; (*ANAT*) pupilla.
puppet ['pʌpɪt] *n* burattino.
puppy ['pʌpɪ] *n* cucciolo/a, cagnolino/a.
purchase ['pəːtʃɪs] *n* acquisto, compera // *vt* comprare; ~**r** *n* compratore/trice.
pure |pjuə*| *a* puro(a).
purely ['pjuəlɪ] *ad* puramente.
purge |pəːdʒ| *n* (*MED*) purga; (*POL*)

epurazione f // vt purgare; (fig) epurare.

puritan ['pjuərɪtən] a, n puritano(a).

purl [pə:l] n punto rovescio.

purple ['pə:pl] a di porpora; viola inv.

purport [pə:'pɔ:t] vi: to ~ to be/do pretendere di essere/fare.

purpose ['pə:pəs] n intenzione f, scopo; on ~ apposta; ~**ful** a deciso(a), risoluto(a).

purr [pə:*] vi fare le fusa.

purse [pə:s] n borsellino // vt contrarre.

purser ['pə:sə*] n (NAUT) commissario di bordo.

pursue [pə'sju:] vt inseguire.

pursuit [pə'sju:t] n inseguimento; (occupation) occupazione f, attività f inv.

purveyor [pə'veɪə*] n fornitore/trice.

push [puʃ] n spinta; (effort) grande sforzo; (drive) energia // vt spingere; (button) premere; (thrust): to ~ sth (into) ficcare qc (in); (fig) fare pubblicità a // vi spingere; premere; **to ~ aside** vt scostare; **to ~ off** vi (col) filare; **to ~ on** vi (continue) continuare; **to ~ through** vt (measure) far approvare; **to ~ up** vt (total, prices) far salire; ~**chair** n (Brit) passeggino; ~**er** n (drug ~er) spacciatore/trice; ~**over** n (col): it's a ~over è un lavoro da bambini; ~**up** n (US: press-up) flessione f sulle braccia; ~**y** a (pej) opportunista.

puss, pussy(-cat) [pus, 'pusɪ(kæt)] n micio.

put, pt, pp **put** [put] vt mettere, porre; (say) dire, esprimere; (a question) fare; (estimate) stimare; **to ~ about** vi (NAUT) virare di bordo // vt (rumour) diffondere; **to ~ across** vt (ideas etc) comunicare; far capire; **to ~ away** vt (return) mettere a posto; **to ~ back** vt (replace) rimettere (a posto); (postpone) rinviare; (delay) ritardare; **to ~ by** vt (money) mettere da parte; **to ~ down** vt (parcel etc) posare, mettere giù; (pay) versare; (in writing) mettere per iscritto; (suppress: revolt etc) reprimere, sopprimere; (attribute) attribuire; **to ~ forward** vt (ideas) avanzare, proporre; (date) anticipare; **to ~ in** vt (application, complaint) presentare; **to ~ off** vt (postpone) rimandare, rinviare; (discourage) dissuadere; **to ~ on** vt (clothes, lipstick etc) mettere; (light etc) accendere; (play etc) mettere in scena; (food, meal) servire; (brake) mettere; **to ~ on weight** ingrassare; **to ~ on airs** darsi delle arie; **to ~ out** vt mettere fuori; (one's hand) porgere; (light etc) spegnere; (person: inconvenience) scomodare; **to ~ up** vt (raise) sollevare, alzare; (pin up) affiggere; (hang) appendere; (build) costruire, erigere; (increase) aumentare;

(accommodate) alloggiare; **to ~ up with** vt fus sopportare.

putt [pʌt] vt (ball) colpire leggermente // n colpo leggero; ~**ing green** n green m inv; campo da putting.

putty ['pʌtɪ] n stucco.

puzzle ['pʌzl] n enigma m, mistero; (jigsaw) puzzle m; (also: crossword ~) parole fpl incrociate, cruciverba m inv // vt confondere, rendere perplesso(a) // vi scervellarsi.

pyjamas [pɪ'dʒɑ:məz] npl (Brit) pigiama m.

pylon ['paɪlən] n pilone m.

pyramid ['pɪrəmɪd] n piramide f.

Pyrenees [pɪrɪ'ni:z] npl: the ~ i Pirenei.

Q

quack [kwæk] n (of duck) qua qua m inv; (pej: doctor) dottoruccio/a.

quad [kwɔd] n abbr = **quadrangle**, **quadruplet**.

quadrangle ['kwɔdræŋgl] n (MATH) quadrilatero; (courtyard) cortile m.

quadruple [kwɔ'drupl] vt quadruplicare // vi quadruplicarsi.

quadruplet [kwɔ'dru:plɪt] n uno/a di quattro gemelli.

quagmire ['kwægmaɪə*] n pantano.

quail [kweɪl] n (ZOOL) quaglia // vi (person) perdersi d'animo.

quaint [kweɪnt] a bizzarro(a); (old-fashioned) antiquato(a); grazioso(a), pittoresco(a).

quake [kweɪk] vi tremare // n abbr = **earthquake**.

Quaker ['kweɪkə*] n quacchero/a.

qualification [kwɔlɪfɪ'keɪʃən] n (degree etc) qualifica, titolo; (ability) competenza, qualificazione f; (limitation) riserva, restrizione f.

qualified ['kwɔlɪfaɪd] a qualificato(a); (able) competente, qualificato(a); (limited) condizionato(a).

qualify ['kwɔlɪfaɪ] vt abilitare; (limit: statement) modificare, precisare // vi: to ~ (as) qualificarsi (come); to ~ (for) acquistare i requisiti necessari (per); (SPORT) qualificarsi (per o a).

quality ['kwɔlɪtɪ] n qualità f inv.

qualm [kwɑ:m] n dubbio; scrupolo.

quandary ['kwɔndrɪ] n: in a ~ in un dilemma.

quantity ['kwɔntɪtɪ] n quantità f inv; ~ **surveyor** n geometra m (specializzato nel calcolare la quantità e il costo del materiale da costruzione).

quarantine ['kwɔrnti:n] n quarantena.

quarrel ['kwɔrl] n lite f, disputa // vi litigare; ~**some** a litigioso(a).

quarry ['kwɔrɪ] n (for stone) cava; (animal) preda // vt (marble etc) estrarre.

quart |kwɔ:t| n ≈ litro.
quarter |'kwɔ:tə*| n quarto; (of year) trimestre m; (district) quartiere m // vt dividere in quattro; (MIL) alloggiare; ~s npl alloggio; (MIL) alloggi mpl, quadrato; a ~ of an hour un quarto d'ora; ~ **final** n quarto di finale; ~**ly** a trimestrale // ad trimestralmente; ~**master** n (MIL) furiere m.
quartet(te) |kwɔ:'tɛt| n quartetto.
quartz |kwɔ:ts| n quarzo; ~ **watch** n orologio al quarzo.
quash |kwɔʃ| vt (verdict) annullare.
quaver |'kweivə*| n (Brit MUS) croma // vi tremolare.
quay |ki:| n (also: ~side) banchina.
queasy |'kwi:zi| a (stomach) delicato(a); to feel ~ aver la nausea.
queen |kwi:n| n (gen) regina; (CARDS etc) regina, donna; ~ **mother** n regina madre.
queer |kwiə*| a strano(a), curioso(a); (suspicious) dubbio(a), sospetto(a); (sick): I feel ~ mi sento poco bene // n (col) finocchio.
quell |kwɛl| vt domare.
quench |kwɛntʃ| vt (flames) spegnere; to ~ one's thirst dissetarsi.
querulous |'kwɛruləs| a querulo(a).
query |'kwiəri| n domanda, questione f; (doubt) dubbio // vt mettere in questione.
quest |kwɛst| n cerca, ricerca.
question |'kwɛstʃən| n domanda, questione f // vt (person) interrogare; (plan, idea) mettere in questione or in dubbio; it's a ~ of doing si tratta di fare; beyond ~ fuori di dubbio; out of the ~ fuori discussione, impossibile; ~**able** a discutibile; ~ **mark** n punto interrogativo.
questionnaire |kwɛstʃə'nɛə*| n questionario.
queue |kju:| (Brit) n coda, fila // vi fare la coda.
quibble |'kwibl| vi cavillare.
quick |kwik| a rapido(a), veloce; (reply) pronto(a); (mind) pronto(a), acuto(a) // ad rapidamente, presto // n: cut to the ~ (fig) toccato(a) sul vivo; be ~! fa presto!; ~**en** vt accelerare, affrettare; (rouse) animare, stimolare // vi accelerare, affrettarsi; ~**ly** ad rapidamente, velocemente; ~**sand** n sabbie fpl mobili; ~-**witted** a pronto(a) d'ingegno.
quid |kwid| n (pl inv) (Brit col) sterlina.
quiet |'kwaiət| a tranquillo(a), quieto(a); (ceremony) semplice; (colour) discreto(a) // n tranquillità, calma // vt, vi (US) = ~**en**; keep ~! sta zitto!; ~**en** (also: ~**en down**) vi calmarsi, chetarsi // vt calmare, chetare; ~**ly** ad tranquillamente, calmamente; sommessamente; discretamente.
quilt |kwilt| n trapunta; (continental ~) piumino.

quin |kwin| n abbr = **quintuplet**.
quinine |kwi'ni:n| n chinino.
quintuplet |kwin'tju:plit| n uno/a di cinque gemelli.
quip |kwip| n frizzo.
quirk |kwɔ:k| n ghiribizzo.
quit, pt, pp quit or **quitted** |kwit| vt lasciare, partire da // vi (give up) mollare; (resign) dimettersi; **notice to** ~ preavviso (dato all'inquilino).
quite |kwait| ad (rather) assai; (entirely) completamente, del tutto; I ~ understand capisco perfettamente; ~ a few of them non pochi di loro; ~ (so)! esatto!
quits |kwits| a: ~ (with) pari (con); let's call it ~ adesso siamo pari.
quiver |'kwivə*| vi tremare, fremere // n (for arrows) faretra.
quiz |kwiz| n (game) quiz m inv; indovinello // vt interrogare; ~**zical** a enigmatico(a).
quota |'kwəutə| n quota.
quotation |kwəu'teifən| n citazione f; (of shares etc) quotazione f; (estimate) preventivo; ~ **marks** npl virgolette fpl.
quote |kwəut| n citazione f // vt (sentence) citare; (price) dare, fissare; (shares) quotare // vi: to ~ from citare.

R

rabbi |'ræbai| n rabbino.
rabbit |'ræbit| n coniglio; ~ **hutch** n conigliera.
rabble |'ræbl| n (pej) canaglia, plebaglia.
rabies |'reibi:z| n rabbia.
RAC n abbr (Brit) = Royal Automobile Club.
race |reis| n razza; (competition, rush) corsa // vt (person) gareggiare (in corsa) con; (horse) far correre; (engine) imballare // vi correre; ~ **car** n (US) = **racing car**; ~ **car driver** n (US) = **racing driver**; ~**course** n campo di corse, ippodromo; ~**horse** n cavallo da corsa; ~ **relations** npl rapporti mpl razziali; ~**track** n pista.
racial |'reifl| a razziale; ~**ist** a, n razzista (m/f).
racing |'reisiŋ| n corsa; ~ **car** n (Brit) macchina da corsa; ~ **driver** n (Brit) corridore m automobilista.
racism |'reisizəm| n razzismo; **racist** a, n razzista (m/f).
rack |ræk| n rastrelliera; (also: **luggage** ~) rete f, portabagagli m inv; (also: **roof** ~) portabagagli // vt torturare, tormentare; **to** ~ **one's brains** scervellarsi.
racket |'rækit| n (for tennis) racchetta; (noise) fracasso; baccano; (swindle) imbroglio, truffa; (organized crime) racket m inv.

racquet ['rækɪt] n racchetta.
racy ['reɪsɪ] a brioso(a); piccante.
radar ['reɪdɑ:*] n radar m // cpd radar inv.
radial5.5 ['reɪdɪəl] a (also: ~-ply) radiale.
radiant ['reɪdɪənt] a raggiante; (PHYSICS) radiante.
radiate ['reɪdɪeɪt] vt (heat) irraggiare, irradiare // vi (lines) irradiarsi.
radiation [reɪdɪ'eɪʃən] n irradiamento; (radioactive) radiazione f.
radiator ['reɪdɪeɪtə*] n radiatore m.
radical ['rædɪkl] a radicale.
radii ['reɪdɪaɪ] npl of **radius**.
radio ['reɪdɪəu] n radio f inv; on the ~ alla radio.
radioactive [reɪdɪəu'æktɪv] a radioattivo(a).
radio station n stazione f radio inv.
radish ['rædɪʃ] n ravanello.
radium ['reɪdɪəm] n radio.
radius ['reɪdɪəs], pl **radii** n raggio; (ANAT) radio.
RAF n abbr = Royal Air Force.
raffle ['ræfl] n lotteria.
raft [rɑ:ft] n zattera; (also: life ~) zattera di salvataggio.
rafter ['rɑ:ftə*] n trave f.
rag [ræg] n straccio, cencio; (pej: newspaper) giornalaccio, bandiera; (for charity) iniziativa studentesca a scopo benefico // vt (Brit) prendere in giro; ~s npl stracci mpl, brandelli mpl; ~-and-bone man n (Brit) = **ragman**; ~ doll n bambola di pezza.
rage [reɪdʒ] n (fury) collera, furia // vi (person) andare su tutte le furie; (storm) infuriare; **it's all the ~** fa furore.
ragged ['rægɪd] a (edge) irregolare; (cuff) logoro(a); (appearance) pezzente.
ragman ['rægmæn] n straccivendolo.
raid [reɪd] n (MIL) incursione f; (criminal) rapina; (by police) irruzione f // vt fare un'incursione in; rapinare; fare irruzione in.
rail [reɪl] n (on stair) ringhiera; (on bridge, balcony) parapetto; (of ship) battagliola; (for train) rotaia; ~s npl binario, rotaie fpl; **by ~** per ferrovia; ~ing(s) n(pl) ringhiere fpl; ~road n (US) = ~way; ~way n (Brit) ferrovia; ~way line n (Brit) linea ferroviaria; ~wayman n (Brit) ferroviere m; ~way station n (Brit) stazione f ferroviaria.
rain [reɪn] n pioggia // vi piovere; **in the ~** sotto la pioggia; **it's ~ing** piove; ~bow n arcobaleno; ~coat n impermeabile m; ~drop n goccia di pioggia; ~fall n (measurement) piovosità; ~y a piovoso(a).
raise [reɪz] n aumento // vt (lift) alzare; sollevare; (build) erigere; (increase)

aumentare; (a protest, doubt, question) sollevare; (cattle, family) allevare; (crop) coltivare; (army, funds) raccogliere; (loan) ottenere; **to ~ one's voice** alzare la voce.
raisin ['reɪzn] n uva secca.
rajah ['rɑːdʒə] n ragià m inv.
rake [reɪk] n (tool) rastrello; (person) libertino // vt (garden) rastrellare; (with machine gun) spazzare.
rally ['rælɪ] n (POL etc) riunione f; (AUT) rally m inv; (TENNIS) scambio // vt riunire, radunare // vi raccogliersi, radunarsi; (sick person, Stock Exchange) riprendersi; **to ~ round** vt fus raggrupparsi intorno a; venire in aiuto di.
RAM [ræm] n abbr (- random access memory) memoria ad accesso casuale.
ram [ræm] n montone m, ariete m; (device) ariete // vt conficcare; (crash into) cozzare, sbattere contro; percuotere; speronare.
ramble ['ræmbl] n escursione f // vi (pej: also: ~ on) divagare; ~r n escursionista m/f; (BOT) rosa rampicante; **rambling** a (speech) sconnesso(a); (BOT) rampicante.
ramp [ræmp] n rampa; **on/off ~** (US AUT) raccordo di entrata/uscita.
rampage [ræm'peɪdʒ] n: **to go on the ~** scatenarsi in modo violento.
rampant ['ræmpənt] a (disease etc) che infierisce.
rampart ['ræmpɑːt] n bastione m.
ramshackle ['ræmʃækl] a (house) cadente; (car etc) sgangherato(a).
ran [ræn] pt of **run**.
ranch [rɑːntʃ] n ranch m inv; ~er n proprietario di un ranch; cowboy m inv.
rancid ['rænsɪd] a rancido(a).
rancour, (US) **rancor** ['ræŋkə*] n rancore m.
random ['rændəm] a fatto(a) or detto(a) per caso // n: **at ~** a casaccio; ~ **access** n (COMPUT) accesso casuale.
randy ['rændɪ] a (Brit col) arrapato(a); lascivo(a).
rang [ræŋ] pt of **ring**.
range [reɪndʒ] n (of mountains) catena; (of missile, voice) portata; (of products) gamma; (MIL: also: **shooting ~**) campo di tiro; (also: **kitchen ~**) fornello, cucina economica // vi: **to ~ over** coprire; **to ~ from ... to** andare da ... a.
ranger ['reɪndʒə*] n guardia forestale.
rank [ræŋk] n fila; (MIL) grado; (Brit: also: **taxi ~**) posteggio di taxi // vi: **to ~ among** essere nel numero di // a puzzolente; vero(a) e proprio(a); **the ~s** (MIL) la truppa; **the ~ and file** (fig) la gran massa.
rankle ['ræŋkl] vi bruciare.
ransack ['rænsæk] vt rovistare; (plunder) saccheggiare.

ransom ['rænsəm] n riscatto; to hold sb to ~ (fig) esercitare pressione su qn.

rant [rænt] vi vociare.

rap [ræp] vt bussare a; picchiare su.

rape [reɪp] n violenza carnale, stupro; (BOT) ravizzone m // vt violentare; ~(seed) oil n olio di ravizzone.

rapid ['ræpɪd] a rapido(a); ~s npl (GEO) rapida; ~ly ad rapidamente.

rapist ['reɪpɪst] n violentatore m.

rapport [ræ'pɔ:*] n rapporto.

rapture ['ræptʃə*] n estasi f inv.

rare [rɛə*] a raro(a); (CULIN: steak) al sangue.

rarefied ['rɛərɪfaɪd] a (air, atmosphere) rarefatto(a).

rarely ['rɛəlɪ] ad raramente.

raring ['rɛərɪŋ] a: to be ~ to go (col) non veder l'ora di cominciare.

rascal ['rɑːskl] n mascalzone m.

rash [ræʃ] a imprudente, sconsiderato(a) // n (MED) eruzione f.

rasher ['ræʃə*] n fetta sottile (di lardo or prosciutto).

raspberry ['rɑːzbərɪ] n lampone m.

rasping ['rɑːspɪŋ] a stridulo(a).

rat [ræt] n ratto.

rate [reɪt] n (proportion) tasso, percentuale f; (speed) velocità f inv; (price) tariffa // vt giudicare; stimare; to ~ sb/sth as valutare qn/qc come; ~s npl (Brit) imposte fpl comunali; (fees) tariffe fpl; ~able value n (Brit) valore, m imponibile or locativo (di una proprietà); ~payer n (Brit) contribuente m/f (che paga le imposte comunali).

rather ['rɑːðə*] ad piuttosto; it's ~ expensive è piuttosto caro; (too much) è un po' caro; there's ~ a lot ce n'è parecchio; I would or I'd ~ go preferirei andare.

ratify ['rætɪfaɪ] vt ratificare.

rating ['reɪtɪŋ] n classificazione f; punteggio di merito; (NAUT: category) classe f; (: Brit: sailor) marinaio semplice.

ratio ['reɪʃɪəu] n proporzione f.

ration ['ræʃən] n (gen pl) razioni fpl // vt razionare.

rational ['ræʃənl] a razionale, ragionevole; (solution, reasoning) logico(a); ~e [-'nɑːl] n fondamento logico; giustificazione f; ~ize vt razionalizzare.

rat race n carrierismo, corsa al successo.

rattle ['rætl] n tintinnio; (louder) strepito; (object: of baby) sonaglino; (: of sports fan) raganella // vi risuonare, tintinnare; fare un rumore di ferraglia // vt scuotere (con strepito); ~snake n serpente m a sonagli.

raucous ['rɔːkəs] a rauco(a).

ravage ['rævɪdʒ] vt devastare; ~s npl danni mpl.

rave [reɪv] vi (in anger) infuriarsi; (with enthusiasm) andare in estasi; (MED) delirare.

raven ['reɪvən] n corvo.

ravenous ['rævənəs] a affamato(a).

ravine [rə'viːn] n burrone m.

raving ['reɪvɪŋ] a: ~ lunatic pazzo(a) furioso(a).

ravioli [rævɪ'əulɪ] n ravioli mpl.

ravishing ['rævɪʃɪŋ] a incantevole.

raw [rɔ:] a (uncooked) crudo(a); (not processed) greggio(a); (sore) vivo(a); (inexperienced) inesperto(a); ~ deal n (col) bidonata; ~ material n materia prima.

ray [reɪ] n raggio; a ~ of hope un barlume di speranza.

rayon ['reɪɔn] n raion m.

raze [reɪz] vt radere, distruggere.

razor ['reɪzə*] n rasoio; ~ blade n lama di rasoio.

Rd abbr = road.

re [ri:] prep con riferimento a.

reach [ri:tʃ] n portata; (of river etc) tratto // vt raggiungere; arrivare a // vi stendersi; out of/within ~ fuori/a portata di mano; to ~ out vi: to ~ out for stendere la mano per prendere.

react [ri:'ækt] vi reagire; ~ion [-'ækʃən] n reazione f.

reactor [ri:'æktə*] n reattore m.

read, pt, pp **read** [ri:d, rɛd] vi leggere // vt leggere; (understand) intendere, interpretare; (study) studiare; to ~ out vt leggere ad alta voce; ~able a (writing) leggibile; (book etc) che si legge volentieri; ~er n lettore/trice; (book) libro di lettura; (Brit: at university) professore con funzioni preminenti di ricerca; ~ership n (of paper etc) numero di lettori.

readily ['rɛdɪlɪ] ad volentieri; (easily) facilmente.

readiness ['rɛdɪnɪs] n prontezza; in ~ (prepared) pronto(a).

reading ['ri:dɪŋ] n lettura; (understanding) interpretazione f; (on instrument) indicazione f.

ready ['rɛdɪ] a pronto(a); (willing) pronto(a), disposto(a); (quick) rapido(a); (available) disponibile // ad: ~-cooked già cotto(a) // n: at the ~ (MIL) pronto a sparare; (fig) tutto(a) pronto(a); to get ~ vi prepararsi // vt preparare; ~-made a prefabbricato(a); (clothes) confezionato(a); ~ money n denaro contante, contanti mpl; ~ reckoner n prontuario di calcolo; ~-to-wear a prêt-à-porter inv.

real [rɪəl] a reale; vero(a); in ~ terms in realtà; ~ estate n beni mpl immobili; ~ism n (also ART) realismo; ~ist n realista m/f; ~istic [-'lɪstɪk] a realistico(a).

reality [ri:'ælɪtɪ] n realtà f inv.

realization |rɪəlaɪˈzeɪʃən| *n* presa di co-scienza; realizzazione *f*.

realize |ˈrɪəlaɪz| *vt* (*understand*) rendersi conto di; (*a project*, *COMM*: *asset*) realizzare.

really |ˈrɪəlɪ| *ad* veramente, davvero.

realm |rɛlm| *n* reame *m*, regno.

realtor |ˈrɪəltɔ:*| *n* (*US*) agente *m* immobiliare.

reap |ri:p| *vt* mietere; (*fig*) raccogliere.

reappear |ri:əˈpɪə*| *vi* ricomparire, riapparire.

rear |rɪə*| *a* di dietro; (*AUT*: *wheel etc*) posteriore // *n* didietro, parte *f* posteriore // *vt* (*cattle*, *family*) allevare // *vi* (*also*: ~ up: *animal*) impennarsi.

rearmament |ri:ˈɑ:məmənt| *n* riarmo.

rearrange |ri:əˈreɪndʒ| *vt* riordinare.

rear-view mirror |ˈrɪəvju.*| *n* (*AUT*) specchio retrovisore.

reason |ˈri:zn| *n* ragione *f*; (*cause*, *motive*) ragione, motivo // *vi*: to ~ with sb far ragionare qn; to have ~ to think avere motivi per pensare; it stands to ~ that è ovvio che; ~**able** *a* ragionevole; (*not bad*) accettabile; ~**ably** *ad* ragionevolmente; ~**ing** *n* ragionamento.

reassurance |ri:əˈʃʊərəns| *n* rassicurazione *f*.

reassure |ri:əˈʃʊə*| *vt* rassicurare; to ~ sb of rassicurare qn di *or* su.

rebate |ˈri:beɪt| *n* (*on product*) ribasso; (*on tax etc*) sgravio; (*repayment*) rimborso.

rebel *n* |ˈrɛbl| ribelle *m/f* // *vi* |rɪˈbɛl| ribellarsi; ~**lion** *n* ribellione *f*; ~**lious** *a* ribelle.

rebound *vi* |rɪˈbaund| (*ball*) rimbalzare // *n* |ˈri:baund| rimbalzo.

rebuff |rɪˈbʌf| *n* secco rifiuto.

rebuke |rɪˈbju:k| *vt* rimproverare.

rebut |rɪˈbʌt| *vt* rifiutare.

recall |rɪˈkɔ:l| *vt* richiamare, (*remember*) ricordare, richiamare alla mente // *n* richiamo.

recant |rɪˈkænt| *vi* ritrattarsi; (*REL*) fare abiura.

recap |ˈri:kæp| *vt* ricapitolare // *vi* riassumere.

recapitulate |ri:kəˈpɪtjuleɪt| *vt*, *vi* = re-**cap**.

rec'd *abbr* = received.

recede |rɪˈsi:d| *vi* allontanarsi; ritirarsi; calare; **receding** *a* (*forehead*, *chin*) sfuggente; he's got a receding hairline sta stempiando.

receipt |rɪˈsi:t| *n* (*document*) ricevuta; (*act of receiving*) ricevimento; ~**s** *npl* (*COMM*) introiti *mpl*.

receive |rɪˈsi:v| *vt* ricevere; (*guest*) ricevere, accogliere.

receiver |rɪˈsi:və*| *n* (*TEL*) ricevitore *m*; (*of stolen goods*) ricettatore/trice; (*LAW*) curatore *m* fallimentare.

recent |ˈri:snt| *a* recente; ~**ly** *ad*

recentemente.

receptacle |rɪˈsɛptɪkl| *n* recipiente *m*.

reception |rɪˈsɛpʃən| *n* ricevimento; (*welcome*) accoglienza; (*TV etc*) ricezione *f*; ~ **desk** *n* (*in hotel*) reception *f inv*; (*in hospital, at doctor's*) accettazione *f*; (*in offices etc*) portineria; ~**ist** *n* receptionist *m/f inv*.

receptive |rɪˈsɛptɪv| *a* ricettivo(a).

recess |rɪˈsɛs| *n* (*in room*) alcova; (*POL etc*: *holiday*) vacanze *fpl*; ~**ion** |-ˈsɛʃən| *n* recessione *f*.

recharge |ri:ˈtʃɑ:dʒ| *vt* (*battery*) ricaricare.

recipe |ˈrɛsɪpɪ| *n* ricetta.

recipient |rɪˈsɪpɪənt| *n* beneficiario/a; (*of letter*) destinatario/a.

recital |rɪˈsaɪtl| *n* recital *m inv*.

recite |rɪˈsaɪt| *vt* (*poem*) recitare.

reckless |ˈrɛkləs| *a* (*driver etc*) spericolato(a).

reckon |ˈrɛkən| *vt* (*count*) calcolare; (*consider*) considerare, stimare; (*think*) I ~ that ... penso che ...; to ~ on *vt fus* contare su; ~**ing** *n* conto; stima.

reclaim |rɪˈkleɪm| *vt* (*land*) bonificare; (*demand back*) richiedere, reclamare.

recline |rɪˈklaɪn| *vi* stare sdraiato(a); re-**clining** *a* (*seat*) ribaltabile.

recluse |rɪˈklu:s| *n* eremita *m*, appartato/a.

recognition |rɛkəgˈnɪʃən| *n* riconoscimento; to gain ~ essere riconosciuto(a); transformed beyond ~ irriconoscibile.

recognize |ˈrɛkəgnaɪz| *vt*: to ~ (by/as) riconoscere (a *or* da/come).

recoil |rɪˈkɔɪl| *vi* (*person*): to ~ (from) indietreggiare (davanti a) // *n* (*of gun*) rinculo.

recollect |rɛkəˈlɛkt| *vt* ricordare; ~**ion** |-ˈlɛkʃən| *n* ricordo.

recommend |rɛkəˈmɛnd| *vt* raccomandare; (*advise*) consigliare.

reconcile |ˈrɛkənsaɪl| *vt* (*two people*) riconciliare; (*two facts*) conciliare, quadrare; to ~ o.s. to rassegnarsi a.

recondition |ri:kənˈdɪʃən| *vt* rimettere a nuovo.

reconnaissance |rɪˈkɒnɪsns| *n* (*MIL*) ricognizione *f*.

reconnoitre, (*US*) **reconnoiter** |rɛkəˈnɔɪtə*| (*MIL*) *vt* fare una ricognizione di // *vi* fare una ricognizione.

reconstruct |ri:kənˈstrʌkt| *vt* ricostruire.

record *n* |ˈrɛkɔ:d| ricordo, documento; (*of meeting etc*) nota, verbale *m*; (*register*) registro; (*file*) pratica, dossier *m inv*; (*also*: police ~) fedina penale sporca; (*MUS*: *disc*) disco; (*SPORT*) record *m inv*, primato // *vt* |rɪˈkɔ:d| (*set down*) prendere nota di, registrare; (*relate*) raccontare; (*MUS*: *song etc*) registrare; in ~ time a tempo di record; to keep a ~ of tener nota di; off the ~ *a* ufficioso(a) // *ad* ufficiosamente; ~ **card** *n* (*in file*) scheda; **~ed delivery** *n* (*Brit POST*): ~**ed delivery letter** *etc* lettera *etc* raccomandata; **~er** *n* (*LAW*) avvocato *che funge da giudice*; (*MUS*) flauto diritto; ~ **holder** *n* (*SPORT*) primatista *m/f*; **~ing** *n* (*MUS*) registrazione *f*; ~ **player** *n* giradischi *m inv*.

recount [rɪ'kaunt] *vt* raccontare, narrare.

re-count *n* ['ri:kaunt] (*POL: of votes*) nuovo computo // *vt* [ri:'kaunt] ricontare.

recoup [rɪ'ku:p] *vt* ricuperare.

recourse [rɪ'kɔ:s] *n* ricorso; rimedio.

recover [rɪ'kʌvə*] *vt* ricuperare // *vi* (*from illness*) rimettersi (in salute), ristabilirsi; (*country, person: from shock*) riprendersi.

recovery [rɪ'kʌvərɪ] *n* ricupero; ristabilimento; ripresa.

recreation [rɛkrɪ'eɪʃən] *n* ricreazione *f*; svago; **~al** *a* ricreativo(a).

recrimination [rɪkrɪmɪ'neɪʃən] *n* recriminazione *f*.

recruit [rɪ'kru:t] *n* recluta // *vt* reclutare.

rectangle ['rɛktæŋgl] *n* rettangolo; **rectangular** [-'tæŋgjulə*] *a* rettangolare.

rectify ['rɛktɪfaɪ] *vt* (*error*) rettificare; (*omission*) riparare.

rector ['rɛktə*] *n* (*REL*) parroco (*anglicano*); **rectory** *n* presbiterio.

recuperate [rɪ'kju:pəreɪt] *vi* ristabilirsi.

recur [rɪ'kɔ:*] *vi* riaccadere; (*idea, opportunity*) riapparire; (*symptoms*) ripresentarsi; **~rent** *a* ricorrente, periodico(a).

red [rɛd] *n* rosso; (*POL: pej*) rosso/a // *a* rosso(a); in the ~ (*account*) scoperto; (*business*) in deficit; ~ **carpet treatment** *n* cerimonia col gran pavese; R**~ Cross** *n* Croce *f* Rossa; **~currant** *n* ribes *m inv*; **~den** *vt* arrossare // *vi* arrossire; **~dish** *a* rossiccio(a).

redeem [rɪ'di:m] *vt* (*debt*) riscattare; (*sth in pawn*) ritirare; (*fig, also REL*) redimere; **~ing** *a* (*feature*) che salva.

redeploy [ri:dɪ'plɔɪ] *vt* (*resources*) riorganizzare.

red-haired [rɛd'hɛəd] *a* dai capelli rossi.

red-handed [rɛd'hændɪd] *a*: to be caught ~ essere preso(a) in flagrante *or* con le mani nel sacco.

redhead ['rɛdhɛd] *n* rosso/a.

red herring *n* (*fig*) falsa pista.

red-hot [rɛd'hɔt] *a* arroventato(a).

redirect [ri:daɪ'rɛkt] *vt* (*mail*) far seguire.

redistribute [ri:dɪ'strɪbju:t] *vt* ridistribuire.

red light *n*: to go through a ~ (*AUT*) passare col rosso; **red-light district** *n* quartiere *m* luce rossa *inv*.

redo [ri:'du:] *vt irg* rifare.

redolent ['rɛdələnt] *a*: ~ of che sa di; (*fig*) che ricorda.

redouble [ri:'dʌbl] *vt*: to ~ one's efforts raddoppiare gli sforzi.

redress [rɪ'drɛs] *n* riparazione *f* // *vt* riparare.

Red Sea *n*: the ~ il Mar Rosso.

redskin ['rɛdskɪn] *n* pellerossa *m/f*.

red tape *n* (*fig*) burocrazia.

reduce [rɪ'dju:s] *vt* ridurre; (*lower*) ridurre, abbassare; "~ **speed now**" (*AUT*) "rallentare"; **reduction** [rɪ'dʌkʃən] *n* riduzione *f*; (*of price*) ribasso; (*discount*) sconto.

redundancy [rɪ'dʌndənsɪ] *n* licenziamento.

redundant [rɪ'dʌndnt] *a* (*worker*) licenziato(a); (*detail, object*) superfluo(a); to be made ~ essere licenziato (per eccesso di personale).

reed [ri:d] *n* (*BOT*) canna; (*MUS: of clarinet etc*) ancia.

reef [ri:f] *n* (*at sea*) scogliera.

reek [ri:k] *vi*: to ~ (of) puzzare (di).

reel [ri:l] *n* bobina, rocchetto; (*TECH*) aspo; (*FISHING*) mulinello; (*CINEMA*) rotolo // *vt* (*TECH*) annaspare; (*also: ~ up*) avvolgere // *vi* (*sway*) barcollare.

ref [rɛf] *n abbr* (*col*: = *referee*) arbitro.

refectory [rɪ'fɛktərɪ] *n* refettorio.

refer [rɪ'fə:*] *vt*: to ~ sth to (*dispute, decision*) deferire qc a; to ~ sb to (*inquirer: for information*) indirizzare qn a; (*reader: to text*) rimandare qn a; to ~ to *vt fus* (*allude to*) accennare a; (*apply to*) riferire a; (*consult*) rivolgersi a.

referee [rɛfə'ri:] *n* arbitro; (*Brit: for job application*) referenza // *vt* arbitrare.

reference ['rɛfrəns] *n* riferimento; (*mention*) menzione *f*, allusione *f*; (*for job application: letter*) referenza; lettera di raccomandazione; (: *person*) referenza; **with ~ to** riguardo a; (*COMM: in letter*) in *or* con riferimento a; ~ **book** *n* libro di consultazione; ~ **number** *n* numero di riferimento.

referendum, *pl* **referenda** [rɛfə'rɛndəm, -də] *n* referendum *m inv*.

refill *vt* [ri:'fɪl] riempire di nuovo; (*pen, lighter etc*) ricaricare // *n* ['ri:fɪl] (*for pen etc*) ricambio.

refine [rɪ'faɪn] *vt* raffinare; **~d** *a* (*person, taste*) raffinato(a).

reflect [rɪ'flɛkt] *vt* (*light, image*) riflettere; (*fig*) rispecchiare // *vi* (*think*) riflettere, considerare; **to ~ on** *vt fus* (*discredit*) rispecchiarsi su; **~ion** [-'flɛkʃən] *n* riflessione *f*; (*image*) riflesso; (*criticism*): **~ion on** giudizio su; attacco a; **on ~ion** pensandoci sopra.

reflex ['ri:flɛks] *a* riflesso(a) // *n* riflesso(a); **~ive** [rɪ'flɛksɪv] *a* (*LING*) riflessivo(a).

reform [rɪ'fɔ:m] *n* riforma // *vt* riformare; **the R~ation** [rɛfə'meɪʃən] *n* la Riforma; **~atory** *n* (*US*) riformatorio.

refrain [rɪ'freɪn] vi: to ~ from doing trattenersi dal fare // n ritornello.

refresh [rɪ'frɛʃ] vt rinfrescare; (subj: food, sleep) ristorare; ~**er course** n (Brit) corso di aggiornamento; ~**ing** a (drink) rinfrescante; (sleep) riposante, ristoratore(trice); ~**ments** npl rinfreschi mpl.

refrigerator [rɪ'frɪdʒəreɪtə*] n frigorifero.

refuel [ri:'fjuəl] vi far rifornimento (di carburante).

refuge ['rɛfju:dʒ] n rifugio; to take ~ in rifugiarsi in.

refugee [rɛfju'dʒi:] n rifugiato/a, profugo/a.

refund n ['ri:fʌnd] rimborso // vt [rɪ'fʌnd] rimborsare.

refurbish [ri:'fɔ:bɪʃ] vt rimettere a nuovo.

refusal [rɪ'fju:zəl] n rifiuto; to have first ~ on avere il diritto d'opzione su.

refuse n ['rɛfju:s] rifiuti mpl // vt, vi [rɪ'fju:z] rifiutare; to ~ to do rifiutare di fare; ~ **collection** n raccolta di rifiuti.

refute [rɪ'fju:t] vt confutare.

regain [rɪ'geɪn] vt riguadagnare; riacquistare, ricuperare.

regal ['ri:gl] a regio(a); ~**ia** [rɪ'geɪlɪə] n insegne fpl regie.

regard [rɪ'gɑ:d] n riguardo, stima // vt considerare, stimare; to give one's ~s to porgere i suoi saluti a; "with kindest ~s" "cordiali saluti"; ~**ing**, as ~s, with ~ to riguardo a; ~**less** ad lo stesso; ~less of a dispetto di, nonostante.

regenerate [rɪ'dʒɛnəreɪt] vt rigenerare.

régime [reɪ'ʒi:m] n regime m.

regiment n ['rɛdʒɪmənt] reggimento // vt ['rɛdʒɪment] irreggimentare; ~**al** [-'mentl] a reggimentale.

region ['ri:dʒən] n regione f; in the ~ of (fig) all'incirca di; ~**al** a regionale.

register ['rɛdʒɪstə*] n registro; (also: electoral ~) lista elettorale // vt registrare; (vehicle) immatricolare; (luggage) spedire assicurato(a); (letter) assicurare; (subj: instrument) segnare // vi iscriversi; (at hotel) firmare il registro; (make impression) entrare in testa; ~**ed** a (design) depositato(a); (Brit: letter) assicurato(a); ~**ed trademark** n marchio depositato.

registrar ['rɛdʒɪstrɑ:*] n ufficiale m di stato civile; segretario.

registration [rɛdʒɪs'treɪʃən] n (act) registrazione f; iscrizione f; (AUT: also: ~ number) numero di targa.

registry ['rɛdʒɪstrɪ] n ufficio del registro; ~ **office** n (Brit) anagrafe f; to get married in a ~ office ≈ sposarsi in municipio.

regret [rɪ'grɛt] n rimpianto, rincrescimento // vt rimpiangere; ~**fully** ad con rincrescimento; ~**table** a de-

plorevole.

regular ['rɛgjulə*] a regolare; (usual) abituale, normale; (soldier) dell'esercito regolare; (COMM: size) normale // n (client etc) cliente m/f abituale; ~**ly** ad regolarmente.

regulate ['rɛgjuleɪt] vt regolare; **regulation** [-'leɪʃən] n (rule) regola, regolamento; (adjustment) regolazione f.

rehabilitation ['ri:həbɪlɪ'teɪʃən] n (of offender) riabilitazione f; (of disabled) riadattamento.

rehearsal [rɪ'hɔ:səl] n prova.

rehearse [rɪ'hɔ:s] vt provare.

reign [reɪn] n regno // vi regnare.

reimburse [ri:ɪm'bɔ:s] vt rimborsare.

rein [reɪn] n (for horse) briglia.

reindeer ['reɪndɪə*] n (pl inv) renna.

reinforce [ri:ɪn'fɔ:s] vt rinforzare; ~**d concrete** n cemento armato; ~**ments** npl (MIL) rinforzi mpl.

reinstate [ri:ɪn'steɪt] vt reintegrare.

reiterate [ri:'ɪtəreɪt] vt reiterare, ripetere.

reject n ['ri:dʒɛkt] (COMM) scarto // vt [rɪ'dʒɛkt] rifiutare, respingere; (COMM: goods) scartare; ~**ion** [rɪ'dʒɛkʃən] n rifiuto.

rejoice [rɪ'dʒɔɪs] vi: to ~ (at or over) provare diletto in.

rejuvenate [rɪ'dʒu:vəneɪt] vt ringiovanire.

relapse [rɪ'læps] n (MED) ricaduta.

relate [rɪ'leɪt] vt (tell) raccontare; (connect) collegare // vi: to ~ to (connect) riferirsi a; (get on with) stabilire un rapporto con; ~**d** a imparentato(a); collegato(a), connesso(a); ~**lating to** prep che riguarda, rispetto a.

relation [rɪ'leɪʃən] n (person) parente m/f; (link) rapporto, relazione f; ~**ship** n rapporto; (personal ties) rapporti mpl, relazioni fpl; (also: family ~ship) legami mpl di parentela.

relative ['rɛlətɪv] n parente m/f // a relativo(a); (respective) rispettivo(a).

relax [rɪ'læks] vi rilasciarsi; (person: unwind) rilassarsi // vt rilasciare; (mind, person) rilassare; ~**ation** [ri:læk'seɪʃən] n rilasciamento; rilassamento; (entertainment) ricreazione f, svago; ~**ed** a rilasciato(a); rilassato(a); ~**ing** a rilassante.

relay ['ri:leɪ] n (SPORT) corsa a staffetta // vt (message) trasmettere.

release [rɪ'li:s] n (from prison) rilascio; (from obligation) liberazione f; (of gas etc) emissione f; (of film etc) distribuzione f; (record) disco; (device) disinnesto // vt (prisoner) rilasciare; (from obligation, wreckage etc) liberare; (book, film) fare uscire; (news) rendere pubblico(a); (gas etc) emettere; (TECH: catch, spring etc) disinnestare; (let go) rilasciare; lasciar andare; sciogliere.

relegate |'rɛləgeɪt| vt relegare; (SPORT):
to be ~d essere retrocesso(a).

relent |rɪ'lɛnt| vi cedere; ~**less** a implacabile.

relevant |'rɛləvənt| a pertinente;
(chapter) in questione; ~ to pertinente
a.

reliability |rɪlaɪə'bɪlɪtɪ| n (of person)
serietà; (of machine) affidabilità.

reliable |rɪ'laɪəbl| a (person, firm)
fidato(a), che dà affidamento; (method)
sicuro(a); (machine) affidabile; **reliably**
ad: to be reliably informed sapere da
fonti sicure.

reliance |rɪ'laɪəns| n: ~ (on) fiducia (in);
bisogno (di).

relic |'rɛlɪk| n (REL) reliquia; (of the
past) resto.

relief |rɪ'li:f| n (from pain, anxiety)
sollievo; (help, supplies) soccorsi mpl;
(of guard) cambio; (ART, GEO) rilievo.

relieve |rɪ'li:v| vt (pain, patient)
sollevare; (bring help) soccorrere; (take
over from: gen) sostituire; (: guard)
rilevare; to ~ sb of sth (load)
alleggerire qn di qc; to ~ o.s. fare i propri bisogni.

religion |rɪ'lɪdʒən| n religione f; **religious** a religioso(a).

relinquish |rɪ'lɪŋkwɪʃ| vt abbandonare;
(plan, habit) rinunziare a.

relish |'rɛlɪʃ| n (CULIN) condimento;
(enjoyment) gran piacere m // vt (food
etc) godere; to ~ doing adorare fare.

relocate |'ri:ləu'keɪt| vt trasferire // vi
trasferirsi.

reluctance |rɪ'lʌktəns| n riluttanza.

reluctant |rɪ'lʌktənt| a riluttante, mal disposto(a); ~**ly** ad di mala voglia, a
malincuore.

rely |rɪ'laɪ|: to ~ on vt fus contare su; (be
dependent) dipendere da.

remain |rɪ'meɪn| vi restare, rimanere;
~**der** n resto; (COMM) rimanenza;
~**ing** a che rimane; ~**s** npl resti mpl.

remand |rɪ'mɑːnd| n: on ~ in detenzione
preventiva // vt: to ~ in custody rinviare
in carcere; trattenere a disposizione
della legge; ~ **home** n (Brit)
riformatorio, casa di correzione.

remark |rɪ'mɑːk| n osservazione f // vt
osservare, dire; (notice) notare; ~**able**
a notevole; eccezionale.

remedial |rɪ'miːdɪəl| a (tuition, classes)
di riparazione.

remedy |'rɛmədɪ| n: ~ (for) rimedio
(per) // vt rimediare a.

remember |rɪ'mɛmbə*| vt ricordare,
ricordarsi di; **remembrance** n
memoria; ricordo.

remind |rɪ'maɪnd| vt: to ~ sb of sth
ricordare qc a qn; to ~ sb to do
ricordare a qn di fare; ~**er** n richiamo;
(note etc) promemoria m inv.

reminisce |rɛmɪ'nɪs| vi: to ~ (about)
abbandonarsi ai ricordi (di).

reminiscent |rɛmɪ'nɪsnt| a: ~ of che fa
pensare a, che richiama.

remiss |rɪ'mɪs| a negligente.

remission |rɪ'mɪʃən| n remissione f; (of
fee) esonero.

remit |rɪ'mɪt| vt (send: money)
rimettere; ~**tance** n rimessa.

remnant |'rɛmnənt| n resto, avanzo; ~**s**
npl (COMM) scampoli mpl; fine f serie.

remorse |rɪ'mɔːs| n rimorso; ~**ful** a
pieno(a) di rimorsi; ~**less** a (fig)
spietato(a).

remote |rɪ'məut| a remoto(a),
lontano(a); (person) distaccato(a); ~
control n telecomando; ~**ly** ad
remotamente; (slightly) vagamente.

remould |'riːməuld| n (Brit: tyre)
gomma rivestita.

removable |rɪ'muːvəbl| a (detachable)
staccabile.

removal |rɪ'muːvəl| n (taking away)
rimozione f; soppressione f; (Brit: from
house) trasloco; (from office: dismissal)
destituzione f; (MED) ablazione f; ~
van n (Brit) furgone m per traslochi.

remove |rɪ'muːv| vt togliere, rimuovere;
(employee) destituire; (stain) far
sparire; (doubt, abuse) sopprimere,
eliminare; ~**rs** npl (Brit: company)
ditta or impresa di traslochi.

Renaissance |rɪ'neɪsɑːns| n: the ~ il
Rinascimento.

render |'rɛndə*| vt rendere; (CULIN: fat)
struggere; ~**ing** n (MUS etc) interpretazione f.

rendez-vous |'rɔndɪvuː| n appuntamento; (place) luogo d'incontro; (meeting)
incontro.

renegade |'rɛnɪgeɪd| n rinnegato/a.

renew |rɪ'njuː| vt rinnovare;
(negotiations) riprendere; ~**al** n
rinnovamento; ripresa.

renounce |rɪ'nauns| vt rinunziare a;
(disown) ripudiare.

renovate |'rɛnəveɪt| vt rinnovare; (art
work) restaurare; **renovation** |-'veɪʃən|
n rinnovamento; restauro.

renown |rɪ'naun| n rinomanza; ~**ed** a
rinomato(a).

rent |rɛnt| n affitto // vt (take for rent)
prendere in affitto; (also: ~ out) dare in
affitto; ~**al** n (for television, car) fitto.

renunciation |rɪnʌnsɪ'eɪʃən| n
rinnegamento; (self-denial) rinunzia.

rep |rɛp| n abbr (COMM: = representative) rappresentante m/f; (THEATRE: = repertory) teatro di repertorio.

repair |rɪ'pɛə*| n riparazione f // vt
riparare; in good/bad ~ in buona/cattiva
condizione; ~ **kit** n corredo per
riparazioni; ~ **shop** n (AUT etc)
officina.

repartee |rɛpɑː'tiː| n risposta pronta.

repatriate [ri:'pætrɪeɪt] vt rimpatriare.

repay [ri:'peɪ] vt irg (money, creditor) rimborsare, ripagare; (sb's efforts) ricompensare; ~**ment** n rimborsamento; ricompensa.

repeal [rɪ'pi:l] n (of law) abrogazione f; (of sentence) annullamento // vt abrogare; annullare.

repeat [rɪ'pi:t] n (RADIO, TV) replica // vt ripetere; (pattern) riprodurre; (promise, attack, also COMM: order) rinnovare // vi ripetere; ~**edly** ad ripetutamente, spesso.

repel [rɪ'pɛl] vt respingere; ~**lent** a repellente // n: insect ~lent prodotto m anti-insetti inv.

repent [rɪ'pɛnt] vi: to ~ (of) pentirsi (di); ~**ance** n pentimento.

repertoire ['rɛpətwɑ:*] n repertorio.

repertory ['rɛpətəri] n (also: ~ theatre) teatro di repertorio.

repetition [rɛpɪ'tɪʃən] n ripetizione f; (COMM: of order etc) rinnovo.

repetitive [rɪ'pɛtɪtɪv] a (movement) che si ripete; (work) monotono(a); (speech) pieno(a) di ripetizioni.

replace [rɪ'pleɪs] vt (put back) rimettere a posto; (take the place of) sostituire; ~**ment** n rimessa; sostituzione f; (person) sostituto/a.

replay ['ri:pleɪ] n (of match) partita ripetuta; (of tape, film) replay m inv.

replenish [rɪ'plɛnɪʃ] vt (glass) riempire; (stock etc) rifornire.

replete [rɪ'pli:t] a ripieno(a); (well-fed) sazio(a).

replica ['rɛplɪkə] n replica, copia.

reply [rɪ'plaɪ] n risposta // vi rispondere; ~ **coupon** n buono di risposta.

report [rɪ'pɔ:t] n rapporto; (PRESS etc) cronaca; (Brit: also: school ~) pagella // vt riportare; (PRESS etc) fare una cronaca su; (bring to notice: occurrence) segnalare, (: person) denunciare // vi (make a report) fare un rapporto (or una cronaca); (present o.s.): to ~ (to sb) presentarsi (a qn); ~ **card** n (US, Scottish) pagella; ~**edly** ad stando a quanto si dice; he ~edly told them to ... avrebbe detto loro di ...; ~**er** n reporter m inv.

repose [rɪ'pəʊz] n: in ~ (face, mouth) in riposo.

reprehensible [rɛprɪ'hɛnsɪbl] a riprensibile.

represent [rɛprɪ'zɛnt] vt rappresentare; ~**ation** [-'teɪʃən] n rappresentazione f; ~**ations** npl (protest) protesta; ~**ative** n rappresentativo/a; (US POL) deputato/a // a rappresentativo(a), caratteristico(a).

repress [rɪ'prɛs] vt reprimere; ~**ion** [-'prɛʃən] n repressione f.

reprieve [rɪ'priːv] n (LAW) sospensione f dell'esecuzione della condanna; (fig) dilazione f.

reprimand ['rɛprɪmɑːnd] n rimprovero // vt rimproverare.

reprisal [rɪ'praɪzl] n rappresaglia.

reproach [rɪ'prəʊtʃ] n rimprovero // vt: to ~ sb with sth rimproverare qn di qc; ~**ful** a di rimprovero.

reproduce [ri:prə'dju:s] vt riprodurre // vi riprodursi; **reproduction** [-'dʌkʃən] n riproduzione f.

reproof [rɪ'pru:f] n riprovazione f.

reprove [rɪ'pru:v] vt (action) disapprovare; (person): to ~ (for) biasimare (per).

reptile ['rɛptaɪl] n rettile m.

republic [rɪ'pʌblɪk] n repubblica; ~**an** a, n repubblicano(a).

repulse [rɪ'pʌls] vt respingere.

repulsive [rɪ'pʌlsɪv] a ripugnante, ripulsivo(a).

reputable ['rɛpjutəbl] a di buona reputazione; (occupation) rispettabile.

reputation [rɛpju'teɪʃən] n reputazione f.

repute [rɪ'pju:t] n reputazione f; ~**d** a reputato(a); ~**dly** ad secondo quanto si dice.

request [rɪ'kwɛst] n domanda; (formal) richiesta // vt: to ~ (of or from sb) chiedere (a qn); ~ **stop** n (Brit: for bus) fermata facoltativa or a richiesta.

require [rɪ'kwaɪə*] vt (need: subj: person) aver bisogno di; (: thing, situation) richiedere; (want) volere; esigere; (order) obbligare; ~**ment** n esigenza; bisogno; requisito.

requisite ['rɛkwɪzɪt] n cosa necessaria // a necessario(a).

requisition [rɛkwɪ'zɪʃən] n: ~ (for) richiesta (di) // vt (MIL) requisire.

rescue ['rɛskju:] n salvataggio; (help) soccorso // vt salvare; ~ **party** n squadra di salvataggio; ~**r** n salvatore/trice.

research [rɪ'sə:tʃ] n ricerca, ricerche fpl // vt fare ricerche su.

resemblance [rɪ'zɛmbləns] n somiglianza.

resemble [rɪ'zɛmbl] vt assomigliare a.

resent [rɪ'zɛnt] vt risentirsi di; ~**ful** a pieno(a) di risentimento; ~**ment** n risentimento.

reservation [rɛzə'veɪʃən] n (booking) prenotazione f; (doubt) dubbio; (protected area) riserva; (Brit: on road: also: central ~) spartitraffico m inv; to make a ~ (in an hotel/a restaurant/on a plane) prenotare (una camera/una tavola/un posto).

reserve [rɪ'zə:v] n riserva // vt (seats etc) prenotare; ~**s** npl (MIL) riserve fpl; in ~ in serbo; ~**d** a (shy) riservato(a); (seat) prenotato(a).

reservoir ['rɛzəvwɑ:*] n serbatoio.

reshuffle [ri:'ʃʌfl] n: Cabinet ~ (POL) rimpasto governativo.

reside [rɪ'zaɪd] vi risiedere.

residence ['rɛzɪdəns] n residenza; ~

permit *n* (*Brit*) permesso di soggiorno.

resident ['rezɪdənt] *n* residente *m/f*; (*in hotel*) cliente *m/f* fisso(a) // *a* residente; ~**ial** [-'denʃəl] *a* di residenza; (*area*) residenziale.

residue ['rezɪdju:] *n* resto; (*CHEM, PHYSICS*) residuo.

resign [rɪ'zaɪn] *vt* (*one's post*) dimettersi da // *vi* dimettersi; to ~ o.s. to rassegnarsi a; ~**ation** [rezɪg'neɪʃən] *n* dimissioni *fpl*; rassegnazione *f*; ~**ed** *a* rassegnato(a).

resilience [rɪ'zɪlɪəns] *n* (*of material*) elasticità, resilienza; (*of person*) capacità di recupero.

resilient [rɪ'zɪlɪənt] *a* (*person*) che si riprende facilmente.

resin ['rezɪn] *n* resina.

resist [rɪ'zɪst] *vt* resistere a; ~**ance** *n* resistenza.

resolution [rezə'lu:ʃən] *n* risoluzione *f*.

resolve [rɪ'zɔlv] *n* risoluzione *f* // *vi* (*decide*): to ~ to do decidere di fare // *vt* (*problem*) risolvere.

resort [rɪ'zɔ:t] *n* (*town*) stazione *f*; (*recourse*) ricorso // *vi*: to ~ to aver ricorso a; as a last ~ come ultimo ricorso.

resounding [rɪ'zaundɪŋ] *a* risonante; (*fig*) clamoroso(a).

resource [rɪ'sɔ:s] *n* risorsa; ~**s** *npl* risorse *fpl*; ~**ful** *a* pieno(a) di risorse, intraprendente.

respect [rɪs'pekt] *n* rispetto // *vt* rispettare; ~**s** *npl* ossequi *mpl*; with ~ to rispetto a, riguardo a; in this ~ per questo riguardo; ~**able** *a* rispettabile; ~**ful** *a* rispettoso(a).

respective [rɪs'pektɪv] *a* rispettivo(a).

respite ['respaɪt] *n* respiro, tregua.

resplendent [rɪs'plendənt] *a* risplendente.

respond [rɪs'pɔnd] *vi* rispondere.

response [rɪs'pɔns] *n* risposta.

responsibility [rɪspɔnsɪ'bɪlɪtɪ] *n* responsabilità *f inv*.

responsible [rɪs'pɔnsɪbl] *a* (*trustworthy*) fidato(a); (*job*) di (grande) responsabilità; (*liable*): ~ (**for**) responsabile (di); **responsibly** *ad* responsabilmente.

responsive [rɪs'pɔnsɪv] *a* che reagisce.

rest [rest] *n* riposo; (*stop*) sosta, pausa; (*MUS*) pausa; (*support*) appoggio, sostegno; (*remainder*) resto, avanzi *mpl* // *vi* riposarsi; (*remain*) rimanere, restare; (*be supported*): to ~ on appoggiarsi su // *vt* (*lean*): to ~ sth on/against appoggiare qc su/contro; **the ~ of them** gli altri; it ~**s with him to decide** sta a lui decidere.

restaurant ['restərɔŋ] *n* ristorante *m*; ~ **car** *n* (*Brit*) vagone *m* ristorante.

restful ['restful] *a* riposante.

rest home *n* casa di riposo.

restitution [restɪ'tju:ʃən] *n* (*act*) restituzione *f*; (*reparation*) riparazione *f*.

restive ['restɪv] *a* agitato(a), impaziente; (*horse*) restio(a).

restless ['restlɪs] *a* agitato(a), irrequieto(a).

restoration [restə'reɪʃən] *n* restauro; restituzione *f*.

restore [rɪ'stɔ:*] *vt* (*building*) restaurare; (*sth stolen*) restituire; (*peace, health*) ristorare.

restrain [rɪs'treɪn] *vt* (*feeling*) contenere, frenare; (*person*): to ~ (**from doing**) trattenere (dal fare); ~**ed** *a* (*style*) contenuto(a), sobrio(a); (*manner*) riservato(a); ~**t** *n* (*restriction*) limitazione *f*; (*moderation*) ritegno.

restrict [rɪs'trɪkt] *vt* restringere, limitare; ~**ion** [-kʃən] *n* restrizione *f*, limitazione *f*.

rest room *n* (*US*) toletta.

restructure [ri:'strʌktʃə*] *vt* ristrutturare.

result [rɪ'zʌlt] *n* risultato // *vi*: to ~ **in** avere per risultato; as a ~ **of** in *or* di conseguenza a, in seguito a.

resume [rɪ'zju:m] *vt, vi* (*work, journey*) riprendere.

résumé ['reɪzjumeɪ] *n* riassunto.

resumption [rɪ'zʌmpʃən] *n* ripresa.

resurgence [rɪ'sə:dʒəns] *n* rinascita.

resurrection [rezə'rekʃən] *n* risurrezione *f*.

resuscitate [rɪ'sʌsɪteɪt] *vt* (*MED*) risuscitare; **resuscitation** [-'teɪʃən] *n* rianimazione *f*.

retail ['ri:teɪl] *n* (vendita al) minuto // *cpd* al minuto // *vt* vendere al minuto; ~**er** *n* commerciante *m/f* al minuto, dettagliante *m/f*; ~ **price** *n* prezzo al minuto.

retain [rɪ'teɪn] *vt* (*keep*) tenere, serbare; ~**er** *n* (*servant*) servitore *m*; (*fee*) onorario.

retaliate [rɪ'tælɪeɪt] *vi*: to ~ (**against**) vendicarsi (di); **retaliation** [-'eɪʃən] *n* rappresaglie *fpl*.

retarded [rɪ'tɑ:dɪd] *a* ritardato(a); (*also*: **mentally** ~) tardo(a) (di mente).

retch [retʃ] *vi* aver conati di vomito.

retire [rɪ'taɪə*] *vi* (*give up work*) andare in pensione; (*withdraw*) ritirarsi, andarsene; (*go to bed*) andare a letto, ritirarsi; ~**d** *a* (*person*) pensionato(a); ~**ment** *n* pensione *f*; **retiring** *a* (*person*) riservato(a).

retort [rɪ'tɔ:t] *n* (*reply*) rimbecco; (*container*) storta // *vi* rimbeccare.

retrace [ri:'treɪs] *vt* ricostruire; to ~ **one's steps** tornare sui passi.

retract [rɪ'trækt] *vt* (*statement*) ritrattare; (*claws, undercarriage, aerial*) ritrarre, ritirare // *vi* ritrarsi.

retrain [ri:'treɪn] *vt* (*worker*) riaddestrare.

retread ['ri:tred] *n* (*tyre*) gomma rigenerata.

retreat |rɪ'triːt| *n* ritirata; (*place*) rifugio // *vi* battere in ritirata; (*flood*) ritirarsi.

retribution |retrɪ'bjuːʃən| *n* castigo.

retrieval |rɪ'triːvəl| *n* (*see vb*) ricupero; riparazione *f*.

retrieve |rɪ'triːv| *vt* (*sth lost*) ricuperare, ritrovare; (*situation, honour*) salvare; (*error, loss*) riparare; (*COMPUT*) ricuperare; ~**r** *n* cane *m* da riporto.

retrospect |'retrəspekt| *n*: in ~ guardando indietro; ~**ive** |-'spektɪv| *a* retrospettivo(a); (*law*) retroattivo(a).

return |rɪ'tɜːn| *n* (*going or coming back*) ritorno; (*of sth stolen etc*) restituzione *f*; (*recompense*) ricompensa; (*FINANCE: from land, shares*) profitto, reddito; (*report*) rapporto // *cpd* (*journey, match*) di ritorno; (*Brit: ticket*) di andata e ritorno // *vi* tornare, ritornare // *vt* rendere, restituire; (*bring back*) riportare; (*send back*) mandare indietro; (*put back*) rimettere; (*POL: candidate*) eleggere; ~**s** *npl* (*COMM*) incassi *mpl*; (*FINANCE*) profitti *mpl*; in ~ (for) in cambio (di); by ~ of post a stretto giro di posta; many happy ~s (of the day)! auguri!, buon compleanno!

reunion |riː'juːnɪən| *n* riunione *f*.

reunite |riːjuː'naɪt| *vt* riunire.

rev |rev| *n abbr* (= revolution: *AUT*) giro // *vb* (*also*: ~ up) *vt* imballare // *vi* imballarsi.

revamp |'riː'væmp| *vt* (*house*) rinnovare; (*firm*) riorganizzare.

reveal |rɪ'viːl| *vt* (*make known*) rivelare, svelare; (*display*) rivelare, mostrare; ~**ing** *a* rivelatore(trice); (*dress*) scollato(a).

reveille |rɪ'vælɪ| *n* (*MIL*) sveglia.

revel |'revl| *vi*: to ~ in sth/in doing dilettarsi di qc/a fare.

revelation |revə'leɪʃən| *n* rivelazione *f*.

revelry |'revlrɪ| *n* baldoria.

revenge |rɪ'vendʒ| *n* vendetta; (*in game etc*) rivincita // *vt* vendicare; to take ~ vendicarsi.

revenue |'revənjuː| *n* reddito.

reverberate |rɪ'vɜːbəreɪt| *vi* (*sound*) rimbombare; (*light*) riverberarsi.

reverence |'revərəns| *n* venerazione *f*, riverenza.

Reverend |'revərənd| *a* (*in titles*) reverendo(a).

reverie |'revərɪ| *n* fantasticheria.

reversal |rɪ'vɜːsl| *n* capovolgimento.

reverse |rɪ'vɜːs| *n* contrario, opposto; (*back*) rovescio; (*AUT: also*: ~ gear) marcia indietro // *a* (*order, direction*) contrario(a), opposto(a) // *vt* (*turn*) invertire, rivoltare; (*change*) capovolgere, rovesciare; (*LAW: judgment*) cassare // *vi* (*Brit AUT*) fare marcia indietro; ~**d charge call** *n* (*Brit TEL*) telefonata con addebito al ricevente; **reversing lights** *npl* (*Brit AUT*) luci *fpl*

per la retromarcia.

revert |rɪ'vɜːt| *vi*: to ~ to tornare a.

review |rɪ'vjuː| *n* rivista; (*of book, film*) recensione *f* // *vt* passare in rivista; fare la recensione di; ~**er** *n* recensore/a.

revile |rɪ'vaɪl| *vt* insultare.

revise |rɪ'vaɪz| *vt* (*manuscript*) rivedere, correggere; (*opinion*) emendare, modificare; (*study*: *subject, notes*) ripassare; **revision** |rɪ'vɪʒən| *n* revisione *f*; ripasso.

revitalize |riː'vaɪtəlaɪz| *vt* ravvivare.

revival |rɪ'vaɪvəl| *n* ripresa; ristabilimento; (*of faith*) risveglio.

revive |rɪ'vaɪv| *vt* (*person*) rianimare; (*custom*) far rivivere; (*hope, courage*) ravvivare; (*play, fashion*) riesumare // *vi* (*person*) rianimarsi; (*hope*) ravvivarsi; (*activity*) riprendersi.

revolt |rɪ'vəult| *n* rivolta, ribellione *f* // *vi* rivoltarsi, ribellarsi // *vt* (far) rivoltare; ~**ing** *a* ripugnante.

revolution |revə'luːʃən| *n* rivoluzione *f*; (*of wheel etc*) rivoluzione, giro; ~**ary** *a*, *n* rivoluzionario(a).

revolve |rɪ'vɒlv| *vi* girare.

revolver |rɪ'vɒlvə*| *n* rivoltella.

revolving |rɪ'vɒlvɪŋ| *a* girevole.

revue |rɪ'vjuː| *n* (*THEATRE*) rivista.

revulsion |rɪ'vʌlʃən| *n* ripugnanza.

reward |rɪ'wɔːd| *n* ricompensa, premio // *vt*: to ~ (for) ricompensare (per); ~**ing** *a* (*fig*) soddisfacente.

rewind |riː'waɪnd| *vt irg* (*watch*) ricaricare; (*ribbon etc*) riavvolgere.

rewire |riː'waɪə*| *vt* (*house*) rifare l'impianto elettrico di.

reword |riː'wɜːd| *vt* formulare or esprimere con altre parole.

rheumatism |'ruːmətɪzəm| *n* reumatismo.

Rhine |raɪn| *n*, the ~ il Reno.

rhinoceros |raɪ'nɒsərəs| *n* rinoceronte *m*.

rhododendron |rəudə'dendrən| *n* rododendro.

Rhone |rəun| *n*: the ~ il Rodano.

rhubarb |'ruːbɑːb| *n* rabarbaro.

rhyme |raɪm| *n* rima; (*verse*) poesia.

rhythm |'rɪðm| *n* ritmo.

rib |rɪb| *n* (*ANAT*) costola // *vt* (*tease*) punzecchiare.

ribald |'rɪbəld| *a* licenzioso(a), volgare.

ribbon |'rɪbən| *n* nastro; in ~**s** (*torn*) a brandelli.

rice |raɪs| *n* riso.

rich |rɪtʃ| *a* ricco(a); (*clothes*) sontuoso(a); the ~ *npl* i ricchi; ~**es** *npl* ricchezze *fpl*; ~**ly** *ad* riccamente; (*dressed*) sontuosamente; (*deserved*) pienamente; ~**ness** *n* ricchezza.

rickets |'rɪkɪts| *n* rachitismo.

rickety |'rɪkɪtɪ| *a* zoppicante.

rickshaw |'rɪkʃɔː| *n* risciò *m inv*.

ricochet |'rɪkəʃeɪ| *n* rimbalzo // *vi* rimbalzare.

rid |rɪd| *pt, pp* **rid** |rɪd| *vt:* to ~ sb of sbarazzare *or* liberare qn di; to get ~ of sbarazzarsi di.

ridden |ˈrɪdn| *pp of* ride.

riddle |ˈrɪdl| *n (puzzle)* indovinello // *vt:* to be ~d with essere crivellato(a) di.

ride |raɪd| *n (on horse)* cavalcata; *(outing)* passeggiata; *(distance covered)* cavalcata; corsa // *vb (pt* **rode**, *pp* **ridden**) *vi (as sport)* cavalcare; *(go somewhere: on horse, bicycle)* andare (a cavallo *or* in bicicletta *etc*); *(journey: on bicycle, motorcycle, bus)* andare, viaggiare // *vt (a horse)* montare, cavalcare; to ~ a horse/bicycle/camel montare a cavallo/in bicicletta/in groppa a un cammello; to ~ at anchor *(NAUT)* essere alla fonda; to take sb for a ~ *(fig)* prendere in giro qn; fregare qn; **~r** *n* cavalcatore/trice; *(in race)* fantino; *(on bicycle)* ciclista *m/f; (on motorcycle)* motociclista *m/f; (in document)* clausola addizionale, aggiunta.

ridge |rɪdʒ| *n (of hill)* cresta; *(of roof)* colmo; *(of mountain)* giogo; *(on object)* riga (in rilievo).

ridicule |ˈrɪdɪkjuːl| *n* ridicolo; scherno // *vt* mettere in ridicolo.

ridiculous |rɪˈdɪkjuləs| *a* ridicolo(a).

riding |ˈraɪdɪŋ| *n* equitazione *f;* ~ school *n* scuola di equitazione.

rife |raɪf| *a* diffuso(a); to be ~ with abbondare di.

riffraff |ˈrɪfræf| *n* canaglia.

rifle |ˈraɪfl| *n* carabina // *vt* vuotare; ~ range *n* campo di tiro; *(at fair)* tiro a segno.

rift |rɪft| *n* fessura, crepatura; *(fig: disagreement)* incrinatura, disaccordo.

rig |rɪg| *n (also:* oil ~: on land) derrick *m inv;* (: at sea) piattaforma di trivellazione // *vt (election etc)* truccare; to ~ out *vt (Brit)* attrezzare; *(pej)* abbigliare, agghindare; to ~ up *vt* allestire; **~ging** *n (NAUT)* attrezzatura.

right |raɪt| *a* giusto(a); *(suitable)* appropriato(a); *(not left)* destro(a) // *n (title, claim)* diritto; *(not left)* destra // *ad (answer)* correttamente; *(not on the left)* a destra // *vt* raddrizzare; *(fig)* riparare // *excl* bene!; to be ~ *(person)* aver ragione; *(answer)* essere giusto(a) *or* corretto(a); by ~s di diritto; on the ~ a destra; to be in the ~ aver ragione, essere nel giusto; ~ now proprio adesso; subito; ~ against the wall proprio contro il muro; ~ ahead sempre diritto; proprio davanti; ~ in the middle proprio nel mezzo; ~ away subito; ~ angle *n* angolo retto; **~eous** |ˈraɪtʃəs| *a* retto(a), virtuoso(a); *(anger)* giusto(a), giustificato(a); **~ful** *a (heir)* legittimo(a); **~-handed** *a (person)* che adopera la mano destra; **~-hand man** *n* braccio destro; **~-hand side** *n* lato destro; **~ly**

ad bene, correttamente; *(with reason)* a ragione; ~ of way *n* diritto di passaggio; *(AUT)* precedenza; **~-wing** *a (POL)* di destra.

rigid |ˈrɪdʒɪd| *a* rigido(a); *(principle)* rigoroso(a).

rigmarole |ˈrɪgmərəul| *n* tiritera; commedia.

rigorous |ˈrɪgərəs| *a* rigoroso(a).

rile |raɪl| *vt* irritare, seccare.

rim |rɪm| *n* orlo; *(of spectacles)* montatura; *(of wheel)* cerchione *m.*

rind |raɪnd| *n (of bacon)* cotenna; *(of lemon etc)* scorza.

ring |rɪŋ| *n* anello; *(also:* wedding ~) fede *f; (of people, objects)* cerchio; *(of spies)* giro; *(of smoke etc)* spirale *m; (arena)* pista, arena; *(for boxing)* ring *m inv; (sound of bell)* scampanio; *(telephone call)* colpo di telefono // *vb (pt* **rang**, *pp* **rung**) *vi (person, bell, telephone)* suonare; *(also:* ~ out: voice, words) risuonare; *(TEL)* telefonare // *vt (Brit TEL: also:* ~ up) telefonare a; to ~ the bell suonare; to ~ back *vt, vi (TEL)* richiamare; to ~ off *vi (Brit TEL)* mettere giù, riattaccare; **~ing** *n (of bell)* scampanio; *(of telephone)* squillo; *(in ears)* ronzio; **~ing tone** *n (Brit TEL)* segnale *m* di libero; **~leader** *n (of gang)* capobanda *m.*

ringlets |ˈrɪŋlɪts| *npl* boccoli *mpl.*

ring road *n (Brit)* raccordo anulare.

rink |rɪŋk| *n (also:* ice ~) pista di pattinaggio.

rinse |rɪns| *n* risciacquatura; *(hair tint)* cachet *m inv* // *vt* sciacquare.

riot |ˈraɪət| *n* sommossa, tumulto // *vi* tumultuare; to run ~ creare disordine; **~ous** *a* tumultuoso(a); che fa crepare dal ridere.

rip |rɪp| *n* strappo // *vt* strappare // *vi* strapparsi; **~cord** *n* cavo di sfilamento.

ripe |raɪp| *a (fruit)* maturo(a); *(cheese)* stagionato(a); **~n** *vt* maturare // *vi* maturarsi; stagionarsi.

rip-off |ˈrɪpɔf| *n (col):* it's a ~! è un furto!

ripple |ˈrɪpl| *n* increspamento, ondulazione *f;* mormorio // *vi* incresparsi.

rise |raɪz| *n (slope)* salita, pendio; *(hill)* altura; *(increase: in wages: Brit)* aumento; (: in prices, temperature) rialzo, aumento; *(fig: to power etc)* ascesa // *vi (pt* **rose**, *pp* **risen** |ˈrɪzn|) alzarsi; levarsi; *(prices)* aumentare; *(waters, river)* crescere; *(sun, wind, person: from chair, bed)* levarsi; *(also:* ~ up: rebel) insorgere; ribellarsi; to give ~ to provocare, dare origine a; to ~ to the occasion essere all'altezza; **rising** *a (increasing: number)* sempre crescente; (: prices) in aumento; *(tide)* montante; *(sun, moon)* nascente, che sorge // n (*uprising*) sommossa.

risk [rısk] n rischio; pericolo // vt rischiare; **to take** *or* **run the ~ of doing** correre il rischio di fare; **at ~ in** pericolo; **at one's own ~** a proprio rischio e pericolo; **~y** *a* rischioso(a).

risqué [ˈriːskeɪ] *a* (*joke*) spinto(a).

rissole [ˈrɪsəul] n crocchetta.

rite [raɪt] n rito; **last ~s** l'estrema unzione.

ritual [ˈrɪtjuəl] *a, n* rituale (m).

rival [ˈraɪvl] n rivale m/f; (*in business*) concorrente m/f // *a* rivale; che fa concorrenza // vt essere in concorrenza con; **to ~ sb/sth in** competere con qn/qc in; **~ry** n rivalità; concorrenza.

river [ˈrɪvə*] n fiume m // cpd (*port, traffic*) fluviale; **up/down ~** a monte/valle; **~bank** n argine m.

rivet [ˈrɪvɪt] n ribattino, rivetto // vt ribadire; (*fig*) concentrare, fissare.

Riviera [rɪvɪˈɛərə] n: **the (French) ~** la Costa Azzurra; **the Italian ~** la Riviera.

road [rəud] n strada; (*small*) cammino; (*in town*) via; **major/minor ~** strada con/senza diritto di precedenza; **~block** n blocco stradale; **~hog** n guidatore m egoista e spericolato; **~ map** n carta stradale; **~ safety** n sicurezza sulle strade; **~side** n margine m della strada; **~sign** n cartello stradale; **~way** n carreggiata; **~works** npl lavori mpl stradali; **~worthy** *a* in buono stato di marcia.

roam [rəum] vi errare, vagabondare // vt vagare per.

roar [rɔ:*] n ruggito; (*of crowd*) tumulto; (*of thunder, storm*) muggito // vi ruggire; tumultuare; muggire; **to ~ with laughter** scoppiare dalle risa; **to do a ~ing trade** fare affari d'oro.

roast [rəust] n arrosto // vt (*meat*) arrostire; **~ beef** n arrosto di manzo.

rob [rɔb] vt (*person*) rubare; (*bank*) svaligiare; **to ~ sb of sth** derubare qn di qc; (*fig: deprive*) privare qn di qc; **~ber** n ladro; (*armed*) rapinatore m; **~bery** n furto; rapina.

robe [rəub] n (*for ceremony etc*) abito; (*also*: **bath ~**) accappatoio; (*US: cover*) coperta // vt vestire.

robin [ˈrɔbɪn] n pettirosso.

robot [ˈrəubɔt] n robot m inv.

robust [rəuˈbʌst] *a* robusto(a); (*material*) solido(a).

rock [rɔk] n (*substance*) roccia; (*boulder*) masso; roccia; (*in sea*) scoglio; (*Brit: sweet*) zucchero candito // vt (*swing gently: cradle*) dondolare; (: *child*) cullare; (*shake*) scrollare, far tremare // vi dondolarsi; scrollarsi, tremare; **on the ~s** (*drink*) col ghiaccio; (*ship*) sugli scogli; (*marriage etc*) in crisi; **~ and roll** n rock and roll m; **~-**

bottom n (*fig*) stremo // *a* bassissimo(a); **~ery** n giardino roccioso.

rocket [ˈrɔkɪt] n razzo; (*MIL*) razzo, missile m.

rock fall n caduta di massi.

rocking [ˈrɔkɪŋ]: **~ chair** n sedia a dondolo; **~ horse** n cavallo a dondolo.

rocky [ˈrɔkɪ] *a* (*hill*) roccioso(a); (*path*) sassoso(a); (*unsteady: table*) traballante.

rod [rɔd] n (*metallic, TECH*) asta; (*wooden*) bacchetta; (*also*: **fishing ~**) canna da pesca.

rode [rəud] pt of **ride**.

rodent [ˈrəudnt] n roditore m.

rodeo [ˈrəudɪəu] n rodeo.

roe [rəu] n (*species: also*: **~ deer**) capriolo; (*of fish, also*: **hard ~**) uova fpl di pesce; **soft ~** latte m di pesce.

rogue [rəug] n mascalzone m.

role [rəul] n ruolo.

roll [rəul] n rotolo; (*of banknotes*) mazzo; (*also*: **bread ~**) panino; (*register*) lista; (*sound: of drums etc*) rullo; (*movement: of ship*) rullio // vt rotolare; (*also*: **~ up**: *string*) aggomitolare; (*also*: **~ out**: *pastry*) stendere // vi rotolare; (*wheel*) girare; **to ~ about** *or* **around** vi rotolare qua e là; (*person*) rotolarsi; **to ~ by** vi (*time*) passare; **to ~ in** vi (*mail, cash*) arrivare a bizzeffe; **to ~ over** vi rivoltarsi; **to ~ up** vi (*col: arrive*) arrivare // vt (*carpet*) arrotolare; **~ call** n appello; **~er** n rullo; (*wheel*) rotella; **~er coaster** n montagne fpl russe; **~er skates** npl pattini mpl a rotelle.

rolling [ˈrəulɪŋ] *a* (*landscape*) ondulato(a); **~ pin** n matterello; **~ stock** n (*RAIL*) materiale m rotabile.

ROM [rɔm] n abbr (= *read only memory*) memoria di sola lettura.

Roman [ˈrəumən] *a, n* romano(a); **~ Catholic** *a, n* cattolico(a).

romance [rəˈmæns] n storia (*or* avventura *or* film m inv) romantico(a); (*charm*) poesia; (*love affair*) idillio.

Romania [rəuˈmeɪnɪə] n = **Rumania**.

Roman numeral n numero romano.

romantic [rəˈmæntɪk] *a* romantico(a); sentimentale.

romanticism [rəˈmæntɪsɪzəm] n romanticismo.

Rome [rəum] n Roma.

romp [rɔmp] n gioco rumoroso // vi (*also*: **~ about**) far chiasso, giocare in un modo rumoroso.

rompers [ˈrɔmpəz] npl pagliaccetto.

roof, pl **~s** [ru:f] n tetto; (*of tunnel, cave*) volta // vt coprire (con un tetto); **~ of the mouth** palato; **~ing** n materiale m per copertura; **~ rack** n (*AUT*) portabagagli m inv.

rook [ruk] n (*bird*) corvo nero; (*CHESS*)

torre *f*.

room |ru:m| *n* (*in house*) stanza; (*also*: **bed~**) camera; (*in school etc*) sala; (*space*) posto, spazio; **~s** *npl* (*lodging*) alloggio; "**~s to let**", (*US*) "**~s for rent**" "si affittano camere"; **~ing house** *n* (*US*) casa in cui si affittano camere o appartamentini ammobiliati; **~mate** *n* compagno/a di stanza; **~ service** *n* servizio da camera; **~y** *a* spazioso(a); (*garment*) ampio(a).

roost |ru:st| *n* appollaiato // *vi* appollaiarsi.

rooster |'ru:stə*| *n* gallo.

root |ru:t| *n* radice *f* // *vt* (*plant, belief*) far radicare; **to ~ about** *vi* (*fig*) frugare; **to ~ for** *vt fus* fare il tifo per; **to ~ out** *vt* estirpare.

rope |rəup| *n* corda, fune *f*; (*NAUT*) cavo // *vt* (*box*) legare; (*climbers*) legare in cordata; **to ~ sb in** (*fig*) coinvolgere qn; **to know the ~s** (*fig*) conoscere i trucchi del mestiere.

rosary |'rəuzərı| *n* rosario; roseto.

rose |rəuz| *pt of* **rise** // *n* rosa; (*also*: **~ bush**) rosaio; (*on watering can*) rosetta // *a* rosa *inv*.

rosé |'rəuzeı| *n* vino rosato.

rose: **~bud** *n* bocciolo di rosa; **~bush** *n* rosaio.

rosemary |'rəuzmərı| *n* rosmarino.

rosette |rəu'zɛt| *n* coccarda.

roster |'rɔstə*| *n*: **duty ~** ruolino di servizio.

rostrum |'rɔstrəm| *n* tribuna.

rosy |'rəuzı| *a* roseo(a).

rot |rɔt| *n* (*decay*) putrefazione *f*; (*col: nonsense*) stupidaggini *fpl* // *vt, vi* imputridire, marcire.

rota |'rəutə| *n* tabella dei turni; **on a ~ basis** a turno.

rotary |'rəutərı| *a* rotante.

rotate |rəu'teıt| *vt* (*revolve*) far girare; (*change round: crops*) avvicendare; (: *jobs*) fare a turno // *vi* (*revolve*) girare; **rotating** *a* (*movement*) rotante.

rote |rəut| *n*: **by ~** (*by heart*) a memoria; (*mechanically*) meccanicamente.

rotten |'rɔtn| *a* (*decayed*) putrido(a), marcio(a); (*dishonest*) corrotto(a); (*col: bad*) brutto(a); (: *action*) vigliacco(a); **to feel ~** (*ill*) sentirsi proprio male.

rouge |ru:ʒ| *n* belletto.

rough |rʌf| *a* aspro(a); (*person, manner*: *coarse*) rozzo(a), aspro(a); (: *violent*) brutale; (*district*) malfamato(a); (*weather*) cattivo(a); (*plan*) abbozzato(a); (*guess*) approssimativo(a) // *n* (*GOLF*) macchia; **to ~ it** far vita dura; **to sleep ~** (*Brit*) dormire all'addiaccio; **to feel ~** sentirsi male; **~age** *n* alimenti *mpl* ricchi in cellulosa; **~-and-ready** *a* rudimentale; **~cast** *n* intonaco grezzo; **~ copy**, **~ draft** *n*

brutta copia; **~ly** *ad* (*handle*) rudemente, brutalmente; (*make*) grossolanamente; (*approximately*) approssimativamente.

roulette |ru:'lɛt| *n* roulette *f*.

Roumania |ru:'meınıə| *n* = **Rumania**.

round |raund| *a* rotondo(a) // *n* tondo, cerchio; (*Brit: of toast*) fetta; (*duty: of policeman, milkman etc*) giro; (: *of doctor*) visite *fpl*; (*game: of cards, in competition*) partita; (*BOXING*) round *m inv*; (*of talks*) serie *f inv* // *vt* (*corner*) girare; (*bend*) prendere; (*cape*) doppiare // *prep* intorno a // *ad*: **all ~** tutt'attorno; **to go the long way ~** fare il giro più lungo; **all the year ~** tutto l'anno; **it's just ~ the corner** (*also fig*) è dietro; **l'angolo**; **~ the clock** *ad* ininterrottamente; **to go ~** fare il giro; **to go ~ to sb's house** andare da qn; **go ~ the back** passi dietro; **to go ~ a house** visitare una casa; **enough to go ~** abbastanza per tutti; **to go the ~s** (*story*) circolare; **~ of ammunition** *n* cartuccia; **~ of applause** *n* applausi *mpl*; **~ of drinks** *n* giro di bibite; **~ of sandwiches** *n* sandwich *m inv*; **to ~ off** *vt* (*speech etc*) finire; **to ~ up** *vt* radunare; (*criminals*) fare una retata di; (*prices*) arrotondare; **~about** *n* (*Brit AUT*) rotatoria; (: *at fair*) giostra // *a* (*route, means*) indiretto(a); **~ers** *npl* (*game*) gioco simile al baseball; **~ly** *ad* (*fig*) chiaro e tondo; **~-shouldered** *a* dalle spalle tonde; **~ trip** *n* (*viaggio di*) andata e ritorno; **~up** *n* raduno; (*of criminals*) retata.

rouse |rauz| *vt* (*wake up*) svegliare; (*stir up*) destare; (*provoke*) risvegliare; **rousing** *a* (*speech, applause*) entusiastico(a).

rout |raut| *n* (*MIL*) rotta.

route |ru:t| *n* itinerario; (*of bus*) percorso; (*of trade, shipping*) rotta; **~ map** *n* (*Brit: for journey*) cartina di itinerario.

routine |ru:'ti:n| *a* (*work*) corrente, abituale; (*procedure*) solito(a) // *n* (*pej*) routine *f*, tran tran *m*; (*THEATRE*) numero; **daily ~** orario quotidiano.

roving |'rəuvıŋ| *a* (*life*) itinerante.

row |rəu| *n* (*line*) riga, fila; (*KNITTING*) ferro; (*behind one another: of cars, people*) fila; |rau| (*noise*) baccano, chiasso; (*dispute*) lite *f* // *vi* (*in boat*) remare; (*as sport*) vogare; |rau| litigare // *vt* (*boat*) manovrare a remi; **in a ~** (*fig*) di fila; **~boat** *n* (*US*) barca a remi.

rowdy |'raudı| *a* chiassoso(a); turbolento(a) // *n* teppista *m/f*.

rowing |'rəuıŋ| *n* canottaggio; **~ boat** *n* (*Brit*) barca a remi.

royal |'rɔıəl| *a* reale; **R~ Air Force** (**RAF**) *n* aeronautica militare britannica.

royalty |'rɔıəltı| *n* (*royal persons*) (membri *mpl* della) famiglia reale; (*payment: to author*) diritti *mpl* d'autore; (: *to inventor*) diritti di brevetto.

r.p.m. *abbr* (= *revolutions per minute*) giri/min.

R.S.V.P. *abbr* (= *répondez s'il vous plait*) R.S.V.P.

Rt Hon. *abbr* (*Brit: = Right Honourable*) ≈ Onorevole.

rub |rʌb| *n* (*with cloth*) fregata, strofinata; (*on person*) frizione *f*, massaggio // *vt* fregare, strofinare; frizionare; to ~ sb up *or* (*US*) ~ sb the wrong way lisciare qn contro pelo; to ~ off *vi* andare via; to ~ off on *vt fus* lasciare una traccia su; to ~ out *vt* cancellare.

rubber |'rʌbə*| *n* gomma; ~ band *n* elastico; ~ plant *n* ficus *m inv*.

rubbish |'rʌbɪʃ| *n* (*from household*) immondizie *fpl*, rifiuti *mpl*; (*fig: pej*) cose *fpl* senza valore; robaccia; sciocchezze *fpl*; ~ bin *n* (*Brit*) pattumiera; ~ dump *n* (*in town*) immondezzaio.

rubble |'rʌbl| *n* macerie *fpl*; (*smaller*) pietrisco.

ruby |'ru:bɪ| *n* rubino.

rucksack |'rʌksæk| *n* zaino.

ructions |'rʌkʃənz| *npl* putiferio, finimondo.

rudder |'rʌdə*| *n* timone *m*.

ruddy |'rʌdɪ| *a* (*face*) fresco(a); (*col: damned*) maledetto(a).

rude |ru:d| *a* (*impolite: person*) scortese, rozzo(a); (: *word, manners*) grossolano(a), rozzo(a); (*shocking*) indecente; ~ness *n* scortesia; grossolanità.

rueful |'ru:ful| *a* mesto(a), triste.

ruffian |'rʌfɪən| *n* briccone *m*, furfante *m*.

ruffle |'rʌfl| *vt* (*hair*) scompigliare; (*clothes, water*) increspare; (*fig: person*) turbare.

rug |rʌg| *n* tappeto; (*Brit: for knees*) coperta.

rugby |'rʌgbɪ| *n* (*also:* ~ football) rugby *m*.

rugged |'rʌgɪd| *a* (*landscape*) aspro(a); (*features, determination*) duro(a); (*character*) brusco(a).

rugger |'rʌgə*| *n* (*Brit col*) rugby *m*.

ruin |'ru:ɪn| *n* rovina // *vt* rovinare; (*spoil: clothes*) sciupare; ~s *npl* rovine *fpl*, ruderi *mpl*; ~ous *a* rovinoso(a); (*expenditure*) inverosimile.

rule |ru:l| *n* regola; (*regulation*) regolamento, regola; (*government*) governo // *vt* (*country*) governare; (*person*) dominare; (*decide*) decidere // *vi* regnare; decidere; (*LAW*) dichiarare; as a ~ normalmente; to ~ out *vt* escludere; ~d *a* (*paper*) vergato(a); ~r *n* (*sovereign*) sovrano/a; (*leader*) capo (dello Stato); (*for measuring*)

regolo, riga; **ruling** *a* (*party*) al potere; (*class*) dirigente // *n* (*LAW*) decisione *f*.

rum |rʌm| *n* rum *m* // *a* (*col*) strano(a).

Rumania |ru:'meɪnɪə| *n* Romania.

rumble |'rʌmbl| *n* rimbombo; brontolio // *vi* rimbombare; (*stomach, pipe*) brontolare.

rummage |'rʌmɪdʒ| *vi* frugare.

rumour, (*US*) **rumor** |'ru:mə*| *n* voce *f* // *vt*: it is ~ed that corre voce che.

rump |rʌmp| *n* (*of animal*) groppa; ~ steak *n* bistecca di girello.

rumpus |'rʌmpəs| *n* (*col*) baccano; (: *quarrel*) rissa.

run |rʌn| *n* corsa; (*outing*) gita (in macchina); (*distance travelled*) percorso, tragitto; (*series*) serie *f*; (*THEATRE*) periodo di rappresentazione; (*SKI*) pista; (*in tights, stockings*) smagliatura // *vb* (*pt* **ran**, *pp* **run**) *vt* (*operate: business*) gestire, dirigere; (: *competition, course*) organizzare; (: *hotel*) gestire; (: *house*) governare; (*COMPUT*) eseguire; (*water, bath*) far scorrere; (*force through: rope, pipe*): to ~ sth through far passare qc attraverso; (*to pass: hand, finger*): to ~ sth over passare qc su // *vi* correre; (*pass: road etc*) passare; (*work: machine, factory*) funzionare, andare; (*bus, train: operate*) far servizio; (: *travel*) circolare; (*continue: play, contract*) durare; (*slide: drawer; flow: river, bath*) scorrere; (*colours, washing*) stemperarsi; (*in election*) presentarsi candidato; there was a ~ on ... c'era una corsa a ...; in the long ~ a lungo andare; on the ~ in fuga; I'll ~ you to the station la porto alla stazione; to ~ a risk correre un rischio; to ~ about *or* around *vi* (*children*) correre qua e là; to ~ across *vt fus* (*find*) trovare per caso; to ~ away *vi* fuggire; to ~ down *vi* (*clock*) scaricarsi // *vt* (*production*) ridurre gradualmente; (*factory*) rallentare l'attività di; (*AUT*) investire; (*criticize*) criticare; to be ~ down (*person: tired*) essere esausto(a); to ~ in *vt* (*Brit: car*) rodare, fare il rodaggio di; to ~ into *vt fus* (*meet: person*) incontrare per caso; (: *trouble*) incontrare, trovare; (*collide with*) andare a sbattere contro; to ~ off *vi* fuggire // *vt* (*copies*) fare; to ~ out *vi* (*person*) uscire di corsa; (*liquid*) colare; (*lease*) scadere; (*money*) esaurirsi; to ~ out of *vt fus* rimanere a corto di; to ~ over *vt* (*AUT*) investire, mettere sotto // *vt fus* (*revise*) rivedere; to ~ through *vt fus* (*instructions*) dare una scorsa a; to ~ up *vt* (*debt*) lasciar accumulare; to ~ up against (*difficulties*) incontrare; ~away *a* (*person*) fuggiasco(a); (*horse*) in libertà; (*truck*) fuori controllo; (*inflation*) galoppante.

rung |rʌŋ| pp of **ring** // n (of ladder) piolo.

runner |'rʌnə*| n (in race) corridore m; (on sledge) pattino; (for drawer etc, carpet: in hall etc) guida; ~ **bean** n (Brit) fagiolo rampicante; ~-**up** n secondo(a) arrivato(a).

running |'rʌnɪŋ| n corsa; direzione f; organizzazione f; funzionamento // a (water) corrente; (commentary) simultaneo(a); to be in/out of the ~ for sth essere/non essere più in lizza per qc; 6 **days** ~ 6 giorni di seguito.

runny |'rʌnɪ| a che cola.

run-of-the-mill |'rʌnəvðə'mɪl| a solito(a), banale.

runt |rʌnt| n (also pej) omuncolo; (ZOOL) animale m più piccolo del normale.

run-through |'rʌnθru:| n prova.

run-up |'rʌnʌp| n: ~ **to** (election etc) periodo che precede.

runway |'rʌnweɪ| n (AVIAT) pista (di decollo).

rupee |ru:'pi:| n rupia.

rupture |'rʌptʃə*| n (MED) ernia.

rural |'ruərl| a rurale.

ruse |ru:z| n trucco.

rush |rʌʃ| n corsa precipitosa; (of crowd) afflusso; (hurry) furia, fretta; (current) flusso // vt mandare or spedire velocemente; (attack: town etc) prendere d'assalto // vi precipitarsi; ~**es** npl (BOT) giunchi mpl; ~ **hour** n ora di punta.

rusk |rʌsk| n biscotto.

Russia |'rʌʃə| n Russia; ~**n** a russo(a) // n russo/a; (LING) russo.

rust |rʌst| n ruggine f // vi arrugginirsi.

rustic |'rʌstɪk| a rustico(a).

rustle |'rʌsl| vi frusciare // vt (paper) far frusciare; (US: cattle) rubare.

rustproof |'rʌstpru:f| a inossidabile.

rusty |'rʌstɪ| a arrugginito(a).

rut |rʌt| n solco; (ZOOL) fregola; to get into a ~ (fig) adagiarsi troppo.

ruthless |'ru:θlɪs| a spietato(a).

rye |raɪ| n segale f; ~ **bread** n pane m di segale.

S

Sabbath |'sæbəθ| n (Jewish) sabato; (Christian) domenica.

sabotage |'sæbətɑ:ʒ| n sabotaggio // vt sabotare.

saccharin(e) |'sækərɪn| n saccarina.

sachet |'sæʃeɪ| n bustina.

sack |sæk| n (bag) sacco // vt (dismiss) licenziare, mandare a spasso; (plunder) saccheggiare; to get the ~ essere mandato a spasso; ~**ing** n tela di sacco; (dismissal) licenziamento.

sacrament |'sækrəmənt| n sacramento.

sacred |'seɪkrɪd| a sacro(a).

sacrifice |'sækrɪfaɪs| n sacrificio // vt sacrificare.

sad |sæd| a triste.

saddle |'sædl| n sella // vt (horse) sellare; to be ~**d with sth** (col) avere qc sulle spalle; ~**bag** n bisaccia; (on bicycle) borsa.

sadistic |sə'dɪstɪk| a sadico(a).

sadness |'sædnɪs| n tristezza.

s.a.e. n abbr = stamped addressed envelope.

safe |seɪf| a sicuro(a); (out of danger) salvo(a), al sicuro; (cautious) prudente // n cassaforte f; ~ **from** al sicuro da; ~ **and sound** sano(a) e salvo(a); (just) to be on the ~ side per non correre rischi; ~-**conduct** n salvacondotto; ~-**deposit** n (vault) caveau m inv; (box) cassetta di sicurezza; ~**guard** n salvaguardia // vt salvaguardare; ~**keeping** n custodia; ~**ly** ad sicuramente; sano(a) e salvo(a); prudentemente.

safety |'seɪftɪ| n sicurezza; ~ **belt** n cintura di sicurezza; ~ **pin** n spilla di sicurezza; ~ **valve** n valvola di sicurezza.

saffron |'sæfrən| n zafferano.

sag |sæg| vi incurvarsi; afflosciarsi.

sage |seɪdʒ| n (herb) salvia; (man) saggio.

Sagittarius |sædʒɪ'tɛərɪəs| n Sagittario.

Sahara |sə'hɑ:rə| n: the ~ (Desert) il (deserto del) Sahara.

said |sed| pt, pp of **say**.

sail |seɪl| n (on boat) vela; (trip): to go for a ~ fare un giro in barca a vela // vt (boat) condurre, governare // vi (travel: ship) navigare; (: passenger) viaggiare per mare; (set off) salpare; (sport) fare della vela; **they** ~**ed into Genoa** entrarono nel porto di Genova; **to** ~ **through** (fig) vt fus superare senza difficoltà // vi farcela senza difficoltà; ~**boat** n (US) barca a vela; ~**ing** n (sport) vela; to go ~**ing** fare della vela; ~**ing boat** n barca a vela; ~**ing ship** n veliero; ~**or** n marinaio.

saint |seɪnt| n santo/a.

sake |seɪk| n: for the ~ of per, per amore di.

salad |'sæləd| n insalata; ~ **bowl** n insalatiera; ~ **cream** n (Brit) (tipo di) maionese f; ~ **dressing** n condimento per insalata.

salary |'sælərɪ| n stipendio.

sale |seɪl| n vendita; (at reduced prices) svendita, liquidazione f; "for ~" "in vendita"; on ~ in vendita; on ~ or return da vendere o rimandare; ~**room** n sala delle aste; ~**s assistant**, (US) ~**s clerk** n commesso/a; ~**sman** n commesso; (representative) rappresentante m; ~**swoman** n commessa.

salient |'seɪlɪənt| a saliente.

sallow ['sæləu] a giallastro(a).

salmon ['sæmən] n (pl inv) salmone m.

saloon [sə'lu:n] n (US) saloon m inv, bar m inv; (Brit AUT) berlina; (ship's lounge) salone m.

salt [sɔlt] n sale m // vt salare // cpd di sale; (CULIN) salato(a); to ~ away vt (col: money) mettere via; ~ cellar n saliera; ~-water a di mare; ~y a salato(a).

salute [sə'lu:t] n saluto // vt salutare.

salvage ['sælvidʒ] n (saving) salvataggio; (things saved) beni mpl salvati or recuperati // vt salvare, mettere in salvo.

salvation [sæl'veiʃən] n salvezza; S~ Army n Esercito della Salvezza.

same [seim] a stesso(a), medesimo(a) // pronoun: the ~ lo(la) stesso(a), gli(le) stessi(e); the ~ book as lo stesso libro di (o che); at the ~ time allo stesso tempo; all or just the ~ tuttavia; to do the ~ fare la stessa cosa; to do the ~ as sb fare come qn; the ~ to you! altrettanto a te!

sample ['sɑ:mpl] n campione m // vt (food) assaggiare; (wine) degustare.

sanctimonious [sæŋkti'məuniəs] a bigotto(a), bacchettone(a).

sanction ['sæŋkʃən] n sanzione f // vt sancire, sanzionare.

sanctity ['sæŋktiti] n santità.

sanctuary ['sæŋktjuəri] n (holy place) santuario; (refuge) rifugio; (for wildlife) riserva.

sand [sænd] n sabbia // vt cospargere di sabbia.

sandal ['sændl] n sandalo.

sandbox ['sændbɔks] n (US) = sandpit.

sandcastle ['sændkɑ:sl] n castello di sabbia.

sandpaper ['sændpeipə*] n carta vc trata.

sandpit ['sændpit] n (for children) buca di sabbia.

sandstone ['sændstəun] n arenaria.

sandwich ['sændwitʃ] n tramezzino, panino, sandwich m inv // vt (also: ~ in) infilare; ~ed between incastrato(a) fra; cheese/ham ~ sandwich al formaggio/ prosciutto; ~ course n (Brit) corso di formazione professionale; ~ man n uomo m sandwich inv.

sandy ['sændi] a sabbioso(a); (colour) color sabbia inv, biondo(a) rossiccio(a).

sane [sein] a (person) sano(a) di mente; (outlook) sensato(a).

sang [sæŋ] pt of sing.

sanitary ['sænitəri] a (system, arrangements) sanitario(a); (clean) igienico(a); ~ towel, (US) ~ napkin n assorbente m (igienico).

sanitation [sæni'teiʃən] n (in house) impianti mpl sanitari; (in town) fognature fpl; ~ department n (US)

nettezza urbana.

sanity ['sæniti] n sanità mentale; (common sense) buon senso.

sank [sæŋk] pt of sink.

Santa Claus [sæntə'klɔ:z] n Babbo Natale.

sap [sæp] n (of plants) linfa // vt (strength) fiaccare.

sapling ['sæpliŋ] n alberello.

sapphire ['sæfaiə*] n zaffiro.

sarcasm ['sɑ:kæzm] n sarcasmo.

sardine [sɑ:'di:n] n sardina.

Sardinia [sɑ:'diniə] n Sardegna.

sash [sæʃ] n fascia; ~ window n fine stra a ghigliottina.

sat [sæt] pt, pp of sit.

Satan ['seitən] n Satana m.

satchel ['sætʃl] n cartella.

sated ['seitid] a (appetite) soddisfatto(a); (person): ~ (with) sazio(a) (di).

satellite ['sætəlait] a, n satellite (m).

satin ['sætin] n raso // a di raso.

satire ['sætaiə*] n satira.

satisfaction [sætis'fækʃən] n soddisfazione f.

satisfactory [sætis'fæktəri] a soddisfacente.

satisfy ['sætisfai] vt soddisfare; (convince) convincere; ~ing a soddisfacente.

Saturday ['sætədi] n sabato.

sauce [sɔ:s] n salsa; (containing meat, fish) sugo; ~pan n casseruola.

saucer ['sɔ:sə*] n sottocoppa m, piattino.

saucy ['sɔ:si] a impertinente.

Saudi ['saudi]: ~ Arabia n Arabia Saudita; ~ (Arabian) a, n arabo(a) saudita.

sauna ['sɔ:nə] n sauna.

saunter ['sɔ:ntə*] vi andare a zonzo, bighellonare.

sausage ['sɔsidʒ] n salsiccia; ~ roll n rotolo di pasta sfoglia · ripieno di salsiccia.

savage ['sævidʒ] a (cruel, fierce) selvaggio(a), feroce; (primitive) primitivo(a) // n selvaggio/a // vt attaccare selvaggiamente.

save [seiv] vt (person, belongings, COMPUT) salvare; (money) risparmiare, mettere da parte; (time) risparmiare; (food) conservare; (avoid: trouble) evitare // vi (also: ~ up) economizzare // n (SPORT) parata // prep salvo, a eccezione di.

saving ['seiviŋ] n risparmio // a: the ~ grace of l'unica cosa buona di; ~s npl risparmi mpl; ~s bank n cassa di risparmio.

saviour, (US) savior ['seivjə*] n salvatore m.

savour, (US) savor ['seivə*] n sapore m, gusto // vt gustare; ~y a saporito(a); (dish: not sweet) salato(a).

saw [sɔ:] *pt of* **see** // *n* (*tool*) sega // *vt* (*pt* **sawed**, *pp* **sawed** *or* **sawn** [sɔ:n]) segare; **~dust** *n* segatura; **~mill** *n* segheria; **~n-off shotgun** *n* fucile *m* a canne mozze.

saxophone ['sæksəfəun] *n* sassofono.

say [seɪ] *n*: to have one's ~ fare sentire il proprio parere; **to have a** *or* **some ~** avere voce in capitolo // *vt* (*pt, pp* **said**) dire; **could you ~ that again?** potrebbe ripeterlo?; **that goes without ~ing** va da sé; **~ing** *n* proverbio, detto.

scab [skæb] *n* crosta; (*pej*) crumiro/a.

scaffold ['skæfəuld] *n* impalcatura; (*gallows*) patibolo; **~ing** *n* impalcatura.

scald [skɔ:ld] *n* scottatura // *vt* scottare.

scale [skeɪl] *n* scala; (*of fish*) squama // *vt* (*mountain*) scalare; **~s** *npl* bilancia; **on a large ~** su vasta scala; **~ of charges** tariffa; **to ~ down** *vt* ridurre (proporzionalmente); **~ model** *n* modello in scala.

scallop ['skɔləp] *n* pettine *m*.

scalp [skælp] *n* cuoio capelluto // *vt* scotennare.

scalpel ['skælpl] *n* bisturi *m inv*.

scamper ['skæmpə*] *vi*: **to ~ away**, **~ off** darsela a gambe.

scampi ['skæmpɪ] *npl* scampi *mpl*.

scan [skæn] *vt* scrutare; (*glance at quickly*) scorrere, dare un'occhiata a; (*poetry*) scandire; (*TV*) analizzare; (*RADAR*) esplorare // *n* (*MED*) ecografia.

scandal ['skændl] *n* scandalo; (*gossip*) pettegolezzi *mpl*.

Scandinavia [skændɪ'neɪvɪə] *n* Scandinavia; **~n** *a, n* scandinavo(a).

scant [skænt] *a* scarso(a); **~y** *a* insufficiente; (*swimsuit*) ridotto(a).

scapegoat ['skeɪpgəut] *n* capro espiatorio.

scar [ska:] *n* cicatrice *f* // *vt* sfregiare.

scarce [skɛəs] *a* scarso(a); (*copy, edition*) raro(a); **~ly** *ad* appena; **scarcity** *n* scarsità, mancanza.

scare [skɛə*] *n* spavento; panico // *vt* spaventare, atterrire; **there was a bomb ~ at the bank** hanno evacuato la banca per paura di un attentato dinamitardo; **to ~ sb stiff** spaventare a morte qn; **~crow** *n* spaventapasseri *m inv*; **~d** *a*: **to be ~d** aver paura.

scarf, *pl* **scarves** [ska:f, ska:vz] *n* (*long*) sciarpa; (*square*) fazzoletto da testa, foulard *m inv*.

scarlet ['ska:lɪt] *a* scarlatto(a).

scathing ['skeɪðɪŋ] *a* aspro(a).

scatter ['skætə*] *vt* spargere; (*crowd*) disperdere // *vi* disperdersi; **~brained** *a* scervellato(a), sbadato(a).

scavenger ['skævəndʒə*] *n* spazzino.

scenario [sɪ'na:rɪəu] *n* (*THEATRE, CINEMA*) copione *m*; (*fig*) situazione *f*.

scene [si:n] *n* (*THEATRE, fig etc*) scena; (*of crime, accident*) scena, luogo; (*sight,*

view) vista, veduta; **~ry** *n* (*THEATRE*) scenario; (*landscape*) panorama *m*; **scenic** *a* scenico(a); panoramico(a).

scent [sɛnt] *n* odore *m*, profumo; (*sense of smell*) olfatto, odorato; (*fig: track*) pista.

sceptical, (*US*) **skeptical** ['skɛptɪkəl] *a* scettico(a).

sceptre, (*US*) **scepter** ['sɛptə*] *n* scettro.

schedule ['ʃɛdju:l, (*US*) 'skɛdju:l] *n* programma *m*, piano; (*of trains*) orario; (*of prices etc*) lista, tabella // *vt* fissare; **on ~** in orario; **to be ahead of/behind ~** essere in anticipo/ritardo sul previsto; **~d flight** *n* volo di linea.

scheme [ski:m] *n* piano, progetto; (*method*) sistema *m*; (*dishonest plan, plot*) intrigo, trama; (*arrangement*) disposizione *f*, sistemazione *f*; (*pension ~ etc*) programma *m* // *vi* fare progetti; (*intrigue*) complottare; **scheming** *a* intrigante // *n* intrighi *mpl*, macchinazioni *fpl*.

schism ['skɪzəm] *n* scisma *m*.

scholar ['skɔlə*] *n* erudito/a; **~ly** *a* dotto(a), erudito(a); **~ship** *n* erudizione *f*; (*grant*) borsa di studio.

school [sku:l] *n* scuola; (*in university*) scuola, facoltà *f inv* // *cpd* scolare, scolastico(a) // *vt* (*animal*) addestrare; **~book** *n* libro scolastico; **~boy** *n* scolaro; **~children** *npl* scolari *mpl*; **~days** *npl* giorni *mpl* di scuola; **~girl** *n* scolara; **~ing** *n* istruzione *f*; **~master** *n* (*primary*) maestro; (*secondary*) insegnante *m*; **~mistress** *n* maestra; insegnante *f*; **~teacher** *n* insegnante *m/f*, docente *m/f*; (*primary*) maestro/a.

sciatica [saɪ'ætɪkə] *n* sciatica.

science ['saɪəns] *n* scienza; **~ fiction** *n* fantascienza; **scientific** [-'tɪfɪk] *a* scientifico(a); **scientist** *n* scienziato/a.

scissors ['sɪzəz] *npl* forbici *fpl*.

scoff [skɔf] *vt* (*Brit col: eat*) trangugiare, ingozzare // *vi*: **to ~ (at)** (*mock*) farsi beffe (di).

scold [skəuld] *vt* rimproverare.

scone [skɔn] *n* focaccina da tè.

scoop [sku:p] *n* mestolo; (*for ice cream*) cucchiaio dosatore; (*PRESS*) colpo giornalistico, notizia (in) esclusiva; **to ~ out** *vt* scavare; **to ~ up** *vt* tirare su, sollevare.

scooter ['sku:tə*] *n* (*motor cycle*) motoretta, scooter *m inv*; (*toy*) monopattino.

scope [skəup] *n* (*capacity: of plan, undertaking*) portata; (: *of person*) capacità *fpl*; (*opportunity*) possibilità *fpl*; **within the ~** of nei limiti di.

scorch [skɔ:tʃ] *vt* (*clothes*) strinare, bruciacchiare; (*earth, grass*) seccare, bruciare.

score [skɔ:*] *n* punti *mpl*, punteggio;

(MUS) partitura, spartito; (twenty) venti // vt (goal, point) segnare, fare; (success) ottenere // vi segnare; (FOOTBALL) fare un goal; (keep score) segnare i punti;. on that ~ a questo riguardo; to ~ 6 out of 10 prendere 6 su 10; to ~ out vt cancellare con un segno; ~board n tabellone m segnapunti.

scorn [skɔːn] n disprezzo // vt disprezzare.

Scorpio ['skɔːpɪəu] n Scorpione m.

scorpion ['skɔːpɪən] n scorpione m.

Scot [skɔt] n scozzese m/f.

scotch [skɔtʃ] vt (rumour etc) soffocare; S~ n whisky m scozzese, scotch m.

scot-free ['skɔt'friː] ad: to get off ~ farla franca.

Scotland ['skɔtlənd] n Scozia.

Scots [skɔts] a scozzese; ~man/woman n scozzese m/f.

Scottish ['skɔtɪʃ] a scozzese.

scoundrel ['skaundrl] n farabutto/a; (child) furfantello/a.

scour ['skauə*] vt (clean) pulire strofinando; raschiare via; ripulire; (search) battere, perlustrare.

scourge [skəːdʒ] n flagello.

scout [skaut] n (MIL) esploratore m; (also: boy ~) giovane esploratore, scout m inv; to ~ around vi cercare in giro.

scowl [skaul] vi accigliarsi, aggrottare le sopracciglia; to ~ at guardare torvo.

scrabble ['skræbl] vi (claw): to ~ (at) graffiare, grattare; (also: ~ around: search) cercare a tentoni // n: S~ ® Scarabeo ®.

scraggy ['skrægi] a scarno(a), molto magro(a).

scram [skræm] vi (col) filare via.

scramble ['skræmbl] n arrampicata // vi inerpicarsi; to ~ out etc uscire etc in fretta; to ~ for azzuffarsi per; ~d eggs npl uova jpl strapazzate.

scrap [skræp] n pezzo, pezzetto; (fight) zuffa; (also: ~ iron) rottami mpl di ferro, ferraglia // vt demolire; (fig) scartare // vi: to ~ (with sb) fare a botte (con qn); ~s npl (waste) scarti mpl; ~book n album m inv di ritagli; ~ dealer n commerciante m di ferraglia.

scrape [skreip] vt, vi raschiare, grattare // n: to get into a ~ cacciarsi in un guaio; to ~ through vi farcela per un pelo; ~r n raschietto.

scrap: ~ heap n mucchio di rottami; ~ merchant n (Brit) commerciante m di ferraglia; ~ paper n cartaccia.

scratch [skrætʃ] n graffio // cpd: ~ team squadra raccogliticcia // vt graffiare, rigare // vi grattare, graffiare; to start from ~ cominciare or partire da zero; to be up to ~ essere all'altezza.

scrawl [skrɔːl] n scarabocchio // vi scarabocchiare.

scrawny ['skrɔːnɪ] a scarno(a), pelle e

ossa inv.

scream [skriːm] n grido, urlo // vi urlare, gridare.

scree [skriː] n ghiaione m.

screech [skriːtʃ] n strido; (of tyres, brakes) stridore m // vi stridere.

screen [skriːn] n schermo; (fig) muro, cortina, velo // vt schermare, fare schermo a; (from the wind etc) riparare; (film) proiettare; (book) adattare per lo schermo; (candidates etc) selezionare; ~ing n (MED) dépistage m inv; ~play n sceneggiatura.

screw [skruː] n vite f; (propeller) elica // vt avvitare; to ~ up vt (paper etc) spiegazzare; (col: ruin) rovinare; to ~ up one's eyes strizzare gli occhi; ~driver n cacciavite m.

scribble ['skribl] n scarabocchio // vt scribacchiare in fretta // vi scarabocchiare.

script [skript] n (CINEMA etc) copione m; (in exam) elaborato or compito d'esame.

Scripture ['skriptʃə*] n sacre Scritture fpl.

scroll [skrəul] n rotolo di carta.

scrounge [skraundʒ] vt (col): to ~ sth (off or from sb) scroccare qc (a qn) // vi: to ~ on sb vivere alle spalle di qn.

scrub [skrʌb] n (clean) strofinata; (land) boscaglia // vt pulire strofinando; (reject) annullare.

scruff [skrʌf] n: by the ~ of the neck per la collottola.

scruffy ['skrʌfɪ] a sciatto(a).

scrum(mage) ['skrʌm(ɪdʒ)] n mischia.

scruple ['skruːpl] n scrupolo.

scrutiny ['skruːtɪnɪ] n esame m accurato.

scuff [skʌf] vt (shoes) consumare strasciando.

scuffle ['skʌfl] n baruffa, tafferuglio.

scullery ['skʌlərɪ] n retrocucina m or f.

sculptor ['skʌlptə*] n scultore m.

sculpture ['skʌlptʃə*] n scultura.

scum [skʌm] n schiuma; (pej: people) feccia.

scupper ['skʌpə*] vt (NAUT) autoaffondare; (fig) far naufragare.

scurrilous ['skʌrɪləs] a scurrile, volgare.

scurry ['skʌrɪ] vi sgambare, affrettarsi; to ~ off andarsene a tutta velocità.

scuttle ['skʌtl] n (NAUT) portellino; (also: coal ~) secchio del carbone // vt (ship) autoaffondare // vi (scamper): to ~ away, ~ off darsela a gambe, scappare.

scythe [saið] n falce f.

SDP n abbr (Brit) = Social Democratic Party.

sea [siː] n mare m // cpd marino(a), del mare; (ship, sailor, port) marittimo(a), di mare; by ~ (travel) per mare; on the ~ (boat) in mare; (town) di mare; to be all at ~ (fig) non sapere che pesci pigliare; out to ~ al largo; (out) at ~ in mare; ~**board** *n* costa; ~**food** *n* frutti *mpl* di mare; ~ **front** *n* lungomare *m*; ~**gull** *n* gabbiano.

seal [si:l] *n* (*animal*) foca; (*stamp*) sigillo; (*impression*) impronta del sigillo // *vt* sigillare; **to ~ off** *vt* (*close*) sigillare; (*forbid entry to*) bloccare l'accesso a.

sea level *n* livello del mare.

seam [si:m] *n* cucitura; (*of coal*) filone *m*.

seaman ['si:mən] *n* marinaio.

seamy ['si:mɪ] *a* orribile.

seance ['seɪɔns] *n* seduta spiritica.

seaplane ['si:pleɪn] *n* idrovolante *m*.

search [sə:tʃ] *n* (*for person, thing*) ricerca; (*of drawer, pockets*) esame *m* accurato; (*LAW: at sb's home*) perquisizione *f* // *vt* perlustrare, frugare; (*examine*) esaminare minuziosamente // *vi:* **to ~ for** ricercare; **in ~ of** alla ricerca di; **to ~ through** *vt fus* frugare; ~**ing** *a* minuzioso(a); penetrante; ~**light** *n* proiettore *m*; ~ **party** *n* squadra di soccorso; ~ **warrant** *n* mandato di perquisizione.

seashore ['si:ʃɔ:*] *n* spiaggia.

seasick ['si:sɪk] *a* che soffre il mal di mare.

seaside ['si:saɪd] *n* spiaggia; ~ **resort** *n* stazione *f* balneare.

season ['si:zn] *n* stagione *f* // *vt* condire, insaporire; ~**al** *a* stagionale; ~**ed** *a* (*fig*) con esperienza; ~**ing** *n* condimento; ~ **ticket** *n* abbonamento.

seat [si:t] *n* sedile *m*; (*in bus, train: place*) posto; (*PARLIAMENT*) seggio; (*buttocks*) didietro; (*of trousers*) fondo // *vt* far sedere; (*have room for*) avere or essere fornito(a) di posti a sedere per; ~ **belt** *n* cintura di sicurezza.

sea water *n* acqua di mare.

seaweed ['si:wi:d] *n* alghe *fpl.*

seaworthy ['si:wə:ðɪ] *a* atto(a) alla navigazione.

sec. *abbr* = **second(s)**.

secluded [sɪ'klu:dɪd] *a* isolato(a), appartato(a).

seclusion [sɪ'klu:ʒən] *n* isolamento.

second ['sekənd] *num* secondo(a) // *ad* (*in race etc*) al secondo posto; (*RAIL*) in seconda // *n* (*unit of time*) secondo; (*in series, position*) secondo/a; (*AUT: also:* ~ **gear**) seconda; (*COMM: imperfect*) scarto; (*Brit SCOL: degree*) laurea con punteggio discreto // *vt* (*motion*) appoggiare; ~**ary** *a* secondario(a); ~**ary school** *n* scuola secondaria; ~**class** *a* di seconda classe; ~**er** *n* sostenitore/trice; ~**hand** *a* di seconda mano, usato(a); ~ **hand** *n* (*on clock*) lancetta dei secondi; ~**ly** *ad* in secondo luogo; ~**ment** [sɪ'kɔndmənt] *n* (*Brit*) distaccamento; ~**rate** *a* scadente; ~ **thoughts** *npl* ripensamenti *mpl*; **on ~**

thoughts *or* (*US*) **thought** ripensandoci bene.

secrecy ['si:krəsɪ] *n* segretezza.

secret ['si:krɪt] *a* segreto(a) // *n* segreto; **in ~** in segreto.

secretariat [sɛkrɪ'tɛərɪət] *n* segretariato.

secretary ['sɛkrətərɪ] *n* segretario/a; **S~ of State** (**for**) (*Brit POL*) ministro (di).

secretive ['si:krətɪv] *a* riservato(a).

sect [sɛkt] *n* setta; ~**arian** [-'tɛərɪən] *a* settario(a).

section ['sɛkʃən] *n* sezione *f*.

sector ['sɛktə*] *n* settore *m*.

secure [sɪ'kjuə*] *a* (*free from anxiety*) sicuro(a); (*firmly fixed*) assicurato(a), ben fermato(a); (*in safe place*) al sicuro // *vt* (*fix*) fissare, assicurare; (*get*) ottenere, assicurarsi.

security [sɪ'kjuərɪtɪ] *n* sicurezza; (*for loan*) garanzia.

sedan [sɪ'dæn] *n* (*US AUT*) berlina.

sedate [sɪ'deɪt] *a* posato(a); calmo(a) // *vt* calmare.

sedation [sɪ'deɪʃən] *n* (*MED*) l'effetto dei sedativi.

sedative ['sɛdɪtɪv] *n* sedativo, calmante *m*.

seduce [sɪ'dju:s] *vt* sedurre; **seduction** [-'dʌkʃən] *n* seduzione *f*; **seductive** [-'dʌktɪv] *a* seducente.

see [si:] *vb* (*pt* **saw**, *pp* **seen**) *vt* vedere; (*accompany*): **to ~ sb to the door** accompagnare qn alla porta // *vi* vedere; (*understand*) capire // *n* sede *f* vescovile; **to ~ that** (*ensure*) badare che + *sub*, fare in modo che + *sub*; ~ **you soon!** a presto!; **to ~ about** *vt fus* occuparsi di; **to ~ off** *vt* salutare alla partenza; **to ~ through** *vt* portare a termine // *vt fus* non lasciarsi ingannare da; **to ~ to** *vt fus* occuparsi di.

seed [si:d] *n* seme *m*; (*fig*) germe *m*; (*TENNIS*) testa di serie; **to go to ~** fare seme; (*fig*) scadere; ~**ling** *n* piantina di semenzaio; ~**y** *a* (*shabby: person*) sciatto(a); (*: place*) cadente.

seeing ['si:ɪŋ] *cj:* ~ (**that**) visto che.

seek [si:k], *pt*, *pp* **sought** *vt* cercare.

seem [si:m] *vi* sembrare, parere; **there ~s to be ...** sembra che ci sia ...; ~**ingly** *ad* apparentemente.

seen [si:n] *pp* of **see.**

seep [si:p] *vi* filtrare, trapelare.

seesaw ['si:sɔ:] *n* altalena a bilico.

seethe [si:ð] *vi* ribollire; **to ~ with anger** fremere di rabbia.

see-through ['si:θru:] *a* trasparente.

segregate ['sɛgrɪgeɪt] *vt* segregare, isolare.

seize [si:z] *vt* (*grasp*) afferrare; (*take possession of*) impadronirsi di; (*LAW*) sequestrare; **to ~ (up)on** *vt fus* ricorrere a; **to ~ up** *vi* (*TECH*) grippare.

seizure ['si:ʒə*] *n* (*MED*) attacco; (*LAW*)

confisca, sequestro.

seldom [ˈsɛldəm] ad raramente.

select [sɪˈlɛkt] a scelto(a) // vt scegliere, selezionare; **~ion** [-ˈlɛkʃən] n selezione f, scelta.

self [sɛlf] n (pl **selves** [sɛlvz]): the ~ l'io m // prefix auto...; **~-catering** a (Brit) in cui ci si cucina da sé; **~-centred**, (US) **~-centered** a egocentrico(a); **~coloured**, (US) **~-colored** a monocolore; **~-confidence** n sicurezza di sé; **~-conscious** a timido(a); **~contained** a (Brit: flat) indipendente; **~-control** n autocontrollo; **~-defence**, (US) **~-defense** n autodifesa; (LAW) legittima difesa; **~-discipline** n autodisciplina; **~-employed** a che lavora in proprio; **~-evident** a evidente; **~governing** a autonomo(a); **~indulgent** a indulgente verso se stesso(a); **~-interest** n interesse m personale; **~ish** a egoista; **~ishness** n egoismo; **~-less** a dimentico(a) di sé, altruista; **~-pity** n autocommiserazione f; **~-portrait** n autoritratto; **~-possessed** a controllato(a); **~-preservation** n istinto di conservazione; **~-respect** n rispetto di sé, amor proprio; **~-righteous** a soddisfatto(a) di sé; **~-sacrifice** n abnegazione f; **~-satisfied** a compiaciuto(a) di sé; **~-service** n autoservizio, self-service m; **~sufficient** a autosufficiente; **~-taught** a autodidatta.

sell [sɛl], pt, pp **sold** vt vendere // vi vendersi; **to ~ at** or **for 1000 lire** essere in vendita a 1000 lire; **to ~ off** vt svendere, liquidare; **to ~ out** vi: **to ~ out** (**to sb/sth**) (COMM) vendere (tutto) (a qn/qc) // vt esaurire; **the tickets are all sold out** i biglietti sono esauriti; **~-by date** n data di scadenza; **~er** n venditore/trice; **~ing price** n prezzo di vendita.

sellotape [ˈsɛləuteɪp] n ® (Brit) nastro adesivo, scotch m ®.

sellout [ˈsɛlaut] n tradimento; (of tickets): **it was a ~** registrò un tutto esaurito.

selves [sɛlvz] npl of **self**.

semblance [ˈsɛmbləns] n parvenza, apparenza.

semen [ˈsiːmən] n sperma m.

semester [sɪˈmɛstə*] n (US) semestre m.

semi... [ˈsɛmɪ] prefix semi...; **~circle** n semicerchio; **~colon** n punto e virgola; **~detached (house)** n (Brit) casa gemella; **~final** n semifinale f.

seminar [ˈsɛmɪnɑ:*] n seminario.

seminary [ˈsɛmɪnərɪ] n (REL) seminario.

semiquaver [ˈsɛmɪkweɪvə*] n semicroma.

semiskilled [ˈsɛmɪˈskɪld] a (worker) parzialmente qualificato(a); (work) che richiede una qualificazione parziale.

senate [ˈsɛnɪt] n senato; **senator** n senatore/trice.

send [sɛnd], pt, pp **sent** vt mandare; **to ~ away** vt (letter, goods) spedire; (person) mandare via; **to ~ away for** vt fus richiedere per posta, farsi spedire; **to ~ back** vt rimandare; **to ~ for** vt fus mandare a chiamare, far venire; **to ~ off** vt (goods) spedire; (Brit SPORT: player) espellere; **to ~ out** vt (invitation) diramare; **to ~ up** vt (person, price) far salire; (Brit: parody) mettere in ridicolo; **~er** n mittente m/f; **~-off** n: **to give sb a good ~-off** festeggiare la partenza di qn.

senior [ˈsiːnɪə*] a (older) più vecchio(a); (of higher rank) di grado più elevato // n persona più anziana; (in service) persona con maggiore anzianità; **~ citizen** n persona anziana; **~ity** [-ˈɔrɪtɪ] n anzianità.

sensation [sɛnˈseɪʃən] n sensazione f; **to create a ~** fare scalpore; **~al** a sensazionale; (marvellous) eccezionale.

sense [sɛns] n senso; (feeling) sensazione f, senso; (meaning) senso, significato; (wisdom) buonsenso // vt sentire, percepire; **~s** npl (sanity) ragione f; **it makes ~** ha senso; **~less** a sciocco(a); (unconscious) privo(a) di sensi.

sensibility [sɛnsɪˈbɪlɪtɪ] n sensibilità; **sensibilities** npl sensibilità sg.

sensible [ˈsɛnsɪbl] a sensato(a), ragionevole.

sensitive [ˈsɛnsɪtɪv] a: **~ (to)** sensibile (a).

sensual [ˈsɛnsjuəl] a sensuale.

sensuous [ˈsɛnsjuəs] a sensuale.

sent [sɛnt] pt, pp of **send**.

sentence [ˈsɛntns] n (LING) frase f; (LAW: judgment) sentenza; (: punishment) condanna // vt: **to ~ sb to death/to 5 years** condannare qn a morte/ a 5 anni.

sentiment [ˈsɛntɪmənt] n sentimento; (opinion) opinione f; **~al** [-ˈmɛntl] a sentimentale.

sentry [ˈsɛntrɪ] n sentinella.

separate a [ˈsɛprɪt] separato(a) // vb [ˈsɛpəreɪt] vt separare // vi separarsi; **~s** npl (clothes) coordinati mpl; **~ly** ad separatamente; **separation** [-ˈreɪʃən] n separazione f.

September [sɛpˈtɛmbə*] n settembre m.

septic [ˈsɛptɪk] a settico(a); (wound) infettato(a); **~ tank** n fossa settica.

sequel [ˈsiːkwl] n conseguenza; (of story) seguito.

sequence [ˈsiːkwəns] n (series) serie f; (order) ordine m.

sequin [ˈsiːkwɪn] n lustrino, paillette f inv.

serene [səˈriːn] a sereno(a), calmo(a).

sergeant [ˈsɑːdʒənt] n sergente m; (POLICE) brigadiere m.

serial ['sɪərɪəl] n (PRESS) romanzo a puntate; (RADIO, TV) trasmissione f a puntate // a (number) di serie; ~ **number** n numero di serie.

series ['sɪərɪːz] n (pl inv) serie f inv; (PUBLISHING) collana.

serious ['sɪərɪəs] a serio(a), grave; ~**ly** ad seriamente.

sermon ['sɔːmən] n sermone m.

serrated [sɪ'reɪtɪd] a seghettato(a).

serum ['sɪərəm] n siero.

servant ['sɔːvənt] n domestico/a.

serve [sɔːv] vt (employer etc) servire, essere a servizio di; (purpose) servire a; (customer, food, meal) servire; (apprenticeship) fare; (prison term) scontare // vi (also TENNIS) servire; (be useful): to ~ as/for/to do servire da/per/ per fare // n (TENNIS) servizio; it ~s him right ben gli sta, se l'è meritata; to ~ out, ~ up vt (food) servire.

service ['sɔːvɪs] n servizio; (AUT: maintenance) assistenza, revisione f // vt (car, washing machine) revisionare; the S~s le forze armate; to be of ~ to sb essere d'aiuto a qn; dinner ~ servizio da tavola; ~**able** a pratico(a), utile; ~ **charge** n (Brit) servizio; ~**man** n militare m; ~ **station** n stazione f di servizio.

serviette [sɔːvɪ'ɛt] n (Brit) tovagliolo.

session ['sɛʃən] n (sitting) seduta, sessione f; (SCOL) anno scolastico (or accademico).

set [sɛt] n serie f inv; (RADIO, TV) apparecchio; (TENNIS) set m inv; (group of people) mondo, ambiente m; (CINEMA) scenario; (THEATRE: stage) scene fpl; (: scenery) scenario; (MATH) insieme m; (HAIRDRESSING) messa in piega // a (fixed) stabilito(a), determinato(a); (ready) pronto(a) // vb (pt, pp set) (place) posare, mettere; (fix) fissare; (adjust) regolare; (decide: rules etc) stabilire, fissare; (TYP) comporre // vi (sun) tramontare; (jam, jelly) rapprendersi; (concrete) fare presa; to be ~ on doing essere deciso a fare; to ~ to music mettere in musica; to ~ on fire dare fuoco a; to ~ free liberare; to ~ sth going mettere in moto qc; to ~ sail prendere il mare; to ~ **about** vt fus (task) intraprendere, mettersi a; to ~ **aside** vt mettere da parte; to ~ **back** vt (in time): to ~ back (by) mettere indietro (di); to ~ **off** vi partire // vt (bomb) far scoppiare; (cause to start) mettere in moto; (show up well) dare risalto a; to ~ **out** vi partire; (aim): to ~ out to do proporsi di fare // vt (arrange) disporre; (state) esporre, presentare; to ~ **up** vt (organization) fondare, costituire; (monument) innalzare; ~**back** n (hitch) contrattempo, inconveniente m; ~

menu n menù m inv fisso.

settee [sɛ'tiː] n divano, sofà m inv.

setting ['sɛtɪŋ] n ambiente m; (of jewel) montatura.

settle ['sɛtl] vt (argument, matter) appianare; (problem) risolvere; (MED: calm) calmare // vi (bird, dust etc) posarsi; (sediment) depositarsi; (also: ~ down) sistemarsi, stabilirsi; calmarsi; to ~ **for** sth accontentarsi di qc; to ~ **on** sth decidersi per qc; **to** ~ **in** vi sistemarsi; **to** ~ **up** vi: to ~ up with sb regolare i conti con qn; ~**ment** n (payment) pagamento, saldo; (agreement) accordo; (colony) colonia; (village etc) villaggio, comunità f inv; ~**r** n colonizzatore/trice.

setup ['sɛtʌp] n (arrangement) sistemazione f; (situation) situazione f.

seven ['sɛvn] num sette; ~**teen** num diciassette; ~**th** num settimo(a); ~**ty** num settanta.

sever ['sɛvə*] vt recidere, tagliare; (relations) troncare.

several ['sɛvərl] a, pronoun alcuni(e), diversi(e); ~ **of us** alcuni di noi.

severance ['sɛvərəns] n (of relations) rottura; ~ **pay** n indennità di licenziamento.

severe [sɪ'vɪə*] a severo(a); (serious) serio(a), grave; (hard) duro(a); (plain) semplice, sobrio(a); **severity** [sɪ'vɛrɪtɪ] n severità; gravità; (of weather) rigore m.

sew [səʊ], pt sewed, pp sewn vt, vi cucire; **to** ~ **up** vt ricucire.

sewage ['suːɪdʒ] n acque fpl di scolo.

sewer ['suːə*] n fogna.

sewing ['səʊɪŋ] n cucitura; cucito; ~ **machine** n macchina da cucire.

sewn [səʊn] pp of **sew**.

sex [sɛks] n sesso; to have ~ with avere rapporti sessuali con; ~**ist** a, n sessista (m/f).

sexual ['sɛksjuəl] a sessuale.

sexy ['sɛksɪ] a provocante, sexy inv.

shabby ['ʃæbɪ] a malandato(a); (behaviour) vergognoso(a).

shack [ʃæk] n baracca, capanna.

shackles ['ʃæklz] npl ferri mpl, catene fpl.

shade [ʃeɪd] n ombra; (for lamp) paralume m; (of colour) tonalità f inv; (small quantity): a ~ of un po' or un'ombra di // vt ombreggiare, fare ombra a; **in the** ~ all'ombra; a ~ **smaller** un tantino più piccolo.

shadow ['ʃædəʊ] n ombra // vt (follow) pedinare; ~ **cabinet** n (Brit POL) governo m ombra inv; ~**y** a ombreggiato(a), ombroso(a); (dim) vago(a), indistinto(a).

shady ['ʃeɪdɪ] a ombroso(a); (fig: dishonest) losco(a), equivoco(a).

shaft [ʃɑːft] n (of arrow, spear) asta; (AUT, TECH) albero; (of mine) pozzo; (of lift) tromba; (of light) raggio.

shaggy |'ʃægı| a ispido(a).

shake |ʃeık| vb (pt **shook**, pp **shaken** |ʃuk. 'ʃeıkn|) vt scuotere; (bottle, cocktail) agitare // vi tremare // n scossa; **to ~ one's head** (in refusal, dismay) scuotere la testa; **to ~ hands with sb** stringere or dare la mano a qn; **to ~ off** vt scrollare (via); (fig) sbarazzarsi di; **to ~ up** vt scuotere; **shaky** a (hand, voice) tremante; (building) traballante.

shale |ʃeıl| n roccia scistosa.

shall |ʃæl| auxiliary vb: I ~ **go** andrò; ~ **I open the door?** apro io la porta?; I'll **get some, ~ I?** ne prendo un po', va bene?

shallow |'ʃæləu| a poco profondo(a); (fig) superficiale.

sham |ʃæm| n finzione f, messinscena; (jewellery, furniture) imitazione f.

shambles |'ʃæmblz| n confusione f, baraonda, scompiglio.

shame |ʃeım| n vergogna // vt far vergognare; **it is a ~ (that/to do)** è un peccato (che + sub/fare); **what a ~!** che peccato!; **~faced** a vergognoso(a); **~ful** a vergognoso(a); **~less** a sfrontato(a); (immodest) spudorato(a).

shampoo |ʃæm'pu:| n shampoo m inv // vt fare lo shampoo a; **~ and set** n shampoo e messa in piega.

shamrock |'ʃæmrɔk| n trifoglio (simbolo nazionale dell'Irlanda).

shandy |'ʃændı| n birra con gassosa.

shan't |ʃɑ:nt| = **shall not.**

shanty town |'ʃæntı-| n bidonville f inv.

shape |ʃeıp| n forma // vt formare; (statement) formulare; (sb's ideas) condizionare // vi (also: ~ **up**) (events) andare, mettersi; (person) cavarsela; **to take ~** prendere forma; **-shaped** suffix: **heart shaped** a forma di cuore; **~less** a senza forma, informe; **~ly** a ben proporzionato(a).

share |ʃeə*| n (thing received, contribution) parte f; (COMM) azione f // vt dividere; (have in common) condividere, avere in comune; **to ~ out** (among or between) dividere (tra); **~holder** n azionista m/f.

shark |ʃɑ:k| n squalo, pescecane m.

sharp |ʃɑ:p| a (razor, knife) affilato(a); (point) acuto(a), acuminato(a); (nose, chin) aguzzo(a); (outline) netto(a); (cold, pain) pungente; (voice) stridulo(a); (person: quick-witted) sveglio(a); (: unscrupulous) disonesto(a); (MUS): **C ~** do diesis // n (MUS) diesis m inv // ad: **at 2 o'clock ~** alle due in punto; **~en** vt affilare; (pencil) fare la punta a; (fig) aguzzare; **~ener** n (also: **pencil ~ener**) temperamatite m inv; **~eyed** a dalla vista acuta; **~ly** ad (turn, stop) bruscamente; (stand out, contrast) nettamente; (criticize, retort) duramen-

te, aspramente.

shatter |'ʃætə*| vt mandare in frantumi, frantumare; (fig: upset) distruggere; (: ruin) rovinare // vi frantumarsi, andare in pezzi.

shave |ʃeıv| vt radere, rasare // vi radersi, farsi la barba // n: **to have a ~** farsi la barba; **~r** n (also: **electric ~r**) rasoio elettrico.

shaving |'ʃeıvıŋ| n (action) rasatura; **~s** npl (of wood etc) trucioli mpl; **~ brush** n pennello da barba; **~ cream** n crema da barba.

shawl |ʃɔ:l| n scialle m.

she |ʃi:| pronoun ella, lei; **~-cat** n gatta; **~-elephant** n elefantessa; NB: for ships, countries follow the gender of your translation.

sheaf |ʃi:f|, pl **sheaves** n covone m.

shear |ʃıə*| vt (pt **~ed**, pp **~ed** or **shorn**) (sheep) tosare; **to ~ off** vi spezzarsi; **~s** npl (for hedge) cesole fpl.

sheath |ʃi:θ| n fodero, guaina; (contraceptive) preservativo.

sheaves |ʃi:vz| npl of **sheaf.**

shed |ʃed| n capannone m // vt (pt, pp **shed**) (leaves, fur etc) perdere; (tears) versare.

she'd |ʃi:d| = **she had, she would.**

sheen |ʃi:n| n lucentezza.

sheep |ʃi:p| n (pl inv) pecora; **~dog** n cane m da pastore; **~ish** a vergognoso(a), timido(a); **~skin** n pelle f di pecora.

sheer |ʃıə*| a (utter) vero(a) (e proprio(a)); (steep) a picco, perpendicolare; (almost transparent) sottile // ad a picco.

sheet |ʃi:t| n (on bed) lenzuolo; (of paper) foglio; (of glass) lastra; (of metal) foglio, lamina; **~ lightning** n lampo diffuso.

sheik(h) |ʃeık| n sceicco.

shelf |ʃelf|, pl **shelves** n scaffale m, mensola.

shell |ʃel| n (on beach) conchiglia; (of egg, nut etc) guscio; (explosive) granata; (of building) scheletro // vt (peas) sgranare; (MIL) bombardare, cannoneggiare.

she'll |ʃi:l| = **she will, she shall.**

shellfish |'ʃelfıʃ| n (pl inv) (crab etc) crostaceo; (scallop etc) mollusco; (pl: as food) crostacei; molluschi.

shelter |'ʃeltə*| n riparo, rifugio // vt riparare, proteggere; (give lodging to) dare rifugio or asilo a // vi ripararsi, mettersi al riparo.

shelve |ʃelv| vt (fig) accantonare, rimandare; **~s** npl of **shelf.**

shepherd |'ʃepəd| n pastore m // vt (guide) guidare; **~'s pie** n timballo di carne macinata e purè di patate.

sheriff |'ʃerıf| n sceriffo.

sherry |'ʃerı| n sherry m inv.

Shetland |'ʃɛtlənd| n (also: **the ~s, the ~ Isles**) le isole Shetland, le Shetland.

shield |ʃiːld| n scudo // vt: **to ~** (**from**) riparare (da), proteggere (da or contro).

shift |ʃɪft| n (change) cambiamento; (of workers) turno // vt spostare, muovere; (remove) rimuovere // vi spostarsi, muoversi; **~less** a: a **~less person** un(a) fannullone(a); **~ work** n lavoro a squadre; **~y** a ambiguo(a); (eyes) sfuggente.

shilling |'ʃɪlɪŋ| n (Brit) scellino (= 12 old pence; 20 in a pound).

shilly-shally |'ʃɪlɪʃælɪ| vi tentennare, esitare.

shimmer |'ʃɪmə*| vi brillare, luccicare.

shin |ʃɪn| n tibia.

shine |ʃaɪn| n splendore m, lucentezza // vb (pt, pp **shone**) vi (ri)splendere, brillare // vt far brillare, far risplendere; (torch): **to ~ sth on** puntare qc verso.

shingle |'ʃɪŋgl| n (on beach) ciottoli mpl; (on roof) assicella di copertura; **~s** n (MED) herpes zoster m.

shiny |'ʃaɪnɪ| a lucente, lucido(a).

ship |ʃɪp| n nave f // vt trasportare (via mare); (send) spedire (via mare); (load) imbarcare, caricare; **~building** n costruzione f navale; **~ment** n carico; **~ping** n (ships) naviglio; (traffic) navigazione f; **~shape** a in perfetto ordine; **~wreck** n relitto; (event) naufragio // vt: **to be ~wrecked** naufragare, fare naufragio; **~yard** n cantiere m navale.

shire |'ʃaɪə*| n (Brit) contea.

shirk |ʃɔːk| vt sottrarsi a, evitare.

shirt |ʃɔːt| n (man's) camicia; **in ~ sleeves** in maniche di camicia.

shit |ʃɪt| excl (col!) merda (!).

shiver |'ʃɪvə*| n brivido // vi rabbrividire, tremare.

shoal |ʃəul| n (of fish) banco.

shock |ʃɔk| n (impact) urto, colpo; (ELEC) scossa; (emotional) colpo, shock m inv; (MED) shock // vt colpire, scioccare; scandalizzare; **~ absorber** n ammortizzatore m; **~ing** a scioccante, traumatizzante; scandaloso(a).

shod |ʃɔd| pt, pp of **shoe**.

shoddy |'ʃɔdɪ| a scadente.

shoe |ʃuː| n scarpa; (also: **horse~**) ferro di cavallo // vt (pt, pp **shod**) (horse) ferrare; **~horn** n calzante m; **~lace** n stringa; **~ polish** n lucido per scarpe; **~shop** n calzoleria; **~string** n (fig): **on a ~string** con quattro soldi.

shone |ʃɔn| pt, pp of **shine**.

shoo |ʃuː| excl sciò!, via!

shook |ʃuk| pt of **shake**.

shoot |ʃuːt| n (on branch, seedling) germoglio // vb (pt, pp **shot**) vt (game) cacciare, andare a caccia di; (person) sparare a; (execute) fucilare; (film) girare // vi (with gun): **to ~ (at)** sparare

(a), fare fuoco (su); (with bow): **to ~ (at)** tirare (su); (FOOTBALL) sparare, tirare (forte); **to ~ down** vt (plane) abbattere; **to ~ in/out** vi entrare/uscire come una freccia; **to ~ up** vi (fig) salire alle stelle; **~ing** n (shots) sparatoria; (HUNTING) caccia; **~ing star** n stella cadente.

shop |ʃɔp| n negozio; (workshop) officina // vi (also: **go ~ping**) fare spese; **~ assistant** n (Brit) commesso/a; **~ floor** n officina; (Brit fig) operai mpl, maestranze fpl; **~keeper** n negoziante m/f, bottegaio/a; **~lifting** n taccheggio; **~per** n compratore/trice; **~ping** n (goods) spesa, acquisti mpl; **~ping bag** n borsa per la spesa; **~ping centre**, (US) **~ping center** n centro commerciale; **~-soiled** a sciupato(a) a forza di stare in vetrina; **~ steward** n (Brit INDUSTRY) rappresentante m sindacale; **~ window** n vetrina.

shore |ʃɔː*| n (of sea) riva, spiaggia; (of lake) riva // vt: **to ~ (up)** puntellare.

shorn |ʃɔːn| pp of **shear**.

short |ʃɔːt| a (not long) corto(a); (soon finished) breve; (person) basso(a); (curt) brusco(a), secco(a); (insufficient) insufficiente // a (also: **~ film**) cortometraggio; (a pair of) **~s** (i) calzoncini; **to be ~ of sth** essere a corto di or mancare di qc; **in ~** in breve; **~ of doing** a meno che non si faccia; **everything ~ of** tutto fuorché; **it is ~ for** l'abbreviazione or il diminutivo di; **to cut ~** (speech, visit) accorciare, abbreviare; (person) interrompere; **to fall ~ of** venir meno a; non soddisfare; **to stop ~** fermarsi di colpo; **to stop ~ of** non arrivare fino a; **~age** n scarsezza, carenza; **~bread** n biscotto di pasta frolla; **~-change** vt: **to ~-change sb** imbrogliare qn sul resto; **~-circuit** n cortocircuito // vt cortocircuitare // vi fare cortocircuito; **~coming** n difetto; **~(crust) pastry** n (Brit) pasta frolla; **~cut** n scorciatoia; **~en** vt accorciare, ridurre; **~fall** n deficit m; **~hand** n (Brit) stenografia; **~hand typist** n (Brit) stenodattilografo/a; **~ list** n (Brit: for job) rosa dei candidati; **~ly** ad fra poco; **~-sighted** a (Brit) miope; **~-staffed** a a corto di personale; **~ story** n racconto, novella; **~-tempered** a irascibile; **~-term** a (effect) di or a breve durata; **~wave** n (RADIO) onde fpl corte.

shot |ʃɔt| pt, pp of **shoot** // n sparo, colpo; (person) tiratore m; (try) prova; (injection) iniezione f; (PHOT) foto f inv; **like a ~** come un razzo; (very readily) immediatamente; **~gun** n fucile m da caccia.

should |ʃud| auxiliary vb: **I ~ go now** dovrei andare ora; **he ~ be there now**

dovrebbe essere arrivato ora; I ~ go if I were you se fossi in te andrei; I ~ like to mi piacerebbe.

shoulder ['ʃəuldə*] n spalla; (Brit: of road): **hard ~** banchina // vt (fig) addossarsi, prendere sulle proprie spalle; **~ bag** n borsa a tracolla; **~ blade** n scapola; **~ strap** n bretella, spallina.

shouldn't ['ʃudnt] = should not.

shout [ʃaut] n urlo, grido // vt gridare // vi urlare, gridare; **to ~ down** vt zittire gridando; **~ing** n urli mpl.

shove [ʃʌv] vt spingere; (col: put): **to ~ sth** in ficcare qc in; **to ~ off** vi (NAUT) scostarsi.

shovel ['ʃʌvl] n pala // vt spalare.

show [ʃəu] n (of emotion) dimostrazione f, manifestazione f; (semblance) apparenza; (exhibition) mostra, esposizione f; (THEATRE, CINEMA) spettacolo // vb (pt **~ed**, pp **shown**) vt far vedere, mostrare; (courage etc) dimostrare, dar prova di; (exhibit) esporre // vi vedersi, essere visibile; **on ~** (exhibits etc) esposto(a); **to ~ in** vt (person) far entrare; **to ~ off** vi (pej) esibirsi, mettersi in mostra // vt (display) mettere in risalto; (pej) mettere in mostra; **to ~ out** vt (person) accompagnare alla porta; **to ~ up** vi (stand out) essere ben visibile; (col: turn up) farsi vedere // vt mettere in risalto; (unmask) smascherare; **~ business** n industria dello spettacolo; **~down** n prova di forza.

shower ['ʃauə*] n (rain) acquazzone m; (of stones etc) pioggia; (also: **~bath**) doccia // vi fare la doccia // vt: **to ~ sb with** (gifts, abuse etc) coprire qn di; (missiles) lanciare contro qn una pioggia di; **~proof** a impermeabile.

showing ['ʃəuiŋ] n (of film) proiezione f.

show jumping n concorso ippico (di salto ad ostacoli).

shown [ʃəun] pp of show.

show-off ['ʃəuɔf] n (col: person) esibizionista m/f.

showroom ['ʃəurum] n sala d'esposizione.

shrank [ʃræŋk] pt of shrink.

shrapnel ['ʃræpnl] n shrapnel m.

shred [ʃrɛd] n (gen pl) brandello // vt fare a brandelli; (CULIN) sminuzzare, tagliuzzare; **~der** n (vegetable ~der) grattugia; (document ~der) distruttore m di documenti.

shrewd [ʃru:d] a astuto(a), scaltro(a).

shriek [ʃri:k] n strillo // vt, vi strillare.

shrill [ʃril] a acuto(a), stridulo(a), stridente.

shrimp [ʃrimp] n gamberetto.

shrine [ʃrain] n reliquario; (place) santuario.

shrink [ʃriŋk] vb (pt **shrank**, pp

shrunk) vi restringersi; (fig) ridursi // vt (wool) far restringere // n (col: pej) psicanalista m/f; **to ~ from doing sth** rifuggire dal fare qc; **~age** n restringimento; **~wrap** vt confezionare con pellicola di plastica.

shrivel ['ʃrivl] (also: **~ up**) vt raggrinzare, avvizzire // vi raggrinzirsi, avvizzire.

shroud [ʃraud] n sudario // vt: **~ed in mystery** avvolto(a) nel mistero.

Shrove Tuesday ['ʃrəuv-] n martedì m grasso.

shrub [ʃrʌb] n arbusto; **~bery** n arbusti mpl.

shrug [ʃrʌg] n scrollata di spalle // vt, vi: **to ~ (one's shoulders)** alzare le spalle, fare spallucce; **to ~ off** vt passare sopra a.

shrunk [ʃrʌŋk] pp of shrink.

shudder ['ʃʌdə*] n brivido // vi rabbrividire.

shuffle ['ʃʌfl] vt (cards) mescolare; **to ~ (one's feet)** strascicare i piedi.

shun [ʃʌn] vt sfuggire, evitare.

shunt [ʃʌnt] vt (RAIL: direct) smistare; (: divert) deviare.

shut, pt, pp **shut** [ʃʌt] vt chiudere // vi chiudersi, chiudere; **to ~ down** vt, vi chiudere definitivamente; **to ~ off** vt fermare, bloccare; **to ~ up** vi (col: keep quiet) stare zitto(a), fare silenzio // vt (close) chiudere; (silence) far tacere; **~ter** n imposta; (PHOT) otturatore m.

shuttle ['ʃʌtl] n spola, navetta; (also: **~ service**) servizio m navetta inv.

shuttlecock ['ʃʌtlkɔk] n volano.

shy [ʃai] a timido(a).

sibling ['sibliŋ] n fratello/sorella.

Sicily ['sisili] n Sicilia.

sick [sik] a (ill) malato(a); (vomiting): **to be ~** vomitare; (humour) macabro(a); **to feel ~** avere la nausea; **to be ~ of** (fig) averne abbastanza di; **~ bay** n infermeria; **~en** vt nauseare // vi: **to be ~ening for sth** (cold etc) cavare qc.

sickle ['sikl] n falcetto.

sick: **~ leave** n congedo per malattia; **~ly** a malaticcio(a); (causing nausea) nauseante; **~ness** n malattia; (vomiting) vomito; **~ pay** n sussidio per malattia.

side [said] n lato; (of lake) riva // cpd (door, entrance) laterale // vi: **to ~ with sb** parteggiare per qn, prendere le parti di qn; **by the ~ of** a fianco di; (road) sul ciglio di; **~ by ~** fianco a fianco; **to take ~s (with)** schierarsi (con); **~board** n credenza; **~boards** (Brit), **~burns** npl (whiskers) basette fpl; **~ effect** n (MED) effetto collaterale; **~light** n (AUT) luce f di posizione; **~line** n (SPORT) linea laterale; (fig) attività secondaria; **~long** a obliquo(a); **~saddle** ad all'amazzone; **~ show** n

attrazione f; ~**step** vt (question)
eludere; (problem) scavalcare; ~
street n traversa; ~**track** vt (fig) distrarre; ~**walk** n (US) marciapiede m;
~**ways** ad (move) di lato, di fianco;
(look) con la coda dell'occhio.

siding ['saɪdɪŋ] n (RAIL) binario di
raccordo.

sidle ['saɪdl] vi: to ~ up (to) avvicinarsi
furtivamente (a).

siege [si:dʒ] n assedio.

sieve [sɪv] n setaccio // vt setacciare.

sift [sɪft] vt passare al crivello; (fig) vagliare.

sigh [saɪ] n sospiro // vi sospirare.

sight [saɪt] n (faculty) vista; (spectacle)
spettacolo; (on gun) mira // vt avvistare; in ~ in vista; out of ~ non
visibile; ~**seeing** n giro turistico; to go
~seeing visitare una località.

sign [saɪn] n segno; (with hand etc) segno, gesto; (notice) insegna, cartello // vt
firmare; **to** ~ **on** vi (MIL) arruolarsi;
(as unemployed) iscriversi sulla lista
(dell'ufficio di collocamento) // vt (MIL)
arruolare; (employee) assumere; **to** ~
over vt: to ~ sth over to sb cedere qc
con scrittura legale a qn; **to** ~ **up**
(MIL) vt arruolare // vi arruolarsi.

signal ['sɪgnl] n segnale m // vi (AUT) segnalare, mettere la freccia // vt (person)
fare segno a; (message) comunicare per
mezzo di segnali; ~**man** n (RAIL)
deviatore m.

signature ['sɪgnətʃə*] n firma; ~ **tune** n
sigla musicale.

signet ring ['sɪgnət-] n anello con sigillo.

significance [sɪg'nɪfɪkəns] n significato;
importanza.

significant [sɪg'nɪfɪkənt] a significativo(a).

signpost ['saɪnpəust] n cartello
indicatore.

silence ['saɪlns] n silenzio // vt far tacere,
ridurre al silenzio; ~**r** n (on gun, Brit
AUT) silenziatore m.

silent ['saɪlnt] a silenzioso(a); (film)
muto(a); to remain ~ tacere, stare zitto;
~ **partner** n (COMM) socio inattivo.

silhouette [sɪlu:'et] n silhouette f inv.

silicon chip ['sɪlɪkən-] n piastrina di
silicio.

silk [sɪlk] n seta // cpd di seta; ~**y** a di
seta.

silly ['sɪlɪ] a stupido(a), sciocco(a).

silt [sɪlt] n limo.

silver ['sɪlvə*] n argento; (money) monete da 5, 10 or 50 pence; (also: ~ware)
argenteria // cpd d'argento; ~ **paper** n
(Brit) carta argentata, (carta) stagnola;
~**plated** a argentato(a); ~**smith** n
argentiere m; ~**y** a (colour)
argenteo(a); (sound) argentino(a).

similar ['sɪmɪlə*] a: ~ (to) simile (a);
~**ly** ad allo stesso modo; così pure.

simile ['sɪmɪlɪ] n similitudine f.

simmer ['sɪmə*] vi cuocere a fuoco lento.

simpering ['sɪmpərɪŋ] a lezioso(a),
smorfioso(a).

simple ['sɪmpl] a semplice; **simplicity**
[-'plɪsɪtɪ] n semplicità.

simultaneous [sɪməl'teɪnɪəs] a
simultaneo(a).

sin [sɪn] n peccato // vi peccare.

since [sɪns] ad da allora // prep da // cj
(time) da quando; (because) poiché,
dato che; ~ then da allora.

sincere [sɪn'sɪə*] a sincero(a); ~**ly** ad:
yours ~ly (in letters) distinti saluti;
sincerity [-'serɪtɪ] n sincerità.

sinew ['sɪnju:] n tendine m; ~s npl (muscles) muscoli mpl.

sinful ['sɪnful] a peccaminoso(a).

sing [sɪŋ], pt **sang**, pp **sung** vt, vi
cantare.

singe [sɪndʒ] vt bruciacchiare.

singer ['sɪŋə*] n cantante m/f.

singing ['sɪŋɪŋ] n canto.

single ['sɪŋgl] a solo(a), unico(a);
(unmarried: man) celibe; (: woman)
nubile; (not double) semplice // n (Brit:
also: ~ ticket) biglietto di (sola) andata;
(record) 45 giri m; ~**s** npl (TENNIS)
singolo; **to** ~ **out** vt scegliere; (distinguish) distinguere; ~ **bed** n letto a
una piazza; ~**breasted** a a un petto; ~
file n: in ~ file in fila indiana; ~**handed** ad senza aiuto, da solo(a); ~**minded** a tenace, risoluto(a); ~ **room**
n camera singola.

singlet ['sɪŋglɪt] n canottiera.

singly ['sɪŋglɪ] ad separatamente.

singular ['sɪŋgjulə*] a (exceptional,
LING) singolare; (unusual) strano(a) // n
(LING) singolare m.

sinister ['sɪnɪstə*] a sinistro(a).

sink [sɪŋk] n lavandino, acquaio // vb (pt
sank, pp **sunk**) vt (ship) (fare)
affondare, colare a picco; (foundations)
scavare; (piles etc): to ~ sth into
conficcare qc in // vi affondare, andare a
fondo; (ground etc) cedere, avvallarsi;
to ~ **in** vi penetrare.

sinner ['sɪnə*] n peccatore/trice.

sinus ['saɪnəs] n (ANAT) seno.

sip [sɪp] n sorso // vt sorseggiare.

siphon ['saɪfən] n sifone m; **to** ~ **off** vt
travasare (con un sifone).

sir [sə*] n signore m; S~ John Smith Sir
John Smith; yes ~ sì, signore.

siren ['saɪərn] n sirena.

sirloin ['sə:lɔɪn] n controfiletto.

sissy ['sɪsɪ] n (col) femminuccia.

sister ['sɪstə*] n sorella; (nun) suora;
(Brit: nurse) infermiera f caposala inv;
~**in-law** n cognata.

sit [sɪt], pt, pp **sat** vi sedere, sedersi;
(assembly) essere in seduta // vt (exam)
sostenere, dare; **to** ~ **down** vi sedersi;
to ~ **in on** vt fus assistere a; **to** ~ **up**

vi tirarsi su a sedere; (*not go to bed*) stare alzato(a) fino a tardi.

sitcom ['sitkɔm] *n abbr* (= *situation comedy*) commedia di situazione.

site [saɪt] *n* posto; (*also*: **building** ~) cantiere *m* // *vt* situare.

sit-in ['sɪtɪn] *n* (*demonstration*) sit-in *m inv*.

sitting ['sɪtɪŋ] *n* (*of assembly etc*) seduta; (*in canteen*) turno; ~ **room** *n* soggiorno.

situated ['sɪtjueɪtɪd] *a* situato(a).

situation [sɪtju'eɪʃən] *n* situazione *f*; "~s vacant" (*Brit*) "offerte *fpl* di impiego".

six [sɪks] *num* sei; ~**teen** *num* sedici; ~**th** *num* sesto(a); ~**ty** *num* sessanta.

size [saɪz] *n* dimensioni *fpl*; (*of clothing*) taglia, misura; (*of shoes*) numero; (*glue*) colla; **to** ~ **up** *vt* giudicare, farsi un'idea di; ~**able** *a* considerevole.

sizzle ['sɪzl] *vi* sfrigolare.

skate [skeɪt] *n* pattino; (*fish*: *pl inv*) razza // *vi* pattinare; ~**board** *n* skateboard *m inv*; ~**r** *n* pattinatore/trice; **skating** *n* pattinaggio; **skating rink** *n* pista di pattinaggio.

skeleton ['skelɪtn] *n* scheletro; ~ **key** *n* passe-partout *m inv*; ~ **staff** *n* personale *m* ridotto.

skeptical ['skeptɪkl] *a* (*US*) = **sceptical**.

sketch [sketʃ] *n* (*drawing*) schizzo, abbozzo; (*THEATRE*) scenetta comica, sketch *m inv* // *vt* abbozzare, schizzare; ~ **book** *n* album *m inv* per schizzi; ~**y** *a* incompleto(a), lacunoso(a).

skewer ['skju:ə*] *n* spiedo.

ski [ski:] *n* sci *m inv* // *vi* sciare; ~ **boot** *n* scarpone *m* da sci.

skid [skɪd] *n* slittamento // *vi* slittare.

skier ['ski:ə*] *n* sciatore/trice.

skiing ['ski:ɪŋ] *n* sci *m*.

ski jump *n* (*ramp*) trampolino; (*event*) salto con gli sci.

skilful ['skɪlful] *a* abile.

ski lift *n* ['ski:lɪft] *n* sciovia.

skill [skɪl] *n* abilità *f inv*, capacità *f inv*; ~**ed** *a* esperto(a); (*worker*) qualificato(a), specializzato(a).

skim [skɪm] *vt* (*milk*) scremare; (*soup*) schiumare; (*glide over*) sfiorare // *vi*: to ~ **through** (*fig*) scorrere, dare una scorsa a; ~**med milk** *n* latte *m* scremato.

skimp [skɪmp] *vt* (*work*) fare alla carlona; (*cloth etc*) lesinare; ~**y** *a* misero(a); striminzito(a); frugale.

skin [skɪn] *n* pelle *f* // *vt* (*fruit etc*) sbucciare; (*animal*) scuoiare, spellare; ~-**deep** *a* superficiale; ~ **diving** *n* nuoto subacqueo; ~**ny** *a* molto magro(a), pelle e ossa *inv*; ~**tight** *a* (*dress etc*) aderente.

skip [skɪp] *n* saltello, balzo; (*container*) benna // *vi* saltare; (*with rope*) saltare la corda // *vt* (*pass over*) saltare.

ski: ~ **pants** *npl* pantaloni *mpl* da sci; ~ **pole** *n* racchetta (da sci).

skipper ['skɪpə*] *n* (*NAUT*, *SPORT*) capitano.

skipping rope ['skɪpɪŋ-] *n* (*Brit*) corda per saltare.

skirmish ['skə:mɪʃ] *n* scaramuccia.

skirt [skə:t] *n* gonna, sottana // *vt* fiancheggiare, costeggiare; ~**ing board** *n* (*Brit*) zoccolo.

ski suit *n* tuta da sci.

skit [skɪt] *n* parodia; scenetta satirica.

skittle ['skɪtl] *n* birillo; ~**s** *n* (*game*) (gioco dei) birilli *mpl*.

skive [skaɪv] *vi* (*Brit col*) fare il lavativo.

skulk [skʌlk] *vi* muoversi furtivamente.

skull [skʌl] *n* cranio, teschio.

skunk [skʌŋk] *n* moffetta.

sky [skaɪ] *n* cielo; ~**light** *n* lucernario; ~**scraper** *n* grattacielo.

slab [slæb] *n* lastra.

slack [slæk] *a* (*loose*) allentato(a); (*slow*) lento(a); (*careless*) negligente // *n* (*in rope etc*) parte *f* non tesa; ~**s** *npl* pantaloni *mpl*; ~**en** (*also*: ~**en off**) *vi* rallentare, diminuire // *vt* allentare.

slag [slæg] *n* scorie *fpl*; ~ **heap** *n* ammasso di scorie.

slain [sleɪn] *pp of* **slay**.

slam [slæm] *vt* (*door*) sbattere; (*throw*) scaraventare; (*criticize*) stroncare // *vi* sbattere.

slander ['slɑ:ndə*] *n* calunnia; diffamazione *f* // *vt* calunniare; diffamare.

slang [slæŋ] *n* gergo, slang *m*.

slant [slɑ:nt] *n* pendenza, inclinazione *f*; (*fig*) angolazione *f*, punto di vista; ~**ed** *a* tendenzioso(a); ~**ing** *a* in pendenza, inclinato(a).

slap [slæp] *n* manata, pacca; (*on face*) schiaffo // *vt* dare una manata a; schiaffeggiare // *ad* (*directly*) in pieno; ~**dash** *a* abborracciato(a); ~**stick** *n* (*comedy*) farsa grossolana; ~-**up** *a*: a ~-**up meal** (*Brit*) un pranzo (or una cena) coi fiocchi.

slash [slæʃ] *vt* squarciare; (*face*) sfregiare; (*fig*: *prices*) ridurre drasticamente, tagliare.

slat [slæt] *n* (*of wood*) stecca; (*of plastic*) lamina.

slate [sleɪt] *n* ardesia // *vt* (*fig*: *criticize*) stroncare, distruggere.

slaughter ['slɔ:tə*] *n* strage *f*, massacro // *vt* (*animal*) macellare; (*people*) trucidare, massacrare.

slave [sleɪv] *n* schiavo/a // *vi* (*also*: ~ **away**) lavorare come uno schiavo; ~**ry** *n* schiavitù *f*.

slay [sleɪ], *pt* **slew**, *pp* **slain** *vt* (*formal*) uccidere.

SLD *n abbr* (*Brit*) = *Social and Liberal Democrats*.

sleazy ['sli:zɪ] *a* trasandato(a).

sledge |slɛdʒ| n slitta; **~hammer** n mazza, martello da fabbro.

sleek |sliːk| a (hair, fur) lucido(a), lucente; (car, boat) slanciato(a), affusolato(a).

sleep |sliːp| n sonno // vi (pt, pp **slept**) dormire; to go to ~ addormentarsi; **to ~ in** vi (lie late) alzarsi tardi; (oversleep) dormire fino a tardi; **~er** n (person) dormiente m/f; (Brit RAIL: on track) traversina; (: train) treno di vagoni letto; **~ing bag** n sacco a pelo; **~ing car** n vagone m letto inv, carrozza f letto inv; **~ing pill** n sonnifero; **~less** a: a ~less night una notte in bianco; **~walker** n sonnambulo/a; **~y** a assonnato(a), sonnolento(a); (fig) addormentato(a).

sleet |sliːt| n nevischio.

sleeve |sliːv| n manica.

sleigh |sleɪ| n slitta.

sleight |slaɪt| n: ~ of hand gioco di destrezza.

slender |'slɛndə*| a snello(a), sottile; (not enough) scarso(a), esiguo(a).

slept |slɛpt| pt, pp of **sleep**.

slew |sluː| vi girare // pt of **slay**.

slice |slaɪs| n fetta // vt affettare, tagliare a fette.

slick |slɪk| a (clever) brillante; (insincere) untuoso(a), falso(a) // n (also: oil ~) chiazza di petrolio.

slide |slaɪd| n (in playground) scivolo; (PHOT) diapositiva; (Brit: also: hair ~) fermaglio (per capelli); (in prices) caduta // vb (pt, pp **slid** |slɪd|) vt far scivolare // vi scivolare; **~ rule** n regolo calcolatore; **sliding** a (door) scorrevole; **sliding scale** n scala mobile.

slight |slaɪt| a (slim) snello(a), sottile; (frail) delicato(a), fragile; (trivial) insignificante; (small) piccolo(a) // n offesa, affronto // vt (offend) offendere, fare un affronto a; not in the ~est affatto, neppure per sogno; **~ly** ad lievemente, un po'.

slim |slɪm| a magro(a), snello(a) // vi dimagrire; fare (or seguire) una dieta dimagrante.

slime |slaɪm| n limo, melma; viscidume m.

slimming |'slɪmɪŋ| n (diet) dimagrante; (food) ipocalorico(a).

sling |slɪŋ| n (MED) benda al collo // vt (pt, pp **slung**) lanciare, tirare.

slip |slɪp| n scivolata, scivolone m; (mistake) errore m, sbaglio; (underskirt) sottoveste f; (of paper) striscia di carta; tagliando, scontrino // vt (slide) far scivolare // vi (slide) scivolare; (move smoothly): to ~ into/out of scivolare in/via da; (decline) declinare; to ~ sth on/off infilarsi/togliersi qc; to give sb the ~ sfuggire qn; a ~ of the tongue un lapsus linguae; to ~ away vi

svignarsela; **~ped disc** n spostamento delle vertebre.

slipper |'slɪpə*| n pantofola.

slippery |'slɪpərɪ| a scivoloso(a).

slip road n (Brit: to motorway) rampa di accesso.

slipshod |'slɪpʃɔd| a sciatto(a), trasandato(a).

slip-up |'slɪpʌp| n granchio (fig).

slipway |'slɪpweɪ| n scalo di costruzione.

slit |slɪt| n fessura, fenditura; (cut) taglio; (tear) squarcio; strappo // vt (pt, pp **slit**) tagliare; (make a slit) squarciare; strappare.

slither |'slɪðə*| vi scivolare, sdrucciolare.

sliver |'slɪvə*| n (of glass, wood) scheggia; (of cheese etc) fettina.

slob |slɔb| n (col) sciattone/a.

slog |slɔg| (Brit) n faticata // vi lavorare con accanimento, sgobbare.

slogan |'sləugən| n motto, slogan m inv.

slop |slɔp| vi (also: ~ over) traboccare; versarsi // vt spandere; versare.

slope |sləup| n pendio; (side of mountain) versante m; (of roof) pendenza; (of floor) inclinazione f // vi: to ~ down declinare; to ~ up essere in salita.

sloppy |'slɔpɪ| a (work) tirato(a) via; (appearance) sciatto(a); (film etc) sdolcinato(a).

slot |slɔt| n fessura // vt: to ~ sth into infilare qc in // vi: to ~ into inserirsi in.

sloth |sləuθ| n (laziness) pigrizia, accidia.

slot machine n (Brit: vending machine) distributore m automatico; (for gambling) slot-machine f inv.

slouch |slautʃ| vi (when walking) camminare dinoccolato(a); she was ~ing in a chair era sprofondata in una poltrona; **to ~ about** vi (laze) oziare.

slovenly |'slʌvənlɪ| a sciatto(a), trasandato(a).

slow |sləu| a lento(a); (watch): to be ~ essere indietro // ad lentamente // vt, vi (also: ~ down, ~ up) rallentare; "~" (road sign) "rallentare"; **~ly** ad lentamente; **~ motion** n: in ~ motion al rallentatore.

sludge |slʌdʒ| n fanghiglia.

slug |slʌg| n lumaca; (bullet) pallottola; **~gish** a lento(a).

sluice |sluːs| n chiusa.

slum |slʌm| n catapecchia.

slumber |'slʌmbə*| n sonno.

slump |slʌmp| n crollo, caduta; (economic) depressione f, crisi f inv // vi crollare.

slung |slʌŋ| pt, pp of **sling**.

slur |slə:*| n pronuncia indistinta; (stigma) diffamazione f, calunnia; (smear): ~ (on) macchia (su); (MUS) legatura // vt pronunciare in modo indistinto.

slush |slʌʃ| n neve f mista a fango; ~ **fund** n fondi mpl neri.

slut |slʌt| n donna trasandata, sciattona.

sly |slaɪ| a furbo(a), scaltro(a).

smack |smæk| n (slap) pacca; (on face) schiaffo // vt schiaffeggiare; (child) picchiare // vi: **to ~ of** puzzare di.

small |smɔːl| a piccolo(a); ~ **ads** npl (Brit) piccola pubblicità; ~ **change** n moneta, spiccioli mpl; ~**holder** n piccolo proprietario; ~ **hours** npl: **in the ~ hours** alle ore piccole; ~**pox** n vaiolo; ~ **talk** n chiacchiere fpl.

smart |smɑːt| a elegante; (clever) intelligente; (quick) sveglio(a) // vi bruciare; **to ~en up** vi farsi bello(a) // vt (people) fare bello(a); (things) abbellire.

smash |smæʃ| n (also: ~-up) scontro, collisione f // vt (break) frantumare, fracassare; (opponent) annientare, schiacciare; (hopes) distruggere; (SPORT: record) battere // vi frantumarsi, andare in pezzi; ~**ing** a (col) favoloso(a), formidabile.

smattering |ˈsmætərɪŋ| n: **a ~ of** un'infarinatura di.

smear |smɪə*| n macchia; (MED) striscio // vt ungere; (fig) denigrare, diffamare.

smell |smɛl| n odore m; (sense) olfatto, odorato // vb (pt, pp **smelt** or **smelled** |smɛlt, smɛld|) vt sentire (l')odore di // vi (food etc): **to ~ (of)** avere odore (di); (pej) puzzare, avere un cattivo odore; **it ~s good** ha un buon odore; ~**y** a puzzolente.

smile |smaɪl| n sorriso // vi sorridere.

smirk |smɔːk| n sorriso furbo; sorriso compiaciuto.

smith |smɪθ| n fabbro; ~**y** n fucina.

smock |smɔk| n grembiule m, camice m.

smog |smɔg| n smog m.

smoke |sməuk| n fumo // vt, vi fumare; ~**d** a (bacon, glass) affumicato(a); ~**r** n (person) fumatore/trice; (RAIL) carrozza per fumatori; ~ **screen** n (MIL) cortina fumogena or di fumo; (fig) copertura; **smoking** n fumo; "no smoking" (sign) "vietato fumare"; **smoky** a fumoso(a); (surface) affumicato(a).

smolder |ˈsməuldə*| vi (US) = **smoulder**.

smooth |smuːð| a liscio(a); (sauce) omogeneo(a); (flavour, whisky) amabile; (movement) regolare; (person) mellifluo(a) // vt lisciare, spianare; (also: ~ **out**: difficulties) appianare.

smother |ˈsmʌðə*| vt soffocare.

smoulder, (US) smolder |ˈsməuldə*| vi covare sotto la cenere.

smudge |smʌdʒ| n macchia; sbavatura // vt imbrattare, sporcare.

smug |smʌg| a soddisfatto(a), compiaciuto(a).

smuggle |ˈsmʌgl| vt contrabbandare; ~**r** n contrabbandiere/a; **smuggling** n contrabbando.

smutty |ˈsmʌtɪ| a (fig) osceno(a), indecente.

snack |snæk| n spuntino; ~ **bar** n tavola calda, snack bar m inv.

snag |snæg| n intoppo, ostacolo imprevisto.

snail |sneɪl| n chiocciola.

snake |sneɪk| n serpente m.

snap |snæp| n (sound) schianto, colpo secco; (photograph) istantanea; (game) rubamazzo // a improvviso(a) // vt (far) schioccare; (break) spezzare di netto; (photograph) scattare un'istantanea di // vi spezzarsi con un rumore secco; **to ~ open/shut** aprirsi/chiudersi di scatto; **to ~ at** vt fus (subj: dog) cercare di mordere; **to ~ off** vt (break) schiantare; **to ~ up** vt afferrare; ~**py** a (col: answer, slogan) d'effetto; **make it ~py!** (hurry up) sbrigati!, svelto!; ~**shot** n istantanea.

snare |snɛə*| n trappola.

snarl |snɑːl| vi ringhiare.

snatch |snætʃ| n (fig) furto con strappo, scippo; (small amount): ~**es of** frammenti mpl di // vt strappare (con violenza); (steal) rubare.

sneak |sniːk| vi: **to ~ in/out** entrare/uscire di nascosto; ~**ers** npl scarpe fpl da ginnastica; ~**y** a falso(a), disonesto(a).

sneer |snɪə*| vi ghignare, sogghignare.

sneeze |sniːz| vi starnutire.

sniff |snɪf| n fiutata, annusata // vi fiutare, annusare; tirare su col naso; (in contempt) arricciare il naso // vt fiutare, annusare.

snigger |ˈsnɪgə*| n riso represso // vi ridacchiare, ridere sotto i baffi.

snip |snɪp| n pezzetto; (bargain) (buon) affare m, occasione f // vt tagliare.

sniper |ˈsnaɪpə*| n (marksman) franco tiratore m, cecchino.

snippet |ˈsnɪpɪt| n frammento.

snivelling |ˈsnɪvlɪŋ| a (whimpering) piagnucoloso(a).

snob |snɔb| n snob m/f inv; ~**bish** a snob inv.

snooker |ˈsnuːkə*| n tipo di gioco del biliardo.

snoop |ˈsnuːp| vi: **to ~ on sb** spiare qn; **to ~ about** curiosare.

snooty |ˈsnuːtɪ| a borioso(a), snob inv.

snooze |snuːz| n sonnellino, pisolino // vi fare un sonnellino.

snore |snɔː*| vi russare.

snorkel |ˈsnɔːkl| n (of swimmer) respiratore m a tubo.

snort |snɔːt| n sbuffo // vi sbuffare.

snotty |ˈsnɔtɪ| a moccioso(a).

snout |snaut| n muso.

snow |snəu| n neve f // vi nevicare; ~**ball** n palla di neve; ~**bound** a bloccato(a) dalla neve; ~**drift** n cumulo di neve (ammucchiato dal vento); ~**drop** n bucaneve m inv; ~**fall** n nevicata; ~**flake** n fiocco di neve; ~**man** n pupazzo di neve; ~**plough**, (US) ~**plow** n spazzaneve m inv; ~**shoe** n racchetta da neve; ~**storm** n tormenta.

snub [snʌb] vt snobbare // n offesa, affronto; ~**-nosed** a dal naso camuso.

snuff [snʌf] n tabacco da fiuto.

snug [snʌg] a comodo(a); (room, house) accogliente, comodo(a).

snuggle ['snʌgl] vi: to ~ up to sb stringersi a qn.

so [səu] ◆ ad 1 (thus, likewise) così; if ~ se è così, quand'è così; I didn't do it — you did ~! non l'ho fatto io — sì che l'hai fatto!; ~ do I, ~ am I etc anch'io; it's 5 o'clock — ~ it is! sono le 5 — davvero!; I hope ~ lo spero; I think ~ penso di sì; ~ far finora, fin qui; (in past) fino ad allora
2 (in comparisons etc: to such a degree) così; ~ big (that) così grande (che); she's not ~ clever as her brother lei non è (così) intelligente come suo fratello
3: ~ much a tanto(a) ◆ ad tanto; I've got ~ much work/money ho tanto lavoro/ tanti soldi; I love you ~ much ti amo tanto; ~ many tanti(e)
4 (phrases): 10 or ~ circa 10; ~ long! (col: goodbye) ciao!, ci vediamo!
◆ cj 1 (expressing purpose): ~ as to do in modo or così da fare; we hurried ~ as not to be late ci affrettammo per non fare tardi; ~ (that) affinché + sub, perché + sub
2 (expressing result): he didn't arrive ~ I left non è venuto così me ne sono andata; ~ you see, I could have gone vedi, sarei potuto andare.

soak [səuk] vt inzuppare; (clothes) mettere a mollo // vi inzupparsi; (clothes) essere a mollo; to ~ in vi penetrare; to ~ up vt assorbire.

so-and-so ['səuəndsəu] n (somebody) un tale.

soap [səup] n sapone m; ~**flakes** npl sapone m in scaglie; ~ **opera** n soap opera f inv; ~ **powder** n detersivo; ~**y** a insaponato(a).

soar [sɔ:*] vi volare in alto.

sob [sɔb] n singhiozzo // vi singhiozzare.

sober ['səubə*] a non ubriaco(a); (sedate) serio(a); (moderate) moderato(a); (colour, style) sobrio(a); to ~ up vt far passare la sbornia a // vi farsi passare la sbornia.

so-called ['səu'kɔ:ld] a cosiddetto(a).

soccer ['sɔkə*] n calcio.

sociable ['səuʃəbl] a socievole.

social ['səuʃl] a sociale // n festa, serata; ~ **club** n club m inv sociale; ~**ism** n socialismo; ~**ist** a, n socialista (m/f);

~**ize** vi: to ~**ize** (with) socializzare (con); ~ **security** n previdenza sociale; ~ **work** n servizio sociale; ~ **worker** n assistente m/f sociale.

society [sə'saɪəti] n società f inv; (club) società, associazione f; (also: **high** ~) alta società.

sociology [səusɪ'ɔlədʒi] n sociologia.

sock [sɔk] n calzino // vt (hit) dare un pugno a.

socket ['sɔkit] n cavità f inv; (of eye) orbita; (Brit ELEC: also: **wall** ~) presa di corrente; (: for light bulb) portalampada m inv.

sod [sɔd] n (of earth) zolla erbosa; (Brit col!) bastardo/a (!).

soda ['səudə] n (CHEM) soda; (also: ~ water) acqua di seltz; (US: also: ~ pop) gassosa.

sodden ['sɔdn] a fradicio(a).

sodium ['səudiəm] n sodio.

sofa ['səufə] n sofà m inv.

soft [sɔft] a (not rough) morbido(a); (not hard) soffice; (not loud) sommesso(a); (kind) gentile; (weak) debole; (stupid) stupido(a); ~ **drink** n analcolico; ~**en** ['sɔfn] vt ammorbidire; addolcire; attenuare // vi ammorbidirsi; addolcirsi; attenuarsi; ~**ly** ad dolcemente; morbidamente; ~**ness** n dolcezza; morbidezza.

software ['sɔftwɛə*] n (COMPUT) software m.

soggy ['sɔgi] a inzuppato(a).

soil [sɔil] n (earth) terreno, suolo // vt sporcare; (fig) macchiare.

solace ['sɔlis] n consolazione f.

solar ['səulə*] a solare.

sold [səuld] pt, pp of sell; ~ **out** a (COMM) esaurito(a).

solder ['səuldə*] vt saldare // n saldatura.

soldier ['səuldʒə*] n soldato, militare m.

sole [səul] n (of foot) pianta (del piede); (of shoe) suola; (fish: pl inv) sogliola // a solo(a), unico(a).

solemn ['sɔləm] a solenne; grave; serio(a).

sole trader n (COMM) commerciante m in proprio.

solicit [sə'lisit] vt (request) richiedere, sollecitare // vi (prostitute) adescare i passanti.

solicitor [sə'lisitə*] n (Brit: for wills etc) ≈ notaio; (: in court) ≈ avvocato.

solid ['sɔlid] a (not hollow) pieno(a); (strong, sound, reliable, not liquid) solido(a); (meal) sostanzioso(a) // n solido.

solidarity [sɔli'dæriti] n solidarietà.

solitaire [sɔli'tɛə*] n (games, gem) solitario.

solitary ['sɔlitəri] a solitario(a); ~ **confinement** n (LAW): in ~ confinement in cella d'isolamento.

solo [ˈsəuləu] *n* assolo; ~**ist** *n* solista *m/f*.

soluble [ˈsɔljubl] *a* solubile.

solution [səˈluːʃən] *n* soluzione *f*.

solve [sɔlv] *vt* risolvere.

solvent [ˈsɔlvənt] *a* (*COMM*) solvibile // *n* (*CHEM*) solvente *m*.

sombre, (*US*) **somber** [ˈsɔmbə*] *a* scuro(a); (*mood, person*) triste.

some [sʌm] ♦ *a* **1** (*a certain amount or number of*): ~ **tea/water/cream** del tè/dell'acqua/della panna; ~ **children/apples** dei bambini/delle mele

2 (*certain: in contrasts*) certo(a), ~ **people say that ...** alcuni dicono che ..., certa gente dice che ...

3 (*unspecified*) un(a) certo(a), qualche; ~ **woman was asking for you** una tale chiedeva di lei; ~ **day** un giorno; ~ **day next week** un giorno della prossima settimana

♦ *pronoun* **1** (*a certain number*) alcuni(e), certi(e); **I've got** ~ (*books etc*) ne ho alcuni; ~ (*of them*) **have been sold** alcuni sono stati venduti

2 (*a certain amount*) un po'; **I've got** ~ (*money, milk*) ne ho un po'; **I've read** ~ **of the book** ho letto parte del libro

♦ *ad:* ~ **10 people** circa 10 persone.

somebody [ˈsʌmbədɪ] *pronoun* = **someone**.

somehow [ˈsʌmhau] *ad* in un modo o nell'altro, in qualche modo; (*for some reason*) per qualche ragione.

someone [ˈsʌmwʌn] *pronoun* qualcuno.

someplace [ˈsʌmpleɪs] *ad* (*US*) = **somewhere**.

somersault [ˈsʌməsɔːlt] *n* capriola; salto mortale // *vi* fare una capriola (*or* un salto mortale); (*car*) cappottare.

something [ˈsʌmθɪŋ] *pronoun* qualcosa, qualche cosa; ~ **nice** qualcosa di bello; ~ **to do** qualcosa da fare.

sometime [ˈsʌmtaɪm] *ad* (*in future*) una volta o l'altra; (*in past*): ~ **last month** durante il mese scorso.

sometimes [ˈsʌmtaɪmz] *ad* qualche volta.

somewhat [ˈsʌmwɔt] *ad* piuttosto.

somewhere [ˈsʌmwɛə*] *ad* in *or* da qualche parte.

son [sʌn] *n* figlio.

song [sɔŋ] *n* canzone *f*.

sonic [ˈsɔnɪk] *a* (*boom*) sonico(a).

son-in-law [ˈsʌnɪnlɔː] *n* genero.

sonnet [ˈsɔnɪt] *n* sonetto.

sonny [ˈsʌnɪ] *n* (*col*) ragazzo mio.

soon [suːn] *ad* presto, fra poco; (*early*) presto; ~ **afterwards** poco dopo; **as** ~ **as possible** prima possibile; **I'll do it as** ~ **as I can** lo farò appena posso; ~**er** *ad* (*time*) prima; (*preference*): **I would** ~**er do** preferirei fare; ~**er or later** prima o poi.

soot [sut] *n* fuliggine *f*.

soothe [suːð] *vt* calmare.

sophisticated [səˈfɪstɪkeɪtɪd] *a* sofisticato(a); raffinato(a); complesso(a).

sophomore [ˈsɔfəmɔː*] *n* (*US*) studente/essa del secondo anno.

sopping [ˈsɔpɪŋ] *a* (*also:* ~ **wet**) bagnato(a) fradicio(a).

soppy [ˈsɔpɪ] *a* (*pej*) sentimentale.

soprano [səˈprɑːnəu] *n* (*voice*) soprano *m*; (*singer*) soprano *m/f*.

sorcerer [ˈsɔːsərə*] *n* stregone *m*, mago.

sore [sɔː*] *a* (*painful*) dolorante; (*col: offended*) offeso(a) // *n* piaga; ~**ly** *ad* (*tempted*) fortemente.

sorrow [ˈsɔrəu] *n* dolore *m*.

sorry [ˈsɔrɪ] *a* spiacente; (*condition, excuse*) misero(a); ~**!** scusa! (*or* scusi! *or* scusate!); **to feel** ~ **for sb** rincrescersi per qn.

sort [sɔːt] *n* specie *f*, genere *m* // *vt* (*also:* ~ **out**: *papers*) classificare; ordinare; (: *letters etc*) smistare; (: *problems*) risolvere; ~**ing office** *n* ufficio *m* smistamento *inv*.

SOS *n abbr* (= *save our souls*) S.O.S. *m inv*.

so-so [ˈsəusəu] *ad* così così.

sought [sɔːt] *pt, pp of* **seek**.

soul [səul] *n* anima; ~**-destroying** *a* demoralizzante; ~**ful** *a* pieno(a) di sentimento.

sound [saund] *a* (*healthy*) sano(a); (*safe, not damaged*) solido(a), in buono stato; (*reliable, not superficial*) solido(a); (*sensible*) giudizioso(a), di buon senso // *ad:* ~ **asleep** profondamente addormentato // *n* (*noise*) suono; rumore *m*; (*GEO*) stretto // *vt* (*alarm*) suonare; (*also:* ~ **out**: *opinions*) sondare // *vi* suonare; (*fig: seem*) sembrare; **to** ~ **like** rassomigliare a; ~ **barrier** *n* muro del suono; ~ **effects** *npl* effetti sonori; ~**ly** *ad* (*sleep*) profondamente; (*beat*) duramente; ~**proof** *vt* insonorizzare, isolare acusticamente // *a* insonorizzato(a), isolato(a) acusticamente; ~**track** *n* (*of film*) colonna sonora.

soup [suːp] *n* minestra; brodo; zuppa; **in the** ~ (*fig*) nei guai; ~ **plate** *n* piatto fondo; ~**spoon** *n* cucchiaio da minestra.

sour [ˈsauə*] *a* aspro(a); (*fruit*) acerbo(a); (*milk*) acido(a), fermentato(a); (*fig*) arcigno(a); acido(a); **it's** ~ **grapes** è soltanto invidia.

source [sɔːs] *n* fonte *f*, sorgente *f*; (*fig*) fonte.

south [sauθ] *n* sud *m*, meridione *m*, mezzogiorno // *a* del sud, sud *inv*, meridionale // *ad* verso sud; **S~ Africa** *n* Sudafrica *m*; **S~ African** *a, n* sudafricano(a); **S~ America** *n* Sudamerica *m*, America del sud; **S~ American** *a, n* sudamericano(a); ~**-east** *n* sud-est *m*; ~**erly** [ˈsʌðəlɪ] *a* del sud; ~**ern** [ˈsʌðən] *a* del sud, meridionale; esposto(a) a sud; **S~ Pole** *n* Polo Sud; **~ward(s)** *ad* verso sud; **~-west** *n* sud-ovest *m*.

souvenir [suːvəˈnɪə*] *n* ricordo, souvenir *m inv.*

sovereign [ˈsɔvrɪn] *a, n* sovrano(a).

soviet [ˈsəʊvɪət] *a* sovietico(a); **the S~ Union** l'Unione *f* Sovietica.

sow *n* [sau] scrofa // *vt* [səu] (*pt* **~ed**, *pp* **sown** [səun]) seminare.

soya [ˈsɔɪə], (*US*) **soy** [sɔɪ] *n*: **~ bean** *n* seme *m* di soia; **~ sauce** *n* salsa di soia.

spa [spaː] *n* (*resort*) stazione *f* termale; (*US*: also: **health ~**) centro di cure estetiche.

space [speɪs] *n* spazio; (*room*) posto; spazio; (*length of time*) intervallo // *cpd* spaziale // *vt* (*also*: **~ out**) distanziare; **~craft** *n* (*pl inv*) veicolo spaziale; **~man/woman** *n* astronauta *m/f*, cosmonauta *m/f*; **~ship** *n* = **~craft**; **spacing** *n* spaziatura.

spacious [ˈspeɪʃəs] *a* spazioso(a), ampio(a).

spade [speɪd] *n* (*tool*) vanga; pala; (*child's*) paletta; **~s** *npl* (*CARDS*) picche *fpl.*

Spain [speɪn] *n* Spagna.

span [spæn] *pt of* **spin** // *n* (*of bird, plane*) apertura alare; (*of arch*) campata; (*in time*) periodo; durata // *vt* attraversare; (*fig*) abbracciare.

Spaniard [ˈspænjəd] *n* spagnolo/a.

spaniel [ˈspænjəl] *n* spaniel *m inv.*

Spanish [ˈspænɪʃ] *a* spagnolo(a) // *n* (*LING*) spagnolo; **the ~** *npl* gli Spagnoli.

spank [spæŋk] *vt* sculacciare.

spanner [ˈspænə*] *n* (*Brit*) chiave *f* inglese.

spar [spaː*] *n* asta, palo // *vi* (*BOXING*) allenarsi.

spare [spɛə*] *a* di riserva, di scorta; (*surplus*) in più, d'avanzo // *n* (*part*) pezzo di ricambio // *vt* (*do without*) fare a meno di; (*afford to give*) concedere; (*refrain from hurting, using*) risparmiare; **to ~** (*surplus*) d'avanzo; **~ part** *n* pezzo di ricambio; **~ time** *n* tempo libero; **~ wheel** *n* (*AUT*) ruota di scorta.

sparing [ˈspɛərɪŋ] *a*: **to be ~ with** sth risparmiare qc; **~ly** *ad* moderatamente.

spark [spaːk] *n* scintilla; **~(ing) plug** *n* candela.

sparkle [ˈspaːkl] *n* scintillio, sfavillio // *vi* scintillare, sfavillare; (*bubble*) spumeggiare, frizzare; **sparkling** *a* scintillante, sfavillante; (*wine*) spumante.

sparrow [ˈspærəu] *n* passero.

sparse [spaːs] *a* sparso(a), rado(a).

spartan [ˈspaːtən] *a* (*fig*) spartano(a).

spasm [ˈspæzəm] *n* (*MED*) spasmo; (*fig*) accesso, attacco; **~odic** [spæzˈmɔdɪk] *a*

spasmodico(a); (*fig*) intermittente.

spastic [ˈspæstɪk] *n* spastico/a.

spat [spæt] *pt, pp of* **spit**.

spate [speɪt] *n* (*fig*): **~ of** diluvio *or* fiume *m* di; **in ~** (*river*) in piena.

spatter [ˈspætə*] *vt, vi* schizzare.

spawn [spɔːn] *vt* deporre // *vi* deporre le uova // *n* uova *fpl.*

speak [spiːk], *pt* **spoke**, *pp* **spoken** *vt* (*language*) parlare; (*truth*) dire // *vi* parlare; **to ~ to** sb/of *or* about sth parlare a qn/di qc; **~ up!** parla più forte!; **~er** *n* (*in public*) oratore/trice; (*also*: **loud~er**) altoparlante *m*; (*POL*): **the S~er** *il presidente della Camera dei Comuni* (*Brit*) *or dei Rappresentanti* (*US*).

spear [spɪə*] *n* lancia; **~head** *vt* (*attack etc*) condurre.

spec [spɛk] *n* (*col*): **on ~** sperando bene.

special [ˈspɛʃl] *a* speciale; **~ist** *n* specialista *m/f*; **~ity** [spɛʃɪˈælɪtɪ] *n* specialità *f inv*; **~ize** *vi*: **to ~ize** (**in**) specializzarsi (in); **~ly** *ad* specialmente, particolarmente.

species [ˈspiːʃiːz] *n* (*pl inv*) specie *f inv.*

specific [spəˈsɪfɪk] *a* specifico(a); preciso(a); **~ally** *ad* esplicitamente; (*especially*) appositamente.

specimen [ˈspɛsɪmən] *n* esemplare *m*, modello; (*MED*) campione *m*.

speck [spɛk] *n* puntino, macchiolina; (*particle*) granello.

speckled [ˈspɛkld] *a* macchiettato(a).

specs [spɛks] *npl* (*col*) occhiali *mpl.*

spectacle [ˈspɛktəkl] *n* spettacolo; **~s** *npl* (*glasses*) occhiali *mpl*; **spectacular** [-ˈtækjulə*] *a* spettacolare // *n* (*CINEMA etc*) film *m inv etc* spettacolare.

spectator [spɛkˈteɪtə*] *n* spettatore *m*.

spectre, (*US*) **specter** [ˈspɛktə*] *n* spettro.

spectrum, *pl* **spectra** [ˈspɛktrəm, -rə] *n* spettro; (*fig*) gamma.

speculation [spɛkjuˈleɪʃən] *n* speculazione *f*; congettura *fpl.*

speech [spiːtʃ] *n* (*faculty*) parola; (*talk*) discorso; (*manner of speaking*) parlata; (*enunciation*) elocuzione *f*; **~less** *a* ammutolito(a), muto(a).

speed [spiːd] *n* velocità *f inv*; (*promptness*) prontezza; **at full** *or* **top ~** a tutta velocità; **to ~ up** *vi, vt* accelerare; **~boat** *n* motoscafo; **~ily** *ad* velocemente; prontamente; **~ing** *n* (*AUT*) eccesso di velocità; **~ limit** *n* limite *m* di velocità; **~ometer** [spɪˈdɔmɪtə*] *n* tachimetro; **~way** *n* (*SPORT*) pista per motociclismo; (*also*: **~way racing**) corsa motociclistica (su pista); **~y** *a* veloce, rapido(a); pronto(a).

spell [spɛl] *n* (*also*: **magic ~**) incantesimo; (*period of time*) (*breve*) periodo // *vt* (*pt, pp* **spelt** (*Brit*) *or* **~ed**

|spelt, speld|) (*in writing*) scrivere (lettera per lettera); (*aloud*) dire lettera per lettera; (*fig*) significare; **to cast a ~** **on sb** fare un incantesimo a qn; **he can't ~** fa errori di ortografia; **~bound** *a* incantato(a); affascinato(a); **~ing** *n* ortografia.

spend, *pt, pp* **spent** |spɛnd, spɛnt| *vt* (*money*) spendere; (*time, life*) passare; **~thrift** *n* spendaccione/a.

sperm |spə:m| *n* sperma *m*.

spew |spju:| *vt* vomitare.

sphere |sfɪə*| *n* sfera.

spice |spaɪs| *n* spezia // *vt* aromatizzare.

spick-and-span ['spɪkən'spæn] *a* impeccabile.

spicy ['spaɪsɪ] *a* piccante.

spider ['spaɪdə*] *n* ragno.

spike |spaɪk| *n* punta.

spill, *pt, pp* **spilt** *or* **~ed** |spɪl, -t, -d| *vt* versare, rovesciare // *vi* versarsi, rovesciarsi; **to ~ over** *vi* (*liquid*) versarsi; (*crowd*) riversarsi.

spin |spɪn| *n* (*revolution of wheel*) rotazione *f*; (*AVIAT*) avvitamento; (*trip in car*) giretto // *vb* (*pt* **spun, span,** *pp* **spun**) *vt* (*wool etc*) filare; (*wheel*) far girare // *vi* girare; **to ~ out** *vt* far durare.

spinach ['spɪnɪtʃ] *n* spinacio; (*as food*) spinaci *mpl*.

spinal ['spaɪnl] *a* spinale; **~ cord** *n* midollo spinale.

spindly ['spɪndlɪ] *a* lungo(a) e sottile, filiforme.

spin-dryer |spɪn'draɪə*| *n* (*Brit*) centrifuga.

spine |spaɪn| *n* spina dorsale; (*thorn*) spina.

spinning ['spɪnɪŋ] *n* filatura; **~ top** *n* trottola; **~ wheel** *n* filatoio.

spin-off |'spɪnɔf| *n* applicazione *f* secondaria; (*product*) prodotto secondario.

spinster ['spɪnstə*] *n* nubile *f*; zitella.

spiral ['spaɪərl] *n* spirale *f* // *a* a spirale // *vi* (*fig*) salire a spirale; **~ staircase** *n* scala a chiocciola.

spire |'spaɪə*| *n* guglia.

spirit ['spɪrɪt] *n* (*soul*) spirito, anima; (*ghost*) spirito, fantasma *m*; (*mood*) stato d'animo, umore *m*; (*courage*) coraggio; **~s** *npl* (*drink*) alcolici *mpl*; **in good ~s** di buon umore; **~ed** *a* vivace, vigoroso(a); (*horse*) focoso(a); **~ level** *n* livella a bolla (d'aria).

spiritual ['spɪrɪtjuəl] *a* spirituale.

spit |spɪt| *n* (*for roasting*) spiedo // *vi* (*pt, pp* **spat**) sputare; (*fire, fat*) scoppiettare.

spite |spaɪt| *n* dispetto // *vt* contrariare, far dispetto a; **in ~ of** nonostante, malgrado; **~ful** *a* dispettoso(a).

spittle ['spɪtl] *n* saliva; sputo.

splash |splæʃ| *n* spruzzo; (*sound*) ciac *m*

inv; (*of colour*) schizzo // *vt* spruzzare // *vi* (*also:* **~ about**) sguazzare.

spleen |spli:n| *n* (*ANAT*) milza.

splendid ['splɛndɪd] *a* splendido(a), magnifico(a).

splint |splɪnt| *n* (*MED*) stecca.

splinter ['splɪntə*] *n* scheggia // *vi* scheggiarsi.

split |splɪt| *n* spaccatura; (*fig: division, quarrel*) scissione *f* // *vb* (*pt, pp* **split**) *vt* spaccare; (*party*) dividere; (*work, profits*) spartire, ripartire // *vi* (*divide*) dividersi; **to ~ up** *vi* (*couple*) separarsi, rompere; (*meeting*) sciogliersi.

splutter ['splʌtə*] *vi* farfugliare; sputacchiare.

spoil, *pt, pp* **spoilt** *or* **~ed** |spɔɪl, -t, -d| *vt* (*damage*) rovinare, guastare; (*mar*) sciupare; (*child*) viziare; **~s** *npl* bottino; **~sport** *n* guastafeste *m/f inv*.

spoke |spəuk| *pt of* **speak** // *n* raggio.

spoken ['spəukn] *pp of* **speak**.

spokesman ['spəuksmən], **spokeswoman** [-wumən] *n* portavoce *m/f inv*.

sponge |spʌndʒ| *n* spugna // *vt* spugnare, pulire con una spugna // *vi*: **to ~ off** *or* **on** scroccare a; **~ bag** *n* (*Brit*) nécessaire *m inv*; **~ (cake)** *n* pan *m* di Spagna.

sponsor ['spɔnsə*] *n* (*RADIO, TV, SPORT etc*) finanziatore/trice (a scopo pubblicitario) // *vt* sostenere; patrocinare; **~ship** *n* finanziamento (a scopo pubblicitario); patrocinio.

spontaneous |spɔn'teɪnɪəs| *a* spontaneo(a).

spooky ['spu:kɪ] *a* che fa accapponare la pelle.

spool |spu:l| *n* bobina.

spoon |spu:n| *n* cucchiaio; **~-feed** *vt* nutrire con il cucchiaio; (*fig*) imboccare; **~ful** *n* cucchiaiata.

sport |spɔ:t| *n* sport *m inv*; (*person*) persona di spirito // *vt* sfoggiare; **~ing** *a* sportivo(a); **to give sb a ~ing chance** dare a qn una possibilità (di vincere); **~ jacket** *n* (*US*) = **~s jacket; ~s car** *n* automobile *f* sportiva; **~s jacket** *n* giacca sportiva; **~sman** *n* sportivo; **~smanship** *n* spirito sportivo; **~swear** *n* abiti *mpl* sportivi; **~swoman** *n* sportiva; **~y** *a* sportivo(a).

spot |spɔt| *n* punto; (*mark*) macchia; (*dot: on pattern*) pallino; (*pimple*) foruncolo; (*place*) posto; (*small amount*): **a ~ of** un po' di // *vt* (*notice*) individuare, distinguere; **on the ~** sul posto; su due piedi; **~ check** *n* controllo senza preavviso; **~less** *a* immacolato(a); **~light** *n* proiettore *m*; (*AUT*) faro ausiliario; **~ted** *a* macchiato(a); a puntini, a pallini; **~ty** *a* (*face*) foruncoloso(a).

spouse |spauz| *n* sposo/a.

spout |spaut| n (of jug) beccuccio; (of liquid) zampillo, getto // vi zampillare.

sprain |spreɪn| n storta, distorsione f // vt: to ~ one's ankle storcersi una caviglia.

sprang |spræŋ| pt of **spring**.

sprawl |sprɔ:l| vi sdraiarsi (in modo scomposto).

spray |spreɪ| n spruzzo; (container) nebulizzatore m, spray m inv; (of flowers) mazzetto // vt spruzzare; (crops) irrorare.

spread |spred| n diffusione f; (distribution) distribuzione f; (CULIN) pasta (da spalmare) // vb (pt, pp **spread**) vt (cloth) stendere, distendere; (butter etc) spalmare; (disease, knowledge) propagare, diffondere // vi stendersi, distendersi; spalmarsi; propagarsi, diffondersi; **~-eagled** |'spredi:gld| a a gambe e braccia aperte; **~sheet** n (COMPUT) foglio elettronico ad espansione.

spree |spri:| n: to go on a ~ fare baldoria.

sprightly |'spraɪtlɪ| a vivace.

spring |sprɪŋ| n (leap) salto, balzo; (coiled metal) molla; (season) primavera; (of water) sorgente f // vi (pt **sprang**, pp **sprung**) saltare, balzare; to ~ from provenire da; to ~ up vi (problem) presentarsi; **~board** n trampolino; **~-clean** n (also: ~ cleaning) grandi pulizie fpl di primavera; **~time** n primavera; **~y** a elastico(a).

sprinkle |'sprɪŋkl| vt spruzzare; spargere; to ~ water etc on, ~ with water etc spruzzare dell'acqua etc su; ~ sugar etc on, ~ with sugar etc spolverizzare di zucchero etc; **~r** n (for lawn) irrigatore m; (to put out fire) sprinkler m inv.

sprint |sprɪnt| n scatto // vi scattare; **~er** n (SPORT) velocista m/f.

sprout |spraut| vi germogliare; **~s** npl (also: Brussels ~s) cavolini mpl di Bruxelles.

spruce |spru:s| n abete m rosso // a lindo(a); azzimato(a).

sprung |sprʌŋ| pp of **spring**.

spry |spraɪ| a arzillo(a), sveglio(a).

spun |spʌn| pt, pp of **spin**.

spur |spə:*| n sperone m; (fig) sprone m, incentivo // vt (also: ~ on) spronare; on the ~ of the moment lì per lì.

spurious |'spjuərɪəs| a falso(a).

spurn |spə:n| vt rifiutare con disprezzo, sdegnare.

spurt |spə:t| vi sgorgare; zampillare.

spy |spaɪ| n spia // vi: to ~ on spiare // vt (see) scorgere; **~ing** n spionaggio.

Sq. abbr (in address) = **square**.

sq. abbr (MATH) = **square**.

squabble |'skwɔbl| vi bisticciarsi.

squad |skwɔd| n (MIL) plotone m; (POLICE) squadra.

squadron |'skwɔdrn| n (MIL) squadrone m; (AVIAT, NAUT) squadriglia.

squalid |'skwɔlɪd| a sordido(a).

squall |skwɔ:l| n raffica; burrasca.

squalor |'skwɔlə*| n squallore m.

squander |'skwɔndə*| vt dissipare.

square |skwɛə*| n quadrato; (in town) piazza; (instrument) squadra // a quadrato(a); (honest) onesto(a); (col: ideas, person) d: vecchio stampo // vt (arrange) regolare; (MATH) elevare al quadrato // vi (agree) quadrare; all ~ pari; a ~ meal un pasto abbondante; 2 metres ~ di 2 metri per 2; 1 ~ metre 1 metro quadrato; **~ly** ad diritto; fermamente.

squash |skwɔʃ| n (SPORT) squash m; (Brit: drink): lemon/orange ~ sciroppo di limone/arancia // vt schiacciare.

squat |skwɔt| a tarchiato(a), tozzo(a) // vi accovacciarsi; **~ter** n occupante m/f abusivo(a).

squawk |skwɔ:k| vi emettere strida rauche.

squeak |skwi:k| vi squittire.

squeal |skwi:l| vi strillare.

squeamish |'skwi:mɪʃ| a schizzinoso(a); disgustato(a).

squeeze |skwi:z| n pressione f; (also ECON) stretta // vt premere; (hand, arm) stringere; to ~ out vt spremere.

squelch |skwɛltʃ| vi fare ciac; sguazzare.

squib |skwɪb| n petardo.

squid |skwɪd| n calamaro.

squiggle |'skwɪgl| n ghirigoro.

squint |skwɪnt| vi essere strabico(a) // n: he has a ~ è strabico; to ~ at sth guardare qc di traverso; (quickly) dare un'occhiata a qc.

squire |'skwaɪə*| n (Brit) proprietario terriero.

squirm |skwə:m| vi contorcersi.

squirrel |'skwɪrəl| n scoiattolo.

squirt |skwə:t| vi schizzare; zampillare.

Sr abbr = **senior**.

St abbr = **saint, street**.

stab |stæb| n (with knife etc) pugnalata; (col: try): to have a ~ at (doing) sth provare a fare qc // vt pugnalare.

stable |'steɪbl| n (for horses) scuderia; (for cattle) stalla // a stabile.

stack |stæk| n catasta, pila // vt accatastare, ammucchiare.

stadium |'steɪdɪəm| n stadio.

staff |stɑ:f| n (work force: gen) personale m; (: Brit SCOL) personale insegnante; (: servants) personale di servizio; (MIL) stato maggiore; (stick) bastone m // vt fornire di personale.

stag |stæg| n cervo.

stage |steɪdʒ| n palcoscenico; (profession): the ~ il teatro, la scena;

(*point*) punto; (*platform*) palco // *vt* (*play*) allestire, mettere in scena; (*demonstration*) organizzare; (*fig*: *perform*: *recovery etc*) effettuare; in ~s per gradi; a tappe; **~coach** *n* diligenza; ~ **door** *n* ingresso degli artisti; ~ **manager** *n* direttore *m* di scena.

stagger ['stægə*] *vi* barcollare // *vt* (*person*) sbalordire; (*hours, holidays*) scaglionare.

stagnate [stæg'neɪt] *vi* stagnare.

stag party *n* festa di addio al celibato.

staid [steɪd] *a* posato(a), serio(a).

stain [steɪn] *n* macchia; (*colouring*) colorante *m* // *vt* macchiare; (*wood*) tingere; **~ed glass window** *n* vetrata; **~less** *a* (*steel*) inossidabile; ~ **remover** *n* smacchiatore *m*.

stair [steə*] *n* (*step*) gradino; ~s *npl* (*flight of* ~s) scale *fpl*, scala; on the ~s sulle scale; **~case, ~way** *n* scale *fpl*, scala.

stake [steɪk] *n* palo, piolo; (*BETTING*) puntata, scommessa // *vt* (*bet*) scommettere; (*risk*) rischiare; to be at ~ essere in gioco.

stale [steɪl] *a* (*bread*) raffermo(a), stantio(a); (*beer*) svaporato(a); (*smell*) di chiuso.

stalemate ['steɪlmeɪt] *n* stallo; (*fig*) punto morto.

stalk [stɔ:k] *n* gambo, stelo // *vt* inseguire // *vi* camminare con sussiego.

stall [stɔ:l] *n* bancarella; (*in stable*) box *m inv* di stalla // *vt* (*AUT*) far spegnere // *vi* (*AUT*) spegnersi, fermarsi; (*fig*) temporeggiare; ~s *npl* (*Brit*: *in cinema, theatre*) platea.

stallion ['stæljən] *n* stallone *m*.

stalwart ['stɔ:lwət] *n* membro fidato.

stamina ['stæmɪnə] *n* vigore *m*, resistenza.

stammer ['stæmə*] *n* balbuzie *f* // *vi* balbettare.

stamp [stæmp] *n* (*postage* ~) francobollo; (*implement*) timbro; (*mark, also fig*) marchio, impronta; (*on document*) bollo; timbro // *vi* (*also*: ~ one's foot) battere il piede // *vt* battere; (*letter*) affrancare; (*mark with a* ~) timbrare; ~ **album** *n* album *m inv* per francobolli; ~ **collecting** *n* filatelia.

stampede [stæm'pi:d] *n* fuggi fuggi *m inv*.

stance [stæns] *n* posizione *f*.

stand [stænd] *n* (*position*) posizione *f*; (*MIL*) resistenza; (*structure*) supporto, sostegno; (*at exhibition*) stand *m inv*; (*in shop*) banco; (*at market*) bancarella; (*booth*) chiosco; (*SPORT*) tribuna // *vb* (*pt, pp stood*) *vi* stare in piedi; (*rise*) alzarsi in piedi; (*be placed*) trovarsi // *vt* (*place*) mettere, porre; (*tolerate, withstand*) resistere, sopportare; to **make** a ~ prendere

posizione; to ~ for parliament (*Brit*) presentarsi come candidato (per il parlamento); to ~ by *vi* (*be ready*) tenersi pronto(a) // *vt fus* (*opinion*) sostenere; to ~ down *vi* (*withdraw*) ritirarsi; to ~ for *vt fus* (*signify*) rappresentare, significare; (*tolerate*) sopportare, tollerare; to ~ in for *vt fus* sostituire; to ~ out *vi* (*be prominent*) spiccare; to ~ up *vi* (*rise*) alzarsi in piedi; to ~ up for *vt fus* difendere; to ~ up to *vt fus* tener testa a, resistere a.

standard ['stændəd] *n* modello, standard *m inv*; (*level*) livello; (*flag*) stendardo // *a* (*size etc*) normale, standard *inv*; ~s *npl* (*morals*) principi *mpl*, valori *mpl*; ~ **lamp** *n* (*Brit*) lampada a stelo; ~ **of living** *n* livello di vita.

stand-by ['stændbaɪ] *n* riserva, sostituto; to be on ~ (*gen*) tenersi pronto(a); (*doctor*) essere di guardia; ~ **ticket** *n* (*AVIAT*) biglietto senza garanzia.

stand-in ['stændɪn] *n* sostituto/a; (*CINEMA*) controfigura.

standing ['stændɪŋ] *a* diritto(a), in piedi // *n* rango, condizione *f*, posizione *f*; of many years' ~ che esiste da molti anni; ~ **order** *n* (*Brit*: *at bank*) ordine *m* di pagamento (permanente); ~ **orders** *npl* (*MIL*) regolamento; ~ **room** *n* posto all'impiedi.

standoffish [stænd'ɔfɪʃ] *a* scostante, freddo(a).

standpoint ['stændpɔɪnt] *n* punto di vista.

standstill ['stændstɪl] *n*: at a ~ fermo(a); (*fig*) a un punto morto; to come to a ~ fermarsi; giungere a un punto morto.

stank [stæŋk] *pt of* **stink**.

staple ['steɪpl] *n* (*for papers*) graffetta // *a* (*food etc*) di base // *vt* cucire; ~r *n* cucitrice *f*.

star [stɑ:*] *n* stella; (*celebrity*) divo/a; (*principal actor*) vedette *f inv* // *vi*: to ~ (in) essere il (*or* la) protagonista (di) // *vt* (*CINEMA*) essere interpretato(a) da.

starboard ['stɑ:bəd] *n* dritta.

starch [stɑ:tʃ] *n* amido.

stardom ['stɑ:dəm] *n* celebrità.

stare [steə*] *n* sguardo fisso // *vi*: to ~ at fissare.

starfish ['stɑ:fɪʃ] *n* stella di mare.

stark [stɑ:k] *a* (*bleak*) desolato(a) // *ad*: ~ **naked** completamente nudo(a).

starling ['stɑ:lɪŋ] *n* storno.

starry ['stɑ:rɪ] *a* stellato(a); **~-eyed** *a* (*innocent*) ingenuo(a).

start [stɑ:t] *n* inizio; (*of race*) partenza; (*sudden movement*) sobbalzo // *vt* cominciare, iniziare // *vi* cominciare; (*on journey*) partire, mettersi in viaggio; (*jump*) sobbalzare; to ~ **doing** *or* to **do sth** (in)cominciare a fare qc; to ~ **off**

vi cominciare; (*leave*) partire; **to ~ up**
vi cominciare; (*car*) avviarsi // *vt*
iniziare; (*car*) avviare; **~er** *n* (*AUT*)
motorino d'avviamento; (*SPORT: official*)
starter *m inv*; (: *runner, horse*) partente
m/f; (*Brit CULIN*) primo piatto; **~ing
point** *n* punto di partenza.

startle |'stɑ:tl| *vt* far trasalire.

starvation |stɑ:'veɪʃən| *n* fame *f*, inedia.

starve |stɑ:v| *vi* morire di fame; soffrire
la fame // *vt* far morire di fame,
affamare.

state |steɪt| *n* stato // *vt* dichiarare,
affermare; annunciare; **the S~s** (*USA*)
gli Stati Uniti; **to be in a ~** essere
agitato(a); **~ly** *a* maestoso(a),
imponente; **~ment** *n* dichiarazione *f*;
(*LAW*) deposizione *f*; **~sman** *n* statista
m.

static |'stætɪk| *n* (*RADIO*) scariche *fpl* // *a*
statico(a).

station |'steɪʃən| *n* stazione *f*; (*rank*)
rango, condizione *f* // *vt* collocare, disporre.

stationary |'steɪʃənərɪ| *a* fermo(a),
immobile.

stationer |'steɪʃənə*| *n* cartolaio/a; **~'s
(shop)** *n* cartoleria; **~y** *n* articoli *mpl*
di cancelleria.

station master *n* (*RAIL*) capostazione
m.

station wagon *n* (*US*) giardinetta.

statistic |stə'tɪstɪk| *n* statistica; **~s** *n*
(*science*) statistica.

statue |'stætju:| *n* statua.

status |'steɪtəs| *n* posizione *f*, condizione *f*
sociale; prestigio; stato; **~ symbol** *n*
simbolo di prestigio.

statute |'stætju:t| *n* legge *f*; **~s** *npl* (*of
club etc*) statuto; **statutory** *a*
stabilito(a) dalla legge, statutario(a).

staunch |stɔ:ntʃ| *a* fidato(a), leale.

stave |steɪv| *n* (*MUS*) rigo // *vt*: **to ~ off**
(*attack*) respingere; (*threat*) evitare.

stay |steɪ| *n* (*period of time*) soggiorno,
permanenza // *vi* rimanere; (*reside*)
alloggiare, stare; (*spend some time*)
trattenersi, soggiornare; **to ~ put** non
muoversi; **to ~ with friends** stare presso
amici; **to ~ the night** passare la notte;
to ~ behind *vi* restare indietro; **to ~
in** *vi* (*at home*) stare in casa; **to ~ on**
vi restare, rimanere; **to ~ out** *vi* (*of
house*) rimanere fuori (di casa); **to ~
up** *vi* (*at night*) rimanere alzato(a);
~ing power *n* capacità di resistenza.

stead |stɛd| *n*: **in sb's ~** al posto di qn;
to stand sb in good ~ essere utile a qn.

steadfast |'stɛdfɑ:st| *a* fermo(a),
risoluto(a).

steadily |'stɛdɪlɪ| *ad* continuamente;
(*walk*) con passo sicuro.

steady |'stɛdɪ| *a* stabile, solido(a),
fermo(a); (*regular*) costante; (*person*)
calmo(a), tranquillo(a) // *vt* stabilizzare;

calmare; **to ~ oneself** ritrovare l'equilibrio.

steak |steɪk| *n* (*meat*) bistecca; (*fish*)
trancia.

steal |sti:l|, *pt* **stole**, *pp* **stolen** *vt, vi*
rubare.

stealth |stɛlθ| *n*: **by ~** furtivamente; **~y**
a furtivo(a).

steam |sti:m| *n* vapore *m* // *vt* trattare
con vapore; (*CULIN*) cuocere a vapore //
vi fumare; (*ship*): **to ~ along** filare; **~
engine** *n* macchina a vapore; (*RAIL*)
locomotiva a vapore; **~er** *n* piroscafo,
vapore *m*; **~roller** *n* rullo compressore;
~ship *n* = **~er**; **~y** *a* (*room*)
pieno(a) di vapore; (*window*)
appannato(a).

steel |sti:l| *n* acciaio // *cpd* di acciaio;
~works *n* acciaieria.

steep |sti:p| *a* ripido(a), scosceso(a);
(*price*) eccessivo(a) // *vt* inzuppare;
(*washing*) mettere a mollo.

steeple |'sti:pl| *n* campanile *m*.

steer |stɪə*| *n* manzo // *vt* (*ship*)
governare; (*car*) guidare // *vi* (*NAUT:
person*) governare; (: *ship*) rispondere
al timone; (*car*) guidarsi; **~ing** *n* (*AUT*)
sterzo; **~ing wheel** *n* volante *m*.

stem |stɛm| *n* (*of flower, plant*) stelo; (*of
tree*) fusto; (*of glass*) gambo; (*of fruit,
leaf*) picciolo // *vt* contenere, arginare;
to ~ from *vt fus* provenire da, derivare
da.

stench |stɛntʃ| *n* puzzo, fetore *m*.

stencil |'stɛnsl| *n* (*of metal, cardboard*)
stampino, mascherina; (*in typing*) matrice *f*.

stenographer |stɛ'nɔgrəfə*| *n* (*US*)
stenografo/a.

step |stɛp| *n* passo; (*stair*) gradino,
scalino; (*action*) mossa, azione *f* // *vi*: **to
~ forward** fare un passo avanti; **~s** *npl*
(*Brit*) = **stepladder**; **to be in/out of ~
(with)** stare/non stare al passo (con); **to
~ down** *vi* (*fig*) ritirarsi; **to ~ off** *vt
fus* scendere da; **to ~ up** *vt*
aumentare; intensificare; **~brother** *n*
fratellastro; **~daughter** *n* figliastra;
~father *n* patrigno; **~ladder** *n* scala a
libretto; **~mother** *n* matrigna; **~ping
stone** *n* pietra di un guado; (*fig*)
trampolino; **~sister** *n* sorellastra;
~son *n* figliastro.

stereo |'stɛrɪəʊ| *n* (*system*) sistema *m*
stereofonico; (*record player*) stereo *m
inv* // *a* (*also*: **~phonic**) stereofonico(a).

sterile |'stɛraɪl| *a* sterile; **sterilize**
|'stɛrɪlaɪz| *vt* sterilizzare.

sterling |'stɜ:lɪŋ| *a* (*gold, silver*) di
buona lega; (*fig*) autentico(a),
genuino(a) // *n* (*ECON*) (lira) sterlina; **a
pound ~** una lira sterlina.

stern |stɜ:n| *a* severo(a) // *n* (*NAUT*)
poppa.

stew |stju:| *n* stufato // *vt, vi* cuocere in

umido.

steward ['stju:əd] n (AVIAT, NAUT, RAIL) steward m inv; (in club etc) dispensiere m; **~ess** n assistente f di volo, hostess f inv.

stick [stɪk] n bastone m; (of rhubarb, celery) gambo // vb (pt, pp **stuck**) vt (glue) attaccare; (thrust): to ~ sth into conficcare or piantare or infiggere qc in; (col: put) ficcare; (col: tolerate) sopportare // vi conficcarsi; tenere; (remain) restare, rimanere; **to ~ out, to ~ up** vi sporgere, spuntare; **to ~ up for** vt fus difendere; **~er** n cartellino adesivo; **~ing plaster** n cerotto adesivo.

stickler ['stɪklə*] n: to be a ~ for essere pignolo(a) su, tenere molto a.

stick-up ['stɪkʌp] n rapina a mano armata.

sticky ['stɪkɪ] a attaccaticcio(a), vischioso(a); (label) adesivo(a).

stiff [stɪf] a rigido(a), duro(a); (muscle) legato(a), indolenzito(a); (difficult) difficile, arduo(a); (cold) freddo(a), formale; (strong) forte; (high: price) molto alto(a); **~en** vt irrigidire; rinforzare // vi irrigidirsi; indurirsi; ~ **neck** n torcicollo.

stifle ['staɪfl] vt soffocare.

stigma ['stɪgmə] n (BOT, fig) stigma m; **~ta** [stɪg'mɑːtə] npl (REL) stigmate fpl.

stile [staɪl] n cavalcasiepe m; cavalcasteccato.

stiletto [stɪ'letəʊ] n (Brit: also: ~ **heel**) tacco a spillo.

still [stɪl] a fermo(a); silenzioso(a) // ad (up to this time, even) ancora; (nonetheless) tuttavia, ciò nonostante; **~born** a nato(a) morto(a); ~ **life** n natura morta.

stilt [stɪlt] n trampolo; (pile) palo.

stilted ['stɪltɪd] a freddo(a), formale; artificiale.

stimulate ['stɪmjʊleɪt] vt stimolare.

stimulus, pl **stimuli** ['stɪmjʊləs, 'stɪmjʊlaɪ] n stimolo.

sting [stɪŋ] n puntura; (organ) pungiglione m // vt (pt, pp **stung**) pungere.

stingy ['stɪndʒɪ] a spilorcio(a), tirchio(a).

stink [stɪŋk] n fetore m, puzzo // vi (pt **stank**, pp **stunk**) puzzare; **~ing** a (fig: col): a **~ing** ... uno schifo di ..., un(a) maledetto(a) ... .

stint [stɪnt] n lavoro, compito // vi: to ~ **on** lesinare su.

stir [stə:*] n agitazione f, clamore m // vt rimescolare; (move) smuovere, agitare // vi muoversi; **to ~ up** vt provocare, suscitare.

stirrup ['stɪrəp] n staffa.

stitch [stɪtʃ] n (SEWING) punto; (KNITTING) maglia; (MED) punto (di sutura); (pain) fitta // vt cucire, attaccare; suturare.

stoat [stəʊt] n ermellino.

stock [stɔk] n riserva, provvista; (COMM) giacenza, stock m inv; (AGR) bestiame m; (CULIN) brodo; (FINANCE) titoli mpl, azioni fpl // a (fig: reply etc) consueto(a); classico(a) // vt (have in stock) avere, vendere; **well-~ed** ben fornito(a); **in ~** in magazzino; **out of ~** esaurito(a); **to take ~ of** (fig) fare il punto di; **~s and shares** valori mpl di borsa; **to ~ up** vi: to ~ up (with) fare provvista (di).

stockbroker ['stɔkbrəʊkə*] n agente m di cambio.

stock cube n (Brit) dado.

stock exchange n Borsa (valori).

stocking ['stɔkɪŋ] n calza.

stockist ['stɔkɪst] n (Brit) fornitore m.

stock: ~ **market** n Borsa, mercato finanziario; ~ **phrase** n cliché m inv; **~pile** n riserva // vt accumulare riserve di; **~taking** n (Brit COMM) inventario.

stocky ['stɔkɪ] a tarchiato(a), tozzo(a).

stodgy ['stɔdʒɪ] a pesante, indigesto(a).

stoke [stəʊk] vt alimentare.

stole [stəʊl] pt of **steal** // n stola.

stolen ['stəʊln] pp of **steal**.

stolid ['stɔlɪd] a impassibile.

stomach ['stʌmək] n stomaco; (abdomen) ventre m // vt sopportare, digerire; ~ **ache** n mal m di stomaco.

stone [stəʊn] n pietra; (pebble) sasso, ciottolo; (in fruit) nocciolo; (MED) calcolo; (Brit: weight) = 6.348 kg.; 14 libbre // cpd di pietra // vt lapidare; ~-**cold** a gelido(a); ~-**deaf** a sordo(a) come una campana; **~work** n muratura.

stood [stʊd] pt, pp of **stand**.

stool [stu:l] n sgabello.

stoop [stu:p] vi (also: have a ~) avere una curvatura; (bend) chinarsi, curvarsi.

stop [stɔp] n arresto; (stopping place) fermata; (in punctuation) punto // vt arrestare, fermare; (break off) interrompere; (also: put a ~ to) porre fine a // vi fermarsi; (rain, noise etc) cessare, finire; **to ~ doing sth** cessare or finire di fare qc; **to ~ dead** fermarsi di colpo; **to ~ off** vi sostare brevemente; **to ~ up** vt (hole) chiudere, turare; **~gap** n (person) tappabuchi m/f inv; (measure) ripiego; **~lights** npl (AUT) stop mpl; **~over** n breve sosta; (AVIAT) scalo.

stoppage ['stɔpɪdʒ] n arresto, fermata; (of pay) trattenuta; (strike) interruzione f del lavoro.

stopper ['stɔpə*] n tappo.

stop press n ultimissime fpl.

stopwatch ['stɔpwɔtʃ] n cronometro.

storage ['stɔːrɪdʒ] n immagazzinamento; (COMPUT) memoria; ~ **heater** n radiatore m elettrico che accumula calore.

store |stɔ:ᵉ| n provvista, riserva; (depot) deposito; (Brit: department ~) grande magazzino; (US: shop) negozio // vt immagazzinare; ~s npl (provisions) rifornimenti mpl, scorte fpl; **to ~ up** vt mettere in serbo, conservare; ~**room** n dispensa.

storey, (US) **story** |'stɔ:rɪ| n piano.

stork |stɔ:k| n cicogna.

storm |stɔ:m| n tempesta, temporale m, burrasca; uragano // vi (fig) infuriarsi // vt prendere d'assalto; ~**y** a tempestoso(a), burrascoso(a).

story |'stɔ:rɪ| n storia; favola; racconto; (US) = **storey**; ~**book** n libro di racconti.

stout |staut| a solido(a), robusto(a); (brave) coraggioso(a); (fat) corpulento(a), grasso(a) // n birra scura.

stove |stəuv| n (for cooking) fornello; (: small) fornelletto; (for heating) stufa.

stow |stəu| vt mettere via; ~**away** n passeggero/a clandestino(a).

straddle |'strædl| vt stare a cavalcioni di.

straggle |'strægl| vi crescere (or estendersi) disordinatamente; trascinarsi; rimanere indietro; ~**r** n sbandato/a.

straight |streɪt| a dritto(a); (frank) onesto(a), franco(a) // ad diritto; (drink) liscio // n: **the ~ la linea retta; (RAIL) il rettilineo; (SPORT) la dirittura d'arrivo; **to put** or **get ~** mettere in ordine, mettere ordine in; ~ **away, ~ off** (at once) immediatamente; ~**en** vt (also: ~**en out**) raddrizzare; ~**faced** a impassibile, imperturbabile; ~**forward** a semplice; onesto(a), franco(a).

strain |streɪn| n (TECH) sollecitazione f; (physical) sforzo; (mental) tensione f; (MED) strappo; distorsione f; (streak, trace) tendenza; elemento // vt tendere; (muscle) sforzare; (ankle) storcere; (friendship, marriage) mettere a dura prova; (filter) colare, filtrare // vi sforzarsi; ~**s** npl (MUS) note fpl; ~**ed** a (laugh etc) forzato(a); (relations) teso(a); ~**er** n passino, colino.

strait |streɪt| n (GEO) stretto; ~**jacket** n camicia di forza; ~**-laced** a bacchettone(a).

strand |strænd| n (of thread) filo; ~**ed** a nei guai; senza mezzi di trasporto.

strange |streɪndʒ| a (not known) sconosciuto(a); (odd) strano(a), bizzarro(a); ~**r** n sconosciuto/a; estraneo/a.

strangle |'stræŋgl| vt strangolare; ~**hold** n (fig) stretta (mortale).

strap |stræp| n cinghia; (of slip, dress) spallina, bretella // vt legare con una cinghia; (child etc) punire (con una cinghia).

strategic |strə'ti:dʒɪk| a strategico(a).

strategy |'strætɪdʒɪ| n strategia.

straw |strɔ:| n paglia; (drinking ~) cannuccia; **that's the last ~!** è la goccia che fa traboccare il vaso!

strawberry |'strɔ:bərɪ| n fragola.

stray |streɪ| a (animal) randagio(a) // vi perdersi; ~ **bullet** n proiettile m vagante.

streak |stri:k| n striscia; (fig: of madness etc): **a ~** of una vena di // vt striare, screziare // vi: **to ~ past** passare come un fulmine.

stream |stri:m| n ruscello; corrente f; (of people) fiume m // vt (SCOL) dividere in livelli di rendimento // vi scorrere; **to ~** in/out entrare/uscire a fiotti.

streamer |'stri:məᵉ| n (of paper) stella filante.

streamlined |'stri:mlaɪnd| a aerodinamico(a), affusolato(a); (fig) razionalizzato(a).

street |stri:t| n strada, via // cpd stradale, di strada; ~**car** n (US) tram m inv; ~ **lamp** n lampione m; ~ **plan** n pianta (di una città); ~**wise** a (col) esperto(a) dei bassifondi.

strength |streŋθ| n forza; (of girder, knot etc) resistenza, solidità; ~**en** vt rinforzare; fortificare; consolidare.

strenuous |'strenjuəs| a vigoroso(a), energico(a); (tiring) duro(a), pesante.

stress |stres| n (force, pressure) pressione f; (mental strain) tensione f; (accent) accento // vt insistere su, sottolineare.

stretch |stretʃ| n (of sand etc) distesa // vi stirarsi; (extend): **to ~ to** or **as far as** estendersi fino a // vt tendere, allungare; (spread) distendere; (fig) spingere (al massimo); **to ~ out** vi allungarsi, estendersi // vt (arm etc) allungare, tendere; (to spread) distendere.

stretcher |'stretʃəᵉ| n barella, lettiga.

strewn |stru:n| a: ~ **with** cosparso(a) di.

stricken |'strɪkən| a (person) provato(a); (city, industry etc) colpito(a); ~ **with** (disease etc) colpito(a) da.

strict |strɪkt| a (severe) rigido(a), severo(a); (precise) preciso(a), stretto(a).

stride |straɪd| n passo lungo // vi (pt **strode**, pp **stridden** |strəud, 'strɪdn|) camminare a grandi passi.

strife |straɪf| n conflitto; litigi mpl.

strike |straɪk| n sciopero; (of oil etc) scoperta; (attack) attacco // vb (pt, pp **struck**) vt colpire; (oil etc) scoprire, trovare // vi far sciopero, scioperare; (attack) attaccare; (clock) suonare; **on ~** (workers) in sciopero; **to ~ a match** accendere un fiammifero; **to ~ down** vt (fig) atterrare; **to ~ out** vt depennare; **to ~ up** vt (MUS) attaccare; **to ~ up a friendship** with fare amicizia con; ~**r** n scioperante m/f; (SPORT) attaccante m; **striking** a che colpisce.

string |strɪŋ| n spago; (row) fila; sequenza; catena; (MUS) corda // vt (pt, pp **strung**): to ~ out disporre di fianco; to ~ together (words, ideas) mettere insieme; the ~s npl (MUS) gli archi; to pull ~s for sb (fig) raccomandare qn; ~ **bean** n fagiolino; ~**(ed) instrument** n (MUS) strumento a corda.

stringent ['strɪndʒənt] a rigoroso(a); (reasons, arguments) stringente, impellente.

strip |strɪp| n striscia // vt spogliare; (also: ~ down: machine) smontare // vi spogliarsi; ~ **cartoon** n fumetto.

stripe [straɪp] n striscia, riga; ~**d** a a strisce or righe.

strip lighting n illuminazione f al neon.

stripper ['strɪpə*] n spogliarellista.

striptease ['strɪptiːz] n spogliarello.

strive, pt **strove**, pp **striven** |straɪv, strəuv, 'strɪvn| vi: to ~ to do sforzarsi di fare.

strode [strəud] pt of **stride**.

stroke [strəuk] n colpo; (MED) colpo apoplettico; (caress) carezza // vt accarezzare; at a ~ in un attimo.

stroll [strəul] n giretto, passeggiatina // vi andare a spasso; ~**er** n (US) passeggino.

strong [strɒŋ] a (gen) forte; (sturdy: table, fabric etc) solido(a); they are 50 ~ sono in 50; ~**box** n cassaforte f; ~**hold** n fortezza, roccaforte f; ~**ly** ad fortemente, con forza; energicamente; vivamente; ~**room** n camera di sicurezza.

strove [strəuv] pt of **strive**.

struck [strʌk] pt, pp of **strike**.

structural ['strʌktʃərəl| a strutturale; (CONSTR) di costruzione; di struttura.

structure ['strʌktʃə*] n struttura; (building) costruzione f, fabbricato.

struggle ['strʌgl] n lotta // vi lottare.

strum [strʌm] vt (guitar) strimpellare.

strung [strʌŋ] pt, pp of **string**.

strut [strʌt] n sostegno, supporto // vi pavoneggiarsi.

stub [stʌb] n mozzicone m; (of ticket etc) matrice f, talloncino // vt: to ~ one's toe urtare or sbattere il dito del piede; **to ~ out** vt schiacciare.

stubble ['stʌbl] n stoppia; (on chin) barba ispida.

stubborn ['stʌbən] a testardo(a), ostinato(a).

stuck [stʌk] pt, pp of **stick** // a (jammed) bloccato(a); ~**up** a presuntuoso(a).

stud [stʌd] n bottoncino; borchia; (of horses) scuderia, allevamento di cavalli; (also: ~ horse) stallone m // vt (fig): ~ded with tempestato(a) di.

student ['stjuːdənt] n studente/essa // cpd studentesco(a); universitario(a); degli studenti; ~ **driver** n (US) conducente

m/f principiante.

studio ['stjuːdɪəu] n studio; ~ **flat**, (US) ~ **apartment** n appartamento monolocale.

studious ['stjuːdɪəs] a studioso(a); (studied) studiato(a), voluto(a); ~**ly** ad (carefully) deliberatamente, di proposito.

study ['stʌdɪ] n studio // vt studiare; esaminare // vi studiare.

stuff [stʌf] n cosa, roba; (belongings) cose fpl, roba; (substance) sostanza, materiale m // vt imbottire; (CULIN) farcire; ~**ing** n imbottitura; (CULIN) ripieno; ~**y** a (room) mal ventilato(a), senz'aria; (ideas) antiquato(a).

stumble ['stʌmbl] vi inciampare; **to ~ across** (fig) imbattersi in; **stumbling block** n ostacolo, scoglio.

stump [stʌmp] n ceppo; (of limb) moncone m // vt sconcertare, lasciare perplesso(a).

stun [stʌn] vt stordire; (amaze) sbalordire.

stung [stʌŋ] pt, pp of **sting**.

stunk [stʌŋk] pp of **stink**.

stunt [stʌnt] n bravata; trucco pubblicitario; (AVIAT) acrobazia // vt arrestare; ~**ed** a stentato(a), rachitico(a); ~**man** n cascatore m.

stupefy ['stjuːpɪfaɪ] vt stordire; intontire; (fig) stupire.

stupendous [stjuː'pɛndəs] a stupendo(a), meraviglioso(a).

stupid ['stjuːpɪd] a stupido(a); ~**ity** [-'pɪdɪtɪ] n stupidità f inv, stupidaggine f.

stupor ['stjuːpə*] n torpore m.

sturdy ['stəːdɪ] a robusto(a), vigoroso(a); solido(a).

sturgeon ['stəːdʒən] n storione m.

stutter ['stʌtə*] n balbuzie f // vi balbettare.

sty [staɪ] n (of pigs) porcile m.

stye [staɪ] n (MED) orzaiolo.

style [staɪl] n stile m; (distinction) eleganza, classe f; **stylish** a elegante; **stylist** n (hair stylist) parrucchiere/a.

stylus ['staɪləs] n (of record player) puntina.

suave [swɑːv] a untuoso(a).

sub... [sʌb] prefix sub..., sotto...; ~**conscious** a, n subcosciente (m); ~**contract** vt subappaltare.

subdue [səb'djuː] vt sottomettere, soggiogare; ~**d** a pacato(a); (light) attenuato(a); (person) poco esuberante.

subject n ['sʌbdʒɪkt] soggetto; (citizen etc) cittadino/a; (SCOL) materia // vt [səb'dʒɛkt]: to ~ to sottomettere a; esporre a; to be ~ to (law) essere sottomesso(a) a; (disease) essere soggetto(a) a; ~**ive** [-'dʒɛktɪv] a soggettivo(a); ~ **matter** n argomento; contenuto.

subjunctive [səb'dʒʌŋktɪv] a

congiuntivo(a) // *n* congiuntivo.

sublet |sʌb'lɛt| *vt* subaffittare.

submachine gun |'sʌbmə'ʃiːn-| *n* mitra *m inv*.

submarine |sʌbmə'riːn| *n* sommergibile *m*.

submerge |səb'məːdʒ| *vt* sommergere; immergere // *vi* immergersi.

submission |səb'mɪʃən| *n* sottomissione *f*.

submissive |səb'mɪsɪv| *a* remissivo(a).

submit |səb'mɪt| *vt* sottomettere // *vi* sottomettersi.

subnormal |sʌb'nɔːməl| *a* subnormale.

subordinate |sə'bɔːdɪnət| *a*, *n* subordinato(a).

subpoena |səb'piːnə| *n* (*LAW*) citazione *f*, mandato di comparizione.

subscribe |səb'skraɪb| *vi* contribuire; **to ~ to** (*opinion*) approvare, condividere; (*fund*) sottoscrivere; (*newspaper*) abbonarsi a; essere abbonato(a) a; **~r** *n* (*to periodical, telephone*) abbonato/a.

subscription |səb'skrɪpʃən| *n* sottoscrizione *f*; abbonamento.

subsequent |'sʌbsɪkwənt| *a* successivo(a), seguente; conseguente; **~ly** *ad* in seguito, successivamente.

subside |səb'saɪd| *vi* cedere, abbassarsi; (*flood*) decrescere; (*wind*) calmarsi; **~nce** |-'saɪdns| *n* cedimento, abbassamento.

subsidiary |səb'sɪdɪərɪ| *a* sussidiario(a); accessorio(a) // *n* filiale *f*.

subsidize |'sʌbsɪdaɪz| *vt* sovvenzionare.

subsidy |'sʌbsɪdɪ| *n* sovvenzione *f*.

subsistence |səb'sɪstəns| *n* esistenza; mezzi *mpl* di sostentamento.

substance |'sʌbstəns| *n* sostanza; (*fig*) essenza.

substantial |səb'stænʃl| *a* solido(a); (*amount, progress etc*) notevole; (*meal*) sostanzioso(a).

substantiate |səb'stænʃɪeɪt| *vt* comprovare.

substitute |'sʌbstɪtjuːt| *n* (*person*) sostituto/a; (*thing*) succedaneo, surrogato // *vt*: **to ~** sth/sb **for** sostituire qc/qn a.

subterfuge |'sʌbtəfjuːdʒ| *n* sotterfugio.

subterranean |sʌbtə'reɪnɪən| *a* sotterraneo(a).

subtitle |'sʌbtaɪtl| *n* (*CINEMA*) sottotitolo.

subtle |'sʌtl| *a* sottile.

subtotal |sʌb'təʊtl| *n* somma parziale.

subtract |səb'trækt| *vt* sottrarre; **~ion** |-'trækʃən| *n* sottrazione *f*.

suburb |'sʌbəːb| *n* sobborgo; **the ~s** la periferia; **~an** |sə'bəːbən| *a* suburbano(a); **~ia** *n* periferia, sobborghi *mpl*.

subversive |sʌb'vəːsɪv| *a* sovversivo(a).

subway |'sʌbweɪ| *n* (*US*: *underground*) metropolitana; (*Brit*: *underpass*) sottopassaggio.

succeed |sək'siːd| *vi* riuscire; avere successo // *vt* succedere a; **to ~ in doing** riuscire a fare; **~ing** *a* (*following*) successivo(a).

success |sək'sɛs| *n* successo; **~ful** *a* (*venture*) coronato(a) da successo, riuscito(a); **to be ~ful** (**in doing**) riuscire (a fare); **~fully** *ad* con successo.

succession |sək'sɛʃən| *n* successione *f*.

successive |sək'sɛsɪv| *a* successivo(a); consecutivo(a).

succumb |sə'kʌm| *vi* soccombere.

such |sʌtʃ| *a* tale; (*of that kind*): **~ a book** un tale libro, un libro del genere; **~ books** tali libri, libri del genere; (*so much*): **~ courage** tanto coraggio // *ad* talmente, così; **~ a long trip** un viaggio così lungo; **~ good books** libri così buoni; **~ a lot of** talmente *or* così tanto(a); **~ as** (*like*) come; **a noise ~ as** to un rumore tale da; **as ~** *ad* come or in quanto tale; **~-and-~** *a* tale (*after noun*).

suck |sʌk| *vt* succhiare; (*breast, bottle*) poppare; **~er** *n* (*ZOOL, TECH*) ventosa; (*BOT*) pollone *m*; (*col*) gonzo/a, babbeo/a.

suction |'sʌkʃən| *n* succhiamento; (*TECH*) aspirazione *f*.

sudden |'sʌdn| *a* improvviso(a); **all of a ~** improvvisamente, all'improvviso; **~ly** *ad* bruscamente, improvvisamente, di colpo.

suds |sʌdz| *npl* schiuma (di sapone).

sue |suː| *vt* citare in giudizio.

suede |sweɪd| *n* pelle *f* scamosciata // *cpd* scamosciato(a).

suet |'suɪt| *n* grasso di rognone.

suffer |'sʌfə*| *vt* soffrire, patire; (*bear*) sopportare, tollerare // *vi* soffrire; **~er** *n* malato/a; **~ing** *n* sofferenza.

suffice |sə'faɪs| *vi* essere sufficiente, bastare.

sufficient |sə'fɪʃənt| *a* sufficiente; **~ money** abbastanza soldi; **~ly** *ad* sufficientemente, abbastanza.

suffocate |'sʌfəkeɪt| *vi* (*have difficulty breathing*) soffocare; (*die through lack of air*) asfissiare.

suffused |sə'fjuːzd| *a*: **~ with** (*colour*) tinto(a) di; **the room was ~ with light** nella stanza c'era una luce soffusa.

sugar |'ʃugə*| *n* zucchero // *vt* zuccherare; **~ beet** *n* barbabietola da zucchero; **~ cane** *n* canna da zucchero; **~y** *a* zuccherino(a), dolce; (*fig*) sdolcinato(a).

suggest |sə'dʒɛst| *vt* proporre, suggerire; indicare; **~ion** |-'dʒɛstʃən| *n* suggerimento, proposta.

suicide |'suɪsaɪd| *n* (*person*) suicida *m/f*; (*act*) suicidio.

suit |suːt| *n* (*man's*) vestito; (*woman's*) completo, tailleur *m inv*; (*CARDS*) seme *m*, colore *m* // *vt* andar bene a *or* per;

essere adatto(a) a or per; (adapt): to ~ sth to adattare qc a; ~**able** a adatto(a); appropriato(a); ~**ably** ad (dress) in modo adatto; (thank) adeguatamente.

suitcase ['su:tkeɪs] n valigia.

suite [swi:t] n (of rooms) appartamento; (MUS) suite f inv; (furniture): bedroom/dining room ~ arredo or mobilia per la camera da letto/sala da pranzo.

suitor ['su:tə*] n corteggiatore m, spasimante m.

sulfur ['sʌlfə*] n (US) = sulphur.

sulk [sʌlk] vi fare il broncio; ~**y** a imbronciato(a).

sullen ['sʌlən] a scontroso(a); cupo(a).

sulphur, (US) **sulfur** ['sʌlfə*] n zolfo.

sultana [sʌl'tɑ:nə] n (fruit) uva (secca) sultanina.

sultry ['sʌltrɪ] a afoso(a).

sum [sʌm] n somma; (SCOL etc) addizione f; **to ~ up** vt, vi riassumere.

summarize ['sʌməraɪz] vt riassumere, riepilogare.

summary ['sʌmərɪ] n riassunto // a (justice) sommario(a).

summer ['sʌmə*] n estate f // cpd d'estate, estivo(a); ~**house** n (in garden) padiglione m; ~**time** n (season) estate f; ~ **time** n (by clock) ora legale (estiva).

summit ['sʌmɪt] n cima, sommità; (POL) vertice m.

summon ['sʌmən] vt chiamare, convocare; **to ~ up** vt raccogliere, fare appello a; ~**s** n ordine m di comparizione // vt citare.

sump [sʌmp] n (Brit AUT) coppa dell'olio.

sumptuous ['sʌmptjuəs] a sontuoso(a).

sun [sʌn] n sole m; **in the ~** al sole; ~**bathe** vi prendere un bagno di sole; ~**burn** n abbronzatura; (painful) scottatura; ~ **cream** n crema solare.

Sunday ['sʌndɪ] n domenica; ~ **school** n ≈ scuola di catechismo.

sundial ['sʌndaɪəl] n meridiana.

sundown ['sʌndaun] n tramonto.

sundry ['sʌndrɪ] a vari(e), diversi(e); **all and ~** tutti quanti; **sundries** npl articoli diversi, cose diverse.

sunflower ['sʌnflauə*] n girasole m.

sung [sʌŋ] pp of **sing**.

sunglasses ['sʌnglɑ:sɪz] npl occhiali mpl da sole.

sunk [sʌŋk] pp of **sink**.

sun: ~**light** n (luce f del) sole m; ~**ny** a assolato(a), soleggiato(a); (fig) allegro(a), felice; ~**rise** n levata del sole, alba; ~ **roof** n (AUT) tetto apribile; ~**set** n tramonto; ~**shade** n parasole m; ~**shine** n (luce f del) sole m; ~**stroke** n insolazione f, colpo di sole; ~**tan** n abbronzatura; ~**tan oil** n olio solare.

super ['su:pə*] a (col) fantastico(a).

superannuation [su:pərænju'eɪʃən] n contributi mpl pensionistici; pensione f.

superb [su:'pə:b] a magnifico(a).

supercilious [su:pə'sɪlɪəs] a sprezzante, sdegnoso(a).

superficial [su:pə'fɪʃəl] a superficiale.

superhuman [su:pə'hju:mən] a sovrumano(a).

superimpose ['su:pərɪm'pəuz] vt sovrapporre.

superintendent [su:pərɪn'tendənt] n direttore/trice; (POLICE) ≈ commissario (capo).

superior [su'pɪərɪə*] a, n superiore (m/f); ~**ity** [-'ɔrɪtɪ] n superiorità.

superlative [su'pə:lətɪv] a superlativo(a), supremo(a) // n (LING) superlativo.

superman ['su:pəmæn] n superuomo.

supermarket ['su:pəmɑ:kɪt] n supermercato.

supernatural [su:pə'nætʃərəl] a soprannaturale.

superpower ['su:pəpauə*] n (POL) superpotenza.

supersede [su:pə'si:d] vt sostituire, soppiantare.

superstitious [su:pə'stɪʃəs] a superstizioso(a).

supervise ['su:pəvaɪz] vt (person etc) sorvegliare; (organization) soprintendere a; **supervision** [-'vɪʒən] n sorveglianza; supervisione f; **supervisor** n sorvegliante m/f; soprintendente m/f; (in shop) capocommesso/a.

supine ['su:paɪn] a supino(a).

supper ['sʌpə*] n cena.

supplant [sə'plɑ:nt] vt (person, thing) soppiantare.

supple ['sʌpl] a flessibile; agile.

supplement n ['sʌplɪmənt] supplemento // vt [sʌplɪ'ment] completare, integrare; ~**ary** [-'mentərɪ] a supplementare.

supplier [sə'plaɪə*] n fornitore m.

supply [sə'plaɪ] vt (provide) fornire; (equip): to ~ (with) approvvigionare (di); attrezzare (con) // n riserva, provvista; (supplying) approvvigionamento; (TECH) alimentazione f; **supplies** npl (food) viveri mpl; (MIL) sussistenza; ~ **teacher** n (Brit) supplente m/f.

support [sə'pɔ:t] n (moral, financial etc) sostegno, appoggio; (TECH) supporto // vt sostenere; (financially) mantenere; (uphold) sostenere, difendere; ~**er** n (POL etc) sostenitore/trice, fautore/trice; (SPORT) tifoso/a.

suppose [sə'pəuz] vt, vi supporre; immaginare; **to be** ~**d to do** essere tenuto(a) a fare; ~**dly** [sə'pəuzɪdlɪ] ad presumibilmente; (seemingly) apparentemente; **supposing** cj se, ammesso che + sub.

suppress [sə'pres] vt reprimere; sop-

primere; tenere segreto(a).
supreme |su'pri:m| *a* supremo(a).
surcharge |'sə:tʃɑ:dʒ| *n* supplemento;
(*extra tax*) soprattassa.
sure |ʃuə*| *a* sicuro(a); (*definite*,
convinced) sicuro(a), certo(a); ~! (*of*
course) senz'altro!, certo!; ~ **enough**
infatti; **to make** ~ **of** sth/that assicurarsi
di qc/che; ~**ly** *ad* sicuramente;
certamente.
surety |'ʃuərətɪ| *n* garanzia.
surf |sə:f| *n* (*waves*) cavalloni *mpl*;
(*foam*) spuma.
surface |'sə:fɪs| *n* superficie *f* // *vt* (*road*)
asfaltare // *vi* risalire alla superficie;
(*fig*: *person*) venire a galla, farsi
vivo(a); ~ **mail** *n* posta ordinaria.
surfboard |'sə:fbɔ:d| *n* tavola per
surfing.
surfeit |'sə:fɪt| *n*: **a** ~ **of** un eccesso di;
un'indigestione di.
surfing |'sə:fɪŋ| *n* surfing *m*.
surge |sə:dʒ| *n* (*strong movement*)
ondata; (*of feeling*) impeto // *vi* (*waves*)
gonfiarsi; (*ELEC*: *power*) aumentare improvvisamente; (*people*) riversarsi.
surgeon |'sə:dʒən| *n* chirurgo.
surgery |'sə:dʒərɪ| *n* chirurgia; (*Brit*:
room) studio *or* gabinetto medico,
ambulatorio; **to undergo** ~ subire un
intervento chirurgico; ~ **hours** *npl*
(*Brit*) orario delle visite *or* di
consultazione.
surgical |'sə:dʒɪkl| *a* chirurgico(a); ~
spirit *n* (*Brit*) alcool *m* denaturato.
surly |'sə:lɪ| *a* scontroso(a), burbero(a).
surname |'sə:neɪm| *n* cognome *m*.
surpass |sə:'pɑ:s| *vt* superare.
surplus |'sə:pləs| *n* eccedenza; (*ECON*)
surplus *m inv* // *a* eccedente, d'avanzo.
surprise |sə'praɪz| *n* sorpresa;
(*astonishment*) stupore *m* // *vt* sorprendere; stupire; **surprising** *a* sorprendente, stupefacente; **surprisingly**
ad (*easy*, *helpful*) sorprendentemente.
surrender |sə'rɛndə*| *n* resa,
capitolazione *f* // *vi* arrendersi.
surreptitious |sʌrəp'tɪʃəs| *a* furtivo(a).
surrogate |'sʌrəgɪt| *n* surrogato; ~
mother *n* madre *f* sostitutiva.
surround |sə'raund| *vt* circondare; (*MIL*
etc) accerchiare; ~**ing** *a* circostante;
~**ings** *npl* dintorni *mpl*; (*fig*) ambiente
m.
surveillance |sə:'veɪləns| *n* sorveglianza,
controllo.
survey *n* |'sə:veɪ| quadro generale;
(*study*) esame *m*; (*in housebuying etc*)
perizia; (*of land*) rilevamento, rilievo
topografico // *vt* |sə:'veɪ| osservare;
esaminare; valutare; rilevare; ~**or** *n*
perito; geometra *m*; (*of land*)
agrimensore *m*.
survival |sə'vaɪvl| *n* sopravvivenza;
(*relic*) reliquia, vestigio.

survive |sə'vaɪv| *vi* sopravvivere // *vt* so-
pravvivere a; **survivor** *n* superstite *m/f*,
sopravvissuto/a.
susceptible |sə'sɛptəbl| *a*: ~ (**to**)
sensibile (a); (*disease*) predisposto(a)
(a).
suspect *a*, *n* |'sʌspɛkt| *a* sospetto(a) // *n*
persona sospetta // *vt* |səs'pɛkt| so-
spettare; (*think likely*) supporre;
(*doubt*) dubitare.
suspend |səs'pɛnd| *vt* sospendere; ~**ed**
sentence *n* condanna con la
condizionale; ~**er belt** *n* reggicalze *m*
inv; ~**ers** *npl* (*Brit*) giarrettiere *fpl*;
(*US*) bretelle *fpl*.
suspense |səs'pɛns| *n* apprensione *f*; (*in*
film etc) suspense *m*.
suspension |səs'pɛnʃən| *n* (*gen AUT*) so-
spensione *f*; (*of driving licence*) ritiro
temporaneo; ~ **bridge** *n* ponte *m* sospeso.
suspicion |səs'pɪʃən| *n* sospetto.
suspicious |səs'pɪʃəs| *a* (*suspecting*) so-
spettoso(a); (*causing suspicion*) so-
spetto(a).
sustain |səs'teɪn| *vt* sostenere;
sopportare; (*LAW*: *charge*) confermare;
(*suffer*) subire; ~**ed** *a* (*effort*)
prolungato(a).
sustenance |'sʌstɪnəns| *n* nutrimento;
mezzi *mpl* di sostentamento.
swab |swɔb| *n* (*MED*) tampone *m*.
swagger |'swægə*| *vi* pavoneggiarsi.
swallow |'swɔləu| *n* (*bird*) rondine *f* //
vt inghiottire; (*fig*: *story*) bere; **to** ~
up *vt* inghiottire.
swam |swæm| *pt of* swim.
swamp |swɔmp| *n* palude *f* // *vt*
sommergere.
swan |swɔn| *n* cigno.
swap |swɔp| *vt*: **to** ~ (**for**) scambiare
(con).
swarm |swɔ:m| *n* sciame *m* // *vi*
formicolare; (*bees*) sciamare.
swarthy |'swɔ:ðɪ| *a* di carnagione scura.
swastika |'swɔstɪkə| *n* croce *f* uncinata,
svastica.
swat |swɔt| *vt* schiacciare.
sway |sweɪ| *vi* (*building*) oscillare; (*tree*)
ondeggiare; (*person*) barcollare // *vt*
(*influence*) influenzare, dominare.
swear |swɛə*|, *pt* **swore**, *pp* **sworn** *vi*
(*witness etc*) giurare; (*curse*) be-
stemmiare, imprecare; **to** ~ **to** sth
giurare qc; ~**word** *n* parolaccia.
sweat |swɛt| *n* sudore *m*, traspirazione *f*
// *vi* sudare.
sweater |'swɛtə*| *n* maglione *m*.
sweatshirt |'swɛtʃə:t| *n* felpa.
sweaty |'swɛtɪ| *a* sudato(a); bagnato(a)
di sudore.
Swede |swi:d| *n* svedese *m/f*.
swede |swi:d| *n* (*Brit*) rapa svedese.
Sweden |'swi:dn| *n* Svezia.
Swedish |'swi:dɪʃ| *a* svedese // *n* (*LING*)

svedese *m*.

sweep |swi:p| *n* spazzata; (*curve*) curva; (*expanse*) distesa; (*range*) portata; (*also*: **chimney ~**) spazzacamino // *vb* (*pt, pp* **swept**) *vt* spazzare, scopare // *vi* camminare maestosamente; precipitarsi, lanciarsi; (e)stendersi; **to ~ away** *vt* spazzare via; trascinare via; **to ~ past** *vi* sfrecciare accanto; passare accanto maestosamente; **to ~ up** *vt, vi* spazzare; **~ing** *a* (*gesture*) largo(a); circolare; **a ~ing** statement un'affermazione generica.

sweet |swi:t| *n* (*Brit*: *pudding*) dolce *m*; (*candy*) caramella // *a* dolce; (*fresh*) fresco(a); (*fig*) piacevole; delicato(a), grazioso(a); gentile; **~corn** *n* granturco dolce; **~en** *vt* addolcire; zuccherare; **~heart** *n* innamorato/a; **~ness** *n* sapore *m* dolce; dolcezza; **~ pea** *n* pisello odoroso.

swell |swel| *n* (*of sea*) mare *m* lungo // *a* (*col*: *excellent*) favoloso(a) // *vb* (*pt* **~ed**, *pp* **swollen**, **~ed**) *vt* gonfiare, ingrossare; aumentare // *vi* gonfiarsi, ingrossarsi; (*sound*) crescere; (*MED*) gonfiarsi; **~ing** *n* (*MED*) tumefazione *f*, gonfiore *m*.

sweltering ['swɛltərɪŋ] *a* soffocante.

swept |swɛpt| *pt, pp of* **sweep**.

swerve |swə:v| *vi* deviare; (*driver*) sterzare; (*boxer*) scartare.

swift |swɪft| *n* (*bird*) rondone *m* // *a* rapido(a), veloce.

swig |swɪg| *n* (*col*: *drink*) sorsata.

swill |swɪl| *n* broda // *vt* (*also*: **~ out, ~ down**) risciacquare.

swim |swɪm| *n*: **to go for a ~** andare a fare una nuotata // *vb* (*pt* **swam**, *pp* **swum**) *vi* nuotare; (*SPORT*) fare il nuoto; (*head, room*) girare // *vt* (*river, channel*) attraversare or percorrere a nuoto; (*length*) nuotare; **~mer** *n* nuotatore/trice; **~ming** *n* nuoto; **~ming cap** *n* cuffia; **~ming costume** *n* (*Brit*) costume *m* da bagno; **~ming pool** *n* piscina; **~suit** *n* costume *m* da bagno.

swindle |'swɪndl| *n* truffa // *vt* truffare.

swine |swaɪn| *n* (*pl inv*) maiale *m*, porco; (*col!*) porco(!).

swing |swɪŋ| *n* altalena; (*movement*) oscillazione *f*; (*MUS*) ritmo; swing *m* // *vb* (*pt, pp* **swung**) *vt* dondolare, far oscillare; (*also*: **~ round**) far girare // *vi* oscillare, dondolare; (*also*: **~ round**: *object*) roteare; (*: person*) girarsi, voltarsi; **to be in full ~** (*activity*) essere in piena attività; (*party etc*) essere nel pieno; **~ door**, (*US*) **~ing door** *n* porta battente.

swingeing ['swɪndʒɪŋ] *a* (*Brit*: *defeat*) violento(a); (*: price increase*) enorme.

swipe |swaɪp| *vt* (*hit*) colpire con forza; dare uno schiaffo a; (*col*: *steal*) sgraffi-

gnare.

swirl |swə:l| *vi* turbinare, far mulinello.

swish |swɪʃ| *a* (*col*: *smart*) all'ultimo grido, alla moda // *vi* sibilare.

Swiss |swɪs| *a, n* (*pl inv*) svizzero(a).

switch |swɪtʃ| *n* (*for light, radio etc*) interruttore *m*; (*change*) cambiamento // *vt* (*change*) cambiare; scambiare; **to ~ off** *vt* spegnere; **to ~ on** *vt* accendere; (*engine, machine*) mettere in moto, avviare; **~board** *n* (*TEL*) centralino.

Switzerland ['swɪtsələnd] *n* Svizzera.

swivel ['swɪvl] *vi* (*also*: **~ round**) girare.

swollen ['swəulən] *pp of* **swell**.

swoon |swu:n| *vi* svenire.

swoop |swu:p| *vi* (*also*: **~ down**) scendere in picchiata, piombare.

swop |swɔp| *n, vt* = **swap**.

sword |sɔ:d| *n* spada; **~fish** *n* pesce *m* spada *inv*.

swore |swɔ:*| *pt of* **swear**.

sworn |swɔ:n| *pp of* **swear**.

swot |swɔt| *vt* sgobbare su // *vi* sgobbare.

swum |swʌm| *pp of* **swim**.

swung |swʌŋ| *pt, pp of* **swing**.

syllable ['sɪləbl] *n* sillaba.

syllabus ['sɪləbəs] *n* programma *m*.

symbol ['sɪmbl] *n* simbolo.

symmetry ['sɪmɪtrɪ] *n* simmetria.

sympathetic |sɪmpə'θɛtɪk| *a* (*showing pity*) compassionevole; (*kind*) comprensivo(a); **~ towards** ben disposto(a) verso.

sympathize ['sɪmpəθaɪz] *vi*: **to ~ with sb** compatire qn; partecipare al dolore di qn; **~r** *n* (*POL*) simpatizzante *m/f*.

sympathy ['sɪmpəθɪ] *n* compassione *f*; **in ~ with** d'accordo con; (*strike*) per solidarietà con; **with our deepest ~** con le nostre più sincere condoglianze.

symphony ['sɪmfənɪ] *n* sinfonia.

symptom ['sɪmptəm] *n* sintomo; indizio.

synagogue ['sɪnəgɔg] *n* sinagoga.

syndicate ['sɪndɪkɪt] *n* sindacato.

synonym ['sɪnənɪm] *n* sinonimo.

synopsis, *pl* **synopses** [sɪ'nɔpsɪs, -si:z] *n* sommario, sinossi *f inv*.

syntax ['sɪntæks] *n* sintassi *f inv*.

synthesis, *pl* **syntheses** ['sɪnθəsɪs, -si:z] *n* sintesi *f inv*.

synthetic |sɪn'θɛtɪk| *a* sintetico(a).

syphilis ['sɪfɪlɪs] *n* sifilide *f*.

syphon ['saɪfən] *n, vb* = **siphon**.

Syria ['sɪrɪə] *n* Siria.

syringe [sɪ'rɪndʒ] *n* siringa.

syrup ['sɪrəp] *n* sciroppo; (*also*: **golden ~**) melassa raffinata.

system ['sɪstəm] *n* sistema *m*; (*order*) metodo; (*ANAT*) organismo; **~atic** |-'mætɪk| *a* sistematico(a); metodico(a); **~ disk** *n* (*COMPUT*) disco del sistema; **~s analyst** *n* analista *m* programmatore.

T

ta |tɑ:| *excl* (*Brit col*) grazie!

tab |tæb| *n* (*loop on coat etc*) laccetto; (*label*) etichetta; **to keep ~s on** (*fig*) tenere d'occhio.

tabby |'tæbɪ| *n* (*also*: **~ cat**) (gatto) soriano, gatto tigrato.

table |'teɪbl| *n* tavolo, tavola // *vt* (*Brit: motion etc*) presentare; **to lay** *or* **set the ~** apparecchiare *or* preparare la tavola; **~cloth** *n* tovaglia; **~ of contents** *n* indice *m*; **~ d'hôte** |tɑ:bl'dəut| *a* (*meal*) a prezzo fisso; **~ lamp** *n* lampada da tavolo; **~mat** *n* sottopiatto; **~spoon** *n* cucchiaio da tavola; (*also*: **~spoonful:** *as measurement*) cucchiaiata.

tablet |'tæblɪt| *n* (*MED*) compressa; (: *for sucking*) pastiglia; (*for writing*) blocco; (*of stone*) targa.

table: **~ tennis** *n* tennis *m* da tavolo, ping-pong *m* ®; **~ wine** *n* vino da tavola.

tabulate |'tæbjuleɪt| *vt* (*data, figures*) tabulare, disporre in tabelle.

tacit |'tæsɪt| *a* tacito(a).

tack |tæk| *n* (*nail*) bulletta; (*stitch*) punto d'imbastitura; (*NAUT*) bordo, bordata // *vt* imbullettare; imbastire // *vi* bordeggiare.

tackle |'tækl| *n* attrezzatura, equipaggiamento; (*for lifting*) paranco; (*RUGBY*) placcaggio // *vt* (*difficulty*) affrontare; (*RUGBY*) placcare.

tacky |'tækɪ| *a* colloso(a), appiccicaticcio(a); ancora bagnato(a).

tact |tækt| *n* tatto; **~ful** *a* delicato(a), discreto(a).

tactical |'tæktɪkl| *a* tattico(a).

tactics |'tæktɪks| *n, npl* tattica.

tactless |'tæktlɪs| *a* che manca di tatto.

tadpole |'tædpəul| *n* girino.

taffy |'tæfɪ| *n* (*US*) caramella *f* mou *inv*.

tag |tæg| *n* etichetta; **to ~ along** *vi* seguire.

tail |teɪl| *n* coda; (*of shirt*) falda // *vt* (*follow*) seguire, pedinare; **to ~ away**, **~ off** *vi* (*in size, quality etc*) diminuire gradatamente; **~back** *n* (*Brit AUT*) ingorgo; **~ coat** *n* marsina; **~ end** *n* (*of train, procession etc*) coda; (*of meeting etc*) fine *f*; **~gate** *n* (*AUT*) portellone *m* posteriore.

tailor |'teɪlə*| *n* sarto; **~ing** *n* (*cut*) stile *m*; **~-made** *a* (*also fig*) fatto(a) su misura.

tailwind |'teɪlwɪnd| *n* vento di coda.

tainted |'teɪntɪd| *a* (*food*) guasto(a); (*water, air*) infetto(a); (*fig*) corrotto(a).

take, *pt* **took,** *pp* **taken** |teɪk, tuk, 'teɪkn| *vt* prendere; (*gain: prize*) ottenere, vincere; (*require: effort, courage*) occorrere, volerci; (*tolerate*)

accettare, sopportare; (*hold: passengers etc*) contenere; (*accompany*) accompagnare; (*bring, carry*) portare; (*exam*) sostenere, presentarsi a; **I ~ it that** suppongo che; **to ~ for a walk** (*child, dog*) portare a fare una passeggiata; **to ~ after** *vt fus* assomigliare a; **to ~ apart** *vt* smontare; **to ~ away** *vt* portare via; togliere; **to ~ back** *vt* (*return*) restituire; riportare; (*one's words*) ritirare; **to ~ down** *vt* (*building*) demolire; (*letter etc*) scrivere; **to ~ in** *vt* (*deceive*) imbrogliare, abbindolare; (*understand*) capire; (*include*) comprendere, includere; (*lodger*) prendere, ospitare; **to ~ off** *vi* (*AVIAT*) decollare // *vt* (*remove*) togliere; (*imitate*) imitare; **to ~ on** *vt* (*work*) accettare, intraprendere; (*employee*) assumere; (*opponent*) sfidare, affrontare; **to ~ out** *vt* portare fuori; (*remove*) togliere; (*licence*) prendere, ottenere; **to ~ sth out of sth** (*drawer, pocket etc*) tirare qc fuori da qc; estrarre qc da qc; **to ~ over** *vt* (*business*) rilevare // *vi*: **to ~ over from sb** prendere le consegne *or* il controllo da qn; **to ~ to** *vt fus* (*person*) prendere in simpatia; (*activity*) prendere gusto a; **to ~ up** *vt* (*one's story*) riprendere; (*dress*) accorciare; (*occupy: time, space*) occupare; (*engage in: hobby etc*) mettersi a; **~away** *a* (*food*) da portar via; **~-home pay** *n* stipendio netto; **~off** *n* (*AVIAT*) decollo; **~out** *a* (*US*) = **~away**; **~over** *n* (*COMM*) assorbimento.

takings |'teɪkɪŋz| *npl* (*COMM*) incasso.

talc |tælk| *n* (*also*: **~um powder**) talco.

tale |teɪl| *n* racconto, storia; (*pej*) fandonia; **to tell ~s** (*fig: to teacher, parent etc*) fare la spia.

talent |'tælnt| *n* talento; **~ed** *a* di talento.

talk |tɔ:k| *n* discorso; (*gossip*) chiacchiere *fpl*; (*conversation*) conversazione *f*; (*interview*) discussione *f* // *vi* (*chatter*) chiacchierare; **~s** *npl* (*POL etc*) colloqui *mpl*; **to ~ about** parlare di; (*converse*) discorrere *or* conversare su; **to ~ sb out of/into doing** dissuadere qn da/convincere qn a fare; **to ~ shop** parlare del lavoro *or* degli affari; **to ~ over** *vt* discutere; **~ative** *a* loquace, ciarliero(a); **~ show** *n* conversazione *f* televisiva, talk show *m inv*.

tall |tɔ:l| *a* alto(a); **to be 6 feet ~** ≈ essere alto 1 metro e 80; **~boy** *n* (*Brit*) cassettone *m* alto; **~ story** *n* panzana, frottola.

tally |'tælɪ| *n* conto, conteggio // *vi*: **to ~ (with)** corrispondere (a).

talon |'tælən| *n* artiglio.

tambourine |tæmbə'ri:n| *n* tamburello.

tame |teɪm| *a* addomesticato(a); (*fig:*

story, style) insipido(a), scialbo(a).

tamper |'tæmpɔ*| *vi*: **to ~ with** manomettere.

tampon |'tæmpɔn| *n* tampone *m*.

tan |tæn| *n* (*also*: **sun~**) abbronzatura // *vt* abbronzare // *vi* abbronzarsi // *a* (*colour*) marrone rossiccio *inv*.

tang |tæŋ| *n* odore *m* penetrante; sapore *m* piccante.

tangent |'tændʒənt| *n* (*MATH*) tangente *f*; **to go off at a ~** (*fig*) partire per la tangente.

tangerine |tændʒə'ri:n| *n* mandarino.

tangle |'tæŋgl| *n* groviglio // *vt* aggrovigliare.

tank |tæŋk| *n* serbatoio; (*for processing*) vasca; (*for fish*) acquario; (*MIL*) carro armato.

tanker |'tæŋkɔ*| *n* (*ship*) nave *f* cisterna *inv*; (*truck*) autobotte *f*, autocisterna.

tantalizing |'tæntəlaızıŋ| *a* allettante.

tantamount |'tæntəmaunt| *a*: **~ to** equivalente a.

tantrum |'tæntrəm| *n* accesso di collera.

tap |tæp| *n* (*on sink etc*) rubinetto; (*gentle blow*) colpetto // *vt* dare un colpetto a; (*resources*) sfruttare, utilizzare; (*telephone*) mettere sotto controllo; **on ~** (*fig*: *resources*) a disposizione; **~ dancing** *n* tip tap *m*.

tape |teɪp| *n* nastro; (*also*: **magnetic ~**) nastro (magnetico) // *vt* (*record*) registrare (su nastro); **~ measure** *n* metro a nastro.

taper |'teɪpɔ*| *n* candelina // *vi* assottigliarsi.

tape recorder *n* registratore *m* (a nastro).

tapestry |'tæpɪstrɪ| *n* arazzo; tappezzeria.

tar |tɑ:*| *n* catrame *m*.

target |'tɑ:gɪt| *n* bersaglio; (*fig*: *objective*) obiettivo.

tariff |'tærɪf| *n* (*COMM*) tariffa; (*taxes*) tariffe *fpl* doganali.

tarmac |'tɑ:mæk| *n* (*Brit*: *on road*) macadam *m* al catrame; (*AVIAT*) pista di decollo.

tarnish |'tɑ:nɪʃ| *vt* offuscare, annerire; (*fig*) macchiare.

tarpaulin |tɑ:'pɔ:lɪn| *n* tela incatramata.

tarragon |'tærəgən| *n* dragoncello.

tart |tɑ:t| *n* (*CULIN*) crostata; (*Brit col*: *pej*: *woman*) sgualdrina // *a* (*flavour*) aspro(a), agro(a); **to ~ up** *vt* (*col*): **to ~ o.s. up** farsi bello(a); (*pej*) agghindarsi.

tartan |'tɑ:tn| *n* tartan *m* *inv*.

tartar |'tɑ:tɔ*| *n* (*on teeth*) tartaro; **~ sauce** *n* salsa tartara.

task |tɑ:sk| *n* compito; **to take to ~** rimproverare; **~ force** *n* (*MIL, POLICE*) unità operativa.

tassel |'tæsl| *n* fiocco.

taste |teɪst| *n* gusto; (*flavour*) sapore *m*, gusto; (*fig*: *glimpse, idea*) idea // *vt* gu-

stare; (*sample*) assaggiare // *vi*: **to ~ of** (*fish etc*) sapere *or* avere sapore di; **it ~s like fish** sa di pesce; **can I have a ~ of this wine?** posso assaggiare un po' di questo vino?; **to have a ~ for sth** avere un'inclinazione per qc; **in good/bad ~** di buon/cattivo gusto; **~ful** *a* di buon gusto; **~less** *a* (*food*) insipido(a); (*remark*) di cattivo gusto; **tasty** *a* saporito(a), gustoso(a).

tatters |'tætəz| *npl*: **in ~** (*also*: **tattered**) a brandelli, sbrindellato(a).

tattoo |tə'tu:| *n* tatuaggio; (*spectacle*) parata militare // *vt* tatuare.

taught |tɔ:t| *pt, pp of* **teach**.

taunt |tɔ:nt| *n* scherno // *vt* schernire.

Taurus |'tɔ:rəs| *n* Toro.

taut |tɔ:t| *a* teso(a).

tawdry |'tɔ:drɪ| *a* pacchiano(a).

tax |tæks| *n* (*on goods*) imposta; (*on services*) tassa; (*on income*) imposte *fpl*, tasse *fpl* // *vt* tassare; (*fig*: *strain*: *patience etc*) mettere alla prova; **~able** *a* (*income*) imponibile; **~ation** |-'seɪʃən| *n* tassazione *f*; tasse *fpl*, imposte *fpl*; **~ avoidance** *n* l'evitare legalmente il pagamento di imposte; **~ collector** *n* esattore *m* delle imposte; **~ disc** *n* (*Brit AUT*) ≈ bollo; **~ evasion** *n* evasione *f* fiscale; **~-free** *a* esente da imposte.

taxi |'tæksɪ| *n* taxi *m* *inv* // *vi* (*AVIAT*) rullare; **~ driver** *n* tassista *m/f*; **~ rank** (*Brit*), **~ stand** *n* posteggio dei taxi.

tax: **~ payer** *n* contribuente *m/f*; **~ relief** *n* agevolazioni *fpl* fiscali; **~ return** *n* dichiarazione *f* dei redditi.

TB *n abbr* = **tuberculosis**.

tea |ti:| *n* tè *m* *inv*; (*Brit*: *snack*: *for children*) merenda; **high ~** (*Brit*) cena leggera (*presa nel tardo pomeriggio*); **~ bag** *n* bustina di tè; **~ break** *n* (*Brit*) intervallo per il tè.

teach |ti:tʃ|, *pt, pp* **taught** *vt*: **to ~ sb sth, ~ sth to sb** insegnare qc a qn // *vi* insegnare; **~er** *n* insegnante *m/f*; (*in secondary school*) professore/essa; (*in primary school*) maestro/a; **~ing** *n* insegnamento.

tea cosy *n* copriteiera *m* *inv*.

teacup |'ti:kʌp| *n* tazza da tè.

teak |ti:k| *n* teak *m*.

team |ti:m| *n* squadra; (*of animals*) tiro; **~work** *n* lavoro di squadra.

teapot |'ti:pɔt| *n* teiera.

tear *n* |tɛə*| strappo; |tɪə*| lacrima // *vb* |tɛə*| (*pt* **tore**, *pp* **torn**) *vt* strappare // *vi* strapparsi; **in ~s** in lacrime; **to ~ along** *vi* (*rush*) correre all'impazzata; **to ~ up** *vt* (*sheet of paper etc*) strappare; **~ful** *a* piangente, lacrimoso(a); **~ gas** *n* gas *m* lacrimogeno.

tearoom |'ti:ru:m| *n* sala da tè.

tease |ti:z| *vt* canzonare; (*unkindly*)

tormentare.

tea set *n* servizio da tè.

teaspoon |'tiːspuːn| *n* cucchiaino da tè; (*also*: ~**ful**: *as measurement*) cucchiaino.

teat |tiːt| *n* capezzolo.

teatime |'tiːtaɪm| *n* ora del tè.

tea towel *n* (*Brit*) strofinaccio (per i piatti).

technical |'tɛknɪkl| *a* tecnico(a); ~**ity** |-'kælɪtɪ| *n* tecnicità; (*detail*) dettaglio tecnico.

technician |tɛk'nɪʃən| *n* tecnico/a.

technique |tɛk'niːk| *n* tecnica.

technological |tɛknə'lɔdʒɪkl| *a* tecnologico(a).

technology |tɛk'nɔlədʒɪ| *n* tecnologia.

teddy (bear) |'tɛdɪ-| *n* orsacchiotto.

tedious |'tiːdɪəs| *a* noioso(a), tedioso(a).

tee |tiː| *n* (*GOLF*) tee *m inv*.

teem |tiːm| *vi* abbondare, brulicare; **to** ~ **with** brulicare di; **it is** ~**ing** (**with rain**) piove a dirotto.

teenage |'tiːneɪdʒ| *a* (*fashions etc*) per giovani, per adolescenti; ~**r** *n* adolescente *m/f*.

teens |tiːnz| *npl*: **to be in one's** ~ essere adolescente.

tee-shirt |'tiː-ʃəːt| *n* = **T-shirt**.

teeter |'tiːtə*| *vi* barcollare, vacillare.

teeth |tiːθ| *npl of* **tooth**.

teethe |tiːð| *vi* mettere i denti.

teething |'tiːðɪŋ|: ~ **ring** *n* dentaruolo; ~ **troubles** *npl* (*fig*) difficoltà *fpl* iniziali.

teetotal |'tiː'təutl| *a* astemio(a).

telegram |'tɛlɪgræm| *n* telegramma *m*.

telegraph |'tɛlɪgrɑːf| *n* telegrafo.

telepathy |tə'lɛpəθɪ| *n* telepatia.

telephone |'tɛlɪfəun| *n* telefono // *vt* (*person*) telefonare a; (*message*) telefonare; ~ **booth**, (*Brit*) ~ **box** *n* cabina telefonica; ~ **call** *n* telefonata; ~ **directory** *n* elenco telefonico; ~ **number** *n* numero di telefono; **telephonist** |tə'lɛfənɪst| *n* (*Brit*) telefonista *m/f*.

telephoto |'tɛlɪ'fəutəu| *a*: ~ **lens** teleobiettivo.

telescope |'tɛlɪskəup| *n* telescopio // *vt* incastrare a cannocchiale.

televise |'tɛlɪvaɪz| *vt* teletrasmettere.

television |'tɛlɪvɪʒən| *n* televisione *f*; ~ **set** *n* televisore *m*.

telex |'tɛlɛks| *n* telex *m inv* // *vt*, *vi* trasmettere per telex; **to** ~ **sb** contattare qn via telex.

tell |tɛl|, *pt*, *pp* **told** *vt* dire; (*relate*: *story*) raccontare; (*distinguish*): **to** ~ **sth from** distinguere qc da // *vi* (*talk*): **to** ~ (**of**) parlare (di); (*have effect*) farsi sentire, avere effetto; **to** ~ **sb to do** dire a qn di fare; **to** ~ **off** *vt* rimproverare, sgridare; ~**er** *n* (*in bank*) cassiere/a; ~**ing** *a* (*remark, detail*)

rivelatore(trice); ~**tale** *a* (*sign*) rivelatore(trice).

telly |'tɛlɪ| *n abbr* (*Brit col*: = *television*) tivù *f inv*.

temerity |tə'mɛrɪtɪ| *n* temerarietà.

temp |tɛmp| *n abbr* (= *temporary*) segretaria temporanea.

temper |'tɛmpə*| *n* (*nature*) carattere *m*; (*mood*) umore *m*; (*fit of anger*) collera // *vt* (*moderate*) temperare, moderare; **to be in a** ~ essere in collera; **to lose one's** ~ andare in collera.

temperament |'tɛmprəmənt| *n* (*nature*) temperamento; ~**al** |-'mɛntl| *a* capriccioso(a).

temperate |'tɛmprət| *a* moderato(a); (*climate*) temperato(a).

temperature |'tɛmprətʃə*| *n* temperatura; **to have** *or* **run a** ~ avere la febbre.

tempest |'tɛmpɪst| *n* tempesta.

template |'tɛmplɪt| *n* sagoma.

temple |'tɛmpl| *n* (*building*) tempio; (*ANAT*) tempia.

temporary |'tɛmpərərɪ| *a* temporaneo(a); (*job, worker*) avventizio(a), temporaneo(a); ~ **secretary** *n* segretaria temporanea.

tempt |tɛmpt| *vt* tentare; **to** ~ **sb into doing** indurre qn a fare; ~**ation** |-'teɪʃən| *n* tentazione *f*.

ten |tɛn| *num* dieci.

tenable |'tɛnəbl| *a* sostenibile.

tenacity |tə'næsɪtɪ| *n* tenacia.

tenancy |'tɛnənsɪ| *n* affitto; condizione *f* di inquilino.

tenant |'tɛnənt| *n* inquilino/a.

tend |tɛnd| *vt* badare a, occuparsi di // *vi*: **to** ~ **to do** tendere a fare.

tendency |'tɛndənsɪ| *n* tendenza.

tender |'tɛndə*| *a* tenero(a); (*delicate*) fragile; (*sore*) dolorante; (*affectionate*) affettuoso(a) // *n* (*COMM*: *offer*) offerta // *vt* offrire.

tendon |'tɛndən| *n* tendine *m*.

tenement |'tɛnəmənt| *n* casamento.

tenet |'tɛnət| *n* principio.

tennis |'tɛnɪs| *n* tennis *m*; ~ **ball** *n* palla da tennis; ~ **court** *n* campo da tennis; ~ **player** *n* tennista *m/f*; ~ **racket** *n* racchetta da tennis; ~ **shoes** *npl* scarpe *fpl* da tennis.

tenor |'tɛnə*| *n* (*MUS, of speech etc*) tenore *m*.

tense |tɛns| *a* teso(a) // *n* (*LING*) tempo.

tension |'tɛnʃən| *n* tensione *f*.

tent |tɛnt| *n* tenda.

tentative |'tɛntətɪv| *a* esitante, incerto(a); (*conclusion*) provvisorio(a).

tenterhooks |'tɛntəhuks| *npl*: **on** ~ sulle spine.

tenth |tɛnθ| *num* decimo(a).

tent: ~ **peg** *n* picchetto da tenda; ~ **pole** *n* palo da tenda, montante *m*.

tenuous |'tɛnjuəs| *a* tenue.

tenure ['tɛnjuə*] *n* (*of property*) possesso; (*of job*) permanenza; titolarità.

tepid ['tɛpɪd] *a* tiepido(a).

term [təːm] *n* (*limit*) termine *m*; (*word*) vocabolo, termine; (*SCOL*) trimestre *m*; (*LAW*) sessione *f* // *vt* chiamare, definire; **~s** *npl* (*conditions*) condizioni *fpl*; (*COMM*) prezzi *mpl*, tariffe *fpl*; **~ of imprisonment** periodo di prigionia; **in the short/long ~** a breve/lunga scadenza; **to come to ~s with** (*problem*) affrontare.

terminal ['təːmɪnl] *a* finale, terminale; (*disease*) nella fase terminale // *n* (*ELEC*) morsetto; (*COMPUT*) terminale *m*; (*AVIAT, for oil, ore etc*) terminal *m* *inv*; (*Brit: also:* **coach ~**) capolinea *m*.

terminate ['təːmɪneɪt] *vt* mettere fine a // *vi:* **to ~ in** finire in *or* con.

terminus, *pl* **termini** ['təːmɪnəs, 'təːmɪnaɪ] *n* (*for buses*) capolinea *m*; (*for trains*) stazione *f* terminale.

terrace ['tɛrəs] *n* terrazza; (*Brit: row of houses*) fila di case a schiera; **the ~s** *npl* (*Brit SPORT*) le gradinate; **~d** *a* (*garden*) a terrazze.

terracotta ['tɛrə'kɔtə] *n* terracotta.

terrain [tɛ'reɪn] *n* terreno.

terrible ['tɛrɪbl] *a* terribile; (*weather*) bruttissimo(a); (*work*) orribile; **terribly** *ad* terribilmente; (*very badly*) malissimo.

terrier ['tɛrɪə*] *n* terrier *m* *inv*.

terrific [tə'rɪfɪk] *a* incredibile, fantastico(a); (*wonderful*) formidabile, eccezionale.

terrify ['tɛrɪfaɪ] *vt* terrorizzare.

territory ['tɛrɪtərɪ] *n* territorio.

terror ['tɛrə*] *n* terrore *m*; **~ism** *n* terrorismo; **~ist** *n* terrorista *m/f*.

terse [təːs] *a* (*style*) conciso(a); (*reply*) laconico(a).

Terylene ['tɛrəliːn] *n* ® terital *m* ®, terilene *m* ®.

test [tɛst] *n* (*trial, check, of courage etc*) prova; (*: of goods in factory*) controllo, collaudo; (*MED*) esame *m*; (*CHEM*) analisi *f* *inv*; (*exam: of intelligence etc*) test *m* *inv*; (*: in school*) compito in classe; (*also:* **driving ~**) esame *m* di guida // *vt* provare; controllare, collaudare; esaminare; analizzare; sottoporre ad esame; **to ~ sb in history** esaminare qn in storia.

testament ['tɛstəmənt] *n* testamento; **the Old/New T~** il Vecchio/Nuovo testamento.

testicle ['tɛstɪkl] *n* testicolo.

testify ['tɛstɪfaɪ] *vi* (*LAW*) testimoniare, deporre; **to ~ to sth** (*LAW*) testimoniare qc; (*gen*) comprovare *or* dimostrare qc; (*: be sign of*) essere una prova di qc.

testimony ['tɛstɪmənɪ] *n* (*LAW*) testimonianza, deposizione *f*.

test: ~ match *n* (*CRICKET, RUGBY*)

partita internazionale; **~ pilot** *n* pilota *m* collaudatore; **~ tube** *n* provetta.

tetanus ['tɛtənəs] *n* tetano.

tether ['tɛðə*] *vt* legare // *n:* **at the end of one's ~** al limite (della pazienza).

text [tɛkst] *n* testo; **~book** *n* libro di testo.

textile ['tɛkstaɪl] *n* tessile *m*.

texture ['tɛkstʃə*] *n* tessitura; (*of skin, paper etc*) struttura.

Thames [tɛmz] *n:* **the ~** il Tamigi.

than [ðæn, ðən] *cj* (*in comparisons*) che; (*with numerals, pronouns, proper names*) di; **more ~** 10/once più di 10/una volta; **I have more/less ~ you** ne ho più/meno di te; **I have more pens ~ pencils** ho più penne che matite; **she is older ~ you think** è più vecchia di quanto tu (*non*) pensi.

thank [θæŋk] *vt* ringraziare; **~ you (very much)** grazie (tante); **~s** *npl* ringraziamenti *mpl*, grazie *fpl* // *excl* grazie!; **~s to** *prep* grazie a; **~ful** *a:* **~ful (for)** riconoscente (per); **~less** *a* ingrato(a); **T~sgiving (Day)** *n* giorno del ringraziamento.

that [ðæt] ♦ *a* (*demonstrative: pl* **those**) quel(quell', quello) *m*; quella(quell') *f*; **~ man/woman/book** quell'uomo/quella donna/quel libro; (*not "this"*) quell'uomo/quella donna/quel libro là; **~ one** quello/quella là

♦ *pronoun* **1** (*demonstrative: pl* **those**) ciò; (*not "this one"*) quello(a); **who's ~?** chi è?; **what's ~?** cos'è quello?; **is ~ you?** sei tu?; **I prefer this to ~** preferisco questo a quello; **~'s what he said** questo è ciò che ha detto; **what happened after ~?** che è successo dopo?; **~ is (to say)** cioè

2 (*relative: direct*) che; (*: indirect*) cui; **the book (~) I read** il libro che ho letto; **the box (~) I put it in** la scatola in cui l'ho messo; **the people (~) I spoke to** le persone con cui *or* con le quali ho parlato

3 (*relative: of time*) in cui; **the day (~) he came** il giorno in cui è venuto

♦ *cj* che; **he thought ~ I was ill** pensava che io fossi malato

♦ *ad* (*demonstrative*) così; **I can't work ~ much** non posso lavorare (così) tanto; **~ high** così alto; **the wall's about ~ high and ~ thick** il muro è alto circa così e spesso circa così.

thatched [θætʃt] *a* (*roof*) di paglia; **~ cottage** *n* cottage *m* *inv* col tetto di paglia.

thaw [θɔː] *n* disgelo // *vi* (*ice*) sciogliersi; (*food*) scongelarsi // *vt* (*food*) (fare) scongelare; **it's ~ing** (*weather*) sta sgelando.

the [ðiː, ðə] *definite article* **1** (*gen*) il(lo, l') *m*; la(l') *f*; i(gli) *mpl*; le *fpl*; **~ boy/girl/ink** il ragazzo/la ragazza/l'inchiostro;

~ books/pencils i libri/le matite; ~ history of ~ world la storia del mondo; give it to ~ postman dallo al postino; I haven't ~ time/money non ho tempo/ soldi; ~ rich and ~ poor i ricchi e i poveri
2 (*in titles*): Elizabeth ~ First Elisabetta prima; Peter ~ Great Pietro il grande
3 (*in comparisons*): ~ more he works, ~ more he earns più lavora più guadagna.

theatre, (*US*) **theater** ['θɪətə*] *n* teatro; ~**-goer** *n* frequentatore/trice di teatri.

theatrical [θɪ'ætrɪkl] *a* teatrale.

theft [θɛft] *n* furto.

their [ðɛə*] *a* il(la) loro, *pl* i(le) loro; ~**s** *pronoun* il(la) loro, *pl* i(le) loro; *see also* **my, mine.**

them [ðɛm, ðəm] *pronoun* (*direct*) li(le); (*indirect*) gli, loro (*after vb*); (*stressed, after prep: people*) loro; (: *people, things*) essi(e); *see also* **me.**

theme [θiːm] *n* tema *m*; ~ **song** *n* tema musicale.

themselves [ðəm'sɛlvz] *pl pronoun* (*reflexive*) si; (*emphatic*) loro stessi(e); (*after prep*) se stessi(e); **between** ~ tra (di) loro; *see also* **oneself.**

then [ðɛn] *ad* (*at that time*) allora; (*next*) poi, dopo; (*and also*) e poi // *cj* (*therefore*) perciò, dunque, quindi // *a*: **the** ~ **president** il presidente di allora; **by** ~ allora; **from** ~ **on** da allora in poi.

theologian [θɪə'ləudʒən] *n* teologo/a.

theology [θɪ'ɔlədʒɪ] *n* teologia.

theorem ['θɪərəm] *n* teorema *m*.

theoretical [θɪə'rɛtɪkl] *a* teorico(a).

theory ['θɪərɪ] *n* teoria.

therapeutic(al) [θɛrə'pjuːtɪk(l)] *a* terapeutico(a).

therapy ['θɛrəpɪ] *n* terapia.

there [ðɛə*] *ad* **1:** ~ **is,** ~ **are** c'è, ci sono; ~ **are 3 of them** (*people*) sono in 3; (*things*) ce ne sono 3; ~ **is no-one here** non c'è nessuno qui; ~ **has been an accident** c'è stato un incidente
2 (*referring to place*) là, lì; **up/in/down** ~ lassù/là dentro/laggiù; **he went** ~ **on Friday** ci è andato venerdì; **I want that book** ~ voglio quel libro là *or* lì; ~ **he is!** eccolo!
3: ~, ~ (*esp to child*) su, su.

thereabouts [ðɛərə'bauts] *ad* (*place*) nei pressi, da quelle parti; (*amount*) giù di lì, all'incirca.

thereafter [ðɛər'ɑːftə*] *ad* da allora in poi.

thereby [ðɛə'baɪ] *ad* con ciò.

therefore ['ðɛəfɔː*] *ad* perciò, quindi.

there's [ðɛəz] = **there is, there has.**

thermal ['θəːml] *a* termico(a).

thermometer [θə'mɔmɪtə*] *n* termometro.

thermonuclear ['θəː'məu'njuːklɪə*] *a* termonucleare.

Thermos ['θəːməs] *n* ® (*also:* ~ **flask**) thermos *m inv* ®.

thermostat ['θəːməstæt] *n* termostato.

thesaurus [θɪ'sɔːrəs] *n* dizionario dei sinonimi.

these [ðiːz] *pl pronoun, a* questi(e).

thesis, pl theses ['θiːsɪs, 'θiːsiːz] *n* tesi *f inv.*

they [ðeɪ] *pl pronoun* essi(esse); (*people only*) loro; ~ **say that ...** (*it is said that*) si dice che ...; ~'**d** = **they had, they would;** ~'**ll** = **they shall, they will;** ~'**re** = **they are;** ~'**ve** = **they have.**

thick [θɪk] *a* spesso(a); (*crowd*) compatto(a); (*stupid*) ottuso(a), lento(a) // *n*: **in the** ~ **of** nel folto di; **it's 20 cm** ~ ha uno spessore di 20 cm; ~**en** *vi* ispessire // *vt* (*sauce etc*) ispessire, rendere più denso(a); ~**ly** *ad* (*spread*) a strati spessi; (*cut*) a fette grosse; (*populated*) densamente; ~**ness** *n* spessore *m*; ~**set** *a* tarchiato(a), tozzo(a); ~**skinned** *a* (*fig*) insensibile.

thief, pl thieves [θiːf, θiːvz] *n* ladro/a.

thigh [θaɪ] *n* coscia.

thimble ['θɪmbl] *n* ditale *m*.

thin [θɪn] *a* sottile; (*person*) magro(a); (*soup*) poco denso(a); (*hair, crowd*) rado(a); (*fog*) leggero(a) // *vt* (*hair*) sfoltire; **to** ~ (**down**) (*sauce, paint*) diluire.

thing [θɪŋ] *n* cosa; (*object*) oggetto; (*contraption*) aggeggio; ~**s** *npl* (*belongings*) cose *fpl*; **for one** ~ tanto per cominciare; **the best** ~ **would be to** la cosa migliore sarebbe di; **how are** ~**s?** come va?

think [θɪŋk] *pt, pp* **thought** *vi* pensare, riflettere // *vt* pensare, credere; (*imagine*) immaginare; **to** ~ **of** pensare a; **what did you** ~ **of them?** cosa ne ha pensato?; **to** ~ **about sth/sb** pensare a qc/qn; **I'll** ~ **about it** ci penserò; **to** ~ **of doing** pensare di fare; **I** ~ **so/not** penso di sì/no; **to** ~ **well of** avere una buona opinione di; **to** ~ **out** *vt* (*plan*) elaborare; (*solution*) trovare; **to** ~ **over** *vt* riflettere su; **to** ~ **through** *vt* riflettere a fondo su; **to** ~ **up** *vt* ideare; ~ **tank** *n* commissione *f* di esperti.

third [θəːd] *num* terzo(a) // *n* terzo/a; (*fraction*) terzo, terza parte *f*; (*Brit SCOL: degree*) laurea col minimo dei voti; ~**ly** *ad* in terzo luogo; ~ **party insurance** *n* (*Brit*) assicurazione *f* contro terzi; ~**rate** *a* di qualità scadente; **the T**~ **World** *n* il Terzo Mondo.

thirst [θəːst] *n* sete *f*; ~**y** *a* (*person*) assetato(a), che ha sete.

thirteen ['θəː'tiːn] *num* tredici.

thirty ['θəːtɪ] *num* trenta.

this [ðɪs] ♦ *a* (*demonstrative: pl* **these**) questo(a); ~ **man/woman/book** quest'uomo/questa donna/questo libro; (*not "that"*) quest'uomo/questa donna/

questo libro qui; ~ **one** questo(a) qui
♦ *pronoun (demonstrative*: *pl* **these)**
questo(a); *(not "that one")* questo(a)
qui; **who/what** is ~? chi è/che cos'è questo?; **I prefer** ~ **to** that preferisco questo
a quello; ~ **is** where **I** live io abito qui;
~ **is** what **he** said questo è ciò che ha
detto; ~ **is** Mr **Brown** *(in introductions*,
photo) questo è il signor Brown; *(on
telephone)* sono il signor Brown
♦ *ad (demonstrative)*: ~ **high/long** *etc*
alto/lungo *etc* così; **I** didn't **know** things
were ~ **bad** non sapevo andasse così
male.

thistle ['θɪsl] *n* cardo.

thong [θɒŋ] *n* cinghia.

thorn [θɔːn] *n* spina.

thorough ['θʌrə] *a (search)*
minuzioso(a); *(knowledge, research)* approfondito(a), profondo(a); *(conscienzioso(a); (cleaning)* a fondo;
~bred *n (horse)* purosangue *m/f inv*;
~fare *n* strada transitabile; "no **~fare**"
"divieto di transito"; **~ly** *ad*
minuziosamente; in profondità; a fondo;
he **~ly agreed** fu completamente
d'accordo.

those [ðəuz] *pl pronoun* quelli(e) // *pl a*
quei(quegli) *mpl*; quelle *fpl*.

though [ðəu] *cj* benché, sebbene // *ad*
comunque.

thought [θɔːt] *pt*, *pp of* **think** // *n*
pensiero; *(opinion)* opinione *f*;
(intention) intenzione *f*; **~ful** *a*
pensieroso(a), pensoso(a); *(considerate)*
premuroso(a); **~less** *a* sconsiderato(a);
(behaviour) scortese.

thousand ['θauzənd] *num* mille; one ~
mille; **~s of** migliaia di; **~th** *num*
millesimo(a).

thrash [θræʃ] *vt* picchiare; bastonare;
(defeat) battere; **to** ~ **about** *vi*
dibattersi; **to** ~ **out** *vt* dibattere.

thread [θɛd] *n* filo; *(of screw)* filetto //
vt (needle) infilare; **~bare** *a* consumato(a), logoro(a).

threat [θrɛt] *n* minaccia; **~en** *vi (storm)*
minacciare // *vt*: **to ~en sb** with sth/to do
minacciare qn con qc/di fare.

three [θriː] *num* tre; **~-dimensional** *a*
tridimensionale; *(film)* stereoscopico(a);
~-piece suit *n* completo (con gilè); **~-
piece suite** *n* salotto comprendente un
divano e due poltrone; **~-ply** *a (wood)* a
tre strati; *(wool)* a tre fili.

thresh [θrɛʃ] *vt (AGR)* trebbiare.

threshold ['θrɛʃhəuld] *n* soglia.

threw [θruː] *pt of* **throw.**

thrifty ['θrɪftɪ] *a* economico(a).

thrill [θrɪl] *n* brivido // *vi* eccitarsi,
tremare // *vt (audience)* elettrizzare; **to
be ~ed** *(with gift etc)* essere
commosso(a); **~er** *n* film *m inv (or
dramma *m or* libro) del brivido; **~ing** *a
(book)* pieno(a) di suspense; *(news,*

discovery) entusiasmante.

thrive, *pt* **thrived, throve,** *pp* **thrived,
thriven** ['θraɪv, θrəuv, 'θrɪvn] *vi* crescere
or svilupparsi bene; *(business)* prosperare; **he ~s on it** gli fa bene, ne
gode; **thriving** *a* fiorente.

throat [θrəut] *n* gola; **to have a sore ~**
avere (un *or* il) mal di gola.

throb [θrɔb] *vi (heart)* palpitare;
(engine) vibrare; *(with pain)* pulsare.

throes [θrəuz] *npl*: in the ~ of alle prese
con; in preda a.

thrombosis [θrɔm'bəusɪs] *n* trombosi *f*.

throne [θrəun] *n* trono.

throng [θrɔŋ] *n* moltitudine *f //* *vt*
affollare.

throttle ['θrɔtl] *n (AUT)* valvola a
farfalla // *vt* strangolare.

through [θruː] *prep* attraverso; *(time)*
per, durante; *(by means of)* per mezzo
di; *(owing to)* a causa di // *a (ticket,
train, passage)* diretto(a) // *ad* attraverso; **to put sb ~ to sb** *(TEL)*
passare qn a qn; **to be ~** *(TEL)* ottenere
la comunicazione; *(have finished)* avere
finito; "no ~ way" *(Brit)* "strada senza
sbocco"; **~out** *prep (place)* dappertutto
in; *(time)* per *or* durante tutto(a) // *ad*
dappertutto; sempre.

throve [θrəuv] *pt of* **thrive.**

throw [θrəu] *n* tiro, getto; *(SPORT)* lancio
// *vt (pt* **threw,** *pp* **thrown** ['θruː,
θrəun]) tirare, gettare; *(SPORT)*
lanciare; *(rider)* disarcionare; *(fig)*
confondere; *(pottery)* formare al tornio;
to ~ a party dare una festa; **to ~ away**
vt gettare *or* buttare via; **to ~ off** *vt*
sbarazzarsi di; **to ~ out** *vt* buttare
fuori; *(reject)* respingere; **to ~ up** *vi*
vomitare; **~away** *a* da buttare; **~-in** *n
(SPORT)* rimessa in gioco.

thru [θruː] *prep, a, ad (US)* = **through.**

thrush [θrʌʃ] *n* tordo.

thrust [θrʌst] *n (TECH)* spinta // *vt (pt,
pp* **thrust)** spingere con forza; *(push in)*
conficcare.

thud [θʌd] *n* tonfo.

thug [θʌg] *n* delinquente *m*.

thumb [θʌm] *n (ANAT)* pollice *m //* *vt
(book)* sfogliare; **to ~ a lift** fare l'autostop; **~tack** *n (US)* puntina da disegno.

thump [θʌmp] *n* colpo forte; *(sound)*
tonfo // *vt* battere su // *vi* picchiare,
battere.

thunder ['θʌndə*] *n* tuono // *vi* tuonare;
(train etc): **to ~ past** passare con un
rombo; **~bolt** *n* fulmine *m*; **~clap** *n*
rombo di tuono; **~ous** ['θʌndrəs] *a*
fragoroso(a); **~storm** *n* temporale *m*;
~y *a* temporalesco(a).

Thursday ['θəːzdɪ] *n* giovedì *m inv*.

thus [ðʌs] *ad* così.

thwart [θwɔːt] *vt* contrastare.

thyme [taɪm] *n* timo.

thyroid ['θaɪrɔɪd] *n* tiroide *f*.

tiara |tɪ'ɑːrə| n (woman's) diadema m.

Tiber |'taɪbə*| n: the ~ il Tevere.

tick |tɪk| n (sound: of clock) tic tac m inv; (mark) segno; spunta; (ZOOL) zecca; (Brit col): **in a ~** in un attimo // vi fare tic tac // vt spuntare; **to ~ off** vt spuntare; (person) sgridare; **to ~ over** vi (engine) andare al minimo; (fig) andare avanti come al solito.

ticket |'tɪkɪt| n biglietto; (in shop: on goods) etichetta; (: from cash register) scontrino; (for library) scheda; **~ collector** n bigliettaio; **~ office** n biglietteria.

tickle |'tɪkl| n solletico // vt fare il solletico a, solleticare; (fig) stuzzicare; piacere a; far ridere.

tidal |'taɪdl| a di marea; **~ wave** n onda anomala.

tidbit |'tɪdbɪt| n (US) = **titbit**.

tiddlywinks |'tɪdlɪwɪŋks| n gioco della pulce.

tide |taɪd| n marea; (fig: of events) corso; **to ~ sb over** dare una mano a qn; **high/low ~** alta/bassa marea.

tidy |'taɪdɪ| a (room) ordinato(a), lindo(a); (dress, work) curato(a), in ordine; (person) ordinato(a) // vt (also: **~ up**) riordinare, mettere in ordine; **to ~ o.s. up** rassettarsi.

tie |taɪ| n (string etc) legaccio; (Brit: also: **neck~**) cravatta; (fig: link) legame m; (SPORT: draw) pareggio // vt (parcel) legare; (ribbon) annodare // vi (SPORT) pareggiare; **to ~ sth in a bow** annodare qc; **to ~ a knot in sth** fare un nodo a qc; **to ~ down** vt fissare con una corda; (fig): **to ~ sb down to** costringere qn a accettare; **to ~ up** vt (parcel, dog) legare; (boat) ormeggiare; (arrangements) concludere; **to be ~d up** (busy) essere occupato or preso.

tier |tɪə*| n fila; (of cake) piano, strato.

tiff |tɪf| n battibecco.

tiger |'taɪgə*| n tigre f.

tight |taɪt| a (rope) teso(a), tirato(a); (clothes) stretto(a); (budget, programme, bend) stretto(a); (control) severo(a), fermo(a); (col: drunk) sbronzo(a) // ad (squeeze) fortemente; (shut) ermeticamente; **~s** npl (Brit) collant m inv; **~en** vt (rope) tendere; (screw) stringere; (control) rinforzare // vi tendersi; stringersi; **~-fisted** a avaro(a); **~ly** ad (grasp) bene, saldamente; **~rope** n corda (da acrobata).

tile |taɪl| n (on roof) tegola; (on wall or floor) piastrella, mattonella.

till |tɪl| n registratore m di cassa // vt (land) coltivare // prep, cj = **until**.

tiller |'tɪlə*| n (NAUT) barra del timone.

tilt |tɪlt| vt inclinare, far pendere // vi inclinarsi, pendere.

timber |'tɪmbə*| n (material) legname m; (trees) alberi mpl da legname.

time |taɪm| n tempo; (epoch: often pl) epoca, tempo; (by clock) ora; (moment) momento; (occasion, also MATH) volta; (MUS) tempo // vt (race) cronometrare; (programme) calcolare la durata di; (remark etc) dire (or fare) al momento giusto; **a long ~** molto tempo; **for the ~ being** per il momento; **4 at a ~** 4 per or alla volta; **from ~ to ~** ogni tanto; **in ~** (soon enough) in tempo; (after some time) col tempo; (MUS) a tempo; **in a week's ~** fra una settimana; **in no ~** in un attimo; **any ~** in qualsiasi momento; **on ~** puntualmente; **5 ~s 5** 5 volte 5, 5 per 5; **what ~ is it?** che ora è?, che ore sono?; **to have a good ~** divertirsi; **~'s up!** è (l')ora!; **~ bomb** n bomba a orologeria; **~ lag** n intervallo, ritardo; (in travel) differenza di fuso orario; **~less** a eterno(a); **~ly** a opportuno(a); **~ off** n tempo libero; **~r** n (~ switch) temporizzatore m; (in kitchen) contaminuti m inv; **~ scale** n periodo; **~ switch** n (Brit) temporizzatore m; **~table** n orario; **~ zone** n fuso orario.

timid |'tɪmɪd| a timido(a); (easily scared) pauroso(a).

timing |'taɪmɪŋ| n sincronizzazione f; (fig) scelta del momento opportuno, tempismo; (SPORT) cronometraggio.

timpani |'tɪmpənɪ| npl timpani mpl.

tin |tɪn| n stagno; (also: **~ plate**) latta; (Brit: can) barattolo (di latta), lattina, scatola; (for baking) teglia; **~foil** n stagnola.

tinge |tɪndʒ| n sfumatura // vt: **~d with** tinto(a) di.

tingle |'tɪŋgl| vi pizzicare.

tinker |'tɪŋkə*| n stagnino ambulante; (gipsy) zingaro/a; **to ~ with** vt fus armeggiare intorno a; cercare di riparare.

tinkle |'tɪŋkl| vi tintinnare.

tinned |tɪnd| a (Brit: food) in scatola.

tin opener |'-əupnə*| n (Brit) apriscatole m inv.

tinsel |'tɪnsl| n decorazioni fpl natalizie (argentate).

tint |tɪnt| n tinta; **~ed** a (hair) tinto(a); (spectacles, glass) colorato(a).

tiny |'taɪnɪ| a minuscolo(a).

tip |tɪp| n (end) punta; (protective: on umbrella etc) puntale m; (gratuity) mancia; (for coal) discarica; (Brit: for rubbish) immondezzaio; (advice) suggerimento // vt (waiter) dare la mancia a; (tilt) inclinare; (overturn: also: **~ over**) capovolgere; (empty: also: **~ out**) scaricare; **~-off** n (hint) soffiata; **~ped** a (Brit: cigarette) col filtro.

Tipp-Ex |'tɪpɛks| n ® correttore m.

tipsy |'tɪpsɪ| a brillo(a).

tiptoe |'tɪptəu| n: **on ~** in punta di piedi.

tiptop ['tɪp'tɔp] a: **in ~ condition** in ottime condizioni.

tire ['taɪə*] n (US) = **tyre** // vt stancare // vi stancarsi; **~d** a stanco(a); **to be ~d of** essere stanco or stufo di; **~some** a noioso(a); **tiring** a faticoso(a).

tissue ['tɪʃuː] n tessuto; (paper handkerchief) fazzoletto di carta; **~ paper** n carta velina.

tit [tɪt] n (bird) cinciallegra; **to give ~ for tat** rendere pan per focaccia.

titbit ['tɪtbɪt], (US) **tidbit** ['tɪdbɪt] n (food) leccornia; (news) notizia ghiotta.

titivate ['tɪtɪveɪt] vt agghindare.

title ['taɪtl] n titolo; **~ deed** n (LAW) titolo di proprietà; **~ role** n ruolo or parte f principale.

titter ['tɪtə*] vi ridere scioccamente.

TM abbr = **trademark**.

to [tuː, tə] ♦ prep **1** (direction) a; **to go ~ France/London/school** andare in Francia/a Londra/a scuola; **to go ~ Paul's/the doctor's** andare da Paul/dal dottore; **the road ~ Edinburgh** la strada per Edimburgo; **~ the left/right** a sinistra/destra

2 (as far as) (fino) a; **from here ~ London** da qui a Londra; **to count ~ 10** contare fino a 10; **from 40 ~ 50 people** da 40 a 50 persone

3 (with expressions of time): **a quarter ~ 5** le 5 meno un quarto; **it's twenty ~ 3** sono le 3 meno venti

4 (for, of): **the key ~ the front door** la chiave della porta d'ingresso; **a letter ~ his wife** una lettera per la moglie

5 (expressing indirect object) a; **to give sth ~ sb** dare qc a qn; **to talk ~ sb** parlare a qn; **to be a danger ~ sb/sth** rappresentare un pericolo per qn/qc

6 (in relation to): **3 goals ~ 2** 3 goal a 2; **30 miles ~ the gallon** ≈ 11 chilometri con un litro

7 (purpose, result): **to come ~ sb's aid** venire in aiuto a qn; **to sentence sb ~ death** condannare a morte qn; **~ my surprise** con mia sorpresa

♦ with vb **1** (simple infinitive): **~ go/eat** etc andare/mangiare etc

2 (following another vb): **to want/try/start ~ do** volere/cercare di/cominciare a fare

3 (with vb omitted): **I don't want ~** non voglio (farlo); **you ought ~** devi (farlo)

4 (purpose, result): **I did it ~ help you** l'ho fatto per aiutarti

5 (equivalent to relative clause): **I have things ~ do** ho da fare; **the main thing is ~ try** la cosa più importante è provare

6 (after adjective etc): **ready ~ go** pronto a partire; **too old/young ~ ...** troppo vecchio/giovane per ...

♦ ad: **to push the door ~** accostare la porta.

toad [təud] n rospo; **~stool** n fungo

(velenoso).

toast [təust] n (CULIN) toast m, pane m abbrustolito; (drink, speech) brindisi m inv // vt (CULIN) abbrustolire; (drink to) brindare a; **a piece or slice of ~** una fetta di pane abbrustolito; **~er** n tostapane m inv.

tobacco [tə'bækəu] n tabacco; **~nist** n tabaccaio/a; **~nist's (shop)** n tabaccheria.

toboggan [tə'bɔgən] n toboga m inv; (child's) slitta.

today [tə'deɪ] ad, n (also fig) oggi (m).

toddler ['tɔdlə*] n bambino/a che impara a camminare.

toddy ['tɔdɪ] n grog m inv.

to-do [tə'duː] n (fuss) storie fpl.

toe [təu] n dito del piede; (of shoe) punta; **to ~ the line** (fig) stare in riga, conformarsi.

toffee ['tɔfɪ] n caramella.

toga ['təugə] n toga.

together [tə'gɛðə*] ad insieme; (at same time) allo stesso tempo; **~ with** insieme a.

toil [tɔɪl] n travaglio, fatica // vi affannarsi; sgobbare.

toilet ['tɔɪlət] n (Brit: lavatory) gabinetto // cpd (bag, soap etc) da toletta; **~ bowl** n vaso or tazza del gabinetto; **~ paper** n carta igienica; **~ries** npl articoli mpl da toletta; **~ roll** n rotolo di carta igienica; **~ water** n acqua di colonia.

token ['təukən] n (sign) segno; (voucher) buono; **book/record ~** (Brit) buono-libro/disco.

told [təuld] pt, pp of **tell**.

tolerable ['tɔlərəbl] a (bearable) tollerabile; (fairly good) passabile.

tolerant ['tɔlərnt] a: **~ (of)** tollerante (nei confronti di).

tolerate ['tɔləreɪt] vt sopportare; (MED, TECH) tollerare.

toll [təul] n (tax, charge) pedaggio // vi (bell) suonare; **the accident ~ on the roads** il numero delle vittime della strada.

tomato, ~es [tə'mɑːtəu] n pomodoro.

tomb [tuːm] n tomba.

tomboy ['tɔmbɔɪ] n maschiaccio.

tombstone ['tuːmstəun] n pietra tombale.

tomcat ['tɔmkæt] n gatto.

tomorrow [tə'mɔrəu] ad, n (also fig) domani (m inv); **the day after ~** dopodomani; **a week ~** domani a otto; **~ morning** domani mattina.

ton [tʌn] n tonnellata (Brit = 1016 kg; US = 907 kg; metric = 1000 kg); (NAUT: also: **register ~**) tonnellata di stazza (= 2.83 cu.m); **~s of** (col) un mucchio or sacco di.

tone [təun] n tono // vi intonarsi; **to ~ down** vt (colour, criticism, sound) attenuare; **to ~ up** vt (muscles) tonificare; **~-deaf** a che non ha orecchio (musicale).

tongs [tɔŋz] npl tenaglie fpl; (for coal) molle fpl; (for hair) arricciacapelli m inv.

tongue [tʌŋ] n lingua; **~ in cheek** ad ironicamente; **~-tied** a (fig) muto(a); **~-twister** n scioglilingua m inv.

tonic [ˈtɔnɪk] n (MED) tonico; (MUS) nota tonica; (also: **~ water**) acqua tonica.

tonight [təˈnaɪt] ad stanotte; (this evening) stasera // n questa notte; questa sera.

tonnage [ˈtʌnɪdʒ] n (NAUT) tonnellaggio, stazza.

tonne [tʌn] n (metric ton) tonnellata.

tonsil [ˈtɔnsl] n tonsilla; **~litis** [-ˈlaɪtɪs] n tonsillite f.

too [tuː] ad (excessively) troppo; (also) anche; **~ much** ad troppo // a troppo(a); **~ many** a troppi(e); **~ bad!** tanto peggio!, peggio così!

took [tuk] pt of **take**.

tool [tuːl] n utensile m, attrezzo // vt lavorare con un attrezzo; **~ box/kit** n cassetta f portautensili/attrezzi inv.

toot [tuːt] vi suonare; (with car horn) suonare il clacson.

tooth [tuːθ], pl **teeth** n (ANAT, TECH) dente m; **~ache** n mal m di denti; **~brush** n spazzolino da denti; **~paste** n dentifricio; **~pick** n stuzzicadenti m inv.

top [tɔp] n (of mountain, page, ladder) cima f; (of box, cupboard, table) sopra m inv, parte f superiore; (lid: of box, jar) coperchio; (: of bottle) tappo; (toy) trottola // a più alto(a); (in rank) primo(a); (best) migliore // vt (exceed) superare; (be first in) essere in testa a; **on ~ of** sopra, in cima a; (in addition to) oltre a; **from ~ to bottom** da cima a fondo; **to ~ up**, (US) **~ off** vt riempire; **~ floor** n ultimo piano; **~ hat** n cilindro; **~-heavy** a (object) con la parte superiore troppo pesante.

topic [ˈtɔpɪk] n argomento; **~al** a d'attualità.

top: ~less a (bather etc) col seno scoperto; **~-level** a (talks) ad alto livello; **~most** a il(la) più alto(a).

topple [ˈtɔpl] vt rovesciare, far cadere // vi cadere; traballare.

top-secret [ˈtɔpˈsiːkrɪt] a segretissimo(a).

topsy-turvy [ˈtɔpsɪˈtəːvɪ] a, ad sottosopra (inv).

torch [tɔːtʃ] n torcia; (Brit: electric) lampadina tascabile.

tore [tɔː*] pt of **tear**.

torment n [ˈtɔːmɛnt] tormento // vt [tɔːˈmɛnt] tormentare; (fig: annoy) infastidire.

torn [tɔːn] pp of **tear**.

tornado, **~es** [tɔːˈneɪdəu] n tornado.

torpedo, **~es** [tɔːˈpiːdəu] n siluro.

torrent [ˈtɔrnt] n torrente m.

tortoise [ˈtɔːtəs] n tartaruga; **~shell** [ˈtɔːtəʃɛl] a di tartaruga.

torture [ˈtɔːtʃə*] n tortura // vt torturare.

Tory [ˈtɔːrɪ] (Brit POL) a dei tories, conservatore(trice) // n tory m/f inv, conservatore/trice.

toss [tɔs] vt gettare, lanciare; (pancake) far saltare; (head) scuotere; **to ~ a coin** fare a testa o croce; **to ~ up for sth** fare a testa o croce per qc; **to ~ and turn** (in bed) girarsi e rigirarsi.

tot [tɔt] n (Brit: drink) bicchierino; (child) bimbo/a.

total [ˈtəutl] a totale // n totale m // vt (add up) sommare; (amount to) ammontare a.

totally [ˈtəutəlɪ] ad completamente.

totter [ˈtɔtə*] vi barcollare.

touch [tʌtʃ] n tocco; (sense) tatto; (contact) contatto; (FOOTBALL) fuori gioco m // vt toccare; **a ~ of** (fig) un tocco di; un pizzico di; **in ~ with** in contatto con; **to get in ~ with** mettersi in contatto con; **to lose ~** (friends) perdersi di vista; **to ~ on** vt fus (topic) sfiorare, accennare a; **to ~ up** vt (paint) ritoccare; **~-and-go** a incerto(a); **~down** n atterraggio; (on sea) ammaraggio; (US FOOTBALL) meta; **~ed** a commosso(a); (col) tocco(a), toccato(a); **~ing** a commovente; **~line** n (SPORT) linea laterale; **~y** a (person) suscettibile.

tough [tʌf] a duro(a); (resistant) resistente; (meat) duro(a), tiglioso(a).

toupee [ˈtuːpeɪ] n parrucchino.

tour [tuə*] n viaggio; (also: package ~) viaggio organizzato or tutto compreso; (of town, museum) visita; (by artist) tournée f inv // vt visitare; **~ing** n turismo.

tourism [ˈtuərɪzəm] n turismo.

tourist [ˈtuərɪst] n turista m/f // a (travel) in classe turistica // cpd turistico(a); **~ office** n pro loco f inv.

tournament [ˈtuənəmənt] n torneo.

tousled [ˈtauzld] a (hair) arruffato(a).

tout [taut] vi: **to ~ for** procacciare, raccogliere; cercare clienti per // n (also: ticket ~) bagarino.

tow [təu] vt rimorchiare; "**on** or (US) **in ~**" (AUT) "veicolo rimorchiato".

toward(s) [təˈwɔːd(z)] prep verso; (of attitude) nei confronti di; (of purpose) per.

towel [ˈtauəl] n asciugamano; (also: tea ~) strofinaccio; **~ling** n (fabric) spugna; **~ rail**, (US) **~ rack** n portasciugamano.

tower [ˈtauə*] n torre f; **~ block** n (Brit) palazzone m; **~ing** a altissimo(a), imponente.

town |taun| n città f inv; **to go to ~** andare in città; (fig) mettercela tutta; **~ centre** n centro (città); **~ clerk** n segretario comunale; **~ council** n consiglio comunale; **~ hall** n ≈ municipio; **~ plan** n pianta della città; **~ planning** n urbanistica.

towrope |'təurəup| n (cavo da) rimorchio.

tow truck n (US) carro m attrezzi inv.

toxic |'tɔksɪk| a tossico(a).

toy |tɔɪ| n giocattolo; **to ~ with** vt fus giocare con; (idea) accarezzare, trastullarsi con.

trace |treɪs| n traccia // vt (draw) tracciare; (follow) seguire; (locate) rintracciare; **tracing paper** n carta da ricalco.

track |træk| n (of person, animal) traccia; (on tape, SPORT, path: gen) pista; (: of bullet etc) traiettoria; (: of suspect, animal) pista, tracce fpl; (RAIL) binario, rotaie fpl // vt seguire le tracce di; **to keep ~ of** seguire; **to ~ down** vt (prey) scovare; snidare; (sth lost) rintracciare; **~suit** n tuta sportiva.

tract |trækt| n (GEO) tratto, estensione f; (pamphlet) opuscolo, libretto.

tractor |'træktə*| n trattore m.

trade |treɪd| n commercio; (skill, job) mestiere m // vi commerciare; **to ~ with/in** commerciare con/in; **to ~ in** vt (old car etc) dare come pagamento parziale; **~ fair** n fiera commerciale; **~-in price** n prezzo di permuta; **~mark** n marchio di fabbrica; **~ name** n marca, nome m depositato; **~r** n commerciante m/f; **~sman** n fornitore m; (shopkeeper) negoziante m; **~ union** n sindacato; **~ unionist** n sindacalista m/f; **trading** n commercio; **trading estate** n (Brit) zona industriale.

tradition |trə'dɪʃən| n tradizione f; **~al** a tradizionale.

traffic |'træfɪk| n traffico // vi: **to ~ in** (pej: liquor, drugs) trafficare in; **~ circle** n (US) isola rotatoria; **~ jam** n ingorgo (del traffico); **~ lights** npl semaforo; **~ warden** n addetto/a al controllo del traffico e del parcheggio.

tragedy |'trædʒədɪ| n tragedia.

tragic |'trædʒɪk| a tragico(a).

trail |treɪl| n (tracks) tracce fpl, pista; (path) sentiero; (of smoke etc) scia // vt trascinare, strascicare; (follow) seguire // vi essere al traino; (dress etc) strusciare; (plant) arrampicarsi; strisciare; **to ~ behind** vi essere al traino; **~er** n (AUT) rimorchio; (US) roulotte f inv; (CINEMA) prossimamente m inv; **~er truck** n (US: articulated lorry) autoarticolato.

train |treɪn| n treno; (of dress) coda, strascico // vt (apprentice, doctor etc) formare; (sportsman) allenare; (dog) addestrare; (memory) esercitare; (point: gun etc): **to ~ sth on** puntare qc contro // vi formarsi; allenarsi; **one's ~ of thought** il filo dei propri pensieri; **~ed** a qualificato(a); allenato(a); addestrato(a); **~ee** |treɪ'niː| n allievo/a; (in trade) apprendista m/f; **~er** n (SPORT) allenatore/trice; (of dogs etc) addestratore/trice; **~ing** n formazione f; allenamento; addestramento; **in ~ing** (SPORT) in allenamento; (fit) in forma; **~ing college** n istituto professionale; (for teachers) ≈ istituto magistrale; **~ing shoes** npl scarpe fpl da ginnastica.

traipse |treɪps| vi girovagare, andare a zonzo.

trait |treɪt| n tratto.

traitor |'treɪtə*| n traditore m.

trajectory |trə'dʒektərɪ| n traiettoria.

tram |træm| n (Brit: also: **~car**) tram m inv.

tramp |træmp| n (person) vagabondo/a; (col: pej: woman) sgualdrina // vi camminare con passo pesante // vt (walk through: town, streets) percorrere a piedi.

trample |'træmpl| vt: **to ~ (underfoot)** calpestare.

trampoline |'træmpəliːn| n trampolino.

tranquil |'træŋkwɪl| a tranquillo(a); **~lizer** n (MED) tranquillante m.

transact |træn'zækt| vt (business) trattare; **~ion** |-'zækʃən| n transazione f; **~ions** npl (minutes) atti mpl.

transatlantic |'trænzət'læntɪk| a transatlantico(a).

transcript |'trænskrɪpt| n trascrizione f.

transfer |'trænsfə*| n (gen, also SPORT) trasferimento; (POL: of power) passaggio; (picture, design) decalcomania; (: stick-on) autoadesivo // vt |træns'fɜː*| trasferire; passare; decalcare.

transform |træns'fɔːm| vt trasformare.

transfusion |træns'fjuːʒən| n trasfusione f.

transient |'trænzɪənt| a transitorio(a), fugace.

transistor |træn'zɪstə*| n (ELEC) transistor m inv; (also: **~ radio**) radio f inv a transistor.

transit |'trænzɪt| n: **in ~** in transito.

transitive |'trænzɪtɪv| a (LING) transitivo(a).

translate |trænz'leɪt| vt tradurre; **translation** |-'leɪʃən| n traduzione f; (SCOL: as opposed to prose) versione f; **translator** n traduttore/trice.

transmission |trænz'mɪʃən| n trasmissione f.

transmit |trænz'mɪt| vt trasmettere; **~ter** n trasmettitore m.

transparency |træns'pɛərnsɪ| n (Brit:

PHOT) diapositiva.
transparent [træns'pærnt] *a* trasparente.
transpire [træn'spaɪə*] *vi* (*happen*)
succedere; (*turn out*): it ~d that si
venne a sapere che.
transplant *vt* [træns'plɑ:nt] trapiantare //
n ['trænsplɑ:nt] (*MED*) trapianto.
transport *n* ['trænspɔ:t] trasporto // *vt*
[træns'pɔ:t] trasportare; ~ation [-'teɪʃən]
n (mezzo di) trasporto; (*of prisoners*)
deportazione *f*; ~ café *n* (*Brit*) trattoria
per camionisti.
trap [træp] *n* (*snare, trick*) trappola;
(*carriage*) calesse *m* // *vt* prendere in
trappola, intrappolare; (*immobilize*)
bloccare; (*jam*) chiudere, schiacciare;
~ door *n* botola.
trapeze [trə'pi:z] *n* trapezio.
trapper ['træpə*] *n* cacciatore *m* di
animali da pelliccia.
trappings ['træpɪŋz] *npl* ornamenti *mpl*;
indoratura, sfarzo.
trash [træʃ] *n* (*pej: goods*) ciarpame *m*;
(: *nonsense*) sciocchezze *fpl*; ~ can *n*
(*US*) secchio della spazzatura.
trauma ['trɔ:mə] *n* trauma *m*; ~tic
[-'mætɪk] *a* traumatico(a).
travel ['trævl] *n* viaggio; viaggi *mpl* // *vi*
viaggiare; (*move*) andare, spostarsi // *vt*
(*distance*) percorrere; ~ **agency** *n*
agenzia (di) viaggi; ~ **agent** *n* agente
m di viaggio; ~**ler**, (*US*) ~**er** *n*
viaggiatore/trice; ~**ler's cheque** *n* assegno turistico; ~**ling**, (*US*) ~**ing** *n*
viaggi *mpl* // *cpd* (*bag, clock*) da
viaggio; (*expenses*) di viaggio; ~ **sickness** *n* mal *m* d'auto (or di mare or
d'aria).
travesty ['trævəstɪ] *n* parodia.
trawler ['trɔ:lə*] *n* peschereccio (a stra-
scico).
tray [treɪ] *n* (*for carrying*) vassoio; (*on
desk*) vaschetta.
treachery ['tretʃərɪ] *n* tradimento.
treacle ['tri:kl] *n* melassa.
tread [tred] *n* passo; (*sound*) rumore *m*
di passi; (*of tyre*) battistrada *m inv* // *vi*
(*pt* **trod**, *pp* **trodden**) camminare; **to
~ on** *vt fus* calpestare.
treason ['tri:zn] *n* tradimento.
treasure ['treʒə*] *n* tesoro // *vt* (*value*)
tenere in gran conto, apprezzare molto;
(*store*) custodire gelosamente.
treasurer ['treʒərə*] *n* tesoriere/a.
treasury ['treʒərɪ] *n* tesoreria; **the T~**,
(*US*) **the T~ Department** il ministero del
Tesoro.
treat [tri:t] *n* regalo // *vt* trattare; (*MED*)
curare; **to ~ sb to sth** offrire qc a qn.
treatise ['tri:tɪz] *n* trattato.
treatment ['tri:tmənt] *n* trattamento.
treaty ['tri:tɪ] *n* patto, trattato.
treble ['trebl] *a* triplo(a), triplice // *vt* tri-
plicare // *vi* triplicarsi; ~ **clef** *n* chiave *f*
di violino.

tree [tri:] *n* albero.
trek [trek] *n* viaggio; camminata; (*tiring
walk*) tirata a piedi // *vi* (*as holiday*)
fare dell'escursionismo.
trellis ['trelɪs] *n* graticcio.
tremble ['trembl] *vi* tremare; (*machine*)
vibrare.
tremendous [trɪ'mendəs] *a* (*enormous*)
enorme; (*excellent*) meraviglioso(a),
formidabile.
tremor ['tremə*] *n* tremore *m*, tremito;
(*also: earth ~*) scossa sismica.
trench [trentʃ] *n* trincea.
trend [trend] *n* (*tendency*) tendenza; (*of
events*) corso; (*fashion*) moda; ~**y** *a*
(*idea*) di moda; (*clothes*) all'ultima
moda.
trepidation [trepɪ'deɪʃən] *n* trepidazione
f, agitazione *f*.
trespass ['trespəs] *vi*: **to ~ on** entrare
abusivamente in; (*fig*) abusare di; "no
~ing" "proprietà privata", "vietato
l'accesso".
trestle ['tresl] *n* cavalletto; ~ **table** *n*
tavolo su cavalletti.
trial ['traɪəl] *n* (*LAW*) processo; (*test: of
machine etc*) collaudo; (*hardship*)
prova, difficoltà *f inv*; (*worry*) cruccio;
by ~ and error a tentoni.
triangle ['traɪæŋgl] *n* (*MATH, MUS*)
triangolo.
tribe [traɪb] *n* tribù *f inv*.
tribunal [traɪ'bju:nl] *n* tribunale *m*.
tributary ['trɪbjutərɪ] *n* (*river*)
tributario, affluente *m*.
tribute ['trɪbju:t] *n* tributo, omaggio; **to
pay ~ to** rendere omaggio a.
trice [traɪs] *n*: **in a ~** in un attimo.
trick [trɪk] *n* trucco; (*joke*) tiro; (*CARDS*)
presa // *vt* imbrogliare, ingannare; **to
play a ~ on sb** giocare un tiro a qn; **that
should do the ~** vedrai che funziona;
~**ery** *n* inganno.
trickle ['trɪkl] *n* (*of water etc*) rivolo;
gocciolio // *vi* gocciolare.
tricky ['trɪkɪ] *a* difficile, delicato(a).
tricycle ['traɪsɪkl] *n* triciclo.
trifle ['traɪfl] *n* sciocchezza; (*Brit CULIN*)
≈ zuppa inglese // *ad*: **a ~ long** un po'
lungo; **trifling** *a* insignificante.
trigger ['trɪgə*] *n* (*of gun*) grilletto; **to
~ off** *vt* dare l'avvio a.
trim [trɪm] *a* ordinato(a); (*house,
garden*) ben tenuto(a); (*figure*) snello(a)
// *n* (*haircut etc*) spuntata, regolata;
(*embellishment*) finiture *fpl*; (*on car*)
guarnizioni *fpl* // *vt* spuntare;
(*decorate*): **to ~ (with)** decorare (con);
(*NAUT: a sail*) orientare; ~**mings** *npl*
decorazioni *fpl*; (*extras: gen CULIN*)
guarnizione *f*.
trinket ['trɪŋkɪt] *n* gingillo; (*piece of
jewellery*) ciondolo.
trip [trɪp] *n* viaggio; (*excursion*) gita,
escursione *f*; (*stumble*) passo falso // *vi*

inciampare; *(go lightly)* camminare con passo leggero; **on a ~** in viaggio; **to ~ up** *vi* inciampare // *vt* fare lo sgambetto a.

tripe |traip| *n (CULIN)* trippa; *(pej: rubbish)* sciocchezze *fpl*, fesserie *fpl*.

triple |'tripl| *a* triplo(a).

triplets |'triplits| *npl* bambini(e) trigemini(e).

tripod |'traipɔd| *n* treppiede *m*.

trite |trait| *a* banale, trito(a).

triumph |'traiʌmf| *n* trionfo // *vi*: **to ~ (over)** trionfare (su).

trivia |'triviə| *npl* banalità *fpl*.

trivial |'triviəl| *a* insignificante; *(commonplace)* banale.

trod |trɔd| *pt of* **tread**; **~den** *pp of* **tread**.

trolley |'trɔli| *n* carrello; **~ bus** *n* filobus *m inv*.

trombone |trɔm'bəun| *n* trombone *m*.

troop |tru:p| *n* gruppo; *(MIL)* squadrone *m*; **~s** *npl (MIL)* truppe *fpl*; **to ~ in/out** *vi* entrare/uscire a frotte; **~er** *n (MIL)* soldato di cavalleria; **~ing the colour** *n (ceremony)* sfilata della bandiera.

trophy |'trəufi| *n* trofeo.

tropic |'trɔpik| *n* tropico; **~al** *a* tropicale.

trot |trɔt| *n* trotto // *vi* trottare; **on the ~** *(Brit: fig)* di fila, uno(a) dopo l'altro(a).

trouble |'trʌbl| *n* difficoltà *f inv*, problema *m*; difficoltà *fpl*, problemi; *(worry)* preoccupazione *f*; *(bother, effort)* sforzo; *(POL)* conflitti *mpl*, disordine *m*; *(MED)*: **stomach** *etc* **~** disturbi *mpl* gastrici *etc* // *vt* disturbare; *(worry)* preoccupare // *vi*: **to ~ to do** disturbarsi a fare; **~s** *npl (POL etc)* disordini *mpl*; **to be in ~** avere dei problemi; **it's no ~!** di niente!; **what's the ~?** cosa c'è che non va?; **~d** *a (person)* preoccupato(a), inquieto(a); *(epoch, life)* agitato(a), difficile; **~maker** *n* elemento disturbatore, agitatore/trice; **~shooter** *n (in conflict)* conciliatore *m*; **~some** *a* fastidioso(a), seccante.

trough |trɔf| *n (also:* **drinking ~)** abbeveratoio; *(also:* **feeding ~)** trogolo, mangiatoia; *(channel)* canale *m*.

trousers |'trauzəz| *npl* pantaloni *mpl*, calzoni *mpl*; **short ~** calzoncini *mpl*.

trousseau, *pl* **~x** *or* **~s** |'tru:səu, -z| *n* corredo da sposa.

trout |traut| *n (pl inv)* trota.

trowel |'trauəl| *n* cazzuola.

truant |'truənt| *n*: **to play ~** *(Brit)* marinare la scuola.

truce |tru:s| *n* tregua.

truck |trʌk| *n* autocarro, camion *m inv*; *(RAIL)* carro merci aperto; *(for luggage)* carrello *m* portabagagli *inv*; **~ driver** *n* camionista *m/f*; **~ farm** *n (US)* orto industriale.

truculent |'trʌkjulənt| *a* aggressivo(a), brutale.

trudge |trʌdʒ| *vi* trascinarsi pesantemente.

true |tru:| *a* vero(a); *(accurate)* accurato(a), esatto(a); *(genuine)* reale; *(faithful)* fedele.

truffle |'trʌfl| *n* tartufo.

truly |'tru:li| *ad* veramente; *(truthfully)* sinceramente; *(faithfully)* fedelmente.

trump |trʌmp| *n* atout *m inv*; **~ed-up** *a* inventato(a).

trumpet |'trʌmpit| *n* tromba.

truncheon |'trʌntʃən| *n* sfollagente *m inv*.

trundle |'trʌndl| *vt, vi*: **to ~ along** rotolare rumorosamente.

trunk |trʌŋk| *n (of tree, person)* tronco; *(of elephant)* proboscide *f*; *(case)* baule *m*; *(US AUT)* bagagliaio; **~s** *npl (also:* **swimming ~s)** calzoncini *mpl* da bagno.

truss |trʌs| *n (MED)* cinto erniario; **to ~ (up)** *vt (CULIN)* legare.

trust |trʌst| *n* fiducia; *(LAW)* amministrazione *f* fiduciaria; *(COMM)* trust *m inv* // *vt (rely on)* contare su; *(entrust)*: **to ~ sth to sb** affidare qc a qn; **~ed** *a* fidato(a); **~ee** |trʌs'ti:| *n (LAW)* amministratore/trice fiduciario(a); *(of school etc)* amministratore/trice; **~ful,** **~ing** *a* fiducioso(a); **~worthy** *a* fidato(a), degno(a) di fiducia.

truth, ~s |tru:θ, tru:ðz| *n* verità *f inv*; **~ful** *a (person)* sincero(a); *(description)* veritiero(a), esatto(a).

try |trai| *n* prova, tentativo; *(RUGBY)* meta // *vt (LAW)* giudicare; *(test: sth new)* provare; *(strain)* mettere alla prova // *vi* provare; **to ~ to do** provare a fare; *(seek)* cercare di fare; **to ~ on** *vt (clothes)* provare; **to ~ out** *vt* provare, mettere alla prova; **~ing** *a (day, experience)* logorante, pesante; *(child)* difficile, insopportabile.

tsar |za:*| *n* zar *m inv*.

T-shirt |'ti:ʃə:t| *n* maglietta.

T-square |'ti:skwɛə*| *n* riga a T.

tub |tʌb| *n* tinozza; mastello; *(bath)* bagno.

tuba |'tju:bə| *n* tuba.

tubby |'tʌbi| *a* grassoccio(a).

tube |tju:b| *n* tubo; *(Brit: underground)* metropolitana, metrò *m inv*; *(for tyre)* camera d'aria.

tubing |'tju:biŋ| *n* tubazione *f*; **a piece of ~** un tubo.

tubular |'tju:bjulə*| *a* tubolare.

TUC *n abbr (Brit: = Trades Union Congress)* confederazione *f* dei sindacati britannici.

tuck |tʌk| *n (SEWING)* piega // *vt (put)* mettere; **to ~ away** *vt* riporre; **to ~ in** *vt* mettere dentro; *(child)* rimboccare // *vi (eat)* mangiare di buon appetito; abbuffarsi; **to ~ up** *vt (child)* rimboccare; ~ **shop** n negozio di pasticceria (in una scuola).

Tuesday ['tju:zdɪ] n martedì m inv.

tuft [tʌft] n ciuffo.

tug [tʌg] n (ship) rimorchiatore m // vt tirare con forza; ~**-of-war** n tiro alla fune.

tuition [tju:'ɪʃən] n (Brit) lezioni fpl; (: private ~) lezioni fpl private; (US: school fees) tasse fpl scolastiche.

tulip ['tju:lɪp] n tulipano.

tumble ['tʌmbl] n (fall) capitombolo // vi capitombolare, ruzzolare; (somersault) fare capriole; to ~ to sth (col) realizzare qc; ~**down** a cadente, diroccato(a); ~ **dryer** n (Brit) asciugatrice f.

tumbler ['tʌmblə*] n bicchiere m (senza stelo); acrobata m/f.

tummy ['tʌmɪ] n (col) pancia.

tumour, (US) **tumor** ['tju:mə*] n tumore m.

tuna ['tju:nə] n (pl inv) (also: ~ **fish**) tonno.

tune [tju:n] n (melody) melodia, aria // vt (MUS) accordare; (RADIO, TV, AUT) regolare, mettere a punto; to be in/out of ~ (instrument) essere accordato(a)/scordato(a); (singer) essere intonato(a)/stonato(a); to ~ in vi: to ~ in (to) (RADIO, TV) sintonizzarsi (su); to ~ up vi (musician) accordare lo strumento; ~**ful** a melodioso(a).

tunic ['tju:nɪk] n tunica.

tuning ['tju:nɪŋ] n messa a punto; ~ **fork** n diapason m inv.

Tunisia [tju:'nɪzɪə] n Tunisia.

tunnel ['tʌnl] n galleria // vi scavare una galleria.

turban ['tə:bən] n turbante m.

turbot ['tə:bət] n (pl inv) rombo gigante.

turbulence ['tə:bjuləns] n (AVIAT) turbolenza.

tureen [tə'ri:n] n zuppiera.

turf [tə:f] n terreno erboso; (clod) zolla // vt coprire di zolle erbose; to ~ out vt (col) buttar fuori.

turgid ['tə:dʒɪd] a (speech) ampolloso(a), pomposo(a).

Turin [tjuə'rɪn] n Torino f.

Turk [tə:k] n turco/a.

Turkey ['tə:kɪ] n Turchia.

turkey ['tə:kɪ] n tacchino.

Turkish ['tə:kɪʃ] a turco(a) // n (LING) turco.

turmoil ['tə:mɔɪl] n confusione f, tumulto.

turn [tə:n] n giro; (in road) curva; (tendency: of mind, events) tendenza; (performance) numero; (MED) crisi f inv, attacco // vt girare, voltare; (milk) far andare a male; (change): to ~ sth **into** trasformare qc in // vi girare; (person: look back) girarsi, voltarsi; (reverse direction) girarsi indietro; (change) cambiare; (become) diventare; to ~ **into** trasformarsi in; a

good ~ un buon servizio; it gave me quite a ~ mi ha fatto prendere un bello spavento; "no left ~" (AUT) "divieto di svolta a sinistra"; it's your ~ tocca a lei; in ~ a sua volta; a turno; to take ~s (at sth) fare (qc) a turno; to ~ **away** vi girarsi (dall'altra parte); to ~ **back** vi ritornare, tornare indietro; to ~ **down** vt (refuse) rifiutare; (reduce) abbassare; (fold) ripiegare; to ~ **in** vi (col: go to bed) andare a letto // vt (fold) voltare in dentro; to ~ **off** vi (from road) girare, voltare // vt (light, radio, engine etc) spegnere; to ~ **on** vt (light, radio etc) accendere; (engine) avviare; to ~ **out** vt (light, gas) chiudere, spegnere // vi: to ~ out to be ... rivelarsi ..., risultare ...; to ~ **over** vi (person) girarsi // vt girare; to ~ **round** vi girare; (person) girarsi; to ~ **up** vi (person) arrivare, presentarsi; (lost object) saltar fuori // vt (collar, sound) alzare; ~**ing** n (in road) curva; ~**ing point** n (fig) svolta decisiva.

turnip ['tə:nɪp] n rapa.

turnout ['tə:naut] n presenza, affluenza.

turnover ['tə:nəuvə*] n (COMM) giro di affari.

turnpike ['tə:npaɪk] n (US) autostrada a pedaggio.

turnstile ['tə:nstaɪl] n tornella.

turntable ['tə:nteɪbl] n (on record player) piatto.

turn-up ['tə:nʌp] n (Brit: on trousers) risvolto.

turpentine ['tə:pəntaɪn] n (also: turps) acqua ragia.

turquoise ['tə:kwɔɪz] n (stone) turchese m // a color turchese; di turchese.

turret ['tʌrɪt] n torretta.

turtle ['tə:tl] n testuggine f; ~**neck (sweater)** n maglione m con il collo alto.

tusk [tʌsk] n zanna.

tussle ['tʌsl] n baruffa, mischia.

tutor ['tju:tə*] n (in college) docente m/f (responsabile di un gruppo di studenti); (private teacher) precettore m; ~**ial** [-'tɔ:rɪəl] n (SCOL) lezione f con discussione (a un gruppo limitato).

tuxedo [tʌk'si:dəu] n (US) smoking m inv.

TV [ti:'vi:] n abbr (= television) tivù f inv.

twang [twæŋ] n (of instrument) suono vibrante; (of voice) accento nasale.

tweed [twi:d] n tweed m inv.

tweezers ['twi:zəz] npl pinzette fpl.

twelfth [twelfθ] num dodicesimo(a).

twelve [twelv] num dodici; at ~ (o'clock) alle dodici, a mezzogiorno; (midnight) a mezzanotte.

twentieth ['twentɪθ] num ventesimo(a).

twenty ['twentɪ] num venti.

twice [twaɪs] ad due volte; ~ as much

due volte tanto.

twiddle |'twɪdl| vt, vi: to ~ (with) sth giocherellare con qc; to ~ one's thumbs (fig) girarsi i pollici.

twig |twɪg| n ramoscello // vt, vi (col) capire.

twilight |'twaɪlaɪt| n crepuscolo.

twin |twɪn| a, n gemello(a) // vt: to ~ one town with another fare il gemellaggio di una città con un'altra; ~-bedded room n stanza con letti gemelli.

twine |twaɪn| n spago, cordicella // vi attorcigliarsi.

twinge |twɪndʒ| n (of pain) fitta; a ~ of conscience/regret un rimorso/rimpianto.

twinkle |'twɪŋkl| n scintillio // vi scintillare; (eyes) brillare.

twirl |twəːl| n piroetta // vt far roteare // vi roteare.

twist |twɪst| n torsione f; (in wire, flex) storta; (in story) colpo di scena // vt attorcigliare; (weave) intrecciare; (roll around) arrotolare; (fig) deformare // vi attorcigliarsi; arrotolarsi; (road) serpeggiare.

twit |twɪt| n (col) minchione/a.

twitch |twɪtʃ| n tiratina; (nervous) tic m inv // vi contrarsi; avere un tic.

two |tuː| num due; to put ~ and ~ together (fig) trarre le conclusioni; ~-door a (AUT) a due porte; ~-faced a (pej: person) falso(a); ~fold ad: to increase ~fold aumentare del doppio; ~-piece (suit) n due pezzi m inv; ~-piece (swimsuit) n (costume m da bagno a) due pezzi m inv; ~-seater n (plane) biposto; (car) macchina a due posti; ~some n (people) coppia; ~-way a (traffic) a due sensi.

tycoon |taɪ'kuːn| n: (business) ~ magnate m.

type |taɪp| n (category) genere m; (model) modello; (example) tipo, (TYP) tipo, carattere m // vt (letter etc) battere (a macchina), dattilografare; ~-cast a (actor) a ruolo fisso; ~face n carattere m tipografico; ~script n dattiloscritto; ~writer n macchina da scrivere; ~written a dattiloscritto(a), battuto(a) a macchina.

typhoid |'taɪfɔɪd| n tifoidea.

typhoon |taɪ'fuːn| n tifone m.

typhus |'taɪfəs| n tifo.

typical |'tɪpɪkl| a tipico(a).

typing |'taɪpɪŋ| n dattilografia.

typist |'taɪpɪst| n dattilografo/a.

tyrant |'taɪərnt| n tiranno.

tyre, (US) **tire** |'taɪə*| n pneumatico, gomma; ~ pressure n pressione f (delle gomme).

tzar |zɑː*| n = **tsar.**

U

U-bend |'juː'bend| n (in pipe) sifone m.

udder |'ʌdə*| n mammella.

UFO |'juːfəu| n abbr (= unidentified flying object) UFO m inv.

ugh |ɔːh| excl puah!

ugly |'ʌglɪ| a brutto(a).

UK n abbr = **United Kingdom.**

ulcer |'ʌlsə*| n ulcera; (also: mouth ~) afta.

Ulster |'ʌlstə*| n Ulster m.

ulterior |ʌl'tɪərɪə*| a ulteriore; ~ motive n secondo fine m.

ultimate |'ʌltɪmət| a ultimo(a), finale; (authority) massimo(a), supremo(a); ~ly ad alla fine; in definitiva, in fin dei conti.

ultrasound |ʌltrə'saund| n (MED) ultrasuono.

umbilical cord |ʌmbɪ'laɪkl-| n cordone m ombelicale.

umbrage |'ʌmbrɪdʒ| n: to take ~ offendersi, impermalirsi.

umbrella |ʌm'brɛlə| n ombrello.

umpire |'ʌmpaɪə*| n arbitro.

umpteen |ʌmp'tiːn| a non so quanti(e); for the ~th time per l'ennesima volta.

UN, UNO n abbr = **United Nations (Organization).**

unable |ʌn'eɪbl| a: to be ~ to non potere, essere nell'impossibilità di; essere incapace di.

unaccompanied |ʌnə'kʌmpənɪd| a (child, lady) non accompagnato(a).

unaccountably |ʌnə'kauntəblɪ| ad inesplicabilmente.

unaccustomed |ʌnə'kʌstəmd| a insolito(a); to be ~ to sth non essere abituato a qc.

unanimous |juː'nænɪməs| a unanime; ~ly ad all'unanimità.

unarmed |ʌn'ɑːmd| a (without a weapon) disarmato(a); (combat) senz'armi.

unassuming |ʌnə'sjuːmɪŋ| a modesto(a), senza pretese.

unattached |ʌnə'tætʃt| a senza legami, libero(a).

unattended |ʌnə'tendɪd| a (car, child, luggage) incustodito(a).

unauthorized |ʌn'ɔːθəraɪzd| a non autorizzato(a).

unavoidable |ʌnə'vɔɪdəbl| a inevitabile.

unaware |ʌnə'wɛə*| a: to be ~ of non sapere, ignorare; ~s ad di sorpresa, alla sprovvista.

unbalanced |ʌn'bælənst| a squilibrato(a).

unbearable |ʌn'bɛərəbl| a insopportabile.

unbeknown(st) |ʌnbɪ'nəun(st)| ad: ~ to all'insaputa di.

unbelievable [ʌnbɪ'liːvəbl] a incredibile.

unbend [ʌn'bɛnd] vb (irg) vi distendersi // vt (wire) raddrizzare.

unbias(s)ed [ʌn'baɪəst] a (person, report) obiettivo(a), imparziale.

unborn [ʌn'bɔːn] a non ancora nato(a).

unbreakable [ʌn'breɪkəbl] a infrangibile.

unbroken [ʌn'brəukən] a intero(a); continuo(a).

unbutton [ʌn'bʌtn] vt sbottonare.

uncalled-for [ʌn'kɔːldfɔː*] a (remark) fuori luogo inv; (action) ingiustificato(a).

uncanny [ʌn'kænɪ] a misterioso(a), strano(a).

unceasing [ʌn'siːsɪŋ] a incessante.

unceremonious ['ʌnsɛrɪ'məunɪəs] a (abrupt, rude) senza tante cerimonie.

uncertain [ʌn'sɜːtn] a incerto(a); dubbio(a); ~ty n incertezza.

unchecked [ʌn'tʃɛkt] a incontrollato(a).

uncivilized [ʌn'sɪvɪlaɪzd] a (gen) selvaggio(a); (fig) incivile, barbaro(a).

uncle ['ʌŋkl] n zio.

uncomfortable [ʌn'kʌmfətəbl] a scomodo(a); (uneasy) a disagio, agitato(a); fastidioso(a).

uncommon [ʌn'kɔmən] a raro(a), insolito(a), non comune.

uncompromising [ʌn'kɔmprəmaɪzɪŋ] a intransigente, inflessibile.

unconcerned [ʌnkən'sɜːnd] a: to be ~ (about) non preoccuparsi (di or per).

unconditional [ʌnkən'dɪʃənl] a incondizionato(a), senza condizioni.

unconscious [ʌn'kɔnʃəs] a privo(a) di sensi, svenuto(a); (unaware) inconsapevole, inconscio(a) // n: the ~ l'inconscio; ~ly ad inconsciamente.

uncontrollable [ʌnkən'trəuləbl] a incontrollabile; indisciplinato(a).

unconventional [ʌnkən'vɛnʃənl] a poco convenzionale.

uncouth [ʌn'kuːθ] a maleducato(a), grossolano(a).

uncover [ʌn'kʌvə*] vt scoprire.

undecided [ʌndɪ'saɪdɪd] a indeciso(a).

under ['ʌndə*] prep sotto; (less than) meno di; al disotto di; (according to) secondo, in conformità a // ad (al) disotto; **from ~ sth** da sotto a or dal disotto di qc; **~ there** là sotto; **~ repair** in riparazione.

under... ['ʌndə*] prefix sotto..., sub...; **~ age** a minorenne; **~carriage** n (Brit) carrello (d'atterraggio); **~charge** vt far pagare di meno a; **~coat** n (paint) mano f di fondo; **~cover** a segreto(a), clandestino(a); **~current** n corrente f sottomarina; **~cut** vt irg vendere a prezzo minore di; **~developed** a sottosviluppato(a); **~dog** n oppresso/a; **~done** a (CULIN) al sangue; (pej) poco cotto(a); **~estimate** vt sottovalutare; **~fed** a

denutrito(a); **~foot** ad sotto i piedi; **~go** vt irg subire; (treatment) sottoporsi a; **~graduate** n studente(essa) universitario(a); **~ground** n (Brit: railway) metropolitana; (POL) movimento clandestino // a sotterraneo(a); (fig) clandestino(a); **~growth** n sottobosco; **~hand(ed)** a (fig) furtivo(a), subdolo(a); **~lie** vt irg essere alla base di; **~line** vt sottolineare; **~ling** ['ʌndəlɪŋ] n (pej) subalterno/a, tirapiedi m/f inv; **~mine** vt minare; **~neath** [ʌndə'niːθ] ad sotto, disotto // prep sotto, al di sotto di; **~paid** a mal pagato(a); **~pants** npl mutande fpl, slip m inv; **~pass** n (Brit) sottopassaggio; **~privileged** a non abbiente; meno favorito(a); **~rate** vt sottovalutare; **~shirt** n (US) maglietta; **~shorts** npl (US) mutande fpl, slip m inv; **~side** n disotto; **~skirt** n (Brit) sottoveste f.

understand [ʌndə'stænd] vb (irg: like stand) vt, vi capire, comprendere; I ~ that ... sento che ...; credo di capire che ...; **~able** a comprensibile; **~ing** a comprensivo(a) // n comprensione f; (agreement) accordo.

understatement [ʌndə'steɪtmənt] n: that's an ~! a dire poco!

understood [ʌndə'stud] pt, pp of understand // a inteso(a); (implied) sottinteso(a).

understudy ['ʌndəstʌdɪ] n sostituto/a, attore/trice supplente.

undertake [ʌndə'teɪk] vt irg intraprendere; to ~ to do sth impegnarsi a fare qc.

undertaker ['ʌndəteɪkə*] n impresario di pompe funebri.

undertaking [ʌndə'teɪkɪŋ] n impresa; (promise) promessa.

undertone ['ʌndətəun] n: in an ~ a mezza voce, a voce bassa.

underwater [ʌndə'wɔːtə*] ad sott'acqua // a subacqueo(a).

underwear ['ʌndəwɛə*] n biancheria (intima).

underworld ['ʌndəwɜːld] n (of crime) malavita.

underwriter ['ʌndəraɪtə*] n (INSURANCE) sottoscrittore/trice.

undies ['ʌndɪz] npl (col) robina, biancheria intima da donna.

undo [ʌn'duː] vt irg disfare; **~ing** n rovina, perdita.

undoubted [ʌn'dautɪd] a sicuro(a), certo(a); **~ly** ad senza alcun dubbio.

undress [ʌn'drɛs] vi spogliarsi.

undue [ʌn'djuː] a eccessivo(a).

undulating ['ʌndjuleɪtɪŋ] a ondeggiante; ondulato(a).

unduly [ʌn'djuːlɪ] ad eccessivamente.

unearth [ʌn'ɜːθ] vt dissotterrare; (fig) scoprire.

unearthly [ʌn'ə:θlɪ] a soprannaturale; (hour) impossibile.

uneasy [ʌn'i:zɪ] a a disagio; (worried) preoccupato(a).

unemployed [ʌnɪm'plɔɪd] a disoccupato(a) // npl: the ~ i disoccupati.

unemployment [ʌnɪm'plɔɪmənt] n disoccupazione f.

unending [ʌn'ɛndɪŋ] a senza fine.

unerring [ʌn'ə:rɪŋ] a infallibile.

uneven [ʌn'i:vn] a ineguale; irregolare.

unexpected [ʌnɪk'spɛktɪd] a inatteso(a), imprevisto(a), ~ly ad inaspettatamente.

unfailing [ʌn'feɪlɪŋ] a (supply, energy) inesauribile; (remedy) infallibile.

unfair [ʌn'fɛə*] a: ~ (to) ingiusto(a) (nei confronti di).

unfaithful [ʌn'feɪθful] a infedele.

unfamiliar [ʌnfə'mɪlɪə*] a sconosciuto(a), strano(a).

unfashionable [ʌn'fæʃnəbl] a (clothes) fuori moda; (district) non alla moda.

unfasten [ʌn'fɑ:sn] vt slacciare; sciogliere.

unfavourable, (US) **unfavorable** [ʌn'feɪvərəbl] a sfavorevole.

unfeeling [ʌn'fi:lɪŋ] a insensibile, duro(a).

unfit [ʌn'fɪt] a inadatto(a); (ill) malato(a), in cattiva salute; (incompetent): ~ (for) incompetente (in); (: work, MIL) inabile (a).

unfold [ʌn'fəuld] vt spiegare; (fig) rivelare // vi (view, countryside) distendersi; (story, plot) svelarsi.

unforeseen ['ʌnfɔ:'si:n] a imprevisto(a).

unforgettable [ʌnfə'gɛtəbl] a indimenticabile.

unfortunate [ʌn'fɔ:tʃnət] a sfortunato(a); (event, remark) infelice; ~ly ad sfortunatamente, purtroppo.

unfounded [ʌn'faundɪd] a infondato(a).

unfriendly [ʌn'frɛndlɪ] a poco amichevole, freddo(a).

ungainly [ʌn'geɪnlɪ] a goffo(a), impacciato(a).

ungodly [ʌn'gɔdlɪ] a empio(a); at an ~ hour a un'ora impossibile.

ungrateful [ʌn'greɪtful] a ingrato(a).

unhappiness [ʌn'hæpɪnɪs] n infelicità.

unhappy [ʌn'hæpɪ] a infelice; ~ with (arrangements etc) insoddisfatto(a) di.

unharmed [ʌn'hɑ:md] a incolume, sano(a) e salvo(a).

unhealthy [ʌn'hɛlθɪ] a (gen) malsano(a); (person) malaticcio(a).

unheard-of [ʌn'hə:dɔv] a inaudito(a), senza precedenti.

uniform ['ju:nɪfɔ:m] n uniforme f, divisa // a uniforme.

uninhabited [ʌnɪn'hæbɪtɪd] a disabitato(a).

union ['ju:njən] n unione f; (also: trade ~) sindacato // cpd sindacale, dei

sindacati; **U~ Jack** n bandiera nazionale britannica.

unique [ju:'ni:k] a unico(a).

unit ['ju:nɪt] n unità f inv; (section: of furniture etc) elemento; (team, squad) reparto, squadra.

unite [ju:'naɪt] vt unire // vi unirsi; ~d a unito(a); unificato(a); (efforts) congiunto(a); **U~d Kingdom (UK)** n Regno Unito; **U~d Nations (Organization) (UN, UNO)** n (Organizzazione f delle) Nazioni Unite (O.N.U.); **U~d States (of America) (US, USA)** n Stati mpl Uniti (d'America) (USA).

unit trust n (Brit) fondo d'investimento.

unity ['ju:nɪtɪ] n unità.

universal [ju:nɪ'və:sl] a universale.

universe ['ju:nɪvə:s] n universo.

university [ju:nɪ'və:sɪtɪ] n università f inv.

unjust [ʌn'dʒʌst] a ingiusto(a).

unkempt [ʌn'kɛmpt] a trasandato(a); spettinato(a).

unkind [ʌn'kaɪnd] a scortese; crudele.

unknown [ʌn'nəun] a sconosciuto(a).

unlawful [ʌn'lɔ:ful] a illecito(a), illegale.

unleash [ʌn'li:ʃ] vt sguinzagliare; (fig) scatenare.

unless [ʌn'lɛs] cj a meno che (non) + sub; ~ otherwise stated salvo indicazione contraria.

unlike [ʌn'laɪk] a diverso(a) // prep a differenza di, contrariamente a.

unlikely [ʌn'laɪklɪ] a improbabile; inverosimile.

unlisted [ʌn'lɪstɪd] a (US TEL): to be ~ non essere sull'elenco.

unload [ʌn'ləud] vt scaricare.

unlock [ʌn'lɔk] vt aprire.

unlucky [ʌn'lʌkɪ] a sfortunato(a); (object, number) che porta sfortuna, di malaugurio; to be ~ essere sfortunato, non avere fortuna.

unmarried [ʌn'mærɪd] a non sposato(a); (man only) scapolo, celibe; (woman only) nubile.

unmistakable [ʌnmɪs'teɪkəbl] a indubbio(a); facilmente riconoscibile.

unmitigated [ʌn'mɪtɪgeɪtɪd] a non mitigato(a), assoluto(a), vero(a) e proprio(a).

unnatural [ʌn'nætʃrəl] a innaturale; contro natura.

unnecessary [ʌn'nɛsəsərɪ] a inutile, superfluo(a).

unnoticed [ʌn'nəutɪst] a: (to go) ~ (passare) inosservato(a).

UNO ['ju:nəu] n abbr = United Nations Organization.

unobtainable [ʌnəb'teɪnəbl] a (TEL) non ottenibile.

unobtrusive [ʌnəb'tru:sɪv] a discreto(a).

unofficial [ʌnə'fɪʃl] a non ufficiale; (strike) non dichiarato(a) dal sindacato.

unpack [ʌn'pæk] vi disfare la valigia (or

le valigie).

unpalatable [ʌn'pælətəbl] a (truth) sgradevole.

unparalleled [ʌn'pærəleld] a incomparabile, impareggiabile.

unpleasant [ʌn'pleznt] a spiacevole.

unplug [ʌn'plʌg] vt staccare.

unpopular [ʌn'pɔpjulə*] a impopolare.

unprecedented [ʌn'presidəntid] a senza precedenti.

unpredictable [ʌnprı'dıktəbl] a imprevedibile.

unprofessional [ʌnprə'feʃənl] a: ~ conduct scorrettezza professionale.

unqualified [ʌn'kwɔlıfaıd] a (teacher) non abilitato(a); (success) assoluto(a), senza riserve.

unquestionably [ʌn'kwestʃənəbli] ad indiscutibilmente.

unravel [ʌn'rævl] vt dipanare, districare.

unreal [ʌn'rıəl] a irreale.

unrealistic [ʌnrıə'lıstık] a (idea) illusorio(a); (estimate) non realistico(a).

unreasonable [ʌn'ri:znəbl] a irragionevole.

unrelated [ʌnrı'leıtıd] a: ~ (to) senza rapporto (con); non imparentato(a) (con).

unreliable [ʌnrı'laıəbl] a (person, machine) che non dà affidamento; (news, source of information) inattendibile.

unremitting [ʌnrı'mıtıŋ] a incessante.

unreservedly [ʌnrı'zə:vıdlı] ad senza riserve.

unrest [ʌn'rest] n agitazione f.

unroll [ʌn'rəul] vt srotolare.

unruly [ʌn'ru:lı] a indisciplinato(a).

unsafe [ʌn'seıf] a pericoloso(a), rischioso(a).

unsaid [ʌn'sed] a: to leave sth ~ passare qc sotto silenzio.

unsatisfactory ['ʌnsætıs'fæktərı] a che lascia a desiderare, insufficiente.

unsavoury, (US) **unsavory** [ʌn'seıvərı] a (fig: person) losco(a); (: reputation, subject) disgustoso(a), ripugnante.

unscathed [ʌn'skeıðd] a incolume.

unscrew [ʌn'skru:] vt svitare.

unscrupulous [ʌn'skru:pjuləs] a senza scrupoli.

unsettled [ʌn'setld] a turbato(a); instabile; indeciso(a).

unshaven [ʌn'ʃeıvn] a non rasato(a).

unsightly [ʌn'saıtlı] a brutto(a), sgradevole a vedersi.

unskilled [ʌn'skıld] a: ~ worker manovale m.

unspeakable [ʌn'spi:kəbl] a (awful) abominevole.

unstable [ʌn'steıbl] a (gen) instabile; (mentally) squilibrato(a).

unsteady [ʌn'stedı] a instabile, malsicuro(a).

unstuck [ʌn'stʌk] a: to come ~ scollarsi; (fig) fare fiasco.

unsuccessful [ʌnsək'sesful] a (writer, proposal) che non ha successo; (marriage, attempt) mal riuscito(a), fallito(a); to be ~ (in attempting sth) non riuscire; non avere successo; (application) non essere considerato(a).

unsuitable [ʌn'su:təbl] a inadatto(a); inopportuno(a); sconveniente.

unsure [ʌn'ʃuə*] a incerto(a); to be ~ of o.s. essere insicuro(a).

unsympathetic [ʌnsımpə'θetık] a (person) antipatico(a); (attitude) poco incoraggiante.

untapped [ʌn'tæpt] a (resources) non sfruttato(a).

unthinkable [ʌn'θıŋkəbl] a impensabile, inconcepibile.

untidy [ʌn'taıdı] a (room) in disordine; (appearance, work) trascurato(a); (person, writing) disordinato(a).

untie [ʌn'taı] vt (knot, parcel) disfare; (prisoner, dog) slegare.

until [ʌn'tıl] prep fino a; (after negative) prima di // cj finché, fino a quando; (in past, after negative) prima che + sub, prima di + infinitive; ~ now finora; ~ then fino ad allora.

untimely [ʌn'taımlı] a intempestivo(a), inopportuno(a); (death) prematuro(a).

untold [ʌn'təuld] a incalcolabile; indescrivibile.

untoward [ʌntə'wɔ:d] a sfortunato(a), sconveniente.

untranslatable [ʌntrænz'leıtəbl] a intraducibile.

unused [ʌn'ju:zd] a nuovo(a).

unusual [ʌn'ju:ʒuəl] a insolito(a), eccezionale, raro(a).

unveil [ʌn'veıl] vt scoprire; svelare.

unwavering [ʌn'weıvərıŋ] a fermo(a), incrollabile.

unwelcome [ʌn'welkəm] a non gradito(a).

unwell [ʌn'wel] a indisposto(a); to feel ~ non sentirsi bene.

unwieldy [ʌn'wi:ldı] a poco maneggevole.

unwilling [ʌn'wılıŋ] a: to be ~ to do non voler fare; ~ly ad malvolentieri.

unwind [ʌn'waınd] vb (irg) vt svolgere, srotolare // vi (relax) rilassarsi.

unwise [ʌn'waız] a poco saggio(a); (decision) avventato(a).

unwitting [ʌn'wıtıŋ] a involontario(a).

unworkable [ʌn'wə:kəbl] a (plan) inattuabile.

unworthy [ʌn'wə:ðı] a indegno(a).

unwrap [ʌn'ræp] vt disfare; aprire.

unwritten [ʌn'rıtn] a (agreement) tacito(a); (law) non scritto(a).

up [ʌp] ♦ prep: he went ~ the stairs/the hill è salito su per le scale/sulla collina; the cat was ~ a tree il gatto era su un albero; they live further ~ the street vivono un po' più su nella stessa strada

◆ ad 1 (upwards, higher) su, in alto; ~ in the sky/the mountains su nel cielo/in montagna; ~ there lassù; ~ above su in alto

2: to be ~ (out of bed) essere alzato(a); (prices, level) essere salito(a)

3: ~ to (as far as) fino a; ~ to now finora

4: to be ~ to (depending on): it's ~ to you sta a lei, dipende da lei; (equal to): he's not ~ to it (job, task etc) non ne è all'altezza; (col: be doing): what is he ~ to? cosa sta combinando?

◆ n: ~s and downs alti e bassi mpl.

up-and-coming [ˌʌpəndˈkʌmɪŋ] a pieno(a) di promesse, promettente.

upbringing [ˈʌpbrɪŋɪŋ] n educazione f.

update [ʌpˈdeɪt] vt aggiornare.

upheaval [ʌpˈhiːvl] n sconvolgimento; tumulto.

uphill [ʌpˈhɪl] a in salita; (fig: task) difficile // ad: to go ~ andare in salita, salire.

uphold [ʌpˈhəʊld] vt irg approvare; sostenere.

upholstery [ʌpˈhəʊlstərɪ] n tappezzeria.

upkeep [ˈʌpkiːp] n manutenzione f.

upon [əˈpɒn] prep su.

upper [ˈʌpə*] a superiore // n (of shoe) tomaia; ~-class a dell'alta borghesia; ~ hand n: to have the ~ hand avere il coltello dalla parte del manico; ~most a il(la) più alto(a); predominante.

upright [ˈʌpraɪt] a diritto(a); verticale; (fig) diritto(a), onesto(a) // n montante m.

uprising [ˈʌpraɪzɪŋ] n insurrezione f, rivolta.

uproar [ˈʌprɔː*] n tumulto, clamore m.

uproot [ʌpˈruːt] vt sradicare.

upset n [ˈʌpsɛt] turbamento // vt [ʌpˈsɛt] (irg: like set) (glass etc) rovesciare; (plan, stomach) scombussolare; (person: offend) contrariare; (: grieve) addolorare; sconvolgere // a [ʌpˈsɛt] contrariato(a); addolorato(a); (stomach) scombussolato(a), disturbato(a).

upshot [ˈʌpʃɒt] n risultato.

upside-down [ˈʌpsaɪdˈdaʊn] ad sottosopra.

upstairs [ʌpˈstɛəz] ad, a di sopra, al piano superiore.

upstart [ˈʌpstɑːt] n parvenu m inv.

upstream [ʌpˈstriːm] ad a monte.

uptake [ˈʌpteɪk] n: he is quick/slow on the ~ è pronto/lento di comprendonio.

uptight [ʌpˈtaɪt] a (col) teso(a).

up-to-date [ˈʌptəˈdeɪt] a moderno(a); aggiornato(a).

upturn [ˈʌptəːn] n (in luck) svolta favorevole; (COMM: in market) rialzo.

upward [ˈʌpwəd] a ascendente; verso l'alto; ~(s) ad in su, verso l'alto.

urban [ˈəːbən] a urbano(a).

urbane [əːˈbeɪn] a civile, urbano(a),

educato(a).

urchin [ˈəːtʃɪn] n monello.

urge [əːdʒ] n impulso; stimolo; forte desiderio // vt: to ~ sb to do esortare qn a fare, spingere qn a fare; raccomandare a qn di fare.

urgency [ˈəːdʒənsɪ] n urgenza; (of tone) insistenza.

urgent [ˈəːdʒənt] a urgente.

urinate [ˈjʊərɪneɪt] vi orinare.

urine [ˈjʊərɪn] n orina.

urn [əːn] n urna; (also: tea ~) bollitore m per il tè.

US, USA n abbr = United States (of America).

us [ʌs] pronoun ci; (stressed, after prep) noi; see also me.

usage [ˈjuːzɪdʒ] n uso.

use n [juːs] uso; impiego, utilizzazione f // vt [juːz] usare, utilizzare, servirsi di; she ~d to do it lo faceva (una volta), era solita farlo; in ~ in uso; out of ~ fuori uso; to be of ~ essere utile, servire; it's no ~ non serve, è inutile; to be ~d to avere l'abitudine di; to ~ up vt consumare; esaurire; ~d a (car) d'occasione; ~ful a utile; ~fulness n utilità; ~less a inutile; ~r n utente m/f; ~r-friendly a (computer) di facile uso.

usher [ˈʌʃə*] n usciere m; (in cinema) maschera; ~ette [-ˈrɛt] n (in cinema) maschera.

USSR n: the ~ l'URSS f.

usual [ˈjuːʒʊəl] a solito(a); as ~ come al solito, come d'abitudine; ~ly ad di solito.

utensil [juːˈtɛnsl] n utensile m; kitchen ~s utensili da cucina.

uterus [ˈjuːtərəs] n utero.

utility [juːˈtɪlɪtɪ] n utilità; (also: public ~) servizio pubblico; ~ room n locale adibito alla stiratura dei panni etc.

utmost [ˈʌtməʊst] a estremo(a) // n: to do one's ~ fare il possibile or di tutto.

utter [ˈʌtə*] a assoluto(a), totale // vt pronunciare, proferire; emettere; ~ance n espressione f; parole fpl; ~ly ad completamente, del tutto.

U-turn [ˈjuːˈtəːn] n inversione f a U.

V

v. abbr = verse, versus, volt; (= vide) vedi, vedere.

vacancy [ˈveɪkənsɪ] n (Brit: job) posto libero; (room) stanza libera.

vacant [ˈveɪkənt] a (job, seat etc) libero(a); (expression) assente; ~ lot n (US) terreno non occupato; (: for sale) terreno in vendita.

vacate [vəˈkeɪt] vt lasciare libero(a).

vacation [vəˈkeɪʃən] n vacanze fpl.

vaccinate [ˈvæksɪneɪt] vt vaccinare.

vacuum |'vækjum| n vuoto; ~ **bottle** n (US) = ~ **flask**; ~ **cleaner** n aspirapolvere m inv; ~ **flask** n (Brit) thermos m inv ®; ~**-packed** a confezionato(a) sottovuoto.

vagina |və'dʒaɪnə| n vagina.

vagrant |'veɪgrnt| n vagabondo/a.

vague |veɪg| a vago(a); (blurred: photo, memory) sfocato(a); ~**ly** ad vagamente.

vain |veɪn| a (useless) inutile, vano(a); (conceited) vanitoso(a); **in** ~ inutilmente, invano.

valentine |'vælɪntaɪn| n (also: ~ **card**) cartolina or biglietto di San Valentino.

valet |'væleɪ| n cameriere m personale.

valiant |'vælɪənt| a valoroso(a), coraggioso(a).

valid |'vælɪd| a valido(a), valevole; (excuse) valido(a).

valley |'vælɪ| n valle f.

valour, (US) **valor** |'vælə*| n valore m.

valuable |'væljuəbl| a (jewel) di (grande) valore; (time) prezioso(a); ~**s** npl oggetti mpl di valore.

valuation |vælju'eɪʃən| n valutazione f, stima.

value |'vælju:| n valore m // vt (fix price) valutare, dare un prezzo a; (cherish) apprezzare, tenere a; ~ **added tax** (**VAT**) n (Brit) imposta sul valore aggiunto (I.V.A.); ~**d** a (appreciated) stimato(a), apprezzato(a).

valve |vælv| n valvola.

van |væn| n (AUT) furgone m; (Brit RAIL) vagone m.

vandal |'vændl| n vandalo/a; ~**ism** n vandalismo.

vanilla |və'nɪlə| n vaniglia // cpd (ice cream) alla vaniglia.

vanish |'vænɪʃ| vi svanire, scomparire.

vanity |'vænɪtɪ| n vanità; ~ **case** n valigetta per cosmetici.

vantage |'vɑ:ntɪdʒ| n: ~ **point** posizione f or punto di osservazione; (fig) posizione vantaggiosa.

vapour, (US) **vapor** |'veɪpə*| n vapore m.

variable |'vɛərɪəbl| a variabile; (mood) mutevole.

variance |'vɛərɪəns| n: **to be at** ~ (**with**) essere in disaccordo (con); (facts) essere in contraddizione (con).

varicose |'værɪkəʊs| a: ~ **veins** varici fpl.

varied |'vɛərɪd| a vario(a), diverso(a).

variety |və'raɪətɪ| n varietà f inv; (quantity) quantità, numero; ~ **show** n varietà m inv.

various |'vɛərɪəs| a vario(a), diverso(a); (several) parecchi(e), molti(e).

varnish |'vɑ:nɪʃ| n vernice f // vt verniciare.

vary |'vɛərɪ| vt, vi variare, mutare.

vase |vɑ:z| n vaso.

vaseline |'væsɪli:n| n ® vaselina.

vast |vɑ:st| a vasto(a); (amount, success) enorme; ~**ly** ad enormemente.

VAT |væt| n abbr = **value added tax**.

vat |væt| n tino.

Vatican |'vætɪkən| n: **the** ~ il Vaticano.

vault |vɔ:lt| n (of roof) volta; (tomb) tomba; (in bank) camera blindata; (jump) salto // vt (also: ~ **over**) saltare (d'un balzo).

vaunted |'vɔ:ntɪd| a: **much-**~ tanto celebrato(a).

VCR n abbr = **video cassette recorder**.

VD n abbr = **venereal disease**.

VDU n abbr = **visual display unit**.

veal |vi:l| n vitello.

veer |vɪə*| vi girare; virare.

vegetable |'vedʒtəbl| n verdura, ortaggio // a vegetale.

vegetarian |vedʒɪ'tɛərɪən| a, n vegetariano(a).

vehement |'vi:ɪmənt| a veemente, violento(a).

vehicle |'vi:ɪkl| n veicolo.

veil |veɪl| n velo // vt velare.

vein |veɪn| n vena; (on leaf) nervatura; (fig: mood) vena, umore m.

velvet |'velvɪt| n velluto.

vending machine |'vendɪŋ-| n distributore m automatico.

veneer |və'nɪə*| n impiallacciatura; (fig) vernice f.

venereal |vɪ'nɪərɪəl| a: ~ **disease** (**VD**) malattia venerea.

Venetian |vɪ'ni:ʃən| a veneziano(a); ~ **blind** n (tenda alla) veneziana.

vengeance |'vendʒəns| n vendetta; **with a** ~ (fig) davvero; furiosamente.

Venice |'venɪs| n Venezia.

venison |'venɪsn| n carne f di cervo.

venom |'venəm| n veleno.

vent |vent| n foro, apertura; (in dress, jacket) spacco // vt (fig: one's feelings) sfogare, dare sfogo a.

ventilate |'ventɪleɪt| vt (room) dare aria a, arieggiare; **ventilator** n ventilatore m.

ventriloquist |ven'trɪləkwɪst| n ventriloquo/a.

venture |'ventʃə*| n impresa (rischiosa) // vt rischiare, azzardare // vi arrischiarsi, azzardarsi.

venue |'venju:| n luogo di incontro; (SPORT) luogo (designato) per l'incontro.

verb |və:b| n verbo; ~**al** a verbale; (translation) letterale.

verbatim |və:'beɪtɪm| a, ad parola per parola.

verdict |'və:dɪkt| n verdetto.

verge |və:dʒ| n (Brit) bordo, orlo; **on the** ~ **of doing** sul punto di fare; **to** ~ **on** vt fus rasentare.

verification |verɪfɪ'keɪʃən| n verifica.

veritable |'verɪtəbl| a vero(a).

vermin |'və:mɪn| npl animali mpl nocivi;

(insects) insetti *mpl* parassiti.

vermouth ['vɜ:məθ] *n* vermut *m inv*.

versatile ['vɜ:sətaɪl] *a* (*person*) versatile; (*machine, tool etc*) (che si presta) a molti usi.

verse [vɜ:s] *n* versi *mpl*; (*stanza*) stanza, strofa; (*in bible*) versetto.

version ['vɜ:ʃən] *n* versione *f*.

versus ['vɜ:səs] *prep* contro.

vertical ['vɜ:tɪkl] *a, n* verticale (*m*); ~**ly** *ad* verticalmente.

vertigo ['vɜ:tɪgəu] *n* vertigine *f*.

verve [vɜ:v] *n* brio; entusiasmo.

very ['verɪ] *ad* molto // *a*: the ~ **book** which proprio il libro che; at the ~ **end** proprio alla fine; the ~ **last** proprio l'ultimo; at the ~ **least** almeno; ~ **much** moltissimo.

vessel ['vesl] *n* (*ANAT*) vaso; (*NAUT*) nave *f*; (*container*) recipiente *m*.

vest [vest] *n* (*Brit*) maglia; (: *sleeveless*) canottiera; (*US*: *waistcoat*) gilè *m inv*; ~**ed interests** *npl* (*COMM*) diritti *mpl* acquisiti.

vestment ['vestmənt] *n* (*REL*) paramento liturgico.

vestry ['vestrɪ] *n* sagrestia.

vet [vet] *n abbr* (= *veterinary surgeon*) veterinario // *vt* esaminare minuziosamente; (*text*) rivedere.

veteran ['vetərn] *n* veterano; (*also*: war ~) reduce *m*.

veterinary ['vetrɪnərɪ] *a* veterinario(a); ~ **surgeon**, (*US*) **veterinarian** *n* veterinario.

veto ['vi:təu] *n, pl* ~**es** veto // *vt* opporre il veto a.

vex [veks] *vt* irritare, contrariare; ~**ed** *a* (*question*) controverso(a), dibattuto(a).

VHF *abbr* (= *very high frequency*) VHF, altissima frequenza.

via ['vaɪə] *prep* (*by way of*) via; (*by means of*) tramite.

viable ['vaɪəbl] *a* attuabile; vitale.

viaduct ['vaɪədʌkt] *n* viadotto.

vibrate [vaɪ'breɪt] *vi*: to ~ (**with**) vibrare (di); (*resound*) risonare (di).

vicar ['vɪkə*] *n* pastore *m*; ~**age** *n* presbiterio.

vicarious [vɪ'kɛərɪəs] *a* indiretto(a).

vice [vaɪs] *n* (*evil*) vizio; (*TECH*) morsa.

vice- [vaɪs] *prefix* vice....

vice squad *n* (squadra del) buon costume *f*.

vice versa ['vaɪsɪ'vɜ:sə] *ad* viceversa.

vicinity [vɪ'sɪnɪtɪ] *n* vicinanze *fpl*.

vicious ['vɪʃəs] *a* (*remark*) maligno(a), cattivo(a); (*blow*) violento(a); ~ **circle** *n* circolo vizioso.

victim ['vɪktɪm] *n* vittima.

victor ['vɪktə*] *n* vincitore *m*.

Victorian [vɪk'tɔ:rɪən] *a* vittoriano(a).

victory ['vɪktərɪ] *n* vittoria.

video ['vɪdɪəu] *cpd* video... // *n* (~ *film*) video *m inv*; (*also*: ~ *cassette*)

videocassetta; (*also*: ~ **cassette recorder**) videoregistratore *m*; ~ **tape** *n* videotape *m inv*.

vie [vaɪ] *vi*: to ~ **with** competere con, rivaleggiare con.

Vienna [vɪ'enə] *n* Vienna.

Vietnam [vjet'næm] *n* Vietnam *m*; ~**ese** *a, n* (*pl inv*) vietnamita (*m/f*).

view [vju:] *n* vista, veduta; (*opinion*) opinione *f* // *vt* (*situation*) considerare; (*house*) visitare; on ~ (*in museum etc*) esposto(a); in full ~ of sotto gli occhi di; in ~ of the fact that considerato che; ~**er** *n* (*viewfinder*) mirino; (*small projector*) visore *m*; (*TV*) telespettatore/trice; ~**finder** *n* mirino; ~**point** *n* punto di vista.

vigil ['vɪdʒɪl] *n* veglia.

vigorous ['vɪgərəs] *a* vigoroso(a).

vile [vaɪl] *a* (*action*) vile; (*smell*) disgustoso(a), nauseante; (*temper*) pessimo(a).

villa ['vɪlə] *n* villa.

village ['vɪlɪdʒ] *n* villaggio; ~**r** *n* abitante *m/f* di villaggio.

villain ['vɪlən] *n* (*scoundrel*) canaglia; (*criminal*) criminale *m*; (*in novel etc*) cattivo.

vindicate ['vɪndɪkeɪt] *vt* comprovare; giustificare.

vindictive [vɪn'dɪktɪv] *a* vendicativo(a).

vine [vaɪn] *n* vite *f*; (*climbing plant*) rampicante *m*.

vinegar ['vɪnɪgə*] *n* aceto.

vineyard ['vɪnjɑ:d] *n* vigna, vigneto.

vintage ['vɪntɪdʒ] *n* (*year*) annata, produzione *f*; ~ **wine** *n* vino d'annata.

vinyl ['vaɪnl] *n* vinile *m*.

violate ['vaɪəleɪt] *vt* violare.

violence ['vaɪələns] *n* violenza; (*POL etc*) incidenti *mpl* violenti.

violent ['vaɪələnt] *a* violento(a).

violet ['vaɪələt] *a* (*colour*) viola *inv*, violetto(a) // *n* (*plant*) violetta.

violin [vaɪə'lɪn] *n* violino; ~**ist** *n* violinista *m/f*.

VIP *n abbr* (= *very important person*) V.I.P. *m/f inv*.

virgin ['vɜ:dʒɪn] *n* vergine *f* // *a* vergine *inv*.

Virgo ['vɜ:gəu] *n* (*sign*) Vergine *f*.

virile ['vɪraɪl] *a* virile.

virtually ['vɜ:tjuəlɪ] *ad* (*almost*) praticamente.

virtue ['vɜ:tju:] *n* virtù *f inv*; (*advantage*) pregio, vantaggio; by ~ of grazie a.

virtuous ['vɜ:tjuəs] *a* virtuoso(a).

virus ['vaɪərəs] *n* virus *m inv*.

visa ['vi:zə] *n* visto.

vis-à-vis [vi:zə'vi:] *prep* rispetto a, nei riguardi di.

visibility [vɪzɪ'bɪlɪtɪ] *n* visibilità.

visible ['vɪzəbl] *a* visibile.

vision ['vɪʒən] *n* (*sight*) vista; (*foresight, in dream*) visione *f*.

visit ['vɪzɪt] n visita; (stay) soggiorno // vt (person) andare a trovare; (place) visitare; **~ing hours** npl (in hospital etc) orario delle visite; **~or** n visitatore/trice; (guest) ospite m/f; (in hotel) cliente m/f; **~ors' book** n libro d'oro; (in hotel) registro.

visor ['vaɪzə*] n visiera.

vista ['vɪstə] n vista, prospettiva.

visual ['vɪzjuəl] a visivo(a); visuale; ottico(a); **~ aid** n sussidio visivo; **~ display unit (VDU)** n visualizzatore m.

visualize ['vɪzjuəlaɪz] vt immaginare, figurarsi; (foresee) prevedere.

vital ['vaɪtl] a vitale; **~ly** ad estremamente; **~ statistics** npl (fig) misure fpl.

vitamin ['vɪtəmɪn] n vitamina.

vivacious [vɪ'veɪʃəs] a vivace.

vivid ['vɪvɪd] a vivido(a); **~ly** ad (describe) vividamente; (remember) con precisione.

V-neck ['viː'nɛk] n maglione m con lo scollo a V.

vocabulary [vəu'kæbjuləri] n vocabolario.

vocal ['vəukl] a (MUS) vocale; (communication) verbale; **~ cords** npl corde fpl vocali.

vocation [vəu'keɪʃən] n vocazione f; **~al** a professionale.

vociferous [və'sɪfərəs] a rumoroso(a).

vodka ['vɔdkə] n vodka f inv.

vogue [vəug] n moda; (popularity) popolarità, voga.

voice [vɔɪs] n voce f // vt (opinion) esprimere.

void [vɔɪd] n vuoto // a (invalid) nullo(a); (empty) vuoto(a); **~ of** privo(a) di.

volatile ['vɔlətaɪl] a volatile; (fig) volubile.

volcano, ~es [vɔl'keɪnəu] n vulcano.

volition [və'lɪʃən] n: of one's own **~** di sua volontà.

volley ['vɔlɪ] n (of gunfire) salva; (of stones etc) raffica, gragnola; (TENNIS etc) volata; **~ball** n pallavolo f.

volt [vəult] n volt m inv; **~age** n tensione f, voltaggio.

voluble ['vɔljubl] a loquace, ciarliero(a).

volume ['vɔlju:m] n volume m; **~ control** n (RADIO, TV) regolatore m or manopola del volume.

voluntarily ['vɔləntrɪlɪ] ad volontariamente; gratuitamente.

voluntary ['vɔləntərɪ] a volontario(a); (unpaid) gratuito(a), non retribuito(a).

volunteer [vɔlən'tɪə*] n volontario/a // vi (MIL) arruolarsi volontario; to **~** to do offrire (volontariamente) di fare.

voluptuous [və'lʌptjuəs] a voluttuoso(a).

vomit ['vɔmɪt] n vomito // vt, vi vomitare.

vote [vəut] n voto, suffragio; (cast) voto; (franchise) diritto di voto // vi votare; **~**

of **thanks** discorso di ringraziamento; **~r** n elettore/trice; **voting** n scrutinio.

vouch [vautʃ]: to **~ for** vt fus farsi garante di.

voucher ['vautʃə*] n (for meal, petrol) buono; (receipt) ricevuta.

vow [vau] n voto, promessa solenne // vi giurare.

vowel ['vauəl] n vocale f.

voyage ['vɔɪdʒ] n viaggio per mare, traversata.

vulgar ['vʌlgə*] a volgare.

vulnerable ['vʌlnərəbl] a vulnerabile.

vulture ['vʌltʃə*] n avvoltoio.

W

wad [wɔd] n (of cotton wool, paper) tampone m; (of banknotes etc) fascio.

waddle ['wɔdl] vi camminare come una papera.

wade [weɪd] vi: to **~ through** camminare a stento in // vt guadare.

wafer ['weɪfə*] n (CULIN) cialda; (REL) ostia; (COMPUT) wafer m inv.

waffle ['wɔfl] n (CULIN) cialda; (col) ciance fpl; riempitivo // vi cianciare; parlare a vuoto.

waft [wɔft] vt portare // vi diffondersi.

wag [wæg] vt agitare, muovere // vi agitarsi.

wage [weɪdʒ] n (also: **~s**) salario, paga // vt: to **~ war** fare la guerra; **~ packet** n busta f paga inv.

wager ['weɪdʒə*] n scommessa.

waggle ['wægl] vt dimenare, agitare // vi dimenarsi, agitarsi.

wag(g)on ['wægən] n (horse-drawn) carro; (Brit RAIL) vagone m (merci).

wail [weɪl] n gemito; (of siren) urlo // vi gemere; urlare.

waist [weɪst] n vita, cintola; **~coat** n (Brit) panciotto, gilè m inv; **~line** n (giro di) vita.

wait [weɪt] n attesa // vi aspettare, attendere; to lie in **~ for** stare in agguato a; to **~ for** aspettare; I can't **~ to** (fig) non vedo l'ora di; to **~ behind** vi rimanere (ad aspettare); to **~ on** vt fus servire; **~er** n cameriere m; **~ing** n: "no **~ing**" (Brit AUT) "divieto di sosta"; **~ing list** n lista di attesa; **~ing room** n sala d'aspetto or d'attesa; **~ress** n cameriera.

waive [weɪv] vt rinunciare a, abbandonare.

wake [weɪk] vb (pt woke, **~d**, pp woken, **~d**) vt (also: **~ up**) svegliare // vi (also: **~ up**) svegliarsi // n (for dead person) veglia funebre; (NAUT) scia; **~n** vt, vi = **wake**.

Wales [weɪlz] n Galles m.

walk [wɔːk] n passeggiata; (short) giretto; (gait) passo, andatura; (path) sentiero; (*in park etc*) sentiero, vialetto // *vi* camminare; (*for pleasure, exercise*) passeggiare // *vt* (*distance*) fare or percorrere a piedi; (*dog*) accompagnare, portare a passeggiare; **10 minutes' ~** from 10 minuti di cammino or a piedi da; **from all ~s** of life di tutte le condizioni sociali; **to ~ out on** *vt fus* (*col*) piantare in asso; **~er** *n* (*person*) camminatore/trice; **~ie-talkie** ['wɔ:kɪ'tɔ:kɪ] *n* walkie-talkie *m inv*; **~ing** *n* camminare *m*; **~ing stick** *n* bastone *m* da passeggio; **~out** *n* (*of workers*) sciopero senza preavviso or a sorpresa; **~over** *n* (*col*) vittoria facile, gioco da ragazzi; **~way** *n* passaggio pedonale.

wall [wɔ:l] *n* muro; (*internal, of tunnel, cave*) parete *f*; **~ed** *a* (*city*) fortificato(a).

wallet ['wɔlɪt] *n* portafoglio.

wallflower ['wɔ:lflauə*] *n* violacciocca; **to be a ~** (*fig*) fare da tappezzeria.

wallop ['wɔləp] *vt* (*col*) pestare.

wallow ['wɔləu] *vi* sguazzare, voltolarsi.

wallpaper ['wɔ:lpeɪpə*] *n* carta da parati.

wally ['wɔlɪ] *n* (*col*) imbecille *m/f*.

walnut ['wɔ:lnʌt] *n* noce *f*; (*tree*) noce *m*.

walrus, *pl* **~** or **~es** ['wɔ:lrəs] *n* tricheco.

waltz [wɔ:lts] *n* valzer *m inv* // *vi* ballare il valzer.

wan [wɔn] *a* pallido(a), smorto(a); triste.

wand [wɔnd] *n* (*also:* **magic ~**) bacchetta (magica).

wander ['wɔndə*] *ni* (*person*) girare senza meta, girovagare; (*thoughts*) vagare; (*river*) serpeggiare // *vt* girovagare per.

wane [weɪn] *vi* (*moon*) calare; (*reputation*) declinare.

wangle [wæŋgl] *vt* (*Brit col*): **to ~ sth** procurare qc con l'astuzia.

want [wɔnt] *vt* volere; (*need*) aver bisogno di; (*lack*) mancare di // *n*: **for ~ of** per mancanza di; **~s** *npl* (*needs*) bisogni *mpl*; **to ~ to do** volere fare; **to ~ sb to do** volere che qn faccia; **~ing** *a*: **to be found ~ing** non risultare all'altezza.

wanton ['wɔntn] *a* sfrenato(a); senza motivo.

war [wɔ:*] *n* guerra; **to go to ~** entrare in guerra.

ward [wɔ:d] *n* (*in hospital: room*) corsia; (*: section*) reparto; (*POL*) circoscrizione *f*; (*LAW: child*) pupillo/a; **to ~ off** *vt* parare, schivare.

warden ['wɔ:dn] *n* (*Brit: of institution*) direttore/trice; (*of park, game reserve*) guardiano/a; (*Brit: also:* **traffic ~**) addetto/a al controllo del traffico e del parcheggio.

warder ['wɔ:də*] *n* (*Brit*) guardia carceraria.

wardrobe ['wɔ:drəub] *n* (*cupboard*) guardaroba *m inv*, armadio; (*clothes*) guardaroba; (*THEATRE*) costumi *mpl*.

warehouse ['wɛəhaus] *n* magazzino.

wares [wɛəz] *npl* merci *fpl*.

warfare ['wɔ:fɛə*] *n* guerra.

warhead ['wɔ:hed] *n* (*MIL*) testata.

warily ['wɛərɪlɪ] *ad* cautamente, con prudenza.

warm [wɔ:m] *a* caldo(a); (*thanks, welcome, applause*) caloroso(a); **it's ~** fa caldo; **I'm ~** ho caldo; **to ~ up** *vi* scaldarsi, riscaldarsi; (*athlete, discussion*) riscaldarsi // *vt* scaldare, riscaldare; (*engine*) far scaldare; **~-hearted** *a* affettuoso(a); **~ly** *ad* caldamente; calorosamente; vivamente; **~th** *n* calore *m*.

warn [wɔ:n] *vt* avvertire, avvisare; **~ing** *n* avvertimento; (*notice*) avviso; **~ing light** *n* spia luminosa; **~ing triangle** *n* (*AUT*) triangolo.

warp [wɔ:p] *vi* deformarsi // *vt* deformare; (*fig*) corrompere.

warrant ['wɔrnt] *n* (*LAW: to arrest*) mandato di cattura; (*: to search*) mandato di perquisizione.

warranty ['wɔrəntɪ] *n* garanzia.

warren ['wɔrən] *n* (*of rabbits*) tana.

warrior ['wɔrɪə*] *n* guerriero/a.

Warsaw ['wɔ:sɔ:] *n* Varsavia.

warship ['wɔ:ʃɪp] *n* nave *f* da guerra.

wart [wɔ:t] *n* verruca.

wartime ['wɔ:taɪm] *n*: **in ~** in tempo di guerra.

wary ['wɛərɪ] *a* prudente.

was [wɔz] *pt of* **be**.

wash [wɔʃ] *vt* lavare // *vi* lavarsi // *n*: **to give sth a ~** lavare qc, dare una lavata a qc; **to have a ~** lavarsi; **to ~ away** *vt* (*stain*) togliere lavando; (*subj: river etc*) trascinare via; **to ~ off** *vi* andare via con il lavaggio; **to ~ up** *vi* (*Brit*) lavare i piatti; (*US*) darsi una lavata; **~able** *a* lavabile; **~basin**, (*US*) **~bowl** *n* lavabo; **~cloth** *n* (*US: face cloth*) pezzuola (per lavarsi); **~er** *n* (*TECH*) rondella; **~ing** *n* (*linen etc*) bucato; **~ing machine** *n* lavatrice *f*; **~ing powder** *n* (*Brit*) detersivo (in polvere); **~ing-up** *n* rigovernatura, lavatura dei piatti; **~ing-up liquid** *n* detersivo liquido (per stoviglie); **~-out** *n* (*col*) disastro; **~room** *n* gabinetto.

wasn't ['wɔznt] = **was not**.

wasp [wɔsp] *n* vespa.

wastage ['weɪstɪdʒ] *n* spreco; (*in manufacturing*) scarti *mpl*; **natural ~** diminuzione *f* di manodopera (*per pensionamento, decesso etc*).

waste [weɪst] *n* spreco; (*of time*) perdita; (*rubbish*) rifiuti *mpl* // *a* (*material*) di scarto; (*food*) avanzato(a)

// vt sprecare; (time, opportunity) perdere; ~s npl distesa desolata; **to lay ~** (destroy) devastare; **to ~ away** vi deperire; ~ **disposal unit** n (Brit) eliminatore m di rifiuti; ~**ful** a sprecone(a); (process) dispendioso(a); ~ **ground** n (Brit) terreno incolto or abbandonato; ~**paper basket** n cestino per la carta straccia; ~**pipe** n tubo di scarico.

watch [wɔtʃ] n orologio; (act of watching) sorveglianza; (guard: MIL, NAUT) guardia; (NAUT: spell of duty) quarto // vt (look at) osservare; (: match, programme) guardare; (spy on, guard) sorvegliare, tenere d'occhio; (be careful of) fare attenzione a // vi osservare, guardare; (keep guard) fare or montare la guardia; **to ~ out** vi fare attenzione; ~**dog** n cane m da guardia; ~**ful** a attento(a), vigile; ~**maker** n orologiaio/a; ~**man** n guardiano (also: **night ~man**) guardiano notturno; ~ **strap** n cinturino da orologio.

water [ˈwɔːtə*] n acqua // vt (plant) annaffiare // vi (eyes) lacrimare; in British ~s nelle acque territoriali britanniche; **to ~ down** vt (milk) diluire; (fig: story) edulcorare; ~**colour** n acquerello; ~**colours** npl colori mpl per acquarello; ~**cress** n crescione m; ~**fall** n cascata; ~ **heater** n scaldabagno; ~ **lily** n ninfea; ~**line** n (NAUT) linea di galleggiamento; ~**logged** a saturo(a) d'acqua; imbevuto(a) d'acqua; (football pitch etc) allagato(a); ~ **main** n conduttura dell'acqua; ~**mark** n (on paper) filigrana; ~**melon** n anguria, cocomero; ~**proof** a impermeabile; ~**shed** n (GEO, fig) spartiacque m; ~**skiing** n sci m acquatico; ~**tight** a stagno(a); ~**way** n corso d'acqua navigabile; ~**works** npl impianto idrico; ~**y** a (colour) slavato(a); (coffee) acquoso(a).

watt [wɔt] n watt m inv.

wave [weɪv] n onda; (of hand) gesto, segno; (in hair) ondulazione f // vi fare un cenno con la mano; (flag) sventolare // vt (handkerchief) sventolare; (stick) brandire; ~**length** n lunghezza d'onda.

waver [ˈweɪvə*] vi vacillare; (voice) tremolare.

wavy [ˈweɪvɪ] a ondulato(a); ondeggiante.

wax [wæks] n cera // vt dare la cera a; (car) lucidare // vi (moon) crescere; ~**works** npl cere fpl; museo delle cere.

way [weɪ] n via, strada; (path, access) passaggio; (distance) distanza; (direction) parte f, direzione f; (manner) modo, stile m; (habit) abitudine f; (condition) condizione f; **which ~?** — **this ~** da che parte or in quale direzione? — da questa parte or per di

qua; **on the ~** (en route) per strada; **to be on one's ~** essere in cammino or sulla strada; **to be in the ~** bloccare il passaggio; (fig) essere tra i piedi or d'impiccio; **to go out of one's ~ to do** (fig) mettercela tutta or fare di tutto per fare; **to lose one's ~** perdere la strada; **in a ~** in un certo senso; **in some ~s** sotto certi aspetti; **by the ~** ... a proposito ...; **"~ in"** (Brit) "entrata", "ingresso"; **"~ out"** (Brit) "uscita".

waylay [weɪˈleɪ] vt irg tendere un agguato a; attendere al passaggio.

wayward [ˈweɪwəd] a capriccioso(a); testardo(a).

W.C. [ˈdʌbljuːˈsiː] n (Brit) W.C. m inv, gabinetto.

we [wiː] pl pronoun noi.

weak [wiːk] a debole; (health) precario(a); (beam etc) fragile; ~**en** vi indebolirsi // vt indebolire; ~**ling** [ˈwiːklɪŋ] n smidollato/a; debole m/f; ~**ness** n debolezza; (fault) punto debole, difetto.

wealth [welθ] n (money, resources) ricchezza, ricchezze fpl; (of details) abbondanza, profusione f; ~**y** a ricco(a).

wean [wiːn] vt svezzare.

weapon [ˈwepən] n arma.

wear [wɛə*] n (use) uso; (deterioration through use) logorio, usura; (clothing): **sports/baby ~** abbigliamento sportivo/per neonati // vb (pt **wore**, pp **worn**) vt (clothes) portare; mettersi; (damage: through use) consumare // vi (last) durare; (rub etc through) consumarsi; **evening ~** abiti mpl or tenuta da sera; **to ~ away** vt consumare; erodere // vi consumarsi; essere eroso(a); **to ~ down** vt consumare; (strength) esaurire; **to ~ off** vi sparire lentamente; **to ~ on** vi passare; **to ~ out** vt consumare; (person, strength) esaurire; ~ **and tear** n usura, consumo.

weary [ˈwɪərɪ] a stanco(a); (tiring) faticoso(a).

weasel [ˈwiːzl] n (ZOOL) donnola.

weather [ˈwɛðə*] n tempo // vt (wood) stagionare; (storm, crisis) superare; **under the ~** (fig: ill) poco bene; ~**beaten** a (person) segnato(a) dalle intemperie; (building) logorato(a) dalle intemperie; ~**cock** n banderuola; ~ **forecast** n previsioni fpl del tempo, bollettino meteorologico; ~ **vane** n = ~**cock**.

weave [wiːv], pt **wove**, pp **woven** vt (cloth) tessere; (basket) intrecciare; ~**r** n tessitore/trice; **weaving** n tessitura.

web [web] n (of spider) ragnatela; (on foot) palma; (fabric, also fig) tessuto.

wed [wed] vt (pt, pp **wedded**) sposare // vi sposarsi.

we'd [wiːd] = **we had**, **we would**.

wedding ['wɛdɪŋ] n matrimonio; **silver/ golden ~ anniversary** n nozze fpl d'argento/d'oro; **~ day** n giorno delle nozze or del matrimonio; **~ dress** n abito nuziale; **~ ring** n fede f.

wedge [wɛdʒ] n (of wood etc) cuneo; (under door etc) zeppa; (of cake) spicchio, fetta // vt (fix) fissare con zeppe; (push) incuneare.

wedlock ['wɛdlɔk] n vincolo matrimoniale.

Wednesday ['wɛnzdɪ] n mercoledì m inv.

wee [wiː] a (Scottish) piccolo(a).

weed [wiːd] n erbaccia // vt diserbare; **~killer** n diserbante m; **~y** a (person) allampanato(a).

week [wiːk] n settimana; **a ~ today/on Friday** oggi/venerdì a otto; **~day** n giorno feriale; (COMM) giornata lavorativa; **~end** n fine settimana m or f inv, weekend m inv; **~ly** ad ogni settimana, settimanalmente // a, n settimanale (m).

weep [wiːp] pt, pp wept vi (person) piangere; **~ing willow** n salice m piangente.

weigh [weɪ] vt, vi pesare; **to ~ down** vt (branch) piegare; (fig: with worry) opprimere, caricare; **to ~ up** vt valutare.

weight [weɪt] n peso; **to lose/put on ~** dimagrire/ingrassare; **~ing** n (allowance) indennità; **~ lifter** n pesista m; **~y** a pesante; (fig) importante, grave.

weir [wɪə*] n diga.

weird [wɪəd] a strano(a), bizzarro(a); (eerie) soprannaturale.

welcome ['wɛlkəm] a benvenuto(a) // n accoglienza, benvenuto // vt accogliere cordialmente, (also: bid ~) dare il benvenuto a; (be glad of) rallegrarsi di; **to be ~** essere il(la) benvenuto(a); **thank you — you're ~!** grazie — prego!

weld [wɛld] n saldatura // vt saldare.

welfare ['wɛlfɛə*] n benessere m; **~ state** n stato assistenziale.

well [wɛl] n pozzo // ad bene // a: **to be ~** andare bene; (person) stare bene // excl allora!; ma!; ebbene!; **as ~** anche; **as ~ as** così come; oltre a; **X as ~ as Y** sia X che Y; **he did as ~ as he could** ha fatto come meglio poteva; **~ done!** bravo(a)!; **get ~ soon!** guarisci presto!; **to do ~ in** sth riuscire in qc; **to ~ up** vi sgorgare.

we'll [wiːl] = we will, we shall.

well: **~-behaved** a ubbidiente; **~-being** n benessere m; **~-built** a (person) ben fatto(a); **~-dressed** a ben vestito(a), vestito(a) bene; **~-heeled** a (col: wealthy) agiato(a), facoltoso(a).

wellingtons ['wɛlɪŋtənz] npl (also: wellington boots) stivali mpl di gomma.

well: **~-known** a noto(a), famoso(a); **~-mannered** a ben educato(a); **~-meaning** a ben intenzionato(a); **~-off** a benestante, danaroso(a); **~-read** a colto(a); **~-to-do** a abbiente, benestante; **~-wisher** n ammiratore/trice.

Welsh [wɛlʃ] a gallese // n (LING) gallese m; **the ~** npl i Gallesi; **~man/woman** n gallese m/f; **~ rarebit** n crostino al formaggio.

went [wɛnt] pt of go.

wept [wɛpt] pt, pp of weep.

were [wəː*] pt of be.

we're [wɪə*] = we are.

weren't [wəːnt] = were not.

west [wɛst] n ovest m, occidente m, ponente m // a (a) ovest inv, occidentale // ad verso ovest; **the W~** l'Occidente m; **the W~ Country** n (Brit) il sudovest dell'Inghilterra; **~erly** a (wind) occidentale, da ovest; **~ern** a occidentale, dell'ovest // n (CINEMA) western m inv; **W~ Germany** n Germania Occidentale; **W~ Indian** a delle Indie Occidentali // n abitante m/f delle Indie Occidentali; **W~ Indies** npl Indie fpl Occidentali; **~ward(s)** ad verso ovest.

wet [wɛt] a umido(a), bagnato(a); (soaked) fradicio(a); (rainy) piovoso(a); **to get ~** bagnarsi; "**~ paint**" "vernice fresca"; **~ blanket** n (fig) guastafeste m/f; **~ suit** n tuta da sub.

we've [wiːv] = we have.

whack [wæk] vt picchiare, battere.

whale [weɪl] n (ZOOL) balena.

wharf [wɔːf], pl **wharves** [wɔːf, wɔːvz] n banchina.

what [wɔt] ♦ ad 1 (in direct/indirect questions) che; quale; **~ size is it?** che taglia è?; **~ colour is it?** di che colore è?; **~ books do you want?** quali or che libri vuole?

2 (in exclamations) che; **~ a mess!** che disordine!

♦ pronoun 1 (interrogative) che cosa, cosa, che; **~ are you doing?** che or (che) cosa fai?; **~ are you talking about?** di che cosa parli?; **~ is it called?** come si chiama?; **~ about me?** e io?; **~ about doing ...?** e se facessimo ...?

2 (relative) ciò che, quello che; **I saw ~ you did/was on the table** ho visto quello che hai fatto/quello che era sul tavolo

3 (indirect use) (che) cosa; **he asked me ~ she had said** mi ha chiesto che cosa avesse detto; **tell me ~ you're thinking about** dimmi a cosa stai pensando

♦ excl (disbelieving) cosa!, come!

whatever [wɔt'ɛvə*] a: **~ book** qualunque or qualsiasi libro + sub // pronoun: **do ~ is necessary/you want** faccia qualunque or qualsiasi cosa sia necessaria/lei voglia; ~ **happens** qualunque cosa accada; **no reason** ~ *or* whatsoever nessuna ragione affatto *or* al mondo; **nothing** ~ proprio niente.

whatsoever |ˈwɔtsəuˈɛvə*| *a – see* **whatever**.

wheat |wiːt| *n* grano, frumento.

wheedle |ˈwiːdl| *vt*: **to** ~ **sb into doing sth** convincere qn a fare qc (con lusinghe); **to** ~ **sth out of sb** ottenere qc da qn (con lusinghe).

wheel |wiːl| *n* ruota; (*AUT*: *also*: steering ~) volante *m*; (*NAUT*) (ruota del) timone *m* // *vt* spingere // *vi* (*also*: ~ round) girare; ~**barrow** *n* carriola; ~**chair** *n* sedia a rotelle; ~ **clamp** *n* (*AUT*) morsa che blocca la ruota di una vettura in sosta vietata.

wheeze |wiːz| *vi* ansimare.

when |wɛn| ◆ *ad* quando; ~ **did it happen?** quando è successo?
◆ *cj* **1** (*at, during, after the time that*) quando; **she was reading** ~ **I came in** quando sono entrato lei leggeva; **that was** ~ **I needed you** era allora che avevo bisogno di te
2 (*on, at which*): **on the day** ~ **I met him** il giorno in cui l'ho incontrato; **one day** ~ **it was raining** un giorno che pioveva
3 (*whereas*) quando, mentre; **you said I was wrong** ~ **in fact I was right** mi hai detto che avevo torto, quando in realtà avevo ragione.

whenever |wɛnˈɛvə*| *ad* quando mai // *cj* quando; (*every time that*) ogni volta che.

where |wɛə*| *ad*, *cj* dove; **this is** ~ è qui che; ~**abouts** *ad* dove // *n*: **sb's** ~**abouts** luogo dove qn si trova; ~**as** *cj* mentre; ~**by** *pronoun* per cui; ~**upon** *cj* al che; **wherever** |-ˈɛvə*| *ad* dove mai // *cj* dovunque + *sub*; ~**withal** *n* mezzi *mpl*.

whet |wɛt| *vt* (*tool*) affilare; (*appetite etc*) stimolare.

whether |ˈwɛðə*| *cj* se; **I don't know** ~ **to accept or not** non so se accettare o no; **it's doubtful** ~ è poco probabile che; ~ **you go or not** che lei vada o no.

which |wɪtʃ| ◆ *a* **1** (*interrogative: direct, indirect*) quale; ~ **picture do you want?** quale quadro vuole?; ~ **one?** quale?; ~ **one of you did it?** chi di voi lo ha fatto?
2: **in** ~ **case** nel qual caso
◆ *pronoun* **1** (*interrogative*) quale; ~ (**of these**) **are yours?** quali di questi sono suoi?; ~ **of you are coming?** chi di voi viene?
2 (*relative*) che; (*: indirect*) cui, il(la) quale; **the apple** ~ **you ate/**~ **is on the table** la mela che hai mangiato/che è sul tavolo; **the chair on** ~ **you are sitting** la sedia sulla quale *or* su cui sei seduto; **he**

said he knew, ~ **is true** ha detto che lo sapeva, il che è vero; **after** ~ dopo di che.

whichever |wɪtʃˈɛvə*| *a*: **take** ~ **book you prefer** prenda qualsiasi libro che preferisce; ~ **book you take** qualsiasi libro prenda.

whiff |wɪf| *n* soffio; sbuffo; odore *m*.

while |waɪl| *n* momento // *cj* mentre; (*as long as*) finché; (*although*) sebbene + *sub*; per quanto + *sub*; **for a** ~ per un po'; **to** ~ **away** *vt* (*time*) far passare.

whim |wɪm| *n* capriccio.

whimper |ˈwɪmpə*| *n* piagnucolio // *vi* piagnucolare.

whimsical |ˈwɪmzɪkl| *a* (*person*) capriccioso(a); (*look*) strano(a).

whine |waɪn| *n* gemito // *vi* gemere; uggiolare; piagnucolare.

whip |wɪp| *n* frusta; (*for riding*) frustino; (*POL*: *person*) capogruppo (*che sovrintende alla disciplina dei colleghi di partito*) // *vt* frustare; (*snatch*) sollevare (*or* estrarre) bruscamente; ~**ped cream** *n* panna montata; ~-**round** *n* (*Brit*) colletta.

whirl |wəːl| *n* turbine *m* // *vt* (far) girare rapidamente; (far) turbinare // *vi* turbinare; ~**pool** *n* mulinello; ~**wind** *n* turbine *m*.

whirr |wəː*| *vi* ronzare; rombare; frullare.

whisk |wɪsk| *n* (*CULIN*) frusta; frullino // *vt* sbattere, frullare; **to** ~ **sb away** *or* **off** portar via qn a tutta velocità.

whiskers |ˈwɪskəz| *npl* (*of animal*) baffi *mpl*; (*of man*) favoriti *mpl*.

whisky, (*US, Ireland*) **whiskey** |ˈwɪskɪ| *n* whisky *m inv*.

whisper |ˈwɪspə*| *n* sussurro; (*rumour*) voce *f* // *vt*, *vi* sussurrare.

whistle |ˈwɪsl| *n* (*sound*) fischio; (*object*) fischietto // *vi* fischiare.

white |waɪt| *a* bianco(a); (*with fear*) pallido(a) // *n* bianco; (*person*) bianco/a; ~ **coffee** *n* (*Brit*) caffellatte *m inv*; ~-**collar worker** *n* impiegato; ~ **elephant** *n* (*fig*) oggetto (*or* progetto) costoso ma inutile; ~ **lie** *n* bugia pietosa; ~ **paper** *n* (*POL*) libro bianco; ~**wash** *n* (*paint*) bianco di calce // *vt* imbiancare; (*fig*) coprire.

whiting |ˈwaɪtɪŋ| *n* (*pl inv*) (*fish*) merlano.

Whitsun |ˈwɪtsn| *n* Pentecoste *f*.

whittle |ˈwɪtl| *vt*: **to** ~ **away**, ~ **down** ridurre, tagliare.

whizz |wɪz| *vi* sfrecciare; ~ **kid** *n* (*col*) prodigio.

who |huː| *pronoun* **1** (*interrogative*) chi; ~ **is it?**, ~'**s there?** chi è?
2 (*relative*) che; **the man** ~ **spoke to me** l'uomo che ha parlato con me; **those** ~ **can swim** quelli che sanno nuotare.

whodunit |huːˈdʌnɪt| *n* (*col*) giallo.

whoever [hu:'ɛvə*] *pronoun*: ~ **finds it** chiunque lo trovi; **ask** ~ **you like** lo chieda a chiunque vuole; ~ **she marries** chiunque sposerà, non importa chi sposerà; ~ **told you that?** chi mai gliel'ha detto?

whole [həul] *a* (*complete*) tutto(a), completo(a); (*not broken*) intero(a), intatto(a) // *n* (*total*) totale *m*; (*sth not broken*) tutto; **the ~ of the time** tutto il tempo; **on the ~, as a ~** nel complesso, nell'insieme; **~hearted** *a* sincero(a); **~meal** *a* (*bread, flour*) integrale; **~sale** *n* commercio *or* vendita all'ingrosso // *a* all'ingrosso; (*destruction*) totale; **~saler** *n* grossista *m/f*; **~some** *a* sano(a); salutare; **~wheat** *a* = **~meal**; **wholly** *ad* completamente, del tutto.

whom [hu:m] *pronoun* **1** (*interrogativo*) chi; ~ **did you see?** chi hai visto?; **to** ~ **did you give it?** a chi lo hai dato? **2** (*relative*) che, *prep* + il (la) quale (*check syntax of Italian verb used*); **the man** ~ **I saw/to** ~ **I spoke** l'uomo che ho visto/al quale ho parlato.

whooping cough ['hu:pɪŋ-] *n* pertosse *f*.

whore [hɔ:*] *n* (*pej*) puttana.

whose [hu:z] ♦ *a* **1** (*possessive: interrogative*) di chi; ~ **book is this?**, ~ **is this book?** di chi è questo libro?; ~ **daughter are you?** di chi sei figlia? **2** (*possessive: relative*): **the man** ~ **son you rescued** l'uomo di cui figlio hai salvato; **the girl** ~ **sister you were speaking to** la ragazza alla cui sorella stavi parlando ♦ *pronoun* di chi; ~ **is this?** di chi è questo?; **I know** ~ **it is** so di chi è.

why [waɪ] *ad, cj* perché // *excl* (*surprise*) ma guarda un po'!; (*remonstrating*) ma (via)!; (*explaining*) ebbene!; ~ **not?** perché no?; ~ **not do it now?** porché non farlo adesso?; **that's not** ~ **I'm here** non è questo il motivo per cui sono qui; **the reason** ~ il motivo per cui; **~ever** *ad* perché mai.

wick [wɪk] *n* lucignolo, stoppino.

wicked ['wɪkɪd] *a* cattivo(a), malvagio(a); maligno(a); perfido(a); (*mischievous*) malizioso(a).

wicker ['wɪkə*] *n* vimine *m*; (*also*: **~work**) articoli *mpl* di vimini.

wicket ['wɪkɪt] *n* (*CRICKET*) porta; area tra le due porte.

wide [waɪd] *a* largo(a); (*area, knowledge*) vasto(a); (*choice*) ampio(a) // *ad*: **to open** ~ spalancare; **to shoot** ~ tirare a vuoto *or* fuori bersaglio; **~-angle lens** *n* grandangolare *m*; **~-awake** *a* completamente sveglio(a); **~ly** *ad* (*differing*) molto, completamente; (*believed*) generalmente; **~ly spaced** molto distanziati(e); **~n** *vt* allargare, ampliare; ~ **open** *a*

spalancato(a); **~spread** *a* (*belief etc*) molto *or* assai diffuso(a).

widow ['wɪdəu] *n* vedova; **~er** *n* vedovo.

width [wɪdθ] *n* larghezza.

wield [wi:ld] *vt* (*sword*) maneggiare; (*power*) esercitare.

wife [waɪf], *pl* **wives** *n* moglie *f*.

wig [wɪg] *n* parrucca.

wiggle ['wɪgl] *vt* dimenare, agitare.

wild [waɪld] *a* selvatico(a); selvaggio(a); (*sea*) tempestoso(a); (*idea, life*) folle; stravagante; **~s** *npl* regione *f* selvaggia; **~erness** ['wɪldənɪs] *n* deserto; ~ **goose chase** *n* (*fig*) pista falsa; **~life** *n* natura; **~ly** *ad* (*applaud*) freneticamente; (*hit, guess*) a casaccio; (*happy*) follemente.

wilful ['wɪlful] *a* (*person*) testardo(a), ostinato(a); (*action*) intenzionale; (*crime*) premeditato(a).

will [wɪl] ♦ *auxiliary vb* **1** (*forming future tense*): **I** ~ **finish it tomorrow** lo finirò domani; **I** ~ **have finished it by tomorrow** lo finirò entro domani; ~ **you do it?** – **yes I** ~**/no I won't** lo farai? – sì (lo farò)/no (non lo farò) **2** (*in conjectures, predictions*): **he** ~ *or* **he'll be there by now** dovrebbe essere arrivato ora; **that** ~ **be the postman** sarà il postino **3** (*in commands, requests, offers*): ~ **you be quiet!** vuoi stare zitto?; ~ **you come?** vieni anche tu?; ~ **you help me?** mi aiuti?, mi puoi aiutare?; ~ **you have a cup of tea?** vorrebbe una tazza di tè?; **I won't put up with it!** non lo accetterò! ♦ *vt* (*pt, pp* **~ed**): **to** ~ **sb to do** volere che qn faccia; **he** ~**ed himself to go on** continuò grazie a un grande sforzo di volontà ♦ *n* volontà; testamento.

willing ['wɪlɪŋ] *a* volonteroso(a); ~ **to do** disposto(a) a fare; **~ly** *ad* volentieri; **~ness** *n* buona volontà.

willow ['wɪləu] *n* salice *m*.

will power *n* forza di volontà.

willy-nilly [wɪlɪ'nɪlɪ] *ad* volente o nolente.

wilt [wɪlt] *vi* appassire.

wily ['waɪlɪ] *a* furbo(a).

win [wɪn] *n* (*in sports etc*) vittoria // *vb* (*pt, pp* **won** [wʌn]) *vt* (*battle, prize*) vincere; (*money*) guadagnare; (*popularity*) conquistare // *vi* vincere; **to** ~ **over**, (*Brit*) ~ **round** *vt* convincere.

wince [wɪns] *n* trasalimento, sussulto // *vi* trasalire.

winch [wɪntʃ] *n* verricello, argano.

wind *n* [wɪnd] vento; (*MED*) flatulenza // *vb* [waɪnd] (*pt, pp* **wound** [waund]) *vt* attorcigliare; (*wrap*) avvolgere; (*clock, toy*) caricare; (*take breath away*: [wɪnd]) far restare senza fiato // *vi* (*road, river*) serpeggiare; **to** ~ **up** *vt* (*clock*) caricare; (*debate*) concludere; **~fall** *n* colpo di fortuna; **~ing** ['waɪndɪŋ] *a* (*road*) serpeggiante; (*staircase*) a chiocciola; ~ **instrument** n (MUS) strumento a fiato; ~**mill** n mulino a vento.

window ['wɪndəu] n finestra; (in car, train) finestrino; (in shop etc) vetrina; (also: ~ **pane**) vetro; ~ **box** n cassetta da fiori; ~ **cleaner** n (person) pulitore m di finestre; ~ **ledge** n davanzale m; ~ **pane** n vetro; ~**sill** n davanzale m.

windpipe ['wɪndpaɪp] n trachea.

windscreen, (US) **windshield** ['wɪndskri:n, 'wɪndʃi:ld] n parabrezza m inv; ~ **washer** n lavacristallo; ~ **wiper** n tergicristallo.

windswept ['wɪndswɛpt] a spazzato(a) dal vento.

windy ['wɪndɪ] a ventoso(a); it's ~ c'è vento.

wine [waɪn] n vino; ~ **cellar** n cantina; ~ **glass** n bicchiere m da vino; ~ **list** n lista dei vini; ~ **tasting** n degustazione f dei vini; ~ **waiter** n sommelier m inv.

wing [wɪŋ] n ala; ~**s** npl (THEATRE) quinte fpl; ~**er** n (SPORT) ala.

wink [wɪŋk] n ammiccamento // vi ammiccare, fare l'occhiolino.

winner ['wɪnə*] n vincitore/trice.

winning ['wɪnɪŋ] a (team) vincente; (goal) decisivo(a); ~**s** npl vincite fpl; ~ **post** n traguardo.

winter ['wɪntə*] n inverno; ~ **sports** npl sport mpl invernali.

wintry ['wɪntrɪ] a invernale.

wipe [waɪp] n pulita, passata // vt pulire (strofinando); (dishes) asciugare; **to ~ off** vt cancellare; (stains) togliere strofinando; **to ~ out** vt (debt) pagare, liquidare; (memory) cancellare; (destroy) annientare; **to ~ up** vt asciugare.

wire ['waɪə*] n filo; (ELEC) filo elettrico; (TEL) telegramma m // vt (house) fare l'impianto elettrico di; (also: ~ **up**) collegare, allacciare.

wireless ['waɪəlɪs] n (Brit) telegrafia senza fili; (set) (apparecchio m) radio f inv.

wiring ['waɪərɪŋ] n impianto elettrico.

wiry ['waɪərɪ] a magro(a) e nerboruto(a).

wisdom ['wɪzdəm] n saggezza; (of action) prudenza; ~ **tooth** n dente m del giudizio.

wise [waɪz] a saggio(a); prudente; giudizioso(a).

...wise [waɪz] suffix: time~ per quanto riguarda il tempo, in termini di tempo.

wish [wɪʃ] n (desire) desiderio; (specific desire) richiesta // vt desiderare, volere; best ~es (on birthday etc) i migliori auguri; with best ~es (in letter) cordiali saluti, con i migliori saluti; to ~ sb good-bye dire arrivederci a qn; he ~ed me well mi augurò di riuscire; to ~ to do/sb to do desiderare or volere fare/che qn faccia; to ~ for desiderare; it's ~ful

thinking è prendere i desideri per realtà.

wishy-washy [wɪʃɪ'wɔʃɪ] a (col: colour) slavato(a); (: ideas, argument) insulso(a).

wisp [wɪsp] n ciuffo, ciocca; (of smoke, straw) filo.

wistful ['wɪstful] a malinconico(a).

wit [wɪt] n (gen pl) intelligenza; presenza di spirito; (wittiness) spirito, arguzia; (person) bello spirito; **to be at one's ~s' end** (fig) non sapere più cosa fare; **to ~** ad cioè.

witch [wɪtʃ] n strega.

with [wɪð, wɪθ] prep **1** (in the company of) con; I was ~ him ero con lui; we stayed ~ friends siamo stati da amici; I'll be ~ you in a minute vengo subito **2** (descriptive) con; a room ~ a view una stanza con vista sul mare (or sulle montagne etc); the man ~ the grey hair/blue eyes l'uomo con il cappello grigio/gli occhi blu **3** (indicating manner, means, cause): ~ tears in her eyes con le lacrime agli occhi; red ~ anger rosso dalla rabbia; **to shake ~ fear** tremare di paura **4**: I'm ~ you (I understand) la seguo; **to be ~ it** (col: up-to-date) essere alla moda; (: alert) essere sveglio(a).

withdraw [wɪθ'drɔ:] vb (irg) vt ritirare; (money from bank) ritirare; prelevare // vi ritirarsi; ~**al** n ritiro; prelievo; (of army) ritirata; (MED) stato di privazione; ~**n** a (person) distaccato(a).

wither ['wɪðə*] vi appassire.

withhold [wɪθ'həuld] vt irg (money) trattenere; (decision) rimettere, rimandare; (permission): **to ~ (from)** rifiutare (a); (information): **to ~ (from)** nascondere (a).

within [wɪð'ɪn] prep all'interno; (in time, distances) entro // ad all'interno, dentro; ~ sight of in vista di; ~ a mile of entro un miglio da; ~ the week prima della fine della settimana.

without [wɪð'aut] prep senza.

withstand [wɪθ'stænd] vt irg resistere a.

witness ['wɪtnɪs] n (person) testimone m/f // vt (event) essere testimone di; (document) attestare l'autenticità di; ~ **box**, (US) ~ **stand** n banco dei testimoni.

witticism ['wɪtɪsɪzm] n spiritosaggine f.

witty ['wɪtɪ] a spiritoso(a).

wives [waɪvz] npl of **wife**.

wizard ['wɪzəd] n mago.

wk abbr = **week**.

wobble ['wɔbl] vi tremare; (chair) traballare.

woe [wəu] n dolore m; disgrazia.

woke [wəuk] pt of **wake**; ~**n** pp of **wake**.

wolf, pl **wolves** [wulf, wulvz] n lupo.

woman ['wumən], pl **women** n donna; ~ **doctor** n dottoressa; **women's lib** n

(*col*) movimento femminista.
womb [wu:m] *n* (*ANAT*) utero.
women ['wɪmɪn] *npl of* **woman**.
won [wʌn] *pt, pp of* **win**.
wonder ['wʌndə*] *n* meraviglia // *vi:* to
~ **whether** domandarsi se; to ~ **at** essere
sorpreso(a) di; meravigliarsi di; to ~
about domandarsi di; pensare a; it's no
~ **that** c'è poco *or* non c'è da meravigliarsi che + *sub*; ~**ful** *a* meravi-
glioso(a).
won't [wəunt] = **will not**.
woo [wu:] *vt* (*woman*) fare la corte a.
wood [wud] *n* legno; (*timber*) legname
m; (*forest*) bosco; ~ **carving** *n* scultura
in legno, intaglio; ~**ed** *a* boschivo(a);
boscoso(a); ~**en** *a* di legno; (*fig*)
rigido(a); inespressivo(a); ~**pecker** *n*
picchio; ~**wind** *npl* (*MUS*): **the** ~**wind** i
legni; ~**work** *n* parti *fpl* in legno;
(*craft, subject*) falegnameria; ~**worm**
n tarlo del legno.
wool [wul] *n* lana; **to pull the** ~ **over sb's**
eyes (*fig*) imbrogliare qn; ~**len**, (*US*)
~**en** *a* di lana; ~**lens** *npl* indumenti
mpl di lana; ~**ly**, (*US*) ~**y** *a* lanoso(a);
(*fig: ideas*) confuso(a).
word [wə:d] *n* parola; (*news*) notizie *fpl*
// *vt* esprimere, formulare; **in other** ~**s**
in altre parole; **to break/keep one's** ~
non mantenere/mantenere la propria
parola; ~**ing** *n* formulazione *f*; ~
processing *n* elaborazione *f* di testi,
word processing *m*; ~ **processor** *n*
word processor *m inv*; ~**y** *a* verboso(a).
wore [wɔ:*] *pt of* **wear**.
work [wə:k] *n* lavoro; (*ART,*
LITERATURE) opera // *vi* lavorare;
(*mechanism, plan etc*) funzionare;
(*medicine*) essere efficace // *vt* (*clay,*
wood etc) lavorare; (*mine etc*)
sfruttare; (*machine*) far funzionare; to
be out of ~ essere disoccupato(a); ~**s** *n*
(*Brit: factory*) fabbrica // *npl* (*of clock,*
machine) meccanismo; **to** ~ **loose** *vi*
allentarsi; **to** ~ **on** *vt fus* lavorare a;
(*principle*) basarsi su; **to** ~ **out** *vi*
(*plans etc*) riuscire, andare bene // *vt*
(*problem*) risolvere; (*plan*) elaborare; it
~**s out at £100 fa 100 sterline; to get** ~**ed**
up andare su tutte le furie; eccitarsi;
~**able** *a* (*solution*) realizzabile; ~**aholic**
n maniaco/a del lavoro; ~**er** *n*
lavoratore/trice, operaio/a; ~**force** *n*
forza lavoro; ~**ing class** *n* classe *f*
operaia *or* lavoratrice; ~**ing-class** *a*
operaio(a); ~**ing man** *n* lavoratore *m*;
~**ing order** *n:* **in** ~**ing order**
funzionante; ~**man** *n* operaio;
~**manship** *n* abilità; lavoro; fattura;
~**sheet** *n* foglio col programma di
lavoro; ~**shop** *n* officina; ~ **station** *n*
stazione *f* di lavoro; ~**-to-rule** *n* (*Brit*)
sciopero bianco.
world [wə:ld] *n* mondo // *cpd* (*champion*)

del mondo; (*power, war*) mondiale; **to**
think the ~ **of sb** (*fig*) pensare un gran
bene di qn; ~**ly** *a* di questo mondo; ~-
wide *a* universale.
worm [wə:m] *n* verme *m*.
worn [wɔ:n] *pp of* **wear** // *a* usato(a);
~**out** *a* (*object*) consumato(a),
logoro(a); (*person*) sfinito(a).
worried ['wʌrɪd] *a* preoccupato(a).
worry ['wʌrɪ] *n* preoccupazione *f* // *vt*
preoccupare // *vi* preoccuparsi.
worse [wə:s] *a* peggiore // *ad, n* peggio;
a change for the ~ un peggioramento; ~
off *a* in condizioni (economiche)
peggiori; ~**n** *vt, vi* peggiorare.
worship ['wə:ʃɪp] *n* culto // *vt* (*God*)
adorare, venerare; (*person*) adorare;
Your W~ (*Brit: to mayor*) signor
sindaco; (: *to judge*) signor giudice.
worst [wə:st] *a* il(la) peggiore // *ad, n*
peggio; **at** ~ al peggio, per male che
vada.
worsted ['wustɪd] *n:* (**wool**) ~ lana
pettinata.
worth [wə:θ] *n* valore *m* // *a:* **to be** ~
valere; it's ~ it ne vale la pena; it is ~
one's while (to do) vale la pena (fare);
~**less** *a* di nessun valore; ~**while** *a*
(*activity*) utile; (*cause*) lodevole.
worthy ['wə:ðɪ] *a* (*person*) degno(a);
(*motive*) lodevole; ~ **of** degno di.
would [wud] *auxiliary vb* **1** (*conditional*
tense): **if you asked him he** ~ **do it** se
glielo chiedesse lo farebbe; **if you had**
asked him he ~ **have done it** se glielo
avesse chiesto lo avrebbe fatto
2 (*in offers, invitations, requests*): ~
you like a biscuit? vorrebbe *or* vuole un
biscotto?; ~ **you ask him to come in?** lo
faccia entrare, per cortesia; ~ **you open**
the window please? apra la finestra, per
favore
3 (*in indirect speech*): **I said I** ~ **do it**
ho detto che l'avrei fatto
4 (*emphatic*): it **WOULD** have to snow
today! doveva proprio nevicare oggi!
5 (*insistence*): **she** ~**n't do it** non ha
voluto farlo
6 (*conjecture*): **it** ~ **have been midnight**
sarà stato mezzanotte; **it** ~ **seem so**
sembrerebbe proprio di sì
7 (*indicating habit*): **he** ~ **go there on**
Mondays andava lì ogni lunedì.
would-be ['wudbi:] *a* (*pej*) sedicente.
wouldn't ['wudnt] = **would not**.
wound *vb* [waund] *pt, pp of* **wind** // *n, vt*
[wu:nd] *n* ferita // *vt* ferire.
wove [wəuv] *pt of* **weave**; ~**n** *pp of*
weave.
wrangle ['ræŋgl] *n* litigio // *vi* litigare.
wrap [ræp] *n* (*stole*) scialle *m*; (*cape*)
mantellina // *vt* (*also:* ~ **up**) avvolgere;
(*parcel*) incartare; ~**per** *n* (*Brit: of*
book) copertina; ~**ping paper** *n* carta
da pacchi; (*for gift*) carta da regali.

wrath [rɔθ] *n* collera, ira.

wreak [ri:k] *vt* (*havoc*) portare, causare; **to ~ vengeance on** vendicarsi su.

wreath, ~s [ri:θ, ri:ðz] *n* corona.

wreck [rɛk] *n* (*sea disaster*) naufragio; (*ship*) relitto; (*pej: person*) rottame *m* // *vt* demolire; (*ship*) far naufragare; (*fig*) rovinare; **~age** *n* rottami *mpl*; (*of building*) macerie *fpl*; (*of ship*) relitti *mpl*.

wren [rɛn] *n* (*ZOOL*) scricciolo.

wrench [rɛntʃ] *n* (*TECH*) chiave *f*; (*tug*) torsione *f* brusca; (*fig*) strazio // *vt* strappare; storcere; **to ~ sth from** strappare qc a *or* da.

wrestle ['rɛsl] *vi*: **to ~ (with sb)** lottare (con qn); **to ~ with** (*fig*) combattere *or* lottare contro; **~r** *n* lottatore/trice; **wrestling** *n* lotta; (*also:* **all-in wrestling**) catch *m*, lotta libera.

wretched ['rɛtʃɪd] *a* disgraziato(a); (*col: weather, holiday*) orrendo(a), orribile; (: *child, dog*) pestifero(a).

wriggle ['rɪgl] *vi* dimenarsi; (*snake, worm*) serpeggiare, muoversi serpeggiando.

wring [rɪŋ], *pt, pp* **wrung** *vt* torcere; (*wet clothes*) strizzare; (*fig*): **to ~ sth out of** strappare qc a.

wrinkle ['rɪŋkl] *n* (*on skin*) ruga; (*on paper etc*) grinza // *vt* corrugare; raggrinzire // *vi* corrugarsi; raggrinzirsi.

wrist [rɪst] *n* polso; **~watch** *n* orologio da polso.

writ [rɪt] *n* ordine *m*; mandato.

write [raɪt], *pt* **wrote**, *pp* **written** *vt, vi* scrivere; **to ~ down** *vt* annotare; (*put in writing*) mettere per iscritto; **to ~ off** *vt* (*debt*) cancellare; (*depreciate*) deprezzare; **to ~ out** *vt* scrivere; (*copy*) ricopiare; **to ~ up** *vt* redigere; **~-off** *n* perdita completa; **~r** *n* autore/trice, scrittore/trice.

writhe [raɪð] *vi* contorcersi.

writing ['raɪtɪŋ] *n* scrittura; (*of author*) scritto, opera; **in ~** per iscritto; **~ paper** *n* carta da scrivere.

written ['rɪtn] *pp of* **write**.

wrong [rɔŋ] *a* sbagliato(a); (*not suitable*) inadatto(a); (*wicked*) cattivo(a); (*unfair*) ingiusto(a) // *ad* in modo sbagliato, erroneamente // *n* (*evil*) male *m*; (*injustice*) torto // *vt* fare torto a; **you are ~ to do it** ha torto a farlo; **you are ~ about that, you've got it ~** si sbaglia; **to be in the ~** avere torto; **what's ~?** cosa c'è che non va?; **to go ~** (*person*) sbagliarsi; (*plan*) fallire, non riuscire; (*machine*) guastarsi; **~ful** *a* illegittimo(a); ingiusto(a); **~ly** *ad* a torto.

wrote [rəʊt] *pt of* **write**.

wrought [rɔ:t] *a*: **~ iron** ferro battuto.

wrung [rʌŋ] *pt, pp of* **wring**.

wry [raɪ] *a* storto(a).

wt. *abbr* = **weight**.

X

Xmas ['ɛksməs] *n abbr* = **Christmas**.

X-ray ['ɛks'reɪ] *n* raggio X; (*photograph*) radiografia // *vt* radiografare.

xylophone ['zaɪləfəun] *n* xilofono.

Y

yacht [jɔt] *n* panfilo, yacht *m inv*; **~ing** *n* yachting *m*, sport *m* della vela.

Yank [jæŋk], **Yankee** ['jæŋkɪ] *n* (*pej*) yankee *m/f inv*.

yap [jæp] *vi* (*dog*) guaire.

yard [jɑ:d] *n* (*of house etc*) cortile *m*; (*measure*) iarda (= 914 mm; 3 feet); **~stick** *n* (*fig*) misura, criterio.

yarn [jɑ:n] *n* filato; (*tale*) lunga storia.

yawn [jɔ:n] *n* sbadiglio // *vi* sbadigliare; **~ing** *a* (*gap*) spalancato(a).

yd. *abbr* = **yard(s)**.

yeah [jɛə] *ad* (*col*) sì.

year [jɪə*] *n* anno; (*referring to harvest, wine etc*) annata; **he is 8 ~s old** ha 8 anni; **an eight-~-old child** un(a) bambino(a) di otto anni; **~ly** *a* annuale // *ad* annualmente.

yearn [jə:n] *vi*: **to ~ for sth/to do** desiderare ardentemente qc/di fare; **~ing** *n* desiderio intenso.

yeast [ji:st] *n* lievito.

yell [jɛl] *n* urlo // *vi* urlare.

yellow ['jɛləu] *a* giallo(a).

yelp [jɛlp] *vi* guaire, uggiolare.

yeoman ['jəumən] *n*: **Y~ of the Guard** guardiano della Torre di Londra.

yes [jɛs] *ad, n* sì (*m inv*); **to say/answer ~** dire/rispondere di sì.

yesterday ['jɛstədɪ] *ad, n* ieri (*m inv*); **~ morning/evening** ieri mattina/sera; **all day ~** ieri per tutta la giornata.

yet [jɛt] *ad* ancora; già // *cj* ma, tuttavia; **it is not finished ~** non è ancora finito; **the best ~** finora il migliore; **as ~** finora.

yew [ju:] *n* tasso (*albero*).

yield [ji:ld] *n* produzione *f*, resa; reddito // *vt* produrre, rendere; (*surrender*) cedere // *vi* cedere; (*US AUT*) dare la precedenza.

YMCA *n abbr* (= *Young Men's Christian Association*) Y.M.C.A. *m*.

yoga ['jəugə] *n* yoga *m*.

yog(h)ourt, yog(h)urt ['jəugət] *n* iogurt *m inv*.

yoke [jəuk] *n* giogo.

yolk [jəuk] *n* tuorlo, rosso d'uovo.

yonder ['jɔndə*] *ad* là.

you [ju:] *pronoun* **1** (*subject*) tu; (: *polite form*) lei; (: *pl*) voi; (: *very formal*) loro; **~ Italians enjoy your food** a voi Italiani piace mangiare bene; **~ and I will go** tu ed io *or* lei ed io andiamo

2 (object: direct) ti; la; vi; loro (after vb); (: indirect) ti; le; vi; loro (after vb); **I know ~** ti or la or vi conosco; **I gave it to ~** te l'ho dato; giel'ho dato; ve l'ho dato; l'ho dato loro

3 (stressed, after prep, in comparisons) te; lei; voi; loro; **I told you** to do it ho detto a TE (or a LEI etc) di farlo; **she's younger than ~** è più giovane di te (or lei etc)

4 (impersonal: one) si; **fresh air does ~ good** l'aria fresca fa bene; **~ never know** non si sa mai.

you'd |juːd| = **you had, you would.**

you'll |juːl| = **you will, you shall.**

young |jʌŋ| a giovane // npl (of animal) piccoli mpl; (people): **the ~** i giovani, la gioventù; **~ster** n giovanotto, ragazzo; (child) bambino/a.

your |jɔː*| a il(la) tuo(a), pl i(le) tuoi(tue); il(la) suo(a), pl i(le) suoi(sue); il(la) vostro(a), pl i(le) vo-stri(e); il(la) loro, pl i(le) loro; see also **my.**

you're |juə*| = **you are.**

yours |jɔːz| pronoun il(la) tuo(a), pl i(le) tuoi(tue); (polite form) il(la) suo(a), pl i(le) suoi(sue); (pl) il(la) vostro(a), pl i(le) vostri(e); (: very formal) il(la) loro, pl i(le) loro; **~ sincerely/faithfully** cordiali/distinti saluti; see also **mine.**

yourself |jɔːˈsɛlf| pronoun (reflexive) ti; si; (after prep) te; sé; (emphatic) tu stesso(a); lei stesso(a); **yourselves** pl pronoun (reflexive) vi; si; (after prep) voi; loro; (emphatic) voi stessi(e); loro stessi(e); see also **oneself.**

youth |juːθ| n gioventù f; (young man; pl **~s** |juːðz|) giovane m, ragazzo; **~club** n centro giovanile; **~ful** a giovane; da giovane; giovanile; **~ hostel** n ostello della gioventù.

you've |juːv| = **you have.**

YTS n abbr (Brit: = Youth Training Scheme) programma di addestramento professionale per giovani.

Yugoslav |ˈjuːgəʊslɑːv| a, n jugo-slavo(a).

Yugoslavia |ˈjuːgəʊslɑːvɪə| n Jugoslavia.

yuppie |ˈjʌpɪ| n, a (col) yuppie (m/f inv).

YWCA n abbr (= Young Women's Christian Association) Y.W.C.A. m.

Z

zany |ˈzeɪnɪ| a un po' pazzo(a).

zap |zæp| vt (COMPUT) cancellare.

zeal |ziːl| n zelo; entusiasmo.

zebra |ˈziːbrə| n zebra; **~ crossing** n (Brit) (passaggio pedonale a) strisce fpl, zebre fpl.

zero |ˈzɪərəʊ| n zero.

zest |zɛst| n gusto; (CULIN) buccia.

zigzag |ˈzɪgzæg| n zigzag m inv // vi zigzagare.

Zimbabwe |zɪmˈbɑːbwɪ| n Zimbabwe m.

zinc |zɪŋk| n zinco.

zip |zɪp| n (also: **~ fastener,** (US) **~per**) chiusura f or cerniera f lampo inv // vt (also: **~ up**) chiudere con una cerniera lampo; **~ code** n (US) codice m di avviamento postale.

zodiac |ˈzəʊdɪæk| n zodiaco.

zombie |ˈzɒmbɪ| n (fig): **like a ~** come un morto che cammina.

zone |zəʊn| n zona; (subdivision of town) quartiere m.

zoo |zuː| n zoo m inv.

zoology |zuːˈɒlədʒɪ| n zoologia.

zoom |zuːm| vi: **to ~ past** sfrecciare; **~ lens** n zoom m inv, obiettivo a tocale variabile.

zucchini |zuːˈkiːnɪ| npl (US: courgettes) zucchine fpl.

ITALIAN VERBS

1 Gerundio *2* Participio passato *3* Presente *4* Imperfetto *5* Passato remoto *6* Futuro *7* Condizionale *8* Congiuntivo presente *9* Congiuntivo passato *10* Imperativo

andare *3* vado, vai, va, andiamo, andate, vanno *6* andrò *etc 8* vada *10* va'!, vada!, andate!, vadano!

apparire *2* apparso *3* appaio, appari *o* apparisci, appare *o* apparisce, appaiono *o* appariscono *5* apparvi *o* apparsi, apparisti, apparve *o* apparì *o* apparse, apparvero *o* apparirono *o* apparsero *8* appaia *o* apparisca

aprire *2* aperto *3* apro *5* aprii *o* apersi, apristi *8* apra

AVERE *3* ho, hai, ha, abbiamo, avete, hanno *5* ebbi, avesti, ebbe, avemmo, aveste, ebbero *6* avrò *etc 8* abbia *etc 10* abbi!, abbia!, abbiate!, abbiano!

bere *1* bevendo *2* bevuto *3* bevo *etc 4* bevevo *etc 8* beva *etc 9* bevessi *etc*

cadere *5* caddi, cadesti *6* cadrò *etc*

cogliere *2* colto *3* colgo, colgono *5* colsi, cogliesti *8* colga

correre *2* corso *5* corsi, corresti

cuocere *2* cotto *3* cuocio, cociamo, cuociono *5* cossi, cocesti

dare *3* do, dai, dà, diamo, date, danno *5* diedi *o* detti, desti *6* darò *etc 8* dia *etc 9* dessi *etc 10* da'!, dia!, date!, diano!

dire *1* dicendo *2* detto *3* dico, dici, dice, diciamo, dite, dicono *4* dicevo *etc 5* dissi, dicesti *6* dirò *etc 8* dica, diciamo, diciate, dicano *9* dicessi *etc 10* di'!, dica!, dite!, dicano!

dolere *3* dolgo, duoli, duole, dolgono *5* dolsi, dolesti *6* dorrò *etc 8* dolga

dovere *3* devo *o* debbo, devi, deve, dobbiamo, dovete, devono *o* debbono *6* dovrò *etc 8* debba, dobbiamo, dobbiate, devano *o* debbano

ESSERE *2* stato *3* sono, sei, è, siamo, siete, sono *4* ero, eri, era, eravamo, eravate, erano *5* fui, fosti, fu, fummo, foste, furono *6* sarò *etc 8* sia *etc 9* fossi, fossi, fosse, fossimo, foste, fossero *10* sii!, sia!, siate!, siano!

fare *1* facendo *2* fatto *3* faccio, fai, fa, facciamo, fate, fanno *4* facevo *etc 5* feci, facesti *6* farò *etc 8* faccia *etc 9* facessi *etc 10* fa'!, faccia!, fate!, facciano!

FINIRE *1* finendo *2* finito *3* finisco, finisci, finisce, finiamo, finite, finiscono *4* finivo, finivi, finiva, finivamo, finivate, finivano *5* finii, finisti, finì, finimmo, finiste, finirono *6* finirò, finirai, finirà, finiremo, finirete, finiranno *7* finirei, finiresti, finirebbe, finiremmo, finireste, finirebbero *8* finisca, finisca, finisca, finiamo, finiate, finiscano *9* finissi, finissi, finisse, finissimo, finiste, finissero *10* finisci!, finisca!, finite!, finiscano!

giungere *2* giunto *5* giunsi, giungesti

leggere *2* letto *5* lessi, leggesti

mettere *2* messo *5* misi, mettesti

morire *2* morto *3* muoio, muori, muore, moriamo, morite, muoiono *6* morirò *o* morrò *etc 8* muoia

muovere *2* mosso *5* mossi, movesti

nascere *2* nato *5* nacqui, nascesti

nuocere *2* nuociuto *3* nuoccio, nuoci, nuoce, nociamo *o* nuociamo, nuocete, nuocciono *4* nuocevo *etc 5* nocqui, nuocesti *6* nuocerò *etc 7* nuoccia

offrire *2* offerto *3* offro *5* offersi *o* offrii, offristi *8* offra

parere *2* parso *3* paio, paiamo, paiono *5* parvi *o* parsi, paresti *6* parrò *etc 8* paia, paiamo, paiate, paiano

PARLARE *1* parlando *2* parlato *3* parlo, parli, parla, parliamo, parlate, parlano *4* parlavo, parlavi, parlava, parlavamo, parlavate, parlavano *5* parlai, parlasti, parlò, parlammo, parlaste, parlarono *6* parlerò, parlerai, parlerà, parleremo, parlerete, parleranno *7* parlerei, parleresti, parlerebbe, parleremmo, parlereste, parlerebbero *8* parli, parli, parli, parliamo, parliate, parlino *9* parlassi, parlassi, parlasse, parlassimo, parlaste, parlassero *10* parla!, parli!, parlate!, parlino!

piacere *2* piaciuto *3* piaccio, piacciamo, piacciono *5* piacqui, piacesti *8* piaccia *etc*

porre *1* ponendo *2* posto *3* pongo, poni, pone, poniamo, ponete, pongono *4* ponevo *etc 5* posi, ponesti *6* porrò *etc 8* ponga, poniamo, poniate, pongano *9* ponessi *etc*

potere *3* posso, puoi, può, possiamo, potete, possono *6* potrò *etc 8* possa, possiamo, possiate, possano

prendere *2* preso *5* presi, prendesti

ridurre *1* riducendo *2* ridotto *3* riduco *etc 4* riducevo *etc 5* ridussi, riducesti *6* ridurrò *etc 8* riduca *etc 9* riducessi *etc*

riempire *1* riempiendo *2* riempito *3* riempio, riempi, riempie, riempiono

rimanere *2* rimasto *3* rimango, rimangono *5* rimasi, rimanesti *6* rimarrò *etc 8* rimanga

rispondere *2* risposto *5* risposi, rispondesti

salire *3* salgo, sali, salgono *8* salga

sapere *3* so, sai, sa, sappiamo, sapete, sanno *5* seppi, sapesti *6* saprò *etc 8* sappia *etc 10* sappi!, sappia!, sappiate!, sappiano!

scrivere *2* scritto *5* scrissi, scrivesti

sedere *3* siedo, siedi, siede, siedono *8* sieda

spegnere *2* spento *3* spengo, spengono *5*

spensi, spegnesti *8* spenga

stare *2* stato *3* sto, stai, sta, stiamo, state, stanno *5* stetti, stesti *6* starò *etc 8* stia *etc 9* stessi *etc 10* sta'!, stia!, state!, stiano!

tacere *2* taciuto *3* taccio, tacciono *5* tacqui, tacesti *8* taccia

tenere *3* tengo, tieni, tiene, tengono *5* tenni, tenesti *6* terrò *etc 8* tenga

trarre *1* traendo *2* tratto *3* traggo, trai, trae, traiamo, traete, traggono *4* traevo *etc 5* trassi, traesti *6* trarrò *etc 8* tragga *9* traessi *etc*

udire *3* odo, odi, ode, odono *8* oda

uscire *3* esco, esci, esce, escono *8* esca

valere *2* valso *3* valgo, valgono *5* valsi, valesti *6* varrò *etc 8* valga

vedere *2* visto *o* veduto *5* vidi, vedesti *6* vedrò *etc*

VENDERE *1* vendendo *2* venduto *3* vendo, vendi, vende, vendiamo, vendete, vendono *4* vendevo, vendevi, vendeva, vendevamo, vendevate, vendevano *5* vendei *o* vendetti, vendesti, vendé *o* vendette, vendemmo, vendeste, venderono *o* vendettero *6* venderò, venderai, venderà, venderemo, venderete, venderanno *7* venderei, venderesti, venderebbe, venderemmo, vendereste, venderebbero *8* venda, venda, venda, vendiamo, vendiate, vendano *9* vendessi, vendessi, vendesse, vendessimo, vendeste, vendessero *10* vendi!, venda!, vendete!, vendano!

venire *2* venuto *3* vengo, vieni, viene, vengono *5* venni, venisti *6* verrò *etc 8* venga

vivere *2* vissuto *5* vissi, vivesti

volere *3* voglio, vuoi, vuole, vogliamo, volete, vogliono *5* volli, volesti *6* vorrò *etc 8* voglia *etc 10* vogli!, voglia!, vogliate!, vogliano!

VERBI INGLESI

present	pt	pp	present	pt	pp
arise	arose	arisen	fly (flies)	flew	flown
awake	awoke	awaked	forbid	forbade	forbidden
be (am, is, are; being)	was, were	been	forecast	forecast	forecast
			forego	forewent	foregone
bear	bore	born(e)	foresee	foresaw	foreseen
beat	beat	beaten	foretell	foretold	foretold
become	became	become	forget	forgot	forgotten
begin	began	begun	forgive	forgave	forgiven
behold	beheld	beheld	forsake	forsook	forsaken
bend	bent	bent	freeze	froze	frozen
beseech	besought	besought	get	got	got, (US) gotten
beset	beset	beset			
bet	bet, betted	bet, betted	give	gave	given
bid	bid, bade	bid, bidden	go (goes)	went	gone
bind	bound	bound	grind	ground	ground
bite	bit	bitten	grow	grew	grown
bleed	bled	bled	hang	hung,	hung,
blow	blew	blown		hanged	hanged
break	broke	broken	have (has; having)	had	had
breed	bred	bred			
bring	brought	brought	hear	heard	heard
build	built	built	hide	hid	hidden
burn	burnt,	burnt,	hit	hit	hit
	burned	burned	hold	held	held
burst	burst	burst	hurt	hurt	hurt
buy	bought	bought	keep	kept	kept
can	could	(been able)	kneel	knelt,	knelt,
cast	cast	cast		kneeled	kneeled
catch	caught	caught	know	knew	known
choose	chose	chosen	lay	laid	laid
cling	clung	clung	lead	led	led
come	came	come	lean	leant, leaned	leant, leaned
cost	cost	cost	leap	leapt, leaped	leapt, leaped
creep	crept	crept	learn	learnt,	learnt,
cut	cut	cut		learned	learned
deal	dealt	dealt	leave	left	left
dig	dug	dug	lend	lent	lent
do (3rd person; he/she/it does)	did	done	let	let	let
			lie (lying)	lay	lain
			light	lit, lighted	lit, lighted
			lose	lost	lost
draw	drew	drawn	make	made	made
dream	dreamed,	dreamed,	may	might	—
	dreamt	dreamt	mean	meant	meant
drink	drank	drunk	meet	met	met
drive	drove	driven	mistake	mistook	mistaken
dwell	dwelt	dwelt	mow	mowed	mown,
eat	ate	eaten			mowed
fall	fell	fallen	must	(had to)	(had to)
feed	fed	fed	pay	paid	paid
feel	felt	felt	put	put	put
fight	fought	fought	quit	quit, quitted	quit, quitted
find	found	found	read	read	read
flee	fled	fled	rid	rid	rid
fling	flung	flung	ride	rode	ridden

present	pt	pp	present	pt	pp
ring	rang	rung	spoil	spoiled, spoilt	spoiled, spoilt
rise	rose	risen			
run	ran	run	spread	spread	spread
saw	sawed	sawn	spring	sprang	sprung
say	said	said	stand	stood	stood
see	saw	seen	steal	stole	stolen
seek	sought	sought	stick	stuck	stuck
sell	sold	sold	sting	stung	stung
send	sent	sent	stink	stank	stunk
set	set	set	stride	strode	stridden
shake	shook	shaken	strike	struck	struck, stricken
shall	should	—			
shear	sheared	shorn, sheared	strive	strove	striven
			swear	swore	sworn
shed	shed	shed	sweep	swept	swept
shine	shone	shone	swell	swelled	swollen, swelled
shoot	shot	shot			
show	showed	shown	swim	swam	swum
shrink	shrank	shrunk	swing	swung	swung
shut	shut	shut	take	took	taken
sing	sang	sung	teach	taught	taught
sink	sank	sunk	tear	tore	torn
sit	sat	sat	tell	told	told
slay	slew	slain	think	thought	thought
sleep	slept	slept	throw	threw	thrown
slide	slid	slid	thrust	thrust	thrust
sling	slung	slung	tread	trod	trodden
slit	slit	slit	wake	woke, waked	woken, waked
smell	smelt, smelled	smelt, smelled	waylay	waylaid	waylaid
			wear	wore	worn
sow	sowed	sown, sowed	weave	wove, weaved	woven, weaved
speak	spoke	spoken			
speed	sped, speeded	sped, speeded	wed	wedded, wed	wedded, wed
			weep	wept	wept
spell	spelt, spelled	spelt, spelled	win	won	won
			wind	wound	wound
spend	spent	spent	withdraw	withdrew	withdrawn
spill	spilt, spilled	spilt, spilled	withhold	withheld	withheld
spin	spun	spun	withstand	withstood	withstood
spit	spat	spat	wring	wrung	wrung
split	split	split	write	wrote	written

I NUMERI

NUMBERS

uno(a)	1	one
due	2	two
tre	3	three
quattro	4	four
cinque	5	five
sei	6	six
sette	7	seven
otto	8	eight
nove	9	nine
dieci	10	ten
undici	11	eleven
dodici	12	twelve
tredici	13	thirteen
quattordici	14	fourteen
quindici	15	fifteen
sedici	16	sixteen
diciassette	17	seventeen
diciotto	18	eighteen
diciannove	19	nineteen
venti	20	twenty
ventuno	21	twenty-one
ventidue	22	twenty-two
ventitré	23	twenty-three
ventotto	28	twenty-eight
trenta	30	thirty
quaranta	40	forty
cinquanta	50	fifty
sessanta	60	sixty
settanta	70	seventy
ottanta	80	eighty
novanta	90	ninety
cento	100	a hundred, one hundred
cento uno	101	a hundred and one
duecento	200	two hundred
mille	1 000	a thousand, one thousand
milleduecentodue	1 202	one thousand two hundred and two
cinquemila	5 000	five thousand
un milione	1 000 000	a million, one million
primo(a), 1°		first, 1st
secondo(a), 2°		second, 2nd
terzo(a), 3°		third, 3rd
quarto(a)		fourth, 4th
quinto(a)		fifth, 5th
sesto(a)		sixth, 6th
settimo(a)		seventh
ottavo(a)		eighth
nono(a)		ninth
decimo(a)		tenth
undicesimo(a)		eleventh
dodicesimo(a)		twelfth

I NUMERI

tredicesimo(a)
quattordicesimo(a)
quindicesimo(a)
sedicesimo(a)
diciassettesimo(a)
diciottesimo(a)
diciannovesimo(a)
ventesimo(a)
ventunesimo(a)
ventiduesimo(a)
ventitreesimo(a)
ventottesimo(a)
trentesimo(a)
centesimo(a)
centunesimo(a)
millesimo(a)
milionesimo(a)

Frazioni etc

mezzo
terzo
due terzi
quarto
quinto
zero virgola cinque, 0,5
tre virgola quattro, 3,4
dieci per cento
cento per cento

Esempi

abita al numero dieci
si trova nel capitolo sette, a pagina
  sette
abita al terzo piano
arrivò quarto
scala uno a venticinquemila

NUMBERS

thirteenth
fourteenth
fifteenth
sixteenth
seventeenth
eighteenth
nineteenth
twentieth
twenty-first
twenty-second
twenty-third
twenty-eighth
thirtieth
hundredth
hundred-and-first
thousandth
millionth

Fractions etc

half
third
two thirds
quarter
fifth
(nought) point five, 0.5
three point four, 3.4
ten per cent
a hundred per cent

Examples

he lives at number 10
it's in chapter 7, on page 7

he lives on the 3rd floor
he came in 4th
scale 1:25,000

L'ORA	THE TIME
che ora è?, che ore sono?	*what time is it?*
è ..., sono ...	*it is ...*
mezzanotte	midnight, twelve pm
l'una (della mattina)	one o'clock (in the morning), one (am)
l'una e cinque	five past one
l'una e dieci	ten past one
l'una e un quarto, l'una e quindici	a quarter past one, one fifteen
l'una e venticinque	twenty-five past one, one twenty-five
l'una e mezzo o mezza, l'una e trenta	half-past one, one thirty
le due meno venticinque, l'una e trentacinque	twenty-five to two, one thirty-five
le due meno venti, l'una e quaranta	twenty to two, one forty
le due meno un quarto, l'una e quarantacinque	a quarter to two, one forty-five
le due meno dieci, l'una e cinquanta	ten to two, one fifty
mezzogiorno	twelve o'clock, midday, noon
l'una, le tredici	one o'clock (in the afternoon), one (pm)
le sette (di sera), le diciannove	seven o'clock (in the evening), seven (pm)
a che ora?	*at what time?*
a mezzanotte	at midnight
all'una, alle tredici	at one o'clock
fra venti minuti	in twenty minutes
venti minuti fa	twenty minutes ago